All in One®

Recommended by **Teachers,** Trusted by **Toppers**

PHYSICS

Class 11

EVERYTHING YOU NEED TO SCORE

- Simplified NCERT Theory
- In-text & Chapter Exercises
- All Types of Exam Pattern Questions
- CBQs; MCQs, A-R, Case Based
- Sample Question Papers

CBSE Exams 2026

Authors

Rahul Kumar
Nitesh Kumar

arihant
SUCCESS AND NOTHING LESS

arihant
SUCCESS AND NOTHING LESS

ARIHANT PRAKASHAN
(School Division Series)

卐 *ADMINISTRATIVE & PRODUCTION OFFICES*

Regd. Office
'Ramchhaya' 4577/15, Agarwal Road, Darya Ganj, New Delhi -110002
Tele: 011- 47630600, 43518550; Fax: 011- 23280316

卐 *Head Office*
Kalindi, TP Nagar, Meerut (UP) - 250002, Tel: 0121-7156203, 7156204

卐 *SALES & SUPPORT OFFICES*
Agra, Ahmedabad, Bengaluru, Bareilly, Chennai, Delhi, Guwahati, Hyderabad, Jaipur, Jhansi, Kolkata, Lucknow, Nagpur & Pune.

PO No : TXT-XX-XXXXXXX-X-XX

Published By Arihant Publications (India) Ltd.

For further information about the books published by Arihant, log on to www.arihantbooks.com or e-mail at info@arihantbooks.com

Follow us on

卐 *PRICE* ₹625.00

PRODUCTION TEAM

Publishing Managers	*Cover Designer*	*Inner Designer*
Mahendra Singh Rawat & Keshav Mohan	Salman Shaikh	Ankit Tyagi
Project Head	*Page Layouting*	*Proof Readers*
Yojna Sharma	Subhash Chaprana	Mansi Tomar, Ishan Khan

Index *cum* Study Planner

One Book- Endless Features

to Help you Succeed

In this Chapter

At the start of each chapter, all the topics of the chapter have been listed, so that students may know what they are going to study.

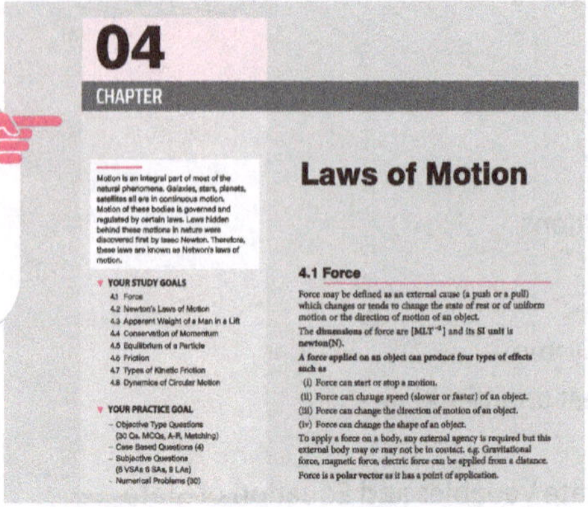
04

CHAPTER

Laws of Motion

Motion is an integral part of most of the natural phenomena. Galaxies, stars, planets, satellites all are in continuous motion. Motion of these bodies is governed and regulated by certain laws. Laws hidden behind these motions in nature were discovered first by Isaac Newton. Therefore, these laws are known as Netwon's laws of motion.

YOUR STUDY GOALS

4.1 Force
4.2 Newton's Laws of Motion
4.3 Apparent Weight of a Man in a Lift
4.4 Conservation of Momentum
4.5 Equilibrium of a Particle
4.6 Friction
4.7 Types of Kinetic Friction
4.8 Dynamics of Circular Motion

YOUR PRACTICE GOAL

- Objective Type Questions (30 Qs. MCQs, A-R, Matching)
- Case Based Questions (4)
- Subjective Questions (6 VSAs 6 SAs, 9 LAs)
- Numerical Problems (30)

4.1 Force

Force may be defined as an external cause (a push or a pull) which changes or tends to change the state of rest or of uniform motion or the direction of motion of an object.

The **dimensions** of force are $[MLT^{-2}]$ and its **SI unit** is **newton(N).**

A force applied on an object can produce four types of effects such as

(i) Force can start or stop a motion.
(ii) Force can change speed (slower or faster) of an object.
(iii) Force can change the direction of motion of an object.
(iv) Force can change the shape of an object.

To apply a force on a body, any external agency is required but this external body may or may not be in contact. e.g. Gravitational force, magnetic force, electric force can be applied from a distance.

Force is a **polar vector** as it has a point of application.

A force applied on an object can produce four types of effects such as

(i) Force can start or stop a motion.
(ii) Force can change speed (slower or faster) of an object.
(iii) Force can change the direction of motion of an object.
(iv) Force can change the shape of an object.

To apply a force on a body, any external agency is required but this external body may or may not be in contact. e.g. Gravitational force, magnetic force, electric force can be applied from a distance.

Force is a **polar vector** as it has a point of application.

Inertia

The inherent property of a material body by virtue of which it resist the change in its state of rest or of uniform motion in a straight line. This term was first used by **Galileo.**

Complete Theory

Each chapter has Complete, Easy to Understand and Simplified theory covering latest syllabus and CBSE Textbook. Theory is developed in such a way that it is suitable for all types of learners.

- **The effect of force on the motion of a body is described by momentum.** This can be understood by the following examples
- We require a greater force to push the truck than the car to bring at the same speed in same time.
  Also, a greater opposing force is required to stop the truck than the car at the same time if they are moving with the same speed. Thus, **mass of a body is an important parameter to determine the effect of force on its motion.**
  Speed is another important parameter to consider.
- A bullet fired by a gun can easily pierce human tissue before it stops, resulting in casuality. The same bullet fired with moderate speed will not cause much damage. Thus, for a given mass, the greater the speed, the greater is the opposing force needed to stop the body in a certain time. **Thus, to describe the effect of force on the motion of a body, the mass and velocity i.e., momentum is an important quantity.**

Boxed Matter

Information in the boxes is given to focus important points related to the concept.

Quick Test 1

Conceptual Questions

1. The distance travelled by a moving body is directly proportional to time. Is any external force acting on it?
2. A body is acted upon by a number of external forces. Can it remain at rest?
3. An impulse is applied to a moving object with a force at an angle of 20° w.r.t. velocity vector, what is the angle between the impulse vector and change in momentum vector?
4. Two bodies of different masses have same linear momentum. Which one of them will move faster?
5. A running bus has several standing passengers is dangerous, why?

Quick Tests

To make students understand the chapter in a smooth part-by-part manner, Quick Tests have been given in each chapter. These Exercises help students to assess the understanding of related concepts at regular interval.

One Book- Endless Features

to Help you Succeed

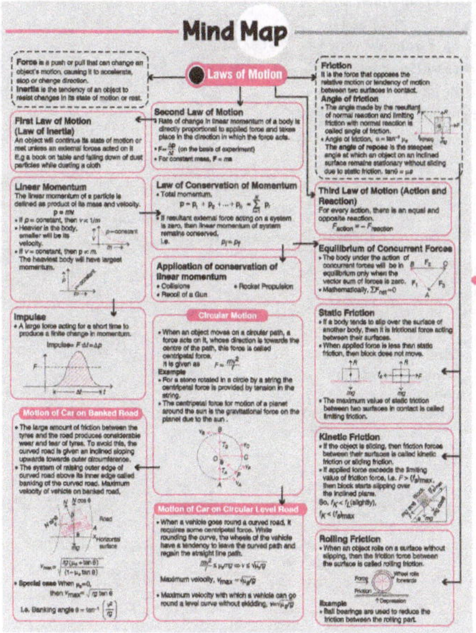

Mind Map

A quick revision visual tool for the complete chapter.

NCERT Exemplar Problems

NCERT Exemplar Problems are considered to be the best problem books for School/Board Examinations. To make students practice of exemplary questions given in this book, each chapter has selected problems from NCERT Exemplar.

Exam Pattern Exercise

To make students completely prepared for examination, this Exercise contains Exam Pattern Questions. This exercise covers all types of questions, like; MCQs, Case Based Questions, Assertion-Reason, VSA, SA & LA Type Questions. All the questions are fully explained helping students to understand, how to write the answers to get full marks in the exam.

8. Conservation of momentum in a collision between particles can be understood from **NCERT Exemplar**
(a) conservation of energy
(b) Newton's first law only
(c) Newton's second law only
(d) both Newton's second and third law

9. A body of mass 2 kg travels according to the law $x(t) = pt + qt^2 + rt^3$ where, $q = 4\ ms^{-2}$, $p = 3\ ms^{-1}$ and $r = 5\ ms^{-3}$. The force acting on the body at $t = 2\ s$ is **NCERT Exemplar**
(a) 136 N (b) 134 N (c) 158 N (d) 68 N

10. A car of mass m starts from rest and acquires a velocity along east, $v = v\hat{i}\ (v > 0)$ in two seconds. Assuming the car moves with uniform acceleration, the force exerted on the car is **NCERT Exemplar**
(a) $\frac{mv}{2}$ eastward and is exerted by the car engine
(b) $\frac{mv}{2}$ eastward and is due to the friction on the tyres exerted by the road
(c) more than $\frac{mv}{2}$ eastward exerted due to the engine and overcomes the friction of the road
(d) $\frac{mv}{2}$ exerted by the engine

EXAM PATTERN QUESTIONS

Objective Type Questions

Multiple Choice Questions (MCQs)

1. Who gave the idea that when a particle is moving with uniform velocity, there is no need of any force, if frictional force is zero?
(a) Aristotle (b) Newton
(c) Galileo (d) Einstein

2. A hockey player is moving northward and suddenly turns westward with the same speed to avoid an opponent. The force that acts on the player is **NCERT Exemplar**
(a) frictional force along westward
(b) muscle force along southward
(c) frictional force along south-west
(d) muscle force along south-west

7. A metre scale is moving with uniform velocity. This implies **NCERT Exemplar**
(a) the force acting on the scale is zero, but a torque about the centre of mass can act on the scale
(b) the force acting on the scale is zero and the torque acting about centre of mass of the scale is also zero
(c) the total force acting on it need not be zero but the torque on it is zero
(d) neither the force nor the torque need to be zero

8. Conservation of momentum in a collision between particles can be understood from **NCERT Exemplar**
(a) conservation of energy
(b) Newton's first law only

One Book- Endless Features

to Help you Succeed

NCERT Questions

To make students completely understand NCERT books, solutions of selected NCERT questions have been given in each chapter.

39. A block of mass 15 kg is placed on a long trolley. The coefficient of static friction between the block and the trolley is 0.18. The trolley accelerates from rest with 0.5 m/s^2 for 20 s and then moves with uniform velocity. Discuss the motion of the block as viewed by

(i) stationary observer on the ground **[1½]**

(ii) an observer moving with the trolley. **NCERT [1½]**

40. Two bodies *A* and *B* of masses 5 kg and 10kg in contact with each other rest on a table against a rigid wall as shown in figure. The coefficient of friction between the bodies and the table is 0.15. A force of 200 N is applied horizontally at *A*.

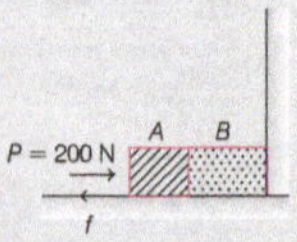

What are (i) the reaction of the partition or wall (ii) the action- reaction forces between *A* and *B*? What happens when the partition is removed? Does the answer to change, when the bodies are in motion? Ignore difference between μ_s and μ_k. **NCERT**

Competency Based Questions

Coverage of competency based questions.

12. The coefficient of friction between tyres and the road is 0.1. Find the maximum speed allowed by traffic police for car to cross a circular turn of radius 10 m to prevent accident. (Take $g = 10 \text{ ms}^{-2}$)

(a) $\sqrt{10} \text{ ms}^{-1}$ (b) $\sqrt{20} \text{ ms}^{-1}$
(c) 5 ms^{-1} (d) 9 ms^{-1}

13. A particle is moving on a circular path of 10 m radius. At any instant of time, its speed is 5 ms^{-1} and the speed is increasing at a rate of 2 ms^{-2}. The magnitude of net acceleration at this instant is

(a) 5 ms^{-2} (b) 2 ms^{-2} (c) 3.2 ms^{-2} (d) 4.3 ms^{-2}

14. A trolley is carrying a box on its surface having coefficient of static friction equal to 0.3. Now, the trolley starts moving with increasing acceleration. Find the maximum acceleration of the trolley so that the box does not slide back on the trolley.

Competency Based Que.

(a) 2 ms^{-2} (b) 3 ms^{-2} (c) 4 ms^{-2} (d) 5 ms^{-2}

SAMPLE QUESTION PAPER 1

A Highly Simulated Sample Question Paper for CBSE Class XI Examination

PHYSICS

Time : 3 Hours **Max. Marks : 70**

General Instructions

1. There are 33 questions in all. All questions are compulsory.
2. This question paper has five sections : Section A, Section B, Section C, Section D and Section E.
3. All the sections are compulsory.
4. Section A contains sixteen questions, twelve MCQ and four Assertion Reasoning based of 1 mark each, **Section B** contains five questions of two marks each, **Section C** contains seven questions of three marks each, **Section D** contains two case study based questions of four marks each and **Section E** contains three long answer questions of five marks each.
5. There is no overall choice. However, an internal choice has been provided in one question in Section B, one question in Section C, one question in each CBQ in Section D and all three questions in Section E. You have to attempt only one of the choices in such questions.
6. Use of calculators is not allowed.
7. You may use the following values of physical constants where ever necessary
   i. $G = 6.67 \times 10^{-11} \text{Nm}^2/\text{kg}^2$
   ii. $R = 8.314 \text{J mol}^{-1}\text{K}^{-1}$
   iii. $k_B = 1.38 \times 10^{-23} \text{J/K}$
   iv. $\sigma = 5.67 \times 10^{-8} \text{Wm}^{-2}\text{K}^{-1}$
   v. $N_A = 6.023 \times 10^{23} \text{mol}^{-1}$

Section-A

1. The displacement-time graphs of two moving particles make angles of ° and ° with the *X*-axis. The ratio of their velocities is

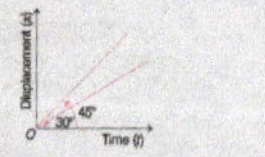

(a) $1:\sqrt{3}$ (b) 1:2 (c) 1:1 (d) $\sqrt{3}:2$

2. Which one of the following statements is true?

(a) A scalar quantity is the one that is conserved in a process
(b) A scalar quantity is the one that can never take negative values
(c) A scalar quantity is the one that does not vary from one point to another in space
(d) A scalar quantity has the same value for observers with different orientation of the axes

3. Conservation of momentum in a collision between particles can be understood from

(a) conservation of energy
(b) Newton's first law only
(c) Newton's second law only
(d) Both Newton's second and third law

4. A ball is travelling with uniform translatory motion. This means that

(a) it is at rest
(b) the path can be a straight line or circular and the ball travels with uniform speed
(c) all parts of the ball have the same velocity (magnitude and direction) and the velocity is constant
(d) the centre of the ball moves with constant velocity and the ball spins about its centre uniformly

Sample Question Papers

To make students practice of examination in real sense, there are 3 Sample Question Papers at the end. All these Sample Questions Papers are exactly prepared on the latest syllabus & pattern of examination.

Latest Course *Structure*

Time: 3 Hrs **Total Marks : 70**

Units	Title	Marks
Unit I	**Physical World and Measurement** Chapter 1 : Units and Measurements	
Unit II	**Kinematics** Chapter 2 : Motion in a Straight Line Chapter 3 : Motion in a Plane	23
Unit III	**Laws of Motion** Chapter 4 : Laws of Motion	
Unit IV	**Work, Energy and Power** Chapter 5 : Work, Energy and Power	
Unit V	**Motion of System of Particles and Rigid Body** Chapter 6 : System of Particles and Rotational Motion	17
Unit VI	**Gravitation** Chapter 7 : Gravitation	
Unit VII	**Properties of Bulk Matter** Chapter 8 : Mechanical Properties of Solids Chapter 9 : Mechanical Properties of Fluids Chapter 10 : Thermal Properties of Matter	
Unit VIII	**Thermodynamics** Chapter 11 : Thermodynamics	20
Unit IX	**Behaviour of Perfect Gases and Kinetic Theory of Gases** Chapter 12 : Kinetic Theory	
Unit X	**Oscillations and Waves** Chapter 13 : Oscillations Chapter 14 : Waves	10
	TOTAL	**70**

UNIT I Physical World and Measurement

Chapter 1 : Units and Measurements

Need for measurement: Units of measurement; systems of units; SI units, fundamental and derived units. significant figures. Determining the uncertainty in result. Dimensions of physical quantities, dimensional analysis and its applications.

UNIT II Kinematics

Chapter 2 : Motion in a Straight Line

Frame of reference, Motion in a straight line: Elementary concepts of differentiation and integration for describing motion, uniform and non-uniform motion, average speed and average velocity and instantaneous velocity, uniformly accelerated motion, velocity - time and position-time graphs. Relations for uniformly accelerated motion (graphical and calculus treatment).

Chapter 3 : Motion in a Plane

Scalar and vector quantities; position and displacement vectors, general vectors and their notations; equality of vectors, multiplication of vectors by a real number; addition and subtraction of vectors, Unit vector; resolution of a vector in a plane, rectangular components, Scalar and Vector product of vectors. Motion in a plane, cases of uniform velocity and uniform acceleration-projectile motion, uniform circular motion.

UNIT III Laws of Motion

Chapter 4 : Laws of Motion

Intuitive concept of force, Inertia, Newton's first law of motion; momentum and Newton's second law of motion; impulse; Newton's third law of motion. Law of conservation of linear momentum and its applications. Equilibrium of concurrent forces, Static and kinetic friction, laws of friction, rolling friction, lubrication. Dynamics of uniform circular motion: Centripetal force, examples of circular motion (vehicle on a level circular road, vehicle on a banked road).

UNIT IV Work, Energy and Power

Chapter 5 : Work, Energy and Power

Work done by a constant force and a variable force; kinetic energy, work-energy theorem, power. Notion of potential energy, potential energy of a spring, conservative forces: non-conservative forces: motion in a vertical circle; elastic and inelastic collisions in one and two dimensions.

UNIT V Motion of System of Particles and Rigid Body

Chapter 6 : System of Particles and Rotational Motion

Centre of mass of a two-particle system, momentum conservation and centre of mass motion. Centre of mass of a rigid body; centre of mass of a uniform rod. Moment of a force, torque, angular momentum, law of conservation of angular momentum and its applications. Equilibrium of rigid bodies, rigid body rotation and equations of rotational motion, comparison of linear and rotational motions. Moment of inertia, radius of gyration, values of moments of inertia for simple geometrical objects (no derivation).

UNIT VI Gravitation

Chapter 7 : Gravitation

Kepler's laws of planetary motion, universal law of gravitation. Acceleration due to gravity and its variation with altitude and depth. Gravitational potential energy and gravitational potential, escape speed, orbital velocity of a satellite, energy of an orbiting satellite.

UNIT VII Properties of Bulk Matter

Chapter 8 : Mechanical Properties of Solids

Elasticity, Stress-strain relationship, Hooke's law, Young's modulus, bulk modulus, shear modulus of rigidity (qualitative idea only), Poisson's ratio; elastic energy. Application of elastic behavior of materials (qualitative idea only).

Chapter 9 : Mechanical Properties of Fluids

Pressure due to a fluid column; Pascal's law and its applications (hydraulic lift and hydraulic brakes), effect of gravity on fluid pressure. Viscosity, Stokes' law, terminal velocity, streamline and turbulent flow, critical velocity, Bernoulli's theorem and its simple applications. Torricelli's law and Dynamic lift. Surface energy and surface tension, angle of contact, excess of pressure across a curved surface, application of surface tension ideas to drops, bubbles and capillary rise.

Chapter 10 : Thermal Properties of Matter

Heat, temperature, thermal expansion; thermal expansion of solids, liquids and gases, anomalous expansion of water; specific heat capacity; *Cp*, *Cv* - calorimetry; change of state - latent heat capacity. Heat transfer-conduction, convection and radiation, thermal conductivity, qualitative ideas of Blackbody radiation, Wein's displacement Law, Stefan's law.

UNIT VIII Thermodynamics

Chapter 11 : Thermodynamics

Thermal equilibrium and definition of temperature, zeroth law of thermodynamics, heat, work and internal energy. First law of thermodynamics, Second law of thermodynamics, Thermodynamic state variable and equation of state, Change of condition of gaseous states of matter, change of condition of gaseous state-isothermal, adiabatic, reversible, irreversible and cyclic processes.

UNIT IX Behaviour of Perfect Gases and Kinetic Theory of Gases

Chapter 12 : Kinetic Theory

Equation of state of a perfect gas, work done in compressing a gas. Kinetic theory of gases - assumptions, concept of pressure. Kinetic interpretation of temperature; rms speed of gas molecules; degrees of freedom, law of equi-partition of energy (statement only) and application to specific heat capacities of gases; concept of mean free path, Avogadro's number.

UNIT X Oscillations and Waves

Chapter 13 : Oscillations

Periodic motion - time period, frequency, displacement as a function of time, periodic functions and their applications. Simple harmonic motion (SHM), uniform circular motion and its equations of motion; phase; oscillations of a loaded spring-restoring force and force constant; energy in SHM Kinetic and potential energies; simple pendulum derivation of expression for its time period.

Chapter 14 : Waves

Wave Motion : Transverse and longitudinal waves, speed of travelling wave, displacement relation for a progressive wave, principle of superposition of waves, reflection of waves, standing waves in strings and organ pipes, fundamental mode and harmonics, Beats.

01

CHAPTER

Measurement is defined as the process of comparison of an unknown quantity with a known or standard Quantity.
Without measurement, any natural phenomena cannot be properly described.

Units and Measurements

▼ **YOUR STUDY GOALS**

▼ **YOUR PRACTICE GOAL**

- Objective Type Questions (26 Qs, MCQs, Matching & A-R)
- Case Based Questions (4)
- Subjective Questions (5 VSAs, 10 SAs, 5 LAs)
- Numerical Problems (26)

1.1 Physical Quantities

All those quantities which can be defined and measured directly or indirectly are called physical quantities. e.g. Length, time, mass, force, etc.

Physical quantities can be further divided into two types

(i) Fundamental Quantities

Those physical quantities which are independent of other physical quantities are called **fundamental quantities** or **base quantities.**

There are seven fundamental or base quantities. These are mass, length, time, temperature, luminous intensity, electric current and the amount of substance.

(ii) Derived Quantities

Those quantities which can be derived from the fundamental quantities are called **derived quantities.** e.g. Velocity, acceleration, linear momentum, etc.

1.2 Physical Units

To measure a physical quantity, a standard is needed, which is called **unit** of that physical quantity.

The result of a measurement of a physical quantity is expressed by a number (numerical value) accompanied by a unit. i.e

Physical quantity = Magnitude × unit

or $$Q = n \times u$$

where, n represents the numerical value and u represents the unit.

Thus while expressing definite amount of physical quantity, as the unit (u) changes, the magnitude (n) will also change but product nu will remain same.

i.e. $\boldsymbol{nu}$ **= constant** or $\boldsymbol{n_1u_1 = n_2u_2}$ **constant.**

Hence $n \propto \frac{1}{u}$, it shows that smaller the unit of physical quantity, larger will be the magnitude and *vice-versa*.

The physical unit can be classified into two ways that can be given as below.

Fundamental Units

The units of fundamental quantities or base quantities, i.e. length, mass and time are called **fundamental units** or **base units.**

Derived Units

The units of measurement of all other physical quantities which can be obtained from fundamental units are called **derived units.**

e.g. $$\text{Speed} = \frac{\text{Distance}}{\text{Time}} = \frac{\text{m}}{\text{s}} = \text{ms}^{-1}$$

Unit of speed (i.e. ms^{-1}) is a derived unit, because it is measured in terms of fundamental units of length and time.

System of Units

A system of units is the complete set of units, both fundamental and derived for all kinds of physical quantities.

The common systems of units used in mechanics are given below.

(i) **FPS System** It is the British engineering system of units, which uses **foot** as the unit of length, **pound** as the unit of mass and **second** as the unit of time.

(ii) **CGS System** It is based on Gaussian system of units, which uses **centimetre, gram** and **second** for length, mass and time, respectively.

(iii) **MKS System** It uses **metre, kilogram** and **second** as the fundamental units of length, mass and time, respectively.

(iv) **International System of Units** (**SI Units**) The system of units, which is accepted internationally for measurement is the System International Units (French for International System of Units) abbreviated as SI.

> **TEACHER TIP**
>
> The advantages of MKS system is that some of the derived units are of convenient size.
>
> The FPS system is not a metric system. This system is not in much use these days.
>
> The drawback of CGS system is that many of the derived units on this system are inconveniently small.

In SI system, there are **seven base units** and **two supplementary units** as listed below.

Basic quantities and SI units

Base quantity	SI Unit	Symbol	Definition
Length	metre	m	The metre is the length of the path travelled by light in vacuum during a time interval of 1/299,792,458 of a second.
Mass	kilogram	kg	The kilogram is equal to the mass of the international prototype of the kilogram (a platinum-iridium alloy cylinder) kept at international Bureau of Weights and Measures at Sevres, near Paris, France.
Time	second	s	The second is the duration of 9,192,631,770 periods of the radiation corresponding to the transition between the two hyperfine levels of the ground state of the cesium-133 atom.

Base quantity	SI Unit	Symbol	Definition
Electric current	ampere	A	The ampere is that constant current which, if maintained in two straight parallel conductors of infinite length, of negligible circular cross-section and placed 1 m apart in vacuum, would produce a force between these conductors equal to 2×10^{-7} N/m of length.
Thermodynamic temperature	kelvin	K	The kelvin is the fraction 1/273.16 of the thermodynamic temperature of the triple point of water.
Amount of substance	mole	mol	The mole is the amount of substance of a system which contains as many elementary entities as there are atoms in 0.012 kg of carbon-12.
Luminous intensity	candela	cd	The candela is the luminous intensity in a given direction of a source that emits monochromatic radiation of frequency 540×10^{12} Hz and that has a radiant intensity in that direction of 1/683 watt per steradian.

Two supplementary quantities and their SI units

Supplementary quantity	SI Unit	Symbol	Definition
Plane angle	radian	rad	One radian is the angle subtended at the centre of a circle by an arc equal in length to the radius of the circle. i.e. $d\theta = \frac{ds}{r}$ 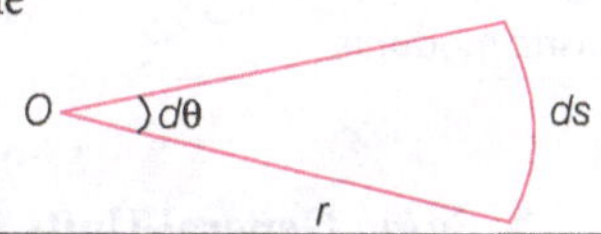
Solid angle	steradian	sr	One steradian is the solid angle subtended at the centre of a sphere, by that surface of the sphere, which is equal in area to the square of radius of the sphere. i.e. $d\Omega = \left(\frac{dA\cos\theta}{r^2}\right)$ 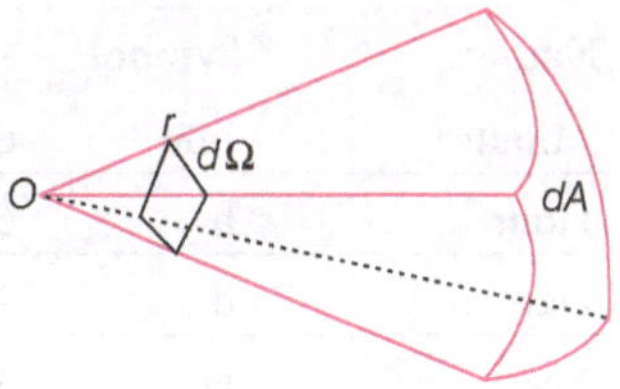

SI derived units with special names

Physical Quantity	SI Unit		
	Name	Symbol	Expression in terms of SI base units
Frequency	Hertz	Hz	s^{-1}
Force	Newton	N	$kg\,m\,s^{-2}$ or $kg\,m/s^2$
Pressure, stress	Pascal	Pa	$kg\,m^{-1}s^{-2}$ or $kg/s^2\,m$
Energy, work, quantity of heat	Joule	J	$kg\,m^2s^{-2}$ or $kg\,m^2/s^2$
Power, radiant flux	Watt	W	$kg\,m^2\,s^{-3}$ or $kg\,m^2/s^3$
Quantity of electricity, electric charge	Coulomb	C	As^{-1}
Electric potential, potential difference, electromotive force	Volt	V	$kg\,m^2\,s^{-3}\,A^{-1}$ or $kg\,m^2/s^3\,A$
Capacitance	Farad	F	$A^2\,s^4\,kg^{-1}m^{-2}$
Electric resistance	Ohm	Ω	$kg\,m^2\,s^{-3}A^{-2}$
Conductance	Siemens	S	$m^{-2}\,kg^{-1}s^3\,A^2$

Some SI derived units expressed through SI units

Physical quantity	SI Unit Name	Symbol	Expression in terms of SI base units
Magnetic moment	Joule per tesla	JT^{-1}	Am^2
Dipole moment	Coulomb metre	C m	s A m
Dynamic viscosity	Poiseuille or pascal second or newton second per square metre	Pl or Pa s or $N\,s\,m^{-2}$	$m^{-1}\,kg\,s^{-1}$
Torque, couple, moment of force	Newton metre	N m	$m^2\,kg\,s^{-2}$
Surface tension	Newton per metre	N/m	$kg\,s^{-2}$
Thermal conductivity	Watt per metre kelvin	$W\,m^{-1}\,K^{-1}$	$m\,kg\,s^{-3}\,K^{-1}$
Energy density	Joule per cubic metre	J/m^3	$kg\,m^{-1}\,s^{-2}$
Electric field strength	Volt per metre	V/m	$m\,kg\,s^{-3}\,A^{-1}$
Electric charge density	Coulomb per cubic metre	C/m^3	$m^{-3}\,A\,s$
Compressibility	Per pascal	Pa^{-1}	$m\,kg^{-1}\,s^2$
Elastic modulus	Newton per square metre	N/m^2 or $N\,m^{-2}$	$kg\,m^{-1}\,s^{-2}$

Some General Units (Outside from SI)

Name	Symbol	Value in SI Unit
Minute	min	60 s
Hour	h	60 min = 3600 s
Day	d	24 h = 86400 s
Year	yr	$365.25\text{ d} = 3.156 \times 10^7$ s
Degree	°	$1° = (\pi/180)$ rad
Litre	L	$1\text{ dm}^3 = 10^{-3}\text{ m}^3$
Tonne	t	10^3 kg
Carat	c	200 mg
Bar	bar	$0.1\text{ MPa} = 10^5$ Pa
Curie	Ci	$3.7 \times 10^{10} s^{-1}$
Roentgen	R	2.58×10^{-4} C/kg
Quintal	q	100 kg
Barn	b	$100\text{ fm}^2 = 10^{-28} m^2$
Area	a	$1\text{ dam}^2 = 10^2 m^2$
Hectare	ha	$1\text{ hm}^2 = 10^4 m^2$
Standard atmospheric pressure	atm	$101325\text{ Pa} = 1.013 \times 10^5$ Pa

Rules for Writing SI Units

- Small letters are used for symbols of units.
- Symbols are not followed by a full stop.
- The initial letter of a symbol is capital only when the unit is named after a scientist.
- The full name of a unit always begins with a small letter even, if it has been named after a scientist.
- Symbols do not take plural form.

Example 1. **How many centimeters are in 1.23×10^{-6} kilometer ?**

Sol. We know that,

1 km = 1000 m

1 m = 100 cm

To find out centimeteres in 1.23×10^{-6} km

$1.23 \times 10^{-6} \times 1000$ m /km $\times$ 100 cm/m

$= 1.23 \times 10^{-6} \times 1000000 = 0.123$ cm

Example 2. **Convert the following measurement into meter (m).**

(a) 280 cm (b) 56100 mm (c) 3.7 km

Sol. (a) 2.8 m (b) 56.1 m (c) 3700m

Order of Magnitude

If we express the magnitude of any physical quantity to its nearest power of 10, then it is called the order of magnitude of that quantity.

For example, a measurement is expressed as then 10^n, then n is the order of magnitude of measurement.

To find the order of magnitude the following rule is used. The quantity less than or equal to $\sqrt{10} = 3.16$ is written as 10^0, while the quantity between $\sqrt{10}$ and 10 is written as 10^1. For example.

$$0.000025 = 2.5 \times 10^{-5} \approx 10^{-5} \quad [\text{because } 2.5 < \sqrt{10}]$$

and $35000 = 3.5 \times 10^4 \approx 10^1 \times 10^4 \approx 10^5$ $[\text{because } 3.5 > \sqrt{10}]$

1.3 Significant Figures

The number of digit in a given value or a measurement necessary to decide the accuracy or precision of measurement are called significant figure or significant digit.

These numbers are sufficient to convey accurate information.

The digits that are known reliably plus the first uncertain digit are known as significant digit or significant figure.

e.g. When a measured distance is reported to be 374.5 m, it has four significant figures 3, 7, 4 and 5. The figures 3, 7, 4 are certain and reliable, while the digit 5 is uncertain.

The rules for determining the number of significant figures are given below.

***Rule* 1** All non-zero digits are significant.

e.g. $x = 1234$ has four significant figures.

***Rule* 2** All the zeros between two non-zero digits are significant.

e.g. $x = 1007$ has four significant figures and $x = 10.07$ also contains four significant figures.

***Rule* 3** If the number is less than one, the zero(s) on the right of decimal point and to the left of first non-zero digit are not significant.

e.g. In $\underline{0}.\underline{0}\,\underline{0}\,5704$, the underlined zeros are not significant. The zero between 7 and 4 is significant. The number of significant figures is 4.

***Rule* 4** In a number without a decimal point, the terminal or trailing zeros are not significant.

e.g. $x = 3210$ has three significant figures, the trailing zero is not significant.

***Rule* 5** The trailing zero(s) in a number with a decimal point are significant.

e.g. 3.500 has four significant figures.

***Rule* 6** The multiplying or dividing factors, which are neither rounded numbers nor numbers representing measured values are exact. They have infinite number of significant digits as per the condition.

e.g. In radius, $r = \frac{d}{2}$ and circumference, $s = 2\pi r$, the factors 2 is an exact number. It can be written as 2.0, 2.00 and 2.000, etc., as required.

***Rule* 7** The number of significant figures does not depend on the system of units, so 16.4 cm, 0.164 m and 0.000164 km, all have three significant figures.

TEACHER TIP

Change of unit should not change number of significant digits.

Example, 4.700 = 470.0 cm = 4700 mm. In this, first two quantities have 4 but third quantity has 2 significant figures.

Use scientific notation to report measurements Numbers should be expressed in powers of 10 like $a \times 10^b$, where b is called **order of magnitude.**

Example, $4.700\text{m} = 4.700 \times 10^{-2}\text{cm}$
$= 4.700 \times 10^3\text{mm} = 4.700 \times 10^{-3}\text{ km}$

In all the above, since power of 10 are irrelevant, number of significant figures are 4.

Example 3. **Write down the number of significant figures in the following.**

(i) 0.072 **(ii) 12.000**
(iii) 0.060 **(iv) 3.08×10^{11}**
(v) 1.2340 **(vi) 0.04**
(vii) 5000

Sol. (i) Two (ii) Five
(iii) Two (iv) Three
(v) Five (vi) One
(vii) One

1.4 Rounding Off

The result of computation with approximate numbers, which contain more than one uncertain digit, should be rounded off. While rounding off measurements, we use the following rules by convention.

***Rule* 1** If the digit to be dropped is less than 5, then the preceding digit is left unchanged.
e.g. $x = 7.82$ is rounded off to 7.8.

***Rule* 2** If the digit to be dropped is more than 5, then the preceding digit is raised by one.
e.g. $x = 6.87$ is rounded off to 6.9.

***Rule* 3** If the digit to be dropped is 5 followed by digits other than zero, then the preceding digit is raised by one.
e.g. $x = 16.351$ is rounded off to 16.4.

***Rule* 4** If the digit to be dropped is 5 or 5 followed by zeros, then the preceding digit is left unchanged, if it is even.
e.g. $x = 3.250$ becomes 3.2 on rounding off.

***Rule* 5** If the digit to be dropped is 5 or 5 followed by zeros, then the preceding digits is raised by one, if it is odd.
e.g. $x = 3.750$ is rounded off to 3.8.

Example 4. Round off the following number as indicated.

(i) 18.35 upto 3 digits = 18.4
(ii) 143.45 upto 4 digits = 143.4
(iii) 189.67 upto 3 digits = 190
(iv) 321.1355 upto 5 digits = 321.14
(v) 31.325×10^{-5} upto 4 digits = 31.32×10^{-5}
(vi) 101.55×10^{6} upto 4 digits = 101.6×10^{6}

Rules for Arithmetical Operations with Significant Figures

Addition and Subtraction

The result should have the same number of significant figures, after rounding-off as the reading, which has the least number of significant digit.

e.g. $2.1\text{m} + 1.78\text{ m} + 2.046\text{ m} = 5.926$

which is rounded off to 5.9 m.

Since, the least precise value is 2.1 m which has 2 significant figures. So the answer will be rounded such that it also has 2 significant digits, i.e. 5.9.

Similarly, if $x = 12.587$ m and $y = 12.5$ m, then $(x - y)$ is $12.587 - 12.5 = 0.087$ m, which is rounded off to 0.1 m.

Multiplication and Division

In multiplication or division, the final result should retain as many significant figures, as are there in the original number with the least significant figures.

e.g. The speed of light is 3.00×10^{8} m/s and one year has 3.1557×10^{7} s, then light year is given by

$$= 3.00 \times 10^{8} \times 3.155 \times 10^{7}$$
$$= 9.4685 \times 10^{15} \text{ m} = 9.5 \times 10^{15} \text{ m}$$

Rounded off upto 2 significant figures

Example 5. Solve the following and express the result to an appropriate number of significant figures.

(i) Add 6.2 g, 4.33 g and 17.456 g
(ii) Subtract 63.54 kg from 187.2 kg
(iii) $75.5 \times 125.2 \times 0.51$
(iv) $\dfrac{2.13 \times 24.78}{458.2}$

Sol. (i) $6.2\text{ g} + 4.33\text{ g} + 17.456\text{ g} = 27.986\text{ g} = 28.0\text{ g}$

Rounded off to first decimal place

(ii) $187.2\text{ kg} - 63.54\text{ kg} = 123.66\text{ kg} = 123.7\text{ kg}$

Rounded off to first decimal place

(iii) $75.5 \times 125.2 \times 0.51 = 4820.826 = 4800$

Rounded off upto two significant figures

(iv) $\dfrac{2.13 \times 24.78}{458.2} = 0.115193 = 0.115$

Rounded off to three significant figures

Rules for Determining Uncertainty in the Results of Arithmetic Calculations

***Rule* 1** Suppose, we use a metre scale to measure length and breadth of a thin rectangular sheets as 15.4 cm and 10.2 cm, respectively.

Each measurement has three significant figures and a precision upto first place of decimal. Therefore,

we can write length $(l) = (15.4 \pm 0.1)$ cm

$$= 15.4 \pm \left(\frac{0.1}{15.4} \times 100\right)$$
$$= 15.4 \text{ cm} \pm 0.6\%$$

Similarly, breadth $(b) = (10.2 \pm 0.1)$ cm

$$=10.2 \pm \left(\frac{0.1 \times 100}{10.2}\right)\%$$

$$= 10.2\text{ cm} \pm 1\%$$

Thus, the error of the product i.e. area of thin sheet is $15.4 \times 10.2 \pm (0.6 + 1.0)\text{ cm}^2$

$$= 157.08\text{ cm}^2 \pm 1.6\%$$

$$= 157.08\text{ cm}^2 \pm \left(\frac{1.6}{100} \times 157.08\right)\text{cm}^2$$

$$= (157.08 \pm 2.51)\text{ cm}^2$$

As per rule, the final value of area can contain only three significant figures and error can contain only one significant figures, we can write the final result as $A = (157 \pm 3)\text{ cm}^2$.

***Rule* 2** If a set of experimental data is specified to n significant figures, then a result obtained by combining the data will also be valid to n significant figures.

e.g. $x = 13.7$ m and $y = 8.08$ m, both have three significant figures.

Now, $x - y = 13.7 - 8.08 = 5.62$ m

So, the final result should retain as many decimal places as, there in the number with least decimal places. Therefore, rounding off to one place of a decimal, we get $x - y = 5.6$ cm

***Rule* 3** The relative error of a value of number specified to n significant figures depend not only on n, but also on the number itself.

e.g. $m_1 = (1.04 \pm 0.01)$ kg

and $m_2 = (9.24 \pm 0.01)$ kg

Relative error in 1.04 kg is

$$\pm\left(\frac{0.01}{1.04}\right) \times 100 = \pm 1\%$$

Similarly, the relative error in 9.24 kg is

$$\pm\left(\frac{0.01}{9.24}\right) \times 100 = \pm 0.1\%$$

Thus, the relative error depends on the number itself.

***Rule* 4** In a multi-step computation, the intermediate results should be calculated to one more significant figure in every measurement, then the number of digits in the least precise measurement.

e.g. $x = 9.58$ has three significant digits. Now, reciprocal of x is $\frac{1}{x} = \frac{1}{9.58} = 0.104$, rounded off to three significant digits. When we take reciprocal of 0.104, we get 9.62, rounded off to three significant digits.

However, if we calculate $\frac{1}{x} = \frac{1}{9.58} = 0.1044$, rounded off to four significant figures, then $\frac{1}{0.1044} = 9.58$, rounded off to three significant digits.

Thus, retaining one more extra digits in intermediate steps of complex calculations would avoid additional errors in the process of rounding off the numbers.

Example 6. **The length, breadth and height of a rectangular block of wood were measured to be**

$l = 12.13 \pm 0.02$ cm, $b = 8.16 \pm 0.01$ cm

and $h = 3.46 \pm 0.01$ cm

Determine the percentage error in the volume of the block.

Sol. Volume of block, $V = lbh$

The percentage error in the volume is given by

$$\frac{\Delta V}{V} \times 100 = \left(\frac{\Delta l}{l} + \frac{\Delta b}{b} + \frac{\Delta h}{h}\right) \times 100$$

$$= \left(\frac{0.02}{12.13} + \frac{0.01}{8.16} + \frac{0.01}{3.46}\right) \times 100$$

$$= \frac{200}{1213} + \frac{100}{816} + \frac{100}{346}$$

$$= 0.1649 + 0.1225 + 0.2890$$

$$= 0.58\% \quad \text{Rounded off to two significant figures}$$

Quick Test 1

Conceptual Questions

1. Is it possible to have length and velocity both as fundamental quantities? Why?

2. How may supplementary units are listed in SI system?

3. If all measurements in an experiment are taken upto same number of significant figures, then which measurement is responsible for maximum error?

4. State the following statement with suitable example. The trailing zero in a number with a decimal point are significant.

Numerical Questions

5. A vehicle moving with a speed of 18 kmh^{-1} covers .... m in 1s.

6. State the number of significant figures in the following. NCERT

(i) 0.007 m^2 (ii) 2.64×10^{24} kg

(iii) 0.2370 g/cm^3 (iv) 6.320 J

(v) 6.032 N/m^2 (vi) 0.0006032 m^2

7. The length, breadth and thickness of a rectangular sheet of metal are 4.234 m, 1.005 m and 2.01 cm, respectively. Give the area and volume of the sheet to correct significant figures. NCERT

Answers

5. 5 7. 8.72 m^2, 0.085 m^3

For Solutions, See QR Code on Pg. 26

1.5 Dimensions of a Physical Quantity

The dimensions of a physical quantity are the powers (or exponents) to which the units of base quantities are raised to represent a derived unit of that quantity.

There are seven base quantities and are represented with **square brackets** [ ] such as length [L], mass [M], time [T], electric current [A], thermodynamic temperature [K], luminous intensity [Cd] and amount of substances [mol].

For example

- The volume occupied by an object is expressed as the product of length, so its dimension is given by
$$V = [L] \times [L] \times [L] = [L^3]$$
As there is no mass and time in volume, so the dimension of volume is expressed as $V = [M^0L^3T^0]$
- Similarly, for force, it is the product of mass and acceleration. It can be expressed as
$$F = \text{mass} \times \text{acceleration}$$
$$= \text{mass} \times \frac{\text{length}}{(\text{time})^2}$$

$\therefore$ The dimension of force is given by
$$F = [M] \times \frac{[L]}{[T]^2} = [MLT^{-2}]$$

Note Using the square bracket [ ], round a quantity means that we are dealing with the **'dimensions of '** the quantity.

Dimensional Formulae and Dimensional Equations

The expression which shows how and which of the fundamental quantities represent the dimension of the physical quantity is called the **dimensional formula** of the given physical quantity.

e.g. Some of the dimensional formulae are as given below.

$$\text{Acceleration} = [M^0L^1T^{-2}]$$
$$\text{Mass density} = [ML^{-3}T^0]$$
$$\text{Volume} = [M^0L^3T^0]$$

The equation obtained by equating a physical quantity with its dimensional formula is called the **dimensional equation** of the given physical quantity.

e.g. Some of the dimensional equations are as given below.

$$\text{Linear momentum} = \text{Mass} \times \text{Velocity} = [M^1L^1T^{-1}]$$
$$\text{Impulse} = \text{Force} \times \text{Time} = [M^1L^1T^{-1}]$$
$$\text{Moment of Inertia} = \text{Mass} \times (\text{Radius of gyration})^2 = [M^1L^2T^0]$$

TEACHER TIP

To solve Numerical Problems

First read the problem carefully and then find out whether we have given with the formulae or any law to describe in it.

Write the formulae of a physical quantity for which the dimensions to be known.

Convert the formulae of derived physical quantity into fundamental quantities, e.g. acceleration
$$= \frac{\text{velocity}}{\text{time}} = \frac{\text{length}}{\text{time}^2}$$

Write the corresponding symbols for fundamental quantities, e.g. mass = [M], length = [L], time = [T], etc.

Make proper algebraic combination and get the result.

Try to arrange the dimensions in order i.e. [M], [L], [T] .....

Example 7. Find out the dimensions of universal gravitational constant used in Newton's law of gravitation.

Sol. According to Newton's law of gravitation, the force F, between two masses m_1 and m_2 separated by distance r can be given as

$$F = G\frac{m_1 m_2}{r^2}$$

where, G = universal gravitational constant

$$G = \frac{Fr^2}{m_1 m_2}$$

$$\Rightarrow \quad G = \frac{\text{newton} \times (\text{metre})^2}{(\text{kg})^2}$$

$$G = \frac{(\text{mass} \times \text{acceleration}) \times (\text{metre})^2}{(\text{mass})^2}$$

$$= \frac{1}{\text{mass}}\left(\frac{\text{change in velocity}}{\text{time}}\right) \times (\text{length})^2$$

$$G = \frac{(\text{length})^2}{\text{mass} \times \text{time}} \times \frac{\text{distance}}{\text{time}}$$

$$G = \frac{[\text{L}]^2}{[\text{M}] \times [\text{T}]} \times \frac{[\text{L}]}{[\text{T}]} = [\text{M}^{-1}\text{L}^3\text{T}^{-2}]$$

Example 8. Derive the dimensional formula of physical quantities.

(i) Tension **(ii) Velocity gradient**

(iii) Linear mass density **(iv) Impulse**

Sol. (i) Tension = Force = Mass × Acceleration

$$[\text{M}] \times [\text{LT}^{-2}] = [\text{MLT}^{-2}]$$

(ii) Velocity gradient $= \dfrac{\text{Velocity}}{\text{Distance}} = \dfrac{[\text{LT}^{-1}]}{[\text{L}]} = [\text{T}^{-1}]$

(iii) Linear mass density $= \dfrac{\text{Mass}}{\text{Length}} = \dfrac{[\text{M}]}{[\text{L}]} = [\text{ML}^{-1}]$

(iv) Impulse = Force × Time = $[\text{MLT}^{-2}] \times [\text{T}] = [\text{MLT}^{-1}]$

Dimensional Variables and Constants

In Physics, we come across many variables and constants. Some of them have dimensions but others are dimensionless. They may be divided into four categories.

- **Dimensional Variables** Physical quantities, that possess dimensions and have variable values are called dimensional variables. For example, length, velocity, acceleration, etc.
- **Non-dimensional Variables** Physical quantities that have no dimensions, but have variable values are called non-dimensional variables. For example, specific gravity, strain, refractive index, etc.
- **Dimensional Constant** Physical quantities that posses dimensions and have constant values are called dimensional constants. For example, gravitational constant, Planck's constant, etc.
- **Non-Dimensional Constant** Physical quantities which have constant values and also have no dimensions are called non-dimensional constant. For example, pure numbers 1, 2, 3, 4………, and mathematical constant π, etc.

1.6 Dimensional Analysis and Its Applications

The dimensional analysis helps us in deducing the relations among different physical quantities and checking the accuracy, derivation and dimensional consistency or its homogeneity of various numerical expressions.

Its applications are as given below

1. Checking the Dimensional Consistency of Equations

The magnitudes of physical quantities may be added together or subtracted from one another only if they have the same dimensions.

The **principle of homogeneity of dimension** states that a physical quantity equation will be dimensionally correct, if the dimensions of all the terms occurring on both sides of the equation are same.

e.g. Let us check the dimensional consistency of the equation of motion as $s = ut + \frac{1}{2}at^2$

Dimensions of different terms are

$$[s] = [\text{L}]$$

$$[ut] = [\text{LT}^{-1}]\ [\text{T}] = [\text{L}]$$

$$\left[\frac{1}{2}at^2\right] = [\text{LT}^{-2}][\text{T}^2] = [\text{L}]$$

As all the terms on both sides of the equations have the same dimensions, so the given equation is dimensionally correct

Example 9. Check whether the given equation is dimensionally correct $\frac{1}{2}mv^2 = mgh$. NCERT

Sol. The dimensions of LHS = $[\text{M}]\ [\text{LT}^{-1}]^2 = [\text{ML}^2\text{T}^{-2}]$

The dimensions of RHS = $[\text{M}]\ [\text{LT}^{-2}][\text{L}] = [\text{ML}^2\text{T}^{-2}]$

The dimensions of LHS and RHS are same, and hence the consistency is verified.

Example 10. Check the dimensional consistency of the following equations.

(i) de-Broglie wavelength, $\lambda = \frac{h}{mv}$

(ii) Escape velocity, $v = \sqrt{\frac{2GM}{R}}$

Sol. (i) Given, $\lambda = \frac{h}{mv}$

LHS as wavelength is a distance, $\lambda = [L]$

Also, RHS $= \frac{h}{mv}$

$$= \frac{\text{Planck's constant}}{\text{Mass} \times \text{Velocity}}$$

$$= \frac{[ML^2T^{-1}]}{[M] \times [LT^{-1}]} = [L]$$

$\therefore$ LHS = RHS

Hence, the given equation is dimensionally correct.

(ii) Here, $v = \sqrt{\frac{2GM}{R}}$

LHS $= v = [LT^{-1}]$, RHS $= \left[\frac{2GM}{R}\right]^{1/2}$

$$G = [M^{-1}L^3T^{-2}], R = [L], M = [M]$$

$$= \left[\frac{M^{-1}L^3T^{-2}M}{L}\right]^{1/2}$$

$$= [L^2T^{-2}]^{1/2} = [LT^{-1}]$$

$\therefore$ Dimensions of LHS = Dimensions of RHS

Hence, the equation is dimensionally correct.

2. Conversion of units from One System into Another

As we know numerical value is inversely proportional to the size of the unit but the magnitude of the physical quantity remains the same, whatever be the system of its measurement.

i.e. $$n_1u_1 = n_2u_2$$

$\Rightarrow$ $$n_2 = \frac{n_1u_1}{u_2} \quad \ldots\text{(i)}$$

where, u_1 and u_2 are two units of measurement of the quantity and n_1 and n_2 are their respective numerical values.

If M_1, L_1 and T_1 are the fundamental units of mass, length and time in one system and while for other system, M_2, L_2 and T_2 are the fundamental units of mass, length and time, then $u_1 = [M_1^aL_1^bT_1^c]$ and $u_2 = [M_2^aL_2^bT_2^c]$

From Eq. (i), $$n_2 = \frac{n_1[M_1^aL_1^bT_1^c]}{[M_2^aL_2^bT_2^c]}$$

$$n_2 = n_1\left[\frac{M_1}{M_2}\right]^a\left[\frac{L_1}{L_2}\right]^b\left[\frac{T_1}{T_2}\right]^c$$

Example 11. A calorie is a unit of heat or energy and it equals about 4.2 J, where $1\text{ J} = 1\text{ kg-m}^2/\text{s}^2$. Suppose we employ a system of units in which the unit of mass equals α kg, the unit of length is β m, the unit of time is γ s. Show that a calorie has a magnitude $4.2\ \alpha^{-1}\beta^{-2}\gamma^2$ in terms of new units. NCERT

Sol. The dimensional formula of energy $= [ML^2T^{-2}]$

Let M_1, L_1, T_1 and M_2, L_2, T_2 are the units of mass, length and time in given two systems.

$\therefore$ $$M_1 = 1\text{ kg}, M_2 = \alpha\text{ kg}$$

$$L_1 = 1\text{ m}, L_2 = \beta\text{ m}, T_1 = 1\text{ s}, T_2 = \gamma\text{ s}$$

For any physical quantity, the product of its magnitude and unit is always constant.

$$n_1u_1 = n_2u_2$$

or $$n_2 = n_1\frac{u_1}{u_2} = 4.2 \times \frac{[M_1L_1^2T_1^{-2}]}{[M_2L_2^2T_2^{-2}]}$$

$$= 4.2\left[\frac{M_1}{M_2}\right] \times \left[\frac{L_1}{L_2}\right]^2 \times \left[\frac{T_1}{T_2}\right]^{-2}$$

$$= 4.2\left[\frac{1}{\alpha}\text{kg}\right] \times \left[\frac{1}{\beta}\text{m}\right]^2 \times \left[\frac{1}{\gamma}\text{s}\right]^{-2}$$

$$n_2 = 4.2\alpha^{-1}\beta^{-2}\gamma^2 \text{ new unit}$$

$\therefore$ $$1\text{ cal} = 4.2\alpha^{-1}\beta^{-2}\gamma^2 \text{ new unit}$$

Example 12. Find the value of 60 J per min on a system that has 100 g, 100 cm and 1 min as the base units.

Sol. Given, $P = \frac{60\text{ J}}{1\text{ min}} = \frac{60\text{ J}}{60\text{ s}} = 1\text{ W}$, which is the SI unit of power

Dimensional formula of power is $[ML^2T^{-3}]$.

$\therefore$ $a = 1, b = 2$ and $c = -3$

SI	New System
$n_1 = 1$	$n_2 = ?$
$M_1 = 1\text{ kg} = 1000\text{ g}$	$M_2 = 100\text{ g}$
$L_1 = 1\text{ m} = 100\text{ cm}$	$L_2 = 100\text{ cm}$
$T_1 = 1\text{s}$	$T_2 = 1\text{min} = 60\text{ s}$

$$n_2 = n_1\left[\frac{M_1}{M_2}\right]^a\left[\frac{L_1}{L_2}\right]^b\left[\frac{T_1}{T_2}\right]^c$$

$$= 1\left[\frac{1000}{100}\right]^1\left[\frac{100}{100}\right]^2\left[\frac{1}{60}\right]^{-3} = 2.16 \times 10^6$$

$\therefore$ $60\text{ J min}^{-1} = 2.16 \times 10^6$ new units of power.

3. Deducing Relation among the Physical Quantities

The method of dimensions is used to deduce the relation among the physical quantities. We should know the dependence of the physical quantity on other quantities.

We will explain with the following illustration.

Consider a simple pendulum having a bob attached to a string that oscillates under the action of the force of gravity.

Suppose, the time period t of oscillation of the simple pendulum depends on its length (l), mass of the bob (m) and acceleration due to gravity (g).

Let $$t = k m^a l^b g^c \quad \text{...(i)}$$

where a, b, c are the unknown powers and k is dimensionless constant of proportionality.

Considering dimensions on both sides in terms of M, L, T, we get

$$[M^0L^0T^1] = [M^aL^b][LT^{-2}]^c$$
$$= [M^aL^{b+c}T^{-2c}]$$

Applying the principle of homogeneity of dimensions, we get

$$a = 0, -2c = 1$$

$\Rightarrow$ $c = \frac{-1}{2}$

and $b + c = 0$

$\Rightarrow$ $b = -c$

$\Rightarrow$ $b = \frac{1}{2}$

Substituting the values of a, b and c in Eq.(i), we get

$$t = k m^0 l^{1/2} g^{-1/2}$$
$$t = k\sqrt{\frac{l}{g}}$$

So, dimensional analysis is very useful in deducing relations among the interdependent physical quantities.

It can only test the dimensional validity but not the exact relationship between physical quantities in any given equation.

Example 13. If velocity of sound v in a gas depends on its elasticity (E) and density (ρ), derive the relation for the velocity of sound in a medium by the method of dimensions.

Sol. Velocity (v) $\propto$ (Elasticity)^a (Density)^b

$$v = KE^a \rho^b \quad \text{...(i)}$$

where, K is a dimensionless proportionality constant.

writing dimensions of both sides of Eq. (i)

$$[M^0L^1T^{-1}] = K[ML^{-1}T^{-2}]^a[M^1L^{-3}]^b$$
$$[M^0L^1T^{-1}] = K[M^{a+b}L^{-a-3b}T^{-2a}]$$

Comparing powers of M, L and T, we get

$$a + b = 0$$
$$-a - 3b = 1$$
$$-2a = -1 \Rightarrow a = 1/2$$
$$\frac{1}{2} + b = 0, \Rightarrow b = -\frac{1}{2}$$

Eq. (i) becomes,

$$v = KE^{1/2}\rho^{-1/2}$$

or $$v = K\sqrt{\left(\frac{E}{\rho}\right)}$$

K cannot be found dimensionally, it can be found experimentally.

Example 14. The frequency ν of vibration of stretched string depends upon

(i) its length l,

(ii) its mass per unit length m and

(iii) the tension T in the string.

Obtain dimensionally an expression for frequency ν.

Sol. Let the frequency of vibration of the string is given by

$$\nu = Kl^a m^b T^c \quad \text{...(i)}$$

where, K is a dimensionless constant.

Dimensions of the various quantities are

$$\nu = [T^{-1}],\ l = [L], T = [T],$$
$$\text{Force} = [MLT^{-2}]$$

and $$m = \frac{\text{mass}}{\text{length}} = [ML^{-1}]$$

Substituting these dimensions in Eq. (i), we get

$$[T^{-1}] = [L]^a[ML^{-1}]^b[MLT^{-2}]^c$$

or $[M^0L^0T^{-1}] = [M^{b+c}L^{a-b+c}T^{-2c}]$

Equating the dimensions of M, L and T,

$$b + c = 0,$$

$$a - b + c = 0 \text{ and } -2c = -1$$

On solving, we get $a = -1, b = -\frac{1}{2}$ and $c = \frac{1}{2}$

$$\therefore \quad \nu = Kl^{-1}m^{-1/2}T^{1/2} \text{ or } \nu = \frac{K}{l}\sqrt{\frac{T}{m}}$$

Limitations of Dimensional Analysis

(i) It does not give any information whether a physical quantity is a scalar or a vector.

(ii) It gives no information about the dimensionless constant in the formula, e.g. 1, 2, 3 ... π etc.

(iii) We cannot derive the formula containing the trigonometrical function, logarithmic function, exponential function which have no dimensions.

(iv) If a physical quantity depends on different quantites having the same dimension, the relation among them cannot be obtain.

Dimensional Formulae of Important Physical Quantities

Quick Test 2

Conceptual Questions

1. Write the dimensional formula of wavelength and frequency of a wave.

2. Express one joule in terms of fundamental unit.

3. Distinguish between dimensional variables and dimensional constants. Give example too.

4. Check the correctness of the relation $v^2 - u^2 = 2as$ by method of dimensions. The symbol have their usual meaning.

Numerical Questions

5. If force F, length L and time T are taken as fundamental units, then what be the dimensions of mass?

6. Find the value of 60 W on a system having 100 g, 20 cm and 1 min as the fundamental units.

7. Find the value of acceleration $8 \, m/s^2$ into km/h^2.

8. The density of a material in SI units is $128 \, kg \, m^{-3}$. In certain units, in which the unit of length is 25 cm and unit of mass is 50 g. Find the numerical unit of density.

Answers

5. $[F^1L^{-1}T^2]$ *6.* 3.24×10^9 units *7.* 10^5 km/h^2 *8.* 40

For Solutions, See QR Code on Pg. 26

Mind Map

Units and Measurements

Measurement

Measurement is the process of comparing an unknown quantity with a known standard quantity (unit).

Physical Quantities

Fundamental Quantities Quantities that cannot be expressed in terms of other quantities (e.g. length, mass, time).

Derived Quantities Quantities derived from fundamental quantities (e.g. velocity, force).

Units of Measurement System of Units

- CGS (Centimeter-Gram-Second) system
- MKS (Metre-Kilogram-Second) system
- SI (International System of Units)

SI Units

SI Units

The SI Unit (International System of Units) is the globally accepted standard system of measurement. It is based on seven fundamental units that define all physical quantities.

Derived Units

Derived units are units of measurement that are formed by combining fundamental (base) units according to algebraic relationships between physical quantities.

SI Units of Fundamental Quanities

- Length → Metre (m)
- Mass → Kilogram (kg)
- Time → Second (s)
- Electric Current → Ampere (A)
- Temperature → Kelvin (K)
- Amount of substance → Mole (mol)
- Luminous intensity → Candela (cd)

Significant Figures

These are the digits in a numerical measurement that are reliable and meaningful in representing the precision of that measurement.

They include all certain digits plus the first uncertain digit (which is estimated).

Purpose

- To express the precision of a measured quantity.
- Reflects the accuracy of the instrument used for measurement.

Importance

- Helps to maintain the precision of results during calculations.
- Avoids overestimation of accuracy

Rules for Counting Significant Figures

- Non-zero digits are always significant.
  Example 123 has 3 significant figures.
- Zeros between non-zero digits are significant.
  Example 1002 has 4 significant figures.
- Leading zeros (zeros before the first non-zero digit) are not significant.
  Example 0.0034 has 2 significant figures.
- Trailing zeros (zeros after the last non-zero digit) are significant if they appear after a decimal point.
  Example 2.300 has 4 significant figures. are not significant if there is no decimal point.
  Example 2300 has 2 significant figures.

Measurement Errors

- **Types of Errors**
  Systematic Error Consistent and predictable errors.
  Random Error Unpredictable variations in measurements.
  Gross Error Human errors.
- Absolute Error
- Relative Error
- Percentage Error

Dimensions of Physical Quantities

Dimensional Formula Expressing physical quantities in terms of fundamental quantities.

Example Force = $[M^1L^1T^{-2}]$

Applications of Dimensional Analysis

- Checking the correctness of equations.
- Deriving relations among physical quantities.

Limitation of Dimensional Analysis

- It cannot establish the formulae containing trigonometrical exponential and logarithmic terms.
- If a physical quantity depends on three physical quantities out of which two quantities have same dimension, then we cannot establish relation among them.

Operations with Significant Figures

Addition/Subtraction

The result should have the same number of decimal places as the quantity with the least decimal places.

Example 12.11+3.2=15.3

Multiplication/Division

The result should have the same number of significant figures as the quantity with the least significant figures.

Example 3.25×2.1=6.8(2 significant figures).

EXAM PATTERN QUESTIONS

Objective Type Questions

Multiple Choice Questions (MCQs)

1. Which one of the following physical quantities is not a fundamental quantity?

(a) Luminous intensity
(b) Thermodynamic temperature
(c) Electric current
(d) Work

2. Among the given following system of unit which is not based on unit of mass, length and time?

(a) CGS (b) FPS
(c) MKS (d) SI

3. Young's modulus of steel is $1.9\times 10^{11}\ \mathrm{N/m^2}$. When expressed in CGS units of dyne/cm^2, it will be equal to ($1\mathrm{N}=10^5$ dyne, $1\ \mathrm{m}^2=10^4\ \mathrm{cm}^2$) NCERT Exemplar

(a) 1.9×10^{10} (b) 1.9×10^{11}
(c) 1.9×10^{12} (d) 1.9×10^{13}

4. Find the value of 12.9 g − 7.05 g.

(a) 5.84 g (b) 5.8 g
(c) 5.86 g (d) 5.9 g

5. The numbers 2.745 and 2.735 on rounding off to 3 significant figures will give NCERT Exemplar

(a) 2.75 and 2.74 (b) 2.74 and 2.73
(c) 2.75 and 2.73 (d) 2.74 and 2.74

6. The length and breadth of a rectangular sheet are 16.2 cm and 10.1 cm, respectively. The area of the in appropriate significant figures is

(a) $164\pm 3\ \mathrm{cm}^2$ (b) $163.62\pm 2.6\ \mathrm{cm}^2$
(c) $163.6\pm 2.6\ \mathrm{cm}^2$ (d) $163.62\pm 3\ \mathrm{cm}^2$

7. The number of significant figures in 0.06900 is NCERT Exemplar

(a) 5 (b) 4
(c) 2 (d) 3

8. The sum of the numbers 436.32, 227.2 and 0.301 in appropriate significant figures is NCERT Exemplar

(a) 663.821 (b) 664
(c) 663.8 (d) 663.82

9. If the unit of force is 100 N, unit of length is 10 m and unit of time is 100 s. What is the unit of mass in this system of units?

(a) 10^5 kg (b) 10^7 kg
(c) 10^2 kg (d) 10^9 kg

10. If P, Q and R are physical quantities, having different dimensions, which of following combinations can never be meaningful quantity? Competency Based Que

(a) $\left(\frac{P-Q}{R}\right)$ (b) $PQ-R$
(c) $\frac{PQ}{R}$ (d) $\frac{PR-Q^2}{R}$

11. If $x=a+bt+ct^2$, where x is in metre and t is in second, then what is the unit of c? Competency Based Que

(a) m/s (b) $\mathrm{m/s^2}$ (c) kg-m/s (d) $\mathrm{m^2/s}$

12. If R and L represent resistance and self- inductance respectively, which of the following combinations has the dimensions of frequency? Competency Based Que

(a) $\frac{R}{L}$ (b) $\frac{L}{R}$
(c) $\sqrt{\frac{R}{L}}$ (d) $\sqrt{\frac{L}{R}}$

13. In the gas equation $\left(p+\frac{a}{V^2}\right)(V-b)=RT$, the dimensions of a are

(a) $[\mathrm{ML^3T^{-2}}]$ (b) $[\mathrm{M^{-1}L^3T^{-1}}]$
(c) $[\mathrm{ML^5T^{-2}}]$ (d) $[\mathrm{M^{-1}L^{-5}T^2}]$

14. The mass and volume of a body are 4.237 g and $2.5\ \mathrm{cm}^3$, respectively. The density of the material of the body in correct significant figures is NCERT Exemplar

(a) $1.6048\mathrm{g\ cm^{-3}}$ (b) $1.69\mathrm{g\ cm^{-3}}$
(c) $1.7\mathrm{g\ cm^{-3}}$ (d) $1.695\mathrm{g\ cm^{-3}}$

15. The mean length of an object is 5 cm. Which of the following measurements is most accurate? NCERT Exemplar

(a) 4.9 cm (b) 4.805 cm (c) 5.25 cm (d) 5.4 cm

16. If x and a stand for distance. Then

$$\int\frac{dx}{\sqrt{a^2-x^2}}=\frac{1}{a}\sin^{-1}\frac{a}{x}$$

(a) is dimensionally correct
(b) is dimensionally incorrect
(c) a and x cannot represent distance
(d) the given equation is numerically and dimensionally incorrect.

17. The dimensional formula of $\frac{e^4}{\varepsilon_0^2 m_p m_e^2 c^3 G}$ is

(where e = charge, m_p, m_e are masses, c = speed of light and G = gravitational constant)

(a) [M] (b) [T] (c) [LT] (d) $[ML^4T^{-2}]$

18. You measure two quantities as $A = 1.0 \text{ m} \pm 0.2 \text{ m}$, $B = 2.0 \text{ m} \pm 0.2 \text{ m}$. We should report correct value for $\sqrt{AB}$ as

(a) 1.4 m ± 0.4 m (b) 1.41 m ± 0.15 m
(c) 1.4 m ± 0.3 m (d) 1.4 m ± 0.2 m

19. Match the following two columns.

	Column I		Column II
A.	Capacitance	P.	Volt $(\text{ampere})^{-1}$
B.	Magnetic induction	Q.	Volt-second $(\text{ampere})^{-1}$
C.	Resistance	R.	Newton $(\text{ampere})^{-1}(\text{metre})^{-1}$
D.	Inductance	S.	$(\text{coulomb})^2(\text{joule})^{-1}$

(a) A-P, B-Q, C-R, D-S (b) A-R, B-S, C-Q, D-P
(c) A-S, B-R, C-P, D-Q (d) A-Q, B-P, C-R, D-S

20. Match the following two columns.

	Column I		Column II
A.	Planck's constant	P.	$[MLT^{-3}K^{-1}]$
B.	Boltzmann constant	Q.	$[ML^2T^{-1}]$
C.	Coefficient of viscosity	R.	$[ML^2T^{-2}K^{-1}]$
D.	Thermal conductivity	S.	$[ML^{-1}T^{-1}]$

(a) A-P, B-R, C-R D-S (b) A-S, B-P, C-Q, D-R
(c) A-D, B-S, C-R, D-Q (d) A-Q, B-R, C-S, D-P

Assertion-Reason

Directions *(Q.No. 21-26) In the following questions, two statements are given- one labelled Assertion (A) and the other labelled Reason (R). Select the correct answer to these questions from the codes (a), (b), (c) and (d) as given below.*

(a) Both Assertion and Reason are true and Reason is the correct explanation of Assertion.

(b) Both Assertion and Reason are true but Reason is not the correct explanation of Assertion.

(c) Assertion is true but Reason is false.

(d) Assertion is false but Reason is true.

21. Assertion (A) The unit based for measuring nuclear cross-section is barn.
Reason (R) 1 barn $= 10^{-14} \text{m}^2$.

22. Assertion (A) Pressure has the dimensions of energy density.
Reason (R) Energy density $= \frac{\text{Energy}}{\text{Volume}}$

23. Assertion (A) The method of dimensional analysis cannot validate the exact relationship between physical quantities in any equation.
Reason (R) It does not distinguish between the physical quantities having same dimensions.

24. Assertion (A) Let us consider an equation

$$(1/2)\, mv^2 = mgh$$

where, m is the mass of the body, v is velocity, g is the acceleration due to gravity and h is the height.
Reason (R) Equation is dimensionally correct.

25. Assertion (A) Number of significant figures in 0.005 is one and that is 0.500 are three.
Reason (R) This is because zeros before decimal are non-significant.

26. Assertion (A) If power of an engine depends on mass, angular speed, torque and angular momentum, then the formula of power is not derived with the help of dimensional method.
Reason (R) In mechanics, if a particular quantity depends on more than three quantities, then we cannot derive the formula of the quantity by the help of dimensional method.

Case Based Questions

Directions *(Q.Nos. 27-30) These questions are case study based questions. Read the following paragraph and answer the questions on the basis of same.*

27. All engineering phenomena deal with definite and measured quantities and so depend on the making of the measurement. We must be clear and precise in making these measurements. To make a measurement, magnitude of the physical quantity (unknown) is compared.

The records of a measurement consist of three parts, i.e the dimension of the quantity, the unit which represents a standard quantity and a number which is the ratio of the measured quantity to the standard quantity.

(i) A device which is used for measurement of light to an accuracy of about 10^{-5} m, is

(a) vernier calliper (b) screw gauge
(c) spherometer (d) Either (b) or (c)

(ii) The mean length of an object is 5 cm. Which of the following measurements is most accurate?
(a) 4.90 cm (b) 4.85 cm
(c) 4.80 cm (d) 4.75 cm

(iii) If the length of rectangle $l = 10.5$ cm, breadth $b = 2.1$ cm and minimum possible measurement by scale = 0.1 cm, then the area is
(a) 22.0 cm^2 (b) 22.5 cm^2
(c) 21.5 cm^2 (d) 21.0 cm^2

(iv) Age of the universe is about 10^{10} yr, whereas the mankind has existed for 10^6 yr. For how many seconds would the man have existed, if age of universe were 1 day?
(a) 7.5 s (b) 8.2 s
(c) 6.6 s (d) 8.6 s

28. All quantities in mechanics are represented in terms of base units of length, mass and time. Additional base unit of temperature (kelvin) is used in heat and thermodynamics. In magnetism and electricity, the additional base unit of electric current is ampere.

(i) The dimensions of universal gravitational constant are
(a) $[ML^{-3}T^2]$ (b) $[ML^2T^{-3}]$
(c) $[M^{-1}L^3T^{-2}]$ (d) $[M^2L^2T^{-2}]$

(ii) The coefficient of thermal conductivity has the dimensions
(a) $[ML^{-1}T^3K^3]$ (b) $[ML^{-1}T^{-3}K^{-1}]$
(c) $[MLT^{-3}K^{-1}]$ (d) $[MLT^{-3}K]$

(iii) Dimensions of resistance are
(a) $[MLT^{-3}A^{-1}]$
(b) $[ML^2T^{-3}A^{-1}]$
(c) $[M^2LT^{-3}A^{-1}]$
(d) $[ML^2T^{-3}A]$

(iv) Given, force $= \dfrac{\alpha}{\text{Density} + \beta^3}$.
What are the dimensions of α and β?
(a) $[ML^2T^{-2}]$, $[ML^{-1/3}]$
(b) $[M^2L^4T^{-2}]$, $[M^{1/3}L^{-1}]$
(c) $[M^2L^{-2}T^{-2}]$, $[M^{1/3}L^{-1}]$
(d) $[M^2L^{-2}T^{-2}]$, $[ML^{-2}]$

(v) Which of the following has unit but no dimension?
(a) Angle (b) Strain
(c) Relative velocity (d) Relative density

29. Dimensions of a physical quantity are the powers to which the fundamental units of mass [M], length [L] and time [T] must be raised to represent the unit of that physical quantity.

In mechanics, the dimensional formula is written in terms of the dimensions of mass, length and time [M, L and T]. In heat and thermodynamics, in addition to M, L and T, we need to mention the dimension of temperature in kelvin [K]. In electricity and magnetism, in addition to M, L and T, we need to mention the dimension of current or charge per unit time [A or QT^{-1}]. There are various applications of dimensional analysis is such as principle of homogeneity, in deriving relationship among various physical quantities, etc.

(i) Find the dimensional formula of the following physical quantities.
(a) Momentum
(b) Surface energy
(c) Force constant

(ii) State the principle of homogeneity of dimension with suitable example.

(iii) Can two physical quantities have the same dimensional formula? If yes, provide an example.

(iv) How can dimensional analysis help in converting units?

30. The dimensional analysis helps us in deducing the relations among different physical quantities and checking the accuracy derivation and dimensional consistency or its homogeneity of various numerical expressions.

The conversion of one system of units into another is an application of dimension. As we know numerical value is inversely proportional to the size of the unit but the magnitude of the physical quantity remains the same whatever be the system of its measurement.

i.e. $$n_1u_1 = n_2u_2 \Rightarrow n_2 = \frac{n_1u_1}{u_2}$$

where, u_1 and u_2 are two units of measurement of the quantity and n_1 and n_2 are their respective numerical values.

The method of dimensions is used to deduce the relation among the physical quantities. We should know the dependence of the physical quantity on other quantities.

(i) How the numerical value of a physical quantity is related to its unit.

(ii) Which method is used to deduce the relation among the physical quantities.

Subjective Questions

Very Short Answer Type Questions

1. Mention two essential requirements of a physical unit.

2. Does the magnitude of a physical quantity depend on system of units chosen for its measurement ?

3. Why length, mass and time are chosen as base quantities in mechanics?

4. Write three pairs of physical quantities which have same dimensional formula.

5. A function $f(\theta)$ is defined as

$$f(\theta) = 1 - \theta + \frac{\theta^2}{2!} - \frac{\theta^3}{3!} + \frac{\theta^4}{4!} + \ldots\ldots\ldots\ldots$$

Why is it necessary for $f(\theta)$ to be dimensionless quantity ? **NCERT Exemplar**

Short Answer Type Questions

6. How do we make the choice of a standard unit of measurement?

7. Write any three significant rules used during rounding off measurements.

8. Obtain the dimensional equation for universal gas constant.

9. Using the relation $E = h\nu$, obtain the dimensions of Planck's constant.

10. The rotational kinetic energy of a body is given by $E = \frac{1}{2}I\omega^2$, where ω is the angular velocity of the body and I is moment of inertia of a body. Use the equation to obtain dimensional formula for moment of inertia I. Also, write its SI unit.

11. In the formula $x = 3yz^2$, x and z have dimensions of capacitance and magnetic induction, respectively. Find the dimensions of y in MKS system.

12. If p represents radiation pressure, c represents the speed of light and q represents the radiation energy per unit area per unit time.

Calculate the non-zero integers such that $p^x q^y c^z$ is dimensionless.

13. During a total solar eclipse the moon almost entirely covers the sphere of the sun. Write the relation between the distances and sizes of the sun and moon. **NCERT Exemplar**

14. The speed of sound in a solid is given by the formula

$$v = \sqrt{\frac{E}{\rho}}$$

where, E is coefficient of elasticity and ρ is density of given solid. Check the relation by method of dimensional analysis.

15. A new system of units is proposed in which unit of mass is α kg, unit of length β m and unit of time γ s. How much will 5 J measure in this new system? **NCERT Exemplar**

Long Answer Type Questions

16. If velocity of sound in air v depends on the modulus of elasticity E and density ρ. Find expression of v. **Competency Based Que**

17. An artificial satellite is revolving around a planet of mass M and radius R in a circular orbit of radius r. From Kepler's third law about the period of a satellite around a common central body, square of the period of revolution T is proportional to the cube of the radius of the orbit r. Show using dimensional analysis, that $T = \frac{k}{R}\sqrt{\frac{r^3}{g}}$, where k is a dimensionless constant and g is acceleration due to gravity. **NCERT Exemplar**

18. (a) If the time period (T) of vibration of a liquid drop depends on surface tension (s) and radius (r) of the drop, and density (ρ) of the liquid. Derive an expression for T using dimensional analysis. **[2½]**

(b) The depth x to which a bullet penetrates a human body depends upon (i) coefficient of elasticity η and (ii) kinetic energy E_k. By the method of dimensions, show

that $x \propto \left[\frac{E_k}{\eta}\right]^{1/3}$. **Competency Based Que** **[2½]**

19. (a) Rule out or accept the following formula for kinetic energy on the basis of dimensional arguments.

(i) $K = \frac{3}{16}mv^2$ (ii) $K = \frac{1}{2}mv^2 + ma$ **[2]**

(b) In the relation $p = (a/b)e^{-(az/\theta)}$, p is the pressure, Z is the distance and θ is the temperature. What is the dimensional formula of p? **Competency Based Que** **[3]**

20. (a) The SI unit of energy is $J = kgm^2s^{-2}$, that of speed v is ms^{-1} and acceleration a is ms^{-2}. Which of the formulae for kinetic energy (K) given below can you rule out on the basis of dimensional arguments (m stands for the mass of the body)? **[2½]**

(i) $K = m^2v^2$ (ii) $K = (1/2)mv^2$

(iii) $K = ma$ (iv) $K = (3/16)mv^2$

(v) $K = \left(\frac{1}{2}\right) mv^2 + ma$ NCERT

(b) How will you convert a physical quantity from one unit system to another by method of dimensions? [2½]

Numerical Problems

System of Units

21. Wavelength of a laser light is 6463 Å. Express it in nm and micron.

22. Find the value of 1 J of energy in CGS system of units.

23. If unit of force, velocity and energy are 100 dyne, 10 cm/s and 400 ergs, respectively. What will be the unit of mass, length and time? Competency Based Que.

24. Convert

(i) 3 ms^{-2} to km h^{-2} [1½]

(ii) $G = 6.67 \times 10^{11}$ $Nm^2 kg^{-2}$ to $cm^3 g^{-1} s^{-2}$ [1½]

Significant Figures and Rounding-off

25. Find the value of the following upto the appropriate significant figures in the following.

(a) 3.27 + 33.5472 (b) 53.312 – 53.3

(c) 2.02 × 23 (d) 3.908 × 5.5

26. How many significant figures are there in the following results for quantities measured in the laboratory?

(a) 3.0120 (b) 123.0 km (c) 0.006235 s

(d) 0.23×10^{-3} (e) 100.007 g (f) 143000 km

27. Solve the following and express the result to an appropriate number of significant figures.

(i) Add 6.2 g, 4.33 g and 17.456 g

(ii) Subtract 63.54 kg from 187.2 kg

(iii) 75.5 × 125.2 × 0.51

(iv) $\frac{2.13 \times 24.78}{458.2}$

28. Measure of two quantities along with the precision of respective measuring instrument is
$A = 2.5\ ms^{-1} \pm 0.5\ ms^{-1}$ and $B = 0.10\ s \pm 0.01\ s$.
The value of AB will be NCERT Exemplar

29. You measure two quantities as $A = 1.0\ m \pm 0.2\ m$, $B = 2.0\ m \pm 0.2\ m$. We should report correct value for $\sqrt{AB}$ as

30. Time for 20 oscillations of a pendulum is measured as $t_1 = 39.6$ s, $t_2 = 39.9$ s and $t_3 = 39.5$ s. What is the precision in the measurements? What is the accuracy of the measurement? NCERT Exemplar

31. A physical quantity X is related to four measurable quantities a, b, c and d as follows $X = a^2 b^3 c^{5/2} d^{-2}$. The percentage error in the measurement of a, b, c and d are 1%, 2%, 3% and 4%, respectively. What is the percentage error in quantity X? If the value of X calculated on the basis of the above relation is 2.763, to what value should you round off the result ? NCERT Exemplar

32. The mass of a box measured by a grocer's balance is 2.3 kg. Two gold pieces of masses 20.15 g and 20.17 g are added to the box. What is (a) the total mass of the box and (b) the difference in the mass of the pieces to correct significant figures? NCERT

33. A new unit of length is chosen such that the speed of light in vacuum is unity. What is the distance between the sun and the earth in terms of the new unit, if light takes 8 min and 20 s to cover this distance? NCERT

34. A student measures the thickness of a human hair by looking at it through a microscope of magnification 100. He makes 20 observations and finds that the average width of the hair in the field of view of the microscope is 3.5 mm. What is the estimate on the thickness of hair? NCERT

Arithmetic Calculations

35. The sides of a rectangle are (10.5 ± 0.2) cm and (5.2 ± 0.1) cm. Calculate its perimeter with error limits.

36. If displacement of a body, $s = (200 \pm 5)$ m and time taken by it $t = (20 + 0.2)$ s, then find the percentage error in the calculation of velocity.

37. The length of a rod as measured in an experiment was found to be 2.48 m, 2.46 m, 2.49 m, 2.50 m and 2.48 m. Find the average length, absolute error and percentage error. Express the result with error limit.

38. The error in the measurement of radius of a sphere is 2%. What would be the error in

(a) volume of sphere? [1½]

(b) surface area of sphere? [1½]

39. Express an acceleration of 10 m/s^2 in km/h^2.

40. Find the relative error in Z, if $Z = \frac{A^4 B^{\frac{1}{3}}}{CD^{\frac{3}{2}}}$ and the percentage error in the measurements of A, B, C and D are 4%, 2%, 3% and 1% respectively.

Dimensional Analysis

41. A famous relation in Physics relates moving mass m to the rest mass m_0 of a particle in terms of its speed v and speed of light c. (This relation first arose as a consequence of special relativity due to Albert Einstein).

A boy recalls the relation almost correctly but forgets where to put the constant c. He writes $m = \frac{m_0}{(1-v^2)^{1/2}}$.

Guess, where to put the missing c? **NCERT**

42. A body of mass m hung at one end of the spring executes SHM. Prove that the relation $T = 2\pi m/k$ is incorrect, where k is the force constant of the spring. Also, derive the correct relation.

43. The time of oscillation T of a small drop of a liquid under surface tension (whose dimensions are those of force per unit length) depends upon the density d, the radius r and the surface tension σ. Derive dimensionally the relationship $T \propto \sqrt{dr^3/\sigma}$.

44. The wavelength λ associated with a moving particle depends on its mass m, its velocity v and Planck's constant h. Show dimensional relation between them. **Competency Based Que**

45. The orbital velocity v of a satellite may depend on its mass m, distance r from the centre of earth and acceleration due to gravity g. Obtain an expression for orbital velocity.

46. A large fluid star oscillates in shape under the influence of its own gravitational field. Using dimensional analysis, find the expression for period of oscillation (T) in terms of radius of star (R). Mean density of fluid (ρ) and universal gravitational constant (G).

Hints & Solutions

Objective Type Questions

1. (d) 2. (d) 3. (c) 4. (b) 5. (d)
6. (a) 7. (b) 8. (b) 9. (a) 10. (a)

11. (b) Use the concept of dimensional analysis, dimension of LHS : L

According to dimensional anylysis, dimension of each term of LHS is equal to that of each term of RHS.

So, Dimension of x = Dimension of ct^2

$$L = [c]T^2$$

$$\therefore \quad [c] = [LT^{-2}]$$

So, unit of c is m/s^2.

12. (a) 13. (c)

14. (c) In this question, density should be reported to two significant figures.

$$\therefore \text{ Density} = \frac{4.237\text{g}}{2.5\text{cm}^3} = 1.6948 \text{ g cm}^{-3}$$

As rounding off the number, we get density = 1.7 g cm^{-3}

15. (a) Given length, $l = 5$ cm

Now, checking the errors with each options one by one, we get

$$\Delta l_1 = 5 - 4.9 = 0.1 \text{ cm}$$
$$\Delta l_2 = 5 - 4.805 = 0.195 \text{ cm}$$
$$\Delta l_3 = 5.25 - 5 = 0.25 \text{ cm}$$
$$\Delta l_4 = 5.4 - 5 = 0.4 \text{ cm}$$

Error, Δl_1 is least.

Hence, 4.9 cm is most precise.

16. (d)

17. (b) We have, $F_g = \frac{Gm_1m_2}{r^2} \Rightarrow [Gm_e^2] = F_g r^2$

Also, $\varepsilon F_e = \frac{1}{4\pi\varepsilon_0}\frac{q_1q_2}{r^2} \Rightarrow \frac{1}{4\pi\varepsilon_0}\frac{e^2}{r^2} = F_e$

$$\Rightarrow \quad \frac{e^2}{\varepsilon_0} = 4\pi F_e r^2$$

$$\Rightarrow \left[\frac{e^2}{\varepsilon_0^2 m_p m_e^2 c^3 G}\right] = \left(\frac{e^2}{\varepsilon_0}\right)^2 \frac{1}{m_p c^3}\left(\frac{1}{Gm_e}\right)$$

$$= (F_e r^2)^2 \frac{1}{m_p c^3}\left(\frac{1}{F_g r^2}\right)$$

$$= \frac{Fr^2}{m_p c^3} = \frac{[MLT^{-2}L^2]}{[M][LT^{-1}]^3} = [T]$$

18. (d) Given, $A = 1.0 \text{ m} \pm 0.2$ m, $B = 2.0 \text{ m} \pm 0.2$ m

Let, $Y = \sqrt{AB} = \sqrt{(1.0)(2.0)} = 1.414$m

Rounding off to two significant digits, $Y = 1.4$ m

$$\frac{\Delta Y}{Y} = \frac{1}{2}\left[\frac{\Delta A}{A} + \frac{\Delta B}{B}\right] = \frac{1}{2}\left[\frac{0.2}{1.0} + \frac{0.2}{2.0}\right] = \frac{0.6}{2 \times 2.0}$$

$$\Rightarrow \Delta Y = \frac{0.6 \times Y}{2 \times 2.0} = \frac{0.6 \times 1.4}{2 \times 2.0} = 0.212$$

Rounding off to one significant digit, $\Delta Y = 0.2$ m

Thus, correct value for $\sqrt{AB} = r + \Delta r = 1.4 \pm 0.2$m

19. (c) Capacitance, $C = \frac{Q}{V} = \frac{Q^2}{W}$ = (coulomb)^2 (joule)$^{-1}$

Magnetic induction, $B = \frac{F}{il} = \frac{\text{Newton}}{\text{ampere} \times \text{metre}}$

$= (\text{Newton})(\text{ampere})^{-1}(\text{metre})^{-1}$

Resistance, $R = \frac{V}{I} = \frac{\text{volt}}{\text{ampere}} = \text{volt (ampere)}^{-1}$

Inductance, $L = \frac{E}{dl/dt} = \frac{\text{volt}}{\text{ampere /second}}$

$= \text{volt-second(ampere)}^{-1}$

20. (*d*) Planck's constant $= \frac{\text{Energy}}{\text{Frequency}}$

$[h] = \frac{[ML^2T^{-2}]}{[T^{-1}]} = [ML^2T^{-1}]$

Boltzmann constant $= \frac{\text{Energy}}{\text{Temperature}}$

$[k_B] = \frac{[ML^2T^{-2}]}{[K]} = [ML^2T^{-2}K^{-1}]$

Coefficient of viscosity $= \frac{\text{Force}}{\text{Area} \times \text{Velocity gradient}}$

$[\eta] = \frac{[MLT^{-2}]}{[L^2][LT^{-1}/L]} = [ML^{-1}T^{-1}]$

Thermal conductivity $= \frac{\text{Heat energy} \times \text{Thickness}}{\text{Area} \times \text{Temperature} \times \text{Time}}$

$[K] = \frac{[ML^2T^{-2}][L]}{[L^2][K][T]} = [MLT^{-3}K^{-1}]$

21. (*c*) Barn is used in nuclear Physics for expressing the cross-sectional area of nuclei and nuclear reaction. It is defined as 10^{-28} m^2 and it is used to measure the probability of interaction between the particles.

22. (*a*) Pressure $= \frac{\text{Force}}{\text{Area}} = \frac{\text{Force} \times \text{Distance}}{\text{Area} \times \text{Distance}}$

$= \frac{\text{Energy}}{\text{Volume}} = \frac{[ML^2T^{-2}]}{[L^3]}$

$= [ML^{-1}T^{-2}] = \text{Energy density}$

23. (*a*) Dimensional analysis is very useful in deducing relations among the interdependent physical quantities. However, dimensionless constants cannot be obtained by this method. The method of dimensions can only test the dimensional validity but not the exact relationship between physical quantities in any equation. It does not distinguish between the physical quantities having same dimensions.

24. (*a*) The dimensions of LHS are

$[M][LT^{-1}]^2 = [M][L^2T^{-2}] = [ML^2T^{-2}]$

The dimensions of RHS are

$[M][LT^{-2}][L] = [M][L^2T^{-2}] = [ML^2T^{-2}]$

The dimensions of LHS and RHS are the same and hence the equation is dimensionally correct.

25. (*c*) Since, zeros placed to the left of the number are never significant, but zeros placed to right of the number are significant.

26. (*a*) If a quantity in mechanics depends on more than three quantities, we shall have more unknown and less equations.

27. (i) (*d*) A screw gauge and a spherometer can be used to measure length accurately as less as 10^{-5} m.

(ii) (*a*) Given length, $l = 5$ cm

Now, checking the errors with each option one-by-one, we get

$\Delta l_1 = 5 - 4.90 = 0.10$ cm

$\Delta l_2 = 5 - 4.85 = 0.15$ cm

$\Delta l_3 = 5 - 4.80 = 0.20$ cm

$\Delta l_4 = 5 - 4.75 = 0.25$ cm

Error, Δl_1 is least.

Hence, 4.9 cm is most precise or accurate.

(iii) (*a*) Area of rectangle, $A = \text{Length} \times \text{Breadth}$

So, $A = l \times b = 10.5 \times 2.1 = 22.05$ cm^2

Minimum possible measurement by scale = 0.1 cm

So, area measured by scale = 22.0 cm^2

(iv) (*d*) Magnification in time $= \frac{\text{Age of mankind}}{\text{Age of universe}}$

$= \frac{10^6}{10^{10}} = 10^{-4}$

Apparent age of mankind $= 10^{-4} \times 1$ day

$= 10^{-4} \times 86400$ s

$= 8.645 \approx 8.65$s

28. (i) (*c*) Universal gravitational constant,

$G = \frac{Fr^2}{m_1 m_2} = \frac{[MLT^{-2}][L^2]}{[M][M]} = [M^{-1}L^3T^{-2}]$

(ii) (*c*) As we know that, rate of heat flow,

i.e., $\frac{\Delta Q}{\Delta t} = KA\frac{dT}{dx}$

$\Rightarrow$ Coefficient of thermal conductivity,

$K = \frac{\Delta Q}{\Delta t} \times \frac{dx}{AdT}$

$= \frac{[ML^2T^{-2}][L]}{[TL^2K]} = [MLT^{-3}K^{-1}]$

(iii) (*b*) Resistance, $R = \frac{V}{I}$

$\Rightarrow \quad V = \frac{W}{Q} = \frac{[ML^2T^{-2}]}{[AT]} = [ML^2T^{-3}A^{-1}]$

(iv) (*c*) Dimensions of β^3 = Dimensions of density

$= [ML^{-3}]$

$$\beta = [M^{1/3}\ L^{-1}]$$

Also, α = Force × Density = $[MLT^{-2}]\ [ML^{-3}]$

$= [M^2L^{-2}T^{-2}]$

(v) (a) Angle has unit of radian but has no dimensions because $\theta = \dfrac{l}{r}$.

29. (i)

Physical quantites	Dimensional formulae
(a) Momentum	$[M^1L^1T^{-1}]$
(b) Surface energy	$[M^1L^2T^{-2}]$
(c) Force constant	$[M^1L^0T^{-2}]$

(ii) Refer to text on Page no. 09

(iii) Yes, two different physical quantities can have the same dimensional formula.

Example : Work and energy both have the dimensional formula $[ML^2T^{-2}]$. While their physical interpretations differ, their dimensions are the same.

(iv) Dimensional analysis ensures that quantities in different unit systems (e.g., SI and CGS) can be converted by comparing their dimensions. For example, energy in SI (Joule) can be converted to CGS (erg) using their dimensional equivalence.

30. (i) The numerical value of a physical quantity is inversely proportional to its unit.

i.e. $n \propto \dfrac{1}{u}$ or nu = constant

(ii) The method of dimensions is used to deduce the relation among the physical quantities.

Subjective Questions

1. Refer to text on page no.2.
2. Yes, the magnitude of a physical quantity depends on the system of units chosen for its mesurement.
3. Length, mass and time are chosen as base quantities in mechanics because
   (i) length, mass and time cannot be derived from one another, i.e. these quantities are independent.
   (ii) all other quantities in mechanics can be expressed in terms of length, mass and time.
4. (i) Work and energy
   (ii) Energy and torque
   (iii) Pressure and stress
5. Since, $f(\theta)$ is a sum of different powers of θ and it is a dimensionless quantity.
   By principle of homogeneity as RHS is dimensionless, hence LHS should also be dimensionless.
6. We make the choice of a standard unit of measurement by keeping in mind the following properties.
   (i) The unit should be of convenient size.
   (ii) It should be possible to define the unit without ambiguity.
   (iii) The unit should be reproducible.
   (iv) The value of unit should not change with space and time.
7. Refer to text on Page no. 6.
8. From ideal gas equation for universal gas constant,

$$pV = nRT$$

where, n = number of moles of gas.

$$\because \quad R = \frac{pV}{nT}$$

$$\Rightarrow \quad [R] = \frac{[ML^{-1}T^{-2}][L^3]}{[mol][K]}$$

$$\Rightarrow \quad [R] = [ML^2T^{-2}mol^{-1}K^{-1}]$$

9. We know that, dimensional formula of energy E of photon is $[M^1L^2T^{-2}]$ and dimensional formula of frequency ν is $[T^{-1}]$.

$$[h] = \frac{[E]}{[\nu]} = \frac{[M^1L^2T^{-2}]}{[T^{-1}]} = [M^1L^2T^{-1}]$$

10. The given relation is $E = \dfrac{1}{2}I\omega^2$

$$I = \frac{[E]}{[\omega^2]} = \frac{[ML^2T^{-2}]}{[T^{-1}]^2}\left[\frac{ML^2T^{-2}}{T^{-2}}\right] = [ML^2]$$

Its SI unit is kg-m^2.

11. Given, $x = 3yz^2$, where

x has dimensions of capacitance, i.e., $x = [M^{-1}L^{-2}A^2T^4]$ and z has dimensions of magnetic induction,

i.e., $\quad z = [M^1A^{-1}T^{-2}]$

Let $\quad y = M^{\alpha}L^{\beta}T^{\gamma}A^{\delta}$

Now considering the given expression and substituting the dimensions, we get

$$[M^{-1}L^{-2}A^2T^4] = [M^{\alpha}L^{\beta}T^{\gamma}A^{\delta}][M^1L^0A^{-1}T^{-2}]^2$$

On comparing and solving further, we get

$$\alpha = -3, \beta = -2, \gamma = 8, \delta = 4$$

$$\therefore \quad [Y] = [M^{-3}L^{-2}T^8A^4]$$

12. Radiation pressure, $p = [ML^{-1}T^{-2}]$

$\because$ Radiation energy,

$$q = \frac{\text{energy / area}}{\text{time}} = \left[\frac{W}{M^2}\right] = [MT^{-3}]$$

c = speed of light $= [LT^{-1}]$

$$[M^0\ L^0\ T^0] = [M^1L^{-1}\ T^{-2}]^x[MT^{-3}]^y[LT^{-1}]$$

On comparing powers, we get

$$x + y = 0 \Rightarrow x = -y \quad \text{...(i)}$$

$$-x + z = 0 \Rightarrow x = z \quad \text{...(ii)}$$

$$-2x - 3y - z = 0 \quad \text{...(iii)}$$

On solving Eqs. (i), (ii) and (iii), we get

$$x = 1,\ y = -1, z = 1$$

13. Consider the diagram given below.

R_{me} = Distance of moon from earth

R_{se} = Distance of sun from earth

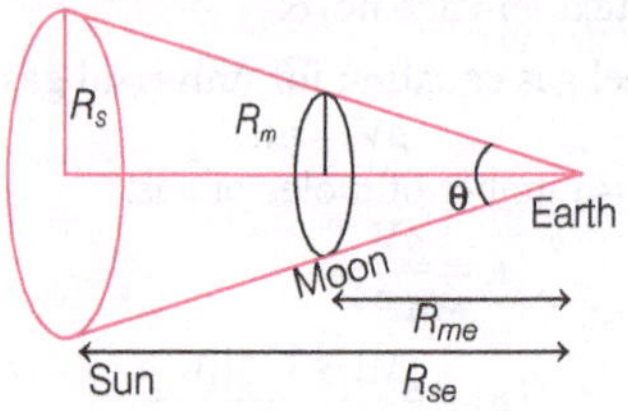

Let angle made by sun and moon is θ, we can write

$$\theta = \frac{A_{sun}}{R_{se}^2} = \frac{A_{moon}}{R_{me}^2}$$

Here, A_{sun} = Area of the sun

A_{moon} = Area of the moon

$$\Rightarrow \quad \theta = \frac{\pi R_s^2}{R_{se}^2} = \frac{\pi R_m^2}{R_{me}^2}$$

$$\Rightarrow \quad \left(\frac{R_s}{R_{se}}\right)^2 = \left(\frac{R_m}{R_{me}}\right)^2$$

$$\Rightarrow \quad \frac{R_s}{R_{se}} = \frac{R_m}{R_{me}} \Rightarrow \frac{R_s}{R_m} = \frac{R_{se}}{R_{me}}$$

Here, radius of sun and moon represents their sizes respectively.

14. In the given relation, dimensions of LHS terms v are $[LT^{-1}]$.

Dimensional formulae for E and ρ are $[ML^{-1}T^{-2}]$ and $[ML^{-3}]$ respectively.

$$\text{Dimensions of RHS} = \sqrt{\frac{ML^{-1}T^{-2}}{ML^{-3}}} = \sqrt{L^2T^{-2}} = [LT^{-1}]$$

As dimensions of LHS and RHS of the equation are same. Hence, the equation is dimensionally correct.

15. We know that dimension of energy = $[ML^2T^{-2}]$

Let M_1, L_1, T_1 and M_2, L_2, T_2 are units of mass, length and time in given two systems.

$\therefore$ $M_1 = 1$ kg, $L_1 = 1$ m, $T_1 = 1$ s

$M_2 = \alpha$ kg, $L_2 = \beta$ m, $T_2 = \gamma$ s

The magnitude of a physical quantity remains the same, whatever be the system of units of its measurement.

i.e., $n_1u_1 = n_2u_2$

$$\Rightarrow n_2 = n_1\frac{u_1}{u_2} = n_1\frac{[M_1 L_1^2 T_1^{-2}]}{[M_2 L_2^2 T_2^{-2}]}$$

$$= 5\left[\frac{M_1}{M_2}\right] \times \left[\frac{L_1}{L_2}\right]^2 \times \left[\frac{T_1}{T_2}\right]^{-2}$$

$$= 5\left[\frac{1}{\alpha}\text{kg}\right] \times \left[\frac{1}{\beta}\text{m}\right]^2 \times \left[\frac{1}{\gamma}\text{s}\right]^{-2} = 5 \times \frac{1}{\alpha} \times \frac{1}{\beta^2} \times \frac{1}{\gamma^{-2}}$$

$$n_2 = \frac{5\gamma^2}{\alpha\beta^2}$$

Thus, new unit of energy will be $\frac{\gamma^2}{\alpha\beta^2}$.

16. According to the question, $v \propto E^a\rho^b$

$$\Rightarrow \quad v = kE^a\rho^b \quad \text{...(i)}$$

where, v = velocity of sound in air

E = modulus of elasticity,

ρ = density

and k = constant of proportionality.

Dimensions are

$$[v] = [LT^{-1}], \quad [\rho] = [ML^{-3}], \quad [E] = [ML^{-1}T^{-2}]$$

Substituting in Eq. (i), we get

$$[LT^{-1}] = [ML^{-3}]^a[ML^{-1}T^{-2}]^b$$

$$[M^0LT^{-1}] = [M^{a+b}L^{-3a-b}T^{-2b}]$$

On comparing powers, we get

$$a + b = 0, \; -3a - 2b = -1 \text{ and } -2b = -1$$

On solving, we get

$$a = -\frac{1}{2}, \; b = \frac{1}{2}$$

$\therefore$ On putting values of a and b in Eq. (i), we get

$$v = \sqrt{E/d}$$

17. By Kepler's third law, $T^2 \propto r^3 \Rightarrow T \propto r^{3/2}$

We know that T is a function of R and g.

Let, $$T \propto r^{3/2}R^a g^b$$

$$\Rightarrow \quad T = kr^{3/2}R^a g^b \quad \text{...(i)}$$

where, k is a dimensionless constant of proportionality.

Substituting the dimensions of each term in Eq. (i), we get

$$[M^0L^0T] = k[L]^{3/2}[L]^a[LT^{-2}]^b$$

$$= k[L^{a+b+3/2}T^{-2b}]$$

On comparing the powers of same terms, we get

$$a + b + 3/2 = 0 \quad \text{...(ii)}$$

$$-2b = 1 \Rightarrow b = -1/2 \quad \text{...(iii)}$$

From Eq. (ii) and (iii), we get

$$a - 1/2 + 3/2 = 0 \Rightarrow a = -1$$

Substituting the values of a and b in Eq. (i), we get

$$T = kr^{3/2}R^{-1}g^{-1/2}$$

$$\Rightarrow \quad T = \frac{k}{R}\sqrt{\frac{r^3}{g}}$$

Note : When we are applying formulae, we should be careful about r (radius of orbit) and R (radius of planet).

18. (a) $T = k(s^a r^b \rho^c)$ (According to the question).

$$\Rightarrow \quad [M^0L^0T^1] = k[MT^{-2}]^a[L]^b[ML^{-3}]^c$$

$\Rightarrow \quad [M^0L^0T^1] = k[M^{a+c}T^{-2a}L^{b-3c}]$

On comparing powers, we get

$$a + c = 0, -2a = 1, b - 3c = 0$$

On solving, we get

$$a = \frac{-1}{2},\ b = \frac{3}{2},\ c = \frac{1}{2}$$

$$\therefore \quad T = k\frac{r^{3/2}.\rho^{1/2}}{s^{1/2}}$$

$$\Rightarrow \quad T = k\sqrt{\frac{r^3\rho}{s}}$$

(b) Let $x \propto E_k^a \eta^b$

where, a and b are the dimensions.

$$x = k E_k^a \eta^b \quad \text{...(i)}$$

where, k is the dimensionless constant of proportionality.

Writing the dimensions in Eq. (i), we get

$$[M^0L^1T^0] = [ML^2T^{-2}]^a[ML^{-1}T^{-2}]^b$$

$$\Rightarrow \quad [M^0L^1T^0] = [M^{a+b}L^{2a-b}T^{-2a-2b}]$$

On comparing powers, we get

$$a + b = 0,\ 2a - b = 1,\ -2a - 2b = 0$$

On solving, we get

$$a = \frac{1}{3},\ b = -\frac{1}{3}$$

On putting the values of a and b in Eq. (i),

we get $x = k\left(\frac{E_k}{\eta}\right)^{1/3}$ or $x \propto \left(\frac{E_k}{\eta}\right)^{1/3}$

19. (a) Dimensions of KE = $[ML^2T^{-2}]$

(i) Dimensions of $\frac{3}{16}mv^2 = [M][LT^{-1}]^2 = [MLT^{-2}]$

(ii) Dimensions of $\frac{1}{2}mv^2 + ma = [ML^2T^{-2}] + [MLT^{-2}]$

$\therefore$ (ii) formula is incorrect as its dimensions are different from the dimensions of kinetic energy.

(b) Since, $e^{-(aZ/\theta)}$ is dimensionless, we have $aZ/\theta = 1$

or $\quad a = \frac{\theta}{Z} = \frac{K}{L} = [L^{-1}K]$

We find that a/b = dimensions of p and $b = [ML^{-1}T^{-2}]$.

Therefore, dimensional formula of p is obtained as

$$p = \frac{a}{[ML^{-1}T^{-2}]} = \frac{[L^{-1}K]}{[ML^{-1}T^{-2}]} = [M^{-1}L^0T^2K]$$

20. (a) As SI unit of energy, J = kgm^{2}s^{-2},

So, $\quad$ [energy] = $[ML^2T^{-2}]$

(i) $[m^2v^2] = [M^2][LT^{-1}]^2 = [M^2L^2T^{-2}]$

(ii) $[1/2mv^2] = [M][LT^{-1}]^2 = [ML^2T^{-2}]$

(iii) $[ma] = [M][LT^{-2}] = [MLT^{-2}]$

(iv) $[3/16mv^2] = [M][LT^{-1}]^2 = [ML^2T^{-2}]$

(v) The quantities $(1/2)mv^2$ and ma have different dimensions and hence cannot be added.

Since, the kinetic energy K has the dimensions of $[ML^2T^{-2}]$, formulae (i), (iii) and (v) are clearly ruled out.

Dimensional analysis cannot tell which of the two, (ii) or (iv) is the correct formula. From the actual definition of kinetic energy, only (ii) is the correct formula for kinetic energy.

(b) If a given quantity is measured in two different unit systems, then $Q = n_1u_1 = n_2u_2$

Let the dimensional formula of the quantity be $[M^aL^bT^c]$, then we have $n_1[M_1^aL_1^bT_1^c] = n_2[M_2^aL_2^bT_2^c]$

Here M_1, L_1, T_1 are the fundamental unit of mass, length and time in first unit system and M_2, L_2, T_2 in the second unit system.

$$\text{Hence,} \quad n_2 = n_1\left[\frac{M_1}{M_2}\right]^a\left[\frac{L_1}{L_2}\right]^b\left[\frac{T_1}{T_2}\right]^c$$

This relation helps us to convert a physical quantity from one unit system to another.

21. Wavelength of a laser light = 6463 Å

$\because \quad 1\text{ Å} = 10^{-10}\text{ m},\ 1\text{ nm} = 10^{-9}\text{ m}$

and $\quad 1\ \mu = 10^{-6}\text{ m}$

$\therefore \quad 6463\text{ Å} = 6463 \times 10^{-10}\text{ m}$

$\Rightarrow \quad 646.3 \times 10^{-9}\text{ m} = 646.3\text{ nm}$

and $0.6463 \times 10^{-6}\text{ m} = 0.6463\mu\text{m}$

22. In CGS system of units, the unit of energy is erg.

$\because$ Energy = Work = Force × Displacement

= Mass × Acceleration × length

$\therefore \quad$ Dimensions of work $[W] = [M^1L^2T^{-2}]$

$\therefore \quad$ we get $a = 1,\ b = 2,\ c = -2$

Now,

SI System	CGS System
$M_1 = 1$ kg	$M_2 = 1$g
$L_1 = 1$m	$L_2 = 1$ cm
$T_1 = 1$s	$T_2 = 1$s

Here, $N_1 = 1$

$$\text{Using } N_2 = N_1\left[\frac{M_1}{M_2}\right]^a\left[\frac{L_1}{L_2}\right]^b\left[\frac{T_1}{T_2}\right]^c$$

$$= 1\left[\frac{1\text{ kg}}{1\text{ g}}\right]^1\left[\frac{1\text{ m}}{1\text{ cm}}\right]^2\left[\frac{1\text{ s}}{1\text{ s}}\right]^{-2}$$

$$= 1\left[\frac{1000\text{ g}}{1\text{ g}}\right]^1\left[\frac{100\text{ cm}}{1\text{ cm}}\right]^2\left[\frac{1\text{ s}}{1\text{ s}}\right]^{-2}$$

$$N_2 = 10^3 \times 10^4 = 10^7\text{ erg}$$

$\therefore$ 1 joule = 10^7 erg or 10^7 CGS units.

23. Force = 100 dyne = $[MLT^{-2}]$ ...(i)

Velocity = 10 cm/s = $[LT^{-1}]$ ...(ii)

Energy = 400 ergs = $[ML^2T^{-2}]$ ...(iii)

Dividing Eq. (iii) by Eq. (i), we get

$$\Rightarrow \frac{\text{Energy}}{\text{Force}} = [L^1] = \frac{400}{100} = 4 \text{ cm}$$

$$\Rightarrow \frac{\text{Energy}}{(\text{Velocity})^2} = [M^1] = \frac{400}{(10)^2} = 4 \text{ g}$$

From Eq. (ii), we have

$$[LT^{-1}] = 10$$

$$\Rightarrow \frac{[L]}{[T]} = 10 \Rightarrow [T] = \frac{[L]}{10}$$

$$\Rightarrow T = \frac{4}{10} = 0.4 \text{ s}$$

24. (i) $3 \text{ ms}^{-2} = \left(\frac{3}{1000} \text{ km}\right)\left(\frac{1}{60 \times 60} \text{ h}\right)^{-2}$

$$= \frac{3 \times (60 \times 60)^2}{1000} = 3.8880 \times 10^4 \text{ km h}^{-2}$$

$$= 3.9 \times 10^4 \text{ km h}^{-2}$$

(ii) $G = 6.67 \times 10^{-11} \text{ N m}^2 \text{ kg}^{-2}$

$$= 6.67 \times 10^{-11} (\text{kg ms}^{-2}) (\text{m}^2 \text{ kg}^{-2})$$

$$= 6.67 \times 10^{-11} \text{ kg}^{-1} \text{ m}^3\text{s}^{-2}$$

$$= 6.67 \times 10^{-11} (1000 \text{ g})^{-1} (100 \text{ cm})^3 (\text{s}^{-2})$$

$$= 6.67 \times 10^{-11} \times \frac{1}{1000} \times 100 \times 100 \times 100 \text{ g}^{-1}\text{cm}^3\text{s}^{-2}$$

$$= 6.67 \times 10^{-8} \text{ g}^{-1}\text{cm}^3\text{s}^{-2}$$

25. (a) $3.27 + 33.5472 = 36.8172 = 36.82$

(b) $53.312 - 53.3 = 0.012 = 0$

(c) $2.02 \times 23 = 46.46 = 46$

(d) $3.908 \times 5.5 = 21.494 = 21$

26. (a) 3.0120 → 5 significant figures

(b) 123.0 km → 4 significant figures

(c) 0.006235 s → 4 significant figures

(d) 0.23×10^{-3} → 3 significant figures

(e) 100.007 g → 6 significant figures

(f) 143000 km → 3 significant figures

27. (i) 6.2 g + 4.33 g + 17.456 g = 27.986 g = 28.0 g

[rounded off to first decimal place]

(ii) 187.2 kg − 63.54 kg = 123.66 kg = 123.7 kg

[rounded off to first decimal place]

(iii) $75.5 \times 125.2 \times 0.51 = 4820.826 = 4800$

[rounded off upto two significant figures]

(iv) $\frac{2.13 \times 24.78}{458.2} = 0.115193 = 0.115$

[rounded off to three significant figures]

28. Given,

$A = 2.5 \text{ ms}^{-1} \pm 0.5 \text{ ms}^{-1}$, $B = 0.10 \text{ s} \pm 0.01 \text{ s}$

$x = AB = (2.5)(0.10) = 0.25$ m

$$\frac{\Delta x}{x} = \frac{\Delta A}{A} + \frac{\Delta B}{B}$$

$$= \frac{0.5}{2.5} + \frac{0.01}{0.10} = \frac{0.05 + 0.025}{0.25} = \frac{0.075}{0.25}$$

$\Delta x = 0.075 = 0.08$ m, rounding off to two significant figures.

$AB = (0.25 \pm 0.08)$ m

29. Given, $A = 1.0 \text{ m} \pm 0.2 \text{ m}$ $B = 2.0 \text{ m} \pm 0.2 \text{ m}$

Let, $Y = \sqrt{AB} = \sqrt{(1.0)(2.0)} = 1.414$ m

Rounding off to two significant digits $Y = 1.4$ m

$$\frac{\Delta Y}{Y} = \frac{1}{2}\left[\frac{\Delta A}{A} + \frac{\Delta B}{B}\right] = \frac{1}{2}\left[\frac{0.2}{1.0} + \frac{0.2}{2.0}\right] = \frac{0.6}{2 \times 2.0}$$

$$\Rightarrow \Delta Y = \frac{0.6 \times Y}{2 \times 2.0} = \frac{0.6 \times 1.4}{2 \times 2.0} = 0.212$$

Rounding off to one significant digit $\Delta Y = 0.2$ m

Thus, correct value for $\sqrt{AB} = r + \Delta r = 1.4 \pm 0.2$m

30. Given, $t_1 = 39.6$ s, $t_2 = 39.9$ s and $t_3 = 39.5$ s

Least count of measuring instrument = 0.1 s

(As measurements have only one decimal place)

Precision in the measurement = Least count of the measuring instrument = 0.1 s

Mean value of time for 20 oscillations is given by

$$t = \frac{t_1 + t_2 + t_3}{3} = \frac{39.6 + 39.9 + 39.5}{3} = 39.7 \text{ s}$$

Absolute errors in the measurements

$$\Delta t_1 = t - t_1 = 39.7 - 39.6 = 0.1 \text{ s}$$

$$\Delta t_2 = t - t_2 = 39.7 - 39.9 = -0.2 \text{ s}$$

$$\Delta t_3 = t - t_3 = 39.7 - 39.5 = 0.2 \text{ s}$$

$$\text{Mean absolute error} = \frac{|\Delta t_1| + |\Delta t_2| + |\Delta t_3|}{3}$$

$$= \frac{0.1 + 0.2 + 0.2}{3} = \frac{0.5}{3} = 0.17 \approx 0.2$$

(rounding off upto one decimal place)

∴ Accuracy of measurement = ± 0.2 s

31. Given, physical quantity is $X = a^2b^3c^{5/2}d^{-2}$

Maximum percentage error in X is

$$\frac{\Delta X}{X} \times 100 = \pm\left[2\left(\frac{\Delta a}{a} \times 100\right) + 3\left(\frac{\Delta b}{b} \times 100\right) + \frac{5}{2}\left(\frac{\Delta c}{c} \times 100\right) + 2\left(\frac{\Delta d}{d} \times 100\right)\right]$$

$$= \pm\left[2(1) + 3(2) + \frac{5}{2}(3) + 2(4)\right]\%$$

$$= \pm\left[2 + 6 + \frac{15}{2} + 8\right] = \pm 23.5\%$$

$\therefore$ Percentage error in quantity $X = \pm\ 23.5\%$

Mean absolute error in $X = \pm\ 0.235$

$= \pm\ 0.24$ (rounding-off upto two significant digits)

The calculated value of x should be round-off upto two significant digits.

$\therefore \quad X = 2.8$

32. Given, mass of the box, $m = 2.3$ kg

Mass of first gold piece, $m_1 = 20.15\text{ g} = 0.0215\text{ kg}$

Mass of second gold piece, $m_2 = 20.17\text{g} = 0.0217\text{kg}$

(a) Total mass of the box, $M = m + m_1 + m_2$

$= 2.3 + 0.02015 + 0.02017$

$= 2.34032$ kg

As the mass of the box has least decimal place, i.e one decimal place, therefore total mass of the box can have only one decimal place. Rounding-off the total mass of the box up to one decimal place, we get

total mass of the box, $M = 2.3$ kg

(b) Difference in masses of gold pieces,

$\Delta m = m_2 - m_1$

$= 20.17 - 20.15 = 0.02\text{g}$

The masses of two gold pieces has two decimal places, therefore it is correct upto two places of decimal.

33. The speed of light in vacuum $(c) = 1$ new unit of length s^{-1}

Time taken by light to reach the earth,

$t = 8\text{ min} + 20\text{ s} = (8 \times 60 + 20)\text{ s} = 500\text{ s}$

$\therefore$ Distance between the sun and the earth

$= \text{Speed of light} \times \text{Time}$

$x = c \times t = 1$ new unit of length $\text{s}^{-1} \times 500$ s

$= 500$ new unit of length

34. Given, magnification of microscope $= 100$

Observed width of the hair $= 3.5$ mm

Estimate on the thickness of hair is given by,

$$\text{Magnification} = \frac{\text{Observed width}}{\text{Real width}}$$

or $$\text{Real width} = \frac{\text{Observed width}}{\text{Magnification}} = \frac{3.5}{100}$$

$= 0.035$ mm

35. $P = 2(l + b) \pm 2(\Delta l + \Delta b) = 2(10.5 + 5.2) \pm 2(0.2 + 0.1)$

$= (31.4 \pm 0.6)$ cm

36. Percentage error in measurement of displacement

$$= \frac{5}{200} \times 100$$

Percentage error in measurement of time $= \dfrac{0.2}{20} \times 100$

$\therefore$ Maximum permissible error $= 2.5 + 1 = 3.5\%$

37. Average length $= \dfrac{2.48 + 2.46 + 2.49 + 2.50 + 2.48}{5}$

$$= \frac{12.41}{5} = 2.48\text{ m}$$

Mean absolute error $= \dfrac{0.00 + 0.02 + 0.01 + 0.02 + 0.00}{5}$

$$= \frac{0.05}{5} = 0.01\text{ m}$$

Percentage error $= \dfrac{0.01}{2.48} \times 100\% = 0.04 \times 100\% = 0.40\%$

38. (a) $V = \dfrac{4}{3}\pi R^3$

$$\frac{\Delta V}{V} = 3\frac{\Delta R}{R} \Rightarrow \frac{\Delta V}{V}\% = 3 \times 2\% = 6\%$$

(b) $A = 4\pi R^2$

$$\frac{\Delta A}{A} = 2\frac{\Delta R}{R} \Rightarrow \frac{\Delta A}{A}\% = 2 \times 2\% = 4\%$$

39. Acceleration $= \dfrac{10\text{ m}}{(1\text{ s})^2} = \dfrac{10 \times 10^{-3}}{\left[\dfrac{1}{60 \times 60}\text{ h}\right]^2}$

$= (3600)^2 \times 10^{-2}\text{ km/h}^2 = 1.29 \times 10^5\text{ km/h}^2$

40. $$\therefore \frac{\Delta Z}{Z} = 4\left(\frac{\Delta A}{A}\right) + \frac{1}{3}\left(\frac{\Delta B}{B}\right) + \frac{\Delta C}{C} + \frac{3}{2}\left(\frac{\Delta D}{D}\right)$$

Given, $\dfrac{\Delta A}{A} \times 100 = 4\%$

$\dfrac{\Delta B}{B} \times 100 = 2\%$, $\dfrac{\Delta C}{C} \times 100 = 3\%$

and $\dfrac{\Delta D}{D} \times 100 = 1\%$

$$\therefore \quad \frac{\Delta Z}{Z} \times 100 = (4 \times 4\%) + \left(\frac{1}{3} \times 2\%\right) + 3\% + \left(\frac{3}{2} \times 1\%\right)$$

$$= \left(16 + \frac{2}{3} + 3 + \frac{3}{2}\right)\% = 21.16\%$$

The percentage error in the measurement of Z is 21.16%. Therefore, the relative error in Z is 0.2116.

41. The relation is written by the boy

$$m = \frac{m_0}{(1 - v^2)^{1/2}}$$

According to the principle of homogeneity of dimensions, the dimensions on either side of a relation must be same i.e., the powers of M, L, T on either side of a relation must be same.

Dimension of m is equal to the dimension of m_0, therefore the denominator $(1 - v^2)^{1/2}$ should be dimensionless. In denominator, 1 is dimensionless but factor v^2 is not dimensionless.

To make it dimensionless, we have to divide it by the same physical quantity with same power, therefore it should be v^2/c^2, to become dimensionless.

Hence, the correct relation should be $m = \dfrac{m_0}{\left(1 - \dfrac{v^2}{c^2}\right)^{1/2}}$

42. Given, $T = \dfrac{2\pi m}{k}$

LHS $\quad T = [T]$

RHS $\quad \dfrac{2\pi m}{k} = \dfrac{[M]}{[MT^{-2}]} = [T^2]$

$$\left[\because k = \frac{\text{Force}}{\text{Length}} = \frac{[MLT^{-2}]}{[L]} = [MT^{-2}]\right]$$

$\therefore \quad$ LHS $\neq$ RHS

Hence, the relation is incorrect.

To find the correct relation, suppose $T = km^a k^b$, then

$$[T]^1 = [M]^a [MT^{-2}]^b = [M^{a+b} T^{-2b}]$$

$\therefore \quad a + b = 0, -2b = 1$

On solving, we get $b = \dfrac{-1}{2}, a = \dfrac{1}{2}$

$\therefore \quad T = km^{1/2} k^{-1/2}$

Hence, $\quad T = k\sqrt{\dfrac{m}{k}}$

43. Let the time of oscillation of a small drop of a liquid is given by

$$T \propto d^a r^b \sigma^c$$

$$T = K d^a r^b \sigma^c \qquad \text{...(i)}$$

where, K = dimensionless constant

Dimension of the various quantities are

$$\sigma = [MT^{-2}],\ d = [ML^{-3}],\ r = [L]$$

Substituting these dimensions in Eq. (i), we get

i.e. $\quad [M^0 L^0 T^1] = K[ML^{-3}]^a [L]^b [MT^{-2}]^c$

$$= [M^{a+c} L^{-3a+b} T^{-2c}]$$

Equating the dimensions of M, L and T, we get

$$a + c = 0, -2c = 1, \ -3a + b = 0$$

We get, $\quad c = -1/2, a = 1/2$ and $b = 3/2$

$$T \propto d^{1/2} r^{3/2} \sigma^{-1/2}$$

i.e. $\quad T \propto \sqrt{\dfrac{dr^3}{\sigma}}$

44. Suppose wavelength λ associated with a moving particle depends on (i) its mass (m), (ii) its velocity (v) and (iii) Planck's constant (h)

$$\lambda = km^a v^b h^c$$

where, k is a dimensionless constant.

Writing dimensions of various terms, we get

$$[M^0 L^1 T^0] = [M]^a [LT^{-1}]^b [ML^2 T^{-1}]^c$$

$$= [M^{a+c} L^{b+2c} T^{-b-c}]$$

Comparing power of M, L and T on two sides of equation, we have

$$a + c = 0, b + 2c = 1, -b - c = 0$$

After solving, we get $a = -1, b = -1, c = +1$

Hence, the relation becomes $\lambda = \dfrac{kh}{mv}$

45. Suppose orbital velocity of satellite be given by the relation $\quad v = km^a r^b g^c$

where, k is a dimensionless constant and a, b, c are unknown powers.

Writing dimensions on two sides of equation, we have

$$[M^0 L^1 T^{-1}] = [M]^a [L]^b [LT^{-2}]^c = [M^a L^{b+c} T^{-2c}]$$

Applying principle of homogeneity of dimensional equation, we find that

$$a = 0 \Rightarrow b + c = 1 \Rightarrow -2c = -1$$

On solving these equations, we find that

$$a = 0, b = +\frac{1}{2} \text{ and } c = +\frac{1}{2}$$

$$v = kr^{1/2} g^{1/2}$$

$\Rightarrow \quad v = k\sqrt{rg}$

46. Suppose period of oscillation T depends on radius of star R, mean density of fluid ρ and universal gravitational constant (G) as

$T = kR^a \rho^b G^c$, where k is a dimensionless constant

$$[M^0 L^0 T^1] = [L]^a [ML^{-3}]^b [M^{-1} L^3 T^{-2}]^c$$

$$= M^{b-c} L^{a-3b+3c} T^{-2c}$$

Comparing powers of M, L and T, we have

$$b - c = 0, \ a - 3b + 3c = 0 \text{ and } -2c = 1$$

On simplifying these equations, we get

$$c = -1/2, \ b = -1/2, \ a = 0$$

Thus, we have $T = k\rho^{-1/2} G^{-1/2} = \dfrac{k}{\sqrt{\rho G}}$

QR Code for Quick Test 1

QR Code for Quick Test 2

SELF ASSESSMENT TEST

Multiple Choice Questions (MCQs)

1. Multiply 107.88 by 0.610 and express the result with correct number of significant figures.
(a) 65.8068 (b) 65.8 (c) 64.807 (d) 65.82

2. The radius of a thin wire is 0.16 mm. The area of cross-section of the wire (in mm^2) with correct number of significant figures is
(a) 0.080384 (b) 0.0804
(c) 0.080 (d) 0.08

3. The velocity v of a particle at time t is given by $v = at + \frac{b}{t+c}$, where a, b and c are constants. The dimensions of a, b and c are, respectively
(a) $[LT^{-2}]$, $[L]$ and $[T]$ (b) $[L]$, $[LT]$ and $[T^2]$
(c) $[L^2]$, $[T]$ and $[LT^2]$ (d) $[LT^2]$, $[LT]$ and $[L]$

4. The density of a liquid is 13.6 g cm^{-3}, its value in SI is
(a) 13.6 kg m^{-3} (b) 136 kg m^{-3}
(c) 13600 kg m^{-3} (d) 1360 kg m^{-3}

5. Which of the following is a dimensionless quantity even when the measured quantity is not dimensionless ?
(a) Absolute error (b) Gross error
(c) Relative error (d) Experiment error

6. Which of the following have same dimension as Plank's constant?
(a) Moment of momentum
(b) Moment of force
(c) Momentum/ Distance
(d) Force/Distance

7. Match the Column I with Column II and select the correct answer.

	Column I		Column II
A.	Spring constant	1.	$[M^1L^2T^{-2}]$
B.	Pascal	2.	$[M^0L^0T^{-1}]$
C.	Hertz	3.	$[M^1L^0T^{-2}]$
D.	Joule	4.	$[M^1L^{-1}T^{-2}]$

(a) A-4, B-2, C-1, D-3 (b) A-2, B-1, C-4, D-3
(c) A-3, B-4, C-2, D-1 (d) A-1, B-4, C-3, D-2

Assertion-Reason

Direction *(Q. Nos. 8-10) In the following questions, two statements are given-one labelled Assertion (A) and the other labelled Reason (R). Select the correct answer to these questions from the codes (a), (b), (c) and (d) as given below.*

(a) Both Assertion and Reason are true and Reason is the correct explanation of Assertion.
(b) Both Assertion and Reason are true but Reason is not the correct explanation of Assertion.
(c) Assertion is true but Reason is false.
(d) Assertion is false but Reason is true.

8. **Assertion** When we change the unit of measurement of a quantity, its numerical value changes.
Reason Smaller the unit of measurement, smaller its numerical value.

9. **Assertion** Speed, distance and acceleration can be taken as basic units.
Reason Speed, distance and acceleration have zero dimensions of mass in their dimensional formula.

10. **Assertion** Dimensional constants are the quantities whose values are constants.
Reason Dimensional constants are dimensionless.

Case Based Questions

Directions *(Q.No. 11) This question is case study based question. Read the following paragraph and answer the questions on the basis of same.*

11. Significant figures in the measured value of a physical quantity tell the number of digits in which we have confidence. Larger the number of significant figures obtained in a measurement, greater is the accuracy of measurement and *vice-versa*. In addition or subtraction, the number of decimal places in the result should equal the smallest number of decimal places in any term in the operation.
In multiplication and division, the number of significant figures in the product or in the quotient is the same as the smallest number of significant figure in any of the terms.

(i) Add 3.8×10^{-6} to 4.2×10^{-5} with regards to significant figures.
(a) 4.6×10^{-5} (b) 4.6×10^{-6}
(c) 4.58×10^{-5} (d) 4.580×10^{6}

(ii) Subtract 2.6×10^{4} from 3.9×10^{5} with regards to significant figures.
(a) 3.64×10^{5} (b) 3.7×10^{5}
(c) 3.6×10^{5} (d) 3.65×10^{6}

(iii) The area enclosed by a circle of diameter 1.06 m with correct number of significant figures is
(a) $0.88\ m^2$ (b) $0.882\ m^2$
(c) $1.88\ m^2$ (d) $0.882026\ m^2$

(iv) The mass of a body is 275.32g and its volume is $36.41\ cm^3$. Express its density upto appropriate significant figures.
(a) $7.5616 g\ cm^{-3}$ (b) $7.56 g\ cm^{-3}$
(c) $7.6 g\ cm^{-3}$ (d) $7.562\ g\ cm^{-3}$

Very Short Answer Type Questions

12. What do you mean by fundamental and derived quantities?

13. What is common between bar and torr?

14. State the dimensional formula for stress, strain and Young's modulus.

15. If the unit of force is 100N, unit of length is 10m and unit of time is 100s, then what is the unit of mass in this system of units?

Short Answer Type Questions

16. When 1m, 1kg and 1 min are taken as the fundamental units, the magnitude of the force is 36 units. What will be the value of this force in CGS system?

17. The equation of state of real gases can be expressed as $\left(p+\frac{a}{V^2}\right)(V-b)=RT$, where p is pressure, V is volume and T is absolute temperature. Find dimensional formula of constants a and b.

Long Answer Type Questions

18. A book with many printing errors contains four different formulae for the displacement y of a particle, undergoing a certain periodic motion

(i) $y = a\sin\frac{2\pi t}{T}$

(ii) $y = a\sin vt$

(iii) $y = \left(\frac{a}{T}\right)\sin\left(\frac{t}{a}\right)$

(iv) $y = \left(\frac{a}{\sqrt{2}}\right)\left(\sin\frac{2\pi t}{T}+\cos\frac{2\pi t}{T}\right)$

where, a = maximum displacement of the particle, v = speed of the particle and T = time period of motion. Rule out the wrong formulae on dimensional grounds.

19. State the principle of homogeneity. Test the dimensional homogeneity of equations -

(i) $s = ut+\frac{1}{2}at^2$

(ii) $s_n = u+\frac{a}{2}(2n-1)$

Answers

1. (b)	2. (c)	3. (a)	4. (a)	5. (c)	6. (a)
7. (c)	8. (c)	9. (d)	10. (c)		

11. (i) (a), (ii) (c), (iii) (b), (iv) (d)

02

CHAPTER

Motion in a straight line is also called rectilinear motion. It involves no change in direction, so its study about is relatively simple. In this chapter, we will study about motion of object either along X-axis or along Y-axis.

YOUR STUDY GOALS

YOUR PRACTICE GOAL

- Objective Type Questions (30 Qs ; MCQs, A-R, Matching)
- Case Based Questions (3)
- Subjective Questions (5 VSAs, 10 SAs, 15 LAs)
- Numerical Problems (23)

Motion in a Straight Line

2.1 General Introduction of Motion

Rest

If the position of an object does not change w.r.t. its surrounding with the passage of time, it is said to be at **rest**. e.g. Book lying on the table, a person sitting on a chair, etc.

Motion

If the position of an object is continuously changing w.r.t. its surrounding with the passage of time, then it is said to be in the **state of motion.**

Thus, **motion can be defined as a change in position of an object with time.** In our daily life, we see a train moving on rails, the walking man, the crawling insects, water flowing down from a dam, etc., showing that the object is in motion. **Rest and motion are relative terms.**

Frame of Reference

It is a set of coordinate axes that defines the position of a particle in two or three dimensional space. The **cartesian coordinate system** is the most basic frame of reference, in which a particle's position is specified by three coordinate axes X, Y and Z. The point of intersection of these three axes is called **origin** (O) and considered as **reference point**.

- This coordinate system along with a clock constitutes a frame of reference.
- There is no meaning of rest or motion without any observer.

Point Object

An object is considered as point object if the size of the object is much smaller than the distance it moves in a reasonable duration of time.

e.g.

(i) A train covering a journey of several hundred kilometres can be regarded as a point object.

(ii) Earth can be regarded as a point object for studying its motion around the sun.

Types of Motion

On the basis of the nature of path followed, motion is classified as

- **Rectilinear Motion** The motion in which a particle moves along a straight line is called rectilinear motion. e.g. Motion of a sliding body on an inclined plane.
- **Circular Motion** The motion in which a particle moves in a circular path is called circular motion. e.g. A string whirled in a circular loop.
- **Oscillatory Motion** The motion in which a particle moves to and fro about a given point is known as oscillatory motion. e.g. Simple pendulum.

On the basis of the number of coordinates required to define the motion, it is classified as

- **One-dimensional Motion** The motion of an object is considered as one-dimensional (1-D) if only one coordinate is needed to specify the position of an object.

  In 1-D motion, the object moves along a straight line. In this type of motion, there are only two directions (backward and forward, upward and downward) in which an object moves and these directions are specified by + and – signs. e.g. A boy running on a straight road, etc.

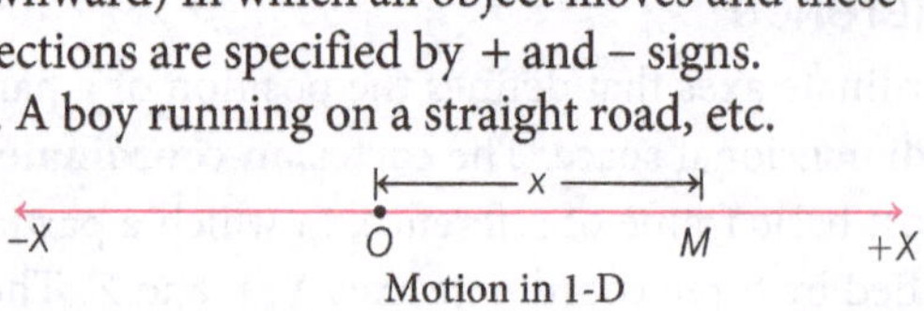

Motion in 1-D

- **Two-dimensional Motion** The motion of an object is considered as two dimensional (2-D) if two coordinates are needed to specify the position of the object. **In 2-D motion, the object moves in a plane.**

  e.g. A satellite revolving around the earth, etc.

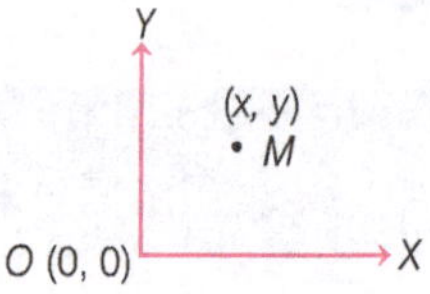

Motion in 2-D

- **Three-dimensional Motion** The motion of an object is considered as three-dimensional (3-D) if all the three coordinates are needed to specify the position of the object.

  e.g. Butterfly flying in garden, the motion of gas molecules in air, etc.

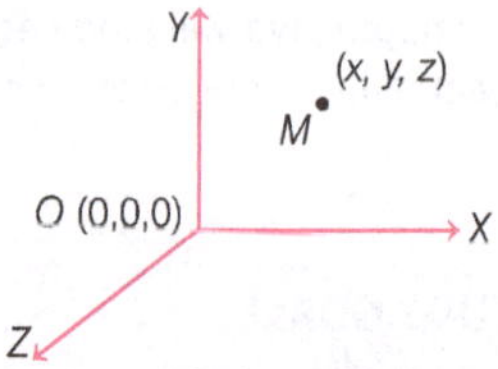

Motion in 3-D

Scalar and Vector Quantities

Physical quantities are studied under two heads, i.e. scalars and vectors. Both types of quantities can be defined as follows.

(i) **Scalar quantity** If only the magnitude is required to specify a physical quantity, that physical quantity is known as scalar quantity or scalars.

e.g. Mass, length, time, speed, etc.

(ii) **Vector quantity** If magnitude as well as direction both are required to specify a physical quantity, that physical quantity is known as vector quantity or vectors.

e.g. Displacement, velocity, acceleration, etc.

2.2 Uniform Motion in a Straight Line

A body is said to be in a uniform motion if it travels equal distance in equal intervals of time along a straight line.

e.g. A vehicle running with the constant speed of 10 m/s will cover equal distance of 10 m in every second, so its motion will be uniform.

Note For a uniform motion along a straight line in a given direction, the magnitude of the displacement is equal to the actual distance covered by an object.

The nature of position-time graph of an object in the following cases are

(i) **When Object is Stationary** The distance of an object will remain unchanged with the passage of time, the position-time graph of such an object will be as shown in figure.

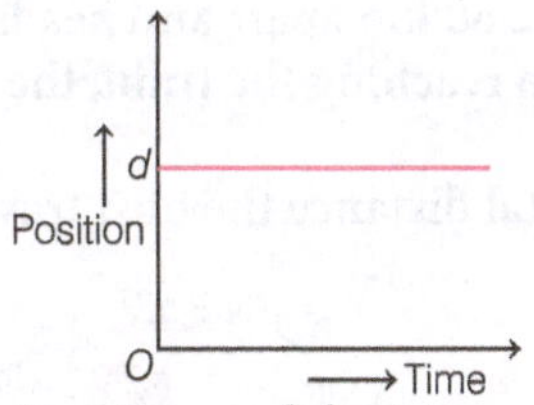

Position-time graph for stationary object

From the graph, it is clear that, **the position of the object remain same w.r.t. time,** i.e. object is at rest position at d distance from origin.

(ii) **When Object is in Variable Motion** The position-time graph of varying motion will not be a straight line as shown below.

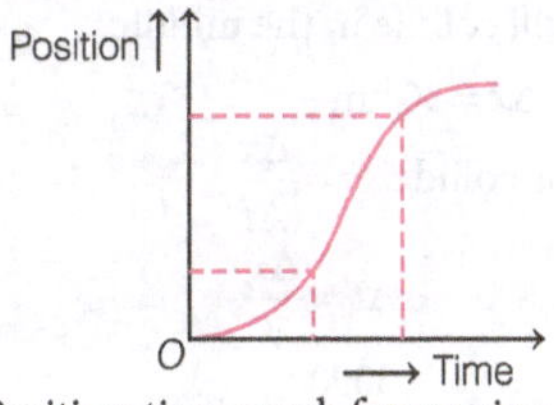

Position-time graph for moving object

From the graph, it is clear that, **object covers unequal distance in equal interval of time.** Initially, it covers less distance and after that, it covers more distance but in same time interval.

Non-uniform Motion

A body is in non-uniform motion if it travels equal displacement in unequal intervals of time.

During the non-uniform motion, the speed of the body or its direction of motion or both change with time.

e.g. The velocity of the vehicle is different at different instants, so it has non-uniform motion.

Example 1. **An object starting from +10 m on the X-axis covers 20 m in first second and 30 m in the next second towards + X-axis. Draw position-time graph for its motion.**

Sol. Just plot the positions of the object at different instants on x-t graph.

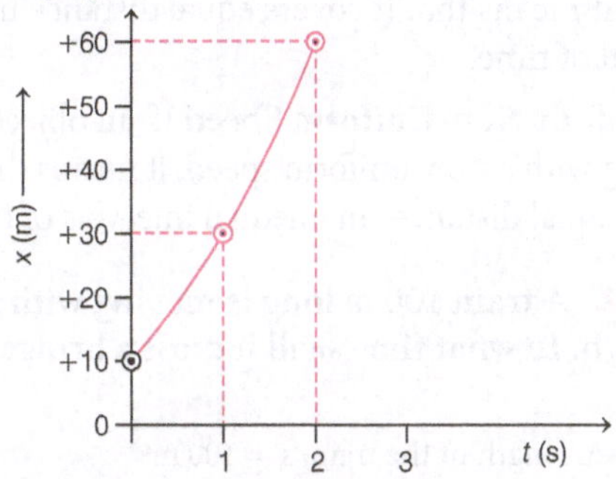

At $t = 0$, the object is at +10 m, at $t = 1$ s, the object will be at +30 m and at $t = 2$ s the object will be at +60 m. One can easily notice that the motion is non-uniform.

Distance or Path Length Covered

The length of the actual path covered by an object is called the distance or path length.

It is a **scalar quantity** and it **can never be zero or negative** during the motion of an object. Its SI unit is **metre**.

Displacement

The shortest distance between the initial and final positions of any object during motion is called displacement. The displacement of an object in a given time can be **positive, zero** or **negative**.

$$\textbf{Displacement, } \Delta x = x_2 - x_1$$

where, x_1 and x_2 are the initial and final positions of object, respectively.

It is a **vector quantity**. Its SI unit is **metre**.

2.3 Speed and Velocity

Speed

The distance covered by an object divided by the time taken by the object to cover that distance is called the speed of that object.

$$\text{Speed} = \frac{\text{Distance travelled}}{\text{Time taken}}$$

Speed is a **scalar quantity**. The speed of the object for a given interval of time is **always positive.**

Unit of speed The unit of speed in MKS (SI) is m/s and in CGS as cm/s.

- **Average Speed** The average speed of an object in a certain time interval is the distance covered by the object in that time interval divided by time.

- **Uniform Speed** If an object is moving with a uniform speed, it means that it covers equal distance in equal interval of time.
- **Variable or Non-Uniform Speed** If an object is moving with a non-uniform speed, it means that it covers equal distances in unequal intervals of time.

Example 2. A train 100 m long is moving with a speed of 60 km/h. In what time shall it cross a bridge of 1 km long?

Sol. Given length of the train, $s_1 = 100$ m

Length of the bridge, $s_2 = 1 \text{ km} = 1000 \text{ m}, t = ?$

Total length, $s = 100 + 1000 = 1100$ m

Speed of train, $s = 60 \text{ km/h} = 60 \times \frac{5}{18} = \frac{50}{3}$ m/s

$\therefore \quad t = \frac{\text{Distance}}{\text{Speed}} = \frac{1100}{\frac{50}{3}} = 66$ s

Velocity

The rate of change of position of an object with time is called the velocity of that object.

i.e. $$\text{Velocity} = \frac{\text{Displacement}}{\text{Time}}$$

It is a **vector** quantity.

The velocity of an object can be **positive, zero** and **negative** according to its displacement.

The unit of velocity is cms^{-1} in CGS and ms^{-1} in MKS or SI.

- **Average velocity** The average velocity of an object in a certain time interval is given as the displacement of an object in that time interval divided by time.
- **Uniform Velocity** If an object covers equal displacement in equal interval of time, it means that it is moving with uniform velocity.
- **Non-uniform Velocity** If an object is moving with a non-uniform velocity, then it will have unequal displacements in equal intervals of time.

Example 3. During a hard sneeze, your eyes might shut for 0.5 s. If you are driving a car at 90 km/h during such a sneeze, how far does the car move during that time?

Sol. Given, $t = 0.5$ s

velocity $(v) = 90$ km/h

$= 90 \times \frac{5}{18} = 25$ m/s

We know that, $v = \frac{\Delta x}{\Delta t}$

$\therefore \quad \Delta x = v\Delta t = (25 \text{ m/s})\ (0.5 \text{ s}) = 12.5 \text{ m} \approx 13 \text{ m}$

Example 4. Two trains, each having a speed of 30 km/h, are headed towards each other on the same track. A bird that can fly 60 km/h flies off infront of one train when they were 60 km apart and heads directly to the other train. On reaching the train, the bird flies back to the first train.
What is the total distance the bird travels before the trains collide?

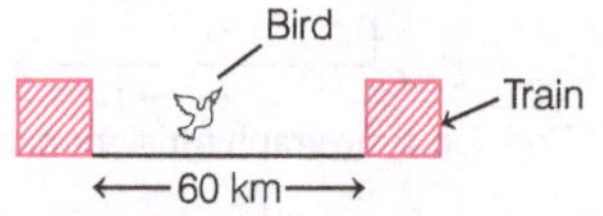

Sol. Given, $v_1 = 30$ km/h, $v_2 = 60$ km/h and $d = 60$ km

$v_1 = 30 \text{ km/h} = 30 \times \frac{5}{18} = 8.33$ m/s

$v_2 = 60 \text{ km/h} = 60 \times \frac{5}{18} = 16.67$ m/s

and $\quad d = 60 \text{ km} = 60 \times 1000 = 60000$ m

The train will collide in the middle.

So, $\quad \Delta x = 30$ km

When trains collide, $v = \frac{\Delta x}{\Delta t}$

$\Rightarrow \quad \Delta t = \frac{\Delta x}{v}$

$\therefore \quad \Delta t = \frac{30000}{8.33} = 3601$ s

Now, $\quad v = \frac{\Delta x}{\Delta t} = \Delta x = v\Delta t$

$\therefore \ \Delta x = (16.67)(3601) \approx 60028.67 \text{ m} = 60 \text{ km}$

Positive Velocity

If the displacement is positive, then the velocity is positive. For positive velocity, the slope of x-t graph will be positive.

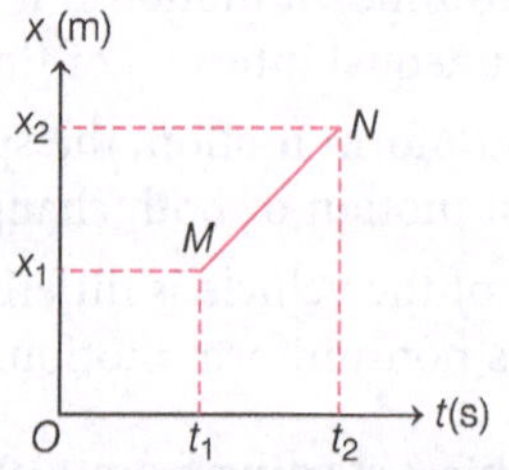

x-t graph for positive velocity

Slope of line $MN = \frac{x_2 - x_1}{t_2 - t_1}$

As $x_2 > x_1$, so $x_2 - x_1 =$ positive. So, **slope is positive.**

Negative Velocity

If the displacement is negative, then the velocity is negative. For negative velocity, the slope of x-t graph will be negative.

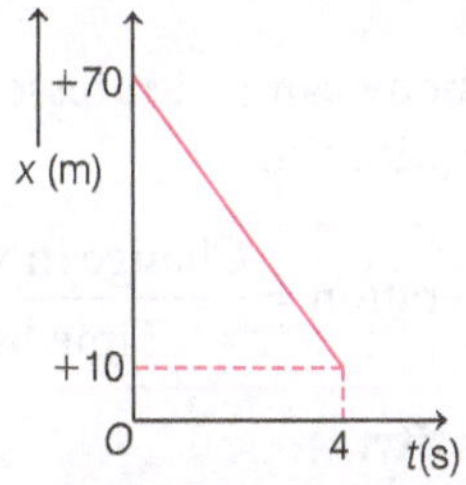

x-t graph for negative velocity

In the above graph, the object is moving towards negative X-axis. At $t=0$, the object is at +70 m and at $t=4$ s the object is at +10 m.

So, the slope of x-t graph $= \dfrac{10-70}{4-0} = \dfrac{-60}{4} = -15$ m/s

Instantaneous Speed and Instantaneous Velocity

Instantaneous Speed

If the speed of an object is variable, then its speed at a given instant of time is called the instantaneous speed.

Speed at an instant is defined as the limit of the average speed as the time interval (Δt) becomes infinitesimally small or approaches to zero.

Mathematically, instantaneous speed at any instant of time (t) is expressed as

$$\text{Instantaneous speed, } s_i = \lim_{\Delta t \to 0} \frac{\Delta s}{\Delta t} \text{ or } s_i = \frac{ds}{dt}$$

[ds is the distance covered in time interval dt]

where, $\dfrac{ds}{dt}$ is the differential coefficient of s w.r.t. t.

Example 5. **If the instantaneous displacement of the particle is $[2t^2\,\hat{i} + 3t\,\hat{j}]$, then find out the instantaneous speed of the particle.**

Sol. Given, position of the particle,

$$s = [2t^2\hat{i} + 3t\hat{j}]$$

$$s_i = \frac{ds}{dt} = \frac{d}{dt}[2t^2\hat{i} + 3t\hat{j}]$$

Instantaneous speed of the particle,

$$s_i = 4t\,\hat{i} + 3\hat{j}$$

Instantaneous Velocity

If the velocity of an object is variable, then its velocity at a given instant is called the instantaneous velocity.

Velocity at an instant is defined as the limit of average velocity as the time interval (Δt) becomes infinitesimally small or approaches to zero.

Mathematically, instantaneous velocity at instant of time (t) is given by

$$v_i = \lim_{\Delta t \to 0} \frac{\Delta x}{\Delta t} \text{ or } v_i = \frac{dx}{dt}$$

where, dx is displacement for time interval dt.

$\lim_{\Delta t \to 0} \dfrac{\Delta x}{\Delta t}$ is called differential coefficient of displacement x w.r.t. time t. i.e. $\dfrac{dx}{dt}$.

Calculation by Graphical Method

Suppose an object is moving along a straight line with variable velocity. Let the position-time graph of this motion is represented by a curve as shown in the figure.

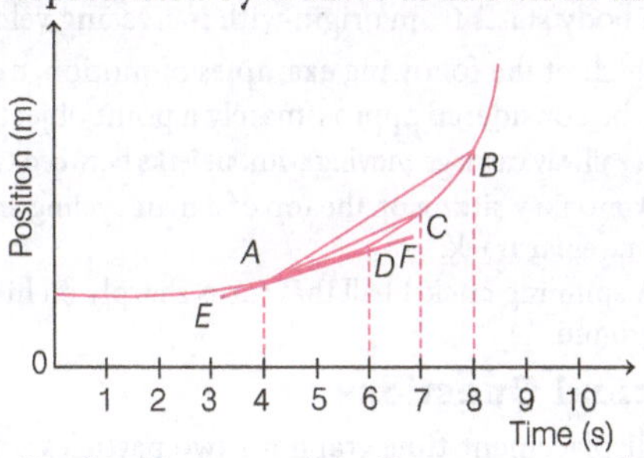

Graphical interpretation of instantaneous velocity

v_{average} over the time interval $\Delta t = 4$s, (i.e. from 4s to 8s) is the slope of straight line AB.

If we decrease the interval of time Δt from 4s to 3s, then the line becomes AC.

Similarly, at time interval $\Delta t = 2$s, the line becomes AD. As Δt approaches to zero, the point B approaches to point A.

Thus, the line AB becomes the tangent EF to the curve at point A. Hence, **the slope of the tangent with time axis gives the value of instantaneous velocity.**

Generally, we use numerical method to find the value of instantaneous velocity as the limiting process becomes clear.

TEACHER TIP

The magnitude of instantaneous velocity is always equal to the instantaneous speed at a particular instant.

Example 6. **The displacement (in metre) of a particle moving along X-axis is given by $x = 18t + 15t^2$. Find the instantaneous velocity at $t = 0$ and $t = 2$ s.**

Sol. Given, Displacement, $x = 18t + 15t^2$

Instantaneous velocity, $v_i = \frac{dx}{dt} = 18 + 30t$

Instantaneous velocity at

$t = 0$, $v = 18 + (30 \times 0) = 18$ m/s

and $t = 2$s, $v = 18 + (30 \times 2) = 78$ m/s

Quick Test 1

Conceptual Questions

1. What is the condition for an object to be considered as a point object?
2. Can a tumbling beaker that has slipped off the edge of a table considered as a point object?
3. Draw position-time graph for a body at rest.
4. With zero speed a particle may have non-zero velocity. Is the statement true or false, explain?
5. Draw position-time graph for a non-uniform motion, when body starts from origin with increasing velocity.
6. In which of the following examples of motion, can the body be considered approximately a point object? *NCERT*
   (i) A railway carriage moving without jerks between two stations.
   (ii) A monkey sitting on the top of a man cycling smoothly on a circular track.
   (iii) A spinning cricket ball that turns sharply on hitting the ground.

Numerical Questions

7. The displacement-time graph for two particles x and y are straight lines making angles of 30° and 60° with the time axis. What is the ratio of the velocities of y and x?
8. The position x of a body is given by $x = A\sin(\omega t)$. Find the time at which the displacement is maximum.
9. A drunkard walking in a narrow lane takes 5 steps forward and 3 steps backward, followed again 5 steps forward and 3 steps backward, and so on. Each step is 1 m long and requires 1 s. Determine how long the drunkard takes to fall in a pit 13 m away from the start. *NCERT*
10. For the motion shown in the figure, find the displacement of car between the time intervals t_1 and t_3.

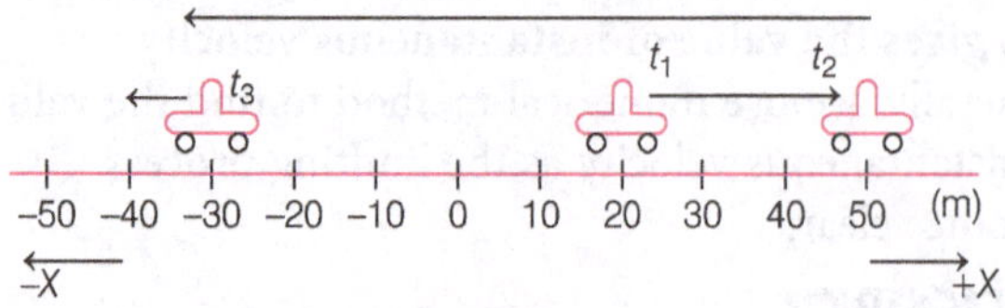

Answers

7. 3 : 1 8. $t = \frac{\pi}{2\omega}$ 9. 37s 10. −50 m

For Solutions, See QR Code on Pg. 66

2.4 Uniformly Accelerated Motion

Acceleration

Acceleration of a body can be expressed as the rate of change of velocity with time.

$$\text{Acceleration} = \frac{\text{Change in velocity}}{\text{Time taken}}$$

It is a **vector quantity.**

Its SI unit is **m/s²** and CGS unit is **cm/s²**.

Its **dimensional formula** is $[M^0L^1T^{-2}]$.

Therefore, **acceleration may result from a change in speed (magnitude), a change in direction or changes in both.**

If the sign of velocity and acceleration is **same** (either both positive or both negative), it means that the body is **accelerating** and when the sign of velocity and acceleration are **opposite**, it means that the body is **retarding.**

Example 7. **Starting from a stationary position, a bus attains a velocity of 6 m/s in 30 s. Then, the driver of the bus applies a brake such that the velocity of the bus comes down to 4 m/s in the next 5 s. Calculate the acceleration of the bus in both the cases.**

Sol. **Case I** Initial velocity of the bus, $u = 0$

Final velocity, $v = 6$ m/s, Time taken, $t = 30$ s

$$\therefore \text{Acceleration} = \frac{\text{Change in velocity}}{\text{Time taken}}$$

$$= \frac{\text{Final velocity} - \text{Initial velocity}}{\text{Time taken}}$$

$$= \frac{v-u}{t} = \frac{6-0}{30} = 0.2\,\text{m/s}^2$$

Case II Initial velocity, $u = 6$ m/s

Final velocity, $v = 4$ m/s

$$\therefore \text{Acceleration} = \frac{v-u}{t} = \frac{4-6}{5} = -0.4\ \text{m/s}^2$$

Thus, the acceleration in both the cases are $0.2\ \text{m/s}^2$ and $-0.4\ \text{m/s}^2$

Average Acceleration

The average acceleration over a time interval is defined as **the change in velocity divided by the time interval.**

Suppose that at any time (t_1) a body has velocity (v_1). At a later time (t_2), it has velocity (v_2). Thus,

Change in velocity, $\Delta v = v_2 - v_1$

Time during which velocity has changed, $\Delta t = t_2 - t_1$

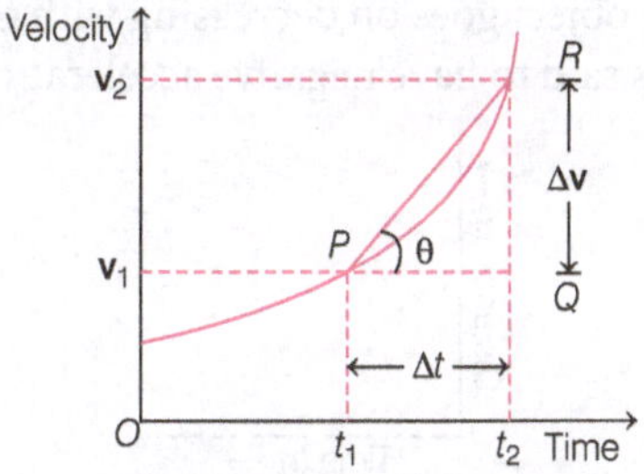

Velocity-time graph to calculate average acceleration

$\mathbf{a}_{av}$ = slope of straight line $PR = \dfrac{RQ}{PQ}$

$$\text{Average acceleration, } \mathbf{a}_{av} = \frac{\Delta \mathbf{v}}{\Delta t} = \frac{\mathbf{v}_2 - \mathbf{v}_1}{t_2 - t_1}$$

Note The slope of velocity-time graph gives acceleration.

Instantaneous Acceleration

It is defined as the acceleration of a body at a certain instant or the **limiting value of average acceleration** when time interval becomes very small or tends to zero.

$$\text{So, Instantaneous acceleration, } \mathbf{a}_{inst} = \lim_{\Delta t \to 0} \frac{\Delta \mathbf{v}}{\Delta t} = \frac{d\mathbf{v}}{dt}$$

where $\dfrac{d\mathbf{v}}{dt}$ is the differential coefficient of v w.r.t. t.

Elementary Concept of Integration for Describing Motion

We know that, $v = \dfrac{ds}{dt}$, $a = \dfrac{dv}{dt}$ or $v\dfrac{dv}{ds}$

If the displacement is given and we have to find the velocity and acceleration, then we use differentiation. If the acceleration is given and we have to find the velocity and displacement, then we use integration. To find the average value of square or any other power of velocity.

$$\overline{v^2} = \frac{\int_{t_1}^{t_2} v^2 dt}{\int_{t_1}^{t_2} dt} \quad \text{Similarly,} \quad \overline{v^4} = \frac{\int_{t_1}^{t_2} v^4 dt}{\int_{t_1}^{t_2} dt}$$

If velocity is a function of displacement, $v = f(x)$, for average of v from $x = x_1$ to $x = x_2$

$$\Rightarrow \qquad \bar{v} = \frac{\int_{x_1}^{x_2} v\,ds}{\int_{x_1}^{x_2} ds}$$

The above procedure can be applied to find the average value of any quantity like velocity, acceleration, force, etc.

Example 8. **From the figure given below, find the average acceleration between points A and B.**

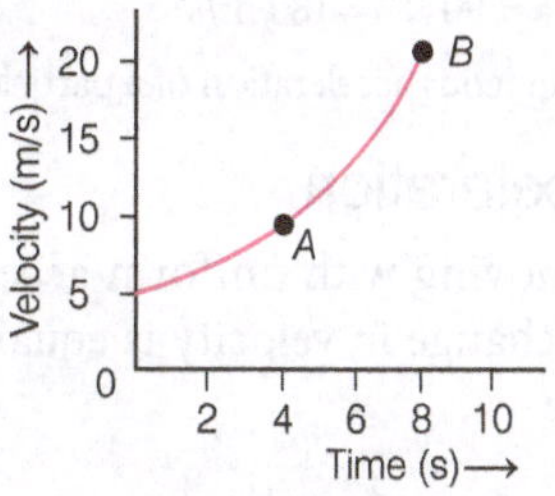

Sol. We draw the graph as

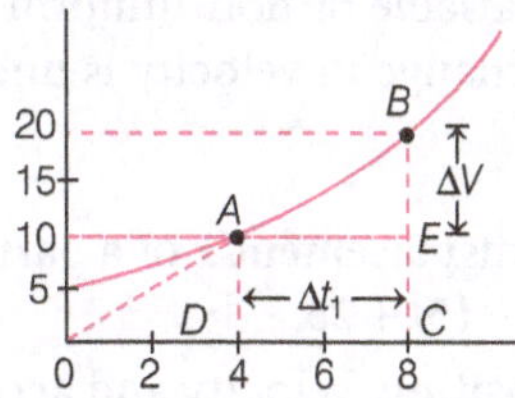

Average acceleration, $\mathbf{a}_{av}$ = slope of line $AB = \dfrac{BE}{AE}$

$$BE = \Delta \mathbf{v} = \mathbf{v}_2 - \mathbf{v}_1 = 20 - 10 = 10 \text{ m/s}$$

$$AE = \Delta t = t_2 - t_1 = 8 - 4 = 4 \text{ s}$$

$$\therefore \qquad \mathbf{a}_{av} = \frac{10}{4} = 2.5 \text{ m/s}^2$$

Example 9. **The velocity of a particle is given by $\mathbf{v} = 2t^2 - 3t + 10$ m/s. Find the instantaneous acceleration at $t = 5$ s.**

Sol. Given, $\mathbf{v} = (2t^2 - 3t + 10)$ m/s

$$\mathbf{a}_{in} = \frac{d\mathbf{v}}{dt} = (4t - 3) \text{ m/s}^2$$

If $t = 5$, $\mathbf{a}_{in} = (5 \times 4) - 3 = 17 \text{ m/s}^2$

Example 10. **A particle is moving in a straight line. Its displacement at any instant t is given by $x = 10t + 15t^3$, where x is in metres and t is in seconds. Find**

(i) the average acceleration in the interval $t = 0$ to $t = 2$ s and

(ii) instantaneous acceleration at $t = 2$ s.

Sol. Given equation, $x = 10t + 15t^3$

(i) Velocity of particle, $\mathbf{v} = \dfrac{dx}{dt}$

$$\mathbf{v} = \frac{d}{dt}(10t + 15t^3) = 10 + 45t^2$$

At $t = 0$, $\mathbf{v}_0 = 10 + 45(0) = 10$ m/s,

At $t = 2$s, $\mathbf{v}_2 = 10 + 45 \times (2)^2 = 10 + 180 = 190$ m/s

$$\Delta \mathbf{v} = \mathbf{v}_2 - \mathbf{v}_0 = 190 - 10 = 180 \text{ m/s}$$

$$\Delta t = 2 - 0 = 2 \text{ s}$$

$$\therefore \qquad \mathbf{a}_{av} = \frac{\Delta \mathbf{v}}{\Delta t} = \frac{180}{2} = 90 \text{ m/s}^2$$

$$a = \frac{d}{dt}(10 + 45t^2) = 90t$$

At $t = 2$ s, $a = 90 \times 2 = 180 \text{ m/s}^2$

The instantaneous acceleration of a particle at 2 s is 180 m/s^2.

Uniform Acceleration

If an object is moving with uniform acceleration, it means that the change in velocity is equal for equal intervals of time.

Non-uniform Acceleration

If an object has variable or non-uniform acceleration, it means that the change in velocity is unequal for equal intervals of time.

Example 11. The displacement x of a particle varies with time t as $x = 4t^2 - 15t + 25$.

(i) Find the position, velocity and acceleration of the particle at $t = 0$.

(ii) Can we call the motion of the particle as one with uniform acceleration?

Sol. (i) Given position, $x = 4t^2 - 15t + 25$

$$\text{Velocity, } v = \frac{dx}{dt} = \frac{d}{dt}(4t^2 - 15t + 25) = (8t - 15) \text{ m/s}$$

$$\text{Acceleration, } a = \frac{dv}{dt} = \frac{d}{dt}(8t - 15)$$

Differentiating gives, $a = 8 \text{ m/s}^2$

At time $t = 0$, we have

$$x = 4t^2 - 15t + 25 = 4(0) - 15(0) + 25 = 25 \text{ m}$$

$$v = 8t - 15 = 8(0) - 15 = -15 \text{ m/s}$$

and $a = 8 \text{ m/s}^2$

(ii) Yes, the particle has a uniform acceleration because it does not depend on time t.

Position-Time Graphs for Positive, Negative and Zero Acceleration

(i) **Positive Acceleration** When distance covered by a moving object goes on increasing with time, the object is said to have positive acceleration.

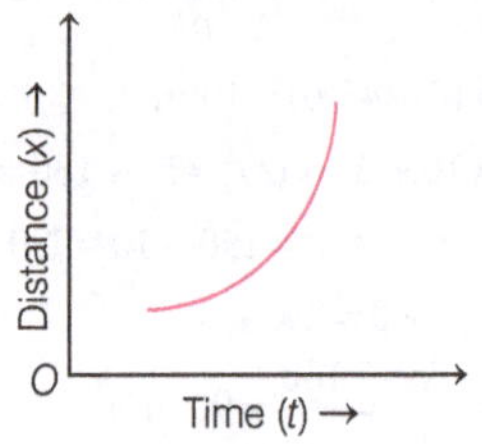

(ii) **Negative Acceleration** When distance covered by a moving object goes on decreasing with time, the object is said to have negative acceleration.

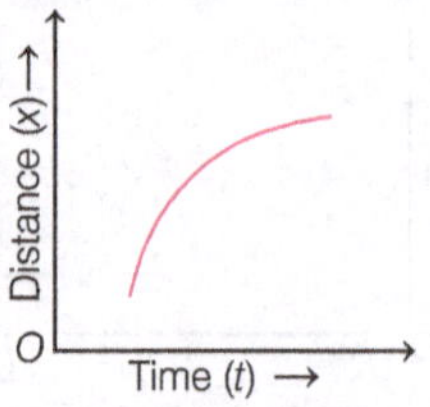

(iii) **Zero Acceleration** When the moving object covers equal distance in equal interval of time, the object is said to have zero acceleration, i.e. for constant velocity, $a = 0$.

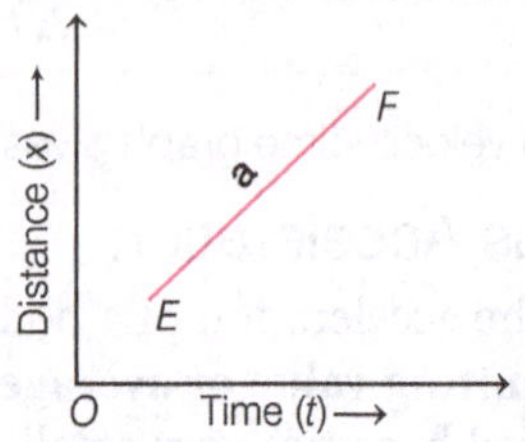

Velocity-Time Graphs for an Accelerated Motion

(i) **Zero Acceleration** In case of zero acceleration, the velocity of the object does not change with time.

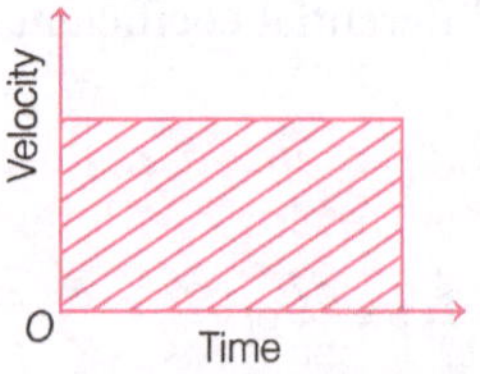

Note The area under v-t graph gives displacement.

(ii) **Positive Acceleration**

(a) If the object is moving with positive acceleration having zero initial velocity, then **the velocity-time graph is a straight line starting from origin.**

In case of positive acceleration, the velocity of the object goes on increasing with time.

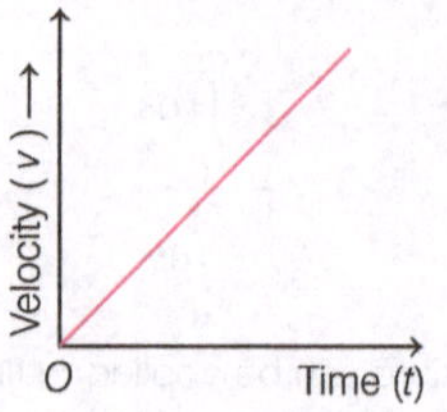

(b) If the object is moving with positive acceleration having some non-zero initial velocity, then **the** velocity-time graph is a straight line starting from **P.**

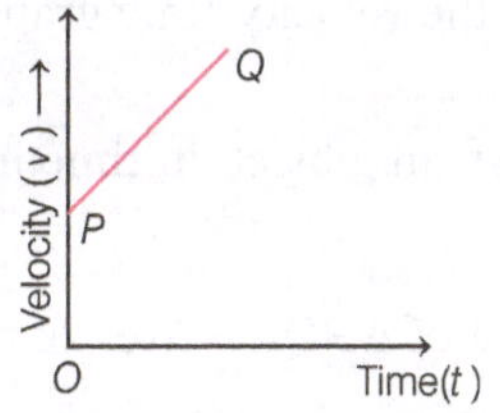

(iii) **Increasing Acceleration** In case of increasing acceleration, the velocity of the object goes on increasing exponentially (non-linearly).

If the object is moving with increasing acceleration having zero initial velocity, then the slope of v-t graph gives the **instantaneous acceleration.**

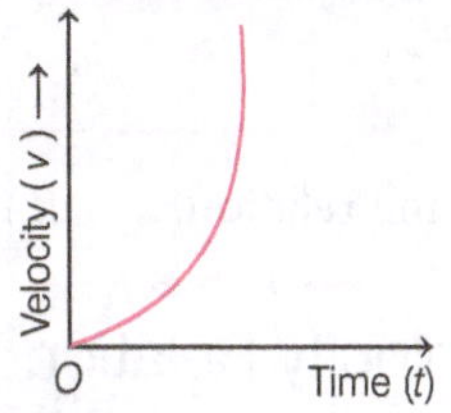

(iv) **Negative Acceleration**

(a) In case of negative acceleration, the velocity of the object decreases linearly with time.

If the object is moving with negative acceleration and having some positive initial velocity, then **the velocity-time graph is a straight line having negative slope.**

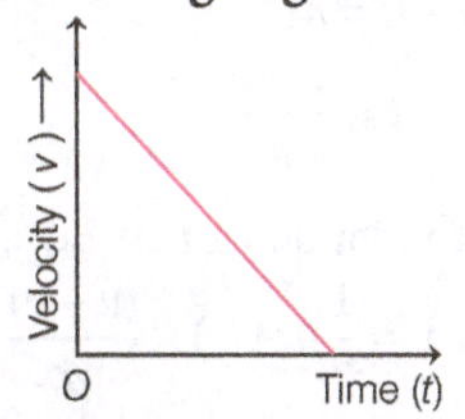

(b) If the object is moving with negative acceleration and having some negative initial velocity, then **the velocity-time graph is a straight line starting from P as point of negative velocity.**

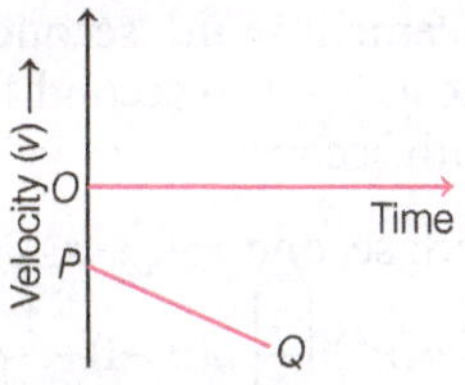

(c) If the object is moving with negative acceleration and having some positive initial velocity, then the direction of its motion can change at time (t). **The slope of velocity-time graph will remain constant for uniform acceleration.**

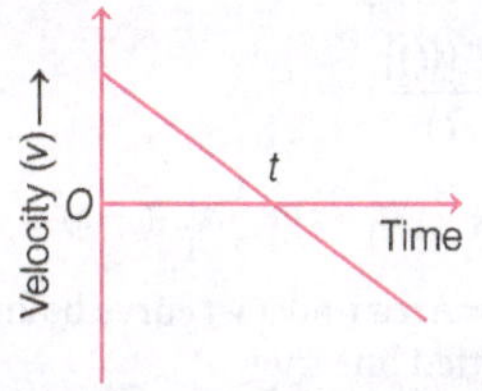

Example 12. With the help of above velocity-time graph, find the

(i) displacement in first three seconds and

(ii) acceleration for the above graph.

Area under the v-t graph gives the measurement of displacement. Thus, displacement = Area under v-t graph.

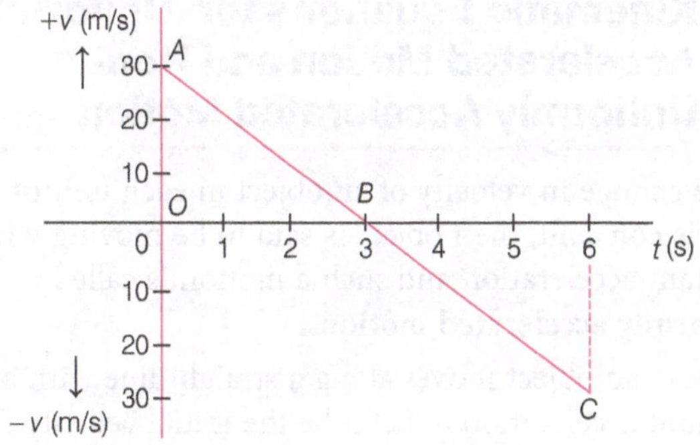

Sol. (i) Displacement in first three seconds = Area of ΔOAB

$$= \frac{1}{2}(OB)\times(OA) = \frac{1}{2}(3)\times(+30) = +45\,\text{m}$$

(ii) Acceleration = Slope of v-t graph

As, v-t graph is a straight line. So, consider the slope of line AB.

$$\therefore \quad \text{Slope of line } AB = \frac{y_2 - y_1}{x_2 - x_1} = \frac{0-30}{3} = -10\,\text{m/s}^2$$

So, the acceleration is negative.

Example 13. The velocity-time graph of a particle in one-dimensional motion is shown in figure. Which of the following formulae are correct for describing the motion of the particle over the time interval t_1 to t_2?

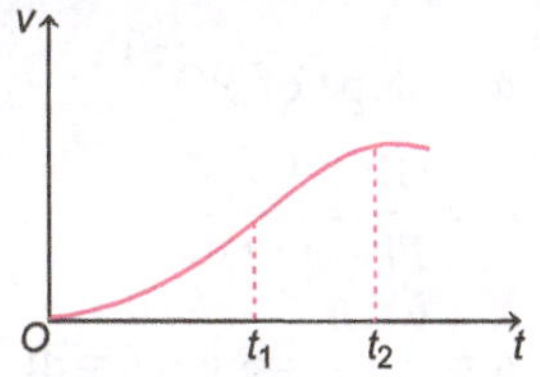

(i) $x(t_2) = x(t_1) + v(t_1)(t_2 - t_1) + \frac{1}{2}a(t_2 - t_1)^2$

(ii) $v(t_2) = v(t_1) + a(t_2 - t_1)$

(iii) $v_{av} = \left[\frac{x(t_2) - x(t_1)}{(t_2 - t_1)}\right]$

(iv) $a_{av} = \frac{[v(t_2) - v(t_1)]}{(t_2 - t_1)}$

(v) $x(t_2) = x(t_1) + v_{av}(t_2 - t_1) + \frac{1}{2}a_{av}(t_2 - t_1)^2$

(vi) $x(t_2) - x(t_1)$ = Area under v-t curve bounded by the t-axis and the dotted line shown. NCERT

Sol. The slope of the given graph over the time interval t_1 to t_2 is not constant and is not uniform. It means acceleration is not constant or uniform, therefore relations (i), (ii) and (v) are not correct which is uniform accelerated motion, but relations (iii), (iv) and (vi) are correct, because these relations are true for both uniform or non-uniform accelerated motion.

2.5 Kinematic Equations for Uniformly Accelerated Motion and Non-Uniformly Accelerated Motion

If the change in velocity of an object in each unit of time is constant, then object is said to be moving with constant acceleration and such a motion is called **uniformly accelerated motion.**

Suppose an object moves along a straight line with a constant acceleration a. Let u be the initial velocity at $t = 0$ and v be the final velocity of the object after time (t).

(i) Velocity-Time Relation

The slope of velocity-time graph gives the acceleration of the object.

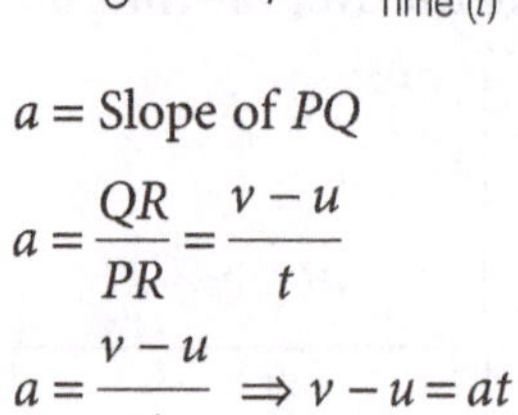

$\therefore$ a = Slope of PQ

$$a = \frac{QR}{PR} = \frac{v-u}{t}$$

$\Rightarrow$ $a = \frac{v-u}{t} \Rightarrow v - u = at$

Velocity-time relation, $v = u + at$

(ii) Position-Time Relation

The area under the velocity-time graph gives the displacement.

Displacement of an object in time interval t is given by

$$x = \text{Area of } \Delta PQR + \text{Area of rectangle } OPRT$$

$$= \frac{1}{2}QR \times PR + OP \times PR = \frac{1}{2}(v-u)t + ut$$

$$= \frac{1}{2}(at)t + ut \qquad [\because v - u = at]$$

$$= \frac{1}{2}at^2 + ut$$

$$\Rightarrow \quad x = \frac{1}{2}at^2 + ut$$

Position-time relation, $x = ut + \frac{1}{2}at^2$

(iii) Position-Velocity Relation

Again the displacement in time interval (t) is given by

$$x = \text{area of trapezium } OPQT.$$

$$= \frac{1}{2}(OP + QT) \times OT$$

$$x = \frac{1}{2}(u + v) \times t \qquad \text{...(i)}$$

From $\quad v - u = at$

$$t = \frac{v-u}{a} \qquad \text{...(ii)}$$

On substituting the value of t in Eq. (i), we get

$$x = \frac{1}{2}(u+v) \times \frac{(v-u)}{a} \Rightarrow v^2 - u^2 = 2ax$$

Position-velocity relation, $v^2 = u^2 + 2ax$

Displacement of the Particle in *n*th Second

Let an object is moving with initial velocity u under constant acceleration a.

To find the displacement in nth second, we subtract the position of particle at $(n-1)$th second from the position of the particle at nth second.

Displacement in nth second $= s_n - s_{n-1}$

$$s\,(n\text{th}) = \left[un + \frac{1}{2}a(n^2)\right] - \left[u(n-1) + \frac{1}{2}a(n-1)^2\right]$$

$$= un + \frac{1}{2}an^2 - un + u - \frac{1}{2}a(n-1)^2$$

$$= u + \frac{a}{2}[n^2 - (n-1)^2]$$

$$= u + \frac{a}{2}(n^2 - n^2 - 1 + 2n)$$

Displacement in the *n*th second, $s(n\text{th}) = u + \frac{a}{2}(2n-1)$

TEACHER TIP

The following steps are recommended for solving problem involving accelerated motion.

Step I Make sure all the units in the problem are consistent. That is, if distances are measured in metres, be sure that velocities have units of metres per second and accelerations have units of metres per second square.

Step II Make a list of all the quantities given in the problem and a separate list of those to be determined.

Step III Think about what is going on physically in the problem and then select relevant equation from the list of kinematic equations that will enable you to determine the unknowns.

Equation of motion for Constant '*a*' using Calculus Method

By definition of acceleration, we have

$$a = \frac{dv}{dt}$$

Integrating both sides from initial to final value

$$\int_{v_0}^{v} dv = \int_0^t a\,dt = a\int_0^t dt \qquad (a = \text{constant})$$

$$v - v_0 = at$$

$$v = v_0 + at \qquad \ldots\text{(i)}$$

Further,

we know, $v = \frac{dx}{dt}$

$$dx = v\,dt$$

Integrating both sides from initial to final value

$$\int_{x_0}^{x} dx = \int_0^t v\,dt$$

$$= \int_0^t (v_0 + at)\,dt \qquad \text{(from Eq. (i))}$$

$$x - x_0 = v_0 t + \frac{1}{2}at^2$$

$$x = x_0 + v_0 t + \frac{1}{2}at^2$$

$$\boxed{x = v_0 t + \frac{1}{2}at^2} \qquad \ldots\text{(ii)} \ (\therefore x_0 = 0)$$

Now, we have

$$a = \frac{dv}{dt} = \frac{dv}{dx}\frac{dx}{dt} = v\frac{dv}{dx}$$

or $\quad v\,dv = a\,dx$

Integrating both sides,

$$\int_{v_0}^{v} v\,dv = \int_{x_0}^{x} a\,dx$$

$$\frac{v^2 - v_0^2}{2} = a(x - x_0)$$

$$v^2 = v_0^2 + 2a(x - x_0)$$

$$\boxed{v^2 = v_0^2 + 2ax} \qquad \ldots\text{(iii)} \ (\because x_0 = 0)$$

This method can be used for motion with non-uniform acceleration also.

Example 14. **Two particles move along *X*-axis. The position of particle 1 is given by $x = 6.00t^2 + 3.00t + 2.00$ (*x* in metre and *t* in seconds), acceleration of particle 2 is given by $a = -8.00t$ (*a* in m/s^2 and *t* seconds) and at $t = 0$, its velocity is 20 m/s. When the velocities of the particles match, find their velocities.**

Sol. List all informations about particle 1 and particle 2.

For particle 1, $x_1 = 6.00t^2 + 3.00t + 2.00$

For particle 2, $a_2 = -8.00t$,

$$v_2 = 20 \text{ m/s at } t = 0 \text{ s}$$

We know that, $v(t) = \frac{dx}{dt}$

$$v(t) = 12t + 3 + 0$$

$$v(t) = 12t + 3$$

For particle 2,

We know that, $\int a(t)\,dt = v(t)$

$$\Rightarrow \quad v(t) = \int -8.00\,t\,dt = -8\int t\,dt = \frac{-8t^2}{2} + C$$

$$v(t) = -4t^2 + C$$

If $v(t) = 20$ m/s and $t = 0$ s, then

$$20 \text{ m/s} = -4(0)^2 + C$$

$$\Rightarrow \quad 20 = 0 + C \Rightarrow C = 20$$

So, $\quad v_2(t) = -4t^2 + 20$

Since the velocities of two particles have to match, you have to set the two equations equal to each other.

$$\therefore \quad v_1(t) = v_2(t)$$

$$12t + 3 = -4t^2 + 20$$

$$4t^2 + 12t - 17 = 0$$

Since, you could not factor out, you probably know to use the quadratic formula

$$= \frac{-b \pm \sqrt{b^2 - 4ac}}{2a} = \frac{-12 \pm \sqrt{(12)^2 - 4(4)(-17)}}{2(4)}$$

$$= \frac{-12 \pm \sqrt{144 + 272}}{8}$$

$$t = \frac{-12 \pm \sqrt{416}}{8} = \frac{-12 \pm 20.3}{8}$$

$$t = -4.04 \text{ s or } t = 1.04 \text{ s}$$

As time cannot be negative, $t = 1.04$ s.

Find the velocities of different particles.

$$v(t_1) = 12(1.04) + 3 = 15.48 \text{ m/s}$$

$$v(t_2) = -4(1.04)^2 + 20 = 15.67 \text{ m/s}$$

Example 15. A motor car starts from rest and accelerates uniformly for 10 s to a velocity of 20 m/s. After that car runs at a constant speed and is finally brought to rest in 40 m with a constant acceleration. Total distance covered is 640 m. Find the value of acceleration, retardation and total time taken.

Sol. Let x_1, x_2 and x_3 be distances covered in three parts of the motion.

For first part of the motion, we have

$$u = 0, t = 10 \text{ s}, v = 20 \text{ m/s}$$

As $v = u + at$

$\therefore$ $20 = 0 + a \times 10$

Acceleration, $a = 2 \text{ m/s}^2$

Distance, $x_1 = ut + \frac{1}{2}at^2 = 0 \times 10 + \frac{1}{2} \times 2 \times (10)^2 = 100 \text{ m}$

For second part of the motion, we have

$$x_1 = 100 \text{ m}, \; x_3 = 40 \text{ m}$$

As $x_1 + x_2 + x_3 = 640$

$\therefore$ $100 + x_2 + 40 = 640$

or $x_2 = 500 \text{ m}$

This distance is covered with a uniform speed of 20 m/s.

$\therefore$ Time taken $= \frac{500}{20} = 25$ s

For third part of the motion, we have

$$u = 20 \text{ m/s}, \; v = 0,$$

$$x = x_3 = 40 \text{ m}$$

As $v^2 - u^2 = 2ax$

$\therefore$ $(0)^2 - (20)^2 = 2 \times a \times 40$

or $a = -\frac{400}{80} = -5 \text{ m/s}^2$

$\therefore$ Retardation $= 5 \text{ m/s}^2$

Time taken, $t = \frac{v-u}{a} = \frac{0-20}{-5} = 4$ s

Total time taken $= 10 + 25 + 4 = 39$ s

Non-uniformly Accelerated Motion

When acceleration of particle is not constant or acceleration is a function of time, then following relations hold for one-dimensional motion.

(i) $v = \frac{ds}{dt}$ (ii) $a = \frac{dv}{dt} = v\frac{dv}{dx}$

(iii) $ds = v\,dt$ and (iv) $dv = a\,dt$ or $v\,dv = a\,dx$

2.6 Equations of Motion for the Motion of an Object under Gravity

When an object is thrown upwards or fall towards the earth, then its motion is called **motion under gravity** because in these conditions (upward or downward), the acceleration of the body is equal to the acceleration due to gravity.

In case of motion under gravity, the equations of motion are given as follows.

$$v = u + (\pm g)t \quad \text{...(i)}$$

$$h = ut + \frac{1}{2}(\pm g)t^2 \quad \text{...(ii)}$$

$$v^2 = u^2 + 2(\pm g)h \quad \text{...(iii)}$$

In case of downward motion, acceleration due to gravity (g) is taken as **positive** and for upward motion, g is taken as **negative.**

Feeling Weightlessness

Actually we feel our weight due to the reaction we get from earth. As in free fall, we are not pushing anything, so we are not getting any reaction (Newton's third law) and feeling weightlessness.

Example 16. A ball is thrown vertically upwards with a velocity of 20 m/s from the top of a multi-storey building. The height of the point from where the ball is thrown is 25 m from the ground.

(i) How high will the ball rise?

(ii) How long will it be before the ball from A to B hits the ground? Take, $g = 10 \text{ m/s}^2$ NCERT

Sol. (i) Consider vertical upward motion of ball from A to B upto highest point, we have

$$u = 20 \text{ m/s}, v = 0, \quad a = -10 \text{ m/s}^2, t = t_1,$$

$h = ?$ (say)

Using theorem, $v^2 = u^2 + 2ah$

$$h = \frac{v^2 - u^2}{2a} = \frac{0 - (20)^2}{2 \times (-10)} = 20 \text{ m}$$

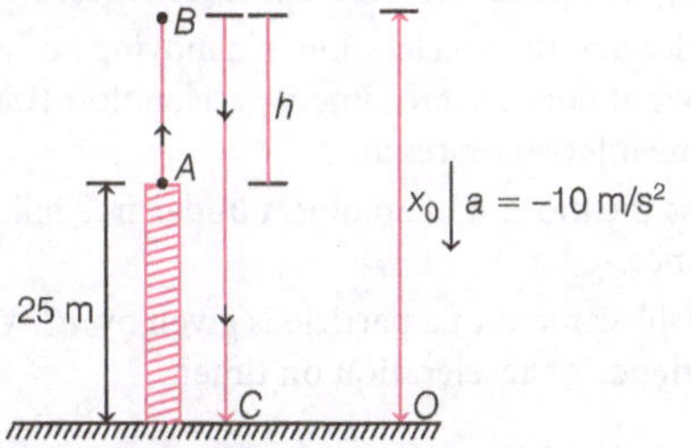

(ii) As shown in figure, we have upward motion A to B in time (t_1) and downward motion (B to C) in time (t_2).

Velocity at B is zero

$\therefore$ $$v = u - gt$$

$$0 = 20 - 10\,t_1 \Rightarrow t_1 = 2 \text{ s}$$

From the top, the ball falls freely under acceleration due to gravity.

$\therefore$ $$x = x_0 + ut + \frac{1}{2} gt_2^2$$

$$x = 0,\ x_0 = 45 \text{ m},\ u = 0$$

and $$g = 10 \text{ m/s}^2$$

$$0 = 45 + 0 + \frac{1}{2}(-10)\,t_2^2 = 45 - 5t_2^2$$

$$t_2^2 = 9 \Rightarrow t_2 = 3 \text{ s}$$

$\therefore$ Total time taken by the ball to hit the ground

$$t = t_1 + t_2 = 2 + 3 = 5 \text{ s}$$

Method II

In this method, we shall consider net displacement = Final position − Initial position = 25m.

Using the formula,

$$x = ut + \frac{1}{2} gt^2$$

$\Rightarrow$ $$-25 = +20t - \frac{1}{2} gt^2 = +20t - 5t^2$$

we get, $$5t^2 - 20t - 25 = 0$$

$\Rightarrow$ $$t^2 - 4t - 5 = 0$$

$$(t - 5)(t + 1) = 0 \Rightarrow t = 5 \text{ s}$$

Galileo's Law of Odd Numbers

Galileo was the first to make quantitative studies of free fall. This law states that **the distances traversed by a freely falling body during equal intervals of time stand to one another in the same ratio as the odd numbers beginning with unity, i.e. 1 : 3 : 5 : 7.**

Stopping Distance for a Vehicle

When brakes are applied to a moving vehicle, the distance it travels before coming to halt is called **stopping distance.**

It is also an important factor for road safety. Its value depends upon the speed at which the vehicle is running and the efficiency of the braking system.

Let the distance travelled by the vehicle before it stops be d_s.

Using the equation of motion,

$$v^2 = u^2 + 2\,ax$$

If $v = 0$ and $x = d_s$, then

$$\text{Stopping distance, } d_s = \frac{-u^2}{2a}$$

Thus, the stopping distance is proportional to the square of the initial velocity. **If we double the initial velocity, its stopping distance increase by a factor of 4 for same deceleration.**

Example 17. **A car moving with a speed of 50 km/h can be stopped by brakes after covering 6 m. What will be the minimum stopping distance, if the same car is moving at a speed of 100 km/h?**

Sol. In first case,

$$u = 50 \text{ km/h} = 50 \times \frac{5}{18}$$

$$= \frac{125}{9} \text{ m/s},\ v = 0,\ x = 6 \text{ m}$$

Using the relation, $v^2 - u^2 = 2ax$

$$0 - \left(\frac{125}{9}\right)^2 = 2a \times 6$$

$\Rightarrow$ $$a = \frac{-125 \times 125}{81 \times 2 \times 6}$$

$$= -16.07 \text{ m/s}^2 \simeq 16 \text{ m/s}$$

In second case,

$$u = 100 \text{ km/h}$$

$$= 100 \times \frac{5}{18} = \frac{250}{9} \text{ m/s}$$

$$v = 0,\ a = -16 \text{ m/s}^2 \text{ and } x = ?$$

Using the relation, $$v^2 - u^2 = 2ax$$

$$0 - \left(\frac{250}{9}\right)^2 = 2 \times (-16)\,x$$

$\Rightarrow$ $$x = \frac{250 \times 250}{81 \times 2 \times 16} = 24.1 \text{ m}$$

Reaction Time

When a situation demands our immediate action, it takes sometime before we really respond. **Reaction time is defined as the time of a person takes to observe, think and act (OTA).**

e.g. If a person is driving a car and suddenly a boy appears on the road, then the time elapsed before he applies the brakes of the car is the reaction time.

Reaction time depends on

(i) an individual presence of mind

(ii) the complexity of the situation

Calculation of Reaction Time

We can find reaction time by the following experiment. Suppose your friend is holding a long rod vertically in the gap between the thumb and fore-finger of your right hand.

He has to drop that rod and you have to catch and hold the falling rod. You will see that rod is caught after moving a distance x.

Let this distance x be 0.21 m. If t is the reaction time, then $u = 0$, $a = 9.8\ \text{m/s}^2$, $x = 0.21\ \text{m}$, $t = ?$

Using the relation,

$$x = ut + \frac{1}{2}at^2$$

$$\Rightarrow \quad 0.21 = 0 + \frac{1}{2} \times 9.8 \times t^2$$

$$\Rightarrow \quad t = \sqrt{\frac{2 \times 0.21}{9.8}} = 0.2\ \text{s}$$

Quick Test 2

Conceptual Questions

1. When a body accelerates by βt, what is the velocity after time t, when it starts from rest ?

2. Consider that the acceleration of a moving body varies with time. What does the area under acceleration-time graph for any time interval represent?

3. Discuss the motion of an object under free fall. Neglect air resistance. NCERT

4. The displacement of a particle is given by at^2. What is dependency of acceleration on time?

5. Points P, Q and R are in a vertical line such that $PQ = QR$. A ball at P is allowed to fall freely. What is the ratio of the times of descent through PQ and QR?

Numerical Questions

6. If position of a particle at instant t is given by $x = 2t^3$, find the acceleration of the particle.

7. Two trains A and B of length 400 m each are moving on two parallel tracks with a uniform speed of 72 km h^{-1} in the same direction with A ahead of B. The driver of B decides to overtake A and accelerates by 1 ms^{-2}. If after 50 s, the guard of B just brushes past the driver of A, what was the original distance between them?

8. A jet plane beginning its take off moves down the runway at a constant acceleration of 4.00 m/s^2. Find the position and velocity of the plane 5.00 s after it begins to move.

Answers

6. $12t$ 7. 450 m 8. (i) 50.0 m, 20.0 m/s

For Solutions, See QR Code on Pg. 66

Mind Map

Motion in a Straight Line

Uniform Motion
- An object travels equal distance in equal intervals along a straight line.

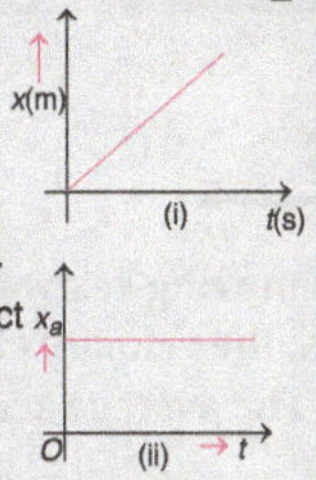

When object is stationary
- From the graph (ii) it is clear that, the position of the object remain same w.r.t. time.

When object is in variable motion
- The position-time graph of varying motion will not be a straight line.

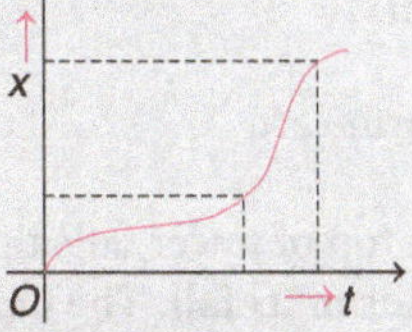

Non-Uniform Motion
- An object travel equal distance in unequal interval of time.
- The speed of the body or its direction of motion or both change with time.

Position
- The point where an object is situated, called position.
- Position determined by the coordinate axis, i.e. marked in units of length and that has positive and negative direction.

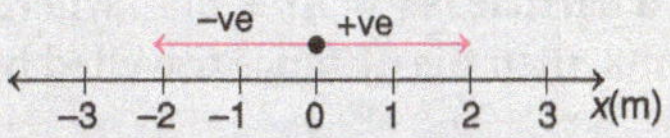

Position in + ve and – ve directions.

Distance
- Length of the path covered by an object in a given time interval is known as its path length or distance travelled.
- Its SI unit is metre.
- **Example**

Displacement
- The change in position of an object in a particular direction.
- Displacement, $\Delta x = x_2 - x_1$

Case I $x_2 > x_1$, Δx is positive
Case II $x_1 > x_2$, Δx is negative
Case III $x_1 = x_2$, Δx is zero

Speed
- The distance covered by an object divided by the time taken by it to cover that distance is called speed.

$$\text{Speed} = \frac{\text{Distance travelled}}{\text{Time taken}}$$

- Speed is a scalar quantity.

Average Speed
- The total distance travelled by the object divided by the total time taken.

$$\text{Average speed} = \frac{\text{Total distance travelled}}{\text{Total time taken}}$$

$$v_{avg} = \frac{s_1 + s_2}{t_1 + t_2}$$

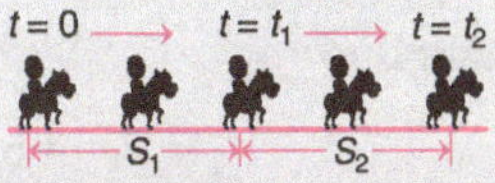

Uniform and Non-Uniform Speed
- **Uniform Speed**
The speed at which an object covers equal distance in equal time interval.
- **Non-Uniform Speed**
The speed at which an object covers equal distance in unequal interval of time.

Velocity
- The rate of change of position of an object with time is called the velocity of that object.

$$\text{Velocity} = \frac{\text{Displacement}}{\text{Time}}$$

- It is a vector quantity.

Average Velocity
- The change in position or displacement divided by the time interval in which that displacement occur. $v = \dfrac{v_i + v_f}{2}$

Relative Velocity
- The velocity of an object A with respect to another object B is called relative velocity.

Example
- If a bus A is moving with velocity vector v_A and another bus B with velocity vector v_B, then velocity of object A relative to bus B is given as $\mathbf{v}_{AB} = \mathbf{v}_A - \mathbf{v}_B$

The relative velocity of bus B, w.r.t. bus A, is
$$\mathbf{v}_{BA} = \mathbf{v}_B - \mathbf{v}_A$$

- **Case I** If $\mathbf{v}_B - \mathbf{v}_A = 0$, then the two objects A and B stay at a constant distance.

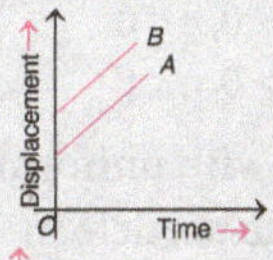

- **Case II** If $\mathbf{v}_A > \mathbf{v}_B$, then one graph is steeper than other and they meet at common point.

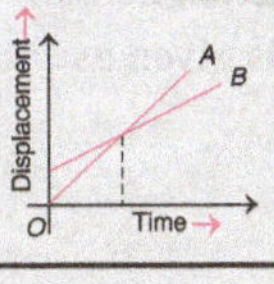

Acceleration
- The rate of change of velocity with time.
- It is a vector quantity.
- SI unit is metre per second square (m/s^2).
- The dimensional formula is $[M^0L^1T^{-2}]$.

Average Acceleration
- The change in velocity divided by time interval.
- Average acceleration $= \dfrac{\Delta \mathbf{v}}{\Delta t} = \dfrac{\mathbf{v}_2 - \mathbf{v}_1}{t_2 - t_1}$

Uniform and Non-Uniform Acceleration
- **Uniform Acceleration** If an object is moving with uniform acceleration, it means that the object velocity is equal for equal interval of time.
- **Non-Uniform Acceleration** If an object has variable or non-uniform acceleration, it means that the change in velocity is unequal in equal interval of time.

Kinematic Equations
- For uniformly accelerated motion, the displacement, time, initial velocity, final velocity and acceleration are related by three simple equations, called kinematic equations of motion.
- **Velocity-Time Relation** $v = u + at$
- **Position-Time Relation** $x = ut + \frac{1}{2}at^2$
- **Position-Velocity Relation** $v^2 = u^2 + 2ax$

Motion of an Object Under Gravity
- When an object is thrown vertically upwards or fall towards the earth, then its motion is called motion under gravity.

$$v = u + (\pm g)t$$
$$h = ut + \frac{1}{2}(\pm g)t^2$$
$$v^2 = u^2 + 2(\pm g)h$$

- In case of upward motion, acceleration due to gravity (g) is taken as negative and for downward motion, g is taken as positive.

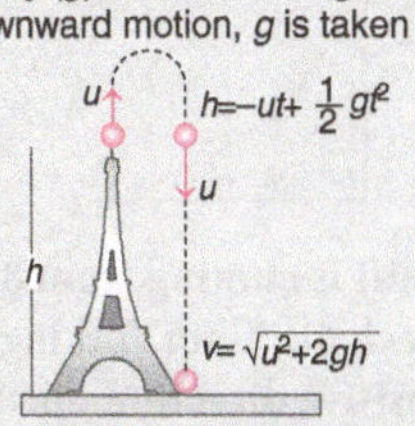

Free Fall
- A situation in which an object moves only under the influence of gravity.
- Free fall is just a downward movement with no initial force or velocity.
- The free fall of any object is just a natural phenomenon on earth without support.

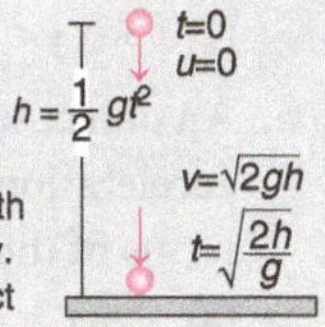

EXAM PATTERN QUESTIONS

Objective Type Questions

Multiple Choice Questions (MCQs)

1. The coordinates of object with respect to a frame of reference at $t = 0$ are $(-1, 0, 3)$. If $t = 5$ s, its coordinates are $(-1, 0, 4)$, then the object is in

(a) motion along Z-axis
(b) motion along X-axis
(c) motion along Y-axis
(d) rest position between $t = 0$ s and $t = 5$ s

2. The velocity of a particle moving along a straight line is described by equation

$$v = 12 - 3t^2$$

where, x is in metre and t in s. The retardation of the particle when its velocity becomes zero, is

Competency Based Que

(a) $24\,\text{ms}^{-2}$ (b) zero
(c) $6\,\text{ms}^{-2}$ (d) $12\,\text{ms}^{-2}$

3. Among the four graphs shown in the figure, there is only one graph for which average velocity over the time interval (O, T) can vanish for a suitably chosen T. Which one is it? **NCERT Exemplar**

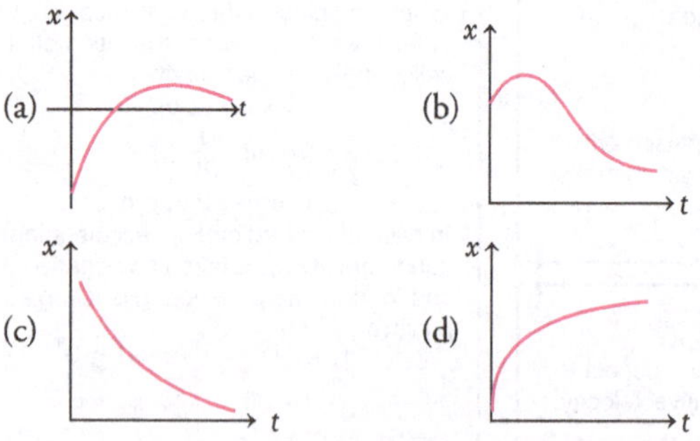

4. A lift is coming from 8th floor and is just about to reach 4th floor. Taking ground floor as origin and positive direction upwards for all quantities, which one of the following is correct? **NCERT Exemplar**

(a) $x < 0, v < 0, a > 0$ (b) $x > 0, v < 0, a < 0$
(c) $x > 0, v < 0, a > 0$ (d) $x > 0, v > 0, a < 0$

5. An object starts from rest and moves with uniform acceleration a. The final velocity of the particle in terms of the distance x covered by it, is given as

(a) $\sqrt{2ax}$ (b) $2ax$
(c) $\sqrt{\frac{ax}{2}}$ (d) $\sqrt{ax}$

6. A particle is moving eastwards with a velocity of 5 m/s. In 10 s, the velocity changes to 5 m/s northwards. The average acceleration in this time is

(a) zero
(b) $\frac{1}{\sqrt{2}}$ m/s^2 towards north-west
(c) $\frac{1}{2}$ m/s^2 towards north
(d) $\frac{1}{\sqrt{2}}$ m/s^2 towards north-east

7. A body dropped from top of tower falls through 60 m during the last 2 seconds of its fall. The height of tower is $(g = 10\text{ m/s}^2)$

(a) 95 m (b) 80 m
(c) 90 m (d) 60 m

8. An object, moving with a speed of 6.25 m/s, is decelerated at a rate given by

$$\frac{dv}{dt} = -2.5\sqrt{v}$$

Where v is the instantaneous speed. The time taken by the object, to come to rest would be

(a) 1 s (b) 2 s (c) 4 s (d) 8 s

9. If the velocity of a particle is $v = At + Bt^2$, where A and B are constants, then the distance travelled by it in 1 s is

(a) $3A + 7B$ (b) $\frac{3}{2}A + \frac{7}{3}B$
(c) $\frac{A}{2} + \frac{B}{3}$ (d) $\frac{3}{2}A + 4B$

10. A train of 150 m in length is going north at a speed of 10 m/s. A parrot flies at a speed of 5 m/s towards south direction parallel to the railway track. The time taken by the parrot to cross the train is equal to

(a) 12 s (b) 8 s
(c) 10 s (d) 15 s

11. At a metro station, a girl walks up a stationary escalator in time t_1. If she remains stationary on the escalator, then the escalator take her up in time t_2. The time taken by her to walk up on the moving escalator will be **NCERT Exemplar**

(a) $(t_1 + t_2)/2$ (b) $t_1 t_2/(t_2 - t_1)$
(c) $t_1 t_2/(t_2 + t_1)$ (d) $t_1 - t_2$

12. In one dimensional motion, instantaneous speed v satisfies $0 \le v < v_0$. **NCERT Exemplar**

(a) The displacement in time T must always take non-negative values.

(b) The displacement x in time T satisfies $-v_0T < x < v_0T$.

(c) The acceleration is always a non-negative number.

(d) The motion has no turning points.

13. A vehicle travels half the distance l with speed v_1 and the other half with speed v_2, then its average speed is **NCERT Exemplar**

(a) $\frac{v_1+v_2}{2}$ (b) $\frac{2v_1+v_2}{v_1+v_2}$ (c) $\frac{2v_1v_2}{v_1+v_2}$ (d) $\frac{L(v_1+v_2)}{v_1v_2}$

14. The displacement of a particle is given by $x = (t-2)^2$, where x is in metre and t in second. The distance covered by the particle in first 4 s is

(a) 4 m (b) 8 m (c) 12 m (d) 16 m

15. An object is moving with an initial velocity of 30 ms^{-1} with uniform acceleration. The velocity of object increases to 40 ms^{-1} in next 5 s. The v-t graph which least represents this situation is

(a)

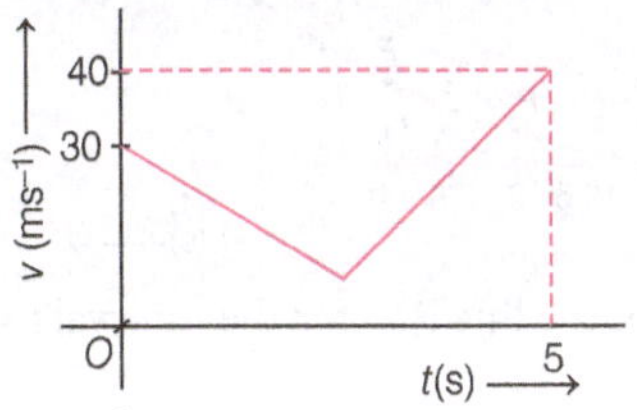

(b)

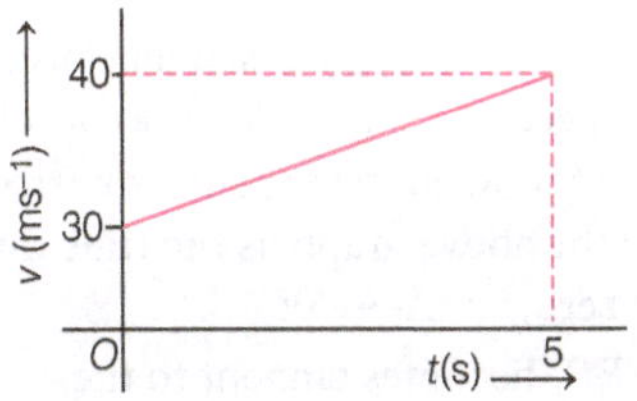

(c)

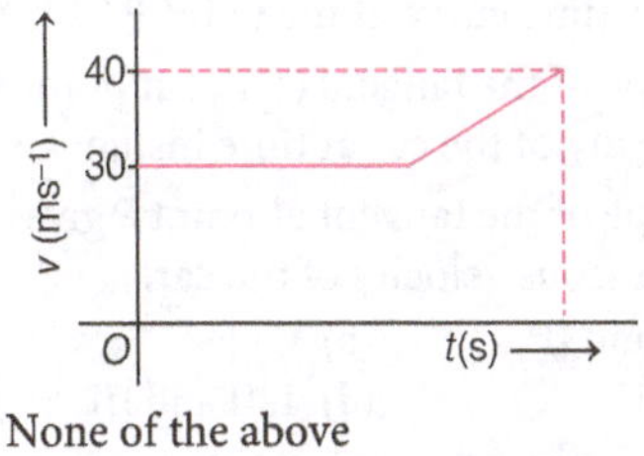

(d) None of the above

16. The relative velocity v_{BA} or v_{AB} is zero for two particles moving along x-axis uniformly. The position-time graph for this situation will be **Competency Based Que.**

(a) straight lines parallel but inclined to time axis

(b) straight lines parallel and also parallel to time axis

(c) straight lines intersecting each other at some point

(d) curves and not straight lines

17. Two trains, each of length 200 m, are running on parallel tracks. One overtakes the other in 20 seconds and one crosses the other in 10 seconds. Calculate the velocities of two trains.

(a) 30 m/s, 10 m/s (b) 20 m/s, 20 m/s
(c) 30 m/s, 20 m/s (d) 20 m/s, 10 m/s

18. A thief snatches a bag from a person and then moves along a straight road with a constant velocity of 36 km/h. A police inspector observed the incident of snatching. He starts his bike within 10s and accelerates it so that he is able to hold the thief after 30s. What is the acceleration of his bike?

(a) 1.5 m/s^2 (b) 2.5 m/s^2 (c) 0.5 m/s^2 (d) 3.5 m/s^2

19. The position of an object moving along X-axis is given by $x(t) = a - bt^2$, where $a = 8.5$ m, $b = 2.5 \text{ ms}^{-2}$ and t is measured in seconds.

For the above situation, match the Column I with Column II and select the correct answer from the options given below.

	Column I		Column II
A.	Velocity of object at $t = 2$s	P.	-15 ms^{-1}
B.	Velocity of object at $t = 0$s	Q.	-10 ms^{-1}
C.	Instantaneous speed of an object at $t = 2$s	R.	0 ms^{-1}
D.	Average velocity between $t = 2$s and $t = 4$s	S.	10 ms^{-1}

(a) A-P, B-S, C-R, D-Q (b) A-S, B-R, C-P, D-Q
(c) A-R, B-Q, C-S, D-P (d) A-Q, B-R, C-S, D-P

20. Given x-t graph represent the motion of an object. Match the column I (parts of graph) with column II (rerepresentation and select the correct answer from the options given below.

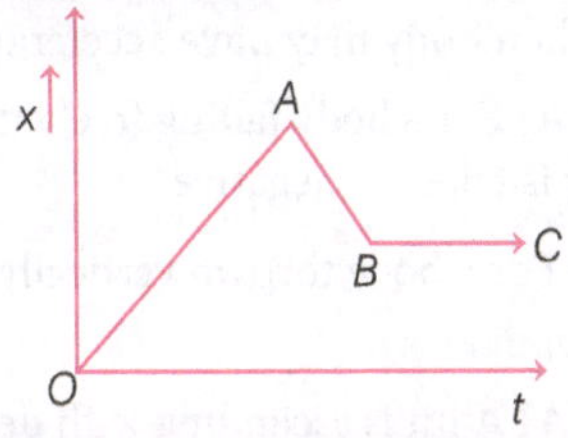

	Column I		Column II
A.	Part OA of graph	P	Positive velocity
B.	Part AB of graph	Q	Object at rest
C.	Part BC of graph	R	Negative velocity
D.	Point A in the graph	S	Change in direction of motion

(a) A-P, B-R, C-Q, D-S (b) A-Q, B-P, C-R, D-S
(c) A-S, B-Q, C-P, D-R (d) A-R, B-S, C-R, D-P

Assertion-Reason

Directions (Q. Nos. 21-30) *In the following questions, two statements are given- one labelled Assertion (A) and the other labelled Reason (R). Select the correct answer to these questions from the codes (a), (b), (c) and (d) as given below.*

(a) Both Assertion and Reason are true and Reason is the correct explanation of Assertion.
(b) Both Assertion and Reason are true but Reason is not the correct explanation of Assertion.
(c) Assertion is true but Reason is false.
(d) Assertion is false but Reason is true.

21. **Assertion (A)** In real life, in a good number of situations, the object is treated as a point object.
Reason (R) The object is treated as point object, as the size of the object is much smaller than the distance it moves in a reasonable duration of time.

22. **Assertion (A)** For uniform motion, velocity is the same as the average velocity at all instants.
Reason (R) In uniform motion along a straight line, the object covers equal distances in equal intervals of time.

23. **Assertion (A)** A body can have acceleration even if its velocity is zero at a given instant of time.
Reason (R) A body is momentarily at rest when it reverses it's direction of motion.

24. **Assertion (A)** In realistic situation, the x-t, v-t and a-t graphs will be smooth. This means physically that acceleration and velocity cannot change values abruptly at an instant.
Reason (R) Changes are always continuous.

25. **Assertion (A)** A body may be accelerated even when it is moving uniformly.
Reason (R) When direction of motion of the body is changing, then body may have acceleration.

26. **Assertion (A)** For a body falling freely under the action of gravity, g is taken as negative.
Reason (R) For a body thrown vertically upward, g is taken as negative.

27. **Assertion (A)** A lift is ascending with decreasing speed means acceleration of lift is downward.
Reason (R) A body always moves in the direction of its acceleration.

28 **Assertion (A)** If acceleration of a particle moving in a straight line varies as $a \propto t^n$, then $s \propto t^{n+2}$.
Reason (R) If a-t graph is a straight line, then s-t graph may be a parabola.

29 **Assertion (A)** Two bodies of different masses are dropped simultaneously from the top of tower and hit the ground simultaneously.
Reason (R) Time taken by a body to fall through certain height is independent of mass of body.

30 **Assertion (A)** The position time (x-t) graph of a stationary object is a straight line parallel to time axis.
Reason (R) For a stationary object the position of object does not change with time.

Case Based Questions

Directions (Q. Nos. 31-33) *These questions are Case Study Based Questions. Read the following paragraph and answer the questions.*

31. **The x-t graph represents the motion of a car at different time instants. With reference to the below graph, choose the correct for the question given below.**

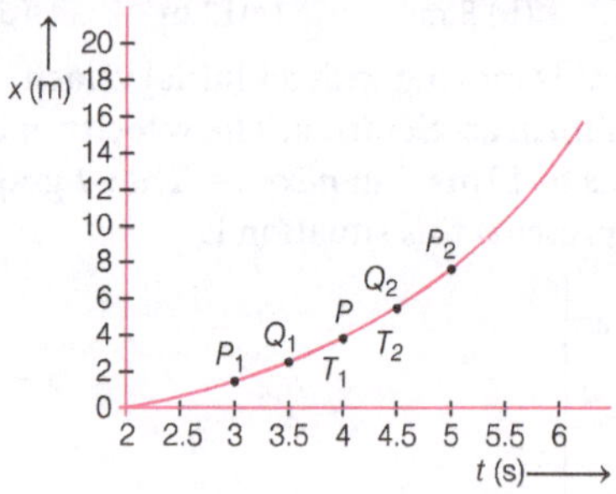

(i) The slope of the line P_1P_2 for the interval $t = 3$ s to $t = 5$ s gives
(a) average velocity (b) instantaneous velocity
(c) average speed (d) Either (a) or (c)

(ii) Which of the following statements is correct with reference to the above graph as the time interval Δt approaches zero, *i.e.*, $\Delta t \to 0$?
I. The line P_1P_2 becomes tangent to the position-time curve at the point P.
II. The slope of the tangent (T_1T_2) at point P gives the velocity of the car at time instant $t = 4$ s.
III. The slope of the tangent at point P gives the instantaneous velocity of the car.
(a) Both I and II (b) Only I
(c) Only III (d) I, II and III

(iii) Figure shows the (x-t) plot of a particle in one-dimensional motion. Two different equal intervals of time are speed in time intervals 1 and 2 respectively. Then,

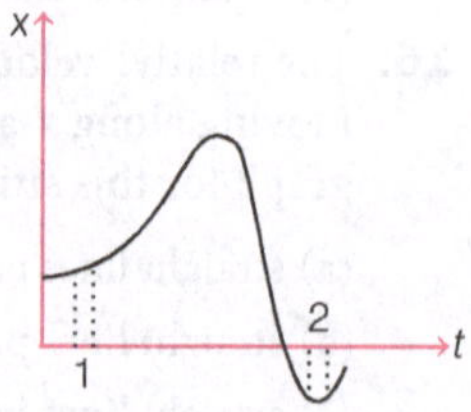

(a) $v_1 > v_2$
(b) $v_2 > v_1$
(c) $v_1 = v_2$
(d) Data insufficient

(iv) Among the four graphs shown in the figure, there is only one graph for which average velocity over the time interval $(0, T)$ can vanish for a suitably chosen T. Which one is it?

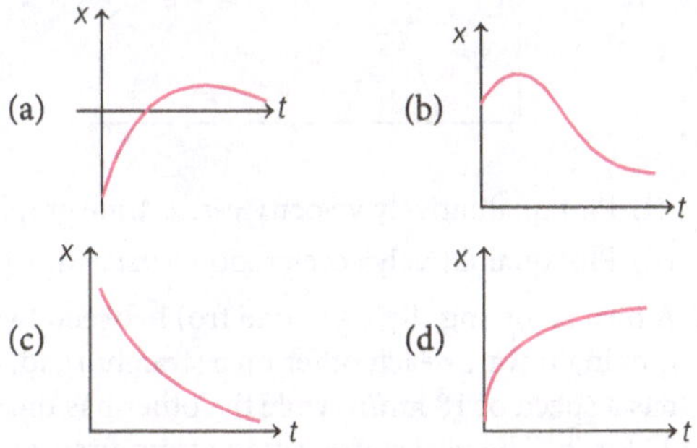

32. **A ball is projected from the ground level in vertically upward direction with an initial velocity u. The ball goes up to a maximum height H and then starts moving downward. Finally the ball falls back on the ground. It is given that motion of the ball under the action of gravity alone and effect of air resistance, if any, is negligible.**

(i) What is the value of maximum height (H) up to which the ball goes?

(a) $H = \frac{u^2}{2g}$ (b) $\frac{u^2}{g}$
(c) $\frac{2u^2}{g}$ (d) $\frac{u}{2g}$

(ii) What time does the ball take to reach the highest point during its motion?

(a) $\frac{2u}{g}$ (b) $\frac{u}{2g}$
(c) $\frac{u}{g}$ (d) $\frac{u^2}{g}$

(iii) What is the acceleration of the body due to gravity

(a) 0 (b) 9.8 m/s^2
(c) 4.9 m/s^2 (d) 19.6 m/s^2

(iv) The motion of ball projected with certain velocity in upward motion is an example of what type of motion?

(a) Uniformly accelerated motion
(b) Uniformly retarded motion
(c) Uniform motion
(d) Non-uniform motion

33. **When an object moves along a straight line with uniform acceleration, it is possible to related its velocity, acceleration During motion and the distance covered by it in a certain time interval by a set of equations known as the equations of motion. For convenience, a set of three such equations are given below**

(I) $v = u + at$; (II) $s = ut = \frac{1}{2}at^2$

(III) $2as = v^2 - u^2$

where, u is the initial velocity of the object which moves with uniform acceleration a for time t, v is the final velocity and s is the distance travelled by the object in time t.

(i) An object takes 4s in falling from the top of the tower to the ground. If acceleration during fall is constant and equal to 9.8 ms^{-2}, find the height of the tower.

(ii) An object of mass 1 kg is relased from the top of a tower of height 125 m. What time will it take to strike the ground. (Take, $g = 10 \text{ m/s}^2$)

(iii) An object is made to fall from the top of a tower of height 78.4 m. Find the distance travelled by it in the Ist second.

(iv) Under what condition is the relation $s = ut$ correct?

(v) What happens to kinematic equations under time reversal?

Subjective Questions

Very Short Answer Type Questions

1. For which condition, the distance and the magnitude of displacement of an object have the same values? **Competency Based Que**

2. Write expression for distance covered in nth second for a uniformly accelerated motion.

3. A uniformly moving cricket ball is turned back by hitting it with a bat for a very short time interval. Show the variation of its acceleration with time (Take, acceleration in the backward direction as positive). **NCERT Exemplar**

4. Give examples of a one-dimensional motion where

(a) the particle moving along positive x-direction comes to rest periodically and moves forward. **[1]**

(b) the particle moving along positive x-direction comes to rest periodically and moves backward. **NCERT Exemplar** **[1]**

5. Give example of a motion where $x > 0, v < 0, a > 0$ at a particular instant. **NCERT Exemplar**

Short Answer Type Questions

6. An object falling through a fluid is observed to have acceleration given by $a = g - bv$, where g = gravitational acceleration and b is constant. After a long time of release, it is observed to fall with constant speed. What must be the value of constant speed? **NCERT Exemplar**

7. From the given example, find if the motion is one or two or three-dimensional.

(i) A kite flying in the sky. **[1]**

(ii) A cricket ball hit by a player. **[1/2]**

(iii) Moon revolving around the earth and. **[1/2]**

(iv) The motion of a stone in a circle. **[1]**

8. (a) The position of an object is given by $x = 2t^2 + 3t$. Find out that its motion is uniform and non-uniform. **[1]**

(b) The distance travelled by a body is proportional to the square of time. What type of motion this body has? **[2]**

9. Two bodies of different masses m_1 and m_2 are dropped from two different heights a and b. What is the ratio of time taken by the two bodies to drop through these distances?

10. (a) Why does a person sitting in one train think that the other train is at rest, when both trains are moving on parallel tracks with the same speed and in the same direction? **Competency Based Que.** **[1½]**

(b) Can a body be said to be at rest as well as in motion at the same time. How? **[1½]**

11. A train covers a distance of 200 km from station A to station B and then covers a distance of 100 km from station B to station C and finally returns to station B covering the same distance. What will be the net displacement of the train,

(i) if A is considered as the starting point of the train.

(ii) if B is considered as the starting point of the train.

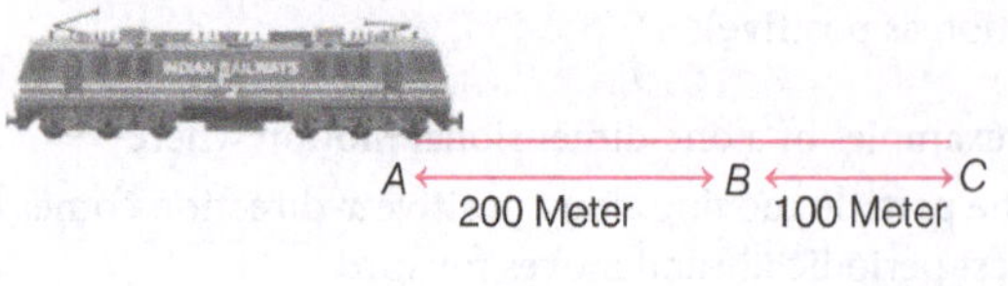

12. A ball is dropped and its displacement *versus* time graph is as shown (Displacement x from ground and all quantities are positive upwards). **NCERT Exemplar**

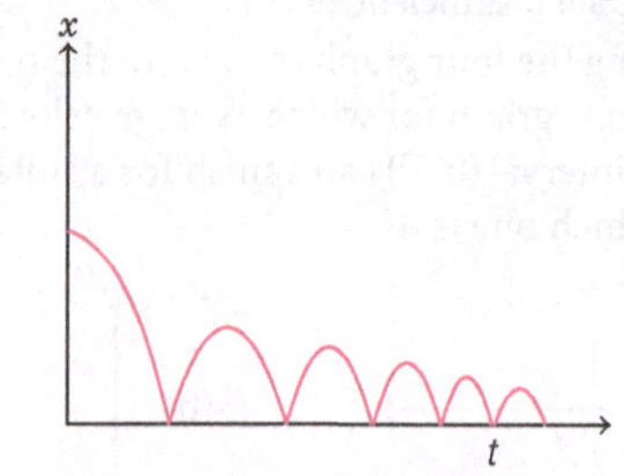

(i) Plot qualitatively velocity *versus* time graph.

(ii) Plot qualitatively acceleration *versus* time graph.

13. A bird is tossing (flying to and fro) between two cars moving towards each other on a straight road. One car has a speed of 18 km/h while the other has the speed of 27 km/h. The bird starts moving from first car towards the other and is moving with the speed of 36 km/h and when the two cars were separated by 36 km. What is the total distance covered by the bird? **NCERT Exemplar**

14. A ball is dropped from a building of height 45 m. Simultaneously another ball is thrown up with a speed 40 m/s. Calculate the relative speed of the balls as a function of time. **NCERT Exemplar**

15. If the displacement of a body is zero, is distance necessarily zero? Answer with one example.

Long Answer Type Questions

16. (a) Derive an expression for stopping distance of a vehicle in terms of initial velocity v_0 and deceleration a. **[3]**

(b) Establish the relation $x(t) = ut + \frac{1}{2}at^2$ by calculus method. **[2]**

17. Prove that the distance travelled by an object in nth second is given by $s_{nth} = u + \frac{a}{2}(2n - 1)$.

18. Look at the graphs (a) to (d) carefully and state with reasons, which of these cannot possibly represent one-dimensional motion of a particle?

(a)

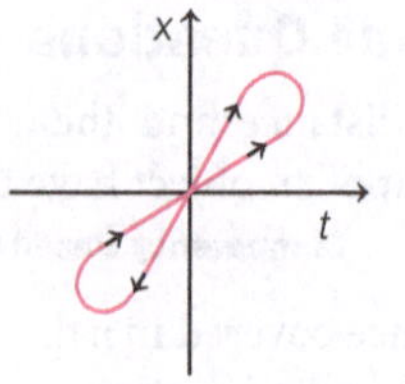

(b)

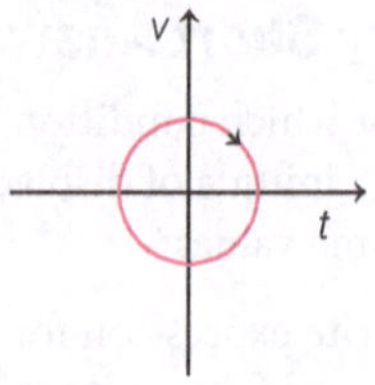

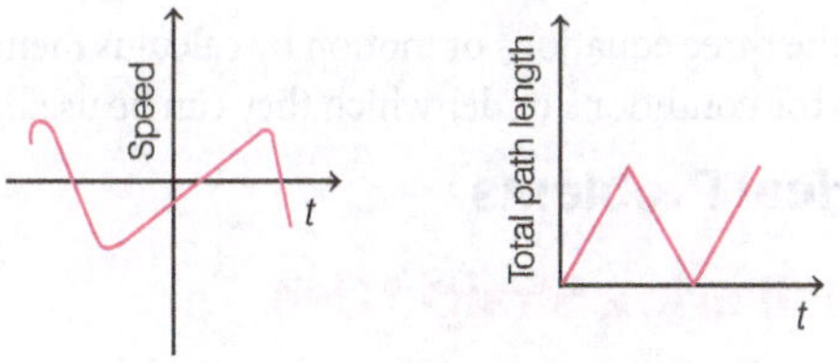

NCERT

19. In a car race, car A takes a time t less than car B and finishes the finishing point with a velocity v more than that of car B. Assuming that the cars start from rest and travel with constant acceleration a_1, and a_2 respectively, show that $v = t\sqrt{a_1 a_2}$

20. (a) The driver of a train moving at a speed v_1 sights another train at a distance d, ahead of him moving in the same direction with a slower speed v_2. He applies the brakes and gives a constant deceleration a to his train. Show that there will be no collision if

$$d > \frac{(v_1 > v_2)^2}{2a}$$ **[3]**

(b) We have carefully distinguished between average speed and magnitude of average velocity. No such distinction is necessary when we consider instantaneous speed and magnitude of velocity. The instantaneous speed is always equal to the magnitude of instantaneous velocity. **[2]**

21. Explain clearly with examples, the distinction between

(i) magnitude of displacement (sometimes called distance) over an interval of time and the total length of the path covered by a particle over the same interval. **[2]**

(ii) magnitude of average velocity over an interval of time and the average speed over the same interval. [Average speed of a particle over an interval of time is defined as the total path length divided by the time interval]. Show in both (a) and (b) that the second quantity is either greater than or equal to first. When is the equality sign true? [For simplicity, consider one-dimensional motion only] NCERT **[3]**

22. Suggest a suitable physical situation for each of the following graph. NCERT

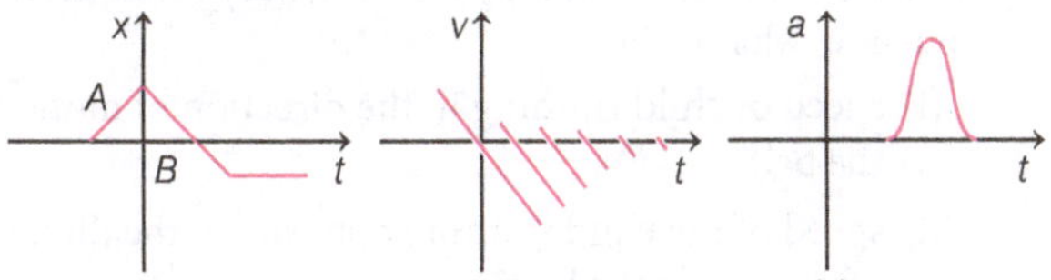

(a) (b) (c)

23. Figure gives the x-t plot of a particle executing one-dimensional simple harmonic motion. Give the signs of position, velocity and acceleration variables of the particles at $t = 0.3$ s, 1.2 s, – 1.2 s. NCERT

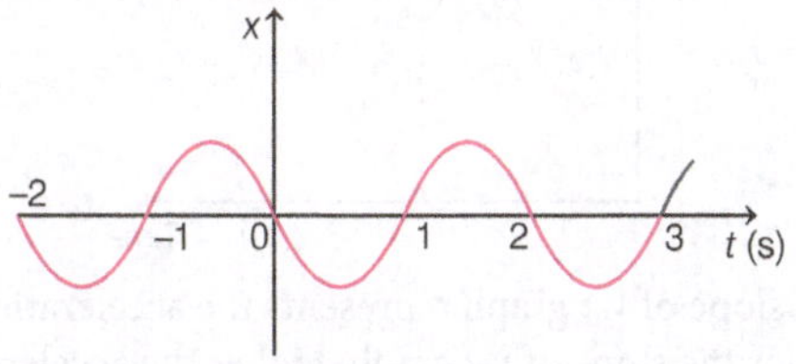

In SHM, the acceleration $a = -\omega^2 x$ i.e. acceleration is directly proportional to the displacement and opposite in direction.

24. (a) Figure shows the x-t plot of a particle in one-dimensional motion. Three different equal intervals of time are shown. In which interval the average speed is greatest and in which it is the least? Give the sign of average speed for each interval. NCERT

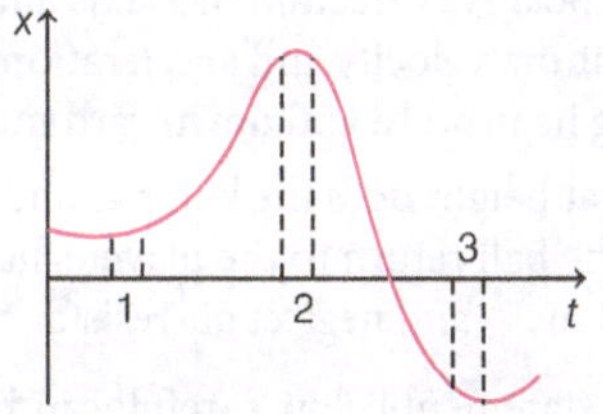

[3]

The slope of x-t graph represents the average speed in that interval of time i.e. higher the slope of x-t graph, higher is the average speed.

(b) Figure shows x-t plot of one-dimensional motion of a particle. Is it correct to say from the graph that the particle moves in a straight line for $t < 0$ and on a parabolic path for $t > 0$?

If not, suggest a suitable physical context for this graph. NCERT

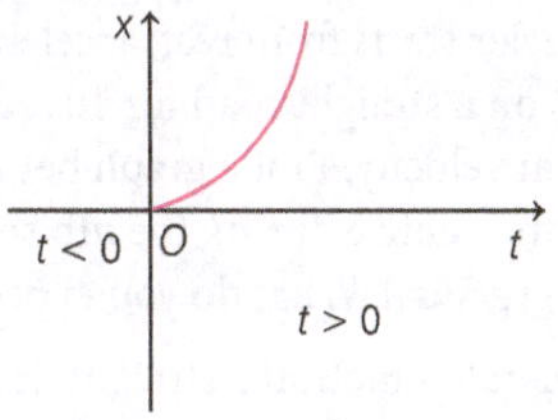

[2]

25. Figure gives a speed-time graph of a particle in one-dimensional motion. Three different equal intervals of time are shown. In which interval is the average acceleration greatest in magnitude? In which interval is the average speed greatest? Choosing the positive direction as the constant direction of motion, give the signs of u and a in the three intervals. What are the accelerations at the points A, B, C and D? NCERT

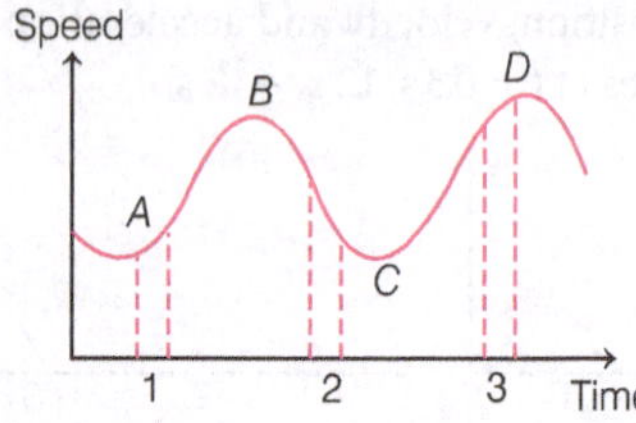

The slope of v-t graph represents the acceleration i.e. higher the slope of v-t graph, higher the acceleration.

26 A player throws a ball upwards with an initial speed of 29.4 ms^{-1}.

(i) What is the direction of acceleration during the upward motion of the ball? [1]

(ii) What are the velocity and acceleration of the ball at the highest point of its motion? [1]

(iii) Choose $x = 0$ and $t = 0$ be the location and time at its highest point, vertically downward direction to be the positive direction of x-axis and give the signs of position, velocity and acceleration of the ball during its upward and downward motion. [1]

(iv) To what height does the ball rise and after how long does the ball return to the player's hands? (Take $g = 9.8 \text{ ms}^{-2}$ and neglect air resistance) NCERT [2]

27. Read each statement below carefully and state with reasons and examples if it is true or false.

A particle in 1-D motion

(i) with zero speed at an instant may have non-zero acceleration at that instant. [1]

(ii) with zero speed may have non-zero velocity. [1]

(iii) with constant speed must have zero acceleration. [1½]

(iv) with positive value of acceleration must be speeding up. NCERT [1½]

28. A three wheeler starts from rest, accelerates uniformly with 1 ms^{-2} on a straight road for 10 s, and then moves with uniform velocity. Plot a graph between the distance covered by the vehicle during the nth second ($n = 1, 2, 3, ...$) *versus* n. What do you expect the plot to be during accelerated motion a straight line or a parabola? NCERT

29. The distance covered by an object between timings t_1 and t_2 is given by area under the v-t graph between t_1 and t_2. Prove that the above statement also holds when an object is moving with negative acceleration has velocities positive at time t_1 and negative at t_2. Competency Based Que.

30. Derive the three equations of motion by calculus method. Express the conditions under which they can be used.

Numerical Problems

Uniform Motion in a Straight Line

31. The data regarding the motion of two different objects P and Q are given in the following table. Examine them carefully and state whether the motion of the objects is uniform or non-uniform.

Time	Distance travelled by object P (in m)	Distance travelled by object Q (in m)
9:30 am	10	12
9:45 am	20	19
10:00 am	30	23
10:15 am	40	35
10:30 am	50	37
10.45 am	60	41
11:00 am	70	44

Speed and Velocity

32. A police van moving on a highway with a speed of 30 km/h fires a bullet at a thief's car speeding away in the same direction with a speed of 192 km/h. If the muzzle speed of the bullet is 150 m/s, with what speed does the bullet hit the thief's car? (Note Obtain that speed which is relevant for damaging the thief's car.) NCERT

33. A man walks on a straight road from his home to a market 2.5 km away with a speed of 5 km/h. Finding the market closed, he instantly turns and walks back home with a speed of 7.5 km/h. What is the

(a) magnitude of average velocity? [2]

(b) average speed of the man over the following interval of time? [3]

(i) 0 to 30 min (ii) 0 to 50 min

(iii) 0 to 40 min NCERT Exemplar

34. On a long horizontal moving belt (as shown in figure), a child runs to and fro with a speed 9 kmh^{-1} (with respect to the belt) between his father and mother located 50 m apart on the moving belt. The belt moves with a speed of 4 kmh^{-1}. For an observer on a stationary platform outside, what is the

(i) speed of child running in the direction of motion of the belt? [1]

(ii) speed of the child running opposite to the direction of motion of the belt? [1]

(iii) time taken by the child in (i) and (ii) to cover the distance of 50 m? [1]

Which of the answers will alter if motion is viewed by one of the parents? **Competency Based Que.**

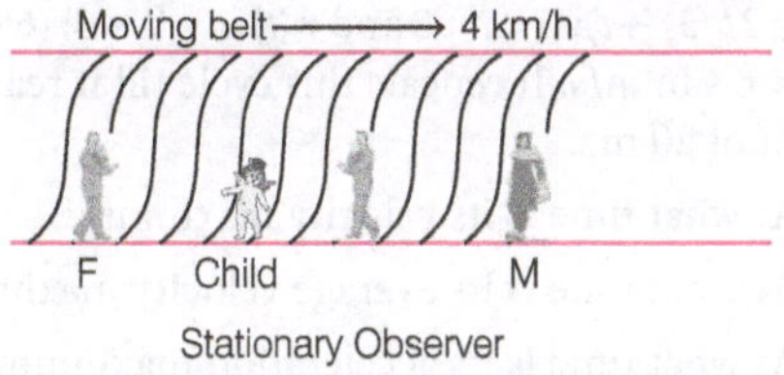

35. Two towns *A* and *B* are connected by a regular bus service with a bus leaving in either direction every *T* min. A man cycling with a speed of 20 km/h in the direction *A* to *B* notices that a bus goes past him every 18 min in the direction of his motion and every 6 min in opposite direction. What is the period *T* of the bus service and with what speed (assumed constant) do the buses ply on the road? **Competency Based Que.**

Uniformly Accelerated Motion

36. A body moving with a uniform acceleration describes 12 m in 3rd second of its motion and 20 m in the 5th second. Find the velocity after 10 s.

37. If the velocity of a particle is given by $v = \sqrt{180 - 16x}$ m/s, what will be its acceleration?

38. A car accelerates from rest at a constant rate α for some time, after which it decelerates at a constant rate β to come to rest. If t is total time elapsed, then calculate

(i) the maximum velocity attained by the car **[1½]**

(ii) the total distance travelled by the car **Competency Based Que. [1½]**

39. A ball is dropped from a height of 90 m on a floor. At each collision with floor, the ball loses one-tenth of its speed. Plot the speed-time graph of its motion between $t = 0$ s and $t = 12$ s. **NCERT**

40. A train moves from one station to another in 2 h time. Its speed during the motion is shown in graph. Determine the maximum acceleration during the journey. Also, calculate the distance covered during the time interval from 0.75 h to 1 h.

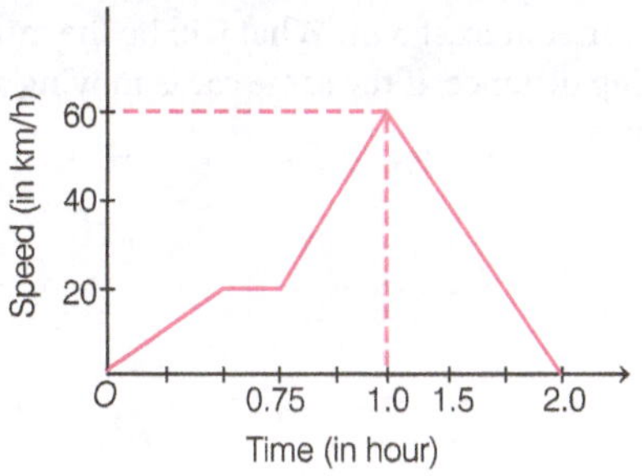

41. The speed-time graph for a car is shown in figure below

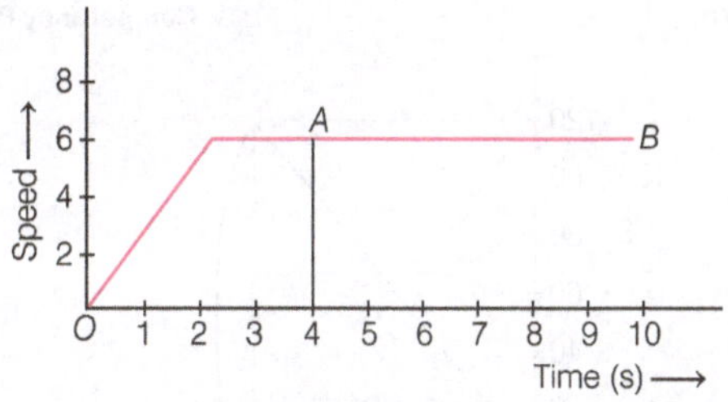

(i) Find how far does the car travel in the first 4s. Shade the area on the graph that represents the distance travelled by the car during the period. **[1½]**

(ii) Which part of the graph represents uniform motion of the car? **Competency Based Que. [1½]**

42. The speed-time graph for a car is shown in figure below.

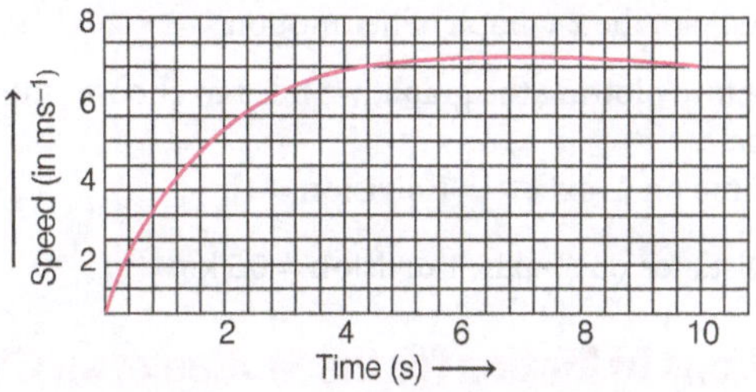

(i) Find how far the car travels in the first 4 s? Shade the area on the graph that represents the distance travelled by the car during the period. **[1½]**

(ii) Which part of the graph represent uniform motion of the car? **[1½]**

43. The velocity-time graph of a particle moving along a straight line as shown in figure by curve *OABCD*. Calculate the distance covered by the particle between (i) $t = 0$ to 18 s (ii) $t = 2$ s to $t = 12$ s and the maximum value of acceleration during this interval. **Competency Based Que.**

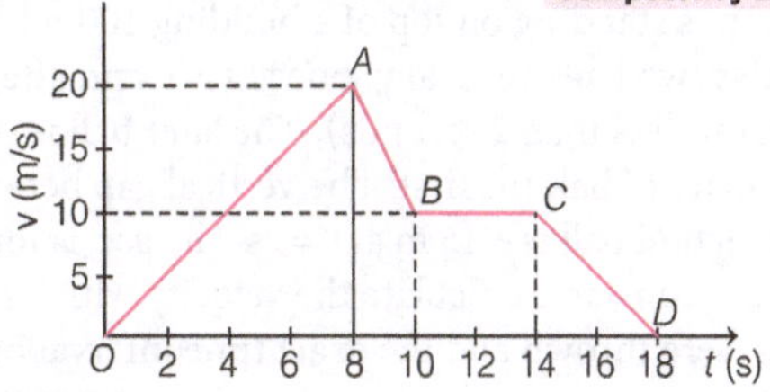

44. Two stones are thrown up simultaneously from the edge of a cliff 200 m high with initial speeds of 15 ms^{-1} and 30 ms^{-1}. Verify that the graph shown in figure, correctly represents the time variation of the relative position of the second stone with respect to the first. Neglect the air resistance and assume that the stones do not rebound after hitting the ground. Take, $g = 10$ ms^{-2}.

Give the equations for the linear and curved part of the plot. **Competency Based Que.**

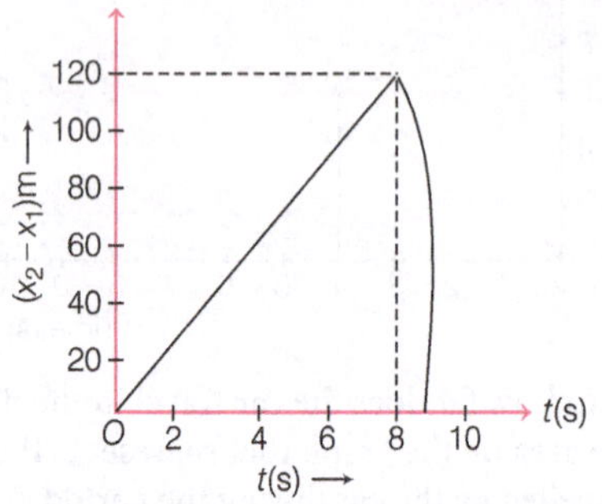

45. A woman starts from her home at 9:00 am walks with a speed of 5 km/h on straight road up to her office 2.5 km away, stays at the office up to 5.00 pm and returns home by an auto with a speed of 25 km/h. Choose suitable scales and plot the x-t graph of her motion. **NCERT**

Before plotting the graph, we need to choose suitable scale.

Time on X-axis, 1 division = 1h

Distance on Y-axis, 1 division = 0.5 km

Equations of Motion for the Motion of an Object Under Gravity

46. A motor boat covers the distance between two spots on the river in $t_1 = 8$ h and $t_2 = 12$ h, downstream and upstream, respectively. What is the time required for the boat to cover this distance in still water?

47. A parachutist bails out from an airplane and after dropping through a distance of 40 m, he opens the parachute and decelerates at 2 m/s^2. If he reaches the ground with a speed of 2 m/s, how long does he float in the air? At what height did he bail out from the plane?

48. A man is standing on top of a building 100m high. He throws two balls vertically, one at $t = 0$ and after a time interval (less than 2 seconds). The later ball is thrown at a velocity of half the first. The vertical gap between first and second ball is + 15 m at $t = 2$s. The gap is found to remain constant. Calculate the velocity with which the balls were thrown and the exact time interval between their throw. **NCERT Exemplar**

49. A monkey climbs up a slippery pole for 3 and subsequently slips for 3 . Its velocity at time t is given by $v(t) = 2t(3s - t)$; $0 < t < 3$ and $v(t) = -(t-3)(6-t)$ for $3 < t < 6$ s in m/s. It repeats this cycle till it reaches the height of 20 m. **NCERT**

(i) At what time is its velocity maximum? **[1]**

(ii) At what time is its average velocity maximum? **[2]**

(iii) At what time is its acceleration maximum in magnitude? **[1]**

(iv) How many cycles (counting fractions) are required to reach the top? **[1]**

50. A car moving along a straight highway with speed of 126 km/h is brought to a stop within a distance of 200 m. What is the retardation of the car (assumed uniform) and how long does it take for the car to stop? **Competency Based Que.**

51. The velocity of a particle is given by equation

$$v = 4 + 2(C_1 + C_2 t)$$

where, C_1 and C_2 are constant. Find the initial velocity and acceleration of the particle.

52. It is a common observation that rain clouds can be at about a kilometre altitude above the ground.

(i) If a rain drop falls from such a height freely under gravity, what will be its speed? Also, calculate in km/h ($g = 10$ m/s^2). **[1]**

(ii) A typical rain drop is about 4 mm diameter. Momentum is mass × speed in magnitude. Estimate its momentum when it hits ground. **[1]**

(iii) Estimate time required to flatten the drop. **[1]**

(iv) Rate of change of momentum is force. Estimate how much force such a drop would exert on you? **[1]**

(v) Estimate the order of magnitude force on umbrella. Typical lateral separation between two rain drops is 5 cm. **[1]**

(Assume that umbrella is circular and has a diameter of 1 m and cloth is not pierced through it.) **NCERT Exemplar**

53. A car moving with a speed of 50 km/h can be stopped by brakes after at least 6 m. What will be the minimum stopping distance, if the same car is moving at a speed of 100km/h?

Hints & Solutions

Objective Type Questions

1. (a) 2. (d) 3. (b) 4. (a) 5. (a)
6. (b) 7. (b) 8. (b) 9. (b)

10. (c) $v_{PT} = 5 - (-10) = 15$ m/s (P = Parrot, T = Train)

So, time taken by the parrot to cross the train is

$$t = \frac{150}{15} = 10 \text{ s}$$

11. (c)

12. (b)

13. (c) Time taken to travel first half distance,

$$t_1 = \frac{l/2}{v_1} = \frac{l}{2v_1}$$

Time taken to travel second half distance $t_2 = \dfrac{l}{2v_2}$

Total time $= t_1 + t_2$

$$= \frac{l}{2v_1} + \frac{l}{2v_2} = \frac{l}{2}\left[\frac{1}{v_1} + \frac{1}{v_2}\right]$$

We know that, v_{av} = Average speed $= \dfrac{\text{total distance}}{\text{total time}}$

$$= \frac{l}{\frac{l}{2}\left[\frac{1}{v_1} + \frac{1}{v_2}\right]} = \frac{2v_1v_2}{v_1 + v_2}$$

14. (b) Given, $x = (t-2)^2$

Velocity, $v = \dfrac{dx}{dt} = \dfrac{d}{dt}(t-2)^2 = 2(t-2)$ m/s

Acceleration, $a = \dfrac{dv}{dt} = \dfrac{d}{dt}[2(t-2)]$

$= 2[1 - 0] = 2 \text{ m/s}^2$

When, $t = 0$; $v = -4$ m/s

$t = 2$s; $v = 0$ m/s

$t = 4$s; $v = 4$ m/s

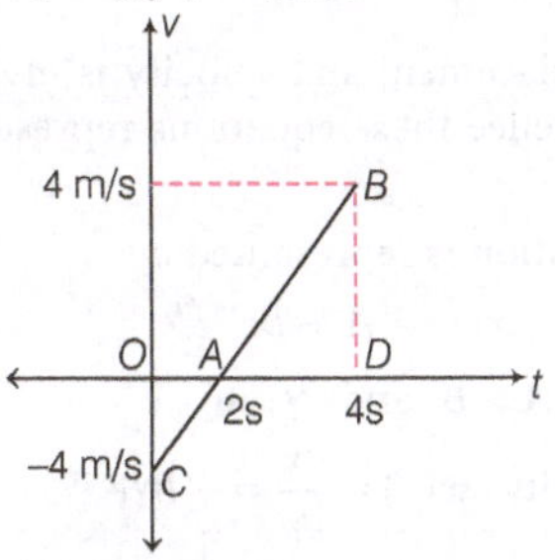

v-t graph is shown above.

Distance travelled = area of the graph.

= area OAC + area ABD

$$= \frac{4 \times 2}{2} + \frac{1}{2} \times 2 \times 4 = 8 \text{ m}$$

15. (b)

16. (a)

17. (a) Let velocity of A and B be u and v.

$$20 = \frac{400}{u - v} \Rightarrow u - v = 20 \qquad \text{...(i)}$$

and $$10 = \frac{400}{u + v} \Rightarrow u + v = 40 \qquad \text{... (ii)}$$

On solving Eqs. (i) and (ii),

$u = 30$ m/s and $v = 10$ m/s

18. (a) Velocity of theif, $v_T = 36$ km/h

$= 10$ m/s, $t = 30$ s

Distance covered by thief

$= s = v_T t = 10 \times 30 = 300$ m

Initial velocity of inspector's bike $= u = 0$

We know, $s = ut + \frac{1}{2}at^2$

$\Rightarrow \quad 300 = 0 \times 20 + \frac{1}{2} \times a \times (20)^2 = 200a$

$\Rightarrow \quad a = 1.5 \text{ m/s}^2$

19. (d) Given, $x(t) = a - bt^2$, $a = 8.5$ m and $b = 2.5 \text{ ms}^{-2}$

$x(t) = 8.5 - 2.5t^2$

Velocity of object $= \dfrac{dx}{dt} = -2bt$

A. Velocity at $t = 2\text{s} = \left.\dfrac{dx}{dt}\right|_{t=2\text{s}} = -4b$

$= -4 \times 2.5 = -10 \text{ ms}^{-1}$

B. Velocity at $t = 0\text{s} = \left.\dfrac{dx}{dt}\right|_{t=0} = 0 \text{ ms}^{-1}$

C. Instantaneous speed at $t = 2$s = Magnitude of velocity

$= |-10 \text{ ms}^{-1}| = 10 \text{ ms}^{-1}$

D. Average velocity $= \dfrac{x(t_2) - x(t_1)}{t_2 - t_1}$

$= \dfrac{x(4) - x(2)}{4 - 2}$

$= \dfrac{[a - b(4)^2] - [a - b(2)^2]}{2}$

$= \dfrac{4b - 16b}{2} = -\dfrac{12b}{2} = -6b$

$= -6 \times 2.5 \text{ ms}^{-1} = -15 \text{ ms}^{-1}$

20. (a) In x-t graph,

$OA \rightarrow$ positive slope $\rightarrow$ positive velocity

$AB \rightarrow$ Negative slope $\rightarrow$ Negative velocity

BC → Zero slope → Object at rest

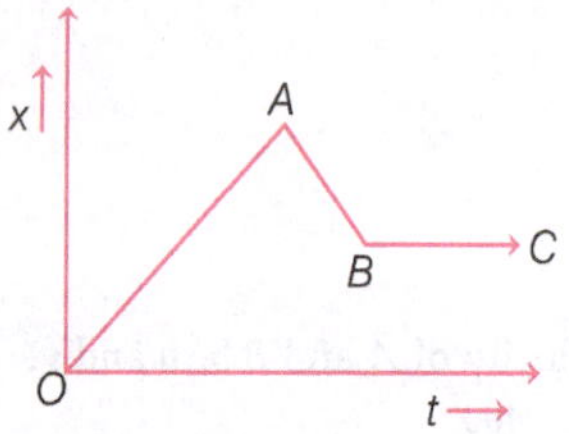

At point A, where change in sign of velocity, hence the direction of motion must have changed at A.

Hence, A-P, B-R, C-Q, D-S.

21. (a) 22. (a) 23. (a) 24. (a) 25. (d)
26. (d) 27. (c) 28. (b) 29. (a) 30. (a)

31. (i) (a), (ii) (d), (iii) (a), (iv) (b)

32. (i) (a), (ii) (c), (iii) (b), (iv) (b)

33. (i) ∵ Object is falling from the top of the tower.

∴ $u = 0$

$g = 9.8$ m/s

$t = 4$s

∵ According to Newton's second equation of motion,

$$s = ut + \frac{1}{2}at^2 = 0\times 4 + \frac{1}{2}\times 9.8\times (4)^2$$

$$= 4.9\times 16 = 78.4\,\text{m}$$

(ii) Given, mass, $m = 1$kg

Initial Velocity, $u = 0$ m/s

Height, $h = 125$m

According to Newton's second equation of motion,

$$\Rightarrow 125 = 0\times t + \frac{1}{2}\times 10\times t^2$$

$$\Rightarrow \quad 125 = 5t^2$$

$$\Rightarrow \quad t^2 = 25 \Rightarrow t = 5\text{s}$$

(iii) Initial velocity of the object will be zero as it was initially at rest.

$u = 0$

$g = 9.8$ m/s^2

from second equation of motion, $h = ut + \frac{1}{2}gt^2$

$$\Rightarrow \quad h = 0(t) + \frac{1}{2}\times gt^2$$

$$\Rightarrow \quad h = 0\times(1) + \frac{1}{2}\times 9.8\times(1)^2$$

$$\Rightarrow \quad h = \frac{1}{2}\times 9.8 = 4.9\text{ m}$$

(iv) The given relation is valid only when the particle moves with uniform velocity and along a straight line.

(v) The kinematic equations of motion do not change in the form under time reversal.

Subjective Questions

1. The distance and the magnitude of displacement of an object have the same values, when the body is moving along a straight line path in a fixed direction.

2. If a is the uniform acceleration, then

$$s(n\text{th}) = u + \frac{1}{2}a(2n-1)$$

where, s (nth) is the distance covered in nth second and u is the initial velocity.

3. If gravity effect is neglected then ball moving uniformly turned back with same speed when a bat hit it. Acceleration of the ball is zero just before it strikes the bat. When the ball strikes the bat, it gets accelerated due to the applied impulsive force by the bat.

The variation of acceleration with time is shown in graph

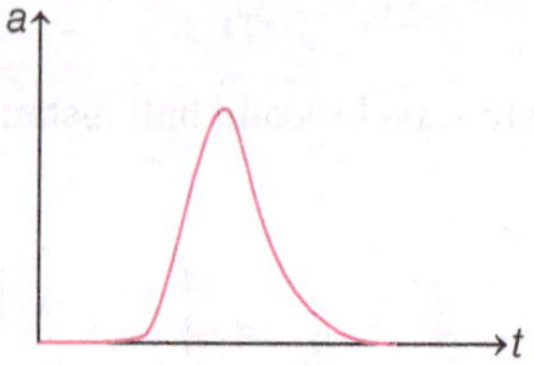

4. When we are writing an equation belonging to periodic nature it will involve sine or cosine function.

(a) The particle will be moving along positive x-direction only if $t > \sin t$

Hence, $x(t) = 1 - \sin t$

Velocity $v(t) = \frac{dx(t)}{dt} = 1 - \cos t$

Acceleration $a(t) = \frac{dv}{dt} = \sin t$

When $t = 0;\ x(t) = 0$

When $t = \pi;\ x(t) = \pi > 0$

When $t = 0;\ x(t) = 2\pi > 0$

(b) Equation can be represented by

$x(t) = \sin t$

$$v = \frac{d}{dt}x(t) = \cos t$$

As displacement and velocity is involving $\sin t$ and $\cos t$, hence these equations represent periodic motion.

5. Let the motion is represented by

$$x(t) = A + Be^{-\gamma t} \quad \text{...(i)}$$

Let $A > B$ and $\gamma > 0$

Now velocity $x(t) = \frac{dx}{dt} = -B\gamma e^{-\gamma t}$

Acceleration $a(t) = \frac{dx}{dt} = B\gamma^2 e^{-\gamma t}$

Suppose we are considering any instant t, then from Eq. (i), we can say that

$$x(t) > 0;\ v(t) < 0 \text{ and } a > 0$$

6. When speed becomes constant acceleration, $a = \frac{dv}{dt} = 0$

Given acceleration $a = g - bv$

where, g = gravitational acceleration

Clearly, from above equation as speed increases acceleration will decrease. At a certain speed say v_0, acceleration will be zero and speed will remain constant.

Hence, $a = g - bv_0 = 0 \Rightarrow v_0 = g/b$

7. (i) A flying kite in the sky comes under three-dimensional motion.

(ii) A cricket ball hit by a player comes under two-dimensional motion.

(iii) Moon revolving around the sun-earth comes under two-dimensional motion.

(iv) The motion of the stone in circular motion comes under two-dimensional motion.

8. (a) As given, $x = 2t^2 + 3t$

By differentiating x w.r.t. t, we get

Velocity, $v = \frac{dx}{dt} = \frac{d}{dt}(2t^2 + 3t)$

$v = (4t + 3)$

As velocity is time dependent, it means that motion is non-uniform.

(b) Let x be the distance travelled in time t. Then,

$x \propto t^2$ [given]

$x = kt^2$ [here, k = constant of proportionality]

We know that velocity is given

$v = \frac{dx}{dt} = 2kt$

and acceleration is given by $a = \frac{dv}{dt} = 2k$ [constant]

Thus, the body has uniform accelerated motion.

9. From second equation of motion, we know

$$s = ut + \frac{1}{2}at^2 \quad \text{...(i)}$$

Given $u = 0, a = g, s_1 = a, s_2 = b$

Using Eq. (i), we get

$$a = \frac{1}{2}gt_1^2$$

$$b = \frac{1}{2}gt_2^2 \Rightarrow \frac{a}{b} = \frac{t_1^2}{t_2^2}$$

$$\Rightarrow \frac{t_1}{t_2} = \sqrt{\frac{a}{b}} \text{ or } t_1 : t_2 = \sqrt{a} : \sqrt{b}$$

10. (a) A person sitting in one train think that other train is at rest, when both trains are moving on parallel tracks with same speed and in same direction. This is because the relative velocity of the train in which the person is sitting with respect to the other train is zero.

(b) Yes, an object can be at rest with respect to one object and can be in motion with respect to another object. For example a body lying on the earth is at rest with respect to earth but the same body is in motion with respect to another planet because earth and the planet are in relative motion.

11. (i) If A is the starting point

Initial position is A

Final position is B

Displacement = AB = 200 km

(ii) If B is the starting point

Initial position is B

Final position is B

Since, initial and final positions are same,

Displacement = 0

12. It is clear from the graph that displacement x is positive throughout. Ball is dropped from a height and its velocity increases in downward direction due to gravity pull. In this condition, v is negative but acceleration of the ball is equal to acceleration due to gravity i.e., $a = -g$.

When ball rebounds in upward direction its velocity is positive but acceleration is $a = -g$.

(i) The velocity-time graph of the ball is shown in figure.

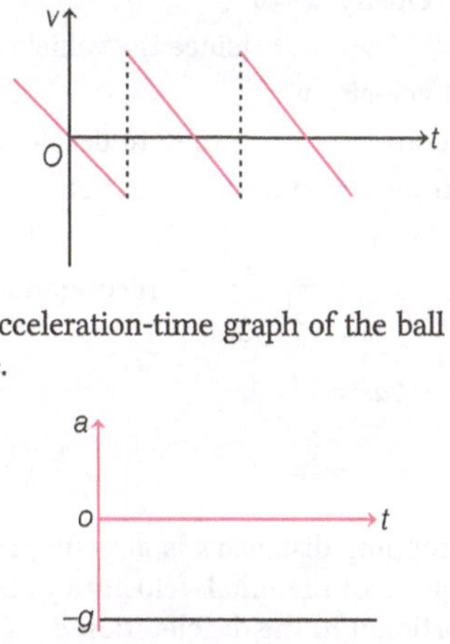

(ii) The acceleration-time graph of the ball is shown in figure.

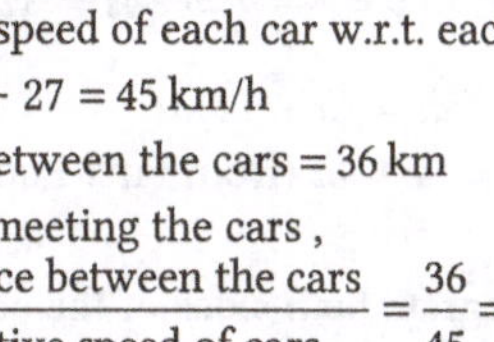

13. Given, speed of first car = 18 km/h

Speed of second car = 27 km/h

∴ Relative speed of each car w.r.t. each other

= 18 + 27 = 45 km/h

Distance between the cars = 36 km

∴ Time of meeting the cars,

$$(t) = \frac{\text{Distance between the cars}}{\text{Relative speed of cars}} = \frac{36}{45} = \frac{4}{5}\text{ h} = 0.8\text{ h}$$

Speed of the bird (v_b) = 36 km/h

∴ Distance covered by the bird = $v_b \times t = 36 \times 0.8$

= 28.8 km

14. For the ball dropped from the building, $u_1 = 0$ and $u_2 = 40\,\text{m/s}$

Velocity of the dropped ball after time t,

$$v_1 = u_1 + gt$$

$$v_1 = gt \quad \text{(downward)}$$

For the ball thrown up, $u_2 = 40$ m/s

Velocity of the ball after time t

$$v_2 = u_2 - gt = (40 - gt) \quad \text{(upward)}$$

∴ Relative velocity of one ball w.r.t. another ball

$$= v_1 - v_2$$

$$= gt - [-(40 - gt)] = 40\,\text{m/s}$$

Note *When we are applying equations for rectilinear motion we should carefully put up the signs for the physical quantities.*

15. No, because the distance covered by an object is the path length of the path covered by the object. The displacement of an object is given by the change in position between the initial position and final position.

e.g. A boy starts from his home and moves towards market along a straight path. Then, he returns to home from the same path. Here, displacement is zero but distance is non-zero.

16. (a) We know the kinematic equation, $v^2 = v_0^2 + 2ad$

Given

Final velocity, $v = 0$

[since the vehicle comes to a stop]

Initial velocity v_0,

Acceleration, $-a$ [due to deceleration, ∵ $a < 0$]

Substitute $v = 0$ into the equation

$$0 = v_0^2 + 2(-a)s$$

[deceleration, a is negative]

$$0 = v_0^2 - 2as$$

$$2as = v_0^2$$

$$s = \frac{v_0^2}{2a}$$

The stopping distance s is directly proportional to the square of the inital velocity v_0 and inversely proportional to the deceleration a.

(b) As we know that, velocity is known as the rate of change of displacement a.

$$v = \frac{ds}{dt} \Rightarrow ds = vdt$$

$$\Rightarrow \quad ds = (u + at)dt$$

{∵ $v = u + at$ (from First Equation of motion)}

$$\Rightarrow \quad ds = u\,dt + at\,dt$$

Now integrate both sides of the above equation, we get

$$\int_0^s ds = \int_0^t udt + \int_0^t atdt$$

$$\therefore \quad s = ut + \frac{1}{2}at^2$$

17. Let S_n and S_{n-1} be the distances covered by an object in n and $n-1$ seconds, respectively.

Let u = its initial velocity

a = acceleration produced in the object

∴ Using the relation $s_t = ut + \frac{1}{2}at^2$,

by putting $t = n$ and $n-1$, we get

$$s_n = un + \frac{1}{2}an^2 \quad \text{...(i)}$$

and $$s_{n-1} = u(n-1) + \frac{1}{2}a(n-1)^2 \quad \text{...(ii)}$$

If $s_{n\text{th}}$ is the distance covered by the object in nth second. Then,

$$s_{n\text{th}} = s_n - s_{n-1}$$

$$= un + \frac{1}{2}an^2 - \left[u(n-1) + \frac{1}{2}a(n-1)^2\right]$$

$$= un + \frac{1}{2}an^2 - \left[un - u + \frac{1}{2}a(n^2 + 1 - 2n)\right]$$

$$= u - \frac{a}{2}(1 - 2n)$$

or $$s_{n\text{th}} = u + \frac{a}{2}(2n - 1)$$

18. (a) No, graph (a) is not representing one-dimensional motion of a particle, because graph shows two different positions of the particle at same instant of time. (At time t_1, particle is at positions P and Q and at time t_2, particle is at positions R and S), which is not possible.

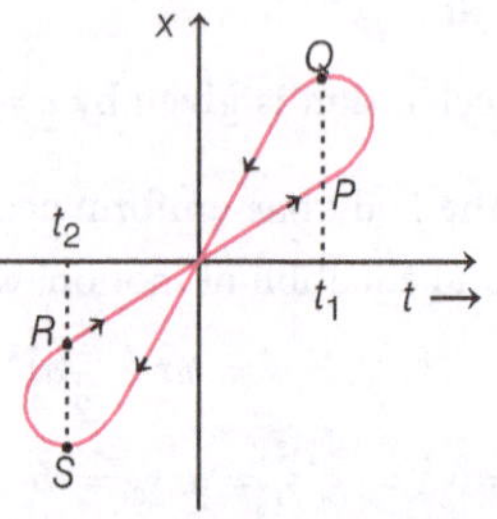

(a)

(b) No, graph (b) cannot represent one-dimensional motion of a particle, because graph shows one positive velocity (v_1) and another negative velocity $(-v_2)$ of the particle at the same instant of time (t_1) which is not possible.

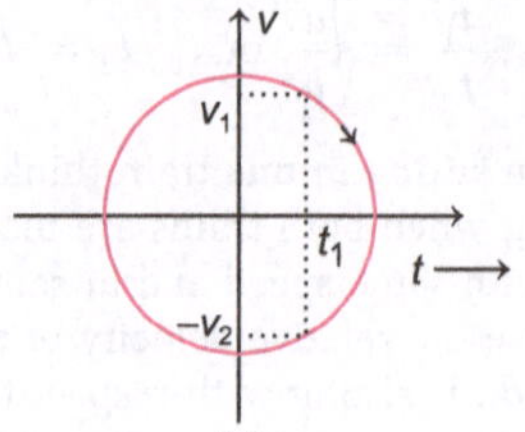

(b)

(c) No, graph (c) cannot represent one-dimensional motion of a particle, because graph shows negative speed of the particle but speed cannot be negative.

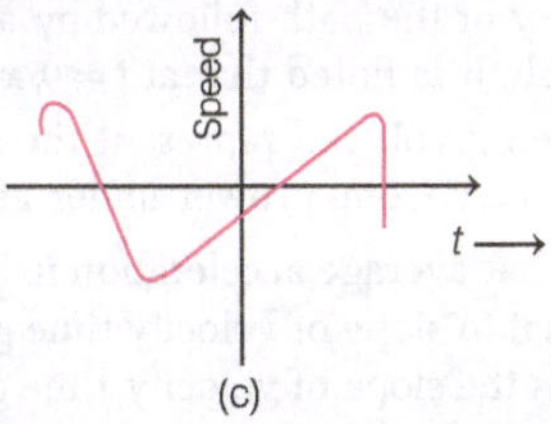

(c)

(d) No, graph (d) cannot represent one-dimensional motion of a particle, because graph shows that total path length increases from time $t = 0$ to $t = t_1$. But total path length of a moving particle can never decrease with time.

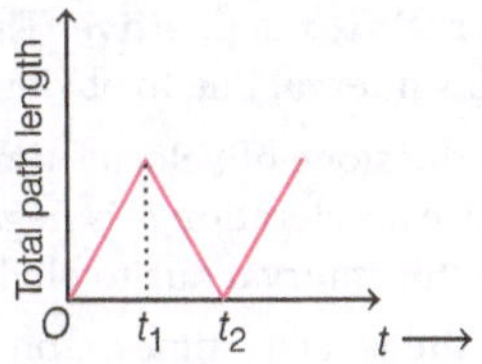

(d)

19. Let v_1, v_2 be the finishing velocities of car A and car B respectively. Let t_1, t_2 be the finishing time intervals for car A and car B respectively.

d = distance travelled by both cars.

∴ According to the statement

$$v = v_1 - v_2 \quad \text{...(i)}$$
$$t = t_2 - t_1 \quad \text{...(ii)}$$

Let d = distance covered during a race by each car

Using equation $s = \left(\frac{u+v}{2}\right)t$, we get

∴ For car A, $d = \left(\frac{0+v_1}{2}\right)t_1 = \frac{v_1t_1}{2}$ $(\because u = 0)$ ...(iii)

For car B, $d = \left(\frac{0+v_2}{2}\right)t_2 = \frac{v_2t_2}{2}$ $(\because u = 0)$ ...(iv)

∴ From Eqs. (iii) and (iv), we get

$$d = \frac{v_1t_1}{2} = \frac{v_2t_2}{2}$$
$$d = \frac{v_1t_1}{2} = \frac{v_2t_2}{2}$$

or $\quad v_1 = \frac{2d}{t_1}$ and $v_2 = \frac{2d}{t_2}$ ...(v)

Also using equation $s = ut + \frac{1}{2}at^2$, we get

$$d = \frac{1}{2}a_1t_1^2 = \frac{1}{2}a_2t_2^2$$

or $\quad a_1 = \frac{2d}{t_1^2}$, and $a_2 = \frac{2d}{t_2^2}$ ...(vi)

(i)/(ii) gives,

$$\frac{v}{t} = \frac{v_1 - v_2}{t_2 - t_1} = \frac{\frac{2d}{t_1} - \frac{2d}{t_2}}{t_2 - t_1} \quad \text{[By using (v)]}$$

$$= \frac{2d(t_2 - t_1)}{t_1t_2(t_2 - t_1)} = \frac{2d}{t_1t_2} = \sqrt{\left(\frac{2d}{t_1t_2}\right)^2}$$

or $\quad \frac{v}{t} = \sqrt{\frac{2d}{t_1^2} \times \frac{2d}{t_2^2}} = \sqrt{a_1 \times a_2}$

∴ $\quad v = t\sqrt{a_1a_2}$

20. (a) Let the collision be just avoided, i.e. the rear train comes to rest after travelling a distance d with a deceleration a.

The initial speed of 1st train = v_1

The initial speed of 2nd train = v_2

If u = initial relative speed of 1st w.r.t. 2nd train, then

$$u = v_1 - v_2$$

Final velocity of rear train, $v = 0$

∴ Using equations, $v_2 - u_2 = 2as$, we get

$$0 - (v_1 - v_2)^2 = 2(-a)d \quad \text{(Here, } a = -a, s = d\text{)}$$

$$d = \frac{(v_1 - v_2)^2}{2a}$$

Thus there will be no collision, if

$$d > \frac{(v_1 - v_2)^2}{2a}$$

(b) Instantaneous speed (v_{ins}) of the particle at an instant is the first derivative of the distance with respect to time at that instant of time i.e. $v_{ins} = \frac{dx}{dt}$.

Since, in instantaneous speed, we take only a small interval of time (dt) during which direction of motion of a body is not supposed to change, hence there is no difference between total path length and magnitude of displacement for small interval of time dt.

Hence, instantaneous speed is always equal to magnitude of instantaneous velocity.

21. (i) Magnitude of displacement of a particle in motion for a given time is the shortest distance between the initial and final position of the particle in that time, whereas, the total length of the path covered by particle is the length of actual path traversed by the particle in the given time.

(ii) Let us consider an example.

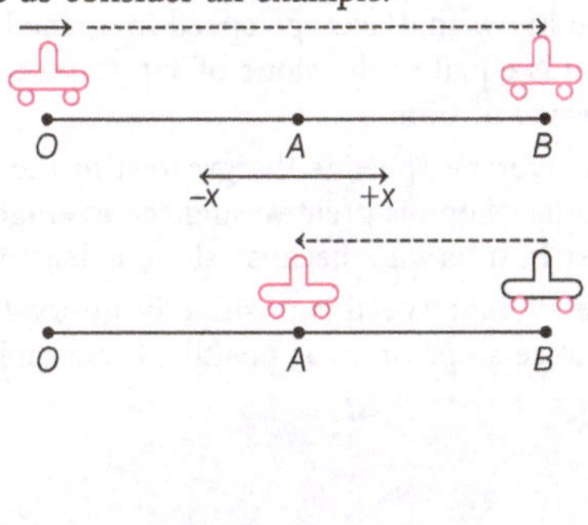

A car starts from O and moves along positive X-axis. The car stops at B and starts moving towards negative X-axis. Finally, the car reaches at A.

For the motion for O to B.

So, [Displacement] =Distance covered

|Average velocity| = Average speed

For the motion from $O \rightarrow B \rightarrow A$

So, |Displacement| < Distance covered

|Average velocity| < Average speed

22. (i) In Fig. (a), the x-t graph shows that initially x is zero i.e. at rest, then it increases with time, attains a constant value and again reduces to zero with time, then it increases in opposite direction till it again attains a constant value i.e. comes to rest.

The similar physical situation arises when a ball resting on a smooth floor is kicked which rebounds from a wall with reduced speed. It then moves to the opposite wall which stops it.

(ii) In Fig. (b), the velocity changes sign again and again with passage of time and every time, some speed is lost. The similar physical situation arises when a ball is thrown up with some velocity, returns back and falls freely. On striking the ground, it rebounds with reduced speed each time it strikes against the ground.

(iii) In Fig. (c), initially the body moves with uniform velocity. Its acceleration increases for a short duration and then falls to zero and thereafter the body moves with a constant velocity. The similar physical situation arises when a cricket ball moving with a uniform speed is hit with a bat for a very short interval of time.

23. In the SHM, acceleration $a = -\omega^2 x$, where ω (i.e. angular frequency) is constant.

(i) At time $t = 0.3$ s, x is negative, the slope of x-t plot is negative, hence position and velocity are negative. Since $a = -\omega^2 x$, hence, acceleration is positive.

(ii) At time $t = 1.2$s, x is positive, the slope of x-t plot is also positive, hence position and velocity are positive. Since $a = -\omega^2 x$, hence acceleration is negative.

(iii) At $t = -1.2$ s, x is negative, the slope of x-t plot is also negative. But since both x and t are negative here, hence velocity is positive. Finally acceleration a is also positive.

24. (a) We know that average speed in a small interval of time is equal to the slope of x-t graph in that interval of time.

The average speed is the greatest in the interval 3 because slope is greatest and the average speed is least in interval 2 because slope is least there.

The average speed is positive in intervals 1 and 2 because slope of x-t is positive there and average speed is negative in interval 3 because the slope of x-t is negative.

(b) No, because the x-t graph does not represent the trajectory of the path followed by a particle. From the graph, it is noted that at $t = 0, x = 0$.

The given graph can represent the motion of a body falling freely from a tower under gravity.

25. We know that average acceleration in a small interval of time is equal to slope of velocity time graph in that interval. As the slope of velocity-time graph is maximum in interval 2 as compared to other intervals 1 and 3, hence the magnitude of average acceleration is greatest in interval 2. The **average speed is greatest in interval 3.** for obvious reasons.

In interval 1, the slope of velocity-time graph is positive, hence **acceleration *a* is positive.** The speed u is positive in this interval due to obvious reasons.

In interval 2, the slope of velocity-time graph is negative, hence acceleration a is negative. The speed u is positive in this interval due to obvious reasons.

In interval 3, the velocity-time graph is parallel to time axis, therefore acceleration a is zero in this interval but v is positive due to obvious reasons.

At points A, B, C and D, the velocity-time graph is parallel to time axis. Therefore, acceleration a **is zero at all the four points.**

26. (i) Since, the ball is moving under the effect of gravity, the direction of acceleration due to gravity is always vertically downwards.

(ii) At the highest point, the velocity of the ball becomes zero and acceleration is equal to the acceleration due to gravity = 9.8 ms^{-2} in vertically downward direction.

(iii) When the highest point is chosen as the location for $x = 0$ and $t = 0$ and vertically downward direction to be the positive direction of X-axis and upward direction as negative direction of X-axis.

During upward motion, sign of position is negative, sign of velocity is negative and sign of acceleration is positive. During downward motion, sign of position is positive, sign of velocity is positive and sign of acceleration is also positive.

(iv) Let t be the time taken by the ball to reach the highest point where height from ground be s.

Taking vertical upward motion of the ball, we have

$$u = -29.4 \text{ms}^{-1},$$

$$a = 9.8 \text{ms}^{-2}, v = 0, s = S, t = ?$$

As, $v^2 - u^2 = 2as$

$\therefore \quad 0 - (-29.4)^2 = 2 \times 9.8 \times S$

or $$S = \frac{-(-29.4)^2}{2 \times 9.8} = -44.1 \text{ m}$$

Here, negative sign shows that the distance is covered in upward direction.

As, $v = u + at$

$\therefore\ 0 = -29.4 + 9.8 \times t$ or $t = \frac{29.4}{9.8} = 3$ s

It means time of ascent = 3 s

When an object moves under the effect of gravity alone, the time of ascent is always equal to the time of descent.

Therefore, total time after which the ball returns to the player's hand = 3 + 3 = 6 s

27. (i) True, when a body is thrown vertically upwards in the space, then at the highest point, the body has zero speed but has downward acceleration equal to the acceleration due to gravity.

(ii) False, because velocity is the speed of body in a given direction. When speed is zero, the magnitude of velocity of body is zero, hence velocity is zero.

(iii) True, when a particle is moving along a straight line with a constant speed, its velocity remains constant with time. Therefore, acceleration (i.e. change in velocity/time) is zero.

(iv) False, if the initial velocity of a body is negative, then even in the case of positive acceleration, the body speeds down. A body speeds up when the acceleration acts in the direction of motion.

Here, $u = 0$, $a = 1\ \text{ms}^{-2}$

28. Distance covered in nth second is

$$D_n = u + \frac{a}{2}(2n - 1)$$

$$D_n = 0 + \frac{1}{2}(2n - 1) = 0.5\,(2n - 1) \qquad \text{...(i)}$$

Putting $n = 1, 2, 3...$, we can find the value of D_n.

The various values of n and corresponding values of D_n are shown below

n	1	2	3	4	5	6	7	8	9	10
D_n	0.5	1.5	2.5	3.5	4.5	5.5	6.5	7.5	8.5	9.5

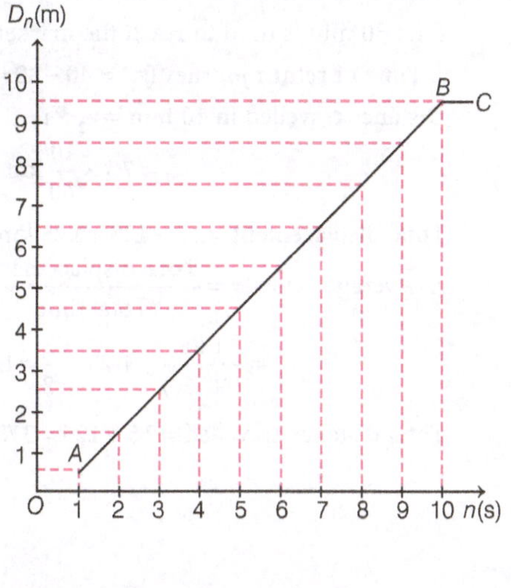

29. Taking vertical downward motion of ball from a height 90 m, we have $u = 0$, $a = 10\ \text{m/s}^2$, $s = 90$ m, $t = ?$; $u = ?$

$$t = \sqrt{\frac{2s}{a}} = \sqrt{\frac{2 \times 90}{10}} = 3\sqrt{2}\ \text{s} = 4.24\ \text{s}$$

$$u = \sqrt{2as} = \sqrt{2 \times 10 \times 90} = 30\sqrt{2}\ \text{m/s}$$

Rebound velocity of ball,

$$u' = \frac{9}{10}u = \frac{9}{10} \times 30\sqrt{2} = 27\sqrt{2}\ \text{m/s}$$

Time to reach the highest point is

$$t' = \frac{u'}{a} = \frac{27\sqrt{2}}{10} = 2.7\sqrt{2} = 2.7\sqrt{2} = 3.81\ \text{s}$$

Total time $= t + t' = 4.24 + 3.81 = 8.05$ s

The ball will take further 3.81 s to fall back to floor, where its velocity before striking the floor $= 27\sqrt{2}$ m/s

Velocity of ball after striking the floor

$$= \frac{9}{10} \times 27\sqrt{2} = 24.3\sqrt{2}\ \text{m/s}$$

Total time elapsed before upward motion of ball

$= 8.05 + 3.81 = 11.86$s

Thus, the speed-time graph of this motion is shown in the following figure.

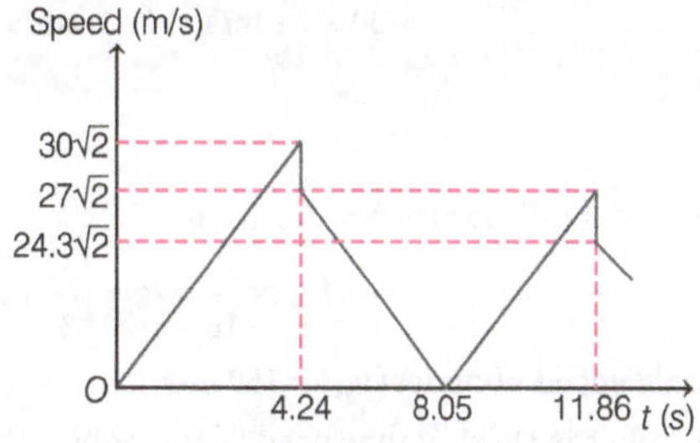

30. Equations of Motion by calculus method.

First equation of motion

Since, we know that acceleration is rate of change of velocity

$$\Rightarrow \quad a = \frac{dv}{dt}$$

$$\Rightarrow \quad a\,dt = dv$$

Integrating both sides,

$$\Rightarrow \quad \int_0^t a\,dt = \int_u^v dv$$

$$\Rightarrow \quad at = v - u$$

$$\Rightarrow \quad v = u + at$$

For second equation of motion, refer to solution (21) of exam pattern exercise.

Third equation of motion,

$\because$ We know that acceleration is the rate of change of velocity, i.e.

$$a = \frac{dv}{dt} \quad \text{...(i)}$$

Velocity is the rate of change of displacement

$$v = \frac{ds}{dt} \quad \text{...(ii)}$$

from Eqs. (i) and (ii), we get

$$a\frac{ds}{dt} = \frac{v\,dv}{dt}$$

$$\Rightarrow \quad \int_0^s a\,ds = \int_u^v v\,dv$$

$$\Rightarrow \quad as = \frac{v^2 - u^2}{2}$$

$$\Rightarrow \quad v^2 - u^2 = 2as$$

$$\Rightarrow \quad v^2 = u^2 + 2as$$

31. We can see that the object P covers a distance of 10 m in every 15 min. In other words, it covers equal distance in equal intervals of time. So, the motion of object P is uniform.

On the other hand, the object Q covers 7 m from 9:30 am to 9:45 am, 4 m from 9:45 am to 10:00 am and so on. In other words, it covers unequal distances in equal intervals of time. So, the motion of object Q is non-uniform.

32. Speed of police van $(v_P) = 30$ km/h

$$= 30 \times \frac{5}{18} \text{ m/s} \quad \left(\because 1 \text{ km/s} = \frac{5}{18} \text{ m/s}\right)$$

$$= \frac{25}{3} \text{ m/s}$$

Speed of thief's car $(v_T) = 192$ km/h

$$= 192 \times \frac{5}{18} \text{ m/s} = \frac{160}{3} \text{ m/s}$$

Muzzle speed of bullet $(v_B) = 150$ m/s

The bullet is sharing the speed of the police van, therefore effective speed of the bullet

$$v_B' = v_B + v_P$$

$$= 150 + \frac{25}{3} = \frac{475}{3} \text{ m/s}$$

Speed of the bullet with which it hits the thief's car = Relative speed of the bullet w.r.t. thief's car (v_{BT})

$$v_{BT} = v_B' - v_T$$

$$= \left(\frac{475}{3} - \frac{160}{3}\right) \text{m/s} = \frac{315}{3} = 105 \text{ m/s}$$

Therefore, bullet will hit the thief's car with a speed 105 m/s.

33. (a) As man return his home, therefore total displacement of the man = 0

$$\therefore \text{ Average velocity} = \frac{\text{Total displacement}}{\text{Total time}} = 0$$

(b) Speed of man during motion from his home to the market $(v_1) = 5$ km/h. Speed of man during motion from market his home $(v_2) = 7.5$ km/h.

Distance between his home and market $(x) = 2.5$ km

(i) **Taking time interval 0 to 30 min**

Time taken by man to reach the market

$$t_1 = \frac{x}{v_1} = \frac{2.5}{5} = \frac{1}{2} \text{ h} = 30 \text{ min}$$

Hence, the man moves from his home to the market in $t = 0$ to 30 min.

$$\therefore \text{ Average velocity} = \frac{\text{Total displacement}}{\text{Total time}}$$

$$= \frac{2.5}{\frac{1}{2}} = 5.0 \text{ km/h}$$

$$\text{Average speed} = \frac{\text{Total distance}}{\text{Total time}} = \frac{2.5}{\frac{1}{2}} = 5.0 \text{ km/h}$$

(ii) **Taking time interval 0 to 50 min**

Time taken by man in returning to his home from the market

$$t_2 = \frac{x}{v_2} = \frac{2.5}{7.5} = \frac{1}{3} \text{ h} = 20 \text{ min}$$

$$\therefore \text{ Total time of journey } (T) = t_1 + t_2 = 30 + 20 = 50 \text{ min}$$

$\therefore$ Total displacement = 0

(as man return to its initial position)

$$\therefore \text{ Average velocity} = \frac{\text{Total displacement}}{\text{Total time}} = 0$$

Total distance $= 2.5 + 2.5 = 5.0$ km

$$\therefore \text{ Average velocity} = \frac{\text{Total distance}}{\text{Total time}}$$

$$= \frac{5.0}{50/60} \text{ km/h} = 6 \text{ km/h}$$

(iii) **Taking time interval 0 to 40 min**

First 30 min is used to reach the market.

$\therefore$ Time of return journey $(t_3) = 40 - 30 = 10$ min

Distance travelled in 10 min $= v_2 \times t_3$

$$= 7.5 \times \frac{10}{60} \text{ km} = 1.25 \text{ km}$$

Total displacement $= 2.5 - 1.25 = 1.25$ km

$$\therefore \text{ Average velocity} = \frac{\text{Total displacement}}{\text{Total time}}$$

$$= \frac{1.25}{(40/60)} = 1.25 \times \frac{3}{2} = 1.875 \text{ km/h}$$

Total distance travelled $= 2.5 + 1.25 = 3.75$ km

$\therefore$ Average speed $= \dfrac{\text{Total distance}}{\text{Total time}}$

$$= \frac{3.75}{\frac{40}{60}} = 3.75 \times \frac{3}{2} \text{ km/h} = 5.625 \text{ km/h}$$

34. Let us consider left to right to be the positive direction of X-axis.

(i) Here, velocity of belt, $v_B = +4 \text{ kmh}^{-1}$, speed of child w.r.t. belt, $v_C = +9 \text{ kmh}^{-1} = 5/2 \text{ ms}^{-1}$

Speed of the child w.r.t. stationary observer,

$$v'_C = v_C + v_B = 9 + 4 = 13 \text{ kmh}^{-1}$$

(ii) Here, $v_B = +4 \text{ kmh}^{-1}$, $v_C = -9 \text{ kmh}^{-1}$

Speed of the child w.r.t. stationary observer,

$$v'_C = v_C + v_B = -9 + 4 = -5 \text{ kmh}^{-1}$$

Here, negative sign shows that the child will appear to run in a direction opposite to the direction of motion of the belt.

(iii) Distance between the parents, $s = 50$ m

Since parents and child are located on the same belt, the speed of the child as observed by stationary observer in either direction (either from mother to father or from father to mother) will be 9 kmh^{-1}.

Time taken by child in case (i) and (ii) is

$$t = \frac{50}{(5/2)} = 20 \text{ s}$$

If motion is observed by one of the parents, answer to case (i) or case (ii) will get altered. It is so because speed of child w.r.t. either of mother or father is 9 kmh^{-1}. But answer (iii) remains unaltered due to the fact that parents and child are on the same belt and as such all are equally affected by the motion of the belt.

35. Let the speed of each bus $= v_b$ km/h

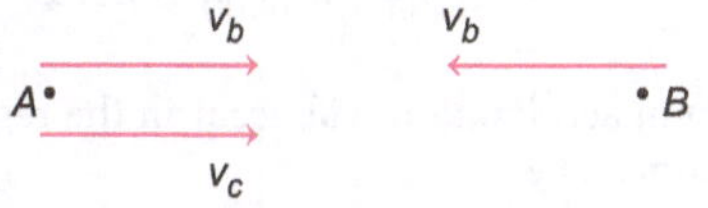

Speed of cyclist = 20 km/h

(a) **In the direction of motion of the cyclist (from A to B)**

Relative velocity of bus w.r.t. cyclist $= v_b - v_c$

$$= (v_b - 20) \text{ km/h}$$

The bus goes past the cyclist after every 18 min.

$\therefore$ Distance covered by the bus w.r.t. the cyclist in this time interval

$$= (v_b - 20) \times \frac{18}{60} \text{ km} \quad \text{...(i)}$$

A bus leaves in either direction after every T min.

$\therefore$ Distance travelled by a bus in T min

$$= v_b \times \frac{T}{60} \text{ km} \quad \text{...(ii)}$$

From Eqs. (i) and (ii), we get

$$(v_b - 20) \times \frac{18}{60} = v_b \times \frac{T}{60}$$

or $$v_b - 20 = \frac{v_b \times T}{18} \quad \text{...(iii)}$$

(b) **In the opposite direction of the cyclist (from B to A)**

Relative velocity of bus w.r.t. cyclist coming from B to A

$$= (v_b + 20) \text{ km/h}$$

The bus goes past the cyclist after every 6 min.

$\therefore$ Distance covered by the bus w.r.t. the cyclist in this time interval

$$= (v_b + 20) \times \frac{6}{60} \text{ km} \quad \text{...(iv)}$$

Distance travelled by the bus in T min

$$= v_b \times \frac{T}{60} \text{ km} \quad \text{...(v)}$$

From Eqs. (iv) and (v), we get

$$(v_b + 20) \times \frac{6}{60} = v_b \times \frac{T}{60}$$

$$v_b + 20 = v_b \times \frac{T}{6} \quad \text{...(vi)}$$

Dividing Eq. (vi) by Eq. (iii), we get

$$\frac{v_b + 20}{v_b - 20} = \frac{18}{6} = 3$$

$$v_b + 20 = 3v_b - 60$$

or $$2v_b = 80, v_b = 40 \text{ km/h}$$

Substituting value of v_b in Eq. (vi), we get

$$(40 + 20) = \frac{40 \times T}{6} \Rightarrow 60 \times 6 = 40 \times T$$

or $$T = \frac{360}{40} = 9 \text{ min}$$

36. $\because$ We know that, $s_n = u + \dfrac{a}{2}(2n - 1)$

$$\Rightarrow \quad 12 = u + \frac{a}{2}(2 \times 3 - 1) \quad \text{...(i)}$$

and $$20 = u + \frac{a}{2}(2 \times 5 - 1) \quad \text{...(ii)}$$

Subtract Eq. (i) from Eq. (ii), we get

$$s = \frac{a}{2}(9 - 5)$$

$$\Rightarrow \quad 2a = 8$$

$$\Rightarrow \quad a = 4 \text{ ms}^{-2}$$

Putting the value of a in Eq. (i),

we get $12 = u + \dfrac{4}{2} \times 5 \Rightarrow u = 2 \text{ ms}^{-1}$

$\because \quad v = u + at$

$\Rightarrow 2 + 4 \times 10 = 42 \text{ ms}^{-1}$

37. $\because$ We know that

$$a = \frac{dv}{dt} = \frac{dx}{dt}\cdot\frac{dv}{dx} = \frac{vdv}{dx}$$

$$v = (180 - 16x)^{1/2}$$

$$v^2 = 180 - 16x$$

Differentiate both sides with respect to x, we get

$$2v\frac{dv}{dx} = -16$$

$$\Rightarrow \quad \frac{vdv}{dx} = as = -8\,\text{ms}^{-2}$$

38. (i) Let maximum velocity be v.

$$\because \quad v = u + at$$

$$\Rightarrow \quad v = 0 + at \quad \{\because u = 0 \text{ m/s}\}$$

$$\Rightarrow \quad v = \alpha t_1$$

$$\Rightarrow \quad t_1 = \frac{v}{\alpha} \quad \text{...(i)}$$

Similarly, $t_2 = \dfrac{v}{\beta}$ ...(ii)

$$\therefore \quad t_1 + t_2 = \frac{v}{\alpha} + \frac{v}{\beta}$$

$$v = \left(\frac{\alpha\beta}{\alpha+\beta}\right)t$$

(ii) The total distance covered is equal to the area under the velocity-time graph.

$$s = \frac{1}{2}\times v \times t$$

$$\Rightarrow \quad s = \frac{1}{2}\left(\frac{\alpha\beta}{\alpha+\beta}\right)t^2$$

39. Let us draw the given situation.

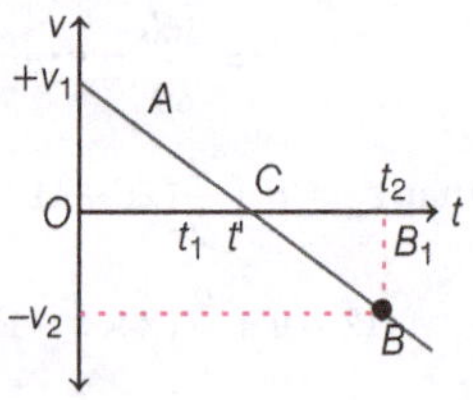

Here, we need to prove that

S = area under the (v-t) curve from t_1 to t_2 ...(i)

Let us consider RHS of Eq. (i),

Area = ar(ΔAB_1C) + ar(ΔBB_1C)

$$\text{Area} = \frac{1}{2}\times(t' - t_1)(+v_1) + \frac{1}{2}(t_2 - t')(-v_2)$$

$$\text{Area} = \frac{v_1}{2}(t' - t_1) - \frac{v_2}{2}[t_2 - t'] \quad \text{...(ii)}$$

$\because$ Slope of graph is constant.

$\Rightarrow$ Slope of ar(ΔAA_1C) = Slope of ar(ΔBB_1C) = a

$$\Rightarrow \quad a = \frac{-v_1}{(t' - t_1)} = \frac{-v_2}{(t_2 - t')}$$

$$\Rightarrow \quad t' - t_1 = \frac{-v}{a} \quad \text{...(iii)}$$

$$t_2 - t' = \frac{-v_2}{a} \quad \text{...(iv)}$$

From Eqs. (ii), (iii) and (iv), we get

$$\text{Area} = \frac{v_1}{2}\left[\frac{-v_1}{a}\right] - \frac{v_2}{2}\left[\frac{-v_2}{a}\right]$$

$$= \frac{v_2^2}{2a} - \frac{v_1^2}{2a} = \frac{v_2^2 - v_1^2}{2a} \quad \text{...(v)}$$

$\because$ We know that from Newtons's 3rd Equation of motion, we have $v^2 = u^2 + 2as$

$$\Rightarrow \quad v^2 - u^2 = 2as$$

If $v = v_2$ and $u = v_1$

$$\therefore \quad v_2^2 - v_1^2 = 2as$$

$$\frac{v_2^2 - v_1^2}{2a} = s \quad \text{...(vi)}$$

From Eqs. (v) and (vi), we get

distance travelled, s = Area under (v-t) curve.

Hence, proved.

40. Consider the given figure.

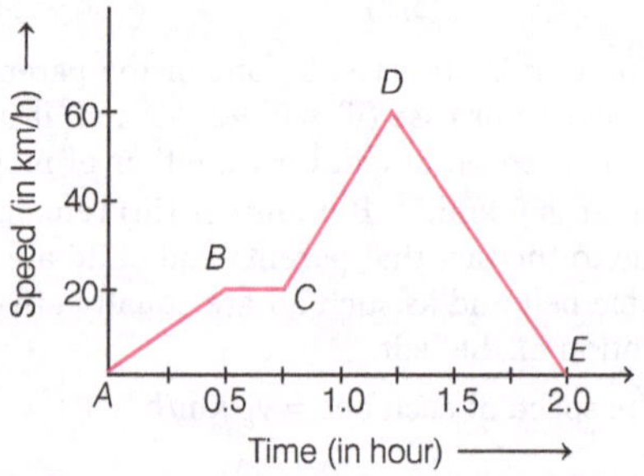

Maximum acceleration will occur in the region with maximum slope.

From the given curve, region CD is having the highest curve.

$\therefore$ Maximum acceleration

$$= \frac{\text{Change in velocity}}{\text{Change in distance}}$$

$$= \frac{60 - 20}{0.25}$$

$$= 160 \text{ km/h}^2$$

Now, total area under the curve between 0.75 h to 1.0 h is given by

$$\left(\frac{1}{2}\times 0.25 \times 40\right) + (20 \times 0.25) = 10\text{km}$$

41. (i) Consider the given graph,

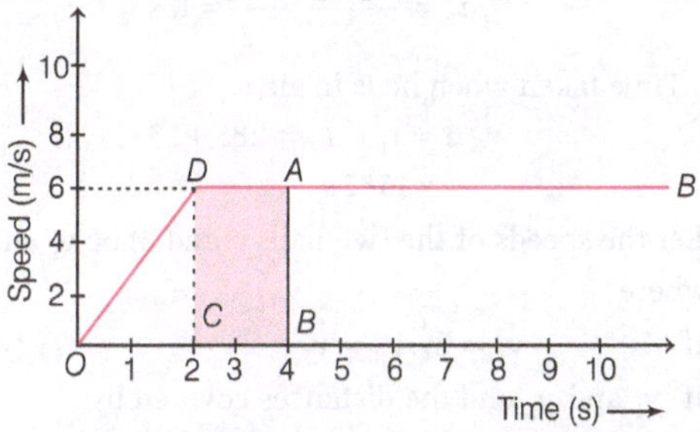

Distance travelled in first 4s = Area under the curve

$= \text{Area}(\Delta\, OCD) + \text{Area}\,(CDAB)$

$= \frac{1}{2} \times 2 \times 6 + 2 \times 6$

$= 6 + 12 = 18\text{m}$

(ii) The car starts moving under the uniform motion after $t = 2$s, because after this instant, speed of the car becomes constant.

42. (i) The shaded portion of the car represents the distance travelled by the car in the first four seconds.

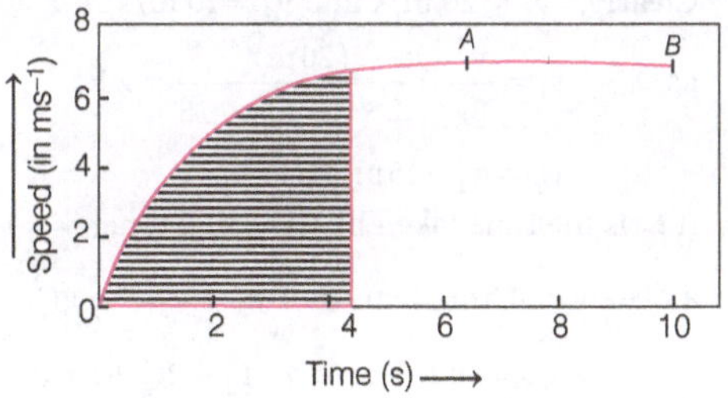

The car travels with a non-uniform speed which is accelerated in nature.

(ii) The straight line portion of the graph represents the uniform motion of the car i.e. from point A to B.

43. Let us draw the given figure.

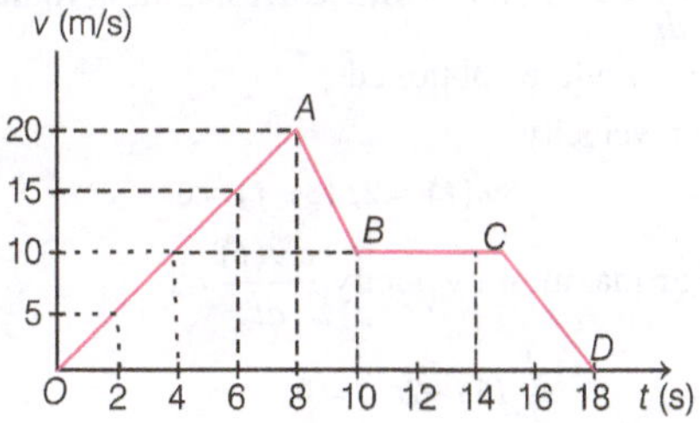

(i) Distance covered by the particle between $t = 0$ to 18s = Area under the curve

(from $t = 0$ to $t = 18$ s)

$= \frac{1}{2} \times 8 \times 20 + \frac{1}{2} \times 2 \times 10 + 6 \times 10 + \frac{1}{2} \times 4 \times 10$

$= 80 + 10 + 60 + 20 = 170$ m

(ii) Distance covered by the particle between $t = 2$s to $t = 12$s = Area under the curve (from $t = 2$s to $t = 12$s)

$= 170 - \frac{1}{2} \times 2 \times 5 - 2 \times 10 - \frac{1}{2} \times 10 \times 4 = 170 - 5 - 20 - 20$

$= 170 - 45 = 125$m

$$a_{max} = \frac{20-10}{8-10} = \frac{10}{-2} = -5 \text{ ms}^{-2}$$

44. Taking vertical upward motion of the first stone for time t, we have

$x_0 = 200$ m, $u = 15$ m/s,

$a = -10\text{m/s}^2$, $t = t$, $x = x_1$

As, $\quad x = x_0 + ut + \frac{1}{2}at^2$

$\therefore \quad x_1 = 200 + 15t + \frac{1}{2}(-10)\,t^2$

or $\quad x_1 = 200 + 15t - 5t^2$ ...(i)

Taking vertical upward motion of the second stone for time t, we have

$x_0 = 200$ m, $u = 30 \text{ ms}^{-1}$,

$a = -10 \text{ ms}^{-2}$, $t = t$, $x = x_2$

Then, $\quad x_2 = 200 + 30\,t - \frac{1}{2} \times 10\,t^2$

$= 200 + 30\,t - 5\,t^2$ ...(ii)

When the first stone hits the ground, $x_1 = 0$, from Eq (i).

So, $\quad t^2 - 3t - 40 = 0$

or $\quad (t-8)(t+5) = 0$

$\therefore$ Either $t = 8$ s or -5 s

Since, $t = 0$ corresponds to the instant, when the stone was projected. Hence, negative time has no meaning in this case. So, $t = 8$ s.

When the second stone hits the ground, $x_2 = 0$, from Eq (ii).

So, $\quad 0 = 200 + 30\,t - 5\,t^2$

or $\quad t^2 - 6\,t - 40 = 0$

or $\quad (t-10)(t+4) = 0$

Therefore, either $t = 10$ s, or $t = -4$ s

Since, $t = -4$ s is meaningless, so $t = 10$ s.

Relative position of second stone w.r.t. first is

$= x_2 - x_1 = 15\,t$ ...(iii)

Since, $(x_2 - x_1)$ and t are linearly related, therefore, the graph is a straight line till $t = 8$ s.

For maximum separation, $t = 8$ s, so maximum separation $= 15 \times 8 = 120$ m

After 8 s only, second stone would be in motion for 2 s, so the graph is in accordance with the quadratic equation, $x_2 = 200 + 30\,t - 5\,t^2$ for the interval of time 8 s to 10 s.

45. Time taken in reaching the office $= \dfrac{\text{Distance}}{\text{Speed}} = \dfrac{2.5}{5} = 0.5$ h

Time taken in returning from office $= \dfrac{2.5}{25} = 0.1$ h $= 6$ min

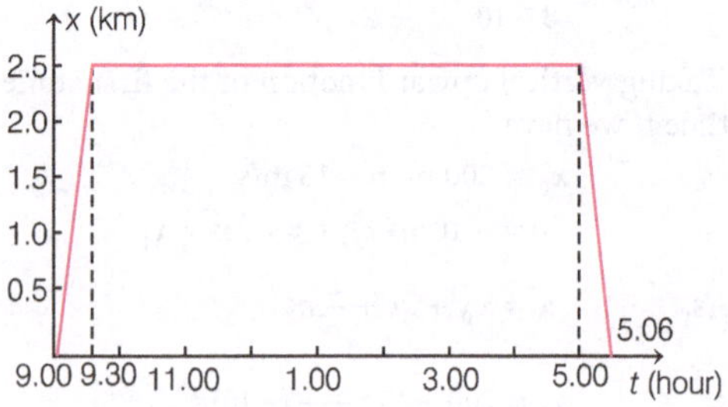

It means that woman reaches the office at 9:30 am and returns home at 5:06 pm.

46. Let the time required in still water be t hours.
Speed of boat be v km/h and stream be v' km/h.

For downstream, $d = (v + v')8$ ...(i)

For upstream, $d = (v - v')12$ ...(ii)

For still water, $d = vt$ ...(iii)

On solving Eqs. (i) and (ii), we get

$$3(v - v') = 2(v + v')$$

$$v = 5v' \quad \text{...(iv)}$$

Putting the value of v in Eq. (i) and also value of t from Eq. (iii), we get

$$vt = \left(v + \frac{v}{5}\right)8 \Rightarrow t = \frac{6 \times 8}{5} = 9.6 \text{ hours}$$

47. Applying third equation of motion to calculate final velocity,

$$v^2 = 0 + 2 \times 9.8 \times 40$$

$$\Rightarrow \quad v = \sqrt{784} = 28 \text{ ms}^{-1}$$

Time taken, $t_1 = \dfrac{28}{9.8} = 2.85$ s

According to question, the parachutist reached the ground with velocity 2 ms^{-1} with deceleration of 2 ms^{-2} and the initial velocity would be which we calculated above, i.e. 28 ms^{-1}.

Let us assume that parachutist travelled a distance of h while falling.

From third equation of motion,

$$2^2 = 28^2 + 2(-2)\,h$$

$$\Rightarrow \quad 4 - 784 = -4h$$

$$\Rightarrow \quad h = 195 \text{m}$$

Time taken, $t_2 = \dfrac{28 - 2}{2} = \dfrac{26}{2} = 13$s

$\therefore$ Time taken when he is in air,

$$t = t_1 + t_2 = 2.85 + 13$$

$$t = 15.85 \text{ s}$$

48. Let the speeds of the two balls (1and 2) be v_1 and v_2 where

if $v_1 = 2v, v_2 = v$

if y_1 and y_2 and the distances covered by the balls 1 and 2 , respectively, before coming to rest, then

$$y_1 = \frac{v_1^2}{2g} = \frac{4v^2}{2g} \text{ and } y_2 = \frac{v_2^2}{2g} = \frac{v^2}{2g}$$

Since, $y_1 - y_2 = 15\text{m}, \dfrac{4v^2}{2g} - \dfrac{v^2}{2g} = 15$ m

or $\dfrac{3v^2}{2g} = 15$ m

or $v^2 = \sqrt{5\text{m} \times (2 \times 10)}$ m/s^2

or $v = 10$ m/s

Clearly, $v_1 = 20$ m/s and $v_2 = 10$ m/s

as $y_1 = \dfrac{v_1^2}{2g} = \dfrac{(20\text{m})^2}{2 \times (10\text{m}) \times 15} = 20\text{m},$

$$y_2 = y_1 - 15\text{m} = 5\text{m}$$

If t_2 is the time taken by the ball 2 toner a distance of 5m, then from $y_2 = v_2 t - \dfrac{1}{2} g t_2^2$

$$5 = 10\,t_2 - 5t_2^2 \text{ or } t_2^2 - 2t_2 + 1 = 0,$$

where, $t_2 = 15$

Since, t_1 (time taken by ball 1 to cover distance of 20m) is 2s, time interval between the two throws

$$= t_1 - t_2 = 2\text{s} - 1\text{s} = 1\text{s}$$

49. It this problem to calculate maximum velocity we will use $\dfrac{dv}{dt} = 0$,then the time corresponding to maximum velocity will be obtained.

Given velocity

$$v(t) = 2t(3 - t) = 6t - 2t^2 \quad \text{...(i)}$$

(i) For maximum velocity $\dfrac{dv(t)}{dt} = 0$

$$\Rightarrow \quad \frac{d}{dt}(6\,t - 2t^2) = 0$$

$$\Rightarrow \quad 6 - 4\,t = 0$$

$$\Rightarrow \quad t = \frac{6}{4} = \frac{3}{2}\text{s} = 1.5 \text{ s}$$

(ii) From Eq. (i) $v = 6\,t - 2t^2$

$$\Rightarrow \quad \frac{ds}{dt} = 6\,t - 2t^2$$

$\Rightarrow \quad ds = (6t - 2t^2)\,dt$

where, s is displacement

$\therefore$ Distance travelled in time interval 0 to 3s.

$$s = \int_0^3 (6t - 2t^2)\,dt$$

$$= \left[\frac{6t^2}{2} - \frac{2t^3}{3}\right]_0^3 = \left[3t^2 - \frac{2}{3}t^3\right]_0^3$$

$$= 3\times 9 - \frac{2}{3}\times 3\times 3\times 3 = 27 - 18 = 9\text{ m}.$$

$$\text{Average velocity} = \frac{\text{Distance travelled}}{\text{Time}}$$

$$= \frac{9}{3} = 3\text{ m/s}$$

Given, $x = 6t - 2t^2$

$\Rightarrow \quad 3 = 6t - 2t^2$

$\Rightarrow \quad 2t^2 - 6t - 3 = 0$

$$\Rightarrow \quad t = \frac{6 \pm \sqrt{6^2 - 4\times 2\times 3}}{2\times 2} = \frac{6\pm\sqrt{36-24}}{4}$$

$$= \frac{6\pm\sqrt{12}}{4} = \frac{3\pm 2\sqrt{3}}{2}$$

Considering positive sign only

$$t = \frac{3+2\sqrt{3}}{2} = \frac{3+2\times 1.732}{2} = \frac{9}{4}\text{ s}$$

(iii) In a periodic motion when velocity is zero acceleration will be maximum putting $v = 0$ in Eq. (i)

$0 = 6t - 2t^2$

$\Rightarrow \quad 0 = t(6-2t) = t\times 2(3-t) = 0$

$\Rightarrow \quad t = 0 \text{ or } 3\text{s}$

(iv) Distance covered in 0 to 3s = 9 m

Distance covered in 3 to 6s $= \int_3^6 (18 - 9t + t^2)\,dt$

$$= \left(18t - \frac{9t^2}{2} + \frac{t^3}{3}\right)_3^6$$

$$= 18\times 6 - \frac{9}{2}\times 6^2 + \frac{6^3}{3} - \left(18\times 3 - \frac{9\times 3^2}{2} + \frac{3^3}{3}\right)$$

$$= 108 - 9\times 18 + \frac{6^3}{3} - 18\times 3 + \frac{9}{2}\times 9 - \frac{27}{3}$$

$$= 108 - 18\times 9 + \frac{216}{3} - 54 + 4.5\times 9 - 9 = -4.5\text{ m}$$

$\therefore$ Total distance travelled in one cycle

$= s_1 + s_2 = 9 - 4.5 = 4.5$ m

Number of cycles covered in total distance to be covered $= \frac{20}{4.5} \approx 4.44 \approx 5.$

50. Initial velocity of the car $(u) = 126$ km/h

$$= 126\times\frac{5}{18}\text{m/s} \qquad \left(\because 1\text{ km/h} = \frac{5}{18}\text{ m/s}\right)$$

$= 35$ m/s

Final velocity of the car $(v) = 0$

Distance travelled $(s) = 200$ m

From equation of motion, $v^2 = u^2 + 2as$

$$\text{or} \quad a = \frac{v^2 - u^2}{2s} = \frac{0-(35)^2}{2\times 200}$$

$$= \frac{-35\times 35}{400} = -\frac{49}{16}\text{ m/s}^2 = -3.06\text{ m/s}^2$$

$\therefore$ Retardation of the car $= -3.06$ m/s^2

From equation of motion, $v = u + at$

$$\text{or} \quad t = \frac{v-u}{a} = \frac{(0-35)}{(-49/16)}$$

$$= \frac{35\times 16}{49} = \frac{5\times 16}{7} = \frac{80}{7}\text{ s} = 11.4\text{ s}$$

$\therefore$ Car will stop after 11.4 s.

51. The given equation is $v = 4 + 2(C_1 + C_2t)$

$\Rightarrow \quad v = (4 + 2C_1) + 2C_2t$

Comparing the above equations with equation of motion $\quad v = u + at$

Initial velocity, $u = 4 + 2C_1\,(t = 0)$

Acceleration of the particle $= 2C_2$

52. Here, height $(h) = 1$ km $= 1000$ m, $g = 10$ m/s^2

(i) Velocity attained by the rain drop in freely falling through a height h.

$$v = \sqrt{2gh} = \sqrt{2\times 10\times 1000} = 100\sqrt{2}\text{ m/s}$$

$$= 100\sqrt{2}\times\frac{60\times 60}{1000}\text{ km/h} = 360\sqrt{2}\text{ km/h} \approx 510\text{ km/h}$$

(ii) Diameter of the drop $(d) = 2r = 4$ mm

$\therefore$ Radius of the drop $(r) = 2$ mm $= 2\times 10^{-3}$ m

Mass of a rain drop $(m) = V\times\rho$

$$= \frac{4}{3}\pi r^3\rho = \frac{4}{3}\times\frac{22}{7}\times(2\times 10^{-3})^3\times 10^3$$

[$\because$ density of water $= 10^3$ kg/m^3]

$\approx 3.4\times 10^{-5}$ kg

Momentum of the rain drop $(p) = mv$

$= 3.4\times 10^{-5}\times 100\sqrt{2} \approx 4.7\times 10^{-3}$ kg-m/s

(iii) Time required to flatten the drop

= time taken by the drop to travel the distance equal to the diameter of the drop near the ground

$$t = \frac{d}{v} = \frac{4\times 10^{-3}}{100\sqrt{2}} = 0.028\times 10^{-3}\text{s} = 2.8\times 10^{-5}\text{s}$$

(iv) Force exerted by a rain drop

$$F = \frac{\text{Change in momentum}}{\text{Time}}$$

$$= \frac{p-0}{t} = \frac{4.7\times 10^{-3}}{2.8\times 10^{-5}} \approx 168\text{ N}$$

(v) Radius of the umbrella $(R) = \frac{1}{2}$ m

$\therefore$ Area of the umbrella $(A) = \pi R^2$

$$= \frac{22}{7} \times \left(\frac{1}{2}\right)^2 = \frac{22}{28} = \frac{11}{14} \approx 0.8 \text{ m}^2$$

Number of drops striking the umbrella simultaneously with average separation of 5 cm or

$$5 \times 10^{-2} \text{ m} = \frac{0.8}{(5 \times 10^{-2})^2} = 320$$

$\therefore$ Net force exerted on umbrella

$$= 320 \times 168 = 53760 \text{ N}$$

53. Given, $u = 50 \text{km/h} = 50 \times \frac{5}{18} = \frac{250}{18} \text{ ms}^{-1}$

$v = 0$

$s = 6\text{m}$

$\because$ We know that

$$v^2 = u^2 + 2as$$

$$\Rightarrow \quad 0 = \left(\frac{250}{18}\right)^2 + 2(-a)(s)$$

$$\Rightarrow \quad 0 = 192.90 - 12a$$

$$\Rightarrow \quad a = -\frac{192.90}{12}$$

$$\Rightarrow \quad a = -16.07 \text{ ms}^{-2}$$

From 3rd equation of motion,

$$v^2 = u^2 + 2as$$

$$\Rightarrow \quad 0 = \left(100 \times \frac{5}{18}\right)^2 + 2(-16.07)s$$

$$\Rightarrow \quad s = \frac{771.10}{32.14}$$

$$\Rightarrow \quad s = 24 \text{ m}$$

QR Code for Quick Test 1

QR Code for Quick Test 2

SELF ASSESSMENT TEST

Multiple Choice Questions (MCQs)

1. The displacement in meters of a body varies with time t in second as $y = t^2 - t - 2$. The displacement is zero for a positive of t equal to

(a) 1s (b) 2s
(c) 3s (d) 4s

2. A boy starts from a point A, travels to a point B at a distance of 1.5 km and returns to A. If he takes one hour to do so, his average velocity is

(a) 3 km/h (b) zero
(c) 1.5 km/h (d) 2 km/h

3. Which of the following is a one dimensional motion?

(a) Motion of train running on a straight track.
(b) Motion of satellite
(c) Motion of air particle
(d) Motion of snake

4. If the displacement-time graph of an object is parallel to the time-axis, then it represents that the object is

(a) at rest
(b) in uniform motion
(c) in acceleration motion
(d) None of the above

5. Look at this graph of two children A and B running together. Who is running faster?

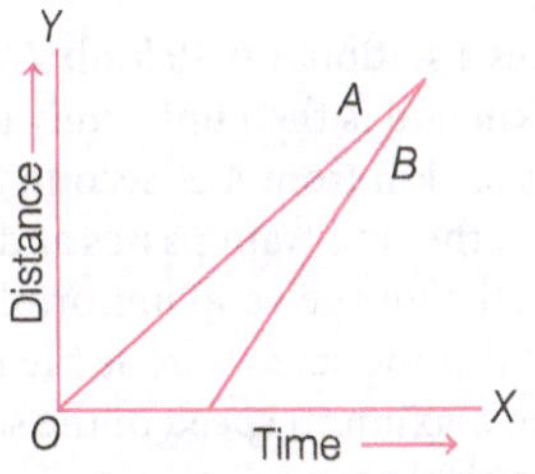

(a) Both are running at the same speed.
(b) A
(c) B
(d) None of the above

6. Vehicle A covers a distance of 100 km in 2 hours and vehicle B covers a distance of 300 km in 5 hour. Which vehicle is faster and by how much?

(a) Vehicle A is faster than vehicle B by 10 km/h
(b) Vehicle B is faster than vehicle A by 10 km/h
(c) Both vehicles have the same speed
(d) Vehicle B is faster by 60 km/h

7. For the velocity - time graph as shown in the figure, in a time interval from $t = 0$ to $t = 6$s, match the following columns and select the correct answer from the options given below.

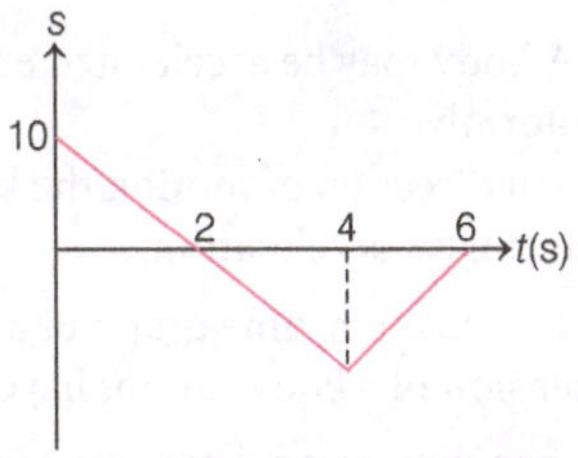

	Column I		Column II
A.	Change in velocity	P	$-5/3$ SI unit
B.	Average acceleration	Q	-20 SI unit
C.	Total displacement	R	-10 SI unit
D.	Acceleration at t=3s	S	-5 SI unit

(a) A-Q, B-S, C-P, D-R (b) A-P, B-S, C-Q, D-R
(c) A-R, B-P, C-R, D-S (d) A-S, B-R, C-P, D-Q

Assertion-Reason

Directions *(Q.Nos. 8-11) In the following questions, two statements are given- one labelled Assertion (A) and the other labelled Reason (R). Select the correct answer to these questions from the codes (a), (b), (c) and (d) as given below.*

(a) Both Assertion and Reason are true and Reason is the correct explanation of Assertion.
(b) Both Assertion and Reason are true but Reason is not the correct explanation of Assertion.
(c) Assertion is true but Reason is false.
(d) Assertion is false but Reason is true.

8. Assertion A body is momentarily at rest at the instant, it reverses the direction.
Reason A body cannot have acceleration, if its velocity is zero at a given instant of time.

9. Assertion In the s -t graph as shown below, the body starts moving in positive direction but not from $s = 0$.

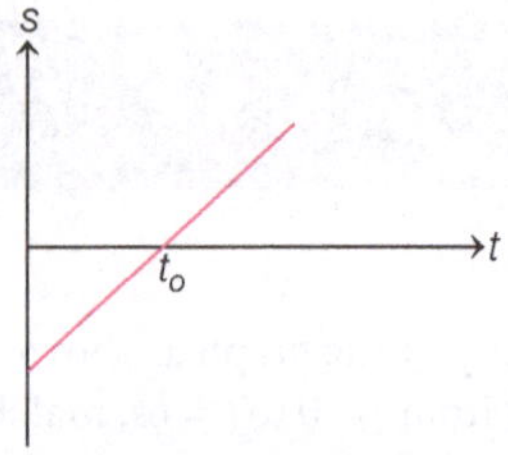

Reason At $t = t_0$, velocity of body changes its direction of motion.

10. **Assertion** A body may be accelerated even when it is moving uniformly.
Reason When direction of motion the body is changing, the body must have acceleration.

11. **Assertion** The position-time graph of a uniform motion in one dimension of a body cannot have negative slope.
Reason In one dimensional motion, the position does not reverse, so it cannot have a negative slope.

Case Based Questions

Directions *(Q.No. 12) This question is case study based question. Read the following paragraph and answer the questions on the basis of same.*

12. Let two objects A and B moving with velocities $\mathbf{v}_A$ and $\mathbf{v}_B$ respectively at a particular instant of time, then velocity of object A w.r.t. velocity of object B (i.e. presuming object B to be at rest) is called the relative velocity of A w.r.t. B and is expressed as $\mathbf{v}_{AB}$, Thus
$\mathbf{v}_{AB} = \mathbf{v}_A - \mathbf{v}_B$
Similarly, relative velocity of object B w.r.t. object A

$$\mathbf{v}_{AB} = \mathbf{v}_A - \mathbf{v}_B$$

Concept of relative velocity is very important in daily life.

(i) If two objects A and B are in motion along a straight path in same direction, then what is the relative velocity of one object with respect to another? Take direction of A as positive.
(a) $\mathbf{v}_{AB} = \mathbf{v}_B - \mathbf{v}_A$ (b) $\mathbf{v}_{AB} = \mathbf{v}_A - \mathbf{v}_B$
(c) $\mathbf{v}_{AB} = \mathbf{v}_A + \mathbf{v}_B$ (d) $\mathbf{v}_{AB} = -\mathbf{v}_A - \mathbf{v}_B$

(ii) What will be the relative velocity of object A w.r.t. directions? Take direction of A as positive direction.
(a) $\mathbf{v}_{AB} = \mathbf{v}_B - \mathbf{v}_A$ (b) $\mathbf{v}_{AB} = \mathbf{v}_A - \mathbf{v}_B$
(c) $\mathbf{v}_{AB} = \mathbf{v}_A + \mathbf{v}_B$ (d) $\mathbf{v}_{AB} = -\mathbf{v}_A - \mathbf{v}_B$

(iii) A thief snatches a bag from a person and then moves along a straight road with a constant velocity of 36 km/h. A police inspector observed the incident of snatching. He starts his bike with in 10s and accelerates it so that he is able to hold the thief after 30s. What is the acceleration of his bike?
(a) $a = 1.5\ \text{m/s}^2$ (b) $2.5\ \text{m/s}^2$
(c) $0.5\ \text{m/s}^2$ (d) $3.5\ \text{m/s}^2$

(iv) What is the average velocity of police inspector's bike?
(a) 25 m/s (b) 20 m/s
(c) 30 m/s (d) 15 m/s

Very Short Answer Type Questions

13. The displacement-time graph of a particle is parallel to time axis, what is the velocity of the particle?

14. Is it possible that a body have a constant velocity but varying speed?

Short Answert Type Questions

15. At $t = 0$, a particle is at rest at origin. Its acceleration is 2 m/s^2 for the first 3s and $-2\ \text{m/s}^2$ for next 3 s.
Plot the acceleration *versus* time and velocity *versus* time graph.

16. The position x of a body is given by $x = A\sin(\omega t)$. Find the time at which the displacement is maximum.

Long Answer Type Questions

17. A train takes 4 min to go between stations 2.25 km apart starting and finishing at rest. The acceleration is uniform for the first 40 s and the deceleration is uniform for the last 20 s.
Assuming the velocity to be constant for the remaining time, calculate the maximum speed, acceleration and retardation, use only the graphical method.

18. A train passes a station A at 40 kmh^{-1} and maintains its speed for 7 km and is then uniformly retarded, stopping at B which is 8.5 km from A. A second train starts from A at the instant, the first train passes and being accelerated some part of the journey and uniformly retarded for the rest, stops at B at the same time as the first train. Calculate the maximum speed of the second train, use only the graphical method.

19 (a) Write an expression for distance covered in nth second for a uniformly accelerated motion.
(b) A bus starting from rest moves with a uniform acceleration of 0.1 m/s^2 for 2 min. Find (i) the speed acquired and (ii) the distance travelled.

Answers

1. (b)	2. (b)	3. (a)	4. (a)	5. (c)
6. (b)	7. (c)	8. (c)	9. (c)	10. (a)

11. (c) 12. (i) (b), (ii) (c), (iii) (a), (iv) (d)

03

CHAPTER

In this chapter, we will study the motion of an object in two dimensions (in plane) and in three dimensions (in space). As a simple case of motion in a plane, we shall discuss motion with constant acceleration and treat it in details as **projectile** and **circular motion**.

YOUR STUDY GOALS

YOUR PRACTICE GOAL

- Objective Type Questions (26 Qs, MCQs, A-R, Matching)
- Case Based Questions (3)
- Subjective Questions (5 VSAs 9 SAs, 12 LAs)
- Numerical Problems (23)

Motion in a Plane

3.1 Scalars and Vectors

On the basis of magnitude and direction, all the physical quantities are classified into two groups as scalars and vectors.

Scalar Quantities

These are the physical quantities which have only magnitude but no direction. e.g. Temperature, mass, length, time, work, etc.

- The rules for combining scalars, follow simple rules of algebra. Scalars can be added, subtracted, multiplied and divided just as the ordinary numbers.
- The quantities with same units can be added or subtracted, but the quantities of different units can be multiplied or divided.

Vector Quantities

These are the physical quantities which have both magnitudes and directions and obey the triangle/ parallelogram laws of addition and subtraction.

e.g. Displacement, acceleration, velocity, momentum, force, etc.

A vector is represented by a **bold face** type and also by **an arrow** placed over a letter.

i.e. $\quad$ **F, a, b** or $\vec{F}, \vec{a}, \vec{b}$

e.g. Suppose a body has a velocity 40 m/s due east. If 1 cm is chosen to represent a velocity of 10 m/s, then a line *OP* of 4 cm in length drawn towards east with arrowhead at *P* will completely represent the velocity of the body (i.e. 40 m/s).

The point *P* is called **head** or **terminal point** and point *O* is called **tail** or **initial point** of the vector **OP**.

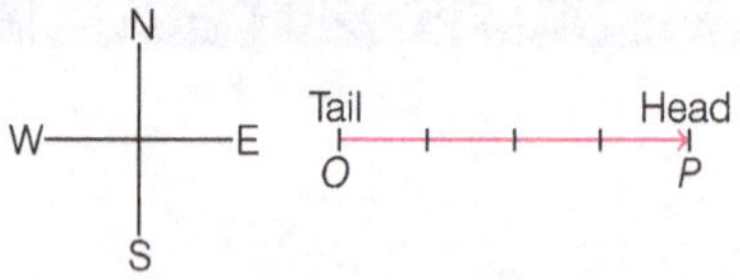

Representation of vector OP

The length of the line gives the magnitude and the arrowhead gives the direction.

Vectors are classified into two types. They are as follows.

(i) **Polar Vectors** Vectors which have a starting point or a point of application are called polar vectors. e.g. Force, displacement, etc.

(ii) **Axial Vectors** Vectors which represent the rotational effect and act along the axis of rotation are called axial vectors. e.g. Angular velocity, angular momentum, torque, etc.
The axial vector will have its direction along its axis of rotation depending on its anti-clockwise or clockwise rotational effect.

Note
- The magnitude of a vector is often called its **absolute value**, indicated by $|\mathbf{v}| = v$.
- The physical quantities which have no specified direction and have different values in different directions are called **tensors**. e.g. Moment of inertia, stress, surface tension, pressure, etc.

Important Definitions Related to Vectors

(i) **Modulus of a Vector** The magnitude of a vector is called modulus of that vector. For a vector **A**, it is represented by $|\mathbf{A}|$ or A.

(ii) **Unit Vector** A vector having magnitude equal to unity but a specific direction is called a unit vector. A unit vector of **A** is written as $\hat{\mathbf{A}}$ and read as A cap.
It is expressed as

$$\hat{\mathbf{A}} = \frac{\mathbf{A}}{|\mathbf{A}|} = \frac{\mathbf{A}}{A} = \frac{\text{Vector}}{\text{Magnitude of the vector}}$$

$$\mathbf{A} = |\mathbf{A}|\hat{\mathbf{A}}$$

Hence, **any vector can be expressed as the magnitude times the unit vector along its own direction.**
In cartesian coordinates, $\hat{\mathbf{i}}$, $\hat{\mathbf{j}}$ and $\hat{\mathbf{k}}$ are the unit vectors along *X*-axis, *Y*-axis and *Z*-axis respectively.

The magnitude of a **unit vector is unity** and has **no unit or dimensions.**

(iii) **Null Vector** A vector with zero magnitude and having an arbitrary direction is called a null vector. This vector is also known as **zero vector** and denoted by 0 (zero). e.g. the acceleration vector of an object moving with uniform velocity.

(iv) **Equal Vectors** Two vectors are said to be equal, if they have equal magnitude and same direction.
Consider two vectors **A** and **B** which are represented by two equal parallel lines drawn in the same magnitude and direction.

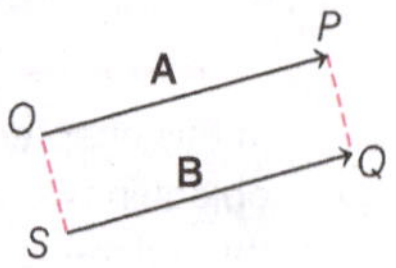

A and **B** are equal vectors

Thus, $\mathbf{OP} = \mathbf{SQ}$ or $\mathbf{A} = \mathbf{B}$
Vectors do not have fixed locations. When we displace a vector parallel to itself, then the vector does not change, such vectors are known as **free vectors.**
e.g. The velocity vector of a particle moving along a straight line is a free vector.

(v) **Negative Vector** Two vectors are said to be the negative of each other, if their magnitudes are equal but directions are opposite.

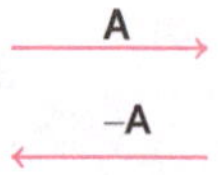

The negative vector of **A** is represented as $-\mathbf{A}$.

(vi) **Collinear Vectors** Two or more vectors are said to be collinear, when they act along the same lines or parallel lines. e.g. Tug of war.

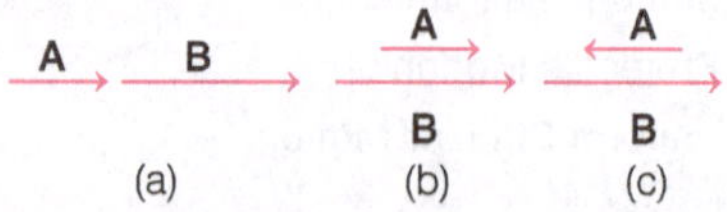

If **A** and **B** are two collinear vectors, then they can be represented along a line in the same direction [Fig. (a)] or along the parallel lines in same direction [Fig.(b)] or along parallel lines in opposite direction [Fig.(c)].

(vii) **Parallel vectors** Two collinear vectors having the same directions are called parallel vectors. In this case, the angle between these two vectors will be zero.

(viii) **Anti-parallel vectors** Similarly, two collinear vectors having the opposite directions are called anti-parallel vectors. In this case, the angle between these two vectors will be 180°.

(ix) **Co-planar Vectors** The vectors lying in the same plane are called co-planar vectors. Three vectors **A, B** and **C** are lying in the same plane of paper as shown in figure, hence they are co-planar vectors.

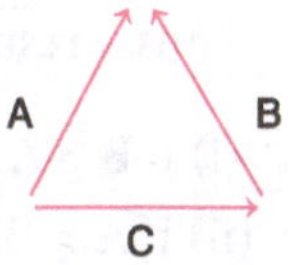

(x) **Co-initial Vectors** The vectors which have the same initial point are called co-initial vectors.

Two vectors **A** and **B** have been drawn from the common initial point O. Therefore, **A** and **B** are called **co-initial vectors.**

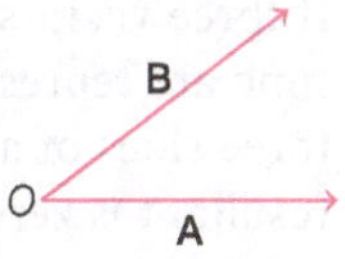

Co-initial vectors

(xi) **Orthogonal Unit Vectors** If two or three unit vectors are perpendicular to each other, they are known as orthogonal unit vectors.

The unit vectors along X-axis, Y-axis and Z-axis are respectively denoted by $\hat{\mathbf{i}}, \hat{\mathbf{j}}$ and $\hat{\mathbf{k}}$. These are orthogonal unit vectors.

$$\hat{\mathbf{i}} = \frac{\mathbf{x}}{x} \Rightarrow \mathbf{x} = x\,\hat{\mathbf{i}}$$

$$\hat{\mathbf{j}} = \frac{\mathbf{y}}{y} \Rightarrow \mathbf{y} = y\,\hat{\mathbf{j}}$$

$$\hat{\mathbf{k}} = \frac{\mathbf{z}}{z} \Rightarrow \mathbf{z} = z\,\hat{\mathbf{k}}$$

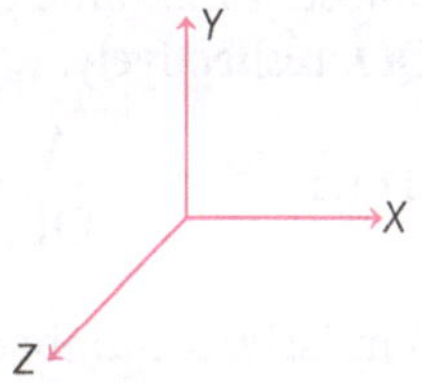

(xii) **Localised Vectors** Those vectors whose initial point is fixed are known as localised vectors. e.g. Position vector of a particle (initial point lies at the origin).

(xiii) **Non-localised Vectors** Those vectors whose **initial point is not fixed** are known as non-localised vectors. e.g. Velocity vector of a particle moving along a straight line.

3.2 Position and Displacement Vectors

Position Vector

A vector which gives position of an object with reference to the origin of a coordinate system is called position vector. It is represented by a symbol **r**.

Consider the motion of an object in XY-plane with origin at O. Suppose an object is at point A at any instant t, then **OA** is the position vector of the object at point A.

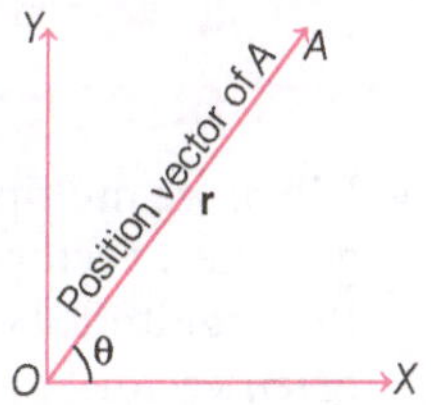

i.e. $\quad\quad \mathbf{OA} = \mathbf{r}$

The position vector provides two informations such as

(i) It tells us about the minimum distance of an object from the origin O.

(ii) It tells us about the direction of the object w.r.t. origin.

Displacement Vector

The vector which tells how much and in which direction an object has changed its position in a given interval of time is called displacement vector.

Displacement vector is the straight line joining the initial and final positions and does not depend on the actual path undertaken by the object between the two positions.

Consider an object moving in the XY-plane. Suppose it is at point A at any instant t and at point B at any later instant t', then vector **AB** is the displacement vector of the object in time t to t'.

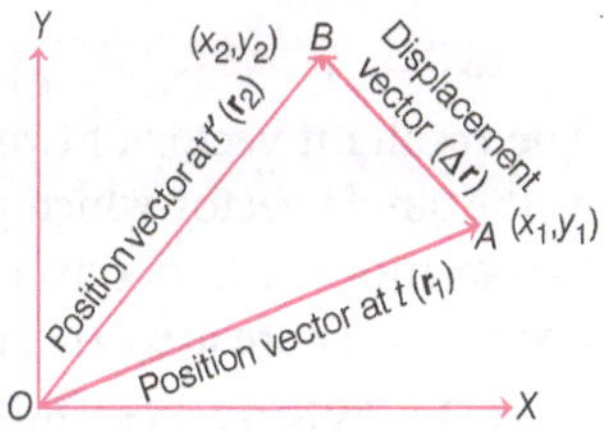

If the coordinates of points A and B are (x_1, y_1) and (x_2, y_2) respectively, then the position vector of the object at point A, $\mathbf{r}_1 = x_1\hat{\mathbf{i}} + y_1\hat{\mathbf{j}}$ and the position vector of the object at point B, $\mathbf{r}_2 = x_2\hat{\mathbf{i}} + y_2\hat{\mathbf{j}}$

∴ The displacement vector for AB can be given as

$$\Delta r = \mathbf{r}_2 - \mathbf{r}_1$$

$$\text{Displacement vector, } \Delta r = (x_2 - x_1)\,\hat{\mathbf{i}} + (y_2 - y_1)\hat{\mathbf{j}}$$

- Magnitude of the displacement vector is given by

$$|\Delta \mathbf{r}| = \Delta r = \sqrt{(x_2 - x_1)^2 + (y_2 - y_1)^2}$$

The magnitude of displacement is either less or equal to the path length of an object between two points.

- Magnitude of vectors for three-dimensional is given by

$$|\Delta \mathbf{r}| = \sqrt{(x_2 - x_1)^2 + (y_2 - y_1)^2 + (z_2 - z_1)^2}$$

Multiplication of a Vector by a Real Number or Scalar

- When we multiply a vector **A** by a real number λ, we get a new vector along the direction of vector **A**. Its magnitude becomes λ times the magnitude of the given vector.
- Similarly, if we multiply vector **A** with a negative real number $-\lambda$, we get a vector whose magnitude is λ times the magnitude of vector **A** but direction is opposite to that of vector **A**.

Hence, $\boxed{\lambda(\mathbf{A}) = \lambda\mathbf{A}}$ and $\boxed{-\lambda(\mathbf{A}) = -\lambda\mathbf{A}}$

e.g. Consider a vector A is multiplied by a real number $\lambda = 3$ or -4, we get 3A or -4A.

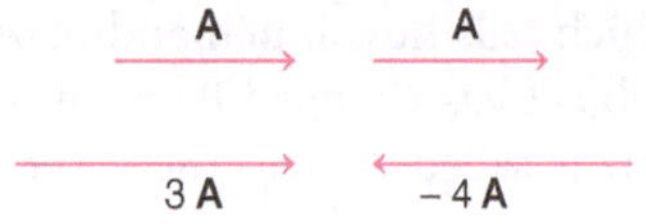

- If we multiply a constant velocity vector by time, we will get a displacement vector in the direction of velocity vector.

Resultant Vector

The resultant vector of two or more vectors is defined as the single vector which produces the same effect as two or more vectors (given vectors) combinedly produces. There are two cases

Case I **When two vectors are acting in the same direction**
Consider the vectors **A** and **B** are acting in the same direction as shown below.

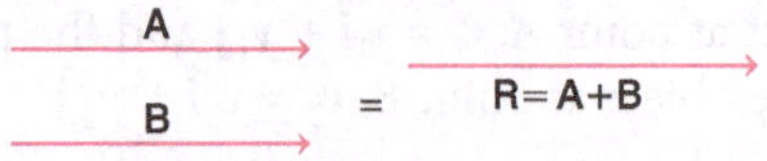

Then, the resultant of these two vectors is given by a vector having direction as same as that of A or B and the magnitude of the resultant vector will be equal to the sum of respective vectors. i.e. $(\mathbf{A}+\mathbf{B})$.

Thus, $\boxed{\text{Resultant vector, } \mathbf{R} = \mathbf{A}+\mathbf{B}}$

Case II **When two vectors are acting in mutually opposite directions** Consider the vectors A and B are acting in mutually opposite direction as shown below.

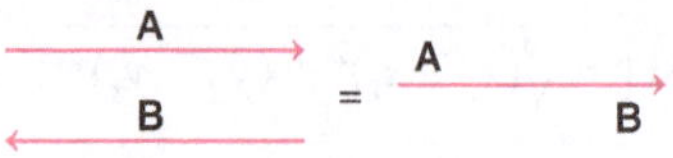

Then, the resultant of these two vectors is given by a vector having direction same as that of vector with larger magnitude. The magnitude of the resultant vector will be equal to $|\mathbf{A}-\mathbf{B}|$.

Thus, $\boxed{\text{resultant vector, } \mathbf{R} = \mathbf{A}-\mathbf{B}}$

(i) If B > A, then **direction of R is along B.**

(ii) If A > B, then **direction of R is along A.**

Conditions for Zero Resultant Vector

If three vectors acting on a point object at the same time are represented in magnitude and direction by the three sides of a triangle taken in the same order, their resultant is zero. The object is said to be in **equilibrium**.

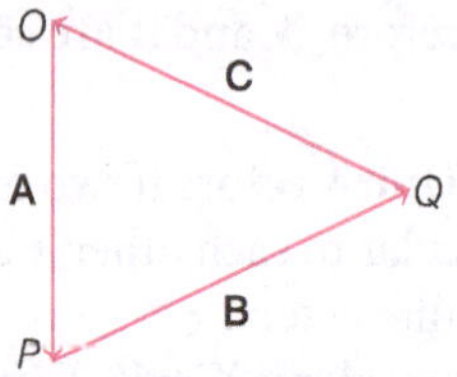

Vectors **A**, **B** and **C** acting along **OP**, **PQ** and **QO** respectively

Consider the three vectors **A**, **B** and **C** acting on an object at the same time represented by **OP**, **PQ** and **QO**, respectively.

Then, $\boxed{\dfrac{A}{OP} = \dfrac{B}{PQ} = \dfrac{C}{QO}}$

Similarly, if number of vectors acting on an object at the same time are represented in magnitude and direction by the various sides of a closed polygon taken in the same order, their resultant vector is zero and the object will be in equilibrium.

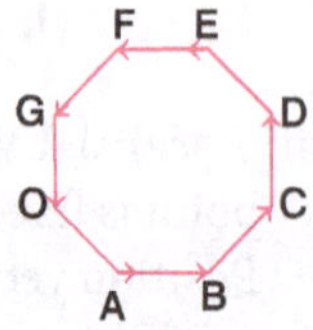

Vectors represented by a closed polygon

$$\boxed{\text{Resultant vector, } \mathbf{R} = \mathbf{OA}+\mathbf{AB}+\mathbf{BC}+\mathbf{CD} + \mathbf{DE}+\mathbf{EF}+\mathbf{FG}+\mathbf{GO} = 0}$$

Conditions for Equilibrium of an Object

(i) There is no linear motion of the object, i.e. the resultant force on the object is zero.

(ii) There is no rotational motion of the object, i.e. the torque due to forces on the object is zero.

(iii) There is minimum potential energy of the object for stable equilibrium.

Example 1. **(a) What is the displacement vector from position (1, 2, 3) to position (4, 5, 6)?**
(b) What angle does that displacement vector make with X-axis?

Sol. (a) The displacement vector is given by

$$d = (4-1)\hat{\mathbf{i}} + (5-2)\hat{\mathbf{j}} + (6-3)\hat{\mathbf{k}} = (3\hat{\mathbf{i}} + 3\hat{\mathbf{j}} + 3\hat{\mathbf{k}})$$

So, the displacement vector is $\mathbf{d} = 3\hat{\mathbf{i}} + 3\hat{\mathbf{j}} + 3\hat{\mathbf{k}}$

(b) We can find angle by taking the scalar product of the displacement vector and unit vector in the x-direction (1, 0, 0).

$$\mathbf{x}\cdot\mathbf{d} = (1)\cdot(3) + (0)\cdot(3) + (0)\cdot(3) = 3$$

$$\mathbf{x}\cdot\mathbf{d} = x\cdot d\cos\theta = (1)(\sqrt{3^2+3^2+3^2})\cos\theta$$

$$3 = \sqrt{27}\cos\theta \Rightarrow 3 = 3\sqrt{3}\cos\theta$$

$$\therefore \quad \cos\theta = \frac{3}{3\sqrt{3}}$$

$$\Rightarrow \quad \theta = \cos^{-1}\left(\frac{1}{\sqrt{3}}\right) \Rightarrow \theta \approx 54.74°$$

3.3 Addition of Vectors (Graphical Method)

Graphical method of addition of vectors helps us in visualising the vectors and the resultant vectors. This method contains following laws

1. Triangle Law of Vector Addition

This law states that **if two vectors can be represented both in magnitude and direction by the two sides of a triangle taken in the same order**, then their resultant is represented completely, both in magnitude and direction, by the third side of the triangle taken in the opposite order.

Consider two vectors **A** and **B** that lie in a plane as shown in Fig. (a). Draw a vector **OM** equal and parallel to vector **A** as shown in Fig. (b).

From head of **OM**, draw a vector **MN** equal and parallel to vector **B**. Then, the resultant vector is given by **ON** which joins the tail of **A** and head of **B**.

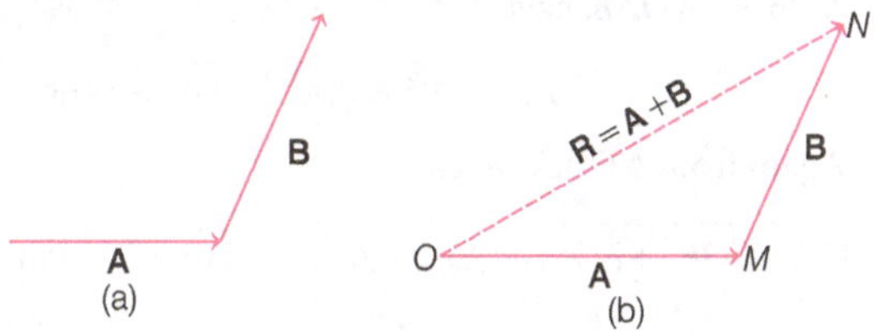

The resultant of **A** and **B** is **ON** = **OM** + **MN**

or $\boxed{\text{Resultant vector, } \mathbf{R} = \mathbf{A} + \mathbf{B}}$

Example 2. **A boy travels 10 m due to North and then 7 m due to east. Find the displacement and direction of the body.**

Sol. Let the boy start moving from point O as shown in figure.

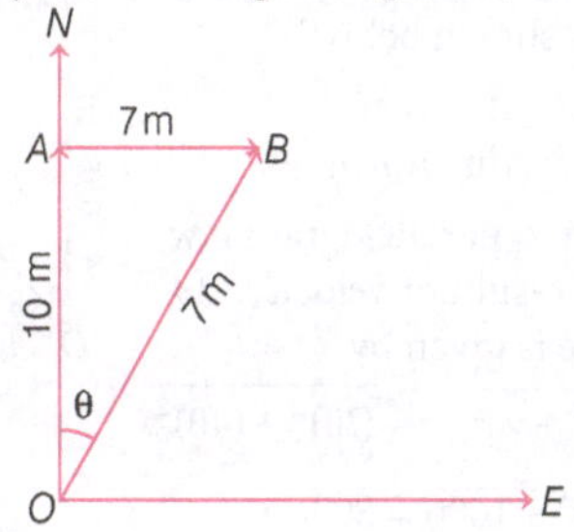

where, **OA** = 10 m, due north

AB = 7 m, due east

According to triangle law of vector addition, **OB** is the resultant displacement.

The magnitude of the resultant displacement,

$$|\mathbf{OB}| = OB = \sqrt{(OA)^2 + (AB)^2} = \sqrt{(10)^2 + (7)^2}$$

$$= \sqrt{100 + 49} = 12.21\,\text{m}$$

Since, the resultant displacement makes an angle θ with the north direction. Then,

$$\theta = \tan^{-1}\left(\frac{AB}{OA}\right) = \tan^{-1}\left(\frac{7}{10}\right) = 35°$$

2. Parallelogram Law of Vector Addition

This law states that if two vectors acting on a particle at the same time are represented in magnitude and direction by two adjacent sides of a parallelogram drawn from a point, then their resultant vector is represented in magnitude and direction by the diagonal of the parallelogram drawn from the same point.

Consider two vectors **A** and **B** that lie in a plane as shown in Fig. (a). From a common point O, draw a vector **OP** equal and parallel to **A** and vector **OR** equal and parallel to **B**. Complete the parallelogram **OPQR** as shown in Fig. (b), then the resultant vector is given by **OQ**.

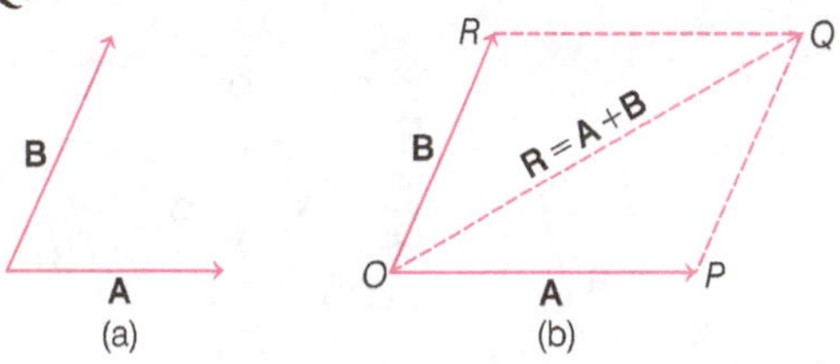

According to parallelogram law of vector addition,

$$\mathbf{OQ} = \mathbf{OP} + \mathbf{OR}$$

or $\boxed{\text{Resultant vector, } \mathbf{R} = \mathbf{A} + \mathbf{B}}$

Example 3. **A body is simultaneously given two velocities of 30 m/s due to east and 40 m/s due to north, respectively. Find the resultant velocity.**

Sol. Let the body be starting from point O as shown below.

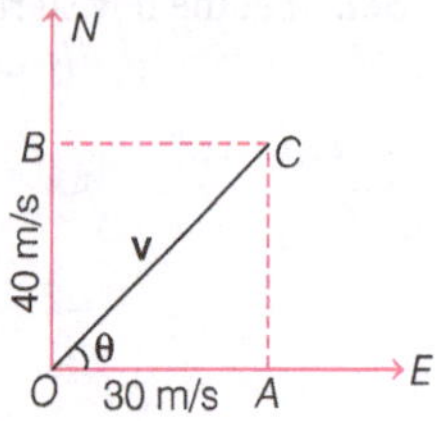

$\mathbf{v}_A = 30\,\text{m/s}$, due east;

$\mathbf{v}_B = 40\,\text{m/s}$, due north

According to parallelogram law, **OC** is the resultant velocity. Its magnitude is given by

$$\mathbf{v} = \sqrt{{v_A}^2 + {v_B}^2} = \sqrt{(30)^2 + (40)^2}$$

$$= \sqrt{900 + 1600} = 50\text{ m/s}$$

Since, the resultant velocity **v** makes an angle θ with the east direction.

$$\text{Then, } \theta = \tan^{-1}\left(\frac{CA}{OA}\right) = \tan^{-1}\left(\frac{40}{30}\right) = 53°8'$$

3. Polygon Law of Vector Addition

This law states that when the number of vectors are represented in both magnitude and direction by the sides of an open polygon taken in an order, then their resultant is represented in both magnitude and direction by the closing side of the polygon taken in opposite order.

Consider four vectors **A**, **B**, **C** and **D** be acting in different directions that lie in a plane as shown in Fig. (a).

Draw a vector **OP** parallel and equal to vector **A**. Move vectors **B, C** and **D** parallel to themselves, so that the tail of **B** touches the head of **A**, the tail of **C** touches the head of **B** and the tail of **D** touches the head of **C** as shown in Fig. (b).

According to the polygon law of vector addition, the closing side OT of the polygon taken in the reverse order represent the resultant **R**.

Thus, $\mathbf{R} = \mathbf{A} + \mathbf{B} + \mathbf{C} + \mathbf{D}$

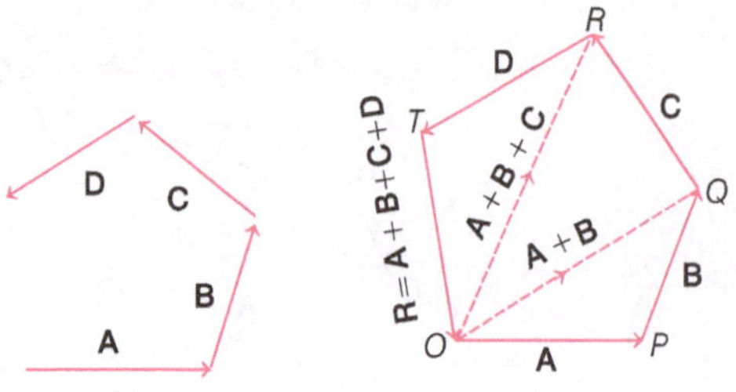

(a) (b)

Properties of Addition of Vectors

(i) Two vectors can be added, if both of them are same of nature. i.e., A displacement vector cannot be added to a force vector but can be added to displacement vector only.

(ii) It follows commutative law, i.e. $\mathbf{A} + \mathbf{B} = \mathbf{B} + \mathbf{A}$

(iii) It follows associative law,

$$(\mathbf{A} + \mathbf{B}) + \mathbf{C} = \mathbf{A} + (\mathbf{B} + \mathbf{C})$$

(iv) It obeys distributive law, $\lambda(\mathbf{A} + \mathbf{B}) = \lambda\mathbf{A} + \lambda\mathbf{B}$

(v) Resultant of two vectors of unequal magnitude can never be zero,

$$A + 0 = A$$

(vi) Resultant of two vector will be maximum when they are parallel and *vice-versa.*

Case 1. Angle between them is zero (parallel vector)

$$R_{\max} = |\mathbf{A} + \mathbf{B}|_{\max} = |\mathbf{A}| + |\mathbf{B}|$$

Case 2. Angle between them is 180° (anti-parallel vector)

$$R_{\max} = |\mathbf{A}| - |\mathbf{B}| = |\mathbf{A}| - |\mathbf{B}|$$

Example 4. **A particle has a displacement of 12 m towards east and 5 m towards the north and then 6 m vertically upwards. Find the magnitude of the sum of these displacements.**

Sol. Suppose initially the particle is at origin O, then its displacement vectors are

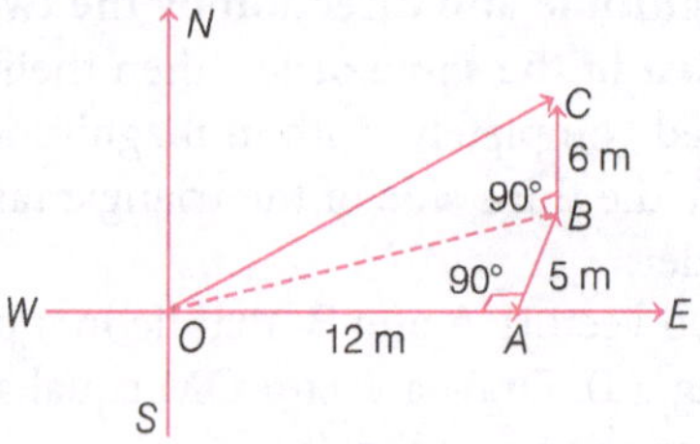

$$OA = 12\text{ m},\ AB = 5\text{ m},\ BC = 6\text{ m}$$

According to polygon law of vector addition, **OC** is the resultant displacement.

∴ From ΔOAB, have

$$\mathbf{OB} = \sqrt{OA^2 + AB^2} = \sqrt{(12)^2 + (5)^2} = 13\text{ m}$$

Again from ΔOBC, we have

$$\mathbf{OC} = \sqrt{OB^2 + BC^2} = \sqrt{(13)^2 + (6)^2} = \sqrt{205} = 14.32\text{ m}$$

3.4 Subtraction of Two Vectors (Graphical Method)

If a vector **B** is to be subtracted from vector **A**, then we have to invert the vector **B** and then add it with vector **A**, according to laws of addition of two vectors.

Hence, the subtraction of vector **B** from a vector **A** is defined as the addition of vector −**B** (i.e. negative of vector **B**) to vector **A**.

It is expressed as $\mathbf{R} = \mathbf{A} + (-\mathbf{B}) = \mathbf{A} - \mathbf{B}$

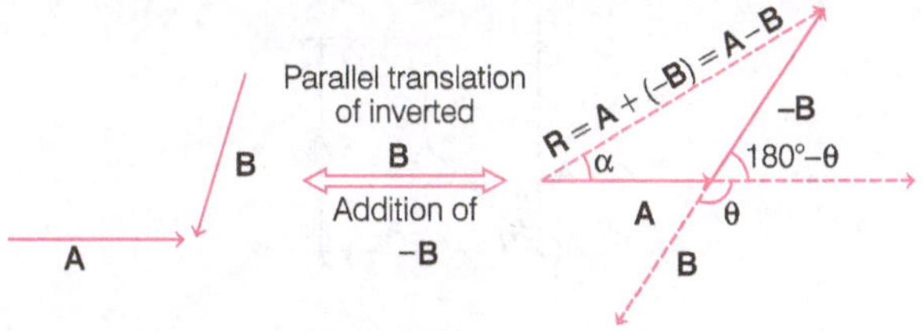

Properties of Subtraction of Vectors

(i) Subtraction of vectors does not follow commutative law, i.e. $\mathbf{A} - \mathbf{B} \neq \mathbf{B} - \mathbf{A}$

(ii) It does not follow associative law, i.e.

$$\mathbf{A} - (\mathbf{B} - \mathbf{C}) \neq (\mathbf{A} - \mathbf{B}) - \mathbf{C}$$

(iii) It follows distributive law, $\lambda(\mathbf{A} - \mathbf{B}) = \lambda\mathbf{A} - \lambda\mathbf{B}$

(iv) If $\vec{\mathbf{A}} + \vec{\mathbf{B}} = \vec{\mathbf{A}} - \vec{\mathbf{B}}$, then $\mathbf{B} = 0$

Example 5. Two forces of 5 N towards east and −7 N towards south acts on a particle. Find the resultant force.

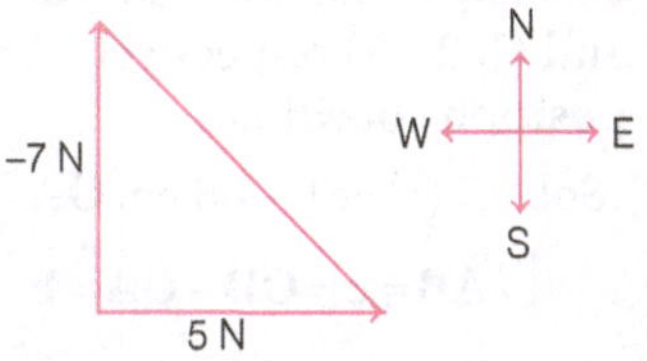

Sol. The two forces be $A = 5$ N and $B = -7$ N

Then, the magnitude of the resultant force is given by

$$F = \sqrt{A^2 + (-B)^2} = \sqrt{5^2 + (-7)^2}$$

$$F = \sqrt{25 + 49} = \sqrt{74} = 8.6 \text{ N}$$

3.5 Resolution of Vectors in Plane (In Two Dimensions)

The process of splitting a single vector into two or more vectors in different directions which collectively produce the same effect as produced by the single vector alone is known as resolution of a vector.

The various vectors into which a single vector is split are known as **components of vectors.**

Any vector **r** can be expressed as a linear combination of two unit vectors $\hat{\mathbf{i}}$ and $\hat{\mathbf{j}}$ at right angle,

i.e. $\mathbf{r} = x\hat{\mathbf{i}} + y\hat{\mathbf{j}}$

The vectors $x\hat{\mathbf{i}}$ and $y\hat{\mathbf{j}}$ are called the **perpendicular components** of **r**. The scalars x and y are called **components or resolved parts** of r in the directions of X-axis and Y-axis.

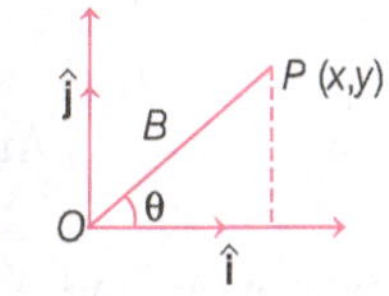

∴ Resultant vector, $\mathbf{r} = \sqrt{x^2 + y^2}$

If θ is the inclination of **r** with X-axis, then

Angle, $\theta = \tan^{-1}\left(\frac{y}{x}\right)$

Resolving a Vector into Two Component Vectors Along Given Directions

Now, draw **OQ** to represent the resultant vector **R** in magnitude and direction. From point O, draw a line **OP** parallel to the vector **A** and from point **P**, draw a line **PQ** parallel to vector **B**.

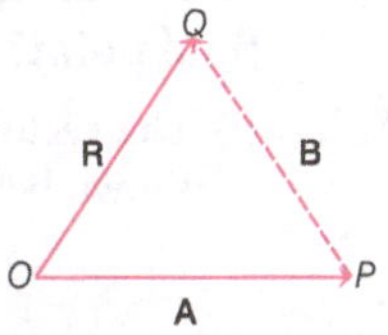

Then, these two lines intersect at point P as shown below.

From triangle law of vector addition, we have

$$\mathbf{OQ} = \mathbf{OP} + \mathbf{PQ}$$

But **OP** and **PQ** are two component vectors of **R** in the direction of **A** and **B**, respectively. Let **OP** = λ**A** and **PQ** = μ**B**, where λ and μ are two real numbers. This is also illustrated in the figure as shown.

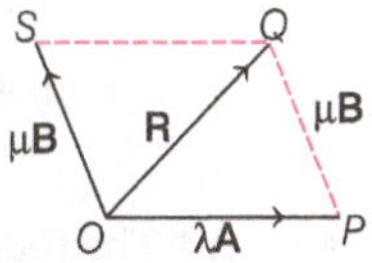

Now, the resultant vector becomes

$$\mathbf{R} = \lambda\mathbf{A} + \mu\mathbf{B}$$

Rectangular Components Resolving a Vector into a Plane

When a vector in a plane is split into two component vectors at right angle to each other, then the component vectors are called rectangular components of that vector. The resultant vector is given by

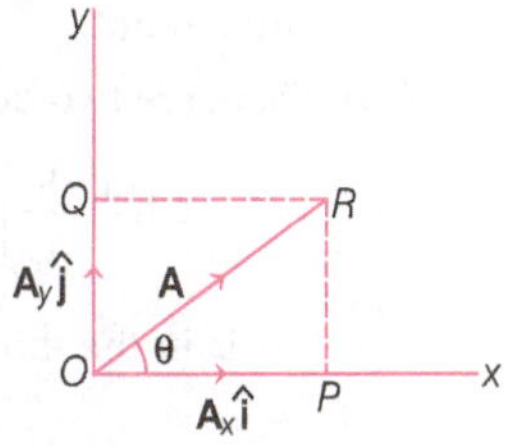

Rectangular components of **A**

$$\mathbf{A} = A_x\hat{\mathbf{i}} + A_y\hat{\mathbf{j}}$$

where, Magnitude of vector, $A = \sqrt{A_x^2 + A_y^2}$

We can also find the angle (θ) between them.

From $$\tan\theta = \left(\frac{A_y}{A_x}\right)$$

$$\Rightarrow \quad \text{Angle, } \theta = \tan^{-1}\left(\frac{A_y}{A_x}\right)$$

where, A_y and A_x are the split vectors component of A in the direction of $\hat{\mathbf{j}}$ and $\hat{\mathbf{i}}$ respectively.

Example 6. A person walks in the following pattern 3.1 km north, then 2.4 km west and finally 5.2 km south.

(i) Sketch the vector diagram that represents this motion.

(ii) How far the person will be from its initial point?

(iii) In what direction, would a bird fly in a straight line from the same starting point to the same final point?

Sol. (i) The vector diagram representing the motion is shown below.

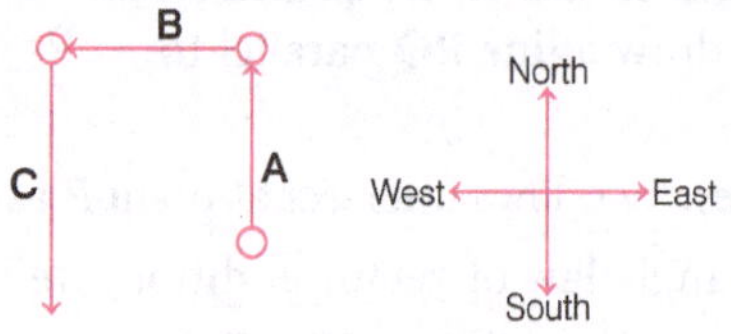

$$\mathbf{A} = 3.1\hat{\mathbf{j}}$$
$$\mathbf{B} = 2.4\hat{\mathbf{i}}$$
$$\mathbf{C} = -5.2\hat{\mathbf{j}}$$

(ii) The final point is represented by

$$\mathbf{r} = \mathbf{A} + \mathbf{B} + \mathbf{C} = 3.1\hat{\mathbf{j}} - 2.4\hat{\mathbf{i}} - 5.2\hat{\mathbf{j}}$$
$$= -2.4\hat{\mathbf{i}} - 2.1\hat{\mathbf{j}}$$

whose magnitude is $|\mathbf{r}| = \sqrt{(-2.4)^2 + (-2.1)^2}$

$$\approx 3.2 \text{ km}$$

Hence, the person will be 3.2 km away from the initial point.

(iii) There are two possibilities for the angle.

$$\theta = \tan^{-1}\left(\frac{A_y}{A_x}\right) = \tan^{-1}\left(\frac{-3.1}{-2.4}\right) = 52.25° \text{ or } 232.25°$$

$\because$ r is in the third quadrant, hence $\theta = 232.25°$

Resolution of a Space Vector (In Three Dimensions)

Similarly, we can resolve a general vector **A** into three components along X, Y and Z-axes in three dimensions (i.e. space).

Let α, β and γ be the angles between **A** and the X, Y and Z-axes, respectively as shown in figure.

Let $\hat{\mathbf{i}}, \hat{\mathbf{j}}, \hat{\mathbf{k}}$ be the unit vectors, along X, Y and Z-axes, respectively.

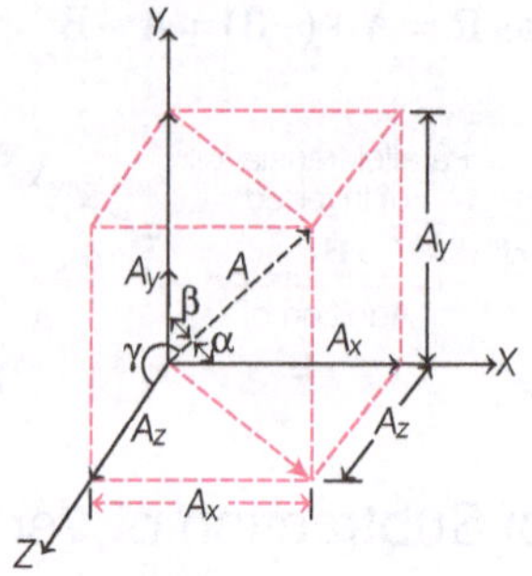

While resolving, we have

$$A_x = A\cos\alpha,\ A_y = A\cos\beta,\ A_z = A\cos\gamma$$

$\therefore$ Resultant vector, $\mathbf{A} = A_x\hat{\mathbf{i}} + A_y\hat{\mathbf{j}} + A_z\hat{\mathbf{k}}$

Magnitude of vector **A**, $A = \sqrt{A_x^2 + A_y^2 + A_z^2}$ ...(i)

Position vector r is given by $\mathbf{r} = x\hat{\mathbf{i}} + y\hat{\mathbf{j}} + z\hat{\mathbf{k}}$

Example 7. Position coordinates of A and B are (−1, 5, 7) and (3, 2−5) respectively. Express AB in term of position coordinates.

Sol. Let O be the origin, **OA** = **a**, **OB** = **b** and

$$\mathbf{AB} = \mathbf{c} = \mathbf{OB} - \mathbf{OA} = \mathbf{b} - \mathbf{a}$$

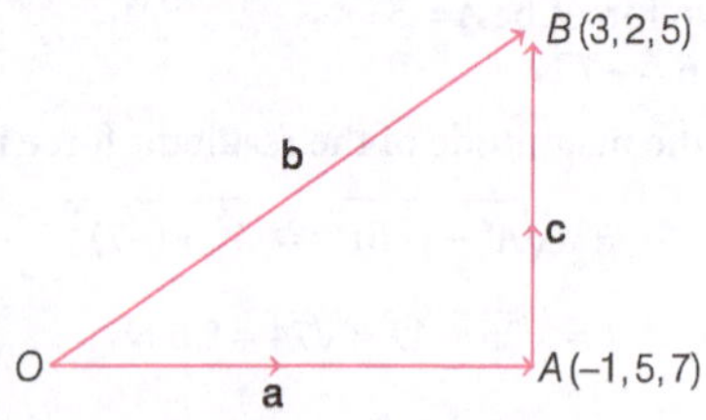

$$\therefore \mathbf{AB} = \mathbf{c} = \mathbf{b} - \mathbf{a}$$
$$= (3\hat{\mathbf{i}} + 2\hat{\mathbf{j}} - 5\hat{\mathbf{k}}) - (-\hat{\mathbf{i}} + 5\hat{\mathbf{j}} + 7\hat{\mathbf{k}})$$
$$= 4\hat{\mathbf{i}} - 3\hat{\mathbf{j}} - 12\hat{\mathbf{k}}$$
$$\mathbf{AB} = 4\hat{\mathbf{i}} - 3\hat{\mathbf{j}} - 12\hat{\mathbf{k}}$$

3.6 Addition of Vectors (Analytical Method)

Consider two vectors **A** and **B** inclined at an angle θ be acting on a particle at the same time.

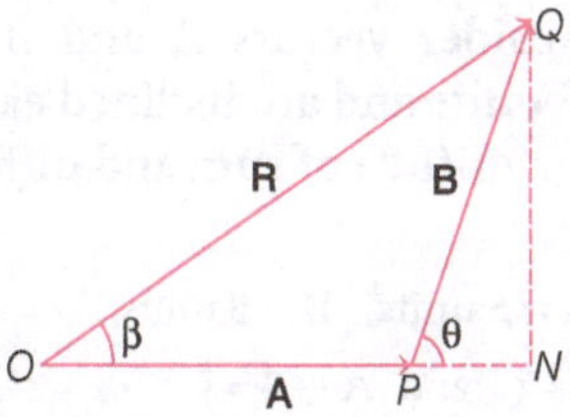

Let them be represented in magnitude and direction by two sides **OP** and **PQ** of ΔOPQ, taken in the same order. Then, according to triangle law of vector addition, the resultant (**R**) is given by the closing side **OQ**, taken in opposite order.

Draw QN perpendicular to OP produced.

From ΔQNP, $\dfrac{PN}{PQ} = \cos\theta$

$\Rightarrow \quad PN = PQ\cos\theta = B\cos\theta \quad [\because PQ = B] \quad \ldots\text{(i)}$

and $\quad \dfrac{QN}{PQ} = \sin\theta$

$\Rightarrow \quad QN = PQ\sin\theta = B\sin\theta \quad \ldots\text{(ii)}$

In right angled ΔONQ, we have

$$OQ^2 = QN^2 + NO^2 = QN^2 + (OP+PN)^2$$

or
$$R^2 = (B\sin\theta)^2 + (A+B\cos\theta)^2$$
$$= B^2\sin^2\theta + A^2 + B^2\cos^2\theta + 2AB\cos\theta$$
$$= A^2 + B^2 + 2AB\cos\theta$$

$\Rightarrow$ Resultant, $R = \sqrt{A^2+B^2+2AB\cos\theta}$

This represents the magnitude of resultant vector **R**.

If the resultant vector **R** makes an angle (β) with the direction of vector **A**, then from right angle ΔQNO,

$$\tan\beta = \frac{QN}{ON} = \frac{QN}{OP+PN} = \frac{B\sin\theta}{A+B\cos\theta}$$

or Direction of resultant **R**, $\tan\beta = \dfrac{B\sin\theta}{A+B\cos\theta}$

Regarding the Magnitude of *R*

(i) When $\theta = 0°$, then $R = A+B$ (maximum).

(ii) When $\theta = 90°$, then $R = \sqrt{A^2+B^2}$.

(iii) When $\theta = 180°$, then $R = A-B$ (minimum).

This can be extended to any number of vectors, if vectors **a**, **b** and **c** are given, then

$$\mathbf{a} = a_x\hat{i} + a_y\hat{j} + a_z\hat{k}$$
$$\mathbf{b} = b_x\hat{i} + b_y\hat{j} + b_z\hat{k}$$
$$\mathbf{c} = c_x\hat{i} + c_y\hat{j} + c_z\hat{k}$$

where, $\mathbf{r}_x = a_x + b_x + c_x,\ \mathbf{r}_y = a_y + b_y + c_y$

$\mathbf{r}_z = a_z + b_z + c_z$

Example 8. **Two vectors C and D having magnitude 5 units and angle θ = 30° with each other. Find the resultant vector.**

Sol. We have to find the resultant of given two vectors **C** and **D**. For the magnitude of resultant vector.

$$R = |\mathbf{R}| = |\mathbf{C}+\mathbf{D}| = \sqrt{C^2 + D^2 + 2CD\cos\theta}$$
$$= \sqrt{(5)^2 + (5)^2 + 2\times5\times5\times\cos30°} \quad \left(\because \cos30° = \frac{\sqrt{3}}{2}\right)$$
$$= \sqrt{25+25+25\sqrt{3}} = 5\sqrt{2+\sqrt{3}} \text{ units}$$

Now, for the direction of resultant vector,

$$\tan\alpha = \frac{D\sin\theta}{C+D\cos\theta}$$
$$= \frac{5\times\sin30°}{5+5\times\cos30°}$$
$$\tan\alpha = \frac{5\times1/2}{5+5\times\frac{\sqrt{3}}{2}}$$
$$= \left(\frac{1}{2+\sqrt{3}}\right) = 2-\sqrt{3}$$
$$= 0.268$$
$$\Rightarrow \alpha = \tan^{-1}(0.268) \simeq 15°$$

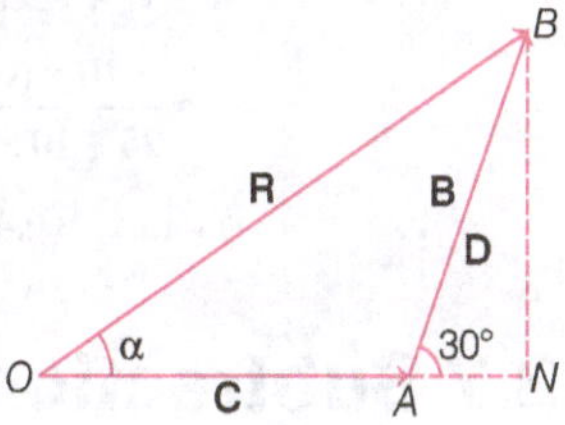

Example 9. **Three vectors are given by**

$$\mathbf{A} = A_x\hat{i} + A_y\hat{j} + A_z\hat{k}$$
$$\mathbf{B} = B_x\hat{i} + B_y\hat{j} + B_z\hat{k}$$
$$\mathbf{C} = C_x\hat{i} + C_y\hat{j} + C_z\hat{k}$$

Determine the magnitude of resultant vector.

Sol. Given, $\mathbf{A} = A_x\hat{i} + A_y\hat{j} + A_z\hat{k}$

$\mathbf{B} = B_x\hat{i} + B_y\hat{j} + B_z\hat{k}$

$\mathbf{C} = C_x\hat{i} + C_y\hat{j} + C_z\hat{k}$

We can add these easily by analytical method.

The resultant of these three vectors are $\mathbf{R} = \mathbf{A}+\mathbf{B}+\mathbf{C}$

$$\mathbf{R} = A_x\hat{i} + A_y\hat{j} + A_z\hat{k} + B_x\hat{i} + B_y\hat{j} + B_z\hat{k} + C_x\hat{i} + C_y\hat{j} + C_z\hat{k}$$
$$= (A_x + B_x + C_x)\hat{i} + (A_y + B_y + C_y)\hat{j} + (A_z + B_z + C_z)\hat{k}$$

The magnitude of **R** is given by

$$R = \sqrt{(A_x + B_x + C_x)^2 + (A_y + B_y + C_y)^2 + (A_z + B_z + C_z)^2}$$

Example 10. **A motor boat is racing towards north at 25 km/h and the water current in that region is 10 km/h in the direction of 60° east to south. Find the resultant velocity of the boat.** NCERT

Sol. Given, velocity of motor boat, $v_b = 25$ km/h (towards north)

Velocity of water current, $v_c = 10$ km/h (towards east to south)

Direction, $\theta = 180° - 60° = 120°$

We know that,

$$v = \sqrt{v_b^2 + v_c^2 + 2v_b v_c \cos\theta}$$

$$v = \sqrt{(25)^2 + (10)^2 + 2 \times 25 \times 10 \times \cos 120°}$$

$$v = \sqrt{625 + 100 + 500\left(-\frac{1}{2}\right)}$$

$\Rightarrow \quad v = 21.8$ km/h

Suppose the resultant velocity v makes angle ϕ with the north direction,

Then, $\tan\phi = \dfrac{v_c \sin 120°}{v_b + v_c \cos 120°}$

$$= \frac{10 \times (\sqrt{3}/2)}{25 + 10 \times (-1/2)} = 0.433$$

$\therefore \quad \phi = \tan^{-1}(0.433) = 23.4°$

3.7 Subtraction of Vectors (Analytical Method)

There are two vectors **A** and **B** at an angle θ. If we have to subtract **B** from **A**, then first invert the vector **B** and then add with **A** as shown in figure.

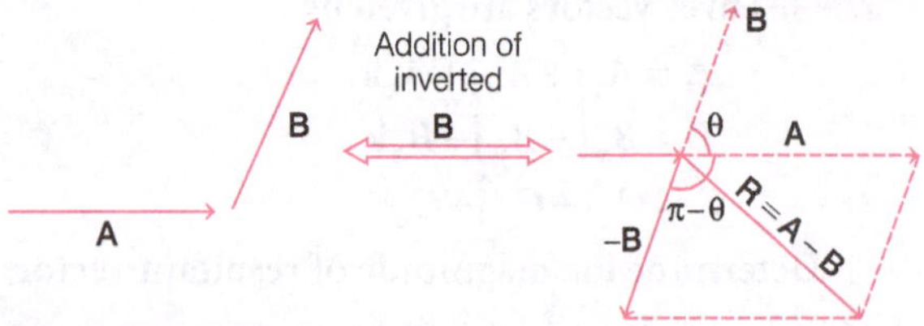

The resultant vector is $\mathbf{R} = \mathbf{A} + (-\mathbf{B}) = \mathbf{A} - \mathbf{B}$

The magnitude of resultant in this case,

$$R = |\mathbf{R}| = \sqrt{A^2 + B^2 + 2AB\cos(\pi - \theta)}$$

$$\text{Resultant, } R = \sqrt{A^2 + B^2 - 2AB\cos\theta}$$

Here, θ = angle between **A** and **B**.

Regarding the magnitude of R

(i) When $\theta = 0°$, then $R = A - B$ (minimum).

(ii) When $\theta = 90°$, then $R = \sqrt{A^2 + B^2}$.

(iii) When $\theta = 180°$, then $R = A + B$ (maximum).

Example 11. **Consider vectors A and B having equal magnitude of 5 units and are inclined each other by 60°. Find the magnitude of sum and difference of these vectors.**

Sol. Given, **A** = 5 units, **B** = 5 units, $\theta = 60°$

A + **B** = ? and **A** − **B** = ?

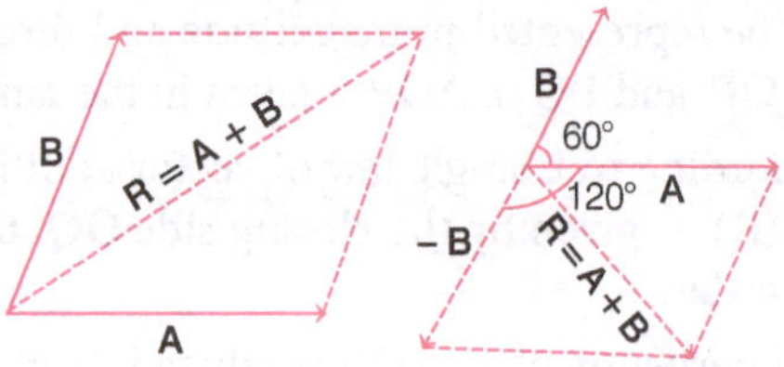

The magnitude of the resultant vectors of the sum,

$$R = \sqrt{A^2 + B^2 + 2AB\cos\theta}$$

$$= \sqrt{5^2 + 5^2 + 2 \times 5 \times 5 \times \cos 60°} = 5\sqrt{3} \text{ units}$$

The magnitude of the resultant vector of the difference,

$$R = \sqrt{A^2 + (-B)^2 + 2AB\cos\theta}$$

$$R = \sqrt{5^2 + 5^2 + 2 \times 5 \times 5 \cos 120°},$$

$$R = 5 \text{ units}$$

3.8 Dot Product or Scalar Product

It is defined as the product of the magnitudes of vectors **A** and **B** and the cosine of the angle θ between them. It is represented by

$$\mathbf{A} \cdot \mathbf{B} = AB\cos\theta$$

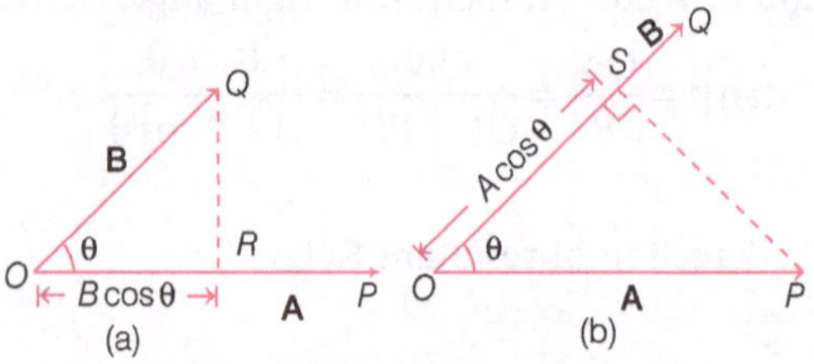

(a) $B\cos\theta$ is the projection of **B** onto **A**.

(b) $A\cos\theta$ is the projection of **A** onto **B**.

Case I When the two vectors are parallel, then $\theta = 0°$.
We have, $\mathbf{A} \cdot \mathbf{B} = AB \cos 0° = AB$

Case II When the two vectors are mutually perpendicular, then $\theta = 90°$.
We have, $\mathbf{A} \cdot \mathbf{B} = AB \cos 90° = 0$

Case III When the two vectors are anti-parallel, then $\theta = 180°$.
We have, $\mathbf{A} \cdot \mathbf{B} = AB \cos 180° = -AB$

Dot Product of Two Vectors in Terms of their Components

It is defined as the product of the magnitude of one vector and the magnitude of the component of other vector in the direction of first vector.

If $\quad \mathbf{a} = a_1\hat{\mathbf{i}} + a_2\hat{\mathbf{j}} + a_3\hat{\mathbf{k}}$ and $\mathbf{b} = b_1\hat{\mathbf{i}} + b_2\hat{\mathbf{j}} + b_3\hat{\mathbf{k}}$,

$$= a_1 \cdot b_1 + a_2 \cdot b_2 + a_3 \cdot b_3$$

where, $\hat{\mathbf{i}} \cdot \hat{\mathbf{i}} = \hat{\mathbf{j}} \cdot \hat{\mathbf{j}} = \hat{\mathbf{k}} \cdot \hat{\mathbf{k}} = 1$

$$\hat{\mathbf{i}} \cdot \hat{\mathbf{j}} + \hat{\mathbf{i}} \cdot \hat{\mathbf{k}} + \hat{\mathbf{j}} \cdot \hat{\mathbf{i}} + \hat{\mathbf{k}} \cdot \hat{\mathbf{i}} = 0$$

Properties of Dot Product

(i) $\mathbf{a} \cdot \mathbf{a} = (\mathbf{a})^2$ (ii) $\mathbf{a} \cdot \mathbf{b} = \mathbf{b} \cdot \mathbf{a}$

(iii) $\mathbf{a} \cdot (\mathbf{b} + \mathbf{c}) = \mathbf{a} \cdot \mathbf{b} + \mathbf{a} \cdot \mathbf{c}$ (iv) $(\mathbf{c} \cdot \mathbf{a}) \cdot \mathbf{b} = \mathbf{c} \cdot (\mathbf{a} \cdot \mathbf{b})$

(v) $\mathbf{a} \cdot \mathbf{b} = |\mathbf{a}||\mathbf{b}| \cos\theta$

Example 12. **Find the angle between the vectors $\mathbf{A} = \hat{\mathbf{i}} + 2\hat{\mathbf{j}} - \hat{\mathbf{k}}$ and $\mathbf{B} = -\hat{\mathbf{i}} + \hat{\mathbf{j}} - 2\hat{\mathbf{k}}$**

Sol. The angle between two vectors is included in the expression of dot product or scalar product.

$$\mathbf{A} \cdot \mathbf{B} = AB \cos\theta \quad \text{...(i)}$$

The magnitude of **A** is given by

$$A = \sqrt{(1)^2 + (2)^2 + (-1)^2} = \sqrt{6} \quad \text{...(ii)}$$

The magnitude of **B** is given by

$$B = \sqrt{(-1)^2 + (1)^2 + (-2)^2} = \sqrt{6} \quad \text{...(iii)}$$

We can separately evaluate the left side of Eq. (i) by writing the vectors in unit vector notation and using the distributive law.

$$\mathbf{A} \cdot \mathbf{B} = (\hat{\mathbf{i}} + 2\hat{\mathbf{j}} - \hat{\mathbf{k}}) \cdot (-\hat{\mathbf{i}} + \hat{\mathbf{j}} - 2\hat{\mathbf{k}})$$

$$= (1 \cdot -1)(\hat{\mathbf{i}} \cdot \hat{\mathbf{i}}) + (1 \cdot 1)(\hat{\mathbf{i}} \cdot \hat{\mathbf{j}}) + (1 \cdot -2)(\hat{\mathbf{i}} \cdot \hat{\mathbf{k}}) + (2 \cdot -1)$$

$$(\hat{\mathbf{j}} \cdot \hat{\mathbf{i}}) + (2 \cdot 1)(\hat{\mathbf{j}} \cdot \hat{\mathbf{j}}) + (2 \cdot -2)(\hat{\mathbf{j}} \cdot \hat{\mathbf{k}}) + (-1 \cdot -1)$$

$$(\hat{\mathbf{k}} \cdot \hat{\mathbf{i}}) + (-1 \cdot 1)(\hat{\mathbf{k}} \cdot \hat{\mathbf{j}}) + (-1 \cdot -2)(\hat{\mathbf{k}} \cdot \hat{\mathbf{k}})$$

$$\mathbf{A} \cdot \mathbf{B} = 3 \begin{bmatrix} \hat{\mathbf{i}} \cdot \hat{\mathbf{i}} = 1, \hat{\mathbf{i}} \cdot \hat{\mathbf{j}} = 0, \hat{\mathbf{i}} \cdot \hat{\mathbf{k}} = 0 \\ \hat{\mathbf{j}} \cdot \hat{\mathbf{j}} = 1, \hat{\mathbf{j}} \cdot \hat{\mathbf{i}} = 0, \hat{\mathbf{j}} \cdot \hat{\mathbf{k}} = 0 \\ \hat{\mathbf{k}} \cdot \hat{\mathbf{k}} = 1, \hat{\mathbf{k}} \cdot \hat{\mathbf{i}} = 0, \hat{\mathbf{k}} \cdot \hat{\mathbf{j}} = 0 \end{bmatrix} \quad \text{...(iv)}$$

Substituting the values of **A** from Eq. (ii) and **B** from Eq. (iii) and $\mathbf{A} \cdot \mathbf{B}$ from Eq. (iv) in Eq. (i), we get

$$3 = (\sqrt{6})(\sqrt{6}) \cos\theta$$

$$\Rightarrow \quad \cos\theta = \frac{3}{6} = \frac{1}{2}$$

$$\Rightarrow \quad \theta = \cos^{-1}\left(\frac{1}{2}\right) = 60°$$

Vector Product or Cross Product

It is defined as the product of the magnitudes of vectors **A** and **B** and the sine of the angle θ between them.

It is represented as

> Cross product of vectors **A** and **B**, $\mathbf{A} \times \mathbf{B} = AB \sin\theta\, \hat{\mathbf{n}}$

where, $\hat{\mathbf{n}}$ is a unit vector in the direction of $\hat{\mathbf{i}}$.

The following figures are representing the vector, product of vectors A and B (using right hand rule).

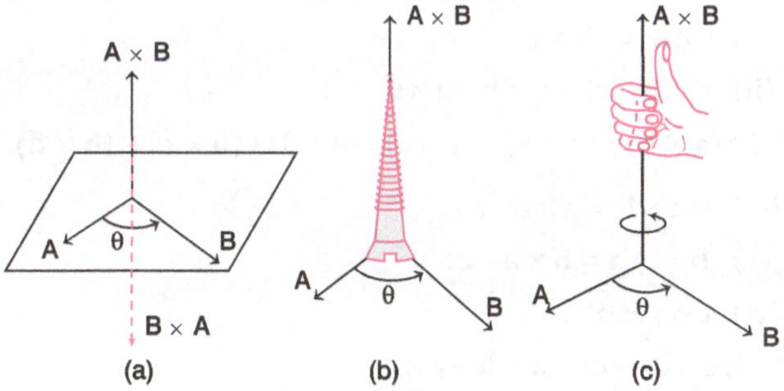

Right hand rules for direction of vector product

Cross Product of Two Vectors in Terms of their Components

- If $\mathbf{a} = a_1\hat{\mathbf{i}} + a_2\hat{\mathbf{j}} + a_3\hat{\mathbf{k}}$ and $\mathbf{b} = b_1\hat{\mathbf{i}} + b_2\hat{\mathbf{j}} + b_3\hat{\mathbf{k}}$, then

$$\mathbf{a} \times \mathbf{b} = \begin{vmatrix} \hat{\mathbf{i}} & \hat{\mathbf{j}} & \hat{\mathbf{k}} \\ a_1 & a_2 & a_3 \\ b_1 & b_2 & b_3 \end{vmatrix}$$

$$= (a_2b_3 - a_3b_2)\hat{\mathbf{i}} - (a_1b_3 - a_3b_1)\hat{\mathbf{j}} + (a_1b_2 - a_2b_1)\hat{\mathbf{k}}$$

where, $\hat{\mathbf{i}} \times \hat{\mathbf{i}} = \hat{\mathbf{j}} \times \hat{\mathbf{j}} = \hat{\mathbf{k}} \times \hat{\mathbf{k}} = 0$;

$$\hat{\mathbf{i}} \times \hat{\mathbf{j}} = \hat{\mathbf{k}},\ \hat{\mathbf{j}} \times \hat{\mathbf{k}} = \hat{\mathbf{i}},\ \hat{\mathbf{k}} \times \hat{\mathbf{i}} = \hat{\mathbf{j}}$$

and $\quad \hat{\mathbf{j}} \times \hat{\mathbf{i}} = -\hat{\mathbf{k}},\ \hat{\mathbf{k}} \times \hat{\mathbf{j}} = -\hat{\mathbf{i}},\ \hat{\mathbf{i}} \times \hat{\mathbf{k}} = -\hat{\mathbf{j}}.$

Case I Cross product of two parallel or anti-parallel vectors is zero.

Case II Cross product of two mutually perpendicular vectors is equal to product of the magnitude of two vectors.

- If A and B are two sides of Δ, then area of $\Delta = \frac{1}{2}|\mathbf{A} \times \mathbf{B}|$

As, area of $\Delta = \frac{1}{2} \times \text{base} \times \text{height} = \frac{1}{2} OS \times PQ$

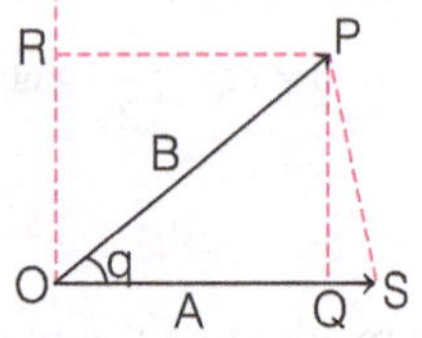

Representation of vectors **A** and **B**

$$\left(\because \sin\theta = \frac{PQ}{OP} \Rightarrow PQ = OP \sin\theta = B\sin\theta \text{ and } OS = A \right)$$

$$= \frac{1}{2} A \times B \sin\theta = \frac{1}{2} AB \sin\theta = \frac{1}{2}|\mathbf{A} \times \mathbf{B}|$$

Properties of Cross Product

(i) $\mathbf{a} \times \mathbf{b} = -\mathbf{b} \times \mathbf{a}$

(ii) $\mathbf{a} \times (\mathbf{b} + \mathbf{c}) = \mathbf{a} \times \mathbf{b} + \mathbf{a} \times \mathbf{c}$

(iii) $(\mathbf{a} \times \mathbf{b}) + (\mathbf{c} \times \mathbf{d}) = (\mathbf{a} \times \mathbf{c}) + (\mathbf{a} \times \mathbf{d}) + (\mathbf{b} \times \mathbf{c}) + (\mathbf{b} \times \mathbf{d})$

(iv) $m\,\mathbf{a} \times \mathbf{b} = \mathbf{a} \times m\,\mathbf{b}$

(v) $(\mathbf{b} + \mathbf{c})\,\mathbf{a} = \mathbf{b} \times \mathbf{a} + \mathbf{c} \times \mathbf{a}$

(vi) $\mathbf{a} \times \mathbf{a} = \mathbf{0}$

(vii) $\mathbf{a} \times (\mathbf{b} - \mathbf{c}) = \mathbf{a} \times \mathbf{b} - \mathbf{a} \times \mathbf{c}$

(viii) $|\mathbf{a} \times \mathbf{b}|^2 = |\mathbf{a}|^2 |\mathbf{b}|^2 - |\mathbf{a} \cdot \mathbf{b}|^2$

(ix) $\mathbf{a} \times (\mathbf{b} \times \mathbf{c}) = (\mathbf{c} \cdot \mathbf{a})\,\mathbf{b} - (\mathbf{b} \cdot \mathbf{a})\,\mathbf{c}$

Example 13. The vector A has a magnitude of 5 units, B has a magnitude of 6 units and the cross product A and B has the magnitude of 15 units. Find the angle between A and B.

Sol. If the angle between **A** and **B** is θ, then cross product will have a magnitude,

$$|\mathbf{A} \times \mathbf{B}| = AB \sin\theta \Rightarrow 15 = 5 \times 6 \sin\theta$$

$$\sin\theta = \frac{1}{2} \Rightarrow \theta = 30^\circ$$

Representation of Unit Vectors in a Circle

Unit vectors along three axes of cartesian coordinate system (i.e. $\hat{i}, \hat{j}, \hat{k}$) can be represented on a circle in such a way that, if we rotate our eyes in anti-clockwise direction, then product of two consecutive vectors will produce the third unit vector.

e.g. $\hat{i} \times \hat{j} = \hat{k}$ and $\hat{j} \times \hat{i} = -\hat{k}$

and similarly for other possibilities.

Scalar Product of Vectors

The scalar product of vectors produce **pseudo scalars**, such as volume, power, etc.

The vector product of two vectors produces a **pseudo vector.** It is also called **axial vector.** The direction of this vector is perpendicular to the plane containing the multiple vectors.

Quick Test 1

Conceptual Questions

1. The total path length is always equal to the magnitude of the displacement vector of a particle. Is it true?
2. Under what condition, the three vectors give zero resultant?
3. When the sum of the two vectors are maximum and minimum?
4. Explain the property of two vectors **A** and **B**, if $|\mathbf{A} + \mathbf{B}| = |\mathbf{A} - \mathbf{B}|$.
5. Can you associate vectors with the following?
   (i) The length of a wire bent into a loop.
   (ii) A plane area.
   (iii) A sphere.

Numerical Questions

6. Two equal forces having their resultant equal to either. At what angle, are they inclined?
7. Suppose you have two forces **F** and **F**. How would you combine them in order to have resultant force of magnitudes?
   (i) Zero (ii) **F**
8. Determine that vector which is added to the resultant of $\mathbf{A} = 3\hat{i} - 5\hat{j} + 7\hat{k}$ and $\mathbf{B} = 2\hat{i} + 4\hat{j} - 3\hat{k}$ gives unit vector along *y*-direction.
9. Two forces 5 kg-wt and 10 kg-wt are acting with an inclination of 120 °between them. Find the angle which the resultant makes with 10 kg-wt.
10. The angle between vectors **A** and **B** is 60°. What is the ratio of $\mathbf{A} \cdot \mathbf{B}$ and $|\mathbf{A} \times \mathbf{B}|$?

Answers

6. 120° 7. (i) 0 (ii)120° 8. $-5\hat{i} + 2\hat{j} - 4\hat{k}$

9. 30° 10. $\frac{1}{\sqrt{3}}$

For Solutions, See QR Code on Pg. 110

3.9 Motion in a Plane

Here, we will discuss how to describe motion of an object in two dimensions using vectors.

Position Vector

Let r be the position vector of a particle P located in a plane with reference to the origin O in XY-plane as shown in figure.

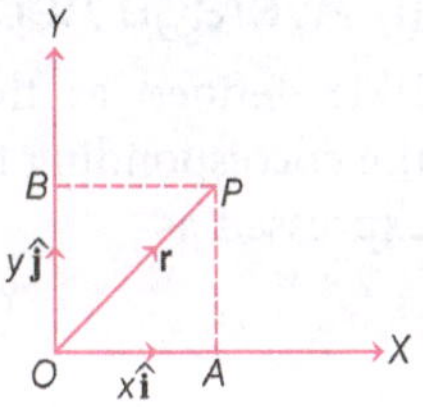

$$\mathbf{OP} = \mathbf{OA} + \mathbf{OB}$$

$$\text{Position vector, } \mathbf{r} = x\hat{\mathbf{i}} + y\hat{\mathbf{j}}$$

In three dimensions, the position vector is represented as

$$r = x\hat{\mathbf{i}} + y\hat{\mathbf{j}} + z\hat{\mathbf{k}}$$

Displacement Vector

Consider a particle moving in XY-plane with a uniform velocity $\mathbf{v}$. Suppose O is the origin for measuring time and position of the particle.

Let the particle be at position A at time t_1 and at position B at time t_2, respectively. The position vectors are $\mathbf{OA} = \mathbf{r}_1 = x_1\hat{\mathbf{i}} + y_1\hat{\mathbf{j}}$ and $\mathbf{OB} = \mathbf{r}_2 = x_2\hat{\mathbf{i}} + y_2\hat{\mathbf{j}}$

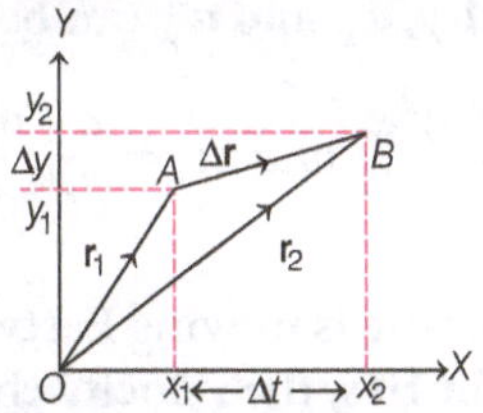

Then, the displacement of the particle in time interval $(t_2 - t_1)$ is **AB**.

$$\text{Displacement, } \mathbf{AB} = (x_2 - x_1)\hat{\mathbf{i}} + (y_2 - y_1)\hat{\mathbf{j}}$$

Similarly, in three dimensions, the displacement can be represented as

$$\Delta\mathbf{r} = (x_2 - x_1)\hat{\mathbf{i}} + (y_2 - y_1)\hat{\mathbf{j}} + (z_2 - z_1)\hat{\mathbf{k}}$$

Velocity Vector

The rate of change of displacement of an object in a particular direction is called its velocity.

It is of two types

Average Velocity

It is defined as the ratio of the displacement and the corresponding time interval.

$$\text{Thus, average velocity} = \frac{\text{displacement}}{\text{time taken}}$$

$$\text{Average velocity, } \mathbf{v}_{av} = \frac{\Delta\mathbf{r}}{\Delta t} = \frac{\mathbf{r}_2 - \mathbf{r}_1}{t_2 - t_1}$$

Velocity can be expressed in the component form as

$$\mathbf{v}_{av} = \frac{\Delta x}{\Delta t}\hat{\mathbf{i}} + \frac{\Delta y}{\Delta t}\hat{\mathbf{j}} = v_x\hat{\mathbf{i}} + v_y\hat{\mathbf{j}}$$

The magnitude of $\mathbf{v}_{av}$ is given by $\mathbf{v}_{av} = \sqrt{v_x^2 + v_y^2}$

and the direction of $\mathbf{v}_{av}$ is given by angle θ,

$$\text{Direction of average velocity, } \theta = \tan^{-1}\left(\frac{v_y}{v_x}\right)$$

Example 14. **A train is moving with a velocity of 30 km/h due east and a car is moving with a velocity of 40 km/h due north. What is the velocity of car as appear to a passenger in the train?**

Sol. Given, $\mathbf{v}_T = 30$ km/h due east

$\mathbf{v}_C = 40$ km/h due north

$\mathbf{v}_{CT} = ?, \theta = ?$

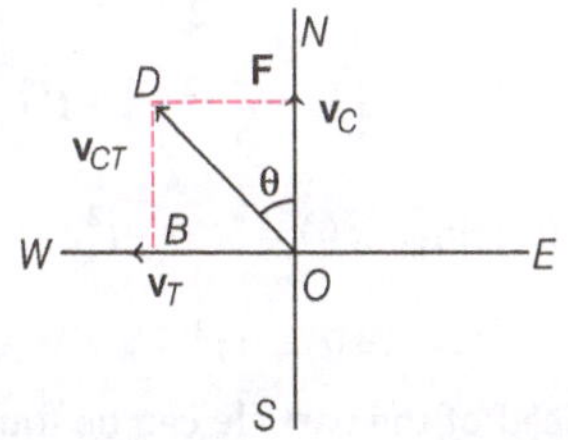

According to question,

In the figure, $\mathbf{v}_{CT} = OD$

$$= \sqrt{OB^2 + BD^2} = \sqrt{v_T^2 + v_C^2}$$

Then, $v_{CT} = \sqrt{(30)^2 + (40)^2} = \sqrt{900 + 1600} = 50$ km/h

$$\tan\theta = \frac{DF}{OF} = \frac{v_C}{v_T} \Rightarrow \tan\theta = \frac{30}{40}$$

$$\theta = \tan^{-1}\left(\frac{30}{40}\right) = 36°52' \text{ west of north}$$

Instantaneous Velocity

The velocity at an instant of time (t) is known as instantaneous velocity.

The average velocity will become instantaneous, if Δt approaches to zero. The instantaneous velocity is expressed as

$$\text{Instantaneous velocity, } \mathbf{v}_i = \lim_{\Delta t \to 0} \frac{\Delta \mathbf{r}}{\Delta t} = \frac{d\mathbf{r}}{dt}$$

TEACHER TIP

The direction of instantaneous velocity at any point on the path of an object is tangential to the path at that point and is in the direction of motion.

Example 15. **A particle starts from origin at t = 0 with a velocity $5\hat{i}$ m/s and moves in XY-plane under action of a force which produces a constant acceleration of $(3\hat{i} + 2\hat{j})$ m/s^2.**

(i) What is the y-coordinate of the particle at the instant its x-coordinate is 84 m?

(ii) What is the speed of the particle at this time? *NCERT*

Sol. (i) Given, $v_0 = 5\hat{i}$ m/s, $a = (3\hat{i} + 2\hat{j})$ m/s^2

We know that, $y(t) = v_0 t + \frac{1}{2}at^2$ and $v = \sqrt{v_x^2 + v_y^2}$

$$y(t) = (5\,\hat{i})\,t + \frac{1}{2}(3\,\hat{i} + 2\,\hat{j})\,t^2$$

$$= \left(5t + \frac{3}{2}t^2\right)\hat{i} + t^2\hat{j}$$

On comparing, $x(t) = 5t + \frac{3}{2}t^2$

$\Rightarrow$ $y(t) = 1t^2$

(ii) The speed of the particle can be found by differentiating the position vector w.r.t. time.

If $x(t) = 84$ m, then $t = 6$ s

$\therefore$ $y(6) = 36$ m

$$v = \frac{dy}{dt} = \frac{d(5t + \frac{3}{2}t^2)\hat{i} + t^2\hat{j}}{dt}$$

$$= (5 + 3t)\hat{i} + 2t\hat{j}$$

At $t = 6$ s, $v = 23\hat{i} + 12\hat{j}$

$\therefore$ $v = \sqrt{(23)^2 + (12)^2} = 26$ m/s

Acceleration

It is defined as the ratio of change in velocity and the corresponding time interval. It can be expressed as

$$\text{Acceleration, } \mathbf{a} = \frac{\text{Change in velocity}}{\text{Time taken}} = \frac{\Delta \mathbf{v}}{\Delta t}$$

$$\text{Acceleration, } \mathbf{a} = \frac{\mathbf{v}_2 - \mathbf{v}_1}{t_2 - t_1}$$

Acceleration is also of two types

(i) Average Acceleration

It is defined as the change in velocity ($\Delta \mathbf{v}$) divided by the corresponding time interval (Δt). It can be expressed as

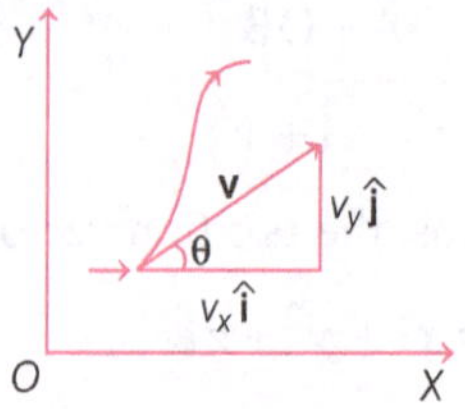

Components of velocity

Average acceleration,

$$\mathbf{a}_{av} = \frac{\Delta \mathrm{v}}{\Delta t} = \frac{\Delta v_x\hat{\mathbf{i}} + \Delta v_y\hat{\mathbf{j}}}{\Delta t} = \frac{\Delta v_x}{\Delta t}\hat{\mathbf{i}} + \frac{\Delta v_y}{\Delta t}\hat{\mathbf{j}}$$

$$\text{Average acceleration, } \mathbf{a}_{av} = a_x\hat{\mathbf{i}} + a_y\hat{\mathbf{j}}$$

which is expressed in component form.

In terms of x and y, a_x and a_y can be expressed as

$$a_x = \frac{d}{dt}\left(\frac{dx}{dt}\right) = \frac{d^2x}{dt^2} \text{ and } a_y = \frac{d}{dt}\left(\frac{dy}{dt}\right) = \frac{d^2y}{dt^2}$$

Example 16. **A particle is moving Eastwards with a velocity of 5 m/s in 10 s, the velocity changes to 5 m/s northwards. Find the average accelaration of the particle in this time interval.**

Sol. According to triangle law of vector addition,

$$\mathbf{OA} + \mathbf{AB} = \mathbf{OB}$$

$$\mathbf{AB} = \mathbf{OB} - \mathbf{OA} = \mathbf{v}_2 - \mathbf{v}_1$$

$$= \text{Change in velocity}$$

$$\therefore \quad |\mathbf{v}_2 - \mathbf{v}_1| = \mathbf{AB} = \sqrt{(\mathbf{OA})^2 + (\mathbf{OB})^2}$$

$$= \sqrt{(5)^2 + (5)^2} = 5\sqrt{2} \text{ m/s}$$

Hence, average acceleration

$$= \frac{|\mathbf{v}_2 - \mathbf{v}_1|}{t}$$

$$= \frac{5\sqrt{2}}{10} = \frac{1}{\sqrt{2}} \text{ m/s}^2$$

Along north-west direction.

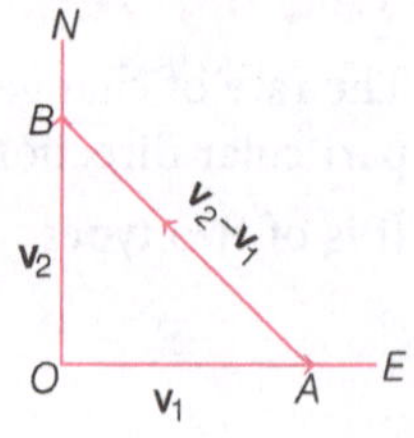

(ii) Instantaneous Acceleration

It is defined as the limiting value of the average acceleration as the time interval approaches to zero.

It can be expressed as

$$\mathbf{a}_i = \lim_{\Delta t \to 0} \frac{\Delta \mathbf{v}}{\Delta t} = \frac{d\mathbf{v}}{dt}$$

$$\boxed{\text{Instantaneous acceleration, } \mathbf{a}_i = a_x \hat{\mathbf{i}} + a_y \hat{\mathbf{j}}}$$

where, $a_x = \frac{dv_x}{dt}, a_y = \frac{dv_y}{dt}$

The magnitude of instantaneous acceleration is given by

$$a_i = \sqrt{a_x^2 + a_y^2}$$

Note In two or three-dimensions, velocity and acceleration vectors can have any angle between 0° to 180°, whereas in one-dimension, the velocity and acceleration of an object are always along the same straight line (may be in same direction or in opposite direction).

Example 17. **The position of a particle is given by $\mathbf{r} = 3.0\, t\, \hat{\mathbf{i}} - 2.0\, t^2\, \hat{\mathbf{j}} + 5.0\, \hat{\mathbf{k}}$ where, t is in seconds and the coefficients have the proper units for r to be in metres.**

(i) Find v(t) and a (t) of the particles.

(ii) Find the magnitude and direction of v(t) at t = 2.0 s. NCERT

Sol. Position of particle, $\mathbf{r} = 3.0\, t\, \hat{\mathbf{i}} - 2.0 t^2 \hat{\mathbf{j}} + 5.0\, \hat{\mathbf{k}}$

(i) $\mathbf{v}(t) = \frac{d\mathbf{r}}{dt} = \frac{d}{dt}(3.0\, t\, \hat{\mathbf{i}} - 2.0 t^2\, \hat{\mathbf{j}} + 5.0\, \hat{\mathbf{k}}) = 3.0\, \hat{\mathbf{i}} - 4.0 t\, \hat{\mathbf{j}}$

$\mathbf{a}(t) = \frac{dv}{dt} = -4.0\, \hat{\mathbf{j}}\ \text{ms}^{-2}$

(ii) At $t = 2.0$ s, $\mathbf{v}(t) = 3.0\, \hat{\mathbf{i}} - 8.0\, \hat{\mathbf{j}}$

$$v = \sqrt{v_x^2 + v_y^2} = \sqrt{(3.0)^2 + (-8)^2} = \sqrt{73} = 8.54\ \text{ms}^{-2}$$

$$\theta = \tan^{-1}\left(\frac{v_y}{v_x}\right) \tan^{-1}\left(\frac{8}{3}\right) = -2.667 = -\tan 69.44°$$

$\theta = 69.44°$ below X-axis

Motion in a Plane with Constant Acceleration

Let an object is moving in XY-plane and its acceleration **a** is constant. At time $t = 0$, the velocity of an object be $\mathbf{v}_0$ (say) and **v** be the velocity at time t.

According to definition of average acceleration, we have

$$\mathbf{a} = \frac{\mathbf{v} - \mathbf{v}_0}{t - 0} = \frac{\mathbf{v} - \mathbf{v}_0}{t} \Rightarrow \boxed{\mathbf{v} = \mathbf{v}_0 + \mathbf{a}t}$$

In terms of rectangular components, we can express it as

$$v_x = v_{ox} + a_x t \text{ and } v_y = v_{oy} + a_y t$$

Let $\mathbf{r}_0$ and **r** be the position vectors of the particle at time $t = 0$ and $t = t$ and their velocities at these instants be $\mathbf{v}_0$ and **v**, then,

$$\mathbf{v}_{av} = \frac{\mathbf{v}_0 + \mathbf{v}}{2}$$

and displacement is given by

$$\mathbf{r} - \mathbf{r}_0 = \left(\frac{\mathbf{v} + \mathbf{v}_0}{2}\right) t$$

$$= \left[\frac{(\mathbf{v}_0 + \mathbf{a}t) + \mathbf{v}_0}{2}\right] t$$

$$\Rightarrow \quad \mathbf{r} - \mathbf{r}_0 = \mathbf{v}_0 t + \frac{1}{2}\mathbf{a}t^2$$

$$\Rightarrow \quad \boxed{\mathbf{r} = \mathbf{r}_0 + \mathbf{v}_0 t + \frac{1}{2}\mathbf{a}t^2}$$

Now, it can be written in component form as

$$\boxed{x = x_0 + v_{0x} t + \frac{1}{2} a_x t^2}$$

$$\boxed{y = y_0 + v_{0y} t + \frac{1}{2} a_y t^2}$$

TEACHER TIP

Motion in a plane can be treated as two separate simultaneous one-dimensional motions with constant acceleration along two perpendicular directions.

It is useful in analysing motion of object in two dimensions.

Example 18. **A particle starts from origin at t = 0 with a velocity $15\,\hat{\mathbf{i}}$ m/s and moves in XY-plane under the action of a force which produces a constant acceleration of $(15\hat{\mathbf{i}} + 10\hat{\mathbf{j}})$ m/s^2. Find the y-coordinate of the particle at the instant. Its x-coordinate is 125 m.**

Sol. The position of the particle is given by

$$r(t) = v_0 t + \frac{1}{2}at^2 = 15\hat{\mathbf{i}}\, t + \frac{1}{2}(15\,\hat{\mathbf{i}} + 10\,\hat{\mathbf{j}})t^2$$

$$= (15t + 7.5t^2)\hat{\mathbf{i}} + 5t^2\hat{\mathbf{j}}$$

$\therefore \quad x(t) = 15t + 7.5t^2,\ y(t) = 5t^2$

If $\quad x(t) = 125$ m, $t = ?$

$125 = 15t + 7.5t^2$

$\Rightarrow \quad 1.5t^2 + 3t - 25 = 0$

$t = 3.2$ s

$\therefore \quad y(t) = 5 \times (3.2)^2 = 51.2$ m

3.10 Projectile Motion

Projectile motion is a form of motion in which an object or particle is thrown with some initial velocity near the earth's surface and it moves along a curved path under the action of gravity alone. The path followed by a projectile is called its **trajectory**.

An object that is in flight after being thrown is called **projectile.**

e.g. A bullet fired from a rifle, a body dropped from the window of a moving train, a jet of water flowing from a hole near the bottom of water tank, a javelin thrown by an athlete, etc.

Assumptions before the Study of Projectile Motion

(i) There is no frictional resistance of air.

(ii) The effect due to rotation of earth and the curvature of the earth is negligible.

(iii) The acceleration due to gravity is constant both in magnitude and direction, at all points during the motion of projectile.

Mathematical Analysis of Projectile Motion

Suppose an object is projected from point O with velocity (u), making an angle (θ) with the horizontal direction OX, such that $x_0 = 0$ and $y_0 = 0$ when $t = 0$.

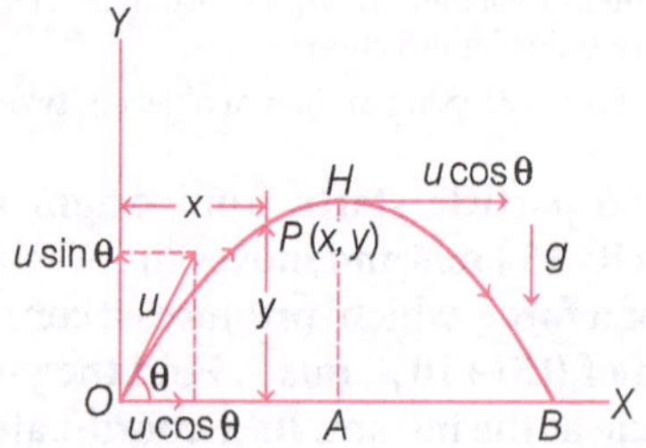

While resolving velocity (u) into two components, we get (a) $u\cos\theta$ along OX and (b) $u\sin\theta$ along OY.

Note The horizontal and vertical components of projectile motion was stated by Galileo.

Motion Along Horizontal Direction (OX)

The velocity of an object in horizontal direction, i.e. OX is constant, so the acceleration a_x in horizontal direction is zero.

$\therefore$ Position of the object at time t along horizontal direction is given by $x = x_0 + u_x t + \frac{1}{2}a_x t^2$

But $x_0 = 0, u_x = u\cos\theta, a_x = 0$ and $t = t$

$$\therefore \quad x = u\cos\theta\, t$$

$$\Rightarrow \quad \text{Time, } t = \frac{x}{u\cos\theta} \quad \text{... (i)}$$

Motion Along Vertical Direction (OY)

The vertical velocity of the object is decreasing from O to H due to gravity, so acceleration a_y is g.

$\therefore$ Position of the object at any time t along the vertical direction, i.e. OY is given by

$$y = y_0 + u_y t + \frac{1}{2}a_y t^2$$

But $\quad y_0 = 0, u_y = u\sin\theta, a_y = -g$ and $t = t$

$$\text{So,} \quad y = u\sin\theta\, t + \frac{1}{2}(-g)t^2$$

$$= u\sin\theta\, t - \frac{1}{2}gt^2 \quad \text{...(ii)}$$

At point H, the object has only horizontal component velocity ($u\cos\theta$). It attains a maximum height at AH. OB is the maximum horizontal range.

Equation of Path of a Projectile

Substituting the value of t from Eq. (i) in Eq. (ii), we get

$$y = u\sin\theta\left(\frac{x}{u\cos\theta}\right) - \frac{1}{2}g\left(\frac{x}{u\cos\theta}\right)^2$$

$$= x\tan\theta - \frac{1}{2}g\left(\frac{x}{u\cos\theta}\right)^2$$

$$\text{Total vertical distance, } y = x\tan\theta - \left(\frac{1}{2}\frac{g}{u^2\cos^2\theta}\right)x^2$$

This equation represents a parabola and is known as equation of trajectory of a projectile.

Time of Flight

It is defined as the total time for which projectile is in flight, i.e. time during the motion of projectile from O to B. It is denoted by T.

$$\text{Total time of flight, } T = \frac{2u\sin\theta}{g}$$

For a projectile, time of ascent is to equal time of descent.

Maximum Height of a Projectile

It is defined as the maximum vertical height attained by an object above the point of projection during its flight. It is denoted by H.

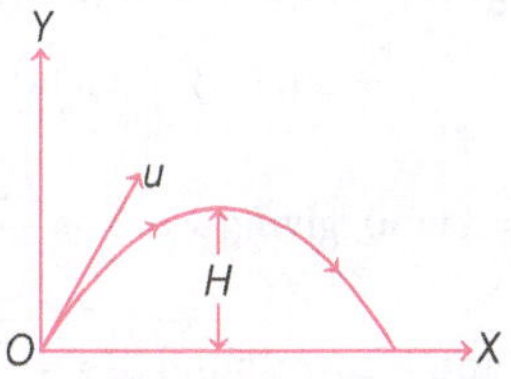

$$\text{Maximum height, } H = \frac{u^2 \sin^2 \theta}{2g}$$

Horizontal Range of a Projectile

The horizontal range of the projectile is defined as the horizontal distance covered by the projectile during its time of flight. It is denoted by R.

$$\text{Horizontal range, } R = \frac{u^2 \sin 2\theta}{g}$$

$[\because \sin 2\theta = 2\sin\theta\cos\theta]$

The horizontal range will be maximum, if

$$\sin 2\theta = \text{maximum} = 1$$
$$\sin 2\theta = \sin 90° \text{ or } \theta = 45°$$

$$\therefore \quad \text{Maximum horizontal range, } R_m = \frac{u^2}{g}$$

Example 19. **A soccer player kicks a ball at an angle of 30° with an initial speed of 20 m/s. Assuming that, the ball travels in a vertical plane. Calculate (i) the time at which the ball reaches the highest point, (ii) the maximum height reached, (iii) the horizontal range of the ball and (iv) the time for which the ball is in the air. ($g = 10 \text{ m/s}^2$).**

Sol. Given, $\theta = 30°, u = 20 \text{ m/s}, g = 10 \text{ m/s}^2$

(i) $t = \frac{T}{2} = \frac{u\sin\theta}{g} = \frac{20 \times \sin 30°}{10} = 2 \times \frac{1}{2} = 1 \text{ s}$

(ii) $H = \frac{u^2 \sin^2\theta}{2g} = \frac{(20)^2 \times \sin^2 30°}{2 \times 10} = 5 \text{ m}$

(iii) $R = \frac{u^2 \sin 2\theta}{g} = \frac{(20)^2 \times \sin 2 \times 30°}{10} = 34.64 \text{ m}$

(iv) $T = \frac{2u\sin\theta}{g} = \frac{2 \times 20 \times \sin 30°}{10} = 2 \text{ s}$

Example 20. **A cricket ball is thrown at a speed of 28 ms^{-1} in a direction 30° above the horizontal. Calculate**

(i) the maximum height,

(ii) the time taken by the ball to return to the same level and

(iii) the distance from the thrower to the point, where the ball returns to the same level. *NCERT*

Sol. (i) The maximum height attained by the ball,

$$H = \frac{(u_0 \sin\theta)^2}{2g} = \frac{(28\sin 30°)^2}{2(9.8)}$$
$$= \frac{14 \times 14}{2 \times 9.8} = 10.0 \text{ m}$$

(ii) The time taken by the ball to return the same level

$$T = (2u_0 \sin\theta)/g = (2 \times 28 \times \sin 30°)/9.8$$
$$= 28/9.8 = 2.9 \text{ s}$$

(iii) The distance from the thrower to the point where the ball returns to the same level,

$$R = \frac{(u_0^2 \sin 2\theta)}{g} = \frac{28 \times 28 \times \sin 60°}{9.8} = 69 \text{ m}$$

Projectile Fired at an Angle with the Vertical

Let a particle be projected at an angle θ with vertical and its muzzle speed (i.e. speed of projection) is u. The projectile has two components of its velocity at all the points during its motion.

The components are along X-axis (horizontal) and along Y-axis (vertical). Clearly, the angle made by the velocity of projectile at point of projection is $(90° - \theta)$ with the horizontal. In this case,

(i) Time of flight $= \frac{2u\sin(90° - \theta)}{g} = \frac{2u}{g}\cos\theta$

(ii) Maximum height $= \frac{u^2 \sin^2(90° - \theta)}{2g}$

$$= \frac{u^2 \cos^2\theta}{2g}$$

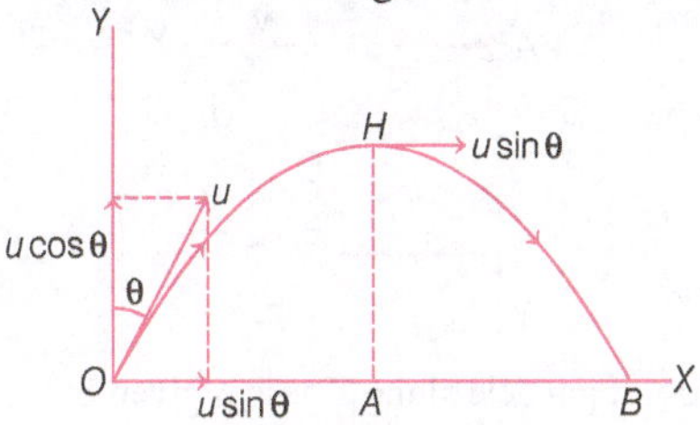

Angle after projection

(iii) Horizontal range $= \dfrac{u^2}{g} \sin 2(90° - \theta)$

$$= \frac{u^2}{g} \sin(180° - 2\theta) = \frac{u^2}{g} \sin 2\theta$$

(iv) Path of projectile

$$y = x \tan(90° - \theta) - \frac{1}{2} \frac{gx^2}{u^2 \cos^2(90° - \theta)}$$

$$= x \cot\theta - \frac{gx^2}{2u^2 \sin^2\theta}$$

(v) Velocity at any time, *t*

$$= \sqrt{[u\cos(90°-\theta)]^2 + [u\sin(90°-\theta) - gt]^2}$$

$$= \sqrt{u^2 + g^2t^2 - 2ugt\sin(90° - \theta)}$$

$$= \sqrt{u^2 + g^2t^2 - 2ugt\cos\theta}$$

This velocity makes an angle β with the horizontal direction, then

$$\tan\beta = \frac{u\sin(90° - \theta) - gt}{u\cos(90° - \theta)} = \frac{u\cos\theta - gt}{u\sin\theta}$$

Effect of Air Resistance on Projectile Motion

- As we have seen that in projectile motion, we assume that air resistance has no effect on its motion.
- A projectile that traverses a parabolic path would slow during its idealised trajectory in the presence of air resistance. It will not hit the ground with the same speed with which it was projected.
- In the absence of air resistance, it is only the *y*-component that undergoes a continuous change. However, in the presence of air resistance, both of *x* and *y*-components would get affected.

Example 21 A particle is projected horizontally with a speed *v* from the top of a plane inclined at angle θ with the horizontal. How far from the point of projection will the particle hit the plane?

Sol. To solve this problem, we take *X* and *Y*-axes as shown in figure.

Consider the motion of particle from *A* to *B*.

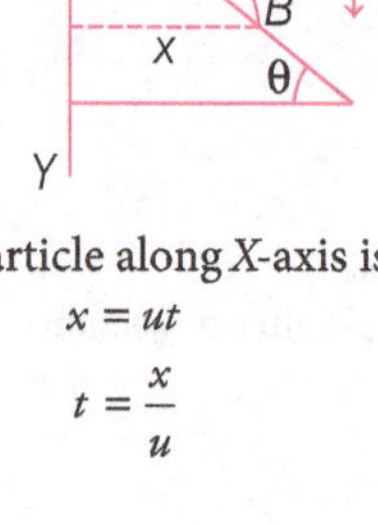

Motion of particle along *X*-axis is given by

$$x = ut \quad \text{...(i)}$$

$$\Rightarrow \quad t = \frac{x}{u}$$

where, t = time to reach the particle from *A* to *B*.

Motion of particle along *Y*-axis is given by

$$y = \frac{1}{2}gt^2 \quad \text{...(ii)}$$

Eliminating t from Eqs. (i) and (ii), we get

$$y = \frac{1}{2}g\frac{x^2}{u^2} \quad \text{and} \quad y = x\tan\theta$$

Thus, $\dfrac{gx^2}{2u^2} = x\tan\theta$, giving $x = 0$ or $\dfrac{2u^2\tan\theta}{g}$, $x = 0$

At points *A* and *B* correspond to $x = \dfrac{2u^2\tan\theta}{g}$, then

$$y = x\tan\theta = \frac{2u^2\tan^2\theta}{g}$$

Now, $AB = \sqrt{x^2 + y^2}$

$$= \frac{2u^2}{g}\tan\theta\sqrt{1 + \tan^2\theta} = \frac{2u^2}{g}\tan\theta\sec\theta$$

3.11 Uniform Circular Motion

When an object follows a circular path at a constant speed, the motion of the object is called uniform circular motion.

Examples

(i) Motion of the tip of the second hand of a clock.

(ii) Motion of a point on the rim of a wheel rotating uniformly.

Terms Related to Circular Motion

Angular Displacement

It is defined as the angle traced out by the radius vector at the centre of the circular path in the given time. It is denoted by $\Delta\theta$ and expressed in radian.

It is a dimensionless quantity. It is a vector quantity, direction is given by **Right-hand rule.**

Angular Velocity

It is defined as the time rate of change of its angular position, denoted by ω and is measured in radian per second.

Its dimensional formula is $[M^0L^0T^{-1}]$. It is a vector quantity.

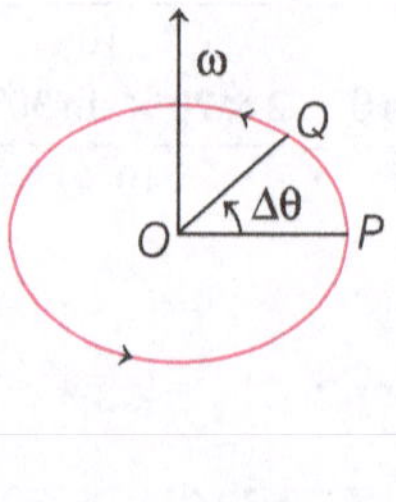

Suppose a point object moving along a circular path, with centre (i.e. axis of rotation) at O. Let the object move from P to Q (as shown in the figure below) in a small time interval Δt, where $\angle POQ = \Delta\theta$.

Now, angular velocity, $\omega = \dfrac{\text{Angle traced}}{\text{Time taken}}$

$$\omega = \lim_{\Delta t \to 0} \frac{\Delta\theta}{\Delta t} = \frac{d\theta}{dt}$$

Time Period

It is defined as the time taken by a particle to complete one revolution along its circular path. It is denoted by T and is measured in second.

Frequency

It is defined as the number of revolutions completed per unit time. It is denoted by f and is measured in Hz.

Angular Acceleration

It is defined as the time rate of change of angular velocity of a particle. It is measured in radian per second square and has dimensions $[M^0L^0T^{-2}]$.

It is denoted by α, where $\alpha = \lim_{\Delta t \to 0} \dfrac{\Delta\omega}{\Delta t} = \dfrac{d\omega}{dt}$

Relation between Time Period and Frequency

Let f be the frequency of an object in circular motion, then the object will complete one revolution in $\dfrac{1}{f}$ second, which is known as time period (T).

$$\text{Time period, } T = \frac{1}{f}$$

Relation among Angular Velocity, Frequency and Time Period

Suppose a point object is illustrating a uniform circular motion with frequency (f) and time period (T). Then, the object completes one revolution and the angle traced at its axis of circular motion is 2π in radian.

If time $t = T, \theta = 2\pi$ radian.

Thus, the angular velocity ω is given by

$$\text{Angular velocity, } \omega = \frac{\theta}{t} = \frac{2\pi}{T} = 2\pi f$$

Relation between Linear Velocity v and Angular Velocity ω

Suppose the particle moving on circular track of radius r is showing angular displacement $\Delta\theta$ in Δt time and in this time period, it covers a distance Δs along the circular track, then

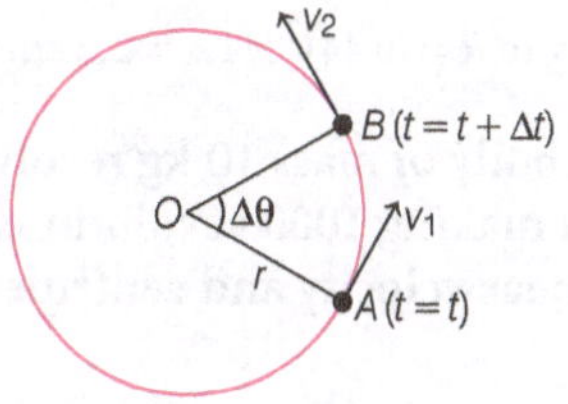

Representation of linear velocity and angular velocity

$$\omega = \frac{\Delta\theta}{\Delta t} \quad \ldots\text{(i)}$$

and
$$v = \frac{\Delta s}{\Delta t} \quad \ldots\text{(ii)}$$

But
$$\Delta s = r\,\Delta\theta \quad \ldots\text{(iii)}$$

(Since, angle = arc/radius)

From above three equations, we get

$$\text{Linear velocity, } v = r\frac{\Delta\theta}{\Delta t} = r\omega$$

Centripetal Acceleration

The acceleration associated with uniform circular motion is called a centripetal acceleration.

Consider a particle of mass (m) moving with a constant speed (v) and uniform angular velocity (ω) on a circular path of radius (r) with centre at O.

$$\text{Centripetal acceleration, } a = \frac{v^2}{r} = \omega^2 r$$

It is towards the centre of circle.

Example 22. **An insect trapped in a circular groove of radius 12 cm moves along the groove steadily and completes 7 revolutions in 100 s.**

(i) What is the angular speed and the linear speed of the motion?

(ii) Is the acceleration vector, a constant vector? What is its magnitude? *(NCERT)*

Sol. The given question is based on uniform circular motion.
Here, radius, $R = 12$ cm.

The angular speed ω is given as

$$\omega = 2\pi / T = 2\pi \times 7 / 100$$
$$= 0.44 \text{ rad/s}$$

and linear speed $v = \omega R = 0.44 \times 12 = 5.3\ \text{cm s}^{-1}$

The direction of velocity v is along the tangent to the circle at every point. The acceleration is directed towards the centre of the circle. Since, this direction changes acceleration continuously, which is not a constant vector.

However, the magnitude of acceleration is constant.

$$a = \omega^2 R = (0.44)^2 \times 12 = 2.3\ \text{cm s}^{-2}$$

Example 23. **A body of mass 10 kg revolves in a circle of diameter 0.4 m making 1000 revolutions per minute. Calculate its linear velocity and centripetal acceleration.**

Sol. Given, $m = 10$ kg, $d = 0.4$ m, $r = 0.2$ m,

Revolutions per min, $v = 1000/\text{min} = \frac{1000}{60}$ s,

Linear velocity, v = ?, centripetal acceleration, a = ?

$$\omega = 2\pi v = 2\pi \times \frac{1000}{60} = \frac{100\,\pi}{3}\ \text{rad/s}$$

$$v = r\omega = 0.2 \times \frac{100\,\pi}{3} = \frac{20\,\pi}{3}\ \text{m/s}$$

$$a = r\omega^2 = 0.2 \times \left(\frac{100\,\pi}{3}\right)^2$$

$$= \frac{2000\,\pi^2}{9}\ \text{m/s}^2$$

Quick Test 2

Conceptual Questions

1. A particle cannot accelerate if its velocity is constant, why?
2. A football is kicked into the air vertically upwards. What is its (i) acceleration and (ii) velocity at the highest point? *NCERT Exemplar*
3. How does the knowledge of projectile help a player in the baseball game?
4. A skilled gun man always keeps his gun slightly tilted above the line of sight while shooting. Why?

Numerical Questions

5. An aircraft is flying at a height of 3400 m above the ground. If the angle subtended at a ground observation point by the aircraft positions 10 s apart is 30°, what is the speed of the aircraft? *NCERT*
6. A passenger arriving in a new town wishes to go from the station to a hotel located 10 km away on a straight road from the station. A dishonest cabman takes him along a circutious path 23 km long and reaches the hotel in 28 min. What is (i) the average speed of the taxi and (ii) the magnitude of average velocity? Are the two equal? *NCERT*
7. A hiker stands on the edge of a cliff 490 m above the ground and throws a stone horizontally with an initial speed of 15 m/s. Neglecting air resistance, find the time taken by the stone to reach the ground and the speed with which it hits the ground. Consider $g = 9.8\ \text{m/s}^2$. *NCERT*

Answers

5. $182.2\ \text{ms}^{-1}$
6. (i) 49.3 km/h, (ii) 21.43 km/h
7. 10 s, 99.14 m/s

For Solutions, See QR Code on Pg. 110

Mind Map

Equality of Vectors Two vectors are said to be equal, if they have the same magnitude and same direction, regardless of their initial positions.

Unit vector is a vector with a magnitude of 1, used to indicate the direction of a vector in space.

Null vector also known as the zero vector. It is a vector with zero magnitude and no specific direction. It is denoted by 0.

Scalars and Vectors

Scalars are quantities that have only magnitude (size or amount) and no direction. e.g distance, mass, speed, etc.

Vectors are quantities that have both magnitude and direction. e.g force and velocity, etc.

Vector Addition

Vector addition combines two or more vectors to form a resultant vector that represents their combined effect. There are two primary methods for vector addition, Graphical Method and Analytical Method.

Graphical Method

(a) Triangle Law of Vector Addition
If two vectors are represented as the sides of a triangle taken in order, their resultant is represented by the closing side of the triangle in the opposite order.

Resultant vector, $\mathbf{R} = \mathbf{A} + \mathbf{B}$

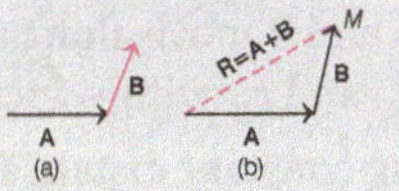

(b) Parallelogram Law of Vector Addition
If two vectors are represented as adjacent sides of a parallelogram, their resultant is represented by the diagonal of the parallelogram starting from the same point.

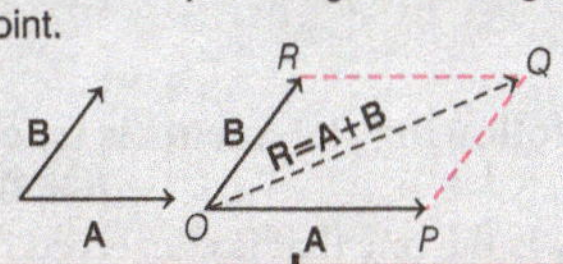

Properties of Addition of Vector

(I) It follows commutative law, i.e.
$\mathbf{A} + \mathbf{B} = \mathbf{B} + \mathbf{A}$

(ii) It follows associative law, i.e.,
$(\mathbf{A} + \mathbf{B}) + \mathbf{C} = \mathbf{A} + (\mathbf{B} + \mathbf{C})$

(iii) It obeys distributive law, i.e.
$\lambda(\mathbf{A} + \mathbf{B}) = \mathbf{A}\lambda + \lambda\mathbf{B}$

(iv) It follows identity law i.e., $\mathbf{A} + 0 = \mathbf{A}$

Substraction of Vector

It is expressed as

$\mathbf{R} = \mathbf{A} + (-\mathbf{B})$

$\mathbf{R} = \mathbf{A} - \mathbf{B}$

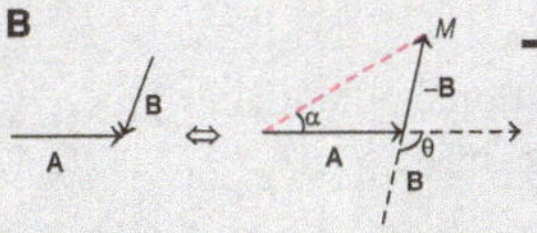

Motion in a Plane

- Vector which gives position of an object with reference to the origin of a coordinate system.
- **Displacement vector** represents the change in position of a point from an initial position to a final position. It is independent of the path taken. Denoted as $\Delta\mathbf{r}$

$$\Delta\mathbf{r} = \mathbf{r}_{final} - \mathbf{r}_{initial}$$

Average Acceleration and Velocity

The average acceleration of an object is the ratio of average velocity and time interval. i.e.

$$\mathbf{a} = \frac{\Delta\mathbf{v}}{\Delta t} = a_x\hat{\mathbf{i}} + a_y\hat{\mathbf{j}}$$

The average velocity of an object is the ratio of the displacement and time interval.

i.e., $\mathbf{v} = \dfrac{\Delta\mathbf{r}}{\Delta t} = v_x\hat{\mathbf{i}} + v_y\hat{\mathbf{j}}$

Resolution of Vector involves breaking a single vector into two or more components that add up to the original vector.where λ and μ are real number

Analytical Method

Analytical Method of vector addition involves calculating the resultant vector by using the components of the vectors to be added

$$\mathbf{A} = A_x\hat{\mathbf{i}} + A_y\hat{\mathbf{j}},\ \mathbf{B} = B_x\hat{\mathbf{i}} + B_y\hat{\mathbf{j}}$$

$$R_x = A_x + B_x,\quad R_y = A_y + B_y$$

$$\mathbf{R} = R_x\hat{\mathbf{i}} + R_y\hat{\mathbf{j}}$$

Magnitude $|\mathbf{R}| = \sqrt{R_x^2 + R_y^2}$

Direction (angle θ) $\theta = \tan^{-1}\left(\dfrac{R_y}{R_x}\right)$

Multiplication of Vector by Real Numbers

- If a vector multiplied by a real number, then the resultant vector is also a vector whose magnitude is changed but the direction remains same.

$$|\lambda\mathbf{A}| = \lambda|\mathbf{A}|, \text{ if } \lambda > 0$$

where, λ is a scalar number.

Properties of Substraction of Vector

(I) It does not follow commutative properties, i.e.,
$\mathbf{A} - \mathbf{B} \neq \mathbf{B} - \mathbf{A}$

(ii) It does not follow associative law, i.e.,
$\mathbf{A} - (\mathbf{B} - \mathbf{C}) \neq (\mathbf{A} - \mathbf{B}) - \mathbf{C}$

(iii) It follows distributive law, i.e.
$\lambda(\mathbf{A} - \mathbf{B}) = \lambda\mathbf{A} - \lambda\mathbf{B}$

(iv) It follows identity law, i.e., $\mathbf{A} - 0 = \mathbf{A}$

Uniform Circular Motion

When an object follows a circular path at a constant speed, the motion of the object is called uniform circular motion.

- Angular Displacement
  The angle traced out by the radius vector at the centre of the circular path in the given time. It is a vector quantity.
- Angular Acceleration
  The time rate of change of angular velocity of a particle.It is denoted by α.

$$\alpha = \lim_{\Delta t \to 0} \frac{\Delta\omega}{\Delta t} = \frac{d\omega}{dt}$$

- Centripetal Acceleration
  The acceleration associated with uniform circular motion is called a centripetal acceleration.
  Centripetal acceleration, $a = \dfrac{v^2}{r}$

Projectile Motion

Projectile motion is a form of motion in which an object is thrown with some initial velocity near the earth's surface and it moves along a curved path under the action of gravity alone.

Equation of Projectile Motion

- **Motion along horizontal direction (*OX*)**

Time, $t = \dfrac{x}{u\cos\theta}$

- **Motion along vertical direction (*OY*)**

Total vertical distance,

$$y = x\tan\theta - \left(\frac{1}{2}\frac{g}{u^2\cos^2\theta}\right)x^2$$

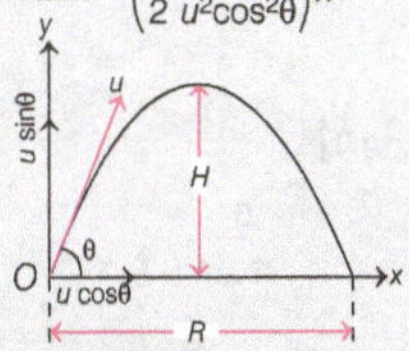

Horizontal Range

The horizontal range is distance covered by the projectile during its time of flight.

Horizontal range, $R = \dfrac{u^2\sin 2\theta}{g}$

Here, maximum horizontal range,

$$R_{max} = \frac{u^2}{g}\quad [\because \theta = 45^\circ]$$

Maximum Height

The maximum vertical height attained by an object above the point of projectile during its flight.

Maximum height, $H = \dfrac{u^2\sin^2\theta}{2g}$

Time of Flight

Total time for which projectile is in flight, i.e. time during the motion of projectile.

Total time of flight, $T = \dfrac{2u\sin\theta}{g}$

EXAM PATTERN QUESTIONS

Objective Type Questions

Multiple Choice Questions

1. The angle between $A = \hat{i} + \hat{j}$ and $B = \hat{i} - \hat{j}$ is **NCERT Exemplar**

(a) 45° (b) 90°
(c) – 45° (d) 180°

2. The quantities A_x and A_y are called x and y-components of the vector A. Note that A_x is itself not a vector, but $A_x\hat{i}$ is a vector and so is $A_y\hat{j}$. Using simple trigonometry, we can express A_x and A_y in terms of the magnitude of A and the angle it makes with the X-axis

$$A_x = A\cos\theta,\ A_y = A\sin\theta$$

Choose the correct figure on the basis of given description.

(a) 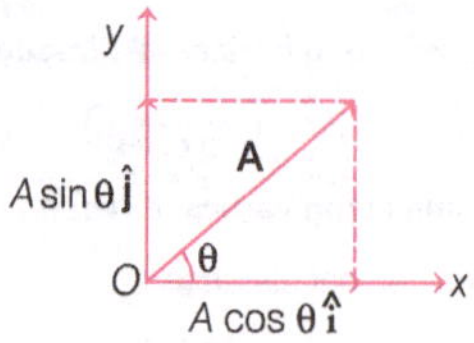

(b) 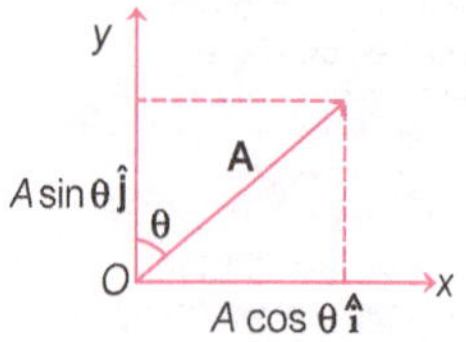

(c) 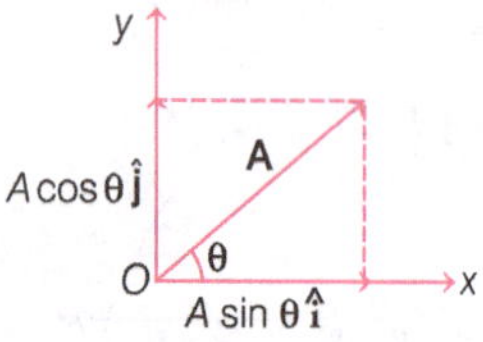

(d) None of these

3. The direction of instantaneous velocity is shown by

(a) 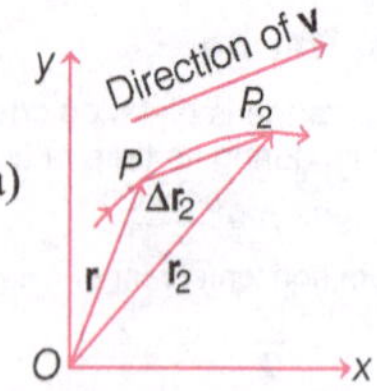

(b) 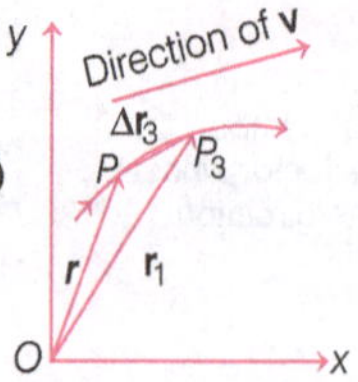

(c) 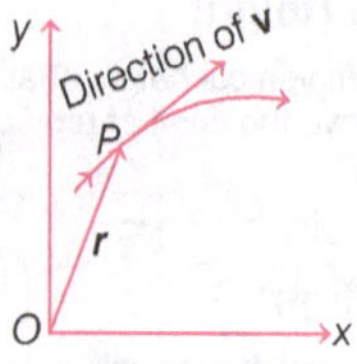

(d) None of these

4. A girl riding a bicycle with a speed of 5 ms^{-1} towards north direction sees raindrops falling vertically downwards. On increasing the speed to 15 ms^{-1}, rain appears to fall making an angle of 45° of the vertical. Find the magnitude of velocity of rain. **Competency Based Que.**

(a) 5 ms^{-1} (b) $5\sqrt{2}$ ms^{-1}
(c) 25 ms^{-1} (d) 10 ms^{-1}

5. The speed of a projectile at the maximum height is half of its initial speed. Find the ratio of range of projectile to the maximum height attained.

(a) $4\sqrt{3}$ (b) $\frac{4}{\sqrt{3}}$ (c) $\frac{\sqrt{3}}{4}$ (d) 6

6. The horizontal range of a projectile fired at an angle of 15° is 50 m. If it is fired with the same speed at an angle of 45°, its range will be

(a) 60 m (b) 71 m (c) 100 m (d) 141 m

7. Two cars A and B move along a concentric circular path of radius r_A and r_B with velocities v_A and v_B maintaining constant distance, then $\frac{v_A}{v_B}$ is equal to **Competency Based Que.**

(a) $\frac{r_B}{r_A}$ (b) $\frac{r_A}{r_B}$ (c) $\frac{r_A^2}{r_B^2}$ (d) $\frac{r_B^2}{r_A^2}$

8. Which one of the following statements is true? **NCERT Exemplar**

(a) A scalar quantity is the one that is conserved in a process.
(b) A scalar quantity is the one that can never take negative values.
(c) A scalar quantity is the one that does not vary from one point to another in space.
(d) A scalar quantity has the same value for observers with different orientation of the axes.

9. Consider the quantities, pressure, power, energy, impulse, gravitational potential, electrical charge, temperature, area. Out of these, the only vector quantities are **NCERT Exemplar**

(a) impulse, pressure and area
(b) impulse and area
(c) area and gravitational potential
(d) impulse and pressure

10. **The component of a vector r along *X*-axis will have maximum value, if** **NCERT Exemplar**

(a) **r** is along positive *Y*-axis
(b) **r** is along positive *X*-axis
(c) **r** makes an angle of 45° with the *X*-axis
(d) **r** is along negative *Y*-axis

11. **In a two dimensional motion, instantaneous speed v_0 is a positive constant. Then, which of the following are necessarily true?** **NCERT Exemplar**

(a) The acceleration of the particle is zero.
(b) The acceleration of the particle is bounded.
(c) The acceleration of the particle is necessarily in the plane of motion.
(d) The particle must be undergoing a uniform circular motion.

12. **Figure shows the orientation of two vectors u and v in the *XY*-plane.** **NCERT Exemplar**

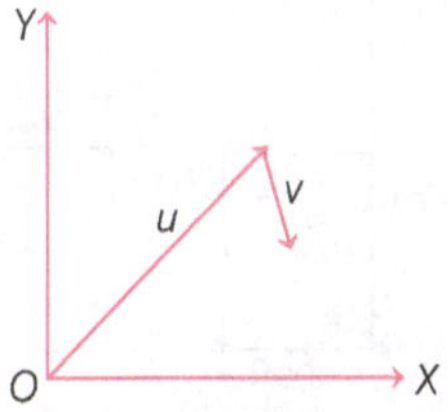

If $\mathbf{u} = a\hat{i} + b\hat{j}$ and $\mathbf{v} = p\hat{i} + q\hat{j}$, which of the following is correct?

(a) *a* and *p* are positive while *b* and *q* are negative
(b) *a*, *p* and *b* are positive while *q* is negative
(c) *a*, *q* and *b* are positive while *p* is negative
(d) *a*, *b*, *p* and *q* are all positive

13. **Match the Column I (magnitude of vectors *A* and *B*) with column II (relationship between *A* and *B*) and select the correct answer from the options given below.**

Column I	Column II
A. $\xrightarrow{\|A\|=l}\xrightarrow{\|B\|=2l}$	P. $A = -B$
B. $\xrightarrow{\|A\|=l}\xleftarrow{\|B\|=l}$	Q. $A = B$
C. $\xrightarrow{\|A\|=2l}\xleftarrow{\|B\|=l}$	R. $2A = B$
D. $\xrightarrow{\|A\|=l}\xrightarrow{\|B\|=l}$	S. $A = -2B$

(a) A-P, B-Q, C-R, D-S (b) A-S, B-P, C-Q, D-R
(c) A-R, B-P, C-S, D-Q (d) A-R, B-S, C-P, D-Q

14. **A particle moves in a plane with a constant acceleration in a direction different from initial velocity. The path of the particle is**

(a) a straight line (b) an arc of the circle
(c) a parabola (d) an ellipse

15. **Given below in Column I are the relations between vectors a, b and c and in Column II are the orientations of a, b and c in the *XY*- plane. Match the relation in Column I to correct orientations in Column II.**

Column I	Column II
A. $\mathbf{a} + \mathbf{b} = \mathbf{c}$	P. 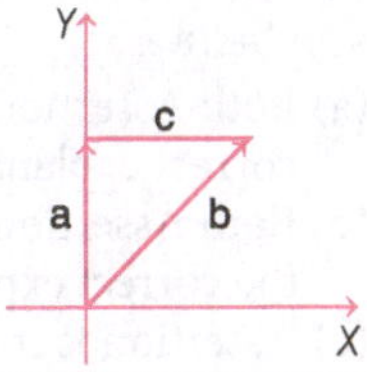
B. $\mathbf{a} - \mathbf{c} = \mathbf{b}$	Q. 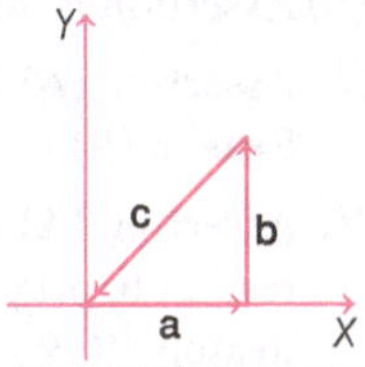
C. $\mathbf{b} - \mathbf{a} = \mathbf{c}$	R. 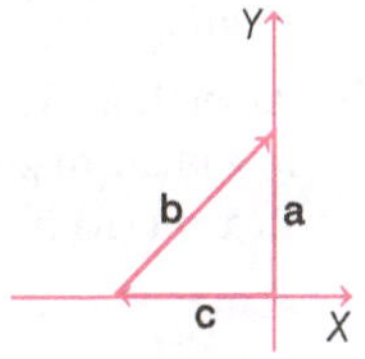
D. $\mathbf{a} + \mathbf{b} + \mathbf{c} = 0$	S. 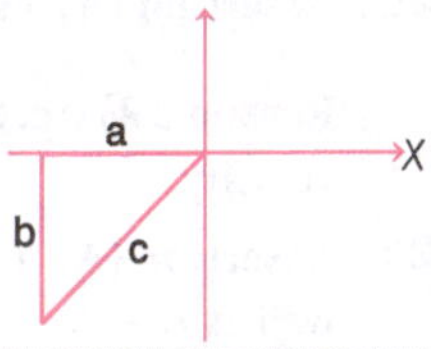

NCERT Exemplar

(a) A-S, B-R, C-P, D-Q
(b) A-Q, B-P, C-R, D-S
(c) A-P, B-Q, C-S, D-R
(d) A-R, B-S, C-P, D-Q

16. **If $|\mathbf{A}| = 2$ and $|\mathbf{B}| = 4$, then match the relations in Column I with the angle θ between *A* and *B* in Column II.**

	Column I		Column II
(A)	$\|\mathbf{A} \times \mathbf{B}\| = 0$	P.	$\theta = 30°$
(B)	$\|\mathbf{A} \times \mathbf{B}\| = 8$	Q.	$\theta = 45°$
(C)	$\|\mathbf{A} \times \mathbf{B}\| = 4$	R.	$\theta = 90°$
(D)	$\|\mathbf{A} \times \mathbf{B}\| = 4\sqrt{2}$	S.	$\theta = 0°$

NCERT Exemplar

(a) A-P, B-R, C-S, D-Q
(b) A-Q, B-P, C-R, D-S
(c) A-R, B-Q, C-S, D-P
(d) A-S, B-R, C-P, D-Q

Assertion and Reason

Direction *(Q.Nos. 17-26) In the following questions, two statements are given- one labelled Assertion (A) and the other labelled Reason (R). Select the correct answer to these questions from the codes (a), (b), (c) and (d) as given below.*

(a) Both Assertion and Reason are true and Reason is the correct explanation of Assertion.
(b) Both Assertion and Reason are true but Reason is not the correct explanation of Assertion.
(c) Assertion is true but Reason is false.
(d) Assertion is false but Reason is true.

17. **Assertion (A)** Force and area are vectors.
Reason (R) Pressure is a vector.

18. **Assertion (A)** Displacement vector is defined with respect to origin.
Reason (R) Position vector is defined with respect to origin.

19. **Assertion (A)** Minimum number of non-equal vectors in a plane to give zero resultant is three.
Reason (R) If $\mathbf{A} + \mathbf{B} + \mathbf{C} = \mathbf{0}$, then they must lie in one plane.

20. **Assertion (A)** The value of a_x depends on $\frac{dv}{dt}$.
Reason (R) Acceleration means rate of change of velocity.

21. **Assertion (A)** $\mathbf{A} \times \mathbf{B}$ is perpendicular to both $\mathbf{A} + \mathbf{B}$ as well as $\mathbf{A} - \mathbf{B}$.
Reason (R) $\mathbf{A} + \mathbf{B}$ as well as $\mathbf{A} - \mathbf{B}$ lie in the plane containing $\mathbf{A}$ and $\mathbf{B}$ but $\mathbf{A} \times \mathbf{B}$ lies perpendicular to the plane containing $\mathbf{A}$ and $\mathbf{B}$.

22. **Assertion (A)** When a body is dropped or thrown horizontally from the same height, it would reach the ground at the same time.
Reason (R) Horizontal velocity has no effect on the vertical direction.

23. **Assertion (A)** The maximum horizontal range of projectile is proportional to square of velocity.
Reason (R) Maximum horizontal range of projectile is equal to maximum height attained by projectile.

24. **Assertion (A)** The range of a projectile is maximum at 45°.
Reason (R) At $\theta = 45°$, the value of $\sin\theta$ is maximum.

25. **Assertion (A)** Speed is constant in uniform circular motion.
Reason (R) Acceleration is constant in uniform circular motion.

26. **Assertion (A)** If the speed of a body is constant, the body cannot have a path other than a circular or straight line path.
Reason (R) It is not possible for a body to have a constant speed in an acceleration motion.

Case Based Questions

Directions *(Q.Nos. 27-28) These questions are case study based questions. Read the following paragraph and answer the questions on the basis of same.*

27. **Projectile motion is a form of motion in which an object or particle is thrown with some initial velocity near the earth's surface and it moves along a curved path under the action of gravity alone. The path followed by a projectile is called its trajectory, which is shown below.**

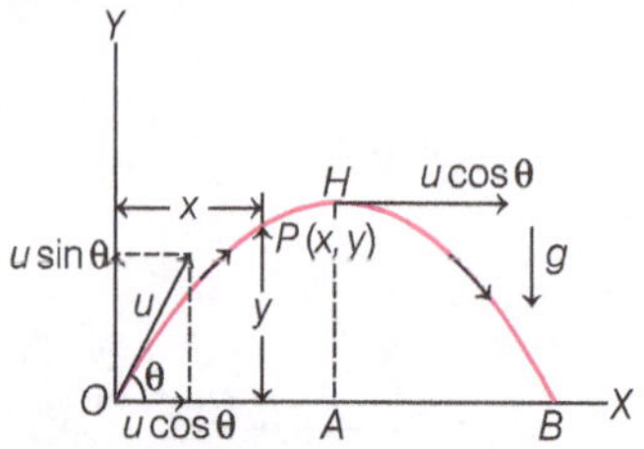

While resolving velocity (u) into two components, we get $u\cos\theta$ along OX and $u\sin\theta$ along OY.

(i) The example of such type of motion is
(a) motion of car on a banked road
(b) motion of boat in sea
(c) a javelin thrown by an athlete
(d) motion of ball thrown vertically upward

(ii) The acceleration of the object in horizontal direction is
(a) constant (b) decreasing
(c) increasing (d) zero

(iii) The vertical component of velocity at point H is
(a) maximum
(b) zero
(c) double to that at O
(d) equal to horizontal component

(iv) A cricket ball is thrown at a speed of 28 m/s in a direction 30° with the horizontal.
The time taken by the ball to return to the same level will be
(a) 2.0 s (b) 3.0 s
(c) 4.0 s (d) 2.9 s

(v) In above case, the distance from the thrower to the point where the ball returns to the same level will be
(a) 39 m (b) 69 m
(c) 68 m (d) 72 m

28. **When an object follows a circular path at a constant speed, the motion of the object is called uniform circular motion. The word uniform refers to the speed which is uniform (constant) throughout the motion. Although, the speed does not vary, the particle is accelerating because the velocity changes its direction at every point on the circular track.**

The figure shows a particle P which moves along a circular track of radius r with a uniform speed v.

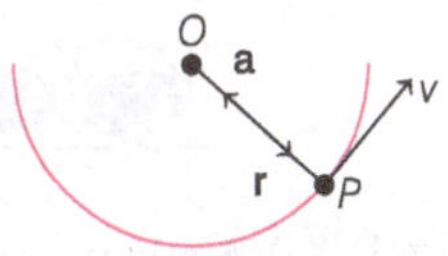

(i) A circular motion
   (a) is one-dimensional motion
   (b) is two-dimensional motion
   (c) it is represented by combination of two variable vectors
   (d) Both (b) and (c)

(ii) The displacement of a particle moving on a circular path when it makes 60° at the centre is
   (a) $2r$ (b) r
   (c) $\sqrt{2}r$ (d) None of these

(iii) A particle is moving with a constant speed v in a circle. What is the magnitude of average velocity after half rotation?
   (a) $2v$ (b) $\frac{2v}{\pi}$
   (c) $\frac{v}{2}$ (d) $\frac{v}{2\pi}$

(iv) What is the centripetal acceleration of a point mass which is moving on a circular path of radius 5 m with speed 23 ms^{-1}?
   (a) 106 ms^{-2} (b) 90 ms^{-2}
   (c) 60 ms^{-2} (d) None of these

29. **A vector quantity is a quantity that has both magnitude and direction and obeys vector law of addition.**

Let A and B be two vectors in a plane, then their vector sum A + B is shown in adjoining figure.

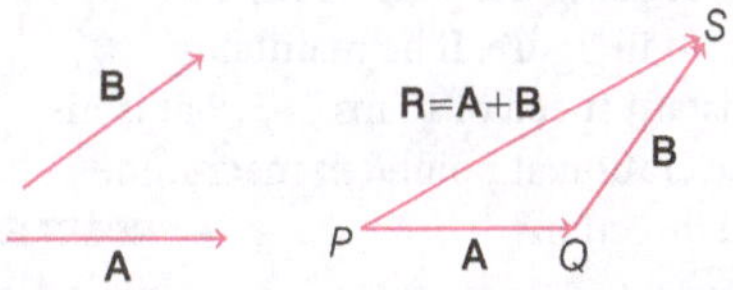

The vector sum of two vector is also known as their resultant vector R. Since in the procedure of vector addition shown, vectors are arranged head to tail method. Since the two vectors and their resultant form three sides of a triangle, this method is also known as triangle method of vector addition.

(i) What is the expression for magnitude of resultant of the two vectors **A** and **B** in terms of their magnitude and angle θ between them?

(ii) Under what condition the magnitude of sum of two vector is equal to sum of magnitudes of these vectors?

(iii) What is the angle between two vectors **A** and **B** when $|\mathbf{A}+\mathbf{B}| = |\mathbf{A}-\mathbf{B}|$?

(iv) Two vectors, both equal in magnitude have their resultant equal in magnitude of either. Find the angle between these vector.

Subjective Questions

Very Short Type Questions

1. Can the walking on a road be an example of resolution of vectors?

2. The direction of the oblique projectile becomes horizontal at the maximum height. What is the cause of it?

3. Why does a tennis ball bounce higher on hills than in plains?

4. A stone is thrown vertically upwards and then it returns to the thrower. Is it a projectile?

5. Can a body move on a curved path without having acceleration? Why?

Short Answer Type Questions

6. (a) A force of $(7\hat{i} + 6\hat{k})$ N makes a body move on a rough plane with a velocity of $(3\hat{i} + 4\hat{k})$ ms^{-1}. Calculate the power (in watt). **[1½]**

(b) The sum and difference of two vectors are perpendicular to each other. Prove that the vectors are equal in magnitude. **[1½]**

7. (a) Two vectors of magnitude 3 units and 4 units are at angle 60° between them. Find the magnitude of their difference. **[1½]**

(b) Determine the vector joining the points $A(2, 3, 0)$ and $B(-1, -2, -4)$ directed from A to B. **[1½]**

8. Galileo, in his book 'Two new sciences', stated that "for elevations which exceed or fall short of 45° by equal amounts, the ranges are equal." Prove this statement. **NCERT**

9. (a) A cyclist starts from centre O of a circular park of radius 1 km and moves along the path $OPRQO$ as shown in figure. If he maintains constant speed of $10\ ms^{-1}$, what is his acceleration at point R in magnitude and direction? **NCERT Exemplar** [1½]

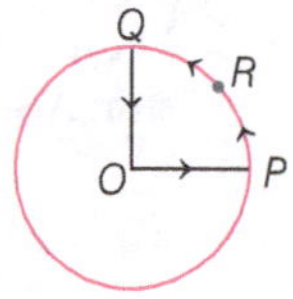

(b) A particle is projected in air at some angle to the horizontal, moves along parabola as shown in figure where x and y indicate horizontal and vertical directions, respectively. Show the direction of velocity and acceleration at points A, B and C. **NCERT Exemplar**

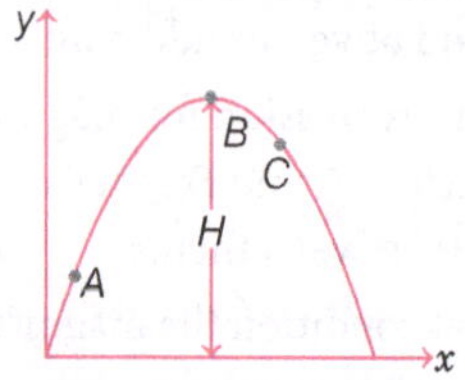

[1½]

10. (a) A boy travelling in an open car moving on a levelled road with constant speed tosses a ball vertically up in the air and catches it back. Sketch the motion of the ball as observed by a boy standing on the footpath. Give explanation to support your diagram. **NCERT Exemplar** [1½]

(b) A boy throws a ball in air at 60° to the horizontal along a road with a speed of 10 m/s (36 km/h). Another boy sitting in a passing car observes the ball. Sketch the motion of the ball as observed by the boy in the car, if car has a speed of (18km/h). Give explanation to support your diagram. [1½] **NCERT Exemplar**

11. (a) In dealing with motion of projectile in air, we ignore effect of air resistance on motion. This gives trajectory as a parabola as you have studied. What would the trajectory look like if air resistance is include? Sketch such a trajectory and explain why you have drawn it that way? **NCERT Exemplar** [1½]

(b) Suppose you are driving in a convertible car with the top removed. The car is moving to the right at a constant velocity. As the figure illustrates, you point a toy rifle straight upward and trigger it. In the absence of air resistance, where would the bullet land (i) behind you, (ii) ahead of you or (iii) in the barrel of the rifle? **Competency Based Que.** [1½]

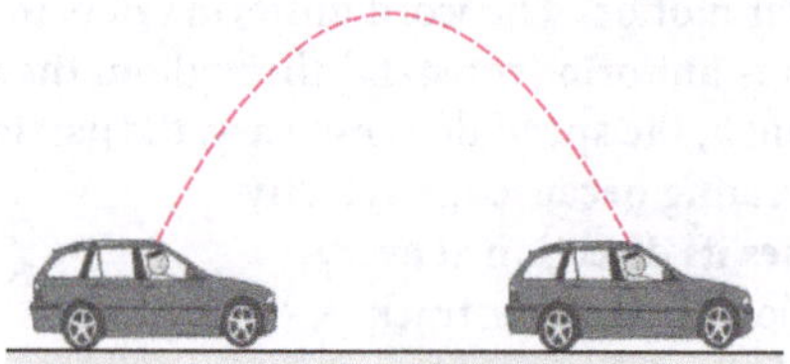

12. (a) A rabbit runs across a parking lot on which a set of coordinates axes has been drawn. The coordinates (in metres) of the rabbit's position as functions of time t (in seconds) are given by
$x = -0.31t^2 + 7.2t + 28$ and $y = 0.22t^2 - 9.1t + 30$
At $t = 15$ s, what is the rabbit's position vector **r** in unit vector notation and in magnitude angle notation?
(i) Draw a graph for rabbit's path for $t = 0$ to 25 s.
(ii) Find the rabbit's velocity **v** at time $t = 15$ s.
(iii) Find the rabbit's acceleration $\boldsymbol{a}$ at time $t = 15$ s. **Competency Based Que.** [1½]

(b) A stone tied at the end of string is whirled in a circle. If the string breaks, the stone flies away tangentially. Why? [1½]

13. A fighter plane is flying horizontally at an altitude of 1.5 km with speed 720 km/h. At what angle of sight (w.r.t. horizontal) when the target is seen, should the pilot drop the bomb in order to attack the target?

14. Earth can be thought of as a sphere of radius 6400 km. Any object (or a person) is performing circular motion around the axis of the earth due to the earth rotation (period 1 day). What is acceleration of object on the surface of the earth (at equator) towards its centre? What is its latitude θ? How does these accelerations compare with $g = 9.8\ m/s^2$?

Long Answer Type Questions

15. (i) $\hat{i}$ and $\hat{j}$ are unit vectors along X and Y-axes, respectively. What is the magnitude and direction of vectors $\hat{i} + \hat{j}$ and $\hat{i} - \hat{j}$? [1½]

(ii) What are the components of a vector $\mathbf{A} = 2\hat{i} + 3\hat{j}$ along the direction $\hat{i} + \hat{j}$ and $\hat{i} - \hat{j}$? (You may use graphical method). [2]

(iii) The modulus of a vector $\mathbf{A} = A_x\hat{\mathbf{i}} + A_y\hat{\mathbf{j}}$ is given by $A = |\mathbf{A}| = \sqrt{A_x^2 + A_y^2}$. If vector is inclined at an angle θ, from X-axis, then $\tan\theta = \frac{A_y}{A}$

Competency Based Que. [1½]

16. (a) Prove that the path of one projectile as seen from another projectile is a straight line. [2½]

(b) A man rows directly across a flowing river in time t_1 and rows an equal distance down the stream in time t_2. If u be the speed of man in still water and v that of stream, then show that

$$t_1 : t_2 = \sqrt{u+v} : \sqrt{u-v}$$ [2½]

17. If R is the horizontal range for θ inclination and h is the maximum height reached by the projectile, show that the maximum range is given by $\frac{R^2}{8h} + 2h$.

18. A hunter aims his gun and fires a bullet directly at a monkey on a tree. At the instant, the bullet leaves the barrel of the gun, the monkey drops. Will the bullet hit the monkey? Substantiate your answer with proper reasoning. **Competency Based Que.** [2½]

19. (a) On a certain day, rain was falling vertically with a speed of 35 m/s. A wind started blowing after sometime with a speed of 12 m/s in east to west direction. In which direction should a boy waiting at a bus stop hold his umbrella? **NCERT** [2½]

(b) If unit vectors $\hat{\mathbf{a}}$ and $\hat{\mathbf{b}}$ are inclined at an angle θ, then prove that $|\hat{\mathbf{a}} - \hat{\mathbf{b}}| = 2\sin\frac{\theta}{2}$. [2½]

20. (a) The position vector of a particle is

$$\mathbf{r} = 2.0\hat{\mathbf{i}} + t^2\hat{\mathbf{j}} + 3.0\hat{\mathbf{k}}$$

where, t is in seconds and the coefficients have the proper units for r to be in metres. What will be the value of $\mathbf{v}(t)$ and $\mathbf{a}(t)$ for the particle and the magnitude and direction of $v(t)$ at $t = 2.0$ s? [2]

(b) A vector has magnitude and direction.

(i) Does it have a location in the space? [1]

(ii) Can it vary with time? [1]

(iii) Will two equal vectors $\mathbf{a}$ and $\mathbf{b}$ at different locations in space necessarily have identical physical effects? Give examples in support of your answer. [1]

21. State with reasons, whether the following algebric operations with scalar and vector physical quantities are meaningful.

(i) Adding any two scalars [1]

(ii) Adding a scalar to a vector of the same dimensions [½]

(iii) Multiplying any vector by any scalar [1]

(iv) Multiplying any two scalars [1]

(v) Adding any two vectors [½]

(vi) Adding a component of a vector to the same vector **NCERT** [1]

22. Establish the following inequalities geometrically or otherwise.

(i) $|\mathbf{A}+\mathbf{B}| \le |\mathbf{A}| + |\mathbf{B}|$ (ii) $|\mathbf{A}+\mathbf{B}| \ge ||\mathbf{A}| - |\mathbf{B}||$ [2½]

(iii) $|\mathbf{A}-\mathbf{B}| \le |\mathbf{A}| + |\mathbf{B}|$ (iv) $|\mathbf{A}-\mathbf{B}| \ge ||\mathbf{A}| - |\mathbf{B}||$ [2½]

When does the equality sign above apply? **NCERT**

23. A particle is projected in air at an angle β to a surface which itself is inclined at an angle α to the horizontal (figure).

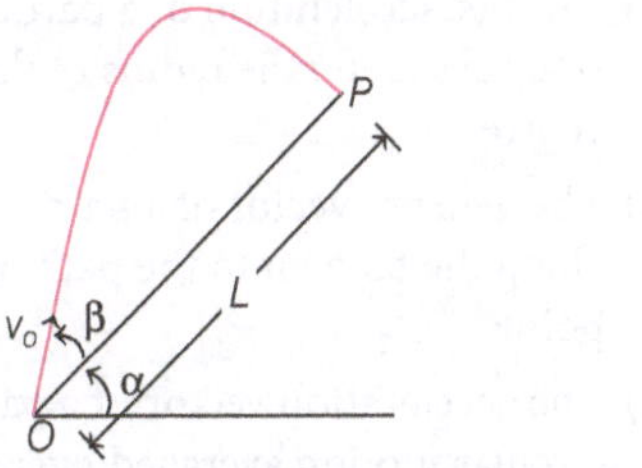

(a) Find an expression of range on the plane surface (distance on the plane from the point of projection at which particle will hit the surface). [2]

(b) Time of flight. [1]

(c) β at which range will be maximum.?

Competency Based Que., NCERT Exemplar [2]

24. (a) Read each statement below carefully and state with reasons, if it is true or false.

(i) The magnitude of a vector is always a scalar. [1/2]

(ii) Each component of a vector is always a scalar. [1/2]

(iii) The average speed of a particle (defined as total path length divided by the time taken to cover the path) is either greater or equal to the magnitude of average velocity of the particle over the same interval of time. [1] **NCERT**

(b) The range of a rifle bullet is 1000 m, when θ is the angle of projection. If the bullet is fired with the same angle from a car travelling at 36 km/h towards the target, show that the range will be increased by $142.9\sqrt{\tan\theta}$ m.

When the bullet is fired from the moving car, the horizontal component velocity of the bullet increases with the velocity of car. But the vertical component of the velocity remains unaffected.

Competency Based Que. [3]

25. (a) A stone tied to the end of a string 80 cm long is whirled in a horizontal circle with a constant speed. If the stone makes 14 revolutions in 25 s, what is the magnitude and direction of acceleration of the stone? **NCERT [2½]**

In uniform circular motion, a centripetal acceleration $a_c = \frac{v^2}{r} = r\omega^2$ acts on the body, whose direction is always towards the centre of the path.

(b) An aircraft executes a horizontal loop of radius 1 km with a steady speed of 900 km h^{-1}. Compare its centripetal acceleration with the acceleration due to gravity. **[2½] NCERT**

26. Read each statement below carefully and state, with reasons, if it is true or false.

(i) The net acceleration of a particle in circular motion is always along the radius of the circle towards the centre. **[2]**

(ii) The velocity vector of a particle at a point is always along the tangent to the path of the particle at that point. **[1]**

(iii) The acceleration vector of a particle in uniform circular motion averaged over one cycle is a null vector. **NCERT [2]**

Numerical Problems

Vectors

27. The greatest and the least resultant of two forces acting at a point are 29 N and 5 N, respectively. If each force is increased by 3 N. Find the resultant of two new forces acting at right angle to each other.

28. In a harbour, wind is blowing at the speed of 72 km/h and the flag on the mast of a boat anchored in the harbour flutters along the north-east direction. If the boat starts moving at a speed of 51 km/h to the north, what is the direction of flag on the mast of the boat? **NCERT**

29. Two billiard balls are rolling on a flat table. One has the velocity components $v_x = 1\ ms^{-1}$, $v_y = \sqrt{3}\ ms^{-1}$ and the other has components $v'_x = 2\ ms^{-1}$ and $v'_y = 2\ ms^{-1}$. If both the balls start moving from the same point, what is the angle between their paths? **Competency Based Que**

30. A ball rolls of the top of a stairway with horizontal velocity of 1.8 m/s. The steps are 0.24 m high and 0.2 m wide. Which step will the ball hit first? Take, $g = 9.8\ m/s^2$

31. A girl riding a bicycle with a speed of 5 m/s towards north direction, observes rain falling vertically down. If she increases her speed to 10 m/s, rain appears to meet her at 45° to the vertical. What is the speed of the rain? In what direction does rain fall as observed by a ground based observer? **NCERT Exemplar**

32. A river is flowing due east with a speed of 3 m/s. A swimmer can swim in still water at a speed of 4 m/s.

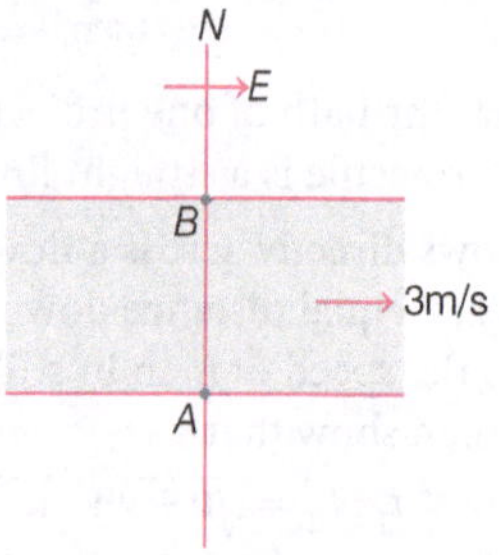

(a) If swimmer starts swimming due north, then what will be his resultant velocity (magnitude and direction)? **[1]**

(b) If he wants to start from point A on south bank and reach opposite point B on north bank,

(i) what will be his resultant speed? **[1/2]**

(ii) which direction should he swim? **[1/2]**

(c) From two different cases as mentioned in (a) and (b) above, in which case will he reach opposite bank in shorter time? **NCERT Exemplar [1]**

33. A particle starts from the origin at $t = 0$ with a velocity of $10.0\,\hat{j}$ m/s and moves in the XY-plane with a constant acceleration of $(8.0\,\hat{i} + 2.0\,\hat{j})\ ms^{-2}$.

(i) At what time the x-coordinate of the particle is 16 m? What is the y-coordinate of the particle at that time ? **[1½]**

(ii) What is the speed of the particle at that time? **NCERT [1½]**

Projectile Motion

34. A cricketer car throw a ball to a maximum horizontal distance of 100 m. With the same speed, how high above the ground can the cricketer throw the same ball?

35. The ceiling of a long hall is 25 m high. What is the maximum horizontal distance that a ball thrown with a speed of 40 m/s can go without hitting the ceiling of the hall? **NCERT**

Maximum height attained by a projectile is given by $H = \frac{u^2 \sin^2\theta}{2g}$ and horizontal range is given by

$R = \frac{u^2 \sin 2\theta}{g}$.

36. A fighter plane flying horizontally at an altitude of 1.5 km with speed 720 km h^{-1} passes directly over an anti-craft gun. At what angle from the vertical should the gun be fired from the shell with muzzle speed 600 ms^{-1} to hit the plane? At what minimum altitude should the pilot fly the plane to avoid being hit? (Take, $g = 10 \text{ ms}^{-2}$) **Competency Based Que.**

37. (i) Show that for a projectile, the angle between the velocity and the X-axis as function of time is given by

$$\theta_{(t)} = \tan^{-1}\left(\frac{v_{oy} - gt}{v_{ox}}\right)$$ **[2½]**

where, the various symbols have their usual meanings.

(ii) Show that projection angle θ_0 for a projectile launched from the origin is given by

$$\theta_0 = \tan^{-1}\left(\frac{4h_m}{R}\right)$$

where the symbols have their usual meanings. **[2½]**

38. Around 1939-1940, Emanuel Zacchini took human-cannon ball act to an extreme. After being shot from a cannon, it soared over three Ferris wheels and into a net as shown in figure. Assume that it is launched with a speed of 26.5 m/s and at an angle of 53.0°.

(i) Treating it as a particle, calculate its clearance over the first wheel. **[1]**

(ii) If he reached maximum height over the middle wheel, by how much did he clear it? **[1]**

(iii) How far from the cannon should the net's centre have been positioned (neglect air drag)? **Competency Based Que.** **[1]**

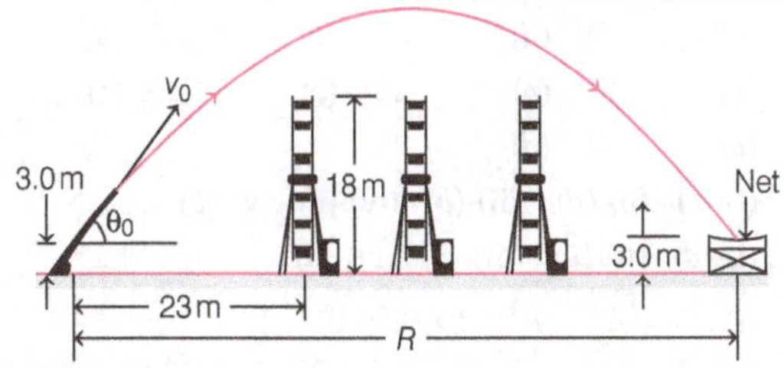

39. A dart is thrown horizontally with an initial speed of 10 m/s toward point P, the bull's eyes on a dart board. It hits at point Q on the rim, vertically below P, 0.19 s later. (i) What is the distance PQ? (ii) How far away from the dart board is the dart released? **Competency Based Que.**

40. A rifle that shoots bullets at 460 m/s is to aim at a target 45.7 m away. If the centre of the target is level with the rifle, how high above the target must the rifle barrel be pointed so that the bullet hits dead centre?

41. Water from a sprinkler comes out with a constant velocity u in all the directions. What is the maximum area of the grassland that can be watered at any time? **Competency Based Que.**

42. A bullet P is fired from a gun when the angle of elevation of the gun is 30°. Another bullet Q is fired from the gun when the angle of elevation is 60°. The vertical height attained in the second case is x times the vertical height attained in the first case. What is the value of x?

43. A hill is 500 m high. Supplies are to be sent across the hill using a canon that can hurl packets at a speed of 125 m/s over the hill. The canon is located at a distance of 800 m from the foot of hill and can be moved on the ground at a speed of 2 m/s, so that its distance from the hill can be adjusted. What is the shortest time in which a packet can reach on the ground across the hill? Take, $g = 10 \text{ m/s}^2$. **NCERT Exemplar**

Circular Motion

44. Earth moves in circular orbit around the sun once every year with an orbital radius of 1.5×10^{11} m. What is the acceleration of the earth (or any object on the surface of the earth) towards the centre of the sun? How does this acceleartion compare with $g = 9.8 \text{ m/s}^2$? **NCERT Exemplar**

45. When a large star becomes a supernova, its core may be compressed so tightly that it becomes a neutron star, with a radius of about 20 km. If a neutron star rotates once every second, what is the

(i) speed of a particle on the star's equator and **[1]**

(ii) Magnitude of the particle's centripetal acceleration? **[1]**

(iii) If the neutron star rotates faster, do the answer to (i) and (ii) increase, decrease or remain the same? **[1]**

46. A woman rides a carnival ferris wheel at radius 15 m, completing five turns about its horizontal axis every minute. What are

(i) the period of the motion, **[1]**

(ii) the magnitude, and **[1]**

(iii) direction of her centripetal acceleration at the highest point, **[1]**

(iv) magnitude and **[1]**

(v) direction of her centripetal acceleration at the lowest point? **[1]**

47. A cyclist starts from the centre O of a circular park of radius 1 km, reaches the edge P of the park, then cycles along the circumference and returns to the centre along QO as shown. If the round trip takes 10 min, what is the

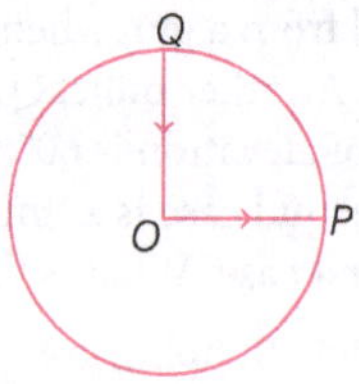

(a) net displacement,
(b) average velocity and
(c) average speed of the cyclist?

48. On an open ground, a motorist follows a track that turns to his left by an angle of 60° after every 500 m. Starting from a given turn, specify the displacement of the motorist at the third, sixth and eighth turn. Compare the magnitude of the displacement with the total path length covered by the motorist in each case.

Competency Based Que.

49. A cyclist is riding with a speed of 27 kmh^{-1}. As he approaches a circular turn on the road of radius 80 m, he applies brakes and reduces his speed at the constant rate of 0.5 ms^{-2}. What is the magnitude and direction of the net acceleration of the cyclist on the circular turn?

Hints & Solutions

Objective Type Questions

1. *(b)* 2. *(b)* 3. *(c)* 4. *(b)* 5. *(c)*
6. *(c)* 7. *(b)* 8. *(d)* 9. *(b)* 10. *(b)*
11. *(c)* 12. *(b)* 14. *(b)*

13. (c) (A) As, $|\mathbf{B}| = 2|\mathbf{A}|$ and they both are in the same direction, so $2\mathbf{A} = \mathbf{B}$.

(B) As, $|\mathbf{A}| = |\mathbf{B}|$ and but both are in opposite direction, so $\mathbf{A} = -\mathbf{B}$.

(C) As, $|\mathbf{A}| = 2|\mathbf{B}|$ but both are in opposite direction, so $\mathbf{A} = -2\mathbf{B}$.

(D) $|\mathbf{A}| = |\mathbf{B}|$ and both are in same direction, so $\mathbf{A} = \mathbf{B}$.

Hence, A-R, B-P, C-S, D-Q

15. (*a*) Consider the adjacent diagram in which vectors **A** and **B** are corrected by head and tail.

Resultant vector $\mathbf{c} = \mathbf{a} + \mathbf{b}$

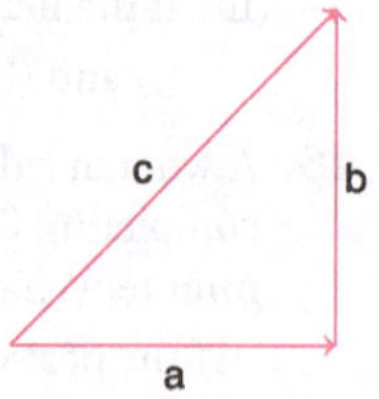

(A) from (S) it is clear that $\mathbf{c} = \mathbf{a} + \mathbf{b}$

(B) from (R) $\mathbf{c} + \mathbf{b} = \mathbf{a} \Rightarrow \mathbf{a} - \mathbf{c} = \mathbf{b}$

(C) from (P) $\mathbf{b} = \mathbf{a} + \mathbf{c} \Rightarrow \mathbf{b} - \mathbf{a} = \mathbf{c}$

(D) from (Q) $-\mathbf{c} = \mathbf{a} + \mathbf{b} \Rightarrow \mathbf{a} + \mathbf{b} + \mathbf{c} = 0$

16. (*d*) Given $|\mathbf{A}| = 2$ and $|\mathbf{B}| = 4$

(A) $|\mathbf{A} \times \mathbf{B}| = AB\sin\theta = 0 \Rightarrow 2 \times 4 \times \sin\theta = 0$

$\Rightarrow \sin\theta = 0 = \sin 0° \Rightarrow \theta = 0°$

∴ Option (A) matches with option (S).

(B) $|\mathbf{A} \times \mathbf{B}| = AB\sin\theta = 8 \Rightarrow 2 \times 4\sin\theta = 8$

$\Rightarrow \sin\theta = 1 = \sin 90° \Rightarrow \theta = 90°$

∴ Option (B) matches with option (R).

(C) $|\mathbf{A} \times \mathbf{B}| = AB\sin\theta = 4 \Rightarrow 2 \times 4\sin\theta = 4$

$\Rightarrow \sin\theta = \frac{1}{2} = \sin 30° \Rightarrow \theta = 30°$

∴ Option (C) matches with option (P).

(D) $|\mathbf{A} \times \mathbf{B}| = AB\sin\theta = 4\sqrt{2} \Rightarrow 2 \times 4\sin\theta = 4\sqrt{2}$

$\Rightarrow \sin\theta = \frac{1}{\sqrt{2}} = \sin 45° \Rightarrow \theta = 45°$

∴ Option (D) matches with option (Q).

17. (c) 18. (*d*) 19. (*b*) 20. (*d*)
21. (*a*) 22. (*a*) 23. (*c*) 24. (*c*)
25. (c) 26. (*d*)
27. (i)-(*c*) (ii)-(*d*) (iii)-(*b*) (iv)-(*d*) (v)-(*b*)
28. (i)-(*d*) (ii)-(*b*) (iii)-(*b*) (iv)-(*a*)
29. (i) $R = \sqrt{A^2 + B^2 + 2AB\cos\theta}$

(ii) When two vectors are in same direction $\theta = 0°$

$$R = \sqrt{A^2 + B^2 + 2AB\cos 0°}$$
$$= \sqrt{(A+B)^2} = A + B$$

(iii) $|\mathbf{A} + \mathbf{B}| = |\mathbf{A} - \mathbf{B}|$

It is possible only when **A** and **B** are in mutually perpendicular direction. So, $\theta = 90°$.

(iv) $R = \sqrt{P^2 + Q^2 + 2PQ\cos\theta}$

$$R = P = Q \quad \text{(given)}$$
$$P = \sqrt{P^2 + P^2 + 2P^2\cos\theta}$$
$$\cos\theta = -\frac{1}{2}$$
$$\theta = 120°$$

Subjective Questions

1. Yes, when a man walks on the road, he presses the road along an oblique direction. The horizontal component of the reaction helps the man to walk on the road.
2. At the maximum height of projectile, the vertical component of velocity becomes zero and only horizontal component of velocity of projectile is there.
3. Maximum height attained by a projectile $\propto 1/g$. As the value of g is less on hills than on plains, so a tennis ball bounces higher on hills than on plains.
4. No, it is not a projectile, because a projectile should have two component velocities in two mutually perpendicular directions, but in this case, the body has velocity only in one direction while going up or coming down.
5. No, a body cannot move on a curved path without acceleration because while moving on a curved path, the velocity of the body changes with time as the direction changes at each point.
6. (a) Using $\hat{\mathbf{k}} \cdot \hat{\mathbf{k}} = 1, \hat{\mathbf{i}} \cdot \hat{\mathbf{j}} = 0$

∴ Power, $P = \mathbf{F} \cdot \mathbf{v} = (7\hat{\mathbf{i}} + 6\hat{\mathbf{k}}) \cdot (3\hat{\mathbf{i}} + 4\hat{\mathbf{k}})$

$= 21 + 24 = 45 \text{ W} \qquad [\because \hat{\mathbf{i}} \cdot \hat{\mathbf{k}} = 0]$

(b) As the vectors $\mathbf{A}+\mathbf{B}$ and $\mathbf{A}-\mathbf{B}$ are perpendicular to each other, therefore

$$(\mathbf{A} + \mathbf{B}) \cdot (\mathbf{A} - \mathbf{B}) = 0$$

$$\mathbf{A} \cdot \mathbf{A} - \mathbf{A} \cdot \mathbf{B} + \mathbf{B} \cdot \mathbf{A} - \mathbf{B} \cdot \mathbf{B} = 0$$

or $\mathbf{A} - \mathbf{B} = 0 \qquad [\because \mathbf{A} \cdot \mathbf{B} = \mathbf{B} \cdot \mathbf{A}]$

$\Rightarrow \mathbf{A} = \mathbf{B}$

7. (a) Let the vectors be $\mathbf{A}$ and $\mathbf{B}$.

Given, $|\mathbf{A}| = 3$ units, $|\mathbf{B}| = 4$ units and $\theta = 60°$

The magnitude of resultant of $\mathbf{A}$ and $\mathbf{B}$,

$$R = |\mathbf{R}| = \sqrt{A^2 + B^2 - 2AB\cos\theta}$$

$$= \sqrt{3^2 + 4^2 - 2 \times 3 \times 4 \cos 60°}$$

$$R = \sqrt{25 - 12}$$

$$= \sqrt{13} = 3.61 \text{ units}$$

(b) Given points are $A(2, 3, 0)$ and $B(-1, -2, -4)$.

Hence, the vector joining the point P and Q is given by

$$\mathbf{AB} = (-1-2)\hat{\mathbf{i}} + (-2-3)\hat{\mathbf{j}} + (-4-0)\hat{\mathbf{k}}$$

$$\mathbf{AB} = -3\hat{\mathbf{i}} - 5\hat{\mathbf{j}} - 4\hat{\mathbf{k}}$$

8. For a projectile launched with velocity v_0 at an angle θ_0, the range is given by $R = \dfrac{v_0^2 \sin 2\theta_0}{g}$. Now, for angles, $(45° + \alpha)$ and $(45° - \alpha)$, $2\theta_0$ is $(90° + 2\alpha)$ and $(90° - 2\alpha)$, respectively. The values of $\sin(90° + 2\alpha)$ and $\sin(90° - 2\alpha)$ are the same, equal to that of $\cos 2\alpha$. Therefore, ranges are equal for elevations which exceed or fall short of 45° by equal amount α.

9. (a) As shown in the adjacent figure. The cyclist covers the path $OPRQO$.

As we know whenever an object performing circular motion, acceleration is called centripetal acceleration and is always directed towards the centre.

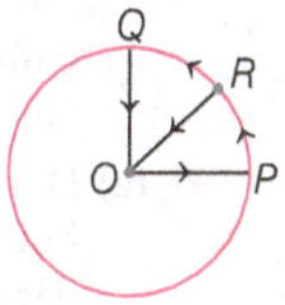

Hence, acceleration at R is $a = \dfrac{v^2}{r}$

$$\Rightarrow a = \frac{(10)^2}{1 \text{ km}} = \frac{100}{10^3} = 0.1 \text{ m/s}^2 \text{ along } RO.$$

(b) Consider the adjacent diagram in which a particle is projected at an angle θ.

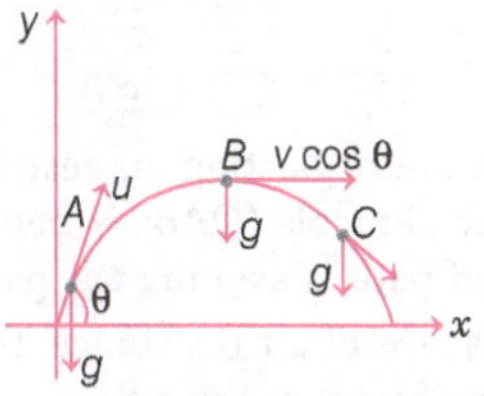

v_x = Horizontal component of velocity

$= v \cos\theta$ = constant.

v_y = Vertical component of velocity $= v \sin\theta$

Velocity will always be tangential to the curve in the direction of motion and acceleration is always vertically downward and is equal to g (acceleration due to gravity).

10. (a) The path of the ball observed by a boy standing on the footpath is parabolic. The horizontal speed of the ball is same as that of the car, therefore, ball as well as car travels equal horizontal distance. Due to its vertical speed, the ball follows a parabolic path.

(b) Consider the diagram below

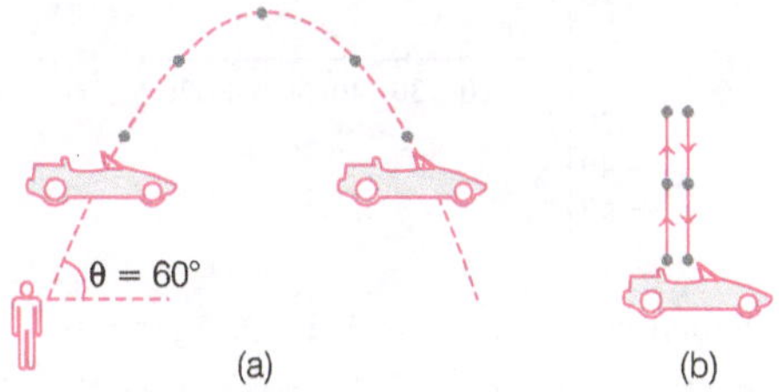

The boy throws the ball at an angle of 60°.

∴ Horizontal component of velocity $= u \cos\theta$

$$= (10 \text{ m/s}) \cos 60° = 10 \times \frac{1}{2} = 5 \text{ m/s}.$$

Speed of the car = 18 km/h = 5 m/s.

As horizontal speed of ball and car is same, hence relative velocity of car and ball in the horizontal direction will be zero.

Only vertical motion of the ball will be seen by the boy in the passing car, as shown in fig. (b)

11. (a) Due to air resistance, particle energy as well as horizontal component of velocity keep on decreasing making the fall steeper than rise as shown in the figure.

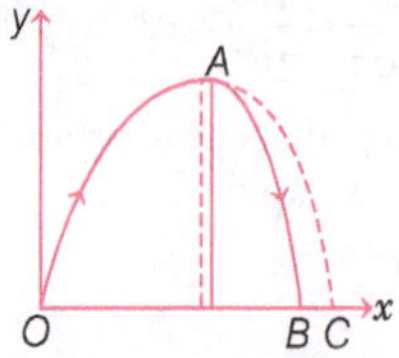

When we are neglecting air resistance path was symmetric parabola (*OAB*). When air resistance is considered path is asymmetric parabola (*OAC*).

(b) In the absence of air resistance, the bullet would land in the barrel of the rifle.

When we are moving in a convertible car with constant speed, so as per inertia, all the objects are moving with the same speed as that of convertible car. So, we can say that bullet when shot from the rifle, it's speed is same as that of convertible car in horizontal direction. We can say that if air friction is absent, then bullet will move the same horizontal distance as the distance moved by you in the convertible car. Therefore, it will reach again at the same position and the displacement of you and bullet is same in horizontal direction.

12. (a) Given $x(t) = -0.31t^2 + 7.2t + 28$

$$y(t) = 0.22\,t^2 - 9.1\,t + 30$$

$\therefore$ Rabbit position at $t = 15\text{s}$, $\mathbf{r} = 64\hat{\mathbf{i}} - 57\hat{\mathbf{j}}$

(i) Rabbit path

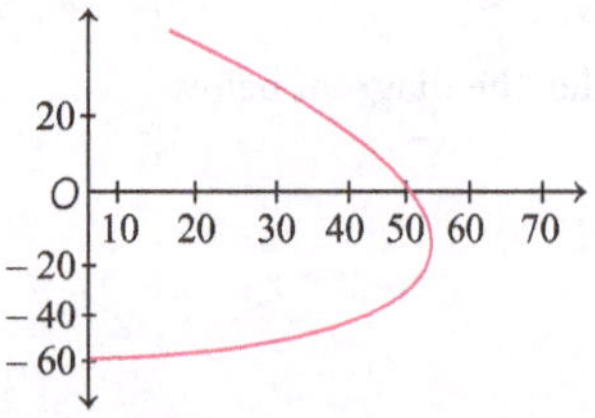

(ii) Rabbit velocity, $\mathbf{v} = -24\hat{\mathbf{i}} - 2.57\hat{\mathbf{j}}$ (m/s)

(iii) Rabbit acceleration, $\mathbf{a} = -0.64\hat{\mathbf{i}} + 0.44\hat{\mathbf{j}}$ (m/s^2)

(b) When a stone is going around a circular path, the instantaneous velocity of stone is acting as tangent to the circle. When the string breaks, the centripetal force stops to act. Due to inertia, the stone continues to move along the tangent to circular path. So, the stone flies off tangentially to the circular path.

13. Consider the adjacent diagram. Let a fighter plane, when it be at position *P*, drops a bomb to hit a target *T*. Let $\angle P'PT = \theta$

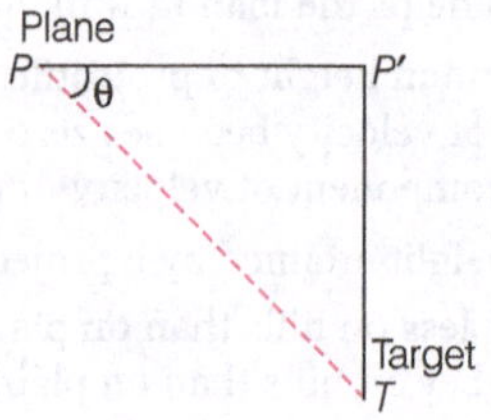

Speed of the plane $= 720 \text{ km/h} = 720 \times \frac{5}{18} \text{ m/s}$

$= 200$ m/s

Altitude of the plane $(P'T) = 1.5 \text{ km} = 1500$ m

If bomb hits the target after time *t*, then horizontal distance travelled by the bomb,

$$PP' = u \times t = 200t \quad \text{...(i)}$$

Vertical distance travelled by the bomb,

$$P'T = \frac{1}{2}gt^2 \Rightarrow 1500 = \frac{1}{2} \times 9.8\,t^2$$

$$\Rightarrow \quad t^2 = \frac{1500}{4.9} \Rightarrow t = \sqrt{\frac{1500}{4.9}} = 17.49 \text{ s}$$

Using value of *t* in Eq. (i),

$$PP' = 200 \times 17.49 \text{ m}$$

Now, $\tan\theta = \frac{P'T}{P'P} = \frac{1500}{200 \times 17.49} = .49287 = \tan 23^\circ 12'$

$$\theta = 23^\circ 12'$$

14. Radius of the earth $(R) = 6400 \text{ km} = 6.4 \times 10^6$ m

Time period $(T) = 1 \text{ day} = 24 \times 60 \times 60 \text{ s} = 86400$ s

Centripetal acceleration $(a_c) = \omega^2 R = R\left(\frac{2\pi}{T}\right)^2 = \frac{4\pi^2 R}{T^2}$

$$= \frac{4 \times (22/7)^2 \times 6.4 \times 10^6}{(86400)^2}$$

$$= \frac{4 \times 484 \times 6.4 \times 10^6}{49 \times (86400)^2} = 0.034 \text{ m/s}^2$$

At equator, latitude $\theta = 0^\circ$

$$\therefore \quad \frac{a_c}{g} = \frac{0.034}{9.8} = \frac{1}{288}$$

15. (i) Magnitude of

$(\hat{\mathbf{i}} + \hat{\mathbf{j}}) = \sqrt{1^2 + 1^2} = \sqrt{2}$

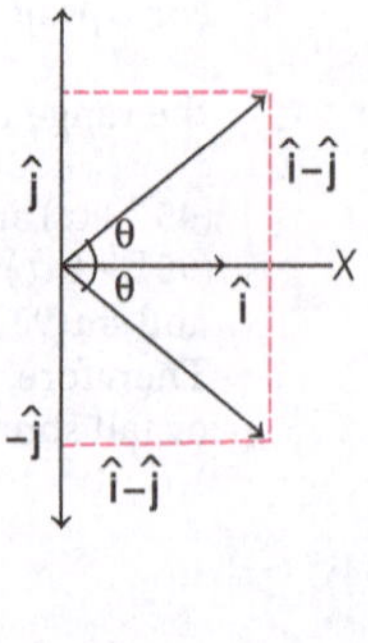

If vector $\hat{\mathbf{i}} + \hat{\mathbf{j}}$ makes an angle θ, with the *X*-axis, then

$$\tan\theta = \frac{A_y}{A_x} = \frac{1}{1} = 1 = \tan 45^\circ$$

or $\quad \theta = 45^\circ$

Magnitude of

$$\hat{\mathbf{i}} - \hat{\mathbf{j}} = \sqrt{1^2 + (-1)^2} = \sqrt{2}$$

If vector $\hat{\mathbf{i}} - \hat{\mathbf{j}}$ makes an angle θ with X-axis,

then $\tan\theta = \dfrac{A_y}{A_x} = -\dfrac{1}{1} = -1$

$= -\tan 45^\circ \Rightarrow \theta = -45^\circ$ with $\hat{\mathbf{i}}$

Hence, vector $(\hat{\mathbf{i}} - \hat{\mathbf{j}})$ makes an angle of 45° from X-axis in negative direction.

(ii) To determine the component of $\mathbf{A} = 2\hat{\mathbf{i}} + 3\hat{\mathbf{j}}$ in the direction of $\hat{\mathbf{i}} + \hat{\mathbf{j}}$

Let $\quad \mathbf{B} = \hat{\mathbf{i}} + \hat{\mathbf{j}}$

$$\mathbf{A} \cdot \mathbf{B} = AB\cos\theta = (A\cos\theta) \cdot B$$

$$A\cos\theta = \frac{\mathbf{A} \cdot \mathbf{B}}{B}$$

$\therefore$ Magnitude of the component of A in the direction of

$$B = A\cos\theta = \frac{\mathbf{A} \cdot \mathbf{B}}{13} = \frac{(2\hat{\mathbf{i}} + 3\hat{\mathbf{j}})(\hat{\mathbf{i}} + \hat{\mathbf{j}})}{\sqrt{1^2 + 1^2}} = \frac{2+3}{\sqrt{2}} = \frac{5}{\sqrt{2}}$$

Unit vector along $(\hat{\mathbf{i}} + \hat{\mathbf{j}})$ = Magnitude of component of A in the direction of

$$(\hat{\mathbf{i}} - \hat{\mathbf{j}}) = \frac{(2\hat{\mathbf{i}} + 3\hat{\mathbf{j}})(\hat{\mathbf{i}} - \hat{\mathbf{j}})}{|\hat{\mathbf{i}} - \hat{\mathbf{j}}|} = \frac{2-3}{\sqrt{2}} = -\frac{1}{\sqrt{2}}$$

Unit vector along $\dfrac{(\hat{\mathbf{i}} - \hat{\mathbf{j}})}{|\hat{\mathbf{i}} - \hat{\mathbf{j}}|} = \dfrac{\hat{\mathbf{i}} - \hat{\mathbf{j}}}{\sqrt{2}}$

$\therefore$ Component of A along $(\hat{\mathbf{i}} - \hat{\mathbf{j}})$ = Magnitude of the component of A along

$$(\hat{\mathbf{i}} - \hat{\mathbf{j}}) = -\frac{1}{\sqrt{2}} \frac{(\hat{\mathbf{i}} - \hat{\mathbf{j}})}{\sqrt{2}} = -\frac{1}{2}(\hat{\mathbf{i}} - \hat{\mathbf{j}})$$

(iii) Modulus of a vector $\mathbf{A} = A_x\hat{\mathbf{i}} + A_y\hat{\mathbf{j}}$

The modulus of a vector is given by

$$|\mathbf{A}| = \sqrt{A_x^2 + A_y^2}$$

For $\quad A = 2\hat{\mathbf{i}} + 3\hat{\mathbf{j}}$

$$|A| = \sqrt{(2)^2 + (3)^2} = \sqrt{4+9} = \sqrt{13}$$

$\therefore$ The angle is calculated as :

$$\tan\theta = \frac{A_y}{A_x} = \frac{3}{2}$$

$$\theta = \tan^{-1}\left(\frac{3}{2}\right)$$

16. (a) The coordinates of first projectile as seen from the second projectile are

$$X = x_1 - x_2$$
$$= u_1\cos\theta_1 t - u_2\cos\theta_2 t$$
$$= (u_1\cos\theta_1 - u_2\cos\theta_2)\,t$$

Similarly, $\quad Y = y_1 - y_2$

$$Y = v_1\sin\theta_1 t - v_2\sin\theta_2 t$$
$$Y = t(v_1\sin\theta_1 - v_2\sin\theta_2)$$

$$\therefore \quad \frac{Y}{X} = \frac{(v_1\sin\theta_1 - v_2\sin\theta_2)\,t}{(u_2\cos\theta_1 - u_2\cos\theta_2)t}$$

$= m$, which is a constant.

$\because Y = mx + c$, which is the equation of a straight line.

(b) Resultant velocity across the river $= \sqrt{u^2 + v^2}$

Resultant velocity down the stream $= u + v$

Let s be the distance covered in each case.

$$\therefore \quad t_1 = \frac{s}{\sqrt{u^2 + v^2}} \quad \text{and} \quad t_2 = \frac{s}{u + v}$$

$$\therefore \quad \frac{t_1}{t_2} = \frac{u + v}{\sqrt{u^2 + v^2}}$$

On rationalising, we will get

$$\frac{t_1}{t_2} = \frac{\sqrt{u + v}}{\sqrt{u - v}}$$

Hence, it means if u be the speed of man in still water and v that of stream, then

$$t_1 : t_2 = \sqrt{u + v} : \sqrt{u - v}$$

17. Let us draw the following figures in order to have more understanding.

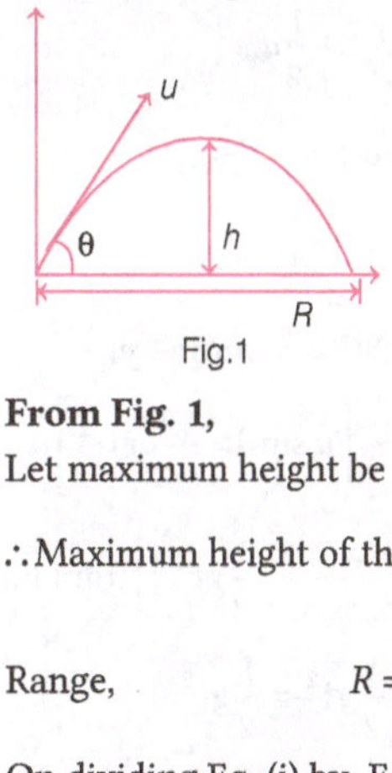

Fig.1

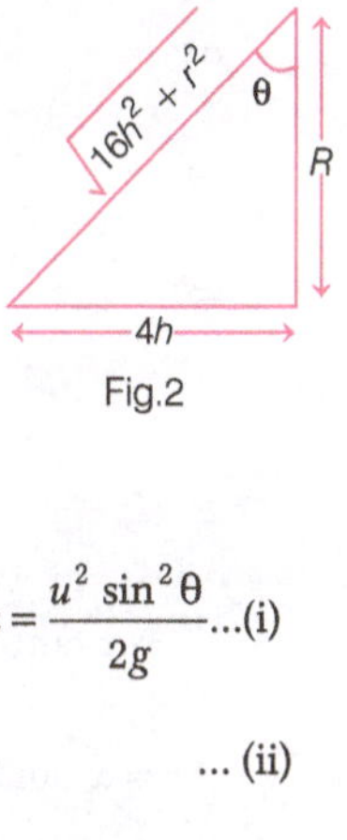

Fig.2

From Fig. 1,

Let maximum height be h.

$\therefore$ Maximum height of the projectile, $h = \dfrac{u^2\sin^2\theta}{2g}$ ...(i)

Range, $\quad R = \dfrac{u^2\sin 2\theta}{g}$ ... (ii)

On dividing Eq. (i) by Eq. (ii), we get

$$\frac{h}{R} = \frac{\sin^2\theta}{2\sin 2\theta} = \frac{\sin^2\theta}{2 \times 2\sin\theta \times \cos\theta} = \frac{\tan\theta}{4}$$

$$\frac{4h}{R} = \sin\theta \qquad \text{... (iii)}$$

From Fig. 2,

Consider Eq. (iii), we can write

$$\sin\theta = \frac{4h}{\sqrt{16h^2 + R^2}} \qquad \text{...(iv)}$$

For maximum range, $\theta = 45^\circ$

$$\Rightarrow \qquad R_{max} = \frac{u^2}{g} \qquad \text{...(v)}$$

From Eqs. (i), (iv) and (v), we get

$$h = \frac{R_{max} \times 16h^2}{2(16h^2 + R^2)} \Rightarrow R_{max} = 2h + \frac{R^2}{8h}$$

18. Let the monkey stationed at A, be fired with a gun from O with a velocity u at an angle θ with the horizontal direction OX.

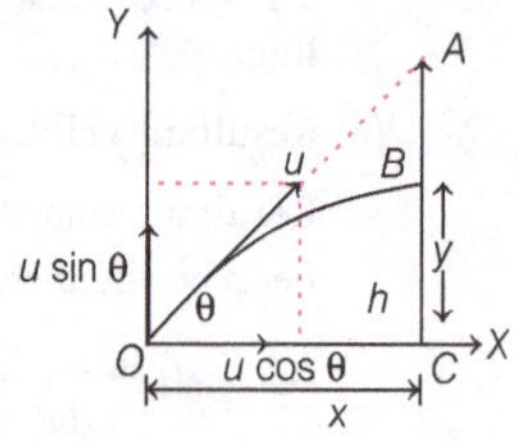

Draw AC, perpendicular to OX. Let the bullet cross the vertical line AC at B after time t and coordinates of $B(x, y)$ with respect to origin O as shown in the figure.

$$\therefore \qquad t = \frac{OC}{u\cos\theta} = \frac{x}{u\cos\theta} \qquad \text{...(i)}$$

[where, $OC = x$]

In ΔOAC, $AC = OC \tan\theta = x\tan\theta$ ...(ii)

Clearly, $CB = y$ = the vertical distance travelled by the bullet in time t.

Taking the motion of the bullet from O to B along X- axis, we have

$$y_o = 0,\ y = y,\ u_y,\ v\sin\theta\ a_y = -g,\ t = t$$

As $\qquad y = y_0 + v_y t + \frac{1}{2}a_y t^2$

$$\Rightarrow \qquad y = 0 + u\sin\theta\, t + \frac{1}{2}(-g)t^2$$

$$\Rightarrow \qquad y = u\sin\theta\, t - \frac{1}{2}gt^2 \qquad \text{... (iii)}$$

$$\therefore \qquad AB = AC - BC = x\tan\theta - y$$

$$= x\tan\theta - \left[u\sin\theta t - \frac{1}{2}gt^2\right]$$

$$= x\tan\theta - \left[u\sin\theta \times \frac{x}{u\cos\theta} - \frac{1}{2}gt^2\right] \text{[from Eq. (i)]}$$

$$AB = x\tan\theta - x\tan\theta + \frac{1}{2}gt^2 = \frac{1}{2}gt^2$$

It means the bullet will pass through the point B on line AC at a vertical distance $\frac{1}{2}gt^2$ below point A.

The distance through which the monkey falls vertically in time $t = \frac{1}{2}gt^2 = AB$. It means that, the bullet and monkey will pass through point B simultaneously. Therefore, the bullet will hit the monkey.

19. (a) In figure

Velocity of rain, $\mathbf{v}_R = \mathbf{OA} = 35$ m/s [vertically downward]

Velocity of wind, $\mathbf{v}_W = \mathbf{OB} = 12$ m/s [east to west]

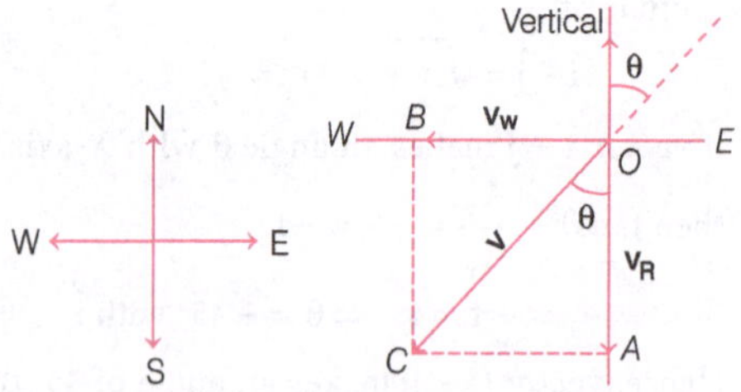

The magnitude of the resultant velocity,

$$v = \sqrt{(v_R)^2 + (v_W)^2} = \sqrt{(35)^2 + (12)^2} = 37\ \text{m/s}$$

Let the resultant velocity $\mathbf{v}(= \mathbf{OC})$ make an angle θ with the vertical, then,

$$\tan\theta = \frac{AC}{OA} = \frac{v_W}{v_R} = \frac{12}{35} = 0.343$$

$$\therefore \qquad \theta = \tan^{-1}(0.343) \simeq 19^\circ$$

Therefore, the boy should hold his umbrella in the vertical plane at an angle of about 19° with the vertical towards the east.

(b) For any vector $\mathbf{a} \Rightarrow |\mathbf{a}|^2 = \mathbf{a}\cdot\mathbf{a}$

$$\therefore \quad |\hat{a} - \hat{b}|^2 = (\hat{a} - \hat{b})\cdot(\hat{a} - \hat{b})$$

$$= \hat{a}\cdot\hat{a} - \hat{a}\cdot\hat{b} - \hat{b}\cdot\hat{a} + \hat{b}\cdot\hat{b}$$

$$= 1 - 2\hat{a}\cdot\hat{b} + 1 \qquad [\because \hat{a}\cdot\hat{a} = 1\times1\times\cos 0^\circ = 1]$$

$$= 2 - 2\times1\times1\times\cos\theta$$

$$= 2(1 - \cos\theta)$$

$$= 2\cdot 2\sin^2\frac{\theta}{2} = 4\sin^2\frac{\theta}{2} \quad [1 - \cos 2\theta = 2\sin^2\theta]$$

Hence, $|\hat{a} - \hat{b}| = 2\sin\frac{\theta}{2}$.

20. (a) The position vector, $\mathbf{r} = 2.0\hat{\mathbf{i}}t + t^2\hat{\mathbf{j}} + 3.0\hat{\mathbf{k}}$

$$\therefore \qquad \mathbf{v}(t) = \frac{d\mathbf{r}}{dt} = \frac{d}{dt}(2.0t\hat{\mathbf{i}} + t^2\hat{\mathbf{j}} + 3.0\hat{\mathbf{k}})$$

$$\mathbf{v}(t) = 2.0\hat{\mathbf{i}} + 2t\hat{\mathbf{j}}$$

$$\mathbf{a}(t) = \frac{d\mathbf{v}(t)}{dt} = \frac{d}{dt}(2.0\hat{\mathbf{i}} + 2t\hat{\mathbf{j}}) = 2\hat{\mathbf{j}}$$

At $t = 2.0$ s, the magnitude of the $\mathbf{v}(t)$ can be given as

$$\mathbf{v}(t) = 2.0\,\hat{\mathbf{i}} + 2\times2\hat{\mathbf{j}} = 2.0\,\hat{\mathbf{i}} + 4\,\hat{\mathbf{j}}$$

$v = \sqrt{4 + 16} = \sqrt{20}$ and direction is

$$\theta = \tan^{-1}\left(\frac{v_y}{v_x}\right) = \tan^{-1}\left(\frac{4}{2}\right) \approx 63^\circ$$

(b) (i) A vector in general has no definite location in space because a vector remains unaffected whenever it is displaced anywhere in space provided its magnitude and direction do not change. However, a position vector has a definite location in space.

(ii) A vector can vary with time, e.g. the velocity vector of an accelerated particle varies with time.

(iii) Two equal vectors at different locations in space do not necessarily have same physical effects, e.g. Two equal forces acting at two different points on a body which can cause the rotation of a body about an axis will not produce equal turning effect.

21. (i) No, adding any two scalars is not meaningful because only the scalars of same dimensions, i.e. having same unit can be added.

(ii) No, adding a scalar to a vector of the same dimensions is not meaningful because a scalar cannot be added to a vector.

(iii) Yes, multiplying any vector by any scalar is meaningful. When a vector is multiplied by a scalar, we get a vector, whose magnitude is equal to the product of magnitude of vector and the scalar and direction remains the same as the direction of the given vector.

e.g. A body of mass 4 kg is moving with a velocity 20 m/s towards east, then product of velocity and mass gives the momentum of the body, which is also a vector quantity.

$$\mathbf{p} = m\mathbf{v} = 4 \text{ kg} \times (20 \text{ m/s}), \text{ east}$$
$$= 80 \text{ kg-m/s, east}$$

(iv) Yes, multiplying any two scalars is meaningful. Density ρ and volume V both are scalar quantities. When density is multiplied by volume, then we get $\rho \times V = m$, mass of the body, which is a scalar quantity.

(v) No, adding any two vectors is not meaningful because only vectors of same dimensions, i.e. having same unit can be added.

(vi) Yes, adding a component of a vector to the same vector is meaningful because both vectors are of same dimensions.

22. Consider two vectors **A** and **B** be represented by the sides **OP** and **OQ** of a parallelogram *OPSQ*. According to parallelogram law of vector addition, (**A** + **B**) will be represented by **OS** as shown in figure.

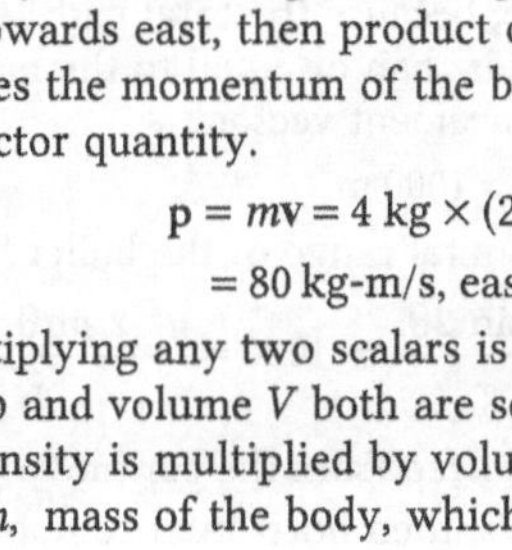

Thus, $OP = |\mathbf{A}|$, $OQ = PS = |\mathbf{B}|$

and $OS = |\mathbf{A} + \mathbf{B}|$

(i) To prove $|\mathbf{A} + \mathbf{B}| \le |\mathbf{A}| + |\mathbf{B}|$

We know that the length of one side of a triangle is always less than the sum of the lengths of the other two sides. Hence, from $\Delta\, OPS$, we have

$$OS < OP + PS$$

$\Rightarrow$ $OS < OP + OQ$

or $|\mathbf{A}+\mathbf{B}| < |\mathbf{A}| + |\mathbf{B}|$ ...(i)

If the two vectors **A** and **B** are acting along the same straight line and in the same direction.

or $|\mathbf{A} + \mathbf{B}| = |\mathbf{A}| + |\mathbf{B}|$ ...(ii)

Combining the conditions mentioned in Eqs. (i) and (ii), we have $|\mathbf{A}+\mathbf{B}| \le |\mathbf{A}|+|\mathbf{B}|$.

(ii) To prove $|\mathbf{A}+\mathbf{B}| \ge ||\mathbf{A}| - |\mathbf{B}||$

From ΔOPS, we have

$$OS + PS > OP \text{ or } OS > |OP - PS|$$

or $OS > |OP - OQ|$ $[\because PS = OQ]$ ... (iii)

The modulus of $(OP - PS)$ has been taken because the LHS is always positive but the RHS may be negative if $OP < PS$. Thus, from Eq. (iii), we have

$|\mathbf{A}+\mathbf{B}| > ||\mathbf{A}| - |\mathbf{B}||$ ...(iv)

If the two vectors **A** and **B** are acting along a straight line in opposite directions, then

$|\mathbf{A}+\mathbf{B}| = ||\mathbf{A}| - |\mathbf{B}||$ ...(v)

Combining the conditions mentioned in Eqs. (iv) and (v) we get

$$|\mathbf{A}+\mathbf{B}| \ge ||\mathbf{A}| - |\mathbf{B}||$$

(iii) To prove $|\mathbf{A}-\mathbf{B}| \le |\mathbf{A}| + |\mathbf{B}|$

In figure, $\mathbf{A} = (\mathbf{OP})$, $-\mathbf{B} = \mathbf{OT} = \mathbf{PR}$

and $(\mathbf{A} - \mathbf{B}) = \mathbf{OR}$

From, ΔORP we note that $OR < OP + PR$.

or $|\mathbf{A} - \mathbf{B}| < |\mathbf{A}| + |-\mathbf{B}|$

or $|\mathbf{A} - \mathbf{B}| < |\mathbf{A}| + |\mathbf{B}|$ ...(vi)

If the two vectors are acting along a straight line. But in the opposite direction, then

$|\mathbf{A} - \mathbf{B}| = |\mathbf{A}| + |\mathbf{B}|$ ...(vii)

Combining the conditions mentioned in Eqs. (vi) and (vii), we get $|\mathbf{A} - \mathbf{B}| \le |\mathbf{A}| + |\mathbf{B}|$

(iv) To prove $|\mathbf{A} - \mathbf{B}| \ge |\mathbf{A}| - |\mathbf{B}|$

In figure from $\Delta\, OPR$, we note that $[\because OT = PR]$

$OR + PR > OP$ or $OR > |OP - PR|$

or $OR > |OP - OT|$ ...(viii)

The modulus of $(OP - OT)$ has been taken because LHS is positive and RHS may be negative, if $OP < OT$.

From Eq. viii , we have

$|\mathbf{A} - \mathbf{B}| > ||\mathbf{A}| - |\mathbf{B}||$ ...(ix)

If the two vectors **A** and **B** are acting along the same straight line in the same direction, then

$|\mathbf{A} - \mathbf{B}| = |\mathbf{A}| - |\mathbf{B}|$ ...(x)

Combining the conditions mentioned in Eqs. (ix) and (x), we get $|\mathbf{A} - \mathbf{B}| \ge |\mathbf{A}| - |\mathbf{B}|$

23. Consider the adjacent diagram.

Mutually perpendicular x and y-axes are shown in the diagram.

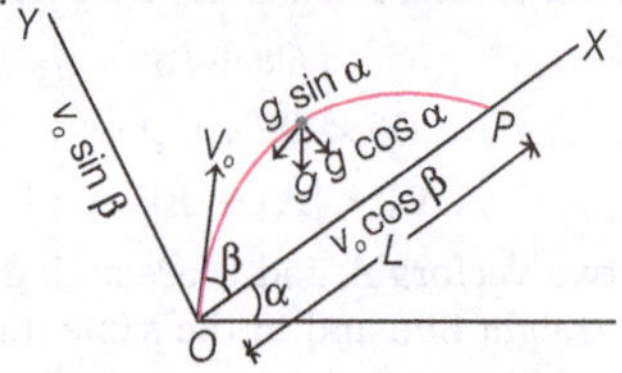

Particle is projected from the point O.

Let time taken in reaching from point O to point P is T.

(a) Considering motion along OX.

$$x = L,\ u_x = v_0 \cos\beta,\ a_x = -g\sin\alpha$$

$$t = T = \frac{2v_0 \sin\beta}{g\cos\alpha}$$

$$x = u_x t + \frac{1}{2}a_x t^2$$

$$\Rightarrow L = v_0 \cos\beta\, T + \frac{1}{2}(-g\sin\alpha)T^2$$

$$\Rightarrow L = v_0 \cos\beta T - \frac{1}{2} g\sin\alpha\, T^2$$

$$= T\left[v_0 \cos\beta - \frac{1}{2} g\sin\alpha\, T\right]$$

$$= T\left[v_0 \cos\beta - \frac{1}{2} g\sin\alpha \times \frac{2v\ \sin\beta}{g\cos\alpha}\right]$$

$$= \frac{2v_0 \sin\beta}{g\cos\alpha}\left[v_0 \cos\beta - \frac{v_0 \sin\alpha \sin\beta}{\cos\alpha}\right]$$

$$= \frac{2v_0^2 \sin\beta}{g\cos^2\alpha}[\cos\beta.\cos\alpha - \sin\alpha.\sin\beta]$$

$$\Rightarrow L = \frac{2v_0^2 \sin\beta}{g\cos^2\alpha}\cos(\alpha + \beta)$$

(b) Considering motion along vertical upward direction perpendicular to OX.

For the journey O to P.

$$y = 0,\ u_y = v_0 \sin\beta,\ a_y = -g\cos\alpha,\ t = T$$

Applying equation, $y = u_y t + \frac{1}{2}a_y t^2$

$$\Rightarrow \quad 0 = v_0 \sin\beta T + \frac{1}{2}(-g\cos\alpha)T^2$$

$$\Rightarrow \quad T\left[v_0 \sin\beta - \frac{g\cos\alpha}{2}T\right] = 0$$

$$\Rightarrow \quad T = 0,\ T = \frac{2v_0 \sin\beta}{g\cos\alpha}$$

As $T = 0$, corresponding to point O

Hence, T = Time of flight $= \frac{2v_0 \sin\beta}{g\cos\alpha}$

(c) For range (L) to be maximum,

$\sin\beta\cos(\alpha + \beta)$ should be maximum.

Let, $Z = \sin\beta\cos(\alpha + \beta)$

$$= \sin\beta[\cos\alpha\cos\beta - \sin\alpha\sin\beta]$$

$$= \frac{1}{2}[\cos\alpha\sin 2\beta - 2\sin\alpha\sin^2\beta]$$

$$= \frac{1}{2}[\sin 2\beta\cos\alpha - \sin\alpha(1 - \cos 2\beta)]$$

$$\Rightarrow \quad z = \frac{1}{2}[\sin 2\beta\cos\alpha - \sin\alpha + \sin\alpha\cos 2\beta]$$

$$= \frac{1}{2}[\sin 2\beta\cos\alpha + \cos 2\beta\sin\alpha - \sin\alpha]$$

$$= \frac{1}{2}[\sin(2\beta + \alpha) - \sin\alpha]$$

For Z to be maximum,

$$\sin(2\beta + \alpha) = \text{maximum} = 1$$

$$\Rightarrow \quad 2\beta + \alpha = \frac{\pi}{2} \text{ or}, \beta = \frac{\pi}{4} - \frac{\alpha}{2}$$

24. (a) (i) **True**, because magnitude is a pure number.

(ii) **False**, each component of a vector is also a vector.

(iii) **True**, because the total path length is either greater than or equal to the magnitude of the displacement vector.

(b) Given, $R = 1000$ m

∴ Horizontal range of the bullet fired at an angle θ,

$$R = \frac{u^2 \sin 2\theta}{g} \Rightarrow 1000 = \frac{u^2\, 2\sin\theta\cos\theta}{g} \quad \text{...(i)}$$

Bullet is fired from the car moving with 36 km/h, i.e. 10 m/s, then horizontal component of the velocity of bullet $= u\cos\theta + 10$

Vertical component of the velocity of the bullet $= u\sin\theta$

then new range of the bullet is

$$R_1 = \frac{2}{g}(u\sin\theta)(u\cos\theta + 10)$$

$$= \frac{2}{g}u^2 \sin\theta\cos\theta + \frac{20}{g}u\sin\theta$$

$$\Rightarrow \quad R_1 = R + \frac{20}{g}u\sin\theta$$

$$\Rightarrow R_1 - R = \frac{20}{g}u\sin\theta \quad \text{...(ii)}$$

From Eq. (i), we have $u = \sqrt{\frac{1000 \times g}{2\sin\theta\cos\theta}}$ ...(iii)

Now, substituting the value of u in Eq. (ii), we get

$$R_1 - R = \frac{20}{g}\sqrt{\frac{1000 \times g}{2\sin\theta\cos\theta}}\sin\theta$$

$$= 20\sqrt{\frac{500 \times \sin\theta}{g\cos\theta}}$$

$$= 20\sqrt{\frac{500}{9.8}\tan\theta} = 142.9\sqrt{\tan\theta}$$

25. (a) Here, $r = 80\,\text{cm} = 0.8\text{ m}, f = (14/25)\,\text{s}^{-1}$

$$\therefore\ \omega = 2\pi f = 2 \times \frac{22}{7} \times \frac{14}{25} = \frac{88}{25}\text{ rad/s}$$

Centripetal acceleration,

$$a = \omega^2 r = \left(\frac{88}{25}\right)^2 \times 0.8 = 9.91\text{ ms}^{-2}$$

(b) Here, $r = 1\text{ km} = 1000\text{ m}$,

$$v = 900\text{ kmh}^{-1} = 900 \times (1000\text{ m})/(60 \times 60\text{ s}) = 250\text{ ms}^{-1}$$

Centripetal acceleration, $a = \frac{v^2}{r} = \frac{(250)^2}{1000}$

Now, $\frac{a}{g} = \frac{(250)^2}{1000} \times \frac{1}{9.8} = 6.38$

26. (i) **False,** because the net acceleration of a particle is towards the centre only in case of a uniform circular motion. In non uniform motion, acceleration has tangential component as well.

(ii) **True,** because while leaving the circular path, the particle moves tangentially to the circular path.

(iii) **True,** because the direction of acceleration vector in a uniform circular motion is directed towards the centre of circular path. It is constantly changing with time. The resultant of all these vectors will be a zero vector.

27. Let P and Q be the two forces.

Greatest resultant, $R_1 = P + Q = 29\text{ N}$ ...(i)

Least resultant, $R_2 = P - Q = 5\text{ N}$ ...(ii)

Solving Eqs. (i) and (ii), we get

$$P = 17\text{ N}, Q = 12\text{ N}$$

When each force is increased by 3 N, then

$$P' = P + 3 = 17 + 3 = 20\text{ N}$$

$$\Rightarrow\ Q' = 12 + 3 = 15\text{ N}$$

The resultant of new forces,

$$R' = \sqrt{(20)^2 + (15)^2} = \sqrt{400 + 225} = 25\text{ N}$$

Let the resultant $\mathbf{R}$, makes an angle θ with $\mathbf{A}$, then

$$\tan\theta = \frac{15}{20} = 0.75$$

$$\Rightarrow\ \theta = \tan^{-1}(0.75) = 36°52'$$

Thus, the resultant of two new forces P' and Q' are 25 N and angle between them is 36°52′.

28. When the boat is anchored in the harbour, the flag flutters along the north-east direction. It shows that the velocity of wind is along the north-east direction. When the boat starts moving, the flag will flutter along the direction of relative velocity of wind w.r.t. boat. Let $\mathbf{v}_{wb}$ be the relative velocity of wind w.r.t. boat and β be the angle between $\mathbf{v}_{wb}$ and $\mathbf{v}_w$, then

$$\mathbf{v}_{wb} = \mathbf{v}_w + (-\mathbf{v}_b)$$

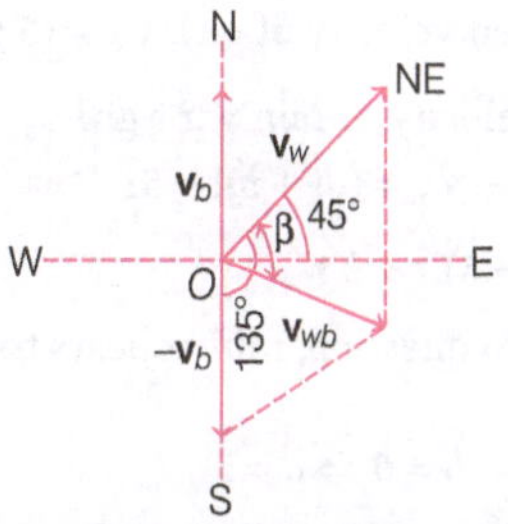

Here, $|\mathbf{v}_w| = 72$ km/h and $|-\mathbf{v}_b| = 51$ km/h

Angle between $\mathbf{v}_w$ and $-\mathbf{v}_b$ is 135° i.e. $\theta = 135°$, then,

$$\tan\beta = \frac{51\sin 135°}{72 + 51\cos 135°} = \frac{51\sin 45°}{72 + 51(-\cos 45°)}$$

$$= \frac{51 \times (1/\sqrt{2})}{72 - 51(1/\sqrt{2})} = 1.0039$$

$$\therefore\ \beta = \tan^{-1}(1.0039) = 45.1°$$

Angle w.r.t. East direction = 45.1° − 45° = 0.1°

It means the flag will flutter almost due East.

29. Components of the relative velocity of the billiard balls are $v_x = 1\text{ ms}^{-1}$

$$v_y = (2 - \sqrt{3})\text{ ms}^{-1}$$

$$\tan\theta = \frac{v_y}{v_x} = \frac{2 - \sqrt{3}}{1}$$

i.e. $\theta = \tan^{-1}(2 - \sqrt{3}) = 15°$

30. Let the ball strike with nth step of stairs.

$\therefore$ Vertical distance travelled $= ny = n \times 0.2 = \frac{1}{2}gt^2$

Horizontal distance travelled $= nx = ut$

$$\Rightarrow\ t = \frac{nx}{u}$$

$$ny = \frac{1}{2}gt^2 = \frac{1}{2}g\left(\frac{nx}{u}\right)^2 = \frac{1}{2}g\frac{n^2x^2}{u^2}$$

$$\Rightarrow\ n = \frac{2u^2y}{gx^2}$$

$$\Rightarrow\ n = \frac{2 \times (1.8)^2 \times 0.2}{9.8 \times (0.2)^2} = 3.3$$

$\therefore$ 4th step will the ball hit first

31. Assume north to be $\hat{\mathbf{i}}$ direction and vertically downward to be $-\hat{\mathbf{j}}$. Let the rain velocity v_r be $a\,\hat{\mathbf{i}} + b\,\hat{\mathbf{j}}$.

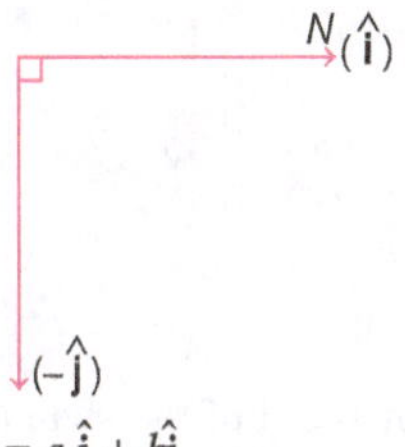

$$\mathbf{v}_r = a\,\hat{\mathbf{i}} + b\hat{\mathbf{j}}$$

***Case* I** Given velocity of girl, $\mathbf{v}_g = (5\ m\ \ s)\,\hat{i}$

Let $\mathbf{v}_{rg}$ = Velocity of rain w.r.t girl

$= \mathbf{v}_r - \mathbf{v}_g = (a\hat{i} + b\hat{j}) - 5\hat{i}$

$= (a-5)\,\hat{i} + b\,\hat{j}$

According to question, rain appears to fall vertically downward.

Hence, $a - 5 = 0 \Rightarrow a = 5$

***Case* II** Given velocity of the girl, $\mathbf{v}_g = (10\ m/s)\,\hat{}$

$\therefore \quad \mathbf{v}_{rg} = \mathbf{v}_r - \mathbf{v}_g$

$= (a\hat{} + b\hat{}) - 10\hat{} = (a-10)\,\hat{i} + b\hat{j}$

According to question rain appears to fall at 45° to the vertical hence $\tan 45° = \dfrac{b}{a-10} = 1$

$\Rightarrow \quad b = a - 10 = 5 - 10 = -5$

Hence, velocity of rain $= a\hat{i} + b\hat{j}$

$\Rightarrow \quad \mathbf{v}_r = 5\hat{i} - 5\hat{j}$

Speed of rain $= |\mathbf{v}_r| = \sqrt{(5)^2 + (-5)^2}$

$= \sqrt{50} = 5\sqrt{2}\ m/s$

32. Given, Speed of the river $(v_r) = 3$ m/s (east)

Speed of swimmer $(v_s) = 4$ m/s (east)

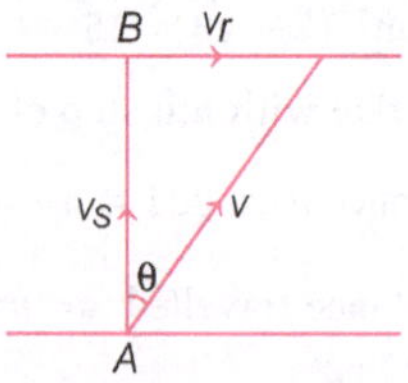

(a) When swimmer starts swimming due north then his resultant velocity,

$$v = \sqrt{v_r^2 + v_s^2} = \sqrt{(3)^2 + (4)^2}$$

$$= \sqrt{9+16} = \sqrt{25} = 5\ m/s$$

$$\tan\theta = \frac{v_r}{v_s} = \frac{3}{4}$$

$$= 0.75 = \tan 36°54'$$

Hence, $\theta = 36°54'$ N

(b) To reach opposite points B, the swimmer should swim at an angle θ of north.

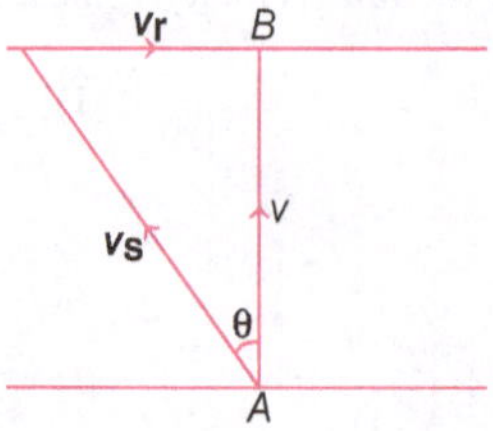

(i) Resultant speed of the swimmer

$$v = \sqrt{v_s^2 - v_r^2} = \sqrt{(4)^2 - (3)^2}$$

$$= \sqrt{16-9} = \sqrt{7}\ m/s$$

(ii) $\tan\theta = \dfrac{v_r}{v} = \dfrac{3}{\sqrt{7}}$

$\Rightarrow \quad \theta = \tan^{-1}\left(\dfrac{3}{\sqrt{7}}\right)$ of north

(c) In case (a),

Time taken by the swimmer to cross the river,

$$t_1 = \frac{d}{v_s} = \frac{d}{4}\,s$$

In case (b),

Time taken by the swimmer to cross the river

$$t_1 = \frac{d}{v} = \frac{d}{\sqrt{7}}$$

As $\dfrac{d}{4} < \dfrac{d}{\sqrt{7}}$, therefore $t_1 < t_2$.

Hence, the swimmer will cross the river in shorter time in case (a).

33. Here, $\mathbf{u} = 10.0\,\hat{j}\ ms^{-1}$ at $t = 0$.

$$\mathbf{a} = \frac{d\mathbf{v}}{dt} = (8.0\,\hat{i} + 2.0\,\hat{j})\ ms^{-2}$$

So, $\quad d\mathbf{v} = (8.0\,\hat{i} + 2.0\,\hat{j})\,dt$

Integrating it within the limits of motion i.e. as time changes from 0 to t, velocity changes from u to v, we have

$$\mathbf{v} - \mathbf{u} = (8.0\,\hat{i} + 2.0\,\hat{j})\,t$$

$\Rightarrow \quad \mathbf{v} = \mathbf{u} + 8.0t\,\hat{i} + 2.0\,t\,\hat{j}$

As, $\quad \mathbf{v} = \dfrac{d\mathbf{r}}{dt} \Rightarrow d\mathbf{r} = \mathbf{v}\,dt$

So, $\quad d\mathbf{r} = (\mathbf{u} + 8.0\,t\,\hat{i} + 2.0t\,\hat{j})\,dt$

Integrating it within the conditions of motion i.e. as time changes from 0 to t, displacement is from 0 to r, we have

$$\mathbf{r} = \mathbf{u}\,t + \frac{1}{2} \times 8.0\,t^2\,\hat{i} + \frac{1}{2} \times 2.0\,t^2\,\hat{j}$$

or $\quad x\,\hat{i} + y\,\hat{j} = 10\,\hat{j}\,t + 4.0\,t^2\,\hat{i} + t^2\,\hat{j}$

$$= 4.0\,t^2\,\hat{i} + (10\,t + t^2)\,\hat{j}$$

Here, we have, $x = 4.0\,t^2$ and $y = 10\,t + t^2$

$\therefore \quad t = (x/4)^{\frac{1}{2}}$

(i) At $x = 16$ m, $t = (16/4)^{\frac{1}{2}} = 2$ s

$\therefore \quad y = 10 \times 2 + 2^2 = 24$ m

(ii) Velocity of the particle at time t is

$$\mathbf{v} = 10\,\hat{j} + 8.0\,t\,\hat{i} + 2.0t\,\hat{j}$$

When $t = 2$ s, then,

$$\mathbf{v} = 10\,\hat{j} + 8.0 \times 2\,\hat{i} + 2.0 \times 2\,\hat{j}$$

$$= 16\,\hat{i} + 14\,\hat{j}$$

$\therefore$ Speed $= |\mathbf{v}| = \sqrt{16^2 + 14^2} = 21.26\ ms^{-1}$

34. Let u be the velocity of projection of the ball. The ball will cover maximum horizontal distance when angle of projection with horizontal, $\theta = 45°$. Then, $R_{max} = u^2/g$.

Here, $u^2/g = 100$ m.

In order to study the motion of the ball along vertical direction, consider a point on the surface of earth as the origin and vertical upward direction as the positive direction of Y-axis. Taking motion of the ball along vertical upward direction, we have

$$u_y = u,\ a_y = -g,\ v_y = 0,\ t = ?,\ y_0 = 0,\ y = \ ?$$

As, $v_y = u_y + a_y t$

$\therefore$ $0 = u + (-g)t \Rightarrow t = u/g$

Also, $y = y_0 + u_y t + \frac{1}{2} a_y t^2$

$$\therefore\quad y = 0 + u(u/g) + \frac{1}{2}(-g)u^2/g^2$$

$$= \frac{u^2}{g} - \frac{1}{2}\frac{u^2}{g} = \frac{1}{2}\frac{u^2}{g} = \frac{100}{2} = 50\text{m}$$

$$\left[\because \frac{u^2}{g} = 100\right]$$

35. Given, initial velocity, $u = 40$ m/s

Height of the hall, $H = 25$ m

Let the angle of projection of the ball be θ, when maximum height attained by it be 25 m.

Maximum height attained by the ball,

$$H = \frac{u^2 \sin^2\theta}{2g} \Rightarrow 25 = \frac{(40)^2 \sin^2\theta}{2 \times 9.8}$$

or $\sin^2\theta = \frac{25 \times 2 \times 9.8}{1600} = 0.3063$

or $\sin\theta = 0.5534 = \sin^{-1}(0.5534)$

or $\theta = 33.6°$

$\therefore$ Horizontal range, $R = \frac{u^2 \sin 2\theta}{g}$

$$= \frac{(40)^2 \sin 2 \times 33.6°}{9.8} = \frac{1600 \times \sin 67.2°}{9.8}$$

$$= \frac{1600 \times 0.9219}{9.8} = 150.5 \text{ m}$$

36. From the figure, let O be the position of gun and A be the position of plane.

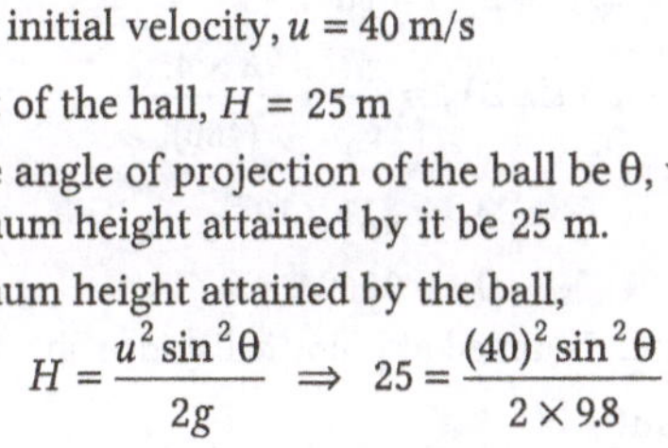

The speed of the plane,

$$v = \frac{720 \times 1000}{60 \times 60} = 200 \text{ ms}^{-1}$$

The speed of the shell, $u = 600$ ms^{-1}

Let the shell hit the plane at B after time t. If fired at an angle θ with the vertical from O, then the horizontal distance travelled by shell in time t is the same as the distance covered by the plane during the same period.

i.e. $u_x \times t = vt$ or $u \sin\theta\, t = vt$

or $\sin\theta = \frac{v}{u} = \frac{200}{600} = 0.33333 = \sin^{-1}(0.33333)$

or $\theta = 19.5°$ with the vertical

The plane will not be hit by the bullet from the gun if it is flying at a minimum height which is the maximum height (H) attained by bullet after firing from gun.

Here, $H = \frac{u^2 \sin^2(90° - \theta)}{2g} = \frac{u^2 \cos^2\theta}{2g}$

$$= \frac{(600)^2 \times (\cos 19.5°)^2}{2 \times 10}$$

$$[\because \sin\theta = 1/3,\ \cos\theta = \sqrt{8}/3]$$

$$= \frac{(600)^2 \times (\sqrt{8}/3)^2}{20} = 16000 \text{ m} = 16 \text{ km}$$

37. (i) Let v_{ox} and v_{oy} be the initial component velocities of the projectile at O along OX direction and OY direction respectively, where OX is horizontal and OY is vertical. Let the projectile go from O to P in time t and v_x, v_y be the component velocity of projectile at P along horizontal and vertical directions as shown in figure.

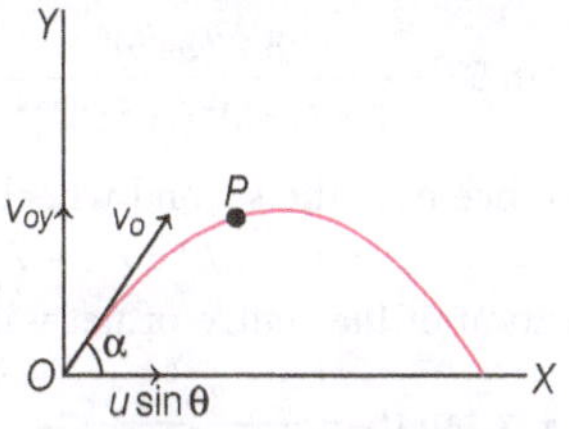

Then, $v_y = v_{oy} - gt$ and $v_x = v_{ox}$

If θ is the angle which the resultant velocity $\mathbf{v}$ makes with horizontal direction, then

$$\tan\theta = \frac{v_y}{v_x} = \frac{v_{oy} - gt}{v_{ax}}$$

$$\Rightarrow \quad \theta = \tan^{-1}\left(\frac{v_{oy} - gt}{v_{ox}}\right)$$

(ii) In angular projection,

Maximum vertical height, $h_m = \frac{u^2 \sin^2\theta_0}{2g}$

Horizontal range,

$$R = \frac{u^2 \sin 2\theta}{g} = \frac{u^2}{g} 2\sin\theta_0 \cos\theta_0$$

So, $\frac{h_m}{R} = \frac{\tan\theta_0}{4}$ or $\tan\theta_0 = \frac{4h_m}{R}$

or $\theta_0 = \tan^{-1}\left(\frac{4h_m}{R}\right)$

38. (i) If the person is considered as a projectile, then he will reach the maximum height over the middle wheel located at

$$x = 23 + \frac{23}{2} = 34.5\text{m}$$

From this, we can deduce the initial launch speed.

$$x = \frac{R}{2} = \frac{v_0^2 \sin 2\theta}{2g}$$

$$\Rightarrow \quad v_0 = \sqrt{\frac{2gx}{\sin 2\theta_0}} = \sqrt{\frac{2 \times 9.8 \times 34.5}{\sin(2 \times 53^\circ)}} = 26.5 \text{ ms}^{-1}$$

On substituting the values, we will obtain

$$y = y_0 + 23 \tan\theta_0 - \frac{gx^2}{2v_0^2 \cos^2\theta_0}$$

$$= 3 + 23 \tan 53^0 - \frac{9.8 \times (23)^2}{2\,(26.5)^2 (\cos 53^0)^2} = 23.3 \text{ m}$$

As, the height of the wheel, $h = 18$ m

The clearence over the first wheel,

$$\Delta y = y - h = 23.3 - 18 = 5.3 \text{ m}$$

(ii) The height of the person when he is standing directly above the second wheel can be found by above equations. Second wheel is located at

$$x = 23 + \frac{23}{2} = 34.5 \text{ m}$$

$$y = y_0 + x \tan\theta_0 - \frac{gx^2}{2v_0^2 \cos^2\theta} = 3\text{m}$$

$$\Rightarrow 34.5 \tan 53^\circ - \frac{9.8 \times (34.5)^2}{2 \times (26.5)^2 (\cos 53^\circ)^2} = 25.9\text{m}$$

∴ Clearance over the second wheel,

$$\Delta y = y - h = 25.9 - 18 = 7.9 \text{ m}$$

(iii) The location of the centre of net will be

$$y = y_0 + x \tan\theta_0 - \frac{gx^2}{2v_0^2 \cos^2\theta_0}$$

$$\Rightarrow y - y_0 = x\tan\theta_0 - \frac{gx^2}{2v_0^2 \cos^2\theta}$$

$$0 = \frac{(26.52)^2 \times \sin(2.53^\circ)}{9.8} = 69 \text{ m}$$

39. The initial velocity is horizontal so, $v_{0y} = 0$

and $v_{ox} = v_0 = 10 \text{ ms}^{-1}$

(i) With the origin at the initial point (where the dart leaves the threwer's hand), the y-coordinate of the dart is given by

$$y = -\frac{1}{2}gt^2, \text{ so that } y = -PQ$$

$$\because \quad PQ = y = \frac{1}{2} \times 9.8 \times (0.19)^2 = 0.18\text{m}$$

(ii) From $x = v_0 t$, we obtain

$$x = 10 \times 0.19 = 1.9\text{m}$$

40. The coordinate origin is at the end of the rifle.

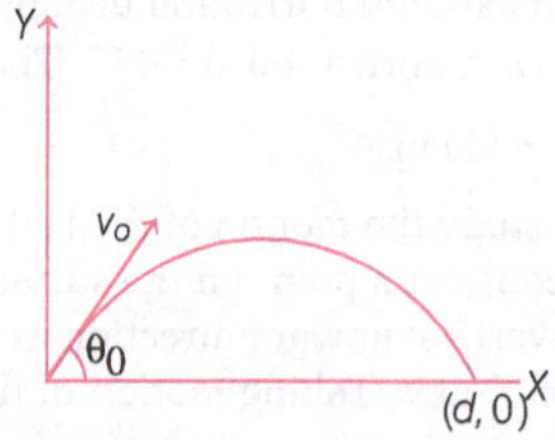

Let θ_0 be the firing angle. If the target is distance d away, then its coordinates are $x = d, y = 0$

The projectile motion equations lead to $d = (v_0 \cos\theta_0)t$

$$\Rightarrow \quad 0 = v_0 t \sin\theta_0 - \frac{1}{2}gt^2$$

The given situation is shown in the following figure. The time at which the bullet strikes the target is

$$t = d/(v_0 \cos\theta_0)$$

Eliminating t leads to

$$2v_0^2 \sin\theta_0 \cos\theta_0 - gd = 0$$

Using $\sin\theta_0 \cos\theta_0 = \frac{1}{2}(\sin 2\theta_0)$, we get

$$v_0^2 \sin(2\theta_0) = gd$$

$$\Rightarrow \quad \sin 2\theta_0 = \frac{gd}{v_0^2} = \frac{9.8 \times 45.7}{(460)^2}$$

$$\Rightarrow \quad \sin 2\theta_0 = 2.11 \times 10^{-3}$$

or $\quad \theta_0 = 0.0604^\circ$

If the gun is aimed at point a distance above the target, then $\tan\theta_0 = \frac{l}{d}$

$$\Rightarrow \quad l = d\tan\theta$$

$$\Rightarrow \quad l = 45.7 \times 0.0606^\circ = 0.0484 \text{ m} = 4.84 \text{ cm}$$

41. Velocity of water that comes out from sprinkler $= v$

Let the radius be r.

∵ Maximum distance d will be at 45° and can be given by

$$d = \frac{v^2 \sin 2\alpha}{g} \Rightarrow d = \frac{v^2 \sin 2(45^\circ)}{g} \Rightarrow d = \frac{v^2}{g}$$

$$\text{Area} = \pi d^2 \Rightarrow A = \pi (v^2/g)^2$$

$$\Rightarrow \quad A = \frac{\pi v^4}{g^2}$$

42. Since the gun is same.

∴ The initial velocity of the two bullets will be equal.

$$H = \frac{u^2 \sin^2\theta}{2g}$$

For P, $H_P = \frac{u^2 \sin^2 30^\circ}{2g} = \frac{u^2}{8g}$

and for Q, $H_Q = \frac{u^2 \sin^2 60^\circ}{2g} = \frac{3u^2}{8g}$

$\because \quad xH_p = H_Q$

$\because \quad H_P = \dfrac{u^2}{8g} \Rightarrow H_Q = 3\left(\dfrac{u^2}{8g}\right) = 3H_P \Rightarrow x = 3$

43. Given, speed of packets = 125 m/s

Height of the hill = 500 m.

To cross the hill, the vertical component of the velocity should be sufficient to cross such height.

$$u_y \geq \sqrt{2gh} \geq \sqrt{2 \times 10 \times 500} \geq 100 \text{ m/s}$$

But $\quad u^2 = u_x^2 + u_y^2$

$\therefore$ Horizontal component of initial velocity,

$$u_x = \sqrt{u^2 - u_y^2} = \sqrt{(125)^2 - (100)^2} = 75 \text{ m/s}$$

Time taken to reach the top of the hill,

$$t = \sqrt{\frac{2h}{g}} = \sqrt{\frac{2 \times 500}{10}} = 10 \text{ s}$$

Time taken to reach the ground from the top of the hill $t' = t = 10$ s. Horizontal distance travelled in 10 s is

$$x = u_x \times t = 75 \times 10 = 750 \text{ m}$$

$\therefore$ Distance through which canon has to be moved

$$= 800 - 750 = 50 \text{ m}$$

Speed with which canon can move = 2 m/s

$\therefore$ Time taken by canon $= \dfrac{50}{2} \Rightarrow t'' = 25$ s

$\therefore$ Total time taken by a packet to reach on the ground $= t'' + t + t' = 25 + 10 + 10 = 45$ s

44. Orbital radius of the earth around the sun (R) $= 1.5 \times 10^{11}$ m

Time period $= 1 \text{ yr} = 365$ day

$$= 365 \times 24 \times 60 \times 60 = 3.15 \times 10^7 \text{ s}$$

Centripetal acceleration $(a_c) = R\omega^2 = \dfrac{4\pi^2 R}{T^2}$

$$= \frac{4 \times (22/7)^2 \times 1.5 \times 10^{11}}{(3.15 \times 10^7)^2} = 5.97 \times 10^{-3} \text{ m/s}^2$$

$$\frac{a_c}{g} = \frac{5.97 \times 10^{-3}}{9.8} = \frac{1}{1642}$$

45. (i) $\because \quad v = \dfrac{2\pi r}{T}$

If we put the values given in the question, we get

$$v = \frac{2\pi(20)}{1} = 126 \text{ km/s}$$

(ii) The magnitude of the acceleration is

$$a = \frac{v^2}{r}$$

Now, putting the values given in the question, we get

$$a = \frac{(126)^2}{20} = 7.9 \times 10^2 \text{ km/s}^2$$

(iii) $\because \quad v \propto \dfrac{1}{T}$ and $a \propto v^2 \Rightarrow a \propto \dfrac{1}{T^2}$

$\Rightarrow$ Both v and a will increase, if T is reduced.

46. (i) Since, the wheel completes 5 turns each minute, its period is one-fifth of a minute or 12 s.

(ii) The magnitude of the centripetal acceleration is given by $a = \dfrac{v^2}{r}$, where r is the radius of the wheel and v is the speed of the passenger.

Since, passenger goes a distance $2\pi R$ for each revolution, his speed,

$$v = \frac{2\pi(15)}{12} = 7.85 \text{ m/s}$$

and his centripetal acceleration,

$$a = \frac{(7.85)^2}{15} = 4.1 \text{ ms}^2$$

(iii) When the passenger is at the highest point, his centripetal acceleration is downward, towards the centre of the orbit.

(iv) The magnitude of centripetal acceleration at lowest point is $a = 4.1 \text{ m/s}^2$.

(v) The direction of centripetal acceleration at lowest point is upward towards the centre of orbit.

47. Given, radius of circular park = 1 km

(a) As cyclist return to its initial state, therefore the net displacement of the cyclist is zero.

(b) Average velocity $= \dfrac{\text{Total displacement}}{\text{Total time taken}}$

$$= \frac{0}{\text{Total time taken}} = 0$$

(c) Total distance travelled by the cyclist

$= OP +$ Actual path length of $PQ + QO$

$$= r + \left(\frac{1}{4} \times 2\pi r\right) + r = 1 + \left(\frac{1}{2} \times \frac{22}{7} \times 1\right) + 1$$

$$= 2 + \frac{11}{7} = \frac{25}{7} \text{ km}$$

Total time taken $= 10 \text{ min} = \dfrac{10}{60} \text{ h} = \dfrac{1}{6} \text{ h}$

$\therefore$ Average speed of the cyclist

$$= \frac{\text{Total distance travelled}}{\text{Total time taken}}$$

$$= \frac{25/7}{1/6} = \frac{150}{7} = 21.43 \text{ km/h}$$

48. The distance after which motorist take a turn = 500 m

As motorist takes a turn at an angle of 60° each time, therefore motorist is moving on a regular hexagonal path. Let the motorist starts from point A and reaches at point D at the end of third turn and at initial point A at the end of sixth turn and at point C at the end of eight turn.

(a) Displacement of the motorist at the third turn = AD

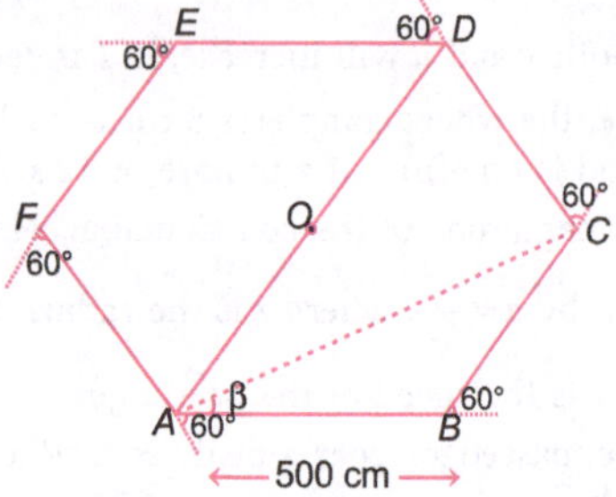

$= AO + OD$

$= 500 + 500 = 1000$ m

Total path length $= AB + BC + CD$

$= 500 + 500 + 500 = 1500$ m

$\therefore \dfrac{\text{Magnitude of displacement}}{\text{Total path length}} = \dfrac{1000}{1500} = \dfrac{2}{3} = 0.67$

(b) At the sixth turn motorist is at the starting point A.

$\therefore$ Displacement of the motorist at the sixth turn = 0

Total path length $= AB + BC + CD + DE + EF + FA$

$= 500 + 500 + 500 + 500 + 500 + 500 = 3000$ m

$\therefore \dfrac{\text{Magnitude of displacement}}{\text{Total path length}} = \dfrac{0}{3000} = 0$

(c) At the eight turn, the motorist is point C.

$\therefore$ Displacement of the motorist = AC

Using triangle law of vector addition,

$$AC = \sqrt{AB^2 + BC^2 + 2AB \cdot BC \cos 60^\circ}$$

$$= \sqrt{(500)^2 + (500)^2 + 2 \times 500 \times 500 \times \frac{1}{2}}$$

$$= \sqrt{3 \times (500)^2} = 500\sqrt{3}\text{m}$$

$$= 500 \times 1.732 \text{ m} = 866 \text{ m}$$

If it is inclined at an angle β from the direction of **AB**, then

$$\tan\beta = \frac{500 \sin 60^\circ}{500 + 500 \cos 60^\circ}$$

$$= \frac{500 \times \frac{\sqrt{3}}{2}}{500 + 500 \times \frac{1}{2}}$$

$$= \frac{500 \times \frac{\sqrt{3}}{2}}{500\left(1 + \frac{1}{2}\right)} = \frac{\frac{\sqrt{3}}{2}}{\frac{3}{2}} = \frac{1}{\sqrt{3}} = \tan 30^\circ$$

or $\beta = 30^\circ$

$\therefore$ Displacement of the motorist at the end of eighth turn is 866 m making an angle 30° with the initial direction of motion.

Total path length $= 8 \times 500 = 4000$ m

$\therefore \dfrac{\text{Magnitude of displacement}}{\text{Total path length}} = \dfrac{500\sqrt{3}}{4000} = \dfrac{\sqrt{3}}{8}$

$= 0.22$

49. Here, $v = 27 \text{ kmh}^{-1}$

$= 27 \times (1000 \text{ m}) \times (60 \times 60 \text{ s})^{-1}$

$= 7.5 \text{ ms}^{-1}$, $r = 80$ m

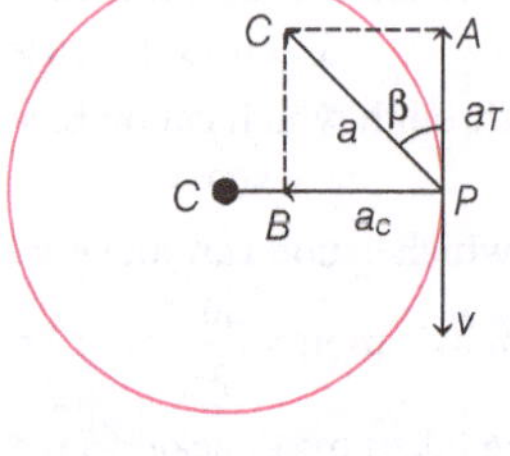

Centripetal acceleration,

$$a_c = \frac{v^2}{r} = \frac{(7.5)^2}{80} = 0.7 \text{ ms}^{-2}$$

Let the cyclist applies the brakes at the point P of the circular turn, then tangential acceleration a_T will act opposite to velocity.

Acceleration along the tangent, $a_T = 0.5 \text{ ms}^{-2}$

Angle between both the accelerations is 90°.

Therefore, the magnitude of resultant acceleration is

$$a = \sqrt{a_c^2 + a_T^2} = \sqrt{(0.7)^2 + (0.5)^2} = 0.86 \text{ ms}^{-2}$$

Let the resultant acceleration make an angle β with the tangent i.e. the direction of net acceleration of the cyclist then, $\tan\beta = \dfrac{a_c}{a_T} = \dfrac{0.7}{0.5} = 1.4$ or $\beta = 54^\circ 28'$

QR Code for Quick Test 1

QR Code for Quick Test 2

SELF ASSESSMENT TEST

Multiple Choice Questions (MCQs)

1. Vectors **A, B** and **C** have magnitudes 12, 5 and 13 units respectively and **A** + **B** = **C**, then angle between **A** and **B** will be

(a) 0 (b) π (c) $\frac{\pi}{2}$ (d) $\frac{\pi}{4}$

2. In uniform circular motion, the acceleration vector

(a) is constant in magnitude and direction both

(b) is constant in magnitude only

(c) is constant in direction only

(d) varies in magnitude and direction both

3. A particle is projected making an angle 60° with the horizon, with K amount of kinetic energy. The kinetic energy of the particle at the highest position is

(a) 0 (b) $\frac{K}{2}$ (c) $\frac{K}{4}$ (d) K

4. A body moving along a circular path of radius r with velocity v, has centripetal acceleration a. If its velocity is made equal to $2v$, then its centripetal acceleration is

(a) $4a$ (b) $2a$ (c) $\frac{a}{4}$ (d) $\frac{a}{2}$

5. A ball thrown by one player reaches the other player in 2s. The maximum height attained by the ball will be (Given, $g = 10\ \text{m/s}^2$)

(a) 3 m (b) 5 m (c) 7 m (d) 9 m

6. If $|\mathbf{A}| = 2$ and $|\mathbf{B}| = 4$, then match the relation in Column I with the angle θ between A and B in column II. Select the correct answer from the options given below.

Column I		Column II	
A.	$A \cdot B = 0$	P.	$\theta = 0$
B.	$A \cdot B = +8$	Q.	$\theta = 90°$
C.	$A \cdot B = 4$	R.	$\theta = 180°$
D.	$A \cdot B = -8$	S.	$\theta = 60°$

(a) A-P, B-S, C-R, D-Q

(b) A-R, B-P, C-Q, D-S

(c) A-Q, B-P, C-S, D-R

(d) A-R, B-Q, C-P, D-S

Assertion-Reason

Direction *(Q. Nos. 7-10) In the following questions, two statements are given-one labelled Assertion (A) and the other labelled Reason (R). Select the correct answer to these questions from the codes (a), (b), (c) and (d) as given below.*

(a) Both Assertion and Reason are true and Reason is the correct explanation of Assertion.

(b) Both Assertion and Reason are true but Reason is not the correct explanation of Assertion.

(c) Assertion is true but Reason is false.

(d) Assertion is false but Reason is true.

7. Assertion (A) In case of projectile motion, the magnitude of rate of change of velocity is variable.

Reason (R) In projectile motion, magnitude of velocity first decreases and then increases during the motion.

8. Assertion (A) At highest point of a projectile, dot product of velocity and acceleration is zero.

Reason (R) At highest point, velocity and acceleration are mutually perpendicular.

9. Assertion (A) Two particle of different mass, projected with same velocity at same angle. The maximum height attained by both the particle will be same.

Reason (R) The maximum height of projectile is independent of particle mass.

10. Assertion (A) Horizontal range is same for angle of projection θ and $(90 - \theta)$.

Reason (R) Horizontal range is independent of angle of projection.

Case Based Questions

Directions *(Q.No. 11) This question is case study based question. Read the following paragraph and answer the questions on the basis of same.*

11. A projectile is projected from a point O on the ground with an initial velocity u at an elevation angle θ from the horizontal direction as shown in the figure. It just crosses two walls A and B of same height h situated symmetrically at times $t_1 = 2$ s and $t_2 = 6$ s respectively.

The horizontal distance between the two walls is $d = 120$ m. (Take $g = 10$ m/s^2)

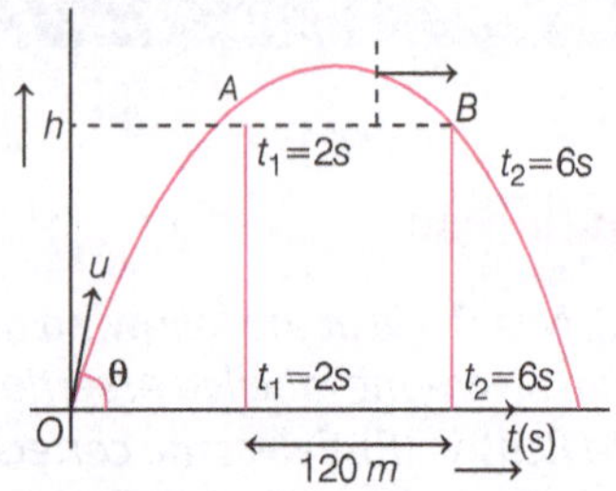

(i) The projectile motion is an example of
- (a) one dimensional motion
- (b) two dimensional motion
- (c) three dimensional motion
- (d) cannot say, precisely

(ii) The total time of flight of the projectile
- (a) 8 s (b) 10 s (c) 4 s (d) 12 s

(iii) The value of angle of projection θ of the projectile is
- (a) $\tan^{-1}\left(\frac{3}{4}\right)$ (b) $\tan^{-1}\left(\frac{4}{5}\right)$
- (c) $\tan^{-1}\left(\frac{4}{3}\right)$ (d) $\tan^{-1}\left(\frac{5}{4}\right)$

(iv) The projectile velocity u of the projectile is
- (a) 30 m/s (b) 40 m/s
- (c) 50 m/s (d) $20\sqrt{3}$ m/s

(v) The height h of either of two walls is
- (a) 120 m (b) 30 m
- (c) 15 m (d) 60 m

Very Short Answer Type Questions

12. Why does the direction of motion of a projectile become horizontal at the highest point of its trajectory?

13. The dot product of two vectors vanishes when vectors are orthogonal and has maximum value when vectors are parallel to each other. Explain.

14. What is the angle between A and B, if A and B denote the adjacent sides of a parallelogram drawn from a point and the area of the parallelogram is (1/2) **AB**?

Short Answer Type Questions

15. Two forces whose magnitudes are in the ratio 3 : 5 give a resultant of 28 N. If the angle of their inclination is 60°, then find the magnitude of each force.

16. A person sitting in a running train throws a ball vertically upwards. What is the nature of the path described by the ball to a person?

(i) Sitting inside the train

(ii) Standing on the ground outside the train.

17. A football is kicked 20 m/s at a projection angle of 45°. A receiver on the goal line 25 m away in the direction of the kick runs the same instant to meet the ball. What must be his speed, if he has to catch the ball before it hits the ground?

Long Answer Type Questions

18. (a) Find the angle of projection for a projectile whose range is n times the maximum height.

(b) A boy stand at 78.4 m from a building and thrown a ball which just enters a window 39.2 m above the ground (where the distance between ground and the window represents the maximum height of the motion). Calculate the velocity of projection of ball.

19. (a) Can a flight of a bird, an example of composition of vectors, why?

(b) A bullet fired at an angle of 30° with the horizontal hits the ground 3 km away. By adjusting its angle of projection, can one hope to hit a target 5 km away? Assume the muzzle speed to be fixed, and neglect air resistance. **NCERT**

20. (a) Rain is falling vertically with a speed of 30 m/s. A woman rides a bicycle with a speed of 10 m/s in the north to south direction. What is the direction in which she should hold her umbrella?

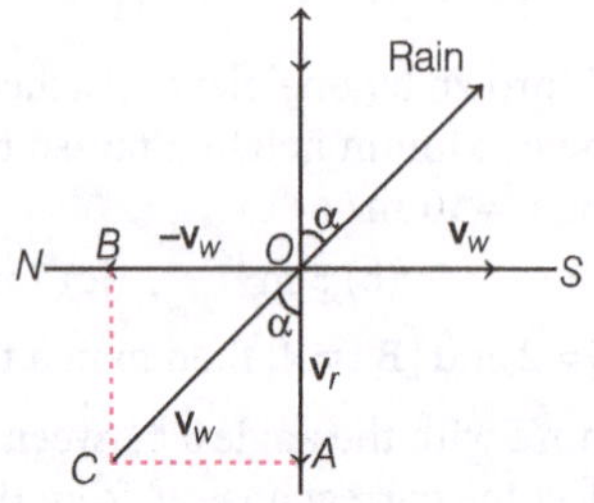

(b) A man can swim with a speed of 4 km/h in still water. How long does he take to cross a river 1 km wide, if the river flows steadily 3 km/h and he makes his strokes normal to the river current? How far down the river does he go when he reaches the other bank?

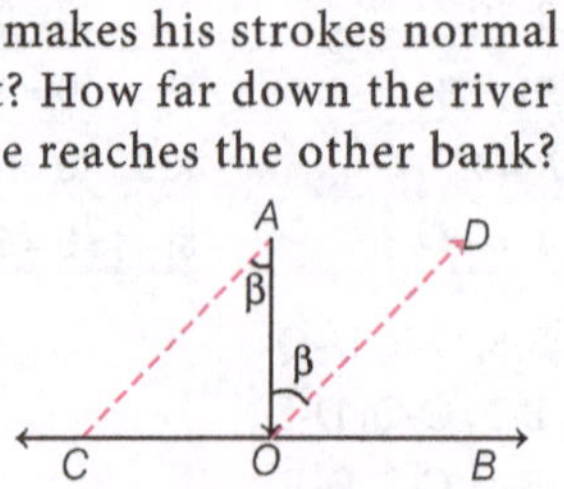

Answers

1. (c) 2. (b) 3. (c) 4. (a) 5. (b)
6. (c) 7. (d) 8. (a) 9. (a) 10. (c)
11. (i) (b), (ii) (a), (iii) (c), (iv) (c), (v) (d)

04

CHAPTER

Motion is an integral part of most of the natural phenomena. Galaxies, stars, planets, satellites all are in continuous motion. Motion of these bodies is governed and regulated by certain laws. Laws hidden behind these motions in nature were discovered first by Issac Newton. Therefore, these laws are known as Netwon's laws of motion.

YOUR STUDY GOALS

YOUR PRACTICE GOAL

- Objective Type Questions (30 Qs, MCQs, A-R, Matching)
- Case Based Questions (4)
- Subjective Questions (6 VSAs 6 SAs, 9 LAs)
- Numerical Problems (30)

Laws of Motion

4.1 Force

Force may be defined as an external cause (a push or a pull) which changes or tends to change the state of rest or of uniform motion or the direction of motion of an object.

The **dimensions** of force are $[MLT^{-2}]$ and its **SI unit** is **newton(N).**

A force applied on an object can produce four types of effects such as

(i) Force can start or stop a motion.
(ii) Force can change speed (slower or faster) of an object.
(iii) Force can change the direction of motion of an object.
(iv) Force can change the shape of an object.

To apply a force on a body, any external agency is required but this external body may or may not be in contact. e.g. Gravitational force, magnetic force, electric force can be applied from a distance.

Force is a **polar vector** as it has a point of application.

Inertia

The inherent property of a material body by virtue of which it resist the change in its state of rest or of uniform motion in a straight line. This term was first used by **Galileo.**

The various types of inertia are as below

1. Inertia of Rest

It is defined as the tendency of a body to remain in its **position of rest.**

e.g. A person standing in a train falls backward when the train suddenly starts moving forward. It depicts, when train moves, the lower part of his body begins to move alongwith the train while the upper part of his body continues to remain at rest due to inertia.

2. Inertia of Motion

It is defined as the tendency of a body to remain in its **state of uniform motion** in a straight line.

e.g. When a moving bus suddenly stops or apply brakes, a person standing in it falls forward. As the bus stops, the lower part of his body comes to rest alongwith the bus while upper part of his body continues to remain in motion due to inertia and falls forward.

3. Inertia of Direction

It is defined as inability of a body by virtue of which it tries to resist the change in its **direction of motion.**

e.g. The rain drops falling vertically downwards cannot change their direction of motion by themselves.

4.2 Newton's Laws of Motion

Sir Isaac Newton arrived at three laws of motion which are called Newton's laws of motion. These laws are as follows

Newton's First Law of Motion

This law states that every body continues in its state of rest or of uniform motion in a straight line unless it is compelled by some external force to change that state.

The first law of motion can be simply expressed as

If the net external force on a body is zero, then its acceleration is zero. Acceleration can be non-zero, only if there is a net external force on the body.

Newton's first law defines force qualitatively.

Newton's first law defines inertia, so it is also known as **law of inertia.**

Momentum

Momentum is a measure of the motion of an object and is define as the product of its mass m and velocity v and is denoted by **p**.

i.e. $\quad$ Momentum, $\mathbf{p} = m\mathbf{v}$

SI unit of momentum = kg-m/s or kg-ms^{-1}
CGS unit of momentum = g cm/s or g cm s^{-1}
The **dimensional formula** of momentum is $[MLT^{-1}]$.
It is a vector quantity.

- **The effect of force on the motion of a body is described by momentum.** This can be understood by the following examples
- We require a greater force to push the truck than the car to bring at the same speed in same time.
  Also, a greater opposing force is required to stop the truck than the car at the same time if they are moving with the same speed. Thus, **mass of a body is an important parameter to determine the effect of force on its motion.**
  Speed is another important parameter to consider.
- A bullet fired by a gun can easily pierce human tissue before it stops, resulting in casuality. The same bullet fired with moderate speed will not cause much damage. Thus, for a given mass, the greater the speed, the greater is the opposing force needed to stop the body in a certain time. **Thus, to describe the effect of force on the motion of a body, the mass and velocity i.e., momentum is an important quantity.**

Example 1. **A block with a mass of 20 g moves at a constant velocity on a rough horizontal floor at a constant velocity if there is an external force of 2 N acts on the block. Determine the magnitude of the friction force experienced by the block.**

Sol. Given Mass $(m) = 20$ g

Force $(F) = 2\text{ N} = v$

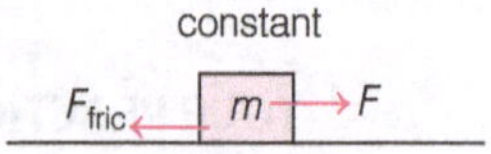

Based on Newton's first law of motion, if a block moves at a constant velocity, then the block has no acceleration. The block moves at a constant velocity and there is no acceleration if

(i) the magnitude of friction force (F_{fric}) same as magnitude of the external force (F).

(ii) The friction force (F_{fric}) has opposite direction with the external force (F).

Apply Newton's first law of motion, $\Sigma F = 0$

$$F - F_{fric} = 0,\ F = F_{fric},\ F_{fric} = 2\text{ N}$$

Newton's Second Law of Motion

This law states that **the rate of change of momentum of a body is directly proportional to the external force applied on the body and the change takes place in the direction of the applied force.**

Let **F** be external force applied on the body in the direction of motion of the body for time interval Δt, then the velocity of a body of mass m changes from **v** to $\mathbf{v}+\Delta\mathbf{v}$, i.e. change in momentum $\Delta\mathbf{p} = m\Delta\mathbf{v}$.

According to Newton's second law,

$$\mathbf{F} \propto \frac{\Delta\mathbf{p}}{\Delta t} \quad \text{or} \quad \mathbf{F} = k\frac{\Delta\mathbf{p}}{\Delta t}$$

where, k is a constant of proportionality.

If limit $\Delta t \to 0$, then the term $\frac{\Delta\mathbf{p}}{\Delta t}$ becomes the derivative $\frac{dp}{dt}$.

Thus, $$\mathbf{F} = k\frac{dp}{dt}$$

For a body of fixed mass m, we have

$$\mathbf{F} = k\frac{d(m\mathbf{v})}{dt} = km\frac{d\,\mathbf{v}}{dt}$$

$$\mathbf{F} = km\mathbf{a} \qquad \left(\because \frac{dv}{dt} = a\right)$$

Let, $k = 1$

So, Force, $\mathbf{F} = m\,\mathbf{a}$

In scalar form, this equation can be written as

$$\boxed{F = ma}$$

$\therefore$ 1 unit force = 1 unit mass × 1 unit acceleration

A unit force may be defined as the force which produces unit acceleration in a body of unit mass.

Units of Force

- The force is a vector quantity and its SI unit is **newton** (N).

$$1\text{ N} = 1\text{ kg m/s}^2$$

- In CGS system, absolute unit of force is **dyne**.

$$1\text{ dyne} = 1\text{ gcm/s}^2$$

- In SI unit, gravitational unit of force is **kilogram weight (kg-wt)**. It is defined as that much force which produces an acceleration of 9.80 m/s^2 in a body of mass 1 kg.

$$1\text{ kg-wt} = 1\text{ kgf}$$
$$= 1\text{ kg} \times 9.8\text{ m/s}^2 = 9.8\text{ N}$$

- In CGS system, gravitational unit of force is **gram weight (g-wt)**

$$1\text{g - wt} = 1\text{ gf} = 1\text{g} \times 980\text{ cm/s}^2 = 980\text{ g cm/s}^2$$

Relation between newton and dyne

$$1\text{ N} = 1\text{ kg} \times 1\text{ m/s}^2 = 1000\text{ g} \times 100\text{ cm/s}^2$$
$$= 10^5\text{ g cm/s}^2 \; [1\text{ dyne} = 1\text{ g cm/s}^2]$$
$$1\text{ N} = 10^5\text{ dyne}$$

TEACHER TIPS

A gravitational unit is g times the corresponding absolute unit.

A gravitational unit of force is used to express the weight of a body. e.g. The weight of a body of mass 10 kg is 10 kg-wt or 10 kgf. For this reason, the gravitational units are also called practical units.

Example 2. **If an electron is subjected to a force of 10^{-25} N in an X-ray machine, then find out the time taken by the electron to cover a distance of 0.2 m. Take mass of the electron = 10^{-30} kg.**

Sol. The acceleration of the electron

$$a = \frac{F}{m} = \frac{10^{-25}}{10^{-30}} = 10^5\text{ m/s}^2$$

The time taken by the electron (t) to cover the distance (s) of 0.2 m can be given by $s = ut + \frac{1}{2}at^2$

$$0.2 = 0 + \frac{1}{2} \times 10^5 \times t^2$$
$$t^2 = 0.4 \times 10^{-5} = 4 \times 10^{-6}\text{ s}^2$$
$$t = 2 \times 10^{-3}\text{ s}$$

Example 3. **A car of mass 800 kg is moving down a hill and reaches a speed of 15 m/s, if it comes to stop in 5 s. Calculate**

(a) momentum of car

(b) the average force that was applied to bring it to rest.

Sol. Momentum is given by

$$p = mv = 800 \times 15 = 12000\text{ kg m/s}$$

We know, $$F = \frac{dp}{dt} \text{ or } \frac{\Delta p}{\Delta t}$$

where, $$\Delta p = p_{\text{final}} - p_{\text{initial}}$$

Since, the car stops, the final momentum is zero.

$$\Delta p = 0 - 12000 = -12000\text{ kg m/s}$$

Then, $$F = ma = m\frac{v}{t} = \frac{p}{t} = \frac{-12000\text{ kg m/s}}{5\text{s}} = -2400\text{ N}$$

Negative sign indicate that the force acting in the opposite direction to the car's initial motion.

Newton's Second Law in Component Form and its Significance

In terms of their rectangular components, the force, momentum and acceleration vectors can be expressed as

$$\mathbf{F} = F_x\hat{i} + F_y\hat{j} + F_z\hat{k}$$

$$\mathbf{p} = p_x\hat{i} + p_y\hat{j} + p_z\hat{k}$$

and $$\mathbf{a} = a_x\hat{i} + a_y\hat{j} + a_z\hat{k}$$

From the formula of force in vector form, for constant m,

$$\mathbf{F} = \frac{d\mathbf{p}}{dt} = m\mathbf{a}$$

$$\therefore \quad F_x\hat{i} + F_y\hat{j} + F_z\hat{k} = \frac{d}{dt}(p_x\hat{i} + p_y\hat{j} + p_z\hat{k})$$

$$= m(a_x\hat{i} + a_y\hat{j} + a_z\hat{k})$$

Equating the components along the three coordinate axes, we get

$$F_x = \frac{dp_x}{dt} = ma_x, \quad F_y = \frac{dp_y}{dt} = ma_y$$

$$F_z = \frac{dp_z}{dt} = ma_z$$

The above three equations represent the component form of Newton's second law.

Example 4. **A hockey puck with a mass of 0.3 kg slides on the horizontal frictionless surface of an ice rink. Two forces act on the puck as shown in figure. The force F_1 has a magnitude of 5 N and F_2 has a magnitude of 8 N. Determine the acceleration of the puck.**

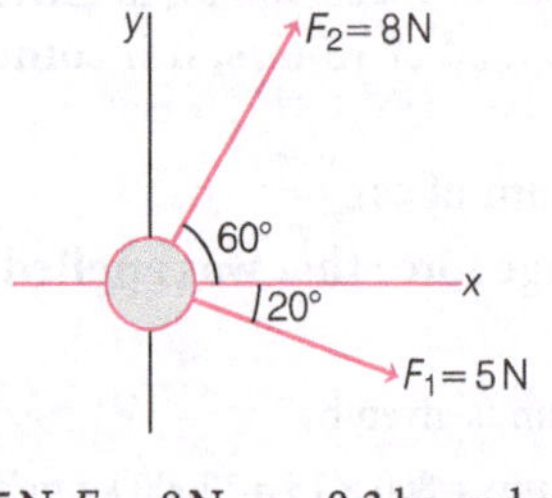

Sol. Given, $F_1 = 5\text{ N}, F_2 = 8\text{ N}, m = 0.3$ kg and acceleration $a = ?$

The resultant force in the x-direction exerted on the puck,

$$\Sigma F_x = F_{1x} + F_{2x} = F_1 \cos 20° + F_2 \cos 60°$$

$$= (5\text{ N})(0.940) + (8\text{ N})(0.500) = 8.70\text{ N}$$

The resultant force in the y-direction exerted on the puck,

$$\Sigma F_y = F_{1y} + F_{2y} = -F_1 \sin 20° + F_2 \sin 60°$$

$$= -(5\text{ N})(0.342) + (8\text{ N})(0.8666) = 5.22\text{ N}$$

Now, we can use Newton's second law in component form to find the x and y-components of acceleration

$$a_x = \frac{\Sigma F_x}{m} = \frac{8.70\text{ N}}{0.3\text{ kg}} = 29.0\text{ m/s}^2$$

and $$a_y = \frac{\Sigma F_y}{m} = \frac{5.22\text{ N}}{0.3\text{ kg}} = 17.4\text{ m/s}^2$$

Magnitude, $a = \sqrt{(29.0)^2 + (17.4)^2}\text{ m/s}^2 = 33.8\text{ m/s}^2$

and its direction is

$$\theta = \tan^{-1}(a_y/a_x) = \tan^{-1}(17.4/29.0) = 31.0°$$

relative to the positive x-axis.

Example 5. **A force applied on an object of mass 1 kg produces an acceleration of 8 m/s². When a force of the same magnitude is applied to a carton of ice cream of mass m_2, it produces an acceleration of 12 m/s². What is the mass of the carton of ice cream and the magnitude of the force?**

Sol. Given, $a_2 = 12\text{ m/s}^2$ and Force $F = ?$

Apply $\Sigma \mathbf{F} = m\mathbf{a}$ to each object.

$$F_1 = m_1a_1 \quad \text{and} \quad F_2 = m_2a_2$$

$$F_1 = F_2 = F \quad \text{or} \quad m_1a_1 = m_2a_2$$

$$\Rightarrow \quad \frac{m_2}{m_1} = \frac{a_1}{a_2} = \frac{8}{12}$$

$$\Rightarrow \quad m_2 = \frac{8}{12} = 0.67\text{ kg} \Rightarrow F = m_1a_1 = 1 \times 8 = 8\text{ N}$$

Example 6. **A bullet of mass 0.04 kg moving with a speed of 90 m/s enters a heavy wooden block and is stopped after a distance of 60 cm. What is the average resistive force exerted by the block on the bullet?** *(NCERT)*

Sol. Given, $s = 60\text{ cm} = 0.6\text{ m}, u = 90\text{ m/s}$

The retardation acceleration of the bullet is given by

$$a = -\frac{u^2}{2s} = \frac{-90 \times 90}{2 \times 0.6} \Rightarrow a = -6750\text{ m/s}^2$$

The retarding force by the second law of motion is

$$F = ma$$

where, $$F = 0.04 \times 6750$$

$$F = 270\text{ N}$$

Actual resistive force and retardation of the bullet may not be uniform. It indicates only average force.

Impulse

The larger force which acts on an object for a very short time producing a finite change in momentum of the object is called **impulsive force.**

Hence, **impulse of a force is defined as the product of the average force and the time interval for which the force acts on the body**. It is denoted by **I**.

Thus, Impulse = Average force × Time or $\boxed{\mathbf{I} = \mathbf{F}\Delta t}$

Impulse is a **vector quantity**. The direction of impulse is same as that of the force.
Its SI unit is **newton-second** (N-s).
Its dimensional formula is $[MLT^{-1}]$.

Note Also, the impulse of a force is equal to the total change in momeutum produced by the force.
Impulse $I = p_2 - p_1$

Daily life Examples of Impulse

Following are some of the **practical aspects of impulse.**

(i) A cricket player lowers his hands while catching a ball to allow a longer time to stop the ball.

As force $= \dfrac{\Delta p}{\Delta t}$, so by increasing time of catch, the player has to apply smaller force on the ball to stop it. So, the ball also exerts a smaller force on his hand and the hands of player are protected from injury.

Change in momentum of the ball

(ii) An athelete is advised to stop slowly after finishing a fast race, so that time of stop increases and hence force experienced by him decreases.

(iii) Boggies of a train are provided with buffers to avoid severe jerks during shunting of the train. Due to presence of buffers, time of impact increases. Thus, force during jerks decreases.

Example 7. A batsman hits back a ball straight in the direction of the bowler without changing its initial speed of 12 m/s. If the mass of the ball is 0.15 kg, determine the impulse imparted to the ball. (Consider a ball in linear motion). (NCERT)

Sol. Given, $m = 0.15$ kg, $v = 12$ m/s, $u = -12$ m/s

Change in momentum $= \mathbf{p}_2 - \mathbf{p}_1 = m[v - u]$

$= 0.15\,[12 - (-12)] = 0.15 \times 24$

$\mathbf{p}_2 - \mathbf{p}_1 = 3.60$ kg-m/s

Impulse, $\quad \mathbf{I} = \mathbf{p}_2 - \mathbf{p}_1 \Rightarrow \mathbf{I} = 3.6$ N-s

Example 8. Consider a ball falling from a height of 2 m and rebounding to a height of 0.5 m. If the mass of the ball is 60 g, find the impulse and the average force between the ball and the ground. The time for which the ball and the ground remained in contact was 0.2 s.

Sol. The initial velocity of the ball at P is zero. Let the final velocity of the ball at Q is v.

Given $s = 2$ m, then $v^2 = u^2 + 2as$

$v^2 = 0 + 2 \times 9.8 \times 2 = 4 \times 9.8$

$v = \sqrt{39.2}$ m/s $= 6.26$ m/s

Let u' be the velocity of rebound of the ball.

Given, $s' = 0.5$ m, the final velocity at R is zero

$v'^2 = u'^2 + 2as$

$0 = u'^2 + 2 \times (-9.8) \times 0.5$

$u' = -\sqrt{9.8}$ m / s

$= -3.13$ m / s

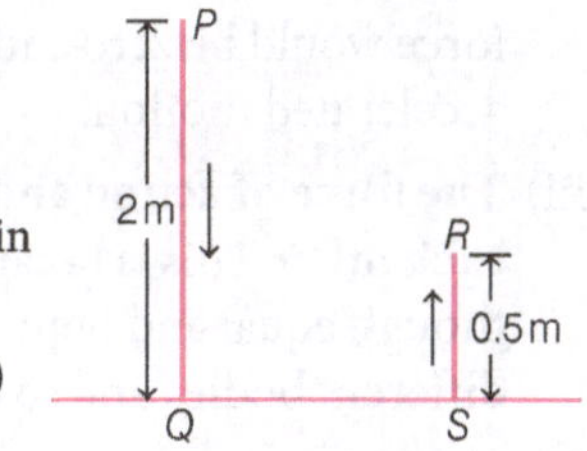

Now, Impulse = Change in momentum

$= mv - (-mu') = m(v + u')$

$= \dfrac{60}{1000}(6.26 + 3.13)$

$= 0.06 \times 9.39 = 0.563$ N-s

$\because$ Average force $= \dfrac{\text{Impulse}}{\text{Time}} = \dfrac{0.563}{0.2} = 2.817$ N

Newton's Third Law of Motion

Newton's third law states that for every action, there is always an equal and opposite reaction.

In simple terms, the third law can be stated as follows

Force in nature always occurs in pairs. Force on body A by body B is equal and opposite to the force on the body B by A.

Explanation

For example, When we press a coiled spring, in turn, the spring exerts a force on our hand and we can feel it.

A book lying on a table applies a force on the table (its weight) and the table exert an equal and opposite force on the book.

Thus, **forces always occur in pairs as a result of mutual interaction between two bodies.**

As shown in figure if $\mathbf{F}_{BA}$ is the force exerted by body A on B and $\mathbf{F}_{AB}$ is the force exerted by B on A, then according to Newton's third law,

$$\mathbf{F}_{AB} = -\mathbf{F}_{BA}$$

Force on A by $B = -$ Force on B by A

The condition is shown in figure.

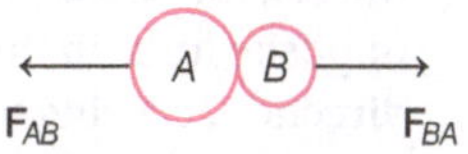

Forces acting on bodies A and B

Some important implications about the third law of motion.

(i) **Newton's third law of motion is applicable irrespective of the nature of the forces.** The forces of action and reaction may be mechanical, gravitational, electric or of any other nature.

(ii) **Action and reaction always act on two different bodies** If they acted on the same body, the resultant force would be zero and there could never be accelerated motion.

(iii) **The force of action and reaction cannot cancel each other** This is because action and reaction, though equal and opposite forces always act on different bodies and so cannot cancel each other.

(iv) **No action can occur in the absence of a reaction** In a tug of war, one team can pull the rope only if the other team is pulling the other end of the rope, no force of action can be exerted if the other end is free.

One team can exert the force of action because the other team provides the force of reaction.

Some Important Concepts about Newton's Third Law of Motion

(i) While walking we press the ground (action) with our feet slightly slanted in the backward direction. The ground exerts an equal and opposite force on us. The vertical component of the force of reaction balances our weight and the horizontal component enables us to move forward as shown in figure.

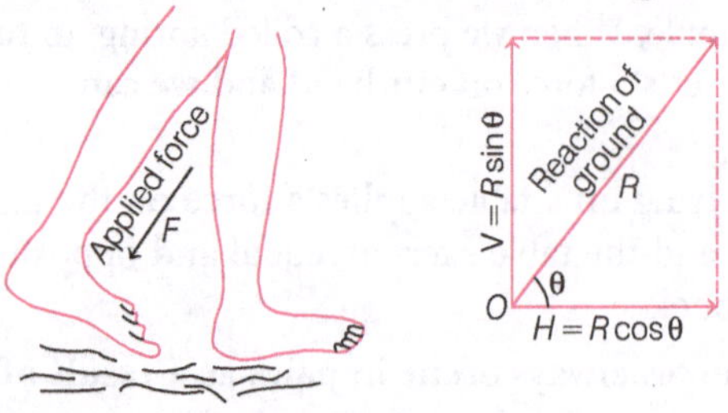

Applied force by the feet and its reaction force along with its components

(ii) **Rotatory lawn sprinkler** The action of rotatory lawn sprinkler is based on third law of motion. As water forces way of the nozzle, it exerts an equal and opposite force in the backward direction, causing the sprinkler to rotate in the opposite direction. Thus, water is scattered in all directions as shown in following figure.

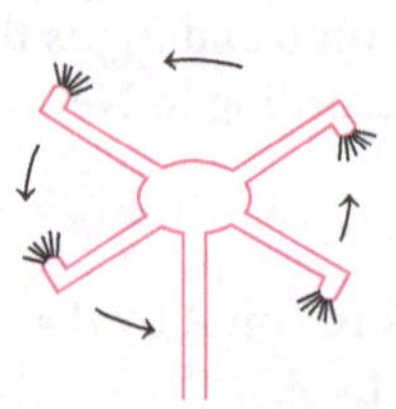

Water Rotatory lawn sprinkler

Example 9. A cat of mass 6 kg jumps on a dining table of mass 30 kg. As the cat walks around on the table, then what is the average force that the table applies to the cat?

Sol. Given, mass of cat = 6 kg.

The force applied by cat on the table is simply its weight.

∴ Force applied by cat on the table,

$$w = mg$$
$$= 6 \times 10 = 60 \text{ N}$$

∴ According to Newton's third law, the average force applied by table to the cat is also 60 N.

Example 10. A truck is moving with a speed of 20 m/s along a straight line. Suddenly, some sand starts falling from the back side of the truck at the rate of 20 g/s. Find the value of external force required to make the truck move with the constant velocity of 20 m/s.

Sol. Since, truck is losing weight or mass without any change in velocity, its momentum changes. When there is a change in momentum, there is creation of force (according to Newton's second law applied in reverse). Since, truck is becoming lighter, it will be accelerated in forward direction. That means force in it will be created in forward direction.

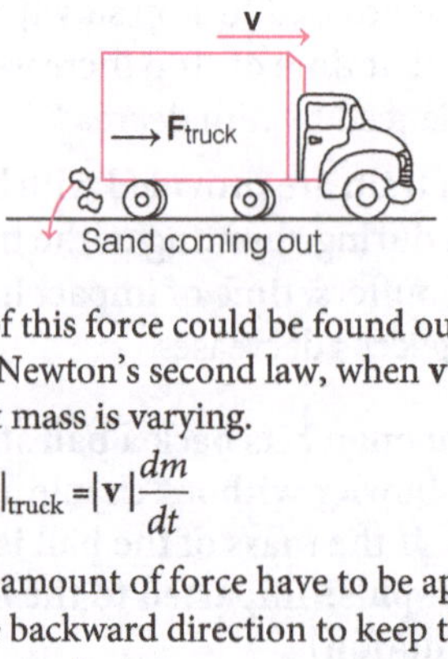

The value of this force could be found out with the formula of Newton's second law, when **v** is constant (at an instant) but mass is varying.

$$|\mathbf{F}|_{truck} = |\mathbf{v}|\frac{dm}{dt}$$

That much amount of force have to be applied on the truck in the backward direction to keep the truck moving with constant velocity.

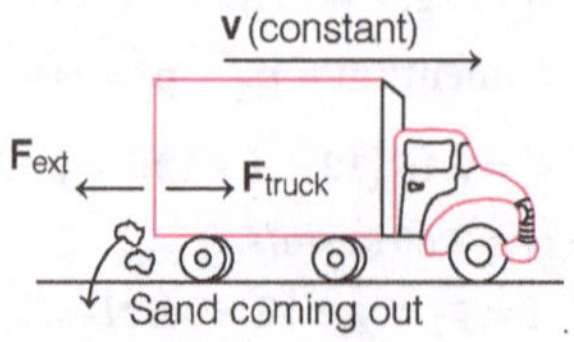

$$F_{ext} = F_{truck} = v\frac{dm}{dt}$$
$$F_{ext} = 20 \text{ m/s}[20 \times 10^{-3} \text{ kg /s}]$$
$$= 0.4 \text{ N (backward)}$$

4.3 Apparent Weight of a Man in a Lift

The reaction exerted by the surface of contact of a weighing machine on a body is called its **apparent weight.**

Let us consider a man of mass m is standing on a weighing machine placed in an elevator/lift. The actual weight mg of the man acts on the weighing machine and offers a reaction R given by the reading of the weighing machine.

This reaction R exerted by the surface of contact on the man is the apparent weight of the man.

Now, we consider how R is related to mg in the different conditions.

(i) **When the lift moves upward with acceleration a as shown in figure**, the net upward force on the man is

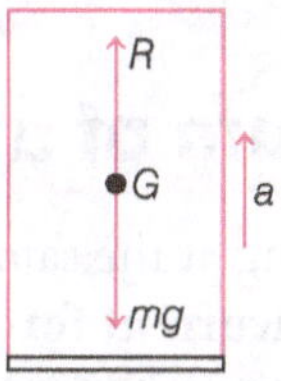

$$R - mg = ma \Rightarrow R = ma + mg$$

$$\boxed{\text{Apparent weight, } R = m(g+a)}$$

So, **when a lift accelerates upward, the apparent weight of the man inside it increases.**

(ii) When the lift moves downward with acceleration a as shown in figure, net downward force on the man is

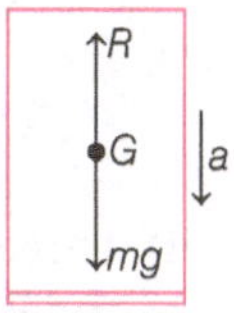

$$mg - R = ma$$

$$\boxed{\text{Apparent weight, } R = m(g-a)}$$

So, **when a lift accelerates downward, the apparent weight of the man inside it decreases.**

(iii) When the lift is at rest or moving with uniform velocity v downward or upward as shown in figure.

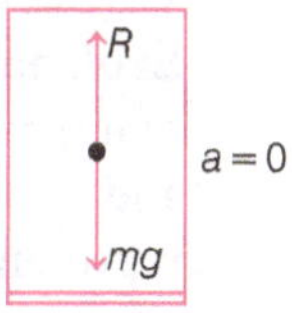

Then, acceleration $a = 0$. So, net force on the man is

$$R - mg = m \times 0 \Rightarrow R = mg$$

or $\boxed{\text{Apparent weight = Actual weight}}$

So, **when the lift is at rest, the apparent weight of the man is the actual weight.**

(iv) When the lift falls freely under gravity if the supporting cable of the lift breaks. Then, $a = g$.

The net downward force on the man is

$$R = m(g-g) \Rightarrow \boxed{R = 0}$$

Thus, **the apparent weight of the man becomes zero.** This is because both the lift and man are moving downwards with the same acceleration g and so there is no force of action and reaction exist between the man and lift. Hence, a **person develops a feeling of weightlessness when the lift falls freely under gravity.**

Example 11. A man of mass 70 kg stands on a weighing scale in a lift which is moving

(i) upwards with uniform speed of 10 m/s.

(ii) downwards with a uniform acceleration of 5 m/s^2.

(iii) upwards with uniform acceleration of 5 m/s^2. What would be the readings on the scale in each case?

(iv) What would be the reading if the lift mechanism failed and it hurtled down freely under gravity? NCERT

Sol. Given, mass of man $(m) = 70$ kg

In each case, the weighing scale will read the reaction R, i.e. the apparent weight.

(i) As lift is moving upward with a uniform speed, therefore, its acceleration $a = 0$

$\therefore$ Normal reaction, $w = R = mg = 70 \times 10 \text{ N} = 700 \text{ N}$

w acts vertically downwards and R acts vertically upwards.

$\therefore$ Reading on weighing scale $= \dfrac{700}{10} = 70$ kg

(ii) Acceleration of the lift, $a = 5 \text{ m/s}^2 (\downarrow)$

$\therefore$ Normal reaction, $R = m(g-a) = 70(10-5)$ N

$= 70 \times 5 \text{ N} = 350$ N

$\therefore$ Reading on weighing scale $= \dfrac{350 \text{ N}}{10 \text{ m/s}^2} = 35$ kg

(iii) Acceleration of the lift, $a = 5 \text{ m/s}^2 (\uparrow)$

$\therefore$ Normal reaction, $R = m(g+a) = 70(10+5)$

$= 1050$ N

$\therefore$ Reading on weighing scale $= \dfrac{1050 \text{ N}}{10 \text{ m/s}^2} = 105$ kg

(iv) Acceleration of the lift when it is falling freely under gravity $a = g \, (\downarrow)$

$\therefore$ Normal reaction, $R = m(g-a) = m(g-g) = 0$

$\therefore$ Reading on weighing scale $= 0$

4.4 Conservation of Momentum

This principle is a consequence of Newton's second and third law of motion. According to this principle,

"In the absence of an external force, the total momentum of a system remains constant or conserved and does not change with time"

If $\mathbf{F}_{ext} = 0$, then the system is called **isolated system.**

Let $\mathbf{F}_{AB}$ and $\mathbf{F}_{BA}$ are the internal forces in the system of bodies A and B in the time Δt.

$\therefore \quad \Delta \mathbf{p}_A$ = change in momentum of $A = \mathbf{F}_{AB} \times \Delta t$

$\therefore \quad \Delta \mathbf{p}_B$ = change in momentum of $B = \mathbf{F}_{BA} \times \Delta t$

As, $\quad \mathbf{F}_{AB} = -\mathbf{F}_{BA}$

$\Rightarrow \quad \mathbf{F}_{AB} \times \Delta t = -\mathbf{F}_{BA} \times \Delta t \quad \Rightarrow \quad \Delta \mathbf{p}_A = \Delta \mathbf{p}_B$

$\Rightarrow \quad \boxed{\Delta \mathbf{p}_A + \Delta \mathbf{p}_B = 0}$

i.e. Change in momentum of the system = 0

$\therefore$ **Vector sum of the linear momentum of the isolated system remains constant.**

This is known as law of conservation of momentum.

Conservation of momentum theorem is applicable for $F_{ext} = 0$, it does not depend on internal forces.

e.g.

(i) Let us consider a bullet fired from a gun. Then, force on the bullet by the gun is F and according to third law of motion, the force on the gun by bullet will be – F. The two forces act for a common interval of time Δt.

According to second law, F Δt is the change in momentum of the bullet and – F Δt is the change in momentum of the gun.

Because bullet and gun are initially at rest and then change in momentum of the system is zero, so the sum of their final momenta must be zero.

Thus, if $\mathbf{p}_b$ is the momentum of the bullet after firing and $\mathbf{p}_g$ is the recoil momentum of the gun, then $\mathbf{p}_g = -\mathbf{p}_b$ or $\boxed{\mathbf{p}_b + \mathbf{p}_g = 0}$

(ii) Let a bomb be at rest, then its momentum will be zero. If the bomb explodes into two equal parts, then the parts fly off in exactly opposite directions with the same speed, so that the total momentum is still zero.

Here, no external force is applied on the system of particles (bomb).

Forces created are internal only.

Note Rocket propulsion is based on the principle of conservation of momentum.

Example 12. **A moving neutron with speed 10^6 m/s collides with a deuteron at rest and sticks to it. Find the speed of the combination if masses of the neutron and deuteron are 1.67×10^{-27} kg and 3.34×10^{-27} kg, respectively.**

Sol. Given, for neutron,

Mass, $m_1 = 1.67 \times 10^{-27}$ kg

Speed, $u_1 = 10^6$ m/s

For deuteron,

Mass, $m_2 = 3.34 \times 10^{-27}$ kg

Speed, $u_2 = 0$ [$\because$ the deuteron is at rest]

From principle of conservation of momentum,

$$m_1 u_1 + m_2 u_2 = (m_1 + m_2) v$$

$$1.67 \times 10^{-27} \times 10^6 + 3.34 \times 10^{-27} \times 0 = (3.34 + 1.67) \times 10^{-27} \times v$$

$$v = \frac{1.67 \times 10^{-27} \times 10^{+6}}{5.01 \times 10^{-27}}$$

$$= 33.33 \times 10^4 \text{ m/s}$$

4.5 Equilibrium of a Particle

Forces which are acting at the same point or on a particle are called **concurrent forces**. These forces are said to be in equilibrium when their resultant is zero.

The equilibrium of concurrent forces can be illustrated by following examples.

(i) If two forces F_1 and F_2 act on a particle, then they will be in equilibrium if $F_1 = -F_2$ i.e. two forces on the particle must be equal and opposite.

Representation of concurrent forces

(ii) Three concurrent forces F_1, F_2 and F_3 will be in equilibrium when the resultant of two forces F_1 and F_2 is equal and opposite to the third force F_3.

Explanation Given figure shows that three concurrent forces F_1, F_2 and F_3 are acting at a point O and represented by OA, OB and OC, respectively.

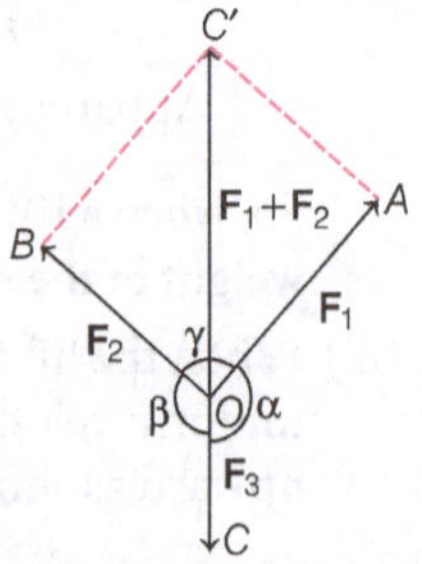

Equilibrium under concurrent forces

Let us complete the parallelogram $OAC'B$.

The diagonal OC' of the parallelogram represents $F_1 + F_2$, the resultant of F_1 and F_2 from law of parallelogram of forces.

If OC' is equal and opposite to OC, then

$$F_1 + F_2 = -F_3 \text{ or } \boxed{F_1 + F_2 + F_3 = 0}$$

i.e. three concurrent forces are in equilibrium when the resultant of any two of them is equal and opposite to the third.

(iii) A particle under the action of forces $F_1, F_2, F_3, \ldots, F_n$ will be in equilibrium if these forces can be represented by the sides of a closed n sided polygon in the same sense, i.e.

$$\boxed{F_1 + F_2 + F_3 + \ldots\ldots + F_n = 0}$$

This equation implies that

$$F_{1x} + F_{2x} + F_{3x} + \ldots\ldots + F_{nx} = 0$$
$$F_{1y} + F_{2y} + F_{3y} + \ldots\ldots + F_{ny} = 0$$
$$F_{1z} + F_{2z} + F_{3z} + \ldots\ldots + F_{nz} = 0$$

where, F_{1x}, F_{1y} and F_{1z} are the rectangular components of F_1 along x, y and z-directions.

Lami's Theorem

According to this theorem, when three concurrent forces F_1, F_2 and F_3 acting on a body are in equilibrium, then

$$\boxed{\frac{F_1}{\sin\alpha} = \frac{F_2}{\sin\beta} = \frac{F_3}{\sin\gamma}}$$

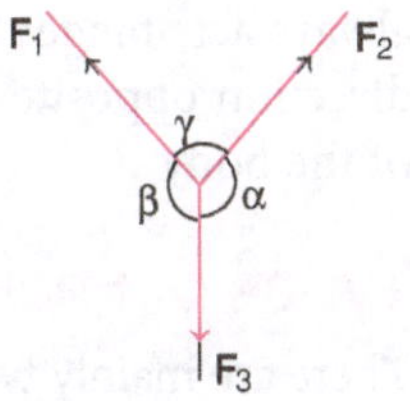

Three concurrent forces acting at some

Example 13. **The below figure is the part of a horizontal stretched net. Section AB is stretched with a force of 10 N, then determine the forces in the sections BC and BF.**

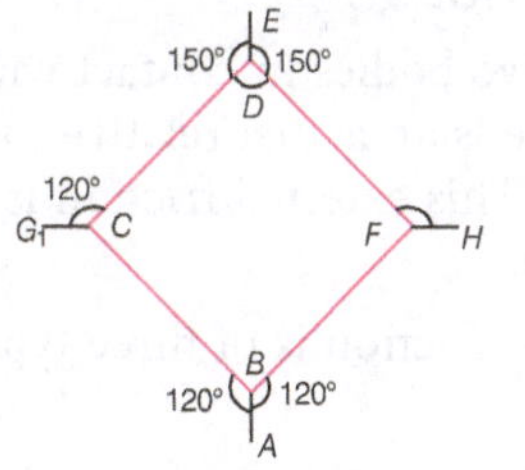

Sol. By drawing the free body diagram of point B.

Let the force in the section BC and BF are F_1 and F_2 respectively.

$$\frac{F_1}{\sin 120°} = \frac{F_2}{\sin 120°} = \frac{F}{\sin 120°}$$

From Lami's theorem

$$F_1 = F_2 = F = 10 \text{ N}$$

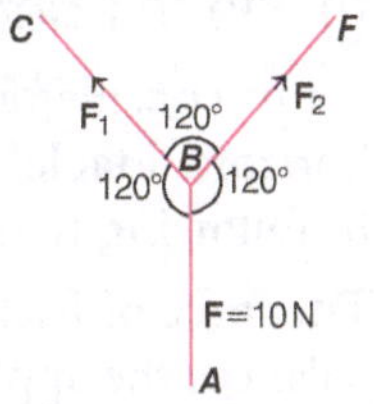

Three concurrent forces acting at

Quick Test 1

Conceptual Questions

1. The distance travelled by a moving body is directly proportional to time. Is any external force acting on it?
2. A body is acted upon by a number of external forces. Can it remain at rest?
3. An impulse is applied to a moving object with a force at an angle of 20° w.r.t. velocity vector, what is the angle between the impulse vector and change in momentum vector?
4. Two bodies of different masses have same linear momentum. Which one of them will move faster?
5. A running bus has several standing passengers is dangerous, why?

Numerical Questions

6. A woman throws an object of mass 500 g with a speed of 25 m/s.
   (i) What is the impulse imparted to the object?
   (ii) If the object hits a wall and rebounds with half the original speed, what is the change in momentum of the object?
7. A person of mass 50 kg stands on a weighing scale on a lift. If the lift is descending with a downward acceleration of 9 m/s^2, what would be the reading of the weighing scale? ($g = 10 \text{ m/s}^2$)
   When a lift descends with a downward acceleration a, the apparent weight of a body of mass m is given by $w' = R = m(g - a)$ *NCERT Exemplar*
8. A stream of water flowing horizontally with a speed of 15 m/s gushes out of a tube of cross-sectional area 10^{-2}m^2 and hits a vertical wall nearby. What is the force exerted on the wall by the impact of water, assuming it does not rebound?
9. A helicopter of mass 1000 kg rises with a vertical acceleration of 15 m/s^2. The crew and the passengers weigh 300 kg. Give the magnitude and direction of the
   (i) force on floor by the crew and passengers.
   (ii) action of the rotor of the helicopter on the surrounding air
   (iii) force on the helicopter due to the surrounding air, take $g = 10 \text{ m/s}^2$.

Answers

6. (i) 12.5 N-s, (ii) – 18.75 N-s 7. 5 kg 8. 2250N
9. (i) 7500 N (upward), (ii) 32500N (downward), (iii) 32500N (upward)

For Solutions, See QR Code on Pg. 152

Common Forces in Mechanics and Circular Motion

In mechanics, we encounter several kinds of forces.

(i) **Gravitational Force** The force of attraction that arises between two bodies having definite masses is called force of gravitation or gravitational force. It is a **non-contact force.**

(ii) **Contact Force** It is a force that is applied by objects in contact with each other. Some of the contact forces are given below.

(a) **Frictional Force** It is a type of contact force which is parallel to surfaces in contact and resists the relative motion of the bodies in contact.

(b) **Normal reaction** It is a type of contact force which is normal to the surfaces in contact.

(c) **Buoyant Force** The upward force exerted by the fluid on the solid immersed in the fluid is called buoyant force. **It is equal to the weight of the fluid displaced by the solid.**

(d) **Spring Force** The force generated in the spring when it is either elongated or compressed for a small displacement.

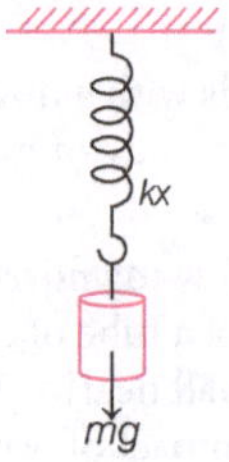

Spring force

(iii) **Tension force** When a body of mass m is fastened with the string, then the weight of the body acts downward while a force acts just opposite to the downward force for balancing the downward force, this force is called tension.

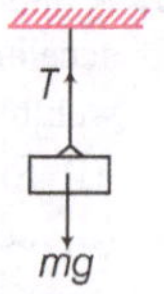

Tension force

$$T = mg$$

where, g = acceleration due to gravity,
T = tension in the string.

Note • Gravitational force is the only non-contact force that we use in mechanics.
• If the rope is not light, we will consider its weight as well.

4.6 Friction

Whenever a body moves or tends to move over the surface of another body, a force comes into play which acts parallel to the surface of contact and opposes the relative motion. This opposing force is called friction.

Explanation Consider a wooden block placed on a horizontal surface and give it a gentle push. The block slides through a small distance and comes to rest, then according to Newton's second law, a retarding force must be acting on the block.

This retarding force or opposing force is called friction or friction force.

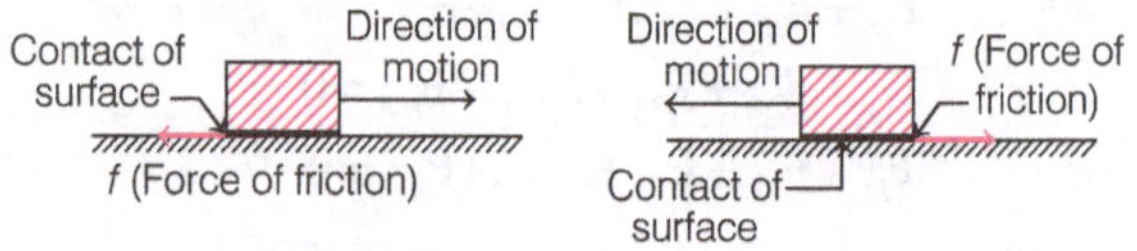

Friction in different directions

As shown in the above figure, the force of friction always acts tangential to the surface in contact and in a direction opposite to the direction of (relative) motion of the body.

Types of Friction

There are mainly two types of friction. They are as follows.

1. Internal Friction

It arises on the account of relative motion between two layers of a liquid. Internal friction is also referred as **viscosity** of liquid.

2. External Friction

It arises when two bodies in contact with each other try to move or there is an actual relative motion between the two bodies. This external friction is also called **contact friction.**

Further, external friction is of three types as given below

(i) Static Friction

Let us consider a wooden block placed over a horizontal table. Apply a small force F on it as shown in following figure. The block does not move.

The force of friction f_s comes into action which balances the applied force F.

Static friction

Thus, force of friction which comes into play between two bodies before one body actually starts moving over the other is called **static friction** and it is denoted by f_s.

Therefore, static friction opposes the **impending motion** i.e. the motion that would take place under the applied force, if friction were absent. The static friction does not exist by itself. When there is no applied force, there is no static friction. It is a self-adjusting force.

(ii) Limiting Friction

As we increase the applied force on the block, static friction f_s also increases to balance the applied force and the block does not move.

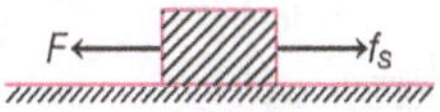

Static friction

Once the applied force is increased beyond a certain limit, the block just begins to move. At this stage, static friction is maximum.

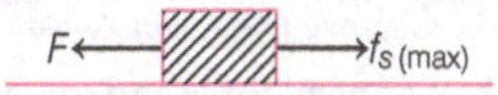

Maximum limiting friction acting on a body

Hence, **maximum force of static friction which comes into play when a body just starts moving over the surface of another body is called limiting friction.** Thus, $f_s \le f_{s(\max)}$.

There are **four laws of limiting friction** such as

(i) The value of the limiting friction depends upon the nature of the two surfaces in contact and their state of roughness.

(ii) The force of limiting friction is tangential (parallel) to the two surfaces in contact and acts opposite to the direction in which the body would start moving on applying the force.

(iii) The value of limiting friction is independent of the area of the surface in contact so long as the normal reaction remains the same.

(iv) The value of limiting friction ($f_{s(\max)}$) between two given surfaces is directly proportional to the normal reaction (R) between the two surfaces

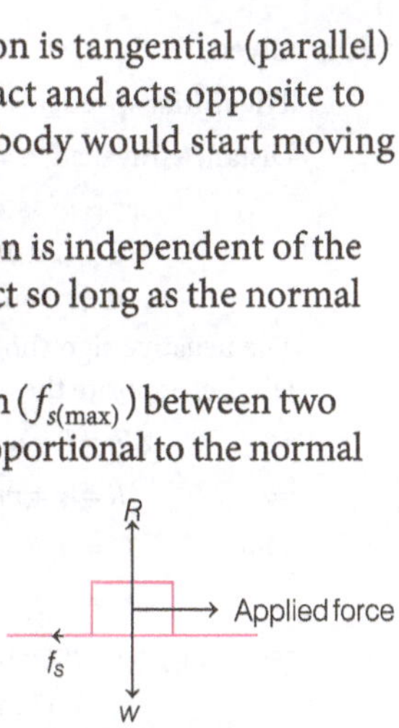

i.e. $f_{s(\max)} \propto R$

or $f_{s(\max)} = \mu_s R$

where, $R = w = mg$,

m = mass of the block

or $\mu_s = \dfrac{f_{s(\max)}}{R} = \dfrac{\text{Limiting friction}}{\text{Normal reaction}}$

The proportionality constant μ_s is called **coefficient of static friction.** It is defined as the ratio of limiting friction to the normal reaction.

Example 14. A block of mass 2 kg is placed on the floor, the coefficient of static friction is 0.4. A force of 2.5 N is applied on the block as shown in figure. Calculate the force of friction between the block and the floor.

Sol. Here $m = 2$ kg, $\mu_s = 0.4$, $g = 9.8$ m/s^2

The value of limiting friction

$$F_{s(\max)} = \mu_s R = \mu_s\, mg = 0.4 \times 2 \times 9.8 = 7.84 \text{ N}$$

As the applied force of 2.5 N is less than the limiting friction (7.84 N), so the block does not move.

In this situation, Force of friction = Applied force = 2.5 N

Angle of Friction

It is the angle made by the resultant of the limiting friction and the normal reaction with the normal reaction is called angle of friction.

In the given figure, OA represents the normal reaction R which balances the weight of the body. OB represents the limiting friction. P is the applied force and OC is the resultant of limiting friction and normal reaction. The angle θ between the normal reaction R and the resultant OC is the angle of friction.

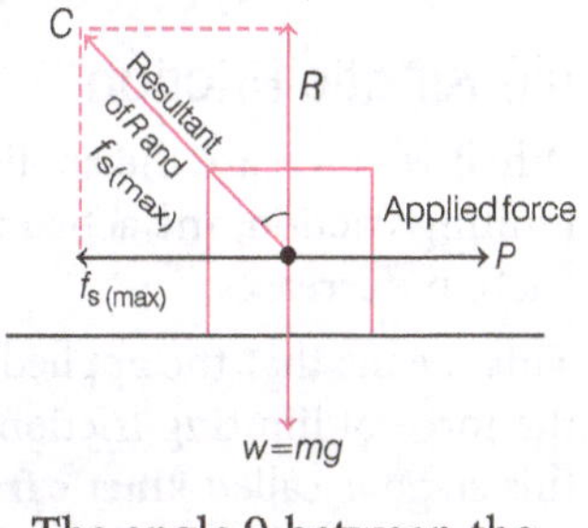

The value of angle of friction depends on the nature of materials of the surfaces in contact and the nature of the surfaces (smooth or rough).

Relation between angle of friction (θ) and coefficient of friction (μ_s) In ΔAOC, $\tan\theta = \dfrac{AC}{OA} = \dfrac{OB}{OA} = \dfrac{f_{s(\max)}}{R}$

But $\dfrac{f_{s(\max)}}{R} = \mu_s$ = coefficient of static friction

$\therefore$ $\tan\theta = \mu_s$ or $\theta = \tan^{-1}(\mu_s)$

Hence, **coefficient of static friction is equal to tangent of the angle of friction.**

Example 15. **A force of 49 N is just sufficient to pull a block of wood weighing 10 kg on a rough horizontal surface, so calculate the coefficient of friction and angle of friction.**

Sol. Here, F = applied force= 49 N

$m = 10$ kg, $g = 9.8$ m/s^2

Coefficient of friction, $\mu = \dfrac{F}{R} = \dfrac{F}{mg} = \dfrac{49}{10 \times 9.8} = 0.5$

As $\tan\theta = \mu = 0.5$

$\therefore \quad \theta = \tan^{-1}(0.5) = 26°34'$

Angle of Repose

Angle of repose is defined as the minimum angle of inclination of a plane with the horizontal, such that a body placed on the plane just begins to slide down the incline.

It is represented by α and its value depends on the material and the nature of the surfaces in contact.

The coefficient of static friction is equal to the tangent of the angle of repose.

As, $\quad \mu_s = \tan\theta = \tan\alpha$

$\theta = \alpha$

Thus, **the angle of friction is equal to the angle of repose.**

(iii) Kinetic Friction

When we increase the applied force slightly beyond limiting friction, the actual motion starts and force of friction decreases.

This means that the applied force is now greater than the force of limiting friction. The force of friction at this stage is called **kinetic friction** or **dynamic friction** which is actually a little bit less than the value of limiting friction.

Hence, kinetic friction or dynamic friction is the opposing force that comes into play when one body is actually moving over the surface of another body. Thus, **kinetic friction opposes the relative motion.**

The kinetic friction does not depend on velocity and is directly proportional to the normal reaction R between the two surfaces.

i.e. $\quad f_k \propto R$

or $\quad f_k = \mu_k R$

The proportionality constant μ_k is called **coefficient of kinetic friction** and it is defined as the ratio of kinetic friction to the normal reaction.

This can be shown as $f_k < f_{s(\max)}$ or $\mu_k R < \mu_s R$

$\therefore \quad \mu_k < \mu_s$

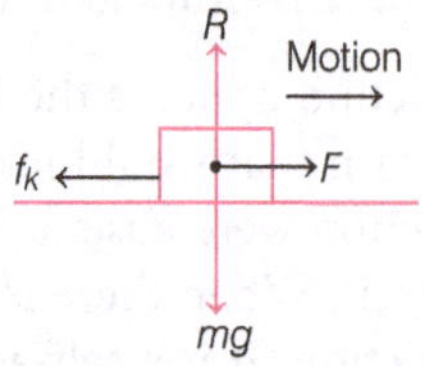

Thus, the coefficient of kinetic friction is less than the coefficient of static friction.

Note The following graph shows the varation of static friction and incrasing the applied force.

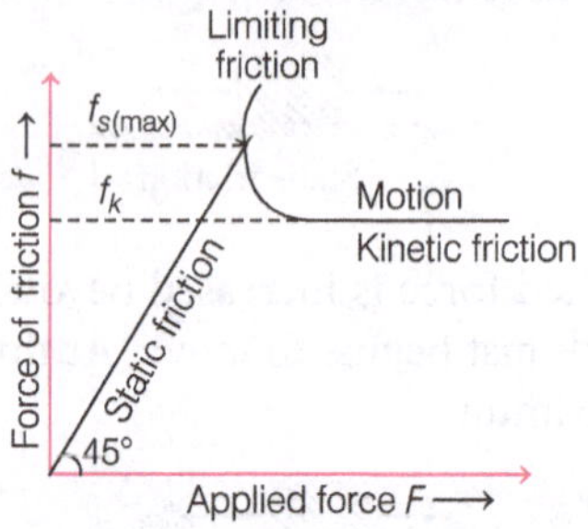

Graph of applied force and force of friction

Example 16. **A hockey puck is given an initial speed of 20 m/s on a frozen pond as shown in figure. The puck remains on the ice and slides 120 m before coming to rest. Determine the coefficient of kinetic friction between the puck and the ice.**

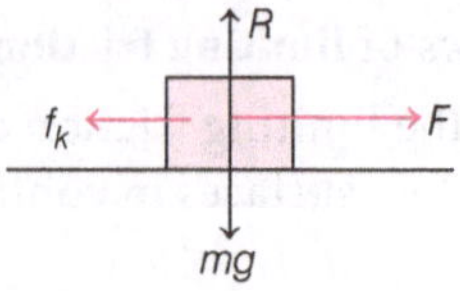

Sol. Given,

The initial speed, $u = 20$ m/s

Distance travelled, $x = 120$ m

$v^2 = u^2 + 2ax \quad$ [third equation of motion]

$0 = (20\text{ m/s})^2 + 2a\,(120\text{ m})$

$a = -1.67\text{ m/s}^2$

The negative sign shows that the acceleration is towards left, i.e. opposite the direction of the velocity.

$\Sigma F_y = R - w = 0$

$\Rightarrow \quad R = w = mg$

Thus, $\quad f_k = \mu_k R = \mu_k mg$

$\Sigma F_x = -f_k = ma$

$\Rightarrow \quad \mu_k mg = m(-1.67\text{ m/s}^2)$

$\mu_k = \dfrac{1.67\text{ m/s}^2}{9.80\text{ m/s}^2} = 0.170$

Example 17. **A block P of mass 4 kg is placed on another block Q of mass 5 kg, and the block Q rests on a smooth horizontal table. For sliding block P on Q, horizontal force of 12 N is required to be applied on P. How much maximum force can applied on Q so that both P and Q move together? Also, find out acceleration produced by this force.**

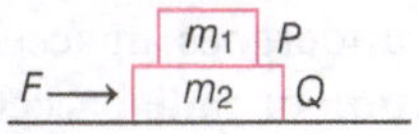

Sol. Here, $m_1 = 4$ kg, $m_2 = 5$ kg

Force applied on block $P = 12$ N

This force must be equal to the kinetic friction applied on P by Q.

$\therefore \quad 12 = F_k = \mu_k R = \mu_k m_1 g$

or $\quad 12 = \mu_k \times 4g$ or $\mu_k = \frac{12}{4g} = \frac{3}{g}$

acceleration of $P = \frac{12}{4} = 3$ m/s

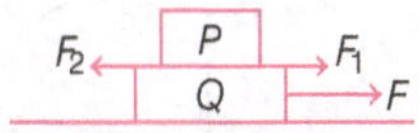

When force F is applied on Q to create common motion in P and Q, the forces created (friction) is shown in the diagram above. F_1 force will be created on P and F_2 force will be created on Q.

Considering forces on Q, we have

$$F - F_2 \text{ (net force)} = m_2 \times a = m_2 \times 3$$

Since, $\quad F_1 = F_2 = \mu_1 m_1 g$

$$F - \mu_k m_1 g = m_2 \times 3$$

$$F = \mu_k m_1 g + m_2 \times 3$$

$$= \frac{3}{g} \times 4 \times g + 5 \times 3$$

$$= 12 + 15 = 27 \text{ N}$$

As this force moves, both the blocks together on a smooth table, so the acceleration produced is

$$a = \frac{F}{m_1 + m_2} = \frac{27}{4+5} = 3 \text{ m/s}$$

4.7 Types of Kinetic Friction

1. Sliding Friction

The force of friction that comes into play when a body slides over the surface of another body is called sliding friction.

e.g. When a flat block is moved over the flat surface of a table, then the opposing force acting on it is known as sliding friction.

Example 18. **What is the acceleration of the block and trolley system shown in a figure. If the coefficient of kinetic friction between the trolley and the surface is 0.04, what is the tension in the string? (take $g = 10\ \text{ms}^{-2}$). Neglect the mass of the string.** NCERT

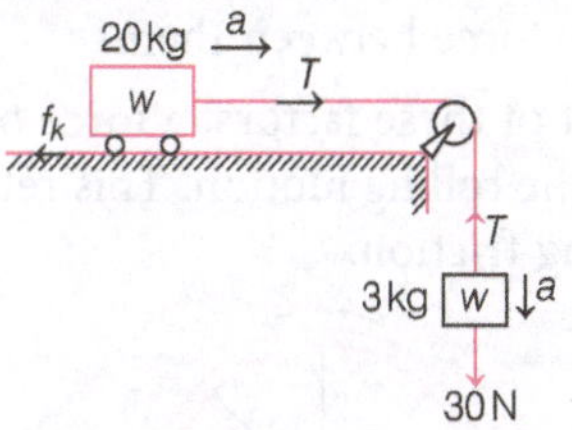

Sol. Applying the second law of motion to the block.

$$30 - T = 3a \quad \text{...(i)}$$

Apply the second law of motion to the trolley.

$$T - f_k = 20a$$

Now, $\quad f_k = \mu_k R = \mu_k mg$

Here, $\quad \mu_k = 0.04$

$$f_k = 0.04 \times 20 \times 10 = 8 \text{ N}$$

Thus, the equation for the motion of the trolley is

$$T - 8 = 20a \quad \text{...(ii)}$$

On adding Eqs.(i) and (ii), we get

$$22 = 23a$$

or $\quad a = \frac{22}{23} = 0.96 \text{ m/s}^2$

From Eq. (i),

$$30 - T = 3 \times 0.96$$

$\Rightarrow \quad T = 30 - 2.88 = 27.12$ N

2. Rolling Friction

The force of friction that comes into play when a body rolls over the surface of another body is called **rolling friction.**

e.g. A car will come to a stop after rolling down hill and reaching a flat road due to opposing force acted between hill and flat road.

The rolling friction is much less than sliding friction and this is why the vehicle runs on wheels.

If there is no slipping, the relative velocity of the point of contact of the wheel with respect to the plane is zero.

i.e; **There is no sliding or static friction in an ideal situation.**

Cause of Rolling Friction

Let us consider a wheel rolling along a road. As the wheel rolls, it exerts a large pressure due to its small area.

This causes a depression in the surface below and a mount or bump in front of it is shown in figure. In addition to this, the rolling wheel has continuously detached itself from the surface on which it rolls. This is opposed by deformation of two surfaces in contact due to adhesive force between them.

On the account of these factors, a force originates which retards the rolling motion. This retarding force is known as rolling friction.

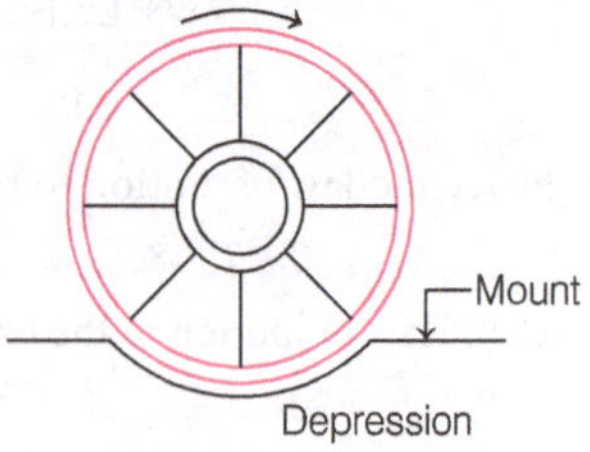

Cause of rolling friction

Ways for Reducing Friction

The various ways of reducing friction are

(i) **Lubrication** They are used to reduce kinetic friction in a machine. Lubricants like oil, grease, etc. fill the irregularities of the surface to make them smoothers. Thus, friction decreases.

(ii) **Polishing** They are used to make the surface smoother.

(iii) **Ball Bearing** The ball bearing arrangement consists of two co-axial cylinders P and R between which suitable number of hard steel balls are arranged. When the wheel rotates the ball B rotates in the direction as shown.

The wheel thus rolls on the balls instead of sliding on the axle. Thus, power dissipation is reduced.

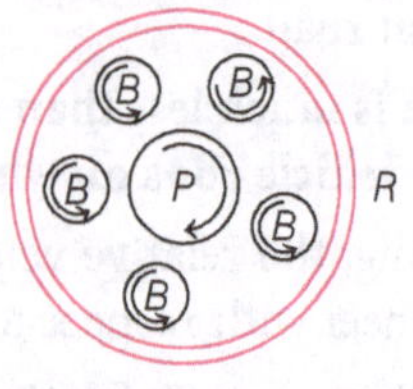

Ball bearing arrangement

(iv) A thin cushion of air is maintained between solid surfaces in relative motion.

(v) **Streamlining** Friction due to air is considerably reduced by streamlining the shape of the body moving through air.

4.8 Dynamics of Circular Motion

When a body moves on a circular path, its direction of motion at any instant of time is along the tangent to the circle. On account of its motion, if the speed of the body remains same and its direction changes continuously, then there is a change in velocity of the body, and hence it undergoes an acceleration, called **centripetal acceleration** or **radial acceleration.**

Thus, **according to Newton's first law of motion, a body cannot be accelerated by itself. An external force is required for this purpose. This external force is called centripetal force.**

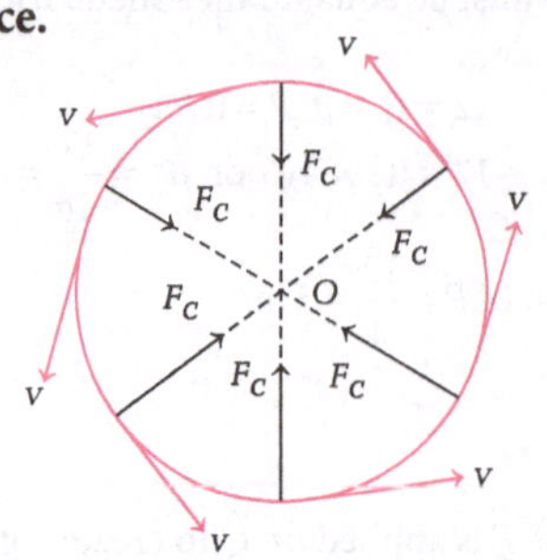

Earlier, we have studied that acceleration of a body moving in a circle of radius r with uniform speed v is $\frac{v^2}{r}$ directed towards the centre.

From second law of motion, the force F_c is given by

$$\text{Centripetal force, } F_c = \frac{mv^2}{r}$$

where, m is the mass of the body. This force directed forward the centre is called **centripetal force.**

But $\frac{v^2}{r}$ is centripetal acceleration or radial acceleration.

$$\therefore \quad \text{Centripetal force, } F_c = mr\omega^2 \qquad [\because v = \omega r]$$

$$= mr(2\pi f)^2 = mr\left(\frac{2\pi}{T}\right)^2$$

Examples

- For a stone rotated in a circle by a string, the centripetal force is provided by the tension in the string.
- The centripetal force for motion of a planet around the sun is the gravitational force on the planet due to the sun.
- For a car taking a circular turn on a horizontal road, the centripetal force act as the force of friction.

Example 19. **An artificial satellite of mass 2500 kg is orbiting around the earth with a speed of $4\ \text{kms}^{-1}$ at a distance of 10^4 km from the earth. Calculate the centripetal force acting on it.**

Sol. Given, $r = 10^4 \text{km} = 10^4 \times 1000 \text{ m} = 10^7 \text{ m}$,

$m = 2500$ kg,

$v = 4\ \text{kms}^{-1} = 4 \times 10^3\ \text{ms}^{-1}$

Now, centripetal force is

$$F = \frac{mv^2}{r}$$

$$F = \frac{2500 \times (4 \times 10^3)^2}{10^7} = \frac{2500 \times 16 \times 10^6}{10^7}$$

$$F = \frac{250 \times 16 \times 10^7}{10^7} = 4000 \text{ N}$$

Interesting Applications of Motion on a Circular Path

Following are the interesting applications of motion of a body on a circular path.

1. Circular Motion of a Car on Level Road

When a vehicle goes round a curved road, it requires some centripetal force. While rounding the curve, the wheels of the vehicle have a tendency to leave the curved path and regain the straight line path. The force of friction between the road and the tyres provided the centripetal force required to keep the car in motion around the curve.

There are three forces acting on the car such as

(i) The **weight of the car *mg*,** acting vertically downwards.

(ii) **Normal reaction *R*** of the road on the car, acting vertically upwards.

(iii) **Frictional force *F*,** along the surface of the road, i.e. towards the centre of the turn.

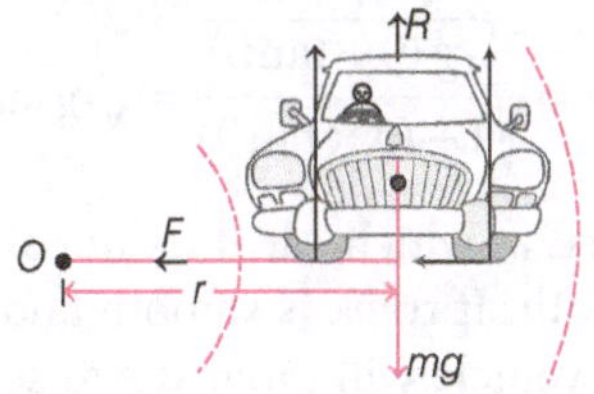

Motion of a car on a circular level road

Let us consider a car of weight *mg* going around a circular level road of radius *r* with velocity *v* as shown in the above figure. While taking the turn, the tyres of the car tend to leave the road and go away from the centre of the curve.

The force of friction *F* is acting on the tyre and *R* is the normal reaction of the ground.

As there is no acceleration in the vertical direction, then

$$R - mg = 0$$

$$\Rightarrow \quad R = mg$$

For circular motion, the centripetal force is along the surface of the road towards the centre of the turn. The static friction opposes the impending motion of the car moving away from the circle. Thus, $\frac{mv^2}{r} \leq F$

where v is the velocity of car while turning and r is the radius of the circular track.

As, $\quad F = \mu_s R = \mu_s mg$

F is limiting friction here to get maximum velocity possible of car, where, μ_s is the coefficient of static friction between the tyres and the road.

$$\therefore \quad \frac{mv^2}{r} \leq \mu_s mg \Rightarrow v \leq \sqrt{\mu_s rg}$$

or $\quad$ Maximum velocity of the vehicle, $v_{\text{max}} = \sqrt{\mu_s rg}$

Hence, the maximum velocity with which a vehicle can go round a level curve without skidding is

$$v = \sqrt{\mu_s rg}.$$

Example 20. **A cyclist speeding at 18 km/h on a level road takes a sharp circular turn of radius 3 m without reducing the speed. The coefficient of static friction between the tyres and the road is 0.1. Will the cyclist slip while taking the turn?** NCERT

Sol. Here, $v = 18 \text{ km/h} = \frac{18 \times 1000}{60 \times 60} = 5 \text{ m/s}$

$r = 3 \text{ m}, \mu_s = 0.1$

On a level road, frictional force alone can provide the centripetal force.

Therefore, condition for the cyclist not to slip is that

$$\frac{mv^2}{r} \leq F_s\ (= \mu_s R = \mu_s\ mg)\ ; v^2 \leq \mu_s rg$$

As $\quad v^2 = (5)^2 = 25 \text{ m}^2\text{s}^{-2}$

and $\quad \mu_s rg = 0.1 \times 3 \times 10 = 3 \text{ m}^2\text{s}^{-2}$

$\therefore$ The condition is not satisfied. Hence, the cyclist will slip.

2. Motion of a Car on a Banked Road

The large amount of friction between the tyres and the road produces **considerable wear** and **tear of the tyres.**

To avoid this, the curved road is given an inclined sloping upward towards the outer circumference. This reduces wearing out of the tyres because the horizontal component of normal reaction provides the necessary centripetal force.

The system of raising the outer edge of a curved road above its inner edge is called **banking of the curved road.**

So, the angle through which the outer edge of the curved road is raised above the inner edge is called **angle of banking.**

Let us consider a car of weight mg going along a curved path of radius r with speed v on a road banked at an angle θ, as shown in the following figure.

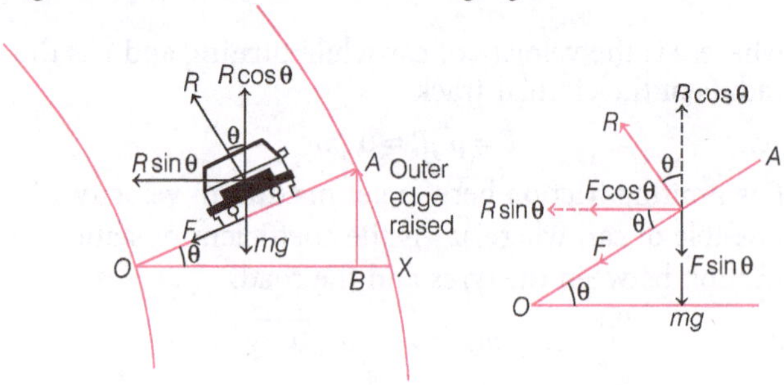

Circular motion of a car on a banked road

The **forces acting on the car** are

(i) **Weight,** mg acting vertically downwards.

(ii) **Normal reaction,** R acting upwards in a direction perpendicular to inclined plane making angle θ with the horizontal plane.

(iii) **Force of friction,** F acting downwards along the inclined plane because car tends to slip outwards.

Reaction, R can be resolved into two rectangular components

(i) $R\cos\theta$, along vertically upward direction.

(ii) $R\sin\theta$, along the horizontal towards the centre of the curved road .

Force of friction F, can also be resolved into two rectangular components.

(i) $F\cos\theta$, along the horizontal, towards the centre of curved road.

(ii) $F\sin\theta$, along vertically downward direction.

Since, there is no motion along vertical, so

$$R\cos\theta = mg + F\sin\theta \quad \text{...(i)}$$

Let v be velocity of the car. The centripetal force is now provided by the components $R\sin\theta$ and $F\cos\theta$, i.e.

$$R\sin\theta + F\cos\theta = \frac{mv^2}{r} \quad \text{...(ii)}$$

We know $F = \mu_s R$, then we can write Eqs. (i) and (ii) as

$$R\cos\theta = mg + \mu_s R\sin\theta \quad \text{...(iii)}$$

and

$$R\sin\theta + \mu_s R\cos\theta = \frac{mv^2}{r} \quad \text{...(iv)}$$

From Eq. (iii), we get

or $R\cos\theta - \mu_s R\cdot\sin\theta = mg$

or $R(\cos\theta - \mu_s \sin\theta) = mg$

or
$$R = \frac{mg}{\cos\theta - \mu_s \sin\theta} \quad \text{...(v)}$$

From Eq. (iv), we get

$$R(\sin\theta + \mu_s \cos\theta) = \frac{mv^2}{r} \quad \text{...(vi)}$$

From Eq. (v) and (vi), we get

$$\frac{mg(\sin\theta + \mu_s\cos\theta)}{\cos\theta - \mu_s \sin\theta} = \frac{mv^2}{r}$$

$$\therefore \quad v^2 = \frac{rg(\sin\theta + \mu_s\cos\theta)}{(\cos\theta - \mu_s\sin\theta)}$$

$$v^2 = \frac{rg\cos\theta\left(\frac{\sin\theta}{\cos\theta} + \frac{\mu_s\cos\theta}{\cos\theta}\right)}{\cos\theta\left(\frac{\cos\theta}{\cos\theta} - \mu_s\frac{\sin\theta}{\cos\theta}\right)}$$

$$v^2 = \frac{rg\cos\theta(\tan\theta + \mu_s)}{\cos\theta(1 - \mu_s\tan\theta)}$$

$$v^2 = \frac{rg(\tan\theta + \mu_s)}{(1 - \mu_s\tan\theta)}$$

Maximum velocity of vehicle on banked rod,

$$v = \sqrt{\frac{rg(\mu_s + \tan\theta)}{(1 - \mu_s\tan\theta)}} \quad \text{...(vii)}$$

Special cases

When there is no friction between the road and the tyres, then the safe limit for maximum velocity is $\mu_s = 0$,

Substituting the value of μ_s in Eq. (vii), we get

$$v = \sqrt{\frac{rg(0 + \tan\theta)}{1 - (0 \times \tan\theta)}} = \sqrt{rg\tan\theta} \quad \text{...(viii)}$$

This is the speed at which car does not slide down even if, track is smooth. If track is smooth and speed is less than $\sqrt{rg\tan\theta}$, vehicle will move down so that r gets decreased and if speed is more than this vehicle, will move up.

The angle of banking θ for minimum wear and tear of tyres is given by Eq. (viii), we get

$$\tan\theta = \frac{v^2}{rg} \quad \text{or} \quad \text{Angle of banking, } \theta = \tan^{-1}\left(\frac{v^2}{rg}\right)$$

Example 21. **A circular race track of radius 300 m is banked at angle of 15°. If the coefficient of friction between the wheels of a race car and the road is 0.2, what is the (i) optimum speed of the race car to avoid wear and tear on its tyres and (ii) maximum permissible speed to avoid slipping? [tan 15° = 0.2679]** NCERT

Sol. (i) The optimum speed v_o is given by equation

$$v_o = (R g \tan\theta)^{1/2}$$

Here, $R = 300$ m, $\theta = 15°$, $g = 9.8$ ms^{-2}, $\mu_s = 0.2$,

We have

$$v_o = 28.1 \text{ ms}^{-1}$$

(ii) The maximum permissible speed v_{max} is given by equation.

$$v_{max} = \left[Rg\left(\frac{\mu_s + \tan\theta}{1 - \mu_s \tan\theta}\right)\right]^{1/2}$$

$$v_{max} = \left(\frac{300 \times 9.8 \times (0.2 + \tan 15°)}{1 - (0.2 \times \tan 15°)}\right)^{1/2}$$

$$v_{max} = \left(\frac{2940 \times (0.4679)}{0.9464}\right)^{1/2}$$

$$= (1453.535)^{1/2} = 38.1 \text{ ms}^{-1}$$

Example 22. **The radius of curvature of a railway track at a place, where the train is moving at a speed of 72 kmh^{-1} is 625 m. The distance between the rails is 1.5 m. Find the angle and the elevation of the out rail so that there may be no side pressure on the rails. Take, g = 9.8 m/s^2 [tan^{-1} (0.0653) = 3.74°, sin 3.74° = 0.06522]**

Sol. Here, $r = 625$ m, $v = 72$ kmh^{-1}

$$v = 72 \times \frac{5}{18} \text{ m/s}$$

$$v = 20 \text{ m/s}, \; g = 9.8 \text{ m/s}^2, \; l = 1.5 \text{ m}$$

Now, angle of elevation of outer rail

i.e. $$\tan\theta = \frac{v^2}{rg}$$

$$\tan\theta = \frac{20 \times 20}{625 \times 9.8} = 0.0653$$

$$\theta = \tan^{-1}(0.0653)$$

$$\theta = 3.74°$$

Also, elevation of outer rail $h = l \sin\theta$

$$h = 1.5 \sin 3.74°$$

$$h = 0.0978 \text{ m} = 9.78 \text{ cm}$$

Example 23. **If a car having speed 50 km/h can round the curve banked at an angle θ. Find out the value of θ, if radius of the curve is 40 m and consider the friction is negligible. [tan^{-1} (0.5) = 26.5]**

Sol. Write the given quantity and the quantity to be known.

$$v = 50 \text{ km/h} = 50 \times \frac{5}{18} \text{ m/s} = 13.88 \text{ m/s}$$

$$r = 40 \text{ m}, \; \theta = ?$$

Draw the FBD of the car.

Now, apply $\Sigma F_y = ma_y$ to the car

$$R\cos\theta - mg = 0$$

$$\Rightarrow \quad R = \frac{mg}{\cos\theta}$$

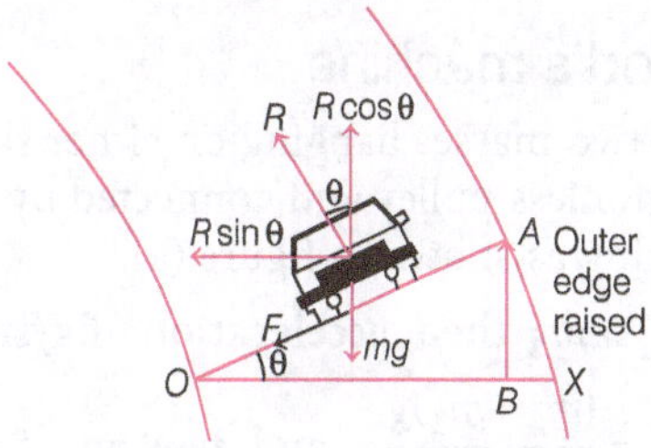

Similarly, apply $\Sigma F_x = ma_x$ to the car

$$R\sin\theta = \frac{mv^2}{r}$$

Put the value of R and then solve for θ.

$$\frac{mg}{\cos\theta} \cdot \sin\theta = \frac{mv^2}{r}$$

$$\Rightarrow \quad \tan\theta = \frac{v^2}{rg}; \theta = \tan^{-1}\left(\frac{v^2}{rg}\right)$$

Put the all given values to get θ.

$$\theta = \tan^{-1}\left[\frac{(13.88)^2}{40 \times 9.8}\right] = \tan^{-1}(0.4917)$$

$$\theta = 26.18°$$

Motion of connected bodies

The motion of different masses connected by a uniform massless string, placed on a smooth horizontal surface can be describe in the following ways.

Case I Two bodies system of mass m_1 and m_2

Let force F is applied on m_2 as shown in figure.

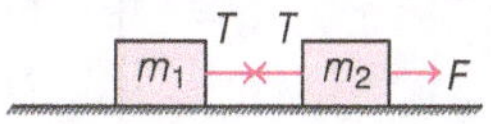

The acceleration and tension produce in the system is given by

$$a = \frac{F}{m_1 + m_2}$$

and $$T = \frac{m_1 F}{m_1 + m_2}$$

Case II Three bodies system of mass m_1, m_2 and m_3

Let force F is applied on mass m_3 as shown in figure.

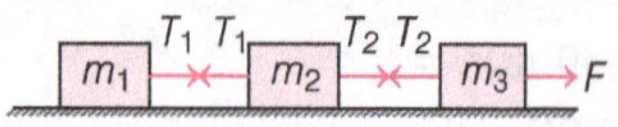

Then, acceleration of system, $a = \dfrac{F}{m_1 + m_2 + m_3}$

Tension, $T_1 = \dfrac{m_1 F}{m_1 + m_2 + m_3}$ and $T_2 = \dfrac{(m_1 + m_2)F}{m_1 + m_2 + m_3}$

The atwood's machine

It consist of two masses hanging on either sides of a smooth frictionless pulley and connected by a light mass less string as shown in figure (a).

Case I If $m_1 > m_2$ then, acceleration of system,

$$a = \frac{(m_1 - m_2)g}{m_1 + m_2} \quad \text{and tension, } T = \frac{2m_1 m_2 g}{m_1 + m_2}$$

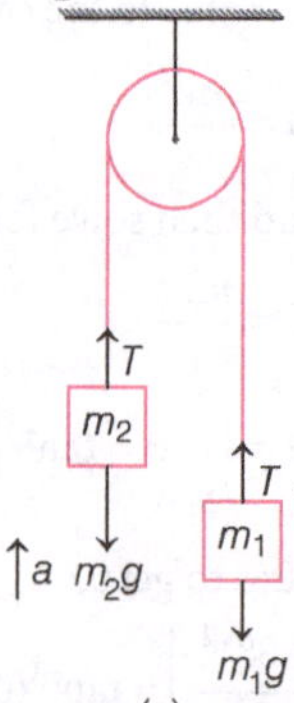

(a)

Case II When one end of string attached to an edge of a horizontable as shown in figure

- Acceleration of the system, $a = \dfrac{m_2 g}{m_1 + m_2}$

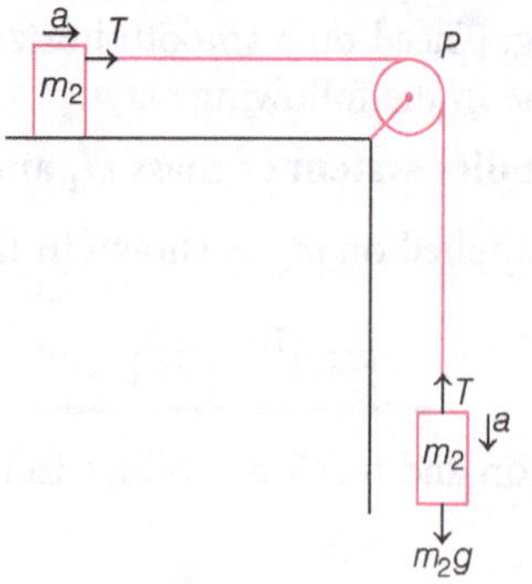

(b)

- Tension in string, $T = \dfrac{m_1 m_2 g}{m_1 + m_2}$

Solving problems in Mechanics

Let us understand the problem solving methods in mechanics by taking few examples.

Example 24. **A wooden block of mass 2 kg rests on a soft horizontal floor. When an iron cylinder of mass 25 kg is placed on top of the block, the floor yields steadily and the block and the cylinder together go down with an acceleration of 0.1 m/s^2. What is the action of the block on the floor (i) before and (ii) after the floor yields? (Take, g = 10 m/s^2). Identify the action-reaction pairs in the problem.** NCERT

Sol. ∵ Mass of the block = 2 kg

Mass of the cylinder = 25 kg

Acceleration of the system = 0.1 m/s^2

$g = 10$ m/s^2

The force of gravitational attraction of the earth, i.e. weight of the block is equal to mg.

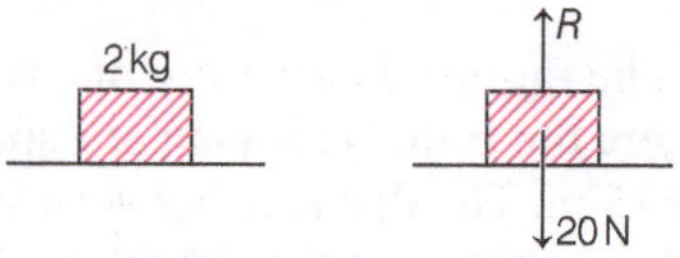

$$w = mg$$
$$\Rightarrow \quad w = 2 \times 10$$
$$\Rightarrow \quad w = 20 \text{ N}$$

According to Newton's first law, net force on the block is zero, i.e. $R = 20$ N

Force of gravity due to the earth, i.e.

$$w = mg = (25 + 2) \times 10 = 270 \text{ N}$$
$$270 - R' = 27 \times 0.1$$
$$\Rightarrow \quad R' = 270 - 2.7$$
$$= 267.3 \text{ N}$$

Example 25. **Consider two masses m_1 and m_2 connected by a light and inextensible string passing over a smooth light pulley which is fixed by a rigid cord, from a rigid support as shown in figure. This**

device is also known as atwood's machine. Find the tension in the rope and acceleration of each block.

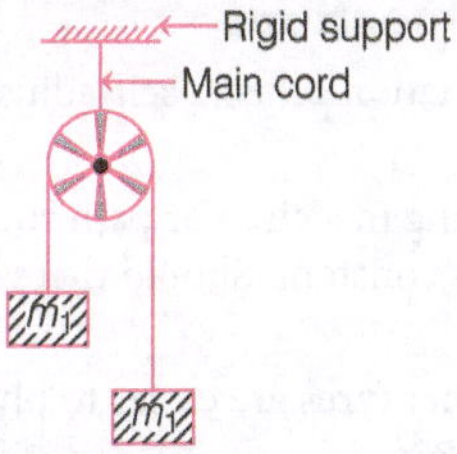

Sol. To study the motion of the blocks, let us draw the free body diagram (FBD) of various parts of the system, by assuming $m_2 > m_1$. FBD and dynamics of block m_1,

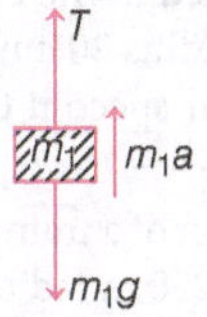

$$T - m_1 g = m_1 a \qquad \text{...(i)}$$

FBD and dynamics of block m_2,

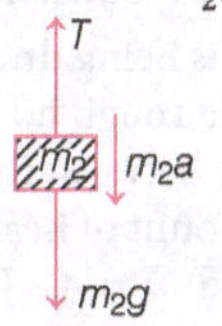

$$m_2 g - T = m_2 a \qquad \text{...(ii)}$$

FBD of pulley,

$$R - 2T = 0 \qquad \text{...(iii)}$$

where, R is reaction on the axle of pulley. Since, pulley is fixed, therefore, $a = 0$ for it.

From the solution of simultaneous Eqs. (i), (ii) and (iii), we get the value of acceleration a, tension T and pressure R on the axle of pulley.

Thus, from adding Eqs. (i) and (ii), we get acceleration a

$$T - m_1 g = m_1 a \quad \text{and} \quad m_2 g - T = m_2 a$$

or $\quad T - m_1 g + m_2 g - T = m_1 a + m_2 a$

$$m_2 g - m_1 g = a(m_1 + m_2)$$

or $$a = \frac{(m_2 - m_1) g}{(m_1 + m_2)}$$

On substituting a in Eqs. (i) or (ii), we get

$$T = \left(\frac{2 m_1 m_2 g}{m_1 + m_2}\right)$$

and pressure on pulley from Eq. (iii), we get

$$R = 2T$$

$$R = 2 \times \frac{2 m_1 m_2 g}{m_1 + m_2} = \frac{4 m_1 m_2 g}{m_1 + m_2}$$

Example 26. **Consider the body of mass m is suspended by two strings making angles α and β with the horizontal as shown in figure. If the body is in equilibrium, then find out the tension in the strings.**

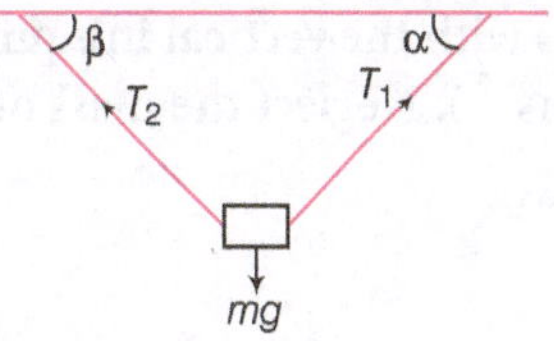

Sol. Draw the free body diagram firstly as shown in figure. Mention all the horizontal and vertical components of tensions T_1 and T_2.

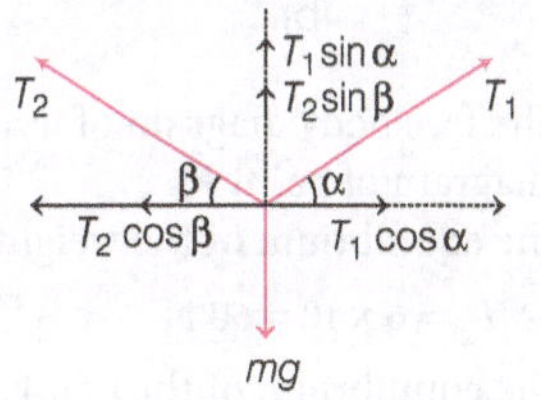

As the body is in equilibrium, the various forces must add to zero. Taking horizontal components of forces.

$$T_1 \cos\alpha = T_2 \cos\beta$$

$$\Rightarrow \quad T_2 = T_1 \frac{\cos\alpha}{\cos\beta}$$

Now, taking the vertical components of forces.

$$T_1 \sin\alpha + T_2 \sin\beta = mg$$

$$T_1 \sin\alpha + T_1 \frac{\cos\alpha}{\cos\beta} \sin\beta = mg$$

Now, solve the equations for T_1 to find out the value of T_1.

$$T_1 = \frac{mg}{\sin\alpha + \frac{\cos\alpha}{\cos\beta}\sin\beta} = \frac{mg\cos\beta}{\sin\alpha\cos\beta + \cos\alpha\sin\beta}$$

$$\therefore \quad T_1 = \frac{mg\cos\beta}{\sin(\alpha + \beta)}$$

[$\because \sin(A+B) = \sin A \cos B + \cos A \sin B$]

$$T_2 = T_1 \frac{\cos\alpha}{\cos\beta}$$

$$= \frac{mg\cos\beta}{\sin(\alpha+\beta)} \times \frac{\cos\alpha}{\cos\beta}$$

$$= \frac{mg\cos\alpha}{\sin(\alpha+\beta)}$$

Example 27. **See in figure a mass of 6 kg is suspended by a rope of length 2 m from the ceiling. A force of 50 N in the horizontal direction is applied at the mid-point *P* of the rope as shown. What is the angle, the rope makes with the vertical in equilibrium? (Take $g = 10\ ms^{-2}$). Neglect the mass of the rope.**

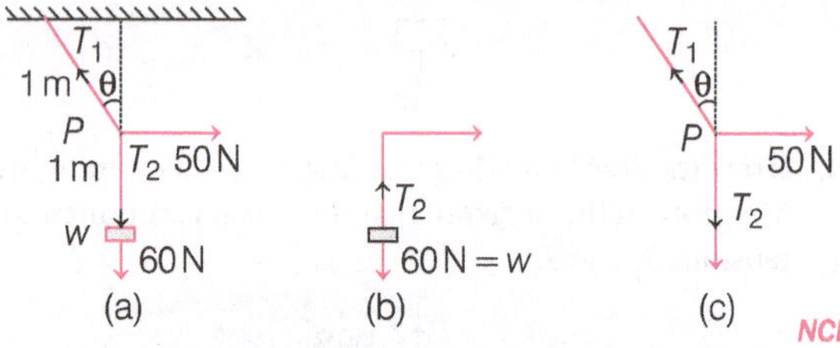

NCERT

Sol. Fig. (b) is the free body diagram of *w* and Fig. (c) is the free body diagram of point *P*.

Consider the equilibrium of the weight *w*. Clearly,

$$T_2 = 6 \times 10 = 60\ \text{N}$$

Consider the equilibrium of the point *P* under the action of three forces, the tensions T_1 and T_2 and the horizontal force 50 N. The horizontal and vertical components of the resultant force must vanish separately.

$$T_1 \cos\theta = T_2 = 60\ \text{N}$$

and $$T_1 \sin\theta = 50\ \text{N}$$

Which gives that $\tan\theta = \frac{5}{6}$

or $$\theta = \tan^{-1}\left(\frac{5}{6}\right)$$

$$= 40°$$

Quick Test 2

Conceptual Questions

1. Why is static friction called a self-adjusting force?
2. A body is moving in a circular path such that its speed always remains constant. Should there be a force acting on the body?
3. Carts with rubber tyres are easier to ply than those with iron tyres. Explain.
4. Why it is easier to pull a lawn roller than to push it?

Numerical Questions

5. A heavy point mass tied to the end of string is whirled in a horizontal circle of radius 20 cm with a constant angular speed. What is angular speed if the centripetal acceleration is 980 cms^{-2}?
6. What is the acceleration of a train travelling at 50 ms^{-1} as it goes round a curve of 250 m radius?
7. A body placed on a rough inclined plane just begins to slide, when the slope of the plane is equal to 1 in 4. Calculate the coefficient of friction.
8. A body of mass 2 kg is being dragged with a uniform velocity of 2 ms^{-1} on a rough horizontal plane. The coefficient of friction between the body and the surface is 0.2. Calculate the amount of heat generated per second. Take $g = 9.8\ ms^{-2}$ and $1\ J = 4.2\ Jcal^{-1}$.
9. An aircraft executes a horizontal loop at a speed of 720 km / h with its wings banked at 15°. What is the radius of the loop? If wings of the aircraft are inclined at an angle θ at turn, then $\tan\theta = \frac{v^2}{rg}$ where *v* is the speed of the aircraft and *r* is the radius of the circular turn.
10. A rocket with a lift-off mass 20000 kg is blasted upward with an initial acceleration of 5.0 m/s^2. Calculate the initial thrust (force) of the blast. NCERT

Answers

5. 7 rad/s *6.* 10 ms^{-2} *7.* 0.258 *8.* 1.87 cal
9. 15.24 km *10.* 2.96×10^5 N

For Solutions, See QR Code on Pg. 152

Mind Map

Laws of Motion

Force is a push or pull that can change an object's motion, causing it to accelerate, stop or change direction.
Inertia is the tendency of an object to resist changes in its state of motion or rest.

First Law of Motion (Law of Inertia)
An object will continue its state of motion or rest unless an external forces acted on it
E.g a book on table and falling down of dust particles while dusting a cloth

Second Law of Motion
- Rate of change in linear momentum of a body is directly proportional to applied force and takes place in the direction in which the force acts.
- $F = \frac{\Delta p}{\Delta t}$ (on the basis of experiment)
- For constant mass, $F = ma$

Friction
It is the force that opposes the relative motion or tendency of motion between two surfaces in contact.

Angle of friction
- The angle made by the resultant of normal reaction and limiting friction with normal reaction is called angle of friction.

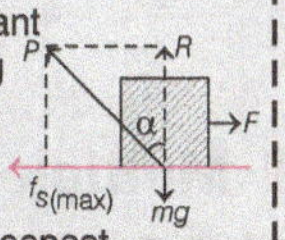

- Angle of friction, $\alpha = \tan^{-1} \mu_s$

The angle of repose is the steepest angle at which an object on an inclined surface remains stationary without sliding due to static friction. $\tan\theta = \mu s$

Linear Momentum
The linear momentum of a particle is defined as product of its mass and velocity.

$$p = mv$$

- If p = constant, then $v \propto 1/m$
- Heavier is the body, smaller will be its velocity.

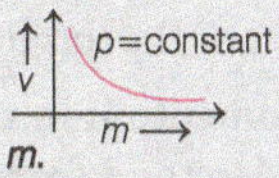

- If v = constant, then $p \propto m$. The heaviest body will have largest momentum.

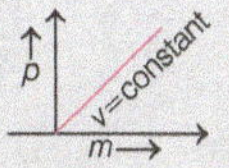

Law of Conservation of Momentum
- Total momentum,

$$p = p_1 + p_2 + \ldots + p_n = \sum_{i=1}^{N} p_i$$

- If resultant external force acting on a system is zero, then linear momentum of system remains conserved.

i.e. $p_i = p_f$

Third Law of Motion (Action and Reaction)
For every action, there is an equal and opposite reaction.

$$F_{action} = -F_{reaction}$$

Equilibrium of Concurrent Forces
- The body under the action of concurrent forces will be in equilibrium only when the vector sum of forces is zero.

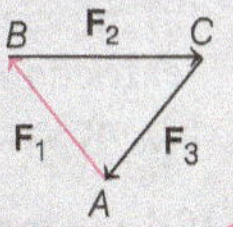

- Mathematically, $\Sigma F_{net} = 0$

Application of conservation of linear momentum
- Collisions
- Recoil of a Gun
- Rocket Propulsion

Impulse
- A large force acting for a short time to produce a finite change in momentum.

Impulse $= F \cdot \Delta t = \Delta p$

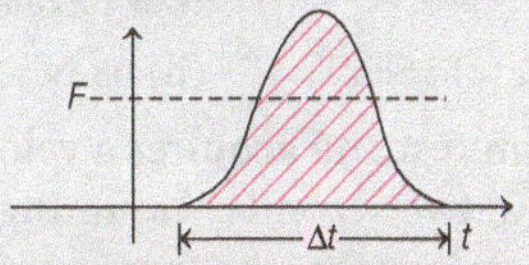

Circular Motion
- When an object moves on a circular path, a force acts on it, whose direction is towards the centre of the path, this force is called centripetal force.

It is given as $F = \frac{mv^2}{r}$

Example
- For a stone rotated in a circle by a string the centripetal force is provided by tension in the string.
- The centripetal force for motion of a planet around the sun is the gravitational force on the planet due to the sun .

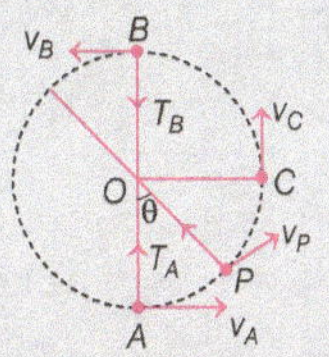

Static Friction
- If a body tends to slip over the surface of another body, then it is frictional force acting between their surfaces.
- When applied force is less than static friction, then block does not move.

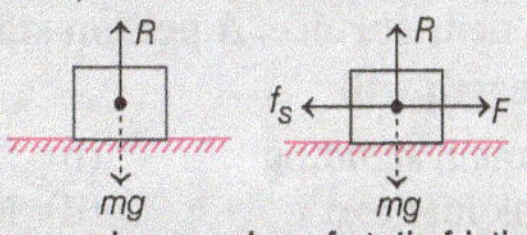

- The maximum value of static friction between two surfaces in contact is called limiting friction.

Motion of Car on Banked Road
- The large amount of friction between the tyres and the road produces considerable wear and tear of tyres. To avoid this, the curved road is given an inclined sloping upwards towards outer circumference.
- The system of raising outer edge of curved road above its inner edge called banking of the curved road. Maximum velocity of vehicle on banked road,

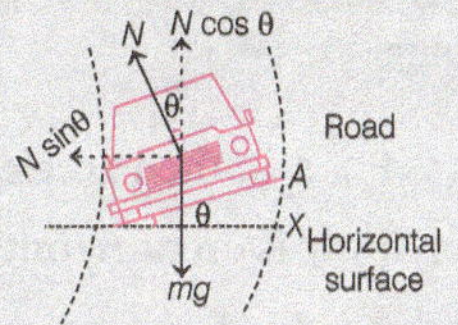

$$v_{max} = \sqrt{\frac{rg(\mu_s + \tan\theta)}{(1 - \mu_s \tan\theta)}}$$

- **Special case** When $\mu_s = 0$, then $v_{max} = \sqrt{rg \tan\theta}$

i.e. Banking angle $\theta = \tan^{-1}\left(\frac{v^2}{rg}\right)$

Kinetic Friction
- If the object is sliding, then friction forces between their surfaces is called kinetic friction or sliding friction.
- If applied force exceeds the limiting value of friction force, i.e. $F > (f_s)_{max}$, then block starts slipping over the inclined plane.

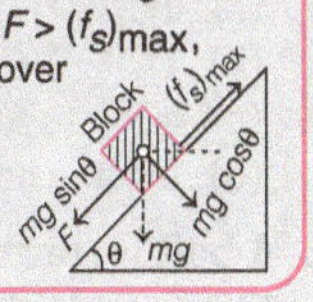

So, $f_K < f_L$(slightly),

$f_K < (f_s)_{max}$

Motion of Car on Circular Level Road
- When a vehicle goes round a curved road, it requires some centripetal force. While rounding the curve, the wheels of the vehicle have a tendency to leave the curved path and regain the straight line path.

$$\frac{mv^2}{r} \le \mu_s mg \Rightarrow v \le \sqrt{\mu_s rg}$$

Maximum velocity, $v_{max} = \sqrt{\mu_s rg}$

- Maximum velocity with which a vehicle can go round a level curve without skidding, $v = \sqrt{\mu_s rg}$

Rolling Friction
- When an object rolls on a surface without slipping, then the friction force between the surface is called rolling friction.

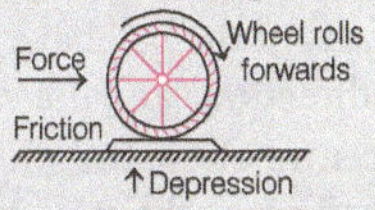

Example
- Ball bearings are used to reduce the friction between the rolling part.

EXAM PATTERN QUESTIONS

Objective Type Questions

Multiple Choice Questions (MCQs)

1. Who gave the idea that when a particle is moving with uniform velocity, there is no need of any force, if frictional force is zero?

(a) Aristotle (b) Newton
(c) Galileo (d) Einstein

2. A hockey player is moving northward and suddenly turns westward with the same speed to avoid an opponent. The force that acts on the player is NCERT Exemplar

(a) frictional force along westward
(b) muscle force along southward
(c) frictional force along south-west
(d) muscle force along south-west

3. If three forces F_1, F_2 and F_3 act on a particle, then in equilibrium

(a) $F_{21} + F_2 + F_3 = 0$ (b) $F_1 + F_2 + F_3 = 0$
(c) $F_{21} + F_2 + F_3$ (d) None of these

4. Suppose the earth suddenly stops attracting objects placed near surface. A person standing on the surface of the earth will

(a) remain standing (b) fly up
(c) sink into earth (d) Either (b) or (c)

5. An astronaut accidentally gets separated out of his small spaceship accelerating in interstellar space at a constant rate of 100 ms^{-2}. What is the acceleration of the astronaut at the instant after he is outside the spaceship? (Assume that there are no nearby stars to exert gravitational force on him)

(a) 0
(b) 1
(c) ∞
(d) Data insufficient

6. A ball is travelling with uniform translatory motion. This means that NCERT Exemplar

(a) it is at rest
(b) the path can be a straight line or circular and the ball travels with uniform speed
(c) all parts of the ball have the same velocity (magnitude and direction) and the velocity is constant
(d) the centre of the ball moves with constant velocity and the ball spins about its centre uniformly

7. A metre scale is moving with uniform velocity. This implies NCERT Exemplar

(a) the force acting on the scale is zero, but a torque about the centre of mass can act on the scale
(b) the force acting on the scale is zero and the torque acting about centre of mass of the scale is also zero
(c) the total force acting on it need not be zero but the torque on it is zero
(d) neither the force nor the torque need to be zero

8. Conservation of momentum in a collision between particles can be understood from NCERT Exemplar

(a) conservation of energy
(b) Newton's first law only
(c) Newton's second law only
(d) both Newton's second and third law

9. A body of mass 2 kg travels according to the law $x(t) = pt + qt^2 + rt^3$ where, $q = 4 \text{ ms}^{-2}$, $p = 3 \text{ ms}^{-1}$ and $r = 5 \text{ ms}^{-3}$. The force acting on the body at $t = 2$ s is NCERT Exemplar

(a) 136 N (b) 134 N (c) 158 N (d) 68 N

10. A car of mass m starts from rest and acquires a velocity along east, $\mathbf{v} = v\hat{\mathbf{i}}\ (v > 0)$ in two seconds. Assuming the car moves with uniform acceleration, the force exerted on the car is NCERT Exemplar

(a) $\frac{mv}{2}$ eastward and is exerted by the car engine
(b) $\frac{mv}{2}$ eastward and is due to the friction on the tyres exerted by the road
(c) more than $\frac{mv}{2}$ eastward exerted due to the engine and overcomes the friction of the road
(d) $\frac{mv}{2}$ exerted by the engine

11. If F is the force applied (as $F > f_k$), then acceleration of the body of mass M when body is on horizontal surface

(a) $\frac{f_k}{M}$ (b) $\frac{F - f_k}{M}$
(c) $\frac{F}{M}$ (d) None of the above

12. The coefficient of friction between tyres and the road is 0.1. Find the maximum speed allowed by traffic police for car to cross a circular turn of radius 10 m to prevent accident. (Take $g = 10\ ms^{-2}$)

(a) $\sqrt{10}\ ms^{-1}$ (b) $\sqrt{20}\ ms^{-1}$
(c) $5\ ms^{-1}$ (d) $9\ ms^{-1}$

13. A particle is moving on a circular path of 10 m radius. At any instant of time, its speed is $5\ ms^{-1}$ and the speed is increasing at a rate of $2\ ms^{-2}$. The magnitude of net acceleration at this instant is

(a) $5\ ms^{-2}$ (b) $2\ ms^{-2}$ (c) $3.2\ ms^{-2}$ (d) $4.3\ ms^{-2}$

14. A trolley is carrying a box on its surface having coefficient of static friction equal to 0.3. Now, the trolley starts moving with increasing acceleration. Find the maximum acceleration of the trolley so that the box does not slide back on the trolley. **Competency Based Que.**

(a) $2\ ms^{-2}$ (b) $3\ ms^{-2}$ (c) $4\ ms^{-2}$ (d) $5\ ms^{-2}$

15. A particle of mass 2 kg is moving on a circular path of radius 10 m with a speed of $5\ ms^{-1}$ and its speed is increasing at rate of $3\ ms^{-1}$. Find the force acting on the particle.

(a) 5 N (b) 10 N (c) 12 N (d) 14 N

16. Two masses $m_1 = 1$ kg and $m_2 = 2$ kg are connected by a light inextensible string and suspended by means of a weightless pulley as shown in figure.

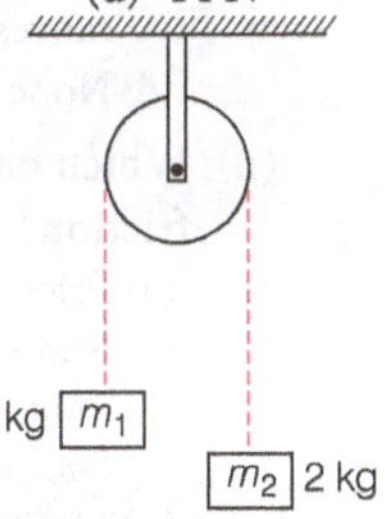

Assuming that both the masses start from rest, the distance travelled by 2 kg mass in 2 s is

(a) $\frac{20}{9}$ m (b) $\frac{40}{9}$ m (c) $\frac{20}{3}$ m (d) $\frac{1}{3}$ m

17. If a box is lying in the compartment of an accelerating train and box is stationary relative to the train. What force cause the acceleration of the box?

(a) Frictional force in the direction of train
(b) Frictional force in the opposite direction of train
(c) Force applied by air
(d) None of the above

18. One end of a string of length l is connected to a particle of mass m and the other to a small peg on a smooth horizontal table. If the particle moves in a circle with speed v the net force on the particle (directed towards the centre) is **Competency Based Que.**

(a) T (b) $T - \frac{mv^2}{l}$
(c) $T + \frac{mv^2}{l}$ (d) 0

T is the tension in the string.

19. Match the Column I (Laws of motion) with Column II (Application) and choose the correct option.

	Column I		Column II
A.	Newton's I law	P.	Stable equilibrium of a body
B.	Newton's II law	Q.	Propulsion of a rocket
C.	Newton's III law	R.	Flying nature of bird
D.	Law of conservation of momentum	S.	Law of force

(a) A → P, B → S, C → R, D → Q
(b) A → P, B → Q, C → R, D → S
(c) A → S, B → P, C → Q, D → R
(d) A → S, B → Q, C → P, D → R

20. Match Column I with Column II and choose the correct answer.

	Column I		Column II
A.	Safe velocity on level curve	P.	$\sqrt{rg\tan\theta}$
B.	Safe velocity on banked road if $\mu_S = 0$	Q.	$\sqrt{\frac{rg(\mu_S + 1)}{1 - \mu_S}}$
C.	Safe velocity on banked road if $\theta = 45°$	R.	$\sqrt{\mu_S rg}$
D.	If angle of banking is θ then $\tan\theta$ is	S.	$\frac{v^2}{rg}$

where, r = radius of curvature, g = acceleration due to gravity, θ = angle of banking and μ_S = coefficient of friction.

(a) A → Q, B → R, C → P, D → S
(b) A → R, B → P, C → Q, D → S
(c) A → R, B → Q, C → P, D → S
(d) A → Q, B → P, C → S, D → R

Assertion and Reason

Directions *(Q.No. 21-30) In the following questions, two statements are given- one labelled Assertion (A) and the other labelled Reason (R). Select the correct answer to these questions from the codes (a), (b), (c) and (d) as given below.*

(a) Both Assertion and Reason are true and Reason is the correct explanation of Assertion.
(b) Both Assertion and Reason are true but Reason is not the correct explanation of Assertion.
(c) Assertion is true but Reason is false.
(d) Assertion is false but Reason is true.

21. **Assertion (A)** A body is momentarily at rest still some force is acting on it at that time.
Reason (R) When a force acts on a body, it may not have some acceleration.

22. **Assertion (A)** During the action of an impulsive force, change in the momentum is very high even though force acts for a very short period.
Reason (R) The amount of force is very high.

23. **Assertion (A)** Action and Reaction forces do not cancel out each other.
Reason (R) It is because both do not act on the same body.

24. **Assertion (A)** Angle of repose is equal to angle of limiting friction.
Reason (R) When a body is just at the point of motion, the force of friction in this stage is called as limiting friction.

25. **Assertion (A)** It is always necessary that external agency of force is in contact with the object while applying force on object.
Reason (R) A stone released from top of a building accelerates downward due to gravitational pull of the earth.

26. **Assertion (A)** At the microscopic level, all bodies are made of charged constituents (nuclei and electrons) and various contact forces arise.
Reason (R) These forces are due to elasticity of bodies, molecular collisions and impacts, etc.

27. **Assertion (A)** Objects in motion generally experience friction, viscous drag, etc.
Reason (R) On the earth, if an object is at rest or in uniform linear motion, it is not because there are no forces acting on it but because the various external forces cancel out, i.e. add upto zero net external force.

28. **Assertion (A)** A seasoned cricketer allows a longer time for his hands to stop the ball, while catching the ball. His hand is not hurt.
Reason (R) The novice (new player) keeps his hand fixed and tries to catch the ball almost instantly. He needs to provide a much greater force to stop the ball instantly and this hurts.

29. **Assertion (A)** Product of mass and velocity (*i.e.* momentum) is basic to the effect of force on motion.
Reason (R) Same force for same time causes the same change in momentum for different bodies.

30. **Assertion (A)** Newton's third law of motion is applicable only when bodies are in motion.
Reason (R) Newton's third law applies to all types of forces, e.g. gravitational, electric or magnetic forces, etc.

Case Based Questions

Directions *(Q.Nos. 31-34) These questions are case study based questions. Read the following paragraph and answer the questions on the basis of same.*

31. **When two bodies are in contact, each experiences a contact force by the other. The component of the contact force parallel to the surfaces in contact, which opposes impending or actual relative motion between the two bodies in contact is opposed by static friction. Kinetic friction opposes actual relative motion between two bodies in contact.**

There is a yet another type of friction which opposes rolling motion of one body over the surface of another body. It is called rolling friction.

We often regard friction as something undesirable. However in many practical situations friction is critically needed.

(i) What is the direction of friction?
(a) Friction always acts tangential to the surface in contact.
(b) Friction acts normal to the surface in contact.
(c) Direction depends upon weight of body which moves over surface of another body.
(d) None of these.

(ii) Which one of the statement is not correct about friction?
(a) Friction is a self adjusting force.
(b) Force of friction is independent of area of contact as long as normal reaction remains same.
(c) Sliding friction is greater than static friction.
(d) Limiting friction is the maximum static friction.

(iii) An automobile is moving on a horizontal road with a speed . If the coefficient of friction between the tyres and the road is μ. What is the shortest distance in which the automobile can be stopped?
(a) $\frac{v^2}{\mu g}$ (b) $\frac{2v^2}{\mu g}$
(c) $\frac{v^2}{4\mu g}$ (d) $\frac{v^2}{2\mu g}$

(iv) What will be the maximum acceleration of the train in which a box lying on the floor will remain stationary? Given that the coefficient of friction between the box and the floor of the train is 0.15. (= 10 m/s)
(a) 2 m/s^2
(b) 2.5 m/s^2
(c) 1 m/s^2
(d) 1.5 m/s^2

(v) In figure, the masses of blocks A and B are 10 kg and 5 kg. Calculate the minimum mass of C which may stop A from slipping. Coefficient of friction between block A and table is 0.2.

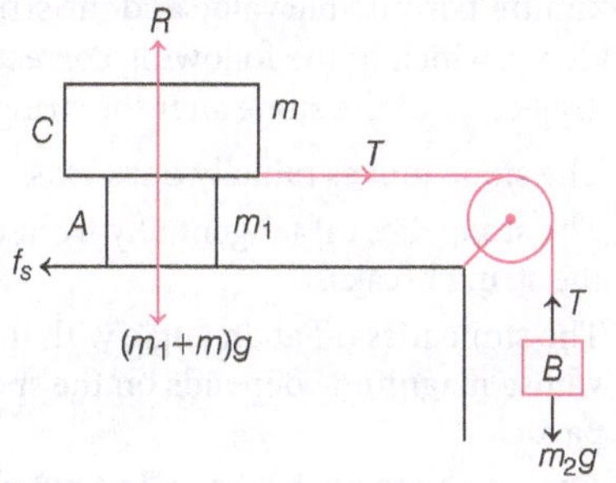

(a) 5 kg (b) 15 kg (c) 25 kg (d) 35 kg

32. **Starting from rest, a body slides down at $\theta = 45°$ inclined plane of length s in twice the time it takes to slide down the same distance in the absence of friction. The coefficient of friction between the body and the inclined plane is μ.**

(i) What is the expression for the acceleration of body?

(a) $a = g(\sin\theta - \mu\cos\theta)$
(b) $a = g(\cos\theta - \mu\sin\theta)$
(c) $a = g\sin\theta$
(d) $a = \mu g\cos\theta$

(ii) Expression for time taken by body to slide down the plane is

(a) $\sqrt{\dfrac{2s}{g(\sin\theta - \mu\cos\theta)}}$ (b) $\sqrt{\dfrac{2s}{g(\sin\theta + \mu\cos\theta)}}$

(c) $\sqrt{\dfrac{2s}{g(\tan\theta - \mu)}}$ (d) None of these

(iii) When friction is absent, time taken to slide down the plane

(a) $\sqrt{\dfrac{2s}{g\sin\theta}}$ (b) $\sqrt{\dfrac{2s}{g\cos\theta}}$

(c) $\sqrt{\dfrac{2s}{g\tan\theta}}$ (d) $\sqrt{\dfrac{2s}{g\cot\theta}}$

(iv) Which of the following relation is correct?

(a) $3\cos\theta = 4\mu\sin\theta$
(b) $3\sin\theta = 4\mu\cos\theta$
(c) $4\cos\theta = 3\mu\sin\theta$
(d) $4\sin\theta = 3\mu\cos\theta$

(v) Coefficient of friction μ is

(a) 0.5 (b) 0.75 (c) 0.25 (d) 0.35

33. **Newton has given three laws to describe the motion of objects. According to Newton's first law, when the net external force on a body is zero, then the body is either at rest or moving with constant velocity. The first law gives the definition of inertia. Inertia means resistance to change in state of rest or motion.**

According to Newton's second law, the rate of change of momentum of a body is directly proportional to the external applied force on the body. The second law gives the measurement of force. According to Newton's third law, For every action, there is always equal and opposite reaction.

(i) Name the property by which any body tries to maintain its original state.

(ii) Why does a cricket player lower his hands while catching a ball?

(iii) An object of mass 50 kg is initially at rest. It gets the speed of 10 m/s in 5 second. Calculate the force applied by engine of the car.

(iv) A object of mass 10 kg jumps on a floor. Calculate the average force applied by the floor to the object.

34. **When a body moves on a circular path with constant speed and changing its direction of motion at every instant of time, then it is called uniform circular motion.**

The change in the direction of motion of the body gives the change in its velocity, and hence the body undergoes an acceleration, called radial acceleration or centripetal acceleration.

Thus, according to Newton's second law of motion, a body cannot be accelerated itself. The external force required to maintain the motion of a body on a circular path is called centripetal force, $F_c = \dfrac{mv^2}{r}$,

where m, v and r are the mass of a body, velocity of the body and the radius of circular path.

(i) Which force provides centripetal force during the motion of the moon around the earth?

(ii) A car is moving on a circular path of radius 25 m. If the coefficient of friction between tyre and road is 0.4, then find the maximum speed of the car without skidding from the circular path.

(iii) Why a cyclist bends during its motion on a circular path?

(iv) The motion of a body on a vertical circle is uniform or non-uniform? Give its explanation.

Subjective Questions

Very Short Answer Type Questions

1. Write two consequences of Newton's second law of motion.

2. The two ends of a spring-balance are pulled by a force of 10 kg each. What will be the reading of the balance?

3. A lift is accelerated upward, will the apparent weight of a person inside the lift increase, decrease or remain the same relative to its real weight? What happen, if the lift is going at a uniform speed?

4. Why does a cyclist lean to one side, while going along a curve? In what direction does he lean?

5. Why does not a heavy gun kick so strongly as a light gun using the same bullets (i.e. cartridges)?

6. The linear velocity of a particle moving on the circumference of the circle is equal to the velocity acquired by a freely falling body through a distance equal to one-fourth the diameter of the circle. What is the centripetal acceleration of the particle moving along the circle?

Short Answer Type Questions

7. (a) Why are porcelain objects wrapped in paper or straw before packing for transportation? **NCERT Exemplar** [1½]

(b) A person driving a car suddenly applies the brakes on seeing a child on the road ahead. If he is not wearing seat belt, he falls forward and hits his head against the steering wheel. Why? **NCERT Exemplar** [1½]

8. Ten one-rupee coins are put on top of each other on a table. Each coin has mass *m*. Give the magnitude and direction of

(a) the force on the 7th coin (counted from the bottom) due to all the coins on its top. [1]

(b) the force on the 7th coin by the eighth coin. [1]

(c) the reaction of the 6th coin on the 7th coin. [1]

9. (a) Why does a child feel more pain when she falls down on a hard cement floor, than when she falls on the soft muddy ground in the garden? **NCERT Exemplar** [1½]

(b) Can a bomb, initially at rest, explode into three pieces which fly in mutually perpendicular directions? [1½]

10. (a) The mountain road is generally made winding upwards rather than going straight up. Why? [1½]

(b) The outer rail of a curved railway track is generally raised over the inner. Why? [1½]

11. (a) If the speed of stone is increased beyond the maximum permissible value and the string breaks suddenly, which of the following correctly describes the trajectory of the stone after the string breaks? [1½]

(i) The stone moves radially outwards.

(ii) The stone flies off tangentially from the instant the string breaks.

(iii) The stone flies off at an angle with the tangent whose magnitude depends on the speed of the particle. **NCERT** [1½]

(b) A boy is trying to push a truck but not able to push it. His friend explains the situation with the help of Newton's third law. His friend says that according to Newton's third law, action-reaction forces are equal and opposite, so they will cancel each other and the net force on the truck will become zero. That's why, the truck will not move.
Analyse the explanation of his friend and comment that his explanation is right or wrong. [1½]

12. A monkey of mass 40 kg climbs on a rope which can stand a maximum tension of 600 N. In which of the following cases will be rope break, when the monkey

(a) climbs up with an acceleration of 6 m/s^2. [1]

(b) climbs down with an acceleration of 4 m/s^2. [1]

(c) climbs up with a uniform speed of 5 m/s. [1]

Long Answer Type Questions

13. A block of mass *m* is held against a rough vertical wall by pressing it with a finger. If the coefficient of friction between the block and the wall is μ and the acceleration due to gravity is *g*, calculate the minimum force required to be applied by finger to hold the block against the wall? **NCERT Exemplar**

14. A body is sliding on a smooth inclined plane as shown in the figure and takes time T to cover some distance. If the smooth surface is replaced by rough surface, then the body takes time pT (where p is some number greater than zero) to cover the same distance then calculate the coefficient of friction. **Competency Based Que**

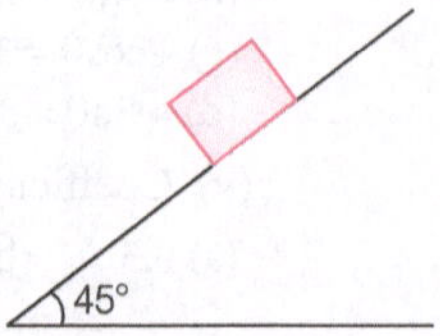

15. (i) What do you mean by inertia? Explain different types of inertia with some examples. **[3]**
(ii) Can you measure inertia? Explain your answer. **[2]**

16. Define the principle of conservation of linear momentum. Deduce the law of conservation of linear momentum from Newton's third law of motion.

17. Why circular roads are banked? Derive an expression for angle of banking for safe circular turn. Consider that coefficient of friction between the tyre and road is μ.

18. Briefly explain static friction, limiting friction and kinetic friction. How do they vary with the applied force?

19. Discuss the equilibrium of concurrent forces acting on a rigid body.

20. For the system below, find the values of T_1, T_2 and T_3. Also, find the acceleration of every block.

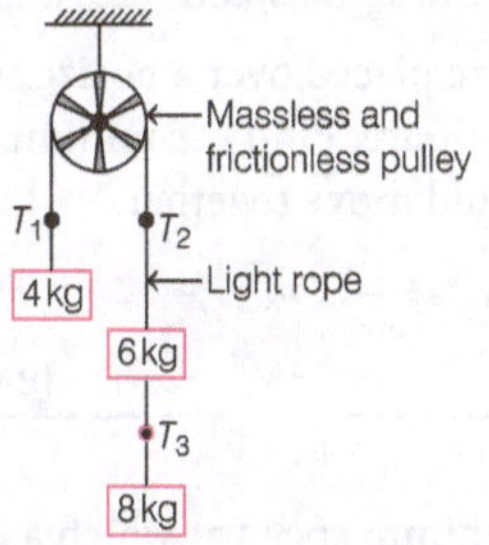

21. A stone of mass m tied to the end of a string revolves in a vertical circle of radius R. The net forces at the lowest and highest points of the circle directed vertically downwards are (choose the correct alternative).

	Lowest point	**Highest point**
(i)	$mg - T_1$	$mg + T_2$
(ii)	$mg + T_1$	$mg - T_2$
(iii)	$mg + T_1 - (mv_1^2)/R$	$mg - T_2 + (mv_2^2)/R$
(iv)	$mg - T_1 - (mv_1^2)/R$	$mg + T_2 + (mv_2^2)/R$

Here, T_1, T_2 and (v_1, v_2) denote the tension in the string (and the speed of the stone) at the lowest and highest point respectively.

Numerical Problems

Concept of Force : Laws of Motion

22. Forces of 16 N and 12 N are acting on a mass of 200 kg in mutually perpendicular direction. Find the magnitude of acceleration produced.

23. A body of mass 0.40 kg moving initially with a consant speed of 10 ms^{-1} to the north is subject to a constant force of 8.0 N directed towards the south for 30 s. Take the instant the force is applied to be $t = 0$, the position of the body at that time to be $x = 0$ and predict its position at $t = -5$ s, 25 s, 100 s. **NCERT**

24. A truck starts from rest and accelerates uniformly at 2.0 ms^{-2}. At $t = 10$ s, a stone is dropped by a person standing on the top of the truck (6 m high from the ground). What are the (a) velocity and (b) acceleration of the stone at $t = 11$ s? (Neglect air resistance) **NCERT**

25. Figure shows (v_x, t), and (v_y, t) diagrams for a body of unit mass. Find the force as a function of time. **NCERT Exemplar**

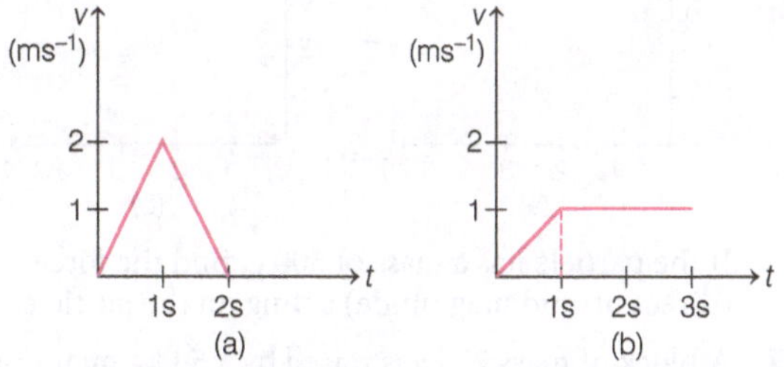

26. A bullet of mass 0.04 kg moving with a speed of 90 m/s enters a heavy wooden block and is stopped after a distance of 60 cm. What is the average resistive force exerted by the block on the bullet?

27. A helicopter of mass 2000 kg rises with a vertical acceleration of 15 ms^{-2}. The total mass of the crew and passengers is 500 kg. Give the magnitude and direction of the ($g = 10$ ms^{-2})
(a) force on the floor of the helicopter by the crew and passengers. **[1]**
(b) action of the rotor of the helicopter on the surrounding air. **NCERT Exemplar** **[1]**
(c) force on the helicopter due to the surrounding air. **[1]**

28. Give the magnitude and direction of the net force acting on
(i) a drop of rain falling down with a constant speed. **[1]**
(ii) a cork of mass 10 g floating on water. **[1]**
(iii) a kite skillfully held stationary in the sky. **[1]**
(iv) a car moving with a constant velocity of 30 km/h on a rough road. **[1]**
(v) a high speed electron in space far from all gravitational (material) objects and free of electric and magnetic fields. **NCERT** **[1]**

29. Give the magnitude and direction of the net force acting on a stone of mass 0.1 kg.
(i) Just after it is dropped from the window of a stationary train. **[1/2]**
(ii) Just after it is dropped from the window of a train running at a constant velocity of 36 km/h. **[1/2]**
(iii) Just after it is dropped from the window of a train accelerating with 1 m/s^2. **[1]**

(iv) Lying on the floor of a train which is accelerating with 1m/s^2, the stone being at rest relative to the train. Neglect air resistance throughout. **NCERT [1]**

30. Figure shows (x, t) and (y, t) diagram of a particle moving in 2-dimensions.

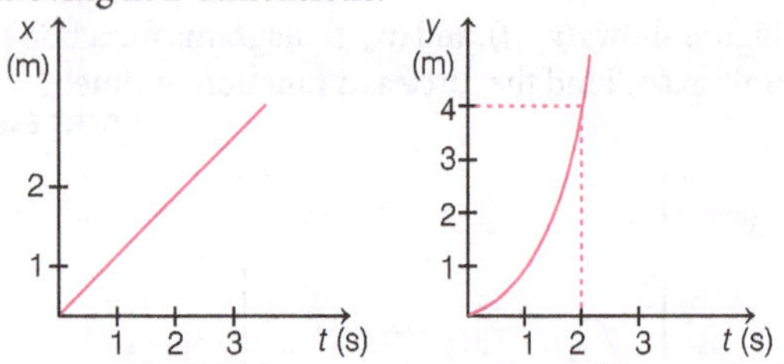

(a) (b)

If the particle has a mass of 500 g, find the force (direction and magnitude) acting on the particle.

31. A block of mass 25 kg is raised by a 50 kg man in two different ways as shown in figure. What is the action on the floor by the man in the two cases? If the floor yields a normal force of 700 N, which mode should the man adopt to lift the block without the floor yielding? **Competency Based Que.**

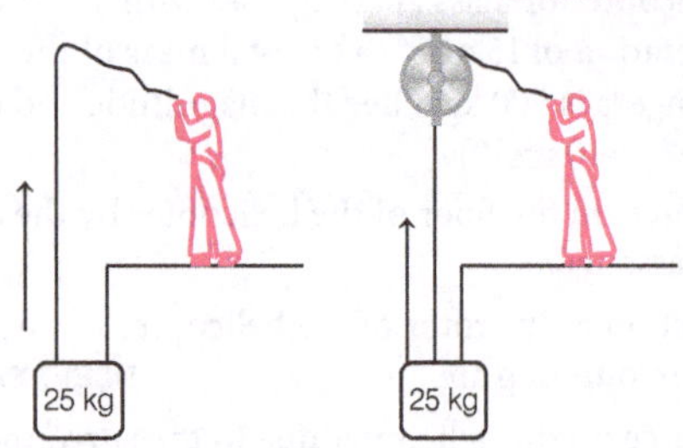

(a) (b)

Momentum and Impulse

32. Following figure shows the position-time graph of a particle of mass 4 kg. What is the (a) force on the particle for $t < 0, t > 4 \text{s}, 0 < t < 4 \text{s}$? (b) Impulse at $t = 0$ and $t = 4 \text{s}$? (Consider one-dimensional motion only). **NCERT**

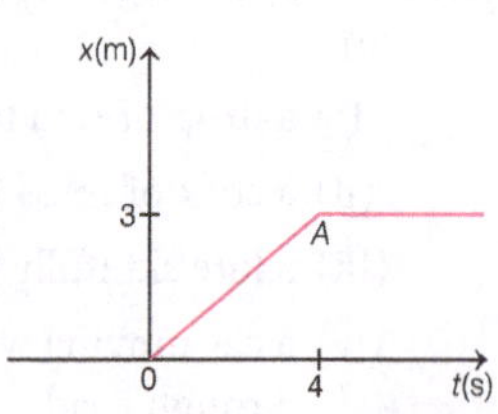

33. Figure shows the position-time graph of a body of mass 0.04 kg. Suggest a suitable physical context for this motion. What is the time between two consecutive impulses received by the body? What is the magnitude of each impulse? **Competency Based Que.**

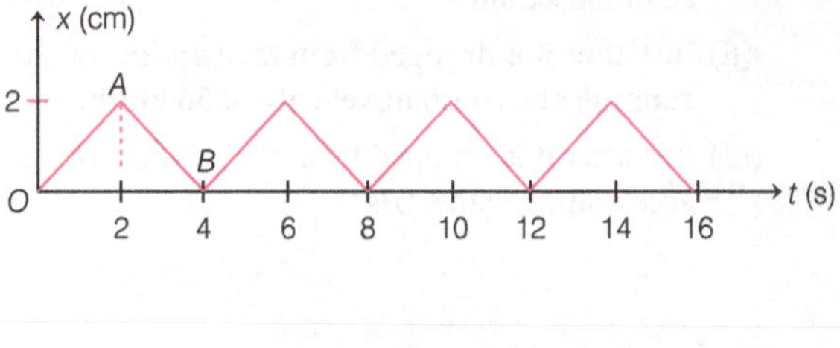

Law of Conservation of Momentum

34. A shell of mass 0.020 kg is fired by a gun of mass 100 kg. If the muzzle speed of the shell is 80 m/s, what is the recoil speed of the gun?

35. A girl riding a bicycle along a straight road with a speed of 5 m/s throws a stone of mass 0.5 kg which has a speed of 15 m/s with respect to the ground along her direction of motion. The mass of the girl and bicycle is 50 kg. Does the speed of the bicycle change after the stone is thrown? What is the change in speed, if so? **NCERT Exemplar**

Friction

36. What is the smallest radius of an unbanked (flat) track around which a bicyclist can move if her speed is 29 km/h and the μ_s between tyres and track is 0.32?

37. Two blocks are placed over a horizontal smooth plane as shown in the figure. Find the minimum value of μ_2, so that block could move together. **Competency Based Que.**

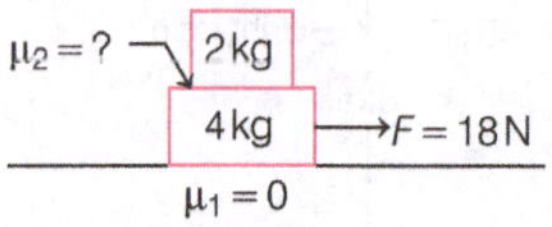

38. Find the maximum speed at which a car can turn around a curve of 30 m radius on a level road, given the coefficient of friction between the tyres and the road is 0.4. $[g = 10 \text{m/s}^2]$

39. A block of mass 15 kg is placed on a long trolley. The coefficient of static friction between the block and the trolley is 0.18. The trolley accelerates from rest with 0.5m/s^2 for 20 s and then moves with uniform velocity. Discuss the motion of the block as viewed by

(i) stationary observer on the ground **[1½]**

(ii) an observer moving with the trolley. **NCERT [1½]**

40. Two bodies A and B of masses 5 kg and 10kg in contact with each other rest on a table is against a rigid wall as shown in figure. The coefficient of friction between the bodies and the table is 0.15. A force of 200 N is applied horizontally at A.

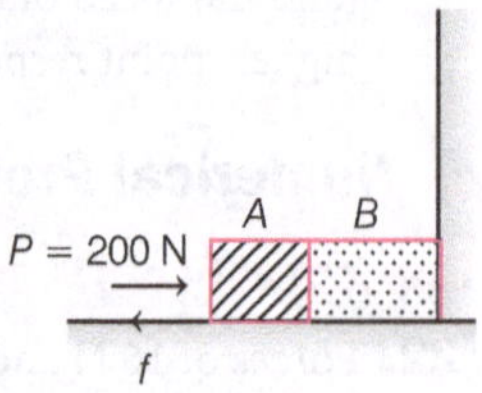

What are (i) the reaction of the partition or wall (ii) the action- reaction forces between A and B? What happens when the partition is removed? Does the answer to change, when the bodies are in motion? Ignore difference between μ_s and μ_k. **NCERT**

41. A 70 kg man stands in contact against the inner wall of a hollow cylindrical drum of radius 3 m rotating about its vertical axis with 200 rev/min. The coefficient of friction between the wall and his clothing is 0.15. What is the minimum rotational speed of the cylinder to enable the man to remain stuck to the wall (without falling) when the floor is suddenly removed? **Competency Based Que.**

42. When a body slides down from rest along a smooth inclined plane making an angle of 45° with the horizontal, it takes time T. When the same body slides down from rest along a rough inclined plane making the same angle and through the same distance, it is seen to take time pT, where p is some number greater than 1. Calculate the coefficient of friction between the body and the rough plane. **NCERT Exemplar**

Dynamic of Circular Motion

43. The wheel of a truck has a radius of $r = 0.29$ m and is being rotated at 830 revolutions per minute (rpm) on a tyre balancing machine. Determine the speed (in m/s) at which the outer edge of the wheel is moving.

44. A disc revolves in a horizontal plane at a steady rate of 3 revolutions per second. A coin of mass 6 g just remains on the disc if kept at a mean distance of 2 cm from the axis of rotation. What is the coefficient of friction between the coin and the disc? ($g = 10\ m/s^2$)

45. You may have seen in a circus a motorcyclist driving in vertical loops inside a death well (a hollow spherical chamber with holes, so the spectators can watch from outside). Explain clearly, why the motorcyclist does not drop down when he is at the uppermost point, with no support from below. What is the minimum speed required at the uppermost position to perform a vertical loop if the radius of the chamber is 25 m? **NCERT**

46. A disc revolves with a speed of $33\frac{1}{3}$ rev/min and has a radius of 15 cm. Two coins are placed at 4 cm and 14 cm away from the centre of the record. If the coefficient of friction between the coins and the record is 0.15, which of the coins will revolve with the record?

47. In a rotor, a hollow vertical cylinder rotates about its axis and a person rests against the inner wall. At a particular speed of the rotor, the floor below the person is removed and the person hangs resting against the wall without any floor.

If the radius of the rotor is 2 m and the coefficient of static friction between the wall and the person is 0.2.

(i) Find the minimum speed at which the floor may be removed. **[1½]**

(ii) What type of speciality is associated with this question? [take, $g = 10\ m/s^2$]

Competency Based Que. [1½]

Vehicle on Banked Road

48. For traffic moving at 60 km/h, if the radius of a curve is 0.1 km, then what is the correct angle of banking of the road? [take $g = 10\ m/s^2$]

49. A train rounds an unbanked circular bend of radius 30 m at a speed of 54 km/h. The mass of the train is 10^6 kg. What provides the centripetal force required for this purpose, the engine or the rails? What is the angle of banking required to prevent wearing out of the rail?

The centripetal force required by the train to cross the circular bend is provided by the lateral thrust exerted by the outer rails on the wheels. According to Newton's third law of motion, the train also exerts an equal and opposite force on the rails causing its wear and tear.

Competency Based Que.

Connected Body Motion

50. Two bodies of masses 10 kg and 20 kg respectively kept on a smooth, horizontal surface are tied to the ends of a light string. A horizontal force $F = 600$ N is applied to (i) A, (ii) B along the direction of string. What is the tension in the string in each case? **NCERT**

51. For the given pulley block system, find the acceleration of 2 kg block.

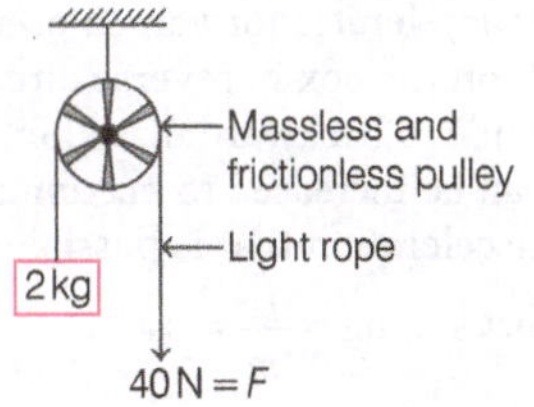

Hints & Solutions

Objective Type Questions

1. (c) 2. (c) 3. (b) 4. (d) 5. (a)
6. (c) 7. (b) 8. (d)

9. (a) Given mass = 2 kg

$$x(t) = pt + qt^2 + rt^3$$

$$v = \frac{dv}{dt} = p + 2qt + 3rt^2$$

$$a = \frac{dv}{dt} = 0 + 2q + 6rt$$

at $t = 2s, a = 2q + 6 \times 2 \times r = 2q + 12r = 2 \times 4 + 12 \times 5$

$$= 8 + 60 = 68 \text{ m/s}$$

Force, $F = ma = 2 \times 68 = 136\text{N}$

10. (b) Given, mass of car = m

$$u = 0$$

$$t = 2\text{s}$$

$$\because \quad v = u + at$$

$$v_i = 0 + a \times 2$$

$$a = \frac{v_i}{2}$$

Force, $F = ma = \frac{mv_i}{2}$

Hence, force acting on car is $\frac{mv}{2}$ towards east.

11. (b)

12. (a) Here, $r = 10$ m, $\mu = 0.1$, $g = 10 \text{ ms}^{-2}$

The maximum speed allowed by traffic police for car to cross a circular turn to prevent accident = $\sqrt{\mu rg}$

$$= \sqrt{0.1 \times (10) \times (10)} = \sqrt{10} \text{ ms}^{-1}$$

13. (c)

14. (b) As trolly accelerates forward, a pseudo force called friction acts on the box in reverse direction. It prevent the box to slide in backward direction. But sliding friction is can be increased to maximum value of μ so, maximum acceleration that is possible for the box before it start sliding = $\frac{f_s}{m} = \mu g$

$$= 0.3 \times 10 = 3 \text{ m/s}^2$$

15. (a) 17. (a) 18. (a) 19. (a) 20. (b)
21. (c) 22. (a) 23. (c) 24. (a) 26. (a)
27. (b) 28. (a) 29. (c) 30. (d)

16. (a) Here, $m_1 = 1$ kg, $m_2 = 2$ kg

The acceleration of the system is

$$a = \frac{(m_2 - m_1)g}{m_1 + m_2} = \frac{(2-1)g}{(1+2)} = \frac{g}{3} = \frac{10}{3}$$

Acceleration of the centre of mass,

$$a_{CM} = \frac{m_1 a_1 + m_2 a_2}{m_1 + m_2} = \frac{1(-a) + 2a}{1+2}$$

$$= \frac{\left(-\frac{g}{3}\right) + 2\left(\frac{g}{3}\right)}{3} = \frac{g}{9} = \frac{10}{9}$$

∴ The distance travelled by the centre of mass in two seconds is

$$s = \frac{1}{2} a_{CM} t^2 = \frac{1}{2} \times \frac{10}{9} \times (2)^2 = \frac{20}{9} \text{ m}$$

25. (d) It is not always necessary that external agency of force is in contact with the object, while applying force on object. Force can be applied on a body/particle without contact or with contact, it depends on the agency, applying force. e.g. Earth pulls (exerts force) from distance. A stone without any physical contact falls due to gravitational pull of the earth.

31. (i) (a)
(ii) (c)
(iii) (d)
(iv) Given, $\mu_s = 0.15$, $g = 10 \text{ ms}^{-2}$

$$a_{max} = ?$$

The frictional force acting between the floor of the train and the surface of the box, will oppose the slipping of the box on the floor of the train.

∴ Limiting friction force,

$$f_s = ma_{max}$$

and $f_s = \mu_s N = \mu_s mg$

$$\therefore \quad m \cdot a_{max} = \mu_s mg$$

$$a_{max} = \mu_s g$$

$$a_{max} = 0.15 \times 10$$

$$\therefore \quad a_{max} = 1.5 \text{ ms}^{-2}$$

(v) (b) Let the mass of block C is m.

For block A, $R = (m_1 + m)$

$$T = fs = \mu R = \mu(m + m_1)g$$

To avoid slipping of A, For block B

$$T = m_2 g$$

or $\mu(m + m_1)g = m_2 g$

$$0.2(m + 10) = 5 \Rightarrow m = 15 \text{ kg}$$

32. (i)-(a) (ii)-(a) (iii)-(a) (iv)-(b) (v)-(b)

33. (i) Inertia is the property of a body by virtue of which the body tries to maintain its either, the state of rest or motion. i.e. original state.

(ii) As, Force = $\frac{\text{Change in momentum}}{\text{Time interval}}$

So, a cricket player lowers his hand while catching a ball in order to increase time interval to reduce velocity. Hence, the force on his hands is reduced and the hands of the players is protected from injury.

(iii) Given, $u = 0, v = 10$ m/s,
$t = 5$s, $m = 50$kg

$$\therefore \quad a = \frac{v-u}{t} = \frac{10-0}{5} = 2 \text{ m/s}^2$$

∴ Force applied by engine of the car is
$F = ma = 50 \times 2 = 100$ N

(iv) Given, $m = 10$kg
∴ According to Newton's third law,
Force applied by floor to the body is the weight of the body.

$$\therefore \quad w = mg = 10 \times 10 = 100 \text{ N}$$

34. (i) The force of gravity between the moon and the earth provides the necessary centripetal force to keep the motion of the moon on the circular path.

(ii) Given, $r = 25$m, $\mu = 0.4$
The frictional force between the tyre and the road provides the centripetal force.

$$\therefore \quad F_c = \frac{mv^2}{r} \le \mu mg$$

$$\therefore \quad v \le \sqrt{\mu rg}$$

$$\therefore \quad v_{max} = \sqrt{\mu rg}$$

$$= \sqrt{0.4 \times 25 \times 10} = 10 \text{ m/s}$$

(iii) When a cyclist moves on a circular path, it bends in order to provide the necessary centripetal force to keep its motion on the circular path. The component of normal reaction gives the required centripetal force during the motion of the cyclist.

(iv) The speed of a body is continuously changing due to gravity while it is moving in a vertical circle. Hence, it is a non-uniform circular motion.

Subjective Questions

1. The two consequences of Newton's Second Law of motion are as follows.
   1. It demonstrates that the motion is only accelerated when force is applied to it.
   2. It introduces the concept of a body's inertial mass.

2. As the spring balancing is based on the tension in the spring, it gauges weight. Now, if both ends are pulled by a 10 kg weight, the tension is 10kg, and reading will be 10 kg.

3. There will be an increase in perceived weight. The apparent weight will the same as the true weight, if the lift moves at a constant pace.

4. A cyclist leans while riding along a curve because a component of the ground's natural response supplies him with the centripetal force he needs to turn.
   He must lean inward from his vertical posture, towards the circular path's centre.

5. The recoil speed of the gun is inversely proportional to its mass. So the recoil speed of the heavy gun is lesser than that of the light gun.

6. a_c = centripetal acceleration $= \frac{v^2}{t}$

But $v^2 - 0^2 = 2g\frac{r}{2}$ $\quad \left(\because s = \frac{2r}{4} = \frac{r}{2}\right)$

$$\therefore \quad a_c = \frac{gr}{r} = g$$

7. (a) Porcelain objects are wrapped in paper or straw before packing to reduce the chances of damage during transportation. During transportation, sudden jerks or even fall can take place. Forces are created at the point of collision and the force takes longer time to reach the porcelain objects through paper or straw for same change in momentum as $F = \Delta p / \Delta t$ and therefore, a lesser force acts on object.

(b) When a person driving a car suddenly applies the brakes, the lower part of the body slower down with the car while upper part of the body continues to move forward due to inertia of motion. If driver is not wearing seat belt, then he falls forward and his head hit against the steering wheel.

8. Mass of each coin $= m$

Number of total coins = 10

(a) Force acting on 7th coin (counted from the bottom)
= weight of the coins above it
= weight of 3 coins
= 3 mg N (downward)

(b) Force acting on 7th coin by the eighth coin = weight of the eighth coin + weight of two coins supported by eight coin
$= mg + 2mg$
$= 3mg$ N (downward)

(c) Reaction of the sixth coin on the seventh coin
= – (force exerted on sixth coin)
= – (weight of four coins)
= –4 mg N (vertically upward)

9. (a) When a child falls on a cement floor, her body comes to rest instantly.
But $F \times \Delta t$ = change in momentum = constant.
As time of stopping Δt decreases, therefore, F increases and hence, child feel more pain. When she falls on a soft muddy ground in the garden, the time of stopping increases and hence F decreases and she feels lesser pain.

(b) Conservation of linear momentum states that linear momentum after explosion should be zero. It means the vector sum of three momentum vectors is zero. Hence, in present case, 3 momentum vectors are not coplanar (i.e. they are not in the same plane), such an explosion cannot take place.

10. (a) When we go up a mountain, the opposing force of friction is $F = \mu R = \mu mg\cos\theta$.

where θ is angle of slope with horizontal. To avoid skidding, F should be large.

$\therefore$ $\cos\theta$ should be large and hence, θ must be small. Therefore, mountain roads are generally made winding upwards. The road straight up would have large slope.

(b) When the outer rail of a curved railway track is raised over the inner, the horizontal component of the normal reaction of the rails, provides the necessary centripetal force for the train to enable it moving along the curved path.

11. (a) The second part (ii) correctly describes the trajectory of the stone after the spring breaks because when a stone tied to one end of a string is whirled round in a circle, then velocity of the stone at any point is along the tangent at that point. If the string breaks suddenly, then stone flies off tangentially, along the direction of its velocity.

(b) The reaction force applied by the truck to the boy is not an external force. So, the net external force on the truck is not zero. The truck is unable to move as the frictional force is greater than the applied force.

Hence, the analysis given by his friend is wrong.

12. Mass of the monkey, $m = 40$ kg

Maximum tension which can be stand by the rope, $(T)_{max} = 600$ N

(a) When monkey climbs up with an acceleration $a = 6\ \text{m/s}^2$, then

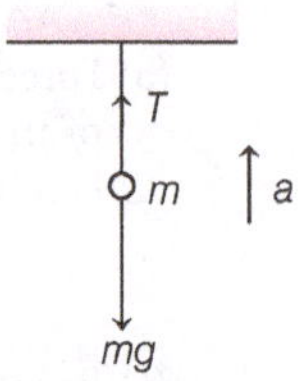

$$T - mg = ma$$
$$T = mg + ma$$
$$T = m(g + a)$$
$$= 40(10 + 6)$$
$$= 640\ \text{N}$$

In this condition $T > T_{max}$, therefore the rope will break.

(b) When monkey descents down with an acceleration m/s^2, then

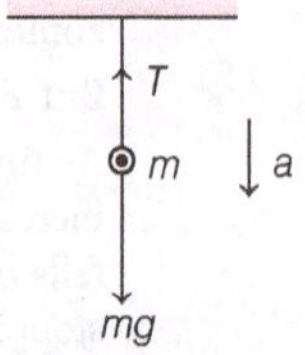

$$mg - T = ma$$
or $$T = mg - ma$$
$$= m(g - a)$$
$$= 40(10 - 4)\ \text{N}$$
$$= 240\ \text{N}$$

In this condition $T < T_{max}$, therefore the rope will not break.

(c) When monkey climbs up with a uniform speed of 5 m/s, then its acceleration a is zero.

$$\therefore \quad T = mg$$
$$= 40 \times 10$$
$$= 400\ \text{N}$$

13. Given, mass of the block $= m$

Coefficient of friction between the block and the wall $= \mu$

Let a force F be applied on the block to hold the block against the wall. The normal reaction of mass be N and force of friction acting upward be f.

In equilibrium, vertical and horizontal forces should be balanced separately.

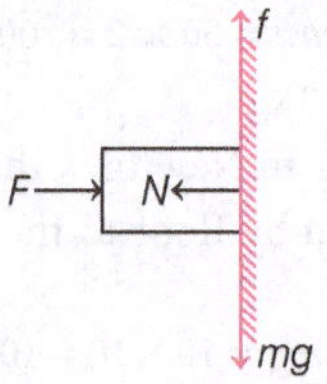

$$\therefore \quad f = mg \quad \text{...(i)}$$
and $$F = N \quad \text{...(ii)}$$

But force of friction $(f) = \mu N$
$$= \mu F \quad \text{[using Eq. (ii)] ...(iii)}$$

From Eqs. (i) and (iii), we get

$$\mu F = mg \quad \text{or} \quad F = \frac{mg}{\mu}$$

14. From relation $s = ut + \frac{1}{2}at^2$

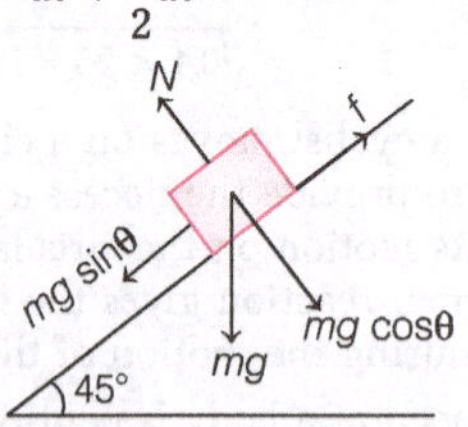

Distance covered by body at time T,

$$s = \frac{1}{2}g\sin\theta T^2 \quad (\because a = g\sin\theta) \text{...(i)}$$

For rough plane,

Upward force, $F = \mu N = \mu mg\cos\theta$

Downward force, $f = mg\sin\theta - \mu mg\cos\theta$

$\Rightarrow \quad a = g\sin\theta - \mu g\cos\theta$

Now, again using equation,

$$s = ut + \frac{1}{2}at^2, \text{ we have}$$
$$s = \frac{1}{2}(g\sin\theta - \mu g\cos\theta)(pT)^2 \quad \text{...(ii)}$$

Equating Eqs. (i) and (ii)

$$\frac{1}{2}g\sin\theta T^2 = \frac{1}{2}(g\sin\theta - \mu g\cos\theta)(pT)^2$$
$$\Rightarrow \quad 1 = (1 - \mu)p^2 \quad (\because \theta = 45°)$$
$$\Rightarrow \quad \mu = 1 - \frac{1}{p^2}$$

15. (i) Refer to text on Pages no. 113 and 114.

(ii) Yes, inertia can be measured by measuring the mass of the body.

e.g. If a football and an iron ball (of same size) are moving on a smooth floor with same velocity, then more force is required to stop the iron ball composed to the football. This implied greater mass means more inertia. Hence, measurement of mass is the measurement of inertia.

16. For definition refer to text on Page no. 120.

Derivation of conservation of momentum from Newton's third law.

Let us consider the momenta of two particles system of masses m_1 and m_2 are $\mathbf{p}_1$ and $\mathbf{p}_2$ respectively, then the net momentum of the whole system is

$$\mathbf{p} = \mathbf{p}_1 + \mathbf{p}_2 \quad \text{...(i)}$$

Suppose $\mathbf{F}_1$ and $\mathbf{F}_2$ are two forces acting on particles of masses m_1 and m_2. Let in a small time interval Δt, the change produced by the forces $\mathbf{F}_1$ and $\mathbf{F}_2$ are $\Delta\mathbf{p}_1$ and $\Delta\mathbf{p}_2$.

Thus, net change in momentum

$$\Delta\mathbf{p} = \Delta\mathbf{p}_1 + \Delta\mathbf{p}_2$$

or $$\frac{\Delta\mathbf{p}}{\Delta t} = \frac{\Delta\mathbf{p}_1}{\Delta t} + \frac{\Delta\mathbf{p}_2}{\Delta t}$$

or $$\frac{d\mathbf{p}}{dt} = \frac{d\mathbf{p}_1}{dt} + \frac{d\mathbf{p}_2}{dt} \quad [\text{as } \Delta t \to 0]$$

or $$\frac{d\mathbf{p}}{dt} = \mathbf{F}_1 + \mathbf{F}_2 \quad \text{...(ii)}$$

where, $\mathbf{F}_1 = \mathbf{F}_{1\,\text{ext}} + \mathbf{F}_{1\,\text{int}}$

and $\mathbf{F}_2 = \mathbf{F}_{2\,\text{ext}} + \mathbf{F}_{2\,\text{int}}$

$$\frac{d\mathbf{p}}{dt} = (\mathbf{F}_{1\,\text{ext}} + \mathbf{F}_{1\,\text{int}}) + (\mathbf{F}_{2\,\text{ext}} + \mathbf{F}_{2\,\text{int}})$$

or $$\frac{d\mathbf{p}}{dt} = (\mathbf{F}_{1\,\text{ext}} + \mathbf{F}_{2\,\text{ext}}) + (\mathbf{F}_{1\,\text{int}} + \mathbf{F}_{2\,\text{int}}) \quad \text{....(iii)}$$

From Newton's third law, the internal forces always occur in pair so

$$(\mathbf{F}_{1\,\text{int}} + \mathbf{F}_{2\,\text{int}}) = 0$$

or $$(\mathbf{F}_{1\,\text{int}} = -\mathbf{F}_{2\,\text{int}})$$

From Eq. (iii), we get

Thus, $$\frac{d\mathbf{p}}{dt} = (-\mathbf{F}_{2\,\text{int}} + \mathbf{F}_{2\,\text{int}}) + (-\mathbf{F}_{1\,\text{ext}} + \mathbf{F}_{2\,\text{ext}})$$

or $$\frac{d\mathbf{p}}{dt} = 0 + \mathbf{F}_{1\,\text{ext}} + \mathbf{F}_{2\,\text{ext}} \text{ or } \frac{d\mathbf{p}}{dt} = \mathbf{F}_{\text{ext}}$$

where, $\mathbf{F} = \mathbf{F}_{1\,\text{ext}} + \mathbf{F}_{2\,\text{ext}}, \mathbf{F}_{\text{ext}} = 0$

Then, $$\frac{d\mathbf{p}}{dt} = 0 \text{ or Momentum, } \mathbf{p} = \text{constant}$$

17. Refer text on Pages no. 127 and 128

18. Refer to text on Pages 123, 124 and 125.

19. Refer to text on Pages 120 and 121.

20. Considering 4 kg and (8 kg + 6 kg) as system

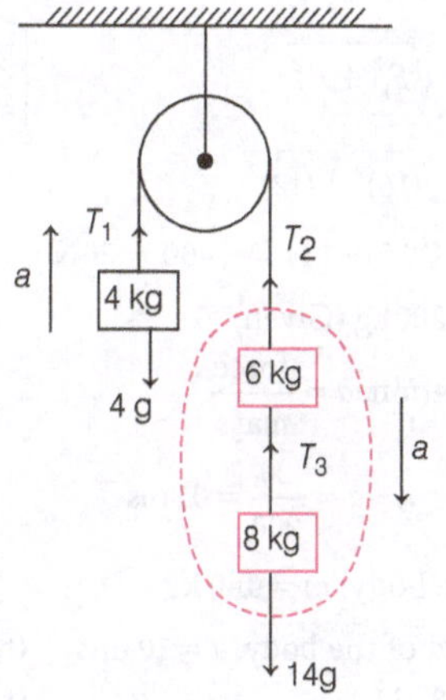

$$\therefore \quad a = \frac{F_{\text{net}}}{m} = \frac{14g - 4g}{4 + 8 + 6}$$

$$\therefore \quad a = \frac{5g}{9}$$

From FBD of 4 kg block,

$$T_1 - 4g = 4a = 4 \times \frac{5g}{9}$$

$$\Rightarrow \quad T_1 = \frac{56g}{9}$$

From FBD of (6kg + 8kg) block,

$$14g - T_2 = 14a = 14 \times \frac{5g}{9} \Rightarrow T_2 = \frac{56g}{9}$$

From FBD of 8 kg block,

$$8g - T_3 = 8a = 8 \times \frac{5g}{9}$$

$$\Rightarrow \quad T_3 = \frac{32g}{9}$$

21. Let tension in the string be T_1 and T_2 at lowest and highest points of the vertical circle.

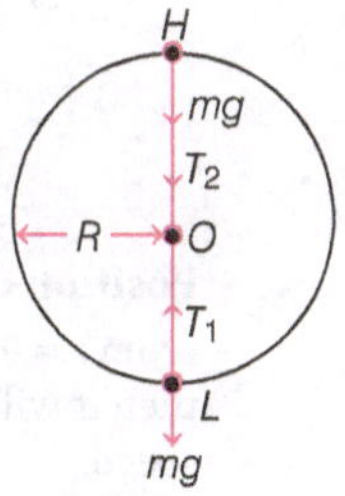

At lowest point T_1 acts towards the centre of the circle

($\because$ at the lowest point, string will be stretched downward due to weight of the stone) and mg acts vertically downward (weight of an object always acts downward).

$\therefore$ Net force acting on the stone in downward direction $(F_L) = mg - T_1$

At highest point Both T_2 and mg act vertically downward ($\because$ at the highest point, string is stretched away from the centre) towards the centre of the vertical circle. Net force acting on the stone in downward direction $(F_H) = mg + T_2$

$\therefore$ Correct option is (i).

22. Force, $F_1 = 16\text{N}$

$F_2 = 12\text{N}$

$\therefore \quad F = \sqrt{F_1^2 + F_2^2 + 2F_1F_2\cos\theta}$

$\Rightarrow \quad F = \sqrt{F_1^2 + F_2^2}$ $\left\{\begin{array}{l}\because \quad \theta = 90^\circ \\ \Rightarrow \cos 90^\circ = 0\end{array}\right\}$

$\Rightarrow \quad F = \sqrt{(16)^2 + (12)^2}$

$\Rightarrow \quad F = \sqrt{256+144} = \sqrt{400} = 20\text{N}$

Mass, $m = 200\text{kg}$ (Given)

$\because$ Acceleration, $a = \dfrac{\text{force}}{\text{mass}}$

$\Rightarrow \quad a = \dfrac{20}{200} = 0.1\,\text{ms}^{-2}.$

23. Mass of the body, $m = 0.40$ kg

Initial speed of the body, $u = 10$ m/s (towards north)

Force, $F = 8.0$ N (towards south)

$= -8.0$ N (Negative sign show that it is retarding force)

Time $t = 30$ s

At time $t = 0$, position of the particle is $x = 0$

Position of the body at $t = -5$ s

From $t = -5$ s to $t = 0$ the motion of the body is unaccelerated motion (towards north).

Distance covered by the body $(x)_{-5} = u \times t$

$(x)_{-5} = 10 \times (-5) = -50$ m

Position of the body at $t = 25$ s

From $t = 0$ to $t = 25$ s, body is in accelerated motion.

Acceleration, $a = \dfrac{F}{m}$

(acceleration produced in the particle towards south for $0 \le t \le 30$)

$= -\dfrac{8.0}{0.40} = -20\text{ m/s}^2$

Using equation of motion $s = ut + \dfrac{1}{2}at^2$

$x_{25} = 10 \times 25 + \dfrac{1}{2}(-20) \times (25)^2$

$= 250 - 6250$

$= -6000$ m

$= -6$ km

Position of the body at $t = 100$ s

From $t = 0$ to $t = 30$ s, body is in accelerated motion after then it will move from $t = 30$ s to $t = 100$ s with constant speed.

Distance travelled in 30 is

$x_{30} = 10 \times 30 + \dfrac{1}{2}(-20) \times (30)^2$

$= 300 - 9000 = -8700$ m

Velocity of the particle at $t = 30$ s

$v = u + at$

$= 10 + (-20) \times 30$

$= 10 - 600 = -590$ m/s

Distance travelled in time interval from $t = 30$ s to $t = 100$ s is $x_{70} = vt = (-590) \times 70 = -41300$ m

$\therefore$ Position at $t = 100$ s is

$x_{100} = x_{30} + x_{70} = -8700 + (-41300)$ m

$= -50000$ m $= -50$ km

24. Initial speed of truck, $u = 0$

Acceleration, $a = 2\text{ m/s}^2$

Time, $t = 10$ s

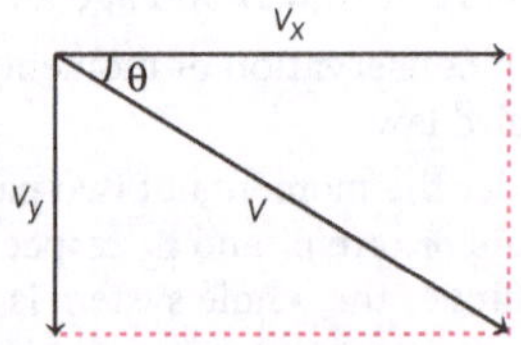

Velocity attained by the truck in 10 s is

$v = u + at = 0 + 2 \times 10 = 20$ m/s

(a) Horizontal velocity of the stone which remains unchanged,

$v_x = 20$ m/s

When stone is dropped from the top of the truck initial vertical velocity, $u_y = 0.$

Velocity attained in vertical direction by the stone in time interval from $t = 10$ s to $t = 11$ s, i.e. in 1 s.

$v_y = u_y + gt = 0 + 9.8 \times 1$

$v_y = 9.8$ m/s

$\therefore$ Resultant velocity of the stone

$v = \sqrt{v_x^2 + v_y^2} = \sqrt{(20)^2 + (9.8)^2} = 22.3$ m/s

If resultant velocity (v) subtends an angle θ with the horizontal, then

$\tan\theta = \dfrac{v_y}{v_x} = \dfrac{9.8}{20} = 0.49 = \tan 26^\circ 12'$

or $\theta = 26^\circ 12'$

(b) Just after the stone is dropped from the truck the horizontal force or acceleration acting on stone due to the truck becomes zero $(a_x = 0)$ and it falls freely under gravity.

$\therefore$ Acceleration of the stone $a_y = g = 9.8\text{ m/s}^2$

25. Consider figure (a),

$v_x = 2t$ for $0 < t < 1$s

$= 2(2-t)$ for $1 < t < 2$s,

$= 0$ for $t < 2$s

From figure (b),

$v_y = t$ for $0 < t < 1$s

$= 1$ for $t > 1$s

$\therefore \quad F_x = ma_x = m\dfrac{dv_x}{dt}$

$= 1 \times 2 = 2$N for $0 < t < 1$s

$= 1(-2) = -2$N for 1s $< t < 2$s

$= 0$ for $t > 2$s

$\therefore \quad F_y = ma_y = m\dfrac{dv_y}{dt}$

$= 1 \times 1 = 1\,\text{N for } 0 < t < 1\text{s}$

$= 0 \text{ for } t > 1\text{s}$

Hence, $F = F_x\hat{\mathbf{i}} + F_y\hat{\mathbf{j}}$

$= (2\hat{\mathbf{i}} + \hat{\mathbf{j}})\text{N for } 0 < t < 1\text{s}$

$= -2\hat{\mathbf{i}}\,\text{N for } 1\text{s} < t < 2\text{s}$

$= 0 \text{ for } t > 2\text{s}$

26. Given,

Mass of bullet, $m = 0.04$ kg

Initial speed of bullet, $u = 90\,\text{ms}^{-1}$

Final speed of bullet, $v = 0\,\text{ms}^{-1}$

Distance covered by bullet, $s = 60\,\text{cm} = 0.06$ m

From Newton's 3rd equation of motion,

$$v^2 = u^2 + 2as$$

$\Rightarrow \quad 0 = (90)^2 + 2 \times a \times 0.6$

$\Rightarrow \quad -(90)^2 = 1.2a$

$\Rightarrow \quad -\dfrac{8100}{1.2} = a \Rightarrow a = -6750\,\text{ms}^{-2}$

$\because$ Resistive force, $F = m \times a$

$\Rightarrow \quad F = -0.04 \times 6750$

$F = -270\text{N}$

27. Given, mass of helicopter $(m_1) = 2000$ kg

Mass of the crew and passengers $m_2 = 500$ kg

Acceleration in vertical direction $a = 15\,\text{m/s}^2\,(\uparrow)$ and $g = 10\,\text{m/s}^2\,(\downarrow)$

(a) Force on the floor of the helicopter by the crew and passengers is

$m_2(g + a) = 500(10 + 15)\text{N}$

$500 \times 25\,\text{N} = 12500\,\text{N}$

(b) Action of the rotor of the helicopter on the surrounding air $= (m_1 + m_2)(g + a)$

$= (2000 + 500) \times (10 + 15) = 2500 \times 25$

$= 62500$ N (downward)

(c) Force on the helicopter due to the surrounding air

= reaction of force applied by helicopter

= 62500 N (upward)

28. (i) As drop of rain is falling downward with a constant speed, therefore its acceleration is zero.

According to Newton's second law of motion, net force acting on drop, $F = ma = 0$.

(ii) In floating condition, the weight of the body is balanced by the upthrust. Therefore, net force acting on a cork floating on water = 0.

(iii) As kite is held stationary in the sky, therefore, acceleration of the kite is zero. Therefore, net force acting on the kite, $F = ma = 0$.

(iv) As car is moving with a constant velocity, therefore its acceleration is zero i.e. $a = 0$, therefore net force acting on the car, $F = ma = 0$.

(v) As electron is in a space, where there is no electric field, magnetic field and gravitational (material) objects, therefore, no electric, magnetic and gravitational force is acting on it. Hence, net force acting on electron is zero.

29. $\because$ Mass of stone $(m) = 0.1$ kg

(i) When stone is dropped from the window of a stationary train, it falls freely under gravity.

$\therefore$ Net force acting on stone (F)

$= mg = 0.1 \times 10 = 1.0$ N (vertical downward)

(ii) Just after the stone is dropped from the window of a train running at a constant velocity, i.e. acceleration of the train is zero. So, no force acts on the stone due to motion and it falls freely under gravity.

The force acts on it is due to its weight only, i.e. acceleration of the train is zero, so no force acts, on the stone due to this motion.

(iii) When the train is accelerating with $1\,\text{ms}^{-2}$ and additional force $F = ma = 0.1 \times 1 = 0.1$ N acts on the stone in the horizontal direction but once the stone is dropped from the train F becomes zero and the net force on the stone is 1N acting vertically downwards.

(iv) As the stone is accelerating with the train, so there must be a net horizontal force on it. Its weight also acts but is balanced by reaction force of the floor.

$$F = m \times a_{(\text{train})} = 0.1 \times 1 = 0.1\,\text{N}$$

30. Given, mass of the particle $(m) = 500\,\text{g} = 0.5$ kg

x-t graph of the particle is a straight line.

Hence, particle is moving with a uniform velocity along X-axis, i.e. its acceleration along X-axis is zero and hence, force acting along X-axis is zero.

y-t graph of particle is a parabola. Therefore, particle is in accelerated motion along Y-axis.

At $\quad t = 0, u_y = 0$

Along Y-axis, at $t = 2\,\text{s}$, $y = 4\text{m}$

Using equation of motion,

$$y = u_y t + \frac{1}{2}a_y t^2$$

$$4 = 0 \times 2 + \frac{1}{2} \times a_y \times (2)^2$$

or $\quad a_y = 2\,\text{m/s}^2$

$\therefore$ Force acting along Y-axis $(f_y) = ma_y$

$= 0.5 \times 2 = 1.0$ N (along Y-axis)

31. $\because$ Mass of block, $m = 25$ kg

Mass of the man, $M = 50$ kg

Force required to lift the block (F) = weight of the block

$$F = mg$$

$= 25 \times 10 = 250\ N$

Weight of the man, $w = Mg = 50 \times 10 = 500\ N$

Case (a)

If the block is raised by the man as shown in Fig. (a), then force is applied by the man in the upward direction, due to which the apparent weight of the man increases. When man applies force on block in upward direction, block applies force on man in downward direction, according to 3rd law of motion. Therefore, action on the floor by the man $= F + w$

$= 250 + 500 = 750\ N$

Case (b)

If the block is raised by the man as shown in Fig. (b), then force is applied by the man in the downward direction due to which apparent weight of the man decreases. Therefore, action on the floor by the man $= mg - F = 500 - 250 = 250\ N$

If the floor can yield to a normal force of 700 N, then the man should adopt the second method to easily lift the block by applying lesser force.

32. (a) **For $t < 0$,** the position-time graph is OO', for which displacement of the particle is zero, therefore, particle is at rest at the origin. Hence, acceleration and force acting on particle will also be zero.

For $t > 4s$, the position-time graph AA' is parallel to time axis. Therefore, for $t > 4s$, particle remains at a fixed distance of 3 m from the origin. It means particle is at rest. Therefore, acceleration and force acting on particle will be zero.

For $0 < t < 4s$, the position-time graph OA is a straight line inclined at an angle from the time axis, which is representing uniform motion of the particle, i.e. the particle is moving with a constant velocity. Therefore, acceleration and force acting on the particle will be zero.

(b) **Impulse at $t = 0$**

Impulse = change in momentum

$= mv - mu = m(v - u)$

Before $t = 0$, particle is at rest, hence $u = 0$

After $t = 0$, particle is moving with a constant velocity.

Velocity of the particle = slope of position-time graph

$$= \frac{3\ m}{4\ s} = 0.75\ m/s$$

$\therefore$ Impulse = change in momentum

$= 4(0.75 - 0) = 3\ kg\text{-}m/s$

Impulse at $t = 4s$

Before $t = 4s$, particle is moving with a constant speed, $u = 0.75\ m/s$

After $t = 4s$, particle is again at rest

$\because \quad v = 0$

$\therefore$ Impulse = Change in momentum $= m(v - u)$

$= 4(0 - 0.75) = -3\ kg\text{-}m/s$

33. Mass of the body, $m = 0.04\ kg$

The position-time graph OA from $t = 0$ to $t = 2s$ is a straight line, therefore body is moving with a constant velocity.

Velocity of the body, v = Slope of x-t graph

$$= \frac{2-0}{2-0} = 1\ cm/s = 10^{-2}\ m/s \quad [\because 1\ cm = 10^{-2}\ m]$$

Part AB of position-time graph is also a straight line, therefore, velocity of the body

$$v' = \frac{0-2}{0-2} = -1\ cm/s = -10^{-2}\ cm/s$$

Negative sign shows that the direction of velocity is reversed after 2 s and it is being repeated.

A suitable physical context for this motion is a ball moving with a constant velocity of 10^{-2} m/s between two walls located at $x = 0$ and at $x = 2$ m and rebounded repeatedly on striking each wall.

Magnitude of the impulse imparted to the ball after every two seconds = change in momentum of the ball

$= mv - mv' = m(v - v')$

$= 0.04\,[10^{-2} - (-10^{-2})] = 8 \times 10^{-4}\ kg\text{-}m/s$

34. Mass of gun $M = 100\ kg$

Mass of shell, $m = 0.020\ kg$

Velocity of shell, $v = 80\ ms^{-1}$

Recoil velocity of gun, v_r = ?

Initial velocities of both gun and shell will be zero.

So, the initial momentum of the system will be zero.

According to law of conservation of momentum,

Initial momentum = final momentum

$$0 = mv - Mv_R$$

$$\Rightarrow \quad v_R = \frac{mv}{M} = \frac{0.020 \times 80}{100} = 0.016\ ms^{-1}$$

$\therefore$ Recoil velocity of gun $= 0.016\ ms^{-1}$.

35. Total mass of girl, bicycle and stone,

$m_1 = (50 + 0.5)\ kg = 50.5\ kg$

Velocity of bicycle, $u_1 = 5\ m/s$

Mass of stone, $m_2 = 0.5\ kg$

Velocity of stone, $u_2 = 15\ m/s$

Mass of girl and bicycle, $m = 50\ kg$

Yes, the speed of the bicycle changes after the stone is thrown.

Let, after throwing the stone, the speed of bicycle be v m/s.

According to the law of conservation of linear momentum,

$$m_1u_1 = m_2u_2 + mv$$

$$50.5 \times 5 = 0.5 \times 15 + 50 \times v$$

$$252.5 - 7.5 = 50v \quad \text{or} \quad v = \frac{245.0}{50}$$

$$v = 4.9 \text{ m/s}$$

Change in speed $= 5 - 4.9 = 0.1$ m/s

36. Given, $v = 29$ km/h, $\mu_s = 0.32$

$\because$ We know that $R_{min} = \frac{v^2}{\mu_s g}$

where, v is the velocity,

g is the acceleration due to gravity

μ_s is the coefficient of friction and

R_{min} is the minimum radius.

$\because$ The maximum value of static friction is

$$f_{s\,max} = \mu_s N = \mu_s mg$$

If the bicycle does not slip, this means

$$\frac{v^2}{R} \le \mu_s g R \ge \frac{v^2}{\mu_s g}$$

$\therefore$ The minimum radius with which a cyclist moving round the curve without slipping is

$$R_{min} = \frac{v^2}{\mu_s g} = \frac{(8.1)^2}{0.32 \times 9.8} = 21 \text{ m}$$

37. Let us draw the given figure.

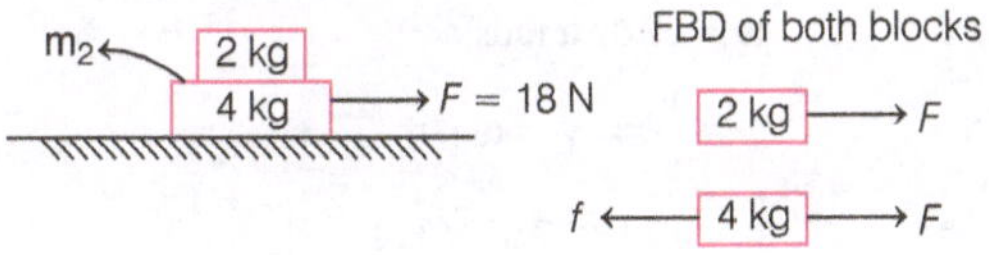

From the above figure,

$$f = \mu_2 N$$

$$\Rightarrow \quad f = \mu_2 \times 20 \quad \text{...(i)}$$

For blocks to move together, both of them must have same acceleration. So,

$$F - f = 4a$$

$$\Rightarrow \quad 180 - 20\mu_2 = 4a \quad \text{...(ii)}$$

$$F = ma \Rightarrow F = 2a \quad \{m = 2\text{kg}\}$$

$$20\mu_2 = 2a \quad [\text{using (i)}]$$

$$\Rightarrow \quad a = 10\mu_2 \quad \text{...(iii)}$$

Putting the value of $a = 10\mu_2$ in Eq. (ii),

$$18 - 20\mu_2 = 40\mu_2 \Rightarrow 18 = 60\mu_2 \Rightarrow \mu_2 = \frac{18}{60}$$

$$\Rightarrow \quad \mu_2 = 0.3$$

38. Given,

Radius of curve, $r = 30$ m

Coefficient of friction, $\mu = 0.4$

$\because$ Maximum speed, $v_{max} = \sqrt{\mu g r} = \sqrt{0.4 \times 9.8 \times 30}$

$$= 10.84 \text{ m/s} \approx 11 \text{ m/s}$$

39. Mass of the block, $m = 15$ kg

Coefficient of friction between the block and the trolley

$$\mu = 0.18$$

Acceleration of the trolley, $a = 0.5 \text{ m/s}^2$

Time, $t = 20$ s

(i) As block is placed on the trolley, therefore friction force is applied on the block by the trolley is

$$F = ma = 15 \times 0.5 = 7.5 \text{ N}$$

Force on the block is the friction applied by trolley on the block, its direction is in the direction of motion of the trolley.

For the stationary observer on the ground, the block will appear to move with acceleration initially and then with uniform velocity as given in the question.

(ii) For an observer on the trolley, the block is always at rest either initially or finally. Trolley always becomes inertial frame with respect to block because both have the same acceleration initially and same velocity finally.

40. Mass of body $A(m_1) = 5$ kg

Mass of body $B(m_2) = 10$ kg

Coefficient of friction between the bodies and the table

$$\mu = 0.15$$

Force applied horizontally at A, $F = 200$ N

(i) **Reaction of partition**

Limiting friction acting to the left

$$f = \mu R = \mu (m_1 + m_2) g$$

$$= 0.15\,(5 + 10) \times 9.8 = 22.05 \text{ N}$$

$\therefore$ Net force acting on the partition towards the right,

$$F' = F - f = 200 - 22.05 = 177.95 \text{ N}$$

According to the Newton's third law of motion,

Reaction of partition = Net force acting on the partition

$$= 177.95 \text{ N} \quad [\text{towards the left}]$$

(ii) **Action-reaction forces between A and B**

Let f_1 be the force of limiting friction acting on body A and F_1 be the net force applied by body A on body B.

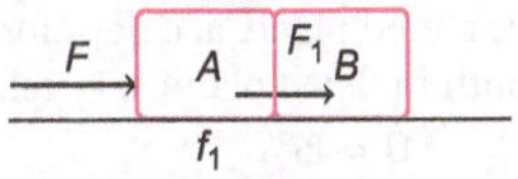

$$f_1 = \mu R_1$$

$$= \mu m_1 g \quad [\because R_1 = m_1 g]$$

$$= 0.15 \times 5 \times 9.8$$

$$= 7.35 \text{ N} \quad (\text{towards the left})$$

$\therefore$ Net force applied by body A on body B,

$$F_1 = F - f_1 = 200 - 7.35$$

$$= 192.65 \text{ N} \quad [\text{towards the right}]$$

According to Newton's third law of motion, reaction force applied by body B on body A

$$F_1 = 192.65 \text{ N} \quad (\text{towards left})$$

When the partition is removed the system of two bodies will move under the action of net force.

$$F'' = 177.95 \text{N}$$

Acceleration produced in the system,

$$a = \frac{F}{m_1 + m_2} = \frac{177.95}{(5+10)} = 11.86 \text{ ms}^{-2}$$

Force producing motion in body A,

$$F_1 = m_1 a = 5 \times 11.83 = 59.3 \text{ N}$$

∴ Net force exerted by body A on B when partition is removed,

$$\Rightarrow \quad F'' - F_1 = 192.65 - 59.3 = 133.35 \text{ N}$$

Hence the reaction of body B on body A when partition is removed = 133.35 N to the left thus answer (ii) do change.

41. Given, radius of the cylindrical drum (r) = 3 m

Coefficient of friction between the wall and his clothing $(\mu) = 0.15$. Frequency (ν) = 200 rev/min

$$= \frac{200}{60} \text{ rev/s} = \frac{10}{3} \text{ rev/s}$$

The normal reaction of the wall on the man acting horizontally provides the required centripetal force.

$$R = mr\omega^2 \quad \text{...(i)}$$

The frictional force F, acting upwards balances his weight

i.e. $$F = mg \quad \text{...(ii)}$$

The man will remain stuck to the wall without slipping, if

$$\mu r \geq F \quad \text{or} \quad F \leq \mu R$$

$$mg \leq \mu \times mr\omega^2 \quad \text{or} \quad \omega^2 \geq \frac{g}{\mu r}$$

$$\omega \geq \sqrt{\frac{g}{\mu r}}$$

For minimum angular speed of rotation,

$$\omega_{\min} = \sqrt{\frac{g}{\mu r}} = \sqrt{\frac{9.8}{0.15 \times 3}} = 4.67 \text{ rad/s}$$

42. On smooth inclined plane, acceleration of a body sliding down a smooth inclined plane, $a = g\sin\theta$

Here, $\theta = 45°$

$$\therefore \quad a = g\sin 45° = \frac{g}{\sqrt{2}}$$

Let the travelled distance be s.

Using the equation of motion, $s = ut + \frac{1}{2}at^2$, we get

$$s = 0.t + \frac{1}{2}\frac{g}{\sqrt{2}}T^2 \quad \text{or} \quad s = \frac{gT^2}{2\sqrt{2}} \quad \text{...(i)}$$

On rough inclined plane

Acceleration of the body,

$$a = g(\sin\theta - \mu\cos\theta) = g(\sin 45° - \mu\cos 45°)$$

$$= \frac{g(1-\mu)}{\sqrt{2}} \quad \left[\text{as } \sin 45° = \frac{1}{\sqrt{2}}\right]$$

Again using equation of motion, $s = ut + \frac{1}{2}at^2$, we get

$$s = 0(pT) + \frac{1}{2}\frac{g(1-\mu)}{\sqrt{2}}(pT)^2$$

or $$s = \frac{g(1-\mu)p^2T^2}{2\sqrt{2}} \quad \text{...(ii)}$$

From Eqs. (i) and (ii), we get

$$\frac{gT^2}{2\sqrt{2}} = \frac{g(1-\mu)p^2T^2}{2\sqrt{2}}$$

or $$(1-\mu)p^2 = 1 \quad \text{or} \quad 1 - \mu = \frac{1}{p^2}$$

or $$\mu = \left(1 - \frac{1}{p^2}\right)$$

43. Wheel of the truck is rotated at 830 revolutions per minute.

∴ Angle swept at the centre in one revolution = 2π

So, the angle swept per second at the centre = $830 \times \frac{2\pi}{60}$

∴ The rate of change in angle at the centre is the angular speed.

$$\therefore \quad \omega = 830 \times \frac{2\pi}{60}$$

$$\Rightarrow \quad \omega = 27.67\,\pi \text{ rads}^{-1}$$

$$\because \quad \omega = \frac{v}{r} \Rightarrow v = \omega \times r$$

$$\Rightarrow \quad v = 0.29 \times 27.67 \times 3.14$$

$$v = 25.2 \text{ ms}^{-1}$$

44. Given, the coin is at a distance 2cm from the axis of rotation, i.e.

$r = 2 \times 10^{-2}$ m

Angular velocity, $\omega = 3 \times 2\pi$

$$\omega = 6\pi \text{ rad/s.}$$

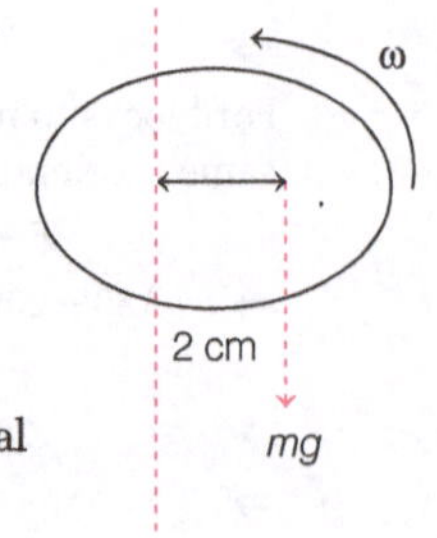

Let the mass of the coin be m.

In this case, the necessary centripetal force is provided by friction, i.e.,

$$f = \frac{m\omega^2}{r} \times r^2 \quad \left[\because \frac{mv^2}{r} = \frac{m(\omega r)^2}{r}\right]$$

$$\therefore \quad \mu mg = \frac{m\omega^2}{r} \times r^2 \Rightarrow \mu mg = \frac{\omega^2 m}{r} \times r^2$$

$$\Rightarrow \quad \mu = \frac{(6\pi)^2 \times 2 \times 10^{-2}}{9.8} \Rightarrow \mu = 0.724$$

45. When the motorcyclist is at the uppermost point of the death well, then weight of the cyclist as well as the normal reaction R of the ceiling of the chamber is in downward direction. These forces are balanced by the outward centrifugal force acting on the motorcyclist.

$$\therefore \quad R + mg = \frac{mv^2}{r}$$

where, v = speed of the motorcyclist
m = mass of (motorcycle + driver)
r = radius of the death well

As the forces acting on the motorcyclist are balanced, therefore, motorcyclist does not fall down.

The minimum speed required to perform a vertical loop is given by

$$mg = \frac{mv_{min}^2}{r}$$

[∵ In the case weight of the object = centripetal force]

$$\text{or} \quad v_{min} = \sqrt{rg} = \sqrt{25 \times 9.8} = 15.65 \text{ m/s}$$

46. Given, $(v) = 33\frac{1}{3} = \frac{100}{3}$ rev/min $= \frac{100}{3 \times 60}$ rev/s $= \frac{5}{9}$ rev/s

$$\therefore \text{ Angular velocity } (\omega) = 2\pi v = 2 \times \frac{22}{7} \times \frac{5}{9} = \frac{220}{63} \text{ rad/s}$$

Radius of the disc $(r) = 15$ cm.

Distance of first coin A from the centre $(x_1) = 4$ cm

Distance of the second coin B from the centre $(x_2) = 14$ cm

Coefficient of friction between the coins and the record = 0.15.

If force of friction between the coin and the record is sufficient to provide the centripetal force, then coil will revolve with the record.

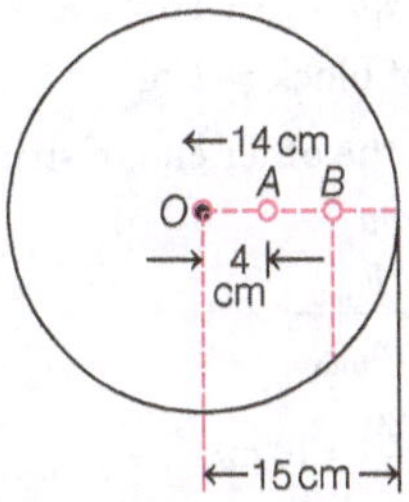

∴ To prevent slipping (or to revolve the coin alongwith record) the force of friction $(f) \geq$ centripetal force (f_c)

$$\text{or} \quad \mu mg \geq mr\omega^2$$

$$\text{or} \quad \mu g \geq r\omega^2$$

For first coin A

$$r\omega^2 = \frac{4}{100} \times \left(\frac{220}{63}\right)^2 = \frac{4 \times 220 \times 220}{100 \times 63 \times 63} = 0.488 \text{ m/s}^2$$

and $\mu g = 0.15 \times 9.8 = 1.47 \text{ m/s}^2$

Here, $\mu g > r\omega^2$, therefore, this coin will revolve with the record.

For second coin B

$$r\omega^2 = \frac{14}{100} \times \left(\frac{220}{63}\right)^2 = \frac{14 \times 220 \times 220}{100 \times 63 \times 63} = 1.707 \text{ m/s}$$

and $\mu g = 1.47$ m/s

Here, $\mu g < r\omega^2$, therefore, centripetal force will not be obtained from the force of friction, hence this coin will not revolve with the record.

47. (i) The situation is shown in figure below.

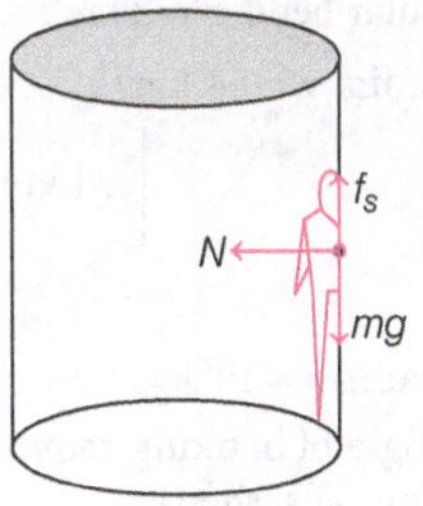

When the floor is removed, the forces on the person are

(a) weight mg downward.

(b) normal force N due to the wall towards the centre.

(c) frictional force (f_s) parallel to the wall, upwards.

The person is moving in a circle with a uniform speed, so its acceleration is v^2/r towards the centre.

Newton's law for the horizontal direction (second law) and for the vertical direction (first law) give

$$N = mv^2/r \quad \text{...(i)}$$

$$\text{and} \quad f_s = mg \quad \text{...(ii)}$$

For the minimum speed, when the floor may be removed, the friction is limiting one and, so equals $\mu_s N$.

This gives $\mu_s N = mg$

$$\text{or} \quad \frac{\mu_s mv^2}{r} = mg \quad \text{[using Eq. (i)]}$$

$$\text{or} \quad v = \sqrt{\frac{rg}{\mu_s}} = \sqrt{\frac{2\text{m} \times 10 \text{ m/s}^2}{0.2}} = 10 \text{ m/s}$$

(ii) Speciality is that without the floor an object, or body may be 0° align with a vertical wall or provided, it is set to be in circular motion (horizontal) with properly required speed.

48. Given, speed of traffic, $v = 60$ km/h

$$60 \times \frac{5}{18} = \frac{50}{3} \text{ ms}^{-1}$$

Radius of curve, $R = 0.1$ km $= 100$ m

∵ Relation between banking angle, speed, radius of circular track is given by

$$\theta = \tan^{-1}\left[\frac{v^2}{rg}\right]$$

$$\Rightarrow \quad \theta = \tan^{-1}\left[\frac{\left(\frac{50}{3}\right)^2}{(100\times 9.8)}\right]$$

$$\Rightarrow \quad \theta = \tan^{-1}\left(\frac{5}{18}\right) \Rightarrow \theta = 15°32'$$

49. Radius of circular bend, $r = 30$ m

Speed of the train, $v = 54$ km/h

$= 54 \times \frac{5}{18}$ m/s $\quad \left[\because 1 \text{ km/h} = \frac{5}{18} \text{ m/s}\right]$

$= 15$ m/s

Mass of the train, $m = 10^6$ kg

Let θ be the angle of banking required to prevent wearing out the rails, then

$$\tan\theta = \frac{v^2}{rg} = \frac{(15)^2}{30\times 9.8} = \frac{225}{30\times 9.8} = 0.7653$$

$$\theta = \tan^{-1}(0.7653) = 37.4°$$

50. Mass of body $A\,(m_1) = 10$ kg

Mass of body $B\,(m_2) = 20$ kg

Force applied $(F) = 600$ N

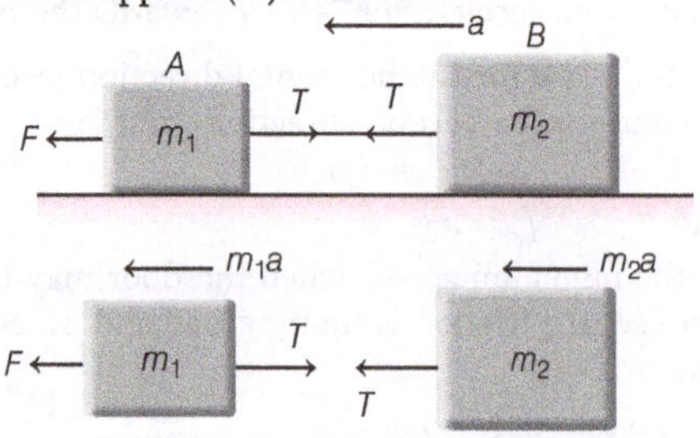

(i) **When force is applied on *A*,** then

For body A,

$$F - T = m_1 a \quad \text{...(i)}$$

For body B,

$$T = m_2 a \quad \text{...(ii)}$$

Adding Eqs. (i) and (ii), we get

$$F = (m_1 + m_2)a$$

or $$a = \frac{F}{m_1 + m_2}$$

$$= \frac{600}{(10+20)} = 20 \text{ m/s}^2$$

Substituting value of a in Eq. (ii), we get

$$T = m_2 a = 20 \times 20 \text{ N}$$

$$= 400 \text{ N}$$

(ii) **When force is applied on *B*,** then

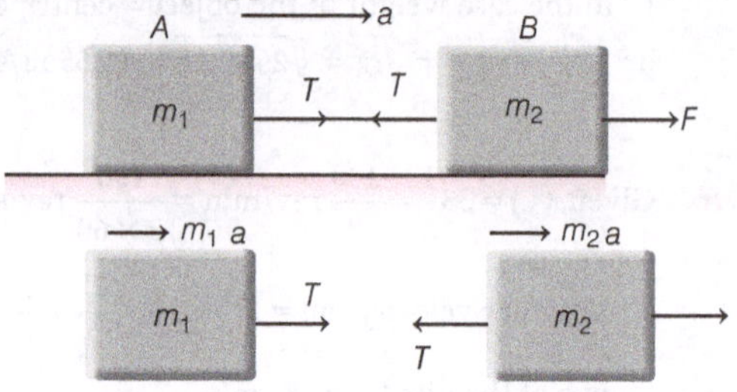

For body A, $\quad T = m_1 a \quad$ ...(iii)

For body B, $\quad F - T = m_2 a \quad$ ...(iv)

Adding Eqs. (iii) and (iv), we get

$$F = (m_1 + m_2)a$$

or $$a = \frac{F}{m_1 + m_2} = \frac{600}{10+20} = 20 \text{ m/s}^2$$

Substituting value of a in Eq. (iii), we get

$$T = m_1 a = 10 \times 20 = 200 \text{ N}$$

51. Given, mass of block = 2 kg

force acting at the other end of string = 40 N

We have, $F = ma$

$$a = \frac{F_{\text{net}}}{m_{\text{total}}}$$

Now, $a = \frac{40-20}{2} = 10 \text{ m/s}^2$

QR Code
for Quick Test 1

QR Code
for Quick Test 2

SELF ASSESSMENT TEST

Multiple Choice Questions (MCQs)

1. The maximum velocity (in m/s) with which a car driver must transverse a flat curve of radius 150 m and coefficient of friction 0.6 to avoid skidding is

(a) 60 (b) 30
(c) 15 (d) 25

2. If the tension in the cable supporting an elevator is equal to the weight of elevator, the elevator may be

(a) going up with increasing speed
(b) going down with increasing speed
(c) going up with uniform speed
(d) elevator falls freely under gravity

3. In a game of tug of wars, a condition of equilibrium exists. Both the team pull the rope with a force of 10^4 N. The tension in the rope is

(a) 10^4 N (b) 10^8 N
(c) 0 N (d) 2×10^4 N

4. The motion of a particle of mass m is described by $y = ut + \frac{1}{2}gt^2$. The force acting on the particle is

(a) mgt (b) gt^2 (c) mg (d) $\sqrt{g}\,um$

5. Match the Column I (terms related to laws of motion) with Column II (properties) and choose the correct option.

	Column I		Column II
A.	Impulse	P.	Depends on material and nature of surface
B.	Angle of repose	Q.	Independent of area of contact between two surface
C.	Momentum	R.	An athlete runs some distance before taking a jump
D.	Kinetic friction	S.	Increases on increasing the applied force

(a) A → P, B → S, C → Q, D → R
(b) A → R, B → P, C → S, D → Q
(c) A → S, B → P, C → R, D → Q
(d) A → R, B → S, C → Q, D → P

6. A bend in a level road has a radius of 100 m. Find the maximum speed which a car turning this bend may have without skidding, if the coefficient of friction between the tyres and road is 0.8.

(a) 30 m/s (b) 20 m/s
(c) 60 m/s (d) 28 m/s

Assertion-Reason

Direction *(Q. Nos. 7-10) In the following questions, two statements are given- one labeled Assertion (A) and the other labeled Reason (R). Select the correct answer to these questions from the codes (a), (b), (c) and (d) as given below.*

(a) Both Assertion and Reason are true and Reason is the correct explanation of Assertion.
(b) Both Assertion and Reason are true but Reason is not the correct explanation of Assertion.
(c) Assertion is true but Reason is false.
(d) Assertion is false but Reason is true.

7. **Assertion (A)** The apparent weight of a body in an elevator moving with some downward acceleration is less than the actual weight of a body.
Reason (R) The part of the weight is spent in producing downward acceleration, when body is in elevator.

8. **Assertion (A)** A table cloth can pulled from a table without disloding the dishes.
Reason (R) To every action there is an equal and opposite reaction.

9. **Assertion (A)** cricketer moves his hands forward to catch a ball so as to catch it easily without hurting.
Reason (R) He tries to decrease the distance travelled by the ball so that it hurts less.

10. **Assertion (A)** rocket works on the principle of conservation of linear momentum.

Reason (R) Whenever there is change in momentum of one body, the same change occurs in the momentum of second body of the same system but in the opposite direction.

Case Based Questions

Directions *(Q.No. 11) This question is case study based question. Read the following paragraph and answer the questions on the basis of same.*

11. The maximum permissible speed for a vehicle to negotiate a turn on a level circular road (without getting slip), depends upon the value of coefficient of friction μ between the tyres and road. But in practice, this limiting value of speed for sharp turn is quite low, especially in hilly areas where the turns are too sharp. In order to move the vehicle at a reasonable speed without getting skid/slip to go around, the sharp turns of the inner one. It is called banking of road.

Banking of roads provide the necessary centripetal force which is needed to make sharp turn with reasonable speed and without getting skid.

(i) Force responsible for the circular motion of the body is
(a) centripetal force
(b) centrifugal force
(c) gravitational force
(d) None of the above

(ii) What is maximum safe speed of car negotiating a circular turn of radius on a frictionless banked track with angle of banking θ?
(a) $\sqrt{r \tan\theta}$
(b) $\sqrt{rg \sin\theta}$
(c) $\sqrt{g \tan\theta}$
(d) $\sqrt{rg \tan\theta}$

(iii) What is maximum safe speed of car in a circular road of radius 3m? The coefficient of friction between the tyres and road is 0.1.
(Take $g = 10 \text{ m/s}^2$)
(a) 1.43 m/s
(b) 1.73 m/s
(c) 1.63 m/s
(d) 1.53 m/s

(iv) Which statement is not correct about banking of roads?
(a) Banking of roads reduces wear and tear on tyres of vehicles.
(b) It provides required centripetal force.
(c) It reduces the friction between road and the tyres.
(d) All are correct

(v) A car sometime overturns while taking a turn. When it overturns, it is
(a) the inner wheel, which leaves the ground first
(b) the outer wheel, which leaves the ground first
(c) both the wheels leaves the ground simultaneously
(d) either wheel, which leaves the ground first

Very Short Answer Type Questions

12. A bird is sitting on the floor of a wire cage and the cage is in the hand of a boy. The bird starts flying in the cage. Will the boy experience any change in the weight of the cage?

13. A force is being applied to a body, but it causes no acceleration. What possibilities might be considered to explain the observation?

14. If force is acting on a moving body perpendicular to the direction of motion, then what will be its effect on the speed and direction of the body?

15. A passenger of mass 72.2 kg is riding in an elevator while standing on a platform scale. What does the scale read when the elevator cab is (i) descending with constant velocity (ii) ascending with constant acceleration, 3.5 m / s^2?

Short Answer Type Questions

16. Determine the tensions T_1 and T_2 in the strings as shown in the figure.

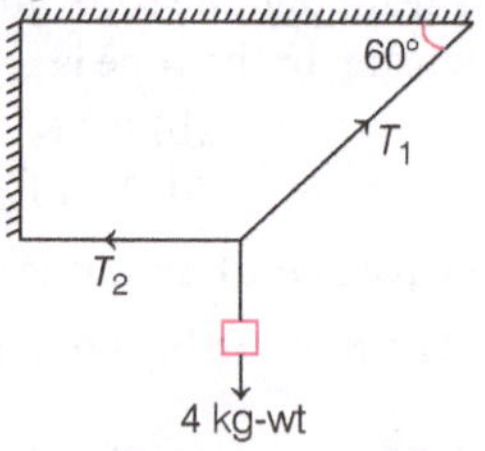

17. Three blocks of masses $m_1 = 10$ kg, $m_2 = 20$ kg and $m_3 = 30$ kg are connected by strings on smooth horizontal surface and pulled by a force of 60 N. Find the acceleration of the system and tension in the string.

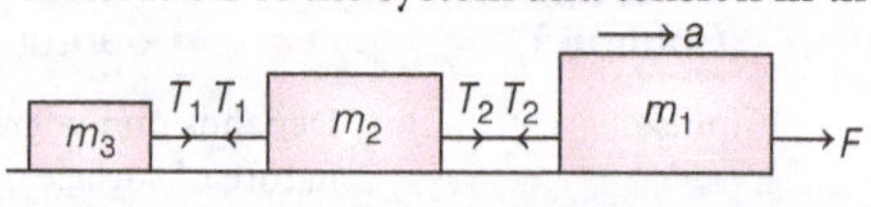

18. The pulley arrangement of figure is identical. The mass of the rope is negligible. In (a) mass m is lifted up by attaching a mass ($2m$) to the other end of the rope. In (b), m is lifted up by pulling the other end of the rope with a constant downward force $F = 2mg$. In which case, the acceleration of m is more?

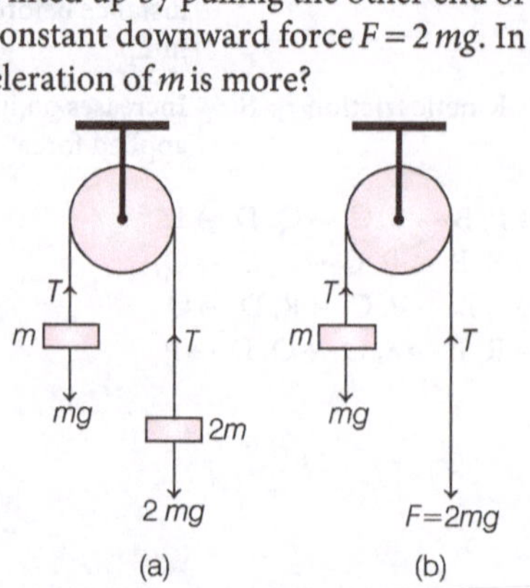

(a) (b)

Long Answer Type Questions

19. A pebble of mass 0.05 kg is thrown vertically upwards. Give the direction and magnitude of the net force on the pebble

(i) during its upward motion

(ii) during its downward motion

(iii) at the highest point where it is momentarily at rest

20. Consider a shuffleboard cue which is being used by a cruise ship passenger. To push the shuffleboard disc of mass 0.50 kg horizontally along the deck so that the disc leaves the cue with a speed of 6 m/s, what will be the coefficient of kinetic friction between the deck and the disc, if the disc slides a distance of 10 m before coming to rest?

21. A body of mass m_1 equal to 20 kg is placed on a smooth horizontal table. This body is connected to a string which passes over a frictionless pulley. The string also carries another body of mass m_2 equals to 10 kg at the other end. Find out the acceleration which will be produced when the nail fixed on the table is removed, also find out the tension in the string during the motion of the bodies. What is the result, when the bodies stop? (Take, $g = 10$ N/kg)

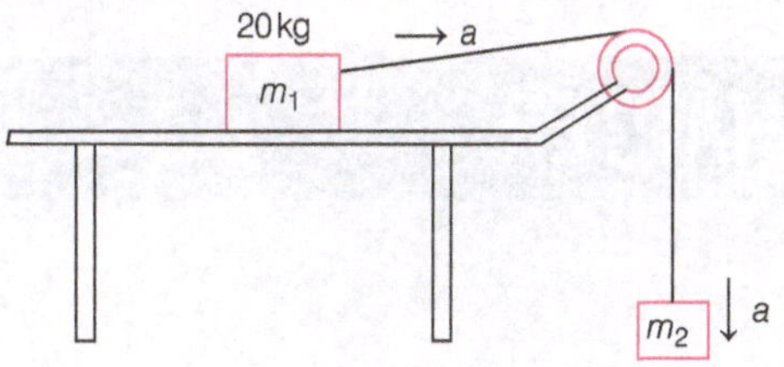

Answers

1. (b) 2. (c) 3. (a) 4. (c) 5. (c) 6. (d)
7. (c) 8. (b) 9. (d) 10. (a)
11. (i) (a), (ii) (d), (iii) (b), (iv) (c), (v) (a)

05

CHAPTER

Work, Energy and Power

Whenever a force acting on a body produces a net displacement in the direction of the applied force, then work is said to be done by the force.
Whereas, energy is our capacity to do work. The word power is also used in everyday life with different shades of meaning. In this chapter, we will study these terms from the vision of science.

YOUR STUDY GOALS

YOUR PRACTICE GOAL

- Objective Type Questions (32 Qs , MCQs, A-R, Matching)
- Case Based Questions (3)
- Subjective Type Questions (5 VSAs, 8 SAs, 9 LAs)
- Numerical Type Questions (17)

5.1 Work Done by a Constant Force

Work done by the force (constant force) is the product of component of force in the direction of the displacement and the magnitude of the displacement.

If a constant force F is applied on a body and the body has a displacement **s** in the direction of the force as shown in figure.

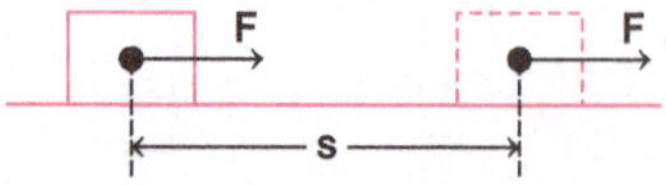

Work done, when force and displacement are in the same

Then, the work done on the body by the force is given by

$$\text{Work done, } W = \mathbf{F} \cdot \mathbf{s}$$

Work Done When Force and Displacement are Inclined to Each Other

Sometimes the displacement **s** is not in the direction of F as shown in figure.

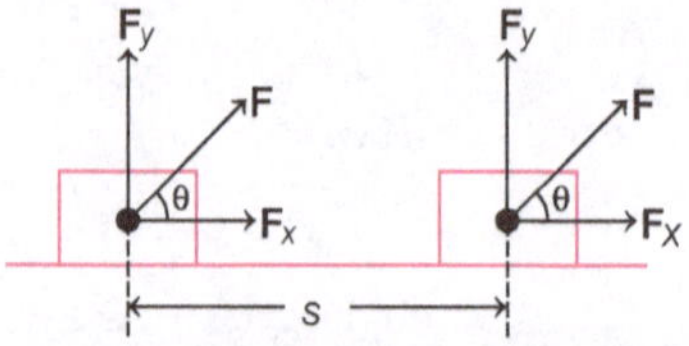

Work done when force and displacement are inclined to each other

In such a case,

Work done, $W = Fs\cos\theta$

Thus, work done is the dot product of force and displacement vector. Hence, work is a **scalar quantity**.

Two cases can be considered for the **maximum and minimum work.**

Case I When **F** and **s** are in the same direction, i.e. $\theta = 0°$, then work done is

$$W = Fs\cos 0° = Fs(1) = Fs$$

i.e. **maximum work is done by the force.**

Case II When **F** and **s** are perpendicular to each other, then

$$W = \mathbf{F}\cdot\mathbf{s} = Fs\cos 90° = Fs(0) = 0$$

i.e. **no work is done by the force, when a body moves in a direction perpendicular to the force.**

Dimensions and Units of Work

As, [work] = [force] × [distance] = $[MLT^{-2}] \times [L]$

Dimensional formula of work $[W] = [ML^2T^{-2}]$

The units of work are of two types

1. Absolute Units

Work done is said to be one absolute unit, if an absolute unit of force displaces a body through a unit distance in the direction of the force.

(i) **Joule** It is the absolute unit of work in SI.

From work done $(W) = Fs\cos\theta$

$$1\text{ J} = 1\text{ N} \times 1\text{ m} \times \cos 0° = 1\text{ N-m}$$

(ii) **Erg** It is the absolute unit of work in CGS system.

From work done $(W) = Fs\cos\theta$

$$1\text{ erg} = 1\text{ dyne} \times 1\text{ cm} \times \cos 0° = 1\text{ dyne-cm}$$

Relation between joule and erg

$$1\text{ J} = 1\text{ N} \times 1\text{ m} = 10^5\text{ dyne} \times 10^2\text{ cm}$$
$$= 10^7\text{ dyne-cm}$$

or $\mathbf{1\ J = 10^7\ erg}$

2. Gravitational Units

Work is said to be one gravitational unit if a gravitational unit of force displaces a body through a unit distance in the direction of the force.

(i) **Kilogram-metre** (kg-m) It is the gravitational unit of work in SI system.

We know that, work done $(W) = Fs\cos\theta$

$$1\text{ kg-m} = 1\text{ kg wt} \times \cos 0° = 9.8\text{ N} \times 1\text{m} \times 1 = 9.8\text{ J}$$

i.e. 1 kg-m = 9.8 J

(ii) **Gram-centimetre** (g-cm) It is the gravitational unit of work in CGS system.

$\therefore$ 1 g-cm = 1 g-wt × 1 cm = 980 dyne × 1 cm

or 1 g-cm = 980 erg

Example 1. A lawn roller has been pushed by a gardener through a distance of 30 m. What will be the work done by him if he applies a force of 30 kg-wt in the direction inclined at 60° to the ground? Take, $g = 10\text{ m/s}^2$

Sol. Given, Displacement $s = 30$ m

Force, $F = 30\text{ kg-wt} = 30 \times 10 = 300\text{N}$

Angle between force and ground, $\theta = 60°$

The work done by the gardener,

$$W = F\cdot s = Fs\cos\theta$$
$$= 300 \times 30 \times \cos 60°$$
$$W = 4500\text{ J}$$

Example 2. A coolie is holding a bag by applying a force of 15 N. He moves forward and covers the horizontal distance of 8 m and then he climbs up and covers the vertical distance of 10 m. What will be the work done by him?

Sol. Given, $F = 15$ N, $s_1 = 8$ m and $s_2 = 10$ m

As coolie is walking horizontally, therefore, the angle between the bag and distance covered is 90°.

$\therefore$ Work done to cover the distance of 8 m.

$$W_1 = Fs_1\cos\theta = 15 \times 8\cos 90° = 0\text{ J}$$

When the coolie climb.

Thus, $\theta = 0°$

The work done, $W_2 = Fs_2\cos\theta$

$$= 15 \times 10 \times \cos 0° = 150\text{ J}$$

The net work done by him

$$W = W_1 + W_2 = 0 + 150 = 150\text{ J}$$

5.2 Nature of Work Done in Different Situations

Although work done is a scalar quantity, its value may be positive, negative or even zero, as discussed below

1. Positive Work

If a force acting on a body has a component in the direction of the displacement, then the work done by the force is positive.

- **For positive work, the angle between direction of force and direction of displacement is acute, i.e. $0° \le \theta < 90°$, so $\cos\theta$ will be positive.**

$\therefore$ Work done $(W) = Fs\cos\theta$ = positive value $[0 \le \theta < 90°]$

e.g. When a horse pulls a cart, the applied force and the displacement are in the same direction. So, work done by horse is positive.

2. Negative Work

If a force acting on the body has a component in the opposite direction of displacement, then work done is negative.

Work done $(W) = Fs\cos\theta$ = negative value $[90° < \theta < 180°]$

e.g. When brakes are applied to a moving vehicle, the work done by the braking force is negative, this is because the braking force and the displacement act in opposite directions.

3. Zero Work

Work done by force is zero, if the body gets displaced in the direction perpendicular to the direction of the applied force or displacement is zero.

Work done $(W) = Fs\cos 90° = Fs \cdot 0$ = zero

e.g. Consider a body sliding over a horizontal surface. The work done by the force of gravity and the normal reaction of the surface will be zero.

This is because both the forces of gravity and reaction act normally to the displacement.

Example 3 **A cyclist comes to a skidding stop in 10 m. During this process, the force on the cycle due to the road is 200 N and is directly opposite to the motion.**

(i) How much work does the road do on the cycle?

(ii) How much work does the cycle do on the road?

NCERT

Sol. (i) The stopping force and the displacement make an angle of 180° with each other. Thus, work done by the road or the work done by the stopping force is

$$W_r = Fs\cos\theta$$
$$= 200 \times 10 \times \cos 180°$$
$$= -2000 \text{ J}$$

(ii) According to Newton's third law, an equal and opposite force acts on the road due to the cycle. Its magnitude is 200 N. However, the road undergoes no displacement. So, work done by the cycle on the road is zero.

5.3 Work Done by a Variable Force

Let a variable force F act on a body along the fixed direction, say X-axis. The magnitude of the force F depends on x, as shown by force-displacement graph in figure.

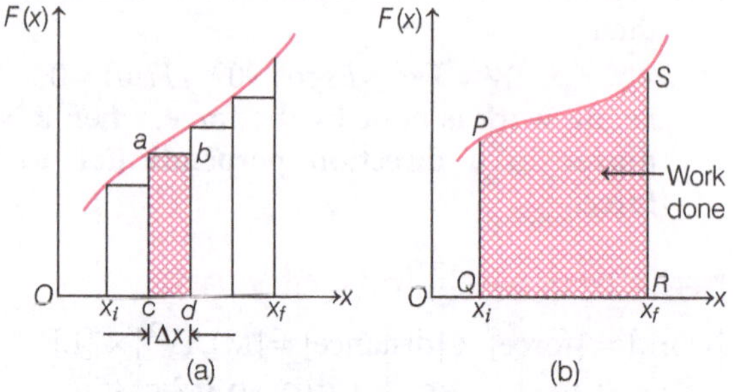

Calculation of work done by a variable force

The work done when the body moves from the initial position x_i to the final position x_f under a force $F(x)$ is

$$\Delta W = F(x)\,\Delta x = \text{Area of } abcd$$

Adding the area of all rectangles in Fig. (a), we get the total work done as

$$W \cong \sum_{x_i}^{x_f} F(x)\,\Delta x$$

If $\Delta x \to 0$, then

$$W_{x_i \to x_f} = \int_{x_i}^{x_f} \mathbf{F} \cdot dx = \int_{x_i}^{x_f} (F\cos\theta) \cdot dx$$
$$= \text{Area of } PQRS$$

$W_{x_i \to x_f}$ = Area under the force-displacement curve

- For a varying force the work done is equal to the definite integral of the force over the given displacement.

If force, $\mathbf{F} = F_x\hat{\mathbf{i}} + F_y\hat{\mathbf{j}} + F_z\hat{\mathbf{k}}$ and displacement,

$$d\mathbf{x} = dx\,\hat{\mathbf{i}} + dy\,\hat{\mathbf{j}} + dz\,\hat{\mathbf{k}}$$

So, work done from (x_i, y_i, z_i) to (x_f, y_f, z_f)

Work done, $W = \int_{x_i}^{x_f} F_x dx + \int_{y_i}^{y_f} F_y dy + \int_{z_i}^{z_f} F_z dz$

where, F_x, F_y and F_z are the rectangular components of force in x, y and z-directions, respectively.

Note When the body is in equilibrium (either static or dynamic), then resultant force is zero. Therefore, work done $W = 0$.

Example 4. **Force $F = [3x^2\,\hat{i} + 4\,\hat{j}]$ N with x in metres, acts on a particle. How much work is done on the particles as it moves from coordinates (2m, 3m) to (3m, 0m)?**

Sol. Given, force $F = 3x^2\,\hat{i} + 4\,\hat{j}$

Coordinates = $(\underset{x_i}{2}\text{m}, \underset{y_i}{3}\text{m})$ to $(\underset{x_f}{3}\text{m}, \underset{y_f}{0}\text{m})$

Here, the force is variable force. Thus, work done is

$$W = \int_{x_i}^{x_f} F_x \cdot dx + \int_{y_i}^{y_f} F_y dy$$

$$= \int_2^3 3x^2\,dx + \int_3^0 4\,dy$$

$$= 3\left[\frac{x^3}{3}\right]_2^3 + 4[y]_3^0$$

$$= \frac{3}{3} \times [27 - 8] + 4[0 - 3] = 19 - 12$$

$$W = 7.0\text{ J}$$

Example 5. **The force applied by a man in pushing a block varies with displacement as shown in figure. If the force is expressed in newton and displacement in metres, find the work done by him.**

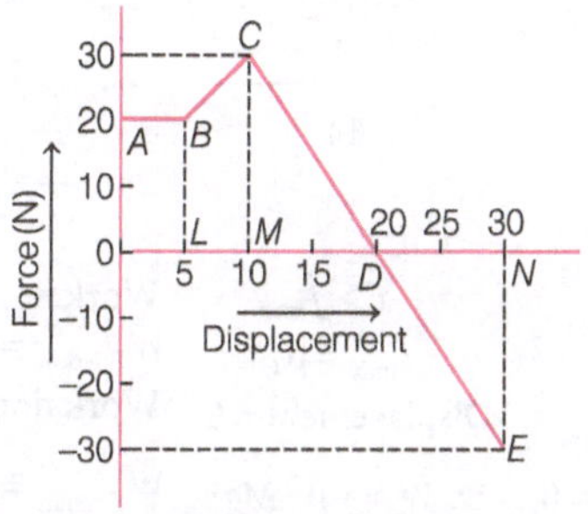

Sol. Given, displacement and forces are

At point B, $d_1 = 5$ m, $f_1 = 20$ N

At point C, $d_2 = 10$ m, $f_2 = 30$ N,

At point D, $d_3 = 20$ m, $f_3 = 0$ N,

At point E, $d_4 = 30$ m, $f_4 = -30$ N

Work done by the man = ?

Area under the rectangle $OABL$ is equal to work done W_{OABL}.

$$W_{OABL} = 20 \times 5 = 100\text{ J}$$

$[\because \text{Area} = \text{length} \times \text{breadth}]$

Area under the trapezium $BCML$ is equal to work done W_{BCML}.

$$W_{BCML} = \frac{1}{2} \times [20 + 30] \times 5$$

$$\left[\because \text{Area} = \frac{1}{2} \times (\text{sum of parallel side}) \times \text{height}\right]$$

$$W_{BCML} = \frac{1}{2} \times 50 \times 5 = 125\text{ J}$$

Area under the $\Delta\,CDM$ is equal to work done W_{CDM}.

$$W_{CDM} = \frac{1}{2} \times 10 \times 30 = 150\text{ J}$$

$$\left[\because \text{Area} = \frac{1}{2} \times \text{base} \times \text{height}\right]$$

Area under the $\Delta\,DEN$ is equal to work done W_{DEN}.

$$W_{DEN} = \frac{1}{2} \times (10) \times -30 = -150\text{ J}$$

$$\left[\because \text{Area} = \frac{1}{2} \times \text{base} \times \text{height}\right]$$

Total amount of work done

$$= 100\text{ J} + 125\text{ J} + 150\text{ J} - 150\text{ J} = 225\text{ J}$$

Conservative Force

If the work done by the force in displacing an object depends only on the initial and final positions of the object and not on the nature of the path followed between the initial and final positions, then such a force is known as conservative force.

e.g. **Gravitational force** is a conservative force.

Properties of Conservative Forces

(i) If only conservative force are acting over a body. Then, the total energy is always conserved.

(ii) The work done by conservative forces is always recovered.

(iii) In a closed loop system, the work done is always zero.

Net Work Done by a Body in Moving Over the Round Trip In case of gravitational force, the work done in moving the body from position P to Q, against the gravity is negative and the work done in moving the body from position Q to P, by gravity, as taken be positive. i.e.

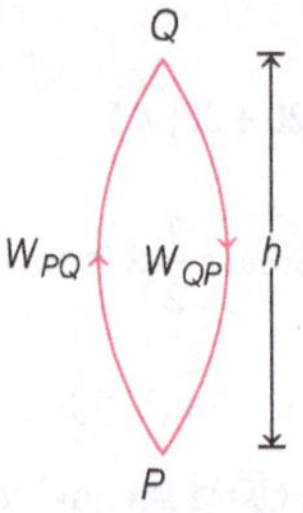

$$W_{PQ} = -W_{QP}, W_{PQ} + W_{QP} = 0$$

Thus, **net work done by the gravitational force in moving the body over the round trip ($P \to Q \to P$) is zero.**

Example 6. **A man weighting 20 kg is standing in a lift. The lift carries the man from point (0m, 2m, 0m) to (0m, 6m, 0m). Calculate the work done by the lift on the man.**

Sol. Given, mass of the person, $m = 20\text{kg}$

$\therefore$ Weight, $w = mg = 20 \times 10 = 200\text{N}$

$\therefore$ $\mathbf{F} = -w\hat{\mathbf{j}} = -200\hat{\mathbf{j}}\text{N}$

Displacement, $\mathbf{r} = (6-2)\hat{\mathbf{j}} = 4\hat{\mathbf{j}}$

$\therefore$ Work done by gravity on the person is

$$W = \mathbf{F}\cdot\mathbf{r} = (-200\hat{\mathbf{j}})\cdot(4\hat{\mathbf{j}}) = -800\text{ J}$$

Hence, the work done by the lift on the person is 800 J.

Non-Conservative Force

If work done by a force in displacing an object from one position to another depends upon the path between the two positions, then such a force is known as non-conservative force.

The **common examples of non-conservative forces** are

(i) Force of friction.

(ii) Viscous force

(iii) Tension

Properties of Non-conservative Forces

(i) It is path dependent.

(ii) In any closed path, the total work done by it in a round trip is not zero.

(iii) The work done by non-conservative forces appear in some other forms of energy like heat, sound, light energy, etc.

Note The law of conservation of energy is true only for conservative force.

Work Done by Non-conservative Forces (Friction Forces)

As we know that friction force is always opposite to the relative motion so that the work done by friction may be positive, zero and negative.

Work Done due to Friction Forces

Case I	Case II	Case III
Fig. (a) shows a situation where a block is pulled by a force F which is insufficient to overcome the friction f_{max}, i.e. $F < f_{max}$ 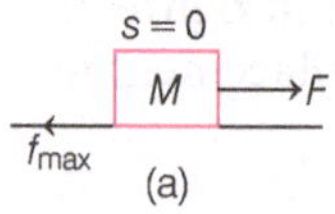 (a)	Fig. (b) shows a situation where a block is pulled by a force F which is large to overcome friction f_{max}, i.e. $F > f_{max}$ Here, the work done by friction force is **negative**. 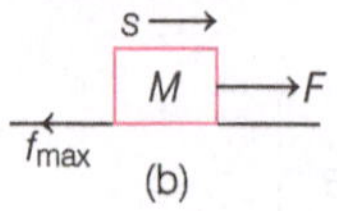 (b)	Fig. (c) shows that block A is placed on block B and when block A is pulled with a force F, friction force does positive work on block B and negative work on block A. 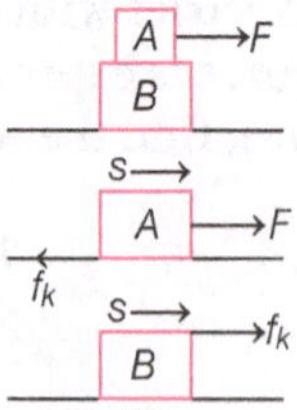 (c)
$F < f_{max}$ $F < \mu_s N$ $F < \mu_s Mg$ $\therefore$ Work done = 0	$F > f_{max}$ $f_{max} = \mu_k M$ Displacement = 5 $\therefore W = -\mu_k Mgs$	Work done $W_{Friction}$ = − ve for A. Work done $W_{Friction}$ = + ve for B.

Example 7. **A wooden block of mass 1 kg is pushed up on a surface inclined to horizontal at angle of 30° by a force of 10 N parallel to the inclined surface [figure]. The coefficient of friction between block and the incline is 0.1. If the block is pushed up by 10 m along the incline. Calculate.**

(i) Work done against gravity.

(ii) Work done against force of friction.

(iii) Acceleration of block when it moves upward.

Sol. Given, $m = 1\,\text{kg}, \theta = 30°, F = 10\text{ N}, \mu = 0.1, s = 10\text{ m}$,

$W_g = ?, W_f = ?, a = ?$

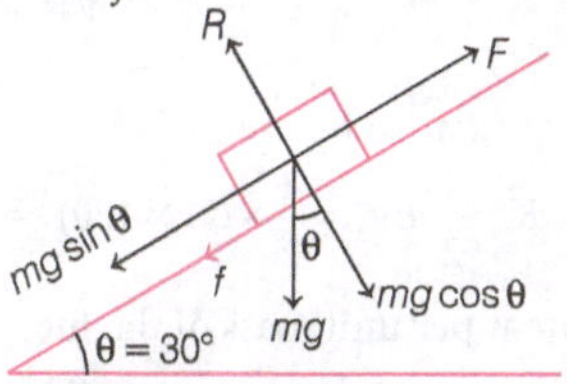

(i) Work done against gravity, $W_g = mg\sin\theta \times s$

$$W_g = mg\sin\theta \times s = 1 \times 10 \sin 30° \times 10 = \frac{100}{2} = 50\text{J}$$

(ii) Work done against friction,

$$W_f = F \times s$$
$$W_f = F \times s = \mu R \times s = \mu mg\cos\theta \times s$$
$$= 0.1 \times 1 \times 10\cos 30° \times 10$$
$$= 10 \times 0.866 = 8.66\text{ J}$$

(iii) Acceleration of block, up the inclined plane is

$$F = ma + (mg\sin\theta + \mu mg\cos\theta)$$
$$\Rightarrow a = \frac{F - (mg\sin\theta + \mu mg\cos\theta)}{m}$$
$$a = \frac{10 - \left(1 \times 10 \times \frac{1}{2} + 0.1 \times 10 \times 0.866\right)}{1} = 4.13\text{ m/s}^2$$

Quick Test 1

Conceptual Questions

1. Can acceleration be produced without doing any work? Give example.

2. In a game of tug of war, one team is slowly giving way to the other. Which team is doing positive work and which team negative?

3. Does the amount of work done depend upon the fact that how fast is a load raised or moved in the direction of force?

4. A mass is moving in a circular path with constant speed. What is the work done in 3/4 th of a rotation?

5. Calculate the work done by a car against gravity in moving along a straight horizontal road. The mass of the car is 400 kg and the distance moved is 2 m. *NCERT Exemplar*

6. Mountain roads wind up gradually instead of going straight up the slope. Why?

Numerical Questions

7. A body constrained to move along the Z-axis of a coordinate system is subjected to a constant force **F** given by $\mathbf{F} = (-\hat{\mathbf{i}} + 2\hat{\mathbf{j}} + 3\hat{\mathbf{k}})$ N, where $\hat{\mathbf{i}}, \hat{\mathbf{j}}$ and $\hat{\mathbf{k}}$ are unit vectors along the X, Y and Z-axes of the system, respectively. What is the work done by this force in moving the body a distance of 4 m along the Z-axis? *NCERT*

8. A man weighing 50 kg supports a body of 25 kg on his head. What is the work done when he moves a distance of 20 m up on an incline of 1 in 10? (Take, $g = 9.8\text{ m/s}^2$)

9. A body of mass of 2 kg initially at rest moves under the action of an applied horizontally force of 7 N on a table with coefficient of kinetic friction = 0.1. Compute the *NCERT*
 (i) work done by the applied force in 10 s,
 (ii) work done by friction in 10 s and
 (iii) work done by the net force on the body in 10 s.

10. A boy has a bag of sand of mass 20 kg. First of all, he keeps the bag on his head and moves 10 m. Second time, he drags the bag through 10 m on a frictionless surface with coefficient of friction $\mu = 0.1$s. In which case, he does more work?

Answers

7. 12 J *8.* 1470 J *9.* (i) 882 J (ii) −247 J (iii) 635 J *10.* Second case

For Solutions, See QR Code on Pg. 190

5.4 Energy

The **energy of a body is defined as its capacity of doing work.**

- Energy is a **scalar quantity.**
- The dimensions of energy are the same as the dimensions of work i.e. $[M^1L^2\ T^{-2}]$.
- It is measured in the same unit as work i.e. **joule in SI** and **erg in CGS system.**

Energy can exist in various forms such as mechanical energy (potential energy and kinetic energy), sound energy, heat energy, light energy, etc. Some practical units of energy and their equivalence to joule is given in the table below.

Some Other Units of Work or Energy

Unit	Symbol	Value in SI
erg	erg	10^{-7} J
electron volt	eV	1.6×10^{-19} J
calorie	cal	4.186 J

Kinetic Energy

The energy possessed by a body by virtue of its motion is called **kinetic energy**. In other words, the amount of work done by a moving object before coming to rest is equal to its kinetic energy.

$$\therefore \text{ Kinetic energy, KE} = \frac{1}{2}mv \cdot v = \frac{1}{2}mv^2$$

where, m is a mass and v is the velocity of a body.

- The units and dimensions of KE are **joule (in SI)** and $[ML^2T^{-2}]$, respectively.
- Kinetic **energy of a body is always positive.** It can never be negative.
- Kinetic energy of a body depends upon the frame of reference, e.g. KE of a person of mass m sitting in a train moving with velocity v is $\left[\frac{1}{2}mv^2\right]$ in the frame of earth and KE of the same person = 0, in the frame of the train.

Example 8. In a ballistics demonstration, a police officer fires a bullet of mass 50.0 g with speed 200 ms^{-1} on soft plywood of thickness 2.00 cm. The bullet emerges with only 10% of its initial kinetic energy. What is the emergent speed of the bullet? NCERT

Sol. Here, $m = 50.0 \text{ g} = 0.05 \text{ kg}, u = 200 \text{ ms}^{-1}$

$$\text{Initial KE} = \frac{1}{2}mu^2 = \frac{1}{2} \times 0.05 \times (200)^2 = 1000 \text{ J}$$

$$\text{Final KE} = 10\% \text{ of } 1000 \text{ J} = \frac{10 \times 1000}{100} = 100 \text{ J}$$

$$\text{or } \frac{1}{2}mv^2 = 100 \text{ J}$$

$$\therefore \quad v = \sqrt{\frac{2 \times 100}{m}} = \sqrt{\frac{2 \times 100}{0.05}} = 63.2 \text{ ms}^{-1}$$

Clearly, the speed reduces nearly by 68% and not by 90% by which the KE reduces.

Example 9. A toy rocket of mass 0.1 kg has a small fuel of mass 0.02 kg which it burns out in 3 s. Starting from rest on horizontal smooth track it gets a speed of 20 ms^{-1} after the fuel is burnt out. What is the approximate thrust of the rocket? What is the energy content per unit mass of the fuel? (Ignore the small mass variation of the rocket during fuel burning).

Sol. Here, $m = 0.1 \text{ kg}, u = 0, v = 20 \text{ ms}^{-1}, t = 3 \text{ s}$

$$\text{Thrust of the rocket} = ma = m\frac{v-u}{t}$$

$$= 0.1 \times \frac{20-0}{3} = \frac{2}{3} \text{ N}$$

$$\left[\because v = u + at \text{ or } a = \frac{v-u}{t}\right]$$

Kinetic energy gained by the rocket

$$K = \frac{1}{2}mv^2 = \frac{1}{2} \times 0.1 \times (20)^2 = 20 \text{ J}$$

Energy content per unit mass of the fuel

$$= \frac{\text{Total energy}}{\text{Mass of the fuel}} = \frac{20 \text{ J}}{0.02 \text{ kg}} = 1000 \text{ Jkg}^{-1}$$

Relation between Kinetic Energy and Linear Momentum

According to linear momentum, we know that, $p = mv$ ...(i)

where, m is mass and v is the velocity of a body.

Then, the kinetic energy of the body is

$$\text{KE} = \frac{p^2}{2m} \quad \text{[from Eq. (i)]}$$

$$= \frac{1}{2m}(mv)^2 = \frac{1}{2m}(m^2v^2)$$

or $p^2 = 2m \text{ KE}$

$\Rightarrow$ Linear momentum, $p = \sqrt{2m\text{KE}}$

Let us consider **three cases** as given below.

(i) Further, if **p = constant,** KE $\propto \frac{1}{m}$. This is shown in Fig. (a).

(ii) If **KE = constant,** $p^2 \propto m$ or $p \propto \sqrt{m}$. This is shown in Fig. (b).

(iii) If **m = constant,** $p^2 \propto$ KE or $p \propto \sqrt{\text{KE}}$. This is shown in Fig. (c).

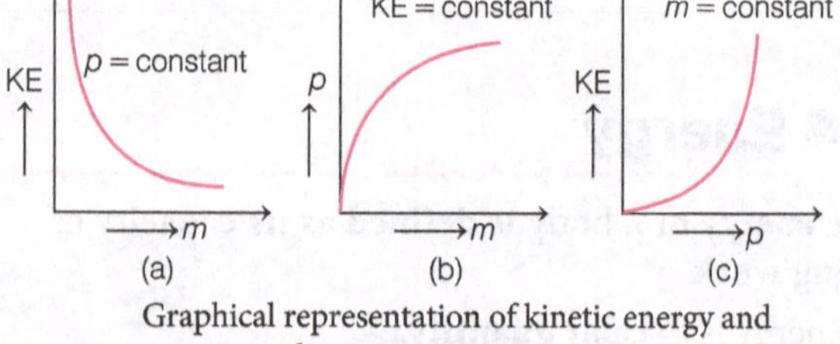

Graphical representation of kinetic energy and linear momentum

Example 10. A nucleus of radium ($^{226}_{88}$Ra) decays to $^{222}_{86}$Rn by the emission of α-particle ($^{4}_{2}$He) of energy 4.8 MeV. If mass of $^{222}_{86}$Rn = 222.0 amu and mass of $^{4}_{2}$He = 4.003 amu, then calculate the recoil energy of the daughter nucleus $^{222}_{86}$Rn.

$^4_2He = 4.003$ amu, then calculate the recoil energy of the daughter nucleus $^{222}_{86}Rn$.

Sol. The nuclear decay may be represented as follows

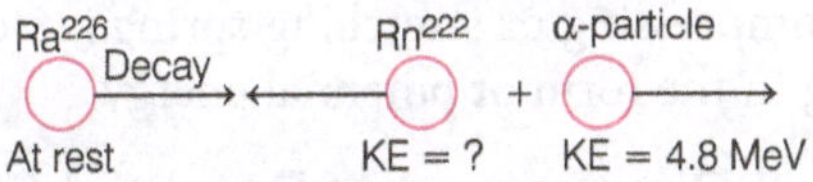

The kinetic energy of a particle is given by $K = \frac{p^2}{2m}$

$$\therefore \quad p = \sqrt{2mK}$$

As momentum is conserved in the absence of an external force, so $mK =$ constant

$$\text{or} \quad m_{Rn}K_{Rn} = m_\alpha K_\alpha$$

$$\text{or} \quad K_{Rn} = \frac{m_\alpha K_\alpha}{m_{Rn}} = \frac{4.003 \times 4.8}{222} = 0.0866 \text{ MeV}$$

Work-Energy Theorem

It states that work done by the net force acting on a body is equal to the change produced in the kinetic energy of the body.

Work-Energy Theorem for a Constant Force

Suppose a force F acting on a body of mass m produces acceleration a in it. After covering distance s, suppose the velocity of the body changes from u to v. Using the equation of motion $v^2 - u^2 = 2as$

Multiplying both sides by $\frac{1}{2}m$, we get

$$\frac{1}{2}mv^2 - \frac{1}{2}mu^2 = mas$$

By Newton's second law, $F = ma$

$$\therefore \quad \frac{1}{2}mv^2 - \frac{1}{2}mu^2 = Fs$$

$$\text{or} \quad \boxed{K_f - K_i = W} \quad [\because W = Fs]$$

where, K_f and K_i are the final and initial kinetic energies of the body.

Work-Energy Theorem for a Variable Force

Suppose a variable force F acts on a body of mass m and produces displacement ds in its own direction $(\theta = 0°)$. Then, the small work done is

$$dW = \mathbf{F} \cdot ds = Fds \cos 0° = Fds$$

The rate of change of kinetic energy is

$$\frac{dK}{dt} = \frac{d}{dt}\left[\frac{1}{2}mv^2\right]$$

$$= \frac{1}{2} \times 2v \times m\frac{dv}{dt}$$

$$= m\frac{dv}{dt}(v) = (ma)\,v$$

$$\left[\because \text{force, } F = ma \text{ and } v = \frac{ds}{dt}\right]$$

$$\therefore \quad \frac{dK}{dt} = F \cdot \frac{ds}{dt}$$

$$\text{Thus,} \quad dK = Fds$$

Integrating from the initial position (x_i) to final position (x_f), we have

$$\int_{K_i}^{K_f} dK = \int_{x_i}^{x_f} Fds$$

where, K_i and K_f are the initial and final kinetic energies corresponding to x_i and x_f, respectively.

$$\text{or} \quad \boxed{\text{Change in kinetic energy, } K_f - K_i = \int_{x_i}^{x_f} Fds}$$

$$\therefore \quad K_f - K_i = \text{work done on the body } (W)$$

$$= \text{increase in KE of body.}$$

This proves the work-energy theorem for a variable force.

Relation between Newton's Second law and Work Energy Theorem

- From Newton's second law, when a net force acts on an object resulting in a **change in velocity over a time** and consequently, a change in KE.
- If you integrate the force over the distance you arrive at the work done which correlates directly to the change in KE.
- Newton's second law is often expressed as a vector equation, focusing on the forces and their direction.
- The work-energy theorem is a scalar equation that deals with energy change. It shows the effect of forces in terms of energy rather than direction and acceleration.

Example 11. Consider a drop of small pebble of mass 1.00 g falling from a cliff of height 1.00 km. It hits the ground with a speed of 50.0 ms^{-1}. What is the work done by the unknown resistive force? NCERT

Sol. We assume that the pebble is initially at rest on the cliff.

$$\therefore \quad u = 0, m = 1.00 \text{ g} = 10^{-3} \text{ kg}$$

$$v = 50 \text{ ms}^{-1}, h = 1.00 \text{ km} = 10^3 \text{ m}$$

The change in KE of the pebble is

$$\Delta K = \frac{1}{2}mv^2 - \frac{1}{2}mu^2$$

$$= \frac{1}{2}\times 10^{-3}\times (50)^2 - 0 = 1.25 \text{ J}$$

Assuming that $g = 10 \text{ ms}^{-2}$ is constant, the work done by the gravitational force is

$$W_g = F\cdot h = mgh = 10^{-3}\times 10\times 10^3 = 10 \text{ J}$$

If W_r is the work done by the resistive force on the pebble, then from the work energy theorem,

$$\Delta K = W_g + W_r$$

or $\quad W_r = \Delta K - W_g = 1.25 - 10.0 = -8.75 \text{ J}$

Example 12. **A block of mass $m = 1$ kg, moving on a horizontal surface with speed $v_i = 2 \text{ ms}^{-1}$ enters a rough patch ranging from $x = 0.10$ m to $x = 2.01$ m. The retarding force F_r on the block in this range is inversely proportional to x over this range.**

$$F_r = \frac{-k}{x} \quad 0.1 < x < 2.01 \text{ m}$$

$$= 0 \text{ for } x < 0.1 \text{ m and } x > 2.01 \text{ m}$$

where, $k = 0.5$ J. What is the final kinetic energy and speed v_f of the block as it crosses this patch? NCERT

Sol. By work-energy theorem,

$$\Delta K = W_r \text{ or } K_f - K_i = \int_{x_i}^{x_f} F_r dx$$

$$\therefore \quad K_f = K_i + \int_{01}^{2.01}\frac{(-k)}{x}dx \qquad [\because F_r = -kx]$$

where, k = spring constant

$$K_f = \frac{1}{2}mv_i^2 - k\int_{01}^{2.01}\frac{1}{x}dx$$

$$= \frac{1}{2}\times 1\times 2^2 - k[\ln x]_{0.1}^{2.01}$$

$$= 2 - 0.5\left[\ln\frac{2.01}{0.1}\right]$$

$$= 2 - 0.5 \ln 20.1$$

$$= 2 - 0.5\times 2.303 \log 20.1$$

$$= 2 - 0.5\times 2.303\times 1.3032$$

$$K_f = 2 - 1.5 = 0.5 \text{ J}$$

Final speed, $v_f = \sqrt{\frac{2K_f}{m}} = \sqrt{\frac{2\times 0.5}{1}} = 1 \text{ ms}^{-1}$

Potential Energy

The potential energy of a body is defined as the energy possessed by the body by virtue of its position or configuration relative to other objects.

If configuration of the system changes, then its potential energy also changes.

e.g. When a spring is compressed or stretched, work done in compressing or stretching spring is stored in the spring in the form of potential energy.

Units and Dimensions of Potential Energy

The units and dimensions of potential energy are same as that of kinetic energy given as,

Dimensions = $[ML^2T^{-2}]$

SI unit = joule (J)

Gravitational Potential Energy

Gravitational potential energy of a body is the energy possessed by the body by virtue of its position above the surface of the earth.

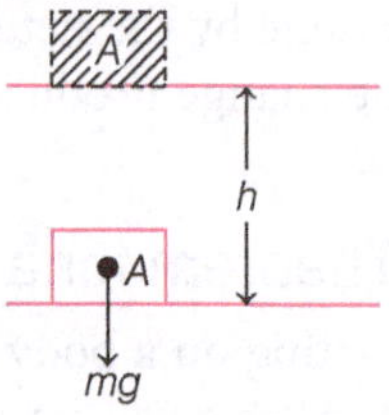

Gravitational potential energy of a body

This work done against gravity is stored as the gravitational potential energy (U) of the body.

$\therefore$ Gravitational potential energy, $U = mgh$

If h is taken as a variable, then the gravitational force F is equal to the negative of derivative of U with respect to h.

Thus, $$F = -\frac{d(U)}{dh} = -mg$$

Here, **the negative sign indicates that the gravitational force is acting downwards.**

- **For gravitational potential energy, the zero of potential energy i.e., reference point is chosen to be the ground.**
- **The work done by the gravitational force does not depend on the angle of inclination of the inclined plane or the path of the falling body.**

  It just depends on the initial and final position. Thus, gravitational force is a conservative force.

$$\therefore \quad F(x) = \frac{-dU}{dx}$$

If x_i and x_f are the initial and final position of the object and U_i and U_f are the corresponding potential energies, then

$$\int_{x_i}^{x_f} F(x)\, dx = -\int_{U_i}^{U_f} dU = U_i - U_f$$

Example 13. **A ball falls from a height of 20 m. Find out the velocity with which the ball hits the ground.**

Sol. Given, $h = 20\,\text{m}, v = ?$

When the ball hits the ground, its kinetic energy is converted into potential energy.

$\therefore$ When it hits the ground KE = PE

$$\frac{1}{2}mv^2 = mgh$$

$$v = \sqrt{2gh}$$

$$= \sqrt{2 \times 9.8 \times 20}$$

$$= \sqrt{392} = 19.798\ \text{m/s}$$

Potential Energy of a Spring

There are many types of spring. Important among these are **helical** and **spiral springs** as shown in figure.

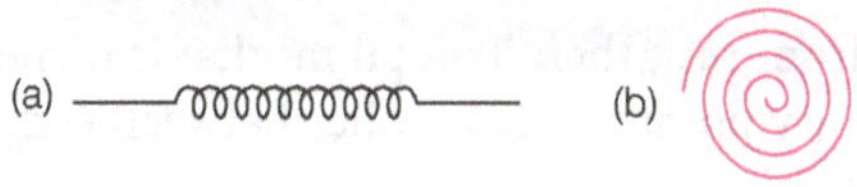

(a) Helical spring and (b) Spiral spring

Usually, we assume that the springs are massless. Therefore, work done is stored in the spring in the form of elastic potential energy of the spring.

Thus, **potential energy of a spring is the energy associated with the state of compression or expansion of an elastic spring.**

Potential Energy of an Ideal Spring

Consider an elastic spring of negligibly small mass with its one end attached to a rigid support and its other end is attached to a block of mass m can slide over a smooth horizontal surface.

At $x = 0$, the position is in the state of equilibrium as shown in Fig. (a), when the spring is stretched in Fig. (b) and compressed by pushing the block as shown in Fig. (c). So, spring force F_s begins to act in equilibrium position.

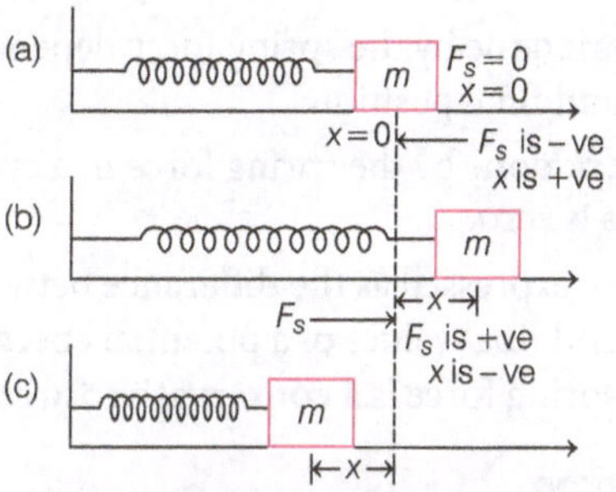

Equilibrium, stretched and compressed states of an elastic spring

For a small stretch [Fig. (b)] or compression [Fig. (c)], spring obeys Hooke's law, i.e. restoring force $\propto$ stretch or compression $-F_s \propto x \Rightarrow F_s = -kx$

where, k is called **spring constant.** Its SI unit is N/m.

The negative sign shows F_s acts in the opposite direction of displacement x. The work done by the spring force for the small extension is

$$dW_s = F_s\, dx = -kx\, dx$$

If the block is moved from an initial displacement x_i to final displacement x_f, then work done by spring force is

$$W_s = \int dW_s = -\int_{x_i}^{x_f} kx\, dx = -k\left[\frac{x^2}{2}\right]_{x_i}^{x_f}$$

or $\quad$ Net work done by the spring, $W_s = U_s = -\frac{1}{2}kx_f^2$

It can also be obtained by calculating the area under the F_s *versus* x graph.

The graph of force-displacement (F_s-x) for a stretched spring is given below

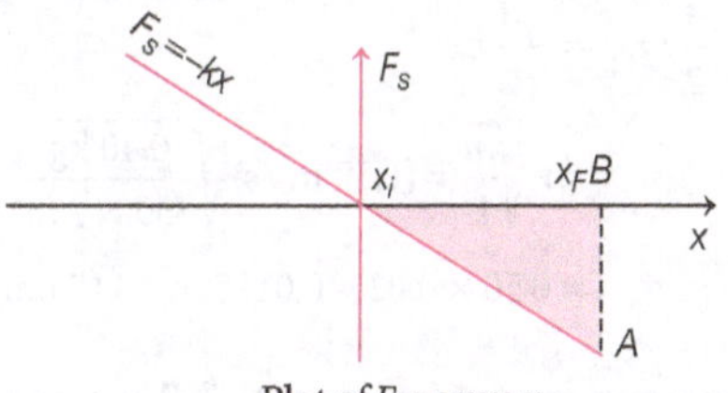

Plot of F_s *versus* x

Conclusion

(i) Spring force F_s is position dependent as it is clear from Hooke's law.

i.e. $\quad F_s = -kx$

(ii) The work done by the spring force depends on initial and final position.

(iii) The work done by the spring force in a cyclic process is zero.

(iv) It can be expressed as the difference between the initial and final values of a potential energy function, hence spring force is a **conservative force.**

TEACHER TIP

The potential energy of a body which is subjected to a conservative force is uncertain upto a certain limit. This is because the point of zero potential energy is a matter of choice.

For the spring potential energy $\frac{1}{2}kx^2$, the zero of the potential energy is the equilibrium position of the oscillating mass.

Example 14. **As shown in figure, a canister of mass $m = 0.40$ kg slides across a horizontal frictionless counter with speed $v = 0.50$ m/s. It then runs into and compresses a spring of spring constant $k = 750$ N / m. When the canister is momentarily stopped by the spring, by what distance d is the spring compressed ?**

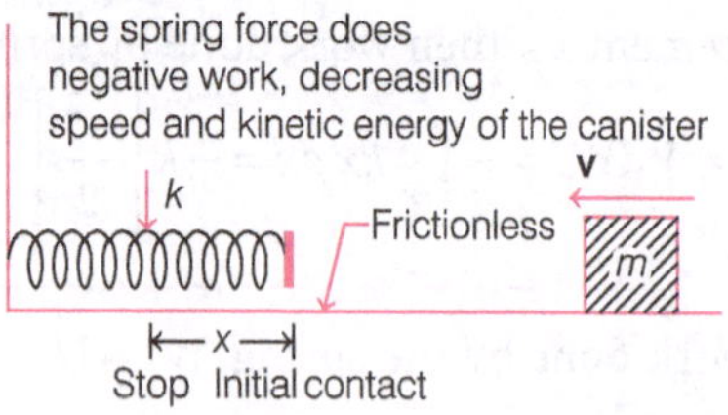

Sol. The work-energy theorem for the canister is

$$K_f - K_i = -\frac{1}{2}kx^2$$

On substituting values

$$0 - \frac{1}{2}mv^2 = -\frac{1}{2}kx^2$$

$$x = v\sqrt{\frac{m}{k}} = (0.50 \text{ m /s})\sqrt{\frac{0.40 \text{ kg}}{750 \text{ N / m}}}$$

$$= 0.50 \times 0.02 = 0.0115 \text{ m} = 1.15 \text{ cm}$$

5.5 Conservation of Mechanical Energy

This principle states that if only the conservative forces are doing work on a body, then its mechanical energy (KE + PE) remains constant.

Suppose that a body undergoes displacement Δx under the action of a conservative force $F(x)$. Then, from work-energy theorem, the change in KE, is $\Delta K = F(x) \cdot \Delta x$.

As the force is conservative, then change in potential energy is given by

$$\Delta U = -F(x)\,\Delta x = \text{Negative of the work done}$$

Combining the above two equations, we get

$$\Delta K = -\Delta U$$

$$\Delta K + \Delta U = 0 \text{ or } \Delta(K + U) = 0$$

i.e. $$K + U = \text{constant} = E$$

$\therefore$ $$K_i + U_i = K_f + U_f$$

The quantity $K + U$, is called the total mechanical energy of the system.

Although, **individually the kinetic energy K and potential energy U may change from one state to another, but their sum or the total mechanical energy of the system remains constant under the conservative forces.**

Conservation of Mechanical Energy of a Stretched Spring

If the block of mass m is extended to position x_m and released from rest, then its total mechanical energy at any arbitrary point x, where x lies between $-x_m$ and $+x_m$ will be given by

$$\frac{1}{2}kx_m^2 = \frac{1}{2}kx^2 + \frac{1}{2}mv^2$$

Thus, speed and kinetic energy will be maximum at the equilibrium position $x = 0$. i.e.

$$\frac{1}{2}mv_m^2 = \frac{1}{2}kx_m^2 \Rightarrow v_m = \sqrt{\frac{k}{m}}\,x_m$$

where, v_m is the maximum speed.

Hence, the kinetic energy is converted to potential energy and *vice-versa.*

However, the total mechanical energy in all positions remains constant.

The variation of PE, KE and TE with distance (x) is shown in the figure below

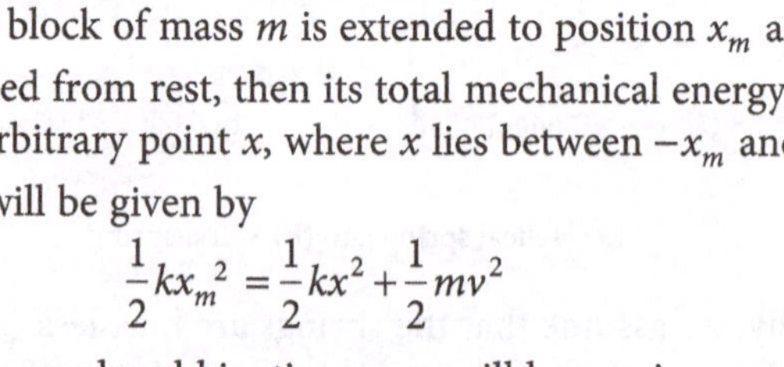

Plots of U, K and E

Example 15. **To simulate car accidents, auto manufacturers study the collisions of moving cars with mounted springs of different spring constants. Consider a typical simulation with a car of mass 1000 kg moving with a speed of 18.0 kmh^{-1} on a smooth road and colliding with a horizontally mounted spring of spring constant 6.25×10^3 Nm^{-1}. What is the maximum compression of the spring?** NCERT

Sol. Here, $m = 1000$ kg,

$$k = 6.25\times 10^3 \text{Nm}^{-1},$$

$$v = 18 \text{ kmh}^{-1} = \frac{18\times 5}{18} \text{ ms}^{-1} = 5 \text{ m/s}$$

At the maximum compression x_m, the kinetic energy of the car is converted entirely into the potential energy of the spring. Therefore,

Gain in PE of the spring = Loss in KE of the car

or $$\frac{1}{2}kx_m^2 = \frac{1}{2}mv^2$$

or $$x_m^2 = \frac{mv^2}{k} = \frac{1000\times 5\times 5}{6.25\times 10^3} = 4$$

$\therefore$ $$x_m = 2.0 \text{ m}$$

Conservation of Mechanical Energy in a Freely Falling Body

Consider a body of mass m lying at position A at a height h above the ground. As the body falls, its kinetic energy increases at the expense of potential energy as shown in figure.

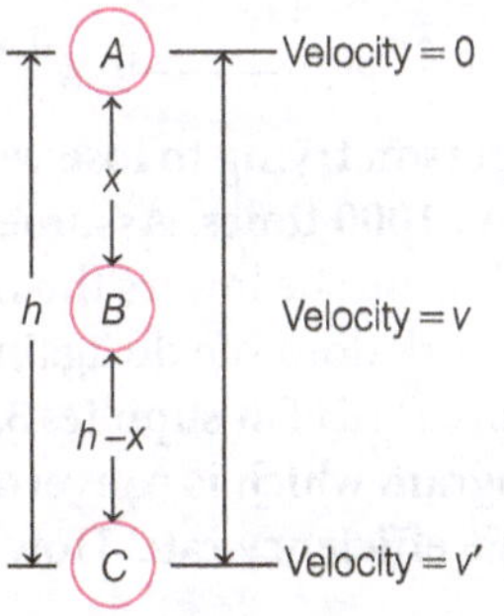

Conservation of energy in a freely falling body

At point A The body is at rest.

KE of the body, $K_A = 0$

PE of the body, $U_A = mgh$

Total mechanical energy $E_A = K_A + U_A = 0 + mgh$

Mechanical energy at position A, $E_A = mgh$

At point B Suppose the body falls freely through height x and reaches the point B with velocity v.

Then, $$v^2 - 0^2 = 2as \qquad [\because \text{using } v^2 - u^2 = 2as]$$

or $$v^2 = 2gx$$

$\therefore$ $$K_B = \frac{1}{2}mv'^2 = \frac{1}{2}\times m\times 2gx = mgx$$

$$U_B = mg(h-x)$$

$$E_B = K_B + U_B = mgx + mg(h-x) = mgh$$

Mechanical energy at position B, $E_B = mgh$

At point C Suppose the body finally reaches at point C on the ground with velocity v'. Then, considering motion from A to C,

$$v'^2 - 0^2 = 2gh$$

or $$v'^2 = 2gh$$

$$K_C = \frac{1}{2}mv'^2 = \frac{1}{2}\times m\times 2gh = mgh$$

$$U_C = mg\times 0 = 0$$

$\therefore$ $$E_C = U_C + K_C = 0 + mgh = mgh$$

Mechanical energy at position C, $E_C = mgh$

Clearly, as the body falls, its PE decreases and KE increases by an equal amount. However, its total mechanical energy remains constant at all points. Thus, **total mechanical energy is conserved during free fall of the body,** as shown in figure.

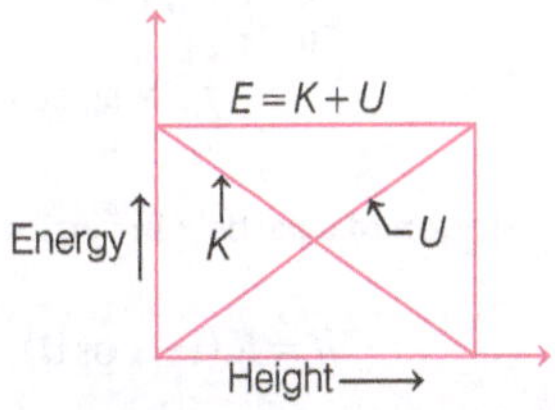

Plot of PE and KE during free fall of a body

$E - U = K$ and K is always positive, therefore for a system to exist. $E - U \geq 0$ or $E \geq U$.

Examples of Conservation of Energy

- When a simple pendulum is pulled to one side at a height h and released, it swings to and fro and reaches equal heights ($= h$) on either side of the mean position.
- At lowest point B, it has maximum speed and hence maximum kinetic energy, but minimum potential energy. i.e. zero
- At the extreme points A and C, it has zero kinetic energy, but has maximum potential energy. At any intermediate state, it has both kinetic and potential energy.

- **The sum of potential energy and kinetic energy i.e. total energy remains constant throughout the swing.**

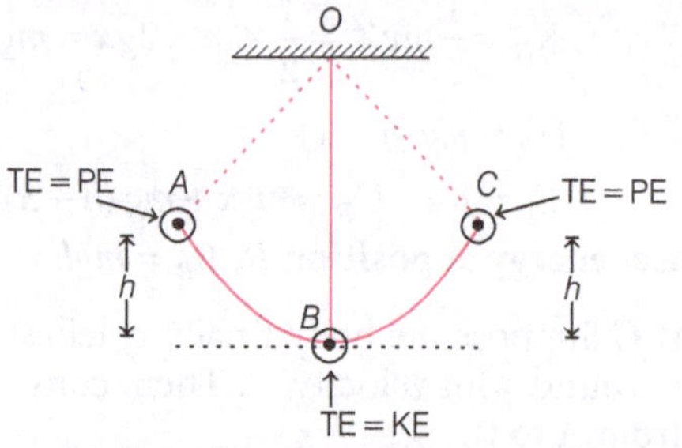

Mechanical energy in a simple pendulum at various points

5.6 Motion in a Vertical Circle

Suppose a particle of mass m is attached to an inextensible light string of length L. The particle is moving in a vertical circle of radius L about a fixed point O.

It is imparted a velocity u in horizontal direction at lowest point A. Let v be its velocity at point B, the circle as shown in figure.

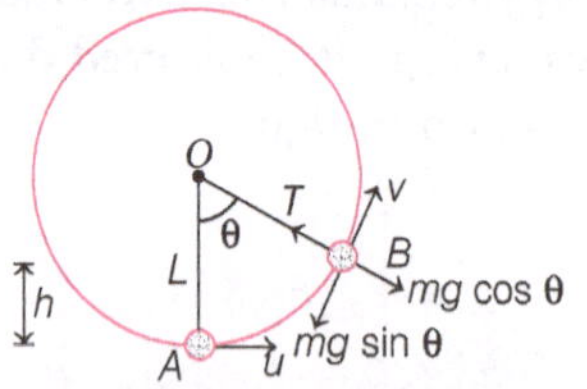

Motion of a particle in vertical circle

Here we have $h = R(1-\cos\theta)$

Now, from conservation of mechanical energy, we have

$$\frac{1}{2}m(u^2 - v^2) = mgh \quad \text{...(i)}$$

The necessary centripetal force is provided by the resultant of tension T and $mg\cos\theta$.

$$\therefore \quad T - mg\cos\theta = \frac{mv^2}{R} \quad \text{...(ii)}$$

As speed of the particle decreases with height, tension in the string is maximum at the bottom. The particle will complete the circle if the string does not slack even at the highest point.

Now following conclusions can be made using above Eqs. (i) and (ii).

(i) **Minimum velocity at highest point** so that particle complete the circle $v_{min} = \sqrt{gL}$, at this velocity, tension in the string is zero.

(ii) **Minimum velocity at lowest point** so that particle complete the circle, $v_{min} = \sqrt{5gL}$, at this velocity, tension in the string is $6\,mg$.

(iii) **When string is horizontal,** then minimum velocity is $\sqrt{3Rg}$ and tension in this condition is $3\,mg$.

(iv) If velocity at lowest point is less than $\sqrt{5\,gR}$, then tension in the string becomes zero before reaching the highest point, now the particle will leave the circle and will move on parabolic path.

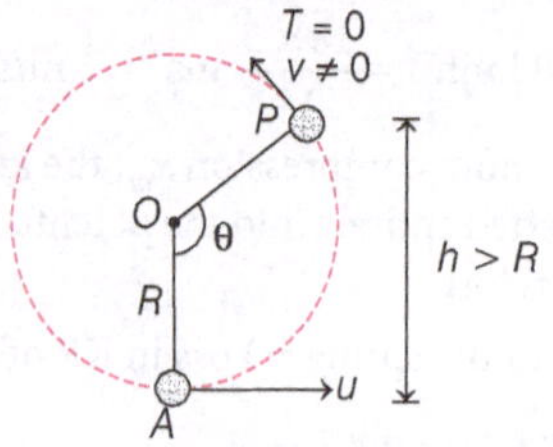

In this condition, if $\sqrt{2gR} < v < \sqrt{5\,gR}$ then tension in the string becomes zero but velocity is not zero, thc particle will leave circle at $90° < \theta < 180°$ or $h > R$

(v) If velocity at lowest point is $0 < v \le \sqrt{2\,gR}$, the particle will oscillate, in this condition velocity becomes zero but tension is not zero. The particle will oscillate in lower half of circle, i.e. $0° < \theta < 90°$.

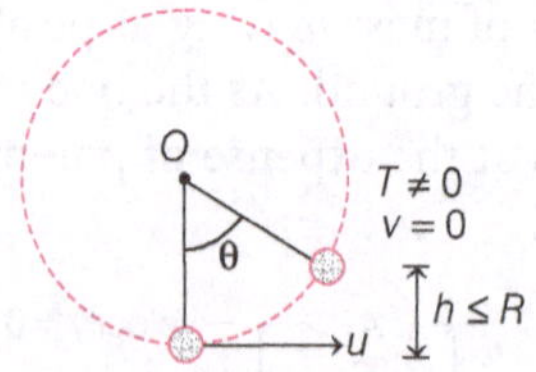

Example 16. **A person trying to lose weight lifts a 10 kg mass upto 0.5 m, 1000 times. Assume that the potential energy lost each time she lowers the mass is dissipated. (i) How much work does she do against the gravitational force? (ii) Fat supplies 3.8×10^7 J of energy per kilogram which is converted to mechanical energy with 20% efficiency rate. How much fat will be dieter use up?** NCERT

Sol. (i) Given, $m = 10$ kg, $h = 0.5$ m, $n = 1000$,

$g = 9.8\ \text{m/s}^2$, $W_g = ?$

Mechanical energy (E_m) = ? and fat consumed?

Work done against the gravitational force

i.e. $W_g = n \times mgh = 1000 \times 10 \times 9.8 \times 0.5 = 49000$ J

(ii) Mechanical energy supplied by 1 kg of fat

$$E_m = 20\%\ \text{of}\ 3.8 \times 10^7\ \text{J} = \frac{20}{100} \times 3.8 \times 10^7 = 76 \times 10^5\ \text{J}$$

$$\text{Consumption of fat} = \frac{1 \times 49000}{76 \times 10^5} = 6.45 \times 10^{-3}\ \text{kg}$$

Example 17. A bob of mass m is suspended by a light string of length L. It is imparted a horizontal velocity v_0 at the lowest point A such that it completes a semi-circular trajectory in the vertical plane with the string becoming slack only on reaching the topmost point, C. This is shown in figure. Obtain an expression for (i) v_0, (ii) the speeds at points B and C and (iii) the ratio of the kinetic energies (K_B/K_C) at B and C. Comment on the nature of the trajectory of the bob after it reaches the point C. NCERT

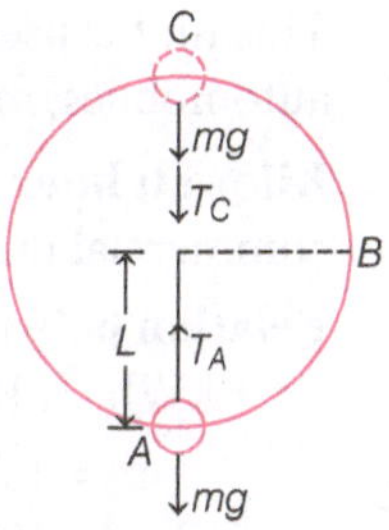

Sol. (i) Two external forces act on the bob, i.e. gravity and tension (T) in the string.

At the lowest point A, the potential energy of the system can be taken zero. So, at point A

Total mechanical energy = Kinetic energy

$$E = \frac{1}{2} m v_0^2 \quad \text{...(i)}$$

If T_A is the tension in the string at point A, then from Newton's second law,

$$T_A - mg = \frac{m v_0^2}{L} \quad \text{...(ii)}$$

At the highest point C, the string slackens, so the tension T_C becomes zero. If v_C is the speed at point C, then by conservation of energy,

$$E = K + U \quad \text{or} \quad E = \frac{1}{2} m v_C^2 + 2\,mgL \quad \text{...(iii)}$$

From Newton's second law, $mg = \dfrac{m v_C^2}{L}$ ...(iv)

or $\quad m v_C^2 = mgL$ ...(v)

Using Eq. (v) in Eq. (iii), we get

$$E = \frac{1}{2} mgL + 2\,mgL = \frac{5}{2} mgL \quad \text{...(vi)}$$

From Eqs. (i) and (vi), we get

$$\frac{5}{2} mgL = \frac{m}{2} v_0^2 \text{ or } v_0 = \sqrt{5\,gL} \quad \text{...(vii)}$$

(ii) From Eq. (iv), we have $v_C = \sqrt{gL}$

The total energy at B is

$$E = \frac{1}{2} m v_B^2 + mgL \quad \text{...(viii)}$$

From Eqs. (i) and (viii), we get

$$\frac{1}{2} m v_B^2 + mgL = \frac{1}{2} m v_0^2$$

$$\frac{1}{2} m v_B^2 + mgL = \frac{1}{2} m \times 5gL \quad \text{[using Eq. (vii)]}$$

$$\therefore \quad v_B = \sqrt{3gL}$$

(iii) The ratio of the kinetic energies at B and C is

$$\frac{K_B}{K_C} = \frac{(1/2)\, m v_B^2}{(1/2)\, m v_C^2} = \frac{3}{1} = 3:1$$

At C, the string becomes slack and the velocity of the bob is horizontal and to the left. Therefore the bob will coninue on its circular path and complete the revolution.

Quick Test 2

Conceptual Questions

1. Is it possible to exert a force which does work on a body without changing its kinetic energy? If, so give example.
2. When an air bubble rises in water, what happens to its potential energy?
3. Is it practically possible to have situation where $(E - U) < 0$?
4. A spring is cut into two equal halves. How is the spring constant of each half affected?
5. Can a body have energy without momentum? If yes, then explain how they are related with each other?

Numerical Questions

6. A body of mass 1.0 kg initially at rest is moved by a horizontal force of 0.5 N on a smooth frictionless table. Calculate the work done by the force in 10 s and show that this is equal to the change in kinetic energy of the body.
7. A body of mass 0.5 kg travels in a straight line with velocity $v = ax^{3/2}$, where $a = 5\text{ m}^{-\frac{1}{2}}\text{ s}^{-1}$. What is the work done by the net force during its displacement from $x = 0$ to $x = 2\text{ m}$? NCERT
8. When a 300 g mass is hung from a vertical spring, it stretches from equilibrium by 10 cm. What work is required to stretch it by next 5 cm?
9. An electron and a proton are detected in a cosmic ray experiment, the electron with kinetic energy 10 keV and the proton with 100 keV. Which is faster, the electron or the proton? Obtain the ratio of their speeds. (Electron mass = 9.11×10^{-31} kg, proton mass = 1.67×10^{-27} kg, 1eV = 1.60×10^{-19} J). NCERT

Answers

6. 12.5 J 7. 50 J 8. 0.1875 J 9. Electron, 13.54

For Solutions, See QR Code on Pg. 190

5.7 Power

- **Power of a person or machine is defined as the rate at which work is done or energy is transferred by it.**

  If a person does work W in time t, then its average power is given by

$$\text{Average power } (P_{av}) = \frac{\text{Work done}}{\text{Time taken}} = \frac{W}{t}$$

- The **instantaneous power** of an agent is defined as the limiting value of the average power of an agent in a small time interval, when the time interval approaches to zero.

  Work done by a force **F** for a small displacement $d\mathbf{r}$ is $dW = \mathbf{F} \cdot d\mathbf{r}$. Then, instantaneous power can be given as

i.e. $$P = \lim_{\Delta t \to 0} \frac{\Delta W}{\Delta t} = \frac{dW}{dt}$$

Now, $dW = \mathbf{F} \cdot d\mathbf{r}$

$\therefore$ $P = \mathbf{F} \cdot \dfrac{d\mathbf{r}}{dt}$

Again $\dfrac{d\mathbf{r}}{dt} = \mathbf{v}$, instantaneous velocity of an agent.

Therefore, $P = \mathbf{F} \cdot \mathbf{v}$

Thus, **the power of an agent at any instant is equal to the dot product of its force and velocity vectors at that instant.**

Dimensional Formula of Power

- Power is a scalar quantity, because it is the ratio of two scalar quantities work (W) and time (t). The dimensional formula of power is $[ML^2T^{-3}]$.

Units of Power

- The SI unit of power is watt (W). **The power of an agent is one watt if it does work at the rate of 1 joule per second.**

$$1 \text{ watt} = \frac{1 \text{ joule}}{1 \text{ second}} = 1 \text{ Js}^{-1}$$

- Another popular units of power are **kilowatt** and **horsepower.**

  1 kilowatt = 1000 watt or 1 kW = 10^3 W

  1 horsepower = 746 watt

  or 1 hp = 746 W

  This unit is used to describe the output of automobiles, motorbikes, engines, etc.

- **Kilowatt hour** (kWh) or **Board of Trade (BOT)** is the commercial unit of electrical energy.

  Relation between kWh and joule

$$1 \text{ kWh} = 1 \text{ kW} \times 1 \text{ h}$$
$$= 1000 \text{ W} \times 1 \text{ h}$$
$$= 1000 \text{ Js}^{-1} \times 3600 \text{ s}$$

or $1 \text{ kWh} = 3.6 \times 10^6 \text{ J}$

Example 18. An elevator which can carry a maximum load of 1800 kg (elevator + passenger) is moving up with a constant speed of 2 ms^{-1}. The frictional force opposing the motion is 4000 N. Determine the minimum power delivered by the motor to the elevator in watts as well as in horsepower.

Sol. The downward force on the elevator is

$$F = mg + F_f$$

where, F_f is the frictional force

$$= 1800 \times 10 + 4000$$
$$= 22000 \text{ N}$$

The motor must supply enough power to balance this force. Hence, $P = Fv = 22000 \times 2 = 44000$ W

$$= \frac{44000}{746} \text{ hp} \simeq 59 \text{ hp}$$

Example 19. A car of mass 2000 kg is lifted up a distance of 30 m by a crane in 1 min. A second crane does the same job in 2 min. Do the cranes consume the same or different amounts of fuel? What is the power supplied by each crane? Neglect power dissipation against friction.

Sol. Here, $m = 2000$ kg, $s = 30$ m

$$t_1 = 1 \text{ min} = 60 \text{ s}, t_2 = 2 \text{ min} = 120 \text{ s}$$

Work done by each crane,

$$W = Fs = mgs$$
$$= 2000 \times 9.8 \times 30$$
$$= 5.88 \times 10^5 \text{ J}$$

As both the cranes do same amount of work, so both consume same amount of fuel.

Power supplied by first crane,

$$P_1 = \frac{W}{t_1} = \frac{5.88 \times 10^5}{60} = 9800 \text{ W}$$

Power supplied by second crane,

$$P_2 = \frac{W}{t_2} = \frac{5.88 \times 10^5}{120} = 4900 \text{ W}$$

5.8 Collision

A collision is an isolated event in which two or more colliding bodies exert strong forces on each other for a relatively short time.

For a collision to take place, the actual physical contact is not necessary (Collision of α-particle with the nucleus)

Collision between particles have been divided into two types

Elastic Collision	Inelastic Collision
A collision in which there is absolutely no loss of kinetic energy.	A collision in which there occurs some loss of kinetic energy.
Forces involved during elastic collision must be conserved in nature.	Some or all forces involved during collision may be non-conservative in nature.
The mechanical energy is not converted into heat, light, sound etc.	A part of the mechanical energy is converted into heat, light, sound, etc.
e.g. Collision between subatomic particles, collision between glass balls, etc.	e.g. Collision between two vehicles, collision between a ball and floor etc.

Conservation of Linear Momentum in Collision

Consider two bodies 1 and 2 collide against each other. They exert mutual impulsive forces on each other during the collision time Δt. The changes produced in momenta of the two bodies will be

$$\Delta p_1 = F_{12}\,\Delta t$$

and $$\Delta p_2 = F_{21}\,\Delta t$$

where, F_{12} is the force exerted on body 1 by body 2 and F_{21} is the force exerted on body 2 by body 1.

According to Newton's third law of motion, we have

$$F_{12} = -F_{21}$$

$\therefore$ $$F_{12}\,\Delta t = -F_{21}\,\Delta t$$

or $$F_{12}\,\Delta t + F_{21}\,\Delta t = 0$$

$$\Delta p_1 + \Delta p_2 = 0$$

$$\Delta (p_1 + p_2) = 0$$

$$\boxed{p_1 + p_2 = \text{constant}}$$

Hence, **total linear momentum is conserved at each instant during collision.**

Elastic Collision in One Dimension

Suppose two bodies A and B of masses m_1 and m_2 are moving along the same straight line with velocities u_1 and u_2, respectively. Let $u_1 > u_2$.

After collision, bodies A and B move with velocities v_1 and v_2 in the same direction such that $v_2 > v_1$ as shown in figure.

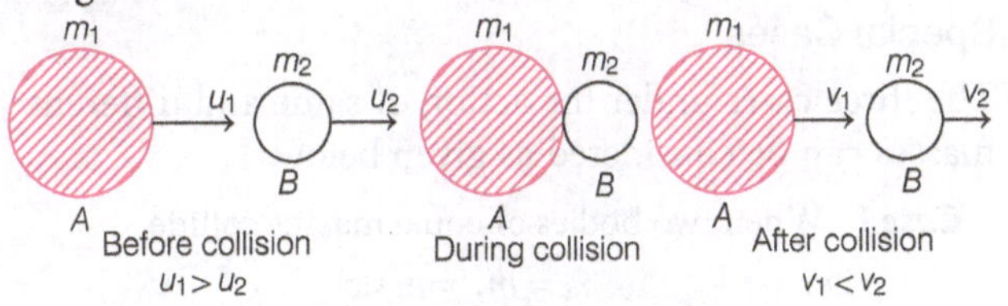

Elastic collision in one dimension

As linear momentum is conserved in any collision, we get

$\therefore$ Initial momentum = Final momentum

$$m_1u_1 + m_2u_2 = m_1v_1 + m_2v_2 \quad \text{...(i)}$$

or $$m_1(u_1 - v_1) = m_2(v_2 - u_2) \quad \text{...(ii)}$$

Since, **KE is also conserved in an elastic collision,** we get

$$\frac{1}{2}m_1u_1^2 + \frac{1}{2}m_2u_2^2 = \frac{1}{2}m_1v_1^2 + \frac{1}{2}m_2v_2^2$$

or $$m_1(u_1 + v_1)(u_1 - v_1) = m_2(v_2 - u_2)(v_2 + u_2) \quad \text{...(iii)}$$

Dividing Eq. (iii) by Eq. (ii), we get

$$u_1 + v_1 = v_2 + u_2$$

or $$u_1 - u_2 = v_2 - v_1 \quad \text{...(iv)}$$

Hence, **in one-dimensional elastic collision, relative velocity of separation after collision is equal to relative velocity of approach before collision.**

Velocities of the Bodies After the Collision

From Eq. (iv), we get

$$v_2 = u_1 - u_2 + v_1 \quad \text{...(v)}$$

Putting this value of v_2 in Eq. (i), we get

$$m_1u_1 + m_2u_2 = m_1v_1 + m_2(u_1 - u_2 + v_1)$$
$$= m_1v_1 + m_2u_1 - m_2u_2 + m_2v_1$$

or $$(m_1 - m_2)u_1 + 2m_2u_2 = (m_1 + m_2)v_1$$

Velocity of body A after collision,

$$v_1 = \left(\frac{m_1 - m_2}{m_1 + m_2}\right)u_1 + \left(\frac{2m_2}{m_1 + m_2}\right)u_2 \quad \text{...(vi)}$$

Putting the value of v_1 in Eq. (v), we get

Velocity of body *B* after collision,

$$v_2 = \left(\frac{m_2 - m_1}{m_1 + m_2}\right)u_2 + \left(\frac{2m_1}{m_1 + m_2}\right)u_1 \quad \text{...(vii)}$$

Eqs. (vi) and (vii) give the **final velocities of the colliding bodies in terms of their initial velocities.**

Special Cases

The three cases under the action of same and different masses can be considered as given below.

***Case* I** When two bodies of equal masses collide.

i.e. $m_1 = m_2 = m$ say

From Eq. (vi), $v_1 = \frac{2mu_2}{2m} = u_2$

From Eq. (vii), $v_2 = \frac{2mu_1}{2m} = u_1$

Hence, **when two bodies of equal masses undergo perfectly elastic collision in one dimension, their velocities are just interchanged.**

***Case* II** (a) When a light body collides against a massive stationary body.

If, $m_1 << m_2$ and $u_2 = 0$

Neglecting m_1 in Eq. (vi), we get

$$v_1 = -\frac{m_2 u_1}{m_2} = -u_1$$

From Eq. (vii), $v_2 \simeq 0$.

(b) If $m_1 >> m_2$ and $u_2 = 0$

Neglecting m_2 in eq. (vi), we get

$$v_1 = u_1$$

From Eq. (vii), $v_2 = 2u_1$

Hence, when a heavy mass (m_1) collides with light mass (m_2) at rest, then the mass m_1 should keep on moving with same velocity while mass m_2 starts moving with velocity double of their initial velocity.

***Case* III** When body having mass m_2 is initially at rest i.e., $u_2 = 0$

From Eqs. (vi) and (vii), we get

$$v_1 = \frac{(m_1 - m_2)u_1}{m_1 + m_2} \Rightarrow v_2 = \frac{2m_1 v_1}{m_1 + m_2}$$

Hence, **when a light body collides against a massive body at rest, the light body rebounds after the collision with an equal and opposite velocity while the massive body practically remains at rest.**

- In an elastic collision, the kinetic energy conservation holds only after the collision is over. **It does not hold during the short duration of actual collision.**
- At the time of collision, the two colliding objects are deformed and may be momentarily at rest with respect to each other.
- **If the initial velocities and final velocities of both the bodies are along the same straight line, then it is called a one-dimensional collision or head-on collision.**

Example 20. Two ball bearings of mass *m* each moving in opposite directions with equal speed collide head-on with each other. Predict the outcome of the collision, assuming it to be perfectly elastic.

Sol. Here, $m_1 = m_2 = m$ (say)

$$u_1 = v, u_2 = -v$$

We have taken $u_1 = v$ and $u_2 = -v$ because both the ball bearings moving with same velocity but in opposite directions.

As the collision is perfectly elastic, velocities after the collision will be

$$v_1 = \frac{m_1 - m_2}{m_1 + m_2} \cdot u_1 + \frac{2m_2}{m_1 + m_2} \cdot u_2$$

$$= \frac{m - m}{m + m} \cdot v + \frac{2m}{m + m}(-v) = 0 - v = -v$$

$$v_2 = \frac{2m_1}{m_1 + m_2} \cdot u_1 + \frac{m_2 - m_1}{m_1 + m_2} \cdot u_2$$

$$= \frac{2m}{m + m} \cdot v + \frac{m - m}{m + m} \cdot (-v) = v + 0 = v$$

Thus, the two balls bounce back with equal speed after the collision.

Example 21. In a nuclear reactor, a neutron of high speed (typically 10^7 ms^{-1}) must be slowed to 10^3 ms^{-1} so that it can have a high probability of interacting with isotope $^{325}_{92}U$ and causing it to fission. Show that a neutron can lose most of its kinetic energy in an elastic collision with a light nucleus like deuterium or carbon which has a mass of only a few times the neutron mass. The material making up the light nuclei, usually heavy water (D_2O) or graphite is called a moderator. NCERT

Sol. Here, m_1 = mass of neutron = m

m_2 = mass of target nucleus = M

$u_1 = u$ and $u_2 = 0$

Now, $v_2 = \frac{2m_1}{m_1 + m_2} \cdot u_1 + \frac{m_2 - m_2}{m_1 + m_2} \cdot u_2$

$$= \frac{2m}{m+M} \cdot u + 0 = \frac{2mu}{m+M}$$

Initial KE of mass m, $K_1 = \frac{1}{2} m_1 u_1^2 = \frac{1}{2} mu^2$

Final KE of mass M,

$$K_2 = \frac{1}{2} m_2 v_2^2 = \frac{1}{2} M \left(\frac{2mu}{m+M} \right)^2 = \frac{2Mm^2u^2}{(m+M)^2}$$

Fraction of the initial KE transferred,

$$f = \frac{K_2}{K_1} = \frac{2Mm^2u^2}{(m+M)^2} \times \frac{2}{mu^2} = \frac{4mM}{(m+M)^2}$$

(i) For deuterium, $M = 2m$, therefore

$$f = \frac{4m \times 2m}{(m+2m)^2} = \frac{8}{9} \simeq 0.9$$

About 90% of the neutron's energy is transferred to deuterium.

(ii) For carbon, $M = 12m$, therefore

$$f = \frac{4m \times 12\,m}{(m+12m)^2} = 0.284$$

About 28.4% of the neutron's energy is transferred to carbon.

Perfectly Inelastic Collision in One Dimension

When the two colliding bodies stick together and move as a single body with a common velocity after the collision, then the collision is **perfectly inelastic.**

As shown in figure, perfectly inelastic collision between two bodies of masses m_1 and m_2. The body of mass m_2 happens to be initially at rest ($u_2 = 0$). After the collision, the two bodies move together with common velocity v.

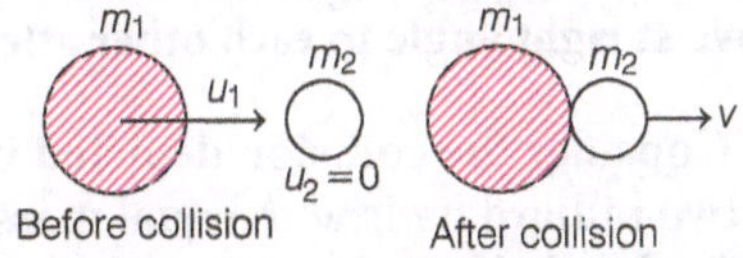

Perfectly inelastic collision

As the total linear momentum of the system remains constant, therefore $p_i = p_f$

i.e. $$m_1u_1 + m_2u_2 = (m_1 + m_2)v$$

$\therefore$ $$v = \frac{m_1u_1}{m_1 + m_2} \quad [\because u_2 = 0]$$

Total KE before collision,

$$E_1 = \frac{1}{2} m_1 u_1^2 + \frac{1}{2} m_2 u_2^2 \quad \text{...(i)}$$

$$E_1 = \frac{1}{2} m_1 u_1^2 \quad [\because u_2 = 0]$$

Total KE after collision,

$$E_2 = \frac{1}{2}(m_1 + m_2)v^2 \quad \text{...(ii)}$$

On putting the value of v in Eq. (ii), we get

$$E_2 = \frac{1}{2}(m_1 + m_2)\left[\frac{m_1u_1}{m_1 + m_2}\right]^2$$

$$= \frac{1}{2} \frac{m_1^2 u_1^2}{(m_1 + m_2)}$$

$$\text{Loss of KE} = E_1 - E_2 = \frac{1}{2} m_1 u_1^2 - \frac{m_1^2 u_1^2}{2(m_1 + m_2)}$$

$$\Delta \text{KE} = \frac{1}{2} m_1 u_1^2 \left[1 - \frac{m_1}{m_1 + m_2}\right] = \frac{1}{2} \frac{m_1 m_2}{m_1 + m_2} u_1^2$$

$$\Delta \text{KE} = \frac{m_1^2 u_1^2 + m_1 m_2 u_1^2 - m_1^2 u_1^2}{2(m_1 + m_2)} = \frac{m_1 m_2 (u_1 - u_2)^2}{2(m_1 + m_2)}$$

$\therefore$ ΔKE is a positive quantity.

Therefore, kinetic energy is lost mainly in the form of light, sound and heat.

Example 22. **A railway carriage of mass 9000 kg moving with a speed of 36 km/h collides with a stationary carriage of the same mass. After the collision, the carriages get coupled and move together. What is their common speed after collision? What type of collision is this ?**

Sol. Given, $m_1 = 9000 \text{ kg}$, $u_1 = 36 \text{ km/h} = 36 \times \frac{5}{18} = 10 \text{ m/s}$

$$m_2 = 9000 \text{ kg}, u_2 = 0, v_1 = v_2 = v$$

By conservation of momentum

$$m_1u_1 + m_2u_2 = (m_1 + m_2)v$$

$$9000 \times 10 + 9000 \times 0 = (9000 + 9000)v$$

or $$v = \frac{90000}{18000} = 5 \text{ m/s}$$

$$\text{Total KE before collision} = \frac{1}{2} m_1 u_1^2 + \frac{1}{2} m_2 u_2^2$$

$$= \frac{1}{2} \times 9000 \times 10 \times 10 + 0$$

$$= 450000 \text{ J}$$

$$\text{Total KE after collision} = \frac{1}{2}(m_1 + m_2)v^2$$

$$= \frac{1}{2} \times 2 \times 9000 \times (5)^2$$

$$= 225000$$

Thus, total KE after collision < total KE before collision

Hence, the collision is inelastic.

Elastic Collision in Two Dimensions or Oblique Collision

Consider two objects A and B of masses m_1 and m_2 kept on the X-axis as shown in figure. Initially, the object B is at rest and A moves towards B with a speed u_1.

Suppose the object A moves with a velocity $\mathbf{v}_1$ making an angle θ with the X-axis and the object B moves with a velocity $\mathbf{v}_2$ making an angle ϕ with the same axis as shown in figure.

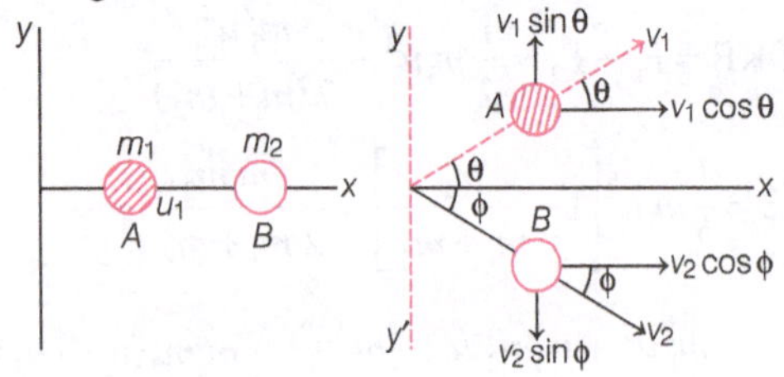

Elastic collision in two dimensions

Also, suppose $\mathbf{v}_1$ and $\mathbf{v}_2$ lie in XY-plane. Using conservation of momentum in x and y-directions, we get

$$m_1 u_1 = m_1 v_1 \cos\theta + m_2 v_2 \cos\phi \qquad [\because u_2 = 0] \quad \ldots(i)$$

$\because$ The initial momentum of m_1 and m_2 along Y-axis is zero, then

$$0 = m_1 v_1 \sin\theta - m_2 v_2 \sin\phi \qquad \ldots(ii)$$

If the collision is elastic, the final kinetic energy is equal to the initial kinetic energy. Thus,

$$KE_i = KE_f$$

$$\frac{1}{2} m_1 u_1^2 = \frac{1}{2} m_1 v_1^2 + \frac{1}{2} m_2 v_2^2$$

or

$$m_1 u_1^2 = m_1 v_1^2 + m_2 v_2^2 \qquad \ldots(iii)$$

The four unknown quantities v_1, v_2, θ and ϕ cannot be calculated by using the three equations (i), (ii) and (iii).

But by measuring one of the four unknowns, say θ experimentally. The value of other three unknowns can be solved.

The three cases can be considered as given below.

Case I **Glancing collision** For such collision, when $\theta \simeq 0°$ and $\phi \simeq 90°$ the incident particle does not lose any kinetic energy and is scattered almost undeflected.

From Eqs. (i) and (ii), we get

$$u_1 = v_1 \text{ and } v_2 = 0$$

$$\text{KE of the target particle} = \frac{1}{2} m_2 v_2^2 = 0$$

Case II **Head-on collision** In this type of collision, the target particle moves in the direction of the incident particle, i.e. $\phi = 0°$. Then, Eqs. (i) and (ii), become

$$m_1 u_1 = m_1 v_1 \cos\theta + m_2 v_2 \text{ and } 0 = m_1 v_1 \sin\theta$$

Eq. (iii) for the kinetic energy remains unchanged.

Case III **Elastic collision of two identical particles** When two particles of same mass undergo perfectly elastic collision in two dimensions, i.e. $m_1 = m_2$.

Let us take $u_1 = u$

From Eq. (iii), $v_1^2 + v_2^2 = u^2$ ...(iv)

From Eq.(i) $v_1 \cos\theta + v_2 \cos\phi = u$ ...(v)

From Eq. (ii), $v_1 \sin\theta - v_2 \sin\phi = 0$ ...(vi)

Using Eq. (v) values, we obtain from Eq.(iv)

$$v_1^2 \sin^2\theta + v_2^2 \sin^2\phi = 2v_1 v_2 \cos\theta\cos\phi \qquad \ldots(vii)$$

From Eq. (vi), $v_2 \sin\phi = v_1 \sin\theta$

Put in Eq. (vii), $2v_1^2 \sin^2\theta = 2v_1 v_2 \cos\theta\cos\phi$

$$\text{or } \cos\theta = \frac{2v_1^2 \sin^2\theta}{2v_1 v_2 \cos\phi} = \left[\frac{v_1}{v_2}\right] \times \frac{\sin^2\theta}{\cos\phi} \qquad \ldots(viii)$$

We know $\cos(\theta + \phi) = \cos\theta\cos\phi - \sin\theta\sin\phi$

Using Eq. (viii) and Eq. (vi), we get

$$\cos(\theta + \phi) = \frac{v_1 \sin^2\theta}{v_2 \cos\phi}\cos\phi - \frac{v_1}{v_2}\sin^2\theta = 0$$

$$\therefore \quad \theta + \phi = 90°$$

Hence, we conclude that in a **perfectly elastic collision, when a moving particle of mass *m* collides elastically in two dimensions with another particle of mass *m*, the two particles move at right angle to each other after collision.**

Example 23. Consider the collision depicted in figure to be between two billiard balls with equal masses $m_1 = m_2$. The first ball is called the cue while the second ball is called the target. The billiard player wants to sink the target ball in a corner pocket, which is at an angle $\theta_2 = 37°$. Assume that the collision is elastic and that friction and rotational motion are not important. Obtain θ_1. NCERT

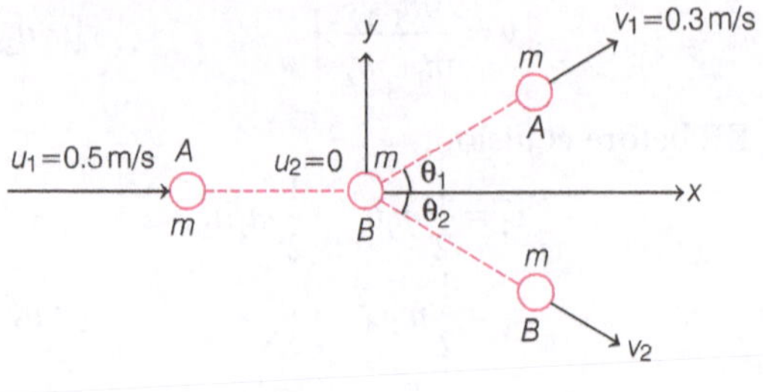

Sol. By conservation of momentum, we have

$$m\mathbf{u}_1 + 0 = m\mathbf{v}_1 + m\mathbf{v}_2$$

or $$\mathbf{u}_1 = \mathbf{v}_1 + \mathbf{v}_2 \quad \text{...(i)}$$

By conservation of energy, we have

$$\frac{1}{2}mu_1^2 = \frac{1}{2}mv_1^2 + \frac{1}{2}mv_2^2$$

or $$u_1^2 = v_1^2 + v_2^2 \quad \text{...(ii)}$$

From Eq. (i), we have

$$\mathbf{u}_1 \cdot \mathbf{u}_1 = (\mathbf{v}_1 + \mathbf{v}_2)\cdot(\mathbf{v}_1 + \mathbf{v}_2)$$
$$= \mathbf{v}_1\cdot\mathbf{v}_1 + \mathbf{v}_1\cdot\mathbf{v}_2 + \mathbf{v}_2\cdot\mathbf{v}_1 + \mathbf{v}_2\cdot\mathbf{v}_2$$
$$u_1^2 = v_1^2 + v_2^2 + 2\mathbf{v}_1\cdot\mathbf{v}_2$$
$$u_1^2 = u_1^2 + 2\mathbf{v}_1\cdot\mathbf{v}_2 \quad \text{[using Eq. (ii)]}$$
$$\mathbf{v}_1\cdot\mathbf{v}_2 = 0$$

Thus, the angle between $\mathbf{v}_1$ and $\mathbf{v}_2$ is 90°.

$$\theta_1 + \theta_2 = 90°$$

$\therefore$ $$\theta_1 = 90° - \theta_2 = 90 - 37° = 53°$$

Inelastic Collision in Two Dimensions

Inelastic collision takes place when two bodies travelling initially along the same straight line collide involving some loss of kinetic energy and move after collision along different directions in a plane.

Example 24. A ball moving with a speed of 9 m/s strikes an identical ball at rest, such that after collision, the direction of each ball makes an angle of 30° with the original line of motion. Find the speed of the two balls after collision.

Sol. Given, $m_1 = m_2 = m$, $u_1 = 9$ m/s, $u_2 = 0$

$$\theta_1 = \theta_2 = 30°, v_1 = ?, v_2 = ?$$

According to principle of conservation of linear momentum.

$$m_1u_1 + m_2u_2 = m_1v_1\cos\theta_1 + m_2v_2\cos\theta_2$$

Along the direction of motion in X-axis

$$m\times 9 + 0 = mv_1\cos 30° + mv_2\cos 30°$$
$$9 = v_1\frac{\sqrt{3}}{2} + v_2\frac{\sqrt{3}}{2} = \frac{(v_1+v_2)\sqrt{3}}{2}$$
$$v_1 + v_2 = \frac{18}{\sqrt{3}} \quad \text{...(i)}$$

Along a direction of motion in Y-axis

$$0 + 0 = m_1v_1\sin\theta_1 - m_2v_2\sin\theta_2$$

$\Rightarrow$ $m_1v_1\sin\theta_1 = m_2v_2\sin\theta_2$

$\Rightarrow$ $mv_1\sin 30° = mv_2\sin 30°$

$\Rightarrow$ $$v_1 = v_2 \quad \text{...(ii)}$$

Substituting value from Eq. (ii) in Eq. (i), then find out values of v_1 and v_2

$$2v_1 = \frac{18}{\sqrt{3}}$$

$\Rightarrow$ $$v_1 = \frac{9}{\sqrt{3}}\times\frac{\sqrt{3}}{\sqrt{3}}$$
$$= \frac{9\sqrt{3}}{3} = 3\sqrt{3}\text{ m/s}$$

Hence, two balls move with same velocity = $3\sqrt{3}$ m/s after collision.

Coefficient of Restitution or Coefficient of Resilience

It is defined as the ratio of relative velocity of separation after collision to the relative velocity of approach before collision. It is denoted by e.

$$e = \left|\frac{\text{Relative velocity of separation (after collision)}}{\text{Relative velocity of approach (before collision)}}\right|$$

$$e = \frac{|v_2 - v_1|}{|u_1 - u_2|} = \frac{v_2 - v_1}{u_1 - u_2}$$

Coefficient of resilience, $e = \dfrac{v_2 - v_1}{u_1 - u_2}$

where u_1, u_2 are velocities of two bodies before collision and v_1, v_2 are their respective velocities after collision.

- The value of e depends on the materials of the colliding bodies.
  For a perfectly elastic collision $e = 1$
  For a perfectly inelastic collision $e = 0$
- For all other collisions, e lies between 0 and 1, i.e. $0<e<1$

Rebouncing of a Ball

If a ball is dropped from certain height h, then it rebounds from a floor as shown in figure.

Rebouncing of a Ball

So, height attained after n impacts is $\boldsymbol{h_n = e^{2n}h}$. Then, total distance travelled before the body comes to rest is

$s = h\left(\dfrac{1+e^2}{1-e^2}\right)$, where e is coefficient of restitution.

Different Types of Collisions

Collision	Kinetic energy	Coefficient of restitution (e)	Main domain
Elastic	Conserved	$e=1$	Between atomic particles
Inelastic	Not conserved	$0<e<1$	Between ordinary objects
Perfectly inelastic	Maximum loss of KE	$e=0$	During Shooting
Super elastic	KE increases	$e>1$	In explosions

Example 24. **A sphere of mass m moving with a velocity u hits another stationary sphere of same mass. What will be the ratio of the velocities of two spheres after the collision. Take e as the coefficient of restitution.**

Sol. Here, $u_1 = u, u_2 = 0$

$$\therefore \quad e = \frac{v_2 - v_1}{u_1 - u_2} = \frac{v_2 - v_1}{u - 0}$$

or $\quad v_2 - v_1 = eu \quad$ ...(i)

According to the law of conservation of momentum, we have

$$mu + m \times 0 = mv_1 + mv_2$$

or $\quad v_1 + v_2 = u \quad$ ...(ii)

On adding Eqs. (i) and (ii), we get

$$2v_2 = u + eu = u(1+e)$$

or $\quad v_2 = \dfrac{u(1+e)}{2} \quad$ ...(iii)

Substituting the value of v_2 in Eq. (ii), we have

$$v_1 = u - v_2 = u - \frac{u(1+e)}{2} = \frac{u(1-e)}{2} \quad \text{...(iv)}$$

Dividing Eq. (iii) by Eq. (iv)

Hence, $\quad \dfrac{v_2}{v_1} = \dfrac{1+e}{1-e}$

Quick Test 3

Conceptual Questions

1. If the momentum and total energy is conserved, then define the collision occurred?
2. Is the total linear momentum conserved during the short time of an elastic collision of two balls ?
3. What is the loss in kinetic energy after collision, if the target body is initially at rest?
4. Fast moving neutrons can be quickly slowed down when passed through water or heavy water, explain why ?

Numerical Questions

5. A pump on the ground floor of a building can pump up water to fill a tank of volume 30 m^3 in 15 min. If the tank is 40 m above the ground and the efficiency of the pump is 30%, then how much electric power is consumed by the pump? NCERT
6. A synchronous motor is used to lift an elevator and its load of 1500 kg to a height of 20 m. The time taken for job is 20 s. What is work done? What is the rate at which work is done? If the efficiency of the motor is 75%, at which rate is the energy supplied to the motor?
7. A particle of mass 1 kg moving with a velocity $\mathbf{v}_1 = (3\hat{\mathbf{i}} - 2\hat{\mathbf{j}})$ m/s experience a perfectly inelastic collision with another particle of mass 2 kg having velocity $\mathbf{v}_2 = (4\hat{\mathbf{j}} - 6\hat{\mathbf{k}})$ m/s. Find the velocity and speed of the particle formed.
8. A trolley of mass 200 kg moves with a uniform speed of 36 km/h on a frictionless track. A child of mass 20 kg runs on the trolley from one end to the other (10 m away) with a speed of 4 ms^{-1} relative to the trolley in a direction opposite to its motion, and jumps out of the trolley. What is the final speed of the trolley? How much has the trolley moved from the time the child begins to run? NCERT

Answers

5. 43.57 kW
6. 2.94×10^5 J, 1.47×10^4 W, 1.96×10^4 W
7. $(\hat{\mathbf{i}} + 2\hat{\mathbf{j}} - 4\hat{\mathbf{k}})$ m/s, $\sqrt{21}$ m/s
8. 10.36 ms^{-1}, 25.9 m

For Solutions, See QR Code on Pg. 190

Mind Map

Work, Energy and Power

Work

If a force applied on a body displaces it, then the work is said to be done.

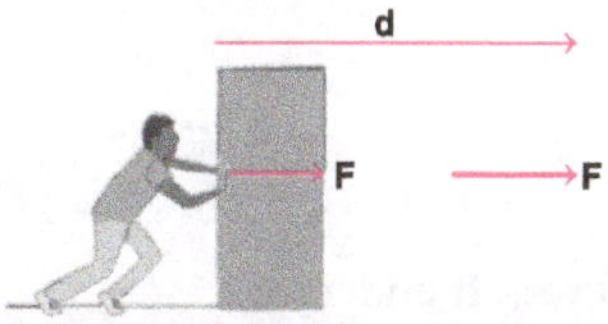

Work Done by Constant Force

When a force F acts on an object over a displacement d in a straight line and the force is constant, the work done is calculated as,

$W = \mathbf{F} \cdot \mathbf{s} \Rightarrow Fs \cos\theta$

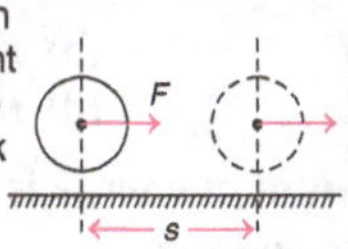

(i) If $\theta = 0°$, $W = Fs \cos 0° = Fs$

(ii) If $\theta = 90°$; $W = Fs \cos 90° = 0$

(iii) If $\theta = 180°$; $W = Fs \cos 180° = -Fs$

Work done by a Variable Force

Let a variable force F acts on a body along the fixed direction, say X-axis.

The magnitude of force F depends on x.

- The work done is $\Delta W = F(x)\,\Delta x$ = Area of rectangle $abcd$
- $W_{x_i - x_f}$ = Area under the F-x curve

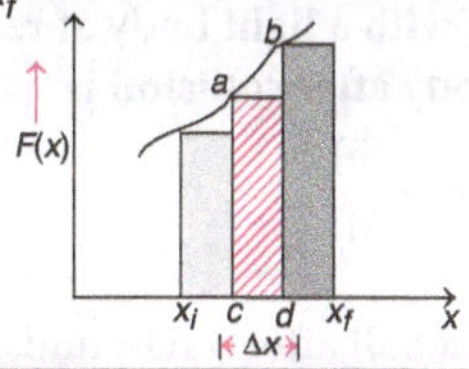

Nature of Positive Work Done

- When applied force and displacement has same direction, then the work is said to be positive work.
- When θ is acute, then $\cos\theta$ is positive $0 \le \theta < 90°$.
- Work done (W) $= Fs \cos\theta$ = Positive

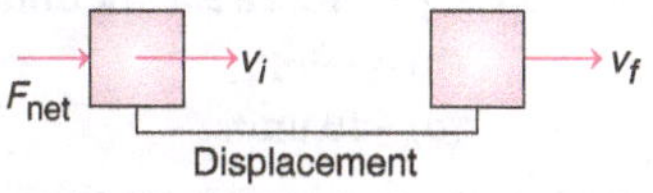

Nature of Negative Work Done

- When force applied and displacement has opposite direction, then it is said to be negative work.
- When θ is obtuse, then $\cos\theta$ is negative, i.e. $90° < \theta < 180°$.

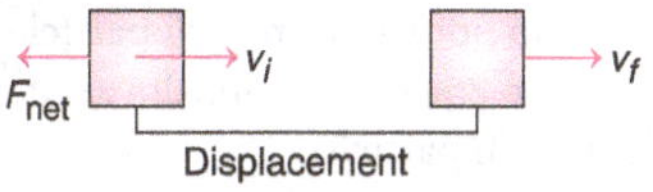

Energy

- The energy of a body is defined as its capacity for doing work.
- It is a scalar quantity.
- Its dimensional formula is $[ML^2T^{-2}]$.
- It is measured in the same units as work. i.e., joule in SI and erg in CGS system.

Potential Energy

- The energy possessed by the body by virtue of its position or configuration in same field.
- Dimensional formula of potential energy is $[ML^2T^{-2}]$.
- The SI unit of potential energy is joule (J).

Kinetic Energy

- The energy possessed by a body by virtue of its motion is called kinetic energy.

  i.e. $KE = \frac{1}{2} mv^2$
- **Relation between kinetic energy and linear momentum**

  Linear momentum, $p = \sqrt{2mKE}$

Work-Energy Theorem

- **For constant force**

  We use the equation of motion, $v^2 - u^2 = 2as$

  or $\frac{1}{2} mv^2 - \frac{1}{2} mu^2 = W$ or $K_f - K_i = W$
- **For variable force**

  Variable force acts on a body of mass m and produce displacement in its own direction ($\theta = 0°$), then small work done,

  i.e. Change in kinetic energy,

Conservation of Mechanical Energy

- If only the conservative forces are doing work on a body, then its mechanical energy (KE + PE) remains constant.

Zero Work

If a body gets displaced in the direction perpendicular to the direction of the applied force.

Work done (W) $= Fs \cos 90°$ $= 0$

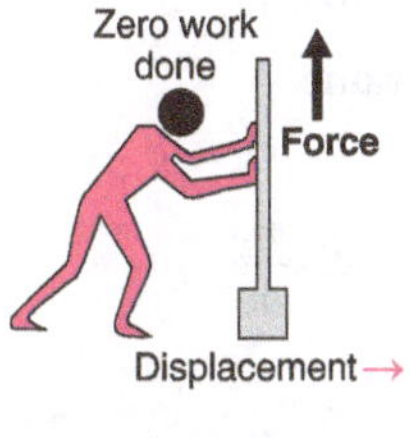

Power

- The rate of doing work is called the power.

Average power (P_{av}) = Rate of doing work.

$P_{av} = \frac{W}{t} \Rightarrow P_{av} = \frac{dW}{dt} = F \cdot \frac{ds}{dt} = \mathbf{F} \cdot \mathbf{v}$

Instantaneous power

- Power is a scalar quantity.
- The dimensional formula of power is $[ML^2T^{-3}]$.
- SI unit of power is watt (W)
- 1 horse power = 746 W

Collision

- Collision between two bodies is defined as mutual interaction of the bodies for a short interval of time as a result of which the energy and momentum of the interacting bodies change.
- **Elastic Collision** Those collisions, in which both momentum and kinetic energy of the system are conserved are called elastic collisions.
- **Inelastic Collision** Those collisions, in which the momentum of the system is conserved but the kinetic energy is not conserved are called inelastic collisions.
- **Perfectly Inelastic Collision** Those collisions, in which the colliding bodies stick together after the collision and then move with a common velocity are called perfectly inelastic collision.

Elastic Collision in One Dimension

- Consider two perfectly elastic bodies A and B of masses M_1 and M_2 moving along the same straight line with velocities u_1 and u_2 respectively.
- If velocity of A is greater than B i.e., $u_1 > u_2$, then two bodies collides.

$$\frac{1}{2} M_1 u_1^2 + \frac{1}{2} M_2 u_2^2 = \frac{1}{2} M_1 v_1^2 + \frac{1}{2} M_2 v_2^2$$

In this type of collision, both momentum and kinetic energy are conserved and the colliding bodies continue to move along the same straight line after collision.

$$v_1 = \frac{(m_1 - m_2)\,u_1 + 2m_2u_2}{m_1 + m_2}, \quad v_2 = \frac{(m_2 - m_1)\,u_2 + 2m_1u_1}{m_1 + m_2}$$

Freely Falling Body

- The mechanical energy of a freely falling body remains constant at all positions.

  $E_A = E_B = E_C$ = Constant

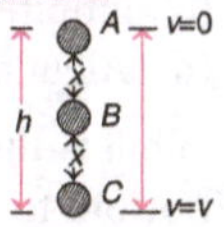

Conservation of Energy in an Elastic Spring

- The kinetic energy is converted to potential energy and *vice-versa*. However, the total mechanical energy remains constant.

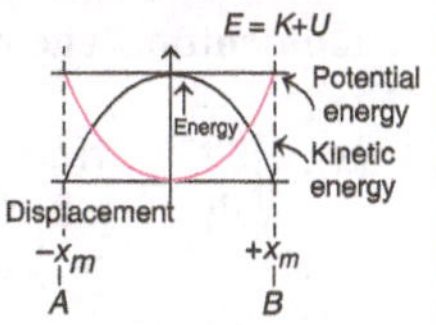

EXAM PATTERN QUESTIONS

Objective Type Questions

Multiple Choice Questions (MCQs)

1. **The earth, moving around the sun in a circular orbit, is acted upon by a force and hence work done on the earth by the force is**

(a) zero (b) positive
(c) negative (d) None of these

2. **A force $F = -k/x^2$ $(x \neq 0)$ acts on a particle in x-direction. Find the work done by the force in displacing the particle from $x = -a$ to $x = 2a$.**

(a) $3k/2a$ (b) $4k/a^2$
(c) $-3k/2a^2$ (d) $\frac{-9k}{a^2}$

3. **A force of 10 N is applied on an object of mass 2 kg placed on a rough surface having coefficient of friction equal to 0.2. Work done by applied force in 4 s is**

(a) 120 J (b) 240 J
(c) 250 J (d) 100 J

4. **A man squatting on the ground gets straight up and stands. The force of reaction of ground on the man during the process is** NCERT Exemplar

(a) constant and equal to mg in magnitude
(b) constant and greater than mg in magnitude
(c) variable but always greater than mg
(d) at first greater than mg and later becomes equal to mg

5. **The potential energy, i.e., $U(x)$ can be assumed zero when**

(a) $x = 0$
(b) gravitational force is constant
(c) infinite distance from the gravitational source
(d) All of the above

6. **What is the ratio of kinetic energy of a particle at the bottom to the kinetic energy at the top when it just loops a vertical loop of radius r?**

(a) 5:1 (b) 2:3 (c) 5:2 (d) 7:2

7. **Two bodies of masses m_1 and m_2 have same momentum. The ratio of their KE is**

(a) $\sqrt{\frac{m_2}{m_1}}$ (b) $\sqrt{\frac{m_1}{m_2}}$ (c) $\frac{m_1}{m_2}$ (d) $\frac{m_2}{m_1}$

8. **A body is initially at rest. It undergoes one-dimensional motion with constant acceleration. The power delivered to it at time t is proportional to** NCERT

(a) $t^{1/2}$ (b) t
(c) $t^{3/2}$ (d) t^2

9. **How much amount of energy is liberated to convert 1 kg of coal into energy?**

(a) 9×10^{16} J (b) 9×10^{15} J
(c) 3×10^{14} J (d) 4×10^{6} J

10. **In a hydroelectric power station, the water is flowing at $2\ ms^{-1}$ in the river which is 100 m wide and 5 m deep. The maximum power output from the river is**

(a) 1.5 MW (b) 2 MW
(c) 2.5 MW (d) 3 MW

11. **In a head-on elastic collision of a very heavy body moving with velocity v with a light body at rest. Then, the velocity of heavy body after collision is**

(a) v (b) $2v$
(c) zero (d) $\frac{v}{2}$

12. **The height attained by a ball after 3 rebounds on falling from a height of h on floor having coefficient of restitution e is**

(a) e^3h (b) e^4h
(c) e^5h (d) e^6h

13. **A particle is pushed by forces $2\hat{i} + 3\hat{j} - 2\hat{k}$ and $5\hat{i} - \hat{j} - 3\hat{k}$ simultaneously and it is displaced from point $\hat{i} + \hat{j} + \hat{k}$ to point $2\hat{i} - \hat{j} + 3\hat{k}$. The work done is**

(a) 7 units (b) −7 units
(c) 10 units (d) −10 units

14. **An electron and a proton are moving under the influence of mutual forces. In calculating the change in the kinetic energy of the system during motion, one ignores the magnetic force of one on another. This is because** NCERT Exemplar

(a) the two magnetic forces are equal and opposite, so they produce no net effect
(b) the magnetic forces do not work on each particle
(c) the magnetic forces do equal and opposite (but non-zero) work on each particle
(d) the magnetic forces are necessarily negligible

15. A body of mass 0.5 kg travels in a straight line by applying a force, $F = m\frac{3}{2}a^2x^2$, where $a = 5\ m^{-1/2}s^{-1}$. The work done by the net force during its displacement from $x = 0$ to $x = 2$ m is **NCERT Exemplar**

(a) 1.5 J (b) 50 J (c) 10 J (d) 100 J

16. A bicyclist comes to a skidding stop in 10 m. During this process, the force on the bicycle due to the road is 200 N and is directly opposed to the motion. The work done by the cycle on the road is **NCERT Exemplar**

(a) +2000J (b) – 200J
(c) zero (d) – 20 000J

17. A force $\mathbf{F} = 5\hat{i} + 6\hat{j} - 4\hat{k}$ acting on a body produces a displacement $\mathbf{s} = 6\hat{i} + 5\hat{k}$. The work done by the force is

(a) 18 units (b) 15 units
(c) 12 units (d) 10 units

18. Which of the diagrams shown in figure most closely shows the variation in kinetic energy of the earth as it moves once around the sun in its elliptical orbit? **NCERT Exemplar; Competency Based Que.**

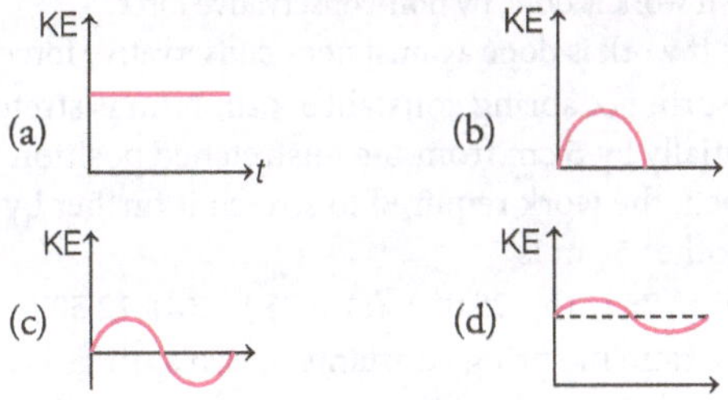

19. Which of the diagrams in figure correctly shows the change in kinetic energy of an iron sphere falling freely in a lake having sufficient depth to impart it a terminal velocity? **NCERT Exemplar**

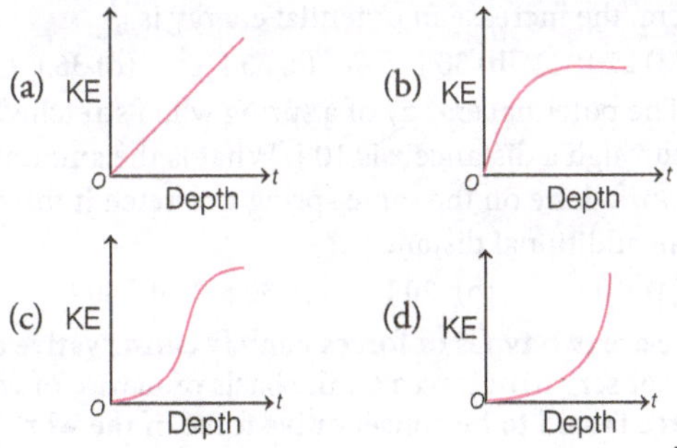

20. A body is falling freely under the action of gravity alone in vaccum. Which of the following quantities remain constant during the fall? **NCERT Exemplar**

(a) Kinetic energy
(b) Potential energy
(c) Total mechanical energy
(d) Total linear momentum

21. A raindrop falling from a height *h* above ground, attains a near terminal velocity when it has fallen through a height (3/4)*h*. Which of the diagrams shown in figure correctly shows the change in kinetic and potential energies of the drop during its fall up to the ground? **NCERT Exemplar, Competency Based Que.**

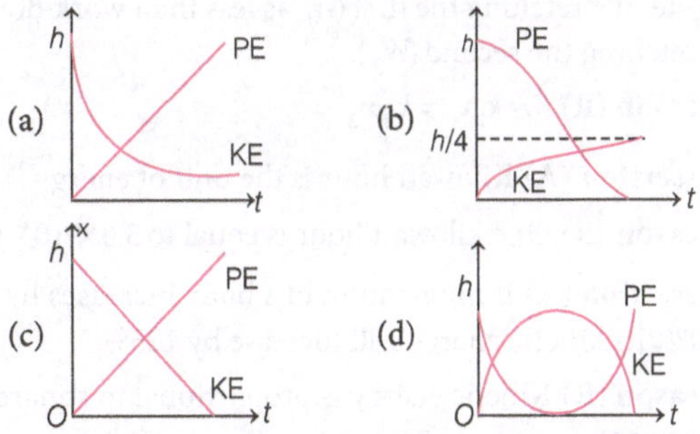

22. Match the Column I (different situation given) with Column II (graph of kinetic energy) and choose the correct option.

	Column I		Column II
A.	A ball is thrown in air at some angle θ.	P.	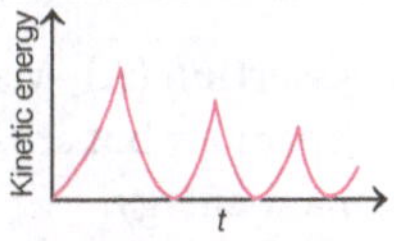
B.	A bouncing ball	Q.	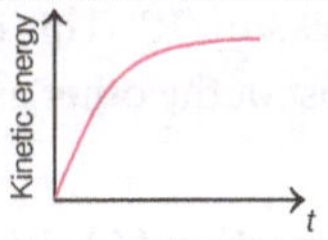
C.	A ball falling in a viscous liquid.	R.	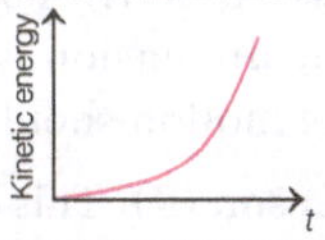
D.	A ball is falling in air under the effect of gravity.	S.	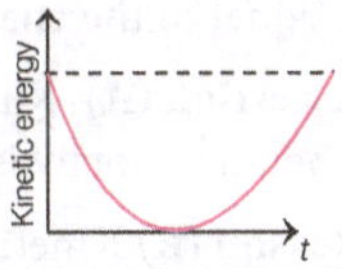

(a) A → P, B → R, C → Q, D → S
(b) A → R, B → P, C → Q, D → S
(c) A → S, B → P, C → Q, D → R
(d) A → S, B → Q, C → R, D → P

Assertion-Reason

Directions *(Q.No. 23-32) In the following questions, two statements are given- one labelled Assertion (A) and the other labelled Reason (R). Select the correct answer to these questions from the codes (a), (b), (c) and (d) as given below.*

(a) Both Assertion and Reason are true and Reason is the correct explanation of Assertion.

(b) Both Assertion and Reason are true but Reason is not the correct explanation of Assertion.
(c) Assertion is true but Reason is false.
(d) Assertion is false but Reason is true.

23. **Assertion (A)** Two springs of force constants k_1 and k_2 are stretched by the same force. If $k_1 > k_2$, then work done in stretching the first (W_1) is less than work done in stretching the second (W_2).

Reason (R) $F = k_1x_1 = k_2x_2$

24. **Assertion (A)** Kilowatt hour is the unit of energy.

Reason (R) One kilowatt hour is equal to 3.6×10^8 J.

25. **Assertion (A)** If momentum of a body increases by 50%, its kinetic energy will increase by 125%.

Reason (R) Kinetic energy is proportional to square of velocity.

26. **Assertion (A)** Stopping distance $= \dfrac{\text{Kinetic energy}}{\text{Stopping force}}$

Reason (R) Work done in stopping a body is equal to change in kinetic energy of the body.

27. **Assertion (A)** Mass and energy are not conserved separately but are conserved as a single entity called mass-energy.

Reason (R) This is because one can be obtained at the cost of the other as per Einstein's equation,

$$E = mc^2$$

28. **Assertion (A)** Force applied on a block moving in one dimension is producing a constant power, then the motion should be uniformly accelerated.

Reason (R) This constant power multiplied with time is equal to the change in kinetic energy.

29. **Assertion (A)** Kinetic energy of a body is quadrupled, when its velocity is doubled.

Reason (R) Kinetic energy is proportional to square of velocity. If velocity is doubled the KE will be quadrupled.

30. **Assertion (A)** If the velocity of a body is tripled, then KE becomes 9 times.

Reason (R) Kinetic energy, KE $= mv^2/2$

31. **Assertion (A)** A spring has potential energy, both when it is compressed or stretched.

Reason (R) In compressing or stretching, work is done on the spring against the restoring force.

32. **Assertion (A)** The change in kinetic energy of a particle is equal to the work done on it by the net force.

Reason (R) Change in kinetic energy of particle is equal to work done only in case of a system of one particle.

Case Based Questions

Directions *(Q.Nos. 33-35) These questions are case study based questions. Read the following paragraph and answer the questions on the basis of same.*

33. **There are many types of spring. Important among these are helical and spiral springs as shown in figure.**

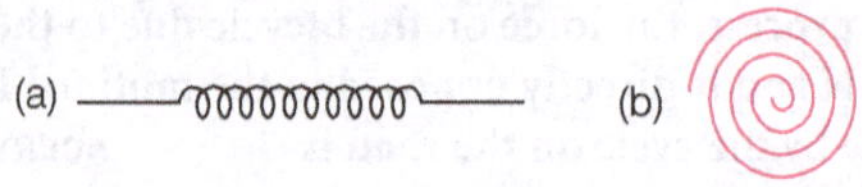

Usually, we assume that the springs are massless. Therefore, work done is stored in the spring in the form of elastic potential energy of the spring. Thus, potential energy of a spring is the energy associated with the state of compression or expansion of an elastic spring.

(i) The potential energy of a body increases in which of the following cases?
(a) If work is done by conservative force.
(b) If work is done against conservative force.
(c) If work is done by non-conservative force.
(d) If work is done against non- conservative force.

(ii) A spring of spring constant 5×10^3 N/m is stretched initially by 5 cm from the unstretched position. Then, the work required to stretch it further by another 5 cm is
(a) 18.75 J (b) 25.00 J (c) 6.25 J (d) 12.50 J

(iii) The ratio of spring constants of two springs is 2 : 3. What is the ratio of their potential energy, if they are stretched by the same force?
(a) 2 : 3 (b) 3 : 2 (c) 4 : 9 (d) 9 : 4

(iv) The potential energy of a spring increases by 15 J when stretched by 3 cm. If it is stretched by 4 cm, the increase in potential energy is
(a) 27 J (b) 30 J (c) 33 J (d) 36 J

(v) The potential energy of a spring when stretched through a distance x is 10 J. What is the amount of work done on the same spring to stretch it through an additional distance x?
(a) 10 J (b) 20 J (c) 30 J (d) 40 J

34. **There are two types of forces namely conservative and non-conservative forces on the basis of nature of work. A force is said to be conservative force, if the work done by this force in moving a body depends only upon initial and final position of the body and is independent of path followed between the initial and final positions. The negative of work done by conservative force give change in potential energy. A force is said to be non-conservative if the work done by this force in moving a body from one position to another, depends on the path followed between two positions. The work done by non-conservative forces**

appear in some other forms of energy like heat, sound, light energy, etc.

(i) A body is moving from point A to B and again comes to point A by an external agent under the effect of gravity. What is the work done by the weight of the body?

(ii) The graph of force-elongation (F-x) of a stretched spring is as shown below.

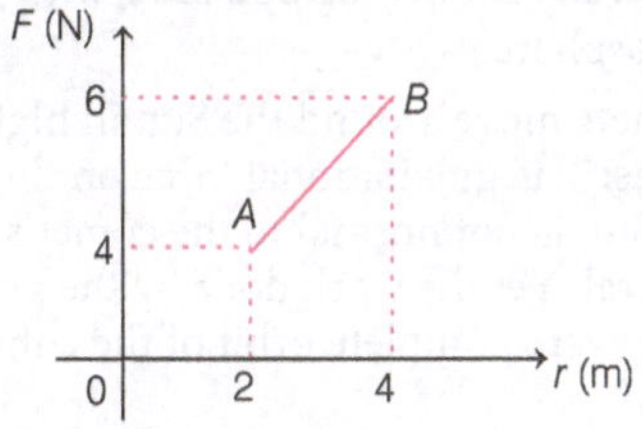

If the potential energy at point A is 22 J, then what is the potential energy at point B?

(iii) A spring is stretched to an elongation of x. Draw the graph of potential energy versus elongation of the spring.

(iv) A block is moved from one point to another point as shown in figure.

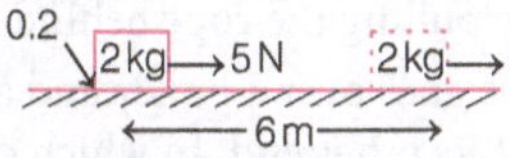

What is the heat produced (in J) between the surfaces of block and the ground?

35. **Collision between two bodies is said to occur when they physically strike against each other or if the path of motion of one is influenced by others. It is of two types namely elastic and inelastic collision. In elastic collision both kinetic energy and momentum is conserved. On the other hand, in inelastic collision, only momentum is conserved, but there is a loss of some kinetic energy.**

The degree of elasticity of a collision is determined by a physical quantity called coefficient of restitution (e). It is the ratio of velocity of separation after collision to velocity of approach before collision. For perfectly elastic collision, e = 1 and for inelastic collision, e = 0.

(i) What is the type of collision in which the two colliding bodies stick together and moves with common velocity?

(ii) Two bodies of masses 1 kg and 2 kg moves with initial velocity 5m/s and 3 m/s. If they are colliding with perfectly elastically. Find the velocities of the bodies.

(iii) Write the range of coefficient of restitution of real collision.

(iv) Name the collision in which the velocity of approach will be equal to velocity of separation of two colliding bodies.

Subjective Questions

Very Short Answer Type Questions

1. A rough inclined plane is placed on a cart moving with a constant velocity u on horizontal ground. A block of mass M rests on the incline. Is any work done by force of friction between the block and incline? Is there then a dissipation of energy? **NCERT Exemplar**

2. Why is electrical power required at all when the elevator is descending? Why should there be a limit on the number of passengers in this case? **NCERT Exemplar**

3. Is it possible for an individual to have

(i) more power and less energy **[1]**

(ii) less power and more energy? **[1]**

4. Two identical ball bearings in contact with each other and resting on a frictionless table are hit head-on by another ball bearing of the same mass moving initially with a speed v. If the collision is elastic, which of the following (figure) is a possible result after collision? **NCERT**

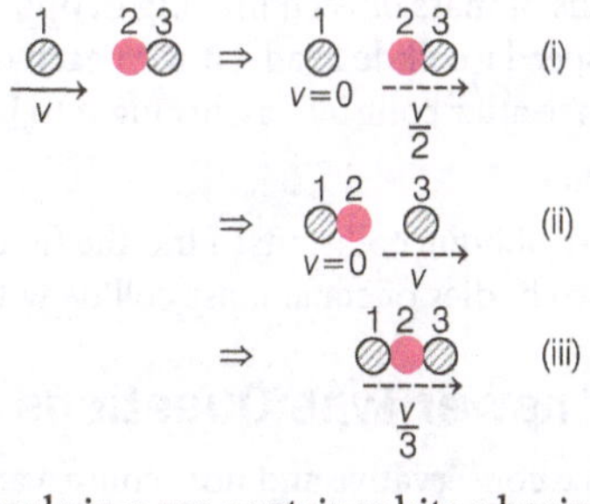

5. A molecule in a gas container hits a horizontal wall with speed 200 ms^{-1} and angle 30° with the normal, and rebounds with the same speed. Is momentum conserved in the collision? Is the collision elastic or inelastic? **NCERT**

Short Answer Type Questions

6. Underline the correct alternative.

(i) When a conservative force does positive work on a body, the potential energy of the body increases/decreases/remains unaltered. **[1]**

(ii) Work done by a body against friction always results in a loss of its kinetic/potential energy. [1]

(iii) The rate of change of total momentum of a many particle system is proportional to the external force/ sum of the internal forces on the system. [1]

7. Consider a one-dimensional motion of a particle with total energy *E*. There are four regions *A*, *B*, *C* and *D* in which the relation between potential energy (*V*), kinetic energy (*K*) and total energy (*E*) is as given below

Region A : $V > E$ **Region B :** $V < E$

Region C : $K > E$ **Region D :** $V > E$

State with reason in each case whether a particle can be found in the given region or not. **NCERT Examplar**

8. A rocket accelerates straight up by ejecting gas downwards. In a small time interval Δt, it ejects a gas of mass Δm at a relative speed u. Calculate KE of the entire system at $(t + \Delta t)$ and t and show that the device that ejects gas does work $=(1/2)\,\Delta m u^2$ in this time interval (negative gravity). **NCERT Exemplar, Competency Based Que.**

9. A family uses 8 kW of power. (i) Direct solar energy is incident on the horizontal surface at an average rate of 200 W per square metre. If 20% of this energy can be converted to useful electrical energy, how large an area is needed to supply 8 kW? (ii) Compare this area to that of the roof of a typical house.

10. Prove that instantaneous power is given by the scalar product of force and velocity.

11. Show that coefficient of restitution for one-dimensional elastic collision is equal to one.

12. Two balls of mass *m*, each moving in opposite direction with a speed *v* collide head-on with each other. How will they move after collision, assuming it to be perfectly elastic?

13. What are oblique collisions? Find the final velocities when two bodies of equal mass collide with each other.

Long Answer Type Questions

14. What is a conservative and non-conservative forces? Explain the properties of conservative and non conservative forces ?

15. The sign of work done by a force on a body is important to understand. State carefully if the following quantities are positive or negative.

(a) Work done by a man in lifting a bucket out of a well by means of a rope tied to the bucket. [1]

(b) Work done by gravitational force in the above case. [1]

(c) Work done by friction on a body sliding down an inclined plane. [1]

(d) Work done by an applied force on a body moving on a rough horizontal plane with uniform velocity. [1]

(e) Work done by the resistive force of air on a vibrating pendulum in bringing it to rest. **NCERT** [1]

16. Answer the following

(i) The casing of a rocket in flight burns up due to friction. At whose expense is the heat energy required for burning obtained, the rocket or the atmosphere? [1½]

(ii) Comets move around the Sun in highly elliptical orbits. The gravitational force on the comet due to the Sun is not normal to the comet's velocity in general. Yet the work done by the gravitational force over every complete orbit of the comet is zero. Why? [1½]

(iii) An artificial satellite orbiting the Earth in very thin atmosphere loses its energy gradually due to dissipation against atmospheric resistance, however small. Why does its speed increase progressively as it comes closer and closer to the earth? [1½]

(iv) In Fig. (a) the man walks 2 m carrying a mass of 15 kg on his hands. In Fig. (b) he walks the same distance pulling the rope behind him.
The rope goes over a pulley and a mass of 15 kg hangs at its other end. In which case is the work done greater? [1½]

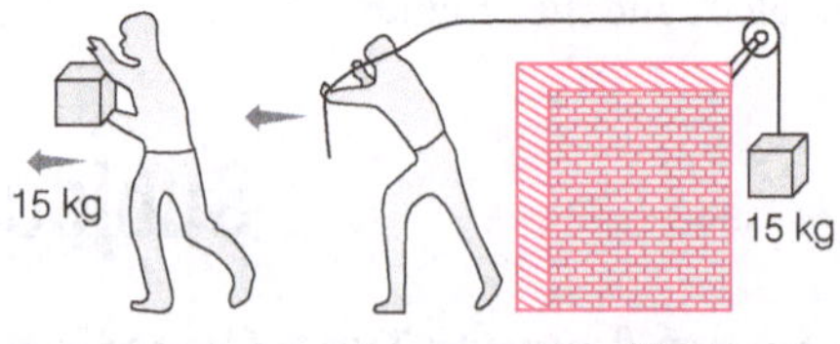

(a) (b)

NCERT

17. A graph of potential energy $V(x)$ *versus* x is shown in figure. A particle of energy E_0 is executing motion in it. Draw graph of velocity and kinetic energy *versus* x for one complete cycle *AFA*. **NCERT Exemplar**

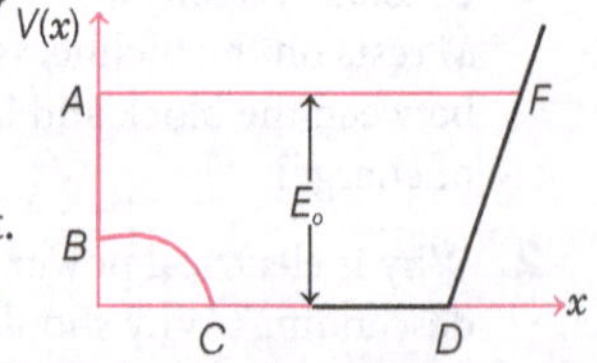

18. What are power, instantaneous power and average power? Write the dimensional formula and unit of power.

19. A rain drop of radius 2 mm falls from the height of 500 m above the ground. It falls with decreasing acceleration (due to viscous resistance of the air) until at half its original height, it attains its maximum (terminal) speed, and moves with uniform speed thereafter. What is the work done by the gravitational force on the drop in the first and second half of its journey? What is the work done by the resistive force in the entire journey if its speed on reaching the ground is 10 ms^{-1} ?

20. Explain perfectly inelastic collision in one dimension.

21. Define the terms elastic and inelastic collision. What is the difference between a partially inelastic collision and a completely inelastic collision?

22. A body of mass m moving with speed v collides elastically head-on with another body of mass m initially at rest. Show that moving body will come to a stop as a result of this collision.

Competency Based Que

Numerical Problems

Work done By a Constant & Variable Force

23. A body of mass 3 kg is under a constant force, which causes a displacement s in metre in it, given by the relation $s = \frac{1}{3}t^2$, where t is in second. Find the work done by the force in 2 s.

24. Find the average frictional force needed to stop a car weighing 800 kg running with an initial speed of 54 km/h with a distance of 25 m.

25. On complete combustion, a litre of petrol gives off heat equivalent to 3×10^7 J. In a test drive, a car weighing 1200 kg including the mass of driver, runs 15 km per litre while moving with a uniform speed on an straight track. Assuming that friction offered by the road surface and air to be uniform, calculate the force of friction acting on the car during the test drive, if the efficiency of the car engine were 0.5. **NCERT Exemplar**

Energy

26. Calculate the kinetic energy of a body of mass 0.1 kg, if its linear momentum is 20 kg-m/s.

27. Momentum of a body is doubled. What is the percentage increase in kinetic energy ?

28. Suppose the average mass of raindrops is 3.0×10^{-5} kg and their average terminal velocity 9 ms^{-1}. Calculate the energy transferred by rain to each square metre of the surface at a place which receives 100cm of rain in a year. **NCERT Exemplar**

Work-Energy Theorem

29. A steel spring of spring constant 150 N/m is compressed from its natural position through a mud wall 1m thick, the speed of bullet drops to 100 m/s. Calculate the average resistance of the wall. Neglect friction of air.

30. A simple pendulum of length 1m has a wooden bob of mass 1 kg. It is struck by a bullet of mass 10^{-2} kg moving with a speed of 2×10^2 m/s. The bullet gets embedded into the bob. Obtain the height to which the bob rises before swinging back. [Take, $g = 10$ m/s^2]

Competency Based Que.

Power

31. An engine of 4.9 kW power is used to pump water from a well 50m deep. Calculate the quantity of water in kilolitres which it can pump out in one hour.

32. (i) What is the power of a centripetal force in circular motion?

(ii) A pump can take out 7200 kg of water per hour from a well 100 m deep. Calculate the power of the pump, assuming that its efficiency is 50%. ($g = 10$ ms^{-2})

33. Calculate the horsepower of a man who can chew ice at the rate of 30 g per minute.
Given 1hp = 746 W, 1 J = 4.2 J/cal and latent heat of ice = 80 cal/gm **Competency Based Que.**

Collission

34. A fast moving neutron make a head-on elastic collision with a stationary deuteron. What fraction of its initial kinetic energy is lost by the neutron during collision?

35. Two balls A and B of masses 0.3 kg and 0.2 kg respectively are moving along positive X-axis and negative X-axis with velocity 20 m/s. They collide and thereafter move in the direction opposite to their original direction. Find the velocity of A and B after collision. Also, calculate total KE of the balls before and after collision.

36. A projectile proton with a speed of 500 m/s collide elastically with a target proton initially at rest. The two protons then move along perpendicular paths, with the projectile path at 60° from the original direction. After collision, what are the speed of (i) the target proton and (ii) the projectile proton?

37. A block of mass 1.2 kg moving at a speed of 20 cm/s collides head-on with a similar block kept at rest. The coefficient of restitution is 3/5, find the loss of kinetic energy during collision.

38. A mass m is moving with a speed u collides with a similar mass m at rest, elastically and obliquely prove that they will move in directions making an angle $\pi/2$ with each other.

39. A body of mass M at rest is struck by a moving body of mass m. Show that the fraction of the initial kinetic energy of moving mass m transferred to the strucked body is $4Mm/(m+M)^2$.

Hints & Solutions

Objective Type Questions

1. (a) 3. (b) 4. (d) 5. (c) 6. (a) 7. (d) 8. (b) 9. (a) 11. (a) 12. (d) 13. (b) 14. (b) 15. (b) 16. (c) 17. (d) 18. (d) 19. (d) 20. (c) 21. (b) 22. (b) 23. (a) 24. (c) 25. (a) 26. (a) 27. (a) 28. (d) 29. (a) 30. (a) 31. (a) 32. (c) 33. (i)-(b) (ii)-(a) (iii)-(b) (iv)-(a) (v)-(c)

2. (*a*) Given, $F(x) = \dfrac{-k}{x^2}$

Work formula,

$$W = \int_{x_1}^{x_2} F(x)dx$$

$$\therefore \quad W = \int_{-a}^{2a} \frac{-k}{x^2}dx$$

$$\therefore \quad W = \left[\frac{k}{x}\right]_{-a}^{2a} = \frac{k}{2a} - \frac{k}{-a}$$

$$\therefore \quad W = \frac{k}{2a} + \frac{2k}{2a} = \frac{3k}{2a}$$

10. (*b*) Given, area of river, $A = 100\,\text{m} \times 5\text{m} = 500\,\text{m}$

$\therefore$ Density of water, $\rho = 10^3\ \text{kg/m}^3$

and $\quad v = 2\,\text{ms}^{-1}$

$\therefore$ Mass of water flowing per second, $m = A\rho v$

$$= 500 \times 10^3 \times 2 = 10^6\ \text{kg/s}$$

Power of power station, P = kinetic energy of water flowing per second

$$= \frac{1}{2}mv^2 = \frac{1}{2} \times 10^6 \times 2^4 = 2\,\text{MW}$$

22. (c) A → S, B → P, C → Q, D → R

34. (i) As, the weight of the body is a conservative force. The body starts from a point and again returns to its original point. So, the body moves round the trip. Hence, the work done by the weight of the body in round trip is zero.

(ii) Given, potential energy at A, $U_A = 22$ J

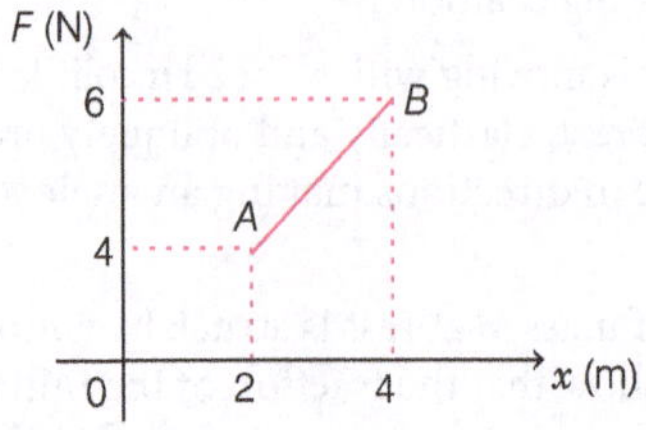

As, work done by conservative force $= -\Delta U$

$\Rightarrow$ Area of F-x diagram $= U_A - U_B$

$$\Rightarrow \quad \frac{1}{2} \times (4 + 6) \times 2 = 22 - U_B$$

$\therefore$ Potential energy at B, $U_B = 12$ J

(iii) The potential energy of a stretched spring of elongation x is given by

$$U = \frac{1}{2}kx^2$$

$\therefore$ The U-x graph will be a parabola which is given below.

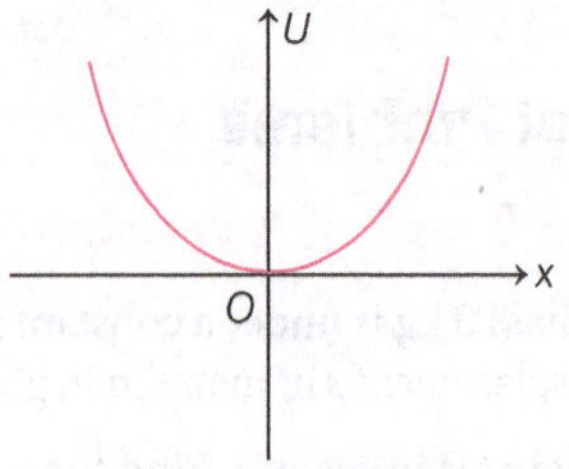

(iv) As, the work done by a non-conservative force appears as heat produced. The frictional force between the surfaces is a non-conservative force.

$\therefore$ Heat produced = Frictional force × displacement

$$= \mu\, mg \times s$$

$$= 0.2 \times 2 \times 10 \times 6 = 24\ \text{J}$$

35. (i) The coefficient of restitution is $e = \dfrac{v_2 - v_1}{u_1 - u_2}$

Given, $v_1 = v_2 = v$ (After collision)

$\therefore e = 0$ (Perfectly inelastic collision)

Hence, in perfectly inelastic collision, the two colliding bodies stick and moves with common velocity after collision.

(ii) Given, $m_1 = 1$ kg, $m_2 = 2$ kg, $u_1 = 5$ m/s, $u_2 = 3$ m/s

$$v_1, v_2 = ?$$

As, $e = 1$ (For perfectly elastic collision)

$$\therefore \quad u_1 - u_2 = v_2 - v_1$$

$$\Rightarrow \quad 5 - 3 = v_2 - v_1$$

$$\therefore \quad v_2 - v_1 = 2 \qquad \text{...(i)}$$

By conservation of momentum,

$$m_1u_1 + m_2u_2 = m_1v_1 + m_2v_2$$

$$\Rightarrow \quad 1 \times 5 + 2 \times 3 = 1 \times v_1 + 2 \times v_2$$

$$\therefore \quad v_1 + 2v_2 = 11 \qquad \text{...(ii)}$$

From Eq. (i) and Eq. (ii), we get

$$v_1 = 2.33\ \text{m/s},\ v_2 = 4.33\ \text{m/s}$$

(iii) Refer to text on Page no. 175.

(iv) We know that,

Coefficient of restitution,

$$e = \left|\frac{\text{Relative velocity of separation}}{\text{Relative velocity of approach}}\right|$$

Hence, $e = 1$

$$\therefore 1 = \left|\frac{\text{Relative velocity of separation}}{\text{Relative velocity of approach}}\right|$$

In elastic collision,

| Relative velocity of approach| = | Relative velocity of separation|

Subjective Questions

1. In the given diagram, the block M is at rest.
Hence, f = frictional force = $Mg \sin \theta$

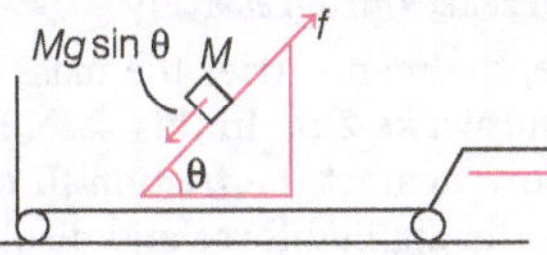

The force of friction acting between the block and incline opposes the tendency of sliding of the block. Since, block is not in motion, therefore no work is done by the force of friction. Hence, no dissipation of energy takes place.

2. When the elevator is descending, then electric power is required to prevent it from falling freely under gravity.
Also, as the weight inside the elevator increases, its speed of descending increases, therefore there should be a limit on the number of passengers in the elevator to prevent the elevator from descending with large velocity.

3. (i) Yes, it is possible in case of a container having greater volume flow rate and a container having more capacity.
(ii) Yes, it is possible in case of capacitor *versus* battery.

4. The situation shown in Fig. (ii) is the correct result of collision, when two bodies of same mass collide, they interchange their velocities. When first ball collides with the combinations of balls 2 and 3, the first ball comes to rest while ball number 2 moves with velocity v again it collides with ball number 3 and hence ball number 2 comes to rest while ball number 3 moves with velocity v.

5. Yes, momentum remains conserved in the collision. To check whether the collision is elastic or inelastic, we consider the kinetic energy of the molecule.
We find that the initial kinetic energy $\left(\frac{1}{2}mu^2\right)$ is same as final KE $\left(\frac{1}{2}mv^2\right)$ of the molecule as $u = v = 200$ m/s
i.e. thus the collision is elastic collision.

6. (i) The potential energy decreases, because $\Delta U = -\int \mathbf{F} \cdot d\mathbf{x}$. If work done by conservative force is positive, then obviously ΔU is – ve.
(ii) Friction always opposes motion. Hence, work done by a body against friction causes loss in its kinetic energy.
(iii) The total (net) momentum can change only when some net external force acts on the system. Hence, its rate of change is proportional to the external force.

7. We know that

Total energy E = PE + KE

$$\Rightarrow \quad E = V + K \quad \text{...(i)}$$

For region A Given, $V > E$, From Eq. (i)

$$K = E - V$$

as $V > E \Rightarrow E - V < 0$

Hence, $K < 0$, this is not possible.

For region B Given, $V < E \Rightarrow E - V > 0$

This is possible because total energy can be greater than PE (V).

For region C Given, $K > E \Rightarrow K - E > 0$

from Eq. (i) PE $= V = E - K < 0$

Which is possible, because PE can be negative.

For region D Given, $V > K$

This is possible because for a system PE (V) may be greater than KE (K).

8. Let M be the mass of rocket at any time t and v_1 the velocity of rocket at the same time t.
Let Δm = mass of gas ejected in time interval Δt.
Relative speed of gas ejected $= u$.
Consider at time $(t + \Delta t)$

$(\text{KE})_{t} + \Delta t$ = KE of rocket + KE of gas

$$= \frac{1}{2}(M - \Delta m)(v + \Delta v)^2 + \frac{1}{2}\Delta m (v - u)^2$$

$$= \frac{1}{2}Mv^2 + Mv\Delta v - \Delta mvu + \frac{1}{2}\Delta mu^2$$

$$(\text{KE})_t = \text{KE of the rocket at time } t = \frac{1}{2}Mv^2$$

$$\Delta K = (\text{KE})_t + \Delta t - (\text{KE})_t$$

$$= (M\Delta v - \Delta mu)\,v + \frac{1}{2}\Delta mu^2$$

Since, action-reaction forces are equal.

$$\text{Hence, } M\frac{dv}{dt} = \frac{dm}{dt}|u| \Rightarrow M\Delta v = \Delta \mu$$

$$\Delta K = \frac{1}{2}\Delta mu^2$$

Now, by work-energy theorem, $\Delta K = \Delta W$

$$\Rightarrow \quad \Delta W = \frac{1}{2}\Delta mu^2$$

9. (i) Power used by family, P = 8 kW = 8000W
As only 20% of solar energy can be converted to useful electrical energy, hence power to be supplied by solar energy $\frac{8000 \text{ W}}{20\%} = 40000$ W

As solar energy is incident at a rate of 200 Wm^{-2}, hence the area needed

$$A = \frac{40000\ W}{200\ Wm^{-2}} = 200\ m^2$$

(ii) The area needed is comparable to roof area of a large sized house.

10. Refer to text on Page no. 170.

11. Refer to text on Pages no. 175 and 176.

12. Given, two balls of mass m

i.e, $m_1 = m_2 = m$

and the speed $u_1 = v$

and $u_2 = -v$ (as they are opposite to each other)

It is a perfectly elastic collision (assumed), hence the velocity after collision will be

$$v_1 = \frac{(m_1 - m_2)u_1}{m_1 + m_2} + \frac{2m_2 u_2}{m_1 + m_2}$$

$$v_1 = 0 + \frac{2m(-v)}{2m}$$

$$v_1 = -v$$

Similarly, $$v_2 = \frac{2mu_1}{(m_1 + m_2)} + \frac{(m_2 - m_1)u_2}{m_1 + m_2}$$

$$v_2 = v$$

∴ According to conservation of momentum.

Total initial and final momentum will be equal and hence, the velocity after collision will be same for the two balls but they move in opposite direction.

13. Refer to text on Page no. 174.

14. Refer to text on Pages no. 159 and 160.

15. (a) **Positive** In the given case, force and displacement are in the same direction. Hence, the sign of work done is positive. In this case, the work is done on the bucket.

(b) **Negative** In the given case, the direction of force (vertically downward) and displacement (vertically upward) are opposite to each other. Hence, the sign of work done is negative.

(c) **Negative** Since the direction to frictional force is opposite to the direction of motion, the work done by frictional force is negative in this case.

(d) **Positive** Here the body is moving on a rough horizontal plane. Frictional force opposes the motion of the body. Therefore, in order to maintain a uniform velocity, a uniform force must be applied to the body. Since, the applied force acts in the direction of motion of the body, the work done is positive.

(e) **Negative** The resistive force of air acts in the direction opposite to the direction of motion of the pendulum. Hence, the work done is negative in this case.

16. (i) Heat energy required for burning of casing of rocket comes from the rocket itself. As a result of work done against friction the kinetic energy of rocket continuously decreases and this work against friction reappears as heat energy.

(ii) The gravitational force is a conservative force, hence, work done by the gravitational force over one complete (closed) orbit of comet is zero.

(iii) As an artificial satellite gradually loses its energy due to dissipation against atmospheric resistance, its potential energy decreases rapidly. As a result, kinetic energy of satellite slightly increases i.e. its speed increases progressively.

(iv) In figure, the man carries the mass of 15 kg on his hands and walks 2 m. In this case, he is actually doing work against the friction force. So, the angle between the applied force and displacement force is 90°.

∴ Work done, $W = Fs\cos 90° = 0$ (∵ $\cos 90° = 0$)

In second case, the man applies a force in horizontal direction and moves also in horizontal direction. So, angle between the applied force and displacement is 0°.

∴ $$W = Fs\cos 0°$$
$$= Fs = mg \times s$$
$$= 15 \times 9.8 \times 2 = 294\ J$$

∴ Work done is greater in second case.

17. **KE *versus* x graph**

We know that, Total ME = KE + PE

⇒ $E_0 = KE + V(x)$

⇒ $KE = E_0 - V(x)$

at $Ax = 0, V(x) = E_0$

⇒ $KE = E_0 - E_0 = 0$

at $B\,V(x) < E_0$

⇒ $KE > 0$ (positive)

at C and D, $V_2(x) = 0$

⇒ KE is maximum at $F_{12}, V(x) = E_o$

Hence, KE = 0

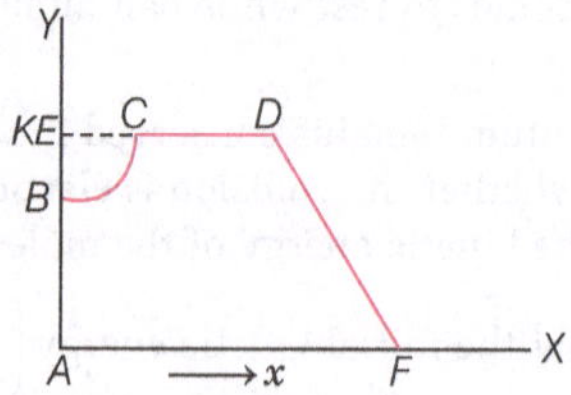

The variation is shown in adjacent diagram.

Velocity *versus* x graph

As $$KE = \frac{1}{2}mv^2$$

∴ At A and F, where KE = 0, $v = 0$.

At C and D, KE is maximum. Therefore, v is $\pm$ max.
At B, KE is positive but not maximum.
Therefore, v is $\pm$ some value (< max.)
The variation is shown in the diagram.

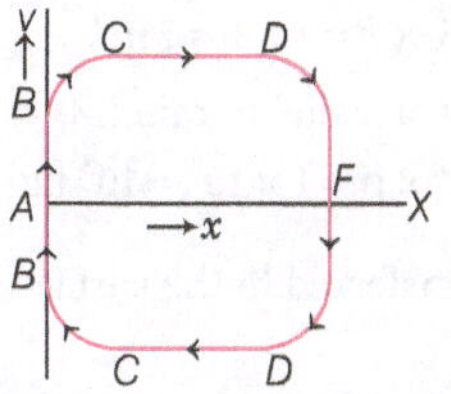

18. Refer to text on Page no. 170.

19. Given, radius of the rain drop,

$$r = 2\text{mm} = 2 \times 10^{-3}\text{ m}$$

Density of water, $\rho = 10^3\ \text{kg/m}^3$

Distance moved in each half of the journey,

$$s = \frac{500}{2} = 250\text{ m}$$

Mass of the rain water, $m = \frac{4}{3}\pi r^3 \times \rho$

$$= \frac{4}{3} \times \pi \times (2 \times 10^{-3})^3 \times 10^3 = 3.35 \times 10^{-5}\text{ kg}$$

$\therefore$ Gravitational force on the rain drop,

$$F = mg = 3.35 \times 10^{-5} \times 9.8\text{ N}$$

$\therefore$ Work done by gravitational force on the rain drop in the first half journey.

$$W = F \cdot s = 3.35 \times 10^{-5} \times 9.8 \times 250 = 0.082\text{ J}$$

The work done on the rain drop in the second-half journey.

$$W = 0.082\text{ J}$$

By work-energy theorem,

$$W_{\text{resistive force}} = E_f - E_i = \frac{1}{2}mv^2 - mgh$$

$$= 3.35 \times 10^{-5} \times \left(\frac{10^2}{2} - 9.8 \times 500\right) = 0.1623\text{ J}$$

20. Refer to text on Page no. 173.

21. **Elastic collision** An elastic collision is a collision between two objects where the total kinetic energy and momentum are conserved. In an elastic collision, there is no net loss of kinetic energy in the system.

Example : Collision between billiard balls or the balls in a Newton's cradle are example of elastic collision.

Inelastic Collision : An inelastic collision is a collision in which the kinetic energy of the system is not conserved but the momentum is conserved.

Example : An showball hits a tree and sticks to it.

Given solution of pratially inelastic collision.

22.

Before Collision **After Collision**

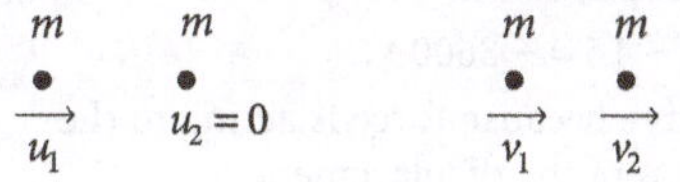

From conservation of linear momentum,

$$\Rightarrow \quad mu_1 + m \times 0 = m \times v_1 + mv_2$$

$$\Rightarrow \quad u_1 = v_1 + v_2$$

Since, the collision is elastic, $e = 1$

$$\Rightarrow \quad \frac{v_2 - v_1}{u_1 - 0} = 1$$

$$\Rightarrow \quad v_2 - v_1 = u_1$$

$$v_2 = u_1 + v_1$$

$$\Rightarrow \quad u_1 = v_1 + v_1 + u_1$$

$$\Rightarrow \quad 2v_1 = 0$$

$$v_1 = 0$$

Hence, the moving body will come to stop.

23. Work done by the force = force × displacement

or $\quad W = F \times s \quad$ ...(i)

But from Newton's 2nd law, we have

Force = mass × acceleration

i.e. $\quad F = ma \quad$ ...(ii)

Hence, from Eqs. (i) and (ii), we get

$$W = m\left(\frac{d^2s}{dt^2}\right)s \quad \left[\because a = \frac{d^2s}{dt^2}\right] \quad \text{...(iii)}$$

Now, we have $s = \frac{1}{3}t^2$

$$\therefore \quad \frac{d^2s}{dt^2} = \frac{d}{dt}\left[\frac{d}{dt}\left(\frac{1}{3}t^2\right)\right]$$

$$= \frac{d}{dt} \times \left(\frac{2}{3}t\right) = \frac{2}{3}\frac{dt}{dt} = \frac{2}{3}$$

Hence Eq. (iii) becomes

$$W = \frac{2}{3}ms = \frac{2}{3} \times m \times \frac{1}{3}t^2 = \frac{2}{9}mt^2$$

We have, $m = 3$ kg, $t = 2s$

$$\therefore \quad W = \frac{2}{9} \times 3 \times (2)^2 = \frac{8}{3}\text{ J}$$

24. Given, mass of car $(m) = 800$kg

Initial speed, $u = 54$ km/h

$$= 54 \times \frac{5}{18} = 15\text{ m/s}$$

Distance covered by car = 25 m

$$\because \quad v^2 = u^2 + 2as$$

$$\Rightarrow \quad (0)^2 - (15)^2 = 2as$$

$$\Rightarrow \quad -\frac{225}{2 \times 25} = a$$

$\Rightarrow$ Acceleration, $a = -4.5 \text{ m/s}^2$

Now, frictional force, $F = m \times a$

$= 800 \times -4.5 = -3600\text{N}.$

Here, F = negative because force is acting in the opposite direction of the displacement.

$\therefore$ Frictional force = 3600N

25. Energy is given by the petrol in the form of heat of combustion.

Thus, by question,

Energy given by 1 litre of petrol $= 3 \times 10^7$ J

Efficiency of the car engine = 0.5

$\therefore$ Energy used by the car $= 0.5 \times 3 \times 10^7$ J

$E = 1.5 \times 10^7$ J

Total distance travelled $(s) = 15 \text{ km} = 15 \times 10^3$ m

If f is the force of friction then,

$E = f \times s$

($\because$ Energy is utilised in working against friction)

$1.5 \times 10^7 = f \times 15 \times 10^3$

$$\Rightarrow \quad f = \frac{1.5 \times 10^7}{15 \times 10^3} = 10^3 \text{ N}$$

$f = 1000$ N

26. Given that mass of body, $m = 0.1$kg

Linear momentum, $p = 20$ kg-m/s

The kinetic energy is given by $K = \frac{p^2}{2m}$

$$\Rightarrow \quad K = \frac{20 \times 20}{2 \times 0.1} = 2000 \text{ J}$$

27. From the relation, $K = \frac{p^2}{2m}$

On doubling the momentum, we get

$$K' = \frac{(2p)^2}{2m} = \frac{2p^2}{m}$$

$\therefore$ Change in kinetic energy $= K' - K$

$$= \frac{2p^2}{m} - \frac{p^2}{2m} = \frac{3p^2}{2m}$$

$$\therefore \% \text{ change in kinetic energy} = \frac{K' - K}{K} \times 100$$

$$= \frac{\frac{2p^2}{m} - \frac{p^2}{2m}}{\frac{p^2}{2m}} \times 100$$

$$= \frac{3p^2}{2m} \times \frac{2m}{p^2} \times 100 = 300\%$$

28. Given, average mass of raindrop,

$m = 3.0 \times 10^{-5}$ kg

Average terminal velocity $(v) = 9$ m/s

Height $(h) = 100 \text{ cm} = 1$ m

Density of water $(\rho) = 10^3 \text{ kg/m}^3$

Area of the surface $(A) = 1 \text{ m}^2$

Volume of the water due to rain (V) = Area $\times$ height

$= A \times h = 1 \times 1 = 1 \text{ m}^3$

Mass of the water due to rain (M) = Volume $\times$ density

$= V \times \rho = 1 \times 10^3 = 10^3$ kg

$\therefore$ Energy transferred to the surface $= \frac{1}{2} mv^2$

$$= \frac{1}{2} \times 10^3 \times (9)^2$$

$$= 40.5 \times 10^3 \text{ J} = 4.05 \times 10^4 \text{ J}$$

29. The potential energy through string, $U = \frac{1}{2} kx^2$

Where x = compression = 1 m (given)

Spring constant, $k = 150$ N/m

$$\therefore \quad U = \frac{1}{2} kx^2 = \frac{1}{2} \times 150 \times (1)^2 = 75\text{J}$$

30. Given, simple pendulum of length = 1 m

Mass of Bob = 1 kg

Mass of Bullet $= 10^{-2}$kg

Speed of bullet $= 2 \times 10^2$m/s

Height to which the bob rises before swinging back = ?

Now, using law of conservation of momentum

$$mv = (m + M)v$$

$$(0.01)(200) = (0.01 + 1)v$$

$$v = 1.98 \text{ m/s}$$

Using conservation of energy

$$(m + M) gh = \frac{1}{2}(m + M)v^2$$

$$v = \sqrt{2gh}$$

$$1.98 = \sqrt{2 \times 10 \times h}$$

$$h = (1.98)^2 / 20 = 0.2 \text{ m}$$

31. Given, power $(P) = 4.9 \text{ kW} = 4.9 \times 10^3 = 4900$W

Depth of wall $(h) = 50$m

Acceleration due to gravity, $g = 9.8 \text{ ms}^{-2}$

Time, $t = 1$h

$= 60 \times 60 \text{ s} = 3600$s

Hence, power $= \frac{mgh}{t}$

$$4900 = \frac{m \times 9.8 \times 50}{3600}$$

$$\therefore \quad m = \frac{3600 \times 4900}{9.8 \times 50} = 36000 \text{ kg}$$

$\therefore$ Volume of water pumped per hour

= 36000 litre = 36 kL

32. (i) In case of circular motion, centripetal force is perpendicular to velocity.

$\therefore$ Power $= \mathbf{F} \cdot \mathbf{v} = F\, v \cos\theta = Fv\cos 90^\circ = 0$

(ii) Given, mass $m = 7200$ kg, $g = 10\,\text{ms}^{-2}$

depth, $h = 100\,\text{m}$, $t = 1\,\text{hr} = 3600\,\text{s}$

Work done, $W = mgh = 7200 \times 10 \times 100 = 7.2 \times 10^6\,\text{J}$

Hence, power $P = \dfrac{W}{t} = \dfrac{7.2 \times 10^6}{3600} = 2 \times 10^3\,\text{W}$

Now, given that efficiency, $\eta = \dfrac{\text{Output power}}{\text{Input power}}$

$$\eta = 50\% = \frac{1}{2}$$

$$\frac{1}{2} = \frac{2 \times 10^3}{P_{in}}$$

Maximum Power, $P_{in} = 2 \times 2 \times 10^3\,\text{W} = 4 \times 10^3\,\text{W}$

33. Given, mass of ice chewed, $m = 30$ g

Time, $t = 1$ min $= 60$ s

Latent heat, $L = 80$ cal / g

Heat, $W = mL$

$= 30 \times 80 = 2400$ cal $= 2400 \times 4.2\,\text{J} = 10080$ J

Power $= \dfrac{W}{t} = \dfrac{10080}{60} = 168\,\text{W} = \dfrac{168}{746}$ hp $= 0.225$ hp

34. After collision, velocity of neutron $= v_1$

Velocity of deutron $= v_2$

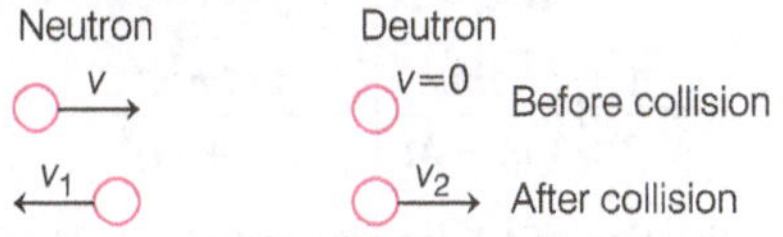

$\because m_d = 2m_n$ let $m_d = 2m$ and $m_n = m$

Applying conservation of momentum

$$mu = mv_1 + 2mv_2$$

$\Rightarrow \quad v_1 + 2v_2 = u \quad$ ...(i)

As collision is elastic, hence $e = 1$

so, $\quad u = v_2 - v_1 \quad$ ...(ii)

By adding Eqs. (i) and (ii), we get

$$v_1 = \frac{-u}{3}$$

$\therefore$ Fractional loss of kinetic energy of neutron

$$= \frac{\frac{1}{2}mu^2 - \frac{1}{2}mv_1^2}{\frac{1}{2}mu^2} = 1 - \left(\frac{v_1}{u}\right)^2 = 1 - \frac{1}{9} = \frac{8}{9}$$

Hence, the fractional loss in KE during collision is $\dfrac{8}{9}$.

35. Here, $m_1 = 0.3$ kg, $m_2 = 0.2$ kg

$u_1 = 20$ m/s, $u_2 = -20$ m/s

Let v_1 = velocity of A after collision along negative X-axis.

v_2 = velocity of B after collision, along postive X-axis.

According to conservation of momentum,

$$m_1v_1 + m_2v_2 = m_1u_1 + m_2u_2$$

$$0.3v_1 + 0.2v_2 = 0.3 \times 20 + 0.2(-20)$$

$$0.3v_1 + 0.2\,v_2 = 6 - 4 = 2$$

$0.3v_1 + 0.2v_2 = 2 \quad$ ...(i)

Relative velocity of separation after collision = Relative velocity of approach before collision

$$v_2 - v_1 = u_1 - u_2 = 20 - (-20) = 40$$

$v_2 = 40 + v_1 \quad$ ...(ii)

Putting in Eq. (i),

$$0.3v_1 = 2 - 0.2(40 + v_1)$$

$$0.3\,v_1 = 2 - 8 - 0.2\,v_1$$

$$0.5v_1 = -6$$

$v_1 = -\dfrac{6}{0.5} = 12\,\text{ms}^{-1}$ along negative X-axis.

From Eq. (ii) $v_2 = 40 - 12 = 28$ m/s along the X-axis.

Total KE of balls before collision,

$$= \frac{1}{2}m_1u_1^2 - \frac{1}{2}m_2u_2^2 = \frac{1}{2}[0.3(20)^2 + 0.2(-20)^2]$$

$$= 100\,\text{J}$$

Total KE of balls after collision

$$= \frac{1}{2}m_1v_1^2 + \frac{1}{2}m_2v_2^2 = \frac{1}{2}[0.3(12)^2 + 0.2(28)^2]$$

$$= 100\,\text{J}$$

Thus, KE of balls is conserved during elastic collision.

36. Given, $v_1 = 500$ m/s and $m_1 = m_2$

Angle made by projectile proton $\theta = 60^\circ$

Angle between target and projectile proton. After collision $= 90^\circ$

$\therefore \quad \phi = 30^\circ$

(i) According to law of conservation of momentum

$m_1v_1 = m_1v'_1 \cos\theta + m_2u'_2 \cos\phi$ along X-axis.

$0 = m_1v'_1 \sin\theta + m_2v'_2 \sin\phi$ along Y-axis.

From the above equations,

$$v'_2 = \frac{v_1 \sin\theta}{\sin(\theta - \phi)} = \frac{(500)\sin 60^\circ}{\sin 90^\circ} = 433\,\text{m/s}$$

(ii) In similar manner,

$$v'_1 = \frac{v_1 \sin\theta}{\sin(\phi - \theta)} = \frac{500 \sin(-30)}{\sin(-90)} = 250\,\text{m/s}$$

37. Here, $m_1 = 1.2$ kg, $u_1 = 20$ cm/s

$m_2 = 1.2$ kg, $u_2 = 0$ (head-on)

Let v_1 and v_2 be the velocities of the two blocks after collision, then according to conservation of momentum.

$$m_1u_1 + m_2u_2 = m_1v_1 + m_2v_2$$

$\Rightarrow \quad 1.2 \times 20 + 0 = 1.2v_1 + 1.2\,v_2 \quad$ ...(i)

$\therefore$ Velocity of approach $= u_1 - u_2 = 20$ cm/s

Velocity of separation $= v_2 - v_1$

$$e = \frac{v_2 - v_1}{u_1 - u_2} = \frac{3}{5} \text{ (given)}$$

$$\therefore \quad v_2 - v_1 = \frac{3}{5} \times 20$$

$$v_2 - v_1 = 12 \quad \text{...(ii)}$$

Now from Eqs. (i) and (ii), we get

$$v_1 = 4 \text{ cm/s}, v_2 = 16 \text{ cm/s}$$

$\therefore$ Loss in kinetic energy KE

$$= \frac{1}{2}m_1u_1^2 - \frac{1}{2}m_1v_1^2 - \frac{1}{2}m_2v_2^2$$

$$= \frac{1}{2} \times 1.2 \times (20 \times 10^{-2})^2$$

$$- \frac{1}{2} \times 1.2 \times (4 \times 10^{-2})^2 - \frac{1}{2} \times 1.2 \times (16 \times 10^{-2})^2$$

$$= 0.768 \times 10^{-2} \text{ J} = 7.7 \times 10^{-3} \text{ J.}$$

38. According to conservation of momentum on X-axis

$$mu = m_1v_1 \cos\theta_1 + mv_2 \cos\theta_2$$

$$\Rightarrow \quad u = v_1 \cos\theta_1 + v_2 \cos\theta_2 \quad \text{...(i)}$$

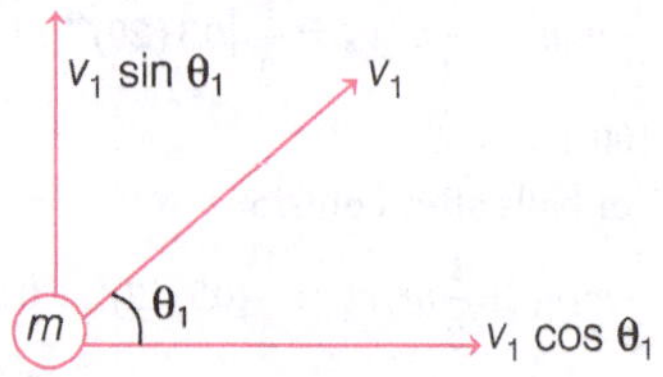

On Y-axis,

$$0 = v_1 \sin\theta_1 + v_2 \cos\theta_2 \quad \text{... (ii)}$$

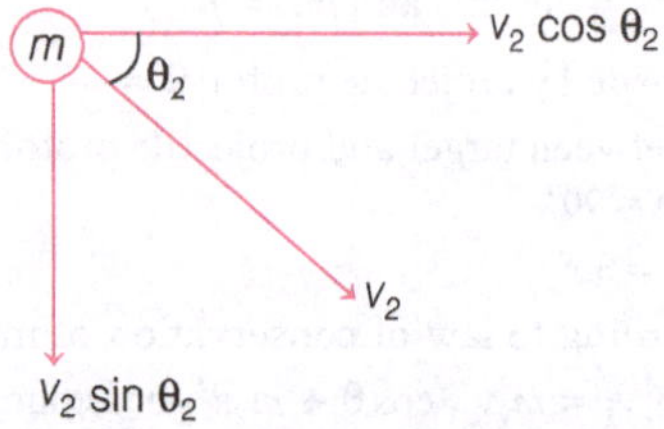

Kinetic energy is also conserved in elastic collision

$$\frac{1}{2}mu^2 = \frac{1}{2}mv_1^2 + \frac{1}{2}mv_2^2$$

$$u^2 = v_1^2 + v_2^2 \quad \text{...(iii)}$$

Squaring and adding Eq. (i) and Eq. (ii), we get

$$\therefore u^2 = v_1^2 + v_2^2 + 2v_1v_2 \cos(\theta_1 + \theta_2)$$

Using (iii), we get

$$2v_1v_2 \cos(\theta_1 + \theta_2) = 0$$

$$\Rightarrow \quad \cos(\theta_1 + \theta_2) = 0$$

$$\theta_1 + \theta_2 = \frac{\pi}{2}$$

Hence, the masses move at right angle with each other.

39. Let, the body of mass m move with velocity u towards mass M at rest.

Initial KE of moving body

$$E_1 = \frac{1}{2}mu_1^2 = \frac{1}{2}mu^2$$

After collision,

$$v_2 = \frac{2m_1u_1}{m_1 + m_2} + \frac{(m_2 - m_1)}{m_1 + m_2}u_2$$

$$= \frac{2\,mu}{m + M} + 0 = \frac{2\,mu}{m + M}$$

Kinetic energy of mass M,

$$E_2 = \frac{1}{2}m_2v_2^2$$

$$= \frac{1}{2}M\left(\frac{2mu}{m + M}\right)^2 = \frac{2Mm^2u^2}{(M + m)^2}$$

Hence, fraction of KE transferred.

$$\frac{E_2}{E_1} = \frac{2Mm^2u^2}{(m + M)^2 \frac{1}{2}mu^2} = \frac{4mM}{(M + m)^2}$$

QR Code for Quick Test 1

QR Code for Quick Test 2

QR Code for Quick Test 3

SELF ASSESSMENT TEST

Multiple Choice Questions (MCQs)

1. A mass of 5 kg is moving along a circular path of radius 1 m. If the mass moves with 300 rev/min its kinetic energy would be (in Joule)

(a) $250\,\pi^2$ (b) $100\,\pi^2$ (c) $5\,\pi^2$ (d) 0

2. An athlete in Olympic games covers a distance of 100 m in 10 s, then kinetic energy can be estimated to be in the range of (assume $m = 60$ kg)

(a) 200 J-500 J (b) 2×0^5 J-3×10^5 J
(c) 20000 J-50000 J (d) 2000 J-5000 J

3. A spring of force constant 800 Nm^{-1} has an extension of 5 cm. The work done is extending it from 5 cm to 15 cm is

(a) 16 J (b) 8 J (c) 35 J (d) 24 J

4. 300 J of work is done in sliding a 2 kg block up on an inclined plane of height 10 m. Work done against friction is ($g = 10\ ms^{-2}$)

(a) 1000 J (b) 200 J (c) 100 J (d) zero

5. A bomb of mass 30 kg at rest explodes into two pieces of masses 18 kg and 12 kg. The velocity of 18 kg mass is 6 ms^{-1}. The kinetic energy of the other mass is

(a) 324 J (b) 486 J (c) 256 J (d) 5245 J

6. Acceleration *a versus x* and potential energy *versus x* graph of a particle moving along *X*-axis are as shown below. Mass of particle is 1 kg and velocity at $x = 0$ is 4 ms^{-1}. Match the following columns for $x = 8$ m and select the correct answer from the options given below.

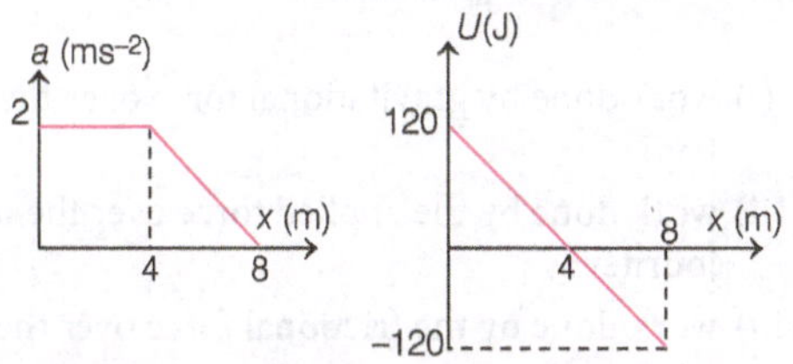

	Column I		Column II
A.	Final kinetic energy	P.	120 J
B.	Work done by conservative forces	Q.	240 J
C.	Total work done	R.	–120 J
D.	Work done by external forces	S.	128 J

(a) A-P, B-S, C-R, D-Q (b) A-S, B-P, C-R, D-Q
(c) A-S, B-Q, C-P, D-R (d) A-P, B-Q, C-R, D-S

Assertion-Reason

Directions *(Q.No. 7-10) In the following questions, two statements are given- one labelled Assertion (A) and the other labelled Reason (R). Select the correct answer to these questions from the codes (a), (b), (c) and (d) as given below.*

(a) Both Assertion and Reason are true and Reason is the correct explanation of Assertion.

(b) Both Assertion and Reason are true but Reason is not the correct e xplanation of Assertion.

(c) Assertion is true but Reason is false.

(d) Assertion is false but Reason is true.

7. Assertion A spring has potential energy, both when it is compressed or stretched.
Reason In compressing or stretching, work is done on the spring against the restoring force.

8. Assertion Friction is a non-conservative force.
Reason This is because work done against friction, in moving a body over a closed path is never zero.

9. Assertion At stable equilibrium position of a body, kinetic energy cannot be zero because it is maximum.
Reason During oscillations of a body, potential energy is minimum at stable equilibrium position.

10. Assertion The change in kinetic energy of a particle is equal to the work done on it by the net force.
Reason Change in kinetic energy of particle is equal to work done only in case of a system of one particle.

Case Based Questions

Directions *(Q.No. 11) This question is case study based question. Read the following paragraph and answer the questions on the basis of same.*

11. The laws of momentum and energy conservation are successfully applied to a commonly encountered phenomenon, namely collisions, several games such as billiards, marble or carrom involve collisions. In all types of collisions, the linear momentum is conserved. On the other hand, the total kinetic energy of the system is not necessarily conserved. The impact and deformation during collision may generate heat and sound. The degree of elasticity of a collision is determined by a quantity called coefficient of restitution (e).

(i) A body of mass M_1 collides elastically with another man M_2 at rest. There is 100% transfer of energy takes place when (assuming perfectly elastic collision)

(a) $M_1 > M_2$
(b) $M_1 < M_2$
(c) $M_1 = M_2$
(d) Same of all values of M_1 and M_2

(ii) A bullet hits and gets embedded in a solid block resting on a frictionless surface. In this process, which one of the following is correct?

(a) Only momentum is conserved
(b) Only KE is conserved
(c) Neither momentum nor KE is conserved
(d) Both momentum and KE ar conserved

(iii) Two identical balls A and B collide head on elastically of velocities of A and B, before the collision are +0.5 m/s and −0.3 m/s respectively, then their velocities after the collision are respectively

(a) −0.5 m/s, +0.3 m/s (b) +0.5 m/s, +0.3 m/s
(c) +0.3 m/s, −0.5 m/s (d) −0.3 m/s, +0.5 m/s

(iv) Two bodies of mass 0.25 kg each moving towards each other with velocities 3 m/s and 1 m/s, respectively. After collision, they stick together. The velocity of the combination will be

(a) 0.1 cm/s (b) 1 cm/s
(c) 1 m/s (d) Cannot be predicted

Very Short Answer Type Questions

12. Under what conditions is the work done by a force zero inspite of displacement not being zero?

13. A man raises a mass m to a height h and then shifts it horizontally by a length x. What is the work done against the force of gravity?

14. Give the conditions under which a force is called conservative force.

15. When ball hits a floor and rebounce after an inelastic collision, what happens total energy and momentum?

Short Answer Type Questions

16. A vertical spring with constant 200 N/m has a light platform on its top. When a 500 g mass is kept on the platform spring compresses 2.5 cm. Mass is now pushed down 7.50 cm further and released. How far above later position will the mass fly? ($g = 10 \text{ ms}^{-2}$)

17. A particle moves along the X-axis from $x = 0$ to $x = 5$ m under the influence of a force given by $f(x) = 7 - 2x + 3x^2$. Calculate the work done.

18. A molecule in a gas container hits a horizontal wall with speed 200 ms^{-1} and angle 30° with the normal and rebounds with the same speed. Is momentum conserved in the collision? Is the collision elastic or inelastic?

19. If momentum of a body increased by 300%, then what will be percentage increase in kinetic energy of a body?

Long Answer Type Questions

20. The blades of a windmill sweep out a circle of area A.

(i) If the wind flows at a velocity v perpendicular to the circle, what is the mass of the air passing through it in time t?

(ii) What is the kinetic energy of the air?

(iii) Assume that the windmill converts 25% of the wind's energy into electrical energy and that $A = 30 \text{ m}^2$, $v = 36$ km/h and the density of the air is 1.2 kg m^{-3}. What is the electrical power produced?

21. Calculate work done in raising a stone of mass 5 kg of specific gravity 3 immersed in water from a depth of 6 m to 1 m below surface of water. ($g = 10 \text{ ms}^{-2}$)

22. A body of mass 0.3 kg is taken up an inclined plane length 10 m and height 5 m and then allowed to slide down the bottom again. The coefficient of friction between the body and the plane is 0.15. What is the

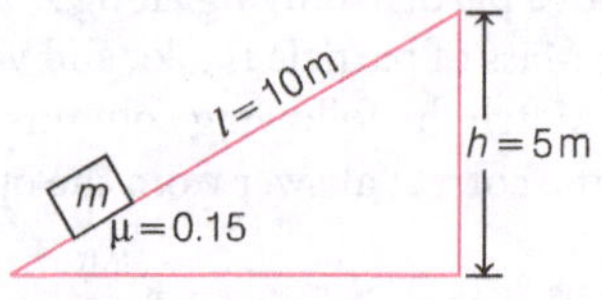

(i) work done by gravitational force over the round trip?

(ii) work done by the applied force over the upward journey?

(iii) work done by the frictional force over the round trip?

(iv) kinetic energy of the body at the end of trip? ($g = 10 \text{ ms}^{-2}$)

Answers

1. (a) *2.* (d) *3.* (b) *4.* (c) *5.* (b) *6.* (c) *7.* (a) *8.* (a) *9.* (d) *10.* (c)
11. (i) (c) (ii) (a) (iii) (d) (iv) (c)

06

CHAPTER

In earlier cases, we considered every object as point mass. Even the finite size objects are considered as point mass to understand their motion.
An extended body (any finite size body) is a system of particles. Hence, now we will consider the motion of system. To understand the motion of a system (extended body), we will understand the concept of centre of mass of a system of particles.

▼ YOUR STUDY GOALS

- 6.1 Rigid body
- 6.2 Centre of Mass
- 6.3 Motion of Centre of Mass
- 6.4 Moment of Force (Torque)
- 6.5 Angular Momentum of a Particle
- 6.6 Equilibrium of a Rigid Body
- 6.7 Moment of Inertia
- 6.8 Kinematic Equations of Rotational Motion about a Fixed Axis
- 6.9 Dynamics of Linear and Rotational Motion

▼ YOUR PRACTICE GOAL

- Objective Type Questions (29 Qs, MCQs, A-R, Matching)
- Case Based Questions-(3)
- Subjective Questions (8 VSAs, 6 SAs, 8 LAs)
- Numerical Problems-(21)

System of Particles and Rotational Motion

6.1 Rigid Body

Ideally, a body is said to be a rigid body when it has a perfectly definite shape and size. The distance between all pairs of particles of such a body do not change while applying any force on it.

e.g. A wheel can be considered as rigid body by ignoring a little change in its shape.

Kinds of Motion of a Rigid Body

A rigid body can possess pure translational motion, pure rotational motion or a combination of both these motions. Let us explore these kinds of motions one by one.

1. Pure Translational Motion

The type of motion in which every particle of the body moves through the same linear distance in a straight line and in a given time interval is known as pure translational motion.

- In pure translational motion, at any instant of time, all particles of the body have the same angular velocity.
- In pure translational motion, all the particles of body move along parallel paths.

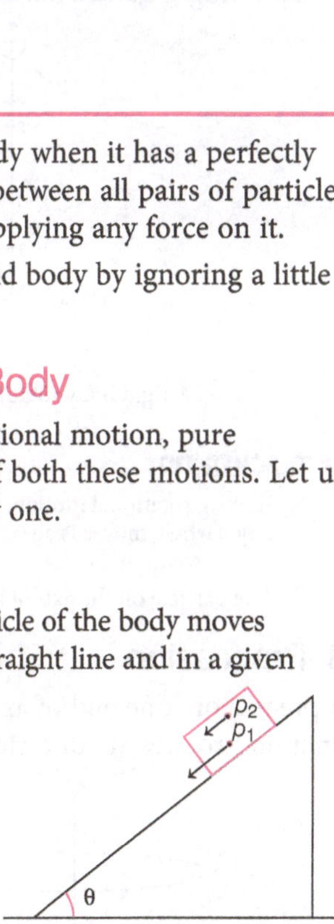

Translational motion of a block down on an inclined plane

2. Rotational Motion (Fixed Axis of Rotation)

In pure rotational motion, every particle of the rigid body moves in circles of different radii about a fixed line, which is known as **axis of rotation**.

The particle lies in a plane perpendicular to the axis of rotation e.g.

(i) Consider a ceiling fan as shown in the figure. When the fan rotates, the particle A revolves in a circle of radius r_1 and particle B revolves in a circle of radius r_2. Hence, the fan is in pure rotational motion.

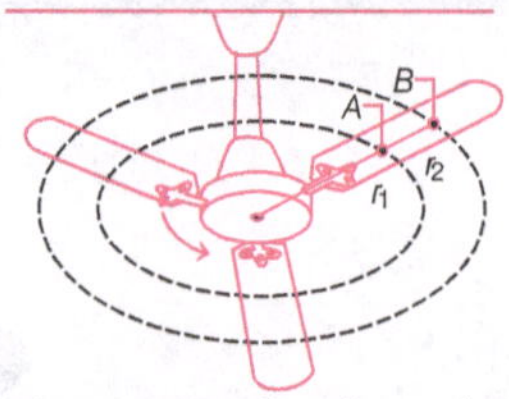

A rotating ceiling fan with the particles A and B moving in circular paths

(ii) The following figure shows the rotational motion of a rigid body about a fixed axis, i.e. Z-axis.

The motion shown in figure focuses on object spinning around a fixed axis or a pivot point.

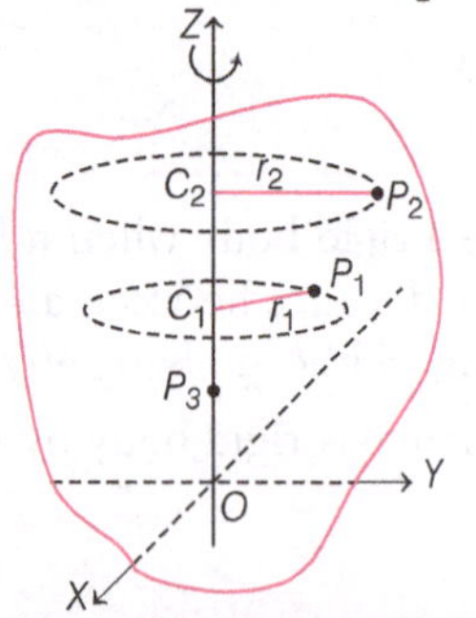

A rigid body rotating about the Z-axis

TEACHER TIP

In pure rotational motion, the plane of the circle in which any particle moves is always perpendicular to the fixed axis of rotation and has its centre on the axis.

The particle on the axis of rotation remains stationary.

3. Precession

In precession, one end of axis of rotation is fixed and other end rotates about a circular path.

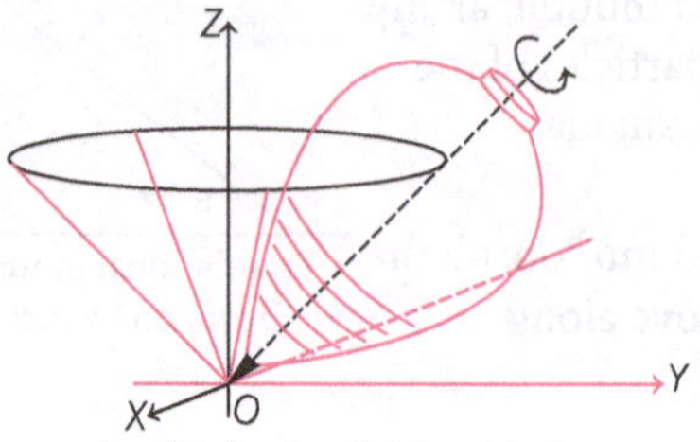

A spinning top is in precession

4. Combination of Translational and Rotational Motion

A rigid body may have a rolling motion, which is a combination of rotation and translation.

e.g. Consider a cylinder rolling down an inclined plane, its motion is the combination of rotation about a fixed axis and translation.

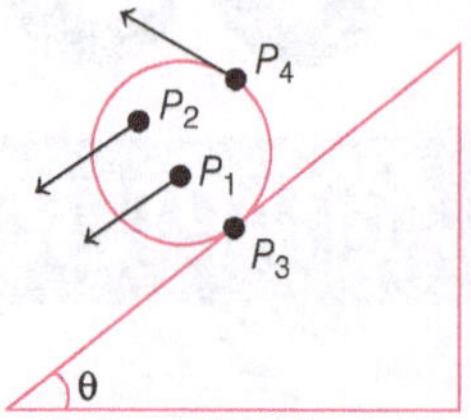

A cylinder rolling down on an inclined plane

6.2 Centre of Mass

A point where the entire mass of the body or system of bodies is supposed to be concentrated is known as the centre of mass.

For a System of Two Particles

Let the distances of the two particles be x_1 and x_2 respectively, from origin O. Let m_1 and m_2 be their masses. The centre of mass of the system is at point C which is at a distance x_{CM} from O, where x_{CM} is given by

$$x_{CM} = \frac{m_1 x_1 + m_2 x_2}{m_1 + m_2}$$

$$\text{Centre of mass, } x_{CM} = \frac{m_1 x_1 + m_2 x_2}{M}$$

where, $M = m_1 + m_2 =$ total mass of system

If two particles have equal mass, then

$$x_{CM} = \frac{x_1 + x_2}{2}$$

i.e., **For two particles of equal mass, the centre of mass lies exactly midway between them.**

The CM of two particles systems (of different masses) divides masses in inverse ratio of their distances from CM

$$\frac{m_1}{m_2} = \frac{r_2}{r_1}$$

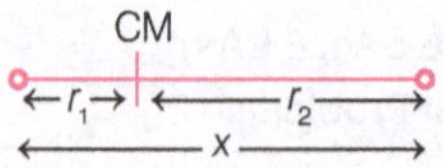

$$\therefore \quad r_1 = \left(\frac{m_2}{m_1 + m_2}\right) x \quad \text{and} \quad r_2 = \left(\frac{m_1}{m_1 + m_2}\right) x$$

Example 1. **Two bodies of masses 1 kg and 2 kg are located at (1, 2) and (−1, 3), respectively. Calculate the coordinates of the centre of mass.**

Sol. Given, $m_1 = 1\text{kg},\ m_2 = 2\text{kg},\ x_1 = 1\text{m},\ x_2 = -1\text{m}$

$$y_1 = 2\text{ m},\ y_2 = 3\text{ m}$$

$$\therefore \quad x_{CM} = \frac{m_1x_1 + m_2x_2}{m_1 + m_2} = \frac{1\times1 + 2\times(-1)}{1+2}$$

$$= \frac{1-2}{3} = \frac{-1}{3} = -0.33$$

and
$$y_{CM} = \frac{m_1y_1 + m_2y_2}{m_1 + m_2}$$

$$= \frac{1\times2 + 2\times3}{1+2} = \frac{2+6}{3} = \frac{8}{3} = 2.66$$

Thus, the coordinates of centre of mass are (−0.33, 2.66).

For a System of n Particles

Consider a system of n particles having masses $m_1, m_2, m_3, \ldots, m_n$ occupying x-coordinates $x_1, x_2, x_3, \ldots, x_n$.

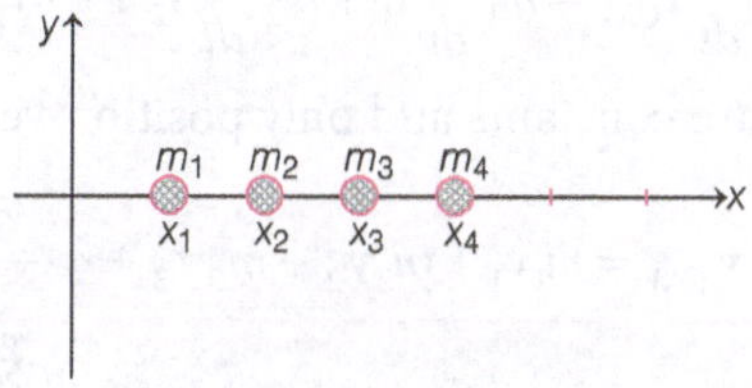

System of n particles

i.e. x_{CM} = x-coordinates of centre of mass of system

$$= \frac{m_1x_1 + m_2x_2 + m_3x_3 + \cdots + m_nx_n}{m_1 + m_2 + m_3 + \cdots + m_n}$$

$$\text{Centre of mass, } x_{CM} = \frac{\sum_{i=1}^{n} m_ix_i}{\Sigma m_i} = \frac{1}{M}\sum_{i=1}^{n} m_ix_i$$

$$y_{CM} = \frac{1}{M}\sum_{i=1}^{n} m_iy_i$$

and
$$z_{CM} = \frac{1}{M}\sum_{i=1}^{n} m_iz_i$$

where, $M = m_1 + m_2 + \cdots = \sum_{i=1}^{n} m_i$ is the total mass of the system. The index i runs from 1 to n, m_i is the mass of the ith particle and the position of the ith particle is given by (x_i, y_i, z_i).

Example 2. **Three masses 3 kg, 4 kg and 5 kg are located at the corners of an equilateral triangle of side 1m. What are the coordinates of centre of mass of this system?**

Sol. Suppose the equilateral triangle lies in the xy-plane with mass 3 kg at the origin. Let (x, y) be the coordinates of centre of mass.

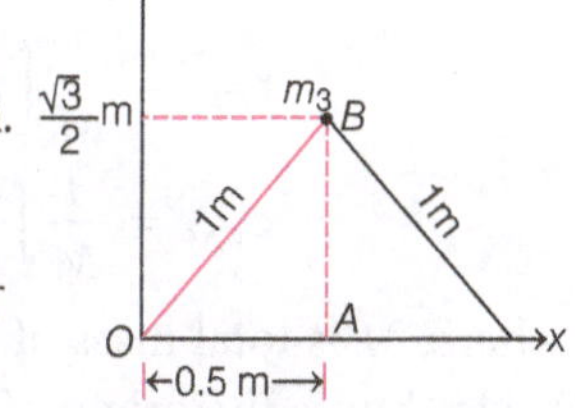

Clearly, $AB = \sqrt{(OB)^2 - (OA)^2}$

$$= \sqrt{(1)^2 - \left(\frac{1}{2}\right)^2} = \frac{\sqrt{3}}{2}\text{m}$$

Now, $x_1 = 0, x_2 = 1\text{m}, x_3 = OA = 0.5\text{ m}$

$$m_1 = 3\text{ kg}, m_2 = 4\text{ kg}, m_3 = 5\text{ kg}$$

$$\therefore \quad x = \frac{m_1x_1 + m_2x_2 + m_3x_3}{m_1 + m_2 + m_3}$$

$$= \frac{3\times0 + 4\times1 + 5\times0.5}{3+4+5} = \frac{6.5}{12} = 0.54\text{ m}$$

Again, $y_1 = 0, y_2 = 0,\ y_3 = AB = \frac{\sqrt{3}}{2}$

$$\therefore \quad y = \frac{m_1y_1 + m_2y_2 + m_3y_3}{m_1 + m_2 + m_3} = \frac{3\times0 + 4\times0 + 5\times\left(\frac{\sqrt{3}}{2}\right)}{3+4+5}$$

$$= \frac{5\times\sqrt{3}}{2\times12} = 0.36\text{ m}$$

Thus, the coordinates of centre of mass are (0.54 m, 0.36 m).

Relation between Position Vectors of Particles and Centre of Mass

We can also define centre of mass in terms of vector. Let r_i be the position vector of the i th particle and $\mathbf{R}$ be the position vector of the centre of mass, then

$$\mathbf{r}_i = x_i\hat{i} + y_i\hat{j} + z_i\hat{k} \quad \text{and } \mathbf{R} = x\hat{i} + y\hat{j} + z\hat{k}$$

$$\text{Position vector of the centre of mass, } \mathbf{R} = \frac{\sum_{i=1}^{n} m_i\mathbf{r}_i}{m}$$

If the origin of the frame of reference is considered at the centre of mass, then

$$\mathbf{R}_{CM} = 0$$

So,
$$\sum_{i=1}^{n} m_i\mathbf{r}_i = 0$$

Centre of Mass of Rigid Continuous Bodies

For a real body which is a continuous distribution of matter, point masses are then differential mass elements dm and centre of mass is defined as

$$x_{CM} = \frac{1}{M}\int x\, dm, \quad y_{CM} = \frac{1}{M}\int y\, dm$$

$$z_{CM} = \frac{1}{M}\int z\, dm$$

where, M is total mass of that real body.

If we choose the origin of coordinate axes at centre of mass, then

$$\int x\, dm = \int y\, dm = \int z\, dm = 0$$

Position of the Centre of Mass in the Absence of External Force

In the absence of an external force, the position of the centre of mass of a stationary system does not change. However, if under the influence of external forces, the position of different particles of masses $m_1, m_2, m_3, \ldots$ changes by $\Delta \mathbf{r}_1, \Delta \mathbf{r}_2, \ldots$, then shift in the position vector of the centre of mass is given by

$$\Delta \mathbf{r}_{CM} = \frac{m_1 \Delta \mathbf{r}_1 + m_2 \Delta \mathbf{r}_2 + \ldots + m_n \Delta \mathbf{r}_n}{m_1 + m_2 + \ldots + m_n} = \frac{\sum_{i=1}^{n} m_i \Delta \mathbf{r}_i}{\sum_{i=1}^{n} m_i}$$

Centre of Mass of a Uniform Thin Rod

Let us consider a uniform thin rod AB of mass M and length L. The rod is held along x-axis with its end A at the origin, where $x = y = 0$, as shown in figure.

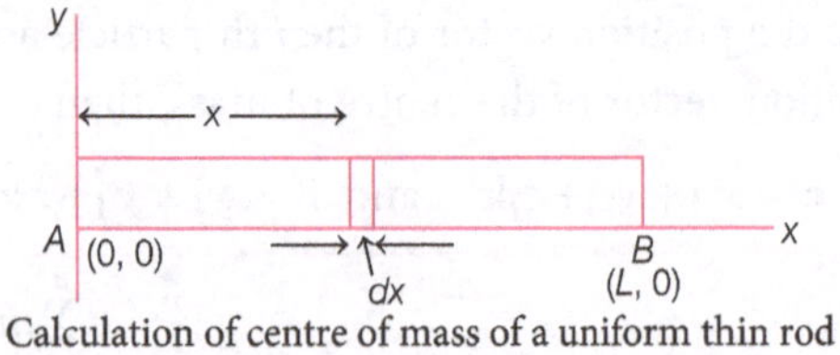

Calculation of centre of mass of a uniform thin rod

Suppose the element is placed side by side of length dx at distance, x from the origin.

Then, mass of element, $dm = \frac{M}{L} dx$

Let (x_{CM}, y_{CM}) be the coordinates of centre of mass of thin rod from origin. Then,

$$x_{CM} = \frac{1}{M}\int_0^L x\, dm = \frac{1}{M}\int_0^L x\left(\frac{M}{L}\right) dx = \frac{1}{L}\left.\frac{x^2}{2}\right|_0^L = \frac{L}{2}$$

Centre of mass, $x_{CM} = \frac{L}{2}$

and $\quad y_{CM} = \frac{1}{M}\int y\, dm = 0 \quad [\because y = 0 \text{ for thin rod}]$

$$y_{CM} = 0$$

Thus, it means that the **centre of mass of thin rod AB lies at point $\left(\frac{L}{2}, 0\right)$ i.e. centre between its ends A and B.** Thus, the centre of mass coincides with the geometric centre.

6.3 Motion of Centre of Mass

As already defined for a system of n particles, we can relate position vector of centre of mass and that of individual masses as

$$M \cdot \mathbf{r}_{CM} = m_1\mathbf{r}_1 + m_2\mathbf{r}_2 + m_3\mathbf{r}_3 + \cdots + m_n\mathbf{r}_n$$

Differentiating with respect to time, we get

$$M \cdot \frac{d}{dt}\mathbf{r}_{CM} = m_1 \frac{d}{dt}\mathbf{r}_1 + m_2 \frac{d}{dt}\mathbf{r}_2 + \cdots + m_n \frac{d}{dt}\mathbf{r}_n$$

As masses are constants and only position vectors are variables

$$\Rightarrow \quad M \cdot \mathbf{v}_{CM} = m_1\mathbf{v}_1 + m_2\mathbf{v}_2 + m_3\mathbf{v}_3 + \cdots + m_n\mathbf{v}_n$$

So, $\quad$ Velocity about centre of mass, $\mathbf{v}_{CM} = \frac{\sum_{i=1}^{n} m_i \mathbf{v}_i}{M}$

where, $\mathbf{v} = \frac{d\mathbf{r}}{dt}$, rate of change of position vector is velocity.

Again, differentiating the result, we get

$$M\frac{d}{dt}\mathbf{v}_{CM} = m_1\frac{d}{dt}\mathbf{v}_1 + m_2\frac{d}{dt}\mathbf{v}_2 + m_3\frac{d}{dt}\mathbf{v}_3 + \cdots + m_n\frac{d}{dt}\mathbf{v}_n$$

$$M\mathbf{a}_{CM} = m_1\mathbf{a}_1 + m_2\mathbf{a}_2 + \cdots + m_n\mathbf{a}_n$$

Acceleration about centre of mass, $\mathbf{a}_{CM} = \frac{S_{i=1}^{n} m_i \mathbf{a}_i}{M}$

But $m_i \mathbf{a}_i$ is the resultant force on the ith particle, so

$$M\mathbf{a}_{CM} = \mathbf{F}_1 + \mathbf{F}_2 + \mathbf{F}_3 + \cdots + \mathbf{F}_n$$

or $\quad M\mathbf{a}_{CM} = \mathbf{F}_{\text{net, ext}} \quad \ldots$(i)

where, $\mathbf{F}_{\text{net, ext}} = \mathbf{F}_1 + \mathbf{F}_2 + \mathbf{F}_3 + \cdots + \mathbf{F}_n$ is net force of all external forces that act on the system.

From the expression (i), it is clear that **the centre of mass of a system of particles moves as if whole mass of the system was concentrated at the centre of mass and all the external forces were applied at that point.**

TEACHER TIP

Internal forces are **action-reaction pairs** and hence, cancel out and only vector sum of external forces remain in the system. The internal forces do not contribute in the motion of centre of mass.

Linear Momentum of a System of Particles

For a system of n particles, total linear momentum is vector sum of linear momenta of individual particles.

So, linear momentum of system is

$$\mathbf{p} = \mathbf{p}_1 + \mathbf{p}_2 + \mathbf{p}_3 + \ldots + \mathbf{p}_n$$

or $$\mathbf{p} = m_1\mathbf{v}_1 + m_2\mathbf{v}_2 + m_3\mathbf{v}_3 + \cdots + m_n\mathbf{v}_n \quad \ldots\text{(i)}$$

From the concept of centre of mass, we know that,

$$m_1\mathbf{v}_1 + m_2\mathbf{v}_2 + m_3\mathbf{v}_3 + \cdots + m_n\mathbf{v}_n = M \cdot \mathbf{v}_{CM} \quad \ldots\text{(ii)}$$

From Eqs. (i) and (ii), we get

$$\text{Total linear momentum, } \mathbf{p} = M\mathbf{v}_{CM} \quad \ldots\text{(iii)}$$

Thus, **the total momentum of a system of particles is equal to the product of the total mass and velocity of its centre of mass.**

Newton's Second Law for System of Particles

Now, differentiating Eq. (iii) with respect to time, we get

or $$\frac{d\mathbf{p}}{dt} = M\frac{d}{dt}\mathbf{v}_{CM} \quad [\text{if } M \text{ is constant}]$$

or $$\frac{d\mathbf{p}}{dt} = M\,\mathbf{a}_{CM} \quad \ldots\text{(iv)}$$

From centre of mass concept, we know that,

$$M\mathbf{a}_{CM} = \text{net external force} \quad \ldots\text{(v)}$$

From Eqs. (iv) and (v), we get

$$\text{Net external force, } \mathbf{F}_{ext} = \frac{d\mathbf{p}}{dt} \quad \ldots\text{(vi)}$$

Above expression represents Newton's second law for system of particles. Here, **p** is net momentum of the system and $\mathbf{F}_{ext}$ is the net external force applied on the system.

Conservation of Linear Momentum for System of Particles

If net external force acting on the system of particles is zero,

i.e. $$\mathbf{F}_{ext} = 0, \text{ then } \frac{d\mathbf{p}}{dt} = 0$$

or **rate of change of momentum is zero. i.e. momentum of system remains constant.**

So, $$\mathbf{p}_{initial} = \mathbf{p}_{final}, \text{ if } \mathbf{F}_{ext} = 0 \quad \ldots\text{(vii)}$$

Above expression represents the law of conservation of linear momentum for system of particles.

- If mass of system assume to be constant the velocity of center of mass of the system will remains constant.
- The vector equation $\frac{d\mathbf{p}}{dt}$ = constant is equivalent to the component of the total linear momentum vector **p** along X, Y and Z-axes are constant.

Example 3. **Two particles of masses $m_1 = 2$ kg and $m_2 = 3$ kg have position vectors $\mathbf{r}_1 = t\hat{i} + 2t^2\hat{j} + 2t\hat{k}$ and $\mathbf{r}_2 = \hat{i} + 2t^3\hat{j} + 5\hat{k}$ respectively, where the position vector of r_1 and r_2 is in metres and time is in seconds. Calculate the velocity and acceleration of centre of mass of two particles system.**

Sol. Here, $m_1 = 2$ kg, $m_2 = 3$ kg, $\mathbf{r}_1 = t\hat{i} + 2t^2\hat{j} + 2t\hat{k}$

and $\mathbf{r}_2 = \hat{i} + 2t^3\hat{j} + 5\hat{k}$

Now, velocity of first particle, $\mathbf{v}_1 = \frac{d}{dt}(\mathbf{r}_1)$

$$= \frac{d}{dt}(t\hat{i} + 2t^2\hat{j} + 2t\hat{k})$$

$$\mathbf{v}_1 = \hat{i} + 4t\hat{j} + 2\hat{k}$$

Velocity of second particle,

$$\mathbf{v}_2 = \frac{d}{dt}(\mathbf{r}_2)$$

$$\mathbf{v}_2 = \frac{d}{dt}(\hat{i} + 2t^3\hat{j} + 5\hat{k}) = 6t^2\hat{j}$$

∴ Velocity of centre of mass of two particles system,

$$\mathbf{v}_{CM} = \frac{m_1\mathbf{v}_1 + m_2\mathbf{v}_2}{m_1 + m_2}$$

$$= \frac{2\times(\hat{i} + 4t\hat{j} + 2\hat{k}) + 3\times(6t^2\hat{j})}{2+3}$$

$$= \frac{2\hat{i} + (8t + 18t^2)\hat{j} + 4\hat{k}}{5}$$

$$= \left[\frac{2}{5}\hat{i} + \frac{(8t+18t^2)}{5}\hat{j} + \frac{4}{5}\hat{k}\right] \text{m/s}$$

Now, acceleration of first particle,

$$a_1 = \frac{d}{dt}(v_1) = \frac{d}{dt}(\hat{i} + 4t\hat{j} + 2\hat{k}) = 4\hat{j}$$

Acceleration of second particle,

$$a_2 = \frac{d}{dt}(v_2) = \frac{d}{dt}(6t^2\hat{j}) = 12t\hat{j}$$

∴ Acceleration of centre of mass of two particles system is calculated as

$$a_{CM} = \frac{m_1 a_1 + m_2 a_2}{m_1 + m_2}$$

$$= \frac{2(4\hat{j}) + 3(12t\hat{j})}{2+3}$$

$$a_{CM} = \left[\frac{(8+36t)}{5}\hat{j}\right] \text{m/s}^2$$

Quick Test 1

Conceptual Questions

1. A cricket bat is cut through its centre of mass into two parts as shown Then, state whether both parts are of same mass or not. Also, give reason.

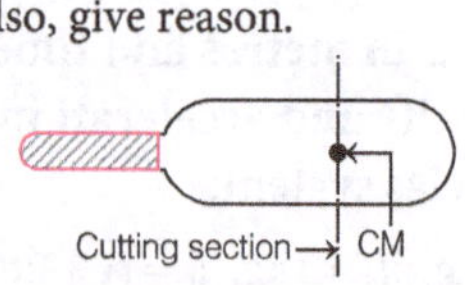

2. The bottom of a ship is made heavy. Why
3. Centre of gravity of a body on the earth coincides with its centre of mass for a small object and for a large object, it may not.
4. If two point masses are placed at (+2 m) and (−2 m), is it necessary that the centre of mass of system must lie at origin?

Numerical Questions

5. Three particles of masses 2kg, 3kg, and 5kg are located at co-ordinates (1,2) (3,4) and (5,6) meters, respectively. Find the co-ordinates of the centre of mass of the system.

Answers

5. (3.6 m, 4.6 m)

For Solutions, See QR Code on Pg. 226

6.4 Moment of Force (Torque)

The moment of force or torque due to a force gives the turning effect of the force about a fixed point or axis.

It is the vector product of position vector (r) of point of application of force and the applied force (F). Let us consider a particle *P* and force F acting on it.

Let the position vector of point of application of force about *O* be r.

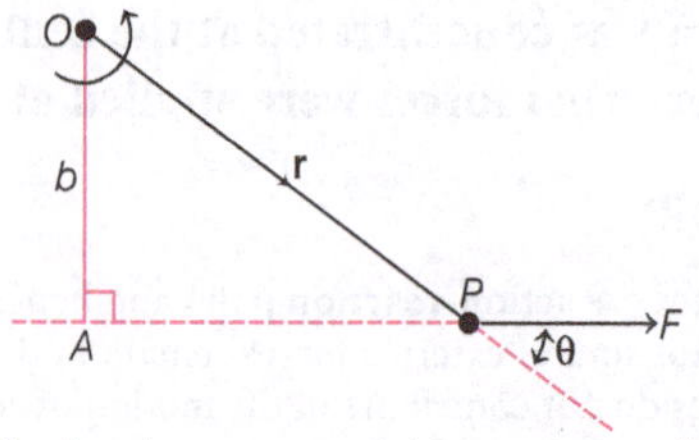

Particle showing torque, position vector and force

From figure, the torque τ acting on the particle relative to the fixed point *O* is a vector quantity and is defined as

$$\text{Torque, } \tau = \mathbf{r} \times \mathbf{F}$$

The magnitude of torque $|\tau|$ is $\tau = rF\sin\theta = Fr\sin\theta$

$$\tau = Fr_{\perp} = Fb \text{ (from figure)}$$

Here, $r_{\perp}$ is the perpendicular distance of the line of action of F from the point *O*.

Torque could be zero, if $r = 0$ or $F = 0$ or $\theta = 0, 180°$

In SI system, torque is expressed in newton-metre (N-m), it has same dimensions as that of work done. Dimensions of torque are $[ML^2T^{-2}]$.

According to vector product, **the direction of torque is perpendicular to the plane of r and F.**

If the body is rotating counterclockwise, then the torque is taken positive otherwise negative.

Example 4. **Find the torque of a force $7\hat{i}+3\hat{j}-5\hat{k}$ about the origin. The force acts on a particle whose position vector is $\hat{i}-\hat{j}+\hat{k}$.**

Sol. Given, position vector, $\mathbf{r} = \hat{i} - \hat{j} + \hat{k}$

Force, $\mathbf{F} = 7\hat{i} + 3\hat{j} - 5\hat{k}$

Torque, $\tau = ?$

$$\therefore \quad \tau = \mathbf{r} \times \mathbf{F} = \begin{vmatrix} \hat{i} & \hat{j} & \hat{k} \\ 1 & -1 & 1 \\ 7 & 3 & -5 \end{vmatrix}$$

$$= (5-3)\hat{i} - (-5-7)\hat{j} + (3+7)\hat{k}$$

$$= 2\hat{i} + 12\hat{j} + 10\hat{k}$$

6.5 Angular Momentum of a Particle

Angular momentum (L) can be defined as **moment of linear momentum** about a point.

The angular momentum of a particle of mass *m* moving with velocity v (having a linear momentum $\mathbf{p} = m\mathbf{v}$)

about a point O is defined by the following vector product.

$$\mathbf{L} = \mathbf{r} \times \mathbf{p}$$

or $\boxed{\text{Angular momentum, } \mathbf{L} = m(\mathbf{r} \times \mathbf{v})}$

$\mathbf{L}$ is the angular momentum of particle about point O,
$\mathbf{r}$ is the position vector of the particle about point O.

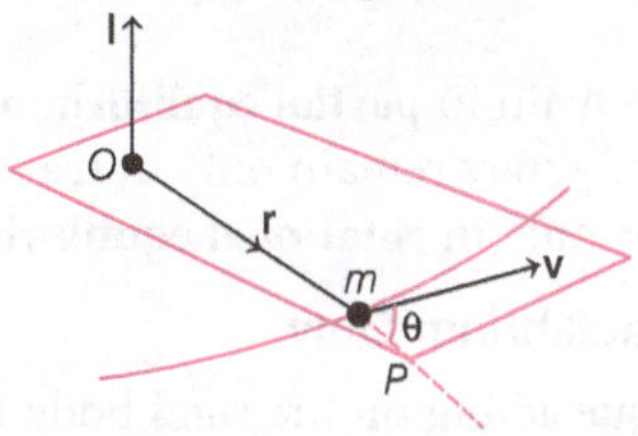

A particle moving about a point O

Magnitude of angular momentum depends on the position of point O and is given by $L = mvr\sin\theta$

where, θ = angle between $\mathbf{r}$ and $\mathbf{v}$

L can be represented as $L = rp\sin\theta = rp_\perp$

where, $p_\perp$ $(p\sin\theta)$ is the component of $\mathbf{p}$ in a direction perpendicular to $\mathbf{r}$.

and $\quad L = pr\sin\theta = pr_\perp$

where, $r_\perp$ is the perpendicular distance of the linear momentum vector ($\mathbf{p}$) from origin.

Example 5. **In a hydrogen atom, electron revolves in a circular orbit of radius 0.53 Å with a velocity of 2.2×10^6 m/s with an angle 30°. If the mass of electron is 9×10^{-31} kg, then find its angular momentum.**

Sol. Given, $r = 0.53\text{Å} = 0.53\times10^{-10}$ m,
$m = 9\times10^{-31}$ kg, $v = 2.2\times10^6$ m/s,
$\theta = 30°$, L = ?

$\therefore \quad L = mvr\sin\theta$
$= 9\times10^{-31}\times2.2\times10^6\times0.53\times10^{-10}\times\sin30°$
$= 5.247\times10^{-35}$ kg-m²/s

Relation between Torque and Angular Momentum

As angular momentum, $\mathbf{L} = \mathbf{r}\times\mathbf{p}$ or $\mathbf{L} = m(\mathbf{r}\times\mathbf{v})$

Differentiating with respect to time,

$$\frac{d\mathbf{L}}{dt} = \frac{d}{dt}m(\mathbf{r}\times\mathbf{v})$$

or $$\frac{d\mathbf{L}}{dt} = m\left(\frac{d\mathbf{r}}{dt}\times\mathbf{v} + \mathbf{r}\times\frac{d\mathbf{v}}{dt}\right)$$

[from product rule of differentiation]

But $\quad \frac{d\mathbf{r}}{dt} = \mathbf{v}$ and $\mathbf{v}\times\mathbf{v} = 0$

So, $$\frac{d\mathbf{L}}{dt} = m\left(\mathbf{r}\times\frac{d\mathbf{v}}{dt}\right)$$

But $\quad \frac{dv}{dt} = a$ = acceleration $= m(\mathbf{r}\times\mathbf{a}) = (\mathbf{r}\times m\mathbf{a}) = \mathbf{r}\times\mathbf{F}$

As $\quad \tau = \mathbf{r}\times\mathbf{F}$

$\therefore$ Rate of change of angular momentum, $\frac{d\mathbf{L}}{dt} = \tau$

Above equation gives Newton's second law of motion in angular form, **rate of change of angular momentum is equal to the torque applied.**

Torque and Angular Momentum for a System of Particles

For a system of particles or a rigid body with n-particles, **the total angular momentum of the system is the vector sum of the angular momenta of the individual particles.**

$$\mathbf{L} = \mathbf{L}_1 + \mathbf{L}_2 + \mathbf{L}_3 + \cdots + \mathbf{L}_n = \sum_{i=1}^{n}\mathbf{L}_i$$

Differentiating the above expression with time,

$$\frac{d\mathbf{L}}{dt} = \sum_{i=1}^{n}\frac{d\mathbf{L}_i}{dt}$$

But $\sum_{i=1}^{n}\frac{d\mathbf{L}_i}{dt}$ is the net torque on the system, so

$$\frac{d\mathbf{L}}{dt} = \tau_{net}$$

i.e. **the net external torque τ_{net} acting on a system of particles is equal to the time rate of change of the system's total angular momentum L.**

For ith particle, the torque is given by

$$\tau = \mathbf{r}_i\times\mathbf{F}_i$$

The force $\mathbf{F}_i$ on the ith particle is the vector sum of external forces $\mathbf{F}_i^{ext}$ acting on the particle and the internal forces $\mathbf{F}_i^{int}$ exerted on it by other particles of the system. Then, total torque is given by

$$\tau = \sum\tau_i = \sum_i\mathbf{r}_i\times\mathbf{F}_i = \tau_{ext} + \tau_{int}$$

where, $\tau_{ext} = \sum_i\mathbf{r}_i\times\mathbf{F}_i^{ext}$ and $\tau_{int} = \sum_i\mathbf{r}_i\times\mathbf{F}_i^{int}$

According to Newton's third law of motion, $\tau_{int} = 0$,

then $\quad \tau_{ext} = \tau$.

$\therefore \quad \tau = \sum\tau_i$

$\boxed{\text{Rate of change of angular momentum, } \frac{d\mathbf{L}}{dt} = \tau_{ext}}$

Thus, **the time rate of the total angular momentum of a system of particles about a point is equal to the sum of the external torques acting on the system taken about the same point.**

Example 6. **At a certain time, a 0.25 kg object has a position vector $\mathbf{r} = (2\hat{i} - 2\hat{k})$ m. At that instant, its velocity is $\mathbf{v} = (-5\hat{i} + 5\hat{k})$ m/s and the force acting on it is $F = 4\hat{j}$ N.**

(i) What is the angular momentum of the object about the origin?

(ii) What is torque on it?

Sol. Angular momentum, $\mathbf{L} = \mathbf{r} \times \mathbf{p} = \mathbf{r} \times m\mathbf{v} = m(\mathbf{r} \times \mathbf{v})$

$$\text{Now, } \mathbf{r} \times \mathbf{v} = \begin{vmatrix} \hat{i} & \hat{j} & \hat{k} \\ 2 & 0 & -2 \\ -5 & 0 & 5 \end{vmatrix}$$

$$= \hat{i}[(0 \times 5) - (0 \times -2)] - \hat{j}[(2 \times 5) - (-2 \times -5)] + \hat{k}[2 \times 0 - (0 \times -5)]$$

$$= 0$$

So, angular momentum of particle is zero

$$\text{and } \tau = \text{torque} = \mathbf{r} \times \mathbf{F} = \begin{vmatrix} \hat{i} & \hat{j} & \hat{k} \\ 2 & 0 & -2 \\ 0 & 4 & 0 \end{vmatrix} = (8\hat{i} + 8\hat{k}) \text{ N-m}$$

6.6 Equilibrium of a Rigid Body

A rigid body is said to be in equilibrium if both of its linear momentum and angular momentum are not changing with time.

This means,

(i) the total force, i.e. the vector sum of all forces acting on the rigid body is zero.

$$\mathbf{F}_1 + \mathbf{F}_2 + \cdots + \mathbf{F}_n = \sum_{i=1}^{n} \mathbf{F}_i = 0$$

It is known as **translatory equilibrium.**

The above equation can be written in scalar form as

$$\sum_{i=1}^{n} \mathbf{F}_{ix} = 0, \sum_{i=1}^{n} \mathbf{F}_{iy} = 0 \text{ and } \sum_{i=1}^{n} \mathbf{F}_{iz} = 0$$

where, $\mathbf{F}_{ix}$, $\mathbf{F}_{iy}$ and $\mathbf{F}_{iz}$ are x, y and z-components of force $\mathbf{F}_i$.

(ii) The total torque, i.e. the vector sum of all torques acting on the body must be zero.

$$\tau_1 + \tau_2 + \tau_3 + \cdots + \tau_n = \sum_{i=1}^{n} \tau_i = 0$$

The above equation can be written in scalar form as

$$\sum_{i=0}^{n} \tau_{ix} = 0, \sum_{i=0}^{n} \tau_{iy} = 0 \text{ and } \sum_{i=0}^{n} \tau_{iz} = 0.$$

where, τ_{ix}, τ_{iy} and τ_{iz} are x, y and z-components of torque τ_i.

Rotational equilibrium condition remains valid for any origin.

A body may remain in **partial equilibrium** as well. It means that body may remain only in **translational equilibrium** or only in **rotational equilibrium.**

Rotational Equilibrium Only

If the net torque acting on the rigid body is zero but net force is non-zero, then rigid body is in rotational equilibrium only.

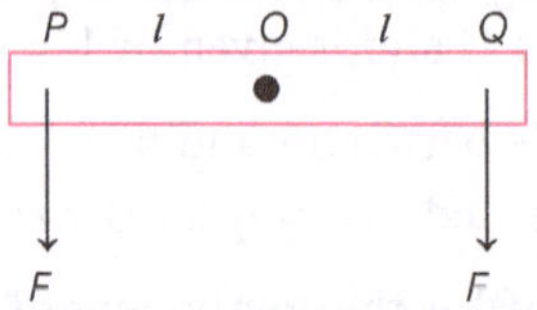

A rod under rotational equilibrium

Two equal forces are acting at the ends of a rod. In this case, the net torque produced by two forces will be zero, but net force is non-zero.

Translational Equilibrium Only

If the net force acting on the rigid body is zero but net torque is non-zero, then the rigid body is in translational equilibrium only.

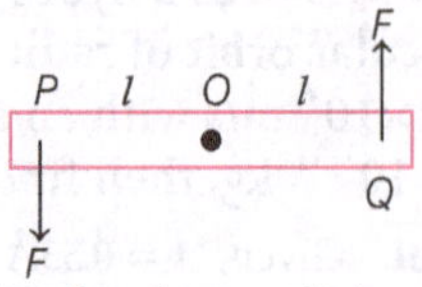

A rod under translational equilibrium

Two equal and opposite forces are acting at the ends of a rod.

In this case, the net force is zero, but both the forces will produce a non-zero torque.

Couple

A pair of equal and opposite forces with parallel lines of action is known as a couple. A couple produces rotation without translation.

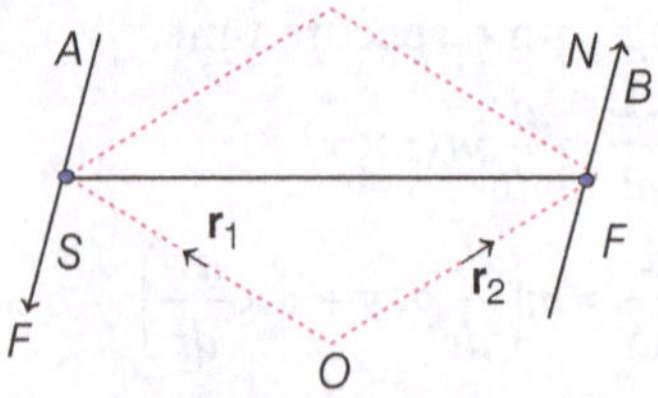

Equal and opposite forces acting at two different points

Let a couple with forces $-\mathbf{F}$ and $\mathbf{F}$ act at points A and B with position vectors $\mathbf{r}_1$ and $\mathbf{r}_2$ with respect to some origin O.

The moment of couple = total torque

$$= \mathbf{r}_1 \times (-\mathbf{F}) + \mathbf{r}_2 \times \mathbf{F}$$
$$= \mathbf{r}_2 \times \mathbf{F} - \mathbf{r}_1 \times \mathbf{F}$$
$$= (\mathbf{r}_2 - \mathbf{r}_1) \times \mathbf{F}$$

$\because$ Moment of couple = $\mathbf{AB} \times \mathbf{F}$

By triangle law, $\mathbf{r}_1 + \mathbf{AB} = \mathbf{r}_2$

So, $\mathbf{AB} = \mathbf{r}_2 - \mathbf{r}_1$

Hence, **moment of couple is independent of origin.** The couple acting an a rigid body cannot produce translatory motion.

Principle of Moment

When an object is in rotational equilibrium, then algebraic sum of all torques acting on it is zero. **Clockwise torques are taken negative and anti-clockwise torques are taken positive.**

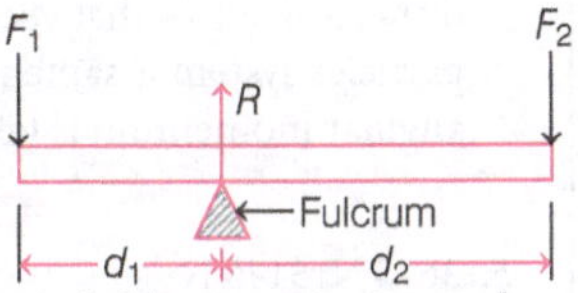

A fulcrum point in a rod

e.g. Consider a rod of negligible mass is provided at some point like a see-saw or a lever. Pivot of lever is called **fulcrum.**

For translational equilibrium,

$$\Sigma F = 0 \text{ or } R - F_1 - F_2 = 0$$

For rotational equilibrium, $\Sigma\tau = 0$ or $F_1 d_1 - F_2 d_2 = 0$

In case of levers, F_1 is called load, d_1 is **load arm,** F_2 is called **effort,** d_2 is **effort arm.**

As, $\quad F_1 d_1 - F_2 d_2 = 0$ or $F_1 d_1 = F_2 d_2$

or $\quad$ load $\times$ load arm = effort $\times$ effort arm.

This is called **principle of moment** for a lever.

Also, $\quad$ Mechanical advantage, $\dfrac{F_1}{F_2} = \dfrac{d_2}{d_1}$

The ratio $\dfrac{F_1}{F_2}$ is called **mechanical advantage** (MA).

Mechanical advantage greater than one is usually required as this means a small effort is required to lift a large load.

Centre of Gravity

If a body is supported at a point such that total gravitational torque about this point is zero, then this point is called centre of gravity of the body.

As, total gravitational torque about centre of gravity (CG) is zero.

Then, $\quad \tau_g = \sum_{i=1}^{n} \tau_i = \Sigma\, \mathbf{r}_i \times m\mathbf{g} = \mathbf{g} \cdot \Sigma m_i\, \mathbf{r}_i = 0$

[if g = constant]

So, $\quad \Sigma m_i \mathbf{r}_i = 0 \quad$ [As, $\mathbf{g} \neq 0$]

Above equation shows that with centre of gravity as origin,

$$\Sigma m_i\, \mathbf{r}_i = 0 \quad \text{...(i)}$$

The position vector of centre of mass $= \dfrac{1}{M} \cdot \Sigma m_i \cdot \mathbf{r}_i$

If centre of mass lies at origin,

$$0 = m_1\mathbf{r}_1 + m_2\mathbf{r}_2 + \dots + m_n\mathbf{r}_n, \quad \Sigma m_i \mathbf{r}_i = 0 \quad \text{...(ii)}$$

So, centre of gravity coincides with centre of mass, if g is constant. But, above statement is not true for very large objects as g will vary and CG does not coincide with CM.

Note CM and CG are two different concepts. For small bodies, g will be constant at all points on the body.

Centre of Gravity of a Body having an Irregular Shape

There is another way of determining the CG of irregular shape. If we suspend the body at point P and draw a vertical line, then it passes through CG of the body.

Similarly, do same thing with another point Q. Thus, the point of intersection of these vertical lines through P and Q gives CG of the body.

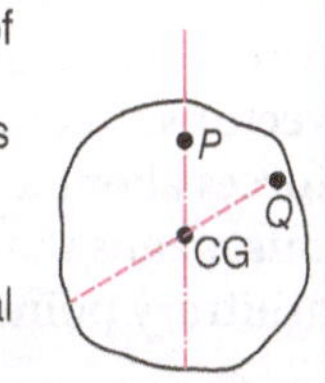

Example 7. **A non-uniform bar of weight w is suspended at rest by two strings of negligible weight as shown in the figure. Angles made by strings with vertical are 36.9° and 53.1°, respectively. If the bar is 2 m long, then calculate the distance x of the centre of gravity of bar from its left end.** *(NCERT)*

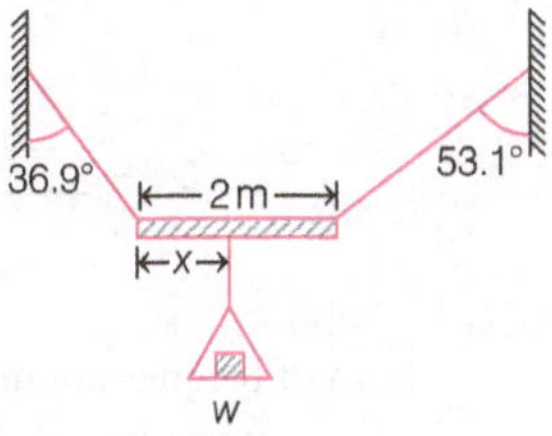

Sol. Bar is in equilibrium, so the total of forces and torque acting on it must be zero.

$$\Rightarrow \quad \Sigma F = 0 \text{ and } \Sigma\tau = 0$$

Let T_1 and T_2 are tensions in strings as shown below

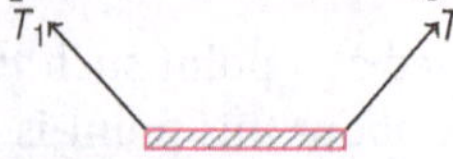

Then, force components are

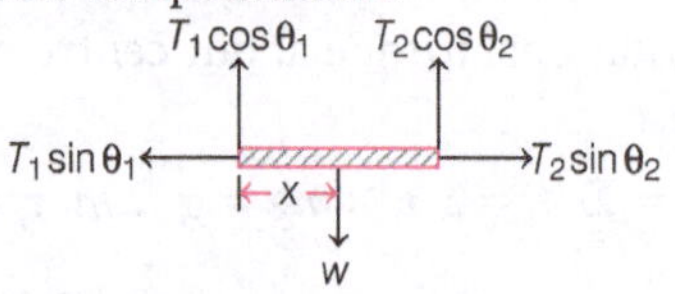

As, sum of vertical components is zero.

$\therefore \quad T_1\cos\theta_1 + T_2\cos\theta_2 - w = 0 \quad$ ...(i)

Sum of horizontal components is zero,

$T_1\sin\theta_1 = T_2\sin\theta_2 \quad$ ...(ii)

Sum of torques must be zero, (taking torque about left hand corner.)

$w \cdot x = T_2\cos\theta_2 \times 4 \quad$ ...(iii)

From Eq. (ii), $T_1 = \dfrac{T_2\sin\theta_2}{\sin\theta_1}$

Substituting in Eq. (i), we get

$T_2 = w\sin\theta_1/\sin\theta_2\cos\theta_1 + \cos\theta_2\sin\theta_1$

So, substituting for T_2 in Eq. (iii), we get

$$x = \frac{L\cdot\sin\theta_1\cos\theta_2}{\sin\theta_2\cos\theta_1 + \cos\theta_2\sin\theta_1} = L\cdot\frac{\sin\theta_1\cos\theta_2}{\sin(\theta_1+\theta_2)}$$

Here, $L = 2$ m, $\theta_1 = 36.9^\circ$, $\theta_2 = 53.1^\circ$

So, $\theta_1 + \theta_2 = 90^\circ$

$\therefore \quad x = 2 \times \sin 36.9^\circ \times \cos 53.1^\circ = 2.20$ m

Example 8. **The vector sum of a system of non-collinear forces acting on a rigid body is given to be non-zero. If vector sum of all the torques due to this system of forces about a certain point is found to be zero, does this means that it is necessarily zero about any arbitrary point.** NCERT Exemplar

Sol. Given that, $\sum_{i=1}^{n} F_i = 0$

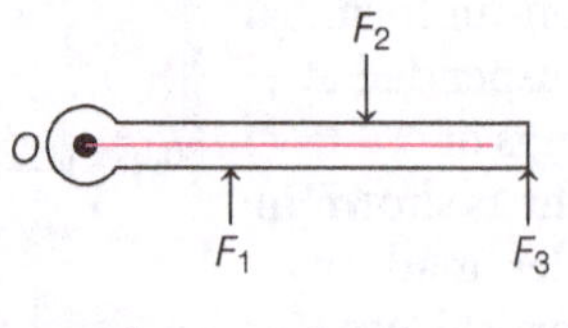

Sum of torques about a point O,

$\Sigma\, \mathbf{r}_i \times \mathbf{F}_i = 0$

Then, sum of torques about any other point A is

$\Sigma\tau = \Sigma(\mathbf{r}_i - \mathbf{a}) \times F_i$

$= \Sigma\, \mathbf{r}_i\mathbf{F}_i - \Sigma\, \mathbf{a}\times\mathbf{F}_i$

Clearly, second term is non-zero. Hence, sum of torques about any other point may not be zero.

Quick Test 2

Conceptual Questions

1. In a flywheel, most of the mass is concentrated at the rim. Explain, why?
2. Which component of linear momentum does not contribute to angular momentum?
3. If net torque on a rigid body is zero, does its linear momentum necessarily remain conserved?
4. Is the angular momentum of a body in translatory motion zero?

Numerical Questions

5. Consider a car of weight 1800 kg. The distance between its front and back axles is 1.8 m. Its centre of gravity is 1.05 m behind the front axle. Determine the force exerted by the level ground on each front wheel and each back wheel. NCERT
6. Two particles each of mass m and speed v travel in opposite direction along parallel lines separated by a distance d. Show that vector angular momentum of the two particles system is same whatever be the point about which angular momentum is taken.

Answers

5. 3675 N, 5145 N

For Solutions, See QR Code on Pg. 226

6.7 Moment of Inertia

The property of a body by the virtue of which it opposes the torque tending to change its state of rest or of uniform rotation about an axis is called **rotational inertia** or **moment of inertia.**

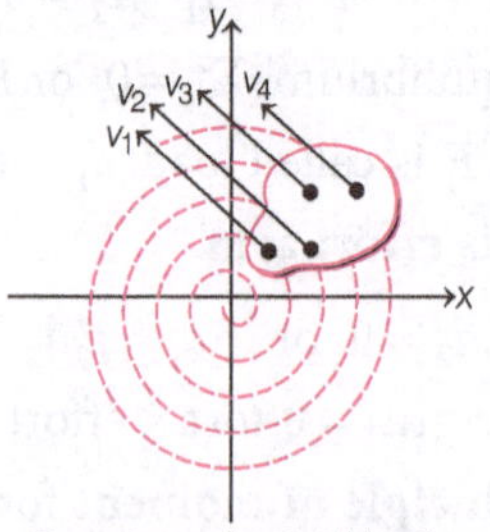

Rotation of a rigid body

To understand moment of inertia, let us consider a rigid body rotating about a fixed axis. For a rotating rigid body, **kinetic energy is the sum of kinetic energies of individual particles.**

So, kinetic energy of a rotating body,

$$K = \frac{1}{2}m_1v_1^2 + \frac{1}{2}m_2v_2^2 + \dots + \frac{1}{2}m_nv_n^2$$

or $$K = \sum_{i=1}^{n} \frac{1}{2}m_iv_i^2$$

Substituting $v = r\omega$,

$$K = \Sigma \frac{1}{2} m_i r_i^2 \omega^2$$

where, m_i is the mass of particle, v_i is its linear velocity. As, the angular velocity ω is same for all the particles of rigid body.

So, $$K = \frac{1}{2}\omega^2 \left(\sum_{i=1}^{n} m_i r_i^2\right) \quad \text{...(i)}$$

The quantity $\Sigma\,(m_i r_i^2)$ depends on distribution of mass around axis of rotation. This quantity is called **moment of inertia** (I).

$$\text{Kinetic energy, } K = \frac{1}{2} I\omega^2 \quad \text{...(ii)}$$

For translational motion, the kinetic energy of a particle of mass m and speed v is

$$\text{KE} = \frac{1}{2} mv^2 \quad \text{...(iii)}$$

By comparing Eqs. (ii) and (iii), we can get that moment of inertia is the rotational analogue of mass. So, for a rotating body, its moment of inertia,

$$I = \sum_{i=1}^{n} m_i r_i^2$$

Hence, **moment of inertia of a rigid body about a fixed axis is defined as the sum of the products of the masses of the particles constituting the body and the squares of their respective distances from the axis of rotation.**

The units of moment of inertia are kg-m^2 (in SI) or g-cm^2 (in CGS). The dimensions of moment of inertia are $[M^1L^2T^0]$.

Example 9. Three masses m_1, m_2 and m_3 are located at the vertices of an equilateral triangle of length a. What is moment of inertia of the system about an axis along the altitude of the triangle passing through m_1?

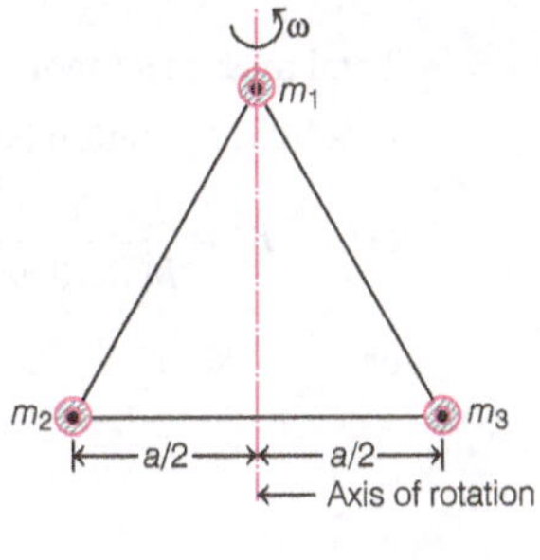

Sol. Moment of inertia of a system containing point masses is

$$I = \sum_{i=1}^{n} m_i r_i^2$$

$$\Rightarrow \quad I = m_1 r_1^2 + m_2 r_2^2 + m_3 r_3^2 + \ldots$$

where, m_i = mass of particle, r_i = distance from axis of rotation.

Now, $$r_1 = 0, r_2 = \frac{a}{2}, r_3 = \frac{a}{2} = \frac{a^2}{4}(m_1 + m_2)$$

Example 10. Two identical rods are connected as shown in the figure. Their axes make angle α. System is placed on a horizontal plane. The system is rotated about an axis passing through O and perpendicular to the plane of the rods. Find the moment of inertia of the system, if the mass of a rod is M and length of the rod is L.

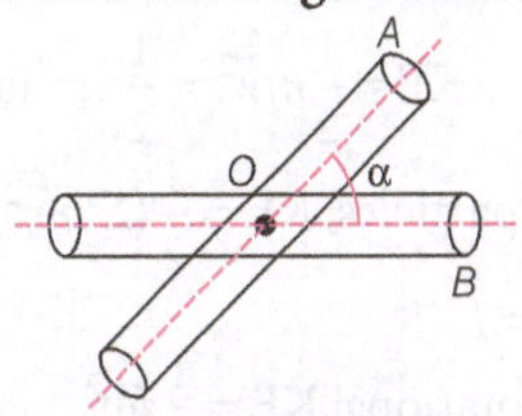

Sol. The moment of inertia of a rod about an axis passing through its centre and perpendicular to its plane is already defined.

$$I_0 = \frac{Ml^2}{12}$$

The moment of inertia of each rod is same for the same axis.

$$(I_A)_0 = (I_B)_0 = \frac{Ml^2}{12}$$

The angle α between their axes could create a confusion but observe carefully that moment of inertia is $\sum_{i=1}^{n} m_i r_i^2$, where r is the perpendicular distance of particles from the axis of rotation.

$$I_{\text{system}} = (I_A)_0 + (I_B)_0$$

So, we can simply add the two moments of inertia to get the moment of inertia of the system.

$$I_{\text{system}} = \frac{Ml^2}{12} + \frac{Ml^2}{12} = \frac{Ml^2}{6}$$

Some Important Points about Moment of Inertia

- Moment of inertia is a measure of rotational inertia and it plays same role as played by mass in translational motion.
- For continuous mass distributions, treating a differentially small mass as a particle, moment of inertia of complete body is

$$I = \int r^2\,dm$$

- A heavy wheel called flywheel is attached to the shaft of steam engine, automobile engine, etc. Because of its large moment of inertia, it acts as an energy reservoir.
  The flywheel opposes the sudden increase or decrease of the speed of the vehicle by supplying or gaining energy and maintains uniform rotation of the shaft.
- In a bicycle, bullock-cart, etc., the moment of inertia is increased by concentrating most of the mass at the rim of the wheel and connecting the rim to the axle through the spokes.
  Even after we stop paddling, the wheels of a bicycle continue to rotate for sometime due to their large moment of inertia.

Relation between Rotational Kinetic Energy and Moment of Inertia

We have rotational kinetic energy

$$KE = \frac{1}{2}(\Sigma mr^2)\,\omega^2$$

$\because$ $$KE = \frac{1}{2}mv^2 = \frac{1}{2}mr^2\omega^2$$

For system of n particles, $KE = \frac{1}{2}(\Sigma\, mr^2)\,\omega^2$

But $\Sigma\, mr^2 = I$

Therefore, rotational $KE = \frac{1}{2}I\omega^2$

When $\omega = 1$, rotational $KE = \frac{1}{2}I$

Moment of inertia, $I = 2 \times$ Rotational KE

Example 11. **An energy of 484 J is spent in increasing the speed of a flywheel from 60 rpm to 360 rpm. Calculate moment of inertia of flywheel.**

Sol. Energy spent, $W = 484$ J

Initial speed, $\omega_1 = 60 \text{ rpm} = \frac{60}{60} \times 2\pi = 2\pi$ rad/s

Final speed, $\omega_2 = 360 \text{ rpm} = \frac{360}{60} \times 2\pi = 12\pi$ rad/s

Moment of inertia, $I = ?$

$\therefore$ Energy spent, $W = E_2 - E_1 = \frac{1}{2}I\omega_2^2 - \frac{1}{2}I\omega_1^2$

$= \frac{1}{2}I[(12\pi)^2 - (2\pi)^2] = 70I\pi^2 \Rightarrow I = \frac{484}{70 \times \pi^2} = 0.7 \text{ kg-m}^2$

Radius of Gyration (K)

The radius of gyration of a body about an axis is defined as the **distance between the axis of rotation and a point at which the whole mass of the body is supposed to be concentrated, so as to possess the same moment of Inertia as that of body.**

When square of radius of gyration is multiplied with the mass of the body, it gives the moment of inertia of the body about the given axis.

$$I = MK^2$$

$$\text{Radius of gyration, } K = \sqrt{\frac{I}{M}}$$

If the body is composed of n particles and $r_1, r_2, \ldots r_n$ are their respective distance from the axis of rotation, then

$$K = \sqrt{\frac{r_1^2 + r_2^2 + \cdots + r_n^2}{n}}$$

Factors on which radius of gyration of a body depend

- Position and direction of the axis of rotation.
- Distribution of mass about the axis of rotation.

Example 12. **Four masses are rotated about an axis as shown. Find radius of gyration of the system.**

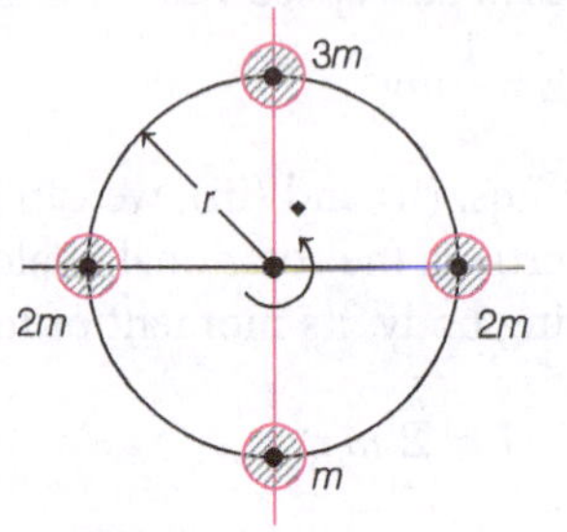

Sol. Moment of inertia of a mass about axis

$= \text{Mass} \times (\text{Distance})^2$

$\therefore$ Moments of inertia of masses are

$I_1 = 2mr^2 \Rightarrow I_2 = 3m \cdot r^2$

$I_3 = 2m \cdot r^2 \Rightarrow I_4 = m \cdot r^2$

So, total moment of inertia of system of masses

$= I_1 + I_2 + I_3 + I_4 = 8\,mr^2$

Total mass of system $= 8m$

If radius of gyration is K, then $I = MK^2$

or $K^2 = \frac{I}{M} = \frac{8\,mr^2}{8\,m}$

or $K = r$

Moment of Inertia in Some Standard Cases

Body	Axis of rotation	Figure	Moment of inertia	K	K^2/R^2
Thin circular ring, radius R	About an axis passing through CG and perpendicular to its plane	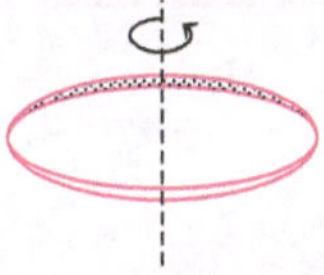	MR^2	R	1
Thin circular ring, radius R	About its diameter	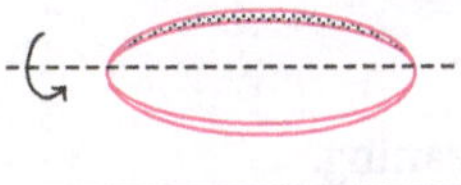	$\frac{1}{2}MR^2$	$\frac{R}{\sqrt{2}}$	$\frac{1}{2}$
Thin rod, length L	Perpendicular to rod at mid-point	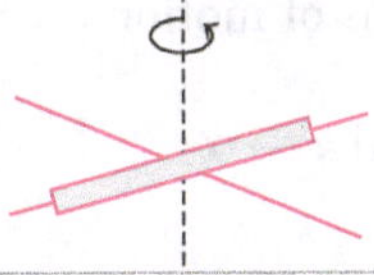	$\frac{1}{12}ML^2$	$\frac{L}{\sqrt{12}}$	
Circular disc, radius R	Perpendicular to disc at centre	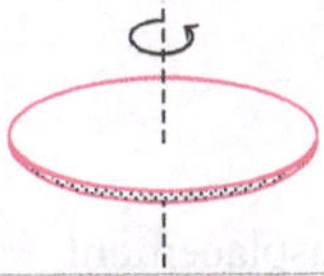	$\frac{1}{2}MR^2$	$\frac{R}{\sqrt{2}}$	$\frac{1}{2}$
Circular disc, radius R	Diameter	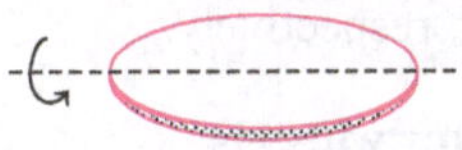	$\frac{1}{4}MR^2$	$\frac{R}{2}$	$\frac{1}{4}$
Hollow cylinder, radius R	About its own axis	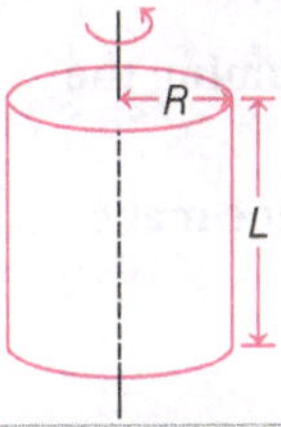	MR^2	R	1
Solid cylinder, radius R	About its own axis	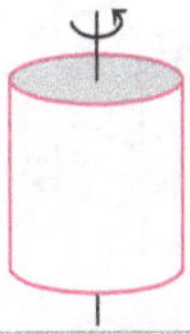	$\frac{MR^2}{2}$	$\frac{R}{2}$	$\frac{1}{2}$
Solid sphere, radius R	About its diametric axis	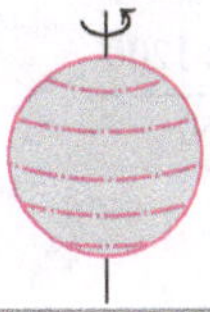	$\frac{2}{5}MR^2$	$\sqrt{\frac{2}{5}}R$	$\frac{2}{5}$

6.8 Kinetic Equations of Rotational Motion about a Fixed Axis

The three equations of linear motion are

(i) $v = u + at$

(ii) $s = ut + \frac{1}{2}at^2$

(iii) $v^2 - u^2 = 2as$

where, the symbols have their usual meaning.

In the similar way, we can write equations of motion for rotational motion such as using transformation $v \rightarrow \omega$, $v \rightarrow \omega_0$ and $a \rightarrow \alpha$

(i) $\omega = \omega_0 + \alpha t$

(ii) $\theta = \omega_0 t + \frac{1}{2}\alpha t^2$

(iii) $\omega^2 - \omega_0^2 = 2\alpha(\theta - \theta_0)$

where, θ_0 and ω_0 are the initial angular displacement and initial angular velocity of the body, respectively.

Example 13. **The angular speed of a motor wheel is increased from 1200 rpm to 3120 rpm in 16 s.**

(i) What is its angular acceleration, assuming the acceleration to be uniform?

(ii) How many revolutions does the engine make during this time? NCERT

Sol. (i) Given, initial revolution of the wheel,

$N_0 = 1200$ rpm

Final revolution of the wheel, $N = 3120$ rpm

Time, $t = 16$ s

Angular acceleration, $\alpha = ?$

Number of revolutions of the engine = ?

Initial angular speed,

$$\omega_0 = \frac{2\pi N_0}{60} = \frac{2\pi \times 1200}{60}$$

$$= 40\pi \text{ rad/s}$$

Final angular speed,

$$\omega = \frac{2\pi N}{60} = \frac{2\pi \times 3120}{60}$$

$$= 104\pi \text{ rad/s}$$

Angular acceleration, $\alpha = \frac{\omega - \omega_0}{t}$

$$\Rightarrow \quad \alpha = \frac{104\pi - 40\pi}{16} = 4\pi \text{ rad/s}^2$$

(ii) Now, evaluate the angular displacement of the motor wheel because the number of revolutions of the wheel of the engine is

$$N_E = \frac{\theta}{2\pi}$$

The angular displacement in time t is

$$\theta = \omega_0 t + \frac{1}{2}\alpha t^2$$

$$\theta = 40\pi \times 16 + \left[\frac{1}{2} \times 4\pi \times (16)^2\right]$$

$$= 1152\pi \text{ rad}$$

The number of revolutions done by the wheel of the engine in time, $t = 16$ s.

$$N_E = \frac{\theta}{2\pi} = \frac{1152\pi}{2\pi}$$

$$\Rightarrow \quad N_E = 576$$

Example 14. **A wheel has a constant angular acceleration of 4.2 rad/s^2. During a certain 8.0 s interval, it turns through angle of 140 rad. Assuming that wheel started from rest, how long it had been in motion before the start of the 8.0 s?**

Sol. Let ω_0 = initial angular speed at $t = 0$

Then, angle turned at end of 8.0 s is 140 rad.

Using $\quad \theta = \omega_0 t + \frac{1}{2}\alpha t^2$,

we have $\quad \omega_0 = \dfrac{\theta - \frac{1}{2}\alpha t^2}{t}$

$$\Rightarrow \quad \omega_0 = \frac{140 - \frac{1}{2}(4.2)(8.0)^2}{8.0}$$

$$\Rightarrow \quad \omega_0 = 0.7 \text{ rad/s}$$

Now, using $\omega = \omega_0 + \alpha t$ and taking $\omega = 0$.

We have,

$$t = \frac{\omega - \omega_0}{\alpha} = \frac{0 - \omega_0}{4.2}$$

$$= -\frac{0.7}{4.2} = -0.16 \text{ s}$$

So, wheel starts from rest 0.16 s before.

6.9 Dynamics of Linear and Rotational Motion

From the given table, we compare linear motion and rotational motion about a fixed axis, i.e. Z-axis.

Comparison of Translational and Rotational Motion

Pure translation	Pure rotational
Position, x	Angular position, θ
Velocity, $v = \dfrac{dx}{dt}$	Angular velocity, $\omega = \dfrac{d\theta}{dt}$
Acceleration, $a = \dfrac{dv}{dt}$	Angular acceleration, $\alpha = \dfrac{d\omega}{dt}$
Mass, m	Rotational inertia, I
Newton's second law, $F = ma$	Newton's second law, $\tau = I\alpha$
Work done, $W = \int F dx$	Work done, $W = \int \tau d\theta$
Kinetic energy, $K = \frac{1}{2}mv^2$	Kinetic energy, $K = \frac{1}{2}I\omega^2$
Power, $P = Fv$	Power, $P = \tau\omega$
Linear momentum, $p = mv$	Angular momentum, $L = I\omega$

Total KE of a body rolling without slipping

Total kinetic energy of a rolling body,

$$K = \frac{1}{2}I\omega^2 + \frac{1}{2}mv_{CM}^2$$

where, v_{CM} is the velocity of centre of mass.

$$\Rightarrow \quad K = \frac{1}{2}mK^2\left(\frac{v_{CM}}{R}\right)^2 + \frac{1}{2}v_{CM}^2$$

$$\Rightarrow \quad K = \frac{1}{2}mv_{CM}^2\left(1 + \frac{K^2}{R^2}\right)$$

Kinetic energy in terms of angular momentum is

$$K = \frac{1}{2}\frac{L^2}{I}$$

It is similar to kinetic energy in linear motion.

$$K = \frac{1}{2}\frac{p^2}{m}$$

Power delivered by a Torque

Consider a rigid body rotating about a fixed axis. Let F_1 be the force acting on a particle of the body at point P_1 with its line of action in a plane perpendicular to the axis.

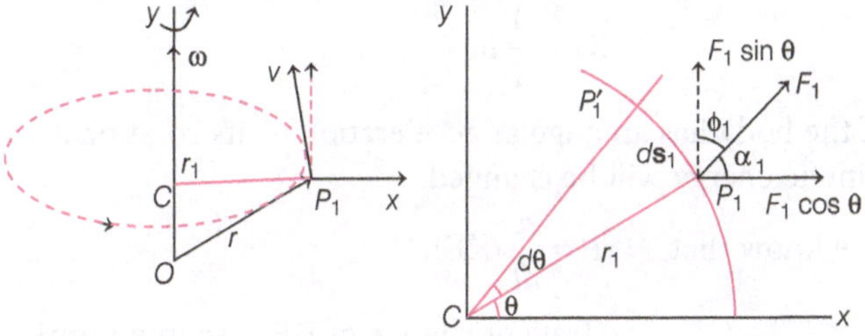

(a) The angular velocity vector ω is directed along the fixed axis (b) Work done by a force acting on a particle of a body

The particle at P_1 describes a circular path of radius r_1 with centre C on the axis, $CP_1 = r_1$.

At time Δt_1, the point moves to the position P_1' and displacement of the particle becomes ds_1.

Work done by the force on the particle is given by

$$dW_1 = \mathbf{F}_1 \cdot d\mathbf{s}_1 = F_1 ds_1 \cos\phi_1$$
$$= F_1(r_1 d\theta)\sin\alpha_1$$

where, ϕ_1 is the angle between $\mathbf{F}_1$ and the tangent at P_1 and α_1 is the angle between $\mathbf{F}_1$ and radius vector $\mathbf{OP}_1$, $\phi_1 + \alpha_1 = 90°$.

Torque due to $\mathbf{F}_1$ about the origin is given by

$$\tau_1 = \mathbf{OP}_1 \times \mathbf{F}_1$$

From Fig. (a), $OP_1 = OC + CP_1$ but OC is along the axis, therefore the torque resulting from it is excluded from our consideration.

Now, the effective torque due to F_1 is given by

$$\tau_1 = \mathbf{CP} \times \mathbf{F}_1$$

$$\therefore \quad dW_1 = \tau_1 d\theta$$

If there are more than one forces acting on the body, then work done is given by

$$dW = (\tau_1 + \tau_2 + \tau_3 + \ldots)d\theta$$
$$= \tau d\theta \qquad [\because \tau_1 + \tau_2 + \tau_3 + \ldots = \tau]$$

Dividing both sides by dt, we get

$$\frac{dW}{dt} = \tau\frac{d\theta}{dt}$$

$\Rightarrow$ Instantaneous power, $P = \tau\omega$

The above expression indicates **instantaneous power**.

Relation between Torque and Moment of Inertia

The rotational kinetic energy of a rigid body is represented by

$$KE = \frac{1}{2} I\omega^2$$

If the body has an angular acceleration α, its rotational kinetic energy will be changed.

We know that, $P = \frac{d}{dt}(KE)$

[rate of change of KE is momentum]

$$= \frac{d}{dt}\left(\frac{1}{2} I\omega^2\right) = \frac{1}{2} I \frac{d}{dt}(\omega^2) \quad \text{[if } I \text{ is constant]}$$

$$= \frac{1}{2} I (2\omega) \frac{d\omega}{dt}$$

$$P = I\omega\alpha \quad \left[\because \alpha = \frac{d\omega}{dt}\right]$$

$$\Rightarrow \quad \tau\omega = I\omega\alpha \quad [\because P = \tau\omega]$$

$$\boxed{\text{Torque, } \tau = I\alpha} \quad [\because I \text{ is constant}]$$

It is similar to the expression of Newton's second law for translational motion with constant mass.

Example 15. **A cord of negligible mass is wound round the rim of a flywheel of mass 20 kg and radius 20 cm. A steady pull of 25 N is applied on the cord. The flywheel is mounted on a horizontal axle with frictionless bearings.**

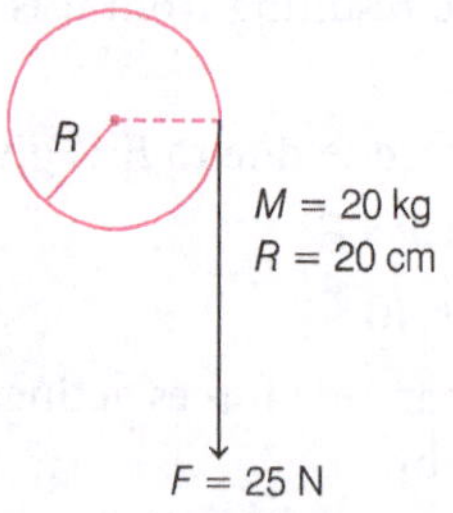

(i) Compute angular acceleration of the flywheel.

(ii) Find the work done by the pull when 2 m of the cord is unwound.

(iii) Also, find the KE of the flywheel at this point. Assume that the flywheel starts from rest.

(iv) Compare the answers of parts (ii) and (iii).

Sol. (i) Torque, $\tau = FR = 25 \times 0.20 = 5$ N-m

$[\because R = 20 \text{ cm} = 0.2 \text{ m}]$

Moment of inertia,

$$I = \frac{MR^2}{2} = \frac{20 \times (0.2)^2}{2} = 0.4 \text{ kg-m}^2$$

Angular acceleration, $\alpha = \frac{\tau}{I} = \frac{5}{0.4} = 12.5 \text{ rad/s}^2$

(ii) Work done by the pull, $W = F \times s = 25 \times 2 = 50$ J

(iii) $KE = \frac{1}{2} I\omega^2$

$$\omega^2 = \omega_0^2 + 2\alpha\theta = 0 + 2 \times 12.5 \times 10 = 250$$

$$\left[\because \omega_0 = 0, \theta = \frac{2}{0.2} = 10 \text{ rad}\right]$$

$$\therefore \quad KE = \frac{1}{2} \times 0.4 \times 250 = 50 \text{ J}$$

(iv) From parts (ii) and (iii), KE = W

$\therefore$ No loss of energy due to friction.

Example 16. **To maintain a rotor at a uniform angular speed of 200 rad s^{-1}, an engine needs to transmit a torque of 180 N-m. What is the power required by engine? Assume 100% efficiency of engine.**

Sol. Work done by torque in turning rotor by angle $d\theta$ is

$= \tau d\theta$

So, power delivered by engine,

$$P = \frac{\text{Work done}}{\text{Time taken}} = \tau \frac{d\theta}{dt}$$

[dt = time for turning by angle $d\theta$]

or $\quad P = \tau\omega$

So, power required $= 180 \times 200 = 36000$ W

$= 36$ kW $\quad [\because 1 \text{ kW} = 1000 \text{ W}]$

Angular Momentum in Case of Rotation about a Fixed Axis

The general expression for total angular momentum of a system of particles is given by

$$\mathbf{L} = \sum_{i=1}^{n} \mathbf{r}_i \times \mathbf{p}_i = \sum_{i=1}^{n} \mathbf{r}_i \times m_i \times \mathbf{v}_i = \sum_{i=1}^{n} \mathbf{r}_i \times m_i \times (\boldsymbol{\omega} \times \mathbf{r}_i)$$

Using vector triple product, we get

$$\mathbf{L} = \sum_{i=1}^{n} m_i[(\mathbf{r}_i \cdot \mathbf{r}_i)\boldsymbol{\omega} - (\mathbf{r}_i \cdot \boldsymbol{\omega}) \cdot \mathbf{r}_i]$$

$$= \sum_{i=1}^{n} m_i[r_i^2 \omega - 0] = \sum_{i=1}^{n} m_i r_i^2 \omega$$

For any individual particle, the vectors of angular momentum and angular velocity are not necessarily parallel. In case of linear motion, linear momentum and linear velocity, vectors are always parallel to each other.

In Z-axis, the moment of inertia, $I = \sum_{i=1}^{n} m_i \cdot r_1^2$ and substituting in the above equation, we get

$$\mathbf{L} = L_z = I\omega\,\hat{\mathbf{k}}$$

The magnitude of angular momentum is given by

$$\boxed{L = I\omega}$$

Conservation of Angular Momentum

As, $\dfrac{d\mathbf{L}}{dt} = \tau_{\text{net}}$ for the rigid body which can be treated as a system of n-particles. If $\tau_{\text{ext}} = 0$, then $\dfrac{d\mathbf{L}}{dt} = 0$, that means $\mathbf{L}$ = constant with time.

Hence, **without any external torque, angular momentum of a system of particles remain constant.** This is known as the conservation of angular momentum.

If $\qquad \tau_{\text{ext}} = 0$

$\Rightarrow \qquad \mathbf{L}_{\text{initial}} = \mathbf{L}_{\text{final}}$

If $\mathbf{L}$ is constant, then its all three components will also be constant.

$$L_x = \text{constant},\ L_y = \text{constant},\ L_z = \text{constant}$$

Applications of Law of Conservation of Angular Momentum

- A circus acrobat performs beats involving spin by bringing her arms and legs closer to her body or *vice-versa*.

  On bringing the arms and legs closer to the body, her moment of inertia I decreases, hence angular velocity ω increases. The same principle is applied by ice skater or a ballet dancer.
- All helicopters are provided with two propellers. If there were only one propeller, the helicopter would rotate itself in opposite direction.
- A diver performs somersaults by jumping from a high diving board keeping his legs and arms out stretched first and then curling his body.

  On doing so, the moment of inertia I of his body decreases. As angular momentum remains constant, therefore angular velocity ω of his body increases. He then performs somersaults. As the diver is about to touch the surface of water, he stretches out his limbs.

Example 17. A child stands at centre of a turntable with his arms out stretched. The turntable is set rotating with an angular speed of 40 rev/min.

(i) How much is the speed of child, if he folds his hands and thereby reduces his moment of inertia to 2/5 times of initial value? Assume turntable is frictionless.

(ii) Show that child's new kinetic energy of rotation is more than the initial kinetic energy. How do you account for this increase in kinetic energy?

NCERT Exemplar

Sol. (i) As no external torque is involved with child + turntable system, so angular momentum of system remains constant.

or $\qquad I_i\omega_i = I_f\omega_f$

where, $I_i\omega_i$ = initial angular momentum
and $I_f\omega_f$ = final angular momentum.

Here, $\qquad \omega_i = 40$ rpm $\Rightarrow I_f = \dfrac{2}{5} I_i$

Substituting, we get

$$I_i \times 40 = \frac{2}{5} I_i \times \omega_f$$

or $\qquad \omega_f = \dfrac{5 \times 40}{2} = 100$ rpm

(ii) Initial $\quad \text{KE} = \dfrac{1}{2} I_i\omega_i^2 = \dfrac{1}{2} \times I_i \times (40)^2$

$$= \frac{1}{2} \times I_i \times 1600 = 800\, I_i$$

$$\text{Final KE} = \frac{1}{2} I_f\omega_f^2 = \frac{1}{2} \times \frac{2}{5} I_i \times (100)^2$$

$$= \frac{1}{2} \times \frac{2}{5} \times I_i \times 100 \times 100 = 2000\, I_i$$

Clearly, final KE > initial KE. This energy is obtained from the conversion of muscular work in KE. Muscular work has to be done in folding of arms.

Example 18. A comet revolves around the sun in a highly elliptical orbit having a minimum distance of 7×10^{10} m and a maximum distance of 1.4×10^{13} m. If its speed while nearest to the sun is 60 kms^{-1}, find its linear speed when situated farthest from the sun.

Sol. Let mass of comet be M and its angular speed be ω when situated at a distance r from the sun, then its angular momentum, $L = I\omega = Mr^2\omega$

If v be the linear speed, then $L = Mr^2\omega = Mrv$

In accordance with conservation law of angular momentum, we can write that

$$mr_1v_1 = mr_2v_2$$

$$\therefore \quad v_2 = \frac{r_1v_1}{r_2} = \frac{7 \times 10^{10} \times 60}{14 \times 10^{13}}$$

$$= 0.3 \text{ km/s or } 300 \text{ m/s}$$

Quick Test 3

Conceptual Questions

1. Why moment of inertia is also called rotational inertia?

2. Two solid spheres of the same mass are made of metals of different densities. Which of them has a larger moment of inertia about the diameter? Why?

3. Why does a solid sphere have smaller moment of inertia than a hollow cylinder of same mass and radius about an axis passing through their axis of symmetry?

Numerical Questions

4. A rope of negligible mass is wound around a hollow cylinder of mass 3 kg and radius 40 cm. What is angular acceleration of the cylinder, if the rope is pulled with a force of 30 N? What is linear acceleration of the rope? Assume no slipping. NCERT

5. A solid cylinder of mass 20 kg rotates about its axis with angular speed (100 rad/s). The radius of cylinder is 0.25 m. What is the kinetic energy associated with the rotation of the cylinder? What is the magnitude of angular momentum of the cylinder about its axis? NCERT

6. A bullet of mass 10 g and speed 500 m/s is fired into a door and gets embedded exactly at the centre of the door. The door is 1.0 m wide and weight 12 kg. It is hinged at one end and rotates about a vertical axis practically without friction. Find the angular speed of the door just after the bullet embeds into it.

Answers

4. 2.5 s^{-2}, 10 m/s^2 5. 3125 J, 62.5 kg-m^2/s 6. 0.625 rad/s

For Solutions, See QR Code on Pg. 226

Mind Map

System of Particles and Rotational Motion

Rigid Body
It is an ideal solid object in which the distance between any two points remains constant, regardless of external forces or torques acting on it

Centre of Mass (CM) of a Rigid Body
It is the point where the entire mass of the body can be considered to be concentrated for analysing translational motion

$$\mathbf{R}_{CM} = \frac{1}{M}\int \mathbf{r}\, dm$$

Motion of Centre of Mass
The motion of the centre of mass describes how the centre of mass of a system moves under the influence of external forces.

The centre of mass obeys Newton's second law

$$M\mathbf{a}_{CM} = \mathbf{F}_{ext}$$

- Velocity of centre of mass,

$$v_{CM} = \frac{\sum_{i=1}^{n} m_i v_i}{M}$$

- Acceleration of centre of mass,

$$a_{CM} = \frac{\sum_{i=1}^{n} m_i a_i}{M}$$

Linear Momentum of a System of Particles
It is the vector sum of the individual momenta of all the particles in the system

$$\mathbf{p} = \sum_{i=1}^{n} m_i \mathbf{v}_i$$

Principle of Moments
It states that for an object to be in rotational equilibrium, the sum of the clockwise moments about a point must equal to the sum of the counter clockwise moments.

Equilibrium of Rigid Body
- A rigid body is said to be in equilibrium, if both of its linear momentum and angular momentum are not changing with time.
- A body in equillbrium does not possess linear acceleration or angular acceleration.

Translational Equilibrium
- If the net force acting on the rigid body is zero but net torque is non-zero, then rigid body is in translational equilibrium.

Rotational Equilibrium
- If the net torque acting on the rigid body is zero but net force is non-zero, then rigid body is in rotational equilibrium only.

Centre of Mass
The point in the system, where the whole mass of the system can be supposed to be concentrated.

Centre of Mass of a Two Particle System
It is the point where the system's total mass is effectively concentrated. It is given by

$$\mathbf{r}_{CM} = \frac{m_1\mathbf{r}_1 + m_2\mathbf{r}_2}{m_1 + m_2}$$

Centre of Mass of n Particle
- Suppose a system of n-particles having masses m_1, m_2, m_3 occupying. x-coordinate x_1, x_2, x_3, x_n
- Centre of mass, $x_{CM} = \dfrac{\sum_{i=1}^{n} m_i x_i}{\sum m_i}$

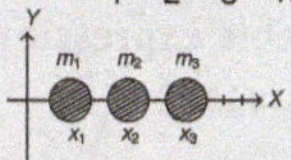

Centre of Mass of a Uniform Rod
- A uniform thin rod AB, mass M and length L.
- For X-axis $X_{CM} = \dfrac{L}{2}$
- For Y-axis, $Y_{CM} = \dfrac{1}{M}\int y\, dm = 0$

$\therefore$ $y = 0$, for thin rod.

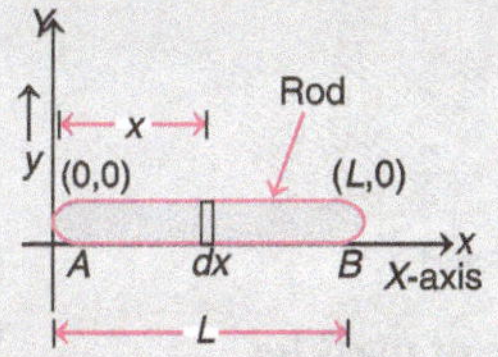

Moment of a Force
It is a measure of the tendency of a force to cause rotational motion about a point or axis. It is also called torque.

$$\tau = rF\sin\theta$$

- When $\theta = 90°$ torque is maximum and for $\theta = 0°$ or $180°$ torque is zero (minimum).

Angular Momentum
- It is defined as the moment of the linear momentum of the particle about fixed axis.
- Angular momentum, $\mathbf{L} = (\mathbf{r} \times \mathbf{v})m$
- SI unit of angular momentum is kg m^2s^{-1}.
- It is a vector quantity.

Principle of Conservation of Angular Momentum
If the net external torque acting on a body is zero,then its angular momentum remains constant. $\dfrac{dL}{dt} = \tau_{ext}$

If $\tau_{ext} = 0$, $\dfrac{d\mathbf{L}}{dt} = 0$, $\mathbf{L}$ = constant.

Translational Motion
The motion of an object in which all points move in the same direction and by the same distance.

Rotational Motion The motion of an object around a fixed axis, where different points on the object move in circular paths.

Rolling Motion The combined motion of translation and rotation, where an object rolls over a surface without slipping.

Kinematics and Dynamics of Rotational motion
(i) Instantaneous power, $P = \tau\omega$

(ii) K.E. $= \frac{1}{2}I\omega^2$

(iii) Torque, $\tau = I\alpha$

Rotational Kinematics Equations

(i) $\omega = \omega_0 + \alpha t$

(ii) $\theta = \omega_0 t + \frac{1}{2}\alpha t^2$

(iii) $\omega^2 - \omega_0^2 = 2\alpha(\theta - \theta_0)$

Moment of Inertia
It is a property of a body by the virture of which it opposes the torque tending to change its state of rest or uniform rotation about an axis.

$$I = \sum_{i=1}^{n} m_i r_i^2$$

Radius of gyration $K = \sqrt{\dfrac{I}{m}}$

Moment of Inertia of Regular Shapes
(i) Thin rod of length L,

$I = \frac{1}{12}ML^2$

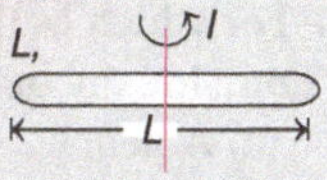

(ii) Circular ring of radius R,

$I = MR^2$

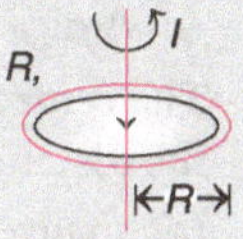

(iii) Solid sphere of radius R,

$I = \frac{2}{5}MR^2$

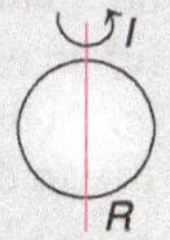

(iv) Circular disc of radius R,

$I = \frac{1}{4}MR^2$

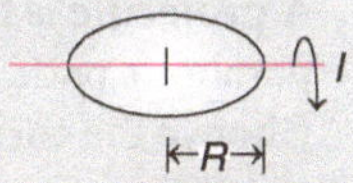

Relation between Angular and Linear Velocities
The linear velocity of a particle rotating about a fixed axis is given by

$$v = \omega r$$

where, ω is angular velocity of particle.

EXAM PATTERN QUESTIONS

Objective Type Questions

Multiple Choice Questions (MCQs)

1. A drum of radius R and mass M rolls down without slipping along an inclined plane of angle θ. The frictional force

(a) converts translational energy into rotational energy
(b) dissipates energy as heat
(c) decreases the rotational motion
(d) decreases the rotational and translational motion

2. For n-particles in a space, the suitable expression for the position vector of centre of mass is

(a) $\frac{\Sigma m_i \mathbf{r}_i}{m_i}$ (b) $m_i \mathbf{r}_i$
(c) $\frac{\Sigma m_i \mathbf{r}_i}{M}$ (d) $\frac{m_i \mathbf{r}_i}{m_i}$

3. Which of the following points is the likely position of the centre of mass of the system shown in figure?

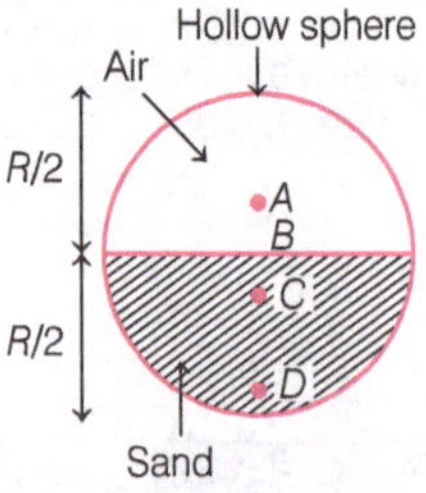

(a) A
(b) B
(c) C
(d) D

4. For which of the following does the centre of mass lie outside the body? NCERT Exemplar

(a) A pencil (b) A shotput
(c) A dice (d) A bangle

5. The centre of mass of a system of two particles divides the distance between them

(a) in inverse ratio of square of masses of particles
(b) in direct ratio of square of masses of particles
(c) in inverse ratio of masses of particles
(d) in direct ratio of masses of particles

6. A projectile is fired at an angle and it was following a parabolic path. Suddenly, it explodes into fragments. Choose the correct option regarding this situation. Competency Based Que.

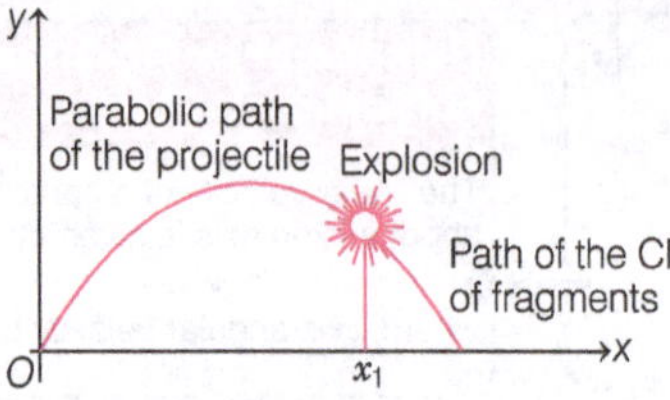

(a) Due to explosion, CM shifts upwards
(b) Due to explosion, CM shifts downwards
(c) Due to explosion, CM traces its path back to origin
(d) CM continues to move along same parabolic path

7. For rotational equilibrium,

(a) $\sum_{i=1}^{n} \mathbf{F}_{\text{net}} = 0$

(b) $\sum_{i=1}^{n} \tau_{\text{net}} = 0$

(c) Both (a) and (b) are the necessary conditions for the rotational equilibrium
(d) Both (a) and (b) are not necessary for rotational equilibrium

8. A rod is rotating about an axis passing through its centre and perpendicular to its length. The radius of gyration for the rod is

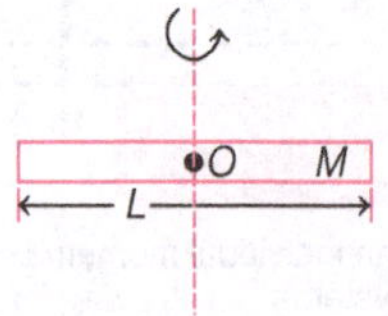

(a) $L/12$ (b) $L/\sqrt{12}$
(c) $L/6$ (d) $L/\sqrt{6}$

9. What is the moment of inertia of a ring about a tangent to the periphery of the ring?

(a) $\frac{1}{2}MR^2$ (b) $\frac{3}{2}MR^2$
(c) MR^2 (d) $MR^2/9$

10. When acrobat bends his body (assume no external torque)

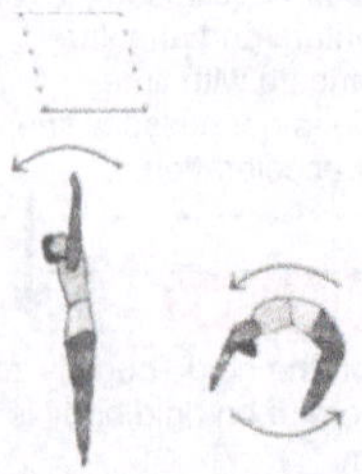

(a) I_{acrobat} decreases
(b) I_{acrobat} increases
(c) ω_{acrobat} increases
(d) Both (a) and (c)

11. Angular velocity vector is directed along
(a) the tangent to the circular path
(b) the inward radius
(c) the outward radius
(d) the axis of rotation

12. In translational equilibrium,
(a) $\sum_{i=1}^{n} \mathbf{F}_{net} = 0$ (b) $\sum_{i=1}^{n} \tau_{net} = 0$
(c) Both (a) and (b) are the necessary conditions for the translational equilibrium
(d) particle may be in equilibrium when (a) and (b) are not fulfilled.

13. A body is rotating with angular velocity $\omega = (3\hat{i} - 4\hat{j} - \hat{k})$. The linear velocity of a point having position vector $\mathbf{r} = (5\hat{i} - 6\hat{j} + 6\hat{k})$ is
(a) $6\hat{i} + 2\hat{j} - 3\hat{k}$ (b) $-18\hat{i} - 23\hat{j} + 2\hat{k}$
(c) $-30\hat{i} - 23\hat{j} + 2\hat{k}$ (d) $6\hat{i} - 2\hat{j} + 8\hat{k}$

14. In the game of see-saw, what should be the displacement of boy *B* from right edge to keep the see-saw in equilibrium? (M_1 = 40 kg, M_2 = 60 kg)
Competency Based Que.

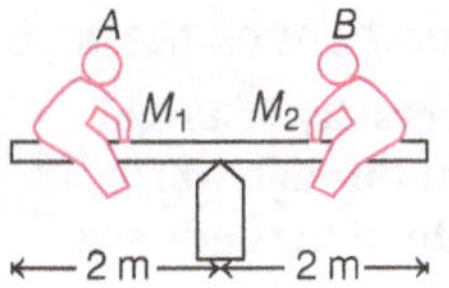

(a) $\frac{4}{3}$ m (b) 1m
(c) $\frac{2}{3}$ m (d) Zero

15. Two masses are joined with a light rod and the system is rotating about the fixed axis as shown in the figure. The MI of the system about the axis is

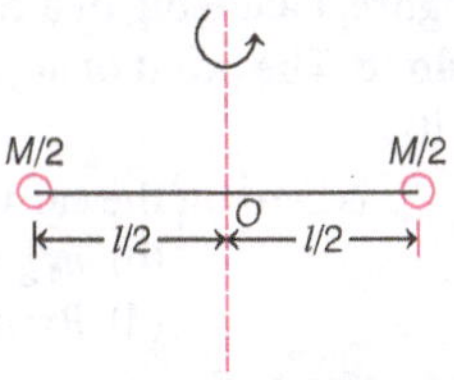

(a) $Ml^2/2$ (b) $Ml^2/4$
(c) Ml^2 (d) $Ml^2/6$

16. The angular velocity of a wheel increases from 100 rps to 300 rps in 10 s. The number of revolutions made during that time is
(a) 600 (b) 1500
(c) 1000 (d) 2000

17. If a girl rotating on a chair bends her hand as shown in figure, the (neglecting frictional force)

(a) I_{girl} will reduce
(b) I_{girl} will increase
(c) ω_{girl} will reduce
(d) None of these

18. When a disc rotates with uniform angular velocity, which of the following is not true? NCERT Exemplar
(a) The sense of rotation remains same.
(b) The orientation of the axis of rotation remains same.
(c) The speed of rotation is non-zero and remains same.
(d) The angular acceleration is non-zero and remain same.

19. A merry-go-round, made of a ring-like platform of radius *R* and mass *M*, is revolving with angular speed ω. A person of mass *M* is standing on it. At one instant, the person jumps off the round, radially away from the centre of the round (as seen from the round). The speed of the round of afterwards is NCERT Exemplar
(a) 2 ω (b) ω (c) $\frac{\omega}{2}$ (d) 0

20. Match Column I (terms) with Column II (definitions) and choose the correct option.

	Column I		Column II
A.	Torque	P.	The rotational analog of mass representing how mass is distributed relative to an axis of rotation.
B.	Moment of inertia	Q.	A state where the net force and net torque acting on a body are zero.
C.	Angular momentum	R.	A measure of the rotational effect of a force applied at a distance from an axis.
D.	Equilibrium	S.	The product of the moment of inertia and angular velocity representing the rotational motion of an object.

(a) A → R, B → S, C → P, D → Q
(b) A → S, B → P, C → R, D → Q
(c) A → S, B → R, C → Q, D → P
(d) A → R, B → P, C → S, D → Q

21. **A uniform sphere of mass m and radius R is placed on a rough horizontal surface (figure). The sphere is struck horizontally at a height h from the floor. Match the following and choose the correct option.**

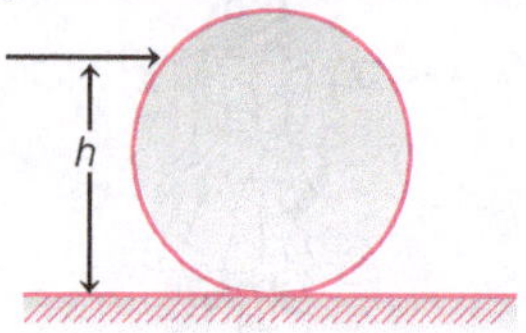

A.	$h = R/2$	P.	Sphere rolls without slipping with a constant velocity and no loss of energy.
B.	$h = R$	Q.	Sphere spins clockwise, loses energy by friction.
C.	$h = 3R/2$	R.	Sphere spins anti-clockwise, loses energy by friction.
D.	$h = 7R/5$	S.	Sphere has only a translational motion, loses energy by friction.

(a) A $\rightarrow$ R, B $\rightarrow$ S, C $\rightarrow$ Q, D $\rightarrow$ P
(b) A $\rightarrow$ S, B $\rightarrow$ P, C $\rightarrow$ R, D $\rightarrow$ Q
(c) A $\rightarrow$ S, B $\rightarrow$ R, C $\rightarrow$ Q, D $\rightarrow$ P
(d) A $\rightarrow$ R, B $\rightarrow$ P, C $\rightarrow$ S, D $\rightarrow$ Q

Assertion and Reason

Directions *(Q.No. 22-29) In the following questions, two statements are given- one labelled Assertion (A) and the other labelled Reason (R). Select the correct answer to these questions from the codes (a), (b), (c) and (d) as given below.*

(a) Both Assertion and Reason are true and Reason is the correct explanation of Assertion.
(b) Both Assertion and Reason are true but Reason is not the correct explanation of Assertion.
(c) Assertion is true but Reason is false.
(d) Assertion is false but Reason is true.

22. **Assertion (A)** The CM of a body must lie on the body.
Reason (R) The CM of a body lie at the geometric centre of body.

23. **Assertion (A)** The motion of the CM describes the translational part of the motion.
Reason (R) Translational motion always means straight line motion.

24. **Assertion (A)** At the centre of earth, a body has centre of mass, but no centre of gravity.
Reason (R) Acceleration due to gravity is zero at the centre of earth.

25. **Assertion (A)** Inertia and moment of inertia are same quantities.
Reason (R) Inertia represents the capacity of a body to oppose its state of motion of rest.

26. **Assertion (A)** Moment of inertia of a particle is same, whatever be the axis of rotation.
Reason (R) Moment of inertia depends on mass and distance of the particle from the axis of rotation.

27. **Assertion (A)** A particle moving on a straight line with a uniform velocity, its angular momentum is constant.
Reason (R) The angular momentum is zero when particle moves with a uniform velocity.

28. **Assertion (A)** For a system of particles under central force field, the total angular momentum is conserved.
Reason (R) The torque acting on such a system is zero.

29. **Assertion (A)** If bodies slide down an inclined plane without rolling, then all bodies reach the bottom simultaneously.
Reason (R) Acceleration of all bodies are equal and independent of the shape.

Case Based Questions

Directions *(Q.Nos. 30-32) These questions are case study based questions. Read the following paragraph and answer the questions on the basis of same.*

30. **The centre of gravity of a rigid body is a point through which the total weight of the body acts. Centre of gravity can lie within the body or not. For small objects, centre of mass always coincides with centre of gravity. But in case of large bodies whose dimensions are comparable to the size of earth, centre of mass and centre of gravity will be at different locations.**

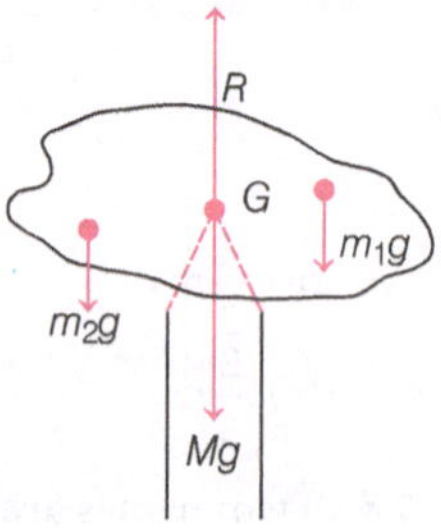

In the given figure, balancing of a cardboard on the tip of a pencil is done. The point of support, G is the centre of gravity.

(i) If the $\mathbf{F}_{\text{net, ext}}$ is zero on the cardboard, it means
(a) $R = Mg$ (b) $m_1 g = Mg$
(c) $m_2 g = Mg$ (d) $R = m_1/g$

(ii) Choose the correct option.
(a) τ_{Mg} about CG = 0
(b) τ_R about CG = 0
(c) Net τ due to $m_1g, m_2g \cdots m_ng$ about CG = 0
(d) All of the above

(iii) The centre of gravity and the centre of mass of a body coincide when
(a) g is negligible (b) g is variable
(c) g is constant (d) g is zero

(iv) If value of g varies, the centre of gravity and the centre of mass will
(a) coincide
(b) not coincide
(c) become same physical quantities
(d) None of the above

(v) Where will be the centre of gravity of the following rigid body?

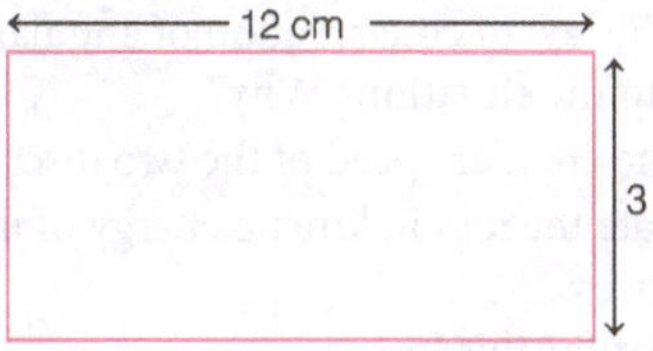

(a) (6,3) (b) (6,6)
(c) (6,1.5) (d) (1.5,3)

31. **The centre of mass of a body or a system of particles is a point at which the entire mass of the body or system of particles is supposed to be concentrated. For a system of n particles, the total sum of moment of mass about centre of mass is zero. If the net external force acting on an object is zero, then the centre of mass of the body is either at rest or moves with constant velocity. In case of net external force acting on the body is not zero, then the motion of the centre of mass of the body is such that the entire mass of the body is concentrated on it and all the external forces are applied on it.**

(i) Two bodies of masses m_1 and m_2 ($m_1 > m_2$) are located on a straight line. Which body is nearest to their centre of mass?

(ii) The forces $\mathbf{F}_1, \mathbf{F}_2$ and $\mathbf{F}_3$ are acting on an object of mass M. What is the acceleration of centre of mass of the object?

(iii) Two bodies of masses 1 kg each are located in XY-plane with position vectors $(2\hat{\mathbf{i}} + 4\hat{\mathbf{j}})$ and $(-3\hat{\mathbf{i}} + \hat{\mathbf{j}})$, respectively. Find the position vector of their centre of mass.

(iv) A uniform disc is located in XY-plane as shown in figure below.

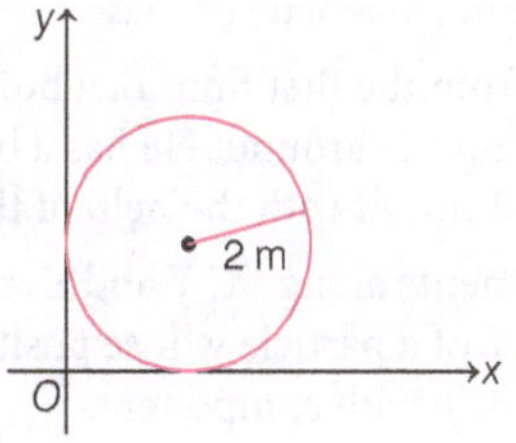

What is the position vector of the centre of mass of the disc?

32. **A quality that measures the inertia of rotational motion of the body is called rotational inertia or moment of inertia of the body. A body at rest tries to maintain the state of rest or a body in rotation tries to maintain the state of rotation due to moment of inertia of the body. It is rotational analogue of mass in linear motion. It is measured by moment of mass about an axis of rotation.**

(i) What are the factors on which moment of inertia depends?

(ii) A hollow and a solid sphere is rotating with uniform angular speed about the axis passing through their centres. Which one will, require more torque to stop?

(iii) Two bodies of masses 1 kg and 2 kg are placed at a distance of 0.5 m and 0.25 m from the axes of rotation. Which one will require more torque for their rotation?

(iv) If the whole mass of a solid sphere is concentrated at a distance x from the axis passing through its centre. Find the value of x.

Subjective Questions

Very Short Answer Type Questions

1. Explain the motion of earth-moon system around the sun in terms of centre of mass concept.

2. A child sits stationary at one end of a long trolley moving uniformly with a speed v on smooth horizontal floor. If child gets up and runs about on the trolley in any manner, what is the speed of CM of the (trolley + child) system? **NCERT**

3. A door is hinged at one end and is free to rotate about a vertical axis. Does its weight cause any torque about its axis? Give reason for your answer. **NCERT Exemplar**

4. Write two differences between centre of mass and centre of gravity.

5. If we apply a force on a door parallel to its axis of rotation, will the door rotate? Also, find the direction of torque generated by this force.

6. Can a body in translational motion have angular momentum? Why?

7. Why is it easier to open a tap with two finger than with one finger?

8. Can the couple acting on a rigid body produce translatory motion?

Short Answer Type Questions

9. Describe moment of inertia. Give two examples about how to find moment of inertia. Hence, describe radius of gyration.

10. Give three illustrations to show that moment of inertia is the rotational analogue of mass.

11. A boy falls from the first floor of a building. He saw a pile of wool on the ground. He has a bag in his hand. Can he save himself with the help of that bag?

12. Find components along X, Y and Z-axes of the angular momentum L of a particle whose position vector is r and momentum is p with components p_x, p_y and p_z. Show if the particle moves only in XY-plane, the angular momentum has only a z-component.

Competency Based Que.

13. Write three practical applications of conservation of angular momentum for a rigid body.

14. (i) It is difficult to open the door by pushing it or pulling it at the hinge. Why ?

(ii) Which physical quantities are expressed by the following

(a) the rate of change of angular momentum?

(b) moment of linear momentum?

Long Answer Type Questions

15. Derive expressions for (i) linear momentum, (ii) Newton's second law and (iii) conservation of linear momentum for the system of particles.

16. (a) Give location of centre of mass of (i) a sphere, (ii) cylinder, (iii) ring and (iv) a cube, each of uniform mass density. Does the centre of mass of a body necessarily lie inside the body?

(b) Locate the centre of mass of uniform triangular lamina and a uniform cone.

17. Explain the concept of torque. Obtain an expression for torque in polar coordinates.

18. Torques of equal magnitude are applied to a hollow cylinder and a solid sphere, both having the same mass and radius. The cylinder is free to rotate about its standard axis of symmetry and the sphere is free to rotate about an axis passing through its centre. Which of the two will acquire a greater angular speed after a given time. **NCERT**

19. (i) Write three equations of motion for the rotational motion about a fixed axis.

(ii) Prove the relation $\tau = I\alpha$, for a rigid body rotating about a fixed axis.

20. A particle of mass m is projected from origin O with speed u at an angle θ with positive X-axis. Find the angular momentum of particle at any time t about O before the particle strikes the ground again.

Competency Based Que.

21. Two discs of moments of inertia I_1 and I_2 about their respective axes (normal to the disc and passing through the centre) and rotating with angular speed ω_1 and ω_2 are brought into contact face to face with their axes of rotation coincident. **Competency Based Que.**

(i) Does the law of conservation of angular momentum apply to the situation? Why?

(ii) Find the angular speed of the two discs system.

(iii) Calculate the loss in kinetic energy of the system in the process.

(iv) Account for this loss.

22. A diver bends his body while jumping in the swimming pool, due to this his angular speed increases. On which law, this incidence is based upon? Explain.

Numerical Problems

Centre of Mass

23. Find position of centre of mass of a semi-circular disc of radius r. **NCERT**

24. From a uniform disc of radius R, a circular section of radius $\frac{R}{2}$ is cut out. The centre of the hole is at $\frac{R}{2}$ from the centre of the original disc. Locate the centre of gravity of the resulting flat body.

Competency Based Que. NCERT

25. Three identical spheres each of radius r and mass m are placed touching each other on a horizontal floor. Locate the position of centre of mass of the system.

26. Find the centre of mass for a solid cone of base radius r and height h.

Centre of Mass of Two-Particles System

27. A disc of radius R is removed from a disc of radius $2R$ as shown.

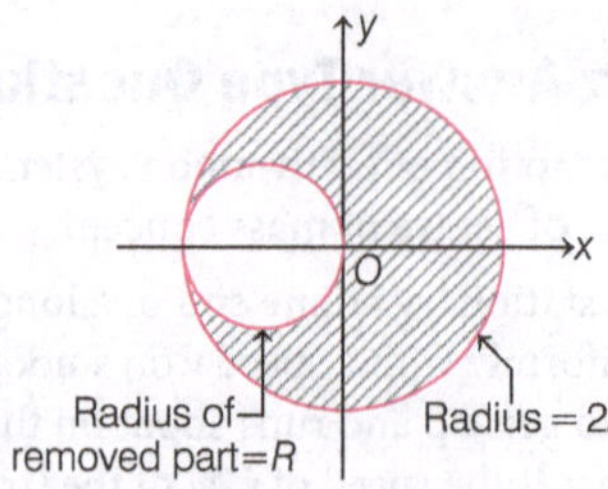

Find centre of mass of above disc with hole. **NCERT**

28. In HCl molecule, separation of nuclei of the two atoms is about 1.27Å (1Å $= 10^{-10}$ m). Find the centre of mass of molecule given that a chlorine atom is about 35.5 times massive than a hydrogen atom. **NCERT**

Momentum of Rigid Body

29. Figure shows momentum *versus* time graph for a particle moving along x-axis. In which region, force on the particle is large. Why?

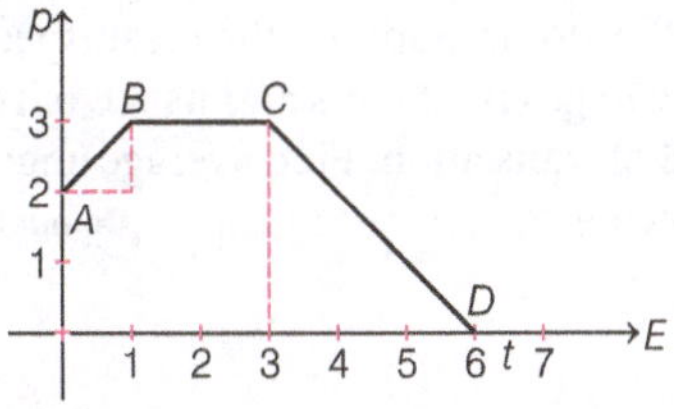

Angular Acceleration

30. In given pulley mass system, mass $m_1 = 500$ g, $m_2 = 460$ g and the pulley has a radius of 5 cm. When released from rest, heavier mass falls through 7.50 cm in 5 s. There is no slipping between pulley and string. **Competency Based Que.**

(i) What is magnitude of acceleration of masses?

(ii) What is magnitude of pulley's angular acceleration?

Torque and Angular Velocity

31. Torques of equal magnitude are applied to a hollow cylinder and a solid sphere, both having the same mass and radius. The cylinder is free to rotate about its standard axis of symmetry and the sphere is free to rotate about an axis passing through its centre. Which of the two will acquire a greater angular speed after a given time?

Moment of inertia of the hollow cylinder about its axis of symmetry is $I_1 = MR^2$

Moment of inertia of the solid sphere about its diameter is $I_2 = \frac{2}{5}MR^2$

32. Two cylindrical hollow drums of radii R and $2R$ and of a common height h, are rotating with angular velocities ω (anti-clockwise) and ω (clockwise), respectively. Their axes, fixed are parallel and in a horizontal plane separated by $3R + \delta$. They are now brought in contact ($\delta \to 0$)

(i) Show the frictional forces just after contact.

(ii) Identify forces and torques external to the system just after contact.

(iii) What would be the ratio of final angular velocities when friction ceases?

Conservation of Angular Momentum

33. Two discs of moment of inertia I_1 and I_2 (about their axes normal to plane of disc and passing through centre) are rotating with angular speeds ω_1 and ω_2 are brought into contact face to face with their axes coinciding.

(i) What is angular speed of two discs system?

(ii) Show that the kinetic energy of combined system is less than the sum of initial kinetic energies of the two discs.

(iii) How do you account for loss of energy?

34. A child stands at the centre of turn table with his two arms out stretched. The turn table is set rotating with an angular speed of 40 rpm. (i) How much is the angular speed of the child if he folds his hands back and thereby reduces his moment of inertia to 2/3 times the initial value? Assume that the turntable rotates without friction. (ii) Show that the child's new kinetic energy of rotation is more than the initial kinetic energy of rotation.

How do you account for this increase in kinetic energy?

Rotational Energy of a Rigid Body

35. A solid sphere is rolling on a frictionless plane surface about its axis of symmetry. Find ratio of its rotational energy to its total energy.

Equilibirium of Rigid Body

36. A car weighs 1800 kg. The distance between its front and back axles is 1.8 m. Its centre of gravity is 1.05 m behind the front axle. Determine the force exerted by the level ground on each front and back wheel.

37. A metal bar 70 cm long and 4 kg in mass supported on two knife edges placed 10 cm from each end. A 6 kg weight is suspended at 30 cm from one end. Find the reactions at the knife edges. Assume the bar to be of uniform cross-section and homogeneous. **Competency Based Que.**

38. A metre stick is balanced on a knife edge at its centre. When two coins, each of mass 5 g are put one on top of the other at the 12 cm mark, the stick is found to be balanced at 45.0 cm. What is the mass of the metre stick? **Competency Based Que.**

Moment of Inertia

39. A man stands on a rotating platform with his arms stretched horizontally holding a 5 kg weight in each hand. The angular speed of the platform is 30 rpm. The man then brings his arms close to his body with the distance of each weight from the axis changing from 90 cm to 20 cm. The moment of inertia of the man together with the platform may be taken to be constant and equal to 7.6 kg-m^2.

(i) What is his new angular speed? (Neglect friction)

(ii) Is kinetic energy conserved in the process? If not, from where does the change come about?

40. Three mass points m_1, m_2 and m_3 are located at the vertices of equilateral triangle of side a. What is moment of inertia of system about an axis along the altitude of Δ passing through m_1 ?

41. A fan of moment of inertia is 0.6 kg-m^2 is to be run upto a working speed of 0.5 rps. What is the angular momentum of the fan?

42. Moment of inertia of a thin rod of length l about an axis passing through its one end and perpendicular to its length is $MR^2/3$. Find the value of radius of gyration for the given scenario.

43. The oxygen molecule has a mass of 5.36×10^{-26} kg and a moment of inertia of 1.94×10^{-46} kg - m^2 about an axis through its centre, perpendicular to the lines joining the atoms. Suppose the mean speed of such a molecule in gas is 500 m/s and its KE of rotation is 2/3 of its KE of translation. Find average angular velocity of the molecule. **Competency Based Que.**

Hints & Solutions

Objective Type Questions

1. (a) 2. (c) 3. (c) 4. (d) 5. (c)

6. (d) Projectile could be consider as rigid body before and after explosion, as its fragments are considered as system of particles. Thus, the concept of CM is applicable to both. Since, the explosion is due to external forces, so the motion of CM after explosion will follow the same parabolic path.

7. (b) 8. (b) 9. (b) 10. (b) 11. (d)
12. (c) 13. (c)

14. (c) Let x be the distance from center, then for rotational equilibrium.

$$M_1 g \times r_A = M_2 g \times x_B$$

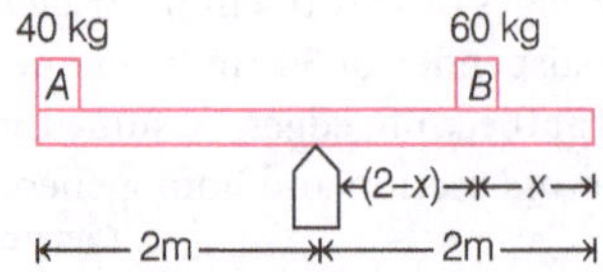

$$(40 \times 10) \times 2 = (60 \times 10) \times (2 - x)$$
$$40 \times 10 \times 2 = 600\,(2 - x)$$
$$4 = 6 - 3x \Rightarrow 3x = 2$$
$$x = \frac{2}{3}\text{ m}$$

15. (b)
16. (d) 17. (a) 18. (d) 19. (a)
20. (d) A → R, B → P, C → S, D → Q

21. (a) Consider the diagram where a sphere of m and radius R, struck horizontally at height h above the floor

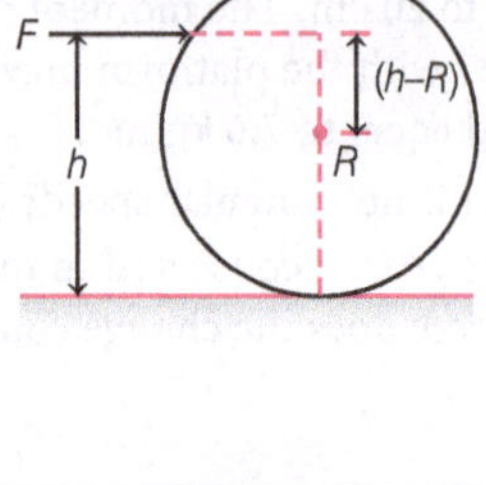

The sphere will roll without slipping when $\omega = \frac{v}{r}$, where v is linear velocity and ω is angular velocity of the sphere.

Now, angular momentum of sphere, about centre of mass is [We are applying conservation of angular momentum just before and after struck]

$$mv(h - R) = I\omega = \left(\frac{2}{5}mR^2\right)\left(\frac{v}{R}\right)$$

$$\Rightarrow \quad mv(h - R) = \frac{2}{5}mvR$$

$$h - R = \frac{2}{5}R \Rightarrow h = \frac{7}{5}R$$

Therefore, the sphere will roll without slipping with a constant velocity and hence, no loss of energy, so (D) → (P)

Torque due to applied force, F about centre of mass

$$\tau = F(h - R) \quad \text{(clockwise)}$$

For $\tau = 0$, $h = R$, sphere will have only translational motion. It would lose energy by friction.

Hence, (B) → (S)

The sphere will spin clockwise when $\tau > 0 \Rightarrow h > R$

Therefore, (C) → (Q)

The sphere will spin anti-clockwise when $\tau < 0 \Rightarrow h < R$

Therefore, (A) → (R)

22. (d)
23. (a) 24. (a) 25. (d) 26. (d) 27. (c)
28. (a) 29. (a)

30. (i)-(a), (ii)-(d), (iii)-(c), (iv)-(b), (v)-(c)

31. (i) As, the moments of all masses about the centre of mass of two bodies are equal.

$$\therefore \quad m_1 r_1 = m_2 r_2$$

i.e. $\quad mr = \text{constant} \Rightarrow m \propto \frac{1}{r}$

Hence, the centre of mass lies the nearest to the heavier body of mass m_1.

(ii) The acceleration of centre of mass is given as

$$\mathbf{a}_{CM} = \frac{\mathbf{F}_{\text{net, external}}}{m} = \frac{\mathbf{F}_1 + \mathbf{F}_2 + \mathbf{F}_3}{m}$$

(iii) Given, $m_1 = m_2 = 1$ kg

$$\mathbf{r}_1 = 2\hat{\mathbf{i}} + 4\hat{\mathbf{j}}, \mathbf{r}_2 = -3\hat{\mathbf{i}} + \hat{\mathbf{j}}$$

$\therefore$ Position of centre of mass for two equal bodies is given by

$$\mathbf{r}_{CM} = \frac{\mathbf{r}_1 + \mathbf{r}_2}{2}$$

$$= \frac{(2\hat{\mathbf{i}} + 4\hat{\mathbf{j}}) + (-3\hat{\mathbf{i}} + \hat{\mathbf{j}})}{2}$$

$$\therefore \quad \mathbf{r}_{CM} = \left(-\frac{1}{2}\hat{\mathbf{i}} + \frac{5}{2}\hat{\mathbf{j}}\right)$$

(iv) The position vector of centre of mass of the disc is given by $\mathbf{r} = (2\hat{\mathbf{i}} + 2\hat{\mathbf{j}})$ m

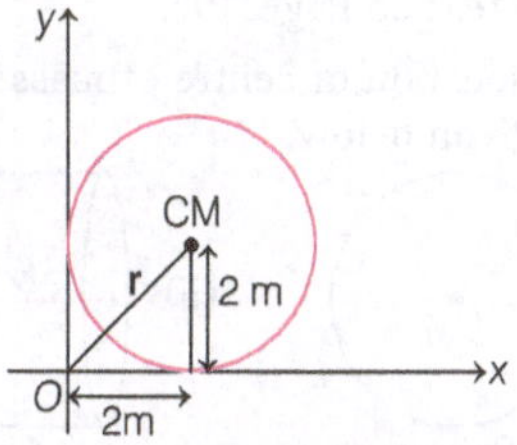

32. (i) The moment of inertia is also given as the moment of mass.

$\therefore \; I = mr^2 = \rho V r^2$

$\therefore$ Moment of inertia of a body depends on the following factors

(a) Density of the body

(b) Shape and size of the body

(c) The perpendicular distance of the body from its axis of rotation

(ii) As, $I_{\text{hollow sphere}} = \frac{2}{3}mr^2$,

$$I_{\text{solid sphere}} = \frac{2}{5}mr^2$$

$$\therefore \quad I_{\text{hollow sphere}} > I_{\text{solid sphere}}$$

Hence, the hollow sphere will require more torque to stop it.

(iii) The moment of inertia of first body,

$$I_1 = m_1 r_1^2 = 1 \times (0.5)^2 = 0.25 \text{ kg-m}^2$$

The moment of inertia of second body,

$$I_2 = m_2 r_2^2 = 2 \times (0.25)^2 = 0.125 \text{ kg-m}^2$$

As $I_1 > I_2$, hence body of mass 1 kg will required more torque to start its rotation.

(iv) $I_{\text{solid sphere}} = \frac{2}{5}mr^2 = mx^2$

$$\therefore \quad x = \sqrt{\frac{2}{5}}\,r$$

Subjective Questions

1. The moon revolves around the earth in an approximate circular orbit and earth revolves around the sun in an elliptical orbit. Hence, earth-moon system revolves about their common CM in elliptical path. The CM of earth-moon lies within the earth because the mass of the earth is very large as compared to that of the moon and it appears that moon revolves around earth but in reality, both revolve about their common centre of mass.

2. When the child gets up and runs on the trolley, he is exerting an internal force on the trolley-child system. Thus, no external force acts on the system. So, centre of mass is not accelerated. Hence, centre of mass of trolley-child system remains same as before, i.e. speed of CM is v.

3. As torque $= \mathbf{r} \times \mathbf{F}$

That means the torque produced by force is in a plane perpendicular to plane containing $\mathbf{r}$ and $\mathbf{F}$.

So, if door is in XY-plane, torque produced by weight is in $\pm z$-direction.

It is never about an axis passing through y- direction.

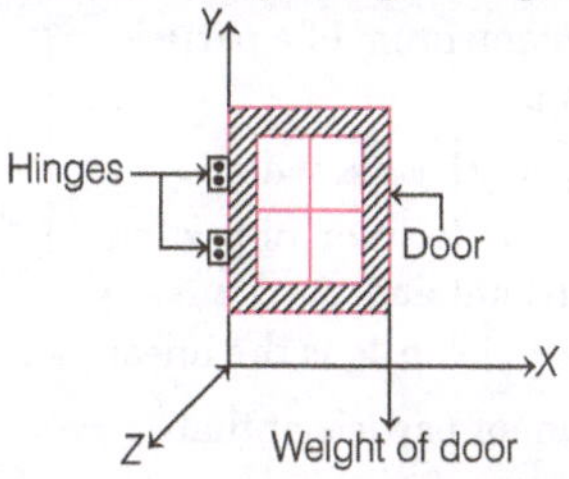

4.

Centre of mass	Centre of gravity
(i) It focuses on the mass of the body.	(i) It focuses on the weight of the body.
(ii) It is used for studying the motion of the body.	(ii) It is used to understand the stability of the body.

5. When we apply a force parallel to the door, it does not rotate about the hinge.

This is because when the force is parallel to the axis, its moment about the axis is zero and hence, it does not produce any turning effect.

The direction of torque, $\tau = r \times F$ is perpendicular to the axis of rotation.

6. Yes, a body in translatory motion can have angular momentum, unless the fixed point about which angular momentum is taken is lies on the line of motion of the body.
7. With two fingers, we are applying a couple whose arm is equal to the length of the handle of the tap. When we apply force with one finger, then the length of arm of couple is halved. Hence, it is easier to open the tap with two fingers.
8. Refer to text on Page.200.
9. Refer to text on Pages. 202, 203 and 204.
10. The three illustration to show that moment of inertia is the rotational analogue of masses are
    1. **Pushing a merry-go-round** When you push a merry-go-round, you can change its angular velocity. The more massive the merry-go-round, the more slowly it well open.
    2. **Spinning a bike wheel** When you spin a bike wheel, you need to apply a force to change its angular velocity. The more massive the wheel, the smaller the angular acceleration.
    3. **Opening a door** Its difficult to open a door from its hinges because the radius is very small there. The more massive the door, the more slowly it opens.
11. Yes, he will be able to save himself because wool is a softer material. So, he will experience relatively lesser amount of pressure exerted on him because he will take more time to loose his velocity.
12. Angular momentum of a particle is $\mathbf{L} = \mathbf{r} \times \mathbf{p}$

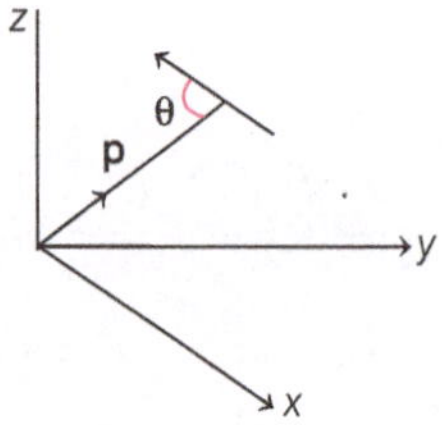

Let $\mathbf{r} = x\hat{\mathbf{i}} + y\hat{\mathbf{j}} + z\hat{\mathbf{k}}$, where (x, y, z) is the location of particle at some instant and $\mathbf{p} = p_x\hat{\mathbf{i}} + p_y\hat{\mathbf{j}} + p_z\hat{\mathbf{k}}$, is the linear momentum of particle at that instant.

Then, angular momentum of particle is given by

$$\mathbf{L} = \mathbf{r} \times \mathbf{p} = \begin{vmatrix} \hat{\mathbf{i}} & \hat{\mathbf{j}} & \hat{\mathbf{k}} \\ x & y & z \\ p_x & p_y & p_z \end{vmatrix}$$

$$= \hat{\mathbf{i}}\,(p_z \cdot y - p_y \cdot z) - \hat{\mathbf{j}}\,(p_z \cdot x - p_x \cdot z) + \hat{\mathbf{k}}\,(p_y \cdot x - p_x \cdot y) \quad \text{...(i)}$$

So, components of angular momentum along X, Y and Z-axes are $\mathbf{L}_x = p_z y - p_y z$

$\mathbf{L}_y = p_z x - p_x z$

and $\mathbf{L}_z = p_y x - p_x y$, respectively

Now, if particle is confined to XY-plane, then

$$\mathbf{r} = x\hat{\mathbf{i}} + y\hat{\mathbf{i}} \Rightarrow z = 0$$

and $$\mathbf{p} = p_x\hat{\mathbf{i}} + p_y\hat{\mathbf{j}} \Rightarrow p_z = 0$$

Substituting in Eq. (i), we get

$$\mathbf{L} = \hat{\mathbf{k}}\,(p_y x - p_x y)$$

So, angular momentum has a z-component only.

As angular momentum is cross-product of **r** and **p**.

∴ It is always perpendicular to plane containing **r** and **p**.

13. Refer to text on Pg. 209.
14. (i) As, torque, τ = force × perpendicular distance. At the hinge of the door, the perpendicular distance is smaller and hence, torque is smaller. So, it is difficult to open the door by pushing or pulling at its hinge.

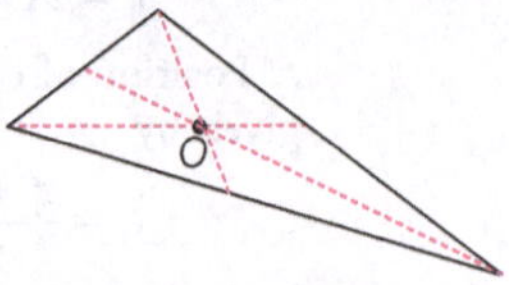

(ii) (a) The rate of change of angular momentum is torque.

(b) The momentum of linear momentum is called angular momentum.

15. Refer to text on Page. 197.
16. (a) The location of centre of masses for different bodies are given below.

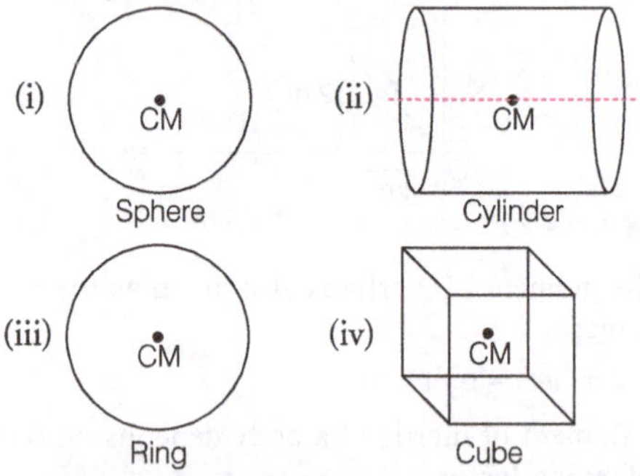

It is not necessary that the centre of mass of a body should lie inside it.

(b) In triangular lamina, the centre of mass is at the intersection of the medians, i.e. the centroid of triangle.

Therefore, the CM in triangular lamina is centroid (as shown in figure.

In uniform cone, the centre of mass is $H/4$ (as shown in figure below)

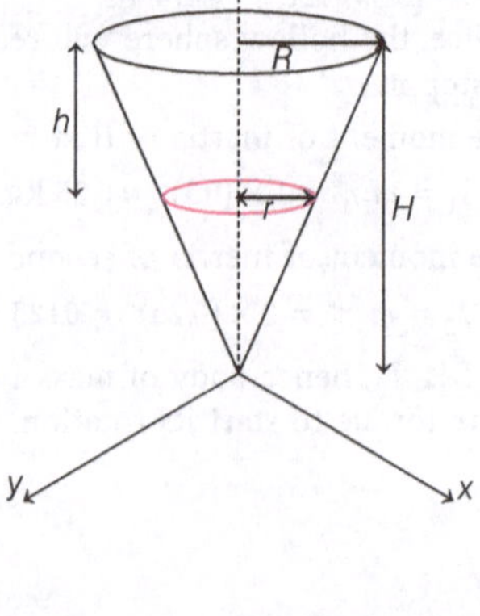

17. Refer to text on Page. 198.

18. Let M and R be the mass and radius of the solid sphere and hollow cylinder.

Moment of inertia of the hollow cylinder about its axis of symmetry,

$$I_1 = MR^2$$

Moment of inertia of the solid sphere about its diameter,

$$I_2 = \frac{2}{5}MR^2$$

Let torque τ of equal magnitude be applied on hollow cylinder and solid sphere. The angular accelerations produced in it are α_1 and α_2 respectively.

$\therefore \quad \tau = I_1\alpha_1$

and $\quad \tau = I_2\alpha_2$

Therefore, $\quad I_1\alpha_1 = I_2\alpha_2$

or $\quad \dfrac{\alpha_1}{\alpha_2} = \dfrac{I_2}{I_1} = \dfrac{\frac{2}{5}MR^2}{MR^2} = \dfrac{2}{5}$

or $\quad \alpha_2 = \dfrac{5}{2}\alpha_1$

$\quad = 2.5\alpha_1 \qquad \ldots\text{(i)}$

Let after time t, ω_1 and ω_2 be the angular speeds of the hollow cylinder and solid sphere respectively.

$\therefore \quad \omega_1 = \omega_0 + \alpha_1 t \qquad \ldots\text{(ii)}$

and $\quad \omega_2 = \omega_0 + \alpha_2 t$

$\quad = \omega_0 + 2.5\,\alpha_1 t \qquad \ldots\text{(iii)}$

From Eqs. (ii) and (iii), we get

$$\omega_2 > \omega_1$$

Therefore, solid sphere will acquire a greater angular speed after a given time.

19. (i) Refer to text on page 206.

(ii) Refer to text on Page. 208.

20. Let particle be P at any instant t and its position vector is $\mathbf{r}$, then $\mathbf{r} = x\hat{\mathbf{i}} + y\hat{\mathbf{j}}$

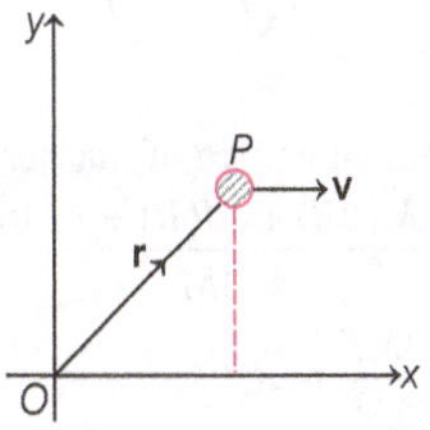

where, $\quad x = u\cos\theta \cdot t$ and $y = u\sin\theta \cdot t - \dfrac{1}{2}gt^2$

and if $\mathbf{v}$ = velocity vector of particle at that instant.

Then, $\mathbf{r} = x\hat{\mathbf{i}} + y\hat{\mathbf{j}}$

where, $\quad x = u\cos\theta \cdot t$

and $\quad y = u\sin\theta \cdot t - \dfrac{1}{2}gt^2$

and if $\quad \mathbf{v}$ = velocity vector of particle at that instant

Then, $\quad \mathbf{v} = \mathbf{v}_x\hat{\mathbf{i}} + \mathbf{v}_y\hat{\mathbf{j}}$

where, $v_x = u\cos\theta \quad$ and $\quad v_y = u\sin\theta - gt$

So, $\mathbf{r} = (u\cos\theta)t\,\hat{\mathbf{i}} + \left((u\sin\theta)\cdot t - \dfrac{1}{2}gt^2\right)\hat{\mathbf{j}}$

and $\quad \mathbf{v} = u\cos\theta\,\hat{\mathbf{i}} + (u\sin\theta - gt)\,\hat{\mathbf{j}}$

So, $\quad \mathbf{L}$ = angular momentum of particle

$= m(\mathbf{r} \times \mathbf{v})$

$$= m\begin{vmatrix} \hat{\mathbf{i}} & \hat{\mathbf{j}} & \hat{\mathbf{k}} \\ u\cos\theta t & \left(u\sin\theta - \frac{1}{2}gt\right)t & 0 \\ u\cos\theta & (u\sin\theta - gt) & 0 \end{vmatrix}$$

$$= -\frac{1}{2}m(u\cos\theta)\,gt^2 \cdot \hat{\mathbf{k}}$$

So, angular momentum is along Z-axis.

21. Consider the diagram below.

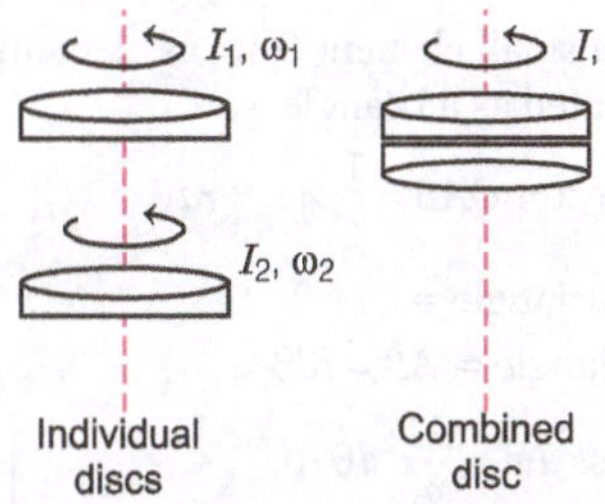

Let the common angular velocity of the system is ω

(i) Yes, the law of conservation of angular momentum can be applied because there is no net external torque on the system of the two discs.

External forces, gravitation and normal reaction, act through the axis of rotation, hence produce no torque.

(ii) By conservation of angular momentum,

$$L_f = L_i \Rightarrow I\omega = I_1\omega_1 + I_2\omega_2$$

$$\Rightarrow \omega = \frac{I_1\omega_1 + I_2\omega_2}{I} = \frac{I_1\omega_1 + I_2\omega_2}{I_1 + I_2} \qquad (\because I = I_1 + I_2)$$

(iii) $K_f = \dfrac{1}{2}(I_1 + I_2)\dfrac{(I_1\omega_1 + I_2\omega_2)^2}{(I_1 + I_2)^2}$

$$= \frac{1}{2}\frac{(I_1\omega_1 + I_2\omega_2)^2}{(I_1 + I_2)}$$

$$K_i = \frac{1}{2}(I_1\omega_1^2 + I_2\omega_2^2)$$

$$\Delta K = K_f - K_i = -\frac{I_1 I_2}{2(I_1 + I_2)}(\omega_1 - \omega_2)^2 < 0$$

(iv) Hence, there is loss in KE of the system. The loss in kinetic energy is mainly due to the work against the friction between the two discs.

22. Refer to text on Page. 208 and 209.

23. As semi-circular disc is symmetrical about its one of diameter, we take axes as shown below. So, now we only have to calculate Y_{CM} ·(As, X_{CM} is zero by symmetry and choice of origin).

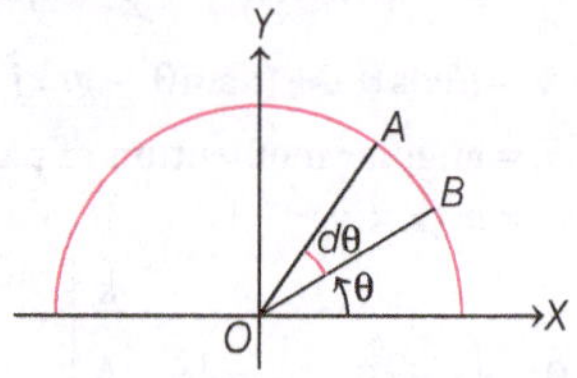

Now, $Y_{CM} = \frac{\int y\,dm}{\int dm}$

From our text, $M \cdot Y_{CM} = \int y\,dm$

$$Y_{CM} = \frac{1}{M}\int y\,dm = \frac{\int y\,dm}{\int dm}$$

Now, for a small element *OAB*, as element is small and it can be treated as a triangle, so

Area of sector $OAB = \frac{1}{2} \times r \times r d\theta$

Height of triangle = r

Base of triangle = $AB = r d\theta$

So, its mass $dm = \frac{1}{2} r^2 d\theta \cdot \rho$ $\quad \left[\because \rho = \frac{\text{mass}}{\text{area}}\right]$

As centre of mass of a triangle is at a distance of $\frac{2}{3}$ from its vertex (at centroid, intersection of medians). So,

$y = \frac{2}{3} r \sin\theta$ (location of CM of small sector *AOB*).

So, $Y_{CM} = \frac{\int_0^\pi y\,dm}{\int_0^\pi \frac{1}{2} r^2 \rho d\theta} = \frac{\int_0^\pi \frac{2}{3} r\sin\theta \times \frac{1}{2} r^2 d\theta \cdot \rho}{\int_0^\pi \frac{1}{2} r^2 \rho d\theta}$

$$= \frac{\frac{1}{2} \times \frac{2}{3} r^3 \cdot \rho \int_0^\pi \sin\theta d\theta}{\frac{1}{2} r^2 \rho \cdot \int_0^\pi d\theta} = \frac{\frac{2r}{3}\int_0^\pi \sin\theta d\theta}{\int_0^\pi d\theta}$$

$$= \frac{\frac{2r}{3}[-\cos\theta]_0^\pi}{[\theta]_0^\pi} = \frac{\frac{-2r}{3}(\cos\pi - \cos 0^\circ)}{(\pi - \theta)} = 4r/3\pi$$

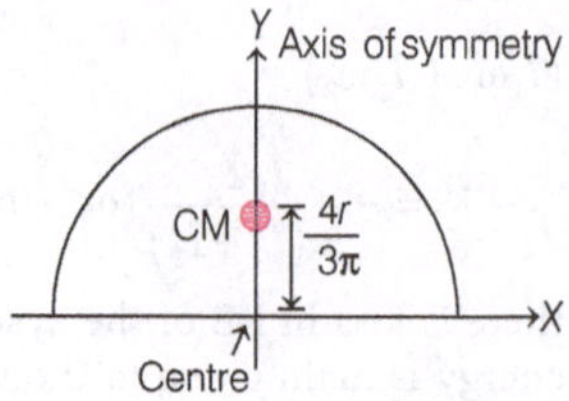

So, CM of disc is at a distance of $\frac{4r}{3\pi}$ from its centre on its axis of symmetry.

24. Let the mass per unit area of the original disc = σ

Radius of the original disc = $2r$

Mass of original disc,

$$m = \pi (2r^2)\sigma = 4\pi r^2 \sigma \quad \text{...(i)}$$

The disc with the cut portion as shown in figure

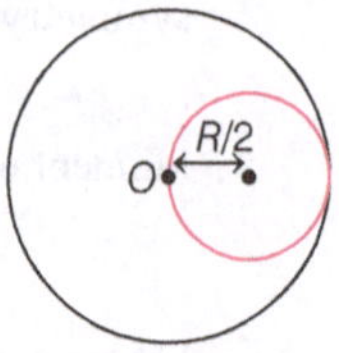

Radius of smaller disc = r

Mass of smaller disc, $m' = \pi r^2 \sigma$

$\Rightarrow \quad m' = m/4$

Let O' and O be the respective centres of the original disc and the disc cut-off from the original. As per the definition of the centre of mass, the centre of mass of the original disc is supposed to be concentrated at O, while for smaller disc is supposed to be concentrated at O'.

$\Rightarrow \quad OO' = R/2 = r_2$

After the smaller circle has been cut out, the left masses,

$$m' = -\frac{M}{4}$$

Let x be the distance of centre of mass from O.

$\Rightarrow \quad x = (m_1 r_1 + m_2 r_2)/m_1 + m_2$

$$x = [m \times 0 - m'(r/2)]/[M + (-M)] = \frac{-R}{6}$$

Negative sign shows that the centre of mass is $\frac{R}{6}$ towards the left of O.

25. Three identical spheres each of radius R are placed touching each other as shown in the below figure.

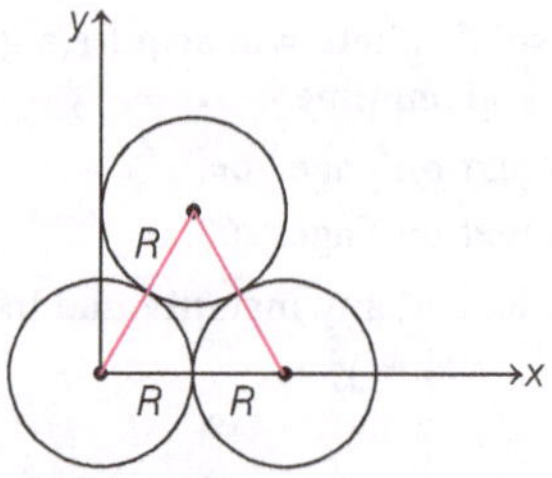

The coordinates of centre of masses,

$$x_{CM} = \frac{M(2R) + M(R) + M(0)}{3M}$$

$$\Rightarrow \quad x_{CM} = \frac{3MR}{3M} = R$$

and $\quad y_{CM} = \frac{M(\sqrt{3}R) + M(0) + M(0)}{3M} = \frac{R}{\sqrt{3}}$

26. Let us consider a uniform solid cone of mass M, radius R and height h.

$$x_{CM} = 0 \text{ (by symmetry)}$$

Let us consider a small element (disc) of dm mass, radius r and thickness dy at a distance y as shown in figure.

Then, $\rho = \dfrac{3M}{\pi R^2 h} = \dfrac{dm}{\pi r^2 dy} \Rightarrow dm = \dfrac{3Mr^2}{R^2 h} dy$

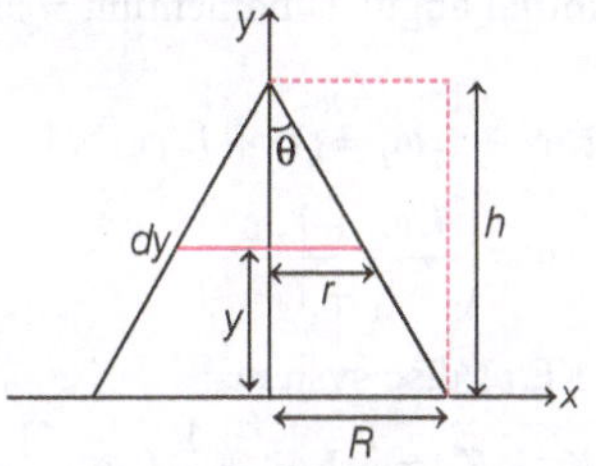

$$y_{CM} = \frac{1}{M}\int y\,dm = \frac{1}{M}\int y \frac{3Mr^2}{R^2 h} dy = \frac{3}{R^2 h}\int y r^2 dy$$

$$= \frac{3}{h}\int_0^h y\left(1 - \frac{y}{h}\right)^2 dy \quad \left[\because \frac{h-y}{r} = \frac{h}{R} \Rightarrow r = \left(1 - \frac{y}{h}\right)R\right]$$

On solving, we get $y_{CM} = \dfrac{h}{4}$

Centre of mass of uniform solid cone is $\dfrac{h}{4}$ from the centre of base.

27. First consider the composite plate

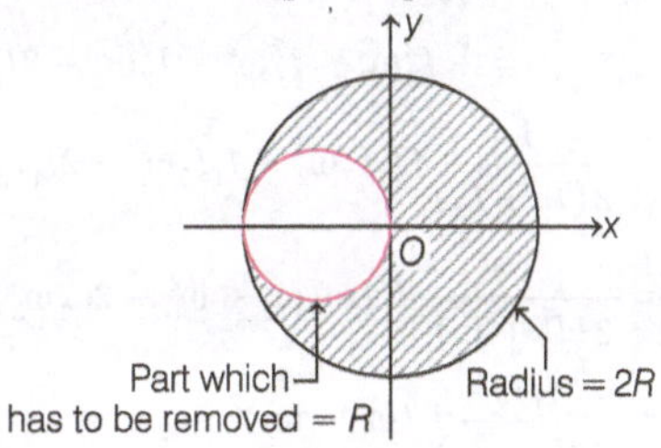

x-coordinate of centre of mass of composite plate is given by $\quad x_{CM} = \dfrac{m_1 x_1 + m_2 x_2}{m_1 + m_2}$

where,

m_1 = mass of disc of radius $2R$,

x_1 = position of centre of mass of disc with hole,

m_2 = mass of part removed of radius R,

x_2 = position of centre of mass of part removed.

Now, as centre of mass of composite plate is at origin, so

$$x_{CM} = 0 = \frac{m_1 x_1 + m_2 x_2}{m_1 + m_2}$$

or $\quad m_1 x_1 + m_2 x_2 = 0$

Now, we are finding x_1.

So, $\quad x_1 = -\dfrac{m_2 x_2}{m_1}$

Now $\quad \dfrac{m_2}{m_1} = \dfrac{\text{density} \times \text{volume of portion 2}}{\text{density} \times \text{volume of portion 1}}$

$$= \frac{\text{thickness} \times \text{area of portion 2}}{\text{thickness} \times \text{area of portion 1}}$$

$$\Rightarrow \frac{m_2}{m_1} = \frac{A_2}{A_1} = \frac{\pi R^2}{\pi(2R)^2 - \pi R^2} = \frac{1}{3}$$

Also, $x_2 = -R$, (negative sign is w.r.t. coordinate axes)

Hence, $\quad x_1 = -\dfrac{m_2}{m_1} \cdot x_2 = -\dfrac{1}{3}(-R) = \dfrac{1}{3}R$

So, centre of mass is located at $\left(x = \dfrac{1}{3}R,\ y = 0\right)$ point.

28.

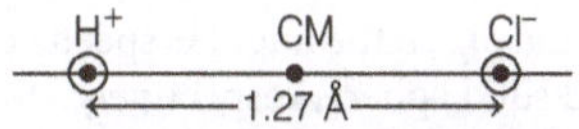

m_1 = mass of hydrogen = 1

m_2 = mass of chlorine = 35.5

$x_1 = 0, x_2 = 1.27$ Å

As the system is symmetrical about X-axis, its centre of mass lies on X-axis.

Using $\quad x_{CM} = \dfrac{m_1 x_1 + m_2 x_2}{m_1 + m_2} = \dfrac{1 \times 0 + 35.5 \times 1.27}{1 + 35.5} = 1.235$ Å

$$= 1.235 \times 10^{-10} \text{ m}$$

29. As, force $= \dfrac{dp}{dt}$ = slope of momentum *versus* time graph.

For region AB,

Force $= \dfrac{3-2}{1-0} = 1$ N

For region BC,

Force $= \dfrac{3-3}{3-1} = 0$

For region CD,

Force $= \dfrac{0-3}{6-3} = -1$ N

Hence, the force in the region AB is maximum.

30. Given, first block mass, $m_1 = 500$ g

Second block mass, $m_2 = 460$ g

Radius of pulley, $R = 5.00$ cm

Time = 5 s

(i) Acceleration of blocks, from kinematical equation

$$s = ut + \frac{1}{2}at^2$$

$$75 \times 10^{-2} = 0 + \frac{1}{2}a(5)^2$$

$$\Rightarrow \quad a = \frac{2 \times 75 \times 10^{-2}}{25} = 6 \times 10^{-2} \text{m/s}^2$$

(ii) The angular acceleration, $\alpha = \dfrac{a}{R}$

$$\Rightarrow \quad \alpha = \frac{6 \times 10^{-2}}{5 \times 10^{-2}} = 1.2 \text{rad/s}^2$$

31. Let M and R be the mass and radius of the solid sphere and hollow cylinder.

Let torque τ of equal magnitude be applied on hollow cylinder and solid sphere. The angular accelerations produced in it are α_1 and α_2, respectively.

$\therefore \quad \tau = I_1\alpha_1$ and $\tau = I_2\alpha_2$

Therefore, $I_1\alpha_1 = I_2\alpha_2$

or $$\frac{\alpha_1}{\alpha_2} = \frac{I_2}{I_1} = \frac{\frac{2}{5}MR^2}{MR^2} = \frac{2}{5}$$

or $$\alpha_2 = \frac{5}{2}\alpha_1 = 2.5\alpha_1 \qquad \text{...(i)}$$

Let after time t, ω_1 and ω_2 be the angular speeds of the hollow cylinder and solid sphere, respectively.

$\therefore$ $$\omega_1 = \omega_0 + \alpha_1 t \qquad \text{...(ii)}$$

and $$\omega_2 = \omega_0 + \alpha_2 t = \omega_0 + 2.5\,\alpha_1 t \qquad \text{...(iii)}$$

From Eqs. (ii) and (iii), we get $\omega_2 > \omega_1$

Therefore, solid sphere will acquire a greater angular speed after a given time.

32. (i)

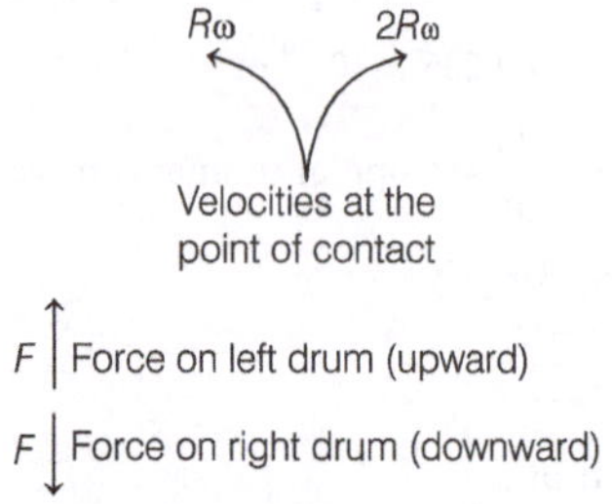

(ii) $F' = F = F''$, where F and F'' are external forces through support.

$$F_{net} = 0$$

External torque = $F \times 3R$, anti-clockwise.

(iii) Let ω_1 and ω_2 be final angular velocities (anti-clockwise and clockwise respectively).

Finally, there will be no friction.

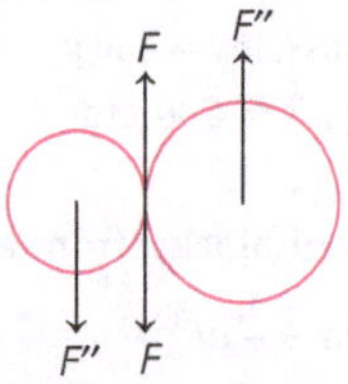

Hence, $R\omega_1 = 2R\omega_2 \Rightarrow \dfrac{\omega_1}{\omega_2} = 2$

33. Let ω be the final angular velocity of two discs system.

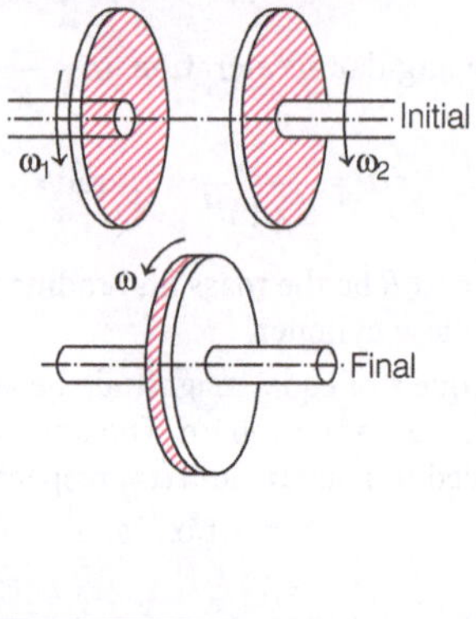

(i) According to conservation of angular momentum, we get

Total initial angular momentum = Final angular momentum

$$\Rightarrow \quad I_1\omega_1 + I_2\omega_2 = (I_1 + I_2)\,\omega$$

$$\Rightarrow \quad \omega = \left(\frac{I_1\omega_1 + I_2\omega_2}{I_1 + I_2}\right)$$

(ii) Initial KE of disc system

$$= K_1 + K_2 = \frac{1}{2}I_1\omega_1^2 + \frac{1}{2}I_2\omega_2^2$$

Final KE of disc system $= \frac{1}{2}(I_1 + I_2)\,\omega^2$

$$= \frac{1}{2}(I_1 + I_2)\cdot\left(\frac{I_1\omega_1 + I_2\omega_2}{I_1 + I_2}\right)^2$$

Loss in KE = Initial KE − Final KE

$$= \left(\frac{1}{2}I_1\omega_1^2 + \frac{1}{2}I_2\omega_2^2\right) - \frac{1}{2}(I_1 + I_2)\cdot\left(\frac{I_1\omega_1 + I_2\omega_2}{I_1 + I_2}\right)^2$$

$$= \frac{1}{2(I_1 + I_2)}(I_1^2\omega_1^2 + I_1I_2\omega_2^2 + I_1I_2\omega_1^2 + I_2^2\omega_2^2 - I_1^2\omega_1^2 - I_2^2\omega_2^2 - 2I_1I_2\omega_1\omega_2)$$

$$= \frac{1}{2(I_1 + I_2)}(I_1I_2\omega_2^2 + I_1I_2\omega_1^2 - 2I_1I_2\omega_1\omega_2)$$

$$= \frac{1}{2(I_1 + I_2)}\cdot I_1I_2\cdot(\omega_2^2 + \omega_1^2 - 2\omega_1\omega_2)$$

$$= \frac{I_1I_2}{2(I_1 + I_2)}\cdot(\omega_1 - \omega_2)^2$$

As above quantity is positive, so a loss of energy occurs.

(iii) When two discs comes in contact, they rub against each other till both reach the same energy.

34. Here $\omega_1 = 40$ rpm, $I_2 = \frac{2}{5}I_1$

(i) By the principle of conservation of angular momentum,

$$I_1\omega_1 = I_2\omega_2$$

or $I_1 \times 40 = \frac{2}{5}I_1\omega_2$ or $\omega_2 = 100$ rpm.

(ii) Initial kinetic energy of rotation,

$$\frac{2}{5}I_1\omega_1^2 = \frac{2}{5}I_1(40)^2 = 800I_1$$

New kinetic energy of rotation,

$$\frac{2}{5}I_2\omega_2 = \frac{1}{2}\times\frac{2}{3}I_1(100)^2 = 200I_1$$

$$\frac{\text{New KE}}{\text{Initial KE}} = \frac{200I_1}{800I_1} = 2.5$$

Thus the child's new kinetic energy of rotation is 2.5 times its initial kinetic energy of rotation. This increase in kinetic energy is due to the internal energy of the child which he uses in folding his hands back from the out stretched position.

35. Rotational KE $= \frac{1}{2} I\omega^2 = \frac{1}{2} \times \frac{2}{5} MR^2 \times \frac{v^2}{R^2}$

$$\left(\text{as } \omega = \frac{v}{R},\ I = \frac{2}{5}MR^2\right)$$

$$= \frac{1}{5}mv^2$$

Total energy = Translational KE + Rotational KE

$$= \frac{1}{2}mv^2 + \frac{1}{5}mv^2 = \frac{7}{10}mv^2$$

$$\therefore \quad \frac{\text{Rotational KE}}{\text{Total Energy}} = \frac{\frac{1}{5}mv^2}{\frac{7}{10}mv^2} = \frac{2}{7}$$

36. For translation equilibrium of car

$N_F + N_B = W = 1800 \times 9.8 = 17640$ N

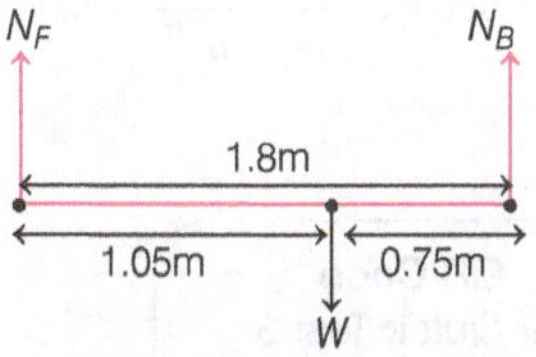

For rotational equilibrium of car

$$1.05N_F = 0.75N_B$$
$$1.05N_F = 0.75(17640 - N_F)$$
$$1.8N_F = 13230$$
$$N_F = \frac{13230}{1.8} = 7350\text{ N}$$
$$N_B = 17640 - 7350 = 10290\text{ N}$$

Force on each front wheel $= \frac{7350}{2} = 3675$ N

Force on each front wheel $= \frac{10290}{2} = 5145$ N

37. Let the normal reactions from the knife edges (K_1 and K_2) be N_1, N_2.

Now, in equilibrium, $N_1 + N_2 = mg$

$$N_1 + N_2 = 10 \times 9.8\text{ N} = 98\text{ N}$$

Also, the system is in rotational equilibrium.

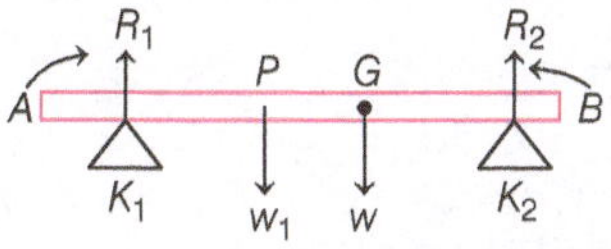

Thus, about the centre of rod, the net torque must be zero.

Hence, $(6 \times 9.8)(5) + N_2(25) = N_1(25) \Rightarrow N_1 = 55$ N

$\Rightarrow \quad N_2 = 98 - 55 = 43$ N

Hence, normal reaction 55 N at K_1 and 43 N at K_2 are formed.

38. Let the total mass of the metre stick be M kg.

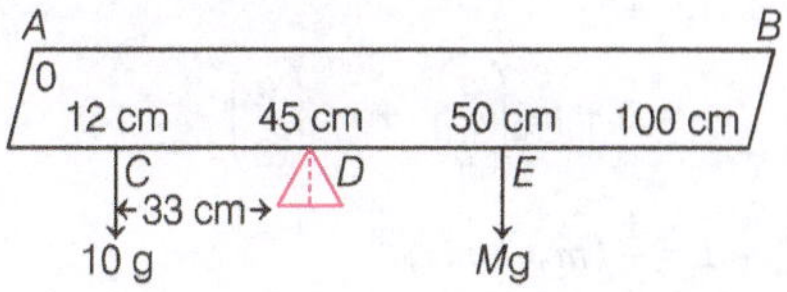

Distance between mid-point E and new centre of gravity

$(DE) = 50 - 45 = 5$ cm

Distance between 12 cm mark and new centre of gravity

$(CD) = 45 - 12 = 33$ cm

From principle of moments in equilibrium,

$$M \times DE = (2 \times 5) \times CD$$
$$\Rightarrow \quad M \times 5 = 10 \times 33$$
$$\Rightarrow \quad M = 66\text{ g}$$

∵ Mass of the metre stick is 66 g.

39. (i) Moment of inertia of man and platform system

$$I_i = 7.6\text{ kg-m}^2$$

Change in moment of inertia of man and platform system when he stretches his hands to a distance of 90 cm $= 2 \times mr^2 = 2 \times 5 \times (0.9)^2 = 8.1$ kg-m^2

$$I_i = I + 8.1 = 7.6 + 8.1 = 15.7\text{ kg-m}^2$$

Initial angular velocity, $\omega_i = 30$ rpm

Initial angular momentum of system,

$$L_i = I_i\omega_i = 15.7\text{ kg-m}^2 \times 30\text{ rpm}$$

When man folds his hands to a distance of 20 cm,

Moment of inertia of man $= 2 \times mr^2$

$$= 2 \times 5 \times (0.2)^2 = 0.4\text{ kg-m}^2$$

So, final moment of inertia of man and platform system

$$= 7.6 + 0.4 = 8\text{ kg-m}^2$$

Final angular momentum of system

$$L_f = I_f\omega_f = 8 \times \omega_f$$

Equating initial and final values

$$L_i = L_f$$

$$\Rightarrow \quad \omega_f = \frac{15.7 \times 30}{8} = 58.88\text{ rpm}$$

(ii) KE is not conserved in process.

$$K_{\text{final}} > K_{\text{initial}}$$

Muscular work done by the man in folding his arms is converted into KE.

40.

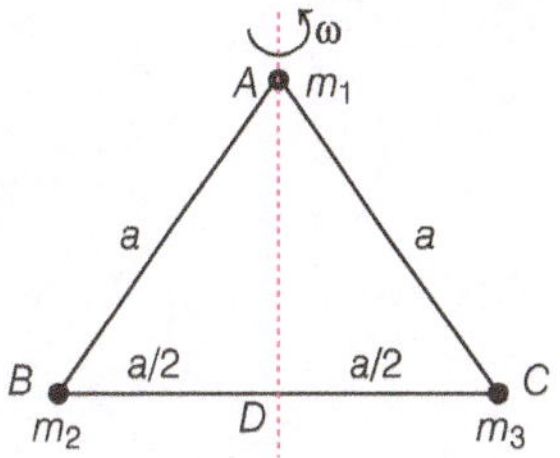

$$I = \sum_{i=1}^{n} m_i r_i^2 = m_1 \times 0 + m_2 \times (BD)^2 + m_3 \times (DC)^2$$

$$= 0 + m_2 \left(\frac{a}{2}\right)^2 + m_3 \left(\frac{a}{2}\right)^2$$

$$I = \frac{1}{4}(m_2 + m_3)a^2$$

41. Given, moment of inertia, $I = 0.6$ kg-m^2

$n = 0.5$ rps, $\omega = 2\pi n = 2\pi \times 0.5$

$\therefore$ Angular momentum $= I\omega = 0.6 \times 0.5 \times 2\pi$

$= 0.6\,\pi$ kg-m^2/s

42. Given that the moment of inertia of thin rod of length l about an axis passing through its one end and perpendicular to its length, $I = \frac{MR^2}{3}$

Radius of gyration is given as $K = \sqrt{\frac{I}{M}}$

So, $K = \sqrt{\frac{MR^2}{3M}} = \frac{R}{\sqrt{3}}$

43. Taking atoms as point masses, moment of inertia of molecule,

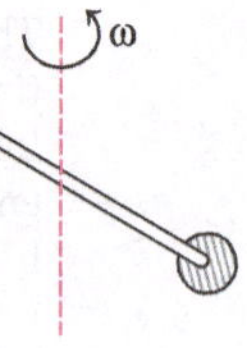

$$I = \frac{m}{2}r^2 + \frac{m}{2}r^2 = mr^2$$

$\Rightarrow$ $I = mr^2$ or $r = \sqrt{\frac{I}{m}}$

Now, given that, $KE_{(rot)} = \frac{2}{3} KE_{(trans.)}$

$$\frac{1}{2} I\omega^2 = \frac{2}{3} \times \frac{1}{2} mv^2$$

$\Rightarrow$ $I\omega^2 = \frac{2}{3} mv^2 \Rightarrow mr^2\omega^2 = \frac{2}{3} mv^2$

or $\omega = \sqrt{\frac{2}{3}}\left(\frac{v}{r}\right) = \sqrt{\frac{2}{3}} \times v \times \sqrt{\frac{m}{I}}$

Here, $v = 500$ m/s, $I = 1.94 \times 10^{-46}$ kg - m^2

$\Rightarrow$ $m = 5.36 \times 10^{-26}$ kg

So, average angular velocity of the molecule is

$$= \sqrt{\frac{2}{3}} \times 500 \times \sqrt{\frac{5.36 \times 10^{-26}}{1.94 \times 10^{-46}}} = 6.7 \times 10^{12} \text{ rad/s}$$

QR Code for Quick Test 1

QR Code for Quick Test 2

QR Code for Quick Test 3

SELF ASSESSMENT TEST

Multiple Choice Questions (MCQs)

1. A uniform square plate has a small piece Q of an irregular shape removed and glued to the centre of the plate leaving a hole behind in figure. The moment of inertia about the Z-axis is

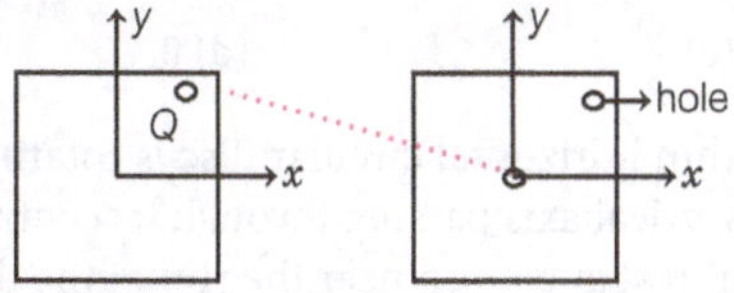

(a) increased
(b) decreased
(c) remain same
(d) changed in unpredicted manner

2. The density of a non-uniform rod of length 1m is given by $\rho(x) = a(1 + bx^2)$, where a and b are constants and $0 \le x \le 1$. The centre of mass of the rod will be at

(a) $\frac{3(2+b)}{4(3+b)}$ (b) $\frac{4(2+b)}{3(3+b)}$
(c) $\frac{3(3+b)}{4(2+b)}$ (d) $\frac{4(3+b)}{3(2+b)}$

3. Two rings of radii R and nR made from the same wire have the ratio of moments of inertia about an axis passing through their centres equal to 1 : 8. The value of n is

(a) 2 (b) $2\sqrt{2}$
(c) 4 (d) 1/2

4. A solid sphere of radius r is rolling with velocity v on a smooth plane. The total kinetic energy of sphere is

(a) $\frac{7}{10}mv^2$ (b) $\frac{3}{4}mv^2$
(c) $\frac{1}{2}mv^2$ (d) $\frac{1}{4}mv^2$

5. Planetary motion in the solar system describes
(a) conservation of kinetic energy
(b) conservation of linear momentum
(c) conservation of angular momentum
(d) All of the above

6. A uniform cube of mass m and side a is placed on a frictionless horizontal surface. A vertical force F is applied to the edge as shown in figure. Match the following (most appropriate choice)

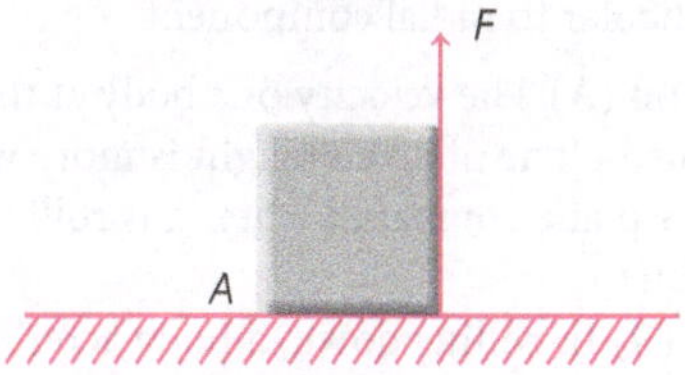

	Column I		Column II
A.	$mg/4 < F < mg/2$	P.	Cube will move up.
B.	$F > mg/2$	Q.	Cube will not exhibit motion.
C.	$F > mg$	R.	Cube will begin to rotate and slip at A.
D.	$F = mg/4$	S.	Normal reaction effectively at $a/3$ from A, no motion.

(a) A-Q, B-R, C-P, D-S
(b) A-S, B-Q, C-P, D-R
(c) A-S, B-P, C-R, D-Q
(d) A-Q, B-R, C-S, D-P

Assertion-Reason

Direction (Q. Nos. 8-10) In the following questions, two statements are given-one labelled Assertion (A) and the other labelled Reason (R). Select the correct answer to these questions from the codes (a), (b), (c) and (d) as given below.

(a) Both Assertion and Reason are true and Reason is the correct explanation of Assertion.
(b) Both Assertion and Reason are true but Reason is not the correct explanation of Assertion.
(c) Assertion is true but Reason is false.
(d) Assertion is false but Reason is true.

7. **Assertion (A)** A wheel moving down a perfectly frictionless inclined plane shall undergo slipping (not rolling).
Reason (R) For rolling torque is required which is provided by tangential frictional force.

8. **Assertion (A)** Torque is due to the transverse component of force only. The radical component has no role to play.
Reason (R) This is because transverse component is not perpendicular to radial component.

9. **Assertion (A)** The velocity of a body at the bottom of an inclined plane of given height is more when it slides down the plane compared when it is rolling down the same plane.
Reason (R) In rolling down, a body acquires both kinetic energy of translation and rotation.

10. **Assertion (A)** Torque is due to the transverse component of force only. The radical component has no role to play.
Reason (R) This is because transverse component is not perpendicular to radial component.

Case Based Questions

Directions *(Q.No. 11) This question is case study based question. Read the following paragraph and answer the questions on the basis of same.*

11. A rigid body is said to be in translational equilibrium, if the net external force acting on the body is zero and it is said to be in rotational equilibrium, if net external torque acting on the body is zero. A rigid body is said to be in partial equilibrium, if either it is in rotational equilibrium but not in translational equilibrium or it is in translational equilibrium but not in rotational equilibrium.

(i) A couple is acting on rigid body, then which statement is true ?
(a) The body is in translational equilibrium but not in rotational equilibrium.
(b) The body is in rotational equilibrium but not in translational equilibrium.
(c) The body is in translational equilibrium as well as in rotational equilibrium.
(d) The body is neither in translational equilibrium nor in rotational equilibrium.

(ii) For a body in translational equilibrium, which of the following option is false ?
(a) $\Sigma \mathbf{F}_{ext} = 0$ (b) $\mathbf{p} = 0$
(c) $\mathbf{v} = 0$ or constant (d) $\mathbf{a} \neq 0$

(iii) For a body in rotational equilibrium, which of the following option is true?
(a) $\Sigma \tau_{ext} = 0$ (b) $\mathbf{L} \neq 0$
(c) $\mathbf{r} \neq 0$ (d) $\omega \neq 0$

(iv) A merry go round, made of a ring like platform of radius R and mass M, is revolving with angular speed ω. A person of mass M is standing on it. At one instant, the person jumps off the round, radially away from the centre of the round (as seen the ground). The speed of the marry go round afterwards is
(a) 2ω (b) ω
(c) $\frac{\omega}{2}$ (d) 0

(v) A thin horizontal circular disc is rotating about a vertical axis passing through its centre. An insect is at rest at a point near the rim of the disc. The insect now moves along a diameter of the disc to reach its other end. During the journey of the insect, the angular speed of the disc
(a) continuously decreases
(b) continuously increases
(c) first increases and then decreases
(d) remains unchanged

Very Short Answer Type Questions

12. Why in hand driven grinding machine, handle is put near the circumference of the stone or wheel?

13. The speed of a whirl wind in a tornado is alarmingly high. Why?

14. From a uniform disc of radius R, a circular disc of radius $R/2$ is cut out. The centre of the hole is at $R/2$ from the centre of original disc. Locate the centre of gravity of the resultant flat body.

Short Answer Type Questions

15. $(n-1)$ equal point masses each of mass m are placed at the vertices of a regular n-polygon. The vacant vertex has a position vector a with respect to the centre of the polygon. Find the position vector of centre of mass.

16. The vector sum of a system of non-collinear forces acting on a rigid body is given to be non-zero. If the vector sum of all the torques due to the system of forces about a certain point is found to be zero, does this mean that it is necessarily zero about any arbitrary point?

17. If earth contracts to half of its radius, what would be the length of the day?

Long Answer Type Questions

18. Six particles are placed at different points of a square as shown in the figure. Find the centre of mass for the system of six particles.

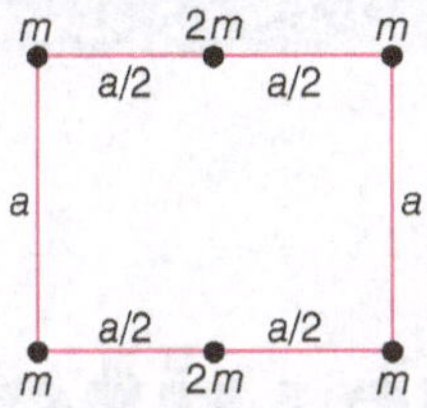

19. A horizontal disc rotating about a vertical axis perpendicular to its plane and passing through centre makes 180 rpm. A small lump of wet mud of mass 10 g falls on disc lightly and sticks to it at a distance of 8 cm from its axis. If now the disc with mud makes 150 rpm only, calculate the moment of inertia of the disc.

20. Three balls of masses 1kg, 2kg and 3kg are arranged at the corners of an equilateral triangle of side 1m. What will be the moment of inertia of the system about an axis through the centroid and perpendicular to the plane of triangle ?

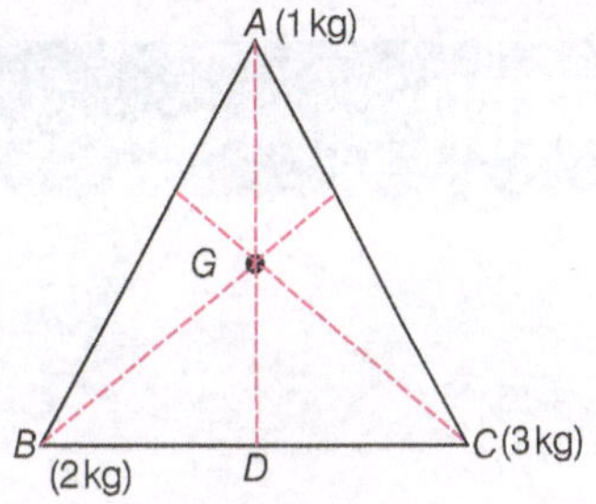

Answers

1. (b) *2.* (a) *3.* (a) *4.* (a) *5.* (c)
6.(a) *7.* (a) *8.* (c) 9. (b) 10. (c)
11.(i) (a) (ii) (d) (iii) (a) (iv) (a) (v) (c)
17. 6 hours *18.* $\frac{a}{2}, \frac{a}{2}$
19. 3.2×10^{-4} kg-m^2 20. 2 kg-m^2

07

CHAPTER

Gravitation

Every object in the universe attracts every other object with a force which is called **force of gravitation.**
Galileo was the first to recognise the fact that all bodies, irrespective of their masses fall towards the earth with a constant acceleration. Kepler believed all heavenly bodies obey a mathematical order unlike anything on the earth.

YOUR STUDY GOALS

7.1 Kepler's Laws of Planetary Motion
7.2 Universal Law of Gravitation
7.3 Acceleration Due to Gravity and Gravitational Potential Energy
7.4 Escape Speed
7.5 Earth Satellites

YOUR PRACTICE GOAL

- Objective Type Questions (34 Qs, MCQs, A-R, Statements, Matching)
- Case Based Questions (4)
- Subjective Questions (6 VSAs, 13 SAs, 6 LAs)
- Numerical Problems (47)

7.1 Kepler's Laws of Planetary Motion

Kepler's laws of planetary motion are three scientific laws describing motion of planets around the sun.

Kepler's First Law of Orbits

According to this law, all planets are move in elliptical orbits with the sun situated at one of the foci of the ellipse.

This law identifies that the distance between the sun and the earth is constantly changing as the earth goes around its orbit as shown in figure.

It shows an ellipse traced out by a planet around the sun S. The closest point is P called the **perihelion** and the farthest point is A called the **aphelion**.

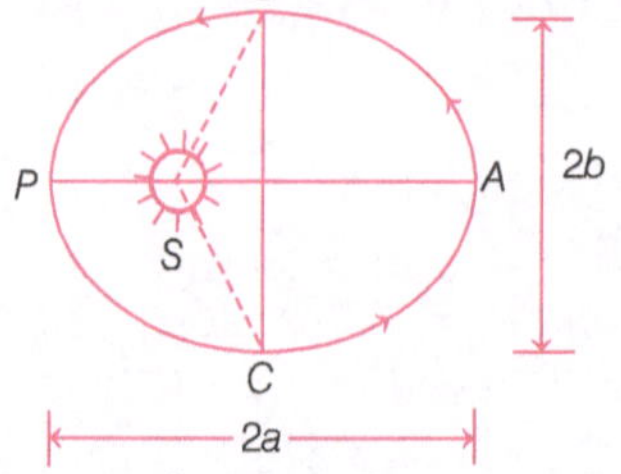

An ellipse traced out by a planet around the sun

Kepler's Second Law of Areas

According to this law, **the speed of planet varies in such a way that the radius vector drawn from the sun to a planet sweeps out equal areas in equal interval of time. i.e. The areal velocity of the planet around the sun is constant.**

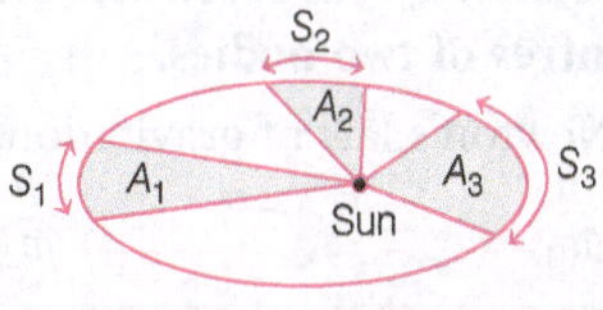

The areas A_1, A_2 and A_3 as shown in figure are swept out by the radius vector in equal intervals of time. According to Kepler's second law, $A_1 = A_2 = A_3$.

Note Areal velocity may be defined as the area swept by the radius vector in unit time.

Proof of Kepler's Second Law

This law is identical with the law of conservation of angular momentum. Consider a small area ΔA described in a small time interval Δt and let the position of the planet be denoted by r.

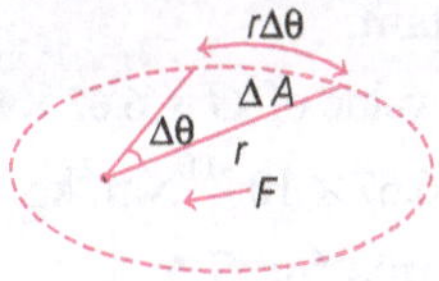

Now, $$\Delta A = \frac{1}{2} r (r\,\Delta\theta)$$

$\therefore$ $$\frac{\Delta A}{\Delta t} = \frac{1}{2} r^2 \frac{\Delta\theta}{\Delta t}$$

Proceeding to limit as $\Delta t \to 0$, we get

$$\lim_{\Delta t \to 0} \frac{\Delta A}{\Delta t} = \frac{1}{2} r^2 \lim_{\Delta t \to 0} \frac{\Delta\theta}{\Delta t}$$

or $$\frac{dA}{dt} = \frac{1}{2} r^2 \omega \quad \left[\because \omega = \frac{\Delta\theta}{\Delta t}\right] \quad \ldots\text{(i)}$$

Instantaneous angular momentum,

$$L = mr^2\omega \quad \ldots\text{(ii)}$$

From Eqs. (i) and (ii), we get

$$\frac{dA}{dt} = \frac{L}{2m}$$

or $$L = 2m \times \frac{dA}{dt} \quad \ldots\text{(iii)}$$

The line of action of the gravitational force passes through the axis. Therefore, angle between **r** and **F** is 180°.

Now, $$\tau_{\text{ext}} = \mathbf{r} \times \mathbf{F} = rF \sin 180°\ \hat{\mathbf{n}} = 0$$

$$\tau_{\text{ext}} = 0$$

$\therefore$ $$L = \text{constant} \quad \left[\because \frac{dL}{dt} = \tau_{\text{ext}}\right] \ldots\text{(iv)}$$

From Eqs. (iii) and (iv), we get

$\therefore$ $$\text{Areal velocity, } \frac{dA}{dt} = \text{constant}$$

i.e. **The areal velocity of the planet around the sun is constant.** This proved the Kepler's second law of planetary motion.

Kepler's Third Law of Period

According to this law, **the square of the time period of revolution of a planet around the sun is proportional to the cube of the semi-major axis of its elliptical orbit.**

i.e. $$\boxed{T^2 \propto a^3} \quad \ldots\text{(i)}$$

T = time period of revolution of a planet

As shown in figure, we have

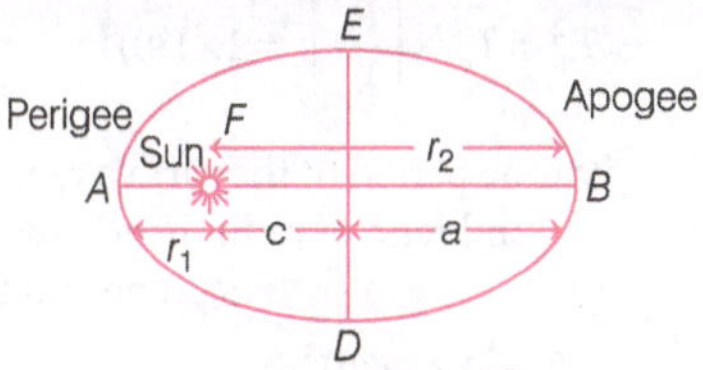

Law of period

$$AB = AF + FB$$

$$2a = r_1 + r_2$$

$\therefore$ $$a = \frac{r_1 + r_2}{2}$$

So, putting the value of a in Eq. (i), we get

$$\boxed{T^2 \propto \left(\frac{r_1 + r_2}{2}\right)^3}$$

where, a = length of semi-major axis,

r_1 = shortest distance of planet from sun (perigee)

and r_2 = longest distance of planet from sun (apogee).

Note Kepler's laws are applicable not only to the solar system but also to the artificial satellites as well as to the moon going around the planets.

Example 1. The distances of two planets from the sun are 10^{14} m and 10^{13} m, respectively. Find the ratio of speeds of the two planets.

Sol. Let d_1 and d_2 are the distances of the planets from the sun and v_1 and v_2 are their orbital speeds, then

$$v_1 = \frac{2\pi d_1}{T_1} \quad \text{and} \quad v_2 = \frac{2\pi d_2}{T_2}$$

$$\therefore \quad \frac{v_1}{v_2} = \frac{d_1}{d_2} \cdot \frac{T_2}{T_1} \quad \text{...(i)}$$

From Kepler's third law, $\frac{T_1}{T_2} = \left(\frac{d_1}{d_2}\right)^{3/2}$ ...(ii)

From Eqs. (i) and (ii), we get

$$\frac{v_1}{v_2} = \left(\frac{d_1}{d_2}\right) \cdot \left(\frac{d_2}{d_1}\right)^{3/2} = \left(\frac{d_2}{d_1}\right)^{1/2} = \left(\frac{10^{13}}{10^{14}}\right)^{1/2} = 1/\sqrt{10}$$

Example 2. Calculate the period of revolution of the neptune around the sun, given that diameter of its orbit is 30 times the diameter of the earth's orbit around the sun. Assume both the orbits to be circular.

Sol. According to Kepler's third law, $\frac{T_n^2}{T_e^2} = \frac{R_n^3}{R_e^3}$

where, subscripts n and e refer to the neptune and the earth, respectively.

$$\therefore \quad T_n^2 = T_e^2 \times \left(\frac{R_n}{R_e}\right)^3 = 1 \times (30)^3$$

[∵ time period of the earth's revolution = 1 year and ratio of radii (hence, diameters) of the neptune and the earth is 30]

$$\therefore \quad T_n = 1 \times \sqrt{(30)^3}$$

$$T_n = 30\sqrt{30} = 164.3 \text{ yr}$$

Example 3. Suppose there existed a planet that went around the sun twice as fast as the earth. What would be its orbital size as compared to that of the earth? NCERT

Sol. Let T_p and T_e denote the time periods of the planet and the earth, respectively. If R_p and R_e denote the corresponding orbital size, then $\frac{T_p^2}{T_e^2} = \frac{R_p^3}{R_e^3}$

or $\left(\frac{R_p}{R_e}\right)^3 = \left(\frac{T_p}{T_e}\right)^2 \Rightarrow \frac{R_p}{R_e} = \left(\frac{T_p}{T_e}\right)^{2/3}$

Since, $T_p = \frac{1}{2}T_e, \frac{T_p}{T_e} = \frac{1}{2}$

Thus, $\frac{R_p}{R_e} = \left(\frac{1}{2}\right)^{2/3} = 0.63$

7.2 Universal Law of Gravitation

It states that, **every body in this universe attracts other body with a force whose magnitude is directly proportional to the product of their masses and inversely proportional to the square of the distance between their centres. This force acts along the line joining the centres of two bodies.**

According to Newton's law of gravitation, we get

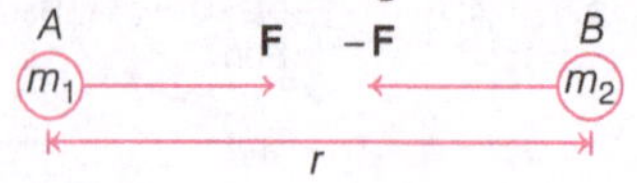

So, $F \propto m_1 m_2$ ...(i)

and $F \propto \frac{1}{r^2}$ ...(ii)

From Eqs. (i) and (ii), we get

$$F \propto \frac{m_1 m_2}{r^2}$$

or $\text{Gravitational force, } F = G\frac{m_1 m_2}{r^2}$ ...(iii)

where, G is a constant of proportionality known as **gravitational constant.** It is also known as **universal gravitational constant.**

In CGS system, the value of G is 6.67×10^{-8} dyne cm^{2}g^{-2} and its SI value is 6.67×10^{-11} Nm^{2}kg^{-2}.

Dimensional formula for G

$$G = \frac{Fr^2}{m_1 m_2} = \frac{[MLT^{-2}][L^2]}{[M^2]}$$

$$= [MLT^{-2}][L^2][M^{-2}] = [M^{-1}L^3T^{-2}]$$

Suppose $m_1 = m_2 = 1$ unit and $r = 1$ unit, then from Eq. (iii), we get

$$F = \frac{G \times 1 \times 1}{(1)^2} \Rightarrow \boxed{F = G}$$

Thus, **universal gravitational constant (G) is numerically equal to the force of attraction acting between two bodies, each of unit mass separated by unit distance apart.**

Important Points about Gravitational Force

- It is always attractive in nature, while electric and magnetic forces can be attractive or repulsive.
- It is independent of the intervening medium between the particles, while electric and magnetic forces depend on the nature of the medium between the particles.

- The gravitational force is a conservative force.
- The value of G does not depend on the nature and size of the masses.
- The force of attraction between a hollow spherical shell of uniform density and a point mass situated outside is just as, if the entire mass of the shell is concentrated at the centre of the shell. Gravitational force possesses spherical symmetry.
- The force of attraction due to a hollow spherical shell of uniform density on a point mass situated inside it, is zero.

Example 4. **A sphere of mass 40 kg is attracted by a second sphere of mass 60 kg with a force equal to 4 mgf. If G is 6×10^{-11} N-m^2/kg^2, then calculate the distance between them. Consider acceleration due to gravity is 10 m/s^2.**

Sol. Given, $M = 40\,\text{kg}, m = 60\,\text{kg}$,

$$F = 4\,\text{mgf} = 4\times10^{-6}\times10 = 4\times10^{-5}\text{N}$$

$$G = 6\times10^{-11}\ \text{N - m}^2/\text{kg}^2, g = 10\text{m/s}^2$$

According to universal law, $F = \dfrac{GMm}{r^2}$

$$\Rightarrow \quad r = \sqrt{\frac{GMm}{F}} = \sqrt{\frac{6\times10^{-11}\times40\times60}{4\times10^{-5}}}$$

$$= 0.06\ \text{m} = 6\ \text{cm}$$

Vector Form of Newton's Law of Gravitation

Consider two particles A and B of masses m_1 and m_2, respectively.

Let $\mathbf{r}_{12}$ = displacement vector from A to B,

$\mathbf{r}_{21}$ = displacement vector from B to A,

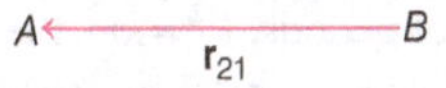

$\therefore \quad \mathbf{r}_{12} = -\mathbf{r}_{21}$

$\mathbf{F}_{21}$ = gravitational force exerted on B by A

$\mathbf{F}_{12}$ = gravitational force exerted on A by B

On vector notation, Newton's law of gravitation is written as follows

$$\mathbf{F}_{12} = G\frac{m_1m_2}{r_{21}^2}\hat{\mathbf{r}}_{12} \quad \ldots\text{(i)}$$

where, $\hat{\mathbf{r}}_{21}$ is a unit vector pointing towards A. The negative sign indicates that the direction of $\mathbf{F}_{12}$ is opposite to that of $\hat{\mathbf{r}}_{21}$. The negative sign also shows that the gravitational force is attractive in nature.

Similarly, $\quad \mathbf{F}_{21} = G\dfrac{m_1m_2}{r_{12}^2}\hat{\mathbf{r}}_{21}$

where, $\hat{\mathbf{r}}_{12}$ is a unit vector pointing towards B.

But $\quad \hat{\mathbf{r}}_{21} = -\hat{\mathbf{r}}_{12}$

Also, $\quad r_{21}^2 = r_{12}^2$

$$\therefore \quad \mathbf{F}_{21} = -G\frac{m_1m_2}{r_{21}^2}\hat{\mathbf{r}}_{12} \quad \ldots\text{(ii)}$$

Equating Eqs. (i) and (ii), we have

$$\mathbf{F}_{12} = -\mathbf{F}_{21}$$

As $\mathbf{F}_{12}$ and $\mathbf{F}_{21}$ are directed towards the centres of the two particles, so **gravitational force is a central force.**

Principle of Superposition

The net force on an object due to number of other masses is the vector sum of the individual forces on that object.

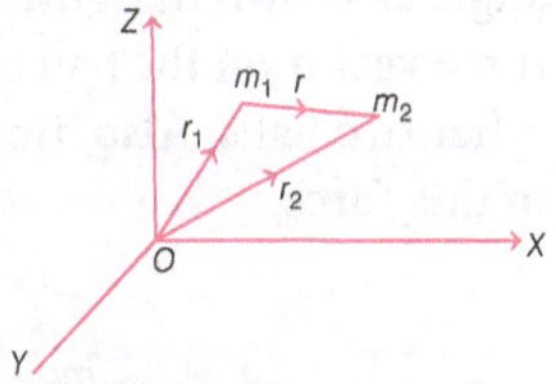

Gravitational force on m_1 due to m_2 is along r, where the vector r is $(r_2 - r_1)$

Suppose $\mathbf{F}_1, \mathbf{F}_2, \ldots, \mathbf{F}_n$ be the individual forces due to the masses $m_1, m_2, \ldots, m_n$ which are given by the universal law of gravitation, then from the principle of superposition, each of these forces acts independently and uninfluenced by the other bodies as shown in figure.

So, the resultant force $\mathbf{F}$ can be expressed in vector addition of various forces

$$\mathbf{F} = \mathbf{F}_{12} + \mathbf{F}_{13} + \mathbf{F}_{14} + \ldots + \mathbf{F}_{1n}$$

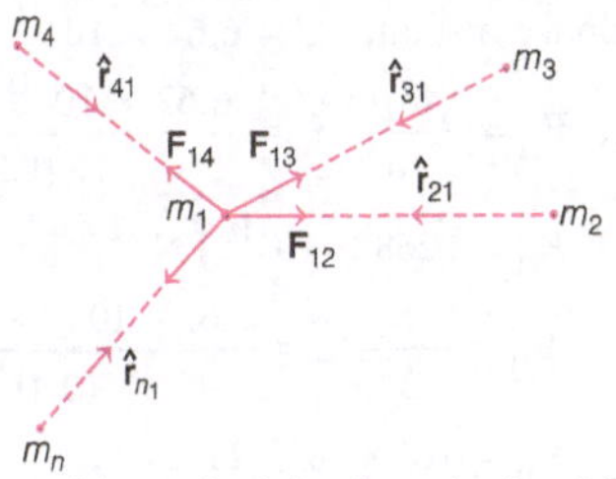

Superposition principle of gravitational forces

$$\text{Clearly, } \mathbf{F} = -G\frac{m_1m_2}{r_{12}^2}\hat{\mathbf{r}}_{21} - G\frac{m_1m_3}{r_{13}^2}\hat{\mathbf{r}}_{31} - \ldots - G\frac{m_1m_n}{r_{1n}^2}\mathbf{r}_{n1}$$

$$\text{Resultant force, } \mathbf{F} = -Gm_1\left[\frac{m_2}{r_{12}^2}\hat{\mathbf{r}}_{21} + \frac{m_3}{r_{13}^2}\hat{\mathbf{r}}_{31} + \ldots \frac{m_n}{r_{1n}^2}\hat{\mathbf{r}}_{n1}\right]$$

Example 5. **Two forces $F_1 = 10$ N and $F_2 = 15$ N are acting on an object of mass $m_1 = 5$ kg. The forces are applied at an angle of 60° to each other. Find the resultant force acting on m_1.**

Sol. We use the principle of superposition to find the resultant force acting on the object. The formula for the resultant force F_R when two forces act at an angle θ is given by

$$F_R = \sqrt{F_1^2 + F_2^2 + 2F_1F_2 \cos\theta}$$

Substitute the given values,

$$F_R = \sqrt{10^2 + 15^2 + 2 \times 10 \times 15 \times \cos 60°}$$

$$F_R = \sqrt{100 + 225 + 2 \times 10 \times 15 \times 0.5}$$

$$F_R = \sqrt{100 + 225 + 150} = \sqrt{475} \approx 21.8 \text{ N}$$

Example 6. **Consider the three billiard balls of masses 400 g are placed on a table at the corners of a right angle as shown in figure. Calculate the gravitational force vector on the ball of the mass m_1 resulting from other two balls. Also, find the magnitude and direction of this force.**

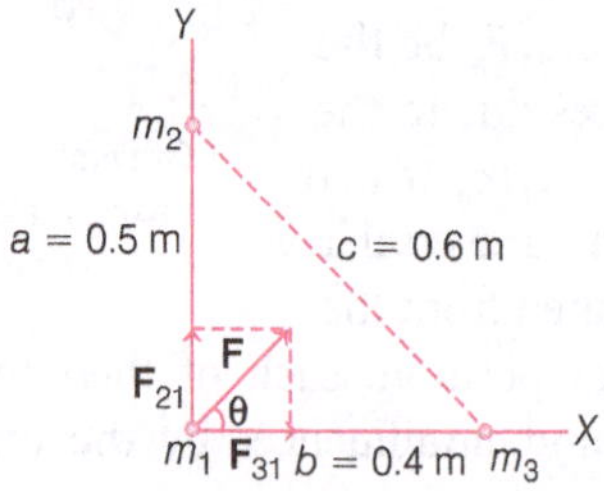

Sol. Force exerted by m_2 on the cue ball of mass m_1.

$$m_1 = m_2 = m_3 = 400 \text{ g} = 0.4 \text{ kg}$$

$$a = 0.5 \text{ m}, b = 0.4 \text{ m and } c = 0.6 \text{ m}$$

Gravitational constant, $G = 6.67 \times 10^{-11}$ Nm^2/kg^2

The force, $\mathbf{F}_{21} = G\dfrac{m_2 m_1}{a^2}\hat{\mathbf{j}} = \dfrac{6.67 \times 10^{-11} \times 0.4 \times 0.4}{(0.5)^2}\cdot\hat{\mathbf{j}}$

$$\mathbf{F}_{21} = 4.268 \times 10^{-11}\,\hat{\mathbf{j}}\text{ N}$$

Similarly, $\mathbf{F}_{31} = \dfrac{Gm_3m_1}{b^2}\hat{\mathbf{i}} = \dfrac{6.67 \times 10^{-11} \times 0.4 \times 0.4}{(0.4)^2}\hat{\mathbf{i}}$

$$\mathbf{F}_{31} = 6.67 \times 10^{-11}\,\hat{\mathbf{i}}\text{ N}$$

The net gravitational force on the one ball,

$$\mathbf{F} = \mathbf{F}_{31} + \mathbf{F}_{21} = (6.67\,\hat{\mathbf{i}} + 4.26\,\hat{\mathbf{j}}) \times 10^{-11} \text{ N}$$

The net gravitational force,

$$F = \sqrt{\mathbf{F}_{31}^2 + \mathbf{F}_{21}^2}$$

$$= \sqrt{(6.67)^2 + (4.268)^2} \times 10^{-11} \text{ N}$$

$$F = 7.918 \times 10^{-11} \text{ N}$$

Also, $\tan\theta = \dfrac{F_y}{F_x} = \dfrac{\mathbf{F}_{21}}{\mathbf{F}_{31}} = \dfrac{4.268 \times 10^{-11}}{6.67 \times 10^{-11}} = 0.639$

$\Rightarrow \quad \theta = 32.6°$

Quick Test 1

Conceptual Questions

1. If earth be at one half its present distance from the sun, then how many days will there be in a year?

2. Do the force of friction and other contact forces arise due to gravitational attraction? If not, then what is the origin of these forces?

3. Draw areal velocity *versus* time graph for mars. *NCERT Exemplar*

4. What is the direction of areal velocity of the earth around the sun? *NCERT Exemplar*

5. Out of aphelion and perihelion, where is the speed of the earth more and why? *NCERT Exemplar*

6. Imagine what would happen if the value of G becomes
(i) 100 times of its present value?
(ii) $\dfrac{1}{100}$ times of its present value?

7. Two identical heavy spheres are separated by a distance 10 times their radius. Will an object be placed at the mid-point of the line joining their centres be in stable equilibrium or unstable equilibrium? Give reasons for your answer. *NCERT Exemplar*

Numerical Questions

8. Two stationary particles of masses M_1 and M_2 are at distance d apart. A third particle lying on the line joining the particles, experiences no resultant gravitational force. What is the distance of this particle from M_1?

9. In Kepler's law of periods, $T^2 = kr^3$, the constant, $k = 10^{-13}$ s^{2}m^{-3}. Express the constant k in days and kilometres. The moon is at a distance of 3.84×10^5 km from the earth. Obtain its time period of revolution in days.

10. A saturn year is 29.5 times the earth year. How far is the saturn from the sun of the earth is 1.50×10^8 km away from the sun? *NCERT*

Answers

8. $r = d\left(\dfrac{\sqrt{M_1}}{\sqrt{M_1} + \sqrt{M_2}}\right)$ 9. 27.3 days 10. 14.3×10^8 km

For Solutions, See QR Code on Pg. 270

7.3 Acceleration Due to Gravity and Gravitational Potential Energy

Acceleration due to Gravity of Earth

The acceleration due to gravity is the rate of increases of velocity of body falling freely towards the earth. It is represented by symbol g and its value is 9.8 m/s^2 on the surface of the earth.

$$\text{Acceleration due to gravity} = \frac{F_{\text{gravity}}}{m_{\text{body}}}$$

$$g = \frac{GM_e m}{mR_e^2}$$

$$g = \frac{GM_e}{R_e^2}$$

where, $G = 6.67 \times 10^{-11} \text{ N-m}^2/\text{kg}^2$, $R_e = 6.4 \times 10^6$ m,

$M_e = 6 \times 10^{24}$ kg

We get value of acceleration due to gravity on earth,

$$g = 9.8 \text{ m/s}^2$$

- The value of acceleration due to gravity differs from place-to-place on the surface of the earth. It also varies with altitude and depth.
- The value of g on the surface of the moon is equal to 1/6 times the value of g on the surface of the earth.
- The value of g is independent of mass, shape, size, etc., of the body and depends upon the mass and radius of the earth.

Example 7. **The acceleration due to gravity at the moon's surface is 1.67 ms^{-2}. If the radius of the moon is 1.74×10^6 m, then calculate the mass of the moon.**

Sol. $g = \frac{GM}{R^2}$ or $M = \frac{gR^2}{G}$

This relation is true not only to the earth but for any heavenly body which is assumed to be spherical.

Now, $g = 1.67 \text{ ms}^{-2}, R = 1.74 \times 10^6$ m

$G = 6.67 \times 10^{-11} \text{ Nm}^{-2} \text{ kg}^{-2}$

$$\therefore \text{ Mass of the moon, } M = \frac{1.67 \times (1.74 \times 10^6)^2}{6.67 \times 10^{-11}} \text{ kg}$$

$$= 7.58 \times 10^{22} \text{kg}$$

Example 8. **A star 2.5 times the mass of the sun and collapsed to a size of 12 km and rotates with a speed of 1.5 revolutions per second. (Extremely compact stars of this kind are known as neutron stars. Certain stellar objects, called pulsars, belong to this category.) Will an object placed on its equator remain stuck to its surface due to gravity?**
(Mass of the sun = 2×10^{30} kg)

Sol. We are given mass of neutron star,

$M = 2.5 \times 2 \times 10^{30} \text{kg} = 5 \times 10^{30}$ kg

Radius of star, $R = 12 \text{ km} = 1.2 \times 10^4$m

Frequency of rotation, $\nu = 1.5$

If g is the acceleration due to gravity on the surface of the star,

$$g = \frac{GM}{R^2} = \frac{6.67 \times 10^{-11} \times 5 \times 10^{30}}{(1.2 \times 10^4)^2} \text{ m/s}^2$$

$$= 2.3 \times 10^{12} \text{ m/s}^2$$

Centrifugal acceleration (a_c) produced in the object at the equator,

i.e. $a_c = R\omega^2 = R \times (2\pi\nu)^2 = 4\pi^2\nu^2 R$

or $a_c = 4 \times 9.87 \times (1.5)^2 \times 1.2 \times 10^4 \text{ m/ s}^2$

$a_c = 1.1 \times 10^6 \text{ m /s}^2$

Since $g > a_c$, the object will remain stuck to its surface due to gravity.

Example 9. **A spherical mass of 20 kg lying on the earth's surface is attracted by another spherical mass of 150 kg with a force equal to the weight of 0.25 mg. The centre of the two masses are 0.3 m apart. Calculate the mass of the earth.**

Sol.

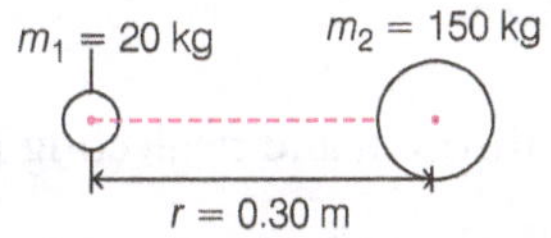

Given, $m_1 = 20$ kg, $m_2 = 150$ kg

$F = 0.25$ mg- wt, $g = 9.80 \text{ ms}^{-2}$, $R = 6 \times 10^6$ m

Now, kg-wt multiply by 9.8 to get in newton.

$F = 0.25 \text{ mg-wt} = 0.25 \times 10^{-3}$ g-wt

$= 0.25 \times 10^{-3} \times 10^{-3} \text{ kg-wt} = 0.25 \times 10^{-6}$ kg-wt

$= 0.25 \times 10^{-6} \times 9.8$ N $\quad [\because 1 \text{ kg-wt} = 9.8 \text{ N}]$

From universal law, $F = G\frac{m_1 m_2}{r^2}$

or $$G = \frac{Fr^2}{m_1 m_2}$$

$$G = \frac{0.25 \times 10^{-6} \times 9.8 \times (0.3)^2}{20 \times 150}$$

$$G = 75 \times 9.80 \times 10^{-13} \text{ Nm}^2 \text{ kg}^{-2}$$

$$\therefore \quad g = \frac{GM}{R^2}$$

$$\therefore \quad M = \frac{g \times R^2}{G} = \frac{9.80 \times (6 \times 10^6)^2}{75 \times 9.80 \times 10^{-13}} = 4.8 \times 10^{24} \text{ kg}$$

Acceleration due to Gravity above the Surface of Earth

Consider a body of mass m lying on the surface of the earth of mass M and radius R. Acceleration due to gravity at the surface of the earth,

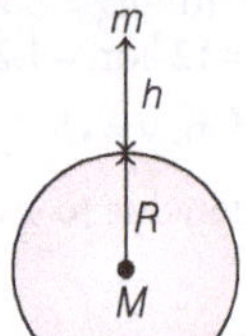

Variation of g with altitude

$$g = \frac{GM}{R^2} \quad \ldots(i)$$

If now the body is taken at height h and g_h is acceleration due to gravity at that height, then

$$g_h = \frac{GM}{(R+h)^2} \quad \ldots(ii)$$

Dividing Eq. (ii) by Eq. (i), we get

$$g_h = \frac{g}{\left(1+\frac{h}{R_e}\right)^2} = g\left(1+\frac{h}{R_e}\right)^{-2}$$

If $h << R$, then $\frac{h}{R} << 1$, so that higher orders of $\frac{h}{R}$ can be neglected.

Using binomial theorem and neglecting higher orders, we get

$$g_h = g\left(1-\frac{2h}{R}\right)$$

Acceleration due to gravity at height h, $g_h = g\left(1-\frac{2h}{R}\right)$

or $$g_h = g - \frac{2h}{R}g \quad \ldots(iii)$$

or $$g - g_h = \frac{2h}{R}g \quad \ldots(iv)$$

From Eq. (iv), we know that the value of acceleration due to gravity decreases with height.

Since, the value of g at a given place on the earth is constant and R is also constant, $g - g_h \propto h$

From the above equation, we note that if h increases, g_h must decrease because g is constant.

Thus, the value of acceleration due to gravity decreases with increase in height above the surface of the earth.

Graphical representation of g outside the earth.

Putting $r = R+h$ in Eq. (ii), we get

$$g_h = \frac{GM}{r^2} \Rightarrow g_h \propto \frac{1}{r^2}$$

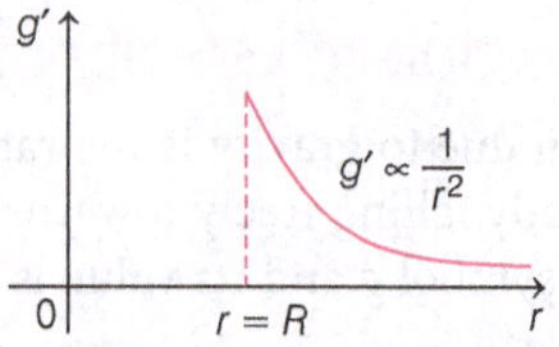

Example 10. If an object at the altitude of the space shuttle's orbit, about 400 km above the earth's surface, then find out the free fall acceleration of that object.

Sol. The acceleration, $g = \frac{F}{m} = \frac{GMm/R^2}{m} = \frac{GM}{R^2}$

If the object is at height h above the earth's surface, then

$$g_h = \frac{GM}{(R+h)^2}$$

$$\Rightarrow \quad g_h = \frac{6.67\times 10^{-11}\times 5.98\times 10^{24}}{(6.4\times 10^6 + 0.4\times 10^6)^2} = 8.70 \text{ m/s}^2$$

Example 11. A body weighs 63 N on the surface of the earth. What is the gravitational force on it due to the earth at a height equal to half the radius of the earth? NCERT

Sol. Let g_h be the acceleration due to gravity at a height equal to half the radius of the earth $\left(h = \frac{R}{2}\right)$ and g is its value on the earth's surface. Let the body have mass m. We know that,

$$\frac{g_h}{g} = \left(\frac{R}{R+h}\right)^2$$

or $$\frac{g_h}{g} = \left(\frac{R}{R+\frac{R}{2}}\right)^2 = \left(\frac{2}{3}\right)^2 = \frac{4}{9}$$

Let w be the weight of body on the surface of the earth and w_h be the weight of the body at height h,

then, $$\frac{w_h}{w} = \frac{mg_h}{mg} = \frac{g_h}{g} = \frac{4}{9}$$

or $$w_h = \frac{4}{9}w = \frac{4}{9}\times 63 \text{ N} = 28 \text{ N}$$

Acceleration due to Gravity below the Earth's Surface

Assume the earth to be a homogeneous sphere (i.e. a sphere of uniform density). Let ρ be the mean density of the earth and a body be lying on the surface of the earth where the value of acceleration due to gravity is g.

Then, $$g = \frac{GM}{R^2}$$

or $$g = \frac{G \times \frac{4}{3}\pi R^3 \rho}{R^2}$$

$$\left[\because \text{mass of the earth, } M = \frac{4}{3}\pi R^3 \rho\right]$$

$$g = \frac{4}{3}\pi G R \rho \qquad \text{...(i)}$$

Now, the body is to be taken to a depth d below the free surface of the earth, where the acceleration due to gravity is g_d. Here, the force of gravity acting on the body is only due to the inner solid sphere of radius $(R-d)$.

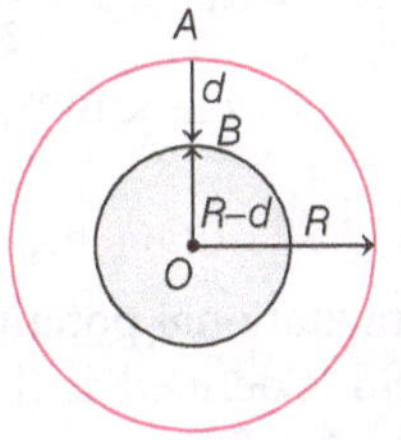

Variation of g with depth

$$\therefore \quad g_d = \frac{GM'}{(R-d)^2}$$

where, M' is the mass of inner solid sphere of radius $(R-d)$.

or $$g_d = \frac{G}{(R-d)^2} \times \frac{4}{3}\pi (R-d)^3 \times \rho$$

or $$g_d = \frac{4}{3}\pi G (R-d)\rho \qquad \text{...(ii)}$$

Dividing Eq. (ii) by Eq. (i), we get

$$\frac{g_d}{g} = 1 - \frac{d}{R}$$

> Acceleration due to gravity at depth d, $g_d = g\left(1 - \frac{d}{R}\right)$

or $$g_d - g = -\frac{d}{R} g$$

or $$g - g_d = \frac{d}{R} g$$

Here, $(g - g_d)$ gives the decrease in the value of g.

Since, g is constant at a given place of the earth and R is also a constant.

$$\therefore \quad (g - g_d) \propto d$$

From the above equation, it is clear that if d increases, g_d must decrease because g is constant. **Hence, the acceleration due to gravity decreases as we move down into the surface of the earth,** i.e. g decreases with the increase in depth d.

At the centre O of the earth, $d = R$

Thus, we get $$g_d = g\left(1 - \frac{R}{R}\right) = 0$$

Hence, acceleration due to gravity at the centre of the earth is zero.

The weight of a body at the centre of the earth is zero though its mass is constant.

Graphical representation of g inside the earth

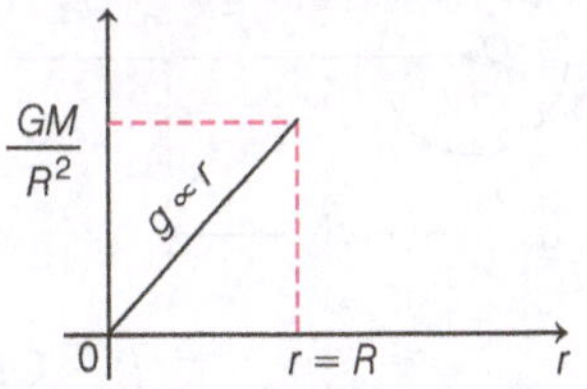

Variation of acceleration due to gravity of the earth is shown in the graph given below.

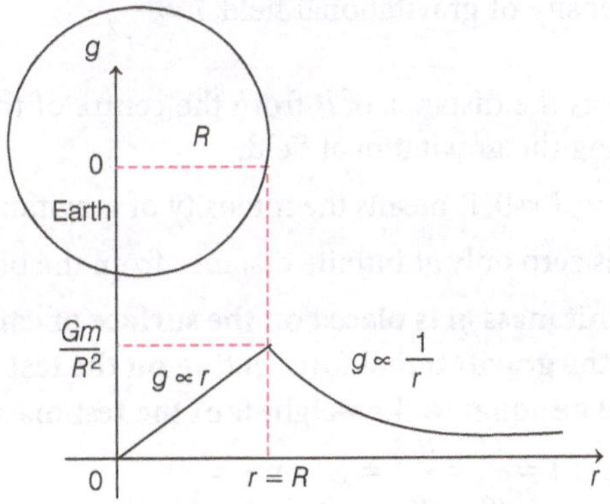

Note Acceleration due to gravity also vary due to the rotation of earth, if a body of mass m lying at a point whose latitude is λ, then rotation of earth (angular speed ω), the apparent acceleration due to gravity on body is given by $g' = g - \omega^2 R\cos^2\lambda$.

Example 12. What will be the value of g at the bottom of sea 7 km deep? Diameter of the earth is 12800 km and g on the surface of the earth is 9.8 ms^{-2}.

Sol. Depth of sea, $d = 7$ km, $g = 9.8$ ms^{-2}

Radius of the earth, $R = \frac{D}{2} = \frac{12800}{2}$ km $= 6400$ km

Value of g at bottom of sea,

$$g_d = g\left(1 - \frac{d}{R}\right) = 9.8\left(1 - \frac{7}{6400}\right) \text{ ms}^{-2}$$

$$g_d = \frac{9.8 \times 6393}{6400} \text{ ms}^{-2}$$

$$= 9.789 \text{ ms}^{-2}$$

Intensity of Gravitational Field at a Point

It is the force experienced by a unit mass placed at that point.

Let M be the mass of a body around which a gravitational field exists. In order to get the gravitational field intensity at a point P in the gravitational field, a test mass m (very small) is placed at the point P.

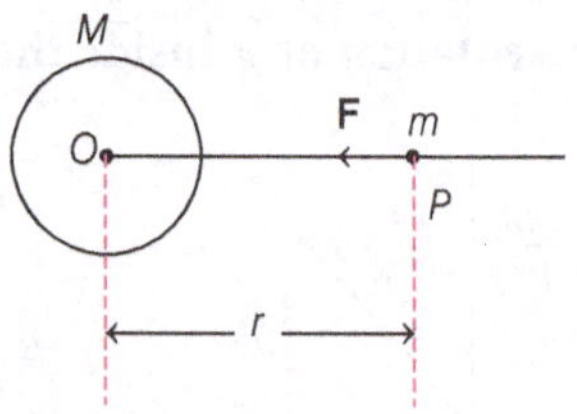

Intensity of gravitational field, $I = \dfrac{F}{m} = \dfrac{GMm/r^2}{m}$

$$\text{Intensity of gravitational field, } I = \frac{GM}{r^2}$$

where, r is the distance of P from the centre of the body producing the gravitational field.

- If $r = \infty$, $I = 0$, it means the intensity of gravitational field is zero only at infinite distance from the body.
- **If a unit mass m is placed on the surface of earth, then the gravitational force acting on the test mass m will be equal to the weight w of the test mass.**

  Now, $I = \dfrac{w}{m} = \dfrac{mg}{m} = g$ or $I = g$

Example 13. **Two masses 800 kg and 600 kg, are at a distance 0.25 m apart. Calculate the magnitude of the gravitational field intensity at a point distance 0.20 m from the 800 kg mass and 0.15 m from the 600 kg mass. (Take, $G = 6.6\times 10^{-11}$ N-m^{2}kg^{-2})**

Sol. Let I_A be the gravitational field intensity at P due to 800 kg mass at A.

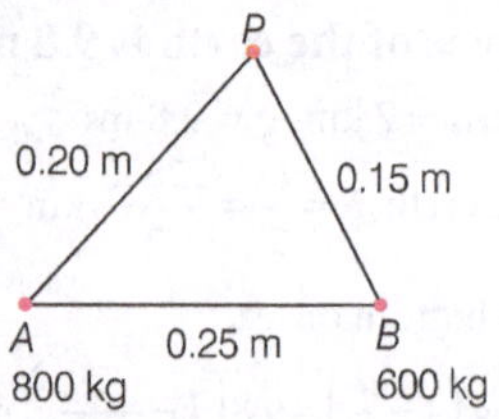

Then, $I_A = G\dfrac{800}{(0.2)^2} = 2\times 10^4 \text{G along } PA$

Let I_B be the gravitational field intensity at P due to 600 kg mass at B, then

$$I_B = G\frac{600}{(0.15)^2} \text{ along } PB = \frac{80000\,G}{3} \text{ along } PB$$

The angle between I_A and I_B is 90°.

If I be the magnitude of the resultant intensity, then

$$I = \sqrt{I_A^2 + I_B^2} = \sqrt{(2\times 10^4 G)^2 + \left(\frac{80000\,G}{3}\right)^2}$$

$$= G\sqrt{4\times 10^8 + \frac{64}{9}\times 10^8} = 6.67\times 10^{-11}\times 2\times 10^4\sqrt{1+\frac{16}{9}}$$

$$= 6.67\times 2\times \frac{5}{3}\times 10^{-7}\ \text{Nkg}^{-1}$$

$$I = 2.22\times 10^{-6}\ \text{Nkg}^{-1}$$

Gravitational Potential

Gravitational potential at a point in the gravitational field is defined as the amount of work done in bringing a body of unit mass from infinity to that point without acceleration, i.e. Gravitational potential,

$$V = -\frac{W}{m} = -\int\frac{\mathbf{F}\cdot d\mathbf{r}}{m} = -\int \mathbf{I}\cdot d\mathbf{r} \qquad \left[\text{as, } \frac{F}{m} = I\right]$$

where, W is the amount of work done in bringing a body of mass m from infinity to that point and I is the intensity of field.

$$\therefore \qquad I = -\frac{dV}{dr}$$

i.e. Negative gradient of potential gives intensity of field or potential which is a scalar function of position whose space derivative gives intensity.

Negative sign indicates that the direction of intensity is in the direction where the potential decreases.

Gravitational potential is a **scalar quantity** and SI unit is **joule/kg** and in CGS system, it is **erg/g.**

Expression for Gravitational Potential

Suppose the earth to be perfect sphere of radius R and mass M, can supposed to be concentrated at its centre O. Then, the gravitational potential at point Q can be calculated, where $OQ = r$ and $r > R$.

Take two points A and B, so $OA = x$ and $AB = dx$ as shown in figure.

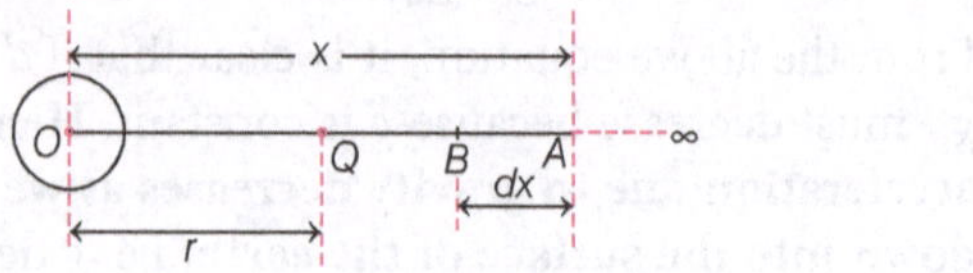

Calculation for gravitational potential

At point A, gravitational force of attraction on a body of unit mass will be $F = \dfrac{GM \times 1}{x^2} = \dfrac{GM}{x^2}$

Small amount of work done in bringing the unit mass body without acceleration through a small distance $(AB = dx)$

$$dW = Fdx = \frac{GM}{x^2}dx$$

Total amount of work done in bringing a body from infinity to point Q, will be

$$\text{Work done, } W = \int_{\infty}^{r} \frac{GM}{x^2}dx = -\left[\frac{GM}{x}\right]_{\infty}^{r}$$

$$= -GM\left[\frac{1}{r} - \frac{1}{\infty}\right] = \frac{-GM}{r}$$

$\because \quad V = W$

$$\text{Gravitational potential, } V = \frac{-GM}{r} \quad \ldots\text{(i)}$$

where, V is total gravitational potential at point Q.

Special Cases

(i) When $r = \infty$ from Eq. (i), then $V_Q = 0$, hence gravitational potential is maximum (zero) at infinity.

(ii) At surface of the earth, $r = R$, then $V_Q = \dfrac{-GM}{R}$.

Potential due to a large number of particles is given by scalar addition of all the potentials as shown in figure.

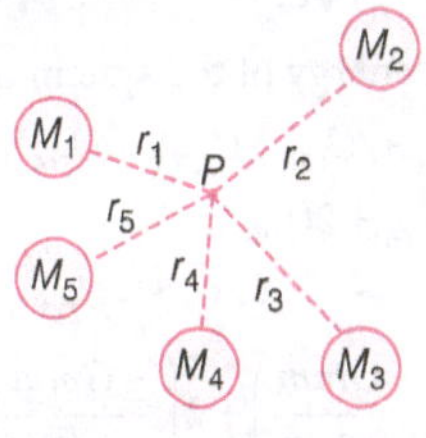

Superposition of different potentials

$$V = V_1 + V_2 + V_3 + \ldots$$
$$= \frac{-GM_1}{r_1} - \frac{GM_2}{r_2} - \frac{GM_3}{r_3} \ldots = -G\sum_{i=1}^{i=n}\frac{M_i}{r_i}$$

Example 14. **As you will learn in the text, a geostationary satellite orbits the earth at a height of nearly 36000 km from the surface of the earth. What is the potential due to the earth's gravity at the site of this satellite? (Take the potential energy at infinity to be zero). Mass of the earth = 6.0×10^{24} kg and radius = 6400 km.**

Sol. We are given that

Mass of the earth, $M = 6.0 \times 10^{24}$ kg

Radius of the earth, $R = 6400$ km

Height of the satellite from the earth's surface,

$h = 36000$ km

Distance of the satellite from the centre of the earth,

$r = R + h = 6400 \text{ km} + 36000 \text{ km}$

$r = 42400 \text{ km} = 4.24 \times 10^7 \text{ m}$

If V is the potential at the site of the satellite,

$$V = -\frac{GM}{r} = -\frac{(6.67 \times 10^{-11}) \times (6.0 \times 10^{24})}{(4.24 \times 10^7)}$$

$V = -9.4 \times 10^6$ J/kg

Example 15. **At a point above the surface of the earth, the gravitational potential is -5.12×10^7 J/kg and the acceleration due to gravity is 6.4 m/s^2. Assuming the mean radius of the earth to be 6400 km, calculate the height of the point above the earth's surface.**

Sol. If r is the distance of the given point from the centre of the earth, then gravitational potential at the point,

$$V = -\frac{GM}{r} = -5.12 \times 10^7 \text{ J/kg}$$

Acceleration due to gravity at this point,

$$g = \frac{GM}{r^2} = 6.4 \text{ m/s}^2$$

Clearly, $\dfrac{|V|}{g} = \dfrac{GM/r}{GM/r^2} = r$

Thus, $r = \dfrac{5.12 \times 10^7 \text{ J/kg}}{6.4 \text{ m/s}^2}$

$= 8 \times 10^6 \text{ m} = 8000$ km

Obviously, height of the point from the earth's surface

$= (r - R) = 8000 \text{ km} - 6400 \text{ km} = 1600$ km

Gravitational Potential Energy

Gravitational potential energy of a body at a point is defined as the amount of work done in bringing the given body from infinity to that point against the gravitational force.

Let a body of mass m is placed at P in the gravitational field of a body of mass M.

Let r be the distance of P from the centre O of the body of mass M as shown in figure, then the total work done W by the gravitational field when a body of mass m is moved from infinity to a distance r from O is given by

$$W = -\frac{GmM}{r}$$

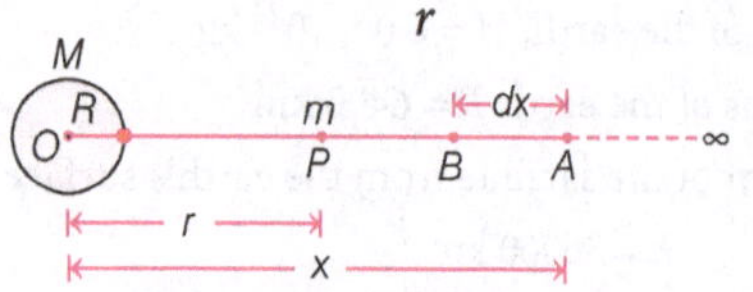

Gravitational potential energy

This work done is equal to the gravitational potential energy U of mass m.

$$\text{Gravitational potential energy, } U = \left(-\frac{GM}{r}\right) \times m$$

∴ **Gravitational potential energy = Gravitational potential × Mass of the body**

Some Cases

(i) According to the superposition principle, if there are three particles of masses m_1, m_2 and m_3 in an isolated system, then total gravitational potential energy of the system is

$$U = -\left(\frac{Gm_1m_2}{r_{12}} + \frac{Gm_2m_3}{r_{23}} + \frac{Gm_1m_3}{r_{13}}\right)$$

(ii) If the body of mass m is moved from the surface of the earth to a point distance h above the surface of the earth, then change in potential energy or work done against gravity will be

$$W = \Delta U = GMm\left(\frac{1}{r_1} - \frac{1}{r_2}\right)$$

Change in gravitational potential energy at height h,

$$\Delta U = GMm\left(\frac{1}{R} - \frac{1}{R+h}\right)$$

[as, $r_1 = R$ and $r_2 = R + h$]

$$\Rightarrow \quad \Delta U = \frac{GMmh}{R^2\left(1+\frac{h}{R}\right)}$$

$$= \frac{mgh}{1+\frac{h}{R}} \qquad \left(\text{as, } \frac{GM}{R^2} = g\right)$$

$$\Delta U = mgh\left(1+\frac{h}{R}\right)^{-1} = mgh\left(1-\frac{h}{R}\right)$$

∵ $h << R$

∴ $\Delta U = mgh$

(iii) When $h = R$, then work done $= \frac{mgR}{1+R/R} = \frac{1}{2}mgR$

Example 16. **A particle of mass 1 kg is placed at a distance of 4 m from the centre and on the axis of a uniform ring of mass 5 kg and radius 3 m. Calculate the work required to be done to increase the distance of the particle from 4 m to $3\sqrt{3}$ m.**

Sol. $U_1 = -\frac{G \times 5 \times 1}{5}$ or $U_1 = -G$

$$U_2 = \frac{-G \times 5 \times 1}{6} = -\frac{5G}{6}$$

$$\text{Work done} = \left(-\frac{5G}{6}\right) - (-G) = G - \frac{5G}{6} = \frac{G}{6}$$

Example 17. **Find the potential energy of a system of four particles placed at the vertices of a square of side l. Also, obtain the potential at the centre of the square.** NCERT

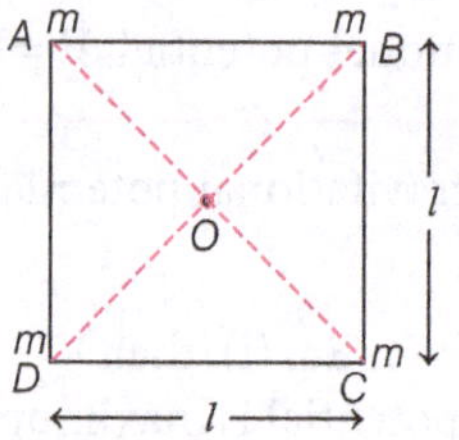

Sol. $AB = BC = CD = DA = l$

Here, $AC = BD = \sqrt{l^2 + l^2} = \sqrt{2l^2} = l\sqrt{2}$

∴ $OA = OB = OC = OD$

$$= \frac{l\sqrt{2}}{2} = \frac{l}{\sqrt{2}}$$

Total potential energy of the system of particles,

$$U = U_{BA} + (U_{CB} + U_{CA}) + (U_{DA} + U_{DB} + U_{DC})$$

$$= 4U_{BA} + 2U_{DB}$$

$[\because U_{BA} = U_{DA} = U_{DC} = U_{CB}, U_{CA} = U_{DB}]$

$$= 4\left(\frac{-Gmm}{l}\right) + 2\left(\frac{-Gmm}{l\sqrt{2}}\right)$$

$$= \frac{-2Gm^2}{l}\left(2 + \frac{1}{\sqrt{2}}\right) = \frac{-2Gm^2}{l}(2 + 0.707)$$

$$U = \frac{-5.41}{l}Gm^2$$

Total gravitational potential at the centre O,

$$V = V_A + V_B + V_C + V_D$$

$$= 4V_A = 4\left(\frac{-Gm}{l_{OA}}\right) = 4 \times \left(\frac{-Gm}{l/\sqrt{2}}\right)$$

$$V = \frac{-4\sqrt{2}\,Gm}{l}$$

Quick Test 2

Conceptual Questions

1. If the earth is regarded as a hollow sphere, then what is the weight of an object below surface of the earth?
2. What is the amount of work done in bringing a mass from the surface of the earth on one side to a point diametrically opposite on the other side?
3. If the force of gravity acts on all bodies in proportion to their masses, then why doesn't a heavy body fall faster than a light body?
4. Define the effect of shape of the earth on the value of g.

Numerical Questions

5. Determine the speed with which the earth would have to rotate on its axis, so that a person on the equator would weigh $\frac{3}{5}$th as much as at present. Take, the equatorial radius as 6400 km.
6. Assuming the earth to be a sphere of uniform mass density, how much would body weigh half way down to the centre of the earth if it weighted 250 N on the surface? *NCERT*

   Hints To calculate the weight of the body down the centre of the earth, we have to calculate the acceleration due to gravity at depth d from earth's surface which is given by $g' = g\left(1 - \frac{d}{R}\right)$.
7. An object of mass m is raised from the surface of the earth to a height equal to the radius of the earth, that is, taken from a distance R to $2R$ from the centre of the earth. What is the gain in its potential energy? *NCERT Exemplar*
8. Two bodies of m and $4m$ are placed at a distance r. The gravitational field is zero at a point on the line joining the two masses. What will be the gravitational potential at this point?
9. What will be the potential energy of a body of mass 67 kg at a distance of 6.6×10^{10} m from the centre of the earth? Find gravitational potential at this distance.

Answers

5. 7.8×10^4 rad/s 6. 125 N 7. $\frac{1}{2} mgR$ 8. $\frac{-9Gm}{r}$

9. -6.1×10^{13} Jkg^{-1}

For Solutions, See QR Code on Pg. 270

7.4 Escape Speed

Escape speed on the earth (or any other planet) is defined as the minimum speed with which a body should be projected vertically upwards from the surface of the earth, so that it just escapes out from gravitational field of the earth and never returns on its own.

e.g. If you fire a projectile upward, usually it will slow down, stop momentarily and return to the earth. A certain minimum initial speed will cause it to move upward forever and coming to rest only at infinity.

Expression for Escape Speed

Consider a body of mass m lying at a distance x from the centre of the earth. Let M be the mass and R be radius of the earth as shown in figure along-side. According to Newton's law of gravitation, **the gravitational force F of attraction between the body and the earth** is given by $F = G\frac{Mm}{x^2}$

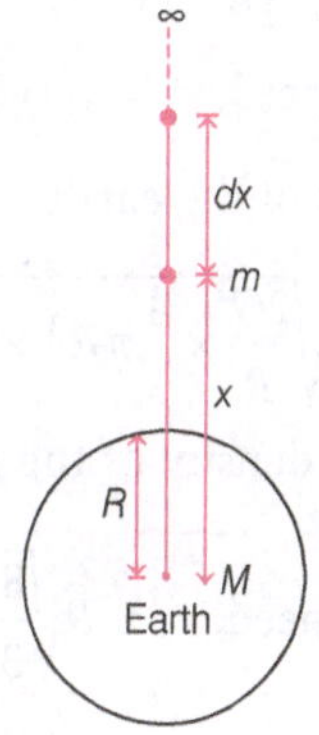

If dW be the work done to displace the body through a small distance dx, then $dW = Fdx = \frac{GMm}{x^2}dx$

Total work done in taking the body from the surface of the earth, i.e. $x = R$ to $x = \infty$ is given by

$$W = \int dW = \int_R^\infty \frac{GMm}{x^2}dx$$

or $$W = GMm\int_R^\infty \frac{1}{x^2}dx$$

[$\because$ GMm is the constant quantity]

$\therefore$ $$W = GMm\int_R^\infty x^{-2}dx = GMm\left(\frac{x^{-2+1}}{-2+1}\right)_R^\infty$$

or $$W = GMm\left[\frac{x^{-1}}{-1}\right]_R^\infty = -GMm\left[\frac{1}{x}\right]_R^\infty$$

$$= -GMm\left[\frac{1}{\infty} - \frac{1}{R}\right]$$

$$W = \frac{GMm}{R} \qquad \left[\because \frac{1}{\infty} = 0\right]$$

If v_e is the required escape speed of the body, then kinetic energy imparted to the body $= \frac{1}{2}mv_e^2$

$$\therefore \quad \frac{1}{2}mv_e^2 = \frac{GMm}{R} \quad \text{or} \quad v_e^2 = \frac{2GM}{R}$$

$$v_e = \sqrt{\frac{2GM}{R}} \quad \text{...(i)}$$

Thus, the escape speed of a body depends on the mass and radius of the planet from which the body is projected.

$$g = \frac{GM}{R^2} \Rightarrow GM = gR^2$$

$$\therefore \quad v_e = \sqrt{\frac{2gR^2}{R}}$$

or $$v_e = \sqrt{2gR} \quad \text{...(ii)}$$

or $$\boxed{\text{Escape speed, } v_e = \sqrt{2gR}}$$

where, R is the radius of the earth.
From Eq. (i),

$$v_e = \sqrt{\frac{2G}{R} \times \frac{4}{3}\pi R^3 \times \rho}$$

where, ρ is the mean density of the earth.

$$\boxed{\text{Escape speed, } v_e = R\sqrt{\frac{8}{3}\pi G\rho}} \quad \text{...(iii)}$$

Escape Speed from Principle of Conservation of Energy

Let the object reach at infinity and its speed be v_f. The energy of an object is the sum of potential energy and kinetic energy, then the total energy of the projectile at infinity is given by

$$E(\infty) = W_1 + \frac{mv_f^2}{2} \quad \text{...(i)}$$

where, W_1 is gravitational potential energy of the object at infinity.

If the object was thrown initially with a speed v_i from a point at a distance $(h+R)$ from the centre of the earth, then its initial energy is given by

$$E(h+R) = \frac{1}{2}m v_i^2 - \frac{GmM}{h+R} + W_1 \quad \text{...(ii)}$$

According to principle of energy conservation, Eqs.(i) and (ii) are equal. So, $\frac{mv_i^2}{2} - \frac{GmM}{(h+R)} = \frac{mv_f^2}{2}$

If $\frac{mv_f^2}{2}$ is zero, then $\frac{mv_i^2}{2} - \frac{GmM}{h+R} = 0$

Thus, the minimum speed required for an object to reach infinity, i.e. escape from the earth corresponds to

$$\frac{1}{2}m(v_i^2)_{\text{min}} = \frac{GmM}{h+R}$$

If the object is thrown from the surface of the earth, h is zero, so we get

$$(v_i)_{\text{min}} = \sqrt{\frac{2GM}{R}}$$

Using the relation, $g = GM/R^2$, we get

$$\boxed{\text{Minimum speed, } (v_i)_{\text{min}} = \sqrt{2gR}}$$

If $g = 9.8 \text{ m/s}^2$ and $R = 6.4 \times 10^6 \text{m}$, then

$$(v_i)_{\text{min}} = 11.2 \text{ km/s}$$

Note Orbital velocity (v_o) of a satellite is the velocity required to put the satellite into its orbit around the earth, $v_o = \sqrt{gR}$, i.e. $v_e = \sqrt{2}v_o$.

Example 18. Calculate the escape speed of a body from the solar system from following data.

(i) Mass of the sun $= 2 \times 10^{30}$ kg.

(ii) Separation of the earth from the sun $= 1.5 \times 10^{11}$ m.

Sol. If M be the mass of the sun and R be the distance of the earth from the sun, then escape velocity,

$$v_e = \sqrt{\frac{2GM}{R}}$$

$$= \sqrt{\frac{2 \times 6.67 \times 10^{-11} \times 2 \times 10^{30}}{1.5 \times 10^{11}}} \text{ ms}^{-1}$$

$$= \sqrt{\frac{4 \times 6.67}{1.5}} \times 10^4 \text{ ms}^{-1}$$

$$= 4.217 \times 10^4 \text{ ms}^{-1}$$

$$v_e = 42.17 \text{ kms}^{-1} \qquad [1 \text{ km} = 1000 \text{ m}]$$

$\therefore$ The escape speed for solar system is 42.17 kms^{-1}.

Example 19. Estimate the size of a rockey sphere with a density of 3.0 g/cm^3 from the surface of which you could barely throw a golf ball and have it never back. (Assume your best throw is 40 m/s)

Sol. Let us consider that the rockey sphere has mass M and radius R. The escape speed for such a sphere is given by

$$v_e = \sqrt{\frac{2GM}{R}}$$

$$= \sqrt{\frac{2G\left(\frac{4\pi}{3}\right)R^3\rho}{R}} = \sqrt{\frac{8\pi G\rho}{3}}R$$

or $\quad R = v_e\sqrt{\frac{3}{8\pi G\rho}}$

Here, $\rho = 3.0\ \text{g/cm}^3 = 3.0 \times 10^3\ \text{kg/m}^3, v_e = 40\ \text{m/s}$

Thus, $R = 40\sqrt{\frac{3}{8 \times 3.14 \times 6.67 \times 10^{-11} \times 3 \times 10^3}}\ \text{m}$

or $\quad R = 40 \times 772.6\ \text{m}$

$= 30904\ \text{m}$

$= 30.904\ \text{km}$

Example 20. **Calculate the escape velocity for an atmospheric particle 1000 km above the earth's surface, given that the radius of the earth = 6.4×10^6 m and acceleration due to gravity on the surface of the earth = $9.8\ \text{m s}^{-2}$.**

Sol. Here, height, $h = 1000$ km,

$R = 6.4 \times 10^6$ m,

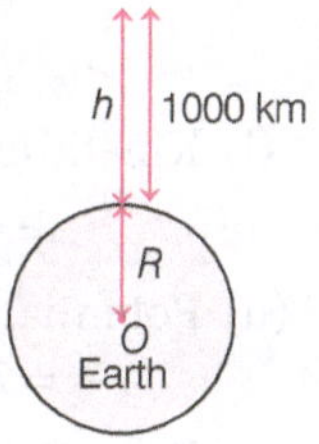

$g = 9.8\ \text{ms}^{-2}$

$h = 1000 \times 1000 = 10^6$ m

Escape velocity at a height h above the earth's surface

$$v_e = \sqrt{2g_h(R+h)}$$

Substitute the value of g_h in the above formula, we get

$$g_h = \frac{gR^2}{(R+h)^2}$$

$$\Rightarrow \quad v_e = \sqrt{\frac{2 \times gR^2}{(R+h)^2}(R+h)} = \sqrt{\frac{2gR^2}{R+h}}$$

$$v_e = \sqrt{\frac{2 \times 9.8 \times (6.4 \times 10^6)^2}{(6.4 + 1)\ 10^6}}\ \text{ms}^{-1}$$

$= 10.42\ \text{kms}^{-1}$

7.5 Earth Satellites

A satellite is a body which is continuously revolving around the earth. e.g. The moon is a natural satellite while INSAT-1B is an artifical satellite of the earth.

Condition for establishment of satellite is that the centre of orbit of satellite must coincide with centre of the earth or satellite must move around great circle of the earth.

Expression for time period of earth satellite

As we have already discussed that, the centripetal force required for circular orbit is given by

$$F_e = \frac{mv^2}{R+h} \quad \text{...(i)}$$

and is directed toward the centre. This centripetal force is provided by the gravitational force which is expressed as,

$$F_c = \frac{GmM}{(R+h)^2} \quad \text{...(ii)}$$

Equating both Eqs. (i) and (ii), we get $v^2 = \frac{GM}{R+h}$

$$\Rightarrow \quad v = \sqrt{\frac{GM}{R+h}} \quad \text{...(iii)}$$

$$v = R\sqrt{\frac{g}{R+h}} \quad \text{...(iv)} \left[\because g = \frac{GM}{R^2}\right]$$

Eqs. (iii) and (iv), give the velocity of revolution of the satellite.

Thus, v decreases as h increases.

When $h = 0$,

Orbital velocity, $v = \sqrt{\frac{GM}{R}} = \sqrt{gR}$

In every orbit, the satellite traverses a distance $2\pi(R+h)$ with speed v.

Then, its time period is given by

$$T = \frac{2\pi(R+h)}{v} = \frac{2\pi(R+h)^{3/2}}{\sqrt{GM}} \quad \text{...(iii)}$$

$$\left[\because v^2 = \frac{GM}{R+h}\right]$$

On squaring both sides in Eq. (iii), we get

$$\boxed{T^2 = k(R+h)^3} \quad \left[\because k = \frac{4\pi^2}{GM}\right]$$

Thus, it is Kepler's law of periods. For a satellite, very close to surface of earth, h can be neglected in comparison to R. If $h = 0$ and T is T_0, then

$$T_0 = 2\pi\sqrt{R/g}$$

For earth, $R = 6400$ km and $g = 9.8\ \text{m/s}^2$

$$T_0 = 2\pi\sqrt{\frac{6.4 \times 10^6}{9.8}} \cong 85\ \text{min}$$

Example 21. **The planet mars has two moons, phobos and delmos.**

(i) Phobos has a period 7h 39 min and an orbital radius of 9.4×10^3 km. Calculate the mass of mars.

(ii) Assume that earth and mars move in circular orbits around the sun with the martian orbit being 1.52 times the orbital radius of the earth. What is the length of the martian year in days?

Sol. (i) Given, $T = 7\text{ h } 39\text{ min} = 459 \times 60\text{ s}$

$$R = 9.4 \times 10^3\text{ km} = 9.4 \times 10^6\text{ m}, \ M_m = ?$$

$$\therefore \text{ Mass of mars, } M_m = \frac{4\pi^2}{G} \cdot \frac{R^3}{T^2}$$

$$= \frac{4 \times (3.14)^2 \times (9.4 \times 10^6)^3}{6.67 \times 10^{-11} \times (459 \times 60)^2}$$

$$= 6.48 \times 10^{23}\text{ kg}$$

(ii) From Kepler's third law, $\frac{T_m^2}{T^2} = \frac{R_{ms}^3}{R_{es}^3}$

where, R_{ms} is the mass-sun distance and R_{es} is the earth-sun distance

$$\therefore \quad T_m = (1.52)^{3/2} \times 365 = 684\text{ days}$$

Energy of an Orbiting Satellite

When a satellite revolves around a planet in its orbit, it possesses both potential energy (due to its position against gravitational pull of the earth) and kinetic energy (due to orbital motion).

If m is the mass of the satellite and v is its orbital velocity, then

KE of the satellite,

$$K = \frac{1}{2}mv^2 = \frac{1}{2}m\frac{GM}{r}$$

$$\boxed{\text{Kinetic energy of satellite, } K = \frac{GMm}{2(R+h)}} \quad \ldots\text{(i)}$$

$$[\because r = R+h]$$

PE of the satellite, $U = mV$

$$\boxed{\text{Potential energy of satellite, } U = -\frac{GMm}{R+h}} \quad \ldots\text{(ii)}$$

Total mechanical energy of satellite, $E = K + U$

or

$$E = \frac{GMm}{2(R+h)} - \frac{GMm}{(R+h)}$$

$$E = -\frac{GMm}{2(R+h)} \quad \ldots\text{(iii)}$$

$$\therefore \quad \boxed{\text{Total energy of satellite, } E = -\frac{GMm}{2(R+h)}}$$

Satellites are always at finite distance from the earth and hence their energy cannot be positive or zero.

Graph for energy of an orbiting satellite

Now, plot the graph between the kinetic, potential and total energies by considering the following conditions.

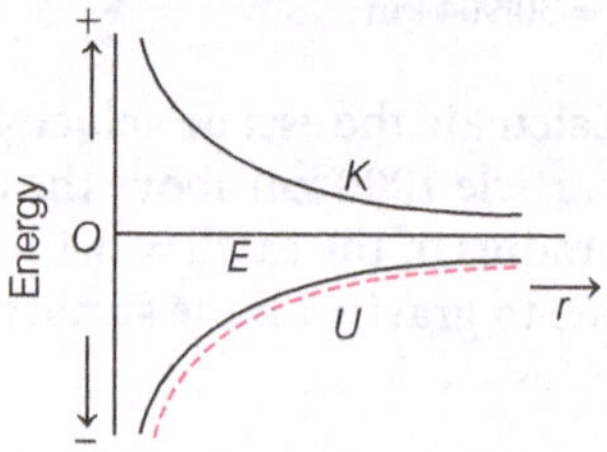

(a) Energy graph for a satellite

(i) Kinetic energy (K)
= – (Total energy)

(ii) Potential energy (U)
= 2(Total energy)

(iii) Potential energy (U) = – 2 (Kinetic energy)
as shown in Fig (a).

The kinetic energy of orbiting satellite is positive, whereas total energy and potential energy are negative. As, total energy of satellite is negative, so the satellite will never be able to escape from the gravitational pull of the planet.

If the orbit of a satellite is elliptical as shown in Fig. (b), then total energy $E = \frac{-GMm}{2a} = \text{constant}$

where a is semi-major axis.

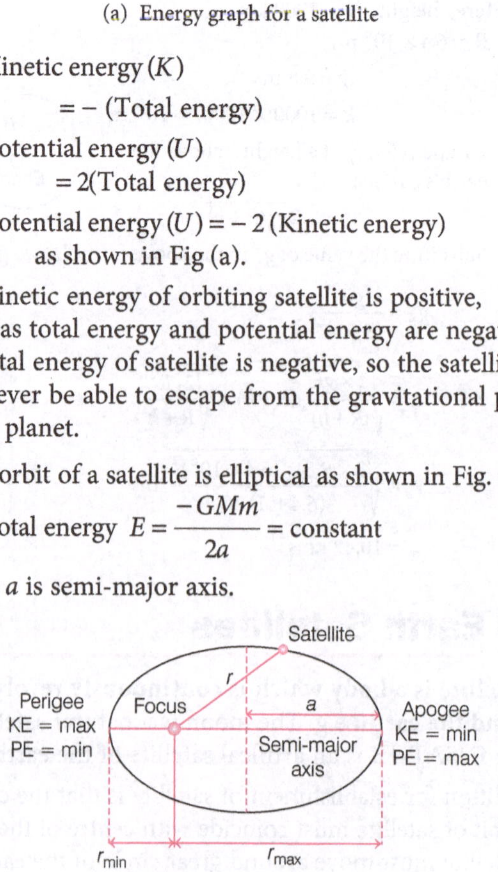

(b) Energy distribution in elliptical orbit

When the satellite is transferred to a higher orbit ($r_2 > r_1$), then work done in changing the orbit,

$$W = E_2 - E_1$$

$$W = \left(\frac{-GMm}{2r_2}\right) - \left(\frac{-GMm}{2r_1}\right)$$

$$W = \frac{GMm}{2}\left[\frac{1}{r_1} - \frac{1}{r_2}\right]$$

Example 22. **A 400 kg satellite is in a circular orbit of radius $2R$ about the earth. How much energy is required to transfer it to a circular orbit of radius $4R$? What are the changes in the kinetic and potential energies?** NCERT

Sol. Given, mass of satellite, $m = 400$ kg

The initial energy is given by

$$E_i = \frac{-GMm}{4R}$$

Final energy is given by

$$E_f = \frac{-GMm}{8R}$$

$\therefore$ Change in the total energy is given by

$$\Delta E = E_f - E_i$$

$$= \frac{-GMm}{8R} - \left(\frac{-GMm}{4R}\right)$$

$$\Delta E = \frac{GMm}{8R} = \left(\frac{GM}{R^2}\right)\frac{mR}{8}$$

$$= \frac{gmR}{8}$$

$$= \frac{9.81 \times 400 \times 6.37 \times 10^6}{8}$$

$$\Delta E = 3.13 \times 10^9 \text{ J}$$

The kinetic energy is reduced,

$\therefore$ $\Delta K = K_f - K_i = -3.13 \times 10^9$ J

Change in potential energy,

$$\Delta U = -2 \times \Delta E$$

$$= -2 \times 3.13 \times 10^9$$

$$= -6.26 \times 10^9 \text{ J}$$

Quick Test 3

Conceptual Questions

1. Why is the atmosphere much rarer on the moon than on the earth?
2. A thief with a box in his hand jumps from the top of a building. What will be the load experienced by him during the state of free fall?
3. An artificial satellite revolving around the earth does not need any fuel. On the other hand, the aeroplane requires fuel to fly at a certain height. Why?
4. If the kinetic energy of a satellite revolving around the earth in any orbit is doubled, then what will happen to it?
5. Show that the orbital velocity of a satellite revolving the earth is 7.92 km s^{-1}.

Numerical Questions

6. A satellite orbits the earth at a height of 400 km above the surface. How much energy must be spent to send the satellite out of the earth's gravitational influence? Mass of the satellite = 200 kg, mass of the earth, $M = 6.0 \times 10^{24}$ kg, radius of the earth $= 6.4 \times 10^6$ m, $G = 6.67 \times 10^{-11}$ Nm^2/kg^2. NCERT
7. The escape speed of a projectile on the earth's surface is 11.2 km/s. A body is projected out with thrice this speed. What is the speed of the body far away from the earth? Ignore the presence of the sun and other planets. NCERT
8. How will you weigh the sun, i.e. estimate its mass? The mean orbital radius of the earth around the sun is 1.5×10^8 km. NCERT
9. Let us assume that our galaxy consists of 2.5×10^{11} stars each of one solar mass. How long will a star at a distance of 50000 ly from the galactic centre take to complete one revolution? NCERT
10. A rocket is fired vertically with a speed of 5 km/s from the earth surface. How far from the earth does the rocket go before returning to the earth? Mass of the earth $= 6.0 \times 10^{24}$ kg. Mean radius of the earth $= 6.4 \times 10^6$ m; $G = 6.67 \times 10^{-11}$ Nm^2/kg^2. NCERT

Answers

6. 5.9×10^9 J *7.* 31.7 km/s *8.* 2.0×10^{30} kg

9. 3.55×10^8 y *10.* 8×10^6 m

For Solutions, See QR Code on Pg. 270

Mind Map

Gravitation

Kepler's First Law : Law of Orbits

- All planets revolve around the sun in elliptical orbits and the sun lies at one of the foci of an ellipse.
- Eccentricity of ellipse, $e = \sqrt{1 - \frac{b^2}{a^2}}$

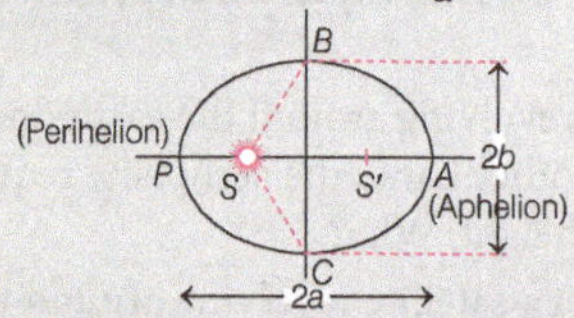

Kapler's Second Law : Law of Areas

- The line joining a planet to the sun sweeps equal area in equal time interval, i.e. areal speed of the planet remain constant in its orbit.
- When a planet is at the farthest position from the sun, its velocity is minimum and when it is nearest to the sun, its velocity is maximum.

Here, $\frac{dA}{dt} = \frac{L}{2m}$ =constant

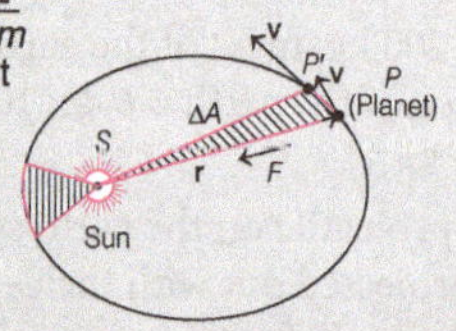

Kepler's Third Law : Law of Periods

- Square of time period of revolution T of a planet about the sun is directly proportional to cube of the semi-major axis a of their elliptical orbit.
  i.e. $T^2 \propto a^3$
- For circular orbit, $a = b = r$ (radius)

$\therefore \quad T^2 \propto r^3$

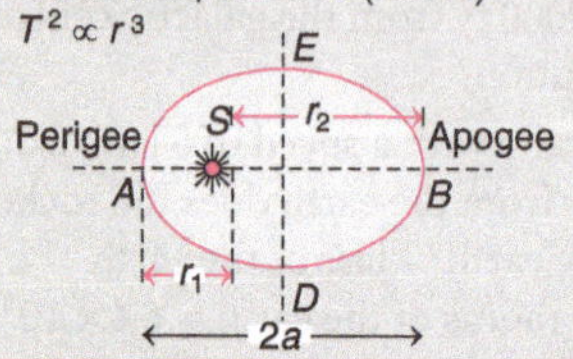

Universal Law of Gravitation

- Every two masses attract each other with a force proportional to their product and inversely proportional to the square of the distance between them.

$F = \frac{-Gm_1m_2}{r^2}$

- **Vector form**

$\mathbf{F} = \frac{-G\, m_1m_2}{r^2}\hat{r}$

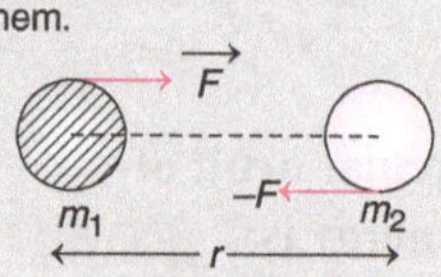

Escape Speed

- That minimum speed with which a body has to be projected vertically upward from the surface of the earth, so that it just crosses the gravitational field of the earth and never return back to earth.
- At infinity, $U_\infty = 0$ and $K_\infty = 0$

Then, $v_e = \sqrt{\frac{2GM_e}{R_e}}$

In terms of acceleration due to gravity, $v_e = \sqrt{2gR_e}$

Thus, $v_e = 11.2 \times 10^3$ m/s or 11.2 km / s

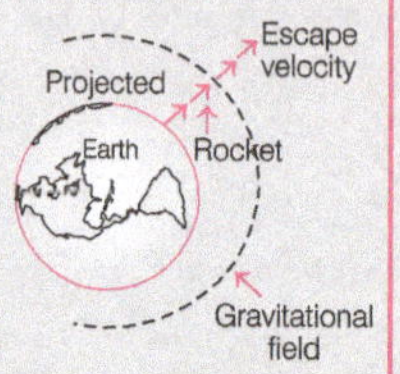

Escape Energy

- The minimum kinetic energy with which the body should be projected upward from earth surface, so that it may move to infinity, crossing gravitational field of earth.
- $U_e = \frac{1}{2}mv_e^2 = \frac{GM_em}{R_e} = mgR_e$

Satellites

- Those bodies which revolve around a planet are called satellites.

Acceleration due to Gravity

- Acceleration experienced by a mass due to Earth's gravity. e.g. A falling apple accelerates at g. $\quad g = G\frac{M}{R^2}$

Variation in g due to Height

- Acceleration due to gravity at height h,

$g' = \frac{GM_e}{(R_e+h)^2}$

$\therefore \quad g' = g\left(1 - \frac{2h}{R_e}\right)$ (if $h << R_e$)

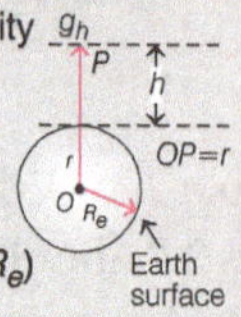

- The decrease in the value of g on going up at height h above the surface of earth by a factor. $\left(1 - \frac{2h}{R_e}\right)$.

Variation in g due to Depth

see below of

- $g' = \frac{GM_e}{R_e^3}(R_e - d)$
- $g' = g\left(\frac{R_e - d}{R_e}\right)$

or $g' = g\left(1 - \frac{d}{R_e}\right)$

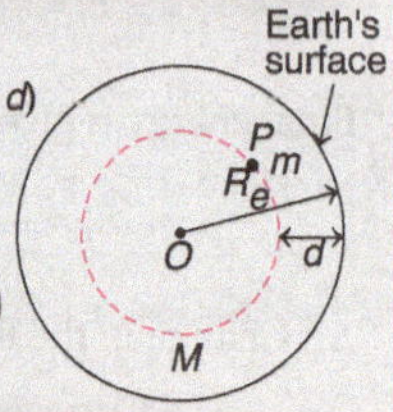

Gravitational Potential

Gravitational potential at a point is the work done per unit mass to bring a test mass from infinity to that point in a gravitational field. $\quad V = -\frac{GM}{r}$

Gravitational Potential Energy

Energy of an object due to its position in a gravitational field.

Example A satellite at height h has gravitational potential energy. $\quad U = -G\frac{m_1m_2}{r}$

Time Period of Satellites

- Time taken by a satellite to complete one cycle around the earth is called its time period or period of revolution (T).

Here,

$T = \frac{2\pi r^{3/2}}{\sqrt{GM_e}}$

$T = 2\pi\sqrt{\frac{(R_e+h)^3}{gR_e^2}}$

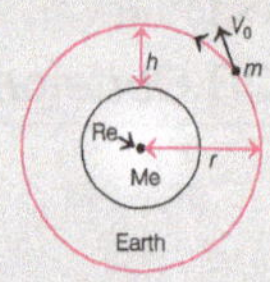

- The variation of time period is $T^2 \propto r^3$
- Therefore, satellite obeys Kepler's third law of planetary motion.

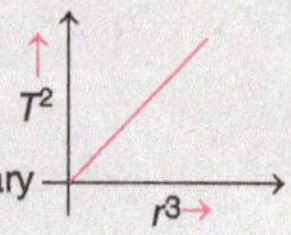

- Greater is the distance of satellite from the earth's surface greater will be its time period of revolution.

Orbital Speed

- Here, orbital speed

$v_o = \sqrt{\frac{Gm_e}{r}}$ (due to centripetal force)

$v_o = \sqrt{\frac{GM_e}{R_e + h}}$ ($\because r = R_e + h$)

Thus, $v_o = \sqrt{\frac{gR_e^2}{(R_e + h)}}$

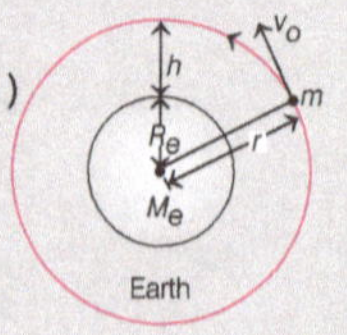

- The variation of orbital speed is given by

$v_o = \sqrt{\frac{GM}{r}}$

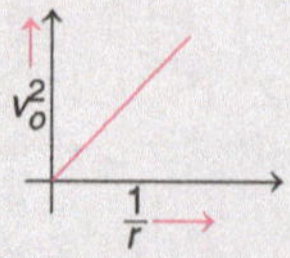

Energy of Satellite

In a circular orbit of radius r around the earth (planet), gravitational potential energy of a satellite,

$U = -\frac{GM_em}{r}$

- Kinetic energy, $K = \frac{1}{2}mv_0^2 = \frac{1}{2}m\left(\sqrt{\frac{GM_e}{r}}\right)^2$

$K = \frac{GM_em}{2r}$

- Total energy, $E = -\frac{GM_em}{2r}$
- Total energy of satellite,

$E = -\frac{GM_em}{2r}$

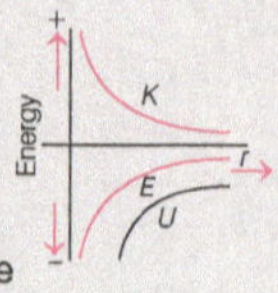

- For a satellite revolving close to the earth's surface,

$U = -\frac{GM_em}{R_e}$, $K = \frac{GM_em}{2R_e}$, $E = -\frac{GM_em}{2R_e}$

EXAM PATTERN QUESTIONS

Objective Type Questions

Multiple Choice Questions

1. **In our solar system, the inter-planetary region has chunks of matter (much smaller in size compared to planets) called asteroids. They** **NCERT Exemplar**

(a) will not move around the sun, since they have very small masses compared to the sun

(b) will move in an irregular way because of their small masses and will drift away into outer space

(c) will move around the sun in closed orbits but not obey Kepler's laws

(d) will move in orbits like planets and obey Kepler's laws

2. **The law of areas can be interpreted as**

(a) $\frac{\Delta A}{\Delta t}$ = constant (b) $\frac{\Delta A}{\Delta t} = \frac{L}{m}$

(c) $\frac{\Delta A}{\Delta t} = \frac{1}{2}(r \times p)$ (d) $\frac{\Delta A}{\Delta t} = \frac{2L}{m}$

3. **Three uniform spheres of mass M and radius R each are kept in such a way that each touches the other two. The magnitude of the gravitational force on any of the spheres due to the other two is**

(a) $\frac{\sqrt{3}}{4}\frac{GM^2}{R^2}$ (b) $\frac{3}{2}\frac{GM^2}{R^2}$

(c) $\frac{\sqrt{3}GM^2}{R^2}$ (d) $\frac{\sqrt{3}}{2}\frac{GM^2}{R^2}$

4. **A point mass m is placed at the centre of the square $ABCD$ of side a unit as shown below.**
The resultant gravitational force on mass m due to masses m_1 and m_2 placed on the vertices of square is

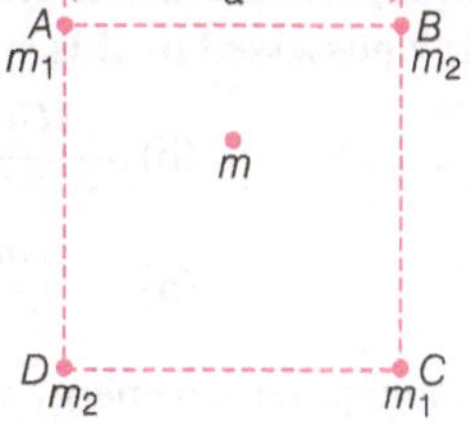

(a) $\frac{Gm_1m_2}{(a\sqrt{2})^2}$ (b) $\frac{2Gm(m_1+m_2)}{a^2}$

(c) zero (d) $\frac{Gm(m_1+m_2)}{(a\sqrt{2})^2}$

5. **Choose the wrong option.** **NCERT Exemplar**

(a) Inertial mass is a measure of difficulty of accelerating a body by an external force whereas the gravitational mass is relevant in determining the gravitational force on it by an external mass

(b) The gravitational mass and inertial mass are equal is an experimental result

(c) The acceleration due to gravity on the earth is the same for all bodies is due to the equality of gravitational mass and inertial mass

(d) Gravitational mass of a particle like proton can depend on the presence of neighbouring heavy objects but the inertial mass cannot

6. **Two spheres of masses m and M are situated in air and the gravitational force between them is F. The space around the masses is now filled with a liquid of specific gravity 3. The gravitational force will now be**

(a) F (b) $\frac{F}{3}$ (c) $\frac{F}{9}$ (d) $3F$

7. **Both the earth and the moon are subjected to the gravitational force of the sun. As observed from the sun, the orbit of the moon** **NCERT Exemplar**

(a) will be elliptical

(b) will not be strictly elliptical because the total gravitational force on it is not central

(c) is not elliptical but will necessarily be a closed curve

(d) deviates considerably from being elliptical due to influence of planets other than the earth

8. **If the gravitational force on body 1 due to 2 is given by $\mathbf{F}_{12}$ and on body 2 due to 1 is given as $\mathbf{F}_{21}$, then**

(a) $\mathbf{F}_{12} = \mathbf{F}_{21}$ (b) $\mathbf{F}_{12} = -\mathbf{F}_{21}$

(c) $\mathbf{F}_{12} = \frac{\mathbf{F}_{21}}{4}$ (d) None of these

9. **As observed from the earth, the sun appears to move in an approximate circular orbit. For the motion of another planet like mercury as observed from the earth, this would** **NCERT Exemplar**

(a) be similarly true

(b) not be true because the force between the earth and mercury is not inverse square law

(c) not be true because the major gravitational force on mercury is due to the sun

(d) not be true because mercury is influenced by forces other than gravitational forces

10. A point mass m is placed outside a hollow spherical shell of mass M and uniform density at a distance d from centre of the big sphere as shown in figure. Gravitational force on point mass m at P is

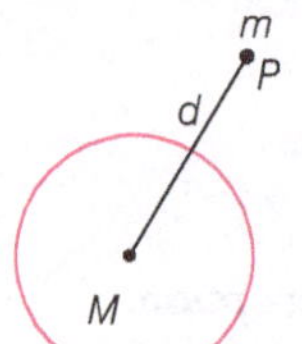

(a) $\frac{GmM}{d^2}$ (b) zero
(c) $\frac{2GmM}{d^2}$ (d) Data insufficient

11. The force of attraction due to a hollow spherical shell of mass M, radius R and uniform density, on a point mass m situated inside it is

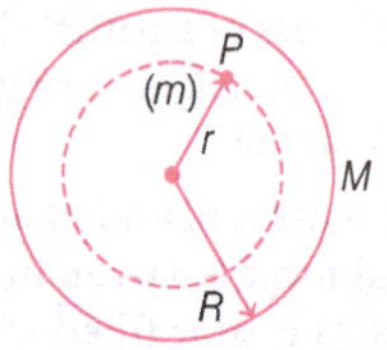

(a) $\frac{GmM}{r^2}$ (b) $\frac{GmM}{R^2}$
(c) zero (d) Data insufficient

12. Particles of masses $2M$, m and M are respectively at points A, B and C with $AB = \frac{1}{2}(BC)$. m is much-much smaller than M and at time $t = 0$, they are all at rest as given in figure.
At subsequent times before any collision takes place,

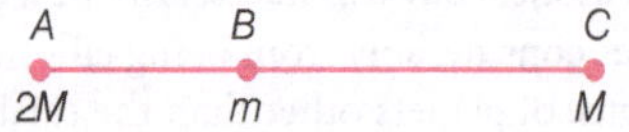

(a) m will remain at rest
(b) m will move towards M
(c) m will move towards $2M$
(d) m will have oscillatory motion

13. A particle is kept at rest at a distance R_e (earth's radius) above the earth's surface. The minimum speed with which it should be projected, so that it does not return is (mass of earth $= M_e$)

(a) $\sqrt{\frac{6M_e}{4R_e}}$ (b) $\sqrt{\frac{GM_e}{2R_e}}$
(c) $\sqrt{\frac{GM_e}{R_e}}$ (d) $\sqrt{\frac{2GM_e}{R_e}}$

14. If the mass of the earth is doubled and its radius is halved, then new acceleration due to the gravity g' is

(a) $4g$ (b) $8g$ (c) g (d) $16g$

15. A planet has twice the density of earth but the acceleration due to gravity on its surface is exactly the same as on the surface of earth. Its radius in terms of radius of earth R will be

(a) $R/4$ (b) $R/2$
(c) $R/3$ (d) $R/8$

16. The earth is an approximate sphere. If the interior contained matter which is not of the same density everywhere, then on the surface of the earth, the acceleration due to gravity **NCERT Exemplar**

(a) will be directed towards the centre but not the same everywhere
(b) will have the same value everywhere but not directed towards the centre
(c) will be same everywhere in magnitude directed towards the centre
(d) cannot be zero at any point

17. The radii of two planets are respectively R_1 and R_2 and their densities are respectively ρ_1 and ρ_2. The ratio of the accelerations due to gravity at their surfaces is

(a) $g_1 : g_2 = \frac{\rho_1}{R_1^2} : \frac{\rho_2}{R_2^2}$ (b) $g_1 : g_2 = R_1R_2 : \rho_1\rho_2$
(c) $g_1 : g_2 = R_1\rho_2 : R_2\rho_1$ (d) $g_1 : g_2 = R_1\rho_1 : R_2\rho_2$

18. What is the value of acceleration caused by force of gravity on a stone placed on ground?

(a) 10 ms^{-2} (b) 9.8 ms^{-2}
(c) 0 (d) -9.81 ms^{-2}

19. A particle of mass m is at the surface of the earth of radius R. It is lifted to a height h above the surface of the earth. The gain in gravitational potential energy of the particle is

(a) $\frac{mgh}{\left(1-\frac{h}{R}\right)}$ (b) $\frac{mgh}{\left(1+\frac{h}{R}\right)}$
(c) $\frac{mghR}{(R+h)}$ (d) Both (b) and (c)

20. Three particles each of mass m are kept at vertices of an equilateral triangle of side L. The gravitational potential energy possessed by this system is

(a) $\frac{-Gm^2}{L}$ (b) $\frac{-3Gm^2}{L}$
(c) $-\frac{2Gm^2}{L}$ (d) $\frac{+3Gm^2}{L}$

21. If the gravitational potential energy at infinity is assumed to be zero, the potential energy at distance $(R_e + h)$ from the centre of the earth is

(a) $\frac{GmM_e}{(R_e+h)}$ (b) $\frac{-GmM_e}{(R_e+h)}$
(c) mgh (d) $\frac{-GmM_e}{2(R_e+h)}$

22. Two point masses m_1 and m_2 are separated by a distance r. The gravitational potential energy of the system is G_1. When the separation between the particles is doubled, the gravitational potential energy is G_2.

Then, the ratio $\frac{G_1}{G_2}$ is

(a) 1 (b) 2 (c) 3 (d) 4

23. The ratio of the magnitude of potential energy and kinetic energy of a satellite is

(a) 1 : 2 (b) 2 : 1 (c) 3 : 1 (d) 1 : 3

24. The radius of the orbit of a satellite is r and its kinetic energy is K. If the radius of the orbit is doubled, then the new kinetic energy K' will be

(a) $2K$ (b) $K/2$
(c) $4K$ (d) Data insufficient

25. Satellites orbitting the earth have finite life and sometimes debris of satellites fall to the earth. This is because **NCERT Exemplar**

(a) the solar cells and batteries in satellites run out
(b) the laws of gravitation predict a trajectory spiralling inwards
(c) of viscous forces causing the speed of satellite and hence height to gradually decrease
(d) of collisions with other satellites

26. Match the Column I with Column II and select the correct answer from the options given below.

	Column I		Column II
A.	Kepler's first law	P.	$T^2 \propto a^3$
B.	Kepler's second law	Q.	Inverse square law
C.	Kepler's third law	R.	Orbit of planet is elliptical
D.	Newton's law of gravitation	S.	Law of conservation of angular momentum

(a) A-R, B-S, C-P, D-Q (b) A-P, B-Q, C-R, D-S
(c) A-S, B-R, C-P, D-Q (d) A-Q, B-P, C-S, D-R

27. Match the Column I with Column II and select the correct answer from the options given below.

	Column I		Column II
A.	The period of a satellite	1.	Does not depend on the mass of the satellite.
B.	The velocity of a satellite	2.	Depends on the radius of the orbit.
C.	The gravitational force on a satellite	3.	Depends on the mass of the planet.
D.	The orbital radius of a satellite	4.	Affects the time it takes for the satellite to complete one orbit.

Codes

(a) A-1,B-2,C-3,D-4 (b) A-4,B-2,C-3,D-1
(c) A-2,B-3,C-1,D-2 (d) A-1,B-3,C-4,D-2

Assertion-Reason

Directions *(Q.No. 28-34) In the following questions, two statements are given- one labelled Assertion (A) and the other labelled Reason (R). Select the correct answer to these questions from the codes (a), (b), (c) and (d) as given below.*

(a) Both Assertion and Reason are true and Reason is the correct explanation of Assertion.
(b) Both Assertion and Reason are true but Reason is not the correct explanation of Assertion.
(c) Assertion is true but Reason is false.
(d) Assertion is false but Reason is true.

28. Assertion (A) The force of attraction due to a hollow spherical shell of uniform density, on a point mass situated inside it is zero.
Reason (R) Various region of the spherical shell attract the point mass inside it in various directions. These forces cancel each other completely.

29. Assertion (A) There is a popular statement regarding Cavendish: 'Cavendish weighed the earth'.
Reason (R) The measurement of G by Cavendish's experiment, combined with the knowledge of g and R_e enables one to estimates M_e from equation.

$$g = \frac{GM_e}{R_e^2}$$

30. Assertion (A) As we go up the surface of the earth, we feel light weighed than on the surface of the earth.
Reason (R) The acceleration due to gravity decreases on going up above the surface of the earth.

31. Assertion (A) The escape speed for the moon is 2.3 kms^{-1} which is five times smaller than that for the earth.
Reason (R) The escape speed depends on acceleration due to gravity on the moon and radius of the moon and both of them are smaller than that of earth.

32. Assertion (A) Moon has no atmosphere.
Reason (R) The escape speed for the moon is much smaller. Gas molecules, if formed on the surface of the moon having velocities larger than escape speed will escape the gravitational pull of the moon.

33. Assertion (A) The velocity of the satellite decreases as its height above earth's surface increases and is maximum near the surface of the earth.
Reason (R) The velocity of the satellite is inversely proportional to its height above the earth's surface.

34. **Assertion (A)** The total energy of the satellite is always negative irrespective of the nature of its orbit i.e., elliptical or circular and it cannot be positive or zero.
Reason (R) If the total energy is positive or zero, the satellite would leave its orbit.

Case Based Questions

Directions *(Q.Nos. 35-38) These questions are case study based questions. Read the following paragraph and answer the questions on the basis of same.*

35. **The figure shows the schematic drawing of Cavendish's experiment to determine the value of the gravitational constant. The bar AB has two small lead spheres attached at its ends. The bar is suspended from a rigid support by a fine wire.**
Two large lead spheres are brought close to the small ones but on opposite sides as shown in figure. The name of G from this experiment came to be 6.67×10^{-11}N-m^2/kg^2.

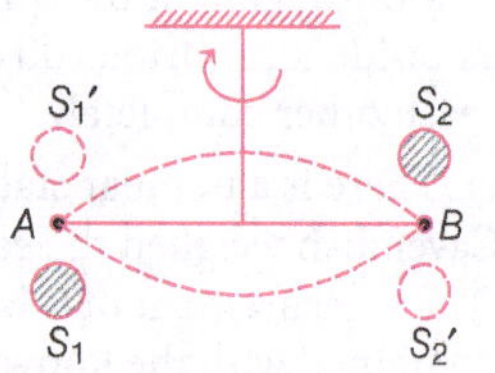

(i) The big spheres attract the nearby small ones by a force which is
(a) equal and opposite (b) equal but in same direction
(c) unequal and opposite (d) None of the above

(ii) The net force on the bar is
(a) non-zero (b) zero
(c) Data insufficient (d) None of these

(iii) The net torque on the bar is
(a) zero
(b) non-zero
(c) F times the length of the bar, where F is the force of attraction between a big sphere and its neighbouring
(d) Both (b) and (c)

(iv) The torque produces twist in the suspended wire. The twisting stops, when
(a) restoring torque of the wire equals the gravitational torque
(b) restoring torque of the wire exceeds the gravitational torque
(c) the gravitational torque exceeds the restoring torque of the wire
(d) None of the above

Or

(iv) After Cavendish's experiment, there have been suggestions that the value of the gravitational constant G becomes smaller when considered over very large time period (in billions of years) in the future. If that happens, for our earth,
(a) nothing will change
(b) we will become hotter after billions of years
(c) we will be going around but not strictly in closed orbits
(d) None of the above

36. **Let the speed of the planet at the perihelion P in following figure be v_P and the sun planet distance SP be r_P. The corresponding quantity at the aphelion A is (r_A, v_A). The mass of the planet in m_P.**

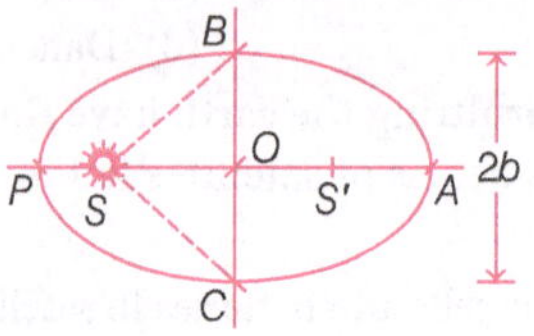

(i) The magnitude of the angular momentum at P is
(a) $L_P = \frac{m_P r_P}{v_P}$ (b) $L_P = \frac{m_P v_P}{r_P}$
(c) $L_P = m_P r_P v_P$ (d) $L_P = m_P v_P$

(ii) The magnitude of the angular momentum at A is
(a) $L_A = m_P r_A v_A$ (b) $L_A = \frac{m_P r_A}{v_A}$
(c) $L_A = m_P v_A$ (d) $L_A = \frac{m_P v_A}{r_A}$

(iii) The vectors $\mathbf{r}_p$ and $\mathbf{v}_p$ are
(a) parallel (b) mutually perpendicular
(c) anti-parallel (d) coincident

(iv) The relation for conservation of angular momentum at P and A is
(a) $m_P r_P v_P = m_P r_A v_A$ (b) $\frac{m_P r_P}{v_P} = \frac{m_P r_A}{v_A}$
(c) $m_P v_P = m_P v_A$ (d) $\frac{m_P v_P}{r_P} = \frac{m_P v_A}{r_A}$

Or

(iv) The magnitude of the angular momentum as the planet goes round the sun
(a) is constant
(b) is variable
(c) depends on magnitude of velocity
(d) increases as planet goes near to the sun

37. **By knowing the Kepler's law of planetary motion, Newton in 1686, has formulated his universal law of gravitation. According to which, the force of attraction between two of objects in this universe is directly proportional to the product of their masses and inversely proportional to the square of distance between them.**

This force of attraction is called gravitational force. If two bodies of masses m_1 and m_2 are separated by a distance r, then the gravitational force between them is given by, $F = G \cdot \frac{m_1 m_2}{r^2}$, where G is universal gravitational constant. The gravitational force is negligibly small compared to the electrical force. The gravitational force does not depend on the medium.

(i) If the distance between two planets is increased by two times, then how will the gravitational force change?

(ii) How the gravitational force depends on the separation between the two objects?

(iii) If the gravitational force between two bodies in air is F, then what will be the gravitational force between the objects, if they are placed in water?

Or (iii) If each mass of the bodies is increased by two times, then find the change in the gravitational force between them.

38. **Acceleration due to gravity is the rate of increase of velocity of a body falling freely towards the earth. At a given place, it is same for all bodies irrespective of their masses. The value of acceleration due to gravity on the surface of the earth is given by $g = 9.8 \text{ m/s}^2$. If we go above the earth surface, its value decreases with increase in the height. The expression for it at height h is, $g_h = g\left(1 - \frac{2h}{R}\right)$. If we go below the earth surface, its value also decreases with increase in depth. The expression for it at depth d, $g_d = g\left(1 - \frac{d}{R}\right)$.**

(i) What will be the value of acceleration due to gravity at the centre of earth?

(ii) How the acceleration due to gravity depends on the radius of the earth at the surface of the earth?

(iii) Draw g *versus* r graph, if we go from centre to the surface of the earth.

Or (iii) What will be the percentage decrease in g, if we go at a depth half of the radius of earth?

Subjective Questions

Very Short Answer Type Questions

1. What would happen if the force of gravity were to disappear suddenly?

2. What would happen to an orbiting planet, if all of a sudden it comes to stand still?

3. We cannot move fingers without disturbing all stars, why?

4. How could we determine the mass of a planet such as venus which has no moon?

5. When a pendulum clock is taken to a mountain, it becomes slow. But a wrist watch controlled by a spring remains unaffected. Explain.

6. Does the speed of a satellite remain constant in a particular orbit (circular)?

Short Answer Type Questions

7. State and explain Kepler's laws of planetary motion. Also, name the physical quantities which remain constant during the planetary motion.

8. The gravitational force between a hollow spherical shell (of radius R and uniform density) and a point mass is F. Show the nature of F *versus* r graph, where r is the distance of the point from the centre of the hollow spherical shell of uniform density. **NCERT Exemplar**

9. You can shield a charge from electrical forces by putting it inside a hollow conductor. Can you shield a body from the gravitational influence of nearby matter by putting it inside a hollow sphere or by some other means? **NCERT**

10. (a) If you compare the gravitational force on the earth due to the sun to that due to the moon, you would find that the sun's pull is greater than the moon's pull. However, the tidal effect of the moon's pull is greater than the tidal effect of the sun. Why? **NCERT**

(b) The acceleration due to gravity on a planet is 196 ms^{-2}. If it is safe to jump from a height of 2 m on the earth, then what will be the corresponding safe height on the planet?

11. Prove that the gravitational field and gravitational potential at any point on the surface of the earth are *g* and *gR*, respectively. The earth may be assumed to be a sphere of uniform density.

12. Find the intensity of gravitational field at a point lying at a distance *x* from the centre on the axis of a ring of radius *a* and mass *M*.

13. Does the change in gravitational potential energy of a body between two given points depend on the nature of path followed, why?

14. Choose the correct alternative.

(i) If the zero of potential energy is at infinity, the total energy of an orbiting satellite is negative of the kinetic/potential energy.

(ii) The energy required to lanuch an orbiting satellite out of earth's gravitational influence is more/less than the energy required to project a stationary object at the same height (as the satellite) out of earth's influence.

15. The gravitational intensity at the centre of a hemispherical shell of uniform mass density (in figure) has the direction indicated by arrow (i) a, (ii) b, (iii) c, (iv) zero. Choose the correct answer. **NCERT**

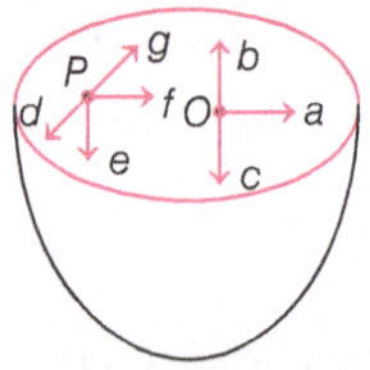

16. If suddenly the gravitational force of attraction between the earth and a satellite revolving around it becomes zero, then what will happen to the satellite?

17. Mean solar day is the time interval between two successive noon when the sun passes through the zenith point (meridian).
Sidereal day is the time interval between two successive transit of distant star through the zenith point (meridian).
By drawing appropriate diagram showing the earth's spin and orbital motion, show that mean solar day is 4 min longer than the sidereal day.
In other words, distant start would rise 4 min early every successive day.

18. A missile is fired radially from the surface of earth (radius 6.4×10^6 m) at a satellite, orbiting the earth. The satellite appears stationary vertically upwards from the point, where the missile is launched. Its distance from the centre of the earth is 25.4×10^6 m. Will the missile actually hit the satellite?

19. What is the angle between the equatorial plane and the orbital plane of

(i) polar satellite?

(ii) geostationary satellite? **NCERT Exemplar**

Long Answer Type Questions

20. Let the speed of the planet at the perihelion *P* in figure be v_P and the sun-planet distance *SP* be r_P. Relate $\{r_P, v_P\}$ to the corresponding quantities at the aphelion $\{r_A, v_A\}$. Will the planet take equal time to traverse *BAC* and *CPB*?

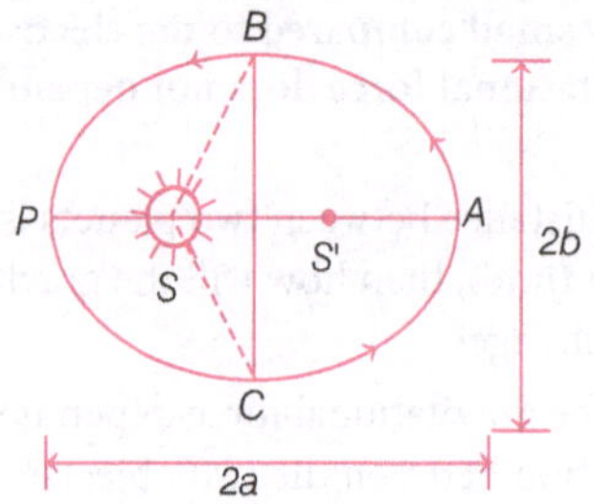

21. What do you understand by gravitational field and intensity of gravitational field? Prove that gravitational intensity at a point is equal to the acceleration due to gravity at that point.

22. A star like the sun has several bodies moving around it at different distances. Consider that all of them are moving in circular orbits. Let *r* be the distance of the body from the centre of the star and let its linear velocity be *v*, angular velocity ω, kinetic energy *K*, gravitational potential energy *U*, total energy *E* and angular momentum *L*. As the radius *r* of the orbit increases, determine which of the above quantities increase and which ones decrease.

23. Does the escape velocity of a body from the earth depend on (a) the mass of the body, (b) the location from which it is projected, (c) the direction of projection, (d) the height of the location from where the body is launched? Explain your answer.

24. Which of the following symptoms is likely to affect an astronaut in space (i) swollen feet, (ii) swollen face, (iii) headache, (iv) orientational problem.

25. Show the nature of the following graph for a satellite orbitting the earth.

(i) KE *versus* orbital radius *R*

(ii) PE *versus* orbital radius *R*

(iii) TE *versus* orbital radius *R* **NCERT Exemplar**

Numerical Problems

Kepler's law of Planetary Motion

26. If the earth be at one half of its present distance from the sun, then how many days will be there in a year?

27. The planet neptune travels around the sun with a period of 165 years. Show that the radius of its orbit is approximately thirty times that of the earth's orbit, both being considered as circular.

28. Calculate the period of revolution of the neptune around the sun. Given that radius of its orbit is 30 times the earth's orbital radius around the sun.

29. The distances of two planets from the sun are 10^{13} m and 10^{12} m, respectively. Calculate the ratio of time period and the speeds of the two planets.

30. If the earth is $\frac{1}{4}$ of its present distance from the sun, then what is the duration of the year?

31. Earth's orbit is an ellipse with eccentricity 0.0167. Thus, earth's distance from the sun and its speed, as it moves around the sun, varies from day-to-day. This means that the length of solar day is not constant throughout the year. Assuming that the earth's spin axis is normal to its orbital plane, find out the length of the shortest and the longest day. A day should be taken from noon to noon. Does this explain variation of length of the day during the year? **NCERT Exemplar**

Universal Law of Gravitation

32. Calculate the force of attraction between two bodies, each of mass 100 kg and 1 m apart on the surface of the earth.

33. Two particles of equal mass m go round a circle of radius R under the action of their mutual gravitational attraction. What is the speed of each particle?

34. A meteor is falling. How much gravitational acceleration would it experience, when its height from the surface of the earth is equal to three times the radius of the earth?

35. A 70 kg boy is standing 1 m away from a 60 kg boy. Calculate the force of gravitational attraction between them.

36. Two steel balls whose masses are 5.2 kg and 0.25 kg are placed with their centres half a metre apart. With what force do they attract each other?

37. A sphere of mass 40 kg is attracted by another sphere of mass 15 kg, with a force of $\frac{1}{40}$ mg-wt. Find the value of the gravitational constant, if their centres are 0.40 m apart.

38. Consider two solid uniform spherical objects of the same density ρ. One has a radius R and the other a radius $2R$. They are in outer space where the gravitational fields from other objects are negligible. If they are at rest with their surfaces touching, then what is the contact force between the objects due to their gravitational attraction?

39. A mass m is placed at P, a distance h along the normal through the centre O of a thin circular ring of mass M and radius r. If the mass is removed further away such that OP becomes $2h$, by what factor the force of gravitation will decrease, if $h = r$? **NCERT Exemplar**

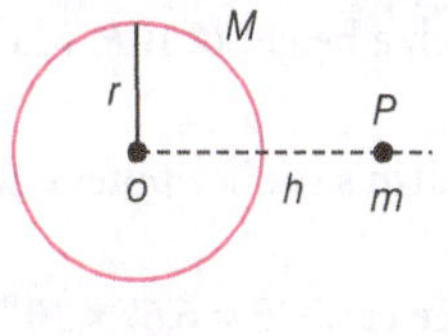

40. A rocket is fired from the earth towards the sun. At what distance from the earth's centre, is the gravitational force on the rocket zero? Mass of the sun $= 2 \times 10^{30}$ kg and mass of the earth $= 6 \times 10^{24}$ kg. Neglect the effect of other planets etc. (Orbital radius $= 1.5 \times 10^{11}$ m). **NCERT**

Superposition Principle

41. The masses and coordinates of the three spheres are as follows; 20 kg, $x = 0.50$ m, $y = 1.0$ m; 40 kg, $x = -1.0$ m, $y = -1.0$ m; 60 kg, $x = 0$ m, $y = -0.50$m. What is the magnitude of the gravitational force on a 20 kg sphere located at the origin due to the other spheres?

42. Six point masses of mass m each are at the vertices of a regular hexagon of side l. Calculate the force on any of the masses.

Acceleration due to Gravity

43. How far away from the surface of the earth does the acceleration due to gravity become 4% of its value on the surface of the earth? [Take, $R_e = 6400$ km]

44. Find the percentage decrease in the weight of a body when taken 10 km below the surface of the earth. [Take radius of the earth of 6400 km]

45. How much below the surface of the earth does acceleration due to gravity become 1% of the value at the earth's surface? [Radius of the earth = 6400 km]

46. The Mount Everest is 8848 m above sea level. Estimate the acceleration due to gravity at this height, given that mean g on the surface of the earth is 9.8 m/s^2. The mean radius of the earth is 6.37×10^8 m.

47. What will be the value of g at the bottom of sea 7 km deep? Diameter of the earth is 12800 km and g on the surface of the earth is 9.8 m/s^2.

48. If the earth was a perfect sphere of radius 6.37×10^6 m, rotating about its axis with a period of 1 day, then how much would the acceleration due to gravity (g) differ from the poles to the equator?

49. At what height above the surface of the earth, value of acceleration due to gravity is 36% of its value on the surface of the earth? Given, radius of the earth = 6400 km.

Gravitational Potential Energy

50. Determine the velocity with which a body must be thrown vertically upward from the surface of earth so that it may reach a height of $10R$, where R is the radius of the earth.

51. Calculate the earth's surface potential from the following data.

(i) Radius of the earth, $R = 6.67 \times 10^6$ m

(ii) Mean density of the earth, $\rho = 5.57 \times 10^3$ kgm^{-3}

(iii) $G = 6.67 \times 10^{-11}$ Nm^2 kg^{-2}

52. At a point above the earth, the gravitational potential is -5.12×10^7 J kg^{-1} and acceleration due to gravity is 6.4 ms^{-2}. Assuming the mean radius of the earth to be 6400 km, calculate the height of this point above the surface of the earth.

53. Two heavy spheres, each of mass 100 kg and radius 0.10 m are placed 1.0 m apart on a horizontal table. What is the gravitational force and potential at the mid-point of the line joining the centres of the spheres? Is an object placed at that point in equilibrium? If so, is the equilibrium stable or unstable? **NCERT**

Escape Speed

54. Determine the speed with which the earth would have to rotate on its axis, so that a person on the equator would weigh 3/5 as much as present.

55. Prove that the moon would depart forever, if its speed were increased by nearly 42%.

56. A body is projected vertically upwards from the bottom of a crater of the moon of depth $\frac{R}{100}$, where R is the radius of the moon, with a velocity equal to the escape velocity on the surface of the moon. Calculate the maximum height attained by the body from the surface of the moon.

57. A body is projected vertically upwards from the surface of the earth so as to reach a height equal to the radius of the earth. Neglecting resistance due to air, calculate the initial speed which should be imparted to the body.

58. If the earth has a mass nine times and radius twice that of the planet mars, calculate the maximum velocity required by a rocket to pull out of the gravitational force of the mars.

59. A spaceship is launched into a circular orbit close to the surface of the earth. What additional velocity has now to be imparted to the spaceship in the orbit to overcome the gravitational pull ?

60. Two stars each of 1 solar mass ($= 2 \times 10^{30}$ kg) are approaching each other for a head-on collision. When they are at a distance of 10^9 km, their speeds are negligible. What is the speed with which they will collide? The radius of each star is 10^4 km. Assume the stars to remain undistorted until they collide (use the known value of G). **NCERT**

61. Two uniform solid spheres of equal radii R, but mass M and $4M$ have a centre of separation $6R$, as shown in figure. The two spheres are held fixed. A projectile of mass m is projected from the surface of the sphere of mass M directly towards the centre of the second sphere. Obtain an expression for the minimum speed v of the projectile, so that it reaches the surface of the second sphere.

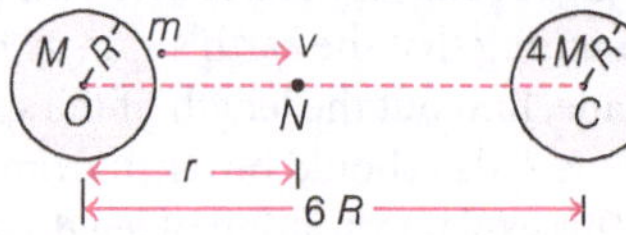

Earth Satellite

62. Calculate the ratio of the kinetic energy required to be given to a satellite, so that it escapes the gravitational field of earth to the kinetic energy required to put the satellite in a circular orbit just above the free surface of the earth.

63. An artificial satellite moving in a circular orbit around the earth has a total energy E_0. What is its potential energy?

64. Two satellites have their masses in the ratio of 3 : 1. The radii of their circular orbits are in the ratio of 1 : 4. What is the ratio of total mechanical energy of A and B?

65. A 400 kg satellite is in circular orbit of radius $2R_e$ about the earth. How much energy is required to transfer it to a circular orbit of radius $4R_e$? What are the changes in the kinetic and potential energies?

66. The world's first artificial satellite (Sputnik-I) launched by USSR was circling the earth at a distance of 896 km. Calculate its orbital speed and period of revolution.

67. An artificial satellite is going round the earth, close to the surface. What is the time taken by it to complete one round?

68. The earth satellite makes a complete circular orbit in 1.5 h. Determine the altitude of satellite above the surface of the earth.

69. Two equal masses of 6.4 kg are separated by a distance of 0.16 m. A small body is released from a point *P* equidistant from the two masses and at a distance of 0.06 m from the line joining them.

(i) Calculate the velocity of this body, when it passes through *Q*.

(ii) Calculate the acceleration of this body at *P* and *Q*, if its mass is 0.1 kg.

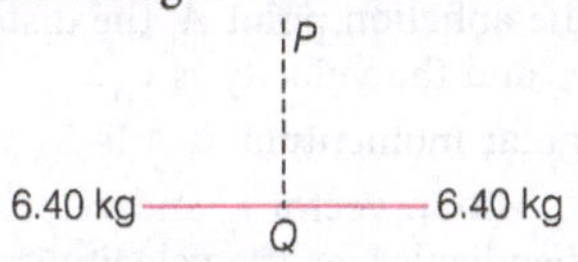

70. A body weighs 90 kg on the surface of the earth. How much will it weigh on the surface of the mars, whose mass is $\frac{1}{9}$ th and radius $\frac{1}{2}$ of that of the earth?

71. The earth-moon distance is 3.8×10^5 km. The mass of the earth is 81 times that of moon. Determine the distance from the earth to the point where the gravitational fields due to the earth and the moon cancel out.

72. A satellite is to be placed in equatorial geostationary orbit around the earth for communication.

(i) Calculate height of such a satellite.

(ii) Find out the minimum number of satellites that are needed to cover entire earth, so that atleast one satellite is visible from any point on the equator.

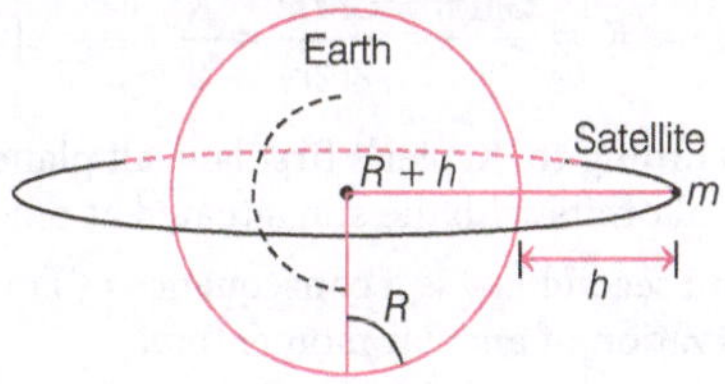

[$M = 6 \times 10^{24}$ kg, $R = 6400$ km, $T = 24$ h, $G = 6.67 \times 10^{-11}$ SI unit]

Hints & Solutions

Objective Type Questions

1. (d)	2. (a)	3. (a)	5 (d)	6. (a)
7. (b)	8. (b)	9. (c)	10. (a)	11. (c)
12. (c)	13. (c)	14. (b)	15. (b)	16 (d)
18. (b)	19. (d)	20. (b)	21. (b)	22. (b)
25 (c)	28. (a)	29. (a)	30. (a)	31. (a)
33 (a)				

4. (c) A point mass *m* is located at the centre of the square *ABCD*. Let gravitational force between *m* and m_1 is

$$|F'| = \left[\frac{Gmm_1}{\frac{a}{(\sqrt{2})^2}}\right]$$

and between *m* and m_2 is $|F_2| = \left[\frac{Gmm_2}{\left(\frac{a}{\sqrt{2}}\right)^2}\right]$ as shown below

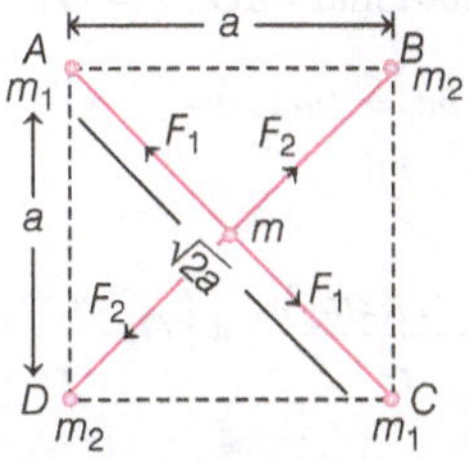

∴ Along *BD*, there are two forces of same magnitude F_2 acting between *m* and m_2 on (*B* or *D*).

Net gravitational force along *BD*,

$$F_{net(BD)} = F_2 - F_2 = 0$$

Similarly, net gravitational force along *AC*,

$$F_{net(AC)} = F_1 - F_1 = 0$$

∴ Net force on *m*, i.e. $|F_{net}|$ = zero

17. (d) The value of *g* at surface

$$g = \frac{GM\rho}{R^2} = \frac{G}{R^2} \cdot \frac{4\pi}{3} R^3 \rho$$

$$g = \frac{4}{3}\pi GR\rho$$

So, $$\frac{g_1}{g_2} = \frac{\frac{4}{3}\pi GR_1\rho_1}{\frac{4}{3}\pi GR_2\rho_2}$$

$$\frac{g_1}{g_2} = \frac{R_1\rho_1}{R_2\rho_2}$$

23. (a) $$\frac{GMm}{R^2} + m\omega^2 R = 0$$

∴ $$\frac{GMm}{R^2} = -m\omega^2 R$$

$$KE = \frac{1}{2} I\omega^2 = \frac{1}{2} mR^2\omega^2 = \frac{GMm}{2R}$$

$$PE = \frac{-GMm}{R}$$

$$\therefore \quad KE = \frac{|PE|}{2}$$

$$\therefore \quad \frac{|KE|}{|PE|} = \frac{1}{2}$$

24. (*b*) KE of a satellite in orbit is given by

$$K = \frac{GMm}{2r}$$

If the radius r is doubled ($r' = 2r$), the new KE (K') becomes

$$K' = \frac{GMm}{2r'} = \frac{GMm}{2(2r)} = \frac{K}{2} \qquad \left[\because K = \frac{GMm}{2r}\right]$$

26. (*a*) According to Kepler's first law, all planets move in elliptical orbits with the sun situated at one of the foci.

Kepler's second law is a consequence of law of conservation of angular momentum.

According to Kepler's third law, the square of the time period of revolution of a planet is proportional to the cube of the semi-major axis of the ellipse traced out by the planet, i.e.

$$T^2 \propto a^3$$

According to Newton's law of gravitation, everybody in the universe attracts every other body with a force which is directly proportional to the product of their masses and inversely proportional to the square of the distance between them.

Hence, A-R, B-S, C-P, D-Q

27. (*b*) A → 4, B → 2, C → 3, D → 1

32. (*a*) Both Assertion (A) and Reason (R) are true and reason is the correct explanation of Assertion.

The moon has a very thin or almost non existent atmosphere due to its low gravity and lack of a significant magnetic field.

The escape velocity on the moon is much smaller than that of the earth, so gas molecules with higher velocities can escape the Moon's gravitational pull.

34. (*a*) Both Assertion (A) and Reason (R) are true and Reason is the correct explanation of Assertion. The total energy of a satellite in orbit is always negative because it is the sum of its kinetic energy (negative due to being bound in the orbit) and gravitational potential energy (also negative), which makes the total energy negative in a stable orbit.

If the total energy were zero or positive, the satellite would have enough energy to escape the gravitational pull of the central body, thus leaving its orbit (escaping the gravitational field).

35. (i) (*a*) The big spheres attract the nearby small ones by a force that is equal and opposite in direction.

(ii) (*b*) The net force on the bar is zero because the forces on both spheres are equal.

(iii) (*b*) The net torque on the bar is non-zero because the gravitational force creates a rotational effect.

(iv) (*b*) The torque produced by the gravitational force stops when the restoring torque exceeds or equals the gravitational torque.

Or (iv) (*a*) We will be going around but strictly in closed orbits. This reflects the expected impact of a charge in G on the earth's orbit over long time scales.

36. (i) (*c*) The formula for angular momentum is given by $L = m \cdot r \cdot v$. At the perihelion point P, the distance from the sun is r_p and the velocity is v_P, so the angular momentum at P is $L_P = m_P \cdot r_P \cdot v_P$

(ii) (*a*) At the aphelion point A, the distance from the sun is r_A and the velocity is v_A.

The angular momentum at A is $L_A = m_P \cdot r_A \cdot v_A$.

(iii) (*b*) The position vector $\mathbf{r}_p$ and velocity $\mathbf{v}_P$ at point P are perpendicular, as the velocity is tangential to the orbit.

(iv) (*b*) Since, angular momentum is conserved in an orbit, we have :

$$m_P \cdot r_P \cdot v_P = m_P \cdot r_A \cdot v_A$$

Or

(iv) (*a*) Since, angular momentum is conserved, its magnitude remains constant as the planet moves in the elliptical orbit.

37. (i) The gravitational force between two masses m_1 and m_2 with separation r is given by

$$F = G \cdot \frac{m_1 m_2}{r^2} \qquad \text{... (i)}$$

If the distance r is increased by two times, then

$$r' = 2r$$

$$\therefore \quad F' = G \cdot \frac{m_1 m_2}{r'^2} = G \cdot \frac{m_1 m_2}{(2r)^2} = \frac{G m_1 m_2}{4r^2}$$

$$\therefore \quad F' = \frac{F}{4} \qquad \text{[from Eq. (i)]}$$

Hence, the new force is decreased by four times.

(ii) The gravitational force between two objects in universe is inversely proportional to the square of distance between them.

(iii) As, the gravitational force is independent of the medium. Hence, the gravitational force between two bodies in water is same as that in the air, which is equal to F.

Or

(iii) The gravitational force, $F = G \cdot \frac{m_1 m_2}{r^2}$

If $m_1' = 2m_1$, $m_2' = 2m_2$, then

$$F' = G \cdot \frac{m_1' m_2'}{r^2}$$

$$= G \cdot \frac{(2m_1)(2m_2)}{r^2} = 4\left(G \cdot \frac{m_1 m_2}{r^2}\right) = 4F$$

Hence, the new gravitational force is increased by four times.

38. (i) The expression for acceleration due to gravity at depth d below the earth surface is given by

$$g_d = g\left(1 - \frac{d}{R}\right)$$

At the centre of the earth, $d = R$

$$\therefore \quad g_d = g\left(1 - \frac{R}{R}\right) = 0$$

(ii) The expression of acceleration due to gravity at the surface of the earth,

$$g = \frac{GM}{R^2} \Rightarrow g \propto \frac{1}{R^2}$$

So, it is inversely proportional to the square of the radius of the earth.

(iii) The expression for g inside the earth,

$$g' = g\left(1 - \frac{d}{R}\right) = g\left(\frac{R-d}{R}\right)$$

Put $\quad R - d = r,\ g' = \left(\frac{g}{R}\right) r \Rightarrow g' \propto r$

$\therefore$ The g' *versus* r graph is

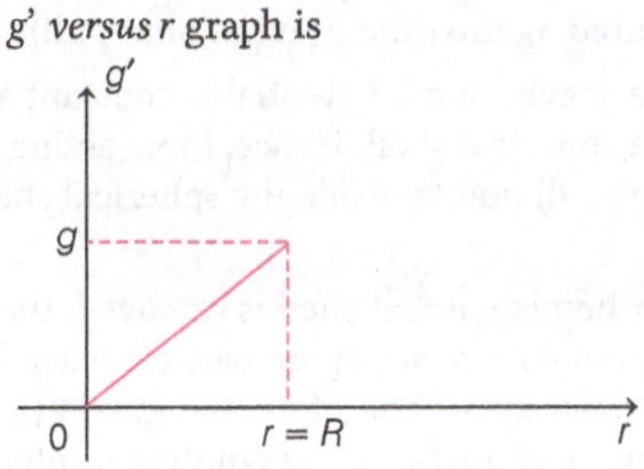

where, g = acceleration due to gravity on the surface of the earth = 9.8 m/s^2 and R = radius of the earth.

Or

(iii) The expression for acceleration due to gravity at depth d from the surface of the earth is given by

$$g_d = g\left(1 - \frac{d}{R}\right) = g - \left(\frac{g}{R}\right) d$$

$\therefore$ % decrease in the value of g

$$= \left(\frac{g - g_d}{g} \times 100\right)\% = \left(\frac{d}{R} \times 100\right)\%$$

$$= \left(\frac{R/2}{R} \times 100\right)\% = 50\% \qquad \left[\because d = \frac{R}{2}\right]$$

Subjective Questions

1. The universe would collapse. We would be thrown away because of the centrifugal force. Eating, drinking and infact all activities would become impossible.

2. If an orbiting planet all of sudden comes to a stand still, then it will lack the velocity to counter the gravitational attraction. Therefore, it will fall towards the centre of path and gobbled up by the star.

3. When we move our finger, the distance of the objects with respect to finger changes, hence the force of attraction changes, disturbing the entire universe, including the stars.

4. The mass of a planet which has no moon is determined by measuring the acceleration due to gravity (g) of the planet.

Its acceleration due to gravity on the venus,

$$g_v = \frac{GM_v}{R_v^2}$$

$$\therefore \text{ Mass of venus,} \quad M_v = \frac{g_v R_v^2}{G}$$

5. At the mountain, g decreases and time period of the pendulum clock increases as $T = 2\pi\sqrt{l/g}$. On the other hand, a spring in the wrist watch remains unaffected by the variation of g.

6. Yes, as $v = \sqrt{\frac{GM}{r}}$, v depends only on r. For a particular orbit, r is constant and so is v.

7. Refer to text on Pages no. 230 and 231.

8. Consider the diagram, density of the shell is constant. Let it is ρ.

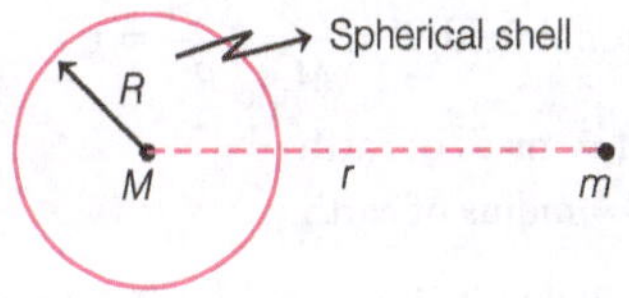

Mass of the shell = (Density) × (Volume)

$$= (\rho) \times \frac{4}{3}\pi R^3 = M$$

As the density of the shell is uniform, it can be treated as a point mass placed at its centre.

Therefore, F = gravitational force between M and $m = \frac{GMm}{r^2}$

$F = 0$ for $r < R$ (i.e. force inside the shell is zero)

$= \frac{GM}{r^2}$ for $r \geq R$

The variation of F *versus* r is shown in the diagram.

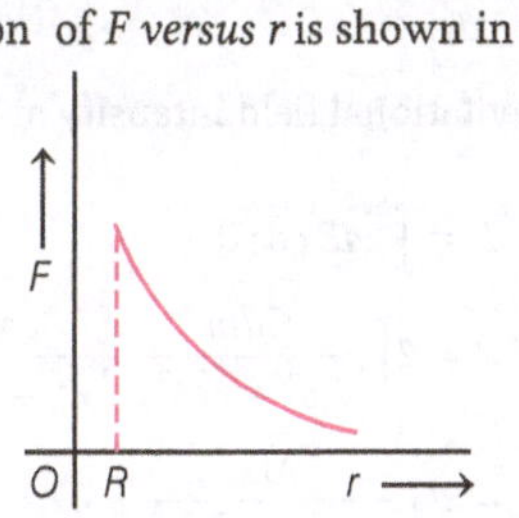

9. No, anybody cannot be shielded from gravitational influence of nearby matter by putting it inside a hollow sphere because gravitational force does not depend

upon the nature of the intervening medium, while electrical forces depend upon the nature of the intervening medium.

10. (a) Tidal effect is not governed by the inverse square law of the gravitational force, but it is inversely proportional to the cube of the distance. Earth-moon distance is very small as compared to the earth-sun distance. Therefore, tidal effect of moon is more effective than the tidal effect of sun.

The ratio of these two effects is

$$\frac{T_m}{T_s} = \left(\frac{d_s}{d_m}\right)^3 = \left(\frac{1.5\times10^{11}}{3.8\times10^8}\right)^3 = 61.5\times10^6$$

(b) The safety limit is final momentum of the man when jumping from either planet should remian same when he reaches the ground. Since the mass of the man is constant, so the velocity with which be jumps should also be same in both planets.

$\therefore \quad V_E^2 = 2g_E h_E \Rightarrow V_E^2 = 2\times 9.8\times 2 = 4\times 9.8\,;$

Since, $V_E = V_P$,

$\therefore \quad V_P^2 = 4\times 9.8 = 2\times g_P\times h_P = 2\times 1.96\times h_p;$

$$\Rightarrow \quad h_P = \frac{4\times 9.8}{2\times 1.96} = 10 \text{ m}$$

11. Gravitational field, $E = \frac{F}{M} = \frac{GM}{R^2} = g$

where, $M =$ mass of earth

and $R =$ radius of earth

Gravitational potential, $V = \int E\cdot dr \Rightarrow V = g\int_0^R dr = gR$

Hence, gravitational potential at any point on the earth surface is gR and the gravitational field at any point on the earth surface is g.

12. Consider a ring of mass M and radius a.

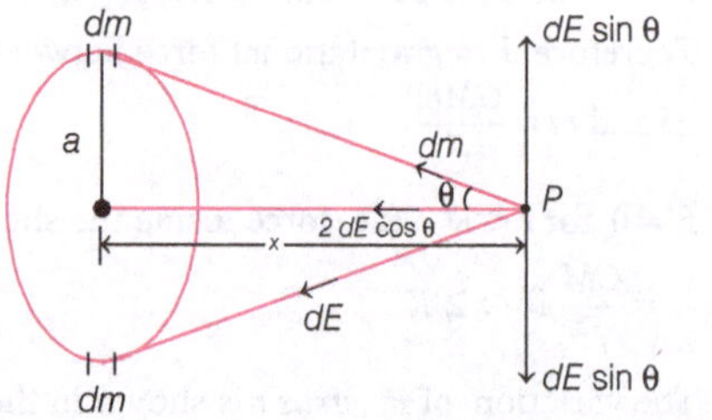

The net gravitational field intensity at point P is given by

$$E = \int 2dE\cos\theta$$

$$= 2\int\left(\frac{Gdm}{(x^2+a^2)^2}\cdot\frac{x}{(x^2+a^2)^{1/2}}\right)$$

$$= 2G.\frac{M_x}{2(x^2+a^2)^{3/2}}$$

$$\therefore \quad E = \frac{GM_x}{(x^2+a^2)^{3/2}}$$

13. The change in gravitational potential energy of a body between two given points depends only on the position of the given points and is independent of the path followed. It is due to the fact that, the gravitational force is a conservative force and work done by a conservative force depends only on the position of initial and final points and is independent of path followed.

14 (i) Potential energy of satellite, $U = -\frac{GMm}{r}$

Kinetic energy of satellite, $K = \frac{GMm}{2r}$

Total energy, $E = U + K$

$$= \frac{-GMm}{r} + \frac{GMm}{2r} = \frac{-GMm}{2r} = -K$$

i.e. negative of kinetic energy.

(ii) The energy required to launch an orbiting satellite out of gravitational influence is less than the energy required to project a stationary object, because in case of orbiting satellite, the gravitational pull of the earth acting on it is balanced by centripetal force, so work is required only in launching it (no work is required against the gravitational pull).

15. (iii) The gravitational potential is constant at all points inside a spherical shell. Hence, force acting on any particle at all points inside the spherical shell will be equal.

If upper hemispherical shell is removed, then gravitational force acting on particle placed at centre O will be downward. Therefore, the gravitational force acting per unit mass, i.e., gravitational intensity will be downward.

16. If suddenly the gravitational force of attraction between the earth and a satellite revolving around it becomes zero, satellite will not be able to revolve around the earth. Instead, the satellite will start moving along a straight line tangentially at that point on its orbit, where it is at the time of gravitational force becoming zero.

17. Consider the diagram below, the earth moves from the point P to Q in one solar day.

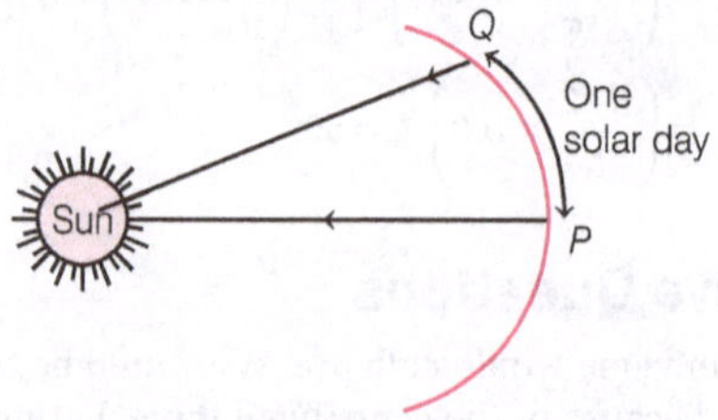

Everyday the earth advances in the orbit by approximately 1°. Then, it will have to rotate by 361° (which we define as 1 day) to have the sun at zenith point again.

$\because$ 361° corresponds to 24 h.

$\therefore$ 1° corresponds to $\frac{24}{361} \times 1 = 0.066$ h

$= 3.99$ min ≈ 4 min

Hence, distant stars would rise 4 min early every successive day.

18. The missile will not hit the satellite. A satellite appears stationary over a point on earth's equator when it is at such a height that its period of revolution about the earth is 24 hours. The missile, after being fired towards the satellite, takes time in covering the distance between the earth and the satellite and in the meantime the satellite changes its position.

19. Consider the diagram where plane of geostationary and polar satellite are shown.

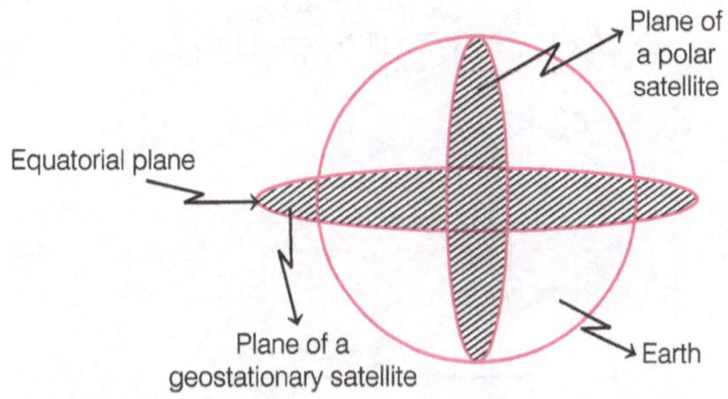

Clearly

(i) Angle between the equatorial plane and orbital plane of a polar satellite is 90°.

(ii) Angle between equatorial plane and orbital plane of a geostationary satellite is 0°.

20. At any point, radius vector and velocity vector of the planet are mutually perpendicular. Angular momentum of the planet at the perihelion P is L_p. Similarly, at the aphelion,

$$L_A = m_A r_A v_A$$

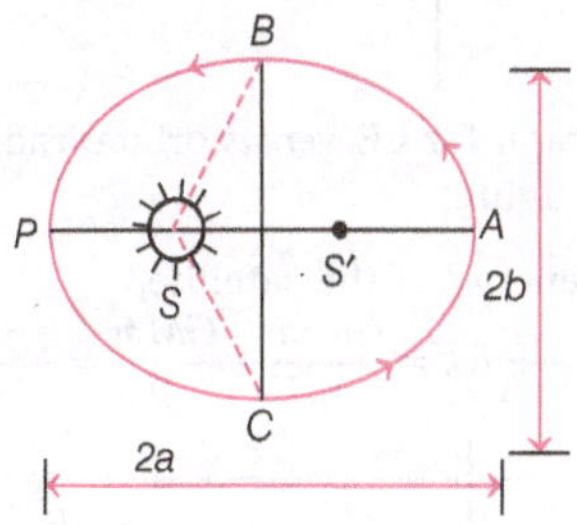

By conservation of angular momentum,

$$L_P = L_A$$

or $m_P r_P v_P = m_A r_A v_A$

or $\frac{v_P}{v_A} = \frac{r_A}{r_P} = \frac{a+c}{a-c} = \frac{1+e}{1-e}$

As, $r_A > r_P$

So, $v_P > v_A$

Here, $r_P = a - c \Rightarrow r_A = a + c$

and eccentricity, $e = \frac{c}{a}$

To traverse BAC, area swept by radius vector = area $SBAC$

To traverse CPB, area swept by radius vector = area $SBPC$.

But, area $SBAC >$ area $SBPC$ as shown in figure.

From Kepler's second law, equal areas are swept in equal time. Hence, the planet will take a longer time to traverse BAC than CPB.

21. Refer to text on Page no. 238.

22. The situation is shown in the diagram, where a body of mass m is revolving around a star of mass M.

Linear velocity of the body $v = \sqrt{\frac{GM}{r}}$

$$\Rightarrow \quad v \propto \frac{1}{\sqrt{r}}$$

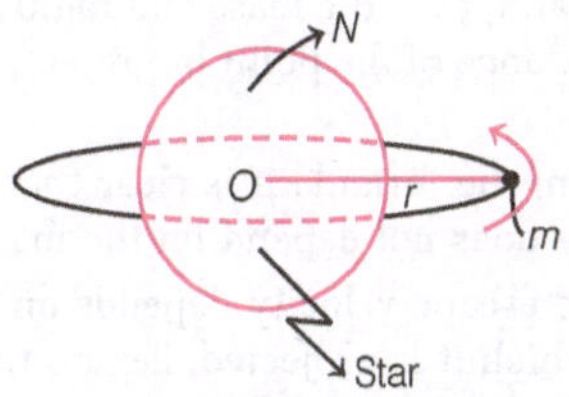

Therefore, when r increases, v decreases.

Angular velocity of the body, $\omega = \frac{2\pi}{T}$

According to Kepler's law of period,

$$T^2 \propto r^3 \Rightarrow T = kr^{3/2}$$

where, k is a constant

$$\therefore \quad \omega = \frac{2\pi}{kr^{3/2}} \Rightarrow \omega \propto \frac{1}{r^{3/2}} \quad \left(\because \omega = \frac{2\pi}{T}\right)$$

Therefore, when r increases, ω decreases.

Kinetic energy of the body, $K = \frac{1}{2}mv^2$

$$= \frac{1}{2}m \times \frac{GM}{r} = \frac{GMm}{2r}$$

$$\therefore \quad K \propto \frac{1}{r}$$

Therefore, when r increases, KE decreases.

Gravitational potential energy of the body,

$$U = -\frac{GMm}{r} \Rightarrow U \propto -\frac{1}{r}$$

Therefore, when r increases, PE becomes less negative i.e., increases.

Total energy of the body, E = KE + PE

$$= \frac{GMm}{2r} + \left(-\frac{GMm}{r}\right) = -\frac{GMm}{2r}$$

Therefore, when r increases, total energy becomes less negative, i.e., increases.

Angular momentum of the body,

$$L = mvr = mr\sqrt{\frac{GM}{r}}$$

$$= m\sqrt{GMr}$$

$$\therefore \quad L \propto \sqrt{r}$$

Therefore, when r increases, angular momentum L increases.

23. Escape velocity is given by

$$v_e = \sqrt{\frac{2GM}{R}} = \sqrt{2gR}$$

At distance r from earth's surface, the escape velocity,

$$v_e = \sqrt{\frac{2GM}{r}}$$

where, M and R are the mass and radius of the earth and r is the distance of the point of projection from earth's centre.

(i) No, from the formula it is clear that the escape velocity does not depend on the mass of the body.

(ii) Yes, the escape velocity depends on the location from which it is projected, i.e., on the altitude and latitude of the point of projection.

Escape velocity $v_e = \sqrt{2gR}$

and the value of g is different at different latitudes and altitudes.

(iii) No, the escape velocity does not depend on the direction of projection.

(iv) Yes, the escape velocity depends on the height of location from where the body is launched.

24. (i) We know that, the legs carry the weight of the body in the normal position due to gravitational pull. The astronaut in space is in weightlessness state. Hence, swollen feet may not affect his working.

(ii) In the conditions of weightlessness, the face of the astronaut is expected to get more supply. Due to it, the astronaut may develop swollen face. As eyes, ears, nose, mouth, etc., are all embedded in the face, hence swollen face may affect to great extent the seeing/hearing/ smelling/eating capabilities of the astronaut in space.

(iii) Headache is due to mental strain. It will persist whether a person is an astronaut in space or he is on earth. It means headache will have the same effect on the astronaut in space as on a person on earth.

(iv) Space also has orientation. We also have the frames of reference in space. Hence, orientational problem will affect the astronaut in space.

25. Consider the diagram, where a satellite of mass m, moving around the earth in a circular orbit of radius R.

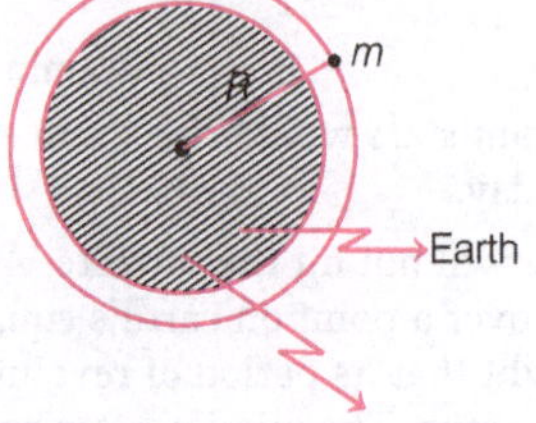

Orbital speed of the satellite orbiting the earth is given by $v_o = \sqrt{\frac{GM}{R}}$

where, M and R are the mass and radius of the earth.

(i) $\therefore$ KE of a satellite of mass m,

$$E_K = \frac{1}{2}mv_o^2 = \frac{1}{2}m \times \frac{GM}{R}$$

$$\therefore \quad E_K \propto \frac{1}{R}$$

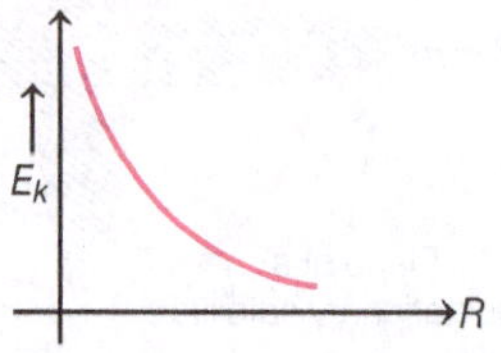

It means the KE decreases exponentially with radius. The graph for KE *versus* orbital radius R is shown in above figure.

(ii) Potential energy of a satellite, $E_P = -\frac{GMm}{R}$

$$E_P \propto -\frac{1}{R}$$

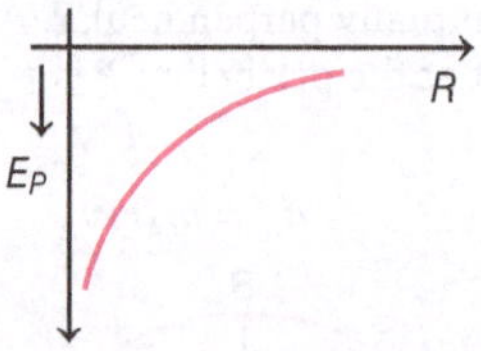

The graph for PE *versus* orbital radius R is shown in above figure.

(iii) Total energy of the satellite,

$$E = E_K + E_P = \frac{GMm}{2R} - \frac{GMm}{R} = -\frac{GMm}{2R}$$

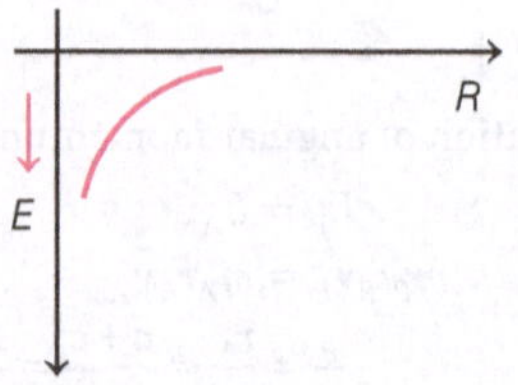

The graph for total energy *versus* orbital radius R is shown in the above figure.

26. From the Kepler's third law of planetary motion, we know that,

$$T^2 = kR^3 \quad ...(i)$$

where, k is constant,

T is orbital time period = 365 days for earth

and R is semi-major axis of orbit.

Now, take $T_1 = 365$ days,

$$R_1 = R,\ R_2 = \frac{R}{2} \text{ (given)}$$

$\therefore$ From Eq. (i),

$$\left(\frac{T_1}{T_2}\right)^2 = \left(\frac{R_1}{R_2}\right)^3$$

$$\Rightarrow \left(\frac{365}{T_2}\right)^2 = \left(\frac{R}{R/2}\right)^3 = 8$$

$$\Rightarrow \frac{365 \times 365}{T_2^2} = 8$$

$$\Rightarrow T_2^2 = \frac{365 \times 365}{8}$$

$$\Rightarrow T_2 = 129 \text{ days}$$

27. From the Kepler's law of planetary motion,

We know that, $T^2 \propto R^3$

$$\Rightarrow T^2 = kR^3$$

Let T_1 be the period of neptune around the sun = 165 years (given),

R_1 be the radius of neptune,

T_2 is the period of the earth and R_2 be its radius.

$$\frac{T_1^2}{T_2^2} = \frac{R_1^3}{R_2^3}$$

$$\frac{(165)^2}{1} = \frac{R_1^3}{R_2^3} \quad (\because T_2 = 1 \text{ year})$$

$$R_1^3 = (165)^2 R_2^3$$

$$R_1 = \sqrt[3]{(165)^2} R_2$$

$$R_1 \approx 30R_2$$

Hence, the radius of neptune orbit is approximately 30 times that of earth's orbit.

28. From the Kepler's law of planetary motion,

$$T^2 = kR^3 \text{ or } T^2 \propto R^3$$

Given that, $R_2 = 30R_1$

where, R_1 is orbital radius of earth around sun

and R_2 = orbital radius of neptune around sun.

Let T_1 = period of earth around sun = 1 year

and T_2 = period of neptune around sun

$$\therefore \frac{T_1^2}{T_2^2} = \frac{R_1^3}{R_2^3}$$

$$\frac{1}{T_2^2} = \left(\frac{1}{30}\right)^3$$

$$T_2^2 = 27000$$

$$T_2 = \sqrt{27000}$$

$$T_2 = 164.3 \text{yr}$$

29. By Kepler's law, $T^2 \propto R^3$

$$\text{or} \quad \frac{T_1^2}{T_2^2} = \left(\frac{R_1}{R_2}\right)^3$$

$$R_1 = 10^{13} \text{ m},$$

$$R_2 = 10^{12} \text{ m}$$

$$\therefore \frac{T_1^2}{T_2^2} = \left(\frac{10^{13}}{10^{12}}\right)^3$$

$$\frac{T_1}{T_2} = 10\sqrt{10}$$

$$\text{Speed,} \quad v = \frac{2\pi R}{T}$$

$$\therefore \frac{v_1}{v_2} = \frac{R_1}{T_1} \times \frac{T_2}{R_2} = \frac{R_1}{R_2} \times \frac{T_2}{T_1}$$

$$= \frac{10^{13}}{10^{12}} \times \frac{1}{10\sqrt{10}}$$

$$\frac{v_1}{v_2} = \frac{1}{\sqrt{10}}$$

30. From Kepler's law, $T^2 \propto R^3$

$$\text{Hence,} \quad \left(\frac{T_1}{T_2}\right)^2 = \left(\frac{R_1}{R_2}\right)^3$$

Given, $R_2 = \frac{R_1}{4}$

$$\therefore \left(\frac{T_1}{T_2}\right)^2 = \left(\frac{R_1}{R_1/4}\right)^3 = (4)^3$$

$$T_2 = \frac{T_1}{4^{3/2}} = \frac{T_1}{8} = \frac{1}{8} = 0.125 \text{ yr}$$

31. From the geometry of the ellipse of eccentricity e and semi-major axis a, the aphelion and perihelion distances are

$$r_a = a(1+e)$$

$$r_p = a(1-e)$$

$$\text{or} \quad \frac{r_a}{r_p} = \frac{1+e}{1-e}$$

Since, angular momentum $(mr^2\omega)$ is conserved.

$$r^2\omega = \text{constant i.e. } r_p^2\omega_p = r_a^2\omega_a$$

$$\text{or} \quad \frac{\omega_p}{\omega_a} = \frac{r_a^2}{r_p^2} = \left(\frac{1+e}{1-e}\right)^2$$

$$= \left(\frac{1 + 0.0167}{1 - 0.0167}\right)^2 = 1.0691$$

or $$\left(\frac{\omega_p}{\omega}\right)\left(\frac{\omega}{\omega_a}\right) = 1.0691 \quad ...(i)$$

where, ω is the angular speed corresponding to mean solar day and can be considered to be the geometric mean of ω_p and ω_a.

i.e. $$\omega_p \cdot \omega_a = \omega^2 \text{ or } \frac{\omega_p}{\omega} = \frac{\omega}{\omega_a} \quad ...(ii)$$

From Eqs. (i) and (ii), we get

$$\frac{\omega_p}{\omega} = \frac{\omega}{\omega_a} = \sqrt{1.0691} = 1.034$$

If $\omega = 1°$/ day (mean angular speed), then

$$\omega_p = 1.034°/\text{day and } \omega_a = \frac{1°}{1.034}/\text{day} = 0.967°/\text{day}$$

Since 361° corresponds to 24 h, (360 + 1.034)° corresponds to 24.0023 h, i.e. 24 h 8.14″ and (360 + 0.967)° corresponds to 23 h 59′ m 52″.

This does not explain the actual variation in the length of the day during the year.

32. We know that, force of attraction between two bodies is given by

$$F = \frac{Gm_1m_2}{r^2}$$

Here, $m_1 = m_2 = 100$ kg, $r = 1$ m

$$\therefore \quad F = (6.67 \times 10^{-11})\left(\frac{100 \times 100}{1^2}\right)$$

$$F = 6.67 \times 10^{-7} \text{ N}$$

33. Given, masses of the two particles,

$$M_1 = M_2 = m$$

and radius of two particles, $r_1 = r_2 = R$

So, the gravitational force of attraction,

$$F_1 = \frac{G \times m \times m}{(2R)^2} \quad ... (i)$$

and the centripetal force, $F_2 = \frac{mv^2}{R}$

Since, $F_1 = F_2$

$$\frac{Gmm}{4R^2} = \frac{mv^2}{R}$$

$$\Rightarrow \quad v^2 = \frac{Gm}{4R} \Rightarrow v = \frac{1}{2}\sqrt{\frac{Gm}{R}}$$

So, the speed of each particle,

$$v = \frac{1}{2}\sqrt{\frac{GM}{R}}$$

34. Given that, height from the surface of earth,

$$h = 3R$$

Gravitational acceleration, $g = \frac{GM}{R^2}$

At above the earth surface, $g' = \frac{GM}{(R+3R)^2}$

$$g' = \frac{GM}{16R^2}$$

$$g' = \frac{g}{16} \quad \left(\text{where, } g = \frac{GM}{R^2}\right)$$

35. Given, mass of boy A, $m_A = 70$ kg

Mass of boy B, $m_B = 60$ kg

Distance of the boys, $R = 1$ m

Hence, the force of attraction,

$$F = \frac{Gm_Am_B}{R^2}$$

$$= \frac{6.67 \times 10^{-11} \times 70 \times 60}{1^2}$$

$$= 2.8 \times 10^{-7} \text{ N}$$

36. Given, $m_A = 5.2$ kg and $m_B = 0.25$ kg

Distance, $R = 0.5$ m

Force of attraction , $F = \frac{Gm_Am_B}{R^2}$

$$= \frac{6.67 \times 10^{-11} \times 5.2 \times 0.25}{(0.5)^2}$$

$$= 34.684 \times 10^{-11} \text{ N}$$

$$= 3.468 \times 10^{-10} \text{ N}$$

37. Given, distance $R = 0.40$ m

Mass $m_1 = 40$ kg, $m_2 = 15$ kg

Force $(F) = \frac{1}{40}$ mg-wt

$$= \frac{1}{40} \times 10^{-3} \times 980 \text{ dyne}$$

$$= \frac{98}{4} \times 10^{-3} \text{ dyne}$$

$$F = 24.5 \times 10^{-8} \text{ N}$$

Also, $F = \frac{Gm_1m_2}{r^2}$

$$24.5 \times 10^{-8} = \frac{G \times 40 \times 15}{(0.40)^2}$$

$$G = \frac{24.5 \times 10^{-8} \times 0.40 \times 0.40}{40 \times 15}$$

$$= 6.53 \times 10^{-11} \text{ Nm}^2 \text{ kg}^{-2}$$

38. Since, the spheres are touching, distance between their centres, $r = R + 2R = 3R$

Mass of sphere of radius R, $m_1 = \rho \frac{4}{3} \pi (R)^3$

Mass of sphere of radius $2R$, $m_2 = \rho \frac{4}{3} \pi (2R)^3$

Force of attraction between spheres $= \dfrac{Gm_1 m_2}{r^2}$

$$= \frac{G\left[\left(\rho \frac{4}{3} \pi (R)^3\right)\left(\rho \frac{4}{3} \pi (2R)^3\right)\right]}{(3R)^2}$$

$$F = \frac{128}{81} G \pi^2 R^4 \rho^2$$

39. Consider a small element of the ring of mass dM, gravitational force between dM and m, distance x apart in figure i.e.

$$dF = \frac{G(dM)m}{x^2}$$

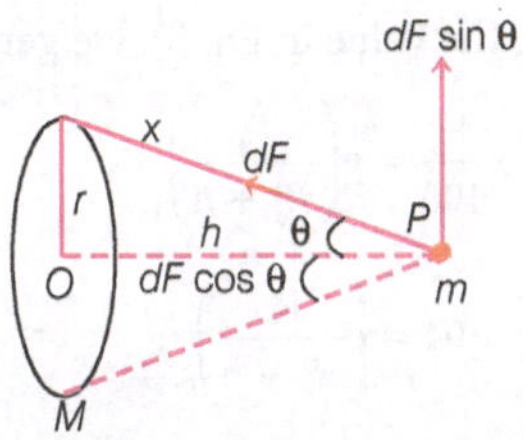

$d\mathbf{F}$ can be resolved into two rectangular components.

(i) $dF \cos\theta$ along PO and

(ii) $dF \sin\theta$ perpendicular to PO (given figure)

The total force (F) between the ring and mass (m) can be obtained by integrating the effects of all the elements forming the ring, whereas all the components perpendicular to PO cancel out, i.e. $\int dF \sin\theta = 0$, the component along PO add together to give F, i.e.

$$F = \int dF \cos\theta = \int \frac{G(dM)m}{x^2}\left(\frac{h}{x}\right) = \frac{Gmh}{x^3}\int dM$$

i.e. $F = \dfrac{GMmh}{(r^2 + h^2)^{3/2}}$ $\quad [\because \int dM = M$ and $x = (r^2 + h^2)^{1/2}]$

Since, $h = r$, $F = GMm\left(\dfrac{r}{2\sqrt{2}r^3}\right) = \dfrac{GMm}{2\sqrt{2}r^2}$

When h becomes $2r$, $F' = \dfrac{GMm(2r)}{(r^2 + 4r^2)^{3/2}} = \dfrac{2GMm}{5\sqrt{5}r^2}$

Thus, $\dfrac{F'}{F} = \left(\dfrac{2GMm}{5\sqrt{5}r^2}\right)\left(\dfrac{2\sqrt{2}r^2}{GMm}\right) = \dfrac{4\sqrt{2}}{5\sqrt{5}}$

40. Given that,

Mass of the sun, $M_s = 2 \times 10^{30}$ kg

Mass of the earth, $M_e = 6 \times 10^{24}$ kg

Distance between the centres of the sun and the earth, $r = 1.5 \times 10^{11}$ m

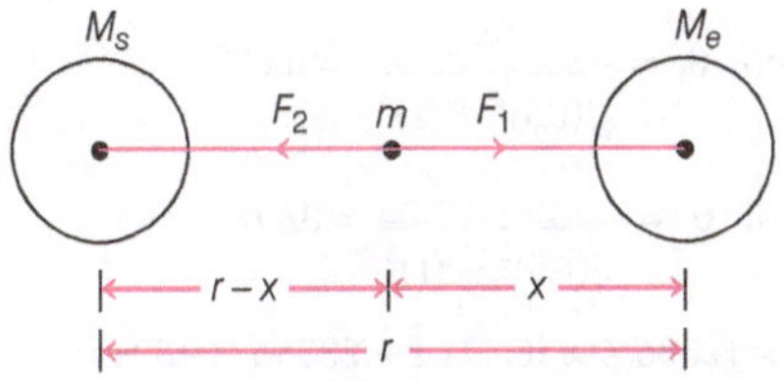

Let x be the distance of the required point from the centre of the earth. Clearly, at this, point the gravitational force (F_1) on the rocket of mass m due to the earth = gravitational force (F_2) on the rocket due to the sun, i.e. $F_1 = F_2$.

or $\dfrac{GmM_e}{x^2} = \dfrac{GmM_s}{(r-x)^2}$

or $\dfrac{(r-x)^2}{x^2} = \dfrac{M_s}{M_e} = \dfrac{2 \times 10^{30} \text{ kg}}{6 \times 10^{24} \text{ kg}} = \dfrac{10^6}{3}$

or $\dfrac{r-x}{x} = \dfrac{10^3}{\sqrt{3}}$ or $\dfrac{r}{x} - 1 = \dfrac{10^3}{\sqrt{3}}$

or $\dfrac{r}{x} = \dfrac{10^3}{\sqrt{3}} + 1 \approx \dfrac{10^3}{\sqrt{3}}$

or $x = \dfrac{\sqrt{3}r}{10^3} = \dfrac{1.732(1.5 \times 10^{11}) \text{ m}}{10^3}$

$= 2.6 \times 10^8$ m

41.

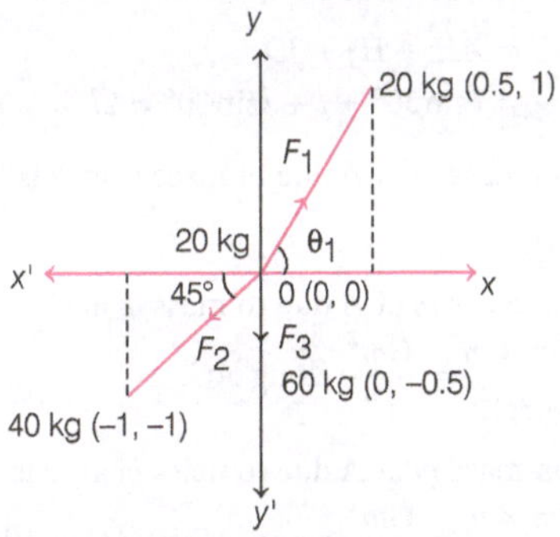

$m_1 = 20$ kg, $m_2 = 40$ kg,

$m_3 = 60$ kg, $m_4 = 20$ kg

The net force on 20 kg mass at origin is given by

$$\mathbf{F} = \mathbf{F}_1 + \mathbf{F}_2 + \mathbf{F}_3$$

$$= (F_1 \cos\theta_1 \hat{\mathbf{i}} + F_1 \sin\theta_1 \hat{\mathbf{j}}) + F_2 \cos 45°(-\hat{\mathbf{i}}) + F_2 \sin 45°(-\hat{\mathbf{j}}) + F_3(-\hat{\mathbf{j}})$$

Now, $F_1 = \dfrac{6.67 \times 10^{-11} \times 20 \times 20}{\sqrt{0.5^2 + (1)^2}} = 2386.4 \times 10^{-11}$ N

$F_2 = \dfrac{6.67 \times 10^{-11} \times 40 \times 20}{\sqrt{1^2 + 1^2}} = 3.773.69 \times 10^{-11}$ N

$F_3 = \dfrac{6.67 \times 10^{-11} \times 20 \times 60}{0.5} = 16008 \times 10^{-11}$ N

$$\cos\theta_1 = \frac{0.5}{\sqrt{(0.5)^2 + (1)^2}} = 0.447$$

$$\sin\theta_1 = \frac{1}{\sqrt{(0.5)^2 + (1)^2}} = 0.894$$

$$\therefore \mathbf{F} = (2386.4 \times 0.4471\,\hat{\mathbf{i}} + 2386.4 \times 0.894\,\hat{\mathbf{j}}$$

$$- 3773.69 \times \frac{1}{\sqrt{2}}\hat{\mathbf{i}} - 3773.69 \times \frac{1}{\sqrt{2}}\hat{\mathbf{j}} - 16008\,\hat{\mathbf{j}}) \times 10^{-11}\text{ N}$$

$$\therefore \quad |\mathbf{F}| = 3.2 \times 10^{-7}\text{ N}$$

42. Consider the diagram below, in which six point masses are placed at six vertices A, B, C, D, E and F.

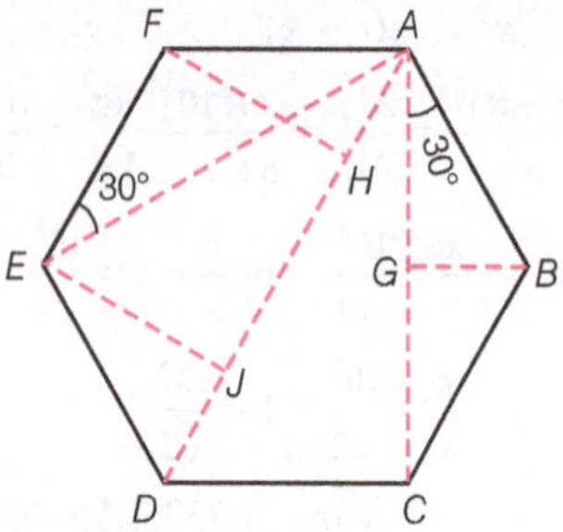

$$AC = AG + GC = 2AG$$
$$= 2l\cos 30° = 2l\sqrt{3}/2$$
$$= \sqrt{3}l = AE$$
$$AD = AH + HJ + JD$$
$$= l\sin 30° + l + l\sin 30° = 2l$$

Force on mass m at A due to mass m at B is, $f_1 = \dfrac{Gmm}{l^2}$ along AB.

Force on mass m at A due to mass m at C is,

$$f_2 = \frac{Gm \times m}{(\sqrt{3}l)^2} = \frac{Gm^2}{3l^2} \text{ along } AC. \qquad [\because AC = \sqrt{3}l]$$

Force on mass m at A due to mass m at D is,

$$f_3 = \frac{Gm \times m}{(2l)^2} = \frac{Gm^2}{4l^2} \text{ along } AD. [\because AD = 2l]$$

Force on mass m at A due to mass m at E is,

$$f_4 = \frac{Gm \times m}{(\sqrt{3}l)^2} = \frac{Gm^2}{3l^2} \text{ along } AE.$$

Force on mass m at A due to mass m at F is,

$$f_5 = \frac{Gm \times m}{l^2} = \frac{Gm^2}{l^2} \text{ along } AF.$$

Resultant force due to f_1 and f_5 is,

$$F_1 = \sqrt{f_1^2 + f_5^2 + 2f_1f_5\cos 120°} = \frac{Gm^2}{l^2} \text{ along } AD.$$

$$[\because \text{ Angle between } f_1 \text{ and } f_5 = 120°]$$

Resultant force due to f_2 and f_4 is,

$$F_2 = \sqrt{f_2^2 + f_4^2 + 2f_2f_4\cos 60°}$$

$$= \frac{\sqrt{3}Gm^2}{3l^2} = \frac{Gm^2}{\sqrt{3}l^2} \text{ along } AD.$$

So, net force along AD

$$= F_1 + F_2 + F_3 = \frac{Gm^2}{l^2} + \frac{Gm^2}{\sqrt{3}l^2} + \frac{Gm^2}{4l^2}$$

$$= \frac{Gm^2}{l^2}\left(1 + \frac{1}{\sqrt{3}} + \frac{1}{4}\right).$$

43. The acceleration due to gravity at height h is given as

$$g' = g\left(\frac{R_e}{R_e + h}\right)^2 \quad \text{...(i)}$$

As the g' becomes 4% of its value at surface of earth.

$$\therefore \quad g' = \frac{4g}{100}$$

Substituting the value in Eq. (i), we get

$$\frac{4g}{100} = g\left(\frac{R_e}{R_e + h}\right)^2$$

$$\Rightarrow \quad 0.04 = \left(\frac{R_e}{R_e + h}\right)^2$$

$$\Rightarrow \quad \frac{R_e}{R_e + h} = 0.2$$

$$\Rightarrow \quad h = 4R_e$$
$$h = 4 \times 6400\text{ km}$$
$$h = 25600 \text{ km}$$

44. Here, $d = 10$ km, $R_e = 6400$ km

Weight of body at depth d is given by

$$mg' = mg\left(1 - \frac{d}{R}\right)$$

% decrease in weight

$$= \frac{mg - mg'}{mg} \times 100 = \frac{d}{R} \times 100$$

$$= \frac{10}{6400} \times 100 = 0.15\%$$

45. Let the depth be d at which g becomes 1%

$$\text{or} \quad \frac{g}{100} = d$$

$$\text{Since,} \quad g' = g\left(1 - \frac{d}{R_e}\right)$$

$$\text{Given,} \quad g' = \frac{g}{100}$$

Also, $R_e = 6400$ km

$$\therefore \quad \frac{g}{100} = g\left(1 - \frac{d}{6400}\right)$$

$$\Rightarrow \quad \frac{d}{6400} = \frac{99}{100} \Rightarrow d = 64 \times 99 \text{ km}$$

$$d = 6336 \text{ km}$$

46. Given, $h = 8848$ m, $g = 9.8$ m/s^2

$R = 6400$ km

Let g' be the acceleration due to gravity on the Mount Everest.

$$\therefore \quad g' = g\left(1 - \frac{2h}{R}\right)$$

$$= 9.8\left(1 - \frac{2 \times 8848}{6400 \times 10^3}\right)$$

$$= 9.8\,(1 - 0.00276)$$

$$g' = 9.773 \text{ m/s}^2$$

47. Given, diameter of earth $= 12800$ km

Hence, radius, $R = \frac{12800}{2}$ km $= 6400$ km

Depth of ocean, $d = 7$ km

$$g = 9.8 \text{ m/s}^2$$

$$\because \quad g' = 9.8\left(1 - \frac{d}{R}\right)$$

$$\therefore \quad g' = 9.8\left(1 - \frac{7}{6400}\right)$$

$$g' = 9.789 \text{ m/s}^2$$

Hence, the value of g at the bottom of sea will be 9.789 m/s^2.

48. Let g_p and g_e are the accelerations due to gravity on poles and equator, respectively.

Radius of earth, $R = 6.37 \times 10^6$ m

Time period of rotation,

$$T = 1 \text{ day} = 86400 \text{ s}$$

$$= 8.64 \times 10^4 \text{ s}$$

Variation of g with latitude due to rotational motion of earth is given by

$$g' = g - \omega^2 R \cos^2 \phi$$

where, ϕ = latitude.

At pole, $\phi = 90°$

$$\therefore \quad g_p = g$$

and at equator, $\phi = 0°$

$$\therefore \quad g_e = g - \omega^2 R$$

So, difference in acceleration due to gravity will be

$$g_p - g_e = g - (g - \omega^2 R) = \omega^2 R$$

$$\Rightarrow \quad g_p - g_e = \left(\frac{2\pi}{T}\right)^2 R$$

$$= \left(\frac{2\pi}{8.64 \times 10^4}\right)^2 \times 6.37 \times 10^6$$

$$\therefore \quad g_p - g_e = 3.37 \times 10^{-2} \text{ m/s}^2$$

49. The acceleration due to gravity above the earth surface,

$$g' = g\left(\frac{R}{R+h}\right)^2$$

Given that $g' = \frac{36}{100} g$, $R = 6400$ km

$$\text{Hence, } \frac{36}{100} g = g\left(\frac{R}{R+h}\right)^2$$

$$\Rightarrow \quad \left(\frac{R}{R+h}\right)^2 = \frac{36}{100}$$

$$\frac{R}{R+h} = \frac{6}{10}$$

$$\Rightarrow \quad 10R = 6R + 6h$$

$$4R = 6h$$

$$h = \frac{4R}{6} = \frac{2}{3}R$$

$$= \frac{2}{3} \times 6400$$

$$h = 4267 \text{ km}$$

50. According to the question,

Kinetic energy of the body will be used for increasing its potential energy

$$\frac{1}{2}mv^2 = -\frac{GMm}{R+h} - \left(-\frac{GMm}{R}\right)$$

Given, $h = 10R$

$$\therefore \quad v^2 = 2\left[-\frac{GM}{11R} + \frac{GM}{R}\right]$$

$$v^2 = 2\left(\frac{10GM}{11R}\right)$$

$$v = \sqrt{\frac{20GM}{11R}}$$

51. Given, radius of the earth, $R = 6.67 \times 10^6$ m

Density, $\rho = 5.57 \times 10^3$ kgm^{-3}

$$G = 6.67 \times 10^{-11} \text{ Nm}^2/\text{kg}^2$$

$$\text{Volume, } V = \frac{4}{3}\pi R^3$$

$$\therefore \quad \text{Mass} = \rho V = \frac{4}{3}\pi R^3 \rho$$

$$\text{Potential} = -\frac{GM}{R} = -\frac{G}{R} \times \frac{4}{3}\pi R^3 \rho$$

$$= -\frac{4}{3} \times 6.67 \times 10^{-11} \times 3.14 \times (6.67 \times 10^6)^2 \times 5.57 \times 10^3$$

$$= -6.84 \times 10^7 \text{ J kg}^{-1}$$

52. Given that, the gravitational potential,

$$V = -5.12 \times 10^7 \text{ J/kg}$$

Mean radius, $R = 6400$ km

Let r be the distance of the given point from the centre of earth, then gravitational potential,

$$V = -\frac{GM}{r} = -5.12 \times 10^7 \text{ J/kg} \quad \text{...(i)}$$

and $$g = \frac{GM}{r^2} = 6.4 \text{ m/s}^2 \quad \text{...(ii)}$$

Dividing Eq. (i) by Eq. (ii), we get

$$r = \frac{5.12 \times 10^7}{6.4} = 8 \times 10^6 \text{ m} = 8000 \text{ km}$$

∴ Height of the point from earth's surface,

$$h = r - R = 8000 - 6400 = 1600 \text{ km}$$

53. Let A and B be the two given spheres and O be the mid-point on the line joining their centres.

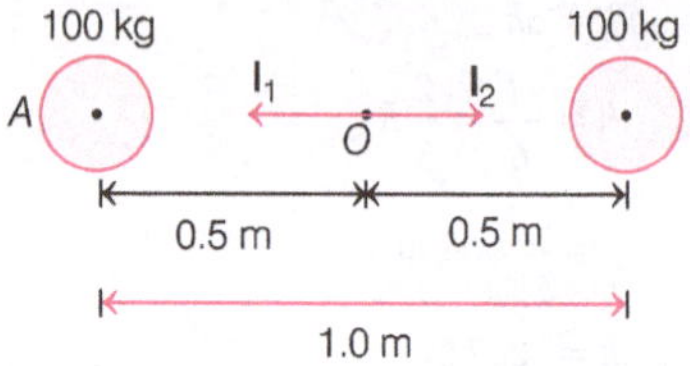

If $\mathbf{I}_1$ and $\mathbf{I}_2$ are the gravitational fields at O due to A and B respectively,

$$I_1 = \frac{G \times 100}{(0.5)^2}, \quad I_2 = \frac{G \times 100}{(0.5)^2}$$

Since, I_1 and I_2 are equal and opposite, then resultant gravitational field at O is zero.

If V is the gravitational potential at O due to A and B,

$$V = -\frac{G \times 100}{0.5} - \frac{G \times 100}{0.5} = -\frac{2G \times 100}{0.5}$$

or $$V = \frac{-2 \times 6.67 \times 10^{-11} \times 100}{0.5}$$

$$= -2.7 \times 10^{-8} \text{ J/kg}$$

The object placed at O is in equilibrium as there is no net force acting on the object. But it will be in an unstable equilibrium as once displaced from O, it will not come back to O.

54. Given, $g' = \frac{3}{5}g$

The value of g at equator is given by equation

$$g' = g - R\omega^2$$

Now, $\frac{3}{5}g = g - R\omega^2$

$$\therefore \quad R\omega^2 = \frac{2}{5}g \quad \text{... (i)}$$

and we know that, speed $v = \omega R$

$$\therefore \quad \omega = \frac{v}{R}$$

Now putting the value of ω in Eq. (i), we get

$$\frac{Rv^2}{R^2} = \frac{2}{5}g$$

$$\Rightarrow \quad \frac{v^2}{R} = \frac{2}{5}g$$

Speed, $v = \sqrt{\frac{2}{5}Rg} = \sqrt{\frac{2}{5} \times 6400 \times 9.8 \times 10^3}$

$$\approx 4.992 \text{ kms}^{-1} = 5 \text{ kms}^{-1}$$

55. We know that, orbital velocity,

$$v_o = \sqrt{\frac{GM}{R}}$$

and escape velocity, $v_e = \sqrt{\frac{2GM}{R}}$

$$\therefore \quad v_e = \sqrt{2}\, v_o$$

Percentage increase of velocity required to reach terminal or escape velocity

$$= \left(\frac{v_e - v_o}{v_o}\right) \times 100$$

$$= \frac{\sqrt{2}v_o - v_o}{v_o} \times 100 = 41.4\%$$

Hence, it is proved that the moon would depart forever, if its speed were raised by 42%.

56. From the figure,

BC is the crater of moon. B denotes bottom of crater.

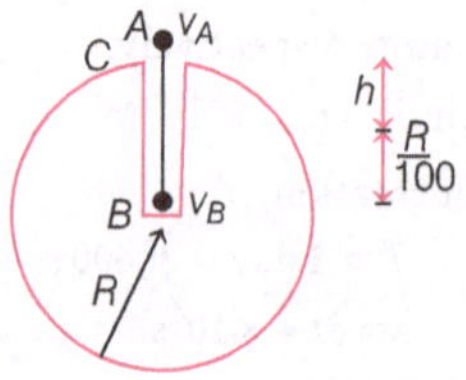

Depth of crater $= \frac{R}{100}$

Radius of moon $= R$

Escape velocity on surface of moon,

$$v_e = \sqrt{\frac{2GM}{R}}$$

At highest point, $v_A = 0$

Since, mechanical energy is conserved in the process.

∴ Decrease in kinetic energy $= \frac{1}{2}mv_B^2$

Increase in PE $= U_A - U_B$

Potential at A, $U_A = -\frac{GM}{R+h}$

where, h = height from surface

Potential at B, $U_B = -\frac{GM}{R^3}\left[\frac{3}{2}R^2 - \frac{1}{2}r^2\right]$ $[\because r = R - d]$

$$= -\frac{GM}{R^3}\left[1.5R^3 - 0.5\left(R - \frac{R}{100}\right)^2\right]$$

$$= -\frac{GM}{R}(1.01)$$

∴ Increase in

$$\text{PE} = -\frac{GMm}{R+h} + \frac{GMm}{R} \times (1.01)$$

∴ Decrease in KE = Increase in PE,

$$\frac{1}{2}mv_B^2 = -\frac{GMm}{R+h} + \frac{GMm}{R} \times 1.01$$

$$\frac{GM}{R} = GM\left[\frac{-1}{R+h} + \frac{1.01}{R}\right]$$

$$\frac{1}{R} = -\frac{1}{R+h} + \frac{1.01}{R}$$

$$\Rightarrow \quad h = 99.5R$$

$$\Rightarrow \quad h \approx 100R$$

57. According to law of conservation of mechanical energy

$$-\frac{GMm}{R} + \frac{1}{2}mv^2 = -\frac{GMm}{(R+R)}$$

$$\Rightarrow \quad \frac{1}{2}mv^2 = \frac{GMm}{R}\left(1 - \frac{1}{2}\right)$$

$$\Rightarrow \quad \frac{1}{2}mv^2 = \frac{GMm}{2R}$$

$$v = \sqrt{\frac{GM}{R}}$$

Now, we know that,

$$G = 6.67 \times 10^{-11}\,\text{Nm}^2\text{kg}^{-2}$$

$$R = 6400\text{ km}$$

$$M = 5.98 \times 10^{24}\text{ kg}$$

Putting these values,

$$v = \sqrt{\frac{6.67 \times 10^{-11} \times 5.98 \times 10^{24}}{6400 \times 10^3}}$$

$$= \sqrt{\frac{39.88}{64} \times 10^8} = 7.89\text{ kms}^{-1}$$

58. Here, $M_e = 9M_m, R_e = 2R_m$

Escape velocity, $v_e = 11.2$ km / s

Let v_m be the speed required to pull out of the gravitational force of mars.

$$v_e = \sqrt{\frac{2GM_e}{R_e}}$$

and $$v_m = \sqrt{\frac{2GM_m}{R_m}}$$

$$\frac{v_m}{v_e} = \sqrt{\frac{2GM_m}{R_m} \times \frac{R_e}{2GM_e}}$$

$$= \sqrt{\frac{M_m}{M_e} \times \frac{R_e}{R_m}}$$

$$= \sqrt{\frac{1}{9} \times 2}$$

$$= \frac{\sqrt{2}}{3}$$

$$\Rightarrow \quad v_m = \frac{\sqrt{2}}{3}v_e$$

$$= \frac{\sqrt{2}}{3} \times 11.2\text{ km / s}$$

$$= 5.28\text{ km / s}$$

59. The orbital velocity in a circular orbit,

$$v = \sqrt{gR}$$

The velocity required to escape,

$$v_e = \sqrt{2gR}$$

$$v_e - v = (\sqrt{2} - 1)\sqrt{gR}$$

$$= 0.414\sqrt{9.8 \times 6400 \times 10^3}$$

$$= 3278.71\text{ m/s} = 3.278\text{ km/s}$$

$$= 3.3\text{ km/s}$$

Hence, the additional velocity required = 3.3km/s

60. Here, mass of each star, $M = 2 \times 10^{30}$ kg

Radius of each star, $r = 10^7$ m

Initial potential energy of the stars when they are 10^{12} m apart $= -\frac{GM \times M}{10^{12}} = -\frac{GM^2}{10^{12}}$

[Distance between two stars = 10^{12} m]

When the stars are just going to collide, the distance between their centres = twice the radius of each star = $2r = 2 \times 10^7$ m

Final potential energy of the stars when they are about to collide $= -G\frac{M \times M}{2 \times 10^7} = -\frac{GM^2}{2 \times 10^7}$

Change in potential energy of stars

$$= -\frac{GM^2}{10^{12}} - \left(-\frac{GM^2}{2 \times 10^7}\right) = \frac{GM^2}{2 \times 10^7} - \frac{GM^2}{10^{12}}$$

$$\approx \frac{GM^2}{2 \times 10^7}\left[\text{as } \frac{GM^2}{10^{12}} << \frac{GM^2}{2 \times 10^7}\right] \quad \text{...(i)}$$

Let v be the speed of each star, just before colliding.

Final KE of the stars $= 2 \times \frac{1}{2}Mv^2 = Mv^2$

Initial KE of the stars = 0

(because when the stars are initially 10^{12} m apart, their speeds are negligible).

Change in KE of the stars $= Mv^2$ ...(ii)

Using the law of conservation of energy, from Eqs. (i) and (ii), we get $\frac{GM^2}{2\times 10^7} = Mv^2$

or $v = \sqrt{\frac{GM}{2\times 10^7}}$ or $v = \sqrt{\frac{6.67\times 10^{-11}\times(2\times 10^{30})}{2\times 10^7}}$

or $v = 2.6\times 10^6$ m/s

61. The two spheres exert gravitational forces on the projectile in mutually opposite directions. At the neutral point N, these two forces cancel out each other. If $ON = r$, then $\frac{GMm}{r^2} = \frac{G(4M)\,m}{(6R-r)^2}$

or $(6R-r)^2 = 4r^2 \Rightarrow 6R - r = \pm 2r$

or $r = 2R$ or $-6R$

The neutral point, $r = -6R$ is inadmissible.

$\therefore$ $ON = r = 2R$

It will be sufficient to project the particle m with a minimum speed v which enables it to reach the point N. Therefore, the particle m gets attracted by the gravitational pull of 4 M.

The total mechanical energy of m at surface of left sphere,

E_i = KE of m + PE due to left sphere + PE due to right sphere

$$= \frac{1}{2}mv^2 - \frac{GMm}{R} - \frac{4\,GMm}{5R}$$

At the neutral point, speed of the particle becomes zero. The energy is purely potential.

$\therefore E_N$ = PE due to left sphere + PE due to right sphere

$$= -\frac{GMm}{2R} - \frac{4GMm}{4R}$$

By conservation of mechanical energy, $E_i = E_N$

or $\frac{1}{2}mv^2 - \frac{GMm}{R} - \frac{4\,GMm}{5R} = -\frac{GMm}{2R} - \frac{4GMm}{4R}$

or $v^2 = \frac{2GM}{R}\left(\frac{4}{5} - \frac{1}{2}\right) = \frac{3GM}{5R}$

$\therefore$ $v = \sqrt{\frac{3GM}{5R}}$

62. Kinetic energy required for satellite to escape from earth's gravitational field,

$$KE_1 = \frac{1}{2}mv_e^2 = \frac{1}{2}m\left(\sqrt{\frac{2GM}{R}}\right)^2 = \frac{GMm}{2R}$$

Kinetic energy required for satellite to move in a circular orbit, $KE_2 = \frac{1}{2}mv_0^2 = \frac{1}{2}m\left(\sqrt{\frac{GM}{R}}\right)^2 = \frac{GMm}{2R}$

$\therefore$ $\frac{KE_1}{KE_2} = \frac{\frac{GM_m}{R}}{\frac{GM_m}{2R}} = 2$

$\therefore$ $\frac{KE_1}{KE_2} = 2$

63. For a satellite, we have

kinetic energy, $KE = \frac{GmM}{2R}$

and potential energy, $U = -\frac{GmM}{R}$

Total energy, $E_0 = KE + PE = \frac{GmM}{2R} - \frac{GmM}{R}$

$$E_0 = -\frac{GmM}{2R} = \frac{PE}{2} = \frac{U}{2}$$

$\therefore$ $U = 2E_0$

64. Given, two satellites A and B

Ratio of their masses, $m_A : m_B = 3:1$

Ratio of their radii, $r_A : r_B = 1:4$

We know that, mechanical energy, $E = -\frac{GMm}{2r}$

$\therefore$ $E \propto \frac{M}{r}$

Let E_A and E_B be the energy of satellites A and B, respectively, then

$$\frac{E_A}{E_B} = \frac{m_A}{m_B}\times\frac{r_B}{r_A} = \frac{3}{1}\times\frac{4}{1}$$

$$\frac{E_A}{E_B} = \frac{12}{1}$$

$\therefore$ $E_A : E_B = 12:1$

65. Here, $m = 400$ kg

$R_e = 6400\text{ km} = 6.4\times 10^6$ m

Initial total energy,

$$E_1 = PE + KE$$

$$= -\frac{GMm}{R} + \frac{1}{2}mv^2$$

$$= -\frac{GMm}{R} + \frac{1}{2}m\left(\frac{GM}{r}\right) = -\frac{GMm}{2r}$$

$$= -\frac{GMm}{2\times 2R_e} = -\frac{GMm}{4R_e}$$

Total energy, $E = -\frac{GMm}{2\times(4R_e)} = -\frac{GMm}{8R_e}$

The change in total energy, $\Delta E = E_f - E_i$

$$= -\frac{GM\,m}{8R_e} - \left(-\frac{GMm}{4R_e}\right)$$

$$= \frac{GMm}{8R_e} = \frac{GM}{(R_e)^2}\times\frac{mR_e}{8} = \frac{g_m mR_e}{8}$$

$$= \frac{9.81\times 400\times 6.4\times 10^6}{8} = 3.13\times 10^9\text{ J}$$

Thus, the energy required to transfer the satellite to the desired orbit $= 3.13 \times 10^9$ J

Decrease in KE,

$$= K_i - K_f = \frac{1}{2} m \left(\frac{GM}{2R_e}\right) - \frac{1}{2} m \left(\frac{GM}{4R_e}\right)$$

$$= \frac{GMm}{8R_E} = \frac{g\,m\,R_E}{8} = 3.13 \times 10^9 \text{ J}$$

Gain in PE $= U_f - U_i$

$$= -\frac{GMm}{4R_E} - \left(-\frac{GMm}{2R_e}\right) = \frac{GMm}{4R_E} = \frac{g\,m\,R_e}{4}$$

$$= 2 \times 3.13 \times 10^9 \text{ J} = 6.26 \times 10^9 \text{ J}$$

66. Let the distance of the satellite, $h = 896$ km

Orbital velocity is given by $v_o = \sqrt{\frac{GM}{R+h}}$

as $gR^2 = GM$

$$v_o = \sqrt{\frac{gR^2}{R+h}} = \sqrt{\frac{9.8 \times (6.4 \times 10^6)^2}{6.4 \times 10^6 + 896 \times 10^3}}$$

$$v_o = 7.417 \text{ km/s}$$

Period of revolution, $T = \frac{2\pi \times h}{v_o} = \frac{2 \times 3.14 \times 896 \times 10^3}{7417 \times 10^3}$

$$= 1 \text{ h } 43 \text{ min } 3 \text{ s}$$

67. Time period of the satellite is given by

$$T = 2\pi \sqrt{\frac{r}{g}}$$

Almost close to surface of earth, $r = R_e$

$\therefore$ Time period,

$$T = 2\pi \sqrt{\frac{R_e}{g}} = 2\pi \sqrt{\frac{6400 \times 10^3}{9.8}}$$

$$T = 5077 \text{ s} = \frac{5044}{3600} \text{ h}$$

$$T = 1.41 \text{ h}$$

68. Time period, $T = 2\pi \sqrt{\frac{r^3}{GM}}$

where, $r = R_e + h$

$$T = 1.5 \text{ h} = 1.5 \times 60 \times 60 = 5400 \text{ s}$$

$\therefore$ $T = 2\pi \sqrt{\frac{(R+h)^3}{gR^2}}$ as

$$GM = gR^2 \Rightarrow R + h = \left[\frac{gR^2T^2}{2\pi^2}\right]^{1/3}$$

$$R + h = \left[\frac{9.8 \times (6400 \times 10^3)^2 \times (5400)^2}{2 \times (3.14)^2}\right]^{1/3}$$

$$R + h = 6668 \text{ km}$$

$$h = 6668 - 6400 = 268 \text{ km}$$

69. In figure, $AP = BP\sqrt{(0.08)^2 + (0.06)^2} = 0.1$ m

Here, $m_1 = 6.4 \text{ kg} = m_2$

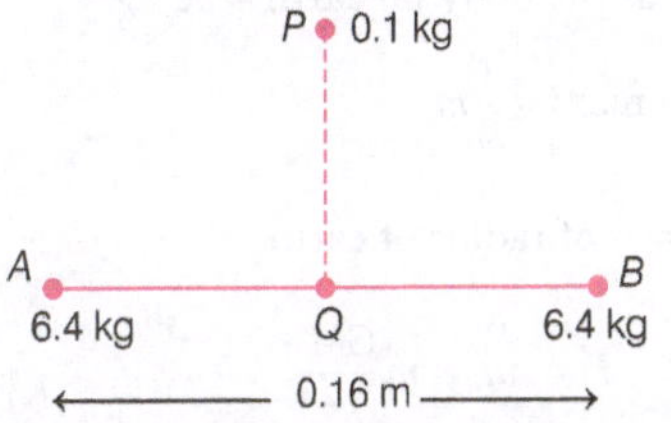

$$m_3 = 0.1 \text{ kg}$$

(i) When body falls from P to Q, the gain in KE of body equals to loss in PE of the system.

$$\therefore \frac{1}{2} m_3 v^2 = -\left[\frac{Gm_1m_2}{0.1} + \frac{Gm_2m_3}{0.1}\right] + \left[\frac{Gm_1m_3}{0.08} + \frac{Gm_2m_3}{0.08}\right]$$

or $$\frac{1}{2} v^2 = -\left[\frac{Gm_1}{0.1} + \frac{Gm_2}{0.1}\right] + \left[\frac{Gm_1}{0.08} + \frac{Gm_2}{0.08}\right]$$

$$v^2 = -2 \times G\left[\left(\frac{6.4}{0.1} + \frac{6.4}{0.1}\right) - \left(\frac{6.4}{0.08} + \frac{6.4}{0.08}\right)\right]$$

$$= -2 \times (6.67 \times 10^{-11}) \times (-32)$$

$$v = [64 \times 6.67 \times 10^{-11}]^{1/2} = 6.53 \times 10^{-5} \text{ m/s}$$

(ii) When the body of mass 0.1 kg is at point P,

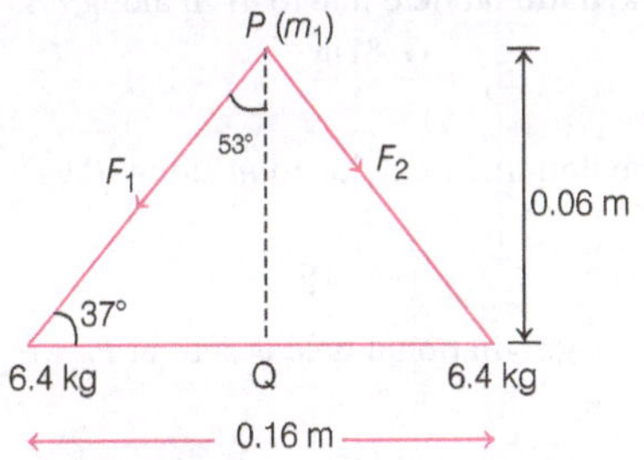

$$F_1 = F_2 = \frac{Gm_1m_2}{(0.1)^2}$$

$$= \frac{6.67 \times 0.1 \times 6.4 \times 10^{-11}}{(0.1)^2} = 426.88 \times 10^{-11} \text{ N}$$

$$\therefore \quad F_P = \sqrt{F_1^2 + F_2^2 + 2F_1F_2\cos(2 \times 53°)}$$

$$= 2F_1 \cos 53° = 2 \times 426.88 \times 10^{-11} \times \frac{0.08}{0.1}$$

$$= 683 \times 10^{-11} \text{ N}$$

$\therefore$ Acceleration at P, $a_P = \frac{F_P}{m} = 683 \times \frac{10^{-11}}{0.1}$

$$= 6.83 \times 10^{-8} \text{ m/s}^2$$

When the body of mass 0.1 kg is at point Q, then net force at Q, $F_Q = F_1 - F_2 = 0$ $[\because F_1 = F_2]$

$\therefore$ Acceleration at Q, $a_Q = \frac{F_Q}{m} = \frac{0}{0.1} = 0$

70. Weight of the body on earth = 90 kg

Mass on mars $= \frac{1}{9}m$

Radius $= \frac{1}{2}$ of radius of earth

$$\therefore \quad F = mg = m\frac{GM}{R_e^2}$$

$$\frac{F_{mars}}{F_{earth}} = \frac{m[GM/R_e^2]_{mars}}{m[GM/R_e^2]_{earth}}$$

$$\frac{F_{mars}}{90\text{kg}} = \frac{M_{earth}/9}{M_{earth}} \times \frac{(R_{earth})^2}{(R_{earth}/2)^2} = \frac{4}{9}$$

$$F_{mars} = 90 \times \frac{4}{9} = 40\,\text{kg}$$

Therefore, mass of body on mars is 40 kg.

71.

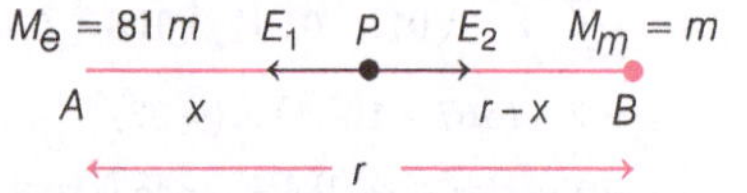

Let gravitational field be zero at distance x from A at P

Gravitational field due to 81 m along PA,

$$E_1 = \frac{G\cdot 81m}{x^2}$$

Gravitational field due to m along PB,

$$E_2 = \frac{G\cdot m}{(r-x)^2}$$

Since, gravitational field is zero at P,

$$\therefore \quad E_1 = E_2$$

$$\frac{81Gm}{x^2} = \frac{Gm}{(r-x)^2} \Rightarrow \frac{9}{x} = \frac{1}{r-x}$$

$$\Rightarrow \quad 9r - 9x = x$$

$$x = \frac{9r}{10} = \frac{9 \times 3.8 \times 10^5}{10} = 3.42 \times 10^5\,\text{km}$$

72. Consider the diagram in the question

Given, mass of the earth, $M = 6 \times 10^{24}$ kg

Radius of the earth, $R = 6400\,\text{km} = 6.4 \times 10^6$ m

Time period, $T = 24\text{ h} = 24 \times 60 \times 60 = 86400$ s

$G = 6.67 \times 10^{-11}\ \text{N-m}^2/\text{kg}^2$

(i) Time period, $T = 2\pi\sqrt{\frac{(R+h)^3}{GM}}$

$$\left[\because v_o = \sqrt{\frac{GM}{R+h}} \text{ and } T = \frac{2\pi(R+h)}{v_o}\right]$$

$$\Rightarrow \quad T^2 = 4\pi^2\frac{(R+h)^3}{GM} \Rightarrow (R+h)^3 = \frac{T^2GM}{4\pi^2}$$

$$\Rightarrow \quad R+h = \left(\frac{T^2GM}{4\pi^2}\right)^{1/3} \Rightarrow h = \left(\frac{T^2GM}{4\pi^2}\right)^{1/3} - R$$

$$\Rightarrow h = \left[\frac{(24 \times 60 \times 60)^2 \times 6.67 \times 10^{-11} \times 6 \times 10^{24}}{4 \times (3.14)^2}\right]^{1/3} - 6.4 \times 10^6$$

$$= 4.23 \times 10^7 - 6.4 \times 10^6 = (42.3 - 6.4) \times 10^6$$

$$= 35.9 \times 10^6 \text{ m} = 3.59 \times 10^7 \text{ m}$$

(ii) If satellite is at height h from the earth's surface, then according to the diagram,

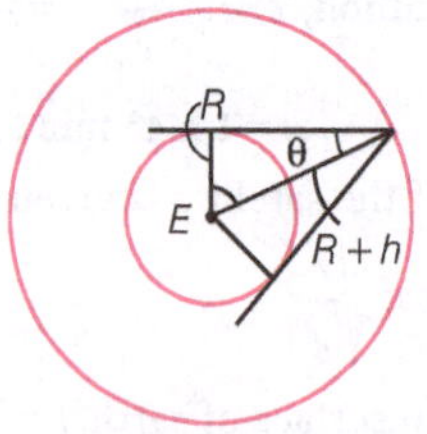

$$\cos\theta = \frac{R}{R+h} = \frac{1}{\left(1+\frac{h}{R}\right)} = \frac{1}{1+\left(\frac{3.59 \times 10^7}{6.4 \times 10^6}\right)}$$

$$= \frac{1}{1+5.61} = \frac{1}{6.61} = 0.513 = \cos 81°18'$$

$$\therefore \quad 2\theta = 2 \times (81°18') = 162°36'$$

If n is the number of satellites needed to cover entire earth then, $n = \frac{360°}{2\theta} = \frac{360°}{162°36'} = 2.31$

$\therefore$ Minimum 3 satellites are required to cover entire earth.

QR Code for Quick Test 1	QR Code for Quick Test 2	QR Code for Quick Test 3

SELF ASSESSMENT TEST

Multiple Choice Questions (MCQs)

1. If both the mass and radius of the earth, each decreased by 50%, the acceleration due to gravity would
(a) remain same (b) decrease by 50%
(c) decrease by 100% (d) increase by 100%

2. A satellite goes along an elliptical path around the earth. The rate of change of area swept by the line joining earth and the satellite is proportional to
(a) $r^{\frac{1}{2}}$ (b) r
(c) $r^{\frac{3}{2}}$ (d) r^2

3. Two bodies of mass m and $4m$ are placed at a distance r. The gravitational potential at a point on the line joining them where the gravitational field is zero, is
(a) zero (b) $-\frac{4Gm}{r}$
(c) $-\frac{6Gm}{r}$ (d) $-\frac{9Gm}{r}$

4. A particle falls from infinity to the earth. Its velocity on reaching the earth surface is
(a) $2Rg$ (b) $\sqrt{Rg}$
(c) $\sqrt{2Rg}$ (d) Rg

5. Match the Column I (quantities) with Column II (approximate values/direction) and select the correct answer from the options given below.

	Column I		Column II
A.	Direction of motion of polar satellite	P.	35800 km
B.	Direction of motion of geo-stationary satellite	Q.	West-East
C.	Height above the surface of the earth for polar satellite	R.	512 km
D.	Height above the surface of the earth for geostationary satellite	S.	North-South

(a) A-Q, B-S, C-P, D-R
(b) A-P, B-R, C-Q, D-S
(c) A-R, B-P, C-S, D-Q
(d) A-S, B-Q, C-R, D-P

6. For which of the following does the graph denote the variation of force of gravity F along a distance r?

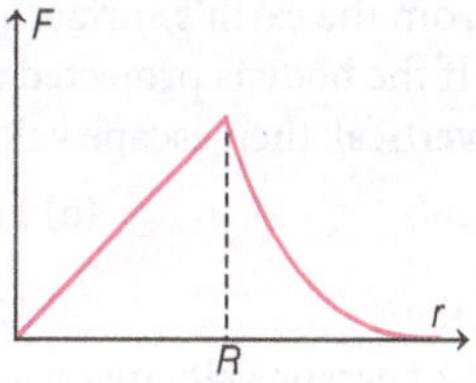

(a) Solid sphere (b) Spherical shell
(c) Plate (d) Point

Assertion-Reason

Directions *(Q.No. 7-8) In the following questions, two statements are given- one labelled Assertion (A) and the other labelled Reason (R). Select the correct answer to these questions from the codes (a), (b), (c) and (d) as given below.*

(a) Both Assertion and Reason are true and Reason is the correct explanation of Assertion.
(b) Both Assertion and Reason are true but Reason is not the correct explanation of Assertion.
(c) Assertion is true but Reason is false.
(d) Assertion is false but Reason is true.

7. **Assertion** (A) In the satellite, everything inside it is in a state of free fall.
Reason (R) Every part and parcel of the satellite has zero acceleration.

8. **Assertion** (A) If earth suddenly stops rotating about its axis, then the value of acceleration due to gravity will become same at all places.
Reason (R) The value of acceleration due to gravity is independent of rotation of earth.

Case Based Question

Directions *(Q.No. 9) This question is case study based question. Read the following paragraph and answer the questions on the basis of same.*

9. If we throw a ball vertically upwards from the surface of the earth; it rises to a certain height and falls back. If we throw it with a greater velocity, it rises to a greater height. If we throw it with a sufficient velocity, it may

never come back. It will escape from the gravitational pull of the earth. This minimum velocity is called escape velocity.

(i) Escape speed of a body of mass m depends upon its mass as

(a) m^0 (b) m (c) m^2 (d) m^3

(ii) The escape velocity for an object projected vertically upward from the earth's surface is approx 11 km/s. If the body is projected at an angle of 45° with the vertical, then escape velocity will be

(a) $\frac{11}{\sqrt{2}}$ km/s (b) 11 km/s

(c) $11\sqrt{2}$ km/s (d) 22 km/s

(iii) The value of escape velocity on a certain planet is 2 km/s. Then, the value of orbital speed of a satellite orbiting close to its surface is

(a) 12 km/s (b) 1 km/s

(c) $\sqrt{2}$ km/s (d) $2\sqrt{2}$ km/s

(iv) The escape speed of the planet is v. If the radius of the planet contracts to $\frac{1}{4}$th of present value, without any change in mass, the escape speed would become

(a) halved (b) doubled

(c) quadrupled (d) one-fourth

Very Short Answer Type Questions

10. Work done in moving a particle round a closed path under the action of gravitational force is zero. Why?

11. Does the concentration of the earth's mass near its centre change the variation of g with height compared with a homogeneous sphere, how?

12. What is the gravitational potential energy of a body at height h from the earth surface?

13. The escape speed on the earth is 11.2 km/s. What is its value for a planet having double the radius and eight times the mass of the earth?

Short Answer Type Questions

14. Derive an expression for work done against gravity.

15. A mass M is broken into two parts, m and $(M - m)$. How is m related to M, so that the gravitational force between two parts is maximum?

16. Calculate the change in the energy of a 500 kg satellite, when it falls from an altitude of 200 km to 199 km. If this change takes place during one orbit. Calculate the retarding force on the satellite.
Given, mass of the earth $= 6 \times 10^{24}$ kg and radius of the earth $= 6400$ km

Long Answer Type Question

17. If one satellite of Jupiter has an orbital period of 1.769 days and the radius of the orbit is 4.22×10^8 m. Show that the mass of jupiter is about one-thousandth that of the sun.

Answers

1. (d) *2.* (a) *3.* (d) *4.* (c) *5.* (d)
6. (a) *7.* (c) *8.* (c)
9. (i) (a), (ii) (b),(iii) (c), (iv) (b)

08

CHAPTER

Mechanical Properties of Solids

The materials having a definite shape and volume are known as solids or rigid bodies. But in reality, these bodies can be deformed by applying force on them. Our aim is to study these materials under loads or forces and their mechanical properties. e.g. Elasticity, plasticity, stress and strain etc., in this chapter.

YOUR STUDY GOALS

- 8.1 Stress
- 8.2 Strain
- 8.3 Hooke's Law
- 8.4 Elastic Modulus
- 8.5 Elastic Potential Energy in a Stretched Wire

YOUR PRACTICE GOAL

- Objective Type Questions (27 Qs, MCQs, A-R, Matching)
- Case Based Questions (4)
- Subjective Questions (7 VSAs, 8 SAs, 4 LAs)
- Numerical Problems (16)

Elastic Body and Elasticity

A body that returns into its original shape and size after the removal of the deforming forces is called an **elastic body.** e.g. Rubber bands, springs, bungee cords, etc.

The property of a body by virtue of which it regains its original shape and size after removal of the deforming forces is called **elasticity**. e.g. If we stretch a spring and release, then it will regain its original size.

Note A **deforming force** is an external force that causes a change in the shape or size of an object. For example, a mild steel rod can be stretched, compressed or bent by applying a deforming force.

Plastic Body and Plasticity

A body that does not regain its original shape and size after the removal of the deforming forces is called a **plastic body.** e.g. Putty, paraffin wax, mud, etc.

The property by virtue of which a body does not restore its natural shape and size after removal of the applied forces is called **plasticity**. e.g. If we stretch a piece of chewing gum and release, it will not regain its original shape and size.

- All rigid bodies are elastic to some extent, which means we can change their dimensions slightly by pulling or pushing them.
- No body is perfectly elastic or perfectly plastic.
- When the elastic behaviour of a body decreases, its plastic behaviour increases.

8.1 Stress

When a body is subjected to a deforming force, an internal restoring force is developed in the body. **This restoring force acting per unit area of a deformed body is called stress.**

$$\text{Stress} = \frac{\text{Restoring force}\,(F)}{\text{Area of cross-section}\,(A)}$$

In equilibrium, the restoring force is equal in magnitude but opposite in direction to the applied force. Thus, quantitatively, stress can be given as

$$\text{Stress, } S = \frac{\text{External deforming force}}{\text{Area of cross-section}}$$

- Its **SI unit** is N/m^2 or **pascal** (Pa).
- The **dimensional formula** of stress is $[ML^{-1}T^{-2}]$.
- Stress is not a vector quantity but a **tensor quantity**.
- The effect of stress is to produce distortion or change in size, volume and shape (i.e. configuration of the body).

Types of Stress

1. Normal or Longitudinal Stress
2. Tangential or Shearing Stress
3. Hydraulic or Bulk Stress

1. Normal or Longitudinal Stress

It is defined as the restoring force per unit area, acting perpendicular to the surface of the body.

It is of two types

(i) Tensile Stress

If the length of a body is increased in the direction of applied force, then the induced stress is called **tensile stress.**

Consider a cylinder of length L, stretched by two equal forces F applied normal to its cross-sectional area A as shown in Fig. (a).The increase in the length of rod is ΔL.

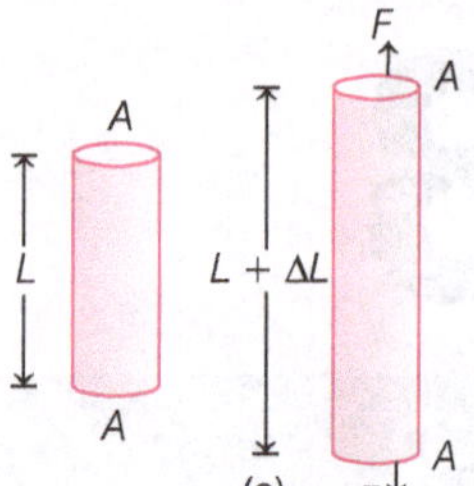

(a)

Tensile stress on a circular rod

A restoring force equal to the applied force F normal to the cross-sectional area A of the rod comes into existence, then the tensile stress is given by

$$\text{Tensile stress} = \frac{F}{A}$$

(ii) Compressive Stress

When the length of a body is decreased due to applied force, the induced stress is called **compressive stress.**

Consider a cylinder of length L, compressed by two equal forces F applied normal to its cross-sectional area A as shown in Fig. (b). The decrease in the length of rod is ΔL .

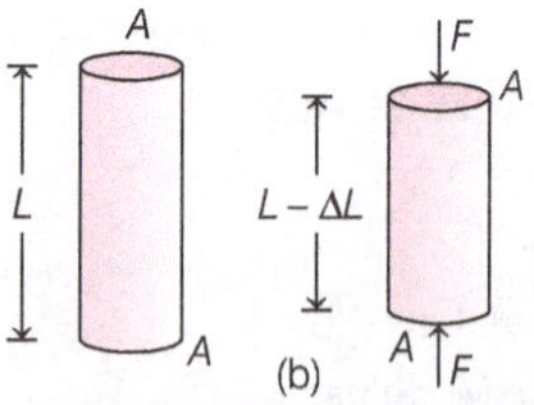

(b)

Compressive stress on a circular rod

A restoring force equal to the applied force F normal to the cross-sectional area A of the rod comes into existence. Then, the compressive stress is given by

$$\text{Compressive stress} = \frac{F}{A}$$

2. Tangential or Shearing Stress

When a deforming force acts tangentially to a body's surface, it changes the body's shape without affecting its volume. This tangential force applied per unit area of cross-section is known as **tangential stress.**

$$\text{Tangential stress} = \frac{F}{A}$$

In case of tangential stress, the deforming force F is applied on top surface of a cylinder in tangential direction due to which the upper face is deformed by an angle θ from its original position as shown in Fig. (c).

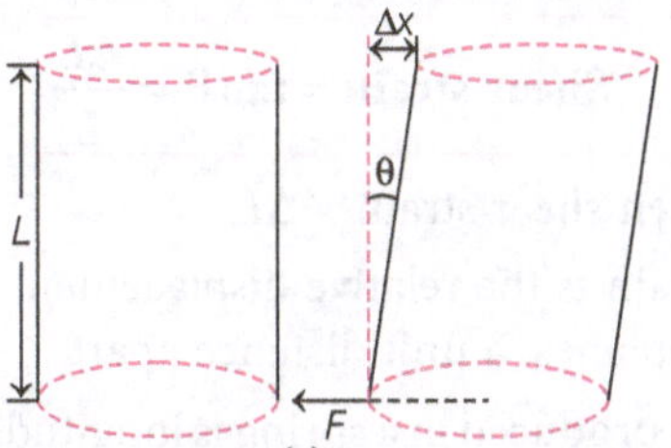

(c)
A body subjected to shearing stress

3. Hydraulic or Bulk Stress

If a body is subjected to a uniform force from all sides, then the corresponding stress is called **hydraulic stress** or **Bulk stress.**

$$\text{Hydraulic or Bulk stress} = \frac{F}{A}$$

- Due to bulk stress, the volume of the body changes but the geometrical shape remains the same.
- The hydraulic stress is equal to magnitude of the hydraulic pressure on the surface.
- It is also known as **volumetric stress.**

In case of hydraulic stress, the force F is applied perpendicular to every point on the surface of body due to which the change in volume ΔV of a body occurred.

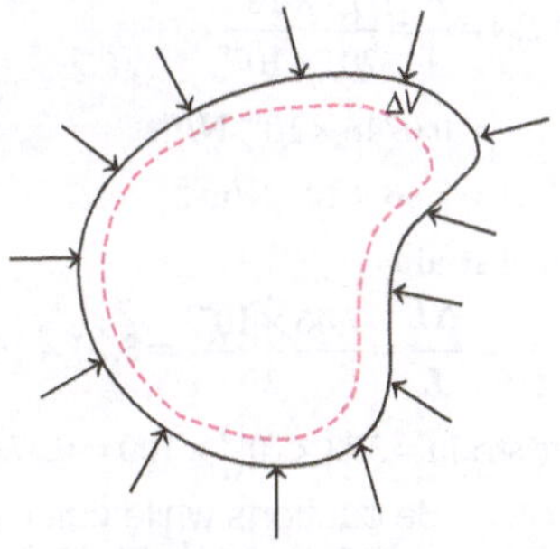

Example 1 **Calculate the value of stress in a wire of steel having radius of 2 mm when 10 kN of force is applied on it.**

Sol. Given, force, $F = 10\text{ kN} = 10^4\text{ N}$

Radius, $r = 2\text{ mm} = 2\times10^{-3}\text{ m}$

Area, $A = \pi r^2 = \pi \times (2\times10^{-3})^2$

$$= 12.56\times10^{-6}\text{ m}^2$$

$$\text{Stress} = \frac{\text{Force}}{\text{Area}} = \frac{10^4}{12.56\times10^{-6}}$$

$$= 0.0796\times10^{10} = 7.96\times10^8\text{ N/m}^2$$

Example 2 **A man carrying mass $M = 125$ kg makes a flying tackle at $v_1 = 4$ m/s on a stationary quarterback of mass $m = 85$ kg and his helmet makes solid contact with quarterback's femur.**

(i) What is the final speed of two athletes immediately after contact and also determine the average force exerted on the quarterback's femur, when last collision occur at 0.1 s?

(ii) If area of cross-section of quarterback's femur is $5\times10^{-4}\text{ m}^2$, then estimate the shear stress exerted on femur in the collision.

Sol. (i) Given, $M = 125$ kg, $v_1 = 4$ m/s, $m = 85$ kg

Applying conservation of linear momentum, we get

$$p_{\text{initial}} = p_{\text{final}}, \text{ i.e. } Mv_i = (M+m)v_f$$

The value of final speed,

$$v_f = \frac{Mv_i}{M+m} = \frac{125\times4}{(125+85)} = 2.38\text{ m/s}$$

(ii) Average force exerted to the quarterback's femur,

So, $F_{av}\times\Delta t = M(v_f - v_i)$

i.e. $$F_{av} = \frac{M(v_f - v_i)}{\Delta t}$$

$$= \frac{125\,(4-2.38)}{0.1}$$

$$= \frac{125\times162}{0.1} = 2.025\times10^3\text{ N}$$

$$\text{Shearing stress} = \frac{F}{A} = \frac{2.025\times10^3}{5\times10^{-4}}$$

$$= 4.05\times10^6\text{ Pa}$$

Mistake Alert *Student generally confuses between the units Pascal (Pa) and N/m². Remember Pascal is equivalent to N/m².*

8.2 Strain

If a deforming force acts on a body, the body undergoes a change in its shape and size. The ratio of the change in size or shape of an object to the original size or shape is called **strain.**

$$\text{Strain} = \frac{\text{Change in size or shape}}{\text{Original size or shape}}$$

The strain is the ratio of two like quantities, i.e. the change in dimension to the original dimension, so it has no unit or dimensional formula.

Types of Strain

- 1. Longitudinal Strain
- 2. Volumetric Strain
- 3. Shear Strain

1. Longitudinal Strain

It is defined as the change in length per unit original length, when the body is deformed by external forces.

$$\text{Longitudinal strain} = \frac{\text{Change in length}}{\text{Original length}} = \frac{\Delta L}{L}$$

2. Volumetric Strain

It is defined as the change in volume per unit original volume, when the body is deformed by external forces.

$$\text{Volumetric strain} = \frac{\text{Change in volume}}{\text{Original volume}} = \frac{\Delta V}{V}$$

3. Shear Strain

If the deforming forces produce a change in the shape of the body, then the strain is called shear strain.

Within elastic limit, it is measured by the ratio of the relative displacement of one plane to its distance from the fixed plane. It can also be measured by the angle through which a line is originally perpendicular to the fixed plane as given below.

Illustration to Show Shear Strain

Consider a cubical body which gets deformed under the effect of tangential force F.

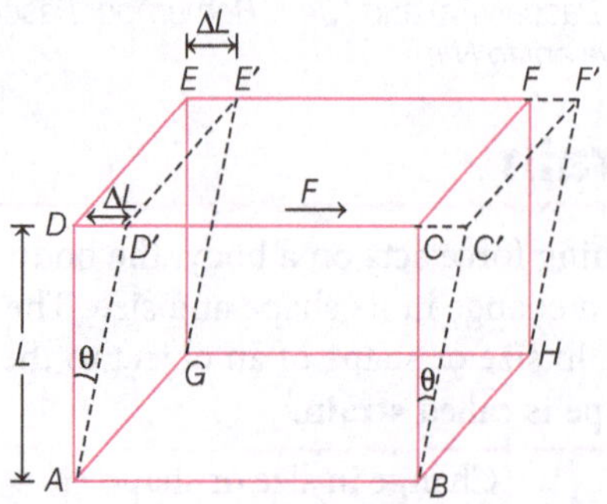

Shear strain

The vertical planes $ADEG$ and $BCFH$ are laterally shifted to positions $AD'E'G$ and $BC'F'H$, respectively through an angle θ. If $AD = L$ and $EE' = \Delta L$ (change in perpendicular distance of the displaced surface from the fixed surface $ADEG$).

The angle θ is called **angle of shear.**

$$\textbf{Shear strain} = \tan\theta = \frac{\Delta L}{L}$$

If $L = 1\,\text{m}$, then shear strain $= \Delta L$.

So, shear strain is the relative displacement between two parallel planes, a unit distance apart.

- The strain produced in a spring is longitudinal as well as shear, if the spring is stretched by suspending a load at its free end.
- The strain persists even when the stress is removed and thus lags behind the stress.

Example 3 **Consider a steel rod having radius of 8 mm and the length of 2 m. If a force of 150 kN stretches it along its length, then calculate the stress and percentage strain in the rod, if the elongation in length is 7.46 mm.**

Sol. If the rod stretches along its length, then the stress produced is the tensile stress, whereas the strain produced is longitudinal strain.

Given, radius, $r = 8\text{ mm} = 8 \times 10^{-3}\text{m}$, length, $L = 2\text{ m}$

Force, $F = 150\text{ kN} = 15 \times 10^4\text{ N}$

Area, $A = \pi r^2 = \pi \times (8 \times 10^{-3})^2 = 201 \times 10^{-6}\text{ m}^2$

$\Delta L = 7.46\text{ mm} = 7.46 \times 10^{-3}\text{ m}$,

Percentage strain = ?

$$\text{Tensile stress} = \frac{F}{A} = \frac{15 \times 10^4}{201 \times 10^{-6}}$$
$$= 0.0746 \times 10^{10}\text{ N/m}^2$$
$$= 7.46 \times 10^8\text{ N/m}^2$$

Longitudinal strain

$$= \frac{\Delta L}{L} = \frac{7.46 \times 10^{-3}}{2} = 3.73 \times 10^{-3}$$

Percentage strain $= 3.73 \times 10^{-3} \times 100 = 0.373\,\%$

Mistake Alert Be cautions while calculating strain. "Strain = Change/Original, Not Final/Original!"

Example 4 **Consider a solid cube which is subjected to a pressure of $6 \times 10^5\ \text{N/m}^2$. Due to this pressure, each side of the cube is shortened by 2%. Find out the volumetric strain of the cube.**

Sol. Let L be the initial length of the each side of the cube.

Volume, $V = L \times L \times L = L^3$

$= \text{Initial volume } (V_i \text{ say})$

If the each side of the cube is shortened by 2%, then final length of the cube $= L - 2\%$ of L

$$= \left(L - \frac{2L}{100}\right) = L\left(1 - \frac{2}{100}\right)$$

$\therefore$ Final volume, $V_f = L^3\left(1-\frac{2}{100}\right)^3 = V\left(1-\frac{2}{100}\right)^3$

Change in volume, $\Delta V = V_f - V_i$

$$= V\left(1-\frac{2}{100}\right)^3 - V$$

$$= V\left[\left(1-\frac{2}{100}\right)^3 - 1\right]$$

$$\frac{\Delta V}{V} = \left(1-\frac{2}{100}\right)^3 - 1 \simeq \left[1-\frac{2\times 3}{100}\right] - 1$$

$[\because (1-x)^n \simeq 1 - nx \text{ for } x << 1]$

$\therefore$ Volumetric strain

$$= \frac{\Delta V}{V} = 1 - 0.06 - 1$$

$= 0.06$ (take positive sign)

Example 5 **If the angle of shear is 30° for a cubical body and the change in length is 250 cm, then what must be the volume of this cubical body?**

Sol. Given, angle of shear = 30°

and change in length, $\Delta L = 250\text{cm} = 2.5 \text{ m}$

$\therefore$ Shear strain, $\tan\theta = \frac{\Delta L}{L} \Rightarrow \tan 30° = \frac{2.5}{L}$

$$L = \frac{2.5}{\tan 30°}$$

$$= \frac{2.5}{0.577} = 4.332 \text{ m}$$

Volume, $V = L^3 = 81.295 \text{ m}^3$

8.3 Hooke's Law

Hooke's law states that,

Within elastic limit, the stress developed is directly proportional to the strain produced in a body.

i.e. Stress ∝ Strain ⇒ Stress = E × Strain

or
$$E = \frac{\text{Stress}}{\text{Strain}}$$

where, E is a constant and is known as **modulus of elasticity** of the material of the body.

TEACHER TIP

To apply Hooke's Law, remember :

"Force proportional to extension, within limits"

This law is applicable to all type of deformation such as compression, bending, twisting etc.

Example 6 **After a fall, a 95 kg rock climber finds himself dangling from the end of a rope that had been 15 m long and 9.6 mm in diameter but has stretched by 2.8 cm. For the rope, calculate**

(i) the strain

(ii) the stress

(iii) the modulus of elasticity

Sol. Given, $L = 1500$ cm is the unstretched length of the rope, $\Delta L = 2.8$ cm is the amount of stretched length.

(i) The strain $= \frac{\Delta L}{L} = \frac{2.8 \text{ cm}}{1500 \text{ cm}} = 1.9 \times 10^{-3}$

(ii) Stress = Force / Area

Force, F = force of gravity on the rock climber

$= mg = 95 \times 9.8$ N

Area, $A = \pi r^2 = \pi \times \left(\frac{D}{2}\right)^2 = \pi \times \left(\frac{9.6}{2} \times 10^{-3} \text{ m}\right)^2$

$$\text{Stress} = \frac{95 \times 9.8}{\pi \times (4.8)^2 \times 10^{-6}} \simeq 1.3 \times 10^7 \text{ N/m}^2$$

(iii) Modulus of elasticity, $E = \frac{\text{Stress}}{\text{Strain}} = \frac{1.3 \times 10^7}{1.9 \times 10^{-3}}$

$= 6.84 \times 10^9 \text{ N/m}^2$

Stress *versus* Strain Curve

When a wire is stretched by a load as in Fig. (a), it is seen that for small value of load, the extension produced in the wire is proportional to the load.

Hence, stress ∝ strain

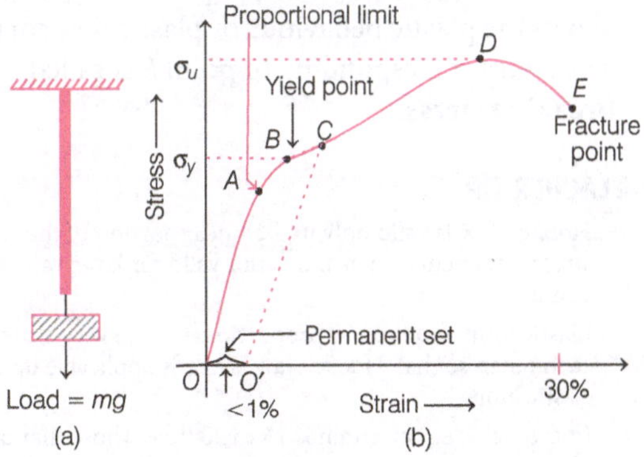

A typical stress-strain curve

The figure given above represents a **stress *versus* strain graph.**

(i) **In region *OA***, the stress is proportional to the strain upto point A (**point of proportional limit**). Thus, Hooke's law is entirely obeyed in this region.

(ii) **In region *AB***, stress is not proportional to strain but the wire still returns to its original dimension when the load is removed.

(iii) The point B in the curve is known as **yield point** (also known as **elastic limit**) and the corresponding stress is known as **yield strength** (σ_y) of the material.

- The material of the wire in the **region** OB shows the elastic behaviour, hence known as **elastic region.**

(iv) In **region** BC, if the load is increased further, the stress developed exceeds the yield strength and strain increases rapidly even for a small change in the stress.

Now, if the load is removed, the wire does not regain its original length, but the increase in the length of the wire is permanent.

In other words, there is a permanent strain equals to OO' even when the stress is zero. This permanent strain in the wire is known as **permanent set**.

(v) Now, as the stress beyond C is increased, there is large strain in the wire.

This large increase in the strain for small stress is represented by CD part of the curve.

The point D on the graph is the **ultimate tensile strength** (σ_u) of the materials beyond this point, the wire breaks at point E which is also known as **fracture point**.

The material of the wire from point C to point D shows the plastic behaviour or plastic deformation. The stress corresponding to point E is called **breaking stress.**

TEACHER TIP

Hooke's law is valid only in the linear portion of the stress-strain curve. The law is not valid for large values of strain.

Elastic limit and limit of proportionality are very close to each other, so that Hooke's law is nearly applicable upto elastic limit.

In the yield region, strain is 15 to 20 times those that takes place upto the proportional limit occur during yielding.

Ductile and Brittle Materials

On the basis of elastic and plastic properties, materials can be classified in two ways.

(i) **Ductile Materials** The materials which have large plastic range of extension are called **ductile materials.**

- **For such material, the ultimate strength and fracture points are widely separated.** They can be drawn into thin wires, e.g. copper, silver, iron, aluminium, etc.

(ii) **Brittle Materials** The materials which have very small range of plastic extension are called brittle materials. Such materials break as soon as the stress is increased beyond the elastic limit.

- **For such materials, the fracture point lies just close to the ultimate strength point**, e.g. cast iron, glass, ceramics, etc.

Elastomers

The materials which can be elastically stretched to large values of strain are called elastomers.
It does not obey Hooke's law over most of the region.

e.g. Rubber can be stretched to several times its original length but still it can regain its original length when the applied force is removed.

- There is no well defined plastic region.
- Elastic region in such cases is very large.

In our body, the elastic tissue of aorta (the large blood vessel carrying blood from the heart) is an elastomer, for which the stress-strain curve is shown in figure.

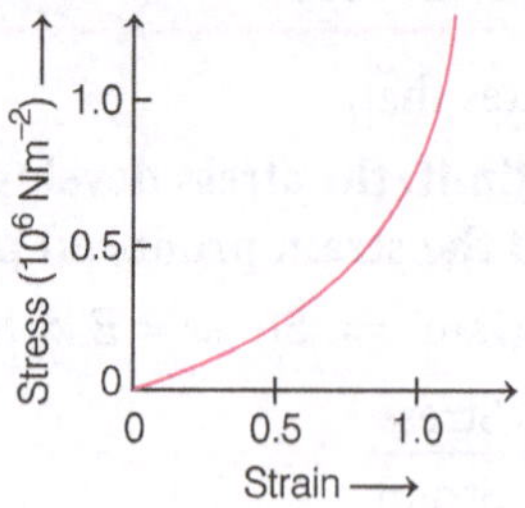

Quick Test 1

Conceptual Questions

1 Two identical solid balls, one of ivory and the other of wet clay, are dropped from the same height on the floor. Which will rise to a greater height after striking the floor and why? *NCERT Exemplar*

2 Stress and pressure both are forces per unit area, then in what respect does stress differ from pressure?

3 A wire fixed at the upper end stretches by length l by applying a force F. What is the work done in stretching the wire?

4 A wire is replaced by another wire of same length and material but of twice diameter.
 (i) What will be the effect on the increase in its length under a given load?
 (ii) What will be the effect on the maximum load which it can bear?

Numerical Questions

5 A steel cable with a radius of 1.5 cm supports a chair lift at a ski area. If the maximum stress is not to exceed $10^8\ \text{N/m}^2$, then what is the maximum load the cable can support? *NCERT*

6 Two strips of metal are riveted together at their ends by four rivets, each of diameter 6 mm. What is the maximum tension that can be exerted by the riveted strip, if the shearing stress on the rivet is not to exceed 6.9×10^7 Pa ? Assume that, each rivet is to carry one-quarter of the load.

7 Anvils made of single crystals of diamond, with the shape as shown in figure are used to investigate the behaviour of materials under very high pressure. Flat faces at the narrow end of the anvil have a diameter of 0.5 mm and the wide end are subjected to a compressional force of 50000 N. What is the pressure at the tip of the anvil?

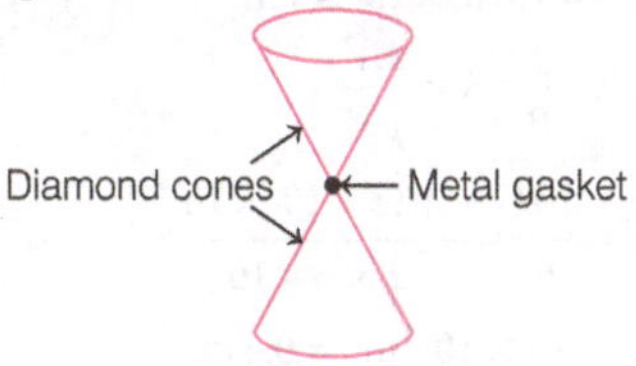

Answers

5. 7.1×10^4 N 6. 7.8×10^3 N 7. 2.5×10^{11} Pa

For Solutions, See QR Code on Pg. 297

8.4 Elastic Modulus

The modulus of elasticity or coefficient of elasticity of a body is defined as the ratio of stress to the corresponding strain within the elastic limit.

$$\text{Modulus of elasticity} = \frac{\text{Stress}}{\text{Strain}}$$

Its SI unit is **Nm^{-2}** or **pascal (Pa)** and its **dimensional formula** is $[\text{ML}^{-1}\text{T}^{-2}]$.

- Modulus of elasticity depends on the nature of the material of the body.
- Modulus of elasticity of a body is independent of its dimensions (i.e. length, area, volume, etc.)
- Dimensional formula of modulus of elasticity is same as that of the stress or pressure.

TEACHER TIP

To remember elastic modulus's concept, think of it as a material's resistance to deformation, i.e. the higher the modulus, the stiffer the material.

There are three types of modulus of elasticity.

1. Young's Modulus of Elasticity

Within the elastic limit, the ratio of longitudinal stress to the longitudinal strain is called Young's modulus of the material of the wire.

i.e. $\text{Young's modulus } (Y) = \dfrac{\text{Longitudinal stress}}{\text{Longitudinal strain}}$

Young's modulus

$$(Y) = \frac{\text{Tensile (or compressive) stress } (\sigma)}{\text{Longitudinal strain } (\varepsilon)} \quad \dots \text{(i)}$$

$\because \text{Longitudinal stress} = \dfrac{\text{Force } (F)}{\text{Area } (A)}$

$\text{Longitudinal strain} = \dfrac{\text{Change in length } (\Delta L)}{\text{Original length } (L)}$

Putting the above values in Eq. (i), we get

$$\therefore \quad \text{Young's modulus}, Y = \frac{F/A}{\Delta L / L} = \frac{FL}{A \Delta L}$$

Example 7 **In a Physics department, a Foucault pendulum consists of a 130 kg steel ball which swings at the end of a 8.0 m long steel cable having the diameter of 3.0 mm. If the ball was first hung from the cable, then determine how much the cable stretched? Young's modulus of the material is $20 \times 10^8\ \text{N/m}^2$.**

Sol. Given, diameter, $D = 3.0\ \text{mm} = 3.0 \times 10^{-3}$ m

Length, $L = 8.0$ m, mass, $m = 130$ kg

Radius, $r = \dfrac{D}{2} = \dfrac{3.0 \times 10^{-3}}{2} = 1.5 \times 10^{-3}$ m

The area of cross-section of the cable,

$$A = \pi r^2 = \pi \times (1.5 \times 10^{-3})^2$$
$$= 7.065 \times 10^{-6} m^2$$

Thus, $F = w = mg = 130 \times 9.8 = 1274$ N

We know that, $Y = \frac{\text{Stress}}{\text{Strain}} = \frac{F/A}{\Delta L/L}$

$$\Rightarrow \Delta L = \frac{LF}{AY} = \frac{8.0 \times 1274}{7.065 \times 10^{-6} \times 20 \times 10^8} = 0.72 \text{ m} = 720 \text{ mm}$$

Example 8 The ball of 200 g is attached to the end of a string of an elastic material (say rubber) and having length and cross-sectional area of 51 cm and 22 mm^2, respectively. Find the Young's modulus of this material if string is whirled round, horizontally at a uniform speed of 50 rpm in a circle of diameter 104 cm.

Sol. Mass of the ball, $m = 200$ g $= 0.2$ kg

Area of cross-section, $A = 22 \text{ mm}^2 = 22 \times 10^{-6} \text{m}^2$

Radius of the circle, $r = \frac{D}{2} = \frac{104}{2} = 52 \text{ cm} = 0.52 \text{ m}$

Length of the string, $l = 51 \text{cm} = 0.51 \text{m}$

Revolution per second, $N = 50 \times 60$ rps $= 3000$ rps

Centripetal force,

$$F = mr\omega^2 = 0.2 \times 0.52 \times (2\pi \times N)^2$$
$$0.2 \times 0.52 \times (2 \times 3.14 \times 3000)^2$$
$$F = 36.91 \times 10^6 \text{ N}$$

The change in length, Δl = radius of the circle – length of the string $= 0.52 - 0.51$

$$\Delta l = 0.01 \text{m}$$

Young's modulus of the material,

$$Y = \frac{F}{A}\frac{l}{\Delta l} = \frac{36.91 \times 10^6}{22 \times 10^{-6}} \times \frac{0.51}{0.01} = 85.56 \times 10^{12} \text{ Nm}^{-2}$$

2. Bulk Modulus of Elasticity

Within the elastic limit, the ratio of normal stress to the volumetric strain is called bulk modulus of elasticity. In other words, **the ratio of hydraulic stress to the hydraulic strain is called bulk modulus.**

If force F is applied normal to a cross-section A to decrease the volume V of the surface by an amount ΔV, the bulk modulus is given by

$$B = \frac{\text{Normal stress}}{\text{Volumetric strain}} = \frac{F/A}{-\Delta V/V}$$

$$\Rightarrow \quad \text{Bulk modulus, } B = -\frac{pV}{\Delta V}$$

where, $p = \frac{F}{A}$ is the normal pressure.

- **Negative sign shows that the volume decreases with the increase in stress.** But for a system in equilibrium, the value of bulk modulus is always positive.
- Bulk modulus for a perfect rigid body and ideal liquid is infinite.

Compressibility

The reciprocal of the Bulk modulus of a material is called its compressibility.

$$\text{Compressibility, } k = \frac{1}{B} = \frac{-\Delta V}{pV}$$

SI unit of compressibility $= \text{N}^{-1}\text{m}^2$

CGS unit of compressibility $= \text{dyne}^{-1}\text{cm}^2$

The **dimensional formula** of compressibility is $[\text{M}^{-1}\text{LT}^2]$.

Example 9 What will be the decrease in volume of 100 cm^3 of water under pressure of 100 atm, if the compressibility of water is 4×10^{-5} per unit atmospheric pressure?

Sol. Bulk modulus $(B) = \frac{1}{\text{Compressibility}} = \frac{1}{k}$

$$= \frac{1}{4 \times 10^{-5}} = 0.25 \times 10^5 \text{atm}$$
$$= 0.25 \times 10^5 \times 1.013 \times 10^5 \text{ N/m}^2$$
$$= 2.533 \times 10^9 \text{ N/m}^2$$

Volume, $V = 100 \text{ cm}^3 = 10^{-4} \text{ m}^3$

Pressure, $p = 100 \text{ atm} = 100 \times 1.013 \times 10^5 \text{ N/m}^2$

$$= 1.013 \times 10^7 \text{N/m}^{-2}$$

Now, apply $\frac{1}{B} = k = \frac{\Delta V}{pV}$

$$\therefore \quad \Delta V = \frac{pV}{B} = \frac{1.013 \times 10^7 \times 10^{-4}}{2.533 \times 10^9}$$

$$\Delta V = 0.4 \times 10^{-6} \text{m}^3 = 0.4 \text{ cm}^3$$

Mistake Alert Student make mistake while relating bulk modulus with compressibility. Remember that both bulk modulus and compressibility are inversely related to each other.

3. Modulus of Rigidity or Shear Modulus

Within the elastic limit, the ratio of tangential stress (shear stress) to corresponding shear strain is called modulus of rigidity. It is denoted as G or η.

$\therefore$ Modulus of rigidity is given by

$$\eta \text{ or } G = \frac{\text{Tangential stress (shear stress)}}{\text{Shear strain}}$$

If a tangential force F is applied on a cross-sectional area A such that there is a lateral shift ΔL of the length L, then

$\because$ Tangential stress $= \frac{F}{A}$ and shear strain $= \frac{\Delta L}{L}$

$$\text{Shear modulus, } \eta = \frac{F}{A} \cdot \frac{L}{\Delta L}$$

- Shear modulus for ideal liquid is zero.
- A solid has all types of moduli of elasticity, i.e. Y, B and η but fluids (i.e. liquids and gases) have only Bulk modulus of elasticity.

Example 10 **Consider an Indian rubber cube having modulus of rigidity of 2×10^7 dyne/cm^2 and of side 8 cm. If one side of the rubber is fixed, while a tangential force equal to the weight of 300 kg is applied to the opposite face, then find out the shearing strain produced and distance through which the strain side moves.**

Sol. Given, modulus of rigidity, $\eta = 2\times10^7$ dyne/cm^2

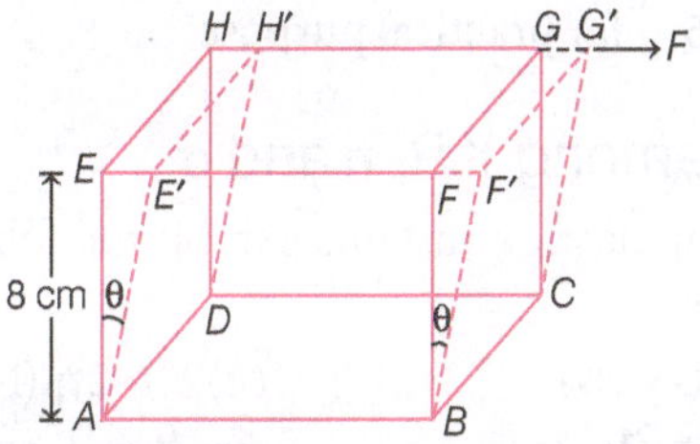

Side of the cube, $l = 8$ cm

Area, $A = l^2 = 64\ \text{cm}^2$

Force or load, $F = 300$ kgf $= 300\times1000\times981$ dyne

As, $\eta = \frac{F}{A\theta} \Rightarrow \theta = \frac{F}{A\eta}$

$$\theta = \frac{300\times1000\times981}{64\times2\times10^7} \simeq 0.23 \text{ rad}$$

As, $\eta = \frac{F}{A}\frac{l}{\Delta l} \Rightarrow \frac{\Delta l}{l} = \theta$

$\Rightarrow$ $\Delta l = l\theta = 8\times0.23$

$\Delta l = 1.84$ cm

Stress, Strain and Various Elastic Moduli

Types of stress	Stress	Strain	Change in Shape	Change in Volume	Elastic modulus	Name of modulus	State of Matter
Tensile or compressive	The deforming force per unit area acting perpendicular to the surface of the body ($\sigma = F/A$)	Elongation or compression in the direction of force ($\Delta L/L$) (longitudinal strain)	Yes	No	$Y = \frac{F\times L}{A\times\Delta L}$	Young's modulus	Solid
Shearing	The deforming force per unit area acting tangentially to the surface of the body ($\sigma_s = F/A$)	Pure shear, θ	Yes	No	$G = \frac{F}{A\times\theta}$	Shear modulus	Solid
Hydraulic	The deforming force per unit area acting normally everywhere to the surface of a solid immersed in a fluid, which changes the volume without change in its shape	Volume change (compression or expansion)($\Delta V/V$)	No	Yes	$B = -\frac{pV}{\Delta V}$	Bulk modulus	Solid, liquid and gas

Poisson's Ratio

The strain produced in the direction of applied force is called longitudinal strain and strain produced in the perpendicular direction is called lateral strain.

When a wire is loaded, its length L increases by ΔL but its diameter D decreases by ΔD. **Within the elastic limit, the ratio of lateral strain to the longitudinal strain is called Poisson's ratio.**

$$\text{Poisson's ratio, } \sigma = \frac{\text{Lateral strain}}{\text{Longitudinal strain}} = \frac{-\Delta D/D}{\Delta L/L}$$

$$\text{Poisson's ratio, } \sigma = \frac{-L}{D} \cdot \frac{\Delta D}{\Delta L}$$

The negative sign indicates that longitudinal and lateral strain are in opposite sense, it has no unit and dimensions.

$$\begin{cases} -1 < \sigma < 0.5 & \text{for theoretical purpose} \\ 0 < \sigma < 0.5 & \text{for practical purpose} \end{cases}$$

Relation among Y, B, η and σ

The different elastic constants exhibit the following relationship.

(i) $Y = 3B(1-2\sigma)$ (ii) $Y = 2\eta(1+\sigma)$

(iii) $\sigma = \dfrac{3B-2\eta}{2\eta+6B}$ (iv) $\dfrac{9}{Y} = \dfrac{1}{B} + \dfrac{3}{\eta}$

Example 11 A material is having Poisson's ratio 0.2. A load is applied on it, due to which it suffers the longitudinal strain 3.0×10^{-3}, then find out the percentage change in its volume.

Sol. Given, Poisson's ratio, $\sigma = 0.2$

Longitudinal strain $= \dfrac{\Delta L}{L} = 3.0 \times 10^{-3}$

As, $\sigma = -\dfrac{\Delta D/D}{\Delta L/L}$ or $\sigma = \dfrac{-\Delta R/R}{\Delta L/L}$

$$\Rightarrow \frac{\Delta R}{R} = -\sigma \times \frac{\Delta L}{L} = -0.6 \times 10^{-3}$$

Volume, $V = \pi R^2 L$

Then, percentage change in volume,

$$\left(\frac{\Delta V}{V} \times 100\right) = \left(\frac{2\Delta R}{R} + \frac{\Delta L}{L}\right) \times 100$$

$$= [2 \times (-0.6 \times 10^{-3}) + 3.0 \times 10^{-3}] \times 100 = 0.18\ \%$$

Mistake Alert Remember that Poisson's ratio is negative for contraction while positive for expansion.

8.5 Elastic Potential Energy in a Stretched Wire

When a wire is stretched, interatomic forces oppose the change in configuration of the wire. Hence, work has to be done against these restoring forces. The work done in stretching the wire will be stored in the form of **elastic potential energy**.

Let a force F applied on a wire of length L to increase its length by ΔL.

Initially, the internal restoring force in the wire is zero.

When the length is increased by ΔL, the internal force increases from 0 to F (applied force).

$\therefore$ Average internal force for an increase in length

$$\Delta L \text{ of wire} = \frac{0+F}{2} = \frac{F}{2}$$

Work done on the wire,

W = Average force × Increase in length

$$= \frac{F}{2} \times \Delta L$$

This work done is stored as elastic potential energy in the wire,

$$U = \frac{1}{2} F \times \Delta L = \frac{1}{2} \text{ Stretching force} \times \text{Increase in length}$$

Let A be the area of cross-section of the wire,

Then, $U = \dfrac{1}{2} \dfrac{F}{A} \times \dfrac{\Delta L}{L} \times AL$

> **Elastic potential energy,**
>
> $$U = \frac{1}{2} \text{ Stress} \times \text{Strain} \times \text{Volume of wire}$$

Elastic potential energy per unit volume of the wire or elastic energy density,

$$u = \frac{U}{\text{Volume}}$$

$$= \frac{1}{2} \text{ Stress} \times \text{Strain}$$

But, stress = Young's modulus × strain

> **Elastic energy density,**
>
> $$u = \frac{1}{2} \text{ Young's modulus} \times (\text{Strain})^2$$

Example 12 When the load of a wire is increased from 3 kg-wt to 5 kg-wt, the length of that wire changes from 0.61 mm to 1.02 mm. Calculate the change in the elastic potential energy of the wire.

Sol. Here, $F_1 = 3 \text{ kg-wt} = 3 \times 9.8 \text{N} = 29.4 \text{N}$

$$\Delta l_1 = 0.61 \text{ mm} = 6.1 \times 10^{-4} \text{m}$$

$$F_2 = 5 \text{ kg-wt} = 5 \times 9.8 = 49 \text{N}$$

$$\Delta l_2 = 1.02 \text{ mm} = 1.02 \times 10^{-3} \text{m}$$

$$\therefore \quad U_1 = \frac{1}{2} F_1 \cdot \Delta l_1 = \frac{29.4 \times 6.1 \times 10^{-4}}{2}$$

$$= 8.96 \times 10^{-3} \text{J}$$

and $U_2 = \dfrac{1}{2} F_2 \cdot \Delta l_2 = \dfrac{49 \times 1.02 \times 10^{-3}}{2}$

$$= 24.99 \times 10^{-3} \text{J}$$

$\therefore$ Change in elastic potential energy of the wire,

$$\Delta U = U_2 - U_1$$

$$= 24.99 \times 10^{-3} - 8.96 \times 10^{-3}$$

$$= 16.03 \times 10^{-3} \text{J}$$

Applications of Elastic Behaviour of Solids

(i) Each metallic part of a machine is subject to stress within its elastic limit. If a metallic part is stressed beyond this limit, it will become permanently deformed and affect its functionality.

(ii) The thickness of metallic ropes used in cranes for lifting and moving heavy weights is determined based on the elastic limit of the rope and the factor of safety.

(iii) When designing a bridge or beam to withstand traffic, wind forces and its own weight, preventing bending or breaking under load is crucial.

The bridge or beam should not bend too much or break.

Consider a beam of length l and of rectangular cross-section having breadth b and depth d.

When the beam is loaded in the middle with a load w, then it gets depressed by an amount δ given by

$$\text{Depression in beam, } \delta = \frac{wl^2}{4Ybd^3}$$

where, Y = Young's modulus of elasticity.

Since, the value of depression δ varies inversely as its breadth (b) and as the cube of its depth (d), the depression can be reduced more effectively by increasing the depth of the beam rather than increasing its breadth.

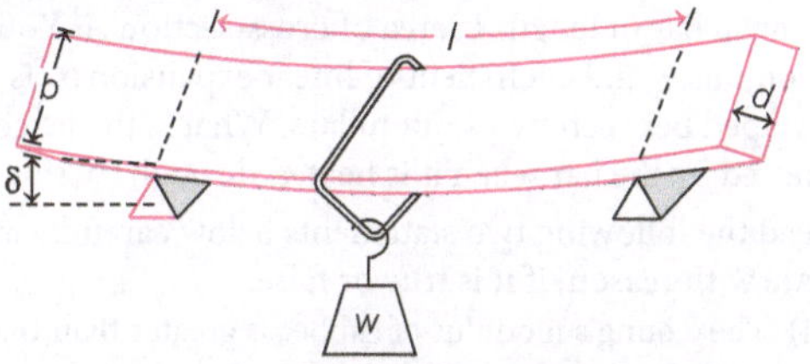

Depression in beam

(iv) Maximum height of a mountain on earth (~10 km) can be estimated from the elastic behaviour of earth.

To illustrate this, consider a mountain of height h, the force per unit area due to the weight of the mountain at its base is $h\rho g$, where ρ is density of material of mountain and g is the acceleration due to gravity.

The material at the bottom experiences this force in the vertical direction. The elastic limit for a typical rock is 30×10^7 Nm^{-2}. Equating this to $h\rho g$.

$$h\rho g = 30 \times 10^7$$

$$h \times 3 \times 10^3 \times 10 = 30 \times 10^7$$

$$= 10 \text{ km}$$

Quick Test 2

Conceptual Questions

1 A metal bar of length L, area of cross-section A, Young's modulus Y and coefficient of linear expansion α, is clamped between two stout pillars. What is the force exerted by the bar when it is heated through t°C?

2 Read the following two statements below carefully and state with reason, if it is true or false.

(i) The Young's modulus of rubber is greater than that of steel.

(ii) The stretching of a coil is determined by its shear modulus.

3 The stress-strain graphs for materials A and B are shown in Fig. (a) and Fig. (b). NCERT

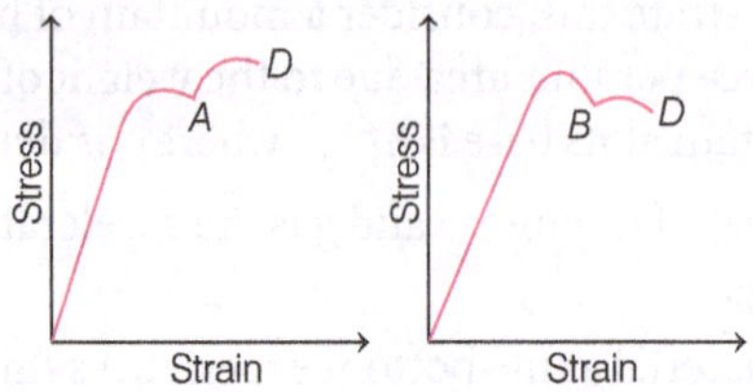

(a) (b)

The graphs are drawn to the same scale.

(i) Which of the materials has greater Young's modulus?

(ii) Which of the two is the stronger material?

4 A wire of length L and radius r is clamped rigidly at one end. When the other end of the wire is pulled by a force F, its length increases by l. Another wire of the same material of length $2L$ and radius $2r$, is pulled by a force $2F$. Find the increase in length of this wire. NCERT Exemplar

Numerical Questions

5 Two wires made of same material are subjected to forces in the ratio 1 : 4. Their lengths are in the ratio 2 : 1 and diameters in the ratio 1 : 3. What is the ratio of their extensions?

6 A truck is pulling a car out of a ditch by means of a steel cable that is 9.1 m long and has a radius of 5 mm. When the car just begins to move, the tension in the cable is 800 N. How much has the cable stretched? (Young's modulus for steel is 2×10^{11} N/m^2) NCERT Exemplar

7 To what depth must a rubber ball be taken in deep sea, so that its volume is decreased by 0.1%? (The Bulk modulus of rubber is 9.8×10^{8} N/m^2 and the density of seawater is 10^3 kg/m^3) NCERT Exemplar

8 A rigid bar of mass 15 kg is supported symmetrically by three wires each 2 m long. Those at each end are of copper and middle one is of iron. Determine the ratio of their diameters if each is to have the same tension. Young's modulus of elasticity for copper and steel are 110×10^9 N/m^2 and 190×10^9 N/m^2, respectively. NCERT

Answers

5. 9 : 2 6. 4.64×10^{-4}m 7. 100 m 8. 1.31 : 1

For Solutions, See QR Code on Pg. 297

Mind Map

Mechanical Properties of Solids

Stress

Stress is the internal force per unit area within a material that arises in response to an applied external force.

$$\text{Stress} = \frac{\text{Restoring force } (F)}{\text{Area of cross-section } (A)}$$

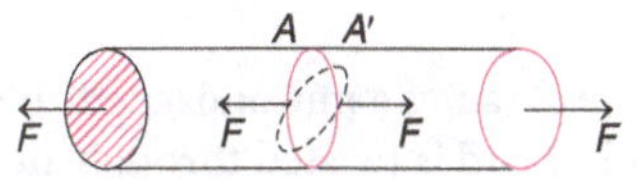

- SI unit is N/m² or pascal (Pa) and CGS system unit is dyne/cm².

Normal Stress

- Restoring force acting normally on any surface inside a body per unit area is called normal stress.

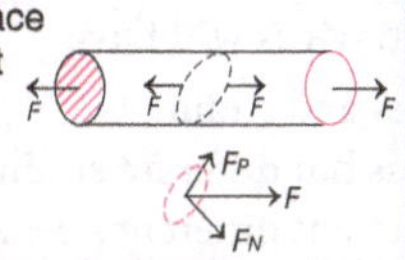

Normal stress $= \frac{F_N}{A}$

Volume Stress

- When a deforming force acting on a body is uniformly acting on each point of the body normal to the surface, then volume of this body is changed.
- Volume stress $= \frac{F}{A}$

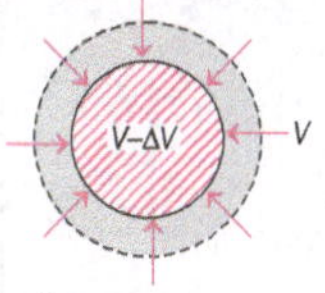

- It is also known as hydraulic stress.

Tangential or Shear Stress

- When a force acting tangentially on the surface of a body, then it changes shape of the body and the body is said to sheared.
- If the cross-sectional area of the cylinder is A and tangential force F, then

Tangential stress $= \frac{F}{A}$

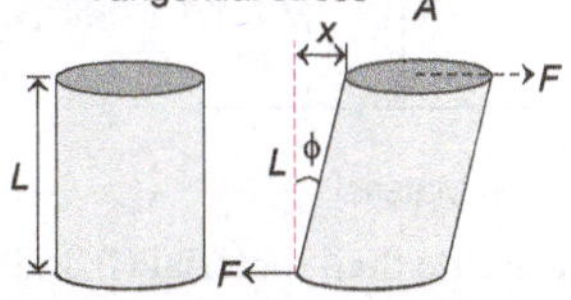

Stationary surface

Elastic Potential Energy

It is the energy stored in an elastic material when it is deformed (stretched or compressed) within its elastic limit. This energy is recoverable when the material returns to its original shape.

$$U = \frac{1}{2}kx^2$$

Strain

Strain is the measure of deformation in a material relative to its original size. It is dimensionless (a ratio)

$$\varepsilon = \frac{\Delta L}{L_0}$$

Longitudinal Strain

- The change in length per unit original length, when the body is deformed by external forces.

$$\text{Longitudinal strain} = \frac{\text{Change in length}}{\text{Original length}} = \frac{\Delta L}{L}$$

Volume Strain

- Fractional change in the volume of a body due to applied deforming force is called volume strain.

$$\text{Volume strain} = \frac{\text{Change in volume}}{\text{Initial volume}} = \frac{\Delta V}{V}$$

Shear Strain

- If the deforming forces produce a change in the shape of the body, then the strain is called shear strain

$$\text{Shearing strain} = \frac{\Delta L}{L} = \tan\theta$$

Elastic and Plastic Behavior

Elastic and plastic behavior of solids describes how materials respond to external forces, focusing on deformation and recovery
In the elastic region, a material deforms when subjected to stress but returns to its original shape and size once the stress is removed.
In the plastic region, a material undergoes permanent deformation when subjected to stress beyond the yield point.

Hooke's law

Within the elastic limit, the deformation of a material is directly proportional to the applied force or stress.
Extension $\propto$ load applied

- Valid only in the elastic region of the material's stress-strain curve.
- Beyond the elastic limit, materials enter the plastic region, where Hooke's law no longer applies.

Elastic Moduli

- The ratio of stress and strain is called modulus of elasticity.
- It has great importance for structural and manufacturing engineering designs.
- Modulus of elasticity $= \frac{\text{Stress}}{\text{Strain}}$

It's SI units is Nm^{-2} or Pascal (Pa).

Bulk Modulus of Elasticity

- The ratio of volume stress to the volume strain produced in a substance is called bulk modulus of elasticity of that substance.

$$B = \frac{\text{Volume or Normal stress}}{\text{Volume strain}}$$

$$B = \frac{-F/A}{\Delta V/V} = -\frac{pV}{\Delta V}$$

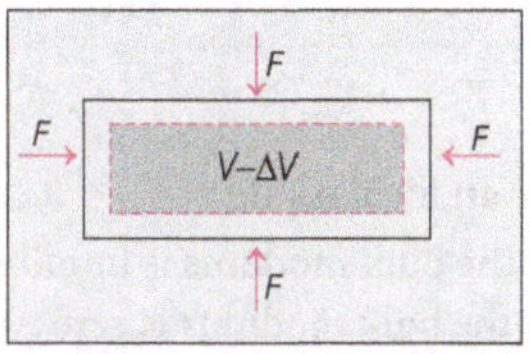

Young's Modulus of Elasticity

- The ratio of longitudinal stress to longitudinal strain produced in the body is called Young's modulus of elasticity of material of body.

$$Y = \frac{\text{Longitudinal stress}}{\text{Longitudinal strain}} = \frac{FL}{A\Delta L}$$

Modulus of Rigidity

- The ratio of produced tangential stress in an object to shear strain called modulus of rigidity.

It is denoted by G or η.

- Tangential stress (Shear stress) $= \frac{F}{A}$
- Modulus of rigidity is given by

$$\eta \text{ or } G = \frac{\text{Tangential stress}}{\text{Shear strain}}$$

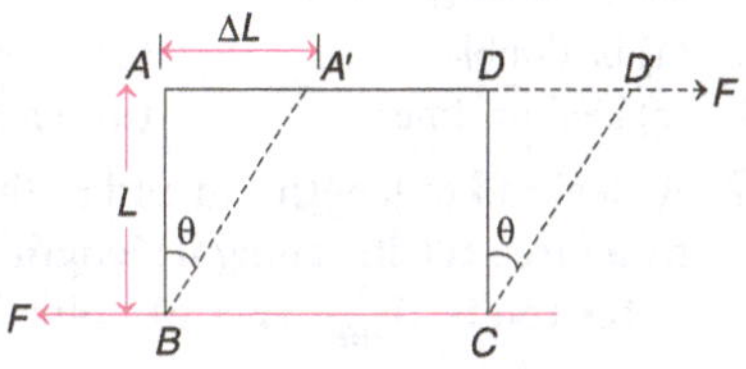

$$\text{Shear modulus,} \quad \eta = \frac{F/A}{\theta} = \frac{F}{A\theta} = \frac{F}{A} \cdot \frac{\Delta L}{L_0}$$

EXAM PATTERN QUESTIONS

Objective Type Questions

Multiple Choice Questions (MCQs)

1. A spring is stretched by applying a load to its free end. The strain produced in the spring is

(a) volumeteric (b) shear
(c) longitudinal and shear (d) longitudinal

2. A mild steel wire of length $2L$ and cross-sectional area A is stretched well within elastic limit, horizontally between two pillars. A mass m is suspended from the mid-point of the wire. Strain in the wire is

(a) $\frac{x^2}{2L^2}$ (b) $\frac{x}{L}$
(c) $\frac{x^2}{L}$ (d) $\frac{x^2}{2L}$

3. For an ideal liquid

(a) the bulk modulus is infinite
(b) the bulk modulus is zero
(c) the shear modulus is infinite
(d) None of these

4. On suspending a weight Mg, the length l of elastic wire having area of cross-section A, becomes double the initial length. The instantaneous stress action on the wire is **Competency Based Que.**

(a) Mg/A (b) $Mg/2A$
(c) $2Mg/A$ (d) $4Mg/A$

5. A cube of aluminium of side 0.1 m is subjected to a shearing force of 100 N. The top face of the cube is displaced through 0.02 cm with respect to the bottom face. The shearing strain would be

(a) 0.02 (b) 0.1
(c) 0.00 (d) 0.002

6. The maximum load a wire can withstand without breaking, when its length is reduced to half of its original length, will **NCERT Exemplar**

(a) be double (b) be half
(c) be four times (d) remains same

7. A steel rod of length 1 m and radius 10 mm is stretched by a force 100 kN along its length. The stress produced in the rod is ($Y_{Steel} = 2 \times 10^{11}\ \text{Nm}^{-2}$).

(a) $3.18 \times 10^6\ \text{N m}^{-2}$ (b) $3.18 \times 10^7\ \text{N m}^{-2}$
(c) $3.18 \times 10^8\ \text{N m}^{-2}$ (d) $3.18 \times 10^9\ \text{N m}^{-2}$

8. The upper end of a wire of radius 4 mm and length 100 cm is clamped and its other end is twisted through an angle of 30°, then angle of shear is

(a) 12° (b) 0.12° (c) 1.2 (d) 0.012°

9. A copper and a steel wire of the same diameter are connected end to end. A deforming force F is applied to this composite wire which causes a total elongation of 1 cm. The two wires will have **NCERT Exemplar**

(a) the same stress and strain
(b) the same stress but different strain
(c) the same strain but different stress
(d) different strains and stress

10. The stress stain graph for this materials are shown below. (Assume scale is same for both graph)

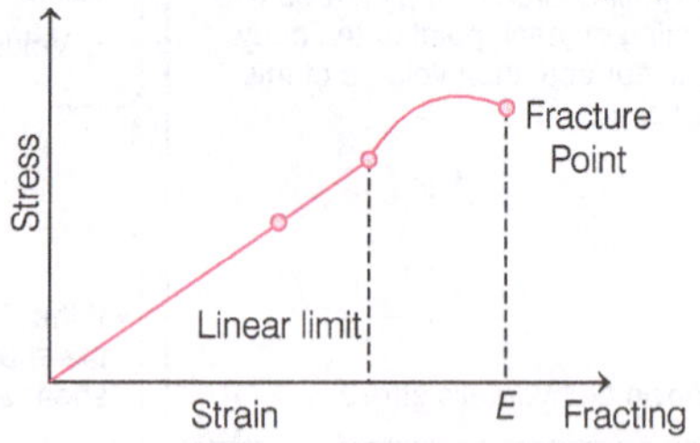

(i) aterial

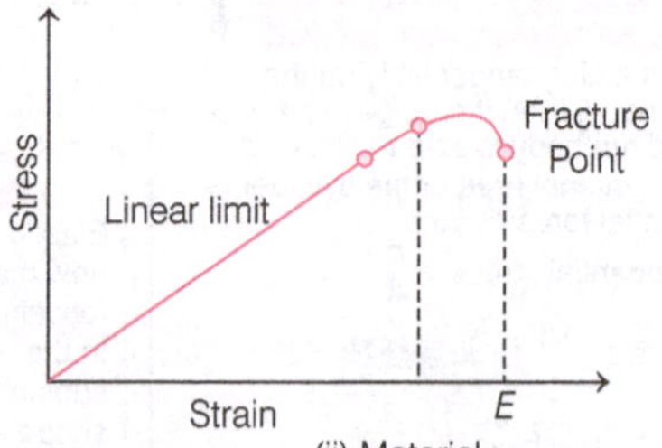

(ii) Material

(a) Material (ii) is more elastic than material (i) and hence material (ii) is more brittle.
(b) Material (i) and (ii) have the same elasticity and the same brittleness.
(c) Material (ii) is elastic over the larger region of stain as compared to material (i)
(d) Materials (ii) is not more brittle than material (i)

11. The material which is most likely to exhibit high tensile strength and low ductility is **Competency Based Que.**

(a) rubber (b) steel
(c) glass (d) aluminium

12. In the given figure, if the dimension of the wire are the same and materials are different, Young's modulus is more for

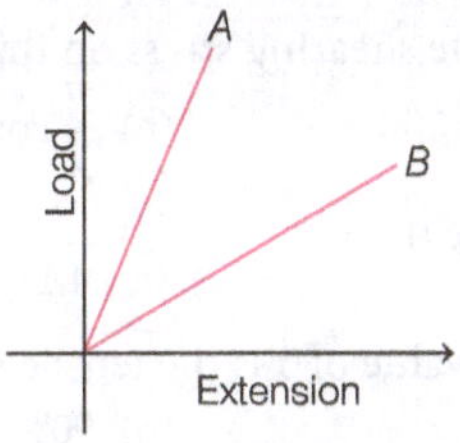

(a) A (b) B
(c) Both (d) None of these

13. A rigid bar of mass M is supported symmertically by three wires each of length L. Those at each end one of Copper and the middle one is of iron. The ratio of their diameters, if each is to have the same tension, is equal to

(a) $\frac{Y_{Copper}}{Y_{iron}}$ (b) $\sqrt{\frac{Y_{iron}}{Y_{Copper}}}$
(c) $\frac{Y^2_{iron}}{Y^2_{Copper}}$ (d) $\frac{Y_{iron}}{Y_{Copper}}$

14. A wire of diameter 1 mm breaks under a tension of 1000 N. Another wire of same material as that of the first one but of diameter 2 mm breaks under a tension of

(a) 500 N (b) 1000 N
(c) 10000 N (d) 4000 N

15. In steel, the Young's modulus and the strain at the breaking point are 2×10^{11} Nm^{-2} and 0.15, respectively. The stress at the breaking point for steel is

(a) 1.33×10^{11} Nm^{-2}
(b) 1.33×10^{12} Nm^{-2}
(c) 7.5×10^{-13} Nm^{-2}
(d) 3×10^{10} Nm^{-2}

16. Two wires of the same material and length but diameter in the ratio 1 : 2 are stretched by the same load. The ratio of elastic potential energy per unit volume for the two wires is

(a) 1 : 1 (b) 2 : 1
(c) 4 : 1 (d) 16 : 1

17. The value of tension in a long thin metal wire has been changed from T_1 to T_2. The lengths of the metal wire at two different values of tension T_1 and T_2 are l_1 and l_2, respectively. The actual length is **NCERT Exemplar**

(a) $\frac{T_1 l_2 - T_2 l_1}{T_1 - T_2}$ (b) $\sqrt{T_1 T_2 l_1 l_2}$
(c) $\frac{l_1 + l_2}{2}$ (d) $\frac{T_1 l_1 - T_2 l_2}{T_1 - T_2}$

18. Match the Column I with Column II.

Column I	Column II
A. Resilience	1. Measure of a material's resistance to localised plastic deformation (e.g. a small dent or scratch
B. Hardness	2. Fluctuating load
C. Fatigue	3. Instantaneous area
D. Trace stress	4. Capacity of a material to absorb energy when it is deformed elastically

(a) A-3, B-1, C-2, D-4 (b) A-2, B-4, C-3, D-1
(c) A-4, B-1, C-2, D-3 (d) A-1, B-2, C-3, D-4

19. Match the Column I with Column II.

Column I (Term)	Column II (Related concept)
A. Elastomers	1. Which have large plastic range of extension
B. Ductile material	2. There no well define plastic region
C. Elastic potential energy	3. The ratio of lateral strain to the longitudinal strain.
D. Poisson's ratio	4. The work done against restoring force is stored in stretched wire

(a) A-2, B-1, C-4, D-3 (b) A-1, B-2, C-4, D-3
(c) A-2, B-1, C-3, D-4 (d) A-4, B-1, C-2, D-3

Assertion-Reason

Directions *(Q.No. 20-27) In the following questions, two statements are given- one labelled Assertion (A) and the other labelled Reason (R). Select the correct answer to these questions from the codes (a), (b), (c) and (d) as given below.*

(a) Both Assertion and Reason are true and Reason is the correct explanation of Assertion.
(b Both Assertion and Reason are true but Reason is not the correct explanation of Assertion.
(c) Assertion is true but Reason is false.
(d) Assertion is false but Reason is true.

20 **Assertion (A)** The bridges declares unsafe after long use.
Reason (R) Elastic strength of bridges losses with time.

21 **Assertion (A)** Strain is a unitless quantity.
Reason (R) Strain is equivalent to force.

22 Assertion (A) Stress is the internal force per unit area of a body.

Reason (R) Rubber is less elastic than steel.

23 Assertion (A) When a solid is deformed, the atoms or molecules are displaced from their equilibrium position.

Reason (R) Due to change in interatomic spacing, intermolecular/interatomic forces arise.

24 Assertion (A) The restoring force F, on a stretched string for extension x is related to potential energy U as

$$F = \frac{-dU}{dx}$$

Reason (R) $F = -kx$ and $U = (1/2)kx^2$, where k is a spring constant for the given stretched string.

25 Assertion (A) The strain produced by a hydraulic pressure is volumetric in nature.

Reason (R) It is a ratio of change in volume (ΔV) to the original volume (V).

26 Assertion (A) Young's modulus for a perfectly plastic body is zero.

Reason (R) For a perfectly plastic body, restoring force is zero.

27 Assertion (A) Ropes are always made of a number of thin wires braided together.

Reason (R) It helps to ease in manufacture, flexibility and strength.

Case Based Questions

Directions *(Q.Nos. 28-31) These questions are case study based questions. Read the following paragraph and answer the questions on the basis of same.*

28 When a bar of cross-section A is subjected to equal and opposite tensile forces at its ends, then a restoring force equals to the applied force normal to its cross-section comes into existence. This restoring force per unit area of cross-section is known as tensile stress. While when the deforming force acts tangentially to the surface, then this tangential force applied per unit area of cross-section is known as tangential stress. Consider a plane section of the bar whose normal makes an angle θ with the axis of the bar.

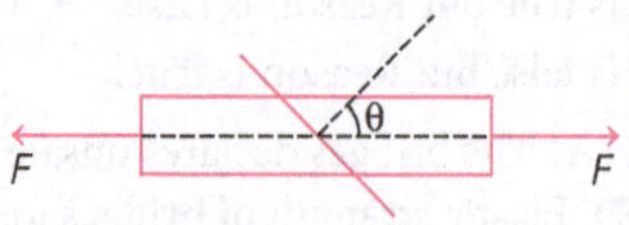

(i) Which of the following property of the bar does not change due to this force?

(a) Area (b) Volume
(c) Shape (d) Size

(ii) What is the tensile stress on this plane?

(a) $(F/A)\cos^2\theta$ (b) F/A
(c) $(F/A)\tan\theta$ (d) $(F/A)\sec^2\theta$

(iii) What is the shearing stress on this plane?

(a) $\frac{F}{2A}\sin 2\theta$ (b) $\frac{F}{A}\cos 2\theta$
(c) $\frac{F}{2A}\cos^2\theta$ (d) $\frac{F}{4A^2}$

(iv) For what value of θ is the tensile stress maximum?

(a) 0° (b) 90°
(c) 45° (d) 30°

Or

(iv) For what value of θ is the shearing stress maximum?

(a) 45° (b) 30°
(c) 90° (d) 60°

29 The property of a body by virtue of which it tends to regain its original shape and size after the removal of applied external force is known as elasticity and the deformation caused is known as elastic deformation. However, if you apply force to a lump of putty or mud, they have no gross tendency to regain their previous shape and they get permanently deformed. Such substances are called plastic and this property is called plasticity. Putty and mud are close to ideal plastics.

(i) What is the value of Young modulus or longitudinal stress by strain for putty and mud ?

(ii) The ratio stress/strain remains constant for a small deformation. What happens to this ratio if deformation is made very large ?

(iii) Both stress and pressure are defined as the force per unit area. Then, how do they differ ?

(iv) Are interatomic forces developed in a deformed body attractive or repulsive ?

Or

(iv) What are the factors on which modulus of elasticity of a material depends ?

30. Elastic modulus are those constants which determine the deformation produced by a given stress system acting on the material. It is the ratio of stress to strain within elastic limit. It is of three types : Young's modulus of elasticity (Y), shear modulus of elasticity (C) and bulk modulus of elasticity (K) and a body with higher value of elastic constant represents more elastic property. They are independent of magnitude of stress and strain but depends on the nature of material of the body and the manner in which the body is deformed.

(i) Why steel is more elastic than rubber?

(ii) How is the Young's modulus of elasticity (Y) depend on the elongation of a rod?

(iii) Two wires are made up of same material. If ratio of their radii is 2 : 1 and they are stretched by equal force, the n find the ratio of stress produced in them.

(iv) When the pressure on a sphere is increased by 80 atm, then its volume is decreased by 0.01%. Find the bulk modulus of elasticity of the sphere.

31 The graph shown below shows qualitatively the relation between the stress and the strain as the deformation gradually increases. Within Hooke's limit for a certain region stress and strain relation is linear. Beyond that up to a certain value of strain the body is still elastic and if deforming forces are removed the body recovers its original shape.

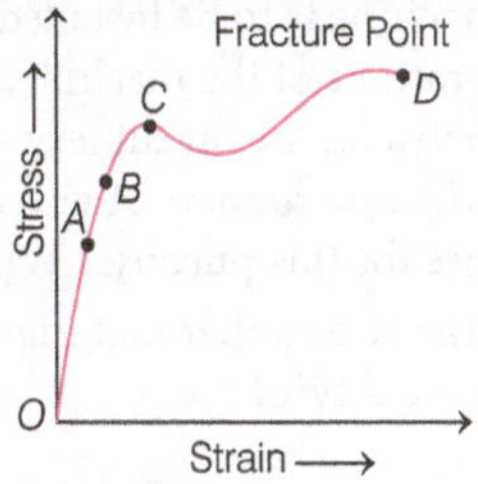

(i) **If deforming forces are removed, up to which point the curve will be retraced?**

(a) upto OA only (b) upto OB
(c) upto C (d) Never retraced its path

(ii) **In the above question, during loading and unloading the force exerted by the material are conservative up to**

(a) OA only (b) OB only
(c) OC only (d) OD only

(iii) **During unloading beyond B, say C, the length at zero stress in now equal to**

(a) less than original length
(b) greater than original length
(c) original length
(d) can't be predicted

(iv) **The breaking stress for a wire of unit cross-section is called**

(a) yield point
(b) elastic fatigue
(c) tensile strength
(d) Young's modulus

Or

(iv) **Substances which can be stretched to cause large strains are called**

(a) isomers (b) plastomers
(c) elastomers (d) polymers

Subjective Questions

Very Short Answer Type Questions

1 Is stress a vector quantity? Explain. **NCERT Exemplar Que.**

2 Which is more elastic steel or rubber? Explain.

3 What does the slope of stress *versus* strain graph indicate? **Competency Based Que.**

4 Is it possible to double the length of a metallic wire by applying a force over it?

5 What is Bulk modulus for a perfectly rigid body? Give one example. **NCERT Exemplar**

6 (i) How are atoms and molecules arranged in a crystalline solid? **[1]**

(ii) What is an elastomer? **[1]**

7 The knowledge of elasticity useful in selecting metal ropes shown its use in cranes for lifting heavy loads, when rope of steel is used (Elastic limit $= 30 \times 10^7 \text{Nm}^{-2}$) if load of 10^5 kg is to be lifted. What should be the radius of steel rope ? What should we do to increase flexibility of such wire ?

Given one example.

Short Answer Type Questions

8 Stress-strain curve for two wires of material A and B are as shown in Fig.

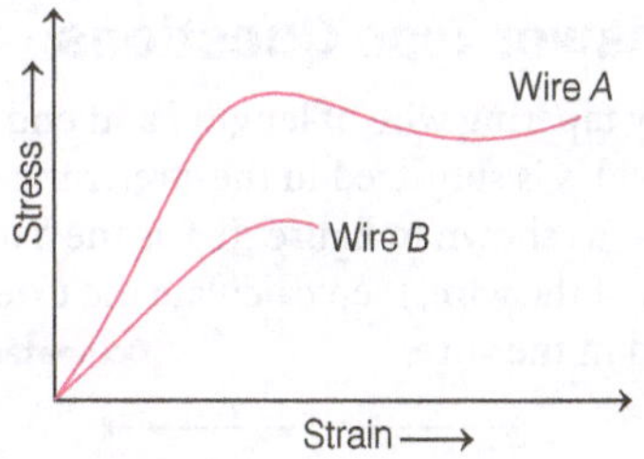

(i) Which material is more ductile ? **[1]**

(ii) Which material has greater value of Young's modulus? **[1]**

(iii) Which of the two is stronger material? **[1]**

9 Two wires P and Q of same diameter are loaded as shown in the figure. The length of wire P is L and its Young's modulus is Y N/m^2 while length of wire Q is twice that of P and material has Young's modulus half that of P. Compute the ratio of their elongation.

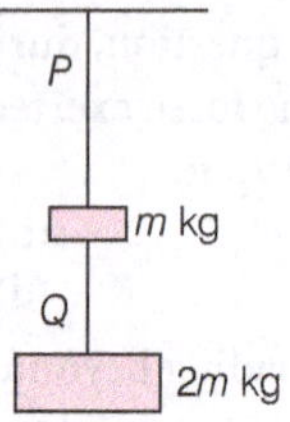

10 What are the Young and Bulk modulii for a perfect rigid body?

11 Identical springs of steel and copper are equally stretched. On which, more work will have to be done ?

12 The shear modulus of a material is always considerably smaller than the Young's modulus for it. What does it signify? **Competency Based Que.**

13 Following are the graphs of elastic materials. Which one correspond to that of brittle material?

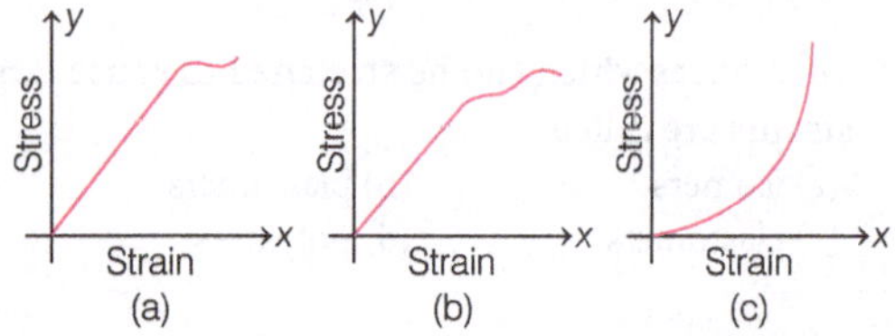

14 A wire of length L and area of cross-section A is stretched by the application of a force. If the Young's modulus is Y, then what is the work done per unit volume?

15 The Young's modulus for steel is much more than that for rubber. For the same longitudinal strain, which one will have greater tensile stress? **NCERT Exemplar**

Long Answer Type Questions

16 A slightly tapering wire of length l and end radii a and b on both sides is subjected to the stretching forces F on both sides as shown in figure. If Y is the Young's modulus of the wire, then calculate the extension produced in the wire. **Competency Based Que.**

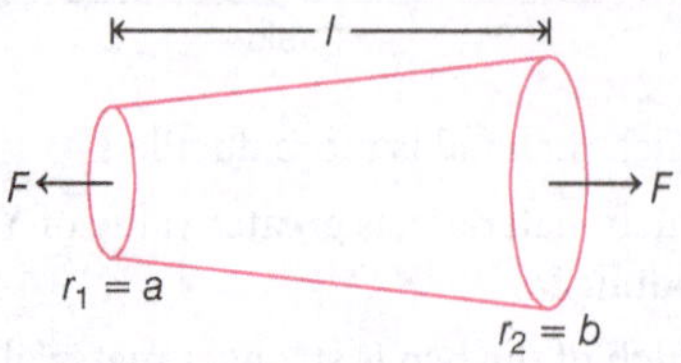

17 A mild steel wire of length $2L$ and cross-sectional area A is stretched, well within elastic limit, horizontally between two pillars (See figure). A mass m is suspended from the mid-point of the wire. Find the strain in the wire.

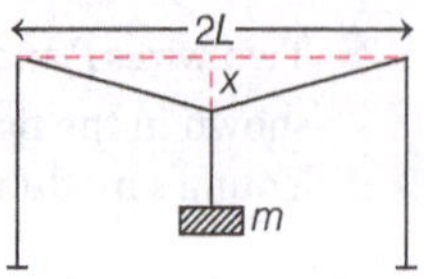

18 A uniform heavy rod of weight w, cross-sectional area A and length l is hanging from a fixed support. Young's modulus of the material of the rod is Y. Neglecting the lateral contraction, find the elongation produced in the rod.

19 Two different types of rubber are found to have the stress-strain curves shown in the given figure. **Competency Based Que.**

(i) In which significant ways do these curves differ from the stress-strain curve of a metal wire?

(ii) A heavy machine is to be installed in a factory. To absorb vibrations of the machine, a block of rubber is placed between the machinery and the floor. Which of the two rubbers A and B would you prefer to use for this purpose? Why?

(iii) Which of the two rubber materials would you choose for a car tyre?

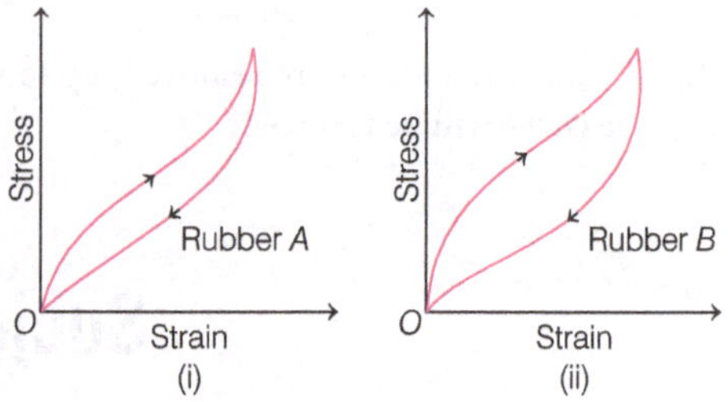

Numerical Problems

Stress and Strain

20 The maximum stress that can be applied to the material of a wire used to suspend on elevator is 1.3×10^8 Nm^{-2}. If the mass of the elevator is 900 kg and it moves up with an acceleration of 2.2 ms^{-2}, then what is the minimum diameter of the wire?

21 Two long metallic strips are joined together by two rivets each of radius 0.1 cm (Fig). Each rivet can withstand a maximum shearing stress of 3.0×10^8 Nm^{-2}. Calculate the maximum tangential force a strip can exert.

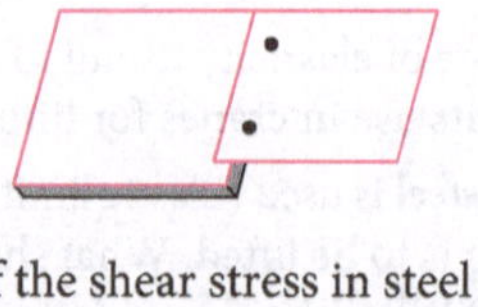

22 Assume that if the shear stress in steel exceeds about 4×10^8 N/m^2, the steel ruptures. Determine the shearing force necessary to (i) shear a steel bolt 1.00 cm in diameter and (ii) punch a 1 cm diameter hole in a steel plate 0.500 cm thick.

23 What is the length of a wire that breaks under its own weight when suspended vertically?
(Breaking stress $= 5\times10^{7}$ Nm^{-2} and density of the material of the wire $= 3\times10^{3}$ kg/m^{3})

Elastic Modulus

24. Figure shows the strain-stress curve for a given material. What are (i) Young's modulus and (ii) approximate yield strength for this material? **NCERT**

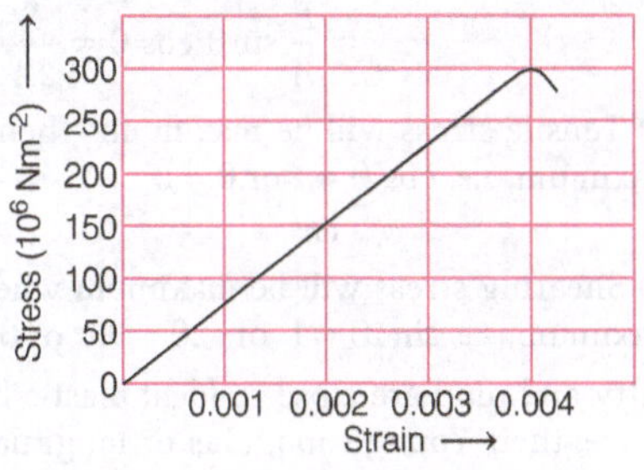

25 A wire elongates by 8 mm when a load of 9 kg is suspended from it. What is the elongation when its radius is doubled, if all other quantities are the same as before? **Competency Based Que.**

26 A piece of copper having a rectangular cross-section of 15.2 mm × 19.1 mm is pulled in tension with 44500 N force, producing only elastic deformation. Calculate the resulting strain? (Y for copper $= 1.1\times10^{11}$ N/m^{2}).

27 Calculate the percentage increase in length of a wire of diameter 2.5 mm stretched by a force of 100 kg weight. Young's modulus of elasticity of wire is 12.5×10^{11}dyne/sq. cm

28 Four identical hollow cylindrical columns of mild steel support a big structure of mass 50000 kg. The inner and outer radii of each column are 30 cm and 60 cm respectively. Assuming the load distribution to be uniform, calculate the compressional strain of each column. Young's modulus, $Y = 2.0\times10^{11}$ Pa.

29 Determine the volume contraction of a solid copper cube, 10 cm on an edge, when subjected to a hydraulic pressure of 7×10^{6} Pa. Bulk modulus for copper $= 140\times10^{9}$Pa.

30 Compute the bulk modulus of water from the following data : initial volume = 100.0 L, pressure increase = 100.0 atm (1 atm $= 1.013\times10^{5}$Pa), final volume = 100.5 L. Compare the bulk modulus of water with that of air (at constant temperature). Explain in simple terms why the ratio is so large?

31 How much should the pressure on a litre of water be changed to compress it by 0.10%. Bulk modulus of elasticity of water $= 2.2\times10^{9}$ N/m^{2}.

32 What is the density of water at a depth where pressure is 80.0 atm, given that its density at the surface is $1.03\times10^{3}$$kg/m^{3}$, compressibility of water is 45.8×10^{-11} Pa^{-1}.

33 To what depth must a rubber ball be taken in deep sea so that its volume is decreased by 0.1%? (The Bulk modulus of rubber is $9.8\times10^{8}$$N/m^{2}$ and the density of seawater is $10^{3}$$kg/m^{3}$.) **NCERT Exemplar**

34 A cube of aluminium of each side 4 cm is subjected to a tangential (shearing) force. The top face of the cube is sheared through 0.012 cm with respect to the bottom face.

Find (i) shearing strain, (ii) shearing stress and (iii) the shearing force. (Given, $\eta = 2.08\times10^{11}$dyne cm^{-2})

35 A square lead slab of side 50 cm and thickness 10 cm is subjected to a shearing force (on its narrow edge) of 9.0×10^{4}N. The lower edge is reveted to the floor. How much will the upper edge be displaced? (Modulus of rigidity of lead $= 5.6\times10^{9}$N/ m^{2})

Hints & Solutions

Objective Type Questions

1.	(b)	2.	(a)	3.	(a)	4.	(c)	5.	(d)
6.	(d)	7.	(c)	8.	(b)	9.	(b)	10.	(c)
11.	(c)	12.	(a)	13.	(b)	14.	(d)	15.	(d)
16.	(d)	16.	(b)	17.	(a)	18.	(c)	19.	(a)
20.	(a)	21.	(c)						

22. (*b*) Stress is defined as internal force per unit area of a body. Also, rubber is less elastic than steel because restoring force is less for rubber than steel.

23. (*a*) When a solid is deformed, the atoms or molecules are displaced from their equilibrium positions causing a change in the interatomic (or intermolecular distances).

24. (*a*) When a string is stretched for an extension *x*, then stored potential energy *U* is given by

$$F = -\frac{dU}{dx} \text{ and } U = \frac{1}{2}kx^2$$

where, *k* is a spring constant.

25. (*a*) The strain produced by a hydraulic pressure is called volume strain as pressure creates a normal force on every point and is defined as the ratio of change in volume (ΔV) to the original volume (V).

i.e. Volume strain $= \dfrac{\Delta V}{V}$

26. (*a*) Young's modulus of a material,

$$Y = \frac{\text{Stress}}{\text{Strain}}$$

$$\therefore \text{ Stress} = \frac{\text{Restoring force}}{\text{Area}}$$

As, restoring force for a perfectly plastic body is zero.

$$\therefore \quad Y = 0$$

27. (*a*) A single wire of this radius would practically be a rigid rod. So, the ropes are always made of a number of thin wires braided together, like in pigtails, for ease in manufacture, flexibility and strength.

28. (i) (*b*) This force produces a change in shape of the body without change in volume.

(ii) (*a*) The resolved part of *F* along the normal is the tensile force on this plane and the resolved part parallel to the plane is the shearing force on the plane.

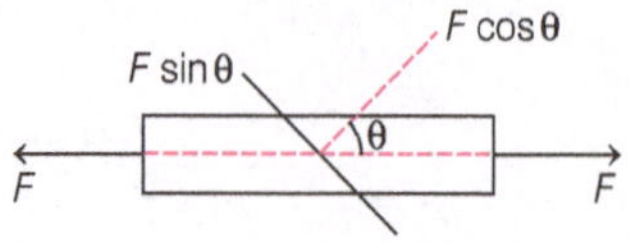

$\because$ Area of plane section $= A \sec\theta$

$$\text{Tensile stress} = \frac{\text{Force}}{\text{Area}} = \frac{F\cos\theta}{A\sec\theta} = \frac{F}{A}\cos^2\theta$$

$$\left(\because \sec\theta = \frac{1}{\cos\theta}\right)$$

(iii) (*a*) $\text{Shearing stress} = \dfrac{\text{Force}}{\text{Area}} = \dfrac{F\sin\theta}{A\sec\theta}$

$$= \frac{F}{A}\sin\theta\cos\theta = \frac{F}{2A}\sin 2\theta$$

(iv) (*a*) Tensile stress will be maximum when $\cos^2\theta$ is maximum, *i.e.* $\cos\theta = 1$ or $\theta = 0°$.

Or

(iv) (*a*) Shearing stress will be maximum when $\sin 2\theta$ is maximum, *i.e.* $\sin 2\theta = 1$ or $2\theta = 90°$ or $\theta = 45°$.

29. (i) Putty and mud are close to ideal plastic bodies hence, their Young's modulus or longitudinal stress by strain is almost zero.

(ii) When the deforming force exceeds the elastic limit, the strain increases more rapidly than stress. Hence the ratio of stress/strain decreases.

(iii) Stress and pressure are different as

(a) pressure is always normal to a surface but stress may be either normal or tangential.

(b) the pressure is always compressive but a stress may be tensile or compressive.

(iv) Interatomic forces are attractive when a body is stressed and repulsive when the body is compressed.

Or

(iv) The modulus of elasticity depends on the nature of a material and the manner of deformation of the body.

30. (i) The Young's modulus of elasticity is given by

$$Y = \frac{F \cdot l}{A \cdot \delta l}$$

$$\Rightarrow \quad Y \propto \frac{l}{\delta l}$$

As, $(\delta l)_{\text{rubber}} > (\delta l)_{\text{steel}} \Rightarrow Y_{\text{rubber}} < Y_{\text{steel}}$

So, higher value of Young's modulus of steel than rubber represents steel is more elastic than the rubber.

(ii) The Young's modulus of elasticity is

$$Y = \frac{F \cdot l}{A \cdot \delta l} \Rightarrow Y \propto \frac{l}{\delta l}$$

Hence, Young's modulus of elasticity of a material is inversely proportional to the elongation of the material.

(iii) Given, $r_1 : r_2 = 2:1$, $F_1 = F_2 = F$

$$\therefore \text{ Stress, } \sigma = \frac{\text{Force}}{\text{Area}} = \frac{F}{\pi r^2} \Rightarrow \sigma \propto \frac{1}{r^2}$$

$$\therefore \quad \frac{\sigma_1}{\sigma_2} = \left(\frac{r_2}{r_1}\right)^2 = \left(\frac{1}{2}\right)^2 = \frac{1}{4}$$

(iv) Given, $p = 80$ atm

$$= 80 \times 1.013 \times 10^5 \text{ N/m}^2$$

$$\frac{\Delta V}{V} = 0.01\% = \frac{0.01}{100}$$

$\therefore$ Bulk modulus,

$$B = \frac{p}{\frac{\Delta V}{V}} = \frac{80 \times 1.013 \times 10^5}{\frac{0.01}{100}}$$

$$= 8.1 \times 10^{10} \text{ N/m}^2$$

31. (i) (*b*)

(ii) (*b*) Point B is the elastic limit.

(iii) (*b*) Beyond B even if deforming forces are removed still some deformation is left.

(iv) (*c*) The breaking stress for a wire of unit cross-section is called tensile strength.

Or

(iv) (*c*) Substances which can be stretched to cause large strains are called elastomers.

Subjective Questions

1. No, stress is a scalar quantity, because it does not combine according to parallelogram law of vector addition. It is a tensor quantity.

$$\text{Stress} = \frac{\text{Magnitude of internal reaction force}}{\text{Area of cross - section}}$$

2. $Y_s = \frac{F}{A}\frac{l}{\Delta l_s}$

$$Y_r = \frac{F}{A}\frac{l}{\Delta l_f}$$

For same force applied to wires made of steel and rubber of same length and same area of cross-section.

$$\Delta l_s = \Delta l_r$$

$$\frac{Y_s}{Y_r} = \frac{\Delta l_r}{\Delta l_s} > 1$$

$$\therefore \quad Y_s > Y_r$$

3. The slope of stress (on Y-axis) and strain (on X-axis) gives modulus of elasticity.

The slope of stress (on X-axis) and strain (on Y-axis) gives the reciprocal of modulus of elasticity.

4. No, it is not possible because within elastic limit, strain is only order of 10^{-3}, wires actually break much before it is stretched to double the length.

5. Bulk modulus $(B) = \frac{p}{\Delta V / V} = \frac{pV}{\Delta V}$

For perfectly rigid body, change in volume, $\Delta V = 0$

$$\therefore \quad B = \frac{pV}{0} = \infty$$

Therefore, Bulk modulus for a perfectly rigid body is ∞.
e.g. A ball bearing made of hardened steel.

6. (i) They are arranged in a definite and regular manner in whole crystal.

(ii) It is a substance which can be elastically stretched to large values of strain.

7. The ultimate stress should not exceed elastic limit of steel (30×10^7 N/m^2)

$$U = \frac{F}{A} = \frac{Mg}{\pi r^2} = \frac{10^5 \times 9.8}{\pi r^2} = 30 \times 10^7$$

$$\therefore \quad r = 3.2 \text{ cm}$$

So, to lift a load of 10^5 kg the crane must be designed to withstand 10^5 kg. To impart flexibility the rope is made of large number of thin wires braided.
e.g. Steel wire ropes used in suspension bridge (like the Golden Gate Bridge) consist of multiple steel strands woven together to enhance flexibility and durability.

8. (i) Wire with larger plastic region is more ductile material A.

(ii) Young's modulus $= \frac{\text{Stress}}{\text{Strain}}$

$$\therefore \quad Y_A > Y_B$$

(iii) For given strain, larger stress is requird for A than that for B.

$\therefore$ A is stronger than B.

9. $\Delta L_p = \frac{3mg}{A} \times \frac{L}{Y}$

$$\Delta L_Q = \frac{2mg}{A} \cdot \frac{2L}{Y/2} = \frac{8mg}{A}\frac{L}{Y} \Rightarrow \frac{\Delta L_p}{\Delta L_q} = \frac{3}{8}$$

10. Young's modulus $(Y) = \frac{F}{A} \times \frac{l}{\Delta l}$

For a perfectly rigid body, change in length, $\Delta l = 0$

$$\therefore \quad Y = \frac{F}{A} \times \frac{l}{0} = \infty$$

Therefore, Young modulus for a perfectly rigid body is ∞.

Bulk modulus $(B) = \frac{p}{\Delta V / V} = \frac{pV}{\Delta V}$

For perfectly rigid body, change in volume, $\Delta V = 0$

$$\therefore \quad B = \frac{pV}{0} = \infty$$

Therefore, Bulk modulus for a perfectly rigid body is ∞.

11. Work done in stretching a wire is given by

$$W = \frac{1}{2} F \times \Delta l$$

As springs of steel and copper are equally stretched.
Therefore, for same force (F),

$$W \propto \Delta l \qquad \text{...(i)}$$

Young's modulus $(Y) = \frac{F}{A} \times \frac{l}{\Delta l}$

or $$\Delta l = \frac{F}{A} \times \frac{l}{Y}$$

As both springs are identical, $\Delta l \propto \frac{1}{Y}$ ...(ii)

From Eqs. (i) and (ii), we get $W \propto \frac{1}{Y}$

$$\therefore \quad \frac{W_{steel}}{W_{copper}} = \frac{Y_{copper}}{Y_{steel}} < 1 \quad [\because Y_{steel} > Y_{copper}]$$

or $$W_{steel} < W_{copper}$$

Therefore, more work will be done for stretching copper spring.

12. Shear modulus η of material is smaller than the Young's modulus Y. As, we know that it is easiser to slide layers of atoms of solids over one another than to pull them apart or to squeeze them to close together

13. Graph (c) is for elastomers because there is no stress ∝ strain region. Material (a) is more brittle than (b) because fracture and elastic points are very close.

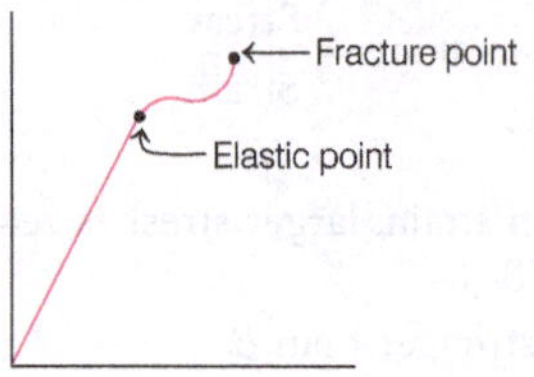

14. Work done is equal to the potential energy stored in the wire.

$$\therefore W = U = \frac{1}{2} \times \text{Stress} \times \text{Strain} \times \text{Volume}$$

$$W = \frac{1}{2} \times Y(\text{Strain})^2 \times \text{Volume}$$

Now, strain $= \frac{x}{L}$ and volume, $V = AL$

$$\therefore \quad W = \frac{1}{2} Y \frac{x^2}{L^2} \times AL$$

$$W = \frac{Yx^2 A}{2L}$$

15. Young's modulus $(Y) = \frac{\text{Stress}}{\text{Longitudinal strain}}$

For same longitudinal strain, $Y \propto$ Stress

$$\therefore \quad \frac{Y_{steel}}{Y_{rubber}} = \frac{(\text{Stress})_{steel}}{(\text{Stress})_{rubber}} \quad \text{...(i)}$$

But $Y_{steel} > Y_{rubber}$

$$\therefore \quad \frac{Y_{steel}}{Y_{rubber}} > 1$$

Therefore, from Eq. (i), we get

$$\frac{(\text{Stress})_{steel}}{(\text{Stress})_{rubber}} > 1$$

or $(\text{Stress})_{steel} > (\text{Stress})_{rubber}$

16. Consider a small element *cdef* of wire of length dx, radius r at a distance x from the end b.

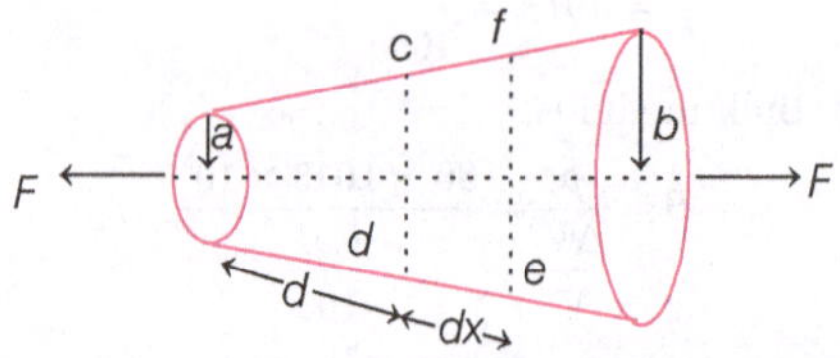

The gradient of radius is constant and is given by

$$K = \frac{b-a}{L} \quad \text{...(i)}$$

If r radius at cd and $(r + dr)$ at fe, then

$$K = \frac{(r+dr) - r}{x + dx - x} = \frac{dr}{dx}$$

or $$dx = \frac{dr}{K} \quad \text{...(ii)}$$

If dL is the extension produced in the wire is given by

$$\Rightarrow \quad I = \int_0^L dl = \int_a^b \frac{F}{Y\pi} \times \frac{dr}{Kr^2} = \frac{-F}{Y\pi K}\left[\frac{1}{r}\right]_a^b$$

$$= \frac{F}{Y\pi K}\left[\frac{1}{a} - \frac{1}{b}\right] = \frac{F(b-a)}{Y\pi Kab}$$

$$I = \frac{FL}{Y\pi ab} \quad \text{[using Eq. (i)]}$$

17. Consider the diagram below

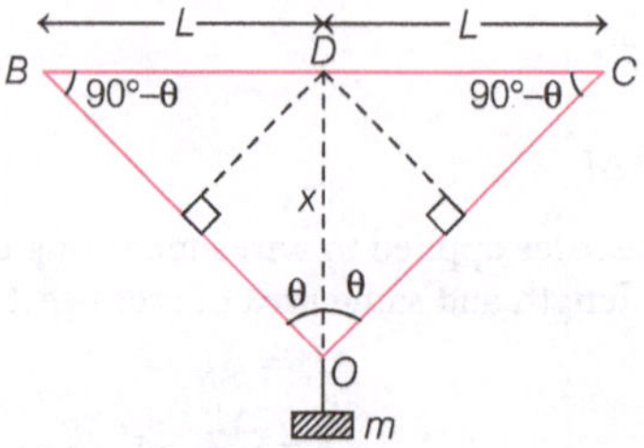

Hence, change in length,

$$\Delta L = BO + OC - (BD + DC)$$

$$= 2BO - 2BD \quad (\because BO = OC, BD = DC)$$

$$= 2[BO - BD] = 2(x^2 + L^2)^{1/2} - L]$$

$$= 2L\left[\left(1 + \frac{x^2}{L^2}\right)^{1/2} - 1\right]$$

$$\approx 2L\left[1 + \frac{1}{2}\frac{x^2}{L^2} - 1\right] = \frac{x^2}{L} \quad [\because x << L]$$

$$\therefore \quad \text{Strain} = \frac{\Delta L}{2L} = \frac{x^2/L}{2L} = \frac{x^2}{2L^2}$$

18. The weight of rod below the element dx is

$$T = \frac{w}{L}(L-x)$$

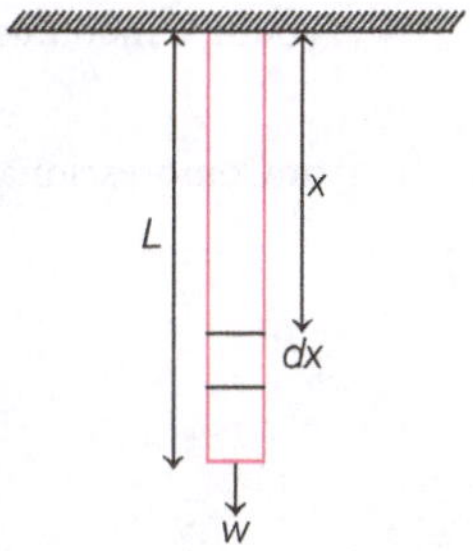

Elongation in $dx = \frac{T\,dx}{A\,Y}$

$$= \frac{\frac{w}{L}(L-x)dx}{AY}$$

Now, total elongation in rod,

$$\Delta L = \int_0^L \frac{w}{LAY}(L-x)\,dx$$

$$= \frac{w}{LAY}\left[Lx - \frac{x^2}{2}\right]_0^L$$

$$= \frac{w}{LAY}\left[L^2 - \frac{L^2}{2}\right] = \frac{wL}{2AY}$$

19. (i) These curves differ from the stress-strain curve of metal wire in the following ways.

(a) Hooke's law is not obeyed.

(b) There is no permanent strain even if a large stress is applied.

(c) When the stress is reduced, the material does not retrace its path back.

(d) Both the materials exhibit elastic hysteresis.

(ii) To absorb vibrations, rubber B is to be preferred. It is because the area enclosed by hysteresis loop of this material is large.

(iii) For making the car tyre, the rubber A should be used, such that it is not heated up quickly. For rubber A, the energy loss is small. Therefore, material A should be chosen.

20. As the elevator moves up, the tension in the wire is

$$F = mg + ma = m(g+a) = 900 \times (9.8 + 2.2) = 10800\text{N}$$

Stress in the wire $= \frac{F}{A} = \frac{F}{\pi r^2}$

Clearly, when the stress is maximum, r is minimum.

$\therefore$ Maximum stress $= \frac{F}{\pi r_{min}^2}$

or $\quad r_{min}^2 = \frac{F}{\pi \times \text{maximum stress}}$

$$= \frac{10800}{3.14 \times 1.3 \times 10^8} = 0.2645 \times 10^{-4}\text{m}$$

or $\quad r_{min} = 0.5142 \times 10^{-2}\text{m}$

Minimum diameter

$$= 2r_{min} = 2 \times 0.5142 \times 10^{-2}$$

$$= 1.0284 \times 10^{-2}\text{m}$$

21. Let F be the tensile force applied. Since, each rivet shares the stretching force equally, so the shearing force on each rivet = $F/2$.

If A is the area of each rivet, then shearing stress on each rivet $= \frac{F}{2A}$. Now, maximum shearing stress on each strip $= 3.0 \times 10^8$ Nm^{-2}

i.e. $\quad \frac{F_{max}}{2A} = 3.0 \times 10^8$ Nm^{-2}

where, F_{max} is maximum tangential force.

or $\quad F_{max} = 3.0 \times 10^8 \times 2A = 6.0 \times 10^8 \times \pi r^2$

$\because \quad r = 0.1$ cm $= 0.1 \times 10^{-2}$ m

$r = 1 \times 10^{-3}$ m

$\Rightarrow \quad F_{max} = 6.0 \times 10^8 \times \frac{22}{7} \times (1 \times 10^{-3})^2 = 1885$ N

22. (i) Force applied, $F = A \cdot$ Stress

$$= \pi(5 \times 10^{-3})^2(4 \times 10^8)$$

$$= 3.14 \times 10^4 \text{ N}$$

(ii) Area over which the shear stress occurs is equal to the circumference of the hole times its thickness.

Thus, $A = (2\pi r)\,t = 2\pi\,(5 \times 10^{-3})\,(5 \times 10^{-3})$

$= 1.57 \times 10^{-4}$ m^2

So, $F = A \cdot \text{Stress} = (1.57 \times 10^{-4})\,(4 \times 10^8)$

$= 6.28 \times 10^4$ N

23. Let length $= l$

Breaking stress $= \frac{\text{Weight}}{\text{Area}}$

Weight, $w = \rho A l \cdot g$

$\Rightarrow$ Breaking stress $= \frac{\rho A l g}{A}$

$$5 \times 10^7 = 3 \times 10^3 \times l \times 9.8$$

$$l = \frac{5 \times 10^7}{3 \times 10^3 \times 9.8} = 0.17 \times 10^4 = 1700 \text{ m}$$

$l = 1.7$ km

24. (i) Young's modulus of the given material (Y)

= Slope of strain-stress curve

$$Y = \frac{150 \times 10^6}{0.002} = 75 \times 10^9 \text{ N/m}^2$$

$= 7.5 \times 10^{10}$ N/m^2

(ii) Yield strength of the given material

= Maximum stress, the material can sustain

$= 300 \times 10^6$ N/m^2 $= 3 \times 10^8$ N/m^2

25. Young's modulus is given by, $Y = \frac{F}{A}\frac{L}{\Delta L}$

where, $\quad A = \pi r^2$

$$Y = \frac{F}{\pi r^2}\frac{L}{\Delta L} \Rightarrow r^2 \Delta L = \frac{FL}{\pi Y} = \text{constant}$$

Hence, $\quad r_1^2 \Delta L_1 = r_2^2 \Delta L_2$

Given, $r_2 = 2r_1$ and $\Delta L_1 = 8$ mm $= 8 \times 10^{-3}$ m

So, $r_1^2 \cdot 8\times10^{-3} = (2r_1)^2 \Delta L_2$

$$\Delta L_2 = \frac{8\times10^{-3}}{4} = 2\times10^{-3} \text{ m or 2 mm}$$

26. Given, cross-section area of copper piece (A)

$$= 15.2 \text{ mm} \times 19.1 \text{ mm}$$
$$= (15.2\times 19.1)\times10^{-6} \text{ m}^2$$

Force applied $(F) = 44500$ N

Young's modulus $(Y) = 1.1\times10^{11}$ Nm^{-2}

$$\text{Young's modulus } (Y) = \frac{\text{Longitudinal stress}}{\text{Longitudinal strain}}$$

$$\text{or Longitudinal strain} = \frac{\text{Longitudinal stress}}{\text{Young's modulus}}$$

$$= \frac{(F/A)}{Y} = \frac{F}{AY}$$

$$= \frac{44500}{15.2\times 19.1\times10^{-6}\times 1.1\times10^{11}}$$

$$= 139.34\times10^{-5}$$
$$= 1.39\times10^{-3}$$

27. Here, $2r = 2.5 \text{ mm} = 0.25 \text{ cm}$ or $r = 0.125$ cm

$$\therefore \quad a = \pi r^2 = \frac{22}{7}\times(0.125)^2 \text{ cm}^2$$

$$F = 100 \text{ kg} = 100\times1000 \text{ g}$$
$$F = 10\times1000\times980 \text{ dyne}$$
$$Y = 12.5\times10^{11} \text{ dyne/sq. cm}$$

As $\quad Y = \dfrac{F\times l}{a\times\Delta l}$

$$\therefore \quad \frac{\Delta l}{l} = \frac{F}{aY}$$

Hence, % increase in length

$$= \frac{\Delta l}{l}\times100 = \frac{F}{aY}\times100$$

$$= \frac{(100\times1000\times980)\times7\times100}{22\times(0.125)^2\times12.5\times10^{11}} = 0.1596\%$$

28. Given, total mass supported by cylindrical columns (m) = 50000 kg

$\therefore$ Total weight supported by cylindrical columns

$$= mg = 50000\times9.8$$
$$= 490000 \text{ N}$$

$\therefore$ Load acting on each cylindrical support,

$$F = \frac{mg}{4} = \frac{490000}{4} \text{ N}$$
$$= 122500 \text{ N}$$

Inner radius of each column $(r_1) = 30$ cm $= 0.3$ m

Outer radius of each column $(r_2) = 60$ cm $= 0.6$ m

$\therefore$ Area of cross-section of each cylindrical column,

$$A = \pi r_2^2 - \pi r_1^2 = \pi(r_2^2 - r_1^2)$$
$$= 3.14\,[(0.6)^2 - (0.3)^2] = 3.14\times0.27 \text{ m}^2$$

Young's modulus $(Y) = 2\times10^{11}$ Pa

Compressional strain of each column = ?

$$\text{Young's modulus } (Y) = \frac{\text{Compressional stress}}{\text{Compressional strain}}$$

$$\text{or Compressional strain} = \frac{\text{Compressional stress}}{\text{Young's modulus}}$$

$$= \frac{F/A}{Y} = \frac{F}{AY}$$

$$= \frac{122500}{(3.14\times0.27)\times2\times10^{11}}$$

$$= 0.722\times10^{-6} = 7.22\times10^{-7}$$

29. Given, each side of cube = 10 cm = 0.1 m

Hydraulic pressure $(p) = 7\times10^6$ Pa

Bulk modulus for copper $(B) = 140\times10^9$ Pa

Volume contraction (ΔV) = ?

Volume of the cube $(V) = l^3 = (0.1)^3 = 1\times10^{-3}$ m^3

$$\text{Bulk modulus for copper } (B) = \frac{p}{\Delta V/V} = \frac{pV}{\Delta V}$$

$$\text{or} \quad \Delta V = \frac{pV}{B} = \frac{7\times10^6\times1\times10^{-3}}{140\times10^9} = \frac{1}{20}\times10^{-6} \text{ m}^3$$

$$= 0.05\times10^{-6} \text{ m}^3 = 5\times10^{-8} \text{ m}^3$$

30. Given, initial volume $(V_1) = 100.0$ L

Final volume $(V_2) = 100.5$ L

$\therefore$ Increase in volume $(\Delta V) = V_2 - V_1$

$$= 100.5 - 100.0 = 0.5 \text{ L}$$
$$= 0.5\times10^{-3} \text{ m}^3 \quad (\because 1 \text{ L} = 10^{-3}\text{m}^3)$$

Increase in pressure $(\Delta p) = 100.0$ atm

$$= 100.0\times1.013\times10^5 \text{ Pa}$$
$$(\because 1 \text{ atm} = 1.013\times10^5 \text{Pa})$$
$$= 1.013\times10^7 \text{ Pa}$$

$$\text{Bulk modulus of water } (K_w) = \frac{\Delta p}{(\Delta V/V)} = \frac{\Delta p\cdot V}{\Delta V}$$

$$= \frac{1.013\times10^7\times100\times10^{-3}}{0.5\times10^{-3}}$$

$$= \frac{10.13}{5}\times10^9 \text{ Pa} = 2.026\times10^9 \text{ Pa}$$

Bulk modulus of air $(K_a) = 1.0\times10^5$ Pa

$$\therefore \quad \frac{\text{Bulk modulus of water } (K_w)}{\text{Bulk modulus of air } (K_a)} = \frac{2.026\times10^9}{1.0\times10^5}$$

$$= 2.026\times10^4$$

This ratio is too large as gases are more compressible than those of liquids. In liquids interatomic forces are more strong than that for gases.

31. Change in volume, $\Delta V = V\times\dfrac{0.10}{100}$

$$\text{or} \quad \frac{\Delta V}{V} = \frac{0.10}{100} = 1\times10^{-3} \quad \text{...(i)}$$

Bulk modulus of water $(K) = 2.2 \times 10^9$ N/m^2

Pressure on water $(\Delta p) = ?$

Bulk modulus of water $(K) = \dfrac{\Delta p}{\Delta V / V}$ or $\Delta p = K \times \dfrac{\Delta V}{V}$

$= 2.2 \times 10^9 \times 1 \times 10^{-3} = 2.2 \times 10^6$ N-m^2

32. Density of water at the surface $(\rho_0) = 1.03 \times 10^3$ kg/m^3

Pressure $(p) = 80.0$ atm

$= 80.0 \times 1.013 \times 10^5$ Pa $\quad (\because 1 \text{ atm} = 1.013 \times 10^5 \text{ Pa})$

Compressibility of water $\left(\dfrac{1}{K}\right) = 45.8 \times 10^{-11}$ Pa^{-1}

Let V and V' be the volumes of certain mass of water at the surface and at a given depth. The density of water at the given depth be ρ'.

Volume of water at the surface, $V = \dfrac{m}{\rho}$

At the given depth, $\quad V' = \dfrac{m}{\rho'}$

$\therefore$ Change in volume, $\quad \Delta V = V - V'$

$$= m\left(\frac{1}{\rho} - \frac{1}{\rho'}\right)$$

$$\text{Volumetric strain} = \frac{\Delta V}{V} = m\left(\frac{1}{\rho} - \frac{1}{\rho'}\right) \times \frac{\rho}{m}$$

$$= \left(1 - \frac{\rho}{\rho'}\right)$$

$$\text{Compressibility} = \frac{1}{\text{Bulk modulus } (K)} = \frac{1}{\dfrac{\Delta p}{(\Delta V / V)}} = \frac{\Delta V}{\Delta p V}$$

$$45.8 \times 10^{-11} = \left(1 - \frac{\rho}{\rho'}\right) \times \frac{1}{80 \times 1.013 \times 10^5}$$

$$45.8 \times 10^{-11} \times 80 \times 1.013 \times 10^5 = 1 - \frac{1.03 \times 10^3}{\rho'}$$

$$3.712 \times 10^{-3} = 1 - \frac{1.03 \times 10^3}{\rho'}$$

$$\frac{1.03 \times 10^3}{\rho'} = 1 - 3.712 \times 10^{-3}$$

or $\quad \rho' = \dfrac{1.03 \times 10^3}{1 - 0.003712} = 1.034 \times 10^3$ kg/m^3

33. Bulk modulus of rubber $(B) = 9.8 \times 10^8$ N/m^2

Density of seawater $(\rho) = 10^3$ kg/m^3

Percentage decrease in volume, $\left(\dfrac{\Delta V}{V} \times 100\right) = 0.1$

or $\quad \dfrac{\Delta V}{V} = \dfrac{0.1}{100}$ or $\dfrac{\Delta V}{V} = \dfrac{1}{1000}$

Let the rubber ball be taken upto depth h.

$\because$ Change in pressure $(p) = h\rho g$

$\therefore$ Bulk modulus $(B) = \dfrac{p}{(\Delta V / V)} = \dfrac{h\rho g}{(\Delta V / V)}$

or $\quad h = \dfrac{B \times (\Delta V / V)}{\rho g} = \dfrac{9.8 \times 10^8 \times \dfrac{1}{1000}}{10^3 \times 9.8} = 100$ m

34. Length of each side, $L = 4$ cm

Length displacement, $x = 0.012$ cm

$\eta = 2.08 \times 10^{11}$ dyne cm^{-2}

(i) Shearing strain, $\theta = \dfrac{x}{L} = \dfrac{0.012}{4} = 0.003$

(ii) From the relation, $\eta = \dfrac{F}{A\theta}$

Shearing stress, $\dfrac{F}{A} = \eta\theta$

$= 2.08 \times 10^{11} \times 3 \times 10^{-3}$

$= 6.24 \times 10^8$ dyne cm^{-2}

(iii) Shearing force = Shearing stress × Area

$= 6.24 \times 10^8 \times L^2$

$= 6.24 \times 10^8 \times 4^2$

$= 9.984 \times 10^9$ dyne

35. Area of face parallel to which the force is applied, $A = 50 \text{ cm} \times 10 \text{ cm} = 500 \text{ cm}^2 = 0.05 \text{ m}^2$

Modulus of rigidity, $\eta = \dfrac{F/A}{\Delta L / L}$

$$\Delta L = \frac{FL}{\eta A}$$

$$\Delta L = \frac{(9 \times 10^4)(0.5)}{5.6 \times 10^9 \times 0.05}$$

$= 1.6 \times 10^{-4}$ m $= 0.16$ mm

QR Code for Quick Test 1

QR Code for Quick Test 2

SELF ASSESSMENT TEST

Multiple Choice Questions (MCQs)

1. In solids, interatomic forces are

(a) totally repulsive

(b) totally attractive

(c) Both (a) and (b)

(d) None of the above

2. The nature of molecular forces resembles with the nature of the

(a) gravitational force (b) nuclear force

(c) electromagnetic force (d) weak force

3. *A* and *B* are two wires. The radius of *A* is twice that of *B*. They are stretched by the same load, then the stress on *B* is

(a) equal to that on *A* (b) four times that on *A*

(c) two times that on *A* (d) half that on *A*

4. A uniform cube is subjected to volume compression. If each side is decreased by 1%, then bulk strain is

(a) 0.01 (b) 0.06 (c) 0.02 (d) 0.03

5. A spring is stretched by applying a load to its free end. The strain produced in the spring is

(a) volumetric (b) shear

(c) longitudinal and shear (d) longitudinal

6. Modulus of rigidity of ideal liquids is

(a) infinity

(b) zero

(c) unity

(d) some finite small non-zero constant value

7. Match the Column I (Physical quantities) with Column II (Units).

	Column I		Column II
A.	Stress × Strain	1.	J
B.	$\frac{YA}{l}$	2.	N/m
C.	Yl^3	3.	J/m^3
D.	$\frac{Fl}{AY}$	4.	m

(a) A-3, B-4, C-2, D-1 (b) A-2, B-1, C-4, D-3

(c) A-1, B-2, C-3, D-4 (d) A-3, B-2, C-1, D-4

Assertion-Reason

Directions *(Q.No. 8-10) In the following questions, two statements are given- one labelled Assertion (A) and the other labelled Reason (R). Select the correct answer to these questions from the codes (a), (b), (c) and (d) as given below.*

(a) Both Assertion and Reason are true and Reason is the correct explanation of Assertion.

(b) Both Assertion and Reason are true but Reason is not the correct e xplanation of Assertion.

(c) Assertion is true but Reason is false.

(d) Assertion is false but Reason is true.

8. **Assertion** Bulk modulus of elasticity (*K*) represents incompressibility of the material.

Reason Bulk modulus of elasticity is proportional to change in pressure.

9. **Assertion** The stretching of a coil is determined by its shear modulus.

Reason Shear modulus change only shape of a body keeping its dimensions unchanged.

10. **Assertion** Identical springs of steel and copper are equally stretched. More work will be done on the steel spring.

Reason Steel is more elastic than copper.

Very Short Answer Type Questions

11. What is the Young's modulus for a perfect rigid body? How are we able to break a wire by repeated bending?

12. If the angle of shear is 30° for a cubical body and the change in length is 250 cm, then what must be the volume of this cubical body?

13. What is the ratio of the normal stress to Young's modulus? A metal is subjected to a stress of 5×10^3 N/m^2. If strain in the metal is 5×10^{-5}, find the value of Young's modulus.

Short Answer Type Questions

14. A lift is tied with thick iron wires and its mass is 1000 kg. If the maximum acceleration of lift is 1.2 ms^{-2} and the maximum safe stress is 1.4×10^8 Nm^{-2}, then

find the minimum diameter of the wire.
(Take, $g = 9.8 \text{ ms}^{-2}$)

15. Determine the fractional change in volume as the pressure of the atmosphere 1.0×10^5 Pa around a metal block is reduced to zero by placing the block in vacuum. The Bulk modulus for the block is $1.25 \times 10^{11} \text{ Nm}^{-2}$.

Long Answer Type Questions

16. Two wires of diameter 0.25 cm, one made of steel and other made of brass are loaded as shown in figure. The unloaded length of steel wire is 1.5 m and that of brass wire is 1.0 m. Young's modulus of steel is 2.0×10^{11} Pa. Compute the elongations of steel and brass wires. ($1 \text{Pa} = 1 \text{ N/m}^2$)

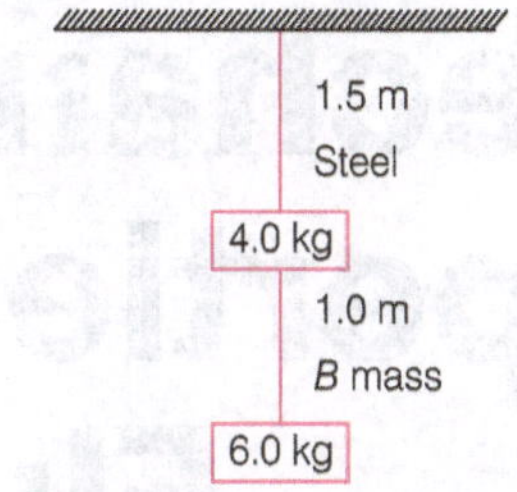

17. A light rod of length 2 m is suspended from the ceiling horizontally by means of two vertical wires of equal length tied to its ends. One of the wires is made of steel and is of cross-sectional area 0.1 sq. cm and the other is of brass of cross-sectional area 0.2 sq. cm. Find out the position along the rod at which a weight may be hung to produce

(i) equal stress in both wires and

(ii) equal strain in both wires.

(Given, Y for steel $= 20 \times 10^{11} \text{dyne cm}^{-2}$ and Y for brass $= 10 \times 10^{11} \text{dyne cm}^{-2}$)

18. The edge of an aluminium cube is 10 cm long. One face of the cube is firmly fixed to a vertical wall. A mass of 100 kg is then attached to the opposite face of the cube. The shear modulus of aluminium is 25 GPa. What is the vertical deflection of this face?

19. A composite wire of diameter 1 cm consisting of copper and steel wire of lengths 2.2 m and 2.0 m, respectively. Total extension of the wire, when stretched by a force is 1.2 mm. Calculate the force, given that Young's modulus for copper is 1.1×10^{11} Pa and for steel is 2.0×10^{11} Pa.

Answers

1. (c) *2.* (c) *3.* (b) *4.* (d) *5.* (c)
6. (b) *7.*(d) *8.* (a) *9.* (a) *10.*(a)
12. 81.309 m^3 *13.* 10^8 N/m^2 *14.* 10^{-2}m
15. 8×10^{-7} *16.* 1.5×10^{-4}m, 1.3×10^{-4} m
17. (i) $\frac{4}{3}$m (ii) 1 m
18. 3.92×10^{-7}m
19. 3142 N

09

CHAPTER

Mechanical Properties of Fluids

Mechanical properties of fluid deals with **viscosity, density and pressure** which describe how fluids respond to external force and influence their behaviour in various situations.

Fluids are substances that can flow under the action of an external force e.g. liquids and gases. Fluid does not have a definite shape, but takes the shape of the containing vessel. Both compressibility and viscosity of an ideal fluid is zero.

YOUR STUDY GOALS

YOUR PRACTICE GOAL

- Objective Type Questions (33 Qs, MCQs, A-R, Matching) Case Based Questions (2)
- Subjective Questions
- (3 VSAs, 3 SAs, 8 LAs)
- Numerical Problems (25)

9.1 Hydrostatics

The study of fluids at rest is known as hydrostatics or **fluid statics.**

Thrust

The molecules of a fluid are always in the state of motion, in result they exert a force on the wall of the container in which they are kept. **The total force exerted by the molecules of a liquid on the surface in contact, is called thrust.** Its SI unit is newton (N).

Thrust always acts in perpendicular direction to surface in contact as shown below.

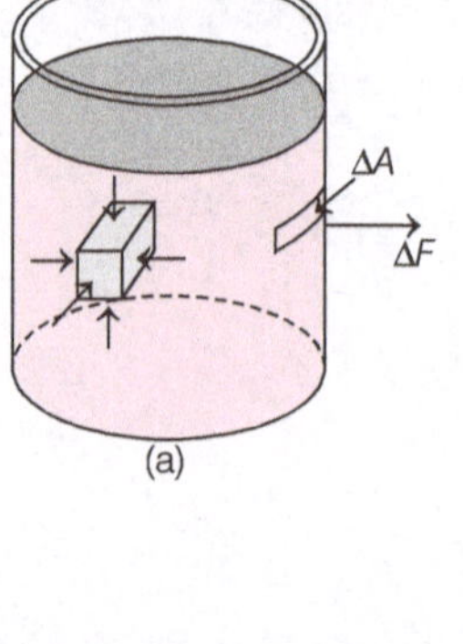

(a)

Pressure

The thrust exerted by a liquid per unit area of the surface in contact is called pressure.

If the total force F acts normally over a flat area A, then the pressure is given by

$$p = \frac{\text{Thrust}}{\text{Area}} = \frac{F}{A}$$

This pressure is also known as **average pressure** (p_{av}).

If the force is not distributed uniformly over the given surface, then pressure will be different at different points. If a force ΔF acts normally on a small area ΔA surrounding a given point, then pressure at that point will be

$$p = \lim_{\Delta A \to 0} \frac{\Delta F}{\Delta A} = \frac{dF}{dA}$$

The unit of pressure is **N/m^2** or **pascal** in SI system and **dyne/cm^2** in CGS system.

1 Pa (or 1 N/m^2) = 10 dyne/cm^2

Pressure is a scalar quantity and its dimensional formula is $[ML^{-1}T^{-2}]$.

Practical Applications of Pressure

(i) A sharp knife cuts better than a blunt one.

(ii) A camel walks easily on sand while it is difficult to walk on sand for a man.

(iii) Railway tracks are laid on large sized wooden or iron sleepers.

(iv) A sharp needle peers the skin easily but not a dull needle although the force applied in both the cases is the same.

Atmospheric Pressure

The pressure exerted by the atmosphere is called atmospheric pressure.

- The force exerted by air column on a unit area on the earth's surface is equal to the atmospheric pressure, it is denoted by p_a.
- Barometer is a device used to measure the atmospheric pressure.

Note A drop in the atmospheric pressure by 10 mm of Hg or more is a sign of an approaching storm.

Different Units of Atmospheric Pressure

- Atmospheric pressure (atm) is the pressure exerted by 76 cm of Hg column (at 0°C, 95° latitude and mean sea level).
- A pressure equivalent of 1 mm of Hg is called a torr named after Torricelli.
- The relation between different units of presssure are given below.

$$1 \text{ bar} = 10^5 \text{ Pa} = 10^6 \text{ dyne/cm}^2$$

$$1 \text{ torr} = 1 \text{ mm of Hg} = 133 \text{ Pa}$$

$$1 \text{ atm} = 1.013 \times 10^5 \text{ N/m}^2 = 1.01 \text{ bar } = 760 \text{ torr}$$

Example 1. The two thigh bones (femurs), each of cross-sectional area 10 cm^2 support the upper part of a human body of mass 40 kg. Estimate the average pressure sustained by the femurs. (NCERT)

Sol. Total area of femurs, $A = 2 \times 10 \text{ cm}^2 = 20 \times 10^{-4} \text{ m}^2$

The weight (mg) of the body is acting downward.

Force on the bones, $F = mg$

$$= (40)(10) = 400 \text{ N} \quad [\because g = 10 \text{ m/s}^2]$$

$$\therefore \quad p_{av} = \frac{F}{A} = \frac{400}{20 \times 10^{-4}} = 2 \times 10^5 \text{ N/m}^2$$

Density and Relative Density

Density of a substance is defined as mass per unit volume of the substance. It is denoted by ρ.

If M be the mass of a substance of volume V, then density of that substance is given by

$$\text{Density, } \rho = \frac{M}{V}$$

The SI unit of density is kg/ m^3 and dimensional formula is $[ML^{-3}]$.

- Liquids are highly incompressible, so density of liquids is almost constant at all pressures.
- As temperature increases, density decreases and *vice versa*.

Relative density (or specific gravity) of substance is defined as the ratio of the density of that substance to the density of water at 4° C, i.e.

$$\text{Relative density} = \frac{\text{Density of substance}}{\text{Density of water at } 4^\circ \text{C}}$$

It has no unit and no dimensions. It is a positive **scalar quantity**. The density of water at 4° C is maximum and equal to 1000 kg/m^3.

Example 2. In making an alloy, a substance of specific gravity s_1 and mass m_1 is mixed with another substance of specific gravity s_2 and mass m_2. Find the specific gravity of the alloy.

Sol. Specific gravity of alloy $= \dfrac{\text{Density of alloy}}{\text{Density of water}}$

$$= \frac{\text{Mass of alloy}}{\text{Volume of alloy} \times \text{Density of water}}$$

$$= \frac{m_1 + m_2}{\left(\dfrac{m_1}{\rho_1} + \dfrac{m_2}{\rho_2}\right) \times \rho_w} = \frac{m_1 + m_2}{\dfrac{m_1}{\rho_1/\rho_w} + \dfrac{m_2}{\rho_2/\rho_w}} = \frac{m_1 + m_2}{\dfrac{m_1}{s_1} + \dfrac{m_2}{s_2}}$$

Pascal's Law

This law states that **the pressure in a fluid at rest is same at all points if they are at the same height**. In other words, for a liquid in equilibrium, the pressure is same at all points in a horizontal plane.

e.g. In the below figure, the pressure of liquid at height A, B and C will be equal because they are at the same height.

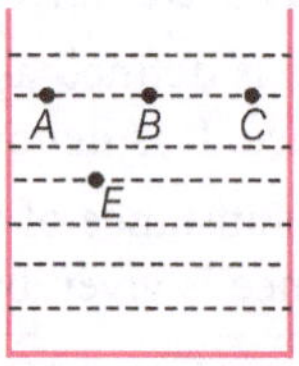

But pressure between points A and E (or B and E, C and E) will be different because they are not at the same height.

Variation of Pressure with Depth

The pressure at a point A inside the liquid is

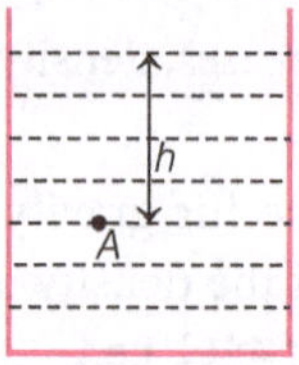

$$p = \rho g h$$

where, ρ = density of liquid,

g = acceleration due to gravity

and h = depth of the point in the liquid

Proof

Consider a fluid at rest having density ρ contained in a cylindrical vessel as shown in figure. Let the two points A and B separated by a vertical distance h.

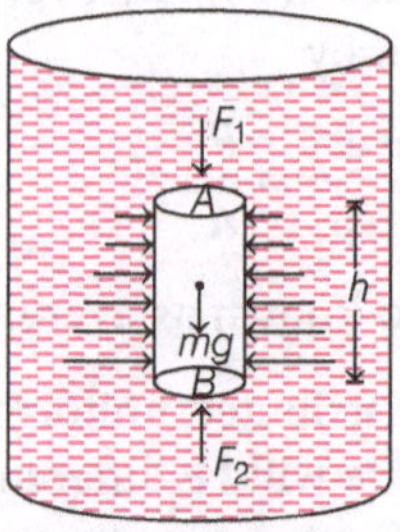

Fluid under gravity

Now, we consider an imaginary cylinder of fluid of cross-sectional area A, such that points A and B lie on its upper and lower circular faces, respectively. Then, weight of fluid cylinder acting downwards,

$$w = m \times g = \text{volume} \times \text{density} \times g = Ah\rho g$$

where, $V = A \times h$

As the fluid is at rest, the resultant horizontal forces should be zero and the resultant vertical forces should balance the weight of the element.

$\therefore$ Net downward force = Net upward force

$$F_1 + w = F_2$$

where, F_1 is the force acting downwards at the top and F_2 is the force acting upwards at the bottom.

$$F_2 - F_1 = w$$

$$p_2 A - p_1 A = Ah\rho g$$

$$\Rightarrow \quad A(p_2 - p_1) = A(h\rho g)$$

Pressure difference, $p_2 - p_1 = h\rho g$

Hence, **the pressure difference depends on the vertical height (i.e. distance between point A and point B), density of the fluid and the acceleration due to gravity.**

If point A is shifted to the fluid surface, which is open to the atmosphere, then replace p_1 by atmospheric pressure p_a and p_2 by p, we get

Pressure, $p = p_a + h\rho g$

Thus, the pressure p at depth below the surface of a liquid open to the atmosphere is greater than atmospheric pressure by an amount ρgh.

Example 3. **What is the pressure on a swimmer 10 m below the surface of a lake? (NCERT) (Take, $\rho = 1000\ \text{kg/m}^3$)**

Sol. Here, $h = 10$ m and $\rho = 1000$ kg/m³

$g = 10\ \text{m/s}^2$

$p = p_a + \rho g h = 1.01 \times 10^5 + 1000 \times 10 \times 10$

$= 2.01 \times 10^5\ \text{Pa} \simeq 2\ \text{atm}$

Hydrostatic Paradox

The principle of hydrostatic paradox states that the pressure exerted by a liquid depends only on the height of fluid column and is independent of the shape of the containing vessel.

As shown in the figure, three vessels *A*, *B*, and *C* are filled with the same height of liquid. The pressure at the bottom of each container will be the same.

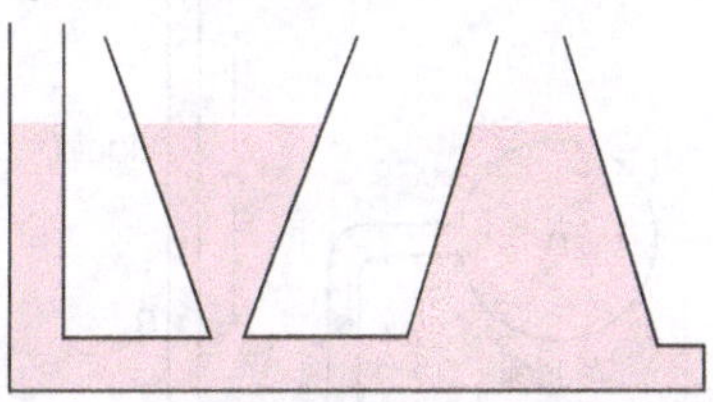

Three vessels *A*, *B* and *C* containing different amounts of liquids

Absolute Pressure and Gauge Pressure

The total or actual pressure *p* at a point is called **absolute pressure.**

Gauge pressure is the difference between the actual pressure (or absolute pressure) at a point and the atmospheric pressure, i.e. $p_g = p - p_a = h\rho g$

- It is proportional to *h*.
- It is measured by devices such as tyre pressure gauge, blood pressure gauge (sphygmomanometer), etc.

TEACHER TIP

The gauge pressure may be positive or negative depending on $p > p_a$ or $p < p_a$.

In inflated tyres or the human circulatory system, the absolute pressure is greater than atmospheric pressure, so gauge pressure is **positive**, called the **over pressure.**

However, when we suck a fluid through a straw, the absolute pressure in our lungs is less than atmospheric pressure and so, the gauge pressure is **negative.**

Example 4. **At a depth 1000 m in an ocean,**

(i) what is the absolute pressure?

(ii) what is the gauge pressure?

(iii) Find the force acting on the window of area 20 cm × 20 cm of a submarine at this depth, the interior of which is maintained at sea-level atmospheric pressure. (The density of sea water is $1.03 \times 10^3\ \text{kgm}^{-3}$ and $g = 10\ \text{ms}^{-2}$) NCERT

Sol. (i) Given, $h = 1000$ m and $\rho = 1.03 \times 10^3\ \text{kg/m}^3$

We know that absolute pressure, $p = p_a + \rho g h$

$p = 1.01 \times 10^5 + 1.03 \times 10^3 \times 10 \times 1000$

$p = 104.01 \times 10^5\ \text{Pa} \approx 104\ \text{atm}$

(ii) Now gauge pressure $p_g = p - p_a \Rightarrow p_g = 104 - 1$

$\because\ p_a = 1$ atm

$\Rightarrow\ p_g = 103$ atm

(iii) $\therefore$ The pressure outside the submarine is *p*, while pressure inside it, is p_a.

Given, $A = 400\ \text{cm}^2 = 0.04\ \text{m}^2$.

The net pressure acting on the window is gauge pressure, then $p_g = \dfrac{F}{A}$

$\Rightarrow\ F = p_g A$

or $F = 103 \times 10^5 \times 0.04 = 4.12 \times 10^5$ N

Example 5. **What are the absolute and gauge pressures of the gas above the liquid surface in the tank shown in figure? Given, density of oil = 820 kg m⁻³, density of mercury = $13.6 \times 10^3\ \text{kgm}^{-3}$ and 1 atm pressure = 1.01×10^5 Pa.**

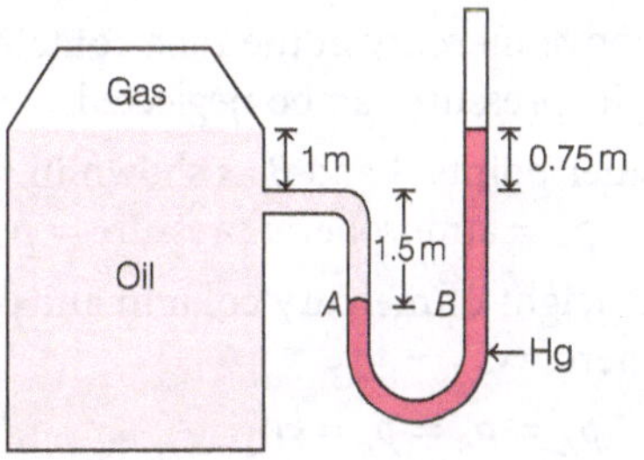

Sol. As the points *A* and *B* are at the same level in the mercury column, so $p_A = p_B$

Now, $p_A = p + (1.50 + 1.00) \times 820 \times 9.8$

where, *p* is the pressure of the gas in the tank.

And $p_B = p' + (1.50 + 0.75) \times 13.6 \times 10^3 \times 9.8$

where, p' is the atmospheric pressure

As, $p_A = p_B$

$p - p' = 2.25 \times 13.6 \times 10^3 \times 9.8 - 2.50 \times 820 \times 9.8$

$= 3 \times 10^5 - 0.2 \times 10^5 = 2.8 \times 10^5\ \text{Pa}$

$\therefore$ Gauge pressure

= Absolute pressure − Atmospheric pressure

$p_g = p - p' = 2.8 \times 10^5$ Pa $\quad [\because p' = p_a]$

Absolute pressure

= Gauge pressure + Atmospheric pressure

$$p = 2.8 \times 10^5 + 1.01 \times 10^5$$
$$= 3.81 \times 10^5 \text{ Pa}$$

Mercury Barometer

An Italian scientist **Evangelista Torricelli** (1608-1647), first devised an instrument to measure atmospheric pressure. It is known as **barometer**.

A long glass tube closed at one end and filled with mercury is inverted into a trough of mercury.

We find that mercury column in the tube has height of about 76 cm above the mercury level in the trough.

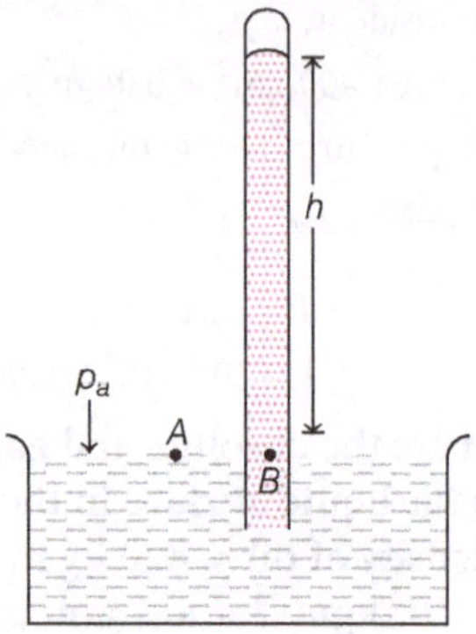

Mercury barometer

The space above mercury in the tube contains mercury vapour and its pressure can be neglected.

Let us consider points A and B as shown in the figure.

Then, $p_A = p_B$ = atmospheric pressure = p_a.

Let h be the height of mercury column and ρ be the density of mercury.

So, $$p_A = p_B = p_a = h\rho g$$
$$h = 0.76 \text{ m}$$
$$\rho = 13.6 \times 10^3 \text{ kg/m}^3$$
$$g = 9.8 \text{ m/s}^2$$

By putting values, atmospheric pressure,

$$p_a = 0.76 \times 13.6 \times 10^3 \times 9.8$$
$$= 1.013 \times 10^5 \text{ N/m}^2$$
$$= 1.013 \times 10^5 \text{ Pa}$$

This is the atmospheric pressure at the sea level.

The pressure can also be stated in terms of cm or mm of mercury (Hg).

- The vertical height of mercury level remains unaffected even if the tube is tilted, raised or lowered in a mercury traugh.

Open Tube Manometer

Open tube manometer is used to measure pressure difference.

It consists of a U-shaped tube containing a liquid having low density such as oil to measure the small pressure difference and mercury as the high density liquid to measure the large pressure difference.

One end of the tube is open to the atmosphere and the other end is joined with a flask, whose pressure we want to know.

The arrangement is shown in the figure below

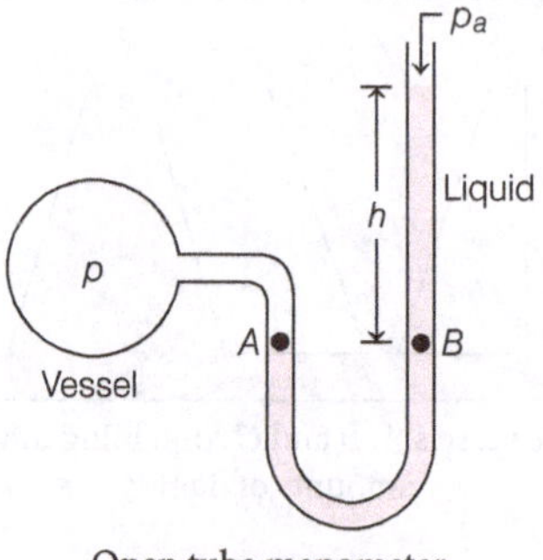

Open tube manometer

The pressure at point A is equal to pressure at point B.

$\therefore$ $$p_A = p_B \text{ (Pascal's law)}$$

As $$p_A = p_a + h\rho g$$

So, $$p_B = p_a + h\rho g$$

> **Height of Atmosphere**
>
> The standard atmospheric pressure is 1.013×10^5 Pa. If the atmosphere of the earth has uniform density $\rho = 1.29 \text{ kg/m}^3$, then the height h of the air column which exerts the standard atmospheric pressure is given by $h\rho g = 1.013 \times 10^5$
>
> $$h = \frac{1.013 \times 10^5}{\rho g} = \frac{1.013 \times 10^5}{1.29 \times 9.8}$$
> $$h = 8.01 \times 10^3 \text{ m} \approx 8 \text{ km}$$
>
> In fact, both the density of air and the value of g decrease with height and the earth's atmosphere extends up to 100 km.

Pascal's Law for Transmission of Fluid Pressure

Pascal's law states that, **whenever external pressure is applied on any part of a fluid contained in a vessel at rest, it is transmitted undiminished and equally in all directions.**

Applications of Pascal's Law

(i) Hydraulic Lift

Hydraulic lift is an application of Pascal's law. It is used to lift heavy loads. It is a force multiplier.

Example Consider a hydraulic lift that consists of two cylinders C_1 and C_2 connected by a pipe E containing a liquid as shown below.

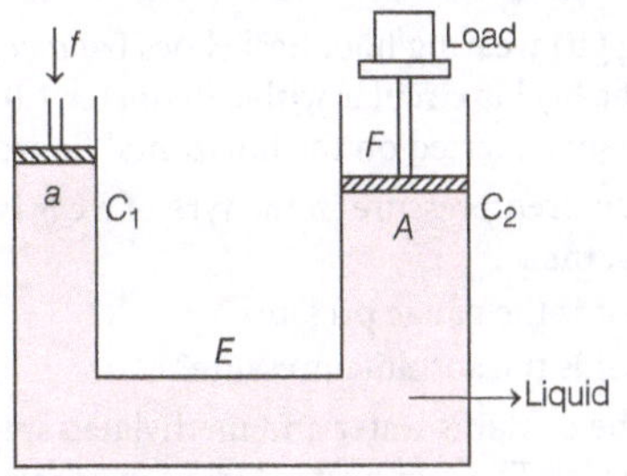

Suppose, a downward force f is applied on the smaller piston of cross-sectional area a. Then, pressure exerted on the liquid,

$$p = \frac{f}{a}$$

According to Pascal's law, this pressure p is transmitted to the larger piston of cross-sectional area A, then upward force on larger piston C_2 is

$$F = p \times A = \frac{f}{a} \times A = \frac{A}{a} \times f$$

> Upward force on the larger piston, $F = \frac{A}{a} f$

As, $A > a$, therefore $F > f$.

- This experiment shows that applied force (f) has been increased by a factor $\frac{A}{a}$ and this factor is called **mechanical advantage** of the hydraulic lift.
- So, a smaller force at the smaller piston can generate a significantly larger force on a larger piston, allowing heavy loads to be lifted efficiently.

Example 6. In a car lift compressed air exerts a force F_1 on a small piston having a radius of 5.0 cm. This pressure is transmitted to a second piston of radius 15 cm. If the mass of the car to be lifted is 1350 kg, calculate F_1. What is the pressure necessary to accomplish this task? ($g = 9.8\ \text{ms}^{-2}$). NCERT

Sol. Given, $r_1 = 5\text{ cm} = 0.05\text{ m}$,

$$r_2 = 15\text{ cm} = 0.15\text{ m},$$
$$m = 1350\text{ kg}$$
$$F_2 = mg = 1350 \times 9.8\text{ N}$$

As the pressure through air is transmitted equally in all directions, so that the pressures p_1 and p_2 will be same.

$$\therefore \quad p_1 = p_2$$

Since, the pressure is transmitted undiminished through the fluid,

$$\Rightarrow \quad \frac{F_1}{A_1} = \frac{F_2}{A_2}$$

$$\Rightarrow \quad \frac{F_1}{\pi r_1^2} = \frac{F_2}{\pi r_2^2}$$

$$\therefore \quad F_1 = F_2 \times \left(\frac{r_1}{r_2}\right)^2$$

$$= 1350 \times 9.8 \times \left(\frac{5}{15}\right)^2$$

$$\simeq 1.47 \times 10^3\text{ N}$$

Now, the required air pressure necessary to lift the car can be calculated.

The air pressure p which will produce the force of 1.47×10^3 N is $p = \frac{F_1}{A_1} = \frac{1.47 \times 10^3}{\pi (0.05)^2}$

$$\Rightarrow \quad p = 1.9 \times 10^5\text{ Pa}$$

(ii) Hydraulic Brakes

The working of the hydraulic brakes is also based on the Pascal's law.

- When brake pedal is pressed by the foot, then the pressure caused is transmitted through the brake oil to act on the piston. Thus, the piston is pushed down and brake shoes expand against brake lining. Thus, the vehicle stops or slows down.
- The advantage of this system is, pressure set up by pressing pedal is transmitted equally to all cylinders attached to all the wheels, i.e. braking effort is equal on all wheels.

Buoyancy

The upward force acting on the body immersed in a fluid is called **upward thrust** or **buoyant force** and the phenomenon is called buoyancy.

- Buoyant force acts through the centre of gravity of the displaced fluid which is called **centre of buoyancy**.
- Upward thrust force does not depend on mass, size or density of immersed body and depends only on volume immersed and nature (density) of displaced liquid.

Archimedes' Principle

The Archimedes' principle gives the magnitude of buoyant force on a body. It states that **when a body is immersed wholly or partially in a liquid at rest, it experiences an upthrust. The upthrust is equal to the weight of the liquid displaced by the immersed part of the body and its upthrust acts through the centre of gravity of the displaced fluid.**

Law of Floatation

The following three cases are possible when the body is immersed in the fluid.

(i) If the weight of the body is greater than the upward force or upthrust by the fluid acting upwards, then the body **sinks**.

(ii) If the weight of the body is equal to the upthrust or the weight of the body is just balanced by upthrust, then the body floats **fully immersed**.

(iii) If the weight of the body is less than the upward force or upthrust, then the body floats **partly immersed**.

When ice floats in a liquid and completely melts, then there could be following cases.

(i) If $\rho_l > \rho_w$, the level of liquid will rise.

(ii) If $\rho_l < \rho_w$, the level of liquid will decrease.

(iii) If $\rho_l = \rho_w$, the level of liquid will remain the same.

where, ρ_l is the density of liquid and ρ_w is the density of water.

Quick Test 1

Conceptual Questions

1. Why the passengers are advised to remove ink from their pens, while going up in an aeroplane?

2. Three vessels have same base area and different neck area. Equal volume of liquid is poured into them, which will possess more pressure at the base?.

3. A mercury barometer is placed in the mercury trough in a way that the angle made with the vertical is 60°. Find the height of mercury column.

4. Why does a hydrogen filled balloon go up ?

5. One gram of iron and 1 cm^3 of aluminium are dropped into water. Which of the two shall experience large buoyant force and why?

Numerical Questions

6. A 50 kg girl wearing high heel shoes balances on a single heel. The heel is circular with a diameter 1.0 cm. What is the pressure exerted on the horizontal floor? NCERT

7. If the required pressure in the tyre of a car is 199 kPa, then

(i) what is the gauge pressure?

(ii) what is the absolute pressure?

8. A U-tube contains water and methylated spirit separated by mercury. The mercury columns in the two arms are in level with 10.0 cm of water in one arm and 12.5 cm of spirit in the other. What is the specific gravity of spirit? NCERT

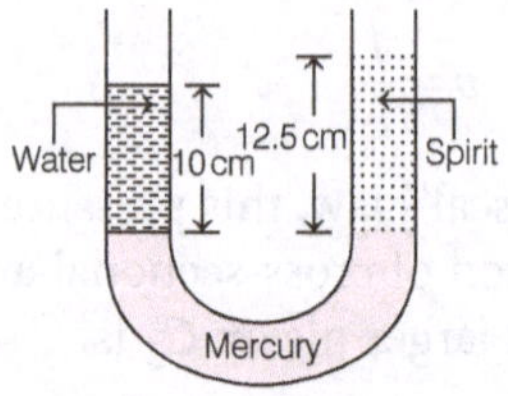

9. Torricelli's barometer used mercury. Pascal duplicated it using French wine of density 948 kg/m^3. Determine the height of the wine column for normal atmospheric pressure. NCERT

10. A hydraulic automobile lift is designed to lift cars with a maximum mass of 3000 kg. The area of cross-section of the piston carrying the load is 425 cm^2. What maximum pressure would the smaller piston have to bear? NCERT

Answers

6. 6.24×10^6 Pa *7.* (i) 199 kPa (ii) 300 k Pa 8. 0.80

9. 10.5 m *10.* 6.92×10^5 Pa

For Solutions, See QR Code on Pg. 333

9.2 Surface Tension and Surface Energy

Surface Tension

The free surface of a liquid acts like a stretched membrane and tends to occupy the minimum surface area. This property of the liquid is called surface tension. It is denoted by S.

Quantitatively, **surface tension can be defined as the force acting per unit length of an imaginary line drawn on the liquid surface.**

$$\text{Surface tension, } S = \frac{\text{Force}}{\text{Length}}$$

The direction of force will be perpendicular to the imaginary line and tangential to the liquid surface.

- It is a scalar quantity.
- Its SI unit is N/m or J/m^2 and CGS unit is dyne/cm or erg/cm^2.
- Its dimensional formula is $[ML^0T^{-2}]$.

Factors Affecting the Surface Tension

- It decreases with increase of temperature.
- It depends on the intermolecular forces and does not depend on the gravity (g).
- The presence of dust, oil or grease on the surface of water reduces surface tension.

Applications of Surface Tension

(i) Rain drops and drops of mercury placed on glass plate are spherical.

(ii) Hair of shaving brush/painting brush, when dipped in water spread out, but as soon as, it is taken out, its hair stick together.

(iii) A greased needle placed gently on the free surface of water in a beaker does not sink.

(iv) Oil drop spreads on cold water but does not change shape on hot water.

Example 7. **A U-shaped wire is dipped in a soap solution and removed. The thin soap film formed between the wire and a light slider supports a weight of 1.5×10^{-2} N (which includes the small weight of the slider). The length of the slider is 30 cm. What is the surface tension of the film?** NCERT

Sol. Length of the slider (l) = 30 cm

As a soap film has two free surfaces, therefore total length of the film to be supported,

$$l' = 2l = 2 \times 30$$
$$= 60 \text{ cm} = 0.60 \text{ m}$$

Let S be the surface tension of the soap solution.

Total force on the slider due to surface tension,

$$F = S \times 2l$$
$$F = S \times 0.60 \text{ N} \quad \ldots \text{(i)}$$

Weight (w) supported by the slider $= 1.5 \times 10^{-2}$ N

In equilibrium,

Force on the slider due to surface tension = Weight supported by the slider

$$\therefore \quad F = w$$
$$S \times 0.60 = 1.5 \times 10^{-2}$$
$$\text{or} \quad S = \frac{1.5 \times 10^{-2}}{0.60} = 2.5 \times 10^{-2} \text{ N/m}$$

Surface Energy

Surface energy is defined as the amount of work done in increasing the area of the liquid surface by unity against the force of surface tension at constant temperature.

Surface energy = Work done

= Surface tension × Surface area of liquid

i.e., $W = S\Delta A$

The SI unit of the surface enegy is J/m^2 and CGS unit is erg/cm^2.

Example 8. **Find the work done required to make a soap bubble of radius 0.02 m. Given, surface tension of soap is 0.03 N/m.**

Sol. Given, $S = 0.03$ N/m

Work done = Surface area × Surface tension

$$= 2 \times 4\pi r^2 \times S$$
$$= 2 \times 4 \times 3.14 \times (0.02)^2 \times 0.03 = 3 \times 10^{-4} \text{ J}$$

Angle of Contact

When the free surface of a liquid comes in contact with a solid, then the surface of liquid becomes curved at the point of contact. **The angle between tangent to the liquid surface at the point of contact and the solid surface inside the liquid is called as angle of contact.** It is denoted by θ.

The value of angle of contact depends on the relative magnitudes of adhesive forces (F_A) between solid-liquid molecules and cohesive force (F_C) between liquid molecules.

Consider the following cases

(a) If adhesive force is greater than cohesive force (i.e., $F_A > F_C$), then the liquid wets the solid and the angle of contact is acute (i.e., $\theta < 90°$).

(b) If adhesive force is less than cohesive force (i.e., $F_A < F_C$), then the liquid will not wet the solid and the angle of contact is obtuse (i.e., $90° < \theta < 180°$).

(c) If adhesive force is equal to cohesive force (i.e., $F_A = F_C$), then the angle of contact will be 90° (i.e., $\theta = 90°$).

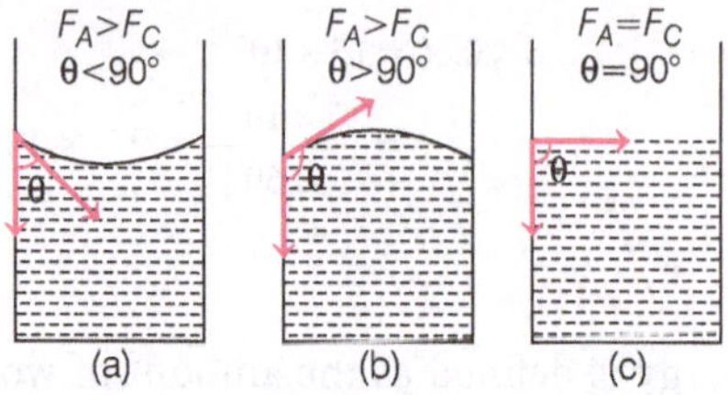

Excess Pressure across a Spherical Surface

The difference between the inside and outside pressure of a spherical surface is called excess pressure.

- The pressure inside a liquid or air drop will be greater than the pressure outside the drop.
- The liquid and air drop have one free surface while soap bubble has two free surfaces.

The excess pressure inside a liquid or air drop is given by

$$\Delta p = \frac{2S}{R}$$

The excess pressure inside a soap bubble is given by

$$\Delta p = \frac{4S}{R}$$

where, R represents the radius and S represents the surface tension.

TEACHER TIP

When an air bubble of radius R lies at a depth h below the free surface of a liquid of density ρ and surface tension S, the excess pressure inside the bubble will be $p = \frac{2S}{R} + h\rho g$

When an ice-skater slides over the surface of smooth ice, some ice melts due to the pressure exerted by the sharp metal edges of the skates. The tiny water droplets act as rigid ball bearings and help the skaters to run along smoothly.

Example 9. Calculate excess pressure in an air bubble of radius 6 mm. Surface tension of liquid is 0.58 N/m.

Sol. Excess pressure in soap bubble,

$$p = \frac{4S}{R} = \left(\frac{4 \times 0.58}{6 \times 10^{-3}}\right)$$

$$= 387 \text{ Nm}^{-2}$$

Example 10. The lower end of a capillary tube of diameter 2 mm is dipped 8 cm below the surface of water in a beaker. What is the pressure required in the tube in order to blow a hemispherical bubble at its end in water? The surface tension of water at temperature of the experiments is 7.30×10^{-2} Nm^{-1}, 1 atm = 1.01×10^5 Pa, density of water = 1000 kg / m^3 and g = 9.80 ms^{-2}. Also, calculate the excess pressure. NCERT

Sol. Given, $h = 0.08$ m, $\rho = 1000$ kg/m^3, $g = 9.80$ m/s^2 and

we know that, $p_0 = p_a + h\rho g$

p_0 is outside pressure

$$p_0 = 1.01 \times 10^5 + 0.08 \times 1000 \times 9.80$$

$$p_0 = 1.01784 \times 10^5 \text{ Pa}$$

Inside pressure,

$$p_i = p_0 + \frac{2S}{r}$$

where, $S = 7.30 \times 10^{-2}$ N/m

$$p_i = 1.01784 \times 10^5 + \frac{2 \times 7.3 \times 10^{-2}}{10^{-3}}$$

$$= (1.01784 + 0.00146) \times 10^5$$

$$\Rightarrow \quad p_i = 1.02 \times 10^5 \text{ Pa}$$

where, the radius of the bubble is taken to be equal to the radius of capillary tube. Since, the bubble is hemispherical the excess pressure in the bubble is 146 Pa.

Capillarity

The term capilla means hair in Latin word. A tube of very fine (hair-like) bore is called a **capillary tube**.

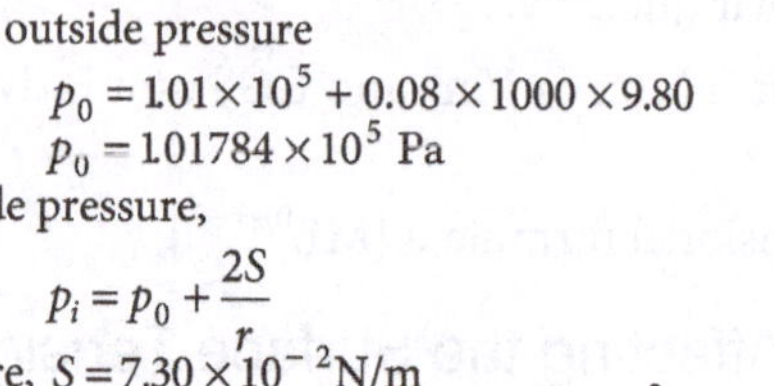

If a capillary tube of glass is dipped in liquid like water, the liquid rises in the tube, but when the capillary tube is dipped in a liquid like mercury, the level of liquid falls in the tube.

This phenomenon of rise or fall of a liquid in the capillary is called capillarity.

Some examples are

(i) We use towels for drying our skin.

(ii) In trees, sap rises due to vessels. It is similar to capillary action.

The liquids which wet the glass surfaces (when their angle of contact is acute) e.g., **water rises in the capillary and the liquids which do not wet the surface (when their angle of contact is obtuse)** falls in the capillary.

Height of rise or fall of liquid in capillary is given by

$$h = \frac{2S\cos\theta}{\rho R g}$$

where, S = Surface tension

θ = Angle of contact,

ρ = Density of liquid,

R = Radius of capillary tube and

g = Acceleration due to gravity.

Example 11. In a glass capillary tube, water rises upto a height of 10.0 cm, while mercury fall down by 5.0 cm in the same capillary. If the angles of contact for mercury glass is 60° and water glass is 0°, then find the ratio of surface tension of mercury and water.

Sol. For water, $h_1 = 10.0 \text{ cm} = 0.1 \text{ m}$

$$\rho_1 = 10^3 \text{ kg/m}^3, \theta = 0°$$

For mercury, $h_2 = 5.0 \text{ cm} = 0.05 \text{ m}$

$$\rho_2 = 13.6 \times 10^3 \text{ kg/m}^3,$$

$$\theta = 60°$$

Suppose S_1 and S_2 are the surface tensions for water and mercury respectively, then

$$S_1 = \frac{h_1 R\rho_1 g}{2\cos\theta_1} \text{ and } S_2 = \frac{h_2 R\rho_2 g}{2\cos\theta_2}$$

The ratio of surface tension of mercury and water,

$$\frac{S_2}{S_1} = \frac{h_2 R\rho_2 g}{2\cos\theta_2} \times \frac{2\cos\theta_1}{h_1 R\rho_1 g}$$

$$\frac{S_2}{S_1} = \frac{h_2\rho_2\cos\theta_1}{h_1\rho_1\cos\theta_2}$$

$$= \frac{0.05 \times 13.6 \times 10^3 \times \cos 0°}{0.1 \times 1000 \times \cos 60°}$$

$$= 13.6 : 1$$

Quick Test 2

Conceptual Questions

1. It becomes easier to spray the water in which some soap is dissolved. Why?

2. A drop of oil placed on surface of water spreads out but a drop of water placed on oil contracts to a spherical shape. Explain both phenomena.

3. How a raincoat becomes waterproof?

4. If a capillary tube is dipped vertically in water in a state of weightlessness, how will the rise of water in it be different to that observed in normal conditions?

5. Why bubbles are emitted when a piece of chalk is immersed in water?

Numerical Questions

6. Find the work done in increasing the radius of a soap bubble from 4 cm to 6 cm. The value of surface tension for the soap solution is 30 dyne cm^{-1}.

7. A capillary tube is dipped vertically in a liquid. The level of liquid in the capillary is the same as that outside the capillary. What is the angle of contact? *NCERT*

8. Two soap bubbles of radii 6 cm and 8 cm coalesce to form a single bubble. Find the radius of the new bubble.

9. Find the work done required to make a soap bubble of radius 0.02 m. Given, surface tension of soap is 0.03 N/m.

10. The sap in trees, which consists mainly of water in summer, rises in a system of capillaries of radius $r = 2.5 \times 10^{-5}$ m. The surface tension of sap is $S = 7.28 \times 10^{-2}$ N/m and angle of contact is 0°. Does surface tension alone account for the supply of water to the top of all trees? *NCERT Exemplar*

Answers

6. 15081.6 erg 7. 90° 8. 10 cm 9. 3×10^{-4} J

For Solutions, See QR Code on Pg. 333

9.3 Hydrodynamics

The branch of physics which deals with the study of fluids in motion is called **fluid dynamics** or hydrodynamics.

Streamline Flow

Streamline flow of a liquid is that flow in which every particle of the liquid follows exactly the path of its preceding particle and has same velocity in magnitude and direction as that of its preceding particle while crossing through that point.

- Streamline is defined as a curve whose tangent at any point is in the direction of the fluid velocity at that point.

Trajectory of a fluid particle

Properties

- Streamlines never cross each other.
- If they do so, the particles of the liquid at the point of intersection will have two different directions for their flow, which will destroy the steady nature of the liquid flow.
- The greater is the crowding of streamline at a place, greater is the velocity of the liquid particles at that place and *vice-versa*.

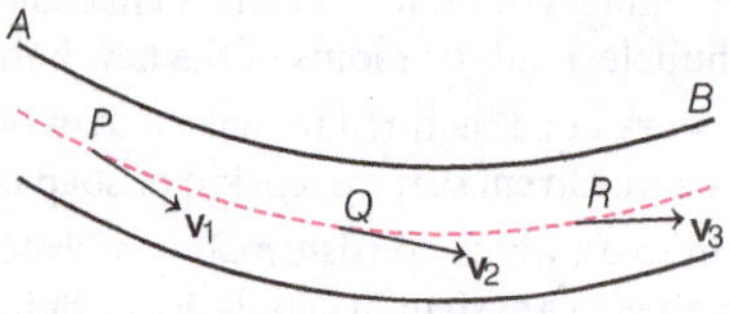

A region of streamline flow

Laminar Flow

If the liquid flows over a horizontal surface in the form of layers of different velocities, then the flow of liquid is called laminar flow.

In laminar flow, the particles of one layer do not enter into another layer. In general, laminar flow is a streamline flow.

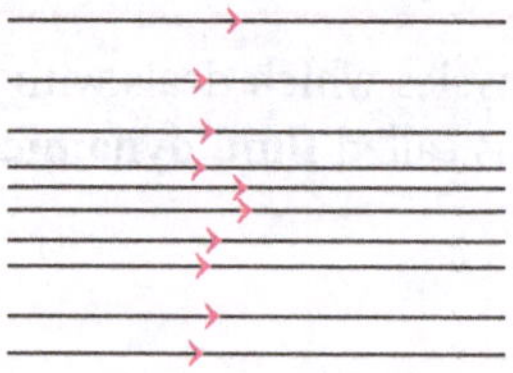
Laminar flow of liquid

Turbulent Flow

When a liquid moves with a high velocity, the motion of its particles becomes disorderly or irregular. Such a flow is called a turbulent flow.

The motion of a liquid in turbulent flow is shown below.

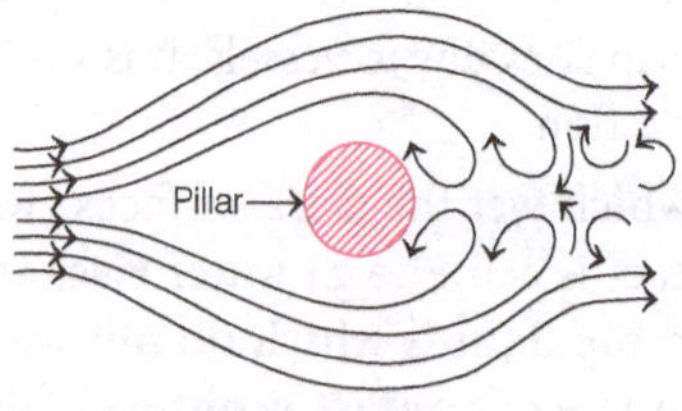

Turbulent flow of liquid

> **Ideal Fluid**
>
> The motion of real fluids is very complicated. To understand fluid dynamics in a simpler manner, we assume that the fluid is ideal. **An ideal fluid** is one which is non-viscous, incompressible, and its flow is steady and irrotational.

Equation of Continuity

It states that, **during the streamline flow of the non-viscous and incompressible fluid through a pipe of varying cross-section, the product of area of cross-section and the normal fluid velocity (av) remains constant throughout the flow.**

$$av = \text{constant} \Rightarrow a \propto \frac{1}{v}$$

The variation of fluid velocity (v) with the cross-sectional area (a) is shown below.

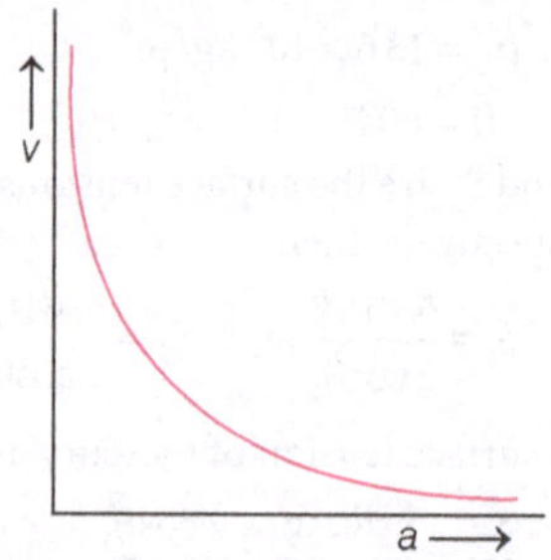

Bernoulli's Theorem

Bernoulli's principle states that **the total energy (pressure energy, kinetic energy and potential energy) per unit volume or mass of an incompressible and non-viscous fluid in steady flow remains constant throughout the flow.**

Mathematically, it can be expressed as

$$p + \frac{1}{2}\rho v^2 + \rho g h = \text{constant}$$

where, p represents pressure, v represents velocity, h represents height and ρ represents density of the fluid.

Proof

Consider an ideal fluid having streamline flow through a pipe of varying area of cross-section as shown in the following figure.

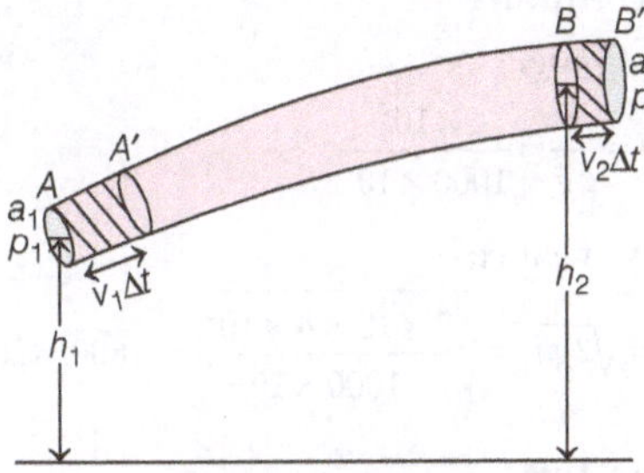

The flow of an ideal fluid in a pipe of varying cross-section

Let p_1, a_1, h_1, v_1 and p_2, a_2, h_2, v_2 be the pressure, area of cross-section, height and velocity of flow at points A and B, respectively.

Distance travelled by the fluid in one second at point A is $\quad d_1 = v_1\Delta t = v_1 \times 1 = v_1$

Work done per second on the fluid at point A

= Force × Distance travelled by fluid in one second

$$W_1 = p_1 a_1 \times v_1$$

Similarly, work done per second by the fluid at point B,

$$W_2 = p_2 a_2 v_2$$

∴ Net work done on the fluid by pressure energy,

$$W = p_1 a_1 v_1 - p_2 a_2 v_2$$

But $\quad a_1 v_1 = a_2 v_2 = \dfrac{m}{\rho}$ (i.e. equation of continuity)

∴ Net work done on the fluid by the pressure energy,

$$W = \left(\frac{p_1 m}{\rho} - \frac{p_2 m}{\rho}\right)$$

Total work done by the pressure energy on the fluid increases the kinetic energy and potential energy of the fluid, when it flows from A to B.

∴ Increase in potential energy of fluid

= KE at B − KE at A

$$= \frac{1}{2}mv_2^2 - \frac{1}{2}mv_1^2 \qquad (\because a_1 > a_2 \Rightarrow v_2 > v_1)$$

Similarly, total increase in potential energy

$$= mgh_2 - mgh_1$$

According to work-energy theorem, work done on the fluid is equal to change in the energy of fluid.

i.e. Work done by the pressure energy = Total increase in energy

$$\therefore \quad \frac{p_1 m}{\rho} - \frac{p_2 m}{\rho} = (mgh_2 - mgh_1) + \left(\frac{1}{2}mv_2^2 - \frac{1}{2}mv_1^2\right)$$

$$\left(\frac{p_1 - p_2}{\rho}\right) = (gh_2 - gh_1) + \frac{1}{2}v_2^2 - \frac{1}{2}v_1^2$$

or $$\frac{p_1}{\rho} + \frac{1}{2}v_1^2 + gh_1 = \frac{p_2}{\rho} + \frac{1}{2}v_2^2 + gh_2$$

Hence, $$\frac{p}{\rho} + gh + \frac{1}{2}v^2 = \text{constant}$$

$$p + \frac{1}{2}\rho v^2 + \rho gh = \text{constant} \qquad \text{...(i)}$$

Dividing both sides of Eq. (i) by ρg, we get

$$\frac{p}{\rho g} + h + \frac{v^2}{2g} = \text{new constant} \qquad \text{...(ii)}$$

Here, $\dfrac{p}{\rho g}$ is called **pressure head,** h is called **gravitational head** and $\dfrac{v^2}{2g}$ is called **velocity head.**

Eq. (ii) enables us to state Bernoulli's theorem in the streamline flow of an ideal liquid as **the sum of pressure head, gravitational head and velocity head is always constant.**

Special Cases

(i) If the fluid is flowing through a horizontal tube, two ends of the tube are at the same level. Therefore, there is no gravitational head. (level difference, i.e. $h = 0$).

$$p_1 + \frac{1}{2}\rho v_1^2 = p_2 + \frac{1}{2}\rho v_2^2$$

So, $$p + \frac{1}{2}\rho v^2 = \text{constant}$$

Bernoulli's principle states that in a horizontal tube with steady streamline flow, an increase in pressure (p) results in a decrease in velocity (v) and *vice-versa*.

(ii) When a fluid at rest, i.e. the velocity is zero everywhere, then the Bernoulli's equation becomes

$$p_1 + \rho gh_1 = p_2 + \rho gh_2$$
$$p_1 - p_2 = \rho g(h_2 - h_1)$$

Limitations of Bernoulli's Theorem

(i) Bernoulli's equation ideally applies to fluids with zero viscosity or non-viscous fluids.

(ii) The fluids must be incompressible, as the elastic energy of the fluid is also not taken into consideration.

(iii) Bernoulli's equation is applicable only to streamline flow of a fluid. It is not valid for non-steady or turbulent flow.

(iv) While deriving the equation, it is assumed that there is no loss of energy when liquid is in motion.

Example 12. A horizontal pipeline carries water in a streamline flow. At a point along the pipe where the cross-sectional area is 10 cm^2, the water velocity is 1 ms^{-1} and the pressure is 2000 Pa. What is the pressure at another point where the cross-sectional area is 5 cm^2?

Sol. According to the equation of continuity, we get

$$a_1v_1 = a_2v_2$$

or $\quad 10 \text{ cm}^2 \times 1\text{ms}^{-1} = 5 \text{ cm}^2 \times v_2$

$\therefore \quad v_2 = 2\text{ms}^{-1}$

Using Bernoulli's theorem for horizontal flow,

$$p_2 + \frac{1}{2}\rho v_2^2 = p_1 + \frac{1}{2}\rho v_1^2$$

or $\quad p_2 + \frac{1}{2} \times 10^3 \times 2^2 = 2000 + \frac{1}{2} \times 10^3 \times 1^2$

or $\quad p_2 = 2000 + 500 - 2000 = 500 \text{ Pa}$

Applications of Bernoulli's Theorem

(i) Velocity of Efflux (Torricelli's Law)

The velocity of efflux refers to the speed at which liquid flows out at some height from the bottom of container filled with liquid. It is equal to the velocity which a body acquires in falling freely from the free liquid surface to the orifice. This result is called **Torricelli's law.**

i.e. velocity of efflux, $v = \sqrt{2gh}$

where, h is depth of orifice from the free surface.

- If a small hole is located at a height y from the base of orifice, the distance at which the stream strikes the floor is $x = 2\sqrt{hy}$.

Example 13. If the water emerges from an orifice in a tank in which the gauge pressure is $4 \times 10^5 \text{ N/m}^2$ before the flow starts, then what will be the velocity of the water emerging out? [Take, density of water as 1000 kg m^{-3}].

Sol. Here, $\rho = 1000 \text{ kgm}^{-3}, p = 4 \times 10^5 \text{ N/m}^2$

and $\quad g = 10 \text{ m/s}^2$

Apply $p = h\rho g$,

$\Rightarrow \quad h = \frac{p}{\rho g} = \frac{4 \times 10^5}{1000 \times 10}$

Velocity of efflux,

$$v = \sqrt{2gh} = \sqrt{\frac{2 \times 10 \times 4 \times 10^5}{1000 \times 10}} = \sqrt{800} = 28.28 \text{ m/s}$$

(ii) Dynamic Lift

Dynamic lift is the force that acts on a body by virtue of its motion through a fluid. It is responsible for the curved path of a spinning ball and the lift of an aircraft wing.

(a) Ball Moving without Spin

When the velocity of the air above the ball is same as below the ball at the corresponding points resulting in zero pressure difference.

The air therefore, exerts no upward or downward force on the ball as shown in Fig. (a).

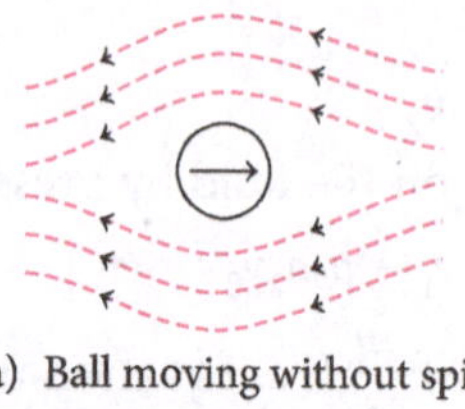

(a) Ball moving without spin

(b) Ball Moving with Spin

When a spinning ball moves through the air, the airflow around it becomes asymmetrical. The spin increases air velocity above the ball and decreases it below, creating a pressure difference. This results in a net upward force, causing the ball to curve in the direction of the spin as shown in Fig. (b).

The difference in lateral pressure, which causes a spinning ball to take a curved path which is curved towards the greater pressure side is called **magnus effect.**

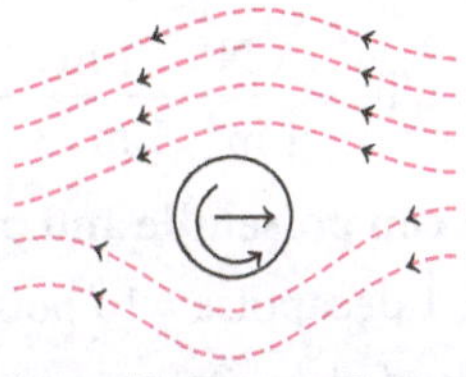

(b) Ball moving with spin

(c) Aerofoil, Lift of an Aircraft Wing

Aerofoil is a solid object shaped to provide an **upward dynamic lift** as it moves horizontally through air. This upward force helps aeroplane fly. The cross-section of the wing of an aeroplane looks like **an aerofoil.**

When the aeroplane moves through air, the air in the region above the wing moves faster than the air below as seen from the streamlines above the wing.

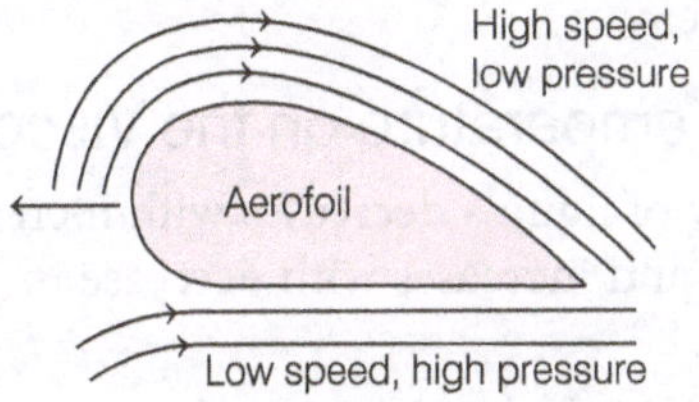

(c) Aerofoil

Example 14. A fully loaded Boeing aircraft has a mass of 3.3×10^5 kg. Its total wing area is 500 m^2. It is in level flight with a speed of 960 km/h.

(i) Estimate the pressure difference between the lower and upper surfaces of the wings.

(ii) Estimate the fractional increase in the speed of the air on the upper surface of the wing relative to the lower surface. (The density of air is $\rho = 1.2\ \text{kgm}^{-3}$) NCERT

Sol. (i) The weight of the Boeing aircraft is balanced by the upward force due to the pressure difference,

$$\Delta p \times A = mg$$
$$= 3.3\times 10^5 \times 9.8$$

So, $$\Delta p = \frac{mg}{A}$$
$$\Delta p = \frac{3.3\times 10^5 \times 9.8}{500}$$
$$= 6.46\times 10^3\ \text{N/m}^2$$
$$\therefore \quad \Delta p \approx 6.5\times 10^3\ \text{N/m}^2$$

(ii) Consider v_1 and v_2 are the speeds of air on lower and upper surfaces of the wings and p_1 and p_2 are the corresponding pressures.

From Bernoulli's principle,

$$p_1 + \frac{1}{2}\rho v_1^2 = p_2 + \frac{1}{2}\rho v_2^2$$
$$\therefore \quad p_1 - p_2 = \Delta p = \frac{\rho}{2}(v_2^2 - v_1^2)$$
$$(v_2 - v_1) = \frac{2\Delta p}{\rho(v_2 + v_1)}$$

Average speed, $$v_{av} = \frac{v_2 + v_1}{2}$$
$$= 960\ \text{km/h}$$
$$= 267\ \text{m/s}$$

So, $$\frac{v_2 - v_1}{v_{av}} = \frac{\Delta p}{\rho v_{av}^2} = \frac{6.5\times 10^3}{1.2\times (267)^2} \approx 0.08 = 8\%$$

Thus, the speed above the wing needs to be only 8% higher than that below.

Viscosity

The property of liquid by virtue of which it opposes the relative motion between adjacent layers is called viscosity.

- It is also called **internal friction** because it is simply the frictional force between the layers of same liquid. The force between the layers opposing the relative motion is **viscous force** or **viscous drag.**

Effects of the viscosity

- For any layer of liquid, its lower layer pulls it backward and its upper layer pulls it in forward direction.
- The velocities of the layers of a liquid increase uniformly from bottom to the top layers.
- When liquid flows in a pipe or a tube, its velocity is maximum along the axis of the tube and decreases gradually as it moves towards the walls where it becomes zero.

Coefficient of Viscosity

Consider the flow of liquid as shown in the following figure. A portion of liquid which at some instant having the shape *MNOP*. After the short interval of time (say Δt), the fluid is deformed and take the shape as *MQRP*, since the fluid has undergone the shear strain, stress in the solid is the force per unit area but in case of fluid, it depends on the rate of change of strain or strain rate.

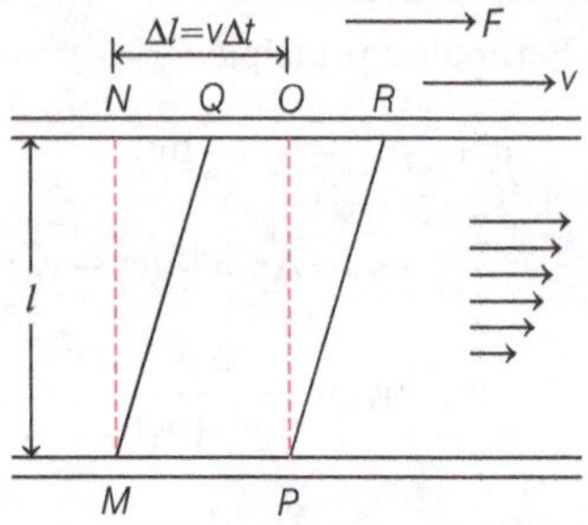

The layer of fluid is deformed under some stress

Strain, $\frac{\Delta l}{l}$ and the rate of change of strain is $\frac{\Delta l}{l\Delta t}=\frac{v}{l}$.

Hence, the coefficient of viscosity is defined as the ratio of shearing stress to the strain rate.

$$\eta=\frac{F/A}{v/l}=\frac{Fl}{vA}$$

Coefficient of viscosity, $\eta=\frac{Fl}{vA}$

or it can be written as, $\eta=\frac{F/A}{\frac{dv}{dx}}$

The term $\frac{dv}{dx}$ is called **velocity gradient.**

- The rate of change of velocity of liquid layers with distance in a direction perpendicular to direction of flow of liquid is called velocity gradient.
- Coefficient of viscosity is a scalar quantity.

Dimensions of η

As we know, $\eta=\frac{F}{A}\cdot\frac{l}{v}$

$$\therefore \quad \eta=\frac{[MLT^{-2}]}{[L^2\ LT^{-1}]}[L]=[ML^{-1}T^{-1}]$$

Units of η

(i) In CGS system, the unit of η is **dyne-s/cm^2** and it is called **poise.**

$$1\text{ poise}=\frac{1\text{ dyne}}{1\text{ cm}^2}\times\frac{1\text{ cm}}{1\text{ cm/s}}$$

1 poise = 1 dyne-s / cm^2

(ii) The SI unit of η is **Ns /m^2** or **kg/ms** and it is called **decapoise** or **poiseuille.**

$$1\text{ poiseuille}=\frac{1\text{ N}}{1\text{ m}^2}\cdot\frac{1\text{ m}}{1\text{ m/s}}=1\text{ Ns/m}^2$$

(iii) **Relation between poiseuille and poise**

1 poiseuille or 1 decapoise = 10 poise

The coefficient of viscosity is a scalar quantity.

Relative Viscosity

Relative viscosity of liquid $=\frac{\eta_{liquid}}{\eta_{water}}$

Relative viscosity of blood remains constant between 0° C and 37°C.

- No fluid has zero viscosity.
- Thin liquids like water, alcohol, etc. are less viscous than thick liquids such as coal tar, blood, honey, glycerine, etc.

Effect of Temperature on the Viscosity

The viscosity of liquids decreases with increase in temperature and increases with decrease in temperature.

On the other hand, the viscosity of gases increases with the increase in temperature and *vice-versa.*

Example 15. A metal block of area 0.10 m^2 is connected to a 0.01 kg mass via a string that passes over an ideal pulley (considered massless and frictionless), as in figure. A liquid with a film thickness of 0.30 mm is placed between the block and the table. When released, the block moves to the right with a constant speed of 0.085 ms^{-1}. Find the coefficient of viscosity of the liquid.

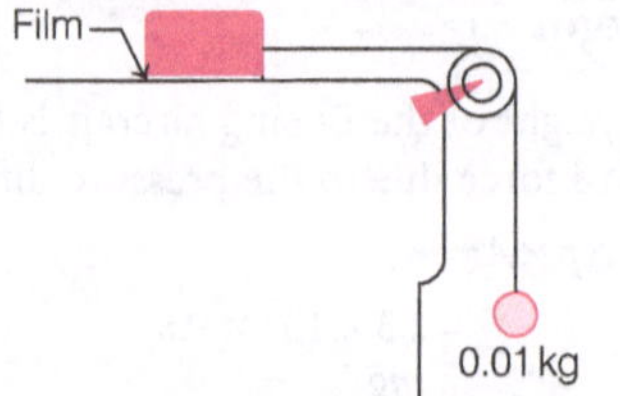

NCERT

Sol. Given, $m=0.010$ kg, $g=9.8$ m/s^2, $A=0.10$ m^2

$$F=T=mg=0.010\times9.8=9.8\times10^{-2}\text{ N}$$

$$\text{Shear stress on the fluid}=\frac{F}{A}=\frac{9.8\times10^{-2}}{0.10}=0.98\text{ N/m}^2$$

$$\text{Strain rate} = \frac{v}{l} = \frac{0.085}{0.30 \times 10^{-3}}$$

Now, the coefficient of viscosity of the liquid is

$$\eta = \frac{\text{Stress}}{\text{Strain rate}} = \frac{F\,l}{Av}$$

$$= \frac{9.8 \times 10^{-2} \times 0.30 \times 10^{-3}}{0.10 \times 0.085}$$

$$\eta = 3.45 \times 10^{-3} \text{Pa-s}$$

Critical Velocity

The critical velocity of a liquid is that limiting value of its velocity of flow upto which the flow is streamlined and above which the flow becomes turbulent.

The critical velocity v_c of a liquid flowing through a tube depends on

(i) coefficient of viscosity of the liquid (η)

(ii) density of the liquid (ρ)

(iii) radius of the tube (r)

Critical velocity, $v_c = \dfrac{k\eta}{\rho r}$

where, k is a constant, known as Reynold's number.

- The flow of liquids of higher viscosity and lower density through narrow pipes tends to be **streamlined.**
- The flow of liquids of lower viscosity and higher density through broad pipes tends to become **turbulent** because in that case, the critical velocity will be very small.

Stoke's Law

When a body moves through a fluid, then the fluid exerts viscous drag on the body to oppose its motion. According to Stoke's law, the viscous or drag force acting on a small spherical body of radius r moving through a fluid is given by

$$F = 6\pi\eta r v$$

where, η is coefficient of viscosity of fluid and v is the speed of spherical body.

Example 15. **Consider a drop of rain having radius 0.4 mm and terminal velocity 2 m/s. Find the viscous force on the rain drops, if viscosity of air is 18×10^{-5} dyne cm^{-2} s.**

Sol. Given, radius, $r = 0.4\text{ mm} = 0.4 \times 10^{-3}$m

Terminal velocity, $v = 2\text{ ms}^{-1}$

and viscosity of air, $\eta = 18 \times 10^{-5}$dyne cm^{-2}s

$= 18 \times 10^{-6}$Pa - s

According to Stoke's law, the viscous force,

$$F = 6\pi\eta r v$$

$$= 6 \times 3.14 \times 18 \times 10^{-6} \times 0.4 \times 10^{-3} \times 2$$

$$F = 2.71 \times 10^{-7}\text{N}$$

Terminal Velocity

The maximum constant velocity acquired by a body while falling through a viscous fluid is called its **terminal velocity.**

Velocity of a spherical body falling in a liquid is directly proportional to square of radius of body. The variation of velocity with time or radius is shown below.

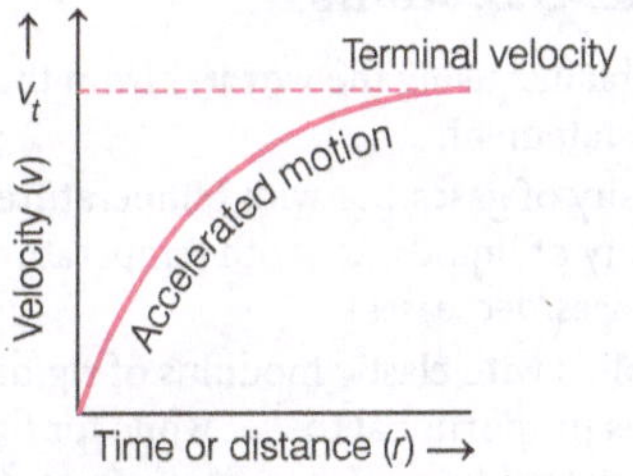

If a body of density ρ is falling through a fluid of density σ, then

$$\text{Terminal velocity, } v = \frac{2}{9} \cdot \frac{r^2(\rho - \sigma)\,g}{\eta}$$

where, r = radius of the spherical body,

v = terminal velocity

and η = coefficient of viscosity of fluid

Example 16. **If 27 drops of rain were to be combined to form one new large spherical drop, then what should be the velocity of this large spherical drop? Consider the terminal velocity of 27 drops of equal size falling through the air is 0.20 ms^{-1}.**

Sol. Let, the radius of the small drop is r and that of big drop is R. The volume of the big drop = 27 × volume of each small drop $= 27 \times \frac{4}{3}\pi r^3 \Rightarrow R = 3r$

Let, the terminal velocities of small and big drops are v_1 and v_2, respectively. Then,

$$v = \frac{2r^2(\rho - \sigma) g}{9\eta} \Rightarrow v \propto r^2$$

Hence, $\frac{v_2}{v_1} = \frac{R^2}{r^2}$

$$\Rightarrow \quad v_2 = v_1 \times \frac{R^2}{r^2} = 0.2\left(\frac{3r}{r}\right)^2 = 0.2 \times 9$$

$$v_2 = 1.8 \text{ m/s}$$

Reynold's number

It is a dimensionless number which determines the nature of the flow of the liquid. For a liquid of viscosity η, density ρ and flowing through a pipe of diameter D, Reynold's number is given by

$$R_e = \frac{\rho v D}{\eta}$$

If $R_e < 2000$, the flow is streamlined or laminar.
If $R_e > 3000$, the flow is turbulent.
If $2000 < R_e < 3000$, the flow is unstable. It may change from laminar to turbulent and *vice-versa*.

Poiseuille's Formula

The volume of a liquid flowing per second through a horizontal capillary tube of length l, radius r under a pressure difference p across its two ends is given by $V = \frac{\pi}{8} \cdot \frac{pr^4}{\eta l}$, where, η is coefficient of viscosity of the liquid.

Quick Test 3

Conceptual Questions

1. Fill in the blanks using the word(s) from the list appended with each statement.
 (i) Viscosity of gases......with temperature whereas viscosity of liquids......with temperature. (increases/decreases)
 (ii) For solids with elastic modulus of rigidity, the shearing force is proportional to......while for fluids, it is proportional to......(shear strain/rate of shear strain).
 (iii) For a fluid in a steady flow, the increase in flow speed at a constriction follows from......while the decrease of pressure there follows from......(conservation of mass/Bernoulli's principle).
 (iv) For the model of a plane in a wind tunnel, turbulence occurs at a......speed than the critical speed for turbulence for an actual plane. (greater/smaller) NCERT

2. Why does the velocity increase when liquid flowing in a wider tube enters a narrow tube? NCERT

3. Does it matter if one uses gauge instead of absolute pressure in applying Bernoulli's equation? Explain.

4. Why the wings of an aeroplane are rounded outwards, while flattened inwards ?

5. A hot liquid moves faster than a cold liquid. Why?

6. Figs. (a) and (b) refer to the steady flow of a non-viscous liquid. Which of two figures is incorrect. Why? NCERT

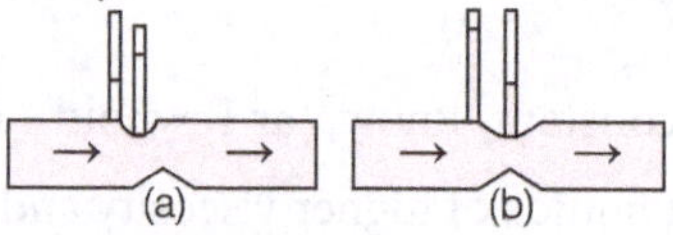

7. Define terminal velocity. Derive an expression for it.

Numerical Questions

8. The height of water level in a tank is $H = 96$ cm. Find the range of water stream coming out of a hole at depth $H/4$ from upper surface of water.

9. The velocity of water in a river is 18 kmh^{-1} near the surface. If the river is 5 m deep, find the shearing stress between horizontal layers of water. The coefficient of viscosity of water is 10^{-2} poise.

10. What should be the average velocity of water in a tube of radius 0.005 m, so that the flow is just turbulent? The viscosity of water is 0.001 Pa-s.

Answers

8. $48\sqrt{3}$ cm 9. 10^{-3} Nm^{-2} 10. 0.3 ms^{-1}

For Solutions, See QR Code on Pg. 333

Mind Map

Mechanical Properties of Fluids

Pressure

The force applied per unit area on a surface, typically measured in units like Pascals (Pa).

Formula $p = F/A$

The unit of pressure is dyne/cm^2 in CGS system and N/m^2 is SI system.

Pascal's Law

In a confined fluid at rest, a pressure change applied at any point is transmitted undiminished to all points within the fluid and acts in all directions.

Atmospheric Pressure The force exerted by the weight of the atmosphere on a surface. Standard atmospheric pressure at sea level is approximately 101,325 Pa or 1 atm.

Application of Pascal's Law

- **Hydraulic Lift**
  It is used to lift the heavy loads. This is made by connecting two cylindrical vessels of different cross-sections. Each cylindrical vessel contains air tight frictionless pistons.
  An incompressible liquid is filled inside the vessel.

$p = \frac{F_1}{A_1}, F_2$

$= pA_2 = \frac{F_1}{A_1} A_2$

$A_2 >> A_1,$

$\therefore F_2 >>> F_1$

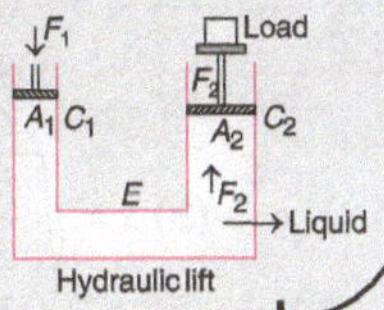

Hydraulic lift

Hydraulic Brake

- The working of the hydraulic brakes is also based on the Pascal's law.

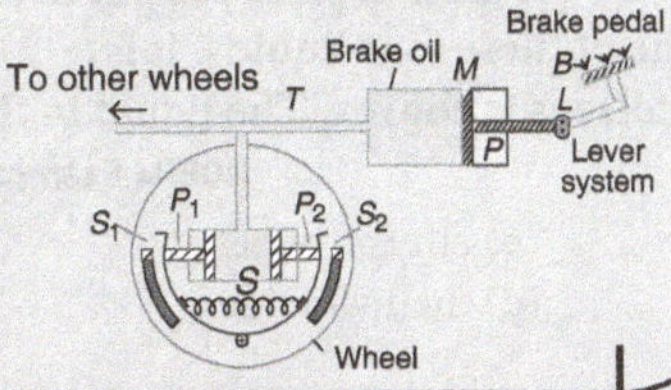

Effect of Gravity on Fluid Pressure

- When the fluid is at rest. The pressure at any given point in a fluid increases with depth due to the weight of the fluid above that point.

Variation of Pressure with Depth

- Consider a fluid at rest having density ρ contained in a cylindrical vessel. So, pressure will distributed all side but depend on height of the vessel.
- Pressure difference, $p_2 - p_1 = h\rho g$
- Pressure, if we shift point A to the liquid surface. $p = p_a + h\rho g$
- Gauge pressure $= p - p_a = h\rho g$

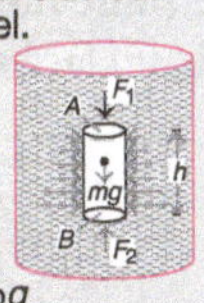

Surface Tension

It is the tendency of a liquid's surface to resist an external force, due to the cohesive forces between the liquid's molecules. It acts like a stretched elastic sheet at the liquid's surface.

$$S = \frac{F}{L}$$

Surface tension is defined as the force per unit length acting along the surface of a liquid.

Factors Affecting Surface Tension

Nature of Liquid Liquids with stronger intermolecular forces (e.g., water) have higher surface tension compared to weaker ones (e.g., alcohol).

Temperature Surface tension decreases as temperature increases because higher thermal energy reduces cohesive forces.

Impurities Adding surfactants (e.g., soap) reduces surface tension by disrupting cohesive forces.

Surface Energy

It is the energy required to increase the surface area of a liquid due to surface tension

Relationship Between Surface Energy and Surface Tension

The work done in increasing the surface area of a liquid is directly related to surface tension (γ).

$$W = \gamma \Delta A$$

Excess Pressure

It refers to the additional pressure exerted inside a curved surface of a liquid, compared to the pressure outside it

- **Excess pressure inside a liquid drop**

$$\Delta p = \frac{2S}{R}$$

In ordinary conditions,

$p = p_0 =$ Atmospheric pressure

$$p_i = p + \frac{2S}{R} = p_0 + \frac{2S}{R}$$

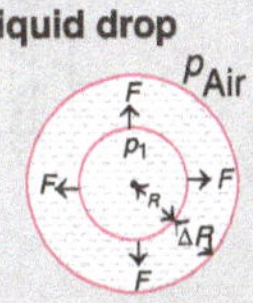

Pressure difference of the pressure on both side of a curved surface of liquid is called excess pressure.

- **Excess pressure inside a soap bubble**

$$\Delta p = \frac{4S}{R}$$

In ordinary conditions,

$p = p_0 =$ Atmospheric pressure

$$p_i = p + \frac{4S}{R} = p_0 + \frac{4S}{R}$$

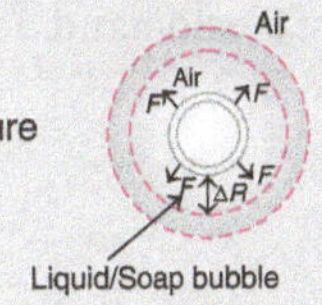

Contact Angle

It is the angle between the tangent to the liquid surface and the solid surface at the point of contact, indicating the wettability of the surface.

Viscosity

It is a measure of a fluid's resistance to flow. It describes the internal friction between layers of the fluid as they move past each other. Fluids with high viscosity (e.g. honey) flow slowly.

Fluids with low viscosity (e.g. water) flow easily.

Coefficient of Viscosity

Newton found that the viscous force acts between two layers of fluid is

(i) $F \propto A$

(ii) $F \propto \frac{dv}{dz}$

Hence, $F = -\eta A \frac{dv}{dz}$

$\eta = \frac{F/A}{dv/dz}$ or $\frac{F/A}{v/z}$

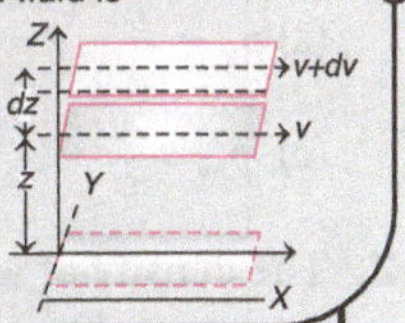

Critical Velocity

The critical velocity is the maximum velocity at which fluid flow remains laminar. Beyond this velocity, the flow transitions to turbulence.

$$v_c = \frac{Re_c \mu}{\rho D}$$

Stokes's Law

Stokes' law describes the drag force experienced by a small spherical object moving through a viscous fluid.

$$F_d = 6\pi\mu r v$$

Terminal Velocity in Fluids

A falling sphere in a fluid reaches terminal velocity when the net force is zero (gravitational force balanced by drag force and buoyant force).

$$v_t = \frac{2r^2 g (\rho_s - \rho_f)}{9\mu}$$

Laminar and Turbulant Flow

Fluid particles move in parallel layers without mixing. Velocity is highest at the center and decreases towards the edges.

Turbulent Flow Chaotic and irregular motion of fluid particles, with eddies and swirls. Velocity distribution is more uniform but unpredictable.

Bernoulli's Principle

In a steady, incompressible flow of an ideal fluid, the total mechanical energy (sum of pressure energy, kinetic energy, and potential energy) remains constant along a streamline.

$$p + \frac{1}{2}\rho v^2 + \rho g h = \text{constant}$$

Capillary Action

Surface tension helps liquid rise in narrow tubes (e.g. water in plants). When angle of contact of liquid with capillary tube is obtuse ($\theta > 90°$), then liquid falls in capillary tube.

Liquid in equilibrium, $h = 2S \cos\theta / R\rho g$

EXAM PATTERN QUESTIONS

Objective Type Questions

Multiple Choice Questions (MCQs)

1. Average pressure p_{av} is defined as

(a) $p_{av} = \frac{F}{A}$ (b) $p_{av} = \frac{V}{F}$

(c) $p_{av} = \frac{A}{F}$ (d) $p_{av} = \frac{F}{V}$

2. The density of water at 4°C is

(a) 1.0×10^3 kgm^{-3} (b) 4×10^2 kgm^{-3}

(c) 6×10^3 kgm^{-3} (d) 3.2×10^3 kgm^{-3}

3. If two liquids of same mass but densities ρ_1 and ρ_2 respectively are mixed, then density of mixture is given by

(a) $\rho = \frac{\rho_1 + \rho_2}{2}$ (b) $\rho = \frac{\rho_1 + \rho_2}{2\rho_1\rho_2}$

(c) $\rho = \frac{2\rho_1\rho_2}{\rho_1 + \rho_2}$ (d) $\rho = \frac{\rho_1\rho_2}{\rho_1 + \rho_2}$

4. Three liquids of densities d, 2d and 3d are mixed in equal proportion of weights. If density of water is d, then the specific gravity of the mixture is

(a) $\frac{11}{7}$ (b) $\frac{18}{11}$ (c) $\frac{13}{9}$ (d) $\frac{23}{18}$

5. A hydraulic lift has 2 limbs of areas A and 2A. Force F is applied over limb of area A to lift a heavy car. If distance moved by piston P_1 is x, then distance moved by piston P_2 is

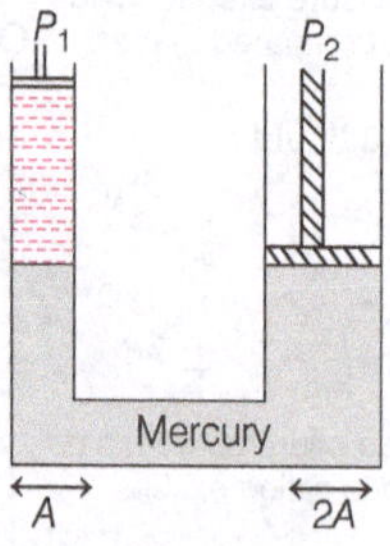

(a) x (b) $2x$

(c) $\frac{x}{2}$ (d) $4x$

6. In given figure, pressure inside a spherical drop is more than pressure outside. (S = surface tension and r = radius of bubble)

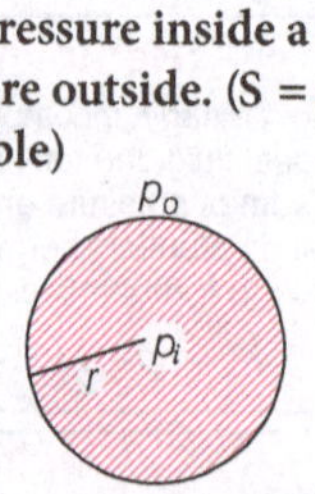

The extra surface energy if radius of bubble is increased by Δr is

(a) $4\pi r\,\Delta r\,S$ (b) $8\pi r\,\Delta r\,S$

(c) $2\pi r\,\Delta r\,S$ (d) $10\pi r\,\Delta r\,S$

7. Radius of a soap bubble is increased from R to 2R. Work done in this process in terms of surface tension is

(a) $24\,\pi R^2 S$ (b) $48\,\pi R^2 S$

(c) $12\pi R^2 S$ (d) $36\pi R^2 S$

8. A tank is filled with water upto a height H. Water is allowed to come out of a hole P in one of the walls at a depth h below the surface of water (see figure). Express the horizontal distance x in terms of H and h.

Competency Based Que.

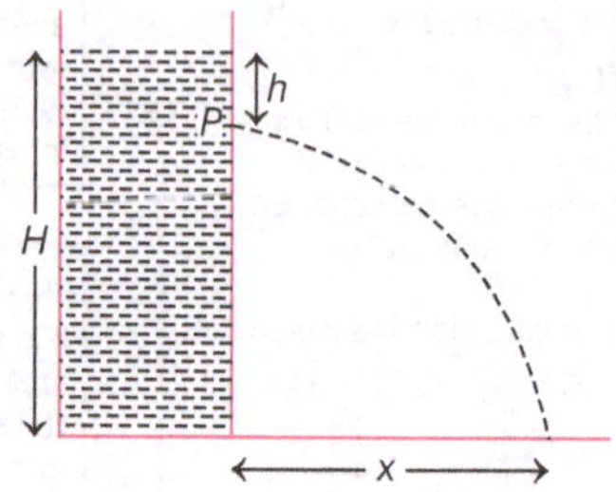

(a) $x = \sqrt{[h(H-h)]}$ (b) $x = \sqrt{\left[\frac{h}{2}(H-h)\right]}$

(c) $x = 2\sqrt{\{h(H-h)\}}$ (d) $x = 4\sqrt{\{h(H-h)}$

9. The angle of contact at the interface of water-glass is 0°, ethyl alcohol-glass is 0°, mercury-glass is 140° and methyliodide-glass is 30°. A glass capillary is put in a trough containing one of these four liquids. It is observed that the meniscus is convex. The liquid in the trough is

NCERT Exemplar

(a) water (b) ethylalcohol

(c) mercury (d) methyliodide

10. In a soap bubble, pressure difference is

(a) $\frac{2S_{la}}{r}$ (b) $\frac{4S_{la}}{r}$

(c) $\frac{S_{la}}{r}$ (d) $\frac{8S_{la}}{r}$

11. The excess pressure inside an air bubble of radius r just below the surface of water is p_1. The excess pressure inside a drop of the same radius just outside the surface is p_2. If T is surface tension, then

Competency Based Que.

(a) $p_1 = 2p_2$ (b) $p_1 = p_2$

(c) $p_2 = 2p_1$ (d) $p_2 = 0, p_1 \neq 0$

12. If two soap bubbles of different radii are connected by a tube,

(a) air flows from the bigger bubble to the smaller bubble till the sizes become equal
(b) air flows from bigger bubble to the smaller bubble till the sizes are interchanged
(c) air flows from the smaller bubble to the bigger
(d) there is no flow of air

13. A 20 cm long capillary tube is dipped in water. The water rises up to 8 cm. If the entire arrangement is put in a freely falling elevator, the length of water column in the capillary tube will be **Competency Based Que.**

(a) 4 cm (b) 20 cm (c) 8 cm (d) 10 cm

14. In a streamline flow,

(a) the speed of a particle always remains same
(b) the velocity of a particle always remains same
(c) the kinetic energies of all the particles arriving at a given point are the same
(d) the potential energies of all the particles arriving at a given point are the same

15. Two water pipes of diameters 2 cm and 4 cm are connected with the main supply line. The velocity of flow of water in the pipe of 2 cm diameter is **Competency Based Que.**

(a) 4 times that in the other pipe
(b) $\frac{1}{4}$ times that in the other pipe
(c) 2 times that in the other pipe
(d) $\frac{1}{2}$ times that in the other pipe

16. Which of the following diagrams does not represent a streamline flow?

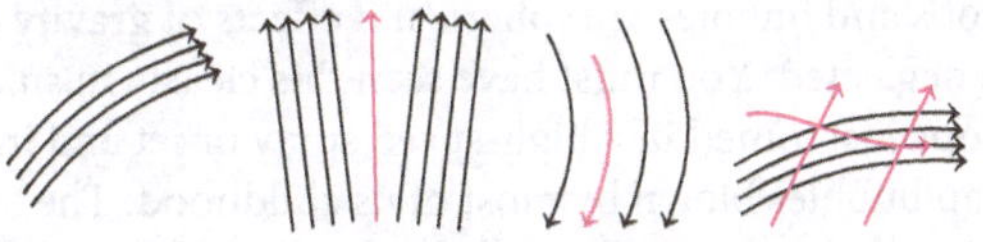

(a) (b) (c) (d)

17. In a turbulent flow, the velocity of the liquid molecules in contact with the walls of the tube is

(a) zero (b) maximum
(c) equal to critical velocity (d) May have any value

18. An ideal fluid flows through a pipe of circular cross-section made of two sections with diameters 2.5 cm and 3.75 cm. The ratio of the velocities in the two pipes is **NCERT Exemplar**

(a) 9 : 4 (b) 3 : 2
(c) $\sqrt{3}:\sqrt{2}$ (d) $\sqrt{2}:\sqrt{3}$

19. A tall cylinder is filled with viscous oil. A round pebble is dropped from the top with zero initial velocity. From the plot shown in figure, indicate the one that represents the velocity (v) of the pebble as a function of time (t). **NCERT Exemplar**

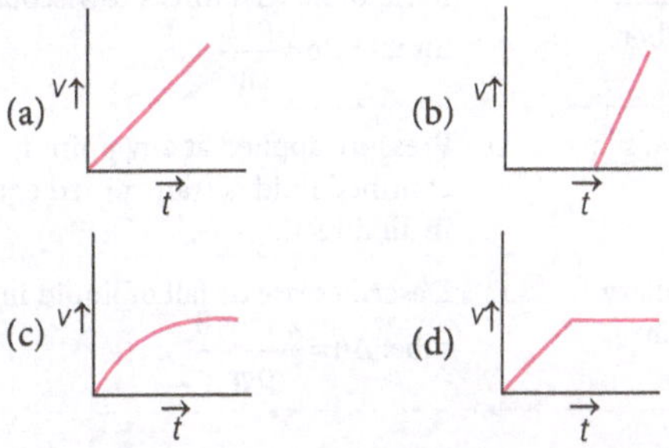

20. A tank with a hole at the bottom is filled with water to a height $h = 5$ m. The tank is open to the atmosphere. What will be the velocity of the water flowing out of the hole?

(a) 5 m/s (b) 7 m/s
(c) 9.9 m/s (d) 10 m/s

21. A small spherical ball of radius r is falling through a viscous fluid under gravity. Which of the following factors does the viscous drag acting on the sphere depend upon?

(a) The mass of the sphere
(b) The viscosity of the fluid
(c) The velocity of the sphere
(d) Both (b) and (c)

22. Match the Column I with Column II.

Column I		Column II
1. Density	A.	Resistance of a fluid to flow
2. Viscosity	B.	The force per unit area exerted by a fluid
3. Pressure	C.	The mass per unit volume of a fluid
4. Surface tension	D.	The tendency of a fluid surface to minimise surface area
5. Compressibility	E.	A measure of the change in volume of a fluid with change in pressure

(a) 1 → C, 2 → A, 3 → B, 4 → D, 5 → E
(b) 1 → A, 2 → B, 3 → C, 4 → D, 5 → E
(c) 1 → B, 2 → C, 3 → B, 4 → D, 5 → E
(d) 1 → E, 2 → A, 3 → C, 4 → B, 5 → D

23. Match the Column I with Column II.

Column I		Column II
1. Continuity equation	A.	$T = \eta\frac{du}{dy}$, where T is shear stress
2. Viscous force	B.	Describes the conservation of mass in fluid flow: $\rho_1 A_1 v_1 = \rho_2 A_2 v_2$

Column I		Column II
3. Reynold's number	C.	Ratio of inertial forces to viscous forces : $Re = \frac{\rho v L}{\eta}$
4. Pascal's law	D.	Pressure applied at any point in a confined fluid is transmitted equally in all directions
5. Capillary action	E.	Describes rise or fall of liquid in a tube: $\Delta h = \frac{2S\cos\theta}{\rho g r}$

(a) $1 \to C, 2 \to A, 3 \to B, 4 \to D, 5 \to E$
(b) $1 \to B, 2 \to A, 3 \to C, 4 \to D, 5 \to E$
(c) $1 \to E, 2 \to D, 3 \to C, 4 \to A, 5 \to D$
(d) $1 \to A, 2 \to B, 3 \to C, 4 \to D, 5 \to E$

Assertion-Reason

Directions *(Q.No. 24-33) In the following questions, two statements are given- one labelled Assertion (A) and the other labelled Reason (R). Select the correct answer to these questions from the codes (a), (b), (c) and (d) as given below.*

(a) Both Assertion and Reason are true and Reason is the correct explanation of Assertion.
(b Both Assertion and Reason are true but Reason is not the correct explanation of Assertion.
(c) Assertion is true but Reason is false.
(d) Assertion is false but Reason is true.

24. **Assertion (A)** A fluid will stick to a solid surface.
Reason (R) Surface energy between fluid and solid is smaller than the sum of surface energies.

25. **Assertion (A)** Smaller drop of liquid resists deforming forces better than the larger drops.
Reason (R) Excess pressure inside a drop is directly proportional to its surface area.

26. **Assertion (A)** The surface of water in the capillary tube is concave.
Reason (R) The pressure difference between two sides of the tube is $\frac{2S}{a}\cos\theta$.

27. **Assertion (A)** Water does not wet wax.
Reason (R) Angle of contact for water-wax is obtuse.

28. **Assertion (A)** The stream of water flowing at high speed from a garden horse pipe tends to spread like a fountain when held vertically up, but tends to narrow down when held vertically down.
Reason (R) In any steady flow of an incompressible fluid, the volume flow rate of the fluid remains constant.

29. **Assertion (A)** The water rises higher in a capillary tube of small diameter than in the capillary tube of large diameter.
Reason (R) Height through which liquid rises in a capillary tube is inversely proportional to the diameter of the capillary tube.

30. **Assertion (A)** Surface tension decreases with an increase in temperature.
Reason (R) Higher temperature reduces intermolecular forces in a liquid.

31. **Assertion (A)** The pressure at the bottom of a container filled with liquid is higher than at the surface.
Reason (R) Pressure in a fluid increases with depth due to the weight of the liquid column above the point of measurement.

32. **Assertion (A)** A fluid at rest cannot sustain a shear stress.
Reason (R) Fluids have a property called viscosity, which resists deformation only when in motion.

33. **Assertion (A)** Streamline flow is always observed at low velocities.
Reason (R) Reynold's number determines whether the flow is laminar or turbulent.

Case Based Questions

Directions *(Q.Nos. 34-35) These questions are case study based questions. Read the following paragraph and answer the questions on the basis of same.*

34. One consequence of surface tension is that free liquid drops and bubbles are spherical if effects of gravity can be neglected. You must have seen this clearly in small drops just joined in a high-speed spray or jet and in soap bubbles blown by most of us childhood. The reason behind the spherical shape of bubbles or drops is that the pressure inside a spherical drop is more than the pressure outside which creates a surface tension.

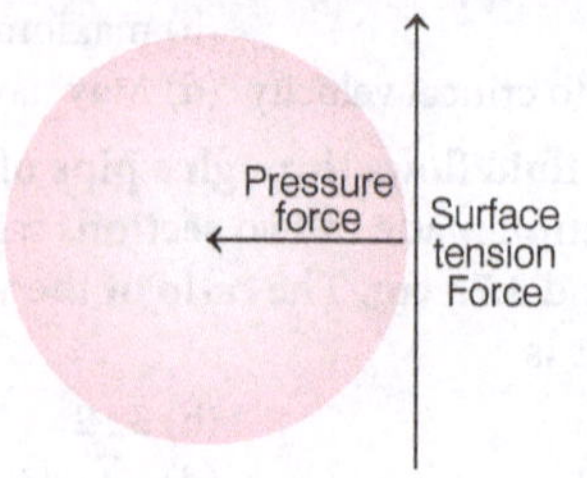

(i) This is a small bubble at one end and bigger bubble at other end of a rod. Then,

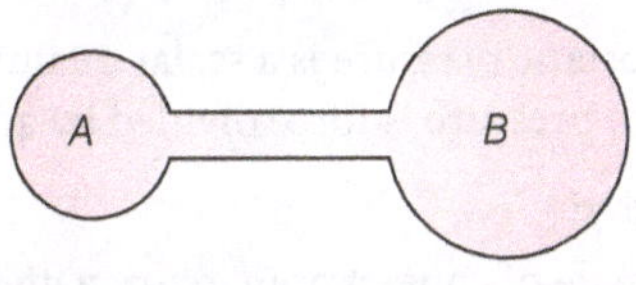

(a) smaller will grow until they collapse
(b) bigger will grow until they collapse
(c) both will remain in equilibrium
(d) None of the above

(ii) 8 mercury drops coalesce to form 1 mercury drop, the energy decreases by a factor of
(a) 1 (b) 2
(c) 4 (d) 6

(iii) One large soap bubble of diameter D breaks into 27 bubbles having surface tension T. The change in surface energy is
(a) $2\pi TD^2$ (b) $4\pi TD^2$ (c) $6\pi TD^2$
(d) $8\pi TD^2$

Or

The surface tension of liquid decreases with rise in
(a) temperature of the liquid
(b) viscosity of the liquid
(c) diameter of container
(d) thickness of container

(iv) The force required to separate the glass plate of area 10^{-2} m^2 from a film of water 0.05 mm thick is (Surface tension of water is 70×10^{-3} N/m)
(a) 25 N (b) 20 N
(c) 14 N (d) 28 N

35. Hydraulic lift is an application of Pascal's law. It is used to lift heavy loads. It is a force multiplier.
So, when small forces applied on the smaller piston (acting downward) will be appearing as a very large force (acting upward) on the larger piston. As a result of it, a heavy load placed on the larger piston is easily lifted upwards.

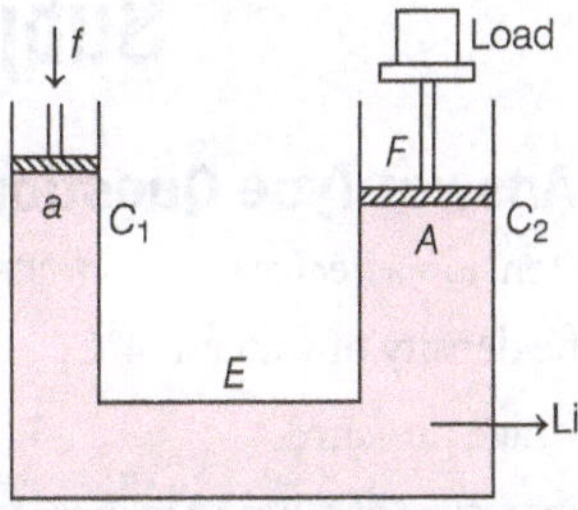

(i) Pascal's law states that pressure in a fluid at rest is the same at all points, if
(a) they are at the same height
(b) they are along same plane
(c) they are along same line
(d) Both (a) and (b)

(ii) Pressure is applied to an enclosed fluid as shown in the above figure. It is
(a) increased and applied to every part of the fluid
(b) diminished and transmitted to the walls of the container
(c) increased in proportion to the mass of the fluid and then transmitted
(d) transmitted unchanged to every portion of the fluid and the walls of container

(iii) Pressure at a point inside a liquid does not depend on
(a) the depth of the point below the surface of the liquid
(b) the nature of the liquid
(c) the acceleration due to gravity at that point
(d) total weight of fluid in the beaker

(iv) If work done by piston in the given figure on fluid is W_1, then work done by fluid in limbs on piston P_2 is
(a) $\frac{W_1}{4}$ (b) $4W_1$
(c) $\frac{W_1}{2}$ (d) W_1

Subjective Questions

Very Short Answer Type Questions

1. (i) Is surface tension a vector? NCERT Exemplar [1]

(ii) What is the density of water at 4°C? [1]

2. (i) Define average pressure. [1]

(ii) If the temperature of a liquid is increased, what will be the effect on its viscosity? [1]

3. (i) Why 2 holes are made to empty an oil tin? [1]

(ii) Why undergarments are usually made of cotton? [1]

Short Answer Type Questions

4. (i) Iceberg floats in water with part of it submerged. What is the fraction of the volume of iceberg submerged, if the density of ice is $\rho_i = 0.917 \text{ cm}^{-3}$? [2] NCERT Exemplar

(ii) A beaker containing a liquid is kept inside a big closed jar. If the air inside the jar is continuously pumped out, how will the pressure change inside the liquid near the bottom? Competency Based Que. [1]

5. Two vessels have same base area but different shapes. The first vessel takes twice the volume of water than the second vessel to fill upto a particular common height. Is the force exerted by the water on the base of the vessel same in the two cases? If so, why do the vessels filled with water to that same height give different reading on a weighing scale? Competency Based Que.

6. What is difference between viscous force and solid friction?

Long Answer Type Questions

7. State and derive equation of continuity.

8. What is Torricelli's law? Derive an expression for speed of efflux.

9. If a drop of liquid breaks into smaller droplets, it results in lowering of temperature of the droplets. Let a drop of radius R breaks into N small droplets each of radius r. Estimate the lowering in temperature. NCERT

10. Explain why ?

(i) The blood pressure in humans is greater at the feet than the brain. [2]

(ii) Atmospheric pressure at a height of about 6 km decreases to nearly half its value at the sea level though the height of the atmosphere is more than 100 km. [2]

(iii) Hydrostatic pressure is a scalar quantity even though pressure is force divided by area. NCERT [1]

11. Explain why?

(i) The angle of contact of mercury with glass is obtuse, while that of water with glass is acute. [2½]

(ii) Water on a clean glass surface tends to spread out while mercury on the same surface tends to form drops. (Put differently, water wets the glass while mercury does not.) NCERT [2½]

12. Explain why?

(i) To keep a piece of paper horizontal, you should blow over, not under it. [1]

(ii) When we try to close a water tap with our fingers, fast jets of water gush through the opening between our fingers. [1]

(iii) The size of the needle of a syringe controls flow rate better than the thumb pressure exerted by a doctor, while administering an injection. [1]

(iv) A fluid flowing out of a small hole in a vessel results in a backward thrust on the vessel. [1]

(v) A spinning cricket ball in air does not follow a parabolic trajectory. NCERT [1]

13. If a number of little droplets of water, each of radius r, coalesce to form a single drop of radius R, and the energy released is converted into kinetic energy, then find out the velocity acquired by the bigger drop. Competency Based Que.

14. If a sphere of radius r falls under gravity through a liquid of viscosity η, its average acceleration is half that of in starting of the motion. Then, show that the time taken by it to attain the terminal velocity is independent of the liquid density. Competency Based Que.

Numerical Problems

Hydrostatics

15. A cube of side $a = 10$ cm is fully submerged in water. The density of water is $\rho_w = 1000 \text{ kg/m}^3$ and the cube has a density of $\rho_c = 800 \text{ kg/m}^3$.

(a) Calculate the buoyant force acting on the cube. [1]

(b) Determine if the cube will float or sink and how much of it will be submerged. [2]

16. If a column of 60 cm height of water supports a 45 cm column of an unknown liquid. Calculate the density of the liquid.

(Given, density of water = 10^3 kg /m^3) **[2]**

17. A container of area 0.02 m^2 is filled with water. Find the pressure at the bottom of the container, if a weight is placed on the piston.

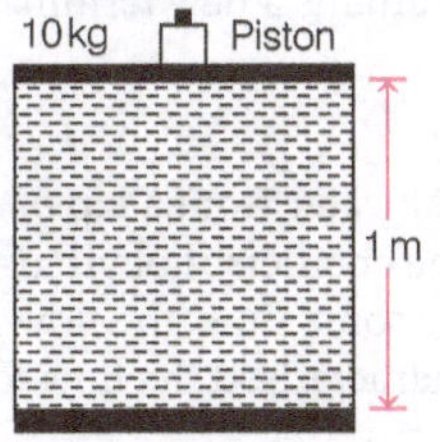

18. A vertical off-shore structure is built to withstand a maximum stress of 10^{10} Pa. Is the structure suitable for putting up on top of an oil well in the ocean? Take the depth of the ocean to be roughly 31 km and ignore ocean currents. **NCERT**

19. Consider the hydraulic lift having small cylindrical piston and larger piston with radii 4.0 cm and 16 cm, respectively. If a truck of mass 3000 kg is placed on the larger piston, then find out the force that must be applied to the small piston to lift the truck. Also, find how far must the small piston move down to lift the truck through a height of 0.20 m. Assume initially these two pistons are at the same height.
(Take g = 10 m/s^2). **Competency Based Que.**

20. A body of mass 6 kg is floating in a liquid with 2/3 of its volume inside the liquid. Find ratio between the density of the body and density of liquid. (Take g = 10 m/s^2).

Surface Tension and Surface Energy

21. A thin wire is bent in the form of a ring of diameter 3.0 cm. The ring is placed horizontally on the surface of soap solution and then raised up slowly. How much upward force is necessary to break the vertical film formed between the ring and the solution?
(Surface tension of soap solution is $S = 3.0 \times 10^{-2}$ Nm^{-1}). **Competency Based Que.**

22. Two mercury droplets of radii 0.1 cm and 0.2 cm collapse into one single drop. What amount of energy is released? The surface tension of mercury is $S = 435.5 \times 10^{-3}$ N/m. **NCERT Exemplar**

23. A thin circular ring of radius R = 5 cm is dipped vertically into a soap solution and then pulled out, forming a soap film. The force required to lift the ring without breaking the film is measured to be F = 0.1 N.

(i) Calculate the surface tension of the soap solution. **[1½]**

(ii) If the film breaks and the ring is again dipped in the solution, but this time forming only a single layer of film, what will be the force required to lift the ring? **[1½]**

24. A liquid drop breaks into 27 small drops. If surface tension of the liquid is S, then find the energy released.

25. A liquid drop of radius 4 mm breaks into 1000 identical drops. Find the change in surface energy.
(S = 0.07 Nm^{-1}).

26. The surface tension and vapour pressure of water at 20°C is 7.28×10^{-2} N / m and 2.33×10^3 Pa, respectively. What is the radius of the smallest spherical water droplet which can form without evaporating at 20°C ? **NCERT**

27. What is the pressure inside the drop of mercury of radius 3.00 mm at room temperature? Surface tension of mercury at that temperature (20°C) is 4.65×10^{-1} N/m. The atmospheric pressure is 101×10^5 Pa. Also, give the excess pressure inside the drop.

28. Two soap bubbles have radii in the ratio 2 : 3. Compare the excess of pressure inside these bubbles. **Competency Based Que.**

29. Two capillary tubes of same diameter are put vertically one each in two liquids whose relative densities are 0.8 and 0.6 and surface tensions are 60 and 50 dyne/cm, respectively. What is the ratio of heights of liquids in the two tubes?

Hydrodynamics

30. The cylindrical tube of a spray pump has a cross-section of 8.0 cm^2 one end of which has 40 fine holes each of diameter 1.00 mm. If the liquid flow inside the tube is 1.5 m/min, what is the speed of ejection of the liquid through the holes? **NCERT**

31. At what speed will the velocity head of stream of water be 40 cm?

32. Water enters a horizontal pipe of non-uniform cross-section with a velocity of 0.6 ms^{-1} and leaves the other end with a velocity of 0.4 ms^{-1}. At the first end, pressure of water is 1200 Nm^{-2}. Calculate the pressure of water at the other end. (Take, density of water = 1000 kgm^{-3}).

33. A non-viscous liquid of constant density 1000 kgm^{-3} flows in a streamline motion along a tube of variable cross-section. The tube is kept inclined in the vertical plane as shown in figure. The area of cross-section of the tube at two points P and Q at heights of 2 m and 5 m are respectively, 4×10^{-3} m^2 and 8×10^{-3} m^2. The velocity of the liquid at point P is 1 ms^{-1}. Find the work done per unit volume by the pressure and the gravity forces as the fluid flows from point P to Q. **Competency Based Que.**

34. 27 identical drops of water are falling down vertically in air each with a terminal velocity of 0.15 ms^{-1}. If they combine to form a single bigger drop, what will be its terminal velocity? **Competency Based Que.**

35. In a test experiment on a model aeroplane in a wind tunnel, the flow speeds on the upper and lower surfaces of the wing are 70 m/s and 63 m/s, respectively. What is the lift on the wing, if its area is 2.5 m^2? Take the density of air to be 1.3 kg/m^3. **Competency Based Que.**

36. Air is streaming past a horizontal aeroplane wing such that its speed is 120 ms^{-1} over the upper surface and 90 ms^{-1} at the lower surface. If the density of air is 1.3 kg m^{-3}, find the difference in pressure between the top and bottom of the wing. If wing is 10 m long and has an average width of 2 m, calculate the gross lift of the wing. **Competency Based Que.**

37. The terminal velocity of a copper ball of radius 2.0 mm falling through a tank of oil at 20°C is 6.5 cms^{-1}. Compute the viscosity of the oil at 20°C. Density of oil is 1.5×10^3 kg m^{-3} and density of copper is 8.9×10^3 kg m^{-3}. **NCERT**

38. Show that, if n equal rain droplets falling through air with equal steady velocity of 10 cms^{-1} coalesce, the resultant drop attains a new terminal velocity of $10\,n^{2/3}$ cms^{-1}. **Competency Based Que.**

39. The flow rate of water from a tap of diameter 1.25 cm is 0.48 L/min. The coefficient of viscosity of water is 10^{-3} Pa-s. After some time, the flow rate is increased to 3 L/min. Characterised the flow for both the flow rates. **NCERT**

Hints & Solutions

Objective Type Questions

1. (a) 2. (a)

3. (c) If two liquids of same mass m but of different densities ρ_1 and ρ_2 are mixed together, then the density of the mixture is given by

$$\rho = \frac{m+m}{\frac{m}{\rho_1}+\frac{m}{\rho_2}} = \frac{2}{\frac{1}{\rho_1}+\frac{1}{\rho_2}} = \frac{2\rho_1\rho_2}{\rho_1+\rho_2}$$

4. (b) $w_1 = w_2 = w_3$

$\Rightarrow$ $m_1 = m_2 = m_3 = m$ (say)

Then, $V_1 = \frac{m}{d}, V_2 = \frac{m}{2d}, V_3 = \frac{m}{3d}$

$\therefore$ $d_{mix} = \frac{\text{Mass}}{\text{Volume}} = \frac{3m}{V_1+V_2+V_3} = \frac{18}{11}d$

So, specific gravity of mixture $= \frac{d_{mix}}{d_{water}} = \frac{18}{11}$

5. (c) As, $V_1 = V_2 \Rightarrow A_1x_1 = A_2x_2$

$\Rightarrow$ $x_2 = \frac{A_1}{A_2}x_1 = \frac{Ax}{2A} = \frac{x}{2}$

6. (b) Suppose a spherical drop of radius r is in equilibrium. If its radius increases by Δr. The extra surface energy is

$$|4\pi(r+\Delta r)^2 - 4\pi r^2|\,S = 8\pi r\,\Delta r\,S$$

7. (a)

8. (c) Time taken by liquid to fall, $t = \sqrt{\frac{2(H-h)}{g}}$

and Speed, $v = \sqrt{2gh}$

Now, horizontal distance,

$$x = vt = \sqrt{2gh} \times \sqrt{\frac{2(H-h)}{g}} = 2\sqrt{h(H-h)}$$

9. (c) According to the question, the observed meniscus is of convex figure shape, which is only possible when angle of contact is obtuse. Hence, the combination will be of mercury-glass (140°).

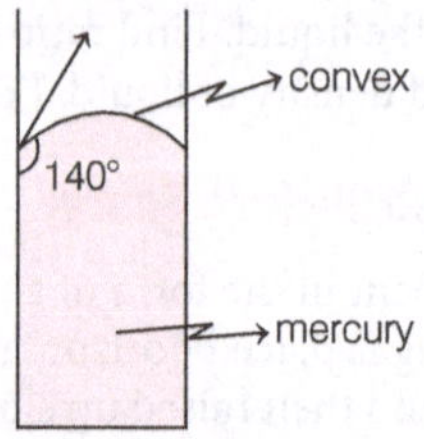

10. (b)

11. (b) Excess pressure inside an air bubble of radius R is given by $p = \frac{2T}{R}$

Both air bubbles have the same radius and surface tension. So, $p_1 = p_2$

12. (c) The excess pressure inside a soap bubble is inversely proportional to its radius. So, the pressure is more inside the smaller bubble than the bigger bubble. When these two bubbles are connected by a tube, air will flow from the smaller bubble to the bigger bubble.

13. (c) In the freely falling elevator, the entire arrangement is in a state of weightlessness, i.e. $g = 0$.

So, water will rise $\left(h = \dfrac{2S\cos\theta}{r\rho g}\right)$.

$$h \propto \frac{1}{g} \text{ and } g = 0$$

Hence, $h = \infty$, which is not possible, hence water will fill the entire tube of length 20 cm.

14. (*b*) Both velocity and direction of flow remain same.

15. (*a*) From equation of continuity, av = constant

$$d_A = 2 \text{ cm} \quad \text{and} \quad d_B = 4 \text{ cm}$$

$$\therefore \quad r_A = 1 \text{ cm} \quad \text{and} \quad r_B = 2 \text{ cm}$$

$$\therefore \quad \frac{v_A}{v_B} = \frac{a_B}{a_A} = \frac{\pi(r_B)^2}{\pi(r_A)^2} = \left(\frac{2}{1}\right)^2$$

$$\Rightarrow \quad v_A = 4v_B$$

16. (*d*) In a streamline flow, at any given point, the velocity of each passing fluid particle remains constant. If we consider a cross-sectional area, then a point on the area cannot have different velocities at the same time, hence two streamlines of flow cannot cross each other.

17. (*d*) In a turbulent flow, the path and the velocity of the particle of the liquid change continuously. So, in this flow, the velocity of the liquid molecules in contact with the walls of the tube may have any value.

18. (*a*) By equation of continuity,

$$A_1v_1 = A_2v_2$$

$$\frac{v_1}{v_2} = \frac{A_2}{A_1} = \frac{\pi r_2^2}{\pi r_1^2} = \frac{r_2^2}{r_1^2} = \frac{(2r_2)^2}{(2r_1)^2} = \frac{d_2^2}{d_1^2} = \frac{(3.75)^2}{(2.5)^2}$$

$$= \frac{14.06}{6.25} = \frac{1406.20}{625} = \frac{9}{4}$$

19. (*c*) When the pebble is falling through the viscous oil, the viscous force is $F = 6\pi\eta rv$

As the force is variable, hence acceleration is also variable, so *v*-*t* graph will not be straight line. First velocity increases and then becomes constant known as terminal velocity.

20. (*c*) Using Torricell's theorem, the velocity of efflux is given by

$$v = \sqrt{2gh}$$

Substituting $g = 9.8 \text{ m/s}^2$ and $h = 5$ m, we have

$$v = \sqrt{2 \times 9.8 \times 5} = \sqrt{98} \approx 9.9 \text{ m/s}$$

21. (*d*) According to Stokes' law, the viscous drag acting on a spherical object moving through a fluid is given by

$$F = 6\pi\eta rv$$

The viscous drag depends on the viscosity (η) and velocity (v) of the sphere, not directly on its mass.

22. (*a*) $1 \to$ C, $2 \to$ A, $3 \to$ B, $4 \to$ D, $5 \to$ E.

23. (*b*) $1 \to$ B, $2 \to$ A, $3 \to$ C, $4 \to$ D, $5 \to$ E

24. (*a*) A fluid will stick to a solid surface, if the surface energy between fluid and the solid is smaller than the sum of surface energies between solid-air and fluid-air, interface.

25. (*c*) The excess pressure inside a liquid drop, we get

$$p = \frac{2S}{R}$$

i.e., $$p \propto \frac{1}{R}$$

Hence, the excess pressure is large in a small drop due to which it can resist the deforming forces.

Also, excess pressure depends on the radius of the drop and not on the surface area.

26. (*a*) Since, the surface of water in the capillary is concave. This means that there is a pressure difference between the two sides of the top surface. This is given by

$$(p_i - p_o) = (2S/r) = 2S/(a \sec\theta) = (2S/a)\cos\theta \quad \text{...(i)}$$

Thus, the pressure of the water inside the tube, just at the meniscus (air-water interface) is less than the atmospheric pressure. Consider the two points *A* and *B*. They must be at the same pressure, namely

$$p_o + h\rho g = p_i = p_A \quad \text{...(ii)}$$

where, ρ is the density of water and h is called the capillary rise. Using Eqs. (i) and (ii), we have

$$h\rho g = (p_i - p_o) = (2S\cos\theta)/a$$

27. (*a*) When angle of contact is an obtuse, then molecules of liquids are attracted strongly to themselves and weakly to those of solids, it costs a lot of energy to create a liquid-solid surface. Hence, liquid does not wet the solid. This is what happens with water on wax and so water does not wet wax.

28. (*a*) As volume flow rate of fluid, i.e. $Q = Av$ = constant.

As speed of upstream decreases, its area of cross-section increases. While, speed of water falling downward increases, then its area of cross-section decreases.

29. (*a*) The height of capillary rise is inversely proportional to radius of capillary tube i.e. $h \propto \frac{1}{r}$

So for smaller *r*, the value of *h* is higher.

30. (*a*) Surface tension depends on intermolecular forces, which weakens with increased temperature.

31. (*a*) The pressure in a liquid increases with depth due to the hydrostatic pressure caused by the weight of the liquid column.

32. (*a*) A fluid at rest cannot sustain shear stress because viscosity acts only when the fluid is in motion.

33. (*a*) Reynold's number predicts the type of flow; low velocities correspond to laminar flow (streamline flow).

34. (i) (*b*) $p = \frac{2S}{R}$ i.e. excess pressure is more in small bubble than in the bigger bubble. Air will flow from smaller to bigger bubble which will grow more until both collapse.

(ii) (*b*) In mercury drop (spherical), $n = 8$

$$nV = V' \Rightarrow 8 \times \frac{4}{3}\pi R^3 = \frac{4}{3}\pi R'^3$$

$\therefore \quad R = 2R$

Now, energy, $U_1 = 8 \times 4\pi R^2 S = 32\,\pi R^2 S$

$U_2 = 4\pi R'^2 S = 4\pi(2R^2)S = 16\,\pi R^2$

$\therefore \quad \frac{U_2}{U_1} = \frac{1}{2}$

So, energy decreases by a factor of 2.

(iii) (*b*) Volume of 27 small bubbles = Volume of larger bubble

or $\quad 27 \times \frac{4}{3}\pi r^3 = \frac{4}{3}\pi\left(\frac{D}{2}\right)^3$

$\therefore \quad r = \frac{D}{6}$

Increase in surface area $= 2\left[27 \times 4\pi\left(\frac{D}{6}\right)^2 - 4\pi\left(\frac{p}{2}\right)^2\right]$

$= 4\pi D^2$

Now, increase is surface energy

= increase in surface area × surface tension

$= 4\pi D^2 T$

Or

(*a*) Temperature of the liquid

(iv) (*d*) Given, $A = 10^{-2}\ \text{m}^2$, $S = 70 \times 10^{-3}$ N/m

$x = 0.05\ \text{mm} = 0.05 \times 10^{-3}$ m

So, $\quad F = \frac{2SA}{x} = \frac{2 \times 70 \times 10^{-3} \times 10^{-2}}{0.05 \times 10^{-3}} = 28$ N

35. (i) (*a*) Pascal's law states that pressure in a fluid at rest is the same at all points, if they are at the same height.

(ii) (*d*) Due to Pascal's law, when the pressure is applied, it will be transmitted unchanged to every portion of fluid and walls of container.

(iii) (*d*) $p = \frac{F}{A} = \rho g h$

$\therefore$ It does not depend on the weight of fluid.

(iv) (*d*) Work done by both pistons is always same.

Subjective Questions

1. (i) No, surface tension is a scalar quantity.

Surface tension $= \frac{\text{Work done}}{\text{Surface area}}$, where work done and surface area both are scalar quantities.

(ii) The density of water at 4°C (277 K) is $1.0 \times 10^3\ \text{kgm}^{-3}$.

2. (i) If F is the magnitude of the normal force acting over an area A, then the average pressure p is defined as the normal force acting per unit area.

i.e. $\quad p_{av} = \frac{F}{A}$

(ii) The viscosity of a liquid decreases with the increase in its temperature.

3. (i) If only one hole is made in tin, then pressure inside tin would be less than atmospheric pressure, hence oil will not come out.

(ii) Cotton threads have large number of capillaries between them. These capillaries help to absorb sweat from the surface of the body due to capillarity action.

4. (i) Given, density of ice $(\rho_{ice}) = 0.917\ \text{g/cm}^3$

Density of water $(\rho_w) = 1\ \text{g/cm}^3$

Let V be the total volume of the iceberg and V' its volume submerged in water;

In floating condition.

Weight of the iceberg = Weight of the water displaced by the submerged part by ice

$V\rho_{ice}\, g = V'\rho_w g$

or $\quad \frac{V'}{V} = \frac{\rho_{ice}}{\rho_w} = \frac{0.917}{1} = 0.917$ ($\because$ Weight $= mg = V\rho g$)

(ii) The total pressure at a point near the bottom is equal to the sum of the pressure due to liquid column and due to air inside the jar. When air of the jar is pumped out, the pressure of air inside the jar decreases. So, pressure near the bottom of the liquid also decreases.

5. The pressure exerted by a liquid column depends on its height. The height of water in both vessels are same, therefore the pressure on the base of each vessel will be same.

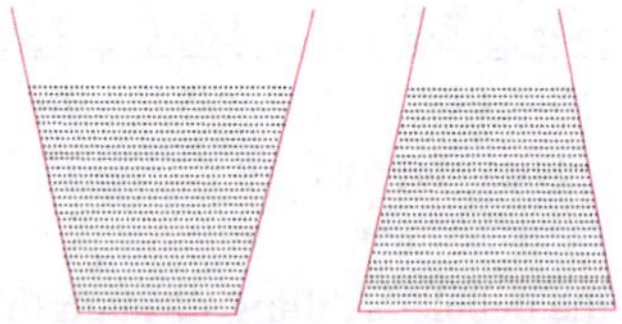

The area of the base of each vessel is also same and hence, force exerted by the water on the base of the vessels is same. Liquid also applies force on the walls of the vessel. As walls of the vessels are not perpendicular to the base, therefore force exerted on the walls by the liquid has a non-zero vertical component, which is more in first vessel. Therefore, the two vessels filled with water to the same height give different readings on a weighing scale.

6. Difference between Viscous force and Solid friction

Viscous force	Solid friction
Viscous force is directly proportional to the area of layers in contact.	Solid friction is independent of the area of the surfaces in contact.
It is directly proportional to the relative velocity between the two liquid layers.	It is independent of the relative velocity between two solid surfaces.
It is independent of the normal reaction between the two liquid layers.	It is directly proportional to the normal reaction between the surfaces in contact.

7. **Equation of Continuity**

It states that "if an ideal liquid (i.e. incompressible and non-viscous) flows through a tube in streamline motion, then the product of cross-section area of tube and velocity of flow is same at every point in the tube."

If A is cross-sectional area and v is the velocity of flow of liquid at any point in the tube, then from equation of continuity, $A \cdot v = \text{constant}$

Derivation

Consider a non-viscous and incompressible liquid flowing through a tube AB of varying cross-section. Let a_1 be the area of cross-section, v_1 be the fluid velocity at section A and the values of corresponding quantities at section B be a_2 and v_2, respectively. The density of flowing fluid is ρ.

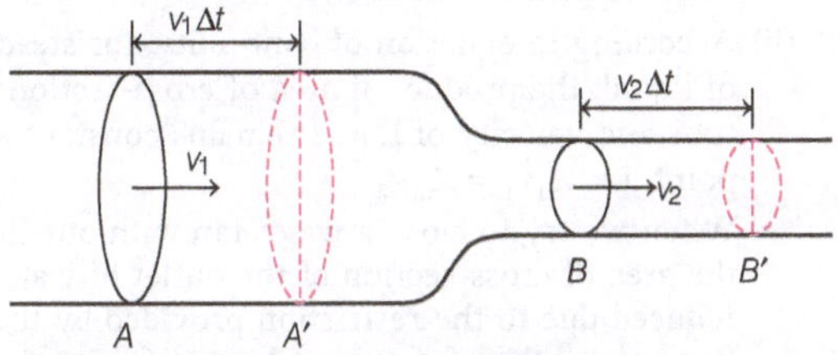

As the fluid is incompressible, density is constant.

Mass = volume × density

= area of cross-section × length × density

∴ Mass of fluid that entering through section A in time Δt,

$$m_1 = a_1 v_1 \Delta t \rho_1$$

Mass of fluid that leaving through section B in time Δt,

$$m_2 = a_2 v_2 \Delta t \rho_2$$

According to conservation of mass, we get

$$m_1 = m_2$$

or $$a_1 v_1 \Delta t \rho = a_2 v_2 \Delta t \rho \quad [\because \rho \text{ is constant}]$$

Hence, $$a_1 v_1 = a_2 v_2$$

or $$\boxed{av = \text{constant}}$$

This is known as **equation of continuity**.

8. The velocity of efflux of a liquid is equal to the velocity which a body acquires in falling freely from the free liquid surface to the orifice. This result is called Torricelli's law.

i.e. Velocity of efflux, $v = \sqrt{2gh}$

where, h is depth of orifice from the free surface.

Derivation

Consider a tank filled with a liquid of density ρ, which has a small hole at a height y_1 from the bottom. Let y_2 be the height of the liquid surface from the bottom and p represents the air pressure above the liquid surface.

If A_1, A_2 are the cross-sectional areas and v_1, v_2 are the velocities of liquid at points 1 and 2 respectively, then from the equation of continuity, we get

$$A_1 v_1 = A_2 v_2 \text{ or } v_2 = \frac{A_1}{A_2} v_1$$

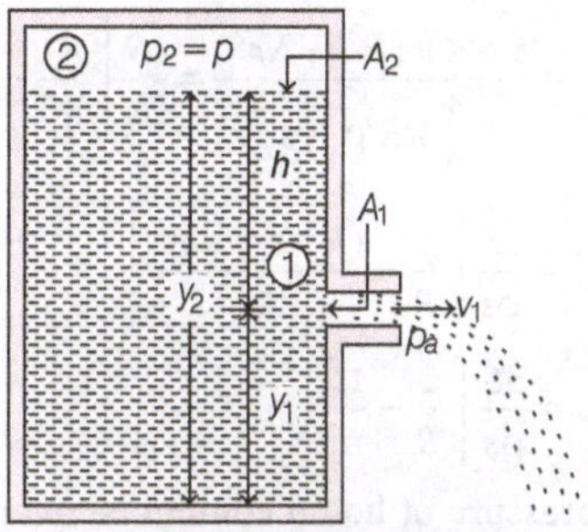

If $A_2 >> A_1$, so the liquid may be taken at rest at the top, i.e. $v_2 \approx 0$.

Applying the Bernoulli's theorem at points 1 and 2. The pressure $p_1 = p_a$ (the atmospheric pressure)

We get, $p_a + \frac{1}{2}\rho v_1^2 + \rho g y_1 = p + \rho g y_2 \quad [\because v_2 \approx 0]$

or $$\frac{1}{2}\rho v_1^2 = \rho g (y_2 - y_1) + (p - p_a)$$

$$y_2 - y_1 = h$$

Hence, $$\frac{1}{2}\rho v_1^2 = \rho g h + (p - p_a)$$

Velocity of the liquid falls from orifice,

$$v_1 = \sqrt{2gh + \frac{2(p - p_a)}{\rho}}$$

When $p >> p_a$ and $2gh$ may be ignored, the speed of efflux is determined by the container pressure. Such a situation occurs in rocket propulsion.

When the tank is open to the atmosphere,

$$p = p_a \text{ and } v_1 = \sqrt{2gh}$$

The above result is called **Torricelli's law**.

9. When a big drop of radius R breaks into N droplets each of radius r, the volume remains constant.

∴ Volume of big drop = N × Volume of small drop

$$\frac{4}{3}\pi R^3 = N \times \frac{4}{3}\pi r^3$$

or $$R^3 = Nr^3 \text{ or } N = \frac{R^3}{r^3}$$

Now, change in surface area $= 4\pi R^2 - N 4\pi r^2$

$= 4\pi (R^2 - Nr^2)$

Energy released $= S \times \Delta A = S \times 4\pi (R^2 - Nr^2)$

Due to releasing of this energy, the temperature is lowered.

If ρ is the density and s is specific heat of liquid and its temperature is lowered by $\Delta\theta$, then

Energy released $= ms\Delta\theta$

$$S \times 4\pi (R^2 - Nr^2) = \left(\frac{4}{3}\pi \times R^3 \times \rho\right) s\Delta\theta$$

$$\Delta\theta = \frac{S \times 4\pi (R^2 - Nr^2)}{\frac{4}{3}\pi R^3 \rho \times s} = \frac{3S}{\rho s}\left[\frac{R^2}{R^3} - \frac{Nr^2}{R^3}\right]$$

$$= \frac{3S}{\rho s}\left[\frac{1}{R} - \frac{(R^3/r^3) \times r^2}{R^3}\right] \qquad \left[\because N = \frac{R^3}{r^3}\right]$$

$$\Delta\theta = \frac{3S}{\rho s}\left[\frac{1}{R} - \frac{1}{r}\right]$$

10. (i) The pressure of liquid column is given by $p = h\rho g$ where, h is depth, ρ is density and g is acceleration due to gravity.

Therefore, pressure of liquid column increases with depth. The height of blood column in human body is more at feet than at the brain. Therefore, the blood pressure in humans is greater at the feet than the brain.

(ii) The density of air is maximum near the surface of the earth and decreases rapidly with height. At a height of 6 km, the density of air decreases to nearly half of its value at the sea level. Beyond 6 km height, the density of air decreases very slowly with height. Hence, the atmospheric pressure at a height of about 6 km decreases to nearly half of its value at the sea level.

(iii) When force is applied on a liquid, the pressure is transmitted equally in all directions inside the liquid. Therefore, hydrostatic pressure has no fixed direction and hence, it is a scalar quantity.

11. (i) When a small quantity of a liquid is poured on a solid, three types of interfaces namely liquid-air, solid-air and solid-liquid are occured. The surface tension corresponding to these three interfaces are S_{la}, S_{sa} and S_{sl}, respectively. If θ is the angle of contact between solid and liquid, then

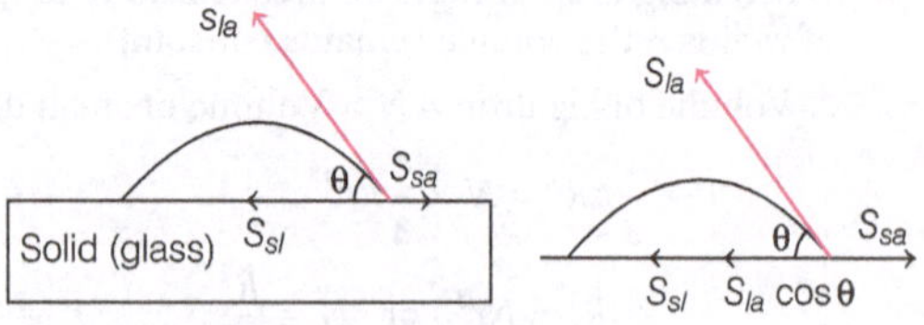

$$S_{sl} + S_{la}\cos\theta = S_{sa}$$

$$\Rightarrow \quad S_{la}\cos\theta = S_{sa} - S_{sl}$$

$$\cos\theta = \frac{S_{sa} - S_{sl}}{S_{la}} \qquad \text{...(i)}$$

For mercury and glass, $S_{sa} < S_{sl}$, therefore from Eq. (i) $\cos\theta$ is negative and therefore, $\theta > 90°$, i.e. obtuse.

For water and glass, $S_{sa} > S_{sl}$, therefore from Eq. (i), $\cos\theta$ is positive and therefore, $\theta < 90°$, i.e. acute.

(ii) For equilibrium of a liquid drop on a solid surface,

$$S_{sl} + S_{la}\cos\theta = S_{sa}$$

In case of mercury and glass, $S_{sl} > S_{sa}$, therefore for equilibrium, $\cos\theta$ should be negative, i.e. θ should be obtuse. In order to achieve this obtuse value of angle of contact, the mercury tends to form a drop. In case of water and glass, $S_{sa} > S_{sl}$, therefore for equilibrium, $\cos\theta$ should be positive, i.e. θ should be acute. In order to achieve this value of angle of contact, the water tends to spread.

12. (i) When we blow over a piece of paper, the velocity of air above the paper increases. So, in accordance with Bernoulli's theorem $\left(p + \frac{1}{2}\rho v^2 = \text{constant}\right)$, the pressure of air decreases above the paper. Due to the pressure difference of air between below and above the paper, a lifting force acts on paper and hence, it remains horizontal.

(ii) According to equation of continuity, for steady flow of liquid, the product of area of cross-section of the tube and velocity of liquid remains constant at each point, i.e. $A_1v_1 = A_2v_2$

When we try to close a water tap with our fingers, the area of cross-section of the outlet of water jet is reduced due to the restriction provided by the fingers and therefore, the velocity of water increases and fast jets of water gush through the openings between our fingers.

(iii) According to Bernoulli's theorem,

$$p + \frac{1}{2}\rho v^2 = \text{constant}$$

In this relation, pressure (p) occurs with one power, while velocity (v) occurs with two powers. Therefore, the influence of velocity is higher than pressure. The size of the needle controls the velocity of flow and the thumb pressure controls pressure.

Therefore, size of the needle of a syringe controls flow rate better than the thumb pressure.

(iv) A fluid flowing out of a small hole in a vessel have a large velocity and therefore, a large momentum. As no external force is acting, therefore according to law of conservation of momentum, equal momentum in opposite direction and hence, a backward velocity is attained by the vessel. Therefore, a backward thrust $\left(F = \frac{dp}{dt}\right)$ acts on the vessel.

(v) A spinning cricket ball in air does not follow a parabolic trajectory due to Magnus effect. Let a spinning cricket ball is moving forward with a velocity v and spinning clockwise with velocity u. As ball moves forward, it leaves lower pressure region behind it.

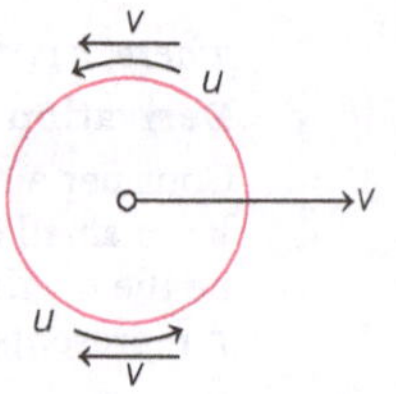

To fill this region, air moves backward with velocity v. The layers of air in contact with the ball spin with velocity u. Therefore, the resultant velocity of air above the ball is $(v - u)$ and below the ball is $(v + u)$. According to Bernoulli's theorem,

$$p + \frac{1}{2}\rho v^2 = \text{constant}$$

Therefore, pressure below the ball becomes lower than above the ball. Due to this pressure difference, a force acts on ball in downward direction. Therefore, the ball follows a curved path in spite of a parabolic trajectory.

13. Let n be the number of little droplets which coalesce to form a single drop. Then,

Volume of n little droplets = Volume of a single drop

or $$n \times \frac{4}{3}\pi r^3 = \frac{4}{3}\pi R^3 \text{ or } nr^3 = R^3$$

Decrease in surface area

$$= n \times 4\pi r^2 - 4\pi R^2 = 4\pi\,[nr^2 - R^2] = 4\pi\left[\frac{nr^3}{r} - R^2\right]$$

$$= 4\pi\left[\frac{R^3}{r} - R^2\right] = 4\pi R^3\left[\frac{1}{r} - \frac{1}{R}\right] \qquad [\because nr^3 = R^3]$$

The energy released,

E = surface tension × decrease in surface area

$$= 4\pi SR^3\left[\frac{1}{r} - \frac{1}{R}\right]$$

The mass of bigger drop,

$$M = \frac{4}{3}\pi R^3 \times 1 = \frac{4}{3}\pi R^3$$

$$\therefore \quad E = \frac{4}{3}\pi SR^3 .3\left[\frac{1}{r} - \frac{1}{R}\right] = 3SM\left[\frac{1}{r} - \frac{1}{R}\right]$$

$$\left[\because M = \frac{4}{3}\pi R^3\right]$$

$\because$ KE of bigger drop = Energy released

$$\frac{1}{2}Mv^2 = 3SM\left[\frac{1}{r} - \frac{1}{R}\right]$$

$$\therefore \quad v = \sqrt{6S\left(\frac{R-r}{Rr}\right)}$$

14. Let the density of sphere's material is ρ and that of liquid is σ. When the sphere just enters in the liquid, downward force on the sphere,

F = Weight of the sphere
− Weight of the fluid displaced by it

$$F = \frac{4}{3}\pi r^3 \cdot \rho g - \frac{4}{3}\pi r^3 \cdot \sigma g$$

$$\because \text{ Mass} = \text{Volume} \times \text{Density} = \frac{4}{3}\pi r^3(\rho - \sigma)g$$

$\therefore$ Acceleration of the sphere at this instant, $a = \frac{F}{m}$

$$a = \frac{\frac{4}{3}\pi r^3(\rho - \sigma)g}{\frac{4}{3}\pi r^3 \rho} = \left(1 - \frac{\sigma}{\rho}\right)g$$

When the sphere approaches to terminal velocity, its acceleration becomes zero.

$\therefore$ Average acceleration of the sphere $= \frac{a+0}{2}$

$$= \frac{\left(1 - \frac{\sigma}{\rho}\right)g}{2} = \left(1 - \frac{\sigma}{\rho}\right)\frac{g}{2}$$

As we know that,

Terminal velocity, $v = \frac{2}{9}\frac{r^2}{\eta}(\rho - \sigma)g$

$\because$ The sphere falls from rest,

$\therefore \quad u = 0$

If time t is taken by the sphere to attain the terminal velocity, then using $v = u + at$

Putting values $\frac{2}{9}\frac{r^2}{\eta}(\rho - \sigma)g = 0 + \left(1 - \frac{\sigma}{\rho}\right)\frac{g}{2} \cdot t$

$$\therefore \quad t = \frac{4}{9}\frac{r^2 \rho}{\eta}$$

Thus, t is independent of the liquid density.

15. (a) Buoyant force, $F_b = \rho_w V g$

$$V = a^3 = (0.1)^3 = 0.001 \text{ m}^3,\ g = 9.8 \text{ m/s}^2$$

$$F_b = (1000)(0.001)(9.8) = 9.8 \text{ N}$$

(b) The cube's weight,

$$W_c = \rho_c V g = (800)(0.001)(9.8) = 7.84 \text{ N}$$

Since, $W_c < F_b$, the cube will float.

$$\text{Fraction submerged} = \frac{\rho_c}{\rho_w} = \frac{800}{1000} = 0.8$$

Thus, 80% of the cube will be submerged.

16. Given, $h_1 = 60$ cm, $h_2 = 45$ cm, $\rho_w = 10^3 \text{ kg/m}^3$

we have, $\rho_w g h_1 = \rho_l g h_2$

$$\rho_l = \frac{\rho_w h_1}{h_2} = \frac{10^3 \times 0.60}{0.45} = 1.3 \times 10^3 \text{ kg/m}^3$$

17. The net force acting on the base $= (\rho g h)A + mg$

$$F = 1000 \times 9.8 \times 1 \times 0.02 + 10 \times 9.8 = 294 \text{ N}$$

$$\therefore \text{ Pressure} = \frac{\text{Thrust}}{\text{Area}} = \frac{294}{0.02} = 14700 \text{ N/m}^2$$

18. Depth, $h = 31 \times 10^3$ m

Density, $\rho = 10^3 \text{ kg/m}^3$

$$g = 9.8 \text{ m/s}^2$$

$$p = h \cdot \rho \cdot g = 31 \times 10^3 \times 10^3 \times 9.8$$

$$= 3 \times 10^8 \text{ Pa}$$

This pressure is less than the maximum stress of 10^9 Pa. So, the structure is suitable for putting up on top of an oil well in the ocean.

19. Given, $r_1 = 4.0$ cm $= 0.04$ m,

$r_2 = 16.0$ cm $= 0.16$ m,

$m = 3000$ kg, $d_2 = 0.20$ m

Force, F_2 = weight of the truck $= mg = 3000 \times 10$

$F_2 = 30000$ N

From Pascal's law, the pressure at given level is same throughout the hydraulic fluid. Since, the piston are at the same level, therefore the downward force on the smaller piston can be determined as $F_1 = \frac{A_1}{A_2} \times F_2$

where, $A_1 = \pi r_1^2 = \pi(0.04)^2 = 0.005024\ \text{m}^2$

$A_2 = \pi r_2^2 = \pi(0.16)^2 = 0.080384\ \text{m}^2$

$$F_1 = \frac{0.005024}{0.080384} \times 30000 = 1875\ \text{N}$$

Hence, a force of 1875 N on small piston can lift a truck weighing 30000 N.

Now, apply the conservation of energy as if we neglect friction, then the amount of work done by the applied force must equal to the work done to lift the truck. Thus,

$$W_1 = W_2$$

$$\Rightarrow \quad F_1 d_1 = F_2 d_2 \quad [\because \text{given, } d_2 = 0.20\ \text{m}]$$

$$1875 \times d_1 = 30000 \times 0.20$$

$$d_1 = \frac{30000 \times 0.20}{1875} = 3.2\ \text{m}$$

20. As we know that for a floating body,

Buoyant force = Weight of liquid displaced

Let V be the volume of the body, then $\frac{2}{3} V\rho_l g = V\rho_b g$

where, ρ_b = density of floating body

and ρ_l = density of liquid.

$$\therefore \quad \frac{\rho_b}{\rho_l} = \frac{2}{3}$$

21. Diameter of the ring of wire = 3 cm = 0.03 m

Radius of the ring of wire $= \frac{0.03}{2} = 0.015$ m

Circumference of circle $= 2\pi r$

$L = 2 \times 3.14 \times 0.015$, $L = 0.0942$ m

Upward force $= 2SL$

$$= 2 \times (3 \times 10^{-2}) \times 0.0942 = 5.652 \times 10^{-3}\ \text{N}$$

22. Radii of mercury droplets, $r_1 = 0.1$ cm $= 1 \times 10^{-3}$ m

$r_2 = 0.2$ cm $= 2 \times 10^{-3}$ m

Surface tension, $S = 435.5 \times 10^{-3}$ N/m

Let the radius of the big drop formed by collapsing be R.

$\therefore$ Volume of big drop = Volume of small droplets

$$\frac{4}{3}\pi R^3 = \frac{4}{3}\pi r_1^3 + \frac{4}{3}\pi r_2^3$$

or $R^3 = r_1^3 + r_2^3 = (0.1)^3 + (0.2)^3 = 0.001 + 0.008 = 0.009$

or $R = 0.21$ cm $= 2.1 \times 10^{-3}$ m

$\therefore$ Change in surface area,

$$\Delta A = 4\pi R^2 - (4\pi r_1^2 + 4\pi r_2^2) = 4\pi\,[R^2 - (r_1^2 + r_2^2)]$$

$\therefore$ Energy released $= S \cdot \Delta A = S \times 4\pi\,[R^2 - (r_1^2 + r_2^2)]$

$$= 435.5 \times 10^{-3} \times 4 \times 3.14\,[(2.1 \times 10^{-3})^2 - (1 \times 10^{-6} + 4 \times 10^{-6})]$$

$$= 435.5 \times 4 \times 3.14\,[4.41 - 5] \times 10^{-6} \times 10^{-3}$$

$$= -32.27 \times 10^{-7} = -3.22 \times 10^{-6}\ \text{J}$$

(Negative sign shows absorption)

Therefore, 3.22×10^{-6} J energy will be absorbed.

23. (i) Given, radius of ring $(R) = 5$ cm $= 0.05$ m

Force $(F) = 0.1$ N

Force due to surface tension of circular ring is given by

$$F = 2 \times T \times \text{Circumference of ring}$$

$$= 2 \times T \times (2\pi R)$$

$$T = \frac{F}{4\pi R}$$

Substituting the values, we get

$$T = \frac{0.1}{4\pi \times 0.05}$$

(ii) If the film breaks and only a single layer remain the force required will be

$$F' = T \times 2\pi R = \frac{0.1}{4\pi \times 0.05} \times (2\pi R)$$

$$= 0.0039 \times 2\pi R = 0.123\ \text{N}$$

24. Let the radius of larger drop $= R$

and radius of each small drop $= r$

Volume of 27 small drops = Volume of the large drop

$$= 27 \times \frac{4}{3} \times \pi r^3 = \frac{4}{3}\pi R^3$$

So, $r = R/3$

Surface area of large drop $= 4\pi R^2$

Surface area of 27 small drops $= 27 \times 4\pi r^2$

$$= 27 \times 4\pi \left(\frac{R}{3}\right)^2 = 12\pi R^2$$

$\therefore$ Increase in surface area $= 12\pi R^2 - 4\pi R^2 = 8\pi R^2$

Increase in energy = Increase in surface area × Surface tension

$$= 8\pi R^2 \times S$$

25. Volume of 1000 small drops = Volume of a large drop

$$1000 \times \frac{4}{3}\pi r^3 = \frac{4}{3}\pi R^3$$

$$r = \frac{R}{10}$$

Surface area of large drop $= 4\pi R^2$

Surface area of 1000 drops $= 4\pi \times 1000\, r^2 = 40\pi R^2$

$\therefore$ Increase in surface area $= (40-4)\pi R^2 = 36\,\pi R^2$

The increase in surface energy

$$= \text{Surface tension} \times \text{Increase in surface area}$$

$$= 36\pi R^2 \times 0.07$$

$$= 36 \times 3.14 \times (4 \times 10^{-3})^2 \times 0.07$$

$$= 1.26 \times 10^{-4}\ \text{J}$$

26. Given, surface tension of water, $S = 7.28 \times 10^{-2}$ N/m

Vapour pressure, $p = 2.33 \times 10^3$ Pa

The drop will evaporate, if the water pressure is greater than the vapour pressure.

Let a water droplet of radius R can be formed without evaporating.

$\therefore$ Vapour pressure = Excess pressure in drop

$$\therefore \quad p = \frac{2S}{R}$$

or $$R = \frac{2S}{p} = \frac{2 \times 7.28 \times 10^{-2}}{2.33 \times 10^3} \approx 6.25 \times 10^{-5}\ \text{m}$$

27. Given, radius of drop $(R) = 3.00$ mm $= 3 \times 10^{-3}$ m

Surface tension of mercury $(S) = 4.65 \times 10^{-1}$ N/m

Atmospheric pressure $(p_0) = 1.01 \times 10^5$ Pa

Pressure inside the drop = Atmospheric pressure + Excess pressure inside the liquid drop $= p_0 + \dfrac{2S}{R}$

$$= 1.01 \times 10^5 + \frac{2 \times 4.65 \times 10^{-1}}{3 \times 10^{-3}}$$

$$= 1.01 \times 10^5 + 3.10 \times 10^2$$

$$= 1.01 \times 10^5 + 0.00310 \times 10^5$$

$$= 1.01310 \times 10^5\ \text{Pa}$$

Excess pressure inside the drop

$$(\Delta p) = \frac{2S}{R} = \frac{2 \times 4.65 \times 10^{-1}}{3 \times 10^{-3}}$$

$$= 3.10 \times 10^2 = 310\ \text{Pa}$$

28. Let R_1 and R_2 be the radii of the two bubbles.

Then, $R_1 / R_2 = 2/3$

If S is the surface tension of soap solution, then excess of pressure inside the soap bubble of radius R_1 is

$p_1 = 4S / R_1$

Excess of pressure inside the soap bubble of radius R_2 is

$$p_2 = 4S / R_2$$

$$\therefore \quad \frac{p_1}{p_2} = \frac{R_2}{R_1} = 3/2$$

29. The capillary rise in a tube is given by the expression,

$$h = \frac{2S\cos\theta}{\rho g r}$$

$$\frac{h_1}{h_2} = \frac{S_1 \rho_2}{S_2 \rho_1} = \frac{60 \times 0.6}{50 \times 0.8} = \frac{9}{10}$$

30. Area of cross-section of tube $(A_1) = 8\ \text{cm}^2 = 8 \times 10^{-4}\ \text{m}^2$

Number of holes, $N = 40$

Diameter of each hole, $2r = 1.0$ mm

$\therefore$ Radius of each hole, $r = 0.5$ mm $= 5 \times 10^{-4}$ m

Velocity of liquid flow in tube $= 1.5$ m/min $= \dfrac{1.5}{60}$ m/s

$$= 2.5 \times 10^{-2}\ \text{m/s}$$

Total area of holes $= N \times \pi r^2 = 40 \times 3.14 \times (5 \times 10^{-4})^2$

$$= 3.14 \times 10^{-5}\ \text{m}^2$$

From equation of continuity, $A_1 v_1 = A_2 v_2$

or $$v_2 = \frac{A_1 v_1}{A_2} = \frac{8 \times 10^{-4} \times 2.5 \times 10^{-2}}{3.14 \times 10^{-5}}$$

$$= \frac{20}{3.14} \times 10^{-1} = 0.64\ \text{m/s}$$

31. Given, $h = 40$ cm, $g = 980\ \text{cm/s}^2$

We know that, velocity head, $h = \dfrac{v^2}{2g}$

$$\therefore \quad v = \sqrt{2gh} = \sqrt{2 \times 980 \times 40} = 280\ \text{cms}^{-1}$$

32. Density of water, $\rho_w = 1000\ \text{kg/m}^3$

$$v_1 = 0.6\ \text{m/s},\ p_1 = 1200\ \text{N/m}^2,\ v_2 = 0.4\ \text{m/s}$$

By Bernoulli's theorem, $\dfrac{1}{2}\rho_w v_1^2 + p_1 = \dfrac{1}{2}\rho_w v_2^2 + p_2$

$$\frac{1}{2} \times 1000 \times (0.6)^2 + 1200 = \frac{1}{2} \times 1000 \times (0.4)^2 + p_2$$

$$p_2 = 1300\ \text{N/m}^2$$

33. Given, $\rho = 1000\ \text{kg/m}^3$, $v_1 = 1$ m/s, $a_1 = 4 \times 10^{-3}\ \text{m}^2$,

$$a_2 = 8 \times 10^{-3}\ \text{m}^2,\ h_1 = 2\ \text{m},\ h_2 = 5\ \text{m}$$

By Bernoulli's theorem,

$$p_1 + \frac{1}{2}\rho v_1^2 + g\rho h_1 = p_2 + \frac{1}{2}\rho v_2^2 + g\rho h_2$$

$$(p_1 - p_2) = \frac{1}{2}\rho(v_2^2 - v_1^2) + \rho g(h_2 - h_1)$$

where, $(p_1 - p_2)$ = work done by pressure per unit volume i.e. $\left(\frac{W}{\text{Volume}}\right)_p = \frac{1}{2}\rho(v_2^2 - v_1^2) + \rho g(h_2 - h_1)$

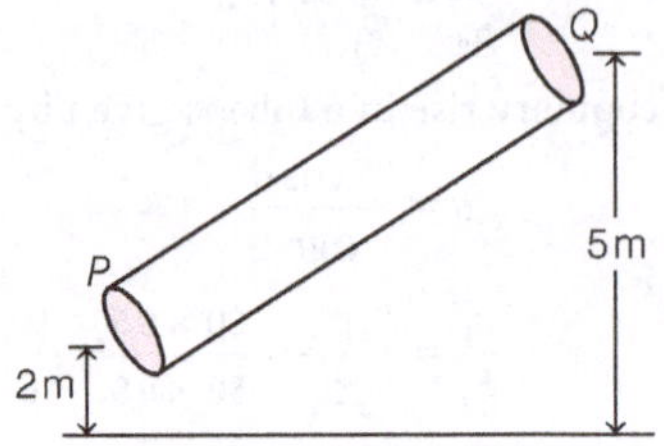

From equation of continuity, $a_1 v_1 = a_2 v_2$

$\Rightarrow \quad v_2 = \frac{a_1 v_1}{a_2} = \frac{4 \times 10^{-3} \times 1}{8 \times 10^{-3}} = 0.5 \text{ m/s}$

$\left(\frac{W}{\text{Volume}}\right)_p = \frac{1}{2} \times 1000\,[0.25 - 1] + 1000 \times 10\,(5 - 2)$

$= -375 + 30000 = 29625 \text{ J/m}^3$

Work done per unit volume by the gravitational force

$= \rho g(h_1 - h_2)$

$= 1000 \times 10\,(2 - 5) = -3 \times 10^4 \text{ J/m}^3$

34. Let R and r be the radii of the big and small drops, respectively.

The volume of the big drop = 27 × Volume of one small drop

$\therefore \quad \frac{4}{3}\pi R^3 = 27 \times \frac{4}{3}\pi r^3$

$\Rightarrow \quad R^3 = 27r^3 \Rightarrow R = 3r$

The terminal velocity of a drop, $v \propto (\text{Radius})^2$

$\therefore \quad \frac{v_2}{v_1} = \frac{R^2}{r^2} = \frac{(3r)^2}{(r)^2} = 9$

$\Rightarrow \quad \frac{v_2}{0.15} = 9$

$\Rightarrow \quad v_2 = 9 \times 0.15 = 1.35 \text{ m/s}$

35. Let the lower and upper surfaces of the wing of the aeroplane be at the same height h and speeds of air on the upper and lower surfaces of the wing be v_1 and v_2.

Speed of air on the upper surface of the wing,

$v_1 = 70 \text{ m/s}$

speed of air on the lower surface of the wing,

$v_2 = 63 \text{ m/s}$

Density of the air, $\rho = 1.3 \text{ kg/m}^3$

Area, $A = 2.5 \text{ m}^2$

According to Bernoulli's theorem,

$$p_1 + \frac{1}{2}\rho v_1^2 + \rho g h = p_2 + \frac{1}{2}\rho v^2 + \rho g h$$

or $\quad p_2 - P_1 = \frac{1}{2}\rho(v_1^2 - v_2^2)$

∴ Lifting force acting on the wings,

$$F = (p_2 - p_1) \times A = \frac{1}{2}\rho(v_1^2 - v_2^2) \times A$$

$\left[\because \text{Pressure} = \frac{\text{Force}}{\text{Area}}\right]$

$= \frac{1}{2} \times 1.3 \times [(70)^2 - (63)^2] \times 2.5$

$= \frac{1}{2} \times 1.3\,[4900 - 3969] \times 2.5$

$= \frac{1}{2} \times 1.3 \times 931 \times 2.5 = 1.51 \times 10^3 \text{ N}$

36. Given, $v_2 = 120$ m/s, $v_1 = 90$ m/s, $\rho_a = 1.3 \text{ kg/m}^3$, $h_1 = 10$ m, $a_1 = 10 \times 2 = 20 \text{ m}^2$

According to Bernoulli's theorem,

$$\frac{p_1}{\rho} + gh_1 + \frac{1}{2}v_1^2 = \frac{p_2}{\rho} + gh_2 + \frac{1}{2}v_2^2$$

For the horizontal flow, $h_1 = h_2$

$\therefore \quad \frac{p_1}{\rho} + \frac{1}{2}v_1^2 = \frac{p_2}{\rho} + \frac{1}{2}v_2^2$

$\therefore \quad \frac{p_1 - p_2}{\rho} = \frac{1}{2}(v_2^2 - v_1^2)$

$(p_1 - p_2) = \frac{\rho(v_2^2 - v_1^2)}{2}$

$= 1.3 \times \frac{(14400 - 8100)}{2} = \frac{1.3 \times 6300}{2}$

$p_1 - p_2 = 4.095 \times 10^3 \text{ N/m}^2$

It is the pressure difference between the top and the bottom of the wing.

Gross lift of wing = $(p_1 - p_2) \times$ Area of the wing

$= 4.095 \times 10^3 \times 10 \times 2 = 8.190 \times 10^4 \text{ N}$

37. Given, $v_t = 6.5 \times 10^{-2}$ m/s

$r = 2 \times 10^{-3}$ m, $g = 9.8 \text{ m/s}^2$

$\rho = 8.9 \times 10^3 \text{ kg/m}^3, \sigma = 1.5 \times 10^3$

$\rho - \sigma = 8.9 \times 10^3 - 1.5 \times 10^3$

$= 7.4 \times 10^3 \text{ kg/m}^3$

As we know, terminal velocity,

$$v_t = \frac{2r^2(\rho - \sigma)}{9\,\eta} g$$

$$\eta = \frac{2}{9} \times \frac{(2 \times 10^{-3})^2 \times 9.8}{(6.5 \times 10^{-2})} \times 7.4 \times 10^3$$

$\eta = 9.9 \times 10^{-1}$ kg/ms

38. Volume of a bigger drop

$= n \times$ Volume of a smaller droplets

or $\frac{4}{3}\pi R^3 = n \times \frac{4}{3}\pi r^3$ or $R^3 = nr^3$ or $R = n^{1/3} r$

Terminal velocity of a small droplet is given by

$$v_s = \frac{2}{9}\frac{r^2}{\eta}(\rho - \rho')g \quad \text{...(i)}$$

Terminal velocity of a bigger drop is given by

$$v_b = \frac{2}{9}\frac{R^2}{\eta}(\rho - \rho')g \quad \text{...(ii)}$$

Dividing Eq. (ii) by Eq. (i), we get

$$\frac{v_b}{v_s} = \frac{R^2}{r^2}$$

But $R = n^{1/3} r$ and $v_s = 10$ cm/s

$$v_b = v_s \times \left(\frac{R^2}{r^2}\right) = 10 \times \frac{n^{2/3} r^2}{r^2}$$

$$v_b = 10\, n^{2/3} \text{cm/s}$$

39. Let the speed of the flow be v.

Given, diameter of tap, $d = 1.25$ cm

Volume of water flowing out per second,

$$Q = V \times \frac{\pi d^2}{4} \Rightarrow V = \frac{4Q}{d^2 \pi}$$

Estimate Reynold's number, $R_e = \frac{4\rho Q}{\pi d \eta}$

$$Q = 0.48 \text{ L/min} = 8 \times 10^{-3} \text{ L/s}$$

$$= 8 \times 10^{-6} \text{ m}^3\text{/s}$$

$$R_e = \frac{4 \times 10^3 \times 8 \times 10^{-6}}{3.14 \times 1.25 \times 10^{-2} \times 10^{-3}}$$

$R_e = 815$ [i.e. below 1000, the flow is steady]

After some time, when $Q = 3$ L/min $= 5 \times 10^{-5}$ m^3/s,

$$R_e = \frac{4 \times 10^3 \times 5 \times 10^{-5}}{3.14 \times 1.25 \times 10^{-2} \times 10^{-3}} = 5095$$

$\therefore$ The flow will be turbulent.

QR Code for Quick Test 1

QR Code for Quick Test 2

QR Code for Quick Test 3

SELF ASSESSMENT TEST

Multiple Choice Questions (MCQs)

1. A wooden block with a coin placed on its top, floats in water as shown in figure.

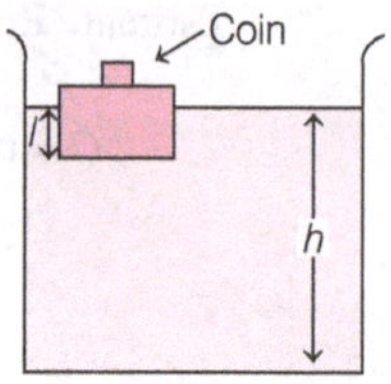

The distance l and h are shown in the figure. After some time, the coin falls into the water. Then,

(a) both l and h decrease
(b) both l and h increase
(c) l decreases and h increases
(d) l increases and h decreases

2. Streamline flow is more likely for liquids with
(a) high density and low viscosity
(b) low density and high viscosity
(c) high density and high viscosity
(d) low density and low viscosity

3. With increase in temperature, the viscosity of
(a) gases and liquids decrease.
(b) gases and liquids increase.
(c) gases increases whereas it decreases for liquids.
(d) gases decreases whereas it increases for liquids.

4. A cylinder of height 20 m is completely filled with water. The velocity of efflux of water (in ms^{-1}) through a small hole on the side wall of the cylinder near its bottom is
(a) 10 (b) 20
(c) 25.5 (d) 5

5. The coefficient of viscosity for hot air is
(a) greater than the coefficient of viscosity for cold air
(b) smaller than the coefficient of viscosity for cold air
(c) same as the coefficient of viscosity for cold air
(d) Increases or decreases depending on the external pressure

6. A ball is moving without spinning in a straight line through a fluid (as shown)

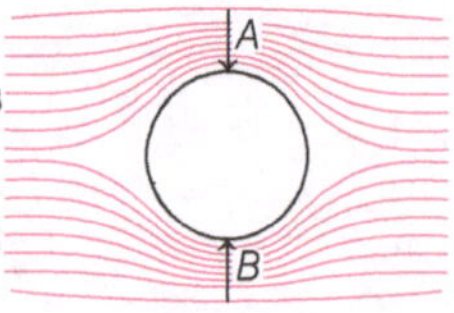

If p_A and p_B are pressures values at A and B, then

(a) $p_A < p_B$
(b) $p_B < p_A$
(c) $p_A \times p_B = 1$
(d) $p_A / p_B = 1$

7. Match the Column I (terms or quantities) with Column II (dimensions) and select the correct answer from the codes given below.

	Column I		Column II
A.	Coefficient of viscosity	1.	$[ML^0T^{-2}]$
B.	Density	2.	$[M^0L^0T^0]$
C.	Surface tension	3.	$[ML^{-1}T^{-1}]$
D.	Reynold's number	4.	$[ML^{-3}T^0]$

(a) A-2, B-3, C-4, D-1 (b) A-1, B-3, C-4, D-2
(c) A-3, B-2, C-1, D-4 (d) A-3, B-4, C-1, D-2

Assertion-Reason

Directions *(Q.No. 8-11) In the following questions, two statements are given- one labelled Assertion (A) and the other labelled Reason (R). Select the correct answer to these questions from the codes (a), (b), (c) and (d) as given below.*

(a) Both Assertion and Reason are true and Reason is the correct explanation of Assertion.
(b) Both Assertion and Reason are true but Reason is not the correct explanation of Assertion.
(c) Assertion is true but Reason is false.
(d) Assertion is false but Reason is true.

8. **Assertion (A)** In steady flow, the velocity of each passing fluid particle remains constant in time.
Reason (R) Each particle follows a smooth path and the paths of the particles do not cross each other.

9. **Assertion (A)** The machine parts are jammed in winter.
Reason (R) The viscosity of the lubricants used in the machine increases at low temperature.

10. **Assertion (A)** Liquid does not overflow due to rise of liquid in a capillary tube of insufficient length.
Reason (R) Rise of liquid in a capillary tube is inversely proportional to the radius of area of cross-section of the tube.

11. **Assertion (A)** An aircraft can gain height due to pressure difference between the upper and lower surfaces of its wings.

Reason (R) The velocity of air on the upper surface of the wings of an aircraft is higher than that on the lower surface of the wings.

Case Based Questions

Directions *(Q.No. 12) This question is case study based question. Read the following paragraph and answer the questions on the basis of same.*

12. A car service station uses a hydraulic lift to raise vehicles for repair. The lift consists of two pistons connected by a pipe filled with an incompressible fluid. The larger piston, used to support the car, has a radius of 20 cm, while the smaller piston, operated by the mechanic, has a radius of 5 cm.

During operation, the mechanic applied a force of 200 N on the smaller piston and the larger piston raises a car weighing 1500 kg. The height difference between the two pistons is negligible.

(i) Verify whether this pressure is sufficient to lift the car by calculating the force exerted by the larger piston.

(ii) If the mechanic increases the applied force on the smaller piston by 20%, determine the new force that the larger piston will exert. Would this increased force be sufficient to raise a car weighing 1800 kg? Justify your answer.

(iii) Assuming no energy losses, if the smaller piston moves downward by 10 cm, calculate the height by which the larger piston will rise.

(iv) Discuss why incompressible fluids are used in hydraulic systems and the what are the potential issues, if the fluid were compressible.

Very Short Answer Type Questions

13. Write any two properties of streamlines.

14. Why are the cars and aeroplanes given streamline shape?

15. What is Torricelli's law?

Short Answer Type Questions

16. A vessel filled with water is kept on a weighing pan and the scale is adjusted to zero. A block of mass M and density ρ is suspended by a massless spring of spring constant k. This block is submerged in the water. What is the reading of the scale?

17. An air bubble of radius r rises steadily through a liquid of density ρ at the rate of v. Neglecting density of air, find the coefficient of viscosity of liquid.

18. Describe how an open tube manometer is used to measure the pressure of a gas. Distinguish between absolute pressure and gauge pressure.

19. Water in a capillary tube rises to a height 6 cm.The area of cross-section of the capillary is made one-fourth. Find the height of rise of the water in the tube.

20. If the terminal speed of a sphere of gold (density $= 19.5\ kg/m^3$) is 0.2 m/s in a viscous liquid (density $= 1.5\ kg/m^3$), then find out the terminal speed of a sphere of silver (density $= 10.5\ kg/m^3$) of the same size in the same liquid.

Long Answer Type Questions

21. (a) Liquid drops are spherical in shape. Why ?

(b) Derive the expression of excess pressure inside the liquid drop.

(c) Give two similarities and dissimilarities between friction and viscosity.

22. (a) Pressure decreases as one ascends the atmosphere. If the density of air is ρ, what is the change in pressure dp over a differential height dh?

(b) Considering the pressure p to be proportional to the density, find the pressure p at a height h if the pressure on the surface of the earth is p_0.

(c) If $p_0 = 1.03 \times 10^5\ Nm^{-2}, \rho_0 = 1.29\ kg\ m^{-3}$ and $g = 9.8\ ms^{-2}$, at what height will be pressure drop to (1/10) the value at the surface of the earth?

(d) This model of the atmosphere works for relatively small distances. Identify the underlying assumption that limits the model.

23. Glycerine flows steadily through a horizontal tube of length 1.5 m and radius 1.0 cm. If the amount of glycerine flowing per second at one end is $4.0 \times 10^{-3}\ kg/s$, what is the pressure difference between the two ends of the tube? (Density of glycerine $= 1.3 \times 10^3\ kg/m^3$ and viscosity of glycerine $= 0.83$ Pa - s). (You may also like to check, if the assumption of laminar flow in the tube is correct).

24. What is the excess pressure inside a bubble of soap solution of radius 5.00 mm, given that the surface tension of soap solution at the temperature (20°C) is $2.50 \times 10^{-2}\ N/m$? If an air bubble of the same dimension were formed at a depth of 40.0 cm inside a container containing the soap solution (of relative density 1.20), what would be the pressure inside the bubble? (1 atm pressure is 1.01×10^5 Pa.)

Answers

1. (c)	*2.* (b)	*3.* (c)	*4.* (b)
5. (a)	*6.* (d)	*7.* (d)	*8.* (a)
9. (a)	*10.* (b)	*11.* (a)	

10 CHAPTER

Thermal properties of matter deals with the characteristics and behavior of substances related to heat and temperature.
These properties play important role in understanding how materials respond to changes in temperature and how they conduct, store or transfer heat.

Thermal Properties of Matter

YOUR STUDY GOALS

10.1 Temperature and Heat
10.2 Ideal Gas Equation and Absolute Temperature
10.3 Thermal Expansion
10.4 Heat Capacity
10.5 Change of State
10.6 Latent Heat
10.7 Heat Transfer

YOUR PRACTICE GOAL

- Objective Type Questions (26 Qs, MCQs, A-R, Matching)
- Case Based Questions (3)
- Subjective Questions (3 VSAs, 8 SAs, 4 LAs)
- Numerical Problems (14)

10.1 Temperature and Heat

- Temperature is the measure of degree of hotness or coldness of a body. It is a relative measure that helps determine the direction of heat flow between objects in contact.
- If two bodies have temperatures T_1 and T_2 (where $T_1 > T_2$), then the body with T_1 is the hotter body and the one with T_2 is the colder body. When a body is heated it may expand or its physical state may be changed.

Heat

Heat is the form of the energy which flows from hotter body to colder body by virtue of temperature difference.

- The SI unit of heat is joule (J) and CGS unit is calorie (cal).
- 1 joule is equal to 4.2 calorie, i.e. $1\ J = 4.186$ cal.
- The ratio of work done (W) to heat produced (Q) is a constant, called **mechanical equivalent of heat** (J). The value of J is 4.186 J/cal.

Note One calorie is equal to heat energy required to raise the temperature of one gram of water through 1°C (From 14.5°C to 15.5° C).

Measurement of Temperature

An instrument used to measure the temperature of a body is called a **thermometer**. Thermometer uses such properties of matter which changes with temperature.

- **Liquid-in-glass thermometers** that use mercury or alcohol, which expand linearly with temperature across a wide range.
- Temperature can be measured using various temperature scales. The most commonly used units of temperature are **Kelvin (K), degree Celsius (°C)** and **degree Fahrenheit (°F)**.
- To define a standard temperature scale, two reference points are used: the **lower fixed point** (LFP) and the **upper fixed point** (UFP). For water, these fixed points are called **ice** or **freezing point** and **steam** or **boiling point** at standard pressure, respectively.

There are following temperature scales, used to measure the temperature of a body

1. Celsius Temperature Scale

It was designed by Celsius in 1710. In this scale, the LFP (freezing point) and UFP (boiling point) are taken as 0°C and 100°C, respectively.

The length between freezing point and boiling point is divided into 100 equal parts and the value of each division is 1°C.

2. Fahrenheit Temperature Scale

It was designed by Fahrenheit in 1717. In this scale, the LFP (freezing point) and UFP (boiling point) are taken as 32°F and 212°F, respectively.

The length between these two fixed points are divided into 180 equal parts. Each smallest division represents 1°F.

If t_F and t_C are the temperatures on celsius and fahrenheit scales respectively, then

$$\frac{t_C - 0}{100} = \frac{t_F - 32}{212 - 32}$$

or $$t_F = \frac{9}{5} t_C + 32$$

The t_F *versus* t_C graph is given as below

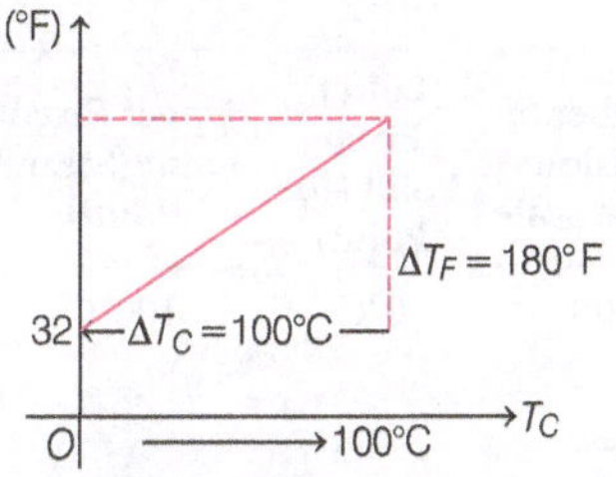

Celsius *versus* fahrenheit scale

3. Kelvin Temperature Scale

This temperature scale was designed by Lord Kelvin. It was also known as **absolute temperature scale.** In this scale, the LFP (freezing point) and UFP (boiling point) are taken as 273.15 K and 373.15 K.

The length between these two fixed points are divided into 100 equal parts and each smallest part represents 1K.

If t_C and t_K are the temperatures on celsius and kelvin scales respectively, then $t_K = t_C + 273.15$

The graph of t_K *versus* t_C is given below

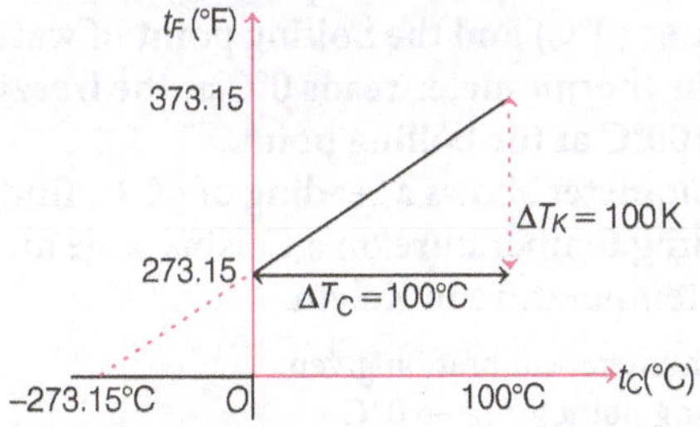

When the graph is extended backward, it meets the kelvin temperature axis at −273.15°C, which corresponds to 0 K. **This is the lowest attainable temperature at which pressure of the gas is zero. This temperature is known as absolute zero.** For the scale of simplicity, we use 273 K in place of 273.15 K.

Relation among the Temperatures Measured by Different Scales

The temperature measured by different scales is given as

$$\frac{C - 0}{100} = \frac{F - 32}{180} = \frac{R - 0}{80} = \frac{K - 273.15}{100}$$

Here, C, F, R and K are the readings of different scales.

The table for the different temperature scales is shown below.

Temperature Scale	Number of Divisions on the Scale	Lower Fixed Point (Ice Point)	Upper Fixed Point (Steam Point)	Remarks
Celsius (°C)	100	0°C	100°C	Equal degree interval in celsius and kelvin scale
Fahrenheit (°F)	180	32°C	212°F	$F = 1.8\ °C + 32$
Kelvin (K)	100	273.15 K	373.15 K	$K = °C + 273.15$

TEACHER TIP

Temperature on one scale can be converted into another scale by using the following identity.

$$\frac{\text{Reading on any scale} - \text{Lower fixed point (LFP)}}{\text{Upper fixed point (UFP)} - \text{Lower fixed point (LFP)}}$$

= Constant for all scales.

Example 1. A mercury thermometer is calibrated by immersing it in two known temperatures: the freezing point of water (0°C) and the boiling point of water (100°C). The thermometer reads 0°C at the freezing point and 100°C at the boiling point.
If the thermometer shows a reading of 40°C, find the corresponding temperature on a Celsius scale and an equivalent temperature in Kelvin.

Sol. Thermometer calibration given,
Freezing point (0°C) → 0°C
Boiling point (100°C) → 100°C
Reading of the thermometer, 40°C

Convert Celsius to Kelvin

$$T(\text{K}) = T(°\text{C}) + 273.15$$

For 40°C

$$T(\text{K}) = 40 + 273.15 = 313.15\text{K}$$

Example 2. The temperature of a body is 25° C. Convert this temperature to
(i) Fahrenheit (°F)
(ii) Kelvin (K)
(iii) Also, if the temperature is 77° F, convert it to Celsius and Kelvin.

Sol. (i) **Converting 25°C to Fahrenheit (°F) and Kelvin (K)**

Given,

Temperature in Celsius $T_C = 25°\text{C}$

To Convert Celsius to Fahrenheit

Use the formula $T_F = \frac{9}{5} T_C + 32$

Substituting the value of $T_C = 25°\text{C}$

$$T_F = \frac{9}{5} \times 25 + 32$$

$$T_F = 45 + 32 = 77°\text{F}$$

To Convert Celsius to Kelvin

Use the formula $T_K = T_C + 273.15$

Substituting $T_C = 25°\text{C}$

$$T_K = 25 + 273.15 = 298.15\text{K}$$

So, 25°C is equal to 298.15K.

(ii) **Converting 77°F to Celsius (°C) and Kelvin (K)**

Given

Temperature in Fahrenheit, $T_F = 77°\text{F}$

To Convert Fahrenheit to Celsius

Use the formula $T_C = \frac{5}{9}(T_F - 32)$

Substituting $T_F = 77°\text{F}$

$$T_C = \frac{5}{9}(77 - 32)$$

$$T_C = \frac{5}{9} \times 45 = 25°\text{C}$$

So, 77°F is equal to 25°C.

(iii) **To Convert Celsius to Kelvin**

We already know that 25°C is equivalent to 298.15 K from the previous part.

10.2 Ideal Gas Equation and Absolute Temperature

Behaviour of a gas is characterised by three properties pressure (p), volume (V) and temperature (T). The following laws regulate the properties of gases.

(i) **Boyle's law** According to this law,

At constant temperature, the pressure (p) of a given mass of a gas is inversely proportional to its volume (V).

$$p \propto \frac{1}{V} \quad \text{(at constant temperature)}$$

i.e. $\boxed{pV = \text{constant}}$

(ii) **Charles' Law** According to this law,

At constant pressure, the volume of a given mass of a gas is directly proportional to its absolute temperature.

$V \propto T$ (at constant pressure)

i.e. $\frac{V}{T} = \text{constant}$

Ideal Gas Equation

On combining these two laws (above mentioned), we get

$\frac{pV}{T} = \text{constant}$ (for a given quantity of gas)

This relation is known as **ideal gas law.** It can be written in more general forms for a given amount of gas as

$$pV = \mu RT$$

where, μ is number of moles of a gas and R is known as **universal gas constant** valued 8.31 J mol^{-1} K^{-1}. This equation is known as **ideal gas equation.**

Absolute Zero Temperature

The lowest temperature of −273.15 °C at which gas is supposed to have zero pressure (or zero volume) and at which entire molecular motion stops is called absolute zero temperature. The lowest attainable temperature is absolute zero.

The absolute zero temperature is regarded as 0 K or − 273.15° C. This implies 273.15 K = 0°C.

The temperature measured in kelvin scale is known as **absolute temperature** and the scale itself is known as **absolute scale.**

p -T Graph

At a constant volume, the ideal gas equation ($pV = \mu RT$) can be written as $p \propto T$

The variation of pressure (p) with temperature T(°C) is shown in figure.

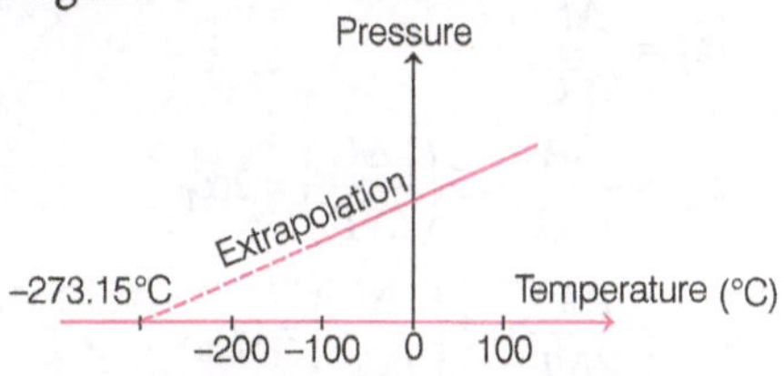

Graph of pressure *versus* temperature of a low density gas kept at constant volume

Note A constant volume gas thermometer based on the principle that, at a fixed volume, the pressure of the gas increases as the temperature increases.
i.e. $p \propto T$

10.3 Thermal Expansion

Most of the substances (solids, liquids and gases) expand on heating and contract on cooling. Few exceptions are water from 0°C to 4°C and silver iodide from 80°C to 141°C, contract on heating and expand on cooling.

The phenomenon of change in dimensions (length, area and volume) due to heat supply is known as thermal expansion.

TEACHER TIP

Thermal expansion is minimum in case of solids but maximum in case of gases because intermolecular forces are maximum in solids and minimum in gases.

Solids can expand in one, two or three dimensions while liquids and gases usually suffer change in volume (i.e. three dimensions) only.

Types of Thermal Expansion

There are three types of thermal expansion.

1. Linear Expansion

The expansion in length of a body due to increase in its temperature is called the linear expansion.

If a rod having initial length l_1 at temperature T_1 and final increased length l_2 at increased temperature T_2, then expansion in length, $\Delta l = \alpha_1 l_1 \Delta T$.

The quantity, α_l is known as **coefficient of linear expansion.**

It is a characteristic of the material of the rod. Normally, metals expand more and hence relatively high values of α_l.

$$\alpha_l = \frac{\Delta l}{l \Delta T} = \frac{\text{Increase in length}}{\text{Original length} \times \text{Rise in temperature}}$$

Hence, **the coefficient of linear expansion of a material of a solid rod is defined as increase in length per unit original length per degree rise in temperature. Its unit is $°C^{-1}$ or K^{-1}.**

Example 3. **A blacksmith fixes iron ring on the rim of the wooden wheel of a bullock cart. The diameters of the rim and the iron ring are 5.243 m and 5.231 m respectively, at 27°C. To what temperature should the ring be heated so as to fit the rim of the wheel? ($\alpha = 1.20 \times 10^{-5} K^{-1}$)** NCERT

Sol. Given, initial temperature, $T_1 = 27°C$

Initial length, $l_1 = 5.231$ m

Final length, $l_2 = 5.243$ m

Now, $\alpha_l = \frac{\Delta l}{l_1 \Delta T} = \frac{l_2 - l_1}{l_1 \Delta T}$

$\Rightarrow \quad l_2 = l_1[1 + \alpha_l (T_2 - T_1)]$

i.e. $\quad 5.243 = 5.231\,[1 + 1.20 \times 10^{-5}(T_2 - 27)]$

$\Rightarrow \quad T_2 = 218°C$

2. Area Expansion

The expansion in the area of a surface due to increase in its temperature is called area expansion.

If a plate having initial area A_1 at temperature T_1 and final area A_2 at temperature T_2, then

expansion in area, $\Delta A = \alpha_A A_1 \Delta T$.

where, α_A is known as **coefficient of area expansion.** It depends on nature of the material of the plate.

$$\alpha_A = \frac{\Delta A}{A_1 \Delta T} = \frac{\text{Increase in surface area}}{\text{Original surface area} \times \text{Rise in temperature}}$$

Hence, **coefficient of area expansion of metal sheet is defined as the increase in its surface area per unit original surface area per degree rise in its temperature. Its unit is °C^{-1} or K^{-1}.**

Example 4. **A metal ball having a diameter of 0.4 m is heated from 273 to 360 K. If the coefficient of area expansion of the material of the ball is 0.000034 K^{-1}, then determine the increase in surface area of the ball.**

Sol. Given, diameter = 0.4 m

Radius, $r = \frac{0.4}{2} = 0.2$ m

$\Delta T = T_2 - T_1$

$= 360 - 273 = 87$ K

$\alpha_A = 0.000034\ K^{-1}$

$\Delta A = ?$

Apply, $\Delta A = \alpha_A A_1 \Delta T$

where, $A_1 = 4\pi r^2 = 4 \times \pi \times (0.2)^2$

$= 0.5024\ m^2$

$\Delta A = 0.000034 \times 0.5024 \times 87$

$\Delta A = 0.001486$

$= 1.486 \times 10^{-3}\ m^2$

3. Volume Expansion

The expansion in the volume of an object due to increase in its temperature is known as volume expansion.

$\Rightarrow$ Expansion in volume, $\Delta V = \alpha_V V_1 \Delta T$

where, α_V is known as **coefficient of volume expansion.**

$$\alpha_V = \frac{\Delta V}{V_1 \Delta T} = \frac{\text{Increase in volume}}{\text{Original volume} \times \text{Rise in temperature}}$$

Hence, **the coefficient of volume (cubical) expansion of a substance is defined as the increase in volume per unit original volume per degree rise in its temperature. Its unit is °C^{-1} or K^{-1}.**

Variation of Coefficient of Volume Expansion with Temperature

It is also a characteristic of material of the object but not strictly a constant. The coefficient of volume expansion α_V depends generally on temperature, its value first increases with temperature and then becomes constant at a high temperature (above 500K). The dependency is as shown below.

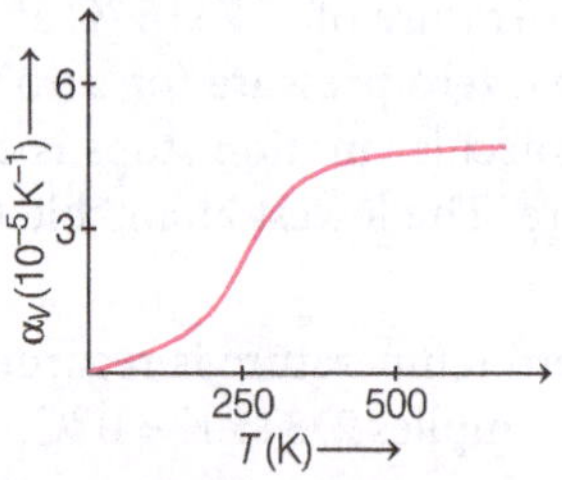

Coefficient of volume expansion with temperature

Note The dimensions of all types of coefficients of expansion is $[K^{-1}]$ and SI unit is per kelvin i.e. K^{-1}.

Relation among the Coefficients of Expansion

The coefficients of thermal expansion are given by

$$\alpha_l = \frac{\Delta l}{l \Delta T}$$

$$\alpha_A = \frac{\Delta A}{A \Delta T} = 2\left(\frac{\Delta l}{l \Delta T}\right) = 2\alpha_l$$

$$\alpha_V = \frac{\Delta V}{V \Delta T} = 3\left(\frac{\Delta l}{l \Delta T}\right) = 3\alpha_l$$

$\therefore$ The ratio of α_l, α_A and α_V is given by

$$\alpha_l : \alpha_A : \alpha_V = \alpha_l : 2\alpha_l : 3\alpha_l = 1 : 2 : 3$$

and $\quad 6\alpha_l = 3\alpha_A = 2\alpha_V$

Coefficient of Thermal Expansion at High Temperature

The coefficients α_l, α_A and α_V for a given solid are constants only at a given temperature. The value of these coefficients, however changes with change in the temperature range and becomes constant only at a high temperature.

Example 5. **The volume of a glass block initially was 15000 cm^3 but when the temperature of that glass block increases from 20°C to 45°C, then its volume increases by 5cm^3. Determine the coefficient of linear expansion.**

Sol. Given, $V_1 = 15000\ \text{cm}^3$,

$$\Delta T = T_2 - T_1 = 45°\text{C} - 20°\text{C} = 25°\text{C}$$

Change in volume, $\Delta V = 5\ \text{cm}^3$

Coefficient of volume expansion,

$$\alpha_V = \frac{\Delta V}{V_1 \Delta T}$$

$$= \frac{5}{15000 \times 25}$$

$$\alpha_V = 0.0133 \times 10^{-3}\ °\text{C}^{-1}$$

Coefficient of linear expansion

$$\alpha_l = \frac{\alpha_V}{3} = \frac{0.0133 \times 10^{-3}}{3}$$

$$\alpha_l = 4.4 \times 10^{-6}\ °\text{C}^{-1}$$

Example 6. **A 100 cm rod of silver at 0°C is heated to 100°C. Its length is increased by 0.19 cm. Find coefficients of area and volume expansion of the silver rod.**

Sol. Given, $L = 100, \Delta L = 0.19\ \text{cm}, \Delta T = 100°\text{C}$

Coefficient of linear expansion,

$$\alpha = \frac{\Delta L}{L \Delta T} = \frac{0.19}{100(100)} = 1.9 \times 10^{-5}\ °\text{C}^{-1}$$

Coefficient of area expansion,

$$\beta = 2\alpha = 2(1.9 \times 10^{-5}\ °\text{C}^{-1}) = 3.8 \times 10^{-5}\ °\text{C}^{-1}$$

Coefficient of volume expansion,

$$\gamma = 3\alpha = 3(1.9 \times 10^{-5}\ °\text{C}^{-1}) = 5.7 \times 10^{-5}\ °\text{C}^{-1}$$

Anomalous Expansion of Water

Generally matter expands on heating and contracts on cooling. In case of water, it expands on heating if its temperature is greater than 4°C.

In the range 0°C to 4°C, water contracts on heating and expands on cooling. This behaviour of water in the range 0°C to 4°C is called **anomalous expansion.**

The figure shows the variation of volume of 1 kg of water with temperature (°C).

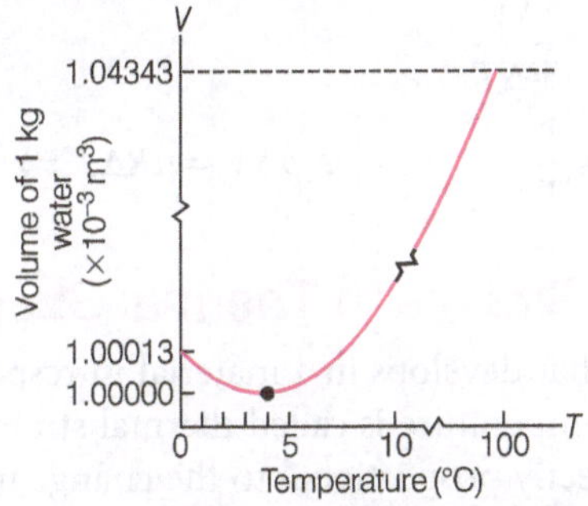

Anomalous behaviour of water

Water reaches its maximum density at 4°C, which has significant environmental implications.

For example

- In lakes and ponds, the surface freezes first.
- As a lake cools to 4°C, the water near the surface loses energy to the atmosphere, becomes denser and sinks, while the warmer, less dense water rises.
- However, when the surface water cools below 4°C, it becomes less dense and stays at the top, where it freezes.
- Without this property, lakes and ponds would freeze from the bottom up, endangering much of their aquatic life.

The curve shows the variation of density of water with respect to temperature from 0°C to 10°C as shown in figure.

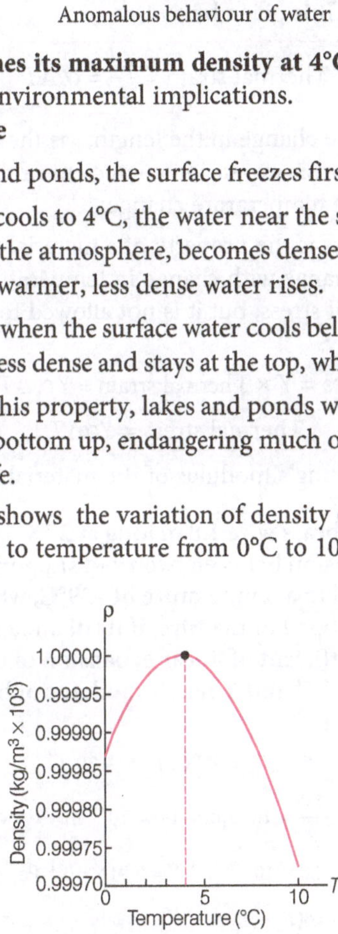

Variation of density of water *versus* temperature

Comparison of Expansions in Solids, Liquids and Gases

- The expansion in solids and liquids is rather small as compared to the gases at ordinary temperature.
- The coefficient of volume expansion for the liquids is relatively independent of the temperature.

For an ideal gas, the coefficient of volume expansion at a constant pressure is given by

$$\alpha_V = \frac{\Delta V}{V\Delta T}$$

$$\alpha_V = \frac{1}{T} \qquad \left[\because p\Delta V = \mu R\Delta T \Rightarrow \frac{\Delta V}{V} = \frac{\Delta T}{T}\right]$$

Thermal Strain and Thermal Stress

The strain that develops in a material in response to a change in temperature is called thermal strain. Thermal strain is directly proportional to the change in temperature. It is given by

$$\text{Thermal strain} = \frac{\Delta l}{l} = \alpha\,\Delta T$$

Here, Δl is the change in the length, l is the original length, α is linear expansion coefficient of the material and ΔT is the temperature change.

Thermal stress is the property of a material when its dimension change with change in temperature and it is called thermal stress, but it is not allowed to expand or contract freely.

Thermal stress = $Y \times$ Thermal strain = $Y\alpha\,\Delta T$

$$\text{Thermal stress} = Y\alpha\Delta T$$

Here, Y is Young's modulus of the material.

Example 7. **A brass wire 1.8 m long at 27°C is held taut with little tension between two rigid supports. If the wire is cooled to a temperature of –39°C, what is the tension developed in the wire, if its diameter is 2.0 mm? Coefficient of linear expansion of brass = 2.0×10^{-5}°C^{-1} and Young's modulus of brass = 0.91×10^{11} Pa.** NCERT

Sol. Here, $l = 1.8$ m, $T_1 = 27°C$, $T_2 = -39°C$

$$r = \frac{2.0}{2} = 1.0 \text{ mm} = 1.0 \times 10^{-3} \text{ m}$$

$$\alpha = 2.0 \times 10^{-5}\,°C^{-1}, Y = 0.91 \times 10^{11} \text{ Pa}$$

As, $\Delta l = l\alpha(T_2 - T_1)$

$\therefore$ Strain, $\frac{\Delta l}{l} = \alpha(T_2 - T_1) = \alpha\Delta T$

Stress = Strain × Young's modulus

$$= \alpha(T_2 - T_1) \times Y = 2.0 \times 10^{-5} \times (-39 - 27) \times 0.91 \times 10^{11}$$

$$= -1.2 \times 10^{8} \text{ Nm}^{-2}$$

$\therefore$ Tension developed in the wire

$$= \text{Stress} \times \text{Area of cross-section} = \text{Stress} \times \pi r^2$$

$$= -1.2 \times 10^{8} \times 3.14 \times (1.0 \times 10^{-3})^2$$

$$= -3.77 \times 10^{2} \text{ N}$$

Quick Test 1

Conceptual Questions

1. The difference between length of a certain brass rod and that of a steel rod is claimed to be constant at all temperatures. Is this possible?

2. There are two spheres of same radius and material at same temperature but one being solid while the other hollow. Which sphere will expand more, if (i) they are heated to the same temperature and (ii) same amount of heat is given to each of them?

3. Two identical rectangular strips-one of copper and the other of steel are riveted to form a bimetallic strip. What will happen on heating?

Numerical Questions

4. Find out the temperature which has same numerical value on celsius and fahrenheit scale. NCERT Exemplar

5. A celsius and fahrenheit thermometers are put in a hot bath. The reading of fahrenheit thermometer is 3/2 times the reading of celsius thermometer. What is the temperature of bath on celsius, fahrenheit and kelvin's scales?

6. The brass scale of a barometer gives correct reading at 0°C. Coefficient of linear expansion of brass is 2.0×10^{-5}/°C. The barometer reads 75.00 cm at 27°C. What is the true atmospheric pressure at 27°C?

7. (i) A brass rod of length 50 cm and diameter 3.0 mm is joined to a steel rod of the same length and diameter. What is the change in length of the combined rod at 250°C, if the original length are at 40.0°C?

(ii) Is there a thermal stress developed at the junction? The ends of the rod are free to expand. Coefficient of linear expansion of brass = 2.0×10^{-5}°C^{-1} and that of steel = 1.2×10^{-5} °C^{-1}. NCERT

8. The coefficient of volume expansion of glycerine is 49×10^{-5} °C^{-1}. What is the fractional change in its density for a 30°C rise in temperature? NCERT

9. A metallic ball has a radius of 9.0 cm at 0°C. Calculate the change in its volume when it is heated to 90°C. Given that, coefficient of linear expansion of metal of ball is 1.2×10^{-5} K^{-1}.

10. The electrical resistance in ohms of a certain thermometer varies with temperature according to the approximate law $R = R_0[1 + 5 \times 10^{-3}(T - T_0)]$. The resistance is 101.6 Ω at the triple point of water and 165.5 Ω at the normal melting point of lead (600.5 K). What is the temperature when the resistance is 123.4 Ω? NCERT

Answers

4. – 40° F *5.* –106.67° C, –160°F, 166.48 K

6. 75.04 cm *7.*(i) 0.34 cm (ii) No

8. 0.0147.9 *9.* 88 cm^3

10. 384.8 K

For Solutions, See QR Code on Pg. 367

10.4 Heat Capacity

The heat capacity of an object is defined as amount of heat needed to raise its temperature by unity. i.e. 1° C. It is denoted by S and having SI unit JK^{-1}.

$$\text{Heat capacity, } S = \frac{\Delta Q}{\Delta T}$$

where, ΔQ = heat absorbed or rejected by body and ΔT = change in temperature.

Specific Heat Capacity

The amount of heat needed to raise the temperature of unit mass of a substance by unity is known as the specific heat capacity or specific heat. It is denoted by s and its SI unit is $Jkg^{-1}K^{-1}$.

$$s = \frac{S}{m} = \frac{\Delta Q}{m\Delta T}$$

$$\Rightarrow \quad \text{Specific heat capacity, } s = \frac{1}{m}\frac{\Delta Q}{\Delta T}$$

where, m = mass of given substance.

- It depends on the nature of the substance and its temperature.
- Mass of water having the same heat capacity as a given body is called **water equivalent** of the body. The unit of water equivalent is gram.

Water has a specific heat capacity of 4186 J $kg^{-1}K^{-1}$, which is higher than that of most other substances. As a result

- Water is commonly used as a coolant in automobile radiators and as a heating medium in hot water bags.
- During the summer, water warms up more slowly than land, which results in a cooling effect from sea breezes.

Note • Specific heat capacity at constant pressure is denoted by S_p

• Specific heat capacity at constant volume is denoted by S_V.

Molar Specific Heat Capacity

The amount of heat needed to raise the temperature of one mole of a substance (gas) by unity is known as the molar specific heat capacity of that substance. It is denoted by C. Its SI unit is $Jmol^{-1}K^{-1}$.

$$\text{Molar specific heat capacity, } C = \frac{\Delta Q}{\mu \Delta T}$$

where, μ = number of moles of substance (gas).

Relation between Specific Heat and Molar Specific Heat Capacity

As, number of moles, $\mu = \frac{m}{M}$

where, m = mass of the substance

and M = molecular mass $m = \mu M$

$$C = \frac{1}{\mu}\left[\frac{\Delta Q}{\Delta T}\right] = M\left[\frac{\Delta Q}{m\Delta T}\right]$$

But, $$\frac{\Delta Q}{m\Delta T} = s$$

Hence, molar specific heat capacity

= molecular mass × specific heat capacity.

$$C = Ms$$

where, s = specific heat capacity,

M = molecular mass of the substance

and C = molar specific heat capacity.

There are two types of molar specific heat capacity.

(i) **Molar specific heat capacity at constant pressure (C_p)** It is molar heat capacity of a gas at constant pressure, i.e. the amount of heat required to raise the temperature of 1 mole of a gas by unity at constant pressure. It is given by $C_p = Ms_p$.

(ii) **Molar specific heat capacity at constant volume (C_V)** It is molar heat capacity of a gas at constant volume i.e., the amount of heat required to raise the temperature of 1 mole of a gas by unity at constant volume. It is given by $C_V = Ms_V$.

Example 8. A 10 kW drilling machine is used to drill a bore in a small aluminium block of mass 8.0 kg. How much is the rise in temperature of the block in 2.5 min, assuming 50% of power is used up in heating the machine itself or lost to the surroundings. (Specific heat of aluminium = 0.91 $Jg^{-1}{}^\circ C^{-1}$) NCERT

Sol. Given, power, $P = 10 \text{ kW} = 10 \times 10^3 \text{ W}$

Time, $t = 2.5 \text{ min} = 2.5 \times 60 \text{ s}$

Total energy used

$= Pt = 10 \times 10^3 \times 2.5 \times 60$
$= 1.5 \times 10^6$ J

Energy absorbed by aluminium block,

$Q = 50\%$ of the total energy

$$= \frac{1.5 \times 10^6}{2} = 0.75 \times 10^6 \text{ J}$$

Also, $m = 8.0$ kg $= 8.0 \times 10^3$ g, $s = 0.91 \text{ Jg}^{-1}{}^\circ\text{C}^{-1}$

As, $Q = ms\,\Delta T$

$$\therefore \quad \Delta T = \frac{Q}{ms} = \frac{0.75 \times 10^6}{8.0 \times 10^3 \times 0.91} = 103.02^\circ\text{C}$$

Example 9. A sample of an ideal gas undergoes an isochoric (constant volume) process. During this process, the internal energy increases by 500 J. The gas consists of 1 mole of an ideal diatomic gas. Calculate the specific heat capacity at constant volume.

Sol. Given,

Change in internal energy,

$$\Delta U = 500 \text{ J}$$

Number of moles, $n = 1$ mol

The gas is diatomic, so $\gamma = \frac{7}{5}$

Formula for change in internal energy,

$$U = nC_V \Delta T$$

Rearranging to solve for C_V.

$$C_V = \frac{\Delta U}{n\Delta T}$$

Internal energy for diatomic ideal gas.

The internal energy change for a diatomic ideal gas is

$$\Delta U = \frac{5}{2} nR\Delta T$$

Where $R = 8.314 \text{ J mol}^{-1}\text{K}$. Substituting the values:

$$500 = \frac{5}{2} \times 1 \times 8.314 \times \Delta T$$

Solve for ΔT,

$$500 = 20.785\Delta T \Rightarrow \Delta T = \frac{500}{20.785} \approx 24.04\text{K}$$

Now, calculate C_V

$$C_V = \frac{500}{1 \times 24.04} = \frac{500}{24.04} \approx 20.8 \text{J mol}^{-1} \text{ K}$$

Calorimetry

It is the branch of science that deals with the measurement of heat. The device used to measure the heat is called calorimeter.

When a body at higher temperature brought in contact with another body at lower temperature, heat flows from the hotter body to the colder body till both bodies acquire the same final temperature.

If there is no heat loss to the surroundings, the principle of calorimetry states that

Heat gained by cold bodies = Heat lost by hot bodies

If there are two bodies of masses m_1 and m_2 and having values of specific heats s_1 and s_2 respectively, then for temperature difference ΔT_1 and ΔT_2.

$$\Rightarrow \quad \boxed{m_1 s_1 \,\Delta T = m_2 s_2 \,\Delta T}$$

TEACHER TIP

A system is said to be isolated one if no exchange of heat takes place between the system and surrounding. During calorimetry, it is assumed that no heat is allowed to escape to the surrounding.

Example 10. In an experiment on the specific heat of a metal, a 0.20 kg block of the metal at 150°C is dropped in a copper calorimeter (of water equivalent 0.025 kg) containing 150 cm³ of water at 27°C. The final temperature is 40°C. Compute the specific heat of the metal.

Sol. Given, mass of metal block, $m = 0.20$ kg $= 200$ g

Fall in temperature of metal block,

$$\Delta T = 150^\circ - 40^\circ = 110^\circ\text{C}$$

Let specific heat of metal block $= 5 \text{ cal g}^{-1}{}^\circ\text{C}^{-1}$

$\therefore$ Heat lost by metal block $= mc\,\Delta T = 200 \times 5 \times 110$ cal

Volume of water in calorimeter $= 150 \text{ cm}^3$

Mass of water, $m' = 150$ g

Water equivalent of calorimeter, $w = 0.025$ kg $= 25$ g

Specific heat of water, $s' = 1 \text{ cal g}^{-1}{}^\circ\text{C}^{-1}$

$\therefore$ Heat gained by water and calorimeter

$$= (m' + w)\, s' \Delta T'$$

$$= (150 + 25) \times 1 \times (40 - 27) = 175 \times 13 \text{ cal}$$

According to the principle of calorimetry, we get

Heat lost = Heat gained

$$\therefore \quad 200 \times s \times 110 = 175 \times 13$$

or $$s = \frac{175 \times 13}{200 \times 110} = 0.1 \text{ cal g}^{-1}{}^\circ\text{C}^{-1}$$

10.5 Change of State

Normally, there are three states of matter : solid, liquid and vapour (or gas). **The transformation of one of these states to another one by absorbing or rejecting heat is called change of state.**

There are two common changes of states of matter.

(i) Solid to liquid (and *vice-versa*)

(ii) Liquid to gas (and *vice-versa*)

The changes can occur when the exchange of heat takes place between substance and its surroundings.

Effect of Heat on Ice

The state of ice (solid) can be changed with time by supplying the heat at a constant rate. The graph between temperature and time is shown below.

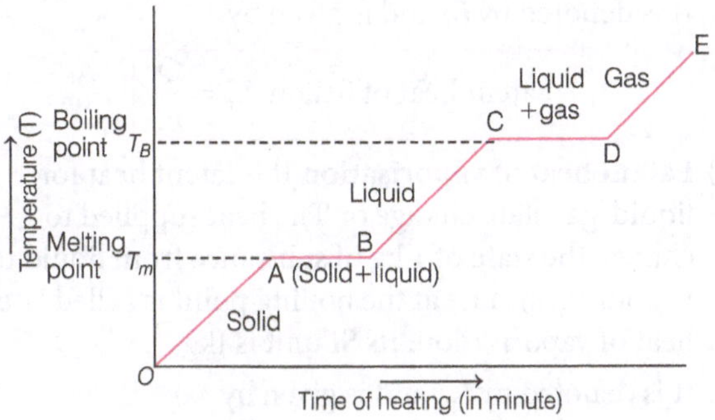

When heat is supplied to ice,

(i) **Heating** The temperature of the ice rises until it reaches 0°C.

(ii) **Melting** At 0°C, the ice (solid) melts into water (liquid), staying at 0°C during this change.

(iii) **Heating Water** After melting, the water's temperature increases to 100°C.

(iv) **Vaporisation** At 100°C, the water (liquid) turns into steam (gas), remaining at 100°C until fully vaporised.

(v) From the graph, it is observed that **the temperature remains constant during the change of state.**

Terms Related to Change of State

There are some important terms related to change of state as given below.

Melting and Melting Point

The process of change of state from solid to liquid is called **melting**. The temperature at which solid starts to liquify is known as the **melting point** of that solid.

The melting point of a substance at standard atmospheric pressure is called **normal melting point.**

Fusion and Freezing Point

The process of change of state from liquid to solid is called **fusion**. The temperature at which liquid starts to freeze is known as the **freezing point** of the liquid.

- When pressure is applied to ice, its melting point is lowered, causing it to melt into water.
- When pressure is released, the water refreezes into ice. This process is called **regelation.**

Vaporisation and Boiling Point

The process of change of state from liquid to vapour (or gas) is called **vaporisation.**

During the change of state (completely), the temperature remains constant which implies both liquid and vapour states of the substance co-exist in thermal equilibrium.

The temperature at which the liquid and the vapour states of the substance co-exist is called the **boiling point** of the liquid.

The boiling point of substance increases with increase in pressure and *vice-versa.*

Hence, cooking is easier in pressure cooker and it is difficult at hill station.

- The boiling point of water is 100°C at 1 atm pressure and it is 128°C at 2 atm pressure.
- The boiling point of a substance at standard atmospheric pressure is called its normal boiling point.

Sublimation

The process of change of state from solid to vapour state without passing through the liquid state is called sublimation and the substance is said to **sublime.**

- The solid and vapour states of a substance co-exist in thermal equilibrium during the sublimation process.

Triple Point

The temperature of a substance remains constant during its phase change (or change of state).

The temperature and pressure at which all three phases of a substance co-exist simultaneously is known as the triple point of the substance. e.g. The triple point for water is represented by temperature 273.16 K and pressure 6.11×10^{-3} Pa.

Two figures below show the phase diagram with triple point for (a) water (b) CO_2.

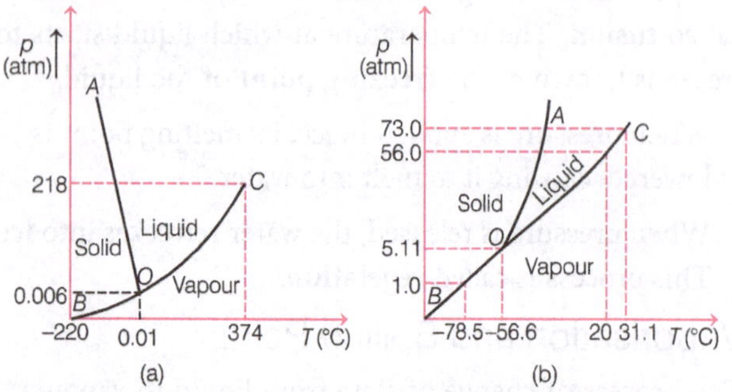

- The graph between temperature and pressure of substance can be plotted which is called **phase diagram** or ***p-T* diagram.**
- The diagram (phase diagram of water and CO_2) shows *p-T* plane divided into three regions i.e. solid region, liquid region and vapour region which are separated by **sublimation curve**, **fusion curve** and **vaporisation curve**.
- These three curves represent the states in which solid and vapour phases, solid and liquid phases and liquid and vapour phases co-exist.
- The point on sublimation curve *BO* represents states in which the solid and vapour phases co-exist. The point on vaporisation curve co-represents the states in which the liquid and vapour phases co-exist.
- The point on the fusion curve *AO* represents the states in which solid and vapour phases co-exist.

10.6 Latent Heat

The amount of heat transferred per unit mass during the change of phase of a substance without any change in its temperature is called latent heat of the substance for particular change.

Latent heat is denoted by *L* and its SI unit is J kg^{-1}. The value of latent heat is usually quoted at standard atmospheric pressure because it also depends upon the pressure.

Thus, if a mass *m* of a substance undergoes a change from one state to the other, then the quantity of heat required is given by

$$Q = mL$$

i.e. $\boxed{\text{Latent heat, } L = Q/m}$

Hence, during the phase change, the heat required by the substance depends on the mass *m* of the substance and heat of transformation *Q*.

Types of Latent Heat

There are two types of latent heat of materials

(i) **Latent heat of fusion** It is latent heat for solid-liquid state change or The heat supplied to change the state of 1 kg of substance from solid (ice) to liquid (water) at the melting point is called latent heat of fusion. Its SI unit is Jkg^{-1}.

It is denoted by L_f and is given by

$$\boxed{\text{Latent heat of fusion, } L_f = \frac{Q}{m}}$$

(ii) **Latent heat of vaporisation** It is latent heat for liquid-gas state change or The heat supplied to change the state of 1 kg of substance from liquid to vapour (gas) state at the boiling point is called latent heat of vaporisation. Its SI unit is Jkg^{-1}.

It is denoted by L_V and is given by

$$\boxed{\text{Latent heat of vaporisation, } L_V = \frac{Q}{m}}$$

- For water, $L_f = 3.33 \times 10^5$ Jkg^{-1} and $L_V = 22.6 \times 10^5$ Jkg^{-1}

Example 11. **A piece of ice of mass 120 g and at a temperature 0°C is put in 150 g of water at 25°C. How much ice will melt as the temperature of water reaches 0°C? The specific heat capacity of water = 4200 $Jkg^{-1}K^{-1}$ and the latent heat of fusion of ice = $3.4 \times 10^5 J\,kg^{-1}$.**

Sol. Mass of ice, $m_i = 120$ g

Mass of water, $m_w = 150$ g

∴ Heat released when the water cools down from 25°C to 0°C, $Q = m_w s_w \Delta\theta = 0.15 \times 4200 \times 25$

∴ The amount of ice melted by this amount of heat is

$$m = \frac{Q}{L} = \frac{0.15 \times 4200 \times 25}{3.4 \times 10^5} = 46.32 \text{ g}$$

Example 12. **The ice of 0.15 kg mass at 0° C is mixed with 0.30 kg of water at 50° C in a container. The resulting temperature of the container (after mixing) is 6.7°C. Determine the heat of fusion of ice, if specific heat (s_w) for the water is 4186 $Jkg^{-1}K^{-1}$.** NCERT

Sol. According to the calorimetry principle, we get

Heat lost by water $= ms_w\,(\theta_f - \theta_i)_w$

$= (0.30)(4186)(50.0 - 6.7) = 54376.14$ J

Heat required to melt ice = mass of ice × L_f

$= m_i L_f = (0.15 \text{ kg}) L_f$

Heat required to raise temperature of ice water to final temperature (from the calorimetry)

$= m_i s_w (\theta_f - \theta_i)_i$

$= (0.15 \text{ kg})(4186 \text{ Jkg}^{-1}\text{K}^{-1})(6.7°\text{C} - 0°\text{C})$

$= 4206.93$ J

Principle of calorimetry, i.e.

heat lost = heat gained

$\Rightarrow \quad 54376.14 \text{ J} = (0.15 \text{ kg})L_f + 4206.93 \text{ J}$

$\Rightarrow \quad L_f = 3.34 \times 10^5 \text{ Jkg}^{-1}$

This is required value of heat of fusion of ice.

Quick Test 2

1. Is it possible to convert water into vapour form without increasing its temperature, if temperature and pressure of water are 30°C and 1 atm, respectively?

2. A sphere made of aluminium of 0.047 kg placed for sufficient time in a vessel containing boiling water, so that the sphere is at 100° C.
After that it is allowed to transform to 0.14 kg copper calorimeter containing 0.25 kg of water kept at the temperature 20° C. The temperature of water rises and attains a steady state at 23° C. Calculate the specific heat capacity of aluminium. *NCERT*

3. Calculate the heat required to convert 3 kg of ice at −12° C kept in a calorimeter to steam at 100° C at atmospheric pressure.
Given, specific heat capacity of ice is 2100 $\text{Jkg}^{-1}\text{K}^{-1}$, specific heat capacity of water is 4186 $\text{Jkg}^{-1}\text{K}^{-1}$, latent heat of fusion of ice is 3.35×10^5 Jkg^{-1} and latent heat of steam is 2.256×10^6 Jkg^{-1}.

4. A copper block of mass 2.5 kg is heated in a furnace to a temperature of 500°C and then placed on a large ice block. What is the maximum amount of ice that can melt? (Specific heat of copper = 0.39 $\text{Jg}^{-1}\,°\text{C}^{-1}$ and heat of fusion of water = 335 Jg^{-1}) *NCERT*

5. A lead bullet penetrates into a solid object and melts. If half of its kinetic energy was used to heat it, calculate the initial velocity of the bullet. The initial temperature of the bullet is 27° C and the melting point of the material of bullet is 327° C. Given that latent heat of fusion of lead is 2.5×10^4 J kg^{-1} and specific heat capacity of lead is 125 J $\text{kg}^{-1}\text{K}^{-1}$.

Answers

2. 0.911 kJ $\text{kg}^{-1}\text{K}^{-1}$ 3. 9.1×10^6 J
4. 1.455 kg 5. 500 ms^{-1}

For Solutions, See QR Code on Pg. 367

10.8 Heat Transfer

Heat is the form of energy which can flow from one body to another due to their temperature difference in the form of radiations, molecular vibrations, molecular displacement, etc. These processes of heat flow are collectively known as heat transfer. The processes of heat transfer are shown in figure.

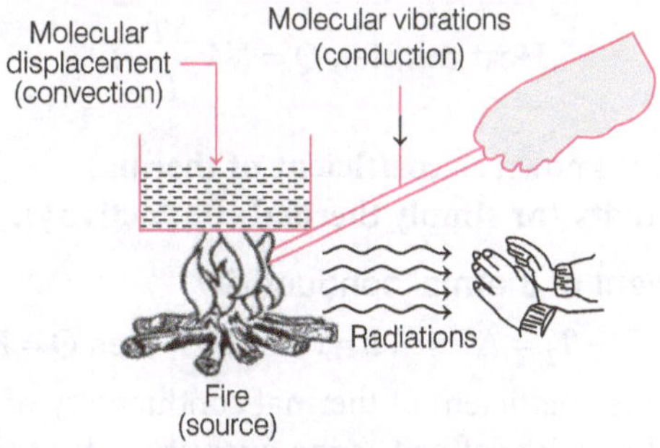

Modes of heat transfer

There are three modes of heat transfer namely
(i) Conduction (ii) Convection (iii) Radiation

Conduction

Conduction is the process in which heat is transmitted from one part of a body to another without any actual movement of its heated particles.

- During conduction, the average position of the molecules will not change.
- The transfer of heat takes place due to molecular vibration (or collisions).
- It is a slow process and generally takes place in solids.

Thermal Conductivity

The ability of a material to conduct the heat through it is known as thermal conductivity. It is denoted by K. It depends upon the nature of material.

- The SI unit of K is $\text{Js}^{-1}\text{m}^{-1}\text{K}^{-1}$ or $\text{Wm}^{-1}\text{K}^{-1}$.
- The dimensional formula of K is $[\text{MLT}^{-3}\text{K}^{-1}]$.
- Greater value of K implies that material will conduct the heat more rapidly.

Heat Current

The rate of flow of heat is known as heat (or thermal) current. It is denoted by H. Its SI unit is J/s or watt (W) and its dimensions are $[\text{ML}^2\text{T}^{-3}]$.

If L be the length of a metal rod and A is the area of cross-section with its ends maintained at temperatures T_1 and T_2, then the rate of flow of heat (or heat current) H is given by

$$H = \frac{\Delta Q}{\Delta t} = \frac{KA(T_1 - T_2)}{L} = KA\frac{\Delta T}{L}$$

Since, $H = \frac{Q}{t}$, the heat transfer is given by

$$\text{Heat transfer, } Q = KA\frac{\Delta T}{L}\cdot t$$

Here, K is known as **coefficient of thermal conductivity (or simply thermal conductivity).**

Coefficient of thermal conductivity

If $A = 1$, $T_1 - T_2 = \Delta T = 1$, $L = 1$ and $t = 1$, then $Q = K$.

Hence, the coefficient of thermal conductivity of a material may be defined as the quantity of heat that flows per unit time through a unit cube of the material when its opposite faces are kept at a temperature difference of one degree.

Temperature Gradient

The rate of change of temperature of the conducting rod with distance along the direction of heat flow is called the temperature gradient.

$$\text{Temperature gradient} = \frac{\Delta T}{L} = \frac{T_1 - T_2}{L}$$

Note Steady state means that the temperature of each part of the body remains constant during the conduction of heat through it.

Thermal Resistance

The hindrance offered by a conductor to the flow of heat is called thermal resistance. Analytically, the ratio of temperature gradient and heat current is called thermal resistance. It is denoted by R.

$$\therefore \quad \text{Thermal resistance, } R = \frac{L}{KA}$$

SI unit of thermal resistance (R) is K-s/J or K/W and its dimensions are $[M^{-1}L^{-2}T^{3}K]$.

Example 13. Calculate the rate of loss of heat through a glass window of area 1000 cm^2 and thickness 0.4 cm. When temperature inside is 37°C and outside is −5° C, coefficient of thermal conductivity of glass is 2.2×10^{-3} cal s^{-1} cm^{-1} K^{-1}.

Sol. Given, $A = 1000 \text{ cm}^2$, $L = 0.4$ cm

$$\Delta T = T_1 - T_2 = 37 - (-5) = 42°\text{C}$$

$$K = 2.2 \times 10^{-3} \text{ cal s}^{-1}\text{cm}^{-1}\text{K}^{-1}$$

Rate of loss of heat, $H = \frac{Q}{T} = \frac{KA(T_1 - T_2)}{L}$

$$= \frac{2.2 \times 10^{-3} \times 1000 \times 42}{0.4}$$

$$H = 231 \text{ cal s}^{-1}$$

Example 14. Two rods A and B are of equal length. Each rod has its ends at temperatures T_1 and T_2. What are the conditions that will ensure equal rates of flow of heat through the rods A and B ?

Sol. Heat transfer rate by rod A is $\frac{\Delta Q_1}{\Delta t}$.

Length of rod A is L and temperature difference,

$$\Delta T = T_1 - T_2$$

Area of cross-section of rod, $A = A_1$

Thermal conductivity, $K_1 \Rightarrow \frac{\Delta Q_1}{\Delta t} = K_1A_1\frac{\Delta T}{L}$

Heat transfer rate by rod B is $\frac{\Delta Q_2}{\Delta t}$.

Length of rod B is L, temperature difference $= T_1 - T_2$ and area of cross-section of rod $B = A_2$.

Thermal conductivity $= K_2$

$$\Rightarrow \quad \frac{\Delta Q_2}{\Delta t} = K_2A_2\frac{\Delta T}{L}$$

For equal rate of heat transfer,

$$\frac{\Delta Q_1}{\Delta t} = \frac{\Delta Q_2}{\Delta t}$$

$$\Rightarrow \quad \frac{K_1A_1\Delta T}{L} = \frac{K_2A_2\Delta T}{L}$$

$$\Rightarrow \quad K_1A_1 = K_2A_2 \Rightarrow \frac{K_2}{K_1} = \frac{A_1}{A_2}$$

This is the required condition for equal rate of heat transferred from both the rods.

Connection of Rods with Different Thermal Conductivities

If two or more rods are connected with one another, the equivalent thermal conductivity of the whole system is changed.

(a) Series combination of conductors

If n conducting rods of same cross-sectional area A are connected in series, then

- The rate of flow of heat in each rod remains the same, i.e. $\frac{Q}{t} = H_1 = H_2 = H_3 \ldots\ldots = H_n$.

- The equivalent thermal resistance will be equal to the sum of thermal resistances of individual rods, i.e. $R_{eq} = R_1 + R_2 + R_3 + ... + R_n$.
- The equivalent thermal conductivity of the combination of rods will be

$$K_{eq} = \frac{L_1 + L_2 + L_3 + ... + L_n}{\frac{L_1}{K_1} + \frac{L_2}{K_2} + \frac{L_3}{K_3} + ... \frac{L_n}{K_n}}$$

where, L represents length and K represents thermal conductivity.

(b) Parallel combination of conductors

If n conducting rods of same length L are connected in parallel, then

- Temperature gradient across each rod will be same.
- The equivalent rate of flow of heat will be equal to the sum of the heat current in individual rods i.e.

$$H_{eq} = H_1 + H_2 + H_3 + ... H_n.$$

The equivalent thermal conductivity of the combination of rods will be

$$K_{eq} = \frac{K_1A_1 + K_2A_2 + K_3A_3 + ... K_nA_n}{A_1 + A_2 + A_3 + ... + A_n}$$

where, A represents area.

Example 15. Two vessels of different materials are identical in size and wall thickness. They are filled with equal quantities of ice at 0° C. If the ice melts completely in 10 and 25 min respectively, compare the coefficients of thermal conductivity of the materials of the vessels.

Sol. Let K_1 and K_2 be the coefficients of thermal conductivity of the materials and t_1 and t_2 be the times in which ice melts in the two vessels.

As the same quantity of ice melts in the two vessels, the quantity of heat flowed into the vessels must be same.

$$\because \quad Q = \frac{K_1A(T_1 - T_2)t_1}{x} = \frac{K_2A(T_1 - T_2)t_2}{x}$$

$$\Rightarrow \quad K_1t_1 = K_2t_2$$

$$\therefore \quad \frac{K_1}{K_2} = \frac{t_2}{t_1} = \frac{25 \text{ min}}{10 \text{ min}} = 5:2$$

Example 16. A brass boiler has a base area of 0.15 m^2 and thickness 1.0 cm. It boils water at the rate of 6.0 kg min^{-1}, when placed on a gas stove. Estimate the temperature of the part of the flame in contact with the boiler. Thermal conductivity of brass = 109 Js^{-1}m^{-1}°C^{-1} and heat of vaporisation of water = 2256 Jg^{-1}.

Sol. Here, $A = 0.15 \text{ m}^2$, $x = 1.0 \text{ cm} = 0.01 \text{ m}$,

$$K = 109 \text{ Js}^{-1}\text{m}^{-1}{}^\circ\text{C}^{-1}, \quad L = 2256 \text{ Jg}^{-1}$$

$$T_2 = 100°\text{C}, t = 1 \text{ min} = 60 \text{ s}$$

Let T_1 be the temperature of the part of the flame in contact with boiler, then amount of heat that flows into water in 1 min.

$$Q = \frac{KA(T_1 - T_2)t}{x} = \frac{109 \times 0.15 \times (T_1 - 100) \times 60}{0.01} \text{ J}$$

Mass of water boiled per min = 6 kg = 6000 g

Heat used to boil water,

$$Q = mL = 6000 \text{ g} \times 2256 \text{ Jg}^{-1} = 6000 \times 2256 \text{ J}$$

$$\therefore \quad \frac{109 \times 0.15 \times (T_1 - 100) \times 60}{0.01} = 6000 \times 2256$$

or $$T_1 - 100 = \frac{6000 \times 2256 \times 0.01}{109 \times 0.15 \times 60} = 138° \text{C}$$

or $$T_1 = 138 + 100 = 238° \text{C}$$

Convection

Convection is the process in which heat is transferred from one point to another by the actual movement of the heated particles of the medium from a region of high temperature to a region of lower temperature. This process of heat transfer takes place only in liquids. There are two types of convections

(a) **Forced convection** It is a type of convection in which heat is transferred by the movement of the particles of the medium due to force given by some external device. For example, a blower is used as a forcing agent for heat transfer.

(b) **Natural or free convection** It is a type of convection in which heat is transferred by the movement of the particles of the medium due to its density difference. For example, heating a liquid in a vessel.

Some natural phenomena like; sea breeze, trade wind, etc. are based on natural convection.

Note Conduction and convection require some material as a transport medium. These modes of heat transfer cannot take place in vacuum.

Radiation

Radiation is the process in which heat is transmitted from one place to the other directly without the necessity of the intervening medium. It is the fastest mode of heat transfer.

- Unlike conduction and convention, radiation does not require a medium, allowing it to occur even in vacuum such as the heat from the sun reaching the Earth.
- Radiation is the transfer of heat through electromagnetic waves which are formed by the oscillating electric and magnetic fields.
- Electromagnetic waves travel with the speed of light (i.e. 3×10^8 m/s) in vacuum.

Thermal Radiation

Thermal radiation is a process by which energy is emitted in the form of electromagnetic radiation by a heated surface in all directions.

The energy transmitted by the electromagnetic waves is called **radiant energy.**

When thermal radiation falls on a body, it may get partly reflected and partly absorbed. The amount of heat that a body absorbs or reflects back by radiation depends on the colour of the body.

Black Body Radiation

A body that absorbs all the radiations falling on it is known as **black body.** It emits the radiations at the fastest rate. The radiations emitted by a black body is known as black body radiation. The black body is also called the **ideal radiator.**

A perfect body absorbs 100% of radiations falling on it. This is only an ideal concept because within the universe, there is no existence of black body.

However, lamp black is close to a black body because it reflects only 1% of radiation falling on it.

Absorptive Power

The ratio of the amount of thermal radiation absorbed by a body in a given time to the total amount of thermal radiations incident on the body in the same time is known as **absorptance** (a) or **absorptive power** of the body.

$$\Rightarrow \quad \boxed{a = \frac{\text{Energy absorbed}}{\text{Energy incident}}}$$

Emissive Power

The emissive power of a body at a given temperature and for a given wavelength λ is defined as the amount of radiant energy per unit time per unit surface area of the body within a unit wavelength range around the wavelength λ.

The ratio of emissive power (e) of a body to the emissive power (E) of a perfect black body at the same temperature is called **emissivity.** It is denoted by ε.

Thus, $$\boxed{\text{emissivity, } \varepsilon = \frac{e}{E}}$$

ε =1 for a perfect radiator (black body).

Stefan-Boltzmann Law

Stefan-Boltzmann law states that the total energy emitted per second by a unit area of a perfect black body is proportional to the fourth power of its absolute temperature.

i.e. $$E \propto T^4$$

$$\boxed{\text{Total energy, } E = \sigma T^4}$$

where, σ is a universal constant called **Stefan-Boltzmann constant.**

$$\sigma = 5.67 \times 10^{-8} \text{ Wm}^{-2} \text{ K}^{-4}$$

If the body is not a perfect black body and has emissivity ε, then above relations get modified as

$$E = \varepsilon \sigma T^4$$

where, ε = emissivity of that body.

If the surface area of a black body is A, the energy emitted per unit time is given by

$$H = A \sigma T^4$$

A body at temperature T, with surroundings at temperatures T_s, emits, as well as receives energy.

For a radiator with emissivity ε, the net rate of loss of radiant energy is

$$H = \sigma \varepsilon A(T^4 - T_s^4)$$

Example 17. Calculate the temperature (in K) at which a perfect black body radiates energy at the rate of 5.67 W/cm^2.
Given, $\sigma = 5.67 \times 10^{-8}$ Wm^{-2} K^{-4}

Sol. Given, $E = 5.67\ \text{W/cm}^2 = 5.67 \times 10^4\ \text{W/m}^2$

$$\sigma = 5.67 \times 10^{-8}\ \text{Wm}^{-2}\ \text{K}^{-4}$$

Apply Stefan-Boltzmann's law, $E = \sigma T^4$

$$T^4 = \frac{E}{\sigma}$$

$$\Rightarrow \quad T = \left(\frac{E}{\sigma}\right)^{1/4} = \left(\frac{5.67 \times 10^4}{5.67 \times 10^{-8}}\right)^{1/4}$$

$$T = (10^{12})^{1/4} = 10^3 = 1000\ \text{K}$$

Example 18. A thin brass rectangular sheet of sides 15.0 cm and 12.0 cm is heated in a furnace to 600°C and taken out. How much electric power is needed to maintain the sheet at this temperature, given that its emissivity is 0.250? Neglect heat loss due to convection. (Stefan-Boltzmann constant, $\sigma = 5.67 \times 10^{-8}$ Wm^{-2} K^{-4}) NCERT

Sol. As the energy is radiated from both surfaces of the sheet, so

$$A = 2 \times 15.0 \times 12.0 \times 10^{-4}\ \text{m}^2 = 3.60 \times 10^{-2}\ \text{m}^2$$

$$T = 600 + 273 = 873\ \text{K}$$

$$\varepsilon = 0.250,$$

$$\sigma = 5.67 \times 10^{-8}\ \text{Wm}^{-2}\ \text{K}^{-4}$$

The rate of heat loss by the sheet,

$$H = \frac{Q}{t} = \varepsilon \sigma A T^4$$

$$= 0.250 \times 5.67 \times 10^{-8} \times 3.60 \times 10^{-2} \times (873)^4$$

$$= 296\ \text{Js}^{-1} = 296\ \text{W}$$

Wien's Displacement Law

Wien's displacement law states that the wavelength (λ_m) corresponding to which the energy emitted by a black body is maximum and is inversely proportional to its absolute temperature (T).

Thus, $$\lambda_m \propto \frac{1}{T}$$

or $$\boxed{\lambda_m T = b}$$

where, b = **Wien's constant**

$$= 2.9 \times 10^{-3}\ \text{m-K}$$

- For moon's surface; $\lambda_m = 14\ \mu\text{m}$ corresponding to its surface temperature $T = 200$ K.
- For sun's surface; $\lambda_m = 4753$Å corresponding to its surface temperature $T = 6060$ K.

Example 19. A hot body having the surface temperature 1327°C. Determine the wavelength at which it radiates maximum energy. Given Wien's constant $= 2.9 \times 10^{-3}$ mK.

Sol. Given, $T = 1327 + 273 = 1600$ K

Wien's constant, $b = 2.9 \times 10^{-3}$ mK

$$\lambda_m = \frac{b}{T} = \frac{2.9 \times 10^{-3}}{1600} = 1.81 \times 10^{-6}\ \text{m}$$

Example 20. Consider a filament which is indirectly heated. The radiating maximum energy having wavelength 3.4×10^{-5} cm. Determine the amount of heat energy lost per second per unit area, if the temperature of surrounding air is 17°C.
Given, $\sigma = 5.67 \times 10^{-8}$ Wm^{-2} K^{-4}, $b = 2.9 \times 10^{-3}$ mK

Sol. Given, wavelength, $\lambda_m = 3.4 \times 10^{-5}\ \text{cm} = 3.4 \times 10^{-7}$ m

Temperature surrounding,

$$T_0 = 17^\circ\text{C} + 273 = 290\ \text{K}$$

$$\sigma = 5.67 \times 10^{-8}\ \text{Wm}^{-2}\ \text{K}^{-4}$$

$$b = 2.9 \times 10^{-3}\ \text{mK}$$

According to Wien's law

$$T = \frac{b}{\lambda_m} = \frac{2.9 \times 10^{-3}\ \text{mK}}{3.4 \times 10^{-7}\text{m}} = 8529.4\ \text{K}$$

According to Stefan-Boltzmann law,

$$E = \sigma(T^4 - T_0^4)$$

$$= 5.67 \times 10^{-8}\ [(8529.4)^4 - (290)^4]$$

$$E = 30016.98 \times 10^4\ \text{W/m}^2$$

Newton's Law of Cooling

Newton's law of cooling states that the rate of cooling of a body is directly proportional to the temperature difference between the body and its surroundings, provided the temperature difference is small.

i.e. Rate of loss of heat ∝ Temperature difference between the body and its surroundings $-\frac{dQ}{dt} \propto (T - T_0)$

Rate of loss of heat, $$\boxed{-\frac{dQ}{dt} = k(T - T_0)}$$

- The negative sign shows that the body temperature decrease with time.

- k is a positive constant which depends on the area and nature of the surface of the body.

Example 21. **A body cools in 7 min from 60°C to 40°C. What will be its temperature after the next 7 min? The temperature of the surroundings is 10°C.**

Sol. According to the Newton's law of cooling, we have

$$\frac{dQ}{dt} = k\left(\frac{T_1 + T_2}{2} - T_0\right)$$

$$\frac{ms\,(T_1 - T_2)}{t} = k\left(\frac{T_1 + T_2}{2} - T_0\right)$$

$$\frac{ms\,(60 - 40)}{7 \times 60} = k\left(\frac{60 + 40}{2} - 10\right)$$

$$\frac{ms \times 20}{420} = k \times 40 \quad \ldots\text{(i)}$$

Suppose, after the next 7 min = 420 s, the temperature is T. Then,

$$\frac{ms\,(40 - T)}{420} = k\left(\frac{40 + T}{2} - 10\right) \quad \ldots\text{(ii)}$$

On dividing Eq. (i) by Eq. (ii), we get

$$\frac{20}{40 - T} = \frac{40}{\left(\frac{40 + T}{2} - 10\right)}$$

On solving, we get $T = 28°\text{ C}$

Quick Test 3

1. Two thermos flasks are of the same height and same capacity. One has a circular cross-section, while the other has a square cross-section. Which of the two is better?
2. On a hot day, a car is left in sunlight with all the windows closed. After sometime, it is found that the inside of the car is considerably warmer than the air outside. Explain, why?
3. Two rods of the same area of cross-section but of lengths l_1 and l_2 and conductivities K_1 and K_2 are joined in series. Show that the combination is equivalent of a material of conducitivity

$$K = \frac{l_1 + l_2}{\left(\frac{l_1}{K_1}\right) + \left(\frac{l_2}{K_2}\right)}$$

4. What is convection current? Explain the role of convection current in relation to the following phenomena. (i) Ventilation (ii) Land and sea breezes
5. Two vessels A and B of different materials but having identical shape, size and wall thickness are filled with ice and kept at the same place. Ice melts at the rate of 100 g min^{-1} and 150 g min^{-1} in A and B, respectively. Assuming that heat enters the vessels through the walls only, calculate the ratio of thermal conductivities of their materials.

Answers

5. 2:3

For Solutions, See QR Code on Pg. 367

Mind Map

Thermal Properties of Matter

Heat

Heat is the form of energy transferred between objects or systems due to a temperature difference, flowing from the higher temperature object to the lower temperature one.
Temperature is a measure of the average kinetic energy of the particles in a substance, indicating how hot or cold the substance is.

- **Measurement of Temperature**
A measure of temperature is obtained using a thermometer on some specified scales.
These scales commonly called unit of temperature.It measure the temperature of body in Kelvin (K), degree centigrade (°C) and degree Fahrenheit (°F).
- **Graph**
The graph of Fahrenheit temperature (T_F) *versus* celsius or centigrade temperature (T_C)

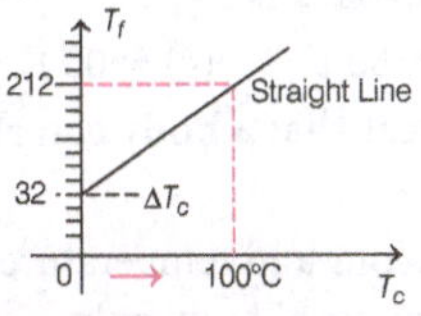

Ideal Gas Equation

- **Ideal Gas Equation**
The ideal gas relationship is

$$pV = R \times (nT) \Rightarrow \frac{pV}{T} = nR \text{ (Constant)}$$

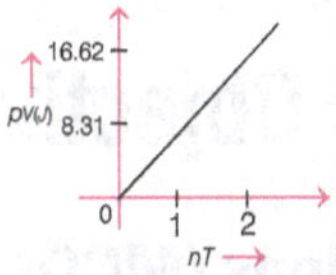

For Two Variables

$$\frac{p_f V_f}{T_f} = \frac{p_i V_i}{T_i} \because R = 8.314 \text{ J/mol K}^{-1}$$

- **Boyle's Law**
It is given by English chemist Robert Boyle. Here, pressure is inversely proportional to the volume at constant temperature.
i.e., $p \propto \frac{1}{V}$

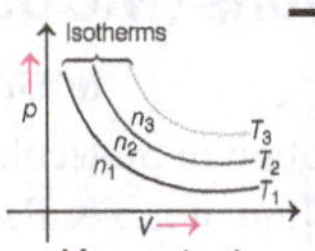

- **Charles' Law**
It is given by French scientist Jacques Charles.
Here, volume of gas is directly proportional to the temperature at constant pressure. i.e., $V \propto T$

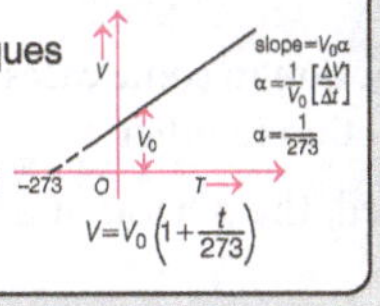

Heat Capacity

The amount of heat needed to change the temperature by unity i.e., 1°C, it is denoted by S and SI unit JK^{-1}

Heat capacity, $S = \frac{\Delta Q}{\Delta T}$

- **Specific Heat Capacity**
The amount of heat needed to raise the temperature of unit mass of a substance by unity is known as the specific heat capacity or specific heat.
SI unit of specific heat capacity $Jkg^{-1} K^{-1}$.
Specific heat capacity, $s = \frac{1}{m} \frac{\Delta Q}{\Delta T}$
- **Relation between specific heat and molar specific heat capacity**
Molar specific heat capacity, $C = \frac{\Delta Q}{n \Delta T}$
- $C = Ms$ (Here, M = Molecular mass of the substance)

Thermal Expansion

Thermal expansion refers to the increase in the size or volume of a substance when it is heated.

Linear Expansion

- The expansion in length of a body due to increase in its temperature is called the linear expansion.
- Expansion in length, $L = L_0(1 + \alpha \Delta T)$

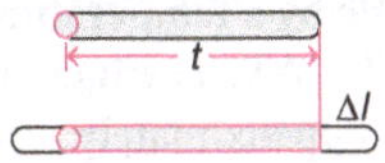

Volume Expansion

The expansion in the volume of an object due to increase in its temperature is known as volume expansion.
Expansion in volume,
$V = V_0(1 + \alpha_V \Delta T)$

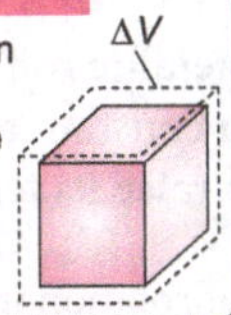

Areas Expansion

- The expansion in the area of surface due to increase in its temperature is called area expansion.
- Expansion in area,
$A = A_0(1 + \alpha_A \Delta T)$

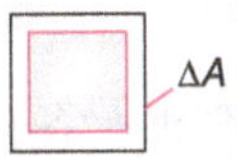

Relation among Coefficients of Expansion

- The coefficient of expansion can be given as

$$\alpha_l = \frac{\Delta l}{l \Delta T}, \alpha_A = \frac{\Delta A}{A \Delta T}, \alpha_V = \frac{\Delta V}{V \Delta T}$$

- The relation among coefficient of expansion is given by
$\alpha_l : \alpha_A : \alpha_V = 1 : 2 : 3$

Calorimetry

Heat lost by hotter body = Heat gained by colder body. $m_1 s_1 \Delta T = m_2 s_2 \Delta T$
Calorimeter is a device used for measuring the quantity of heat .

Latent Heat

- Latent heat is the amount of heat required to change the phase of a substance without changing its temperature. It is associated with phase transitions, such as melting, freezing, boiling, or condensation.

Change of State

Change of state refers to the transformation of a substance from one phase to another, such as from solid to liquid, liquid to gas, or vice versa, due to the addition or removal of heat. These phase changes occur at specific temperatures and involve latent heat without a change in temperature.
Melting Solid to liquid (e.g., ice to water).
Freezing Liquid to solid (e.g., water to ice).
Boiling (Vaporisation) Liquid to gas (e.g., water to steam).
Condensation Gas to liquid (e.g., steam to water).
Sublimation Solid to gas (e.g., dry ice to carbon dioxide gas).

Black Body Readiation

It is the electromagnetic radiation emitted by a perfect black body, which absorbs and emits all wavelengths of radiation, and its emission depends only on its temperature.
Wein's Displacement Law
States that the wavelength at which the intensity of radiation from a black body is maximum is inversely proportional to the temperature of the body.
Stefan's Law
States that the total energy radiated per unit surface area of a black body is directly proportional to the fourth power of its absolute temperature.

Absolute Temperature

It is the temperature measured on the Kelvin scale, where the zero point (0 K) represents absolute zero, the theoretical temperature at which the motion of particles comes to a complete stop.

Newton's Law of Cooling

The rate of cooling of a body is directly proportional to temperature difference between the body and its surroundings,

$$-\frac{dQ}{dt} \propto (T - T_0)$$

Rate of loss of heat, $-\frac{dQ}{dt} = k(T - T_0)$

EXAM PATTERN QUESTIONS

Objective Type Questions

Multiple Choice Questions (MCQs)

1. Heat is associated with NCERT Exemplar

(a) kinetic energy of random motion of molecules
(b) kinetic energy of orderly motion of molecules
(c) total kinetic energy of random and orderly motion of molecules
(d) kinetic energy of random motion in some cases and kinetic energy of orderly motion in other

2. As the temperature is increased, the period of a pendulum

(a) increases as its effective length increases even though its centre of mass still remains at the centre of the bob
(b) decreases as its effective length increases even though its centre of mass still remains at the centre of the bob
(c) increases as its effective length increases due to shifting to centre of mass below the centre of the bob
(d) decreases as its effective length remains same but the centre of mass shifts above the centre of the bob

3. An aluminium sphere is dipped into water. Which of the following is true? NCERT Exemplar

(a) Buoyancy will be less in water at 0°C than that in water at 4°C.
(b) Buoyancy will be more in water at 0°C than that in water at 4°C.
(c) Buoyancy in water at 0°C will be same as that in water at 4°C.
(d) Buoyancy may be more or less in water at 4°C depending on the radius of the sphere.

4. A normal diet furnishes 200 kcal to a 60 kg person in a day. If this energy was used to heat the person with no losses to the surroundings, how much would the person's temperature increases? The specific heat of the human body is 0.83 cal $g^{-1}\,°C^{-1}$.

(a) 8.2°C
(b) 4.016°C
(c) 6.0°C
(d) 5.03°C

5. When water boils or freezes, during these processes its temperature

(a) increases
(b) decreases
(c) does not change
(d) sometimes increase and sometimes deceases

6. A furnace emits radiation with maximum intensity at wavelength 11×10^{-7} m. The temperature of the sun is 5500 K and it emits maximum intensity radiuation in the yellow region of wavlength 5.5×10^{-7} m. Then the temperature of furnace is

(a) 1125 K (b) 2750 K (c) 5500 K (d) 11000 K

7. The amount of heat that a body can absorb by radiation

(a) depends on colour and temperature both of body
(b) depends on colour of body only
(c) depends on temperature of body only
(d) depend on density of body

8. Due to the change in main voltage, the temperature of an electric bulb rises from 3000K to 4000K. What is the percentage rise in electric power consumed? Competency Based Que.

(a) 216 (b) 100 (c) 150 (d) 178

9. The radius of a metal sphere at room temperature T is R and the coefficient of linear expansion of the metal is α. The sphere heated a little by a temperature ΔT, so that its new temperature is $T+\Delta T$. The increase in the volume of the sphere is approximately NCERT Exemplar

(a) $2\pi R\alpha\,\Delta T$ (b) $\pi R^2\alpha\,\Delta T$
(c) $4\pi R^3\alpha\,\Delta T/3$ (d) $4\pi R^3\alpha\,\Delta T$

10. A uniform metallic rod rotates about its perpendicular bisector with constant angular speed. If it is heated uniformly to raise its temperature slightly NCERT Exemplar

(a) its speed of rotation increases
(b) its speed of rotation decreases
(c) its speed of rotation remains same
(d) its speed increases because its moment of inertia increases

11. 2 litre of water at 27°C is heated by 1 kW heater in an open container. On an average heat is lost to surroundings at the rate 160 J/s. The time required for the temperature to reach 77°C.

(a) 8 min 20 s (b) 10 min (c) 14 min (d) 7 min

12. A black body at temperature 300 K radiates heat at the rate E. If its temperature is increased by 900 K, the rate of radiation will increase to

(a) 16 *E* (b) 64 *E*
(c) 81 *E* (d) 256 *E*

13. A black body at temperature 227°C radiates heat at a rate of 20 cal/cm^2 s^{-1}. At a temperature of 727°C the rate of heat radiated per unit area will be

(a) 50 cal/cm^2 s^{-1}
(b) 250 cal/cm^2 s^{-1}
(c) 80 cal/cm^2 s^{-1}
(d) 320 cal/cm^2 s^{-1}

14. A sphere, a cube and a thin circular plate, all of same material and same mass are initially heated to same high temperature.

(a) Plate will cool fastest and cube the slowest
(b) Sphere will cool fastest and cube the slowest
(c) Plate will cool fastest and sphere the slowest
(d) Cube will cool fastest and plate the slowest

15. Match the Column I with Column II.

Column I	Column II
1. Latent heat	A. Increase in the length or volume of a substance due to a temperature change.
2. Thermal Expansion	B. Heat required to raise the temperature of 1 kg of substance by 1°C.
3. Boiling point	C. The temperature at which a substance changes from solid to liquid.
4. Melting point	D. The temperature at which a substance changes from liquid to gas.

Codes

	1 2 3 4		1 2 3 4
(a)	B A D C	(b)	A B C D
(c)	D A B C	(d)	A C B D

16. Match the Column I with Column II.

Column I	Column II
1. Boiling a water in a pot	A. Heat transfer through the moment of air.
2. Heat from the sun	B. Heat transfer through solids by particle vibrations.
3. Heating a metal rod at one end	C. Heat transfer through electromagnetic induction.
4. A radiator in a room	D. Heat transfer through fluids by the motion of particles.

Codes

	1 2 3 4		1 2 3 4
(a)	A B C D	(d)	D C A B
(c)	D C B A	(d)	A D B C

Assertion-Reason

Directions *(Q.No. 17-26) In the following questions, two statements are given- one labelled Assertion (A) and the other labelled Reason (R). Select the correct answer to these questions from the codes (a), (b), (c) and (d) as given below.*

(a) Both Assertion and Reason are true and Reason is the correct explanation of Assertion.
(b) Both Assertion and Reason are true but Reason is not the correct explanation of Assertion.
(c) Assertion is true but Reason is false.
(d) Assertion is false but Reason is true.

17. Assertion (A) Heat transfer by conduction occurs only in solids.
Reason (R) In solids, molecules are closely packed, allowing them to transfer energy efficiently through collisions.

18. Assertion (A) The coefficient of linear expansion of a material is the fractional increase in its length per degree rise in temperature.
Reason (R) The increase in the length of a material is directly proportional to its original length and the temperature change.

19. Assertion (A) The coefficient of thermal expansion of a gas is independent of its pressure.
Reason (R) For an ideal gas, the coefficient of thermal expansion is directly related to the temperature and volume, not pressure.

20. Assertion (A) At room temperature, water does not sublimate from ice to steam.
Reason (R) The critical point of water is much above the room temperature.

21. Assertion (A) When heat transfer takes place between a system and surroundings, the total heat content of system or surroundings separately remains same.
Reason (R) Heat is a form of energy which follows the principle of conservation of energy.

22. Assertion (A) The triple point of water is a standard fixed point in modern thermometry.
Reason (R) Melting point of ice and the boiling point of water change due to change in atmospheric pressure but triple point of water does not change.

23. Assertion (A) Water kept in an open vessel will quickly evaporate on the surface of the moon.
Reason (R) The temperature at the surface of the moon is much higher than boiling point of water.

24. Assertion (A) Houses made of concrete roofs get very hot during summer days.

Reason (R) Thermal conductivity of concrete is much smaller than metal.

25. Assertion (A) A black body at higher temperature T radiates energy U. When temperature falls to one-third, the radiated energy will be $U/81$.

Reason (R) $U \propto T^4$

Competency Based Que.

26. Assertion (A) The melting point of ice decreases with increase of pressure.

Reason (R) Ice contracts on melting.

Case Based Questions

Directions *(Q.Nos. 27-29) These questions are case study based questions. Read the following paragraph and anwer the questions.*

27 **An iron bar ($L_1 = 0.1$ m, $A_1 = 0.02$ m^2, $K_1 = 79$ Wm^{-1}K^{-1}) and a brass bar ($L_2 = 0.1$ m, $A_2 = 0.02$ m^2, $K_2 = 109$ Wm^{-1}K^{-1}) are soldered end to end as shown in figure. The free ends of the iron bar and brass bar are maintained at 373 K and 273K, respectively.**

Competency Based Que.

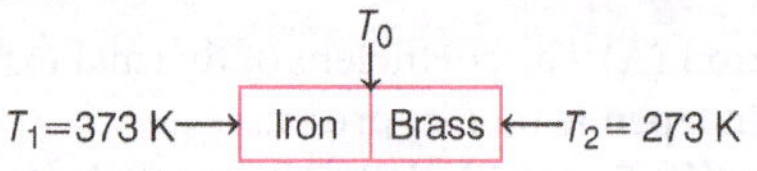

(i) What is the temperature of the junction of two bars in steady state?

(a) 315 K (b) 420 K
(c) 520 K (d) 600 K

(ii) Compute the equivalent thermal conductivity of the compound bar.

(a) 100 Wm^{-1} K^{-1} (b) 9.16 Wm^{-1} K^{-1}
(c) 110 Wm^{-1} K^{-1} (d) 120 Wm^{-1} K^{-1}

(iii) How much heat current flows through the compound bar?

(a) 920 W (b) 916.1 W
(c) 102.5 W (d) 112.5 W

(iv) Two rods of same length and material transfer a given amount of heat in 12 s, when they are joined end to end (i.e., in series). But when they are joined in parallel, they will transfer same heat under same temperature difference across thier ends in

(a) 24 s (b) 6 s
(c) 38 s (d) 1.5 s

(v) The two ends of a metal rod are maintained at temperatures 100°C and 110°C. The rate of heat flow in the rod is found to be 4.0 J/s. If the ends are maintained at temperatures 200°C and 210°C, the rate of heat flow will be

(a) 44.0 Js^{-1} (b) 16.8 Js^{-1}
(c) 8.0 Js^{-1} (d) 4.0 Js^{-1}

28 **Ferry's Black Body : It consists of a hollow copper sphere blackened inside with a small fine hole, O is the surface. When the radiations enter the hole, they suffer a number of reflections at the inner walls of the sphere unitll it is completely absorbed. To avoid direct reflection of the radiation from the inner surface a pointed projection is made in front of the hole as shown in figure. Thus the small hole acts as a black-body absorber. When this spere is placed in a bath at a fixed temperature, the heat radiations come out of the hole. It is to be noted that only the hole and not the walls of the sphere acts as a black-body radiator.**

A perfectly black-body is one which absorbs all the heat radiations of whatever wavelength, incident on it. It neither reflects nor transmits any of the incident radiation.

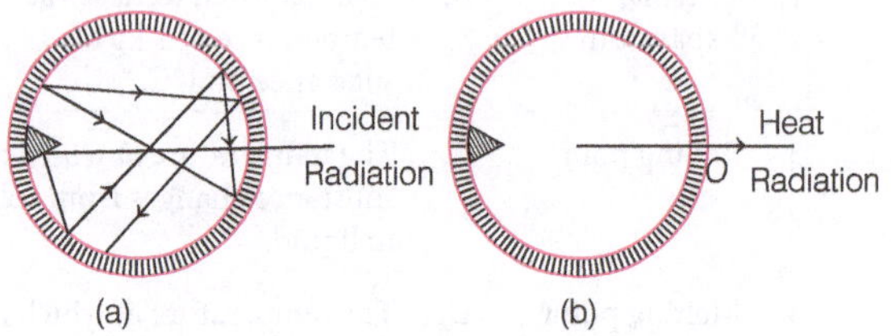

(i) Which of the following is best close to an ideal black body ?

(a) Platinum black
(b) Black lamp
(c) Cavity maintained at constant temperature
(d) A lamp of charcoal heated to high temperature

(ii) Which of the following graphs correctly represents the relation between E and T, where E is the amount of radiation emitted per unit time from unit area of body and T is the absolute temperatrue.

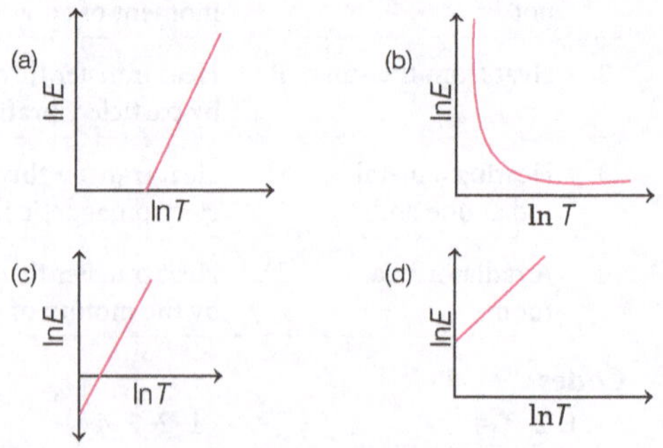

(iii) A black body emits radiaton of maximum intensity of wavelength λ at 2,000 K. Its corresponding wavelength at 3,000 K will be

(a) $16\lambda/81$ (b) $81\lambda/16$ (c) $2\lambda/3$ (d) $4\lambda/3$

(iv) If the temperature of the sun were to increase from T to $2T$ and its radius from R to $2R$, then the ratio of the radiant energy received on earth to energy received previously, will be

(a) 4 (b) 16 (c) 32 (d) 64

Or

A black body is heated from 27°C to 127°C. The ratio of their energies of radiations emitted will be

(a) 81 : 256 (b) 27 : 6
(c) 9 : 16 (d) 3 : 4

29. **A railway track is laid out in a region where the seasonal temperature variation ranges from −5°C in winter to 40°C in summer. The track is made of steel and each section of the track is 10 metres long. The coefficient of linear expansion of steel is $\alpha = 12 \times 10^{-6}$ per °C.**

In the winter, the temperature is very low and the track is contracted. In the summer, the track expands due to the rise in temperature. This causes a problem in the functioning of the railway track, as the track sections might either buckle or create gaps, potentially leading to accidents.

(i) Calculate the change in length of the railway track during the seasonal temperature variation from −5°C to 40°C.

(ii) Explain why the railway track sections are made with gaps between them. How does this help in dealing with the thermal expansion?

(iii) What could be the consequences of ignoring the thermal expansion of materials when designing structures like bridges or railway tracks?

(iv) If the railway track were made of a material with a lower coefficient of thermal expansion, how would that affect the design and performance of the track?

Subjective Questions

Very Short Answer Type Questions

1. (i) Why felt rather than air is employed for thermal insulation? **[1]**

(ii) Air is a bad conductor of heat, why is it so that we do not feel warm without cloth? **[1]**

2. (i) Why snow is a better heat insulator than ice ? **[1]**

(ii) These days people use steel utensiles with copper bottom. This is supposed to be good for uniform heating of food. Explain this effect using the fact that copper is the better conductor **[1] NCERT Exemplar**

3. The plots of intensity *versus* wavelength for three black body at temperature T_1, T_2 and T_3 respectively are shown.

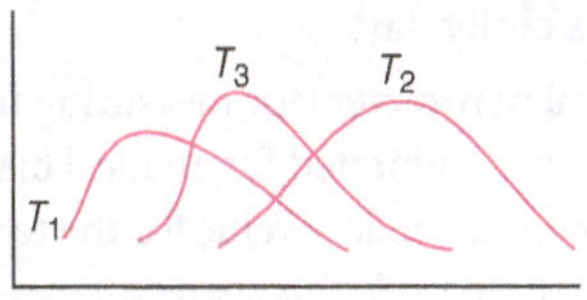

Arrange the temperature in decreasing order. Justify your answer. **[2]**

Short Answer Type Questions

4. Show that the coefficient of volume expansion for a soild substance is three times its coefficient of linear expansion.

5. Given below are observations on molar specific heats at room temperatures of some common gases.

Gas	Molar specific heat (C_V) [cal/mol-K]
Hydrogen	4.87
Nitrogen	4.97
Oxygen	5.02
Nitric oxide	4.99
Carbon monoxide	5.01
Chlorine	6.17

The measured molar specific heats of these gases are markedly different from those for monoatomic gases (typically molar specific heat of a monoatomic gas is 2.92 cal/mol-K). Explain this difference. What can you infer from the somewhat larger (than the rest) value for chlorine?

6. What is calorimetry? Describe briefly the construction of calorimeter.

7. Why does it take significantly more time to completely convert a given quantity of water into steam (starting from room temperature, say 25°C) as compared to simply heating it to its boiling point? Explain with relevant calculations.

8. (i) Pendulum clocks generally go fast in winter and slow in summer. Why? **[1½]**

(ii) Ice is put into a tumbler containing water at room temperature. For faster cooling, should the ice be allowed to float naturally in the water or be pushed to the bottom of the container with a stick and held there? Explain. **[1½]**

9. Pieces of copper and glass are heated to the same temperature. Why does the piece of copper feel hotter on touching?

10. The graph below depicts the cooling curve of a substance as it cools from higher to a lower temperature.

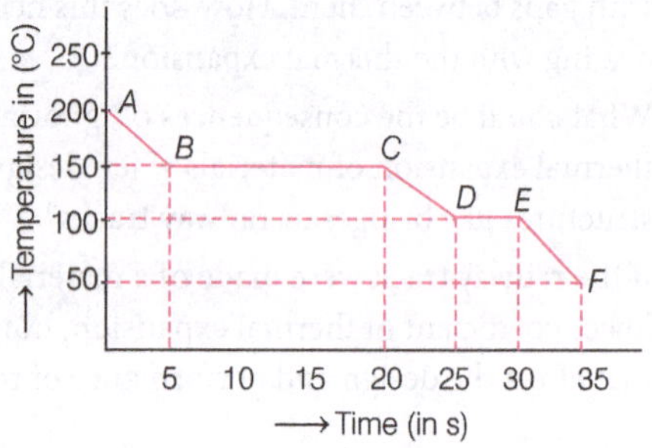

(i) What is the boiling point of the given substance? **[1]**

(ii) Describe the process occuring in the region marked as *DE*. **[1]**

(iii) Why is the duration of the region *DE* shorter compared to the region *BC*? **[1]**

11. Explain the following

(i) Hot tea cools rapidly when poured into the saucer from the cup. **[1]**

(ii) Temperature of a hot liquid falls rapidly in the beginning but slowly afterwards. **[1]**

(iii) A hot liquid cools faster if outer surface of the container is blackened. **[1]**

Long Answer Type Questions

12. Answer the following **NCERT**

(i) The triple point of water is a standard fixed point in modern thermometry. Why? What is wrong in taking the melting point of ice and the boiling point of water as standard fixed points (as was originally done in the celsius scale)? **[1]**

(ii) There were two fixed points in the original celsius scale as mentioned above which were assigned the number 0°C and 100°C, respectively. On the absolute scale, one of the fixed points is the triple point of water, which on the kelvin absolute scale is assigned the number 273.16 K. What is the other fixed point on this (kelvin) scale? **[1]**

(iii) The absolute temperature (kelvin scale) *T* is related to the temperature t_K on the celsius scale by $t_C = T - 273.15$. Why do we have 273.15 in this relation and not 273.16? **[1]**

(iv) What is the temperature of the triple point of water on an absolute scale whose unit interval size is equal to that of the fahrenheit scale? **Competency Based Que.** **[2]**

13. (i) Name three coefficient of thermal expansion of solid. Establish relation between them. **[3]**

(ii) Establish the relation $\rho' = \rho(1 - \gamma \Delta T)$, where the symbols have their usual meanings. **[2]**

14. Answer the following questions based on the *p*-*T* phase diagram of CO_2. **Competency Based Que.**

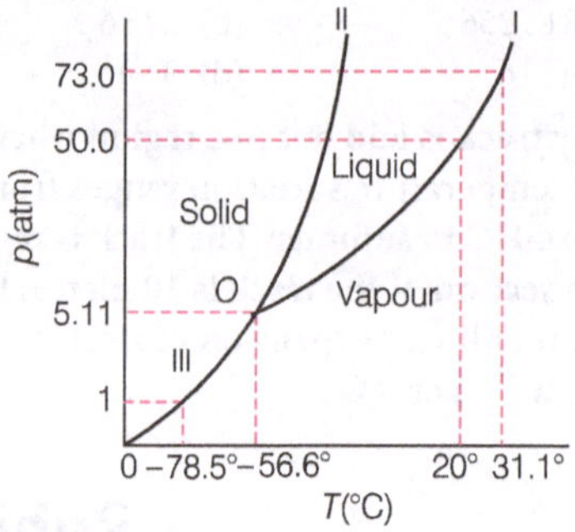

(i) CO_2 at 1 atm pressure and temperature – 60°C is compressed isothermally. Does it go through the liquid phase? **[1]**

(ii) What happens when CO_2 at 4 atm pressure is cooled from room temperature at constant pressure? **[1]**

(iii) Describe qualitatively the changes in a given mass of solid CO_2 at 10 atm pressure and temperature – 65°C as it heated upto room temperature at constant pressure. **[2]**

(iv) CO_2 is heated to a temperature 70°C and compressed isothermally. What changes in its properties do you expect to observe? **[1]**

15. Explain why?

(i) A body with large reflectivity is a poor emitter. **[1]**

(ii) A brass tumbler feels much colder than a wooden tray on a chilly day. **[1]**

(iii) An optical pyrometer (for measuring high temperature) calibrated for an ideal black body radiation gives too low value for the temperature of a red hot iron piece in the open, but gives a correct value for the temperature when the same piece is in the furnace. **[1]**

(iv) The earth without its atmosphere would be inhospitably cold. **[1]**

(v) Heating systems based on circulation of steam are more efficient in warming a building than those based on circulation of hot water. **[1]**

Numerical Problems

Temperature and Heat

16. A specific book describes a new temperature scale called Z, in which boiling and freezing points of water are referred as 65°Z and – 15°Z, respectively.

(i) To what temperature on fahrenheit scale would a temperature – 95°Z correspond? [1½]

(ii) What temperature change on the Z scale would correspond to a change of 40° on celsius scale? [1½]

Thermal Expansion

17. A resistance thermometer reads the resistance $R = 20.0\ \Omega$, $27.5\ \Omega$ and $50.0\ \Omega$ at the ice point (0°C), the steam point (100°C), the zinc point (420°C), respectively. Assuming that the resistance varies with temperature as $R_t = R_0(1 + \alpha t + \beta t^2)$, where t is temperature in Celsius scale. Determine the value R_0, α and β.

Competency Based Que.

18. An aluminium cube 10 cm on a side at 0°C is heated to 30°C. Find the change in its density. Given that coefficient of volume expansion of aluminium $= 7.2 \times 10^{-5}$ /°C and density of aluminium at 0°C $= 2700\ \text{kg/m}^3$. **Competency Based Que.**

19. Calculate the stress developed inside a tooth cavity filled with copper when hot tea at temperature of 57°C is drunk. You can take body (tooth) temperature to be 37°C and $\alpha = 1.7 \times 10^{-5}$/°C bulk modulus for copper $= 140 \times 10^9\ \text{N/m}^2$. **NCERT Exemplar**

20. A clock with an iron pendulum keeps correct time at 20°C. How much will it lose or gain in a day, if temperature changes to 40°C? Coefficient of cubical expansion of iron is $36 \times 10^{-6}\ °\text{C}^{-1}$.

21. A circular disc made by iron is rotating about its axis of rotation with a uniform angular speed ω.

Determine the change in the linear speed of particle at the rim in percentage. The disc of rim is slowly heated from 20°C to 50°C keeping the angular speed uniform. Given that coefficient of linear expansion for the material of iron is $1.2 \times 10^{-5}\ °\text{C}^{-1}$. **Competency Based Que.**

Calorimetry

22. A copper block of mass 2.5 kg is heated in a furnace to a temperature of 500°C and then placed on a large ice block. What is maximum amount of ice that can melt? Given that specific heat of water = 390 $\text{J kg}^{-1}\text{K}^{-1}$ and latent heat of fusion of water $= 3.35 \times 10^5\ \text{J kg}^{-1}$

23. A metal piece of 50 g specific heat 0.6 cal/g°C initially at 120°C is dropped in 1.6 kg of water at 25°C. Find the final temperature of mixture.

24. 100 g of ice at 0°C is mixed with 100 g of water at 80°C. The resulting temperature is 6°C. Calculate heat of fusion of ice.

25. Calculate heat required to convert 3 kg of water at 0°C to steam at 100°C. Given specific heat capacity of $H_2O = 4186\ \text{J kg}^{-1}\text{K}^{-1}$ and latent heat of steam $= 2.256 \times 10^6$ J/kg.

Heat Transfer

26. A box having total surface area 0.05 m^2 and of 6 mm thick side walls is filled with melting ice and kept in a room. Calculate the thermal conductivity of the box material if 0.5 kg of ice melts in 1 h. The room temperature is 40°C and latent heat of fusion of ice $= 3.33 \times 10^5\ \text{J kg}^{-1}$. [3]

27. Three rods of identical cross-sectional area and made from the same metal from the sides of an isosceles triangle ABC (shown in figure), right-angled at B. The points A and B are maintained at temperatures T and $\sqrt{2}T$, respectively. In the steady state, the temperature of the point C is T_C. Assuming that only heat conduction takes place. Then, determine the value of $\frac{T_C}{T}$. Given, a, a and $\sqrt{2}a$ are the respective side lengths. [3]

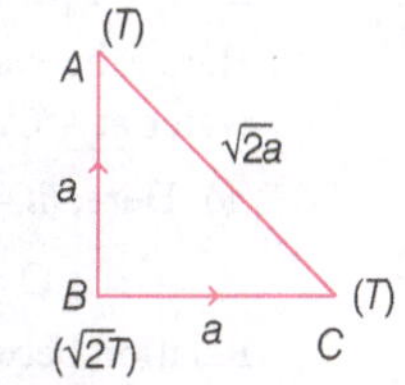

28. A pan filled by hot food cools from 94°C to 86°C in 120 s when the room temperature is 293 K. How long will it take to cool from 71°C to 69°C? **NCERT**

29. According to Stefan's law of radiation, a black body radiates energy σT^4 from its unit surface area every second where T is the surface temperature of the black body and $\sigma = 5.67 \times 10^{-8}\ \text{W/m}^2\text{K}^4$ is known as Stefan's constant. A nuclear weapon may be though of as a ball of radius 0.5 m. When detonated, it reaches temperature of 10^6 K and can be treated as a black body.

(i) Estimate the power it radiates. [1]

(ii) If surrounding has water at 30°C, how much water can evaporate in 1s by 10% of energy produced by weapon?
$[S_w = 4186.0\ \text{J/kg}$ and $L_v = 22.6 \times 10^5\ \text{J/kg}]$ [2]

(iii) If all this energy U is in the form radiation corresponding momentum is $p = U/c$. How much momentum per unit time does it impart on unit area at a distance of 1 km? [2] **NCERT Exemplar**

Hints & Solutions

Objective Type Questions

1. (a)
2. (a) As the temperature is increased length of the pendulum increases.

We know that, time period of pendulum, $T = 2\pi\sqrt{\frac{L}{g}}$

$\Rightarrow \quad T \propto \sqrt{L}$

As L, increases so, time period (T) also increases.

3. (a) Let volume of the sphere is V and ρ is the density of water, then we can write buoyant force

$F = V\rho g$ (g = acceleration due to gravity)

$\Rightarrow F \propto \rho$ ($\because$ V and g are almost constant)

$\Rightarrow \frac{F_{4°C}}{F_{0°C}} = \frac{\rho_{4°C}}{\rho_{0°C}} > 1 \quad (\because \rho_{4°C} > \rho_{0°C})$

$\Rightarrow \quad F_{4°C} > F_{0°C}$

Hence, buoyancy will be less in water at 0°C than that in water at 4°C.

4. (b) Here, $m = 60$ kg $= 60 \times 10^3$ g, $c = 0.83$ cal g^{-1} °C^{-1}

$Q = 200$ kcal $= 2 \times 10^5$ cal

Relation between heat and temperature

$Q = mc\Delta T$

$\Rightarrow \quad \Delta T = \frac{Q}{mc} = \frac{2 \times 10^5}{60 \times 10^3 \times 0.83} = 4.016°$ C

5. (c)
6. (b) According to Wien's displacment, $\lambda_m T$ = constant.

$\lambda_{mL} T_1 = \lambda_{m_2} T_2$

$\Rightarrow 5.5 \times 10^{-7} \times 5500 = 11 \times 10^{-7} T_2$

$\therefore \quad T_2 = 5.5 \times 500$

$= 2750$ K.

7. (a)
8. (a) Electric power consumed in first case,

$P_1 = \sigma T_1^4 = \sigma (3000)^4$ ...(i)

Electric power consumed in second case,

$P_2 = \sigma T_2^4 = \sigma (4000)^4$ ...(ii)

On dividing Eq. (ii) by Eq. (i), we get

$\frac{P_2}{P_1} = \frac{(4000)^4}{(3000)^4} = \frac{256}{81}$

As we know percentage rise in power

$= \frac{P_2 - P_1}{P_1} \times 100 = \frac{256 - 81}{81} \times 100$

$= \frac{175}{81} \times 100 = 216\%$

9. (d) As $\gamma = \frac{\Delta V}{V \times \Delta T}$ and $\gamma = 3\alpha$

$\therefore \quad 3\alpha = \frac{\Delta V}{\left(\frac{4}{3}\pi R^3\right)\Delta T}$

Hence $\Delta V = (4\pi R^3 \alpha \Delta T)$

10. (b)
11. (a) Change in tempertrue, $\Delta\theta = 77 - 27 = 50°$ C

By the law of conservation of energy

Energy given by heater = Energy gain by water + Energy lost from the lid

$\Rightarrow \quad Pt = ms\,\Delta\theta$ + Energy lost

$\Rightarrow 1000t = 2 \times 4.2 \times 10^3 \times 50 + 160\,t$

$\Rightarrow 840t = 8.4 \times 10^3 \times 50$

$\therefore \quad t = 500$ sec $= 8$ min 20 sec

12. (d) The rate of radiation of a black body is given by Stefan-Boltzmann law.

$P \propto T^4$

Given, $\quad T_1 = 300$ K

$T_2 = 300 + 900 = 1200$ K

Ratio of radiation rates

$\frac{P_2}{P_1} = \left(\frac{T_2}{T_1}\right)^4 = \left(\frac{1200}{300}\right)^4 = 4^4 = 256$

Thus, the new rate of radiation is 256 E.

13. (d) The temperature of the black body is

$T_1 = 227°C = 500$ K

$\therefore$ Using Stefan's law, the rate of heat radiation per unit area per unit time is

$E_1 = \sigma T^4 \Rightarrow 20 = \sigma(500)^4$

$\Rightarrow \quad \sigma = \frac{20}{(500)^4}$ ...(i)

Now, the temperature of the black body is raised to

$T_2 = 727°C = 1000$ K

$\therefore$ Rate of heat radiation per unit area is

$E_2 = \sigma T_2^4$

From Eq. (i),

$\Rightarrow \quad \frac{20}{(500)^4} \times (1000)^4 = 20 \times 2^4 = 320$ cal m^{-2} s^{-1}

14. (c) Consider the diagram where all the three objects are heated to same temperature T. We know that density,

$\rho = \frac{\text{mass}}{\text{volume}}$ as ρ is same for all the three objects hence, volume will also be same.

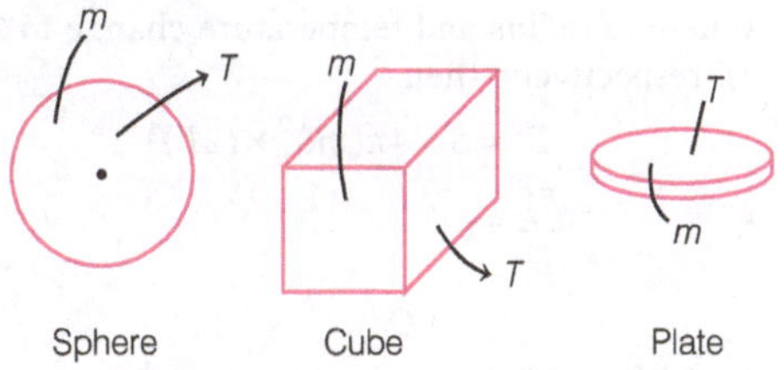

As thickness of the plate is least hence, surface area of the plate is maximum.

We know that, according to Stefan's law of heat loss

$$H \alpha AT^4$$

where, A is surface area of the object and T is temperature.

As A_{plate} is maximum.

Hence, the plate will cool fastest.

As, the sphere is having minimum surface area hence, the sphere cools slowest.

15. (*a*) 1-B, 2-A, 3-D, 4-C

16. (*c*) 1-D, 2-C, 3-B, 4-A

17. (*d*) Assertion is false because conduction also occurs in liquids and gases, although less efficiently than in solids.

Reason is true because the close packing of molecules in solids indeed allows efficient energy transfer through collisions, making solids better conductors as compared to liquids and gases.

18. (*a*) Assertion is correct because the coefficient of linear expansion (α) is defined as the fractional increase in length per degree rise in temperature.

$\Delta L = L_0 \alpha \Delta T$ where ΔL is the change in length, L_0 is the initial length, α is the coefficient of linear expansion and ΔT is the temperature change.

Reason is also correct. The increase in length is indeed directly proportional to the initial length and the temperature change, which is the principle behind linear expansion.

19. (*d*) Assertion is false because the coefficient of thermal expansion for gases does depend on the pressure (at constant volume) or temperature (at constant pressure). Reason is true in describing the ideal gas law, where volume depends on temperature and pressure. The reasoning here is generally correct for ideal gases in specific conditions, but the Assertion itself is incorrect.

20. (*a*)

21. (*a*)

22. (*a*) Assertion is correct. The triple point of water is used as a reference point in modern thermometry (0.01°C and 611.657 Pa)

Reason is correct. The triple point of water remains constant, unlike the melting and boiling points, which vary with atmospheric pressure.

23. (*c*) Since, the escape velocity on the surface of the moon is much less than that on earth, so the water molecules get evaporated faster.

24. (*c*) Houses made of concrete roofs get very hot during summer days, because thermal conductivity of concrete is much smaller than that of a metal still it is significant.

25. (*a*)

26. (*b*)

27. Given,

Iron bar, $L_1 = 0.1$ m, $A_1 = 0.02$ m^2

$K_1 = 79$ W/mK

Brass bar, $L_2 = 0.1$ m, $A_2 = 0.02$ m^2

$K_2 = 109$ W/mK

Temperature, $T_1 = 373$ K (iron end)

$T_2 = 273$ K (brass end)

(i) (*a*) We use the formula of steady state heat flow.

$$\frac{Q}{T} = \frac{KA\Delta T}{L}$$

For steady state the heat current through both bars must be the same.

$$\frac{K_1A_1(T_1 - T_j)}{L_1} = \frac{K_2A_2(T_j - T_2)}{L_2}$$

Substitute the known values

$$\frac{79 \times 0.02 \times (373 - T_j)}{0.1} = \frac{109 \times 0.02 \times (T_j - 273)}{0.1}$$

$$\Rightarrow 79(373 - T_j) = 109(T_j - 273)$$

$$29467 - 79T_j = 109T_j - 29757$$

Solving for T_j

$$29467 + 29757 = 109T_j + 79T_j$$

$$59224 = 188T_j$$

$$T_j = \frac{59224}{188} = 315 \text{ K}$$

(ii) (*b*) The equivalent thermal conductivity for two bars in series is given by

$$\frac{1}{K_{eq}} = \frac{L_1}{K_1A_1} + \frac{L_2}{K_2A_2}$$

Substituting the values,

$$\frac{1}{K_{eq}} = \frac{0.1}{79 \times 0.02} + \frac{0.1}{109 \times 0.02}$$

Calculating

$$\frac{1}{K_{eq}} = \frac{0.1}{1.58} + \frac{0.1}{2.18}$$

$$\frac{1}{K_{eq}} = 0.0633 + 0.0459 = 0.1092$$

$$K_{eq} = \frac{1}{0.1092} = 9.16 \text{ W/mK}$$

(iii) (*b*) The heat current through the compound bar is given by

$$\frac{Q}{t}=\frac{K_{eq}A\Delta T}{L_{total}}$$

Where, $L_{total}=L_1+L_2=0.1+0.1=0.2$ m

$\Delta T=T_1-T_2=373-273=100$ K

Substituting the values

$$\frac{Q}{t}=\frac{9.16\times0.02\times100}{0.2}$$

$$\frac{Q}{t}=\frac{183.2}{0.2}=916.1\text{ W}$$

(iv) (*b*) For two rods in series, the heat current is given by

$$\frac{Q}{t_{series}}=\frac{K_{eq}A\Delta T}{L_{total}}$$

for rods in parallel, the heat current is

$$\frac{Q}{t_{total}}=\frac{K_1A_1\Delta T}{L_1}+\frac{K_2A_2\Delta T}{L_2}$$

If the heat flow in series is the same as in parallel, we can solve for the time ratio.

∵ The heat currents are equal.

$$\frac{t_{parallel}}{t_{series}}=2$$

Hence, the time in parallel is half that in series.

Therefore, the time in parallel is $\frac{12}{2}$ =6 seconds.

(v) (*c*) The rate of heat flow is proportional to the temperature difference. If the temperature difference doubles, the rate of heat flow will also double.

$$\frac{Q_2}{Q_1}=\frac{\Delta T_2}{\Delta T_1}=\frac{200-100}{110-100}=2$$

∴ The new rate of boat flow is

$$Q_2=4.0\text{ J}\times2\text{s}=8.0\text{ J/s}$$

28. (i) (*c*) A cavity maintained at a constant temperature acts as an ideal black body.

(ii) (*c*) According to Stefan's law,

$$E=\sigma AT^4$$

$$\therefore\quad \ln E=4\ln T+\ln\sigma$$

This shows that graph between ln*E* and ln*T*, a straight line with $m=4$. Also, value of $\sigma(5.67\times10^{-8}$ $\text{Wm}^{-2}\text{ K}^{-4})$ is quite samll, *y*- intercept (= lnσ) must be on negative side.

(iii) (*c*) By Wien's displacement law,

$$\lambda_m' T'=\lambda_m T$$

$$\therefore\quad \lambda_m'=\frac{\lambda_m T}{T'}=\frac{\lambda\times2000}{3000}=\frac{2\lambda}{3}$$

(iv) (*d*) Energy radiated by the sun per second,

$$E=\sigma AT^4$$

$$=\sigma\times4\pi R^2\times T^4$$

When its radius and temperature change to 2*R* and 2*T* respectively, then

$$E'=\sigma\times4\pi(2R)^2\times(2T)^4$$

$$\therefore\quad \frac{E'}{E}=64$$

Or

(*a*) By Stefan's law,

$$E\propto T^4\Rightarrow\frac{E_2}{E_1}=\left(\frac{T_2}{T_1}\right)^2=\left(\frac{273+27}{273+127}\right)^4=\left(\frac{300}{400}\right)^4$$

$$=81:256$$

29. (i) The change in length ΔL can be calculated using the formula.

$$\Delta L=L_0\alpha\Delta T$$

where

$L_0=10$ m (initial length of the track),

$\alpha=12\times10^{-6}$ per° C

(coefficient of linear expansion of steel),

$\Delta T=40°\text{C}-(-5°\text{C})=45°\text{C}$ (temperature change).

Substituting the values

$$\Delta L=10\times12\times10^{-6}\times45=0.0054\text{ m}$$

$$=5.4\text{ mm}$$

Thus, the track will expand by 5.4 mm.

(ii) The gaps between the railway track sections allow the track to expand and contract freely without causing stress that could lead to track damage or buckling. If the track sections were joined rigidly without gaps, the expansion in summer would cause the metal to buckle due to the inability of the track to expand outward. Similarly in winter, the lack of gaps could cause tension as the metal contracts. These expansion gaps absorb the changes in length and ensure the track remains safe and operational.

(iii) Ignoring the thermal expansion could lead to significant structural problems. For example, in railway tracks, lack of provision for expansion could result in the track sections pushing against each other, causing buckling or warping. In bridges, the lack of expansion joints could lead to cracks or even the collapse of parts of the bridge due to the unaccounted-for stress caused by temperature fluctuations. In extreme cases, the entire structure could become unstable, posing a risk to human lives and causing expensive repairs.

(iv) If the railway track were made of a material with a lower coefficient 'of thermal expansion, the track would expand and contract less for a given temperature change. This would reduce the size of the expansion gaps needed and potentially improve the stability of the track, as there would be less thermal strain.

However, it could also lead to a reduction in flexibility, which might make the track more vulnerable to fractures under extreme temperature fluctuations. A careful balance would be required to choose a material that both minimizes expansion and maintains structural integrity.

Subjective Questions

1. (i) The actual motion of air is discontinued by catching air in between its delicate fibres.
Therefore, convection is suppressed out of this, the felt displays better thermal insulator than air.
(ii) This is because when we are without clothes, air carriers away heat from our body due to convection and hence, we feel cold.

2. (i) Snow is better heat insulator than ice because snow contains air packets inside it and air is a good insulator of heat. Due to this, snow takes longer time to melt than ice of same mass.
(ii) As copper is a good conductor of heat as compared to steel. The steel utensils with copper bottom absorbs heat more quickly than steel and give it to the food in utensil. As as result, of it the food in utensil is heated uniformly and quickly.

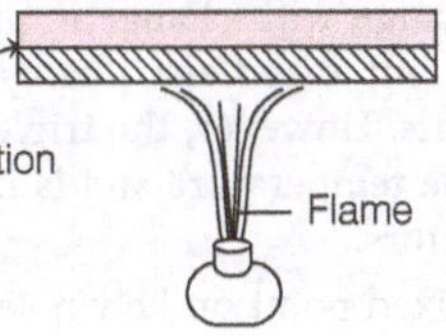

3. According to Wein's displacement law, $\lambda_m T$ = constant
So, $\lambda_1 < \lambda_3 < \lambda_2$
$\therefore \quad T_1 > T_3 > T_2$

4. Consider a solid in the form of a rectangular parallelopiped of sides a, b and c respectively, so that its volume $V = abc$.
If the solid is heated so that its temperature rises by ΔT, then increase in its sides will be

$$\Delta a = a \cdot \alpha \cdot \Delta T, \Delta b = b \cdot \alpha \cdot \Delta T \text{ and } \Delta c = c \cdot \alpha \cdot \Delta T$$

or $a' = a + \Delta a = a(1 + \alpha \cdot \Delta T)$
$b' = b + \Delta b = b(1 + \alpha \cdot \Delta T)$
and $c' = c + \Delta c = c(1 + a \cdot \Delta T)$
$\because$ New volume, $V' = V + \Delta V = a'b'c'$
$= abc(1 + \alpha \cdot \Delta T)^3$
$\therefore$ Increase in volume,

$$\Delta V = V' - V = [abc(1 + \alpha \cdot \Delta T)^3 - abc]$$

$\therefore$ Coefficient of volume expansion,

$$\gamma = \frac{\Delta V}{V \cdot \Delta T} = \frac{abc(1 + \alpha \cdot \Delta T)^3 - abc}{abc \cdot \Delta T}$$

$$\therefore \quad \gamma = \frac{(1 + \alpha \cdot \Delta T)^3 - 1}{\Delta T}$$

$$= \frac{(1 + 3\alpha \cdot \Delta T + 3\alpha^2 \cdot \Delta T^2 + \alpha^3 \cdot \Delta T^3) - 1}{\Delta T}$$

$$= 3\alpha + 3\alpha^2 \Delta T + \alpha^3 \cdot \Delta T^2.$$

However, as α has an extremely small value for solids, hence terms containing higher powers of α may be neglected. Therefore, we obtain the relation $\gamma = 3\alpha$,
i.e. coefficient of volume expansion of a solid is three times of its coefficient of linear expansion.

5. All the gases given in the list are diatomic gases. Diatomic gases have 5 degrees of freedom. While monoatomic gases have 3 degrees of freedom. Therefore, molar specific heat of diatomic gas $= 5 \times \frac{R}{2} = 5 \times \frac{1.98}{2} = 4.95$ cal/mol-K. It agrees with the molar specific heats of the given gases except chlorine.
Monoatomic gases has only translational motion while diatomic gas molecules has translational, vibrational and rotational motion. Therefore, to increase the temperature of diatomic gas through 1°C, heat energy is supplied to increase its translational, vibrational and rotational energies and hence, molar specific heat of diatomic gases are higher than the molar specific heat of monoatomic gases. The molar specific heat of chlorine is higher due to translational motion along with rotational motion while other gases molecule have only translational and rotational motion at room temperature.

6. **Calorimetry** It is the branch of physics which deals with the measurement of heat. A device in which heat measurement can be done is called a **calorimeter.**
Construction
- It consists of a copper cylindrical vessel equipped with a stirrer, which is kept inside a wooden jacket.
- The space between the calorimeter and the jacket is insulated with materials like glass wool as shown below.

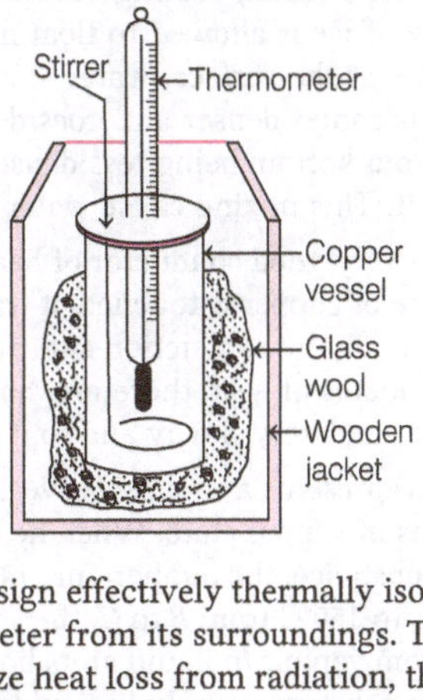

- This design effectively thermally isolates the calorimeter from its surroundings. To further minimize heat loss from radiation, the outer surface of the calorimeter and the inner surface of the jacket are polished.

- The lid contains holes for inserting a thermometer and a stirrer into the calorimeter.

7. Water have high value of specific latent heat of vaporisation as compared to its specific heat capacity. The specific heat capacity of water is 4200 J/kg°C, while the specific latent heat of steam is 2268×10^3 J/kg.
$\therefore$ Heat required to raise the temperature of m kg of water to its boiling point.

$$Q_1 = mC_w \times \Delta t = m \times 4200 \times (100 - 25)$$
$$= m \times 4200 \times 75 \text{ J}$$

Heat required to boil m kg of water at 100°C into steam

$$Q_2 = mL = m \times 2268 \times 10^3 \text{ J}$$
$$\frac{Q_2}{Q_1} = \frac{m \times 2268 \times 10^3}{m \times 4200 \times 75} = 7.2$$

Clearly, the heat required to boil off a certain quantity of water is 7.2 times the heat required to bring the water to its boiling point from room temperature. Hence, it takes a longer time to boil off water rather than to bring it to its boiling point from room temperature.

8. (i) The time period of a pendulum is given by

$$t = 2\pi\sqrt{\frac{L}{g}}$$

where, L is the length of the pendulum. Thus, t is directly proportional to $\sqrt{L}$. In summer, L increases with increase in temperature while in winter, L decreases with fall in temperature. As a result, pendulum clocks go fast in winter and slow in summer.

(ii) To cool water quickly, ice should be allowed to float naturally in water.

Justification

When ice melts, water in the vicinity gets cooled and becomes denser. If ice is made to stay at the bottom of the tumbler, water at bottom becomes cold. But colder water being denser remains at bottom. As a result, cooling occurs slowly. On the contrary, if ice is allowed to float naturally in the water, i.e. at the surface, water at surface becomes cold. It becomes denser and goes down and warmer water from bottom being less dense rises up to replace it. This mixing cause water to cool quickly.

9. Copper is a very good conductor of heat. When the heated piece of copper is touched, it transfers heat to our hand rapidly by conduction and we feel hot. Glass is a poor conductor of heat, therefore, hot glass conducts heat to our hand very slowly and so it appears less hot.

10. The graph represents a cooling curve. At A the substance is in vapour state. When heat is withdrawn from the substance, the temperature of vapour falls from 200°C to 150°C from B to C, the state of substance changes from vapour to liquid at its boiling point. At point D the substance purely in liquid state.

(i) Thus, the boiling point of substance is 150°C. From C to D there is fall of temperature of liquid.

(ii) From D to E the liquid state changes into solid state. At D, substance is in liquid state and at E it is in solid state.
Thus, in region DE the liquid state is being changed in solid state.

(iii) The region DE is shorter than the region BC because the latent heat of fusion of substance is less than the latent heat of vaporisation of the substance.

11. (i) As surface area increases on pouring hot tea in saucer from the cup and the rate of loss of heat is directly proportional to surface area of the radiating surface, so the tea will cool faster in the saucer.

(ii) Temperature of a hot liquid falls exponentially in accordance with Newton's law of cooling. In other words, rate of cooling is directly proportional to the temperature difference between hot liquid and the surroundings. It is due to this reason that a hot liquid cools rapidly in the beginning but slowly afterwards.

(iii) When outer surface of container is blackened, the surface becomes good emitter of heat and so the hot liquid in it cools faster.

12. (i) The melting point of ice as well as the boiling point of water change with change in pressure. The presence of impurities also changes the melting and boiling points. However, the triple point of water has a unique temperature and is independent of external factors.

(ii) The other fixed point on kelvin scale is absolute zero, which is the temperature at which the volume and pressure of any gas become zero.

(iii) As the triple point of water on celsius is 0.01°C (and not 0°C) and on kelvin scale 273.16 and the size of degree on the two scales is same, so

$$t_C - 0.01 = T - 273.16$$
$$\therefore \quad t_C = T - 273.15$$

(iv) One degree on fahrenheit scale

$$= \frac{180}{100} = \frac{9}{5} \text{ divisions on celsius scale.}$$

But one celsius scale division is equal to one division on kelvin scale.

$\therefore$ Triple point on kelvin scale (whose size of a degree is equal to that of the fahrenheit scale).

$$= 273.16 \times 9/5$$
$$= 491.69$$

13. (i) Thermal expansion of solids are of three types

(a) linear expansion, α

(b) Area expansion, β

(c) Volume expansion, γ

Relation between them is as follows

Let us consider a cube of side I, its original volume is $V = I^3$

Suppose the cube is heated, so that its temperature increased by ΔT. Its each side will become

$$l' = l + \Delta l = l + \alpha l \Delta T = l(1 + \alpha \Delta T)$$

The new volume of the cube will be

$$V' = l'^3 = l^3 (1 + \alpha \Delta T)^2 = V(1 + \alpha \Delta T)^3$$

$$V' = V(1 + 3\alpha \Delta T + 3\alpha^2 \Delta T^2 + \alpha^3 \Delta T^3)$$

α small. So the terms containing α^2 and α^3 can be neglected,

$$\therefore \quad V' = V(1 + 3\alpha \Delta T)$$

According to the definition of coefficient of cubical expansion,

$$\gamma = \frac{\Delta V}{V \Delta T} = \frac{V' - V}{V \Delta T}$$

$$\Rightarrow \quad \gamma = \frac{V(1 + 3\alpha \Delta T)}{V \Delta T} = 3\alpha$$

Similarly we get, $\beta = 2\alpha$

Hence, $\frac{\alpha}{1} = \frac{\beta}{2} = \frac{\gamma}{3}$

(ii) When a given mass of a solid or liquid is heated, its volume increases and hence density decreases.

If V and V' are the volumes and ρ and ρ' are the densities of a given mass M at temperature T and $(T + \Delta T)$ respectively, then

$$V' = V(1 + \gamma \Delta T)$$

$$\Rightarrow \quad \frac{M}{\rho'} = \frac{M}{\rho}(1 + \gamma \Delta T) = \rho' = \rho(1 + \gamma \Delta T)^{-1}$$

By using binomial theorem in the above equation and neglecting the higher power of $\gamma \Delta T$, we get

$$\rho' = \rho(1 - \gamma \Delta T)$$

So, $\rho' < \rho$ i.e. density of a solid or liquid decreases with the increase in temperature.

14. (i) No; At 1 atm pressure and at –60°C, CO_2 lies to the left of –56.6°C (triple point O). Hence, it lies in the region of vaporous and solid phases.

(ii) At 4 atm pressure, CO_2 lies below 5.11 atm (triple point O). Hence, it lies in the region of vaporous and solid phases. Thus, it condenses into the solid state directly, without passing through the liquid state.

(iii) When the temperature of a mass of solid CO_2 (at 10 atm pressure and at –65°C) is increased, it changes to the liquid phase and then to the vaporous phase. It forms a line parallel to the temperature axis at 10 atm. The fusion and boiling points are given by the intersection point where this parallel line cuts the fusion and vaporisation curves.

(iv) If CO_2 is heated to 70°C and compressed isothermally, then it will not exhibit any transition to the liquid state. This is because 70°C is higher than the critical temperature of CO_2. It will remain in the vapour state, but will depart from its ideal behaviour as pressure increases.

15. (i) A body with large reflectivity is a poor absorber of heat. According to Kirchhoff's law, a poor absorber of heat is a poor emitter. Hence, a body with large reflectivity is a poor emitter.

(ii) Brass is a good conductor of heat. When a brass tumbler is touched, heat quickly flows from human body to tumbler. Consequently, the tumbler appears colder. Wood is a bad conductor. So, heat does not flow from the human body to the tray in this case. Thus, it appears comparatively hotter.

(iii) Let T be the temperature of the hot iron in the furnace.

Heat radiated per second per unit area, $E = \sigma T^4$

When the body is placed in the open at temperature T_0, the heat radiated per second/unit area,

$E' = \sigma (T_4 - T_0^4)$.

Clearly, $E' < E$. So, the optical pyrometer gives too low value for the temperature in the open.

(iv) Heat radiated out by the earth is reflected back by the atmosphere. In the absence of atmosphere, at night all heat would escape from the earth's surface and thereby the earth's surface would be inhospitably cold. Also, atmosphere helps in maintaining the temperature through convection current.

(v) Though steam and boiling water are at the same temperature but each unit mass of steam contains a larger amount of additional heat called the latent heat. e.g. Each gram of steam has 540 cal of more heat than each gram of boiling water. Hence, steam loses more heat than boiling water.

16. Freezing Point = –15° Z

Boiling Point = 65° Z

(i) $[T° F] = [T° Re] \times \frac{9}{4} + 32$

$$[T° F] = [-95° Z] \times \frac{9}{4} + 32$$

$$[T° F] = -181.75° F$$

$$\therefore \quad -95° Z = -181.75° F$$

(ii) $[T° Z] = [T° C] \times \frac{4}{5} = 40° C \times \frac{4}{5}$

$$T° Z = 32° C$$

$$\therefore \quad 40°C = 32°Z$$

17. R at ice point $(R_0) = 20\ \Omega$

R at steam point $(R_{100}) = 27.5\ \Omega$

R at zinc point $(R_{420}) = 50\ \Omega$

The resistance at particular value of temperature is given as

$$R_t = R_0 (1 + \alpha t + \beta t^2)$$

$$\Rightarrow \quad R_{100} = R_0 + R_0 \alpha t + R_0 \beta t^2$$

$$\Rightarrow \quad \frac{R_{100} - R_0}{R_0} = \alpha t + \beta t^2$$

$$\Rightarrow \frac{27.5 - 20}{20} = \alpha \times 100 + \beta \times 10000$$

$$\Rightarrow \frac{7.5}{20} = 100\alpha + 10000\beta \quad \text{...(i)}$$

$$R_{420} = R_0(1 + \alpha t + \beta t^2)$$

$$\Rightarrow \frac{50 - R_0}{R_0} = \alpha t + \beta t^2$$

$$\Rightarrow \frac{50 - 20}{20} = 420\alpha + 176400 \times \beta$$

$$\Rightarrow \frac{3}{2} = 420\alpha + 176400\beta \quad \text{...(ii)}$$

From Eq. (i) and (ii), we get

$$\alpha = 3.5 \times 10^{-3} /°C$$

$$\beta = -5.6 \times 10^{-7} /°C$$

$$R_0 = 20°C$$

18. Volume coefficient of expansion is given by

$$\gamma = \frac{\Delta\rho}{\rho\,(\Delta t)}$$

$$\therefore \Delta\rho = \gamma\rho\Delta t = 7.2 \times 10^{-5} \times 2700 \times 30 = 5.83 \text{ kg m}^{-3}$$

19. Given, decrease in temperature $(\Delta t) = 57 - 37 = 20°C$

Coefficient of linear expansion $(\alpha) = 1.7 \times 10^{-5}/°C$

Bulk modulus for copper $(B) = 140 \times 10^9 \text{ N/m}^2$

Coefficient of cubical expansion $(\gamma) = 3\alpha = 5.1 \times 10^{-5}/°C$

Let initial volume of the cavity be V and its volume increase by ΔV due to increase in temperature.

$$\therefore \quad \Delta V = \gamma V \Delta t \Rightarrow \frac{\Delta V}{V} = \gamma\,\Delta t$$

Thermal stress produced = $B \times$ Volumetric strain

$$= B \times \frac{\Delta V}{V} = B \times \gamma\,\Delta t = 140 \times 10^9 \times (5.1 \times 10^{-5} \times 20)$$

$$= 1{,}428 \times 10^8 \text{ N/m}^2$$

This is about 10^3 times of atmopheric pressure.

20. Initial time period, $T = 2\pi\sqrt{\frac{l}{g}}$

Change in temperatue, $\Delta t = 40 - 20 = 20°C$

New length of pendulum, $L' = L(1 + \alpha\Delta T)$

$$\text{where,} \quad \alpha = \frac{\gamma}{3} = \frac{36 \times 10^{-6}}{3} = 12 \times 10^{-6}\,°C^{-1}$$

Now, new length of pendulum, $l' = l[1 + (12 \times 10^{-6})(20)]$

$$= l[1 + 0.00024]$$

Now, new time period,

$$T' = 2\pi\sqrt{\frac{l'}{g}} = 2\pi\sqrt{\frac{l}{g}}\sqrt{1 + 0.00024} = T(1 + 0.00012)$$

$$\Rightarrow \quad T' - T = T(0.00012)$$

Given that, $T = 24 \times 3600$ s (Time period for one day)

$$\Rightarrow \quad T' - T = (86400) \times (0.00012) = 10.368$$

At higher temperature length of pendulum clock will be more. So, time period will be more and it will lose the time.

21. Let initial radius of the circular disc at 20°C = r_{20}

Let final radius of the circular disc at 50°C = r_{50}

Coefficient of linear expansion, $\alpha = 1.2 \times 10^{-5}/°C$

Change in temperature,

$$\Delta T = 50 - 20 = 30°C$$

If v and v' be the linear speed at 50°C and 20°C respectively, as ω remains constant.

$$\therefore \quad \omega = \frac{v}{r} = \frac{v'}{r'}$$

Changed distance of particle is given by

$$r' = r(1 + \alpha\Delta T)$$

$$\Rightarrow \quad r' = r(1 + 1.2 \times 10^{-5} \times 30)$$

$$r' = 1.00036 \text{ r}$$

Changed linear velocity $\Rightarrow v' = r\omega$

$$v' = r(1 + \alpha\,\Delta T)\omega = v(1 + \alpha\Delta T)$$

$$\% \text{ change} \Rightarrow \frac{v' - v}{v} \times 100$$

$$= \frac{0.00036v - v}{v} \times 100 = 0.00036 \times 100 = 3.6 \times 10^{-2}$$

22. Mass of copper block, $M = 2.5$ kg

Specific heat of copper, $C = 390 \text{ J kg}^{-1}\text{K}^{-1}$

Fall in temperature, $\Delta T = 500 - 0 = 500°C$

Heat loss by copper block = $mC\Delta T = 2.5 \times 390 \times 500$ J

Let mass of ice melted = M kg

Latent heat of fusion of ice, $L = 3.35 \times 10^5$ J/kg

Heat gained by ice = $ML = M \times 3.35 \times 10^5$

$\because$ Heat gained = Heat lost

$$M \times 3.35 \times 10^5 = 2.5 \times 390 \times 500$$

$$M = \frac{2.5 \times 390 \times 500}{3.35 \times 10^5} = 1.455 \text{ kg}$$

23. $m_1c_1(\theta_1 - \theta) = m_2c_2(\theta - \theta_2)$

$$\therefore \quad c_2 = 1\text{cal/gm°C}$$

$$\therefore 50 \times 0.6 \times (120 - \theta) = 1.6 \times 10^3 \times 1 \times (\theta - 25)$$

$$\theta = 26.8°\text{ C}$$

24. Ice + Water → Water

at 0°C at 80°C at 6°C

$$m_1c_1(80 - 6) = m_2L + m_2c_2(6 - 0)$$

$$100 \times 1 \times 74 = 100L + 100 \times 1 \times 6$$

$$L = (1 \times 74) - 6 = 68 \text{ cal/g}$$

25. Heat required to convert H_2O at 0° to H_2O at 100°

$$= m_1c_1t$$

$$= 30 \times 4186 \times 100 = 1255800 \text{ J}$$

Heat required to convert H_2O at 100°C to steam at 100°C = mL

$$= 3 \times 2.256 \times 10^6 = 6768000 \text{ J}$$

Total heat = 8023800 J

26. Given, surface area, $A = 0.05 \text{ m}^2$

Thickness, $x = 6 \text{ mm} = 6 \times 10^{-3}$ m

Temperature difference,

$$\Delta T = 40^\circ \text{C} - 0^\circ \text{C} = 40^\circ\text{C}$$

time, $t = 1 \text{ h} = 1 \times 60 \times 60 \text{ s} = 3600$ s

Latent heat, $L = 3.33 \times 10^5$ J/kg

Amount of heat into the box

$$Q = mL = 0.5 \times 3.33 \times 10^5 = 1.665 \times 10^5 \text{ J}$$

Now, we know that $Q = \dfrac{KA\Delta Tt}{x}$

Thermal conductivity, $K = \dfrac{Q \cdot x}{A\Delta T \cdot t}$

$$= \frac{1.665 \times 10^5 \times 6 \times 10^{-3}}{0.05 \times 3600 \times 40} = \frac{9.99 \times 10^2}{7200}$$

$$= 0.138 \text{ Wm}^{-1}\text{K}^{-1}$$

27. At steady state, the temperature at point $C = T_C$

From the fig. given in question

$$\left(\frac{\Delta Q}{\Delta t}\right)_{BC} = \left(\frac{\Delta Q}{\Delta t}\right)_{CA}$$

$$\Rightarrow \frac{KA(\sqrt{2}T - T_C)}{a} = \frac{KA(T_C - T)}{\sqrt{2}a}$$

$$\sqrt{2}(\sqrt{2}T - T_C) = T_C - T$$

$$\Rightarrow \quad 2T - \sqrt{2}T_C = T_C - T$$

$$3T = T_C(\sqrt{2} + 1)$$

$$\Rightarrow \quad \frac{T_C}{T} = \frac{3}{\sqrt{2} + 1}$$

28. According to Newton's cooling law,

$$\frac{T_1 - T_2}{t} = K\left(\frac{T_1 + T_2}{2} - T_0\right)$$

$$\frac{94 - 86}{120} = K\left[\frac{94 + 86}{2} - 20\right]$$

$$\frac{8}{120} = K[90 - 20] = K[70]$$

$$K = \frac{1}{1050}$$

Again, $\dfrac{71 - 69}{t'} = \dfrac{1}{1050}\left[\dfrac{71 + 69}{2} - 20\right]$

$$\frac{2}{t'} = \frac{1}{1050}[50] \Rightarrow t' = \frac{1050 \times 2}{50} = 42 \text{ s}$$

29. Given, $\sigma = 5.67 \times 10^{-8}$ W/m² Kg

Radius, = $R = 0.5$m, $T = 10^6$ K

(i) Power radiated by Stefan's law,

$$P = \sigma AT^4 = (4\pi R^2)T^4$$

$$= (5.67 \times 10^{-4} \times 4 \times (3.14) \times (0.5)^2 \times (10^6)^4$$

$$= 1.78 \times 10^{17} \text{J/s} = 1.8 \times 10^{17} \text{J/s}$$

(ii) Energy available per second, $U = 1.8 \times 10^{17}$ J/s

$$= 18 \times 10^{16} \text{J/s}$$

Actual energy required to evaporate water = 10% of 1.8×10^{17} J/s

$$= 1.8 \times 10^{16} \text{ J/s}$$

Energy used per second to raise the temperature of m kg of water from 30°C to 100°C and then into vapour at 100°C

$$= ms_w\Delta\theta + mL_v = m \times 4186 \times (100 - 30) + m \times 22.6 \times 10^5$$

$$= 2.93 \times 10^5 m + 22.6 \times 10^5 \ m = 25.53 \times 10^5 \text{ m J/s}$$

As per question $25.53 \times 10^5 \text{ m} = 1.8 \times 10^{16}$

or $m = \dfrac{1.8 \times 10^{16}}{25.53 \times 10^5} = 7.0 \times 10^9$ kg

(iii) Momentum per unit time,

$$p = \frac{U}{c} = \frac{1.8 \times 10^{17}}{3 \times 10^8} = 6 \times 10^8 \text{ kg-m/s}^2$$

[p = Momentum, U = energy c = velocity of Light]

Momentum per unit time per unit area

$$d = \frac{P}{4\pi R^2} = \frac{6 \times 10^8}{4 \times 3.14 \times (10^3)^2}$$

$$\Rightarrow \quad d = 47.7 \text{ N/m}^2 \quad [4\pi R^2 = \text{Surface area}]$$

QR Code for Quick Test 1

QR Code for Quick Test 2

QR Code for Quick Test 3

SELF ASSESSMENT TEST

Multiple Choice Questions (MCQs)

1. Temperature of atmosphere in Kashmir falls below $-10°C$ in winter. Due to this water animal and plant life of Dal-lake

(a) is destroyed in winters

(b) frozen in winter and regenerated in summers

(c) survives as only top layer of lake is frozen

(d) None of the above

2. At atmospheric pressure, water boils at 100°C. If pressure is reduced, then it

(a) still boils at same temperature

(b) boils at a lower temperature

(c) boils at a higher temperature

(d) does not boil at all

3. A uniform metallic rod rotates about its perpendicular bisector with constant angular speed. If it is heated uniformly to raise its temperature slightly, then

(a) its speed of rotation increases

(b) its speed of rotation decreases

(c) its speed of rotation remains same

(d) its speed increase because its moment of interia increases

4. The graph between two temperature scales A and B is shown in figure between upper fixed point and lower fixed point there are 150 equal divsion on scale A and 100 on scale B. The relationship for conversion between the two scales is given by

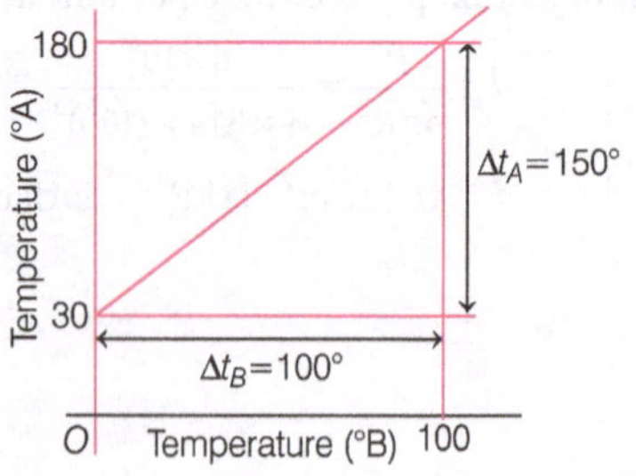

(a) $\frac{t_A - 180}{100} = \frac{t_B}{150}$ (b) $\frac{t_A - 30}{150} = \frac{t_B}{100}$

(c) $\frac{t_B - 180}{150} = \frac{t_A}{150}3$ (d) $\frac{t_B - 40}{100} = \frac{t_A}{180}$

5. Match the Column I and Column II.

	Column I		Column II
A	Specific heat capacity (s)	1	$l_1 - l_2 =$ constant for $l_1\alpha_1 = l_2\alpha_2$
B	Two metals (l_1, a_1) and (l_2, a_2) are heated	2.	Y is same
C	Thermal stress	3.	$s = \infty$ for $\Delta T = 0$
D	Four wires of same material	4.	$Y \propto \Delta t$

(a) $A \to 3$; $B \to 1$; $C \to 4$; $D \to 2$

(b) $A \to 1$; $B \to 2$; $C \to 3$; $D \to 4$

(c) $A \to 2$; $B \to 1$; $C \to 4$; $D \to 3$

(d) $A \to 3$; $B \to 4$; $C \to 2$; $D \to 1$

6. Hot water cools from 60°C to 50°C in first 10 minutes and from 50°C to 42°C in next 10 minuts. The temperature of surrounding is

(a) 5°C (b) 10°C

(c) 15°C (d) 20°C

Assertion-Reason

Directions *(Q.No. 7-10) In the following questions, two statements are given- one labelled Assertion (A) and the other labelled Reason (R). Select the correct answer to these questions from the codes (a), (b), (c) and (d) as given below.*

(a) Both Assertion and Reason are true and Reason is the correct explanation of Assertion.

(b) Both Assertion and Reason are true but Reason is not the correct explanation of Assertion.

(c) Assertion is true but Reason is false.

(d) Assertion is false but Reason is true.

7. **Assertion (A)** A flannel keeps the ice cold but keeps people warm.

Reason (R) Bad conductors do not permit heat to flow through them.

8. **Assertion (A)** A piece of ice, with a stone frozen inside it, floats on water in a beaker, when the ice melts, the level of water in the beaker decreases.

Reason (R) Density of stone is more than that water.

9. **Assertion (A)** Heat energy is transferred through conduction only in solids.
Reason (R) In conduction, energy is transferred through the vibration of particles in a medium.

10. **Assertion (A)** Water has a higher specific heat capacity than metals.
Reason (R) Water requires more energy to raise its temperature by 1°C compared to metals.

Case Based Questions

Directions *(Q.No. 11) This question is case study based question. Read the following paragraph and answer the questions on the basis of same.*

11. During a winter evening, a scientist in a laboratory is studying the thermal properties of different materials. He decides to conduct an experiment using three materials: a metal rod, a glass tube and a rubber strip. The scientist places all three materials in the same hot water bath, which has a constant temperature. After some time, he observes that the metal rod feels very hot at the ends, the glass tube feels a bit warm, and the rubber strip remains at a similar temperature as it was initially.

The scientist recalls the principles of heat transfer and begins to analyse why the materials behave differently despite being in the same hot water bath.

(i) Why does the metal rod feel very hot at the ends faster than the other materials?
(a) Metal has a high specific heat capacity.
(b) Metal is a good conductor of heat.
(c) Metal has a low coefficient of linear expansion.
(d) Metal absorbs less heat.

(ii) What can be inferred about the behavior of the rubber strip in the experiment?
(a) Rubber has a high thermal conductivity.
(b) Rubber has a low specific heat capacity.
(c) Rubber is a poor conductor of heat.
(d) Rubber is in thermal equilibrium with the water immediately.

(iii) If the scientist wanted to improve the temperature rise in the rubber strip, which property should he focus on?
(a) Decrease the specific heat capacity of the rubber.
(b) Increase the coefficient of linear expansion of the rubber.
(c) Increase the thermal conductivity of the rubber.
(d) Decrease the mass of the rubber strip.

(iv) What is the likely reason why the glass tube feels only a bit warm compared to the metal rod?
(a) Glass has a very high specific heat capacity.
(b) Glass is a better conductor than rubber.
(c) Glass has a low thermal conductivity compared to metal.
(d) Glass does not absorb heat at all.

Very Short Answer Type Questions

12. Animal curl their bodies into a ball when they feel very cold. Why?

13. In which method of heat transfer, gravity does not play any part?

14. Calorimeters are made of metals not glass. Why?

15. The earth constantly receives heat radiation from the sun and gets warmed up. Why does the earth not get as hot as the sun?

16. Two absolute scales *A* and *B* have triple points of water defined to be 200 *A* and 350 *B*. What is relation between T_A and T_B? **NCERT**

Short Answer Type Questions

17. Three rods of equal lengths of thermal conductivities *K*, 2*K* and 3*K* are symmetrically joined a point.If temperatures of ends are 0°C, 50°C and 100°C respectively, determine the temperature of junction point.

18. 100 g of water is supercooled to −10°C. At this point, due to some disturbance mechanised or otherwise some of it suddenly freezes to ice. What will be the temperature of the resultant mixture and how much mass would freeze? [Specific heat of water = 1 cal/g/°C and latent heat of fusion of water = 80 cal/g] **NCERT Exemplar**

Long Answer Type Questions

19. A copper cube of mass 200 g slides down on a rough inclined plane having inclination 37° at a constant speed. If any loss in mechanical energy goes into the copper block as thermal energy. Find the increase in the temperature of the block as it slides down through 60 cm. Given, specific heat of copper is 420 J $kg^{-1}K^{-1}$.

20. What should be the length of steel and copper rods at 0°C, so that the length of the steel rod is 5 cm longer than the copper rod at any temperature? Given that linear expansion coefficient of steel $= 12 \times 10^{-5}$ /°C and for copper= 1.6×10^{-5} /°C.

Answers

1. (c) *2.* (b) *3.* (b) *4.* (b) *5.* (a)
6. (b) *7.* (a) *8.* (a) *9.* (a) *10.* (a)
11. (i) (b) (ii) (c) (iii) (c) (iv) (c)

11

CHAPTER

Thermodynamics is a branch of science which deals with exchange of heat and energy between bodies and conversion of the heat energy into mechanical energy and *vice versa*.
It provides a macroscopic frame work for understanding now energy interacts with matter and influences physical properties such as temperature, pressure and volume.

YOUR STUDY GOALS

YOUR PRACTICE GOAL

- Objective Type Questions (28 Qs ; MCQs, A-R, Matching)
- Case Based Questions (3)
- Subjective Questions (4 VSAs, 8 SAs, 2 LAs)
- Numerical Problems (17)

Thermodynamics

11.1 Thermodynamic System

The collection of an extremely large number of atoms or molecules is called a thermodynamic system. It can be represented in the form of pressure (p), volume (V) and temperature (T).

- Anything outside the thermodynamic system to which energy or matter is exchanged is called its **surroundings**.
- A system is separated from its surroundings by a **boundary**. It may be real or imaginary.

Classification of Thermodynamic System

On the basis of transfer of heat and matter across the boundary, a thermodynamic system can be classified as open, closed and isolated systems.

(i) **Open System** It exchanges both energy and matter with the surroundings.

(ii) **Closed System** It exchanges only energy (not matter) with its surroundings.

(iii) **Isolated System** It exchanges neither energy nor matter with its surroundings.

Thermodynamic Equilibrium

A thermodynamic system is said to be in thermodynamic equilibrium when macroscopic variables (like pressure, volume, temperature, mass, composition, etc.) that characterise the system do not change with time.

A system in the state of thermodynamic equilibrium possesses the following equilibrium simultaneously.

- If there is no unbalanced force and torque is acting on the system, then the system is said to be in **mechanical equilibrium.**
- If the system does not undergo any spontaneous change in its internal structure due to chemical reaction, diffusion, etc., then the system is said to be in **chemical equilibrium.**
- Two systems are said to be in **thermal equilibrium**, if there is no net flow of heat between them when they are brought into thermal contact.

Zeroth Law of Thermodynamics

Zeroth law states that, **if two systems *A* and *B* are separately in thermal equilibrium with a third system *C*, then *A* and *B* are in thermal equilibrium with each other**. This law leads to the concept of temperature.

Concept of Temperature

Zeroth law of thermodynamics implies that temperature is a physical quantity which has the same value for all systems which are in thermal equilibrium with each other.

Hence, zeroth law says that if systems *A* and *B* are separately in thermal equilibrium with *C*, then

$$T_A = T_C \text{ and } T_B = T_C \Rightarrow T_A = T_B$$

So, systems *A* and *B* will also be in thermal equilibrium with each other.

Some Definitions of Temperature

Temperature is that thermodynamic variable which determines whether the two systems in contact will be in thermal equilibrium or not.

Temperature of a body is that parameter which determine the degree of hotness or coldness of a body.

Temperature of a body is that parameter which determines the direction of flow of heat when the body is brought in contact with another body.

11.2 Internal Energy, Heat and Work

Internal Energy

Internal energy of a system is defined as the total energy possessed by the system due to molecular motion and molecular configuration. It is represented by U.

The energy due to molecular motion is called **internal kinetic energy** (U_K).

The energy due to molecular configuration is called **internal potential energy** (U_P). Then,

$$\text{Internal energy, } U = U_K + U_P$$

Thus, the internal energy of a system is the sum of molecular kinetic and potential energies in the frame of reference relative to which the centre of mass of the system is at rest.

Properties of Internal Energy

(i) The internal energy is a microscopic variable of a system.

(ii) It depends only on the state of the system and is independent of path followed.

(iii) For the given mass of a gas, the internal energy depends on its state described by specific values of pressure, volume and temperature.

(iv) In thermodynamics, the KE of the system as a whole is not relevant. It means if the container of the gas is moving as a whole with some velocity as shown in figure, the KE of the container is not to be included in internal energy.

Container is moving

(v) Internal energy in a cyclic process is always zero.

(vi) Internal energy of an ideal gas is totally kinetic and depends on the temperature of the gas.

Heat

Heat is the energy which is transferred between a system and its environment because of the temperature difference between them. It flows from the body at a higher temperature to the one at lower temperature.

- Its **SI unit is Joule (J)** and its **dimensional formula is** $[ML^2T^{-2}]$.
- **It is a scalar and a path dependent quantity.**
- If temperature of a body of mass m is increased from T_i to T_f, then the change in heat of the body is given by

$$\Delta Q = ms\,(T_f - T_i)$$

where, s = specific heat capacity of the body

Work

Work is the energy transfer to or from an object *via* the application of force along its displacement, such as motion of the piston of a cylinder containing gas, by raising or lowering some weight connected to it.

It is a **scalar quantity** and its SI unit is **joule.**

Suppose a gas is confined in a cylinder with a movable piston. If p is the pressure on the piston and A is area of piston, then force exerted by the gas on the piston of cylinder, $F = pA$.

When the piston is pushed outward an infinitesimal distance dx, then the work done by the gas,

$$dW = Fdx = pA\,dx = p\,dV \qquad [\because A dx = dV]$$

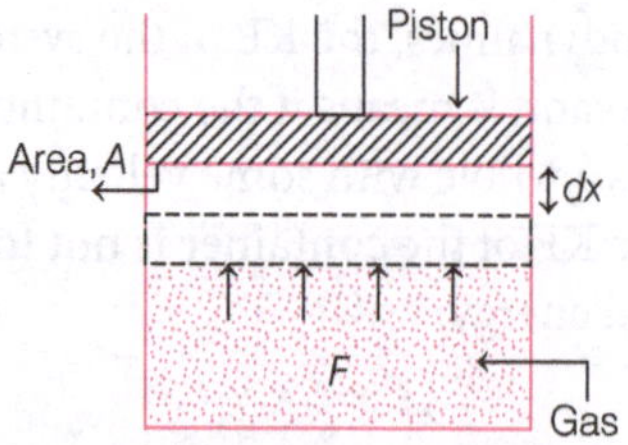

and for a finite volume change from V_i to V_f,

$$\text{Work done, } W = \int_{V_i}^{V_f} dW$$

A diagram represented by a plot between pressure and volume of a gas is called an **indicator diagram.** It is shown below

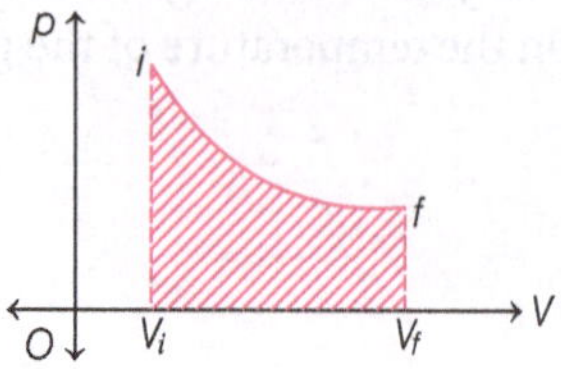

p-V diagram

If system expands, $V_f > V_i$, **i.e.** W **= positive**

If system contracts, $V_f < V_i$, **i.e.** W **= negative**

Like heat, work done is also path dependent and so it is not a state function. In case of a cyclic process, work done is equal to the area enclosed under *p-V* diagram and it is positive, if cycle is clockwise and negative, if the cycle is anti-clockwise.

Note Heat and work are two different modes to change the state and internal energy of a system.

Sign Convention of Heat, Work and Internal Energy

ΔQ	Positive	When heat is supplied to a system
	Negative	When heat is taken out from a system
ΔW	Positive	When work is done by the system (expansion)
	Negative	When work is done on the system (compression)
ΔU	Positive	When temperature of the system increases
	Negative	When temperature of the system decreases

Example 1 A diatomic gas has a total internal energy of 2000 J. If 60% of the total internal energy is due to internal kinetic energy, then calculate both U_K (kinetic energy) and U_P (potential energy).

Sol. $U_K = 0.6 \times U \Rightarrow U_K = 0.6 \times 2000 = 1200\text{ J}$

$U_P = U - U_K$

$U_P = 2000 - 1200 = 800\text{ J}$

First Law of Thermodynamics

First law of thermodynamics is a statement of conservation of energy applied to any system in which energy transfer from or to the surroundings is taken into account.

It states that heat given to a system is either used in doing external work or it increases the internal energy of the system or both.

i.e. $$\text{Heat supplied, } \Delta Q = \Delta U + \Delta W$$

where,

ΔQ = heat supplied to the system by the surroundings,

ΔW = work done by the system on the surroundings

and ΔU = change in internal energy of the system.

e.g. Suppose a gas at initial pressure and volume (p, V) in a cylinder. If gas expands by a very small volume ΔV, the work done by the gas is given by $\Delta W = p\Delta V$

So, first law of thermodynamics can also be written as

$$\Delta Q = \Delta U + p\Delta V$$

Example 2. **1 g of water at 100°C is converted into steam at the same temperature. If the volume of steam is 1551 cm^3, find out the change in internal energy of the water. Latent heat of steam = 2256×10^3 J/kg. Consider atm pressure.**

Sol. Given, mass of water, $m = 1\ g = 1 \times 10^{-3}$ kg

Hence, atmospheric pressure, $p = 1.013 \times 10^5 N/m^2$

Volume of steam, $V_s = 1551\ cm^3 = 1551 \times 10^{-6} m^3$

Volume of water, $V_w = \frac{\text{Mass}}{\text{Density}}$

$$= \frac{1 \times 10^{-3}}{10^3} = 1 \times 10^{-6} m^3$$

First law of thermodynamics gives

$$\Delta Q = \Delta U + p\Delta V$$

$$\Rightarrow \quad mL = \Delta U + p(V_s - V_w)$$

$\therefore$ Change in internal energy,

$$\Delta U = mL - p(V_s - V_w)$$

$$= 1 \times 10^{-3} \times 2256 \times 10^3 - 1.013 \times 10^5 \times (1551 \times 10^{-6} - 10^{-6})$$

$$= 2256 - 0.1013 \times 1550 \cong 2099\ J$$

Example 3. **The quantities in the following table represent four different paths for same initial and final states. Find the values of *a, b, c, d, e, f* and *g*.**

S. No.	Q(J)	W(J)	ΔU(J)
Path I	– 80	–120	*d*
Path II	90	*c*	*e*
Path III	*a*	40	*f*
Path IV	*b*	– 40	*g*

Sol. For path I, $\Delta Q = \Delta W + \Delta U \Rightarrow \Delta U = \Delta Q - \Delta W$

$$= -80 - (-120) = 40\ J$$

As, ΔU = a state function, so $d = e = f = g = 40$ J

Now for path II, $\Delta Q = \Delta W + \Delta U$

$$90 = c + 40 \Rightarrow c = 50\ J$$

Similarly, $a = 80$ J, $b = 0$

11.3 Heat Capacity

If an amount of heat ΔQ is needed to change its temperature by ΔT, then heat capacity can be defined as

$$\text{Heat capacity, } S = \frac{\Delta Q}{\Delta T}$$

Heat capacity is numerically equal to the heat energy required to change the temperature of a body by unity. Its unit is J/K.

Specific Heat Capacity

The amount of heat required to change the temperature of unit mass of a substance by unity is known as specific heat capacity of heat substance.

$$s = \frac{S}{m} = \frac{1}{m}\frac{\Delta Q}{\Delta T}$$

$$\text{Specific heat capacity, } s = \frac{1}{m}\frac{\Delta Q}{\Delta T}$$

where, s = specific heat capacity of the substance.

It depends on the nature of substance and its temperature. Its unit is J/kg-K. **Heat capacity per kg is known as specific heat capacity.**

Molar Specific Heat Capacity

The amount of heat required to raise the temperature of one gram mole of a substance through a unit is called molar specific heat capacity of the substance.

$$C = \frac{S}{\mu} = \frac{1}{\mu}\left(\frac{\Delta Q}{\Delta T}\right)$$

$$\text{Molar specific heat capacity, } C = \frac{1}{\mu}\frac{\Delta Q}{\Delta T}$$

where, μ = number of moles.

C depends on the nature of the substance, its temperature and the conditions under which heat is supplied. Its unit is J/mol-K.

Note The molar specific heat capacity for solids is $C = 3R$.

Specific and molar heat capacities of some solids at room temperature and atmospheric pressure

Substance	Specific heat ($Jkg^{-1}K^{-1}$)	Molar specific Heat ($J\ mol^{-1}K^{-1}$)
Aluminium	900.0	24.4
Carbon	506.5	6.1
Copper	386.4	24.5
Lead	127.7	26.5
Silver	236.1	25.5
Tungsten	134.4	24.9

Specific Heat Capacity of Water

In the past, calorie was used as a unit of heat, defined as the amount of heat needed to raise the temperature of 1 g of water by 1°C.

However, it was later observed that the specific heat of

water varies slightly with temperature, as shown in the figure below.

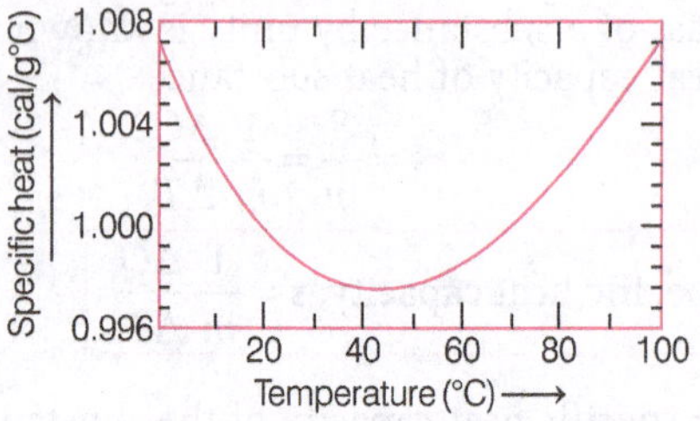

Specifically, **one calorie is defined to be the amount of heat required to raise the temperature of 1 g of water from 14.5°C to 15.5°C.**

In SI unit, the specific heat capacity of water is 4186 J/kg-K or 4.186 J/g-K.

Mechanical Equivalent of Heat

Mechanical equivalent of heat is defined as the amount of work needed to produce 1 calorie of heat.

It is just a conversion factor.

$$1 \text{ calorie (heat energy)} = 4.186 \text{ J} \simeq 4.2 \text{ J}$$

Specific Heat Capacities of Gases

For gases, specific heat capacities depends on the process under which, heat exchanges between the gases and the surrounding.

There are two main specific heat capacities for a gas and defined as

(i) **Molar heat capacity at constant volume** The amount of heat required to increase the temperature of one mole of the gas by 1°C (or 1K) at constant volume is known as molar heat capacity at constant volume. **It is denoted by C_V.**

(ii) **Molar heat capacity at constant pressure** The amount of heat required to increase the temperature of one mole of the gas by 1°C (or 1K) at constant volume is known as molar heat capacity at constant pressure. **It is denoted by C_p.**

Note For a gas, $C_p > C_V$ always, because at constant pressure, more heat is required to increase the temperature of one mole of the gas by 1°C (or 1K) as compare to that of at constant volume.

Relation between C_p and C_V (Mayer's Formula)

For an ideal gas, the relation between C_p and C_V is

$$C_p - C_V = R \quad \ldots\text{(i)}$$

This relation is known as **Mayer's formula.**

The ratio of C_p and C_V is notified by γ.

$$\gamma = C_p / C_V$$

It is also known as heat capacity ratio, then

$$C_V = \frac{R}{\gamma - 1} \text{ and } C_p = \frac{\gamma R}{\gamma - 1}$$

Example 4. A gaseous mixture enclosed in a vessel consists of 1 g mole of a gas A $\left(\gamma = \frac{5}{3}\right)$ and some amount of gas B $\left(\gamma = \frac{7}{5}\right)$ at a temperature T. The gases A and B do not react with each other and are assumed to be ideal. Find number of gram moles of the gas B, if γ for the gaseous mixture is $\left(\frac{19}{13}\right)$.

Sol. For an ideal gas,

$$\frac{C_p}{C_V} = \gamma \text{ and } C_p - C_V = R$$

So, combining above equations, we get

$$C_V = \frac{R}{\gamma - 1}$$

$$(C_V)_A = \frac{R}{\frac{5}{3} - 1} = \frac{R}{\left(\frac{2}{3}\right)} = \frac{3R}{2}$$

and $(C_V)_B = \frac{5}{2}R$ and $(C_V)_{\text{mix}} = \frac{R}{\frac{19}{13} - 1} = \frac{13}{6}R$

Now, from conservation of energy,

$$U_{\text{mix}} = U_A + U_B$$

or $$\Delta U_{\text{mix}} = \Delta U_A + \Delta U_B$$

$$\Rightarrow (\mu_A + \mu_B)(C_V)_{\text{mix}} \Delta T = \mu_A (C_V)_A \Delta T + \mu_B (C_V)_B \Delta T$$

$$\Rightarrow (C_V)_{\text{mix}} = \frac{\mu_A (C_V)_A + \mu_B (C_V)_B}{\mu_A + \mu_B}$$

$$\Rightarrow \frac{13}{6}R = \frac{1 \times \frac{3}{2}R + \mu_B \times \frac{5}{2}R}{1 + \mu_B}$$

$$\Rightarrow 13 + 13\mu_B = 9 + 15\mu_B$$

$$\Rightarrow \mu_B = 2 \text{ g-mol}$$

Example 5. Find molar specific heat for the process $p = \frac{a}{T}$ for a monoatomic gas. $\left(a = \text{constant}, C_V = \frac{3}{2}R\right)$

Sol. From first law of thermodynamics,

$$\Delta Q = \Delta W + \Delta U$$

$$\Delta Q = \Delta W + \Delta U$$

$$\Rightarrow \quad C = \frac{\Delta Q}{\Delta T} = \frac{\Delta W}{\Delta T} + \frac{\Delta U}{\Delta T}$$

$$\text{or} \quad C = \frac{\Delta W}{\Delta T} + C_V \qquad [\because \Delta U = C_V \Delta T]$$

$$C = \frac{p\Delta V}{\Delta T} + C_V \qquad [\because \Delta W = p\Delta V] \ldots \text{(i)}$$

For the process,

$$pV = RT \qquad [\because \text{for monoatomic gas, } \mu = 1]$$

$$\Rightarrow \quad V = \frac{RT}{p} = \frac{RT^2}{a} \qquad \left[\because p = \frac{a}{T}\right]$$

$$\Rightarrow \quad \frac{\Delta V}{\Delta T} = \frac{dV}{dT} = \frac{2RT}{a} \qquad \ldots \text{(ii)}$$

On substituting value of Eq. (ii) in Eq. (i), we get

$$= p\left(\frac{2RT}{a}\right) + C_V = \frac{a}{T}\left(\frac{2RT}{a}\right) + C_V \qquad \left[\because p = \frac{a}{T}\right]$$

$$\Rightarrow \quad C = 2R + C_V = 2R + \frac{3}{2}R = \frac{7}{2}R$$

11.4 Thermodynamic State Variables and Equation of State

Equilibrium State

Every equilibrium state of a thermodynamic system is completely described by specific values of some macroscopic variables and these are called **state variables.**

e.g. Pressure, volume, temperature and mass.

A system is not always in a equilibrium state but with time, it comes in mechanical and thermal equilibrium state.

Equation of State

The various state variables are not necessarily independent. The equation which represents the relationship between the state variables of a system is called its equation of state.

e.g. For an ideal gas, the equation of state is the ideal gas equation,

$$\boxed{pV = \mu RT}$$

For a fixed amount of gas given, there are only two independent variables, say p and V or T and V.

The pressure-volume curve for a fixed temperature is called an **isotherm.**

Extensive and Intensive State Variables

State variables are of two types, i.e. extensive and intensive.

Extensive State Variables

Extensive state variables indicate the size of the system. Let us consider that a system in equilibrium is divided into two equal parts. The variable whose values get halved in each part are **extensive.** e.g. Internal energy (U), volume (V), total mass (M) are extensive variables.

Intensive State Variables

These are state variables that do not depend on the size of the system. Again consider a system in equilibrium divided into two equal parts. The variables that remain unchanged for each part are **intensive.**

e.g. Pressure (p), temperature (T) and density (ρ) are intensive variables.

Note The extensive variables change with the size of the system, but the intensive variables do not change with size.

Quick Test 1

1. Explain the relationship between heat, work and internal energy in the context of the first law of thermodynamics.
2. What is the difference between intensive and extensive thermodynamic variables? Give examples of each and explain their significance.
3. Why does the internal energy of an ideal gas depend only on temperature and not on volume or pressure?
4. In an adiabatic process, explain how the first law of thermodynamics applies when no heat is exchanged?
5. A gas is heated and absorbs 100 J of heat. During this process, it does 40 J of work. Calculate the change in internal energy of the gas.

Answer

5. 60 J

For Solutions, See QR Code on Pg. 398

11.5 Thermodynamic Processes

When state of a system changes or the state variables changes with time, then this process is known as thermodynamic process.

Quasi-Static Process

A quasi-static process is an infinitely slow process such that the system remains in thermal and chemical equilibrium with the surroundings.

TEACHER TIP

The processes that do not involve accelerated motion of piston-large temperature gradient and pressure gradient are quasi-static.

Some Important Processes

(i) An **isothermal process** occurs at constant temperature.
e.g. Freezing of water at 0°C to form ice at 0°C.

(ii) An **isobaric process** occurs at constant pressure.
e.g. Boiling of water in an open container.

(iii) An **isochoric process** is one in which volume is kept constant, meaning that the work done by the system will be zero.
e.g. Heat given to a system with fixed walls.

(iv) An **adiabatic process** does not allow transfer of heat by or to the system.
e.g. Rapid compression, like filling of a cycle tube by a hand pump.

(v) **Cyclic and non-cyclic process** In cyclic process, initial and final states are same while in non-cyclic processes, they are different.

The graph between pressure and volume for different processes is shown below.

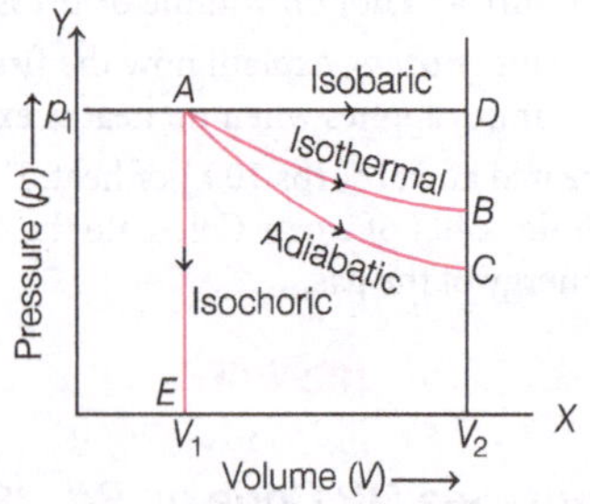

Work Done in an Isothermal Process

For an isothermal process, temperature remains constant.

For an ideal gas, the equation of state is given by

$$pV = \text{constant}$$

So, gas follows Boyle's law

$$p_iV_i = p_fV_f, \text{ for isothermal process}$$

p-V Diagram

On a p-V diagram, an isotherm is a curve that connects points of same temperature.

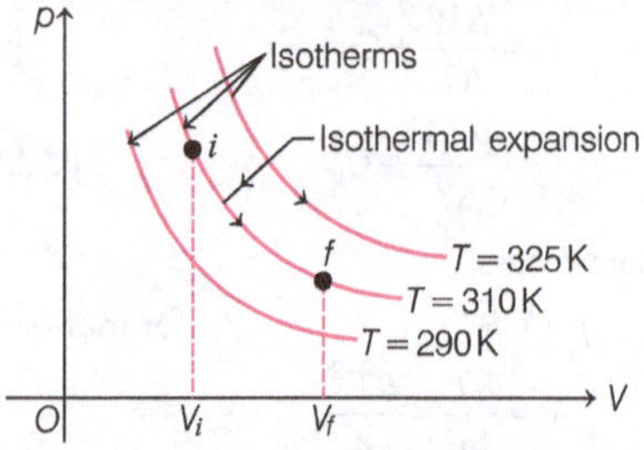

An isothermal expansion process

Work Done

Work done in an isothermal process

$$= \text{Area under } p\text{-}V \text{ graph}$$

$$= \int_{V_i}^{V_f} p\,dV = \mu RT \int_{V_i}^{V_f} \frac{dV}{V}$$

$$\left[\because pV = \mu RT \Rightarrow p = \frac{\mu RT}{V}\right]$$

$$= \mu RT \ln(V)_{V_i}^{V_f} = \mu RT(\ln V_f - \ln V_i)$$

$$W_{\text{iso}} = \mu RT \ln\left(\frac{V_f}{V_i}\right)$$

Work done, $W_{\text{iso}} = 2.303\,\mu RT \log\left(\frac{V_f}{V_i}\right)$

As temperature of ideal gas remains constant.

$\therefore \quad \Delta U = 0$

So, by first law of thermodynamics

$$\Delta Q = \Delta W + \Delta U$$

$$\Rightarrow \quad \Delta Q = \Delta W = \mu RT \ln\left(\frac{V_f}{V_i}\right)$$

where, μ = number of moles, R = gas constant and T = temperature.

V_f and V_i are the final and initial volumes of the gas, respectively.

i.e. Heat supplied in an isothermal change is used to do work against surroundings or if the work is done on the system, then the equal amount of heat energy will be liberate by the system.

Let us consider two cases for finding the nature of the work done.

Case I If $V_f > V_i$, then $W > 0$.
Thus, it is an **isothermal expansion** which means the gas absorbs heat.

Case II If $V_f < V_i$, then $W < 0$.
Thus, it is an **isothermal compression,** work is done on the gas by the environment and heat is released.

Example 6. Three moles of an ideal gas kept at constant temperature of 300 K are compressed from a volume of 4 L to 1 L. Calculate the work done in the process. Take R as 8.31 J/mol-K.

Sol. Given, $\mu = 3$ mol, $T = 300$ K,

$V_i = 4$ L, $V_f = 1$ L,

$R = 8.31$ J/mol-K, $W = ?$

Work done in isothermal process is given by

$$W = 2.303 \mu RT \log \frac{V_f}{V_i}$$

$$= 2.303 \times 3 \times 8.31 \times 300 \log \frac{1}{4}$$

$$= -1.037 \times 10^4 \text{ J}$$

Work Done in an Adiabatic Process

In an adiabatic process, there is no exchange of heat between system and the surroundings.

By first law, $\Delta Q = \Delta U + \Delta W$ ...(i)

For adiabatic process, $\Delta Q = 0$

$\therefore$ $\Delta U = -\Delta W$

For adiabatic process,

$$\boxed{pV^\gamma = \text{constant}}$$

where, $\gamma = \dfrac{C_p}{C_V}$

Thus, if we consider an ideal gas with the adiabatic range from (p_i, V_i) to (p_f, V_f), then

$$p_i V_i^\gamma = p_f V_f^\gamma = \text{constant}$$

or $p^{1-\gamma} \cdot T^\gamma = \text{constant}$ and $V^{\gamma-1} \cdot T = \text{constant}$

p-V Diagram

On a p-V diagram, the process is represented by an adiabatic curve as shown below.

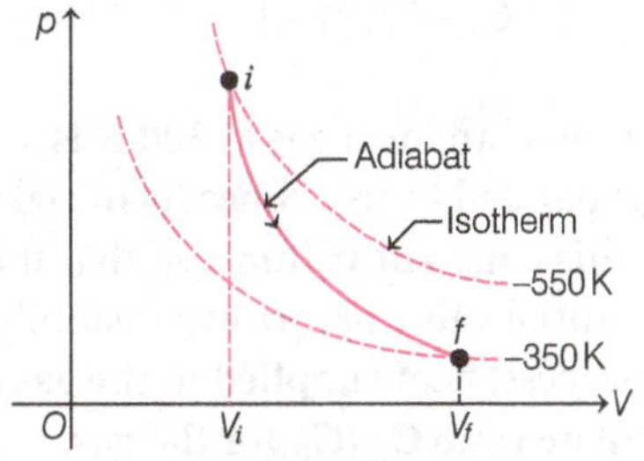

An adiabatic expansion process

A curve representing an adiabatic process is called an **adiabatic.** If we differentiate $pV^\gamma =$ constant, we get

$$dp\, V^\gamma + p\gamma V^{\gamma-1} dV = 0$$

$$\Rightarrow \quad \frac{dp}{dV} = -\gamma\left(\frac{p}{V}\right)$$

So, **slope of adiabatic curve** $= -\gamma\left(\dfrac{p}{V}\right)$**, which is γ times more than slope of an isotherm.**

By definition of specific heat,

$$C = \frac{\Delta Q}{m\Delta T} = \frac{Q}{m\Delta T}, \Delta Q = 0 \text{ in adiabatic process.}$$

So, $C = 0$ (adiabatic process)

So, **specific heat of a gas in adiabatic compression or expansion is zero.**

Work Done

Also, work done in an adiabatic process,

$$W = \int_{V_i}^{V_f} p\,dV = \int_{V_i}^{V_f} \frac{K}{V^\gamma} dV$$

$\because$ $pV^\gamma = K$ [K = constant]

$\therefore$ $p_i V_i^\gamma = p_f V_f^\gamma = K$

where, $pV^\gamma = \text{constant} = K$

$$\Rightarrow \quad W = K\left|\frac{V^{-\gamma+1}}{-\gamma+1}\right|_{V_i}^{V_f} = \frac{K}{1-\gamma}\left[\frac{1}{V_f^{\gamma-1}} - \frac{1}{V_i^{\gamma-1}}\right]$$

$$\text{Thus, } W = \frac{1}{1-\gamma}\left[\frac{p_f V_f^\gamma}{V_f^{\gamma-1}} - \frac{p_i V_i^\gamma}{V_i^{\gamma-1}}\right] = \frac{p_i V_i - p_f V_f}{\gamma - 1}$$

$$pV = \mu RT, \; p_i V_i = \mu R T_i \text{ and } p_f V_f = \mu R T_f$$

$$\boxed{\text{Work done, } W = \frac{\mu R (T_i - T_f)}{\gamma - 1}}$$

Now, by first law of thermodynamics

$$\Delta Q = \Delta U + \Delta W$$

As, $\Delta Q = 0 \Rightarrow \Delta U = -\Delta W$

So, if work is done by the system, the internal energy and so the temperature of system falls, i.e. $W > 0$, $T_f < T_i$. Conversely, if work is done on the system, the internal energy and so the temperature of system increases.

i.e. $W < 0$, $T_f > T_i$

All nearly practical adiabatic processes occur so rapidly that no transfer of energy as heat occurs between the system and surroundings.

e.g. Sudden bursting of bicycle tube and propagation of sound waves in air.

The p-V curves of an ideal gas for two adiabatic processes connecting two isotherms is shown in the figure.

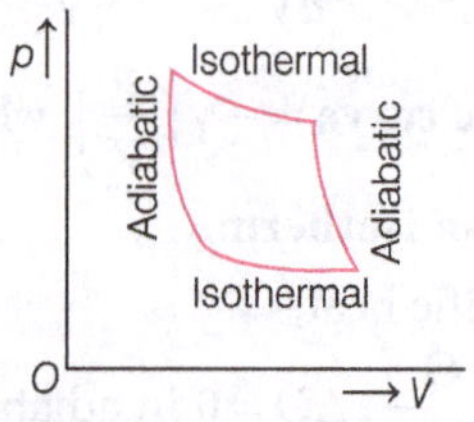

Example 7. **A cylinder containing one gram molecule of the gas was compressed adiabatically until its temperature goes from 27°C to 97°C. Calculate the work done and heat produced in the gas. Take, γ as 1.5.**

Sol. Given, $T_i = 27°C = 27 + 273 = 300$ K

$$T_f = 97°C = 97 + 273 = 370 \text{ K}, \gamma = 1.5$$

Work done in adiabatic compression is given by

$$W = \frac{R}{1-\gamma}(T_i - T_f) = \frac{8.31}{1-1.5}(300 - 370) = 1163.4 \text{ J}$$

$$\text{Heat produced, } H = \frac{W}{J} = \frac{1163.4}{4.2} = 277 \text{ cal}$$

Work Done in an Isochoric Process

In case of an isochoric process, volume of the system remains constant. So, if heat is added to system, its pressure increases and if heat is extracted from the system, pressure will be decreases.

Equation of State

In this process, p and T changes but V = constant, Gay-Lussac's law is obeyed.

$$\Rightarrow \quad p \propto T \Rightarrow \frac{p_1}{T_1} = \frac{p_2}{T_2}$$

where, V = constant

So, $\boxed{\text{Work done, } \Delta W = 0}$

$$\Rightarrow \quad \Delta W = p\,\Delta V = 0 \quad [\because \Delta V = 0]$$

From first law of thermodynamics, $\Delta Q = \Delta U$

Hence, in an isochoric process, the entire heat given to or taken from the system goes to change its internal energy and temperature of the system.

The change in temperature can be determined by the equation.

$$\boxed{\Delta U = \mu C_V \Delta T}$$

Work Done in an Isobaric Process

When a thermodynamic system undergoes a physical change at constant pressure, then this thermodynamic process is known as **isobaric process.**

Suppose the pressure p of a gas remains constant and its volume changes from V_i to V_f, then the work done by the gas is

$$W = \int_{V_i}^{V_f} p\,dV = p\int_{V_i}^{V_f} dV = p(V_f - V_i)$$

$$\boxed{\text{Work done, } W = \mu R(T_f - T_i)}$$

$$[\because pV = \mu RT]$$

Example 8. **If 70 cal of heat is required to raise the temperature of 2 mol of an ideal gas at constant pressure from 30°C to 35°C, calculate**

(i) work done by the gas

(ii) increase in internal energy of gas. (Take, R = 2 cal/mol-K)

Sol. (i) In isobaric process, p = constant

and ΔW = work done = $p\Delta V$

$$= nR(\Delta T) = 2 \times 2 \times (35 - 30) = 20 \text{ cal}$$

(ii) $\Delta U = \Delta Q - \Delta W$ [from first law of thermodynamics]

$$= 70 - 20 = 50 \text{ cal}$$

Example 9. **Find the ratio of $\frac{\Delta Q}{\Delta U}$ and $\frac{\Delta Q}{\Delta W}$ in an isobaric process. The ratio of molar specific heats is $\frac{C_p}{C_V} = \gamma$.**

Sol. In an isobaric process, p = constant

$$\therefore \quad C = C_p$$

and $$\frac{\Delta Q}{\Delta U} = \frac{nC_p\Delta T}{nC_V\Delta T} = \frac{C_p}{C_V} = \gamma$$

also $$\frac{\Delta Q}{\Delta W} = \frac{\Delta Q}{\Delta Q - \Delta U}$$

$$= \frac{nC_p\Delta T}{nC_p\Delta T - nC_V\Delta T}$$

$$= \frac{C_p}{C_p - C_V} = \frac{\gamma}{\gamma - 1}$$

Example 10. **3 mol of an ideal gas at 300 K is isothermally expanded to five times its initial volume and heated at this constant volume, so that the pressure is raised to its initial value before expansion. In the whole process, heat supplied to the gas is 83.14 kJ. Calculate ratio C_p/C_V for the gas. [$\log_e 5$ = 1.61 and R = 8.31 J mol^{-1} K^{-1}]**

Sol. Process is shown in the given diagram.

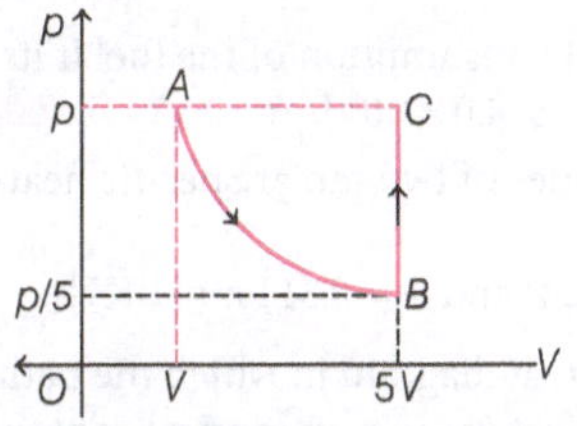

For isothermal process AB,

$$\Delta W = \mu RT \log_e (V_f/V_i)$$
$$= 3 \times 8.31 \times 300 \times \log_e 5$$
$$= 12.03 \text{ kJ}$$

As for isothermal process,

$$\Delta T = 0$$
$$\Rightarrow \quad \Delta U = 0$$

and by first law, $\Delta Q = \Delta W = 12.03$ kJ

For isochoric process BC,

$$V = \text{constant}$$
$$\Rightarrow \quad \Delta W = 0$$
$$\Delta U = \mu C_V \Delta T = 3 C_V \Delta T$$

Now, for process BC, $\dfrac{p_B}{T_B} = \dfrac{p_C}{T_C}$

$$\Rightarrow \quad \frac{P/5}{300} = \frac{P}{T_C}$$
$$\Rightarrow \quad T_C = 1500 \text{ K}$$
$$\Rightarrow \quad \Delta T_{BC} = T_C - T_B$$
$$= 1500 - 300 = 1200 \text{ K}$$

So, $\quad \Delta U = \mu C_V \Delta T$
$$= 3 \times C_V \times 1200 = 3.6\, C_V \text{ kJ}$$

$\therefore \quad (\Delta Q)_{\text{isochoric}} = 3.6\, C_V$ kJ

Now, given that $\Delta Q_{\text{process } ABC} = 83.14$ kJ

$$\Rightarrow \Delta Q_{ABC} = \Delta Q_{\text{isothermal}} + \Delta Q_{\text{isochoric}}$$
$$\Rightarrow \quad 83.14 = 12.03 + 3.6\, C_V$$
$$\Rightarrow \quad C_V = 19.75 \text{ J/mol-K}$$

and $\quad C_p = C_V + R = 19.75 + 8.31$
$$= 28.05 \text{ J/mol -K}$$

$$\therefore \quad \gamma = \frac{C_p}{C_V} = \frac{28.05}{19.75} = 1.42$$

Work Done in a Cyclic Process

When a system returns back to its initial state after undergoing a series of changes, then this process is called **cyclic process**.

As both initial and final states are same in a cyclic process, $\Delta U = U_f - U_i = 0$.

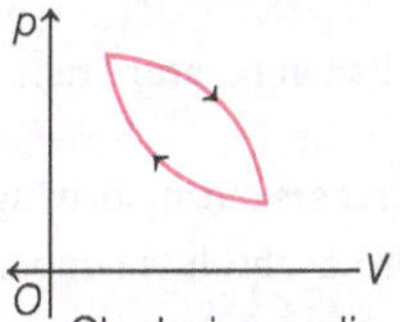

Clockwise cyclic process

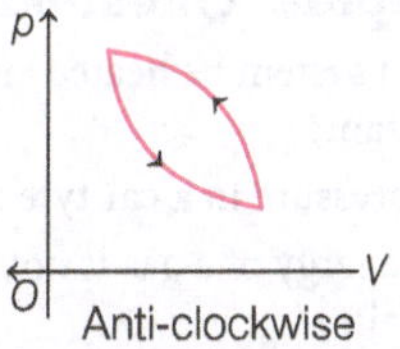

Anti-clockwise cyclic process

For a cyclic process, *p-V* graph is a closed curve and area enclosed by the curve is equal to the work done.

From first law of thermodynamics, $\Delta Q = \Delta U + \Delta W$

For cyclic process, $\Delta U = 0$ or $\Delta Q = \Delta W$

So, heat supplied to the system is converted into work done and *vice-versa.*

- If the cycle is clockwise, work done is positive and if the cycle is anti-clockwise, the work done is negative.
- A process in which the system do not return to its initial state after undergoing a series of change is known as **non-cyclic process.**

Example 11. **When a system goes from state *A* to state *B*, it is supplied with 400 J of heat and it does 100 J of work.**

(i) For process $A \rightarrow B$, what is the change in internal energy ?

(ii) If the system moves from *B* to *A*, what will be change in system, internal energy?

(iii) If in moving from *A* to *B* along a different path, where work done on the system is 400 J, how much heat does it absorb for this path?

Sol. (i) From first law of thermodynamics,

$$\Delta U_{AB} = \Delta Q_{AB} - \Delta W_{AB}$$
$$= (400 - 100) \text{ J} = 300 \text{ J}$$

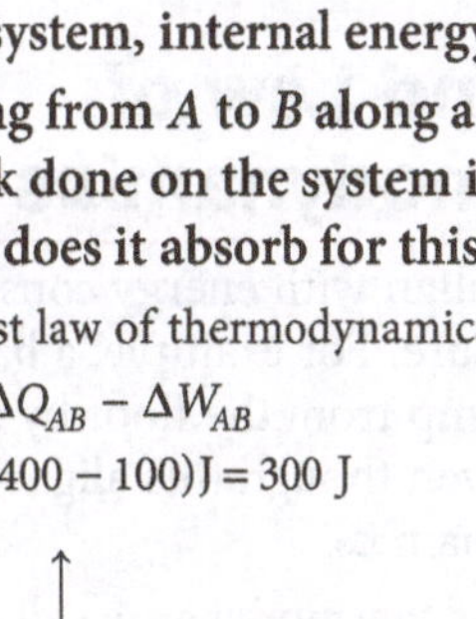

(ii) As ΔU for a closed path is zero, $\Delta U_{AB} + \Delta U_{BA} = 0$

$$\Delta U_{BA} = -\Delta U_{AB} = -300 \text{ J}$$

(iii) As ΔU_{AB} is same for any other paths so

$$\Delta U_{AB} = \Delta Q - \Delta W \Rightarrow 300 \text{ J} = \Delta Q - (-400 \text{ J})$$
$$\Rightarrow \quad \Delta Q = -100 \text{ J}$$

Quick Test 2

Conceptual Questions

1. Can a system be heated and its temperature remain constant? NCERT Exemplar
2. Air pressure in a car tyre increases during driving. Why?
3. The energy of a gas is not zero at absolute temperature. Explain
4. When ice melts, then change in internal energy is greater than the heat supplied, why?
5. Two isothermal curves do not intersect each other, why?
6. In the given p-V diagrams, find which curve represents
   (i) isothermal process,
   (ii) adiabatic process for
   (a) monoatomic
   (b) diatomic
   (c) triatomic gas.

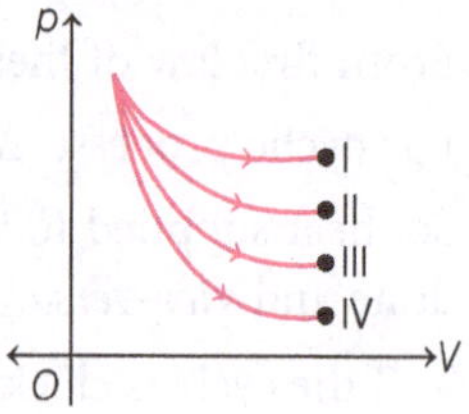

Numerical Questions

7. A person of mass 60 kg wants to lose 5 kg by going up and down a 10 m high stairs. Assume he burns twice as much fat while going up than coming down. If 1 kg of fat is burnt on expending 7000 kcal, how many times must he go up and down to reduce his weight by 5 kg?
8. A geyser heats water flowing at the rate of 3.0 L/min from 27°C to 77°C. If the geyser operates on a gas burner, what is the rate of consumption of the fuel if its heat of combustion is 4.0×10^4 J/g? NCERT
9. Find the values of two molar specific heats of nitrogen.
   Given, $\gamma = 1.41$ and $R = 8.31\text{ J mol}^{-1}\text{K}^{-1}$.
10. Consider a p-V diagram in which the path followed by one mole of perfect gas in a cylindrical container is shown.
   (i) Find the work done when the gas is taken from state 1 to state 2.
   (ii) What is the ratio of temperatures T_1/T_2, if $V_2 = 2V_1$?

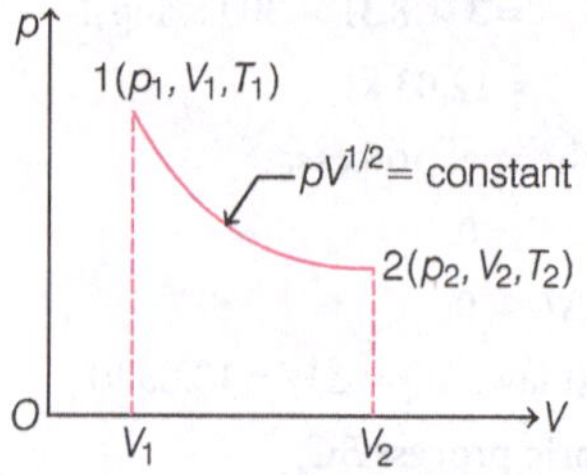

   (iii) Given the internal energy for one mole of gas at temperature T is $(3/2)RT$, find the heat supplied to the gas when it is taken from states 1 to 2, with $V_2 = 2V_1$.

Answers

7. 16.3×10^3 times 8. 15.75 g/min 9. 28.623 J/mol-K

For Solutions, See QR Code on Pg. 398

11.6 Second Law of Thermodynamics

Many processes align with energy conservation but are impossible in nature. For example, a ball cannot spontaneously jump from the floor by gaining heat energy from it, even though this aligns with the first law of thermodynamics.

The second law of thermodynamics disallows some processes consistent with the first law of thermodynamics. It has two statetments which are given below.

(i) Kelvin-Planck's Statement

It is impossible to design an engine that extract heat and fully utilizes into work without producing any other effect.

(ii) Clausius Statement

It is impossible for a self acting machine to transfer heat from a colder body to a hotter one without the aid of an external agency.

Reversible and Irreversible Process

Reversible Process

A process which could be reserved in such a way that the system and its surrounding returns exactly to their initial states with no other changes in the universe is known as **reversible process.**

A process is reversible only if it is Quasi-Static and there are no dissipative effects.

The **conditions for reversibility** are

(i) There must be complete absence of dissipative forces such as friction, viscosity, electric resistance, etc.

(ii) The direct and reverse processes must take place infinitely slowly.

(iii) The temperature of the system must not differ appreciably from its surroundings.

Some examples of reversible process are

(i) All isothermal and adiabatic changes are reversible, if they are performed very slowly.

(ii) When a certain amount of heat is absorbed by ice, it melts. If the same amount of heat is removed from it, the water formed in the direct process will be converted into ice.

(iii) An extremely slow extension or contraction of a spring without setting up oscillations.

(iv) When a perfectly elastic ball falls from some height on a perfectly elastic horizontal plane, the ball rises to the initial height.

(v) Very slow evaporation or condensation.

Irreversible Process

Any process which is not reversible exactly is an irreversible process. All natural processes such as conduction, radiation, radioactive decay etc., are irreversible processes.

All practical processes such as free expansion, Joule-Thomson expansion, electrical heating of a wire are also irreversible.

Irreversibility Arises Mainly From Two Causes

(i) Many processes (like diffusion of gases, decay of organic matter) take the system to non-equilibrium states.

(ii) Many processes involve the dissipative forces like friction, viscosity, inelasticity, etc.

Some examples of irreversible processes are given below

(i) When a steel ball is allowed to fall on an inelastic lead sheet, its kinetic energy changes into heat energy by friction. The heat energy raises the temperature of lead sheet. No reverse transformation of heat energy occurs.

(ii) The sudden and fast stretching of a spring may produce vibrations in it. Now, a part of the energy is dissipated. This is the case of irreversible process.

(iii) Sudden expansion or contraction and rapid evaporation or condensation are examples of irreversible processes.

(iv) The passage of an electric current through a resistor is irreversible.

(v) Heat transfer between bodies at different temperatures is also irreversible.

(vi) Joule-Thomson effect is irreversible because on reversing the flow of gas, a similar cooling or heating effect is not observed.

Carnot Engine

A reversible heat engine operating between two temperatures is called a Carnot engine.

- A Carnot engine is free from all the limitations of a practical engine.
- While it cannot be realised in real-world applications, it serves as a standard against which the performance of actual engines can be measured.

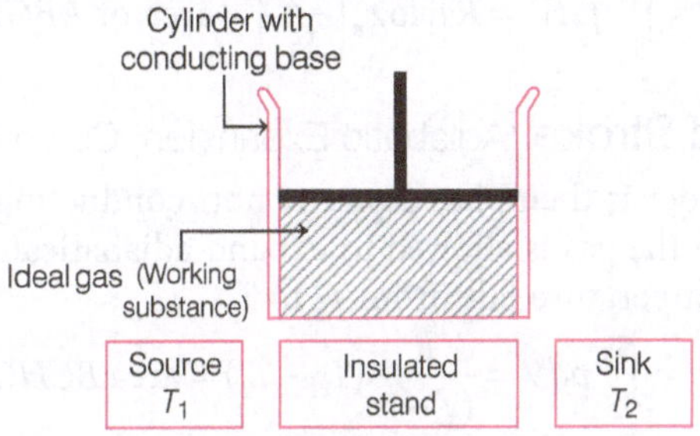

A Carnot engine

The main parts of a Carnot engine are as follows

(i) A **cylinder** contains perfectly non-conducting walls and a perfectly conducting base. Also, it contains a perfect gas as working substance fitted with a non-conducting frictionless piston.

(ii) A **source** of infinite thermal capacity maintained at constant higher temperature T_1.

(iii) A **sink** of infinite thermal capacity maintained at constant lower temperature T_2.

(iv) A perfectly non-conducting i.e. insulated stand for the cylinder.

(v) An ideal gas used as a working substance in the cylinder.

Carnot Cycle

As the engine works, the working substance of the engine undergoes a cycle known as Carnot cycle.

The Carnot cycle consists of the following four strokes.

First Stroke (Isothermal Expansion, Curve AB)

The cylinder containing one mole of an ideal gas as working substance allowed to expand slowly at the constant temperature T_1 by putting it on the source.

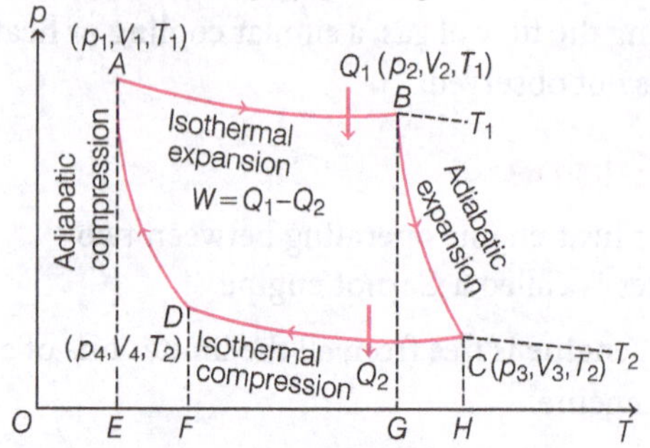

Various processes in Carnot cycle

Work done = heat absorbed by the system

$$W_1 = Q_1 = \int_{V_1}^{V_2} pdV = RT_1 \log_e\left(\frac{V_2}{V_1}\right) = \text{area of } ABGEA$$

Second Stroke (Adiabatic Expansion, Curve BC)

The cylinder is then placed on the non-conducting stand and the gas is allowed to expand adiabatically till the temperature falls from T_1 to T_2.

$$W_2 = \int_{V_2}^{V_3} pdV = \frac{R}{(\gamma - 1)}(T_1 - T_2) = \text{area } BCHGB$$

Third Stroke (Isothermal Compression, Curve CD)

The cylinder is placed on the sink and the gas is compressed at constant temperature T_2.

Work done = Heat released by the system

$$W_3 = Q_2 = -\int_{V_3}^{V_4} pdV = -RT_2 \log_e \frac{V_4}{V_3}$$

$$= RT_2 \log_e \frac{V_3}{V_4} = \text{area } CDFHC$$

Fourth Stroke

(Adiabatic Compression, Curve DA)

Finally, the cylinder is again placed on non-conducting stand and the compression is continued so that gas returns to its initial stage.

$$W_4 = -\int_{V_4}^{V_1} pdV = -\frac{R}{\gamma - 1}(T_2 - T_1)$$

$$= \frac{R}{\gamma - 1}(T_1 - T_2) = \text{area of } ADFEA$$

Efficiency of Carnot Cycle

The efficiency of engine is defined as the ratio of work done to the heat supplied, i.e.

$$\eta = \frac{\text{Work done}}{\text{Heat input}} = \frac{W_{net}}{Q_1}$$

Net work done during the complete cycle is

$$W = W_1 + W_2 + (-W_3) + (-W_4)$$

$$= W_1 - W_3 = \text{area } ABCDA \qquad (\text{as } W_2 = W_4)$$

$$\therefore \quad \eta = \frac{W}{Q_1} = \frac{W_1 - W_3}{W_1} = \frac{Q_1 - Q_2}{Q_1} = 1 - \frac{Q_2}{Q_1}$$

or $$\eta = 1 - \frac{RT_2 \log_e (V_3/V_4)}{RT_1 \log_e (V_2/V_1)} \qquad \ldots \text{(i)}$$

Since, points B and C lie on same adiabatic curve

$$\therefore \quad T_1 V_2^{\gamma-1} = T_2 V_3^{\gamma-1}$$

or $$\frac{T_1}{T_2} = \left(\frac{V_3}{V_2}\right)^{\gamma-1} \qquad \ldots \text{(ii)}$$

Also, points D and A lie on the same adiabatic curve

$$\therefore \quad T_1 V_1^{\gamma-1} = T_2 V_4^{\gamma-1}$$

or $$\frac{T_1}{T_2} = \left(\frac{V_4}{V_1}\right)^{\gamma-1} \qquad \ldots \text{(iii)}$$

From Eqs. (ii) and (iii), we get $\frac{V_3}{V_2} = \frac{V_4}{V_1}$

or $$\frac{V_3}{V_4} = \frac{V_2}{V_1} \Rightarrow \log_e\left(\frac{V_3}{V_4}\right) = \log_e\left(\frac{V_2}{V_1}\right)$$

On substituting values in Eq. (i), we get

> Efficiency of Carnot engine, $\eta = 1 - \frac{T_2}{T_1}$

- The efficiency of the Carnot engine depends only on the temperatures of source and sink.
- The efficiency of Carnot engine does not depend on the nature of the working substance.
- The efficiency of Carnot engine will be 100%, if the temperature of the sink is 0 K. As practically, we cannot attain a sink at 0 K, so it is not possible to have 100% efficiency.
- No engine operating between two temperatures can have efficiency greater than that of the Carnot engine.

Carnot Theorems

According to Carnot theorem,

(i) A heat engine working between the two given temperatures T_1 of hot reservoir i.e. source and T_2 of cold reservoir i.e. sink cannot have efficiency more than that of the Carnot engine.

(ii) The efficiency of the Carnot engine is independent of the nature of working susbtance.

Coefficient of Performance of Carnot Engine

For Carnot refrigerator, $\frac{Q_1}{Q_2} = \frac{T_1}{T_2}$

$$\Rightarrow \quad \frac{Q_1 - Q_2}{Q_2} = \frac{T_1 - T_2}{T_2} \text{ or } \frac{Q_2}{Q_1 - Q_2} = \frac{T_2}{T_1 - T_2}$$

So, Coefficient of performance, $\beta = \frac{T_2}{T_1 - T_2}$

where, T_1 = temperature of surrounding
and T_2 = temperature of cold body.

It is clear that $\beta = 0$ when $T_2 = 0$, i.e. the coefficient of performance will be zero, if the cold body is at the temperature equal to absolute zero.

Example 12. Consider a Carnot cycle operating between $T_1 = 500$ K and $T_2 = 300$K producing 1 kJ of mechanical work per cycle. Find the heat transferred to/by the engine by/to the reservoir. NCERT Exemplar

Sol. Here, $T_1 = 500$ K, $T_2 = 300$ K, $W = 1$ kJ $= 1000$ J

As, efficiency, $\eta = \frac{W}{Q} = \frac{T_1 - T_2}{T_1}$

So, heat transferred to engine by the hot reservoir in cycle.

$$\therefore \quad Q_1 = \frac{WT_1}{T_1 - T_2} = \frac{1000 \times 500}{500 - 300}$$

$$= 2500 \text{ J or } 2.5 \text{ kJ}$$

and heat transferred by the engine to the cold reservoir in one cycle,

$$Q_2 = Q_1 - W = 2.5 \text{ kJ} - 1 \text{ kJ} = 1.5 \text{ kJ}$$

Example 13. A Carnot engine takes 10^6 cal of heat from a source at 827°C and exhaust it to a sink 27°C. How much work does it give or output? What is engine efficiency? Also, find out the coefficient of performance of the engine, if it is used in reverse direction.

Sol. Given, $T_1 = 827 + 273 = 1100$ K

$$T_2 = 27 + 273 = 300 \text{ K}, Q_1 = 10^6 \text{ cal}$$

$$Q_2 = \frac{T_2}{T_1} \times Q_1 = \frac{300}{1100} \times 10^6$$

$$= 2.72 \times 10^5 \text{ cal}$$

$$\text{Efficiency} (\eta) = \left(1 - \frac{T_2}{T_1}\right) \times 100\%$$

$$= \left(1 - \frac{300}{1100}\right) \times 100 = 72.72\%$$

As, coefficient of performance,

$$\beta = \frac{T_2}{T_1 - T_2} = \frac{300}{1100 - 300} = \frac{300}{800} = 0.375$$

Quick Test 3

Conceptual Questions

1. Which thermodynamic law put restrictions on the complete conversion of heat into work?
2. If the temperature of the sink is increased, what will happen to the efficiency of Carnot engine?
3. Find the efficiency of the Carnot engine working between boiling point and freezing point of water.
4. Draw p-V diagram of a Carnot cycle.
5. Explain why the efficiency of a reversible engine is maximum?

Numerical Questions

6. Consider a Carnot cycle operating between $T_1 = 500$ K and $T_2 = 300$ K producing 1 kJ of mechanical work per cycle. Find the heat transferred to the engine by the reservoirs. *NCERT Exemplar*
7. A Carnot engine is operating between 600 K and 200 K. Consider that the actual energy produced is 2 kJ per kilocalorie of heat absorbed. Compare the real efficiency with the efficiency of Carnot engine.
8. A Carnot engine with ideal gas is used for freezing water which is at 0°C. The engine is operated by a 600 W electric motor having an efficiency of 50%. Find time to freeze 25 kg of water. Take 25°C and 0°C as the source and sink. Latent heat of ice $= 333 \times 10^3 \text{ J kg}^{-1}$
9. The efficiency of a Carnot engine is 1/2. If the sink temperature is reduced by 100°C, then engine efficiency becomes 2/3. Find
   (i) sink temperature
   (ii) source temperature
   (iii) Explain, why a Carnot engine cannot have 100% efficiency?
10. Two Carnot engines A and B are operated in series. The first one A receives heat at 800 K and rejects to a reservoir at temperature T K. The second engine B receives the heat rejected by the first engine and in turn rejects to a heat reservoir at 300 K. Calculate the temperature T K for the following cases.
    (i) When the outputs of the two engines are equal.
    (ii) When the efficiencies of the two engines are equal.

Answers

6. 2500 J *7.* 0.71 *8.* 3049.45 s *9.* (i) 300 K (ii) 600 K
10. (i) 550 K (ii) 489.9 K

For Solutions, See QR Code on Pg. 398

Mind Map

Thermodynamics

Zeroth Law of Thermodynamics

- If two systems *A* and *B* are in thermodynamic equilibrium with a system *C*, they will also be in thermodynamic equilibrium mutually.

Internal Energy

- Energy due to the configuration and motion of the molecules of thermodynamical system is called internal energy.
- **Internal Kinetic Energy U_K** This is due to the motion of molecules.
- **Internal Potential Energy U_P** This is due to the configuration of molecules.

Thus, total internal energy, $U = U_K + U_P$

First Law of Thermodynamics

- Heat given to a system is equal to the sum of work done by the system and increase in the internal energy of the system.

$Q = \Delta U + \Delta W$

- **Change in Internal Energy,**

$\Delta U = dQ - \Delta W$

- **Limitation** This law does not explain the direction of flow of heat, whether it flows from hot rod to cold rod or *vice-versa*.

It is impossible to convert entire heat into work.

Second Law of Thermodynamics

- The principle that put a restriction on the first law of thermodynamics is known as second law of thermodynamics.

Mathematically, this law is represented as

$$\Delta S_{uni} > 0$$

where, ΔS_{uni} is the change in the entropy of the universe.

Example The process of decaying organisms is showcase the tendency of nature towards increasing entropy.

Carnot Engine

- Carnot engine is an ideal heat engine which is proposed by Sadi Carnot in 1824. The reversible engine which operates between two temperatures.

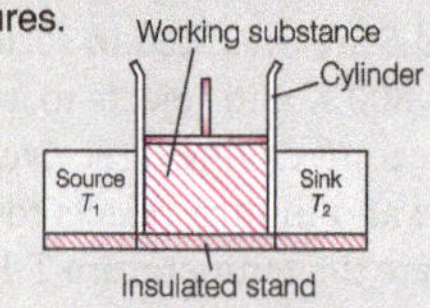

- **Efficiency of Carnot Engine**

The ratio of work done to the heat supplied

i.e., $\eta = \dfrac{\text{Work done}}{\text{Heat input}} = \dfrac{W_{net}}{Q_1}$

In cyclic process $\Delta U = 0$, therefore

$$\Delta W = \Delta Q$$

Final efficiency of Carnot engine,

$$\eta = 1 - \frac{T_2}{T_1} = 1 - \frac{Q_2}{Q_1}$$

Thermodynamics Processes

Quasi-Statics Process

- A hypothetical process in which at every stage the system remains in equilibrium.

Practically, a process that are sufficiently slow are consider as quasi-static process.

Isothermal Process

- That process in which temperature of a thermodynamical system remains constant.

Example Melting of ice (or any solid) at melting point.

- ***p*-*V* Diagram**

Follows Boyle's law,

$p_i V_i = p_f V_f$

Thus, pV = constant

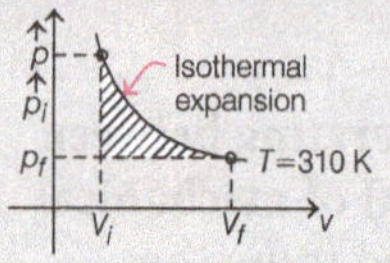

- **Work done**

Work done=Area under *p*-*V* graph

$$W_{iso} = 2.303\, nRT \log \left(\frac{V_f}{V_i}\right)$$

If $V_f > V_i$, then $W > 0$ (Isothermal expansion)

If $V_f < V_i$, then $W < 0$ (Isothermal compression)

Isobaric Process

- Pressure of the system remains constant.
- Work done,

$W = \mu R (T_f - T_i)$

- As temperature of the gas changes, so its internal energy also changes.

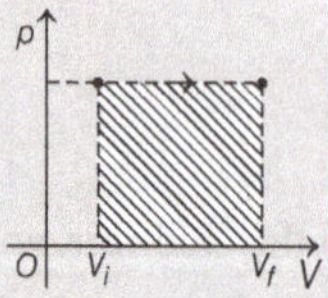

Adiabatic Process

- The process, in which there is no exchange of heat between system and the surrounding take place.

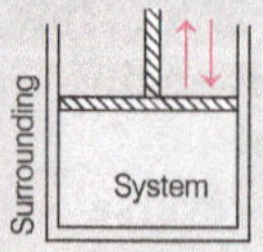

- ***p*-*V* Diagram**

From first law of thermodyamics,

$\Delta Q = \Delta U + \Delta W$

Adiabatic process,

pV^{γ} = Constant

Thus, $p_i V_i^{\gamma} = p_f V_f^{\gamma}$

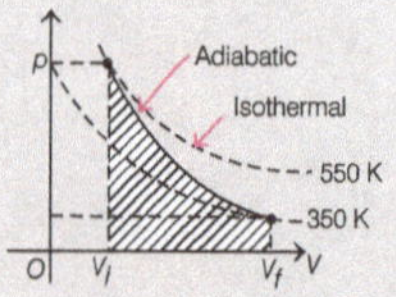

- **Work done**

Work done in an adiabatic process,

$$W = \int_{V_i}^{V_f} p\,dV = \int_{V_i}^{V_f} \frac{K}{V^{\gamma}}\,dV$$

Work done, $W = \dfrac{\mu R (T_i - T_f)}{\gamma - 1}$

Heat

- The energy that exchanged between a system and its surrounding because of the temperature difference between them.
- SI unit of heat is joule.

Work

- By work, we mean work done by the system or on the system.
- Work done, $W = \int_{V_i}^{V_f} dW = \int_{V_i}^{V_f} p\,dV$
- If system expands, $V_f > V_i$ i.e., W = positive
- If system contracts, $V_f < V_i$ i.e., W = negative

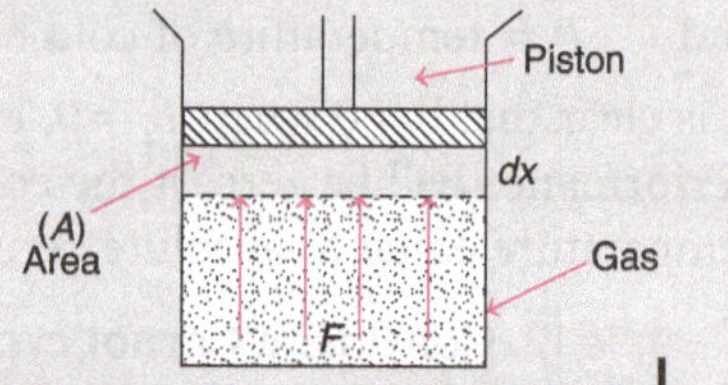

Specific Heat Capacity

- The amount of heat required to change the temperature of unit mass of a substance by unity. $s = \dfrac{1}{m}\left(\dfrac{\Delta Q}{\Delta T}\right)$

Molar Specific Heat Capacity

- Heat capacity per mole is known as molar specific heat capacity.

$$C = \frac{S}{\mu} = \frac{1}{\mu}\left(\frac{\Delta Q}{\Delta T}\right)$$

- SI unit of molar specific heat capacity is J/mol-K

Relation Between C_p and C_V

- For an ideal gas, the relation between C_p and C_V is given as,

$$C_p - C_V = R$$

This is called **Mayer's formula**.

- The ratio of C_p and C_V is notified by γ.

i.e., $\gamma = C_p / C_V$

Here, $C_p = \left(\dfrac{\Delta Q}{\Delta T}\right)_p$ and $C_V = \left(\dfrac{\Delta Q}{\Delta T}\right)_V$

Isochoric Process

- Volume of the system remains constant. If heat added to system, its pressure increases and if heat extracted, pressure will be reduced.
- Work done, $\Delta W = 0$
- Change in internal energy, $\Delta U = \mu C_V \Delta T$

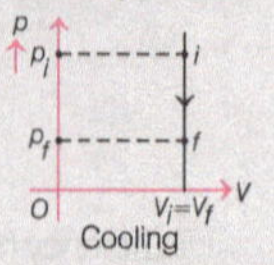

EXAM PATTERN QUESTIONS

Objective Type Questions

Multiple Choice Questions (MCQs)

1. If two systems are in thermal equilibrium with each other, it means their

(a) masses are equal, temperatures may be unequal
(b) temperatures are equal
(c) masses and temperatures are equal
(d) None of the above

2. Three copper blocks of masses M_1, M_2 and M_3 kg respectively are brought into thermal contact till they reach equilibrium. Before contact, they were at T_1, T_2, T_3 ($T_1 > T_2 > T_3$). Assuming there is no heat loss to the surroundings, the equilibrium temperature T is (s is specific heat of copper) **Competency Based Que.**

(a) $T = \dfrac{T_1 + T_2 + T_3}{3}$

(b) $T = \dfrac{M_1T_1 + M_2T_2 + M_3T_3}{M_1 + M_2 + M_3}$

(c) $T = \dfrac{M_1T_1 + M_2T_2 + M_3T_3}{3(M_1 + M_2 + M_3)}$

(d) $T = \dfrac{M_1T_1s + M_2T_2s + M_3T_3s}{M_1 + M_2 + M_3}$

3. A system is provided with 200 cal of heat and the work done by the system on the surroundings is 40 J, then its internal energy

(a) increases by 600 J
(b) decreases by 800 J
(c) increases by 800 J
(d) decreases by 50 J

4. Which of the following is not a state function?

(a) Temperature (b) Entropy
(c) Pressure (d) Work

5. In the following indicator diagram, the net amount of work done will be **Competency Based Que.**

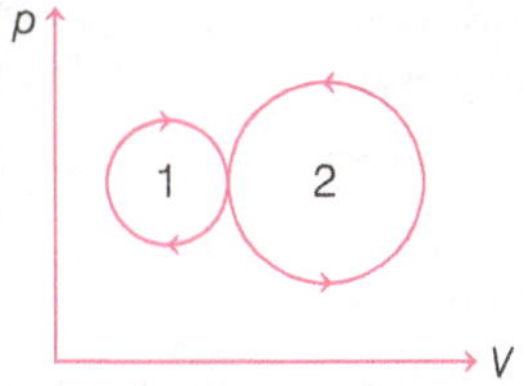

(a) positive (b) negative (c) zero (d) infinity

6. Based on the first law of thermodynamics, which one of the following is correct?

(a) For an isothermal process, $Q = +W$
(b) For an isochoric process, $\Delta U = -Q$
(c) For an adiabatic process, $\Delta U = -W$
(d) For a cyclic process, $Q = -W$

7. An ideal gas undergoes cyclic process ABCDA as shown in given p-V diagram. The amount of work done by the gas is **NCERT Exemplar**

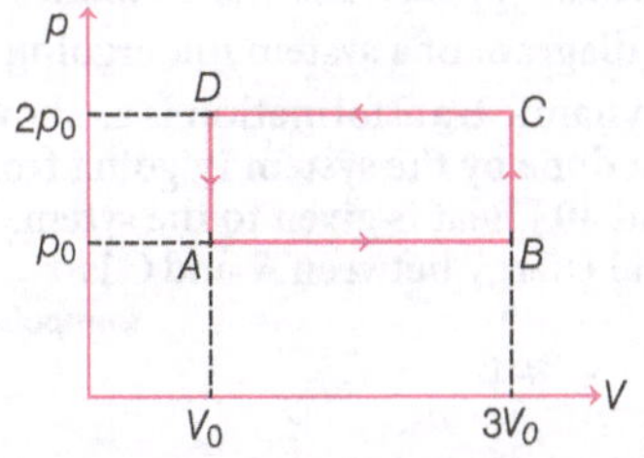

(a) $6p_0V_0$ (b) $-2p_0V_0$ (c) $+2p_0V_0$ (d) $+4p_0V_0$

8. For isothermal expansion of an ideal gas,

(a) ΔU = positive (b) ΔQ = positive
(c) ΔW = positive (d) Both (b) and (c)

9. In the following figure, four curves A, B, C and D are shown. The curves are

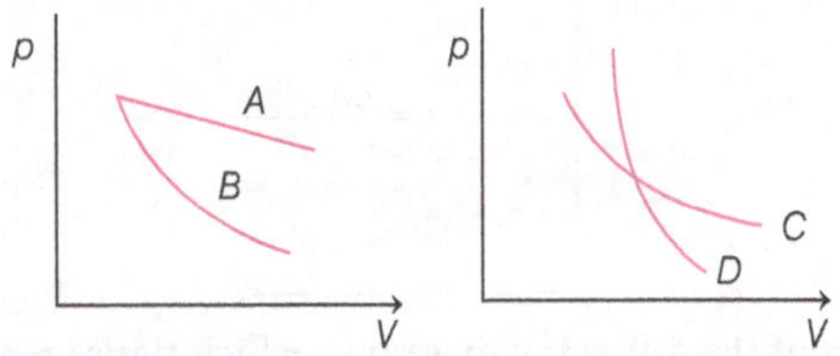

(a) isothermal for A and D while adiabatic for B and C
(b) adiabatic for A and C while isothermal for B and D
(c) isothermal for A and B while adiabatic for C and D
(d) isothermal for A and C while adiabatic for B and D

10. Two samples A and B of a gas initially at the same pressure and temperature are compressed from volume V to V/2 (A isothermally and B adiabatically). The final pressure of A is **Competency Based Que.**

(a) greather than the final pressure of B
(b) equal to the final pressure of B
(c) less than the final pressure of B
(d) twice the final pressure of B

11. An ideal gas undergoes a four step cycle as shown in p-V diagram. During this cycle, heat is absorbed by gas in

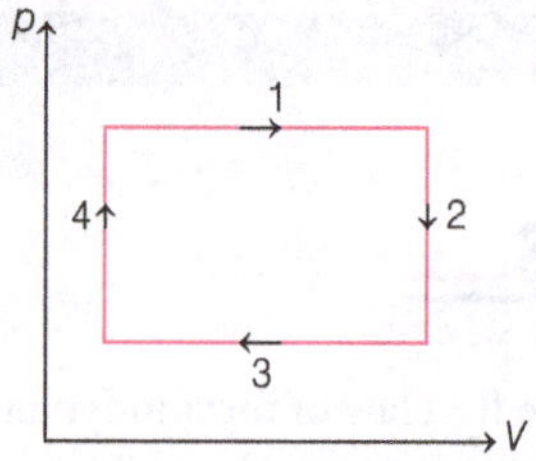

(a) Steps 1 and 2 (b) Steps 1 and 3
(c) Steps 1 and 4 (d) Steps 2 and 4

12. Cylinders A and B of equal capacity are conceded each other via a stopcock. A contains an ideal gas at standard temperature and pressure. B is completely evacuated. The entire system is thermally insulated. The stopcock is suddenly opened. The process is

(a) isothermal (b) adiabatic (c) isochoric (d) isobaric

13. The p-V diagram of a system undergoing thermodynamic transformation is as shown in figure. The work done by the system in going from A→B→C is 30 J and 40 J heat is given to the sytem. The change in internal energy between A and C is **Competency Based Que.**

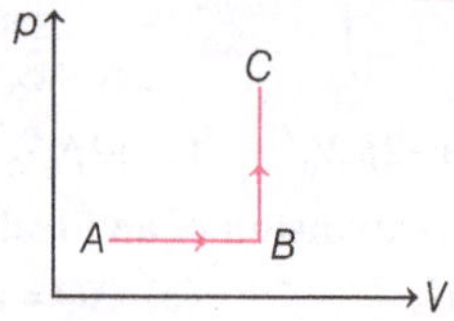

(a) 10 J (b) 70 J (c) 84 J (d) 134 J

14. Consider p-V diagram for an ideal gas shown in figure.

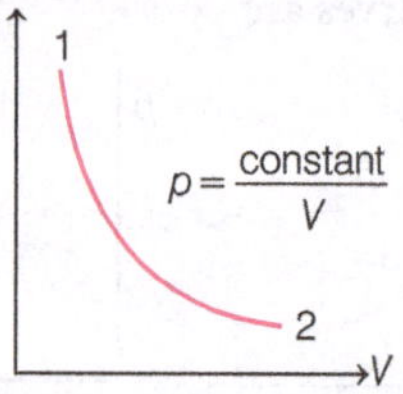

Out of the following diagrams, which figure represents the T-p diagram? **NCERT Exemplar**

(a)
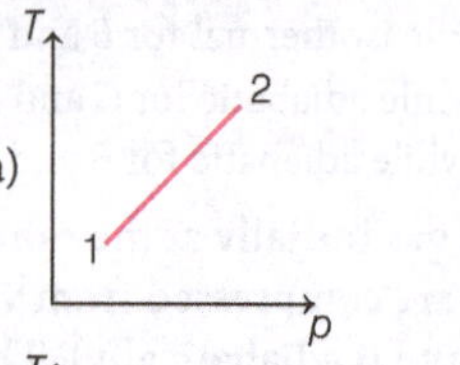

(b)
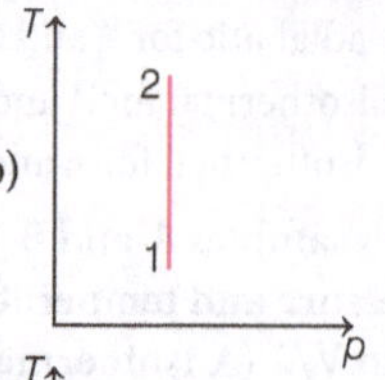

(c)
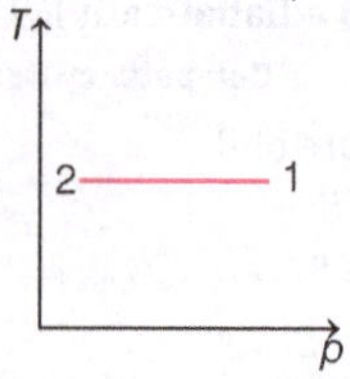

(d)
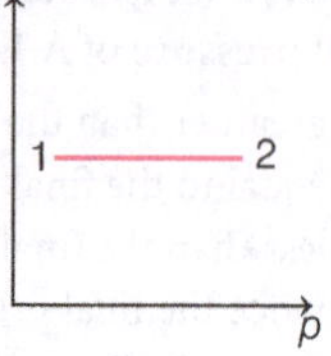

15. If an average person jogs, he produces 14.5×10^3 cal/min. This is removed by the evaporation of sweat. The amount of sweat evaporated per minute is (assuming 1 kg requires 580×10^3 cal for evaporation) **NCERT Exemplar**

(a) 0.25 kg (b) 2.25 kg (c) 0.05 kg (d) 0.20 kg

16. Consider two containers A and B containing identical gases at the same pressure, volume and temperature. The gas in container A is compressed to half of its original volume isothermally while the gas in container B is compressed to half of its original value adiabatically. The ratio of final pressure of gas in B to that of gas in A is **NCERT Exemplar**

(a) $2^{\gamma-1}$ (b) $\left(\frac{1}{2}\right)^{\gamma-1}$

(c) $\left(\frac{1}{1-\gamma}\right)^2$ (d) $\left(\frac{1}{\gamma-1}\right)^2$

17. According to Carnot, which type of engine working between two temperatures T_1 and T_2 have maximum efficiency?

(a) Reversible engine
(b) Irreversible engine
(c) External combustion engine
(d) Diesel engine

18. Match the Column I with Column II.

Column I	Column II
A. First law of thermodynamics	1. $\Delta U = Q + W$
B. Second law of thermodynamics	2. Entropy of an isolated system always increases
C. Enthalpy (H)	3. $H = U + pV$
D. Isothermal process	4. Temperature remains constant during the process

(a) A-1, B-2, C-3, D-4 (b) A-4, B-2, C-3, D-1
(c) A-2, B-1, C-4, D-3 (d) A-3, B-4, C-2, D-1

19. Match the Column I with Column II.

Column I	Column II
A. Work done in an isothermal process	1. $p_{ext}\Delta V$
B. Heat capacity at constant pressure	2. $C_p = \frac{\Delta Q}{\Delta T}$
C. Adiabatic process	3. $\Delta Q = 0$
D. Specific heat at constant volume	4. $C_V = \frac{R}{\gamma - 1}$

(a) A-1, B-2, C-3, D-4 (b) A-4, B-1, C-3, D-2
(c) A-2, B-3, C-4, D-1 (d) A-3, B-2, C-1, D-4

Assertion–Reason

Directions *(Q.No. 20-28) In the following questions, two statements are given- one labelled Assertion (A) and the other labelled Reason (R). Select the correct answer to these questions from the codes (a), (b), (c) and (d) as given below.*

(a) Both Assertion and Reason are true and Reason is the correct explanation of Assertion.

(b Both Assertion and Reason are true but Reason is not the correct explanation of Assertion.

(c) Assertion is true but Reason is false.

(d) Assertion is false but Reason is true.

20. **Assertion (A)** The ratio of specific heat of a gas at constant pressure and specific heat at constant volume for a diatomic gas is more than that for a monoatomic gas.

Reason (R) The molecules of a monoatomic gas have more degree of freedom than those of a diatomic gas.

Competency Based Que.

21. **Assertion (A)** When a bottle of cold carbonated drink is opened, a fog forms around opening.

Reason (R) Adiabatic expansion of gas causes lowering of temperature and condensation of water vapours.

Competency Based Que.

22. **Assertion (A)** Work done by a gas in isothermal expansion is more than the work done by the gas in the adiabatic expansion.

Reason (R) Temperature remains constant in isothermal expansion and not in adiabatic expansion.

23. **Assertion (A)** State variables are required to specify the equilibrium state of the system.

Reason (R) Pressure is an intensive state variable.

24. **Assertion (A)** In isothermal process for ideal gas, change in internal energy is zero.

Reason (R) No heat is supplied to system or rejected by system, in an isothermal process.

25. **Assertion (A)** Reversible Carnot engine with one particular substance cannot be more efficient than the one using another substance.

Reason (R) Efficiency of Carnot engine = T_2/T_1.

Competency Based Que.

26. **Assertion (A)** We cannot change the temperature of a body without giving (or taking) heat to (or from) it.

Reason (R) According to principle of conservation of energy, total energy of a system should remains conserved.

27. **Assertion (A)** Thermodynamic processes in nature are irreversible.

Reason (R) Dissipative effects cannot be eliminated.

28. **Assertion (A)** The Zeroth law said that, when two systems A and B, are in thermal equilibrium, there must be a physical quantity that has the same value for both.

Reason (R) The physical quantity which is same for both system is temperature.

Case Based Questions

Directions *(Q.Nos. 29-31) These questions are case study based questions. Read the following paragraph and answer the questions on the basis of same.*

29. **First law of thermodynamics is a statement of conservation of energy applied to any system in which energy transfer from or to the surroundings is taken into account.**

It states that heat given to a system is either used in doing external work or it increases the internal energy of the system or both.

i.e. Heat supplied, $\Delta Q = \Delta U + \Delta W$

where, ΔQ = heat supplied to the system by the surroundings,

ΔW = work done by the system on the surroundings

and ΔU = change in internal energy of the system.

(i) For an ideal gas, internal energy depends on
(a) only molecular kinetic energy
(b) only potential energy of the molecules
(c) both kinetic and potential energies of the molecules
(d) None of the above

(ii) The internal energy of a system could be changed
(a) by extracting heat from the system
(b) by doing work done on the system
(c) if system do some work on the surroundings
(d) All of the above

(iii) $(\Delta Q - \Delta W)$ is
(a) path dependent (b) path independent
(c) equal to ΔU (d) Both (b) and (c)

(iv) Using first law of thermodynamics, which is true for isothermal expansion of an ideal gas?
(a) ΔU = positive (b) ΔQ = positive
(c) ΔW = positive (d) Both (b) and (c)

(v) A system is provided with 200 cal of heat and the work done by the system on the surroundings is 40 J, then its internal energy
(a) increases by 600 J (b) decreases by 800 J
(c) increases by 800 J (d) decreases by 50 J

30. **A heat engine is a device by which a system is made to undergo a cyclic process that results in conversion of heat in to work. Basically a heat engine consists of**

(i) hot reservation maintain at a higher temperature T_1

(ii) cold reservation maintained at a lower temperature T_2 and (iii) a working substance.

If in one cycle of it's operation the system draw, Q_1 heat from the hot reservoir, does W work and releases Q_2 heat to the cold reservoir than.

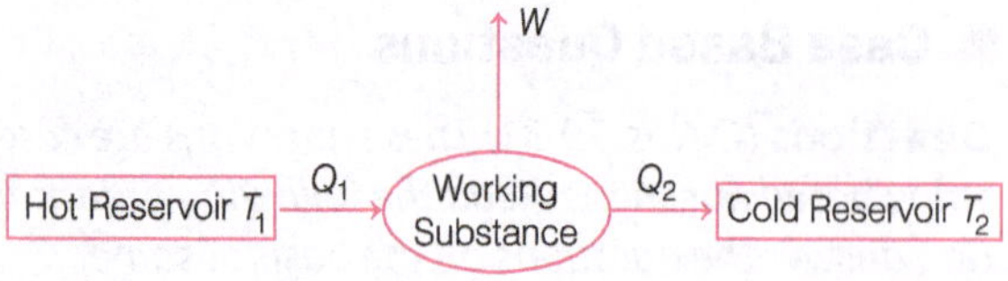

Efficiency of engine, $\eta_1 = \frac{W}{Q_1} = \frac{Q_1 - Q_2}{Q_1} = 1 - \frac{Q_2}{Q_1}$

(i) The area enclosed by a Carnot cycle represents.
(a) heat absorbed
(b) heat released
(c) amount of work done
(d) None of the above

(ii) A reversible heat engine *A* operates between 223°C and 123°C. The efficiency of engine is
(a) 15% (b) 20% (c) 25% (d) 30%

(iii) Another reversible engine *B* operates between temperature 123°C and T°C and has the efficiency 30%. The value of *T* will be
(a) 7°C (b) 10°C (c) 280°C (d) 320°C

(iv) Even Carnot engine cannot give 100% efficiency, because we cannot
(a) prevent radiation
(b) find ideal source
(c) eliminate friction
(d) reach absolute zero temperature

(v) The efficiency of heat engine
(a) more in plane area than hilly areas
(b) less in plane area than hilly areas
(c) remains same in both areas
(d) depends upon nature of working substance

31. An equilibrium state of a gas is completely specified by the values of pressure, volume, temperature and mass (and composition, if there is a mixture of gases). A gas allowed to expand freely against vacuum is not an equilibrium state.

During the rapid expansion, pressure of the gas may not be uniform throughout. Similarly, a mixture of gases undergoing an explosive chemical reaction is not an equilibrium state, again its temperature and pressure are not uniform. Now consider following system.

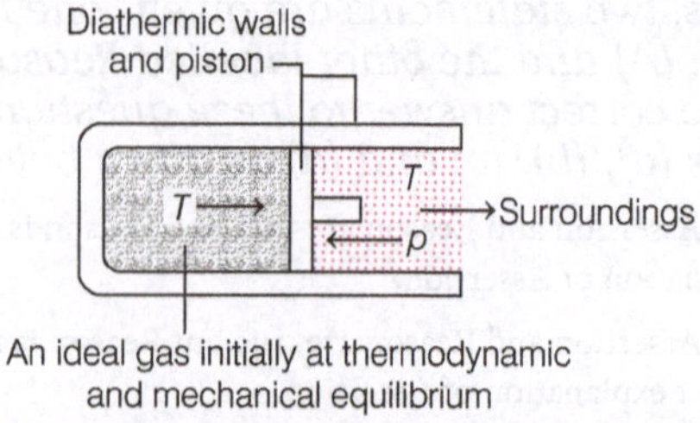

(i) If the external pressure is reduced suddenly, then
(a) the gas will expand suddenly which has non-equilibrium intermediate stages
(b) the piston will accelerate outwards
(c) Both (a) and (b)
(d) Neither (a) nor (b)

(ii) If a finite temperature difference exists between system and surroundings, then
(a) there will be a rapid exchange of heat between system and surroundings with non-equilibrium intermediate stages
(b) after sometime, the temperature and pressure of surroundings and system will become same
(c) Both (a) and (b)
(d) Neither (a) nor (b)

(iii) Choose the correct option.
(a) Thermodynamics is a microscopic science
(b) Thermodynamics results based on molecular description of the molecules of the gas
(c) *p*, *V* and *T* are state variables
(d) *Q* is a state variable

(iv) The internal energy of the given system could be changed
(a) by extracting heat from the system
(b) by doing work done on the system
(c) if system do some work on the surroundings
(d) All of the above

(v) A mixture of gases undergoing explosive chemical reaction
(a) is in equilibrium state during explosion
(b) have constant temperature and pressure values during explosion
(c) finally the gas will attained equilibrium state with its surroundings
(d) Both (b) and (c)

Subjective Questions

Very Short Answer Type Questions

1. (i) When work done is positive? **[1]**

(ii) Can a system be heated and its temperature remains constant? **NCERT Exemplar [1]**

2. (i) Is the internal energy of a gas a function of pressure? **[1]**

(ii) Can a ship be moved with the energy of the sea water? **[1]**

3. When we rub our palms, the temperature rises to a certain extent, why ?

4. What do you mean by an adiabatic wall and a diathermic wall ?

Short Answer Type Questions

5. Two bodies at different temperatures T_1 and T_2 are brought in contact. Under what condition, they settle to mean temperature (after they attain equilibrium) ? **NCERT Exemplar**

6. (i) Is it possible to increase the temperature of a gas without heating it? **[1½]**

(ii) Which one a solid, a liquid or a gas of same mass and at the same temperature has greatest internal energy? Give reason. **Competency Based Que. [1½]**

7. Arrange four paths shown in ascending order on the basis of (i) change in internal energy (ii) work done by the gas (iii) magnitude of energy transferred or heat.

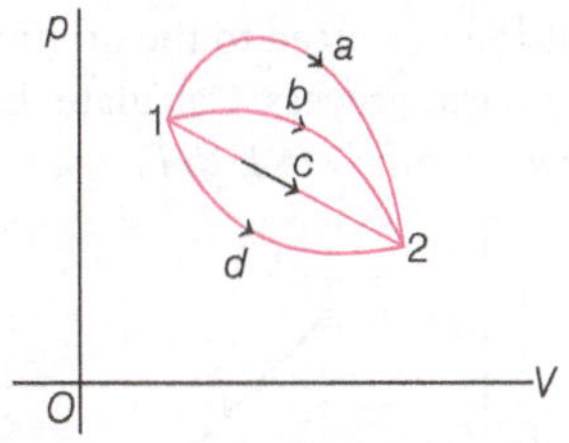

8. (i) First law of thermodynamics does not forbid flow of heat from lower temperature to higher temperature. Comment. **[1½]**

(ii) Find value of specific heat of a gas in isothermal process. **[1½]**

9. Consider a cycle tyre being filled with air by a pump. Let V be the volume of the tyre (fixed) and at each stroke of the pump $\Delta V (<< V)$ of air is transferred to the tube adiabtically. What is the work done when the pressure in the tube is increased from p_1 to p_2? **NCERT Exemplar**

10. (i) 500 J of work is done on a gas to reduce its volume by compression adiabatically. What is the change in internal energy of the gas? **[1]**

Explain, why?

(ii) The coolant in a chemical or a nuclear plant, i.e. the liquid used to prevent the different parts of a plant from getting too hot should have high specific heat. **[1]**

(iii) The climate of a harbour town has more temperature than that of a town in a desert at the same latitude. **[1]**

Long Answer Type Questions

11. A cycle followed by an engine (made of one mole of an ideal gas in a cylinder with a piston) is shown in figure. Find heat exchanged by the engine with the surroundings for following sections of the cycle. $[C_V = (3/2)R]$ **NCERT Exemplar**

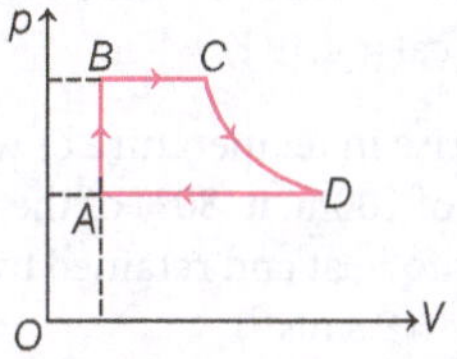

(i) AB : constant volume **[1]**

(ii) BC : constant pressure **[1]**

(iii) CD : adiabatic **[1]**

(iv) DA : constant pressure **[2]**

12. Consider that an ideal gas (n moles) is expanding in a process given by $p = f(V)$, which passes through a point (V_0, p_0). Show that the gas is absorbing heat at (p_0, V_0), if the slope of the curve $p = f(V)$ is larger than the slope of the adiabat passing through (p_0, V_0). **NCERT Exemplar**

13. Find work done during the cyclic process shown in indicator diagram.

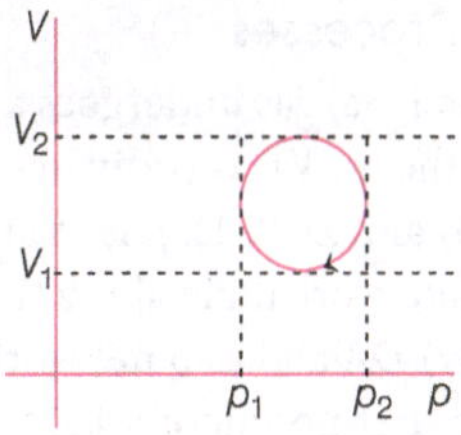

14. Explain with the suitable example that a reversible process must be carried slowly and a fast process is necessarily irreversible.

Numerical Problems

Internal Energy, Heat and Work

15. An electric heater supplies heat to a system at a rate of 100 W. If the system performs work at a rate of 75 J/s, at what rate, is the internal energy increasing? **NCERT**

16. The work of 146 kJ is performed in order to compress one kilo mole of gas adiabatically and in this process the temperature of the gas increases by 7° C. Identify the atomicity of the gas. (Take, $R = 8.3 \text{ J mol}^{-1}\text{K}^{-1}$)

17. Specific heat of argon at constant pressure is $0.125 \text{ cal g}^{-1}\text{K}^{-1}$ and at constant volume is $0.075 \text{ cal g}^{-1}\text{K}^{-1}$. Calculate the density of argon at STP. Given, $J = 4.18 \times 10^7 \text{ erg cal}^{-1}$ and normal pressure $= 1.01 \times 10^6 \text{ dyne cm}^{-2}$. **Competency Based Que.**

18. In changing the state of a gas adiabatically from an equilibrium state A to another equilibrium state B, an amount of work equal to 22.3 J is done on the system. If the gas is taken from state A to B *via* a process in which the net heat absorbed by the system is 9.35 cal, how much is the net work done by the system in the latter case? (Take, 1 cal = 4.19 J). **NCERT**

19. Calculate the rise in temperature of water which falls from a height of 100m, if 80% of the energy due to falls is converted into heat and retained by water. ($J = 4.2$ J/cal, $g = 9.8 \text{ ms}^{-2}$)

20. An ideal gas is taken through a cyclic thermodynamic process through four steps. The amounts of heat involved in these steps are $Q_1 = 5960$ J, $Q_2 = -5585$ J, $Q_3 = -2980$ J and $Q_4 = 3645$ J respectively. The corresponding works involved are $W_1 = -2200$ J, $W_2 = -825$ J, $W_3 = -1100$ J and W_4 respectively. Find (i) W_4 and (ii) efficiency of the cycle.

21. 1 mole of monoatomic ideal gas is heated from 0° to 80°C at constant normal pressure. Find out the work done by the gas and change in its internal energy. The heat given to the gas is 1.0 kJ. Given, gas constant, $R = 8.3 \text{ J/mol K}^{-1}$.

Thermodynamic Processes

22. One mole of an ideal gas undergoes a cyclic change $ABCD$, where the (p, V) co-ordinates are $A(5, 1)$ $B(5, 3)$, $C(2, 3)$ and $D(2, 1)$. p is in atmosphere and V is in litre. Calculate work done along (i) AB, (ii) BC (iii) CD and (iv) DA and also net work done in the process. Given, 1 atmosphere $= 1.01 \times 10^5 / \text{Nm}^{-2}$. **Competency Based Que.**

23. A monoatomic ideal gas of two moles is taken through a cyclic process starting from A as shown in figure.

The volume ratios are $\frac{V_B}{V_A} = 2$ and $\frac{V_D}{V_A} = 4$.

If the temperature T_A at A is 27°C, calculate

(i) the temperature of the gas at point B, **[1]**

(ii) heat absorbed or released by the gas in each process and **[3]**

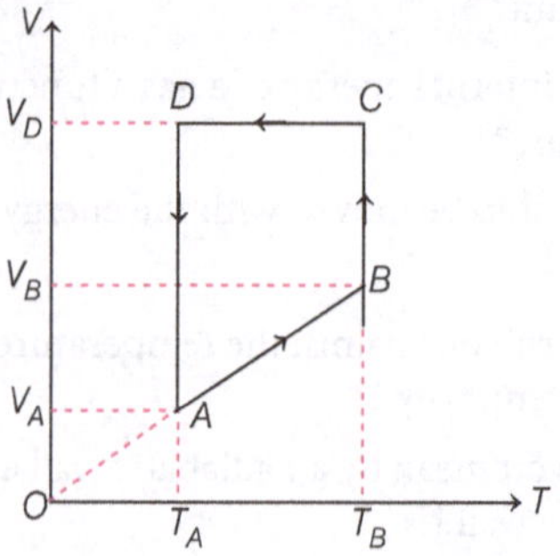

(iii) the total work done by the gas during the complete cycle. **[1]**

Express your answer in terms of the gas constant R.

24. An ideal gas having initial pressure p, volume V and temperature T is allowed to expand adiabatically until its volume becomes 5.66 V while its temperature falls to $T/2$. (i) How many degrees of freedom do the gas molecules have? (ii) Obtain the work done by the gas during the expansion as a function of the initial pressure p and volume V. **Competency Based Que.**

Work Done in Cyclic Process

25. A thermodynamic system is taken from an original state to an intermediate state by the linear process shown in figure.

Its volume is then reduced to the original value from E to F by an isobaric process. Calculate the total work done by the gas from D to E to F.

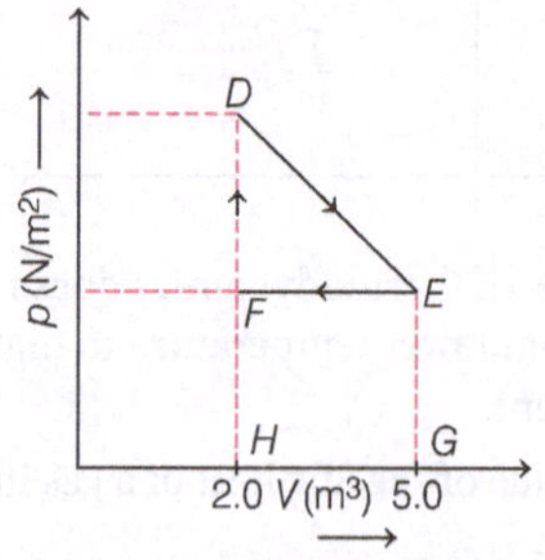

26. A cylinder with a movable piston contains 3 moles of hydrogen at standard temperature and pressure. The walls of the cylinder are made of a heat insulator and the piston is insulated by having a pile of sand on it. By what factor, does the pressure of the gas increase, if the gas is compressed to half of its original volume? **NCERT**

Second Law of Thermodynamics

27. A Carnot engine whose heat sink is at 27°C has an efficiency of 40%. By how many degrees should the temperature of the source be changed to increase the efficiency by 10% of the original efficiency?

Competency Based Que.

28. A Carnot cycle is performed by air initially at 327°C. Each stage represents a compression or expansion in the ratio 1 : 6. Calculate (i) the lowest temperature and (ii) efficiency of the cycle. (Given, $\gamma = 14$). **[1½]**

Competency Based Que. [1½]

29. Two Carnot engines *A* and *B* are operated in series. The first one *A* receives heat at 900 K and reject to a reservoir at temperature *T* K.
The second engine B receives the heat rejected by the first engine and in turn rejects to a heat reservoir at 400 K. Calculate the temperature *T* when

(i) the efficiencies of the two engines are equal and

(ii) the work output of the two engines are equal

30. The temperatures T_1 and T_2 of the two heat reservoirs in an ideal Carnot engine be 1500°C and 500°C respectively. Which of these increasing T_1 by 100°C or decreasing T_2 by 100°C would result in a greater improvement in the efficiency of the engine?

p-V Diagram

31. A system goes from *P* to *Q* by two different paths in the *p-V* diagram as shown in figure. Heat given to the system in path 1 is 1000 J. The work done by the system along path 1 is more than path 2 by 100 J.
What is the heat exchanged by the system in path 2?

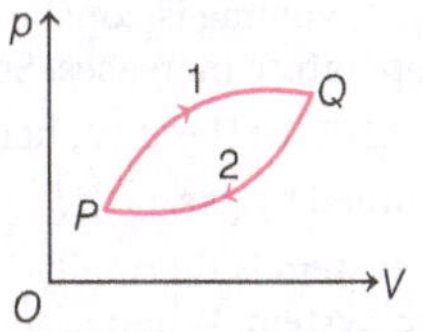

Hints & Solutions

Objective Type Questions

1. (*b*) If two systems are in thermal equilibrium with each other, it means their temperatures must be same. Masses may be equal or unequal.

2. (*b*) Let the equilibrium temperature of the system is *T*.
Let us assume that $T_1, T_2 < T < T_3$.
According to question, there is no heat loss to the surroundings.
Heat lost by M_1 = Heat gained by M_2 + Heat gained by M_3
$\Rightarrow M_1 s(T_1 - T) = M_2 s(T - T_1) + M_3 s(T - T_2)$
(where, *s* is specific heat of the copper material)
$$T[M_1 + M_2 + M_3] = M_3T_3 + M_1T_1 + M_2T_2$$
$$T = \frac{M_1T_1 + M_2T_2 + M_3T_3}{M_1 + M_2 + M_3}$$

3. (*c*) Given, $dQ = +200$ cal
$$= 200 \times 4.2 = 840\text{ J}, dW = +40\text{ J}$$
From first law of thermodynamics,
$$dQ = dU + dW$$
$$dU = dQ - dW = 840 - 40 = 800\text{ J}$$
So, the internal energy of the system increases by 800 J.

4. (*d*) Work is not a state function because it does not describe the state of system.

5. (*b*) Figure shows that loop 2 is anti-clockwise, therefore W_2 is negative, loop 1 is clockwise, therefore W_1 is positive. Also, loop 2 is bigger.
$$W_2 > W_1$$
Hence, net work done,
$$W = W_1 - W_2 = \text{negative}$$

6. (*d*) For a cyclic process, $\Delta U = 0$. Hence, $Q = -W$

7. (*b*) Consider the *p-V* diagram given in the question.
Work done in the process *ABCD* = Area of rectangle *ABCDA*
$$= (AB) \times BC = (3V_0 - V_0) \times (2p_0 - p_0)$$
$$= 2V_0 \times p_0 = 2p_0V_0$$
As the process is going anti-clockwise, hence there is a net compression in the gas. So, work done by the gas
$$= -2p_0V_0$$

8. (*d*) For isothermal expansion,
$$\Delta U = 0 \Rightarrow \Delta Q = \Delta W$$
Here, $\Delta W \to$ positive $\Rightarrow \Delta Q \to$ positive

9. (*d*) Adiabatic curves are more stepper than isothermal curves.

10. (*c*) *A* is compressed isothermally, hence
$$p_1V = p_2\frac{V}{2} \Rightarrow p_2 = 2p_1$$
and *B* is compressed adiabatically, hence
$$p_1V^\gamma = p_2\left(\frac{V}{2}\right)^\gamma \Rightarrow p_2 = (2)^\gamma p_1$$
Since $\gamma > 1$, hence final pressure of *A* is less than final pressure of *B*.

11. (*c*) During process 1, pressure is constant, so volume increases, hence temperature also increases.

So, $\Delta W > 0, \Delta U > 0$

So, by law, thermodynamics,

$$\Delta Q = \Delta U + \Delta W \Rightarrow \Delta U > 0,$$

So, heat is absorbed by gas.

During process 2, V = constant and pressure decreases, so temperature also decreases.

$$W = \int p\,dV = 0, \text{ so } \Delta T < 0, \text{ hence } \Delta U < 0$$

$$\Delta Q = \Delta U + \Delta W \quad \because \quad \Delta Q < 0$$

So, heat is ejected by gas.

During process 3. pressure = constant, volume decreases, temperature also decreases.

So, $\Delta U < 0, \Delta W < 0.$

So, heat is ejected by gas.

During process 4, volume is constant, pressure increases and hence temperature increases. So, $\Delta W = 0, \Delta U > 0.$

$$\Delta Q = \Delta U + \Delta W, \text{ hence } \Delta Q > 0.$$

So, heat is absorbed by gas.

12. (*b*) The entire system is thermally insulated, hence no heat flows into system. When stopcock is removed, the gas expands adiabatically.

13. (*a*) Heat given, $\Delta Q = 40$ J

Work done, $\Delta W = 30\text{ J} \Rightarrow \Delta U = \Delta Q - W = 40 - 30 = 10$ J

14. (c) According to the question given that pV = constant

Hence, we can say that the gas is going through an isothermal process.

Clearly, from the graph that between process 1 and 2 temperature is constant and the gas expands and pressure decreases i.e., $p_2 < p_1$ which corresponds to diagram (c).

15. (*a*) Amount of sweat evaporated/minute

$$= \frac{\text{Sweat produced / minute}}{\text{Number of calories required for evaporation / kg}}$$

$$= \frac{\text{Amount of heat produced per minute in jogging}}{\text{Latent heat (in cal / kg)}}$$

$$= \frac{14.5 \times 10^3}{580 \times 10^3} = \frac{145}{580} = 0.025 \text{ kg}$$

16. (*a*) Consider the *p-V* diagram shown for the container *A* (isothermal) and for container *B* (adiabatic).

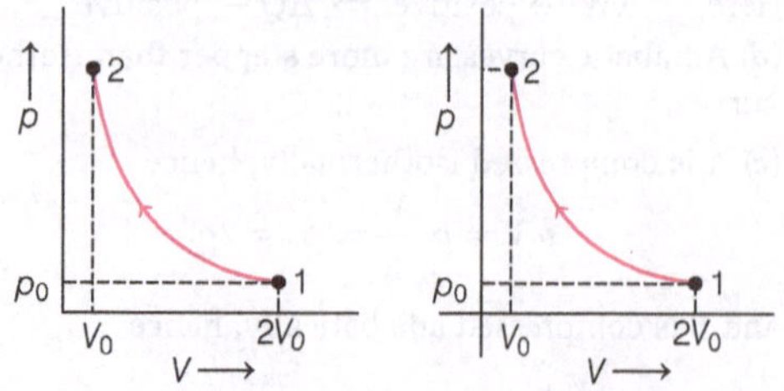

Container *A* (Isothermal) Container *B* (Adiabatic)

Both the process involving compression of the gas.

For isothermal process (gas *A*) (during $1 \rightarrow 2$)

$$p_1V_1 = p_2V_2$$

$$\Rightarrow p_0(2V_0) = p_2(V_0)$$

$$\Rightarrow p_2 = 2p_0$$

For adiabatic process, (gas *B*) (during $1 \rightarrow 2$)

$$p_1V_1^\gamma = p_2V_2^\gamma$$

$$\Rightarrow p_0(2V_0)^\gamma = p_2(V_0)^\gamma$$

$$\Rightarrow p_2 = \left(\frac{2V_0}{V_0}\right)^\gamma p_0 = (2)^\gamma p_0$$

Hence, $\frac{(p_2)_B}{(p_2)_A}$ = Ratio of final pressure $= \frac{(2)^\gamma p_0}{2p_0} = 2^{\gamma - 1}$

where, γ is ratio of specific heat capacities for the gas.

17. (*a*) According to Carnot, for a reversible engine, efficiency is maximum.

18. (*a*)

A. The first law of thermodynamics is the principle of energy conservation, which states that the change in internal energy (ΔU) of a system is equal to the heat added to the system (Q) and the work done on the system (W).

$$\Delta U = Q + W$$

B. The second law of thermodynamics states that the entropy of an isolated system will always increase or remain constant, it never decreases.

Entropy increases in any spontaneous process.

C. Enthalpy is a thermodynamic quantity defined as $H = U + pV$, where U is internal energy, p is pressure, and V is volume.

$$H = U + pV$$

D. In an isothermal process the temperature of the system remains constant.

Hence, A $\rightarrow$ 1, B $\rightarrow$ 2, C $\rightarrow$ 3, D $\rightarrow$ 4.

19. (*a*)

A. In an isothermal process, the temperature remains constant and the work done can be expressed as $W = p_{ext}\Delta V$, where p_{ext} is the external pressure.

B. The heat capacity at constant pressure is defined as $C_p = \frac{\Delta Q}{\Delta T}$, where ΔQ is the heat added, and ΔT is the change in temperature.

C. In adiabatic process no, heat is exchanged with the surroundings, i.e., $\Delta Q = 0$.

D. The specific heat at constant volume for an ideal gas is given by $C_V = \frac{R}{\gamma - 1}$, where γ is the adiabatic index, and R is the universal gas constant.

Hence, A $\rightarrow$ 1, B $\rightarrow$ 2, C $\rightarrow$ 3, D $\rightarrow$ 4.

20. (*d*) For a monoatomic gas, number of degree of freedom, $n = 3$ and for a diatomic gas, $n = 5$

As, $\dfrac{C_p}{C_V} = x = 1 + \dfrac{2}{n}$

So, for monoatonic gas, $\dfrac{C_p}{C_V} = \dfrac{5}{3} = 1.66$

and for diatomic gas, $\dfrac{C_p}{C_V} = \dfrac{7}{5} = 1.4$

$\therefore \quad \left(\dfrac{C_p}{C_V}\right)_{\text{mono}} > \left(\dfrac{C_p}{C_V}\right)_{\text{di}}$

21. (*a*) Change is fast and also adiabatic expansion causes cooling.

22. (*b*)

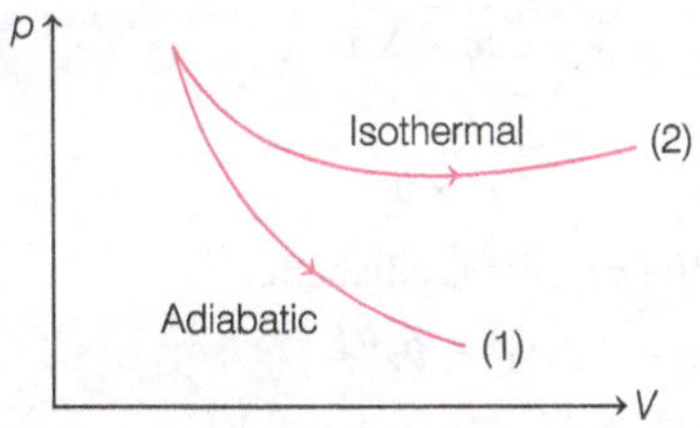

As from the curve, area covered under *p-V* curve is equal to work done.

Area under curve (2) > Area under curve (1)

23. (*b*) State variables are required to specify the equilibrium state of a system. When values of some state variables are given and relation between state variables is known, then values of other state variables can be calculated. Pressure is an intensive state variable.

24. (*c*) For isothermal process, $\Delta T = 0$, $\Delta U = 0$ but $\Delta Q \neq 0$.

In isothermal process,

Temperature, $T =$ constant

Change in temperature, $\Delta T = 0$

Change in internal energy, $\Delta U = 0$
(internal energy depends on temperature only)

$\therefore$ Assertion is true.

To keep temperature constant, container is kept totally submerged in constant temperature source. From source, system in container takes heat during expansion

$\therefore$ Reason is false.

25. (*c*) Efficiency of Carnot engine, $\eta = 1 - \dfrac{T_2}{T_1}$

where, $T_2 =$ sink temperature

and $T_1 =$ source temperature

This expression of η does not include working substance information.

So, η is independent of working substance.

All reversible Carnot engines have same efficiency , if source and sink temperatures are same, it does not matter what substance they use.

26. (*d*) We can change the temperature of a body without giving (or taking) heat to (or from) it. For example in an adiabatic compression temperature rises and in an adiabatic expansion temperature falls, although no heat is given or taken from the system in the respective changes.

27. (*a*) In reversible process, there is always some loss of energy. This is because energy spent in working against the dissipative force is not recovered back. Some irreversible process occur in nature such as friction where extra work to cancel the effect of friction. Salt dissolves in water but a salt does not separate by itself into pure salt and pure water. Hence, all thermodynamic processes are irreversible.

28. (*a*) If *A* and *B* are separately in equilibrium with *C*, $T_A = t_B$ and $T_B = t_C$. It means $T_A = T_B$ i.e. the systems *A* and *B* are also in thermal equilibrium.

29. (i) (*a*) For an ideal gas, internal energy depends only on the molecular kinetic energy.

(ii) (*d*) By heat and work, we can change the internal energy of the system.

(iii) (*d*) $\Delta Q - \Delta W = \Delta U$ and it is path independent.

(iv) (*d*) For isothermal expansion, $\Delta U = 0$

From first law of thermodynamics, $\Delta Q = \Delta U + \Delta W$

$\Rightarrow \Delta Q = \Delta W$

Here, $\Delta W \to$ positive (for expansion)

$\Rightarrow \quad \Delta Q \to$ positive

(v) (*c*) Given, $dQ = +200 \text{ cal} = 200 \times 4.2 = 840 \text{ J}$

$dW = +40 \text{ J}$

From first law of thermodynamics,

$$dQ = dU + dW$$

$$dU = dQ - dW = 840 - 40 = 800 \text{ J}$$

So, the internal energy of the system increases by 800 J.

30. (i) (*c*), (ii) (*b*), (iii) (*a*), (iv) (*d*), (v) (*b*)

31. (i) (*c*) Free expansion of gas is the example of non-equilibrium states. When outside, pressure is less, piston accelerates outward.

(ii) (*c*) Finite temperature difference between system and surroundings causes rapid exchange of heat between them with non-equilibrium intermediate stages. After sometime, equilibrium is attained.

(iii) (*c*) Only option (c) is correct as *p*, *V* and *T* are state variables. Thermodynamics is a macroscopic science and result are based on macroscopic or measurable variables.

(iv) (*d*) Internal energy is a state variable. Heat and work are not state variables. Heat and work are related to changing the state but not to actual state of system. So, by changing heat and work, we can change the internal energy of the system.

(v) (*c*) A mixture of gases undergoing an explosive chemical reaction is not in equilibrium because during explosion, temperature rises abruptly. When explosions are over with time, it attains equilibrium with surroundings.

Subjective Questions

1. (i) If system is doing some work.
(ii) If the system does work against the surrounding, so that it compensates for the heat supplied, the temperature can remain constant.

2. (i) Yes, the internal energy of an ideal gas depends only on the temperature of gas, while for real gas depends on the temperature and volume. The temperature and volume depends on the pressure.
(ii) No, a ship cannot be moved in a sea by the use of the energy of sea water because it is against the second law of thermodynamics.

3. By rubbing palms, work is converted into heat due to which the temperature rises. After a certain temperature, further produced heat is dissipated to the surroundings and hence, temperature does not rise further.

4. Adiabatic wall is an insulating wall that does not allow flow of energy or heat from one to another.
Diathermic is a wall that allows energy flow or heat from one to another.

5. Let m_1 and m_2 are masses of bodies with specific heats s_1 and s_2, and if their temperature T is equal, then they are in thermal equilibrium.

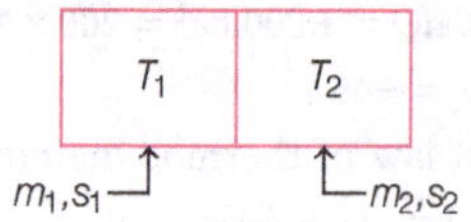

Then, if $T_1 > T > T_2$ and assuming no heat loss.
Heat lost by hot body = Heat gained by cold body

$$m_1s_1(T_1 - T) = m_2s_2(T - T_2)$$

$$\Rightarrow \frac{m_1s_1T_1 + m_2s_2T_2}{m_1s_1 + m_2s_2} = T \text{ [equilibrium temperature]}$$

So for bodies to settle down to mean temperature,

$$m_1 = m_2 \text{ and } s_1 = s_2$$

means bodies have same specific heat and have equal masses.

Then, $T = \frac{T_1 + T_2}{2}$ [mean temperature]

6. (i) Yes it is possible to increase the temperature of a gas without adding heat to it. This is possible during adiabatic compression.
(ii) A gas has greatest value of internal energy because negative potential energy of its molecules is smallest.

7. (i) As, ΔU depends on initial and final states but not on path, so for all a, b, c and d paths, ΔU is same.
(ii) Work done is given by area under curve and above volume axis, so in ascending order, work done is *d, c, b, a.*
(iii) By first law, $\Delta Q = \Delta U + \Delta W$
and ΔU is same for all so, ΔQ is greatest for which ΔW is greatest. So, ascending order for ΔQ is *d, c, b, a.*

8. (i) First law of thermodynamics simply tells about the conversion of mechanical energy into heat energy and *vice-versa.* It does not put any condition as to why heat cannot flow from lower temperature to higher temperature.
(ii) For isothermal process,

$$\Delta T = 0$$

$$C = \frac{\Delta Q}{m \times \Delta T}$$

$$C = \frac{\Delta Q}{m \times 0} = \infty$$

9. Since, the process is adiabatic

$$p_1V_1^\gamma = p_2V_2^\gamma$$

$$p(V + \Delta V)^\gamma = (p + \Delta p)V^\gamma$$

$$pV^\gamma\left[1 + \frac{\Delta V}{V}\right]^\gamma = pV^\gamma\left[1 + \frac{\Delta p}{p}\right]$$

$$1 + \gamma\frac{\Delta V}{V} = 1 + \frac{\Delta p}{p}$$

$$\gamma\frac{\Delta V}{V} = \frac{\Delta p}{p}$$

$$p\,\Delta V = \frac{V}{\gamma}\Delta p$$

$$\int p\,dV = \int_{p_1}^{p_2}\frac{V\,dp}{\gamma} \Rightarrow \int dW = \frac{V}{\gamma}\int(p_2 - p_1)$$

$$W = \frac{V}{\gamma}(p_2 - p_1)$$

$$W = \frac{V(p_2 - p_1)}{\gamma}$$

10. (i) $\because$ Process is adiabatic

$\therefore \quad \Delta Q = 0$

Work done on the gas, $\Delta W = -500\text{J}$
According to the first law of thermodynamics,

$$\Delta Q = \Delta U + \Delta W$$

$$\Rightarrow \quad \Delta U = -\Delta W = 500\text{ J}$$

(ii) This is because heat absorbed by a substance (coolant) is directly proportional to the specific heat of the substance.
(iii) This is because in a harbour town, the relative humidity is more than in a desert town. Hence, the climate of a harbour town is without extremes of hot and cold.

11. (i) In figure, portion AB of the cycle involved increases in pressure/temperature of gas at constant volume. Therefore, the system gains heat from the surroundings.

$$Q_{AB} = U_{AB} \qquad [\because W = 0]$$
$$= \frac{3}{2}R(T_B - T_A)$$
$$= \frac{3}{2}(p_B V_B - p_A V_A) \quad [\because \Delta U = nC_V \Delta T]$$
$$= \frac{3}{2}(p_B - p_A) V_A \qquad [\because V_B = V_A]$$

(ii) In the portion BC, the gas increases in volume at constant pressure. Heat required for this is gained from surroundings.

$$Q_{BC} = U_{BC} + W_{BC}$$
$$= \frac{3}{2}(p_C V_C - p_B V_B) + p_B(V_C - V_B)$$
$$= \frac{5}{2}p_B(V_C - V_B) \qquad [\because p_C = p_B]$$
$$Q_{BC} = \frac{5}{2}p_B(V_C - V_B)$$

(iii) As CD represents an adiabatic change, therefore $Q_{CD} = 0$.

(iv) DA involves compression of gas from V_D to V_A at constant pressure p_A. Work is done on the gas (negative).

$$\Delta Q_{DA} = \Delta U_{DA} + \Delta W_{DA}$$
$$= \frac{3}{2}R(T_A - T_D) + p_A(V_A - V_D)$$
$$= \frac{3}{2}p_A(V_A - V_D) + p_A(p_A - V_D)$$
$$= \frac{5}{2}p_A(V_A - V_D)$$

12. Slope of $p = f(V)$, curve at $(V_0, p_0) = f(V_0)$

Slope of adiabat at $(V_0, p_0) = K(-\gamma) V_0^{-1-\gamma} = -\gamma p_0 / V_0$

Now, heat absorbed in the process $p = f(V)$

$$dQ = dU + dW = nC_V dT + pdV$$

Since, $T = (1/nR)\, pV = (1/nR)\, V\, f(V)$

$\therefore \quad dT = (1/nR)\,[f(V) + Vf'(V)]\, dV$

Thus, $$\left.\frac{dQ}{dV}\right|_{V = V_0} = \frac{C_V}{R}[f(V_0) + V_0 f'(V_0)] + f(V_0)$$
$$= \left[\frac{1}{\gamma - 1} + 1\right] f(V_0) + \frac{V_0 f'(V_0)}{\gamma - 1}$$
$$= \frac{\gamma}{\gamma - 1}p_0 + \frac{V_0}{\gamma - 1}f'(V_0)$$

Heat is absorbed when $dQ/dV > 0$ when gas expands, that is when $\gamma p_0 + V_0 f'(V_0) > 0$

$$f'(V_0) > -\gamma\, p_0 / V_0$$

13.

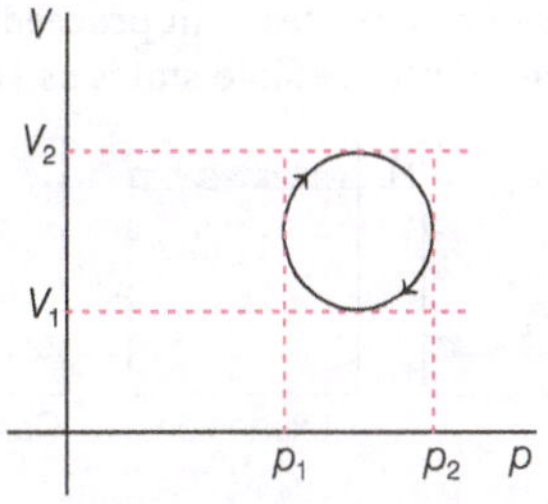

Area under the curve = Work done

Area of circle = πr^2

Diameter = $V_2 - V_1 = p_2 - p_1$

Radius, $r = \frac{1}{2}(V_2 - V_1) = \frac{1}{2}(p_2 - p_1)$

Work done = πr^2

$$= \pi\left(\frac{p_2 - p_1}{2}\right)^2$$

To express work done in terms of pressure and volume substitute

$$\frac{p_2 - p_0}{2} \text{ for } \frac{V_2 - V_1}{2}$$

$$\text{Work done} = \pi r^2 = \pi\left(\frac{V_2 - V_1}{2}\right)\left(\frac{V_2 - V_1}{2}\right)$$
$$= \pi\left(\frac{V_2 - V_1}{2}\right)\left(\frac{p_2 - p_1}{2}\right)$$
$$= \frac{\pi}{4}(V_2 - V_1)(p_2 - p_1)$$

14. A reversible process must pass through equilibrium states which are very close to each other so that when process is reversed, it passes back through these equilibrium states.

Then, it is again decompressed or it passes through same equilibrium states, system can be restored to its initial state without any change in surroundings.

e.g. If a gas is compressed as shown

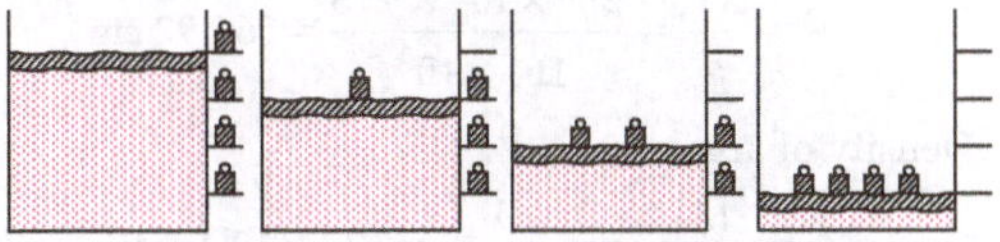

In the above case, the gas is compressed very slowly and two neighbouring states are in equilibrium. The similar process is shown below for the expansion.

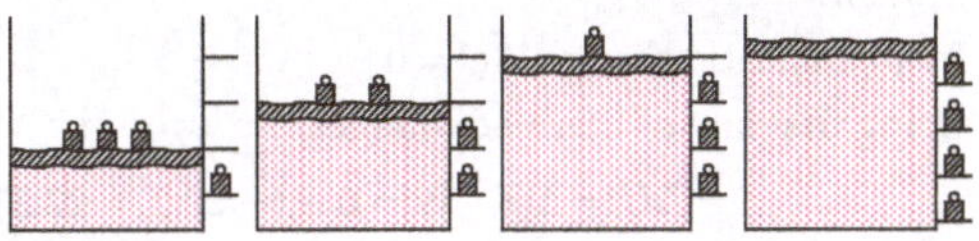

But an irreversible process can proceed without reaching equilibrium in intermediate states as shown below.

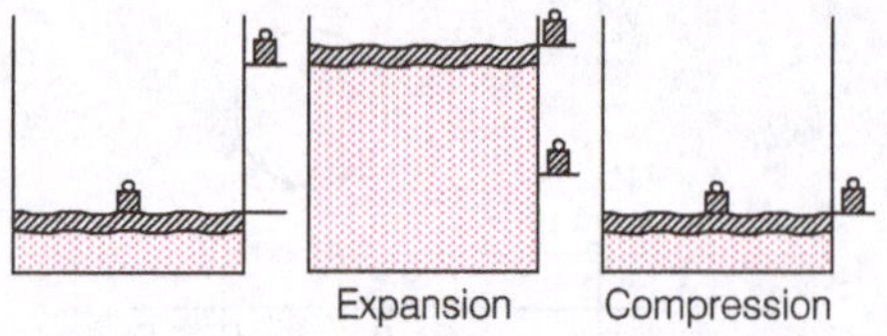

15. Heat energy supplied per second by the heater,

$$\Delta Q = 100 \text{ W} = 100 \text{ J/s}$$

Work done by the system, $\Delta W = +75$ J/s

Rate of change in internal energy, $\Delta U = ?$

According to first law of thermodynamics,

$$\Delta U = \Delta Q - \Delta W = 100 - 75 = 25 \text{ J/s} = 25 \text{ W}$$

16. By first law of thermodynamics,

$$\Delta Q = \Delta U + \Delta W$$

For an adiabatic process, $\Delta Q = 0$

$\therefore \quad \Delta U = -\Delta W = -(-146 \text{ kJ}) = +146 \text{ kJ}$

As, $\Delta U = nC_V\Delta T$

$$\therefore \quad C_V = \frac{\Delta U}{n\Delta T} = \frac{146 \times 10^3}{1 \times 10^3 \times 7} \qquad [\because \Delta T = 7°\text{C} = 7\text{K}]$$

$$= 20.8 \text{ J mol}^{-1}\text{K}^{-1}$$

For a diatomic gas,

$$C_V = \frac{5}{2}R = \frac{5}{2} \times 8.3 = 20.8 \text{ J mol}^{-1}\text{K}^{-1}$$

Hence, the gas is diatomic.

17. Here, $C_p = 0.125 \text{ cal g}^{-1}\text{K}^{-1}$

$$C_V = 0.075 \text{ cal g}^{-1}\text{K}^{-1},$$

$$J = 4.18 \times 10^6 \text{ erg cal}^{-1}$$

For 1 g of a gas, $C_p - C_V = \dfrac{R}{J}$

$$\therefore \quad R = J(C_p - C_V) = 4.18 \times 10^7 \times (0.125 - 0.075)$$

$$= 4.18 \times 10^7 \times 0.05 = 2.09 \times 10^6 \text{ erg g}^{-1}\text{K}^{-1}$$

$\therefore$ Volume of 1 g of argon at STP,

$$V = \frac{RT}{p} = \frac{2.09 \times 10^6 \times 273}{1.01 \times 10^6} = 564.92 \text{ cm}^3$$

Density of argon,

$$\rho = \frac{\text{Mass}}{\text{Volume}} = \frac{1}{564.92} = 1.77 \times 10^{-3} \text{gcm}^{-3}$$

18. Given, work done, $W = -22.3$ J

Work done is taken negative as work is done on the system.

In an adiabatic change, $\Delta Q = 0$

Using first law of thermodynamics,

$$\Delta U = \Delta Q - W = 0 - (-22.3) = 22.3 \text{ J}$$

For another process between states A and B,

Heat absorbed $(\Delta Q) = +9.35$ cal

$$= +(9.35 \times 4.19) \text{ J} = +39.18 \text{ J}$$

Change in internal energy between two states *via* different paths are equal.

$$\therefore \quad \Delta U = 22.3 \text{ J}$$

$\therefore$ From first law of thermodynamics,

$$\Delta U = \Delta Q - W$$

or $\quad W = \Delta Q - \Delta U = 39.18 - 22.3 = 16.88 \text{ J} \approx 16.9 \text{ J}$

19. Let m kg of water falls from a height h,

Then loss of potential energy is

$$U = mgh = mg \times 100$$

80% of energy is converted into heat.

$$\therefore \quad Q = \frac{80}{100} \times mg \times 100 = 80 \, mg \text{ joule}$$

$$= \frac{80 \, mg}{4.2} \text{ calorie}$$

If C $(1 \times 10^3 \text{cal / kg°C})$ is specific heat of water and ΔT is rise in temperature of water then

$$nC\Delta T = \frac{80 \, mg}{4.2}$$

$$\Delta T = \frac{80 \times 9.8}{4.2 \times 10^3} = 0.186° \text{C}$$

20. By the first law of thermodynamics, $Q = \Delta U + W$

$$\Delta U = Q - W$$

$$\Delta U_1 = Q_1 - W_1 = 5960 - 2200$$

$$= 3760 \text{ J}$$

$$\Delta U_2 = Q_2 - W_2 = -5585 + 825$$

$$= -4760 \text{ J}$$

$$\Delta U_3 = Q_3 - W_3 = -2980 + 1100 = -1880 \text{ J}$$

$$\Delta U_4 = Q_4 - W_4 = 3645 \text{ J} - W_4$$

For a cyclic process, $\Delta U = 0$

$\therefore \quad 3760 \text{ J} - 4760 \text{ J} - 1880 \text{ J} + 3645 \text{ J} - W_4 = 0$

$$W_4 = 765 \text{J}$$

Now, efficiency

$$= \frac{\text{Work output}}{\text{Heat energy input}}$$

$$= \frac{W_1 + W_2 + W_3 + W_4}{Q_1 + Q_4}$$

$$= \frac{2200 - 825 - 1100 + 765}{5960 + 3645}$$

$$= \frac{1040}{9605} = 0.108 = 10.8\%$$

21. Increase in internal energy of μ mole of the gas is

$$\Delta U = \mu C_V \Delta T$$

For monoatomic gas, $C_V = \dfrac{3}{2}R$

$$\therefore \Delta U = \mu\left(\frac{3}{2}R\right)\Delta T = 1 \text{ mol} \times \left(\frac{3}{2} \times 8.31 \text{ J / mol / K}\right) \times 80 \text{ K}$$

$$= 996 \text{ J}$$

From the first law of thermodynamics, we have

$$Q = \Delta U + W$$

Here, $Q = 1\text{ kJ} = 1000\text{ J}$

$\therefore$ Work done by the gas,

$$W = Q - \Delta U = 1000\text{ J} - 996\text{ J} = 4\text{ J}$$

22. (i) Work done along AB,

$$W_1 = \text{area } ABFEA = EA \times EF$$
$$= (3 \times 1.01 \times 10^5) \times 2 \times 10^{-3} = 606\text{ J}$$

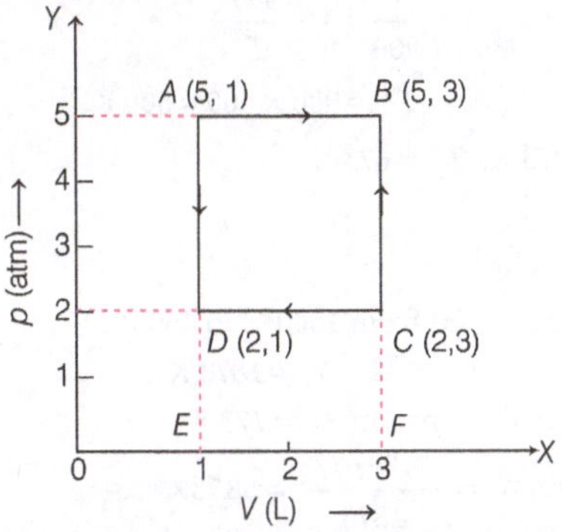

(ii) Work done along BC, $W_2 = pdV = 0$.

(iii) Work done along CD

$$W_3 = -\text{ area } CDEFC = -EF \times CF$$
$$= -2 \times 1.01 \times 10^5 \times 2 \times 10^{-3} = -404\text{ J}.$$

(iv) Work done along DA, $W_4 = pdV = 0$.

Net work done in the process,

$$W = W_1 + W_2 + W_3 + W_4$$
$$= 606 + 0 - 404 + 0 = 202\text{ J}.$$

23. (i) The process $A \to B$ is isobaric.

$\therefore$ $V/T = \text{constant}$

Hence, $\dfrac{V_A}{T_A} = \dfrac{V_B}{T_B}$

or $T_B = \dfrac{V_B}{V_A} \cdot T_A = 2 \times 300 = 600\text{ K} = 327°\text{C}$

(ii) The heat absorbed in the process $A \to B$ is given by

$Q_1 + nC_p dT = (5R)(600 - 300) = 1500\, R.$

The process $B \to C$ is isothermal. The heat absorbed is given by

$$Q_2 = W_2 = nRT_B \log(V_D / V_B)$$
$$= 2 \times R \times 600 \log_e 2$$
$$= 1200R \times 0.693 = 831.6\, R$$

The process $C \to D$ is isochoric. The heat released is given by

$$Q_3 = nC_V dT = 2 \times \frac{3}{2} R \times (300 - 600) = -900\, R$$

The process $D \to A$ is isothermal.

The heat released is given by

$$Q_4 = nRT_A \log_e \frac{V_A}{V_D} = 2\, R \times 600 \log_e \frac{1}{4}$$
$$= -1200R \log_e 2 = -831.6R$$

(iii) The total work done by the gas during the complete cycle,

$$W = Q_1 + Q_2 + Q_3 + Q_4$$
$$= 1500R + 831.6R - 900R - 831.6R = 600R$$

24. (i) For an adiabatic expression,

$$T_1 V_1^{\gamma - 1} = T_2 V_2^{\gamma - 1}$$

$\therefore$ $TV^{\gamma - 1} = \dfrac{T}{2} \times (5.66V)^{\gamma - 1}$

or $(5.66)^{\gamma - 1} = 2$

Taking logarithms, $(\gamma - 1)\log 5.66 = \log 2$

or $\gamma - 1 = \dfrac{\log 2}{\log 5.66} = \dfrac{0.3010}{0.7528} = 0.4$

or $\gamma = 1.4$

Let f be the degrees of freedom of the gas, then

$$\gamma = 1 + \frac{2}{f} \text{ or } 1.4 = 1 + \frac{2}{f}$$

or $\dfrac{2}{f} = 1.4 - 1 = 0.4$ or $f = \dfrac{2}{0.4} = 5$

(ii) Work done by the gas in adiabatic expansion from temperature $T_1\ (= T)$ to $T_2 (= T/2)$ is

$$W = \frac{R}{\gamma - 1}(T_1 - T_2)$$
$$= \frac{R}{0.4}\left(T - \frac{T}{2}\right) = \frac{5}{4}RT = \frac{5}{4}pV$$

25. Total work done by the gas from D to E to F.

$W = W_{DE} + W_{EF}$

= Area of trapezium $DEGHD$

− Area of rectangle $EFHG$

= Area of triangle $DEG = \dfrac{1}{2} DE \times FE$

$$= \frac{1}{2}(600 - 300)\text{ Nm}^{-2} \times (5.0 - 2.0)\text{ m}^3 = 450\text{ J}$$

26. As no heat is allowed to be exchanged, the process is adiabatic.

$$\therefore\ p_2 V_2^\gamma = p_1 V_1^\gamma \text{ or } \frac{p_2}{p_1} = \left(\frac{V_1}{V_2}\right)^\gamma$$

As $V_2 = \dfrac{1}{2}V_1$ or $\dfrac{p_2}{p_1} = \left(\dfrac{V_1}{\frac{1}{2}V_1}\right)^{1.4} = 2^{1.4} = 2.64$

27. Here, $T_2 = 27 + 273 = 300\text{ K}, \eta = 40\%, T_1 = ?$

As $\eta = 1 - \dfrac{T_2}{T_1}$

$\therefore$ $\dfrac{T_2}{T_1} = 1 - \eta = 1 - \dfrac{40}{100} = \dfrac{60}{100} = \dfrac{3}{5}$

or $T_1 = \frac{5}{3} \times T_2 = \frac{5}{3} \times 300 = 500$ K

Increase in efficiency = 10% of 40 = 4%.

$\therefore$ New efficiency, $\eta' = 40 + 4 = 44\%$

Let new temperature of the source = T_1 K, then

$$\eta' = 1 - \frac{T_2}{T_1'} \text{ or } \frac{44}{100} = 1 - \frac{300}{T_1'}$$

or $$\frac{300}{T_1'} = 1 - \frac{44}{100} = \frac{56}{100}$$

$$\therefore \quad T_1' = \frac{100 \times 300}{56} = 535.7\text{K}$$

Increase in temperature of the source

$= 535.7 - 500 = 35.7$ K or 35.7°C

28. Here, $T_1 = 327 + 273 = 600\text{K}$,

$V_1 / V_2 = 1/6, \gamma = 1.4$

(i) As, $T_2 V_2^{\gamma - 1} = T_1 V_1^{\gamma - 1}$

$$\therefore \quad T_2 = \left(\frac{V_1}{V_2}\right)^{\gamma - 1} \times T_1$$

$$= \left(\frac{1}{6}\right)^{1.4 - 1} \times 600 = 293 \text{ K or } 20°\text{C}$$

(ii) Efficiency, $\eta = 1 - \frac{T_2}{T_1} = 1 - \frac{293}{600} = 0.512 = 51.2\%$

29. $W_A = W_B$

$$\frac{W}{Q_1} = \left(1 - \frac{T_2}{T_1}\right)$$

$$W = Q_1\left(1 - \frac{T_2}{T_1}\right)$$

$$Q_2\left(1 - \frac{T_3}{T_2}\right) = Q_1\left(1 - \frac{T_2}{T_1}\right)$$

$$\left(1 - \frac{T}{900}\right)Q_1 = \left(1 - \frac{400}{T}\right)Q_2$$

$$\left(1 - \frac{T}{900}\right)Q_1 = \left(1 - \frac{400}{T}\right)\frac{T}{900}$$

$$1 - \frac{T}{900} = \frac{T}{900} - \frac{400}{900}$$

$$\frac{2T}{900} = \frac{13}{9}$$

$$T = 650 \text{ K}$$

$$\eta_A = \eta_B$$

$$1 - \frac{T}{900} = 1 - \frac{400}{T}$$

$$T^2 = 900 \times 400 = 600 \text{ K}$$

$T_1 = 273$ K, $T_2 = 673$ K

30. $\eta = 1 - \frac{T_2}{T_1}$

T_1 is increased from 1500°C to 1600°C

$T_1 = 1873$ K

T_2 remain constant $T_2 = 773$ K

$$\eta_1 = \frac{1873 - 773}{1873} = 58.73\%$$

T_1 remain constant = 1500° C

$T_1 = 1500 + 273 = 1773$ k

T_2 is decreased by 100 i.e., 400°C

$T_2 = 400 + 273 = 673$ K

$$\eta_2 = \frac{1773 - 673}{1773} = \frac{1100}{1773} = 62.04\%$$

31. For path 1, Heat given $Q_1 = +1000$ J

Work done $= W_1$ [let]

For path 2, Work done $W_2 = (W_1 - 100)$ J

Heat given $Q_2 = ?$

As change in internal energy between two states for different path is same.

$$\Delta U = Q_1 - W_1 = Q_2 - W_2$$

$$1000 - W_1 = Q_2 - (W_1 - 100)$$

$$Q_2 = 1000 - 100 = 9900 \text{ J}$$

QR Code for Quick Test 1	QR Code for Quick Test 2	QR Code for Quick Test 3

SELF ASSESSMENT TEST

Multiple Choice Questions (MCQs)

1. If the amount of heat given to a system be 35 J and the amount of work done by the system be −15 J, then the change in the internal energy of the system is

(a) −50 J (b) 20 J (c) 30 J (d) 50 J

2. In an isothermal reversible expansion, if the volume of 96 g of oxygen at 27°C is increased from 70 L to 140 L then the work done by the gas will be

(a) $300\,R\log_{10}2$ (b) $81\,R\log_e 2$
(c) $900\,R\log_{10}2$ (d) $2.3\times 900\,R\log_{10}2$

3. An ideal gas at 27°C is compressed adiabatically to $\frac{8}{27}$ of its original volume. If $\gamma = \frac{5}{3}$, then the rise in temperature is

(a) 400 K (b) 375 K (c) 225 K (d) 405 K

4. A Carnot engine working between 300 K and 600 K has work output of 800 J per cycle. What is the amount of heat energy supplied to the engine from source per cycle?

(a) 1800 J/Cycle (b) 1000 J/Cycle
(c) 2000 J/Cycle (d) 1600 J/Cycle

5. Thermodynamic processes are indicated in the following diagram.

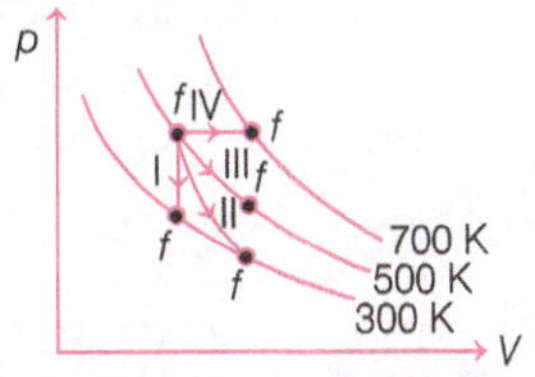

Column-I		Column-II	
(A)	Process -I	(P)	Adiabatic
(B)	Process -II	(Q)	Isobaric
(C)	Process -III	(R)	Isochoric
(D)	Process -IV	(S)	Isothermal

(a) A-S, B-Q, C-P, D-R
(b) A-P, B-R, C-S, D-Q
(c) A-R, B-P, C-S, D-Q
(d) A-R, B-S, C-Q, D-P

Assertion-Reason

Directions *(Q.No. 6-7) In the following questions, two statements are given- one labelled Assertion (A) and the other labelled Reason (R). Select the correct answer to these questions from the codes (a), (b), (c) and (d) as given below.*

(a) Both Assertion and Reason are true and Reason is the correct explanation of Assertion.
(b) Both Assertion and Reason are true but Reason is not the correct e xplanation of Assertion.
(c) Assertion is true but Reason is false.
(d) Assertion is false but Reason is true.

6. Assertion (A) A room can be cooled by opening the door of a refrigerator in closed room.
Reason (R) Heat flows from lower temperature (refrigerator) to higher temperature (room).

7. Assertion (A) Efficiency of Carnot engine increase on reducing the temperature of sink
Reason (R) The efficiency of Carnot engine is defined as ratio of net mechanical work done per cycle by the gas to the amount of heat absorbed per cycle from the source.

Case Based Questions

Directions *(Q.No.8) This question is case study based question. Read the following paragraph and answer the questions on the basis of same.*

8. Two cylinders *A* and *B* of equal capacity are connected to each other *via* a stopcock. *A* contains a gas at standard temperature and pressure. *B* is completely evacuated. The entire system in thermally insulated. The stopcock is suddenly opened.

(i) What is final pressure of the gas in cylinders *A* and *B*?
(ii) What is the change in internal energy of the gas?
(iii) What is the change in temperature of the gas?
(iv) Do the intermediate states of the system (before settling to the final equilibrium state) lie on its *p-V-T* surface?

Very Short Answer Type Questions

9. Refrigerator transfers heat from cold body to a hot body. Does this violate the second law of thermodyamics?

10. Under what ideal condition, the efficiency of a Carnot engine be 100%.

11. Plot a graph between internal energy (U) and temperature (T) of an ideal gas.

Short Answer Type Questions

12. No real engine can have an efficiency greater than that of a Carnot engine working between the same temperatures. Why?

13. A gas undergoes a change of state during which 100 J of heat is supplied to it and it does 20 J of work. The system is brought back to its original state through a process during which 20 J of heat is released by the gas. Find the work done by the gas in the second process.

14. A gas expands with temperature according to the relation $V = kT^{2/3}$. What is the work done when the temperature changes by 30°C?

Long Answer Type Questions

15. (i) A mole of an ideal gas at 300 K is expanded from a volume of 10 L to 20 L at constant pressure of 1 atm. Calculate the work done by the gas during the expansion.

(ii) A certain amount of gas undergoes an isothermal expansion from 5 L to 10 L at a constant temperature of 300 K. If the pressure of the gas is 2 atm, calculate the work done by the gas during the expansion.

15. When a system is taken from state A to state B along the path ACB, 80 k cal of heat flows into the system and 30 kcal of work is done.

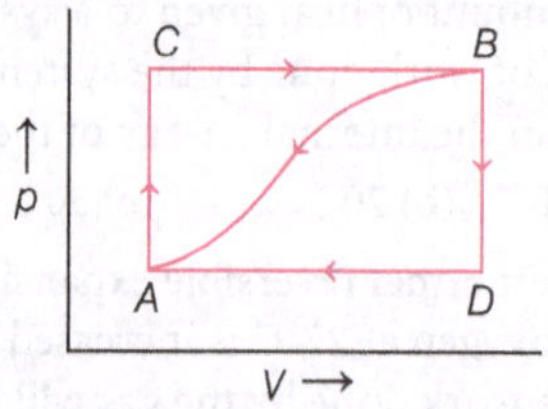

(a) How much heat flows into the system along path ADB, if the work done is 10 kcal?

(b) When the system is returned from B to A along the curved path, the work done is 20 kcal. Does the system absorb or liberate heat?

(c) If $U_A = 0$ and $U_D = 40$ kcal, find the heat absorbed in the process AD.

Answers

1. (d) 2. (d) 3. (b) 4. (d) 5. (c)
6. (d) 7. (b) 13. 60 J 14. 20R
15. (i) 1013 J (ii) 753.23 J
16. (i) 60 kcal (ii) −70 kcal (iii) 50 kcal

12

CHAPTER

The **Kinetic Theory of Gases** is a scientific theory that explains the behaviour of gases in terms of the motion of their constituent particles, such as atoms or molecules. According to modern theories, atoms are not elementary; they consist of a nucleus and electrons. Nucleus made up of protons and neutrons, which are further composed of quarks.

▼ **YOUR STUDY GOALS**

▼ **YOUR PRACTICE GOAL**

- Objective Type Questions (27 Qs ; MCQs, A-R, Matching)
- Case Based Questions (2)
- Subjective Questions (4 VSAs, 12 SAs, 6 LAs)
- Numerical Problems (18)

Kinetic Theory of Gases

12.1 Molecular Nature of Matter

John Dalton proposed atomic theory (also called **molecular theory**) to explain the formation of a compound. According to this theory

- The smallest constituent of an element is **atom.**
- Atoms combine to form a molecule of the **compound.**
- The molecules of a given gas are all identical but are different than those of another gas.

According to **atomic hypothesis**, all substances are made up of atoms, which are small particles in constant motion. Atoms attract each other when distant and repel when compressed.

The observation of molecules with electron microscope and scanning tunneling microscope shows that the **size of an atom is around (1 Å) 10^{-10} m.**

States of Matter

- Solids are the substances which have definite shape and volume. In solid, the interatomic spacing is least (about 2 Å) and interatomic force of attraction is maximum.
- **Liquids** possess a definite volume but no fixed shape. Their interatomic spacing is greater than in solids but less than in

gases, leading to weaker attractive forces that allow them to flow.

- Gases are the substances which do not have fixed shape and volume. In gases, the interatomic spacing is maximum (about 10 Å). Interatomic force of attraction is least in comparison to solids and liquids.

Ideal Gas Equation

- The ideal gas equation can be written as

$$pV = \mu RT$$

where, μ is number of moles and $R = N_A k_B$ is universal constant and T is absolute temperature in kelvin.

- Let N be the number of molecules in mass M of a gas and N_A be the number of molecules in the molecular weight M_0 of the gas,

then $$\mu = \frac{M}{M_0} = \frac{N}{N_A}$$

- In terms of density, ideal gas equation is $p = \frac{\rho RT}{M_0}$

where, ρ = mass density of the gas,

M_0 = molar mass of the gas (mass of one mole of the gas),

$R = 8.314 \text{ J mol}^{-1}\text{K}^{-1}$

Example 1. Molar volume is the volume occupied by 1 mol of any (ideal) gas at standard temperature and pressure (STP : 1 atm pressure, 0°C). Show that, it is 22.4 L.

Sol. As, for one mole of ideal gas, $pV = \mu RT$ $[\mu = 1]$

$$pV = RT \Rightarrow V = \frac{RT}{p}$$

Putting, $R = 8.31 \text{ J mol}^{-1}\text{ K}^{-1}, T = 273\text{K}$

$p = 1 \text{ atm} = 1.013 \times 10^5 \text{ N-m}^{-2}$

$$V = \frac{8.31 \times 273}{1.013 \times 10^5} = 0.0224 \text{ m}^3 = 22.4 \text{ L} \quad [\because 1\text{m}^3 = 10^3 \text{L}]$$

Example 2. The density of water is 1000 kgm^{-3}. The density of water vapour at 100°C and 1 atm pressure is 0.6 kg m^{-3}. The volume of a molecule multiplied by the total number gives, which is called, molecular volume. Estimate the ratio of the molecular volume to the total volume occupied by the water vapour under the above conditions of temperature and pressure. NCERT

Sol. For a given mass of water molecule, Volume $\propto \frac{1}{\text{Density}}$

$\therefore$ Ratio of the molecular volume to the total volume of water vapour

$$= \frac{\text{Density of water vapour}}{\text{Density of water}} = \frac{0.6 \text{ kgm}^{-3}}{1000 \text{ kgm}^{-3}} = 6 \times 10^{-4}$$

Example 3. Estimate the volume of a water molecule using the data in example 2. NCERT

Sol. Molecular mass of water = 18

$\therefore$ Number of molecules in 18 g or 0.018 kg of water $= 6 \times 10^{23}$

Mass of 1 molecule of water $= \frac{0.018}{6 \times 10^{23}} = 3 \times 10^{-26}\text{kg}$

In the liquid phase, the molecules of water are closely packed, so density of water molecules may be taken equal to the density of bulk water = 1000 kgm^{-3}

$\therefore$ Volume of a water molecule

$$= \frac{\text{Mass}}{\text{Density}}$$

$$= \frac{3 \times 10^{-26}}{1000} = 3 \times 10^{-29} \text{m}^3$$

12.2 Behaviour of Real Gas and Ideal Gas

A gas which strictly obeys the gas laws, is called an **ideal gas** or **perfect gas**. An ideal gas is a theoretical model of a gas and no real gas is truly ideal.

However, a **real gas behaves as an ideal gas most closely at low pressure and high temperature**. This is because at low pressure and high temperature, the molecules of gas are far apart due to which molecular force of attraction is negligible.

As, $pV = \mu RT$ (ideal gas equation)

$$\therefore \frac{pV}{\mu T} = R = \text{constant}$$

There is a graph drawn between $\frac{pV}{\mu T}$ and p as shown in the figure below.

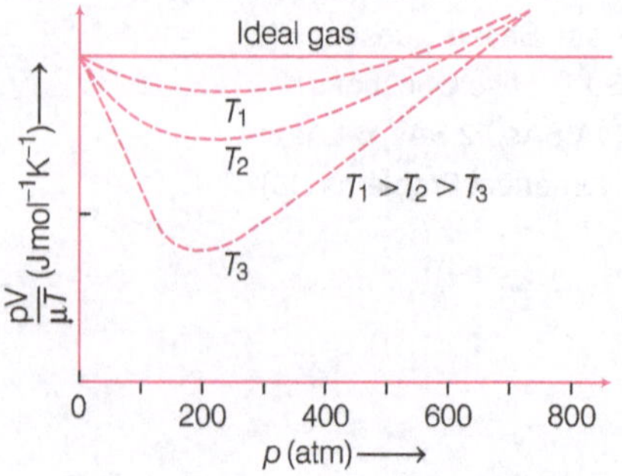

Behaviour of real gases approach ideal gas at low pressure and high temperature

In the given graph

- The dotted lines signifies the behaviour of real gases at temperatures T_1, T_2 and T_3.
- On increasing the temperature, the behaviour of real gases approaches the ideal gas behaviour.

Example 4. **An air bubble of volume 1.0 cm^3 rises from the bottom of a lake 40 m deep at a temperature of 12°C. To what volume does it grow when it reaches the surface, which is at a temperature of 35°C? (Given, 1 atm = 1.01×10^5 Pa)** NCERT

Sol. Initially, when air bubble is at 40 m deep. Then,

$$V_1 = 1\,\text{cm}^3 = 1\times 10^{-6}\,\text{m}^3,$$
$$T_1 = 12\,°\text{C} = 273+12 = 285\,\text{K}$$
$$p_1 = 1\,\text{atm} + h\rho g$$
$$= 1.01\times 10^5 + 40\times 10^3\times 9.8$$
$$= 493000\,\text{Pa}$$

Firstly, when air bubble reaches at the surface, then

$$T_2 = 35°\text{C} = 273+35 = 308\,\text{K}$$
$$p_2 = 1\,\text{atm} = 1.01\times 10^5\,\text{Pa}, V_2 = ?$$

As we know, $\dfrac{p_1V_1}{T_1} = \dfrac{p_2V_2}{T_2}$

$$\Rightarrow \quad V_2 = \frac{p_1V_1T_2}{T_1p_2}$$

Final volume,

$$V_2 = \frac{(493000)\times(1\times 10^{-6})\times 308}{285\times 1.01\times 10^5}$$
$$= 5.275\times 10^{-6}\,\text{m}^2$$

12.3 Laws for an Ideal Gas

Boyle's Law

It states that for a given mass of a gas at constant temperature, the volume of that mass of gas is inversely proportional to its pressure. i.e. $V\propto\dfrac{1}{p}$

According to ideal gas equation, we get $pV=\mu RT$

At constant temperature, pV = constant

$\Rightarrow$ Boyle's law, $p_1V_1 = p_2V_2 = p_3V_3 \cdots =$ constant

The figure below shows the comparison between experimental p-V curves and the theoretical curves predicted by Boyle's law.

The graphs between (a) p **and** V, and (b) p **and** $\dfrac{1}{V}$ at constant temperature are shown below.

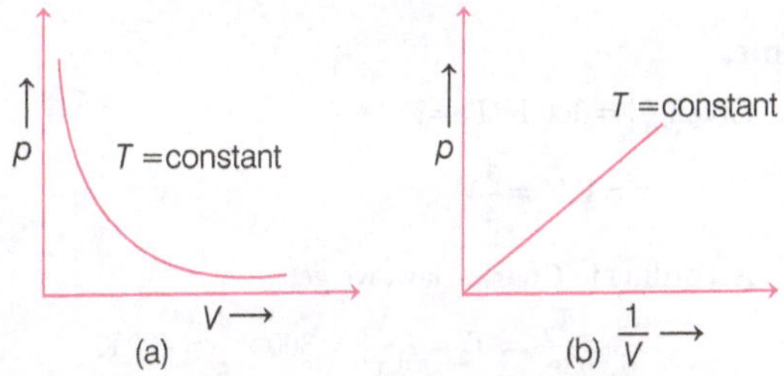

Example 5. **A gas at 27°C in a cylinder has a volume of 4 L and pressure 100 N/m^2. If the gas is first compressed at constant temperature, so that the pressure is 150 N/m^2. Estimate the change in volume.**

Sol. Given, $V_1 = 4$ L, $V_2 = ?$, $p_1 = 100$ N/m^2

$$p_2 = 150\,\text{N/m}^2, \Delta V = ?$$

Using Boyle's law for constant temperature, we have

$$p_1V_1 = p_2V_2$$
$$\Rightarrow \quad V_2 = \frac{p_1V_1}{p_2} = \frac{100\times 4}{150} = 2.667\,\text{L}$$

$\therefore$ Change in volume, $\Delta V = V_1 - V_2 = 4 - 2.667 = 1.33$ L

Charles' Law

It states that for a given mass of an ideal gas at constant pressure, volume (V) of a gas is directly proportional to its absolute temperature (T).

i.e. $\quad V\propto T$

From ideal gas equation, $\quad \dfrac{V}{T} = \dfrac{\mu R}{p}$

At constant pressure, $\dfrac{V}{T}$ = constant

$\Rightarrow$ Charles' law, $\dfrac{V_1}{T_1} = \dfrac{V_2}{T_2} = \dfrac{V_3}{T_3} = \cdots =$ constant

The graph between V and T at constant pressure is shown below.

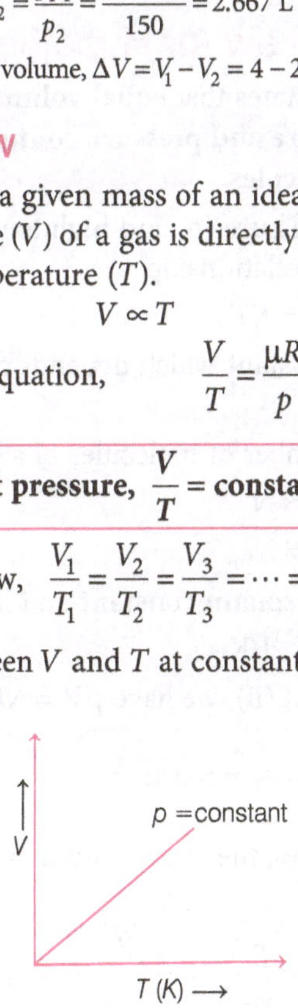

Example 6. **A gas is filled in a cylinder at 300K. Calculate the temperature upto which it should be heated, so that its volume becomes $\frac{4}{3}$ of its initial volume.**

Sol. Given, $T_1 = 300$ K, $T_2 = ?$

$$V_1 = V, V_2 = \frac{4}{3}V$$

According to Charles' law, we get

$$\frac{V_2}{V_1} = \frac{T_2}{T_1} \Rightarrow T_2 = T_1\frac{V_2}{V_1} = 300 \times \frac{4}{3} = 400 \text{ K}$$

Gay Lussac's Law

It states that at constant volume, pressure of the given mass of a gas is directly proportional to its absolute temperature.

$$p \propto T$$

At constant volume, $\frac{p}{T} = \text{constant}$

Avogadro's Law (or Hypothesis)

Avogadro's law states that **equal volume of all gases at same temperature and pressure contain equal number of molecules.**

Proof At low pressure (p) and high temperature (T), gases follow the relationship

$$pV = KT \quad \text{...(i)}$$

where, K is a constant which depends on the volume (V) of the gas.

Let N be the number of molecules of a gas sample, then

$$K \propto N$$

i.e. $$K = Nk_B \quad \text{...(ii)}$$

where, k_B is **Boltzmann constant** and its value in SI units is 1.38×10^{-23} J/K.

From Eqs. (i) and (ii), we have $pV = Nk_BT$

or $$\frac{pV}{NT} = k_B = \text{constant}$$

For different gases, the above equation can be written as

$$\frac{p_1V_1}{N_1T_1} = \frac{p_2V_2}{N_2T_2} = \frac{p_3V_3}{N_3T_3} \cdots = k_B = \text{constant}$$

If p, V and T are same, then N will be same for all gases and this is **Avogadro's hypothesis.**

TEACHER TIP

At STP (Standard Temperature 273 K and Pressure 1 atm), 22.4 L of any gas has a mass equal to its molecular weight in grams. The amount of substance is called a mole.

The number of atoms present in 1 mole of a substance is known as **Avogadro's number.** Its symbol is N_A.

Avogadro's number (N_A) = 6.023×10^{23}

Dalton's Law of Partial Pressure

It states that the total pressure of a mixture of non-interacting ideal gases is equal to the sum of partial pressures exerted by individual gases in the mixture.

i.e. $$p = p_1 + p_2 + p_3 + \cdots$$

where, p_1, p_2, p_3 are the partial pressures of component gases.

Example 7. **Two non-reactive gases are kept in a container. The ratio of their partial pressures is given 5 : 3. Find the ratio of number of molecules.**

Sol. As two non-reactive gases are mixed in a container, so the value of V and T will be same for both with partial pressures p_1 and p_2.

For gas I $p_1V = \mu_1RT$ ...(i)

For gas II $p_2V = \mu_2RT$ ...(ii)

Dividing Eq. (i) by Eq. (ii), we get

$$\frac{p_1}{p_2} = \frac{\mu_1}{\mu_2} \quad \text{...(iii)}$$

$$\mu_1 = N_1/N_A \quad \text{...(iv)}$$

$$\mu_2 = N_2/N_A \quad \text{...(v)}$$

Dividing Eq. (iv) by Eq. (v), we get

$$\frac{\mu_1}{\mu_2} = \frac{N_1}{N_2} \quad \text{...(vi)}$$

From Eqs. (iii) and (vi), we get

$$\frac{N_1}{N_2} = \frac{\mu_1}{\mu_2} = \frac{p_1}{p_2} \Rightarrow \frac{N_1}{N_2} = \frac{p_1}{p_2} \text{ or } \frac{N_1}{N_2} = \frac{5}{3}$$

Graham's Law of Diffusion

It states that the rate of diffusion of a gas is inversely proportional to the square root of its density.

$$r \propto \frac{1}{\sqrt{\rho}} \quad \text{...(i)}$$

If p is the pressure, M_0 is the molecular mass and T is the temperature of a gas, the density is given by

$$\rho = \frac{pM_0}{RT} \quad \text{...(ii)}$$

So $$r \propto \frac{1}{\sqrt{M_0}} \quad \text{[from Eqs. (i) and (ii)]}$$

Let r_1 and r_2 be the rates of diffusion of gases 1 and 2 respectively, then

$$\boxed{\frac{r_1}{r_2} = \sqrt{\frac{\rho_2}{\rho_1}} = \sqrt{\frac{M_{02}}{M_{01}}}}$$

where, ρ_1 is density of gas 1 and ρ_2 is density of gas 2.

Example 8. From a certain apparatus, the diffusion rate of hydrogen has an average value of 28.7 $cm^3 s^{-1}$. The diffusion of another gas under the same conditions is measured to have an average rate of 7.2 $cm^3 s^{-1}$. Identify the gas. NCERT

Sol. According to Graham's law of diffusion, we get

$$\frac{r_1}{r_2} = \sqrt{\frac{M_2}{M_1}}$$

where, r_1 = rate of diffusion of hydrogen = 28.7 $cm^3 s^{-1}$

r_2 = rate of diffusion of unknown gas = 7. 2 $cm^3 s^{-1}$

M_1 = molecular mass of hydrogen = 2 unit

M_2 = molecular mass of unknown gas = ?

$$\therefore \quad \frac{28.7}{7.2} = \sqrt{\frac{M_2}{2}}$$

$$\Rightarrow M_2 = \left(\frac{28.7}{7.2}\right)^2 \times 2 = 31.78 \approx 32$$

which is molecular mass of oxygen, so unknown gas is oxygen.

12.4 Kinetic Theory of Ideal Gas

Kinetic theory of gases is based on the molecular picture of matter. It correlates the macroscopic properties (e.g. pressure and temperature) of gases to microscopic properties (e.g. speed and kinetic energy) of gas molecules.

Assumptions of Kinetic Theory of Gases

- A given amount of gas consists of a very large number of molecules (of the order of Avogadro's number 10^{23}) and all molecules are identical in all respect.
- **Assumptions Regarding Motion** The molecules of a gas are in a state of continous random motion in all directions with different speeds. They move freely in straight lines following **Newton's first law.**
- **Assumptions Regarding Pressure** The size of a molecule is much smaller than the average separation between the molecules. At ordinary pressure and temperature, the average distance between molecules is about 20 Å, whereas size of a molecule is 2 Å.
- **Assumptions Regarding Force** There is no intermolecular forces between molecules of gas except during collision.
- **Assumptions Regarding Collisions** The collision between molecules among themselves or between molecules and walls are perfectly elastic. i.e. Total momentum and total kinetic energy of molecules are conserved, however only their velocities will change.
- The duration of collision between two molecules is negligible as compared to time interval of two successive collisions, i.e. collisions are instantaneous.
- **Assumptions Regarding Density** The density and the distribution of molecules is uniform throughout the gas.

Pressure of an Ideal Gas

Using kinetic theory of gases, the pressure exerted by an ideal gas is gives by

$$p = \frac{1}{3}\left(\frac{N}{V}\right) m\bar{v}^2 = \frac{1}{3} nm\bar{v}^2$$

$$\boxed{p = \frac{1}{3}\rho\bar{v}^2}$$

where, N is number of molecules, V is volume, m is the mass, n is number density, ρ is density and $\bar{v}^2$ is the mean square speed of the gas molecules.

Example 9. A container is filled with a gas at a pressure of 76 cm of mercury at a certain temperature. The mass of a gas is increased by 50% by introducing more gas in the container at same temperature. Calculate the final pressure of the gas.

Sol. According to kinetic theory of gases,

$$pV = \frac{1}{3}Mv_{rms}^2$$

At constant temperature, v_{rms}^2 is constant. As V is also constant.

$$\therefore \quad p \propto M$$

When the mass of the gas is increased by 50%, pressure also increased by 50%.

$\therefore$ Resultant pressure $= 76 + \frac{50}{100} \times 76 = 114$ cm of Hg

Kinetic Interpretation of Temperature

The molecules of an ideal gas are considered to have only translational motion, so they have only translation kinetic energy.

The total translational kinetic energy of an ideal gas is given by

$$E = N\left(\frac{1}{2}m\bar{v}^2\right) = \frac{3}{2}pV = \frac{3}{2}Nk_BT$$

where, N is number of molecules, m is the mass, p is pressure, V is volume, T is temperature and $\bar{v}^2$ is the mean square speed of the gas molecules .

The **average kinetic energy** of a molecule is given by

$$E = \frac{1}{2}m\bar{v}^2 = \frac{3}{2}k_BT$$

Average kinetic energy, $\frac{1}{2}m\bar{v}^2 \propto T$

So, the **average kinetic energy of a molecule is directly proportional to the absolute temperature of the gas.** It is independent of pressure, volume and the nature of the ideal gas.

Note Absolute zero of temperature is defined as that temperature at which the velocities of the gas molecules become zero. The value of absolute zero for an ideal gas is −273°C.

Example 10. A balloon has 5.0 g mole of helium at 7°C. Calculate NCERT Exemplar

(i) the number of atoms of helium in the balloon.

(ii) the total internal energy of the system.

Sol. (i) Here, $\mu = 5.0$, $T = 7\,°C = 273 + 7 = 280$ K

Number of atoms $= \mu N_A = 5.0 \times 6.02 \times 10^{23}$

$\approx 30 \times 10^{23}$

(ii) Average kinetic energy per molecule $= \frac{3}{2}k_BT$

$\therefore$ Total internal energy $= \frac{3}{2}k_BT \times N$

$= \frac{3}{2} \times 30 \times 10^{23} \times 1.38 \times 10^{-23} \times 280$

$= 1.74 \times 10^4$ J

Root Mean Square Speed

The square root of the mean square speed $\bar{v}^2$ of molecules is known as root mean square speed.

i.e. $$v_{rms} = \sqrt{\bar{v}^2} = \sqrt{\frac{v_1^2 + v_2^2 + v_3^2 + \ldots\ldots v_n^2}{N}}$$

From kinetic interpretation,

$$\frac{1}{2}m\bar{v}^2 = \frac{3}{2}k_BT$$

So, $$\bar{v}^2 = \frac{3k_BT}{m}$$

Taking square root of both the sides, we get

$$\sqrt{\bar{v}^2} = \sqrt{\frac{3k_BT}{m}}$$

Root mean square speed, $$v_{rms} = \sqrt{\frac{3k_BT}{m}} = \sqrt{\frac{3RT}{M}}$$

where, m = mass of one molecule,

k_B = Boltzmann constant

and T = absolute temperature.

Most probable speed

The speed possessed by the maximum number of molecules in a gas at a given temperature.

$$v_{mp} = \sqrt{\frac{2k_BT}{m}}$$

Mean or Average speed

The arithmetic mean of the speed of the molecules of a gas at a given temperature.

$$v_{av} = \frac{v_1 + v_2 + v_3 + \ldots\ldots + v_n}{N}$$

$$\Rightarrow \quad v_{av} = \sqrt{\frac{8k_BT}{\pi m}}$$

According to Maxwell's speed distribution, the three speeds are related as $v_{rms} > v_{av} > v_{amp}$.

Example 11. Find root mean square speed of a nitrogen molecule at 300 K.

Sol. Molar mass of nitrogen molecule, $M = 28 \times 10^{-3}$ kg/mol

$$v_{rms} = \sqrt{\frac{3RT}{M}} = \sqrt{\frac{3 \times 8.31 \times 300}{28 \times 10^{-3}}}$$

$= 516.82$ m/s

Example 12. **A sample of oxygen gas (O_2) is at a temperature of 300 K. Given that the molar mass of oxygen is 32 g/mol, calculate the following.**

(i) Root mean square (rms) speed

(ii) Most probable speed (v_{mp})

(iii) Average speed (v_{avg})

Take the gas constant $R = 8.314$ J/mol-K

Sol. Convert molar mass into kilogram,

$$M = 32 \text{ g/mol} = 0.032 \text{ kg/mol}$$

(i) The rms speed is given by

$$v_{rms} = \sqrt{\frac{3k_B T}{m}}$$

On putting the values,

$$v_{rms} = \sqrt{\frac{3 \times 8.314 \times 300}{0.032}} = \sqrt{\frac{7482.6}{0.032}}$$

$$v_{rms} = \sqrt{233{,}831.25} \approx 483.56 \text{ m}$$

(ii) The most probable speed is given by

$$v_{mp} = \sqrt{\frac{2k_B T}{m}}$$

$$v_{mp} = \sqrt{\frac{2 \times 8.314 \times 300}{0.032}}$$

$$v_{mp} = \sqrt{\frac{4988.4}{0.032}}$$

$$v_{mp} = \sqrt{155{,}887.5} \approx 394.82 \text{ m/s}$$

(iii) The average speed is given by

$$v_{avg} = \sqrt{\frac{8k_B T}{\pi m}}$$

$$v_{avg} = \sqrt{\frac{8 \times 8.314 \times 300}{\pi \times 0.032}}$$

$$v_{avg} = \sqrt{\frac{19953.6}{0.10048}}$$

$$v_{avg} \approx 445.62 \text{ m/s}$$

Quick Test 1

Conceptual Questions

1. The given graph shows the variation of pV *versus* p graph for different gases at constant temperature. Which of the following gas is ideal and why?

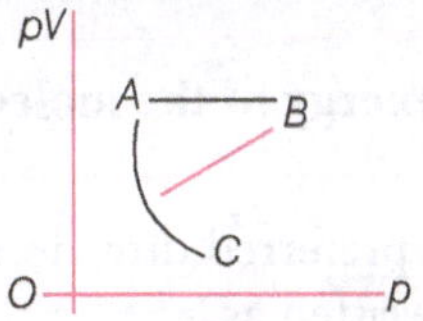

2. Explain Dalton's law of definite and multiple proportion.

3. (i) How does the pressure of a gas depend on its number of molecules?

(ii) If number of molecules of gas in a vessel is doubled, how is the pressure of gas affected?

4. What would be the effect on rms velocity of gas molecules, if the temperature of the gas is increased by a factor 4?

5. A gas mixture consists of molecules of types A, B and C with masses, $m_A > m_B > m_C$. Rank the three types of molecules in decreasing order of (i) average KE and (ii) rms speed. *NCERT Exemplar*

Numerical Questions

6. Estimate the total number of air molecules (inclusive of oxygen, nitrogen, water vapour and other constituents) in a room of capacity 25.0 m^3 at a temperature of 27°C and 1 atm pressure. (Take, $k_B = 1.38 \times 10^{-23}$ JK^{-1}) *NCERT*

7. Calculate the number of atoms in 39.4 g gold. Molar mass of gold is 197g mol^{-1}. *NCERT Exemplar*

8. Two molecules of a gas have speeds of 9×10^6 ms^{-1} and 1×10^6 ms^{-1}, respectively. What is the root mean square speed of these molecules? *NCERT Exemplar*

9. Estimate the average thermal energy of a helium atom at (i) room temperature (27° C) (ii) the temperature on the surface of the sun (6000 K), (iii) the temperature of 10 million kelvin (the typical core temperature in the case of a star). *NCERT*

Answers

6. 6.10×10^{26} 7. 1.2×10^{23} 8. $\sqrt{41} \times 10^6$ ms^{-1}

9. (i) 6.21×10^{-21} J (ii) 1.242×10^{-19} (iii) 2.07×10^{-16} J

For Solutions, See QR Code on Pg. 426

12.5 Motion of Gas Molecules

Degree of Freedom

The total number of coordinates or independent quantities required to describe completely the position and configuration of a dynamical system is known as **number of degrees of freedom** of the system.

It is represented by f and expressed as

$$\boxed{f = 3N - K}$$

where, N is the number of particles in a system and K is number of independent relations between the particles.

The degree of freedom can be **translational, rotational** or **vibrational** or **any combination of these.**

The degrees of freedom are of three types

- **Translational degree of freedom** — Maximum three degree of freedom are there corresponding to translational motion.
- **Rotational degree of freedom** — The number of degrees of freedom in this case depends on the structure of the molecule.
- **Vibrational degree of freedom** — It is exhibited at high temperature.

The table for the value of degree of freedom for different gases is shown below

Atomicity of gas	Arrangement of atoms	N	λ	f
Monoatomic He, Ne, Ar, etc.		1	0	3
Diatomic H_2, N_2, O_2, CO, etc.		2	1	5
Triatomic (linear) CO_2, HCN, etc.,		3	2	7
Triatomic (non-linear) SO_2, H_2O, etc.	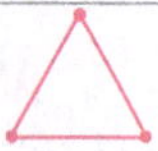	3	3	6

Degrees of freedom for different gases according to atomicity of gases

Atomicity of gas	Transl-ational	Rotati-onal	Vibrat-ional	Total	
Monoatomic He, Ar, Ne, ideal gas etc.	3	0	0	3	
Diatomic	3	2	0	5	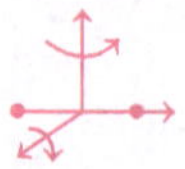
Triatomic or (Triatomic CO_2, C_2H_2)	3	2	2	7	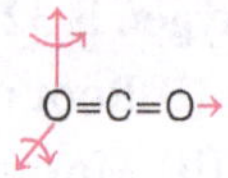
Polyatomic (Triangular H_2O, NH_3 CH_4)	3	3	0	6	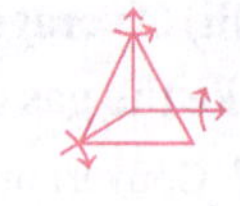

Law of Equipartition of Energy

It states that **'for a dynamic system in thermal equilibrium, the total energy is distributed equally amongst all the degree of freedom and the energy associated with each molecule per degree of freedom is $\frac{1}{2}k_BT$.**

where, $k_B = 1.38 \times 10^{-23} \text{JK}^{-1}$ is Boltzmann constant and T is absolute temperature of system on the kelvin scale.

For a monoatomic gas in thermal equilibrium at temperature T, the average value of translational energy of the molecule

$$\langle E_t \rangle = \left\langle \frac{1}{2}mv_x^2 \right\rangle + \left\langle \frac{1}{2}mv_y^2 \right\rangle + \left\langle \frac{1}{2}mv_z^2 \right\rangle$$

Translational energy of the molecules $\langle E_t \rangle = \frac{3}{2}k_BT$

Since, there is no preferred direction, then the above equation can be written as

$$\left\langle \frac{1}{2}mv_x^2 \right\rangle = \frac{1}{2}k_BT, \left\langle \frac{1}{2}mv_y^2 \right\rangle = \frac{1}{2}k_BT, \left\langle \frac{1}{2}mv_z^2 \right\rangle = \frac{1}{2}k_BT$$

Thus, energy associated with each molecule per degree of freedom is $\frac{1}{2}k_BT$, which is **law of equilibrium of energy.**

Therefore, total energy of a diatomic gas molecule is the sum of translational energy E_t and rotational energy E_r.

- In case of diatomic/polyatomic gas, molecules may not be a **rigid rotator** having no vibration. Molecules like CO at moderate temperatures have a mode of vibration and contributes a vibrational energy E_v to total energy

$$E_v = \frac{1}{2}m\left(\frac{dy}{dt}\right)^2 + \frac{1}{2}ky^2$$

where, k = force constant of the oscillator

and y = vibrational coordinate.

$\therefore$ Total energy, $E = E_t + E_v + E_r$

Molar Heat Capacity (C)

Molar heat capacity (C) is the heat required to raise the temperature of 1 mole of a gas by 1°C (or 1K).

Monoatomic Gases

In monoatomic gases, a molecule has **three translational degrees** of freedom, i.e. $f = 3$.

The total energy of one mole of a monoatomic gas is given by

$$U = \frac{f}{2}k_B T N_A = \frac{3}{2}k_B T N_A$$

$$= \frac{3}{2}RT \quad (\text{as } R = N_A k_B)$$

The specific heat at constant volume is given by

$$C_v = \frac{dU}{dT} = \frac{f}{2}R = \frac{3}{2}R$$

Using Mayer's formula ($C_p - C_V = R$) the specific heat at constant pressure is given by

$$C_p = \left(\frac{f}{2}+1\right)R = \frac{5}{2}R$$

The ratio of specific heat capacities for monoatomic gases is

$$\gamma = \frac{C_p}{C_V} = \frac{5}{3} = 1.67$$

Example 13. **Calculate the molecular kinetic energy of 1 g of helium (molecular weight 4) at 127° C. (Given, $R = 8.31\ \text{Jmol}^{-1}\text{K}^{-1}$)**

Sol. Given, $T = 273 + 127 = 400$ K

Helium is monoatomic gas.

$\therefore$ Average kinetic energy per mole of helium $= \frac{3}{2}RT$

Average kinetic energy of 1 g of helium

$$= \frac{3}{2}\frac{RT}{M} = \frac{3 \times 8.31 \times 400}{2 \times 4} = 1246.5\ \text{J}$$

Diatomic Gases

If vibrational mode is neglected in diatomic gases, a molecule has **five translational degrees** of freedom. i.e. $f = 5$.

The total energy of one mole of a diatomic gas is given by

$$U = \frac{5}{2}RT$$

Specific heat at constant volume, $C_V = \frac{dU}{dT} = \frac{5}{2}R$

Specific heat at constant pressure, $C_p = \frac{7}{2}R$

The ratio of specific heat capacities for the rigid diatomic gases is

$$\gamma = \frac{C_p}{C_V} = \frac{7}{5} = 1.40$$

Example 14. **Calculate the total number of degrees of freedom possessed by the molecules in 1 cm^3 of H_2 gas at temperature 273 K and 1 atm pressure?** NCERT Exemplar

Sol. At 273 K temperature and 1 atm pressure mean STP condition.

$\therefore$ Number of H_2 molecules on 22400 cm^3 at STP

$= 6.02 \times 10^{23}$

$\therefore$ Number of H_2 molecules in 1 cm^3 at STP

$$= \frac{6.02 \times 10^{23}}{22400} = 2.6875 \times 10^{19}$$

Number of degrees of freedom associated with each H_2 (diatomic) molecule = 5

$\therefore$ Total number of degrees of freedom associated with 1 cm^3 of gas $= 2.6875 \times 10^{19} \times 5 = 1.34375 \times 10^{20}$

Example 15. **A gas mixture consists of 2.0 moles of oxygen and 4.0 moles of neon at temperature T. Neglecting all vibrational modes, calculate the total internal energy of the system. (Oxygen has two rotational modes)** NCERT Exemplar

Sol. O_2 has five degrees of freedom,

therefore energy per mole $= \frac{5}{2}RT$

$\therefore$ For 2 moles of O_2, energy $= 5RT$

Neon has three degrees of freedom

$\therefore$ Energy per mole $= \frac{3}{2}RT$

$\therefore$ For 4 moles of neon, energy $= 4 \times \frac{3}{2}RT = 6RT$

$\therefore$ Total energy $= 5RT + 6RT = 11RT$

Triatomic Gases

In triatomic linear gases, a molecule has **seven translational degrees of freedom**, i.e. $f = 7$

Total energy of one mole of a diatomic gas,

$$U = \frac{7}{2}RT$$

Specific heat at constant volume,

$$C_V = \frac{dU}{dT} = \frac{7}{2}R$$

Specific heat at constant pressure,

$$C_p = \frac{9}{2}R$$

The ratio of specific heat capacities for triatomic linear gases is

$$\gamma = \frac{C_p}{C_V} = \frac{9}{7} = 1.28$$

Similarly, the ratio of specific heat capacities for triatomic non-linear gases,

$$\gamma = \frac{C_p}{C_V} = \frac{\frac{8}{2}R}{\frac{6}{2}R} = 1.33$$

Polyatomic Gas

A polyatomic gas molecule in general has three translational, three rotational degrees of freedom and with certain number (let f) of vibrational modes. Using law of equipartition of energy, total internal energy of one mole of such gases,

$$U = \left[\frac{3}{2}k_BT + \frac{3}{2}k_BT + fk_BT\right] \times N_A$$

$$\Rightarrow \quad U = (3 + f)RT$$

Now, $$C_V = \frac{dU}{dT} = \frac{d(3+f)RT}{dT} = (3+f)R$$

$$\Rightarrow \quad C_V = (3+f)R$$

$$\therefore \quad C_p = C_V + R = (3+f)R$$

$$\Rightarrow \quad C_p = (4+f)R$$

So, $$\gamma = \frac{C_p}{C_V} = \frac{(4+f)}{(3+f)}$$

Specific Heat Capacity of Solids

In solids, each atom vibrates about its mean position, let us consider one mole of solid containing N_A atoms. By law of equipartition of energy, average energy associated with an atom due to its oscillation in one dimension $= 2 \times \left(\frac{1}{2}k_BT\right) = k_BT$

$\therefore$ In three dimension (3D), average energy per atom

$$= 3k_BT$$

$\therefore$ Total energy of one mole of solid,

$$U = (3k_BT) \times N_A = 3RT \; (\because k_BN_A = R)$$

According to first law of thermodynamics,

$$\Delta Q = \Delta U + \Delta W$$

In case of solid, ΔV is negligible

$$\therefore \quad \Delta Q \approx \Delta U$$

Molar specific heat of solid,

$$C = \frac{\Delta Q}{\Delta T} = \frac{\Delta U}{\Delta T}$$

Specific heat capacity of solids, $C = 3R$

$$\Rightarrow \quad C = 24.93 \text{ J mol}^{-1}\text{K}^{-1} \quad (\because R = 8.31 \text{ Jmol}^{-1}\text{K})^{-1}$$

Specific Heat Capacities of Some Solids at Room Temperature and Atmospheric Pressure

Substance	Specific Heat (J kg^{-1}K^{-1})	Molar Specific Heat (J mol^{-1}K^{-1})
Aluminium	900.0	24.4
Carbon	506.5	6.1
Copper	386.4	24.5
Lead	127.7	26.5
Silver	236.1	25.5
Tungsten	134.4	24.9

From this table, it is clear that the prediction generally agrees with experimental values at ordinary temperature except, i.e. carbon.

Note The temperature at which all metals have constant C_V is called **debye temperature**.

Mean Free Path (λ)

The average distance travelled by a molecule between two successive collisions is known as mean free path of the molecule. It is given by

$$\lambda = \frac{1}{\sqrt{2}\,n\pi d^2}$$

$$\Rightarrow \quad \lambda \propto \frac{1}{n}$$

where, d = diameter of each molecule

and n = number of molecules per unit volume.

Mean free path, $\lambda = \frac{k_BT}{\sqrt{2}\pi d^2 p}$ (**in terms of temperature and pressure**).

The mean free path of a given gas is (i) directly proportional to its absolute temperature and (ii) inversely proportional to its pressure.

Basic Assumptions on Mean Free Path

(i) The molecules of gas are considered as hard spheres, each of diameter d.

(ii) The collision between gas molecules are perfectly elastic.

(iii) All molecules of a gas except the molecules under consideration are at rest.

(iv) A molecule of the gas under consideration collides with all those molecules whose centre are at distance d from centre of molecules under consideration.

Example 16. The average speed of air molecules is 485 m/s. At STP, the number density is $2.7\times 10^{25}\ /m^3$ and diameter of the air molecule is 2×10^{-10} m. Find the value of mean free path (λ) for the air molecule and average time (τ) between successive collisions.

Sol. To find the mean free path, we need the values of d and n. Just put these values in the formula of mean free path.

$$\lambda = \frac{1}{\sqrt{2}n\pi d^2} = \frac{1}{\sqrt{2}\times 2.7\times 10^{25}\times 3.14\times (2\times 10^{-10})^2}$$

$$= 2.9\times 10^{-7}\text{m}$$

The value of $\tau = \frac{l}{v}$

Now, put the values and get the value of τ.

$$\tau = \frac{2.9\times 10^{-7}}{485} = 5.9\times 10^{-10}\text{s}$$

Brownian Motion

It is a continuous *zig-zag* motion of particles of macroscopic size (in order of 10^{-5}m) suspended in fluid.

The Brownian motion depends upon the following factors as

(i) Size of the suspended particle

(ii) Density of the fluid

(iii) Temperature of the medium

(iv) Viscosity of the medium

Quick Test 2

Conceptual Questions

1. How degree of freedom of a gas molecule is related with the temperature?

2. What is basic law followed by equipartition of energy?

3. If there are f degrees of freedom with n moles of a gas, then find the internal energy possessed at a temperature T.

4. At room temperature, diatomic gas molecule has five degrees of freedom. At high temperature, it has seven degrees of freedom, explain?

Numerical Questions

5. Calculate the number of degrees of freedom in 15 cm^3 of nitrogen at NTP.

6. If one mole of ideal monoatomic gas ($\gamma = 5/3$) is mixed with one mole of diatomic gas ($\gamma = 7/5$). What is the value of γ for the mixtures?
(Here, γ represents the ratio of specific heat at constant pressure to that at constant volume)

7. A diatomic gas is heated in a vessel to a temperature of 10000 K. If each molecule possess an average energy E_1. After sometime, a few molecule escape into the atmosphere at 300 K. Due to which, their energy changes to E_2. Calculate the ratio of $\frac{E_1}{E_2}$.

8. Calculate the ratio of the mean free paths of the molecules of two gases having molecular diameters 1Å and 2Å. The gases may be considered under identical conditions of temperature, pressure and volume. *NCERT Exemplar*

9. A cylinder of fixed capacity contains 44.8 L of helium gas at STP. Calculate the amount of heat required to raise the temperature of container by 15°C? (Given, $R = 8.31\,\text{J mol}^{-1}\text{K}^{-1}$)

10. What will be the mean free path of nitrogen gas at STP of given diameter of nitrogen molecule = 2 Å?

Answers

5. 2.015×10^{21}	6. 1.5	7. 140 : 3
8. 4 : 1	9. 374 J	10. 2.1×10^{-7} m

For Solutions, See QR Code on Pg. 426

Mind Map

Kinetic Theory of Gases

Behaviour of Gases

- In a gas, molecules are far from each other and their mutual interactions are negligible except when two molecules collide.
- Gases at low pressures and high temperature, well above, their liquifaction temperatures, obey the equation $PV = Nk_BT$, observation tell that k_B remains constant for all gases.
- **For different gases**

$$\frac{p_1V_1}{N_1T_1} = \frac{p_2V_2}{N_2T_2} = \frac{p_3V_3}{N_3T_3} \ldots\ldots = k_B = \text{constant.}$$

Boltzmann's constant, $k_B = 1.38 \times 10^{-23}$ J/K

Behaviour of Real Gas and Ideal Gas

- A real gas behaves as an ideal gas most closely at low pressure and high temperature.

$$pV = \mu RT$$

$$\frac{pV}{\mu T} = R = \text{Constant}$$

- Behaviour of real gas approach ideal gas at low pressure.

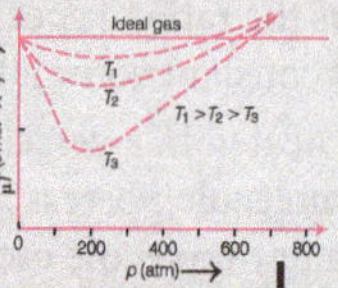

Boyle's Law

- At constant temperature, volume of definite quantity of a gas is inversely proportional to its pressure (p).
- Therefore, $V \propto \frac{1}{p}$ (constant temperature)

$p_1V_1 = p_2V_2 =$ Constant

- p-V curve for temperatures T_1 and T_2 is as shown.

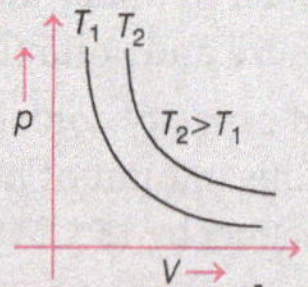

Charles' Law

- At constant pressure, volume of definite quantity of a gas is directly proportional to absolute temperature (T) of the gases. Therefore,

$V \propto T$ (constant pressure)

- $\frac{V_1}{T_1} = \frac{V_2}{T_2} = \frac{V_3}{T_3} = \ldots. =$ Constant

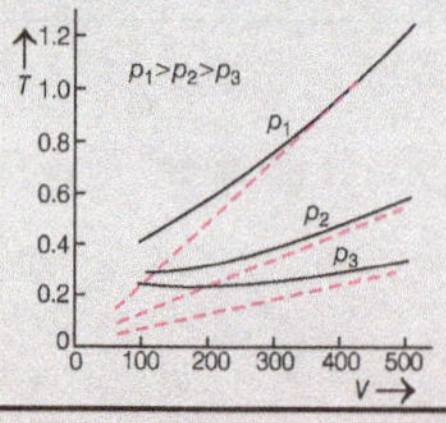

Dalton's Law of Partial Pressure

- Total pressure of mixture of non-interacting ideal gas is equal to the sum of partial pressures exerted by individual gases in the mixture. $p = p_1 + p_2 + p_3 + \ldots$

Kinetic Theory of an Ideal Gas

- A gas which obeys all gaseous laws under all conditions of pressure and temperature is called ideal gas.

Assumption of Kinetic Theory of Gases

- The density and the distribution of molecules is uniform throughout the gas.
- There is no intermolecular forces between molecules of gas except during collision.
- Specific heat capacities C_p and C_V of an ideal gas do not depend on the temperature.

Kinetic Interpretation of Temperature

- In kinetic theory, the kinetic interpretation of temperature states that the average kinetic energy of the gas molecules of an ideal gas is directly proportional to absolute temperature of the molecules.
- Molecular arrangements in solid, liquids and gases.

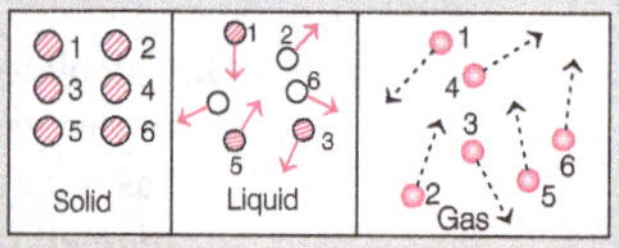

Pressure of an Ideal Gas

- The force exerted by the gas molecules on unit area of the walls of container is called pressure of gas.
- Impulse = Change in momentum

$F\Delta t = \Delta p_x = -2mv_x$

- Average force exerted,

$$F = -\frac{2mv_x}{\Delta t} = \frac{(-2mv_x)}{\left(\frac{2l}{v_x}\right)}$$

$$F = -\frac{mv_x^2}{l}$$

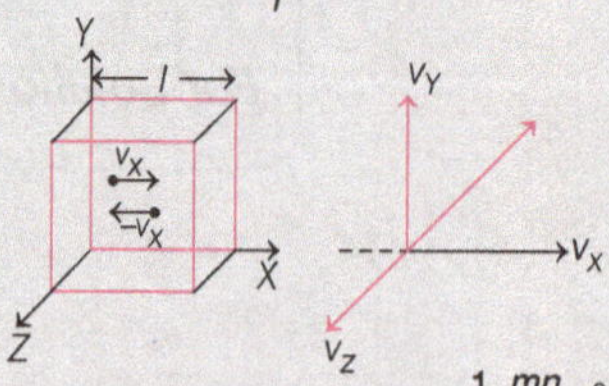

- Pressure of an ideal gas, $p = \frac{1}{3}\frac{mn}{V}v_{rms}^2$

$n \rightarrow$ number of moleculus

Most Probable Speed

The speed with which most of the molecules move is called most probable speed.

$$v_{mp} = \sqrt{\frac{2RT}{M}} = \left(\sqrt{\frac{2}{3}}\right) v_{rms} = 0.816 v_{rms}$$

Concept of Temperature

- **Relation between temperature and rms speed** $\frac{1}{3}Mv_{rms}^2 = RT \Rightarrow v_{rms} = \sqrt{\frac{3RT}{M}}$
- **Relation between temperature and molecular kinetic energy**

$$E = \frac{3}{2}kT$$

- Temperature of gas is directly proportional to square of root of mean square velocity.

Law of Equipartition of Energy

- For a dynamic system in thermal equilibrium, the total energy is distributed equally amongst all the degree of freedom and the energy associated with each molecule per degree of freedom is (1/2) k_BT.
- Translational energy $< E_t > = (3/2)\ k_B T$.

Mean Free Path

- The average distance travelled by a molecule between two successive collisions is known as the mean free path of molecule.
- Mean free path, $\lambda = \frac{1}{\sqrt{2}n\pi d^2}$

Here,

d = Diameter of each molecule and

n = Number of molecules per unit volume.

- The mean free path in gases is of the order of thousand of angstroms.

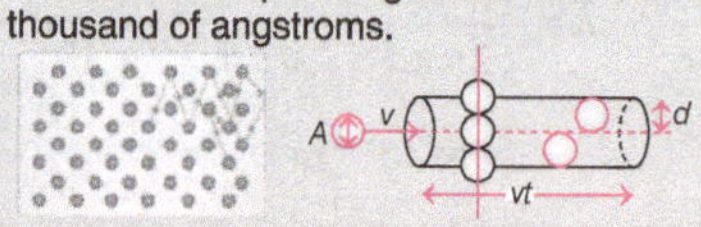

Degree of Freedom

- Total number of coordinates or independent quantities required to describe completely the position and configuration of a dynamical system.

Degree of freedom, $f = 3N - k$

- **For monoatomic gas**, such as helium, neon, argon, have translational degree of freedom. If $N = 1$ and $k = 0$, then $f = 3 \times 1 - 0 = 3$
- **For diatomic gas**, such as oxygen, hydrogen, nitrogen etc. $f = 5$
- **For triatomic gas**, such as H_2S, SO_2 have translational degree of freedom.

$f = 7$, $f = 6$ (for non-linear)

Average Speed

This is equal to average of the speed of molecules i.e.,

$$v_{av} = \frac{v_1 + v_2 + \ldots. + v_n}{n}$$

- The relation among most probable speed, average speed and rms speed is given by

$$v_{mp} : v_{av} : v_{rms} = \sqrt{\frac{2RT}{M}} : \sqrt{\frac{8RT}{\pi M}} : \sqrt{\frac{3RT}{M}}$$

Root Mean Square Speed

This speed is equal to the square root of the mean value of square of the velocities.

$$v_{rms} = \sqrt{\left(\frac{v_1^2 + v_2^2 + v_3^2 + \ldots v_n^2}{n}\right)}$$

EXAM PATTERN QUESTIONS

Objective Type Questions

Multiple Choice Questions (MCQs)

1. **The collisions of the molecules of an ideal gas are**

(a) elastic
(b) inelastic
(c) completely inelastic
(d) partially elastic

2. **A gas is found to obey the law p^2V = constant. The initial temperature and volume are T_0 and V_0. If the gas expands to a volume $3V_0$. Its final temperature becomes** Competency Based Que.

(a) $\frac{T_0}{3}$ (b) $\frac{T_0}{\sqrt{3}}$
(c) $3T_0$ (d) $\sqrt{3}T_0$

3. **A gas behaves as an ideal gas at**

(a) low pressure and high temperature
(b) low pressure and low temperature
(c) high pressure and low temperature
(d) high pressure and high temperature

4. **During an experiment, an ideal gas is found to obey an additional law Vp^2 = constant. The gas is initially at temperature T and volume V. What will be the temperature of the gas when it expands to a volume $2V$?** Competency Based Que.

(a) $T' = \sqrt{4}T$ (b) $T' = \sqrt{2}T$
(c) $T' = \sqrt{5}T$ (d) $T' = \sqrt{6}T$

5. **Boyle's law is applicable for an** NCERT Exemplar

(a) adiabatic process (b) isothermal process
(c) isobaric process (d) isochoric process

6. **An inflated rubber balloon contains one mole of an ideal gas, has a pressure p, volume V and temperature T. If the temperature rises to 1.1 T and the volume is increased to 1.05 V, the final pressure will be** NCERT Exemplar

(a) 1.1 p (b) p
(c) less than p (d) between p and 1.1 p

7. **If number of molecules of hydrogen gas is double the number of molecules of oxygen gas. The ratio of total KE of hydrogen gas to the total KE of oxygen gas at 300K will be**

(a) 1 : 1 (b) 1 : 2
(c) 2 : 1 (d) 1 : 16

8. **A cylinder containing an ideal gas is in vertical position and has a piston of mass M, i.e. able to move up or down without friction (figure). If the temperature is increased,** NCERT Exemplar

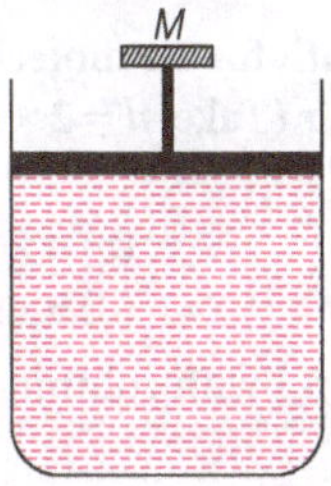

(a) Both p and V of the gas will change
(b) Only p will increase according to charles law
(c) V will change but not p
(d) p will change but not V

9. **The number of molecules in 1L of an ideal gas at 300K and 2 atm pressure with KE 2×10^{-9}J per molecule is**

(a) 6×10^{11} (b) 3×10^{11}
(c) 0.75×10^{11} (d) 1.5×10^{11}

10. **The average energy associated with each translational degree of freedom is**

(a) $\frac{3}{2}k_BT$ (b) k_BT
(c) $\frac{1}{2}k_BT$ (d) $2k_BT$

11. **At what temperature is the rms velocity of hydrogen molecules equal to that of an oxygen molecule at 47°C?**

(a) −73 K (b) 3K
(c) 20 K (d) 80 K

12. **The average kinetic energy of a gas molecule at 27° C is 621×10^{-1} J. The average kinetic energy of gas molecule at 227° will be** Competency Based Que.

(a) 52.2×10^{-21}J (b) 5.22×10^{-21} J
(c) 10.35×10^{-21} J (d) 11.35×10^{-21}J

13. **A gas is filled in a container at pressure p_0. If the mass of molecules is halved and their rms speed is doubled. The resultant pressure would be**

(a) $2p_0$ (b) $4p_0$
(c) $\frac{p_0}{4}$ (d) $\frac{p_0}{2}$

14. For a rigid diatomic molecule, universal gas constant $R = nC_p$, where C_p is molar specific heat at constant pressure and n is a number. Here, n is equals to

(a) 0.2257 (b) 0.4 (c) 0.2857 (d) 0.3557

15. The total energy for one mole of solid is

(a) $2RT$ (b) $3RT$
(c) $4RT$ (d) $(3/2)RT$

16. If γ is the ratio of specific heats of a perfect gas, the number of degrees of freedom of a molecules of the gas is

(a) $\frac{3}{\gamma+1}$ (b) $\frac{1}{\gamma-1}$ (c) $\gamma+1$ (d) $\frac{2}{\gamma-1}$

17. The mean free path for air molecule with average speed 485 ms^{-1} at STP is (Take, $d = 2\times10^{-10}$ m and $n = 2.7\times10^{25}\ m^{-3}$)

(a) 3.5×10^{-7} m (b) 4×10^{-7} m
(c) 2.08×10^{-7} m (d) 5×10^{-7} m

18. Match the column I with column II

	Column A		Column B
1.	Root mean square speed (v_{rms})	A.	$\sqrt{\frac{2kT}{m}}$
2.	Average speed of gas molecules	B.	$\sqrt{\frac{3kT}{m}}$
3.	Most probable speed (v_{mp})	C.	$\frac{1}{2}mv_{rms}^2$
4.	kinetic energy of a gas molecule	D.	$\sqrt{\frac{3RT}{m}}$

Codes

	1 2 3 4		1 2 3 4
(a)	A B D C	(b)	B A D C
(c)	A B C D	(d)	D A B C

19. Match the column I with column II

	Column I		Column II
1.	Ideal gas law constant (R)	A.	$\frac{3}{2}\cdot\frac{p}{n}$
2.	Relation of pressure with kinetic energy	B.	Average distance between collisions
3.	Mean free path	C.	8.314 J/ mol-K
4.	Ideal gas equation for 2 moles	D.	Product of R and T divided by molar mass

Codes

	1 2 3 4		1 2 3 4
(a)	C A B D	(b)	A B C D
(c)	D A C B	(d)	A C B D

Assertion-Reason

Directions *(Q.No. 20-27) In the following questions, two statements are given-one labelled Assertion (A) and the other labelled Reason (R). Select the correct answer to these questions from the codes (a), (b), (c) and (d) as given below*

(a) Both Assertion and Reason are true and Reason is the correct explanation of Assertion.

(b Both Assertion and Reason are true but Reason is not the correct explanation of Assertion.

(c) Assertion is true but Reason is false.

(d) Assertion is false but Reason is true.

20. **Assertion (A)** A bubble comes from the bottom of a lake to the top.
Reason (R) Its radius increases.

21. **Assertion (A)** Total KE of any gas at temperature T would be $\frac{1}{2}mv_{rms}^2$.
Reason (R) Translational KE of any type of gas at temperature T would be $\frac{3RT}{2}$ for one mole.

22. **Assertion (A)** In gases, the molecules move faster and move long distances without colliding.
Reason (R) In gases, the interatomic forces are negligible.

23. **Assertion (A)** A gas can be liquified at any temperature by increase of pressure alone.
Reason (R) On increasing pressure, the temperature of gas increases.

24. **Assertion (A)** Internal energy of an ideal gas does not depend upon volume of the gas.
Reason (R) Internal energy of ideal gas depends on temperature of gas.

25. **Assertion (A)** Specific heat of a gas at constant pressure is greater than its specific heat at constant volume.
Reason (R) This is because at constant pressure, some heat is spent in expansion of the gas.

26. **Assertion (A)** Mean free path of a gas molecule is inversely proportional to the density of gas.
Reason (R) Mean free path of gas molecules varies inversely as pressure of the gas.

27. **Assertion (A)** If a gas container is in motion is suddenly stopped, the temperature of the gas rises.
Reason (R) The kinetic energy of ordered mechanical motion is converted into the kinetic energy of random motion of gas molecules.

Case Based Questions

Directions *(Q.Nos. 28-29) These questions are case study based questions. Read the following paragraph and anwer the questions.*

28 **A molecule of gas collides with the wall of a container elastically.**

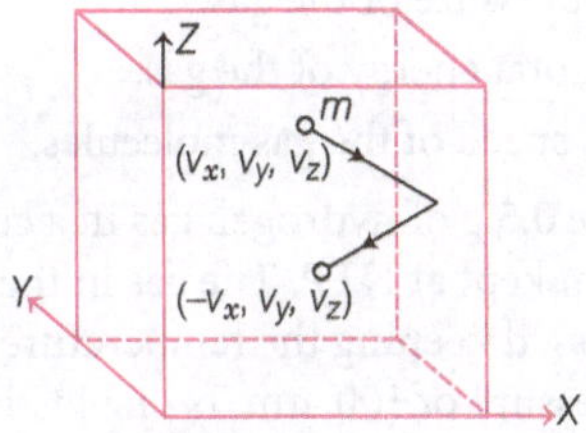

As collision is elastic only the x-component of the velocity changes after collision. It become reversed y and z-components of velocity do not change.

(i) Momentum imparted to the wall due to collision of the molecule is

(a) $2mv_y$ (b) $2mv_x$

(c) $2mv_z$ (d) mv_x

(ii) The total momentum imparted to the wall in time Δt on the area A of the wall due to molecules of velocity v_x, is

(a) $nmv_x^2 A\Delta t$ (b) $nmv_x A\Delta t$

(c) $\frac{1}{2}nmv_x^2 A\,\Delta t$ (d) $\frac{1}{2}nmv_x A\Delta t$

(iii) The expression of pressure due to the collision of molecules of velocity v_x is

(a) nmv^2 (b) nmv_x^2

(c) nmv_x (d) $\frac{1}{2}nmv_x^2$

(iv) The expression of total pressure to the group of molecules having velocities along the X- axis is

(a) nmv_x^2 (b) $nm\bar{v}_x^2$

(c) nmv_x^2 (d) None of these

(v) The general expression of pressure due to a gas is

(a) $\frac{1}{2}nm\bar{v}^2$ (b) $\frac{1}{3}nm\bar{v}^2$

(c) $nm\bar{v}$ (d) None of these

where, $\bar{v}^2$ is mean of the square speed of a molecule.

29 **According to this law, for any system in thermal equilibrium, then total energy is equally distributed its various degree of freedom. And each degree of freedom is assoicated with energy $\frac{1}{2}kT$ (where $k = 1.3\times10^{-23}$ J/K, T = absolute temperatrue of the system.**

At a given temperature T; all ideal gas molecules no matter what their mass have the same averge translational kinetic energy; namely, $\frac{3}{2}kT$. When measure the temperature of a gas, we are also measuring the average translational kinetic energy of its's molecules.

At same temperature gases with different degrees of freedom (e.g. He and H) will have different average energy or internal energy namely $\frac{f}{2}kT$. (f is different for different gases)

(i) Relation between pressure p and average kinetic energy E per unit volume of a gas is

(a) $p=\frac{2E}{3}$ (b) $p=\frac{E}{3}$

(c) $p=\frac{3E}{2}$ (d) $p=3E$

(ii) At 0 K, which of the following properties of a gas will be zero ?

(a) Kinetic energy

(b) Potential energy

(c) Vibrational energy

(d) Density

(iii) The root mean square velocity of a gas molecule of mass m at a given temperature is proportional to

(a) m^0 (b) m

(c) $\sqrt{m}$ (d) $m^{-1/2}$

(iv) An ant is walking on the horizontal surface. The number of degrees of freedom of ant will be

(a) 1 (b) 2

(c) 3 (d) 6

(v) The number of degrees of freedom for a diatomic gas molecules is

(a) 2 (b) 3 (c) 5 (d) 6

Subjective Questions

Very Short Answer Type Questions

1 Why temperature less than 0 K is not possible?

2 What is the volume of a gas at absolute zero of temperature?

3 Draw the graph between p and $1/v$ (reciprocal of volume) for a perfect gas at a constant temperature.

4 (i) If the number of molecules in a container is doubled, what will be the effect on the rms speed of the molecules ? **Competency Based Que.**

(ii) Name of the factors on which the degree of freedom of gas depends.

Short Answer Type Questions

5 Show that the root mean square speed of the molecules of a gas is directly proportional to the square root of the absolute temperature of the gas.

6 State Charles' law, obtain it from kinetic theory of gases.

7 Two thermally insulated vessels 1 and 2 are filled, with air at temperatures (T_1, T_2), volume (V_1, V_2) at pressure (p_1, p_2) respectively. If the value joining the two vessels is opened what is the temperature of the vessel at equilibrium?

Competency Based Que.

8 State Grahm's law of diffusion. How do you obtain this form kinetic theory of gases ?

9 When air is pumped into a cycle tyre the volume and pressure of the air in the tyre both are increased. What about Boyle's law in this case?

10 A partition divides a container having insulated walls into two compartments I and II. The same gas fills the two compartments. What is the ratio of the number of molecules in compartments I and II ?

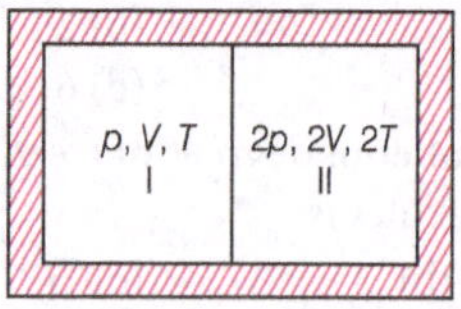

Competency Based Que.

11 From kinetic theory of gases, can we obtain ideal gas equation? If yes, how?

12 Equal masses of oxygen and helium gases are supplied equal amount of heat. Which gas will undergo a greater temperature rise and why? **Competency Based Que.**

13 An insulated container containing monoatomic gas of molar mass m is moving with a velocity v_0. If the container is suddenly stopped, find the change in temperature.

14 Write the difference between ideal gas and real gas.

15 There are n molecules of a gas in a container. If the number of molecules is increased to $2n$, what will be

(a) the pressure of the gas.

(b) the total energy of the gas.

(c) rms speed of the gas molecules.

16 We have 0.5 g of hydrogen gas in a cubic chamber of size 3 cm kept at NTP. The gas in the chamber is compressed keeping the temperature constant till a final pressure of 100 atm. Is one justified in assuming the ideal gas law, in the final state? (Hydrogen molecules can be consider as spheres of radius 1 Å).

Long Answer Type Questions

17 Derive an expression for the pressure exerted by an ideal gas.

18 Three vessels of equal capacity have gases at the same temperature and pressure. The first vessel contains neon (monoatomic), the second contains chlorine (diatomic) and the third contains uranium hexafluoride (polyatomic). Do the vessels contain equal number of respective molecules? Is the root mean square speed of molecules, the same in the three cases? If not, in which case is v_{rms} the largest?

NCERT

19 Explain, why

(i) there is no atmosphere on moon.

(ii) there is fall in temperature with altitude.

NCERT Exemplar

20 What is Maxwell Boltzmann law with regard to speed distribution amongst molecules, state and explain?

Competency Based Que.

21 Using the law of equipartition of energy, show that for an ideal gas having f degrees of freedom is given by $\gamma = 1 + 2/f$.

22 (i) Define mean free path.

(ii) Derive an expression for mean free path of a gas molecule.

Numerical Problems

Behaviour of Real Gas and Ideal Gas

23 An air bubble of volume 1.0 cm^3 rises from the bottom of a lake 40 m deep at a temperature of 12°C. To what volume does it grow when it reaches the surface, which is at a temperature of 35°C?

24 A vessel is filled with a gas at a pressure of 76 cm of mercury at a certain temperature. The mass of the gas is increased by 50% by introducing more gas in the vessel at the same temperature. Find out the resultant pressure of the gas.

25 An oxygen cylinder of volume 30 L, has an initial gauge pressure of 15 atm and a temperature of 27 °C. After some oxygen is withdrawn from the cylinder, the gauge pressure drops to 11 atm and its temperature drops to 17 °C. Estimate the mass of oxygen taken out of the cylinder ($R = 8.31\ \text{mol}^{-1}\text{K}^{-1}$, molecular mass of $O_2 = 32$ u).

26 Figure shows plot of pV/T *versus* p for 1.00×10^{-3} kg of oxygen gas at two different temperatures. **NCERT**

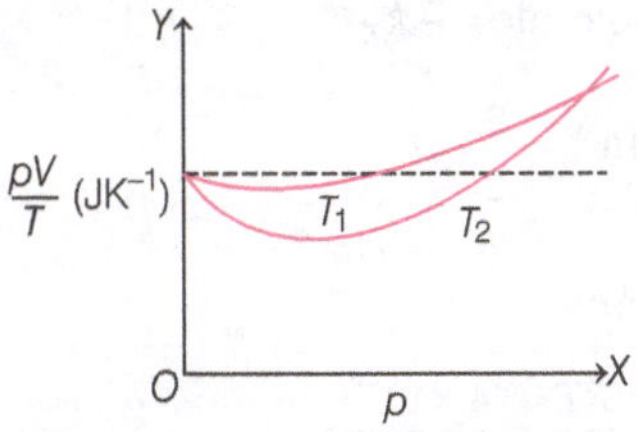

(i) What does the dotted plot signify?
(ii) Which is true, $T_1 > T_2$ or $T_1 < T_2$?
(iii) What is the value of pV/T, where the curves meet on the Y-axis?
(iv) If we obtain similar plots for 1.00×10^{-3} kg of hydrogen, would we get the same value of pV/T at the point where the curves meet on the Y-axis? If not, what mass of hydrogen yields the same value of pV/T (for low pressure, high temperature region of the plot)? (Molecular mass of $H_2 = 2.02$ u, $O_2 = 32.0$ u and $R = 8.31\ \text{Jmol}^{-1}\text{K}^{-1}$)

27 Estimate the total number of molecules inclusive of oxygen, nitrogen, water vapour and other constituents in a room of capacity $25.0\ \text{m}^3$ at a temperature of 27° C and 1 atmospheric pressure. **Competency Based Que.**

Kinetic Theory of Ideal Gas

28 A gas is filled in a vessel at a certain temperature and at a pressure of 80 cm of mercury. At the same temperature, more gas is filled in the vessel, so that its mass increases by 60%. Determine the resultant pressure in the vessel.

29 Find the temperature at which rms speed of a gas is half of its value of 0°C, pressure remaining constant.

30 You are given, the following data about a group of particles, where n_i represents the number of molecules with speed v_i.

n_i	2	4	8	6	3
v_i (ms^{-1})	1.0	2.0	3.0	4.0	5.0

Calculate
(i) average speed,
(ii) rms speed and
(iii) most probable speed.

31 What is the kinetic energy of translation of one molecule of a gas at 300 K ? Gas is having three degree of freedom and $k_B = 1.38 \times 10^{-23}\ \text{JK}^{-1}$.

32 At what temperature the rms speed of oxygen atom equal to rms speed of helium gas atom at −10° C?
Atomic mass of helium = 4
Atomic mass of oxygen = 32 **Competency Based Que.**

33 Find the root mean square velocity of the molecules of oxygen (molecular weight = 32) at 27°C and also the kinetic energy of 4 g gas. (Gas constant $R = 8.31$ joule/mol-K)

34 The density of carbon dioxide gas at 0°C and at a pressure of $1.0 \times 10^5\ \text{N m}^{-2}$ is $1.98\ \text{kg m}^{-3}$. Find the root mean square speed of its molecules at 0°C and 30°C. Pressure is constant.

35 A flask contains argon and chlorine in the ratio of 2 : 1 by mass. The temperature of the mixture is 27°C. Obtain the ratio of
(i) average kinetic energy per molecule and
(ii) root mean square speed (v_{rms}) of the molecules of the two gases. Atomic mass of argon = 39.9 u; Molecular mass of chlorine = 70.9 u. **NCERT**

Degree of Freedom

36 2 mole oxygen and 4 mole helium are in a gas mixture at 27°C. Calculate the total internal energy of the system. Degrees of freedom of oxygen and helium are 5 and 3, respectively.

37 One mole of a monoatomic gas is mixed with three moles of a diatomic gas. What is the molar specific heat of the mixture at constant volume? ($R = 8.31\ \text{J mol}^{-1}\ \text{K}^{-1}$)

38 An ideal diatomic gas undergoes a process where the pressure and volume are related by $pV^{3/2}$ = constant. If the initial temperature of the gas is 300 K, calculate the final temperature after the volume changes by a factor of 2. **Competency Based Que.**

39 0.014 kg of nitrogen is enclosed in a vessel at a temperature of 27°C. How much heat has to be transferred to the gas to double the rms speed of its molecules. **Competency Based Que.**

40 Calculate the mean free path of nitrogen gas at STP. Given the diameter of nitrogen molecule is 4 Å.

Hints & Solutions

Objective Type Questions

1. (*a*) According to kinetic theory of gases, the collision among molecules and the collision of molecule with the walls of container are elastic.

2. (*d*) It is given that,

$$p^2V = \text{constant} = K$$

From ideal gas law, $pV = nRT$

$$\Rightarrow \quad p = \frac{nRT}{V}$$

$$\Rightarrow \quad \left(\frac{nRT}{V}\right)^2 V = K$$

$$\Rightarrow \quad \frac{T^2}{V} = K'$$

$$\Rightarrow \quad \left(\frac{T'}{T_0}\right)^2 = \frac{V'}{V_0}$$

$$\Rightarrow \quad T' = \sqrt{3}T_0$$

3. (*a*) Generally, a gas behaves more like an ideal gas at higher temperature and lower pressure, as the potential energy due to intermolecular forces becomes less significant compared with the particle's kinetic energy and the size of the molecules becomes less significant compared to the empty space between them.

4. (*b*) $pV = RT \Rightarrow p = \dfrac{RT}{V}$

$$Vp^2 = \text{constant}$$

$$\therefore \quad V\left(\frac{RT}{V}\right)^2 = \text{constant}$$

$$\frac{T^2}{V} = \text{constant}$$

$$\therefore \quad \frac{T'^2}{2V} = \frac{T^2}{V}$$

$$T' = \sqrt{2}T$$

5. (*b*) Boyle's law is applicable when temperature is constant.

i.e. $pV = nRT = \text{constant}$

$\Rightarrow \quad pV = \text{constant (at constant temperature)}$

i.e., $p \propto \dfrac{1}{V}$ (where, p =pressure and V= volume)

So, this process can be called as isothermal process.

6. (*d*) $\dfrac{p_1V_1}{T_1} = \dfrac{p_2V_2}{T_2}$

$$p_2 = \frac{p_1V_1T_2}{V_2T_1} = \frac{pV \times 1.1T}{1.05V \times T}$$

$p_2 = 1.05p$ (between p and $1.1\,p$)

7. (*c*) $\dfrac{E_H}{E_O} = \dfrac{\frac{3}{2}n_HkT}{\frac{3}{2}n_OkT} \Rightarrow \dfrac{n_H}{n_O} = \dfrac{2}{1} = 2:1$

8. (*c*) Pressure $= \dfrac{\text{Force}}{\text{Area}} = \dfrac{Mg}{\text{Area of piston}} = \text{constant}$

If the temperature is increased, only the volume increased, as the piston moves up without friction. Recall $V \propto T$ as constant pressure.

9. (*d*) Volume $V = 1\text{L}$

$$T = 300\text{K}$$

$$p = 2\text{ atm}$$

$$\text{KE per molecule} = \frac{3}{2}k_BT$$

$$2\times10^{-9} = \frac{3}{2}k_BT$$

$$k_BT = \frac{2\times2\times10^{-9}}{3}$$

$$\frac{RT}{N_A} = \frac{4\times10^{-9}}{3}$$

We have, $pV = \dfrac{N}{N_A}RT$

$$pV = \frac{4\times10^{-3}}{3}N$$

$$N = \frac{3pV}{4\times10^{-3}} = \frac{3\times2\times1.013\times10^5\times10^{-3}}{4}$$

$$N = 1.5\times10^{-11}\text{ molecules}$$

10. (*c*) Average energy associated with each translational degree of freedom is $\frac{1}{2}k_BT$.

11. (*c*) $v_1 = \sqrt{\dfrac{3RT_1}{M_1}}$, $v_2 = \sqrt{\dfrac{3RT_2}{M_2}}$, i.e

$$T_1 = \frac{M_1}{M_2}T_2 = \frac{2}{32}\times320 = 20\text{ K}$$

12. (*c*) We know that, the KE of one mole of a gas molecules at a temperature T is given by

$$K = \frac{3}{2}kT$$

Now, $T_1 = 27°\text{C} = 300\text{ K}$

$$k_1 = 6.21\times10^{-21}\text{J}$$

$$T_2 = 227°\text{C} = 500\text{ K}$$

$$k_2 = ?$$

We have,

$$\frac{k_1}{k_2} = \frac{T_1}{T_2}$$

$$k_2 = \frac{T_2}{T_1} \times k_1 = \frac{500}{300} \times 6.21 \times 10^{-21}$$
$$= 10.35 \times 10^{-21} \text{J}$$

13. (a) $p_0 = \frac{1}{3}\frac{Nm}{V}v_{rms}^2$

where, m = mass of each molecule and V = volume of the gas.

Now, $m' = \frac{1}{2}m$

$$v'_{rms} = 2v_{rms}$$
$$p' = \frac{1}{3}\frac{Nm.4v_{rms}^2}{2v}$$
$$= 2.\frac{1}{3}\frac{Nm}{V}v_{rms}^2 = 2p_0$$

14. (c) For a rigid diatomic molecule,

$$\frac{C_p}{C_V} = \frac{7}{5} \text{ and } C_V = \frac{5}{7}C_p$$
$$C_p - C_V = R$$
$$C_p - \frac{5}{7}C_p = nC_p \Rightarrow \frac{2}{7}C_p = nC_p$$
$$\Rightarrow \quad n = \frac{2}{7} = 0.2857$$

15. (b) The total energy for mole of solid is $3RT$.

16. (d) $\gamma = \frac{C_p}{C_V} = \frac{\left(\frac{f+2}{2}\right)R}{\frac{f}{2}R}$

$$= \frac{f+2}{f} = 1 + \frac{2}{f}$$
$$f = \frac{2}{\gamma - 1}$$

17. (c) For air at STP, $n = 2.7 \times 10^{25}$ m^{-3}

$$d = 2\times 10^{-10} \text{ m}$$
$$\Rightarrow \quad l = \frac{1}{\sqrt{2}n\pi d^2}$$

On putting values $l = \frac{1}{\sqrt{2}\pi \times 2.7 \times 10^{25}(2\times 10^{-10})^2}$

$$l = 2.08 \times 10^{-7} \text{ m}$$

18. (b) 1 → B, 2 → A, 3 → D, 4 → C

19. (a) 1 → C, 2 → A, 3 → B, 4 → D

20. (b) Pressure decreases as bubble comes to top, hence volume increases, thus radius also increases.

21. (b) Only translational PE is mv_{rms}^2 and translational KE or (degree of freedom is 3) one mole is $\frac{3RT}{2}$.

22. (a) The interatomic forces are negligible in gases. Therefore, in gases, the molecules are free and move large distance before colliding.

23. (d) A vapour above the critical temperature is a gas and gas below the critical temperature for the substance is a vapour. A gas cannot be liquified by the application of pressure alone, however large the pressure may be while vapour can be liquified under pressure alone. To liquify a gas, it must be cooled upto or below its critical temperature.

24. (b) Internal energy of an ideal gas does not depend upon volume of the gas because there are no force of attraction/repulsion amongst the molecules an ideal gas. Also, internal energy of ideal gas depends on temperature.

25. (a) At constant pressure, some heat is used to expand the gas. So, specific heat of constant pressure is greater than specific heat at constant volume.

$\therefore \quad C_p - C_V = R$

26. (b) Mean free path in terms of temperature and pressure is given by $\lambda = \frac{k_B T}{\sqrt{2}\pi d^2 p}$

Hence, the mean free path of a given gas is inversely proportional to its pressure and density.

27. (a) The motion of the container is known as the ordered motion of the gas and *zig-zag* motion of gas molecules within the container is called disordered motion. When the container suddenly stops, ordered kinetic energy gets convereted into disordered kinetic energy which increases the temperatrue of the gas.

28. (i) (b) As only x-component of velocity changes, change in momentum of molecule

$$= -mv_x - (mv_x) = -2mv_x$$

As collision is elastic, the total momentum of molecule and wall is conserved.

So, change in momentum of wall (momentum imparted to wall) = $2mv_x$.

(ii) (a) Force = Momentum imparted to the wall in unit time

In time Δt, the number of molecules with velocity v_x that could reach the wall = $nA\, v_x\Delta t$ = volume of cylinder of length $v_x\Delta t$, where n = number density.

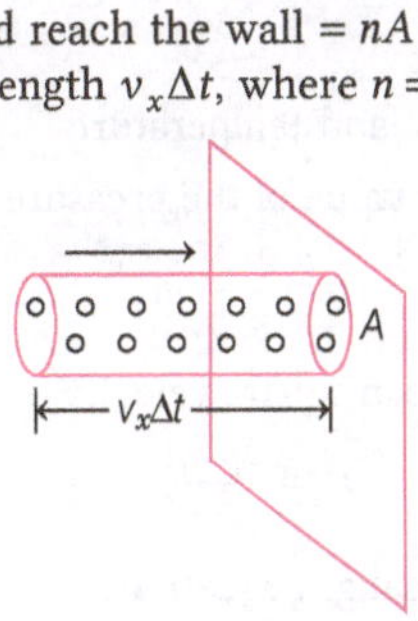

But on an average half of these molecules will hit the wall in time,

$$\Delta t = \frac{1}{2} n A v_x \Delta t$$

The total momentum transferred to the wall in time Δt

$$= (2mv_x)\left(\frac{1}{2} n A v_x \Delta t\right) = (nmv_x^2) A\, \Delta t$$

(iii) (*b*) Pressure $= \frac{F}{A} = \frac{(nmv_x^2) A\, \Delta t}{A\, \Delta t} = nmv_x^2$

(iv) (*a*) As the *x*-component of velocities of all the molecules are not same so, we take average of v_x^2.

Total pressure, $p = nm\overline{v_x^2}$

(v) (*b*) As, gas is isotropic, $\overline{v_x^2} = \overline{v_y^2} = \overline{v_z^2} = \frac{\overline{v^2}}{3}$

$$\Rightarrow \quad \overline{v^2} = (\overline{v_x^2} + \overline{v_y^2} + \overline{v_z^2}) \Rightarrow p = \frac{1}{3} nm\, \overline{v^2}$$

29. (i) (*a*) $p = \frac{2E}{3}$

(ii) (*a*) At 0 K, all molecular motion stops, so kinetic energy becomes zero.

(iii) (*d*) $v_{rms} = \sqrt{\frac{3K_3 T}{m}}$ i.e. $v_{rms} \propto m^{-1/2}$

(iv) (*b*) As the ant can move on a plane, it has 2 degree of freedom.

(v) (*c*) A diatomic molecule has 3 degree of freedom due to translatory motion and 2 degrees of freedom due to rotatory motion.

Subjective Questions

1. The thermal motion of gas molecules reaches at absolute zero, so the temperature less than 0K is not possible.

2. Zero

3.

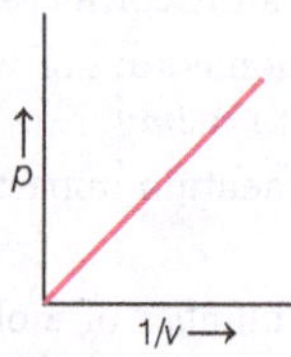

4. (i) No effect

(ii) Atomicity and temperature

5. The average value of the pressure of the gas is

$$p = \frac{1}{3} \frac{N}{V} m\overline{v^2}$$

Thus, the mean square velocity of the molecule will be

$$\overline{v^2} = \frac{3pV}{Nm}$$

Using the ideal gas equation,

$$pV = nRT$$

$$\overline{v^2} = \frac{3nRT}{Nm}$$

But, $n = \frac{N}{N_A}$

$$\therefore \quad \overline{v^2} = \frac{3NRT}{N_A N m}$$

Also, $mN_A = M_0$ (Molar mass of the gas)

$$\overline{v^2} = \frac{3RT}{M_0}$$

$$\sqrt{\overline{v^2}} = v_{rms} = \sqrt{\frac{3RT}{M_0}}$$

As R and M_0 in the above equation are constant,

$$\therefore \quad v_{rms} \propto \sqrt{T}$$

6. According to Charle's law, for a given mass of an ideal gas at constant pressure, volume (V) of a gas is directly proportional to its absolute temperature.

$$V \propto T$$

Now, according to kinetic theory of gases, pressure of an ideal gas is given by

$$p = \frac{1}{3} \rho \overline{v}^2$$

$$p = \frac{1}{3} \frac{M}{V} \overline{v}^2$$

$$V = \frac{1}{3} \frac{M}{p} \overline{v}^2$$

At constant pressure for a given mass of gas, $V \propto \overline{v}^2$

We know that,

(mean of the squared speed) $\overline{v}^2 \propto T$

$$V \propto T$$

Therefore, at constant pressure, $V \propto T$

7. For the system, the total number of moles remains constant.

$$\therefore \quad \frac{p_1 V_1}{RT_1} + \frac{p_2 V_2}{RT_2} = \frac{p(V_1 + V_2)}{RT}$$

or

$$T = \frac{p(V_1 + V_2) T_1 T_2}{p_1 V_1 T_2 + p_2 V_2 T_1}$$

Apply Boyle's law,

$$p_1 V_1 + p_2 V_2 = p(V_1 + V_2)$$

$$\therefore \quad T = \frac{(p_1 V_1 + p_2 V_2) T_1 T_2}{(p_1 V_1 T_2 + p_2 V_2 T_1)}$$

8. Refer to text Pages no 404 and 405.

9. When air is pumped, more molecules are pumped and Boyle's law is stated for situation where number of molecules remains constant.

In this case, as the number of air molecules keep increasing. Hence, this is a case of variable mass. Boyle's law (and even Charle's law) is only applicable in situations, where number of gas molecules remains fixed.

Hence, in this case Boyle's law is not applicable.

10. Compartment I : $p, V\ T$ no. of molecules $= N_1$ (say)

Compartment II : $2p$, $2V$, T no. of molecules N_2(say)

As $$pV = NK_BT$$

$$(pV/NT) = \text{Constant}$$

$$\therefore (N_1/N_2) = \{(p_1V_1)/T_1\}\cdot\{T_2/(p_2/V_2)\}$$

$$\therefore (N_1/N_2) = (pV/T)\times\{T/(2p\times 2V) = (1/4)$$

11. Yes;

From kinetic theory of gas, $p = \dfrac{Nmv^{-2}}{3V}$

We know that, $E_k = \dfrac{3}{2}kT = \dfrac{1}{2}mv^{-2}$

$$mv^{-2} = 3kT$$

$$p = \frac{N3kT}{3V} = \frac{NkT}{V}$$

The Boltzmann constant k is also ratio of the gas constant (R) to the Avogadro's constant (N_A).

Substituting $k = \dfrac{R}{N_A}$ in the above equation.

$$p = \frac{NRT}{N_A \cdot V}$$

$$p = \frac{nRT}{V} \qquad \left[\because \frac{N}{N_A} = n\right]$$

$$pV = nRT$$

Therefore, the ideal gas equation $pV = nRT$ is derived using the kinetic theory of gas.

12. Heat supplied to oxygen = Heat supplied to helium

$$mc_1\Delta T_1 = mc_2\Delta T_2$$

$$\frac{\Delta T_1}{\Delta T_2} = \frac{c_2}{c_1}, \text{ As } c \times \frac{1}{m}, m = \text{molecular mass}$$

$$\frac{\Delta T_1}{\Delta T_2} = \frac{c_2}{c_1} = \frac{m_1}{m_2}, \text{ As } m_1 > m_2$$

$$\Delta T_1 = \Delta T_2$$

13. According to kinetic interpretation of temperature, absolute temperature of a given sample of a gas is proportional to the total translational kinetic energy of its molecules.

Hence, any change in absolute temperature of a gas will contribute to corresponding change in translational KE and *vice-versa*.

Assuming n = number of moles.

Given, m = molar mass of the gas.

When, the container stops, its total KE is transferred to gas molecules in the form of translational KE, thereby increasing the absolute temperature.

If ΔT = change in absolute temperature.

Then, KE of molecules due to velocity v_o,

$$\text{KE} = \frac{1}{2}(mn)\,v_0^2 \qquad \text{...(i)}$$

Increase in translational

$$\text{KE} = n\frac{3}{2}R(\Delta T) \qquad \text{...(ii)}$$

According to kinetic theory Eqs. (i) and (ii) are equal

$$\Rightarrow \quad \frac{1}{2}(mn)\,v_0^2 = n\frac{3}{2}R(\Delta T)$$

$$(mn)\,v_0^2 = n3R(\Delta T)$$

$$\Rightarrow \quad \Delta T = \frac{(mn)\,v_0^2}{3nR}$$

$$\Rightarrow \quad \Delta T = \frac{mv_0^2}{3R}$$

14.

Ideal Gas	Real Gas
It obeys ideal gas equation $pV = \mu RT$ at all temperatures and pressures.	It does not obey $pV = \mu RT$ at all values of temperature and pressure.
The volume of the molecules of an ideal gas is zero.	The volume of the molecules of a real gas is non-zero.
There is no intermolecular force between the molecules.	There is intermolecular force of attraction or repulsion depending on whether intermolecular separation is larger or small.
There is no intermolecular potential energy (U) because intermolecular force (F) is zero.	Potential energy (U) does not equal to zero as intermolecular force (F) is not zero.
It has only kinetic energy.	It has both kinetic and potential energies.
At absolute zero, the volume, pressure and internal energy become zero.	All real gases get liquified before reaching absolute zero. The internal energy of the liquified gas is not zero.

15. (a) We know that

$$p = \frac{1}{3}mnC^2$$

where n = number of molecules per unit volume. Thus, when no. of molecules is increased from n to $2n$, number of molecules per unit volume (n) will increase from n to $2n$.

nv to $2nv$, hence, pressure will become double.

(b) The KE of a gas molecule, $\dfrac{1}{2}mnC^2 = \dfrac{3}{2}NkT$

If the number of molecules is increased from n to $2n$. There is no effect on the average KE of a gas molecule, but the total energy is doubled.

(c) Rms speed of gas is $C_{\text{rms}} = 3P\rho$ ..... $\sqrt{=3Pmn}$

When n increased from n to $2n$. both n and p become double and the ratio Pn remains unchanged. So there will be no effect of increasing the number of molecules from n to $2n$ on rms speed of gas molecules.

16. Assuming hydrogen molecules as spheres of radius 1 Å.

So, $r = 1\text{ Å} =$ radius

The volume of hydrogen molecules $= \frac{4}{3}\pi r^3$

$$= \frac{4}{3}(3.14)(10^{-10})^3 \approx 4 \times 10^{-30}\ \text{m}^3$$

Number of moles of $H_2 = \frac{\text{Mass}}{\text{Molecular mass}}$

$$= \frac{0.5}{2} = 0.25$$

Molecules of H_2 present = Number of moles of H_2 present $\times 6.023 \times 10^{23}$

$$= 0.25 \times 6.023 \times 10^{23}$$

$\therefore$ Volume of molecules present = Molecules number $\times$ Volume of each molecule

$$= 0.25 \times 6.023 \times 10^{23} \times 4 \times 10^{-30}$$

$$= 6.023 \times 10^{23} \times 10^{-30}$$

$$\approx 6 \times 10^{-7}\ \text{m}^3 \quad \text{.... (i)}$$

Now, if ideal gas law is considered to be constant.

$$p_i V_i = p_f V_f$$

$$V_f = \left(\frac{p_i}{p_f}\right) V_i = \left(\frac{1}{100}\right)(3 \times 10^{-2})^3$$

$$= \frac{27 \times 10^{-6}}{10^2} = 2.7 \times 10^{-7}\ \text{m}^3 \quad \text{...(ii)}$$

Hence, on compression the volume of the gas is of the order of the molecular volume [from Eq. (i) and Eq. (ii)]. The intermolecular forces will play role and the gas will deviate from ideal gas behaviour.

17. Consider an ideal gas consisting of N molecules in a container of volume V. The container is a cube with edges of length l. Consider a molecule of mass m moving with velocity (v_x, v_y, v_z).

As molecule collides with the wall parallel to YZ-plane elastically, its x-component of velocity is reversed, while its y and z-components of velocity remain unaltered, i.e. velocity after collision is $(-v_x, v_y, v_z)$.

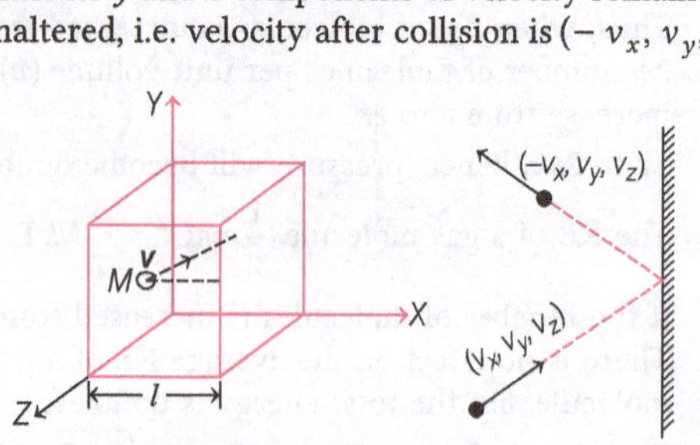

So, the change in momentum of the molecule,

$$\Delta p_x = (p_x)_{\text{final}} - (p_x)_{\text{initial}}$$

$$\Delta p_x = -mv_x - (mv_x)$$

$$\Delta p_x = -2mv_x$$

$\because$ Impulse = Change in momentum of molecule

$$\Rightarrow \quad F\,\Delta t = \Delta p_x = -2mv_x$$

where, F is the average force on the molecule by the wall in time interval Δt.

For molecule to collide second time with same wall, it must travel a distance $2l$ in x-direction.

So, time interval between two collisions with same wall,

$$\Delta t = \frac{2l}{v_x}$$

The average force exerted on a molecule by the wall for each collision,

$$F = \frac{-2mv_x}{\Delta t} = \frac{(-2mv_x)}{(2l/v_x)} = \frac{-mv_x^2}{l}$$

By Newton's third Law, the average force exerted by a molecule on the wall is $\frac{mv_x^2}{l}$. If there are N molecules, so total force on the wall will be

$$F_{\text{wall}} = \frac{m}{l}(v_{x_1}^2 + v_{x_2}^2 + \dots + v_{x_N}^2)$$

It can be rewritten as

$$F_{\text{wall}} = \frac{Nm}{l}\bar{v}_x^2 \quad \text{...(i)}$$

where, $\bar{v}_x^2 = \frac{v_{x_1}^2 + v_{x_2}^2 + \dots + v_{x_N}^2}{N}$

Now, $\bar{v}^2 = \bar{v}_x^2 + \bar{v}_y^2 + \bar{v}_z^2$

[as velocity has 3 components v_x, v_y, v_z]

Since, motion is completely random, so average values $\bar{v}_x^2$, $\bar{v}_y^2$ and $\bar{v}_z^2$ are equal to each other

i.e. $\bar{v}_x^2 = \bar{v}_y^2 = \bar{v}_z^2$

$$\therefore \quad \bar{v}^2 = 3\bar{v}_x^2 \text{ or } \bar{v}_x^2 = \frac{1}{3}\bar{v}^2 \quad \text{...(ii)}$$

From Eqs. (i) and (ii), we get $F_{\text{wall}} = \frac{N}{3}\left(\frac{m}{l}\bar{v}^2\right)$

Here, F_{wall} is normal force on the wall.

Pressure on the wall, $p = \frac{F_{\text{wall}}}{A} = \frac{F_{\text{wall}}}{l^2}$

$$\Rightarrow \quad p = \frac{1}{l^2}\left(\frac{N}{3}\frac{m\bar{v}^2}{l}\right)$$

or $$p = \frac{1}{l^3}\left(\frac{Nm\bar{v}^2}{3}\right)$$

or, $$p = \frac{1}{V}\left(\frac{Nm\bar{v}^2}{3}\right) \quad [\because \text{volume, } V = l^3]$$

or, $$p = \frac{1}{3}\left(\frac{N}{V}\right)m\bar{v}^2$$

$\Rightarrow$ Pressure exerted by an ideal gas,

$$p = \frac{1}{3} nm\bar{v}^2 \quad \text{...(iii)}$$

where, p = pressure exerted on wall,

n = number density (i.e. number of molecules per unit volume) of gas,

m = mass of one molecule,

$\bar{v}^2$ = mean square speed

and $p = \frac{1}{3} nm\bar{v}^2$ is known as expression for pressure exerted by an ideal gas and also called **kinetic gas equation.**

18. As three vessels are identical, i.e. they have same volume. Now at constant pressure, temperature and volume, the three vessels will contain equal number of molecules (by Avogadro's law) and is equal to Avogadro's number, $N_A = 6.023 \times 10^{23}$.

$$\because \quad v_{\text{rms}} = \sqrt{\frac{3k_BT}{m}}$$

$$\Rightarrow \quad v_{\text{rms}} \propto \frac{1}{\sqrt{m}}$$

where, m is mass of single gas molecule as neon has the smallest mass, so rms speed will be greatest in case of neon.

19. (i) The moon has small gravitational force and hence the escape velocity is small. As the moon is in the proximity of the earth as seen from the sun, the moon has the same amount of heat per unit area as that of the earth. The air molecules have large range of speeds.

Even though the rms speed of the air molecules is smaller than escape velocity on the moon, a significant number of molecules have speed greater than escape velocity and they escape.

Now, rest of the molecules arrange the speed distribution for the equilibrium temperature. Again, a significant number of molecules escape as their speeds exceed escape speed. Hence, over a long time, the moon has lost most of its atmosphere.

(ii) As the molecules move higher, their potential energy increases and hence, kinetic energy decreases and hence, temperature reduces.

At greater height, more volume is available and gas expands and hence, some cooling takes place.

20. **Maxwell's Speed Distribution**

In a given sample of gas, all molecules don't move with same speed. They move randomly in different directions but the distribution of velocities among the molecules remain fixed. Maxwell first studied molecular speed distribution and derived an equation giving distribution of molecules as follows.

If dN represents the number of molecules having speed between v and $v + dv$, then

$$dN = 4\pi N\left(\frac{m}{2\pi k_BT}\right)^{3/2} v^2 e^{-\frac{mv^2}{2k_BT}} dv$$

where, v = molecular speed of the gas,

m = the molecular mass of the gas,

T = temperature of the gas in kelvin,

N = total number of molecules of the gas

and k_B = Boltzmann constant.

The fraction of molecules with speed v and dv is equal to area of strip shown in figure.

i.e. $\frac{dN}{N} = f(v)\,dv$ = area of the strip

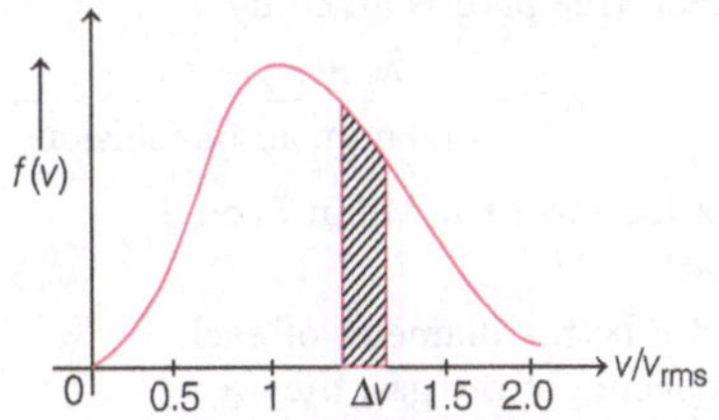

Total area of the curve will be unity, as it represents all molecules.

Figure shows the Maxwell's distribution function $f(v)$ of a gas at three different temperatures. Each graph has a peak which represents the maximum fraction of total molecules having maximum speed (v_{max}) due to this reason v_{max} is also called most probable speed. As the temperature increases, the curve become flatter and its maximum points (peak points) shifts towards higher speed.

21. **Law of Equipartition of Energy**

It states that '**For a dynamic system in thermal equilibrium, the total energy is distributed equally amongst all the degree of freedom and the energy associated with each molecule per degree of freedom is $\frac{1}{2} k_BT$.**

where, $k_B = 1.38 \times 10^{-23} \text{JK}^{-1}$ is Boltzmann constant and T is absolute temperature of system on the kelvin scale.

If a polyatomic gas molecule has f degrees of freedom, then internal energy of one mole of the gas,

$$U = f \times \left(\frac{1}{2}k_BT\right) \times N_A = \frac{f}{2}RT$$

Now, $$C_V = \frac{dU}{dT} = \frac{d}{dT}\left(\frac{f}{2}RT\right) = \frac{f}{2}R$$

$$C_V = \frac{f}{2}R$$

$$\therefore \quad C_p = C_V + R = \frac{f}{2}R + R = \left(\frac{f}{2} + 1\right)R$$

$$C_p = \left(\frac{f}{2} + 1\right)R$$

So, specific heat ratio, $\gamma = \frac{C_p}{C_V} = \frac{\left(\frac{f}{2}+1\right)R}{\frac{f}{2}R} \Rightarrow \gamma = \left(1+\frac{2}{f}\right)$

which is required relation between γ and f.

22. (i) The mean free path of a gas molecule is defined as the average distance travelled by a molecule between two successive collisions.

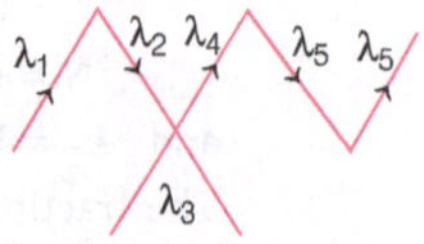

According to figure, if a molecule covers free path $\lambda_1, \lambda_2, \lambda_3 \cdots$ after successive collisions, then its mean free path is given by

$$\lambda = \frac{\lambda_1 + \lambda_2 + \lambda_3 \cdots}{(\text{total number of collisions})}$$

(ii) **Expression for Mean Free Path**

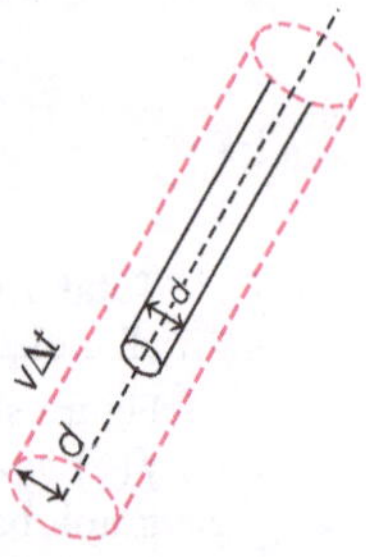

Let d be the diameter of each molecule of the gas, then a particular molecule will suffer collision with any molecule that comes within a distance d between centres of two molecules.

If v is average speed of molecule, then from figure, the volume swept by the molecule in small time Δt in which any molecule will collide with it

$$= \pi d^2 \langle v \rangle \Delta t$$

If n is number of molecules per unit volume of the gas, then number of collision suffered by the molecule in time $\Delta t = \pi d^2 \langle v \rangle \Delta t \times n$

So, number of collisions per second

$$= \frac{\pi d^2 \langle v \rangle \Delta t \times n}{\Delta t} = n \pi d^2 \langle v \rangle$$

$\therefore$ Average time between two successive collisions,

$$\tau = \frac{1}{n \pi d^2 \langle v \rangle}$$

$\therefore$ Mean free path = Average distance between two successive collisions

$$\Rightarrow \lambda = \tau \times \text{mean velocity} = \frac{1}{n \pi d^2 \langle v \rangle} \times \langle v \rangle = \frac{1}{n \pi d^2}$$

Mean free path, $\lambda = \frac{1}{n \pi d^2}$

where, d = diameter of each molecule

and n = number of molecules per unit volume.

23. $V_1 = 10^{-6} \text{m}^3$

Pressure on bubble p_1 = water pressure + Atmospheric pressure

$$= \rho g h + p_{\text{atm}} = 4.93 \times 10^5 \text{ Pa}$$

$T_1 = 285$ K and $T_2 = 308$ K

$$\frac{p_1 V_1}{T_1} = \frac{p_2 V_2}{T_2}$$

$$V_2 = \frac{4.93 \times 10^5 \times 1 \times 10^{-6} \times 308}{285 \times 1.01 \times 10^5} = 5.3 \times 10^{-6} \text{m}^3$$

24. According to kinetic theory of gases, $pV = \frac{1}{3} m v_{\text{rms}}^2$

At constant temperature, v_{rms}^2 is constant. As v is also constant, so $p \propto m$. When the mass of the gas increased by 50% pressure also increases by 50%,

$\therefore$ Final pressure $= 76 + \frac{50}{100} \times 76 = 114$ cm of Hg.

25. $V_1 = 30 \text{ L} = 30 \times 10^3 \text{ cm}^3 = 3 \times 10^{-2} \text{ m}^3$

$p_1 = 15 \times 1.013 \times 10^5 \text{ N/m}^2$

$T_1 = 300$ K

$R = 8.314 \text{ J mol}^{-1}\text{K}^{-1} \Rightarrow \mu_1 = \frac{p_1 V_1}{R T_1} = 18.3$

$p_2 = 11 \times 1.013 \times 10^5 \text{ N/ m}^2$

$V_2 = 3 \times 10^{-2} \text{m}^3 \Rightarrow T_2 = 290 \text{ K}$

$\mu_2 = \frac{p_2 V_2}{R T_2} = 13.9$

$\mu_2 - \mu_1 = 18.3 - 13.9 = 4.4$

Mass of gas taken out of cylinder

$$= 4.4 \times 32 \text{ g} = 140.8 \text{ g} = 0.140 \text{ kg}$$

26. (i) Dotted plot shows that $\frac{pV}{T}$ is a constant quantity $\left(\frac{pV}{T} = mR\right)$ which is independent of pressure. It signifies the ideal gas behaviour.

(ii) As curve at temperature T_1 is closer to the dotted plot than the curve at temperature T_2. Since, the behaviour of a real gas approaches the behaviour of perfect gas when temperature is increased, so $T_1 > T_2$.

(iii) The value of $\frac{pV}{T}$, where the curves meet on Y-axis is equal to μR.

Now, given mass of oxygen gas

$$= 1.00 \times 10^{-3} \text{ kg} = 1 \text{ g}$$

$$\therefore \quad \frac{pV}{T} = \mu R = \left(\frac{1}{32}\right) \times 8.31 \text{ JK}^{-1}$$

$$= 0.26 \text{ JK}^{-1}$$

(iv) If we use 1.00×10^{-3} kg of hydrogen, then we will not get same value of $\frac{pV}{T}$ at the point, where the curves meet on Y-axis because molecular mass of hydrogen is different from oxygen.

Now, to get same value of $\frac{pV}{T}$, mass of hydrogen required is obtained from

$$\frac{pV}{T} = \mu R = \frac{m}{2.02} \times 8.31 = 0.26$$

$$\Rightarrow \quad m = \frac{2.02 \times 0.26}{8.31} = 6.32 \times 10^{-2}\text{g}$$

27. As Boltzmann's constant, $k_B = \frac{R}{N}$,

$\therefore \quad R = k_B N$

Now, $\quad pV = nRT = nk_B NT$

$\therefore$ The number of molecules in the room

$$-nN = \frac{pV}{Tk_B} = \frac{1.013 \times 10^5 \times 25.0}{300 \times 1.38 \times 10^{-23}} = 6.117 \times 10^{26}$$

28. According to the kinetic theory, we have for 1 gram-molecule of a gas, $pV = \frac{1}{2} M \bar{v}^2$

At constant temperature the value $\bar{v}^2$ will remain constant. Then, if V is constant, we have $p \propto M$

on increasing the mass of gas by 60%, the pressure will also increase by 60%. Hence, the final pressure of the gas

$= 80 \text{ cm} + \left(80 \times \frac{60}{100}\right) \text{cm} = 128 \text{ cm (of mercury)}.$

29. $T_1 = 0°\text{C} = (0 + 273)\text{K} = 273\text{K}$

$$T_2 = ?, \quad v_2 = \frac{1}{2} v_1$$

$$\frac{v_2}{v_1} = \sqrt{\frac{T_2}{T_1}} = \frac{1}{2} = \frac{T_2}{T_1} = \left(\frac{1}{2}\right)^2$$

$$T_2 = \frac{T_1}{4} = \frac{273}{4} = 68.25 \text{ K}$$

30. (i) Average speed

$$= \frac{n_1 v_1 + n_2 v_2 + n_3 v_3 + n_4 v_4 + n_5 v_5}{n_1 + n_2 + n_3 + n_4 + n_5}$$

$$= \frac{2 \times 1 + 4 \times 2 + 8 \times 3 + 6 \times 4 + 3 \times 5}{2 + 4 + 8 + 6 + 3} = 3.17 \text{ m/s}$$

(ii) Root mean square speed

$$= \sqrt{\frac{n_1 v_1^2 + n_2 v_2^2 + n_3 v_3^2 + n_4 v_4^2 + n_5 v_5^2}{n_1 + n_2 + n_3 + n_4 + n_5}}$$

$$= \sqrt{\frac{2 \times 1^2 + 4 \times 2^2 + 8 \times 3^2 + 6 \times 4^2 + 3 \times 5^2}{2 + 4 + 8 + 6 + 3}}$$

$= 3.36$ m/s

(iii) The most probable speed is that speed which is possessed by maximum number of molecules.

Most probable speed (v_{mp})

$$= \sqrt{\frac{2k_BT}{m}} = \sqrt{\frac{3k_BT}{m}} \times 2/3$$

$$v_{mp} = \sqrt{\frac{2}{3}} \times \sqrt{\frac{3k_BT}{m}} = \sqrt{\frac{2}{3}} v_{rms} = \sqrt{\frac{2}{3}} \times 3.36 \text{ m/s}$$

$$= 0.816 \times 3.36 \text{ m/s} = 2.74 \text{ m/s}$$

31. Given, $k_B = 1.38 \times 10^{-23}$ J/K

$$T = 300 \text{ K}$$

$$E = \frac{3}{2} k_B T = \frac{3}{2} \times 1.38 \times 10^{-23} \times 300 = 6.21 \times 10^{-21} \text{J}$$

32. $v_{rms} = \left[\frac{3pV}{M}\right]^{1/2} = \left[\frac{3RT}{M}\right]^{1/2}$

Let rms speed of oxygen is $(v_{rms})_1$ and of helium is $(v_{rms})_2$ is equal at temperatures T_1 and T_2, respectively.

$$\frac{(v_{rms})_1}{(v_{rms})_2} = \sqrt{\frac{M_2 T_1}{M_1 T_2}}$$

$$\left[\frac{4T_1}{32 \times 263}\right]^{1/2} = 1$$

$$T_1 = \frac{32 \times 263}{4} = 2104 \text{ K}$$

33. The root mean square velocity of a oxygen molecule at absolute temperature T is given by $v_{rms} = \sqrt{\frac{3RT}{M}}$

where M is molecular weight of oxygen molecule $M = 32 \times 10^{-3}$kg.

$$v_{rms} = \sqrt{\frac{3 \times 8.31 \times 300}{32 \times 10^{-3}}} = 483.44 \text{ m/s}$$

The kinetic energy of 4 g gas

$$= \frac{1}{2} m v_{rms}^2 = \frac{1}{2} \times 4 \times 10^{-3} \times (483.44)^2 = 467.43 \text{ J}$$

34. According to the kinetic theory, the pressure p of a gas is given by $p = \frac{1}{3} \rho \bar{v}^2$

where, ρ is the density of the gas and $\bar{v}^2$ the mean square speed of its molecules.

$$\therefore \quad v_{rms} = \sqrt{\bar{v}^2} = \sqrt{\frac{3p}{\rho}}$$

Here, $p = 1.0 \times 10^5 \text{ Nm}^{-2}$ and $\rho = 1.98 \text{ kg m}^{-3}$

$$\therefore \quad v_{rms} = \sqrt{\frac{3 \times 1.0 \times 10^5}{1.98}} = 389 \text{ ms}^{-1}$$

Again, from the kinetic theory, the root mean square speed is directly proportional to the square root of the absolute temperature.

$$v_{rms} \propto \sqrt{T}$$

$$\therefore \quad \frac{(v_{rms})_{30}}{(v_{rms})_0} = \sqrt{\frac{273 + 30}{273 + 0}} = \sqrt{\frac{303}{273}} = 1.053$$

$$\therefore \quad (v_{rms})_{30} = (v_{rms})_0 \times 1.053$$

$$= (389 \text{ ms}^{-1}) \times 1.053 = 410 \text{ ms}^{-1}$$

35. (i) The average kinetic energy per molecule of any gas is $3/2k_BT$. It depends only on temperature and not on the nature of the gas. As both argon and chlorine have the same temperature in the flask, the ratio of average KE per molecule of the two gases is 1 : 1.

(ii) If m is mass of single molecule and M is the molecular mass, then

$$\frac{1}{2}mv_{rms}^2 = \frac{3}{2}k_BT = \text{constant at a given temperature}$$

$$\therefore \frac{(v_{rms}^2)_{Ar}}{(v_{rms}^2)_{Cl_2}} = \frac{(m)_{Cl_2}}{(m)_{Ar}} = \frac{M_{Cl_2}}{M_{Ar}} = \frac{70.9}{39.9} = 1.777$$

or $$\frac{(v_{rms})_{Ar}}{(v_{rms})_{Cl_2}} = \sqrt{1.777} = 1.333$$

36. The internal energy of μ mole of a gas at temperature T, is given by $U = \frac{1}{2}\mu f\, RT$

The internal energy of 2 mole oxygen,

$$U_1 = \frac{1}{2} \times 2 \times 5RT = 5RT$$

The internal energy of 4 mole helium,

$$U_2 = \frac{1}{2} \times 4 \times 3RT = 6RT$$

The total internal energy of the system,

$$U = 5RT + 6RT = 11\ RT = 11 \times 8.31 \times 300\ \text{J} = 2.74 \times 10^4\ \text{J}$$

Now, Substitute the value of

$$R(c_v)_{mix} \frac{9}{4} \times 8.31 = 18.69\ \text{JK}^{-1}\text{mol}^{-1}$$

37. $n = 1$ mole $C_V = \frac{3}{2}R$, $n' = 3$ mole

$$C_V' = \frac{5}{2}R$$

From conservation of energy for the mixture,

$$(C_V)_{mix} = \frac{n \times C_V + n'C_V'}{n + n'} = \frac{1 \times \frac{3}{2}R + 3 \times \frac{5}{2}R}{1 + 3} = \frac{9}{4}R$$

Now, substitute value of R

$$(C_V)_{mix} = \frac{9}{4} \times 8.31 = 18.69\ \text{JK}^{-1}\text{mol}^{-1}$$

38. For a polytropic process, the relation between pressure and volume is pV^n = constant

when n is the polytropic index, In this case, $pV^{3/2}$ = cosntant, so $n = \frac{3}{2}$.

Using the ideal gas law, $pV = nRT$, and for the process to remain polytropic, the temperature.

Volume are related as $T_1V_1^{n-1} = T_2V_2^{n-1}$

Since, $n = \frac{3}{2}$, we have, $T_1V_1^{1/2} = T_2V_2^{1/2}$

Now, the initial and final temperatures can be related by

$$\frac{T_2}{T_1} = \left(\frac{V_1}{V_2}\right)^{1/2}$$

Since, the volume changes by a factor of 2,

we have $\frac{V_2}{V_1} = 2$,

So, $$\frac{T_2}{300} = \left(\frac{1}{2}\right)^{1/2}, \frac{T_2}{300} = \frac{1}{\sqrt{2}} = 0.707$$

$$T_2 = 300 \times 0.707 = 212.1\ \text{K}$$

Thus, the final temperature is $T_2 = 212.1$ K.

39. Number of moles in 0.014 kg of nitrogen,

$$n = \frac{0.014 \times 10^3}{28} = \frac{1}{2}\ \text{mol}$$

$$C_V = \frac{5}{2}R$$

Further, according to the given problem, $\frac{V_2}{V_1} = \sqrt{\frac{T_2}{T_1}} = 2$

$$\therefore T_2 = 4T_1$$

$$\Delta T = T_1 - T_2 = 4T - T = 3T$$

$$= 3 \times 300 = 900k$$

$$\Delta Q = nC_v\Delta T = \frac{1}{2} \times 5 \times 900 = 2250\ \text{cal}$$

40. Given, $p = 1\ \text{atm} = 1.01 \times 10^5$ Pa

$$k_B = 1.38 \times 10^{-23}\ \text{J/K}$$

$$T = 273\ \text{K}$$

From an ideal gas law, $n = \frac{p}{k_BT}$

$$n = \frac{1.01 \times 10^5}{1.38 \times 10^{-23} \times 273} = \frac{1.01 \times 10^5 \times 10^{23}}{376.74}$$

$$= 2.68 \times 10^{25}\ \text{mole/m}^3$$

Mean free path of the air molecule,

$$T = \frac{1}{\sqrt{2}\pi nd^2} = \frac{1}{1.414 \times 3.14 \times 2.68 \times 10^{25} \times (4 \times 10^{-10})^2}$$

$$= 5.2 \times 10^{-8}\text{m}$$

QR Code for Quick Test 1

QR Code for Quick Test 2

SELF ASSESSMENT TEST

Multiple Choice Questions (MCQs)

1. For a gas, the rms speed at 800 K is
   (a) four times the value at 200 K
   (b) half the value at 200 K
   (c) twice the value at 200 K
   (d) same at 200 K
2. The average kinetic energy of a helium atom at 30°C is
   (a) less than 1 eV (b) a few keV
   (c) 50-60 eV (d) 13-6 eV
3. Fire molecules of a gas have speeds 1, 2, 3, 4 kms^{-1}. The value of the root mean square speed of the gas molecules is
   (a) 3 kms^{-1} (b) $\sqrt{11}$ kms^{-1}
   (c) $\frac{1}{2}\sqrt{11}$ kms^{-1} (d) 2.738 kms^{-1}
4. A gas filled in a closed vessel is heated through 1K and its pressure increases by 0.4%. What was the initial temperature of the gas ?
   (a) 250 K (b) 350 K
   (c) 450 K (d) 500 K
5. An ant is walking on the horizontal surface. The number of degrees of freedom of ant will be
   (a) 1 (b) 2
   (c) 3 (d) 6
6. Match Column I and Column II and choose the correct match from the given choices.

	Column I		Column II
(A)	Root mean square speed of gas molecules	(P)	$\frac{1}{3}nm\bar{v}^2$
(B)	Pressure exerted by ideal gas	(Q)	$\sqrt{\frac{3RT}{M}}$
(C)	Average kinetic energy of a molecule	(R)	$\frac{5}{2}RT$
(D)	Total internal energy of 1 mole of a diatomic gas	(S)	$\frac{3}{2}k_BT$

   (a) A-Q, B-R, C-S, D-P (b) A-Q, B-P, C-S, D-R
   (c) A-R, B-Q, C-P, D-S (d) A-R, B-P, C-S, D-Q

Assertion-Reason

Direction *(Q. Nos. 7-10) In the following questions, two statements are given-one labelled Assertion (A) and the other labelled Reason (R). Select the correct answer to these questions from the codes (a), (b), (c) and (d) as given below.*

(a) Both Assertion and Reason are true and Reason is the correct explanation of Assertion.
(b) Both Assertion and Reason are true but Reason is not the correct e xplanation of Assertion.
(c) Assertion is true but Reason is false.
(d) Assertion is false but Reason is true.

7. **Assertion** In pressure-temperature (p-T) phase diagram of water, the slope of the melting curve is found to be negative
   Reason Ice contracts on melting to water
8. **Assertion** For gas atom the number of degrees of freedom is 3.
   Reason $\frac{C_p}{C_V} = \gamma$
9. **Assertion (A)** The pressure exerted by an ideal gas on the walls of its container indeed arises from the constant collisions of gas molecules with the walls.
   Reason (R) According to the kinetic theory of gases, gas molecules are in continuous random motion and their collisions with the container walls produce a force, which results in pressure.
10. **Assertion (A)** The pressure of an ideal gas increases when its temperature increases, provided the volume is constant.
    Reason (R) Increasing temperature increases the speed of the gas molecules, which leads to more frequent and forceful collisions with the walls, thus increasing pressure.

Case Based Question

Directions *(Q.Nos. 11) This question is case study based question. Read the following paragraph and answer the questions on the basis of same.*

11. A sample of an ideal gas is contained in a rigid, sealed container. The gas molecules are moving with a range of velocities and the gas is in thermal equilibrium at temperature T. The container has a fixed volume and is initially at a pressure p_1. The gas is then heated to a higher temperature T_2, causing the average kinetic energy of the molecules to increase.

(i) What happens to the pressure of the gas when it is heated from temperatures T_1 to T_2 assuming the volume remains constant?

(a) the pressure decreases
(b) the pressure remains constant
(c) the pressure increases
(d) the pressure fluctuates

(ii) Which of the following describes the relationship between pressure and temperature for a fixed volume in this case?

(a) $p \propto T^2$ (b) $p \propto T$
(c) $p \propto \frac{1}{T}$ (d) $p \propto \frac{1}{T^2}$

(iii) How does the root mean square (rms) speed of the gas molecules change when the temperature increases?

(a) The rms speed decreases
(b) The rms speed increases
(c) The rms speed remains constant
(d) The rms speed becomes zero

(iv) What will happen to the mean free path of the gas molecules when the temperature is increased, assuming the pressure remains constant?

(a) The mean free path will increase
(b) The mean free path will decrease
(c) The mean free path will remain unchanged
(d) The mean free path will become zero

Very Short Answer Type Questions

12. If the temperature of a gas is doubled, what happens to the volume and pressure of the gas if it behaves ideally?

13. The absolute temperatrue of a gas is increased 3 times what is the effect on the root mean square velocity of the molecules?

14. What is the ratio of rms velocity to most probable velocity?

15. Why does the pressure exerted by a gas increases with temperature according to the kinetic theory?

Short Answer Type Questions

16. On what parameters does the λ (mean free path) depends.

17. Is it possible to increase the temperature of a gas while keeping its pressure and volume constant? Explain it.

18. What is the kinetic energy of translation of one molecules of a gas at 300 K? Gas is having three dergree of freedom and $k_B = 1.38 \times 10^{-23}$ JK^{-1}

Long Answer Type Questions

19. State Dalton's law of partial pressure. Obtain it from kinetic theory of gases.

20. Uranium has two isotopes of masses 235 and 238 units. If both are present in uranium hexafluoride gas, which would have the larger average speed? If atomic mass of fluorine is 19 units, estimate the percentage difference in speeds at any temperature. How is the above concept of difference in speeds utilised in the enrichment of uranium needed for nuclear fission?

Answers

1. (c) *2.* (a) *3.* (d) *4.* (a) *5.* (b)
6. (b) *7.* (a) *8.* (b) *9.* (a) *10.* (a)
11. (i) (c), (ii) (b), (iii) (b), (iv) (a)
18. 6.21×10^{-21} J

13

CHAPTER

Oscillations are repetitive periodic motions in which an object or a system moves back and forth around an equilibrium position.
This type of motion is common in nature and forms the basis of many physical phenomena, ranging from the swinging of a pendulum to the vibrations of atoms in a solid.
If forms the basis for studing wave phenomena vibrations in mechanical systems.

YOUR STUDY GOALS

YOUR PRACTICE GOAL

- Objective Type Questions (27 Qs ; MCQs, A-R, Matching)
- Case Based Questions (02)
- Subjective Questions (6 VSAs, 9 SAs, 6 LAs)
- Numerical Problems (20)

Oscillations

13.1 Introduction of Oscillation

Periodic Motion

A motion that repeats itself after regular intervals of time is called periodic motion. e.g. Motion of planets around the sun, motion of a ball in a bowl, etc.

Oscillatory Motion

A motion in which a body moves to and fro or back and forth repeatedly about a fixed point in a regular interval of time is called **oscillatory motion.** This fixed point is known as **mean/equilibrium position** or **centre of oscillation.**

e.g. Motion of a simple pendulum as it moves to and fro about its mean position.

- Oscillatory motion is also called as **harmonic motion.**
- If the body is given a small displacement from its mean position, a force called **restoring force,** comes into play which tries to bring the body back to the equilibrium point. **This process repeats itself again and again causing oscillation.**

  A ball placed in a bowl will be in equilibrium at the bottom. If it is displaced a little from the mean position, it will start oscillatory motion in the bowl.

Note Every oscillatory motion is periodic but every periodic motion needs not to be oscillatory. e.g. Circular motion is periodic but not oscillatory.

Period and Frequency

Period

The smallest interval of time after which a periodic motion is repeated, is called its period. Its SI unit is second and it is denoted by the symbol T.

Period of oscillation should have a very high range of accuracy, so its unit varies with the necessity.

Frequency

The number of oscillations executed by body per second is called frequency.

Frequency can also be defined as reciprocal of time period, it is denoted by ν.

Thus, Frequency, $\nu = \frac{1}{T}$

The SI unit of frequency is Hertz (Hz), where $1\text{ Hz} = 1$ oscillation per sec $= 1\text{ s}^{-1}$

When frequency of an oscillatory motion is very high, then motion is called **vibrational motion**.

Example 1. **Human heart on an average, is found to beat 75 times in a minute. Calculate its beat frequency and period.** NCERT

Sol. The beat frequency of heart

$$= \frac{\text{Number of beats}}{\text{Time taken}} = \frac{75}{60} = 1.25\text{ s}^{-1} = 1.25\text{ Hz}$$

$$\text{Beat period, } T = \frac{1}{\text{Frequency}} = \frac{1}{1.25\text{ s}^{-1}} = 0.8\text{ s}$$

Displacement

In general, the name displacement is given to a change in position of a particle with respect to origin. In oscillation, **we use term displacement as the change in position with respect to mean position (or equilibrium position) or reference position.**

Illustrations for Displacement of a Particle

(i) Consider that a block is attached to a spring at one of its end, the other end of which is fixed to a ring wall. Generally, it is convenient to measure the displacement variable (x) as the deviation of the block from the mean position of the oscillation with time, as given in the diagram along side.

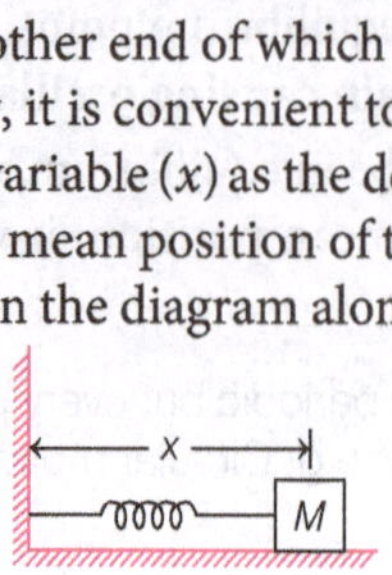

(ii) In a simple pendulum, the displacement variable is its angular deviation (θ) from the vertical axis during oscillations with time as given in the diagram below.

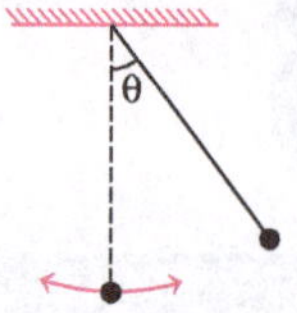

Note Displacement variable is measured as a function of time having both positive and negative values.

Periodic Function

The function which repeats its value at regular intervals of time or period is called periodic function. A function $f(t)$ with period T will be periodic, if

$$f(t) = f(t + T)$$

The periodic function with period $T = \frac{2\pi}{\omega}$ is given by

- $f(t) = A\sin\omega t$ [when time is measured from the mean position]
- $f(t) = A\cos\omega t$ [when time is measured from the extreme position]

It means **any periodic function can be expressed as a superposition of sine and cosine functions of different time periods with suitable coefficients.**

i.e. $f(t) = A\sin\omega t + B\cos\omega t$

If $A = D\cos\phi$ and $B = D\sin\phi$, the periodic function is given by

$$f(t) = D\sin(\omega t + \phi)$$

where, $D = \sqrt{A^2 + B^2}$

and $\phi = \tan^{-1}\left(\frac{B}{A}\right)$

Example 2. **Which of the following functions of time represent (a) periodic and (b) non-periodic motion? Give the period for each case of periodic motion. (ω is any positive constant)** NCERT

(i) $\sin\omega t + \cos\omega t$

(ii) $\sin\omega t + \cos 2\omega t + \sin 4\omega t$

(iii) $e^{-\omega t}$

(iv) $\log(\omega t)$

Sol. (i) Given, $x(t) = \sin\omega t + \cos\omega t$

$$= \sqrt{2}\left[\sin\omega t\cos\frac{\pi}{4} + \cos\omega t\sin\frac{\pi}{4}\right]$$

$$x(t) = \sqrt{2}\sin\left(\omega t + \frac{\pi}{4}\right)$$

Moreover, $x\left(t + \frac{2\pi}{\omega}\right) = \sqrt{2}\sin\left[\omega\left(t + \frac{2\pi}{\omega}\right) + \frac{\pi}{4}\right]$

$$= \sqrt{2}\sin\left(\omega t + 2\pi + \frac{\pi}{4}\right)$$

$$= \sqrt{2}\sin\left(\omega t + \frac{\pi}{4}\right) = x(t)$$

$[\because \sin(2\pi + \theta) = \sin\theta]$

Hence, $\sin\omega t + \cos\omega t$ is a periodic function with time period equal to $\frac{2\pi}{\omega}$.

(ii) Given, $x(t) = \sin\omega t + \cos 2\omega t + \sin 4\omega t$

$\sin\omega t$ is a periodic function with period

$$= \frac{2\pi}{\omega} = T$$

$\cos 2\omega t$ is a periodic function with period

$$= \frac{2\pi}{2\omega} = \frac{\pi}{\omega} = \frac{T}{2}$$

$\sin 4\omega t$ is a periodic function with period

$$= \frac{2\pi}{4\omega} = \frac{\pi}{2\omega} = \frac{T}{4}$$

Clearly, the function $x(t)$ repeats after a minimum time, $T = \frac{2\pi}{\omega}$. Hence, the given function is periodic.

(iii) The function $e^{-\omega t}$ decreases monotonically to zero as $t \to \infty$. It is an exponential function with a negative exponent of e, where $e \approx 2.71828$. It never repeats its value. So, it is non-periodic.

(iv) The function $\log(\omega t)$ increases monotonically with time. As $t \to \infty$, $\log(\omega t) \to \infty$. It never repeats its value. So, it is non-periodic.

Example 3. The equation of a wave is given by $y = 6\sin 10\pi t + 8\cos 10\pi t$, where y is in centimetre and t in second. Determine the constants involved in the standard equation of the wave.

Sol. Given, $y = 6\sin 10\pi t + 8\cos 10\pi t$ ...(i)

The general equation of wave is $y = A\sin(\omega t + \phi)$

$$= A\sin\omega t\cos\phi + A\cos\omega t\sin\phi$$

$$= (A\cos\phi)\sin\omega t + (A\sin\phi)\cos\omega t \quad \text{...(ii)}$$

Comparing Eqs. (i) and (ii), we get

$$A\cos\phi = 6 \quad \text{...(iii)}$$

$$A\sin\phi = 8 \quad \text{...(iv)}$$

and $\omega t = 10\pi t$ or $\omega = 10\pi$

$\therefore$ Time period, $T = \frac{2\pi}{\omega} = \frac{2\pi}{10\pi} = 0.2$ s

Squaring and adding Eqs. (iii) and (iv), we get

$$A^2(\cos^2\phi + \sin^2\phi) = 6^2 + 8^2 = 36 + 64 = 100$$

or $A^2 = 100$

$\therefore$ $A = 10$ cm

Dividing Eq. (iv) by Eq. (iii), we get

$$\tan\phi = \frac{8}{6} = 1.3333$$

$\therefore$ $\phi = \tan^{-1}(1.3333) = 53°8'$

13.2 Simple Harmonic Motion

A special type of periodic motion in which a particle moves to and fro repeatedly about a mean position under the influence of a restoring force is known as Simple Harmonic Motion (SHM).

Characteristic of Restoring Force in SHM

The restoring force is always directed towards the mean position and its magnitude at any instant is directly proportional to the displacement of the particle from its mean position at that instant.

$$F \propto -x$$

$$F = -kx$$

where, k is a force constant having **SI unit N/m**.

The negative sign shows that the restoring force F is always directed towards the mean position.

The relation $F = -kx$ is known as **force law** for SHM.

Equation of SHM

Consider a particle oscillating back and forth about the origin of an X-axis between the limits $+A$ and $-A$ as shown in the figure below.

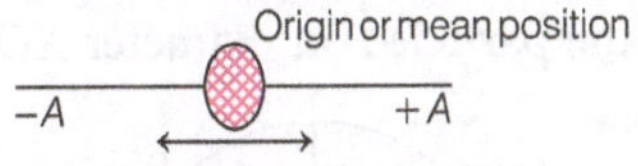

A particle executing SHM

This oscillatory motion of the particle is said to be SHM, if the displacement x of the particle from the origin varies with time as

Displacement, $x(t) = A\cos(\omega t + \phi)$

where, A, ω and ϕ are constants.

Example 4. Which of the following functions of time represent (a) simple harmonic motion (b) periodic but not simple harmonic?
Give the period for each function when functions are

(i) $\sin\omega t - \cos\omega t$ (ii) $\sin^2\omega t$ NCERT

Sol. (i) Given, function is

$$\sin\omega t-\cos\omega t=\sin\omega t-\sin\left(\frac{\pi}{2}-\omega t\right)$$

$$=2\sin\left(\frac{\omega t+\frac{\pi}{2}-\omega t}{2}\right)\sin\left(\frac{\omega t-\frac{\pi}{2}+\omega t}{2}\right)$$

$$\text{Given function}=2\sin\left(\frac{\pi}{4}\right)\sin\left(\omega t-\frac{\pi}{4}\right)$$

$$=\sqrt{2}\sin\left(\omega t-\frac{\pi}{4}\right)$$

This function represents a simple harmonic motion having a period of $T=\frac{2\pi}{\omega}$.

(ii) Also, $\sin^2\omega t=\frac{1-\cos 2\omega t}{2}=\frac{1}{2}-\frac{1}{2}\cos 2\omega t$

The function is periodic having a period of $T=\frac{\pi}{\omega}$. It also represents a harmonic motion with the point of equilibrium occurring at 1/2 instead of zero.

Simple Harmonic Motion and Uniform Circular Motion (Geometrical Interpretation of SHM)

Simple harmonic motion is also defined as the projection of uniform circular motion on any diameter of circle of reference.

e.g. Consider that a particle P starting from X is moving with a uniform speed along the circumference of a circle of radius A, with centre at O. This circle is known as **circle of reference**, while the particle P is known as **reference particle.**

Let P' be the foot of perpendicular drawn from the point P to the diameter XOX'. P' is known as **projection** of the particle P at diameter XOX'.

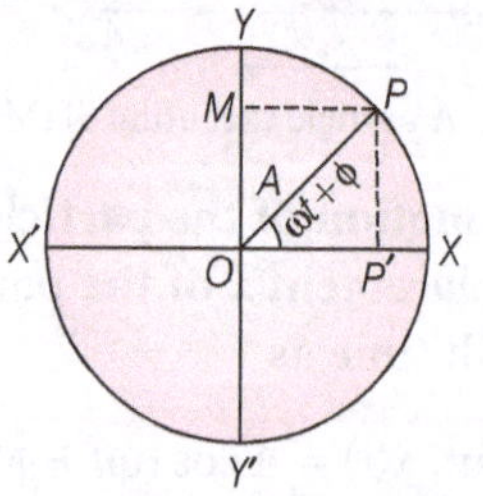

Circular representation of SHM

In the above figure, point P' is executing SHM while particle P is executing uniform circular motion.

The displacement of the particle as a function of time is given by $OP'=A\cos(\omega t+\phi)$

Characteristics of Simple Harmonic Motion

(i) Displacement

The displacement of a particle executing SHM at an instant is given by the distance of the particle from the mean position at that instant.

The values of displacement as a continuous function of time can be represented as the following graph.

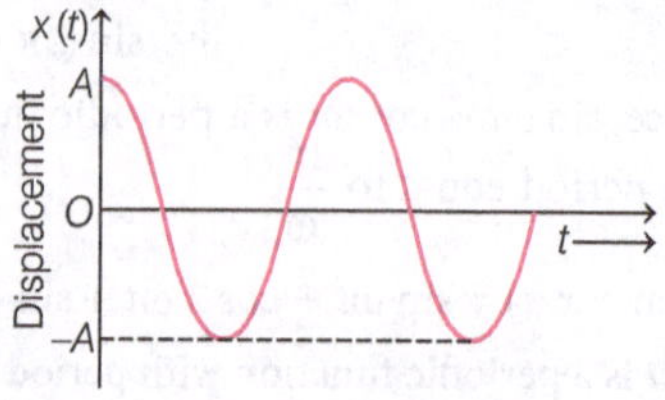

Displacement as a continuous function of time

Here, Displacement, $x(t)=A\cos(\omega t+\phi)$

where, A is amplitude, ω is angular frequency and ϕ is phase constant.

Note Displacement variable is measured as a function of time having both positive and negative values.

(ii) Amplitude

The magnitude of maximum displacement of a particle executing SHM is called amplitude of the oscillation of that particle. Amplitude is measured on either side of mean position.

The displacement varies between the extremes $+A$ and $-A$ because the sinusoidal function of time varies from +1 to −1.

Two SHM may have same ω (angular frequency) and ϕ (phase constant) but different amplitudes A and B as shown below

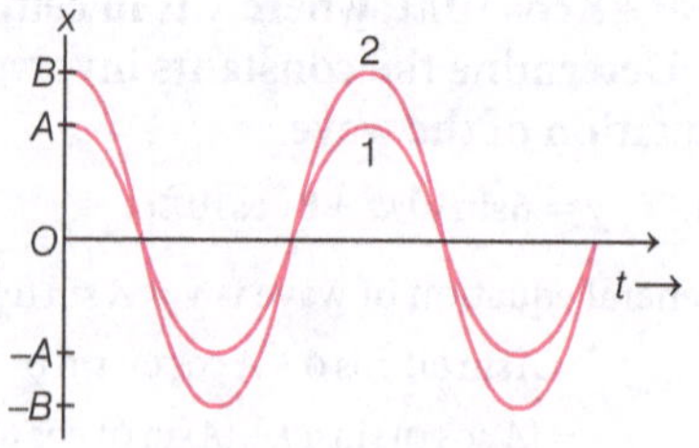

Different amplitudes in SHM at same time

(iii) Phase

The phase of a vibrating particle at any instant gives the state of the particle with regard to its position and the direction of motion at that instant.

If amplitude A is fixed for a given SHM, then the state of motion, i.e. position and velocity of the particle at any time t is determined by the argument $(\omega t + \phi)$ in the sinusoidal function. The quantity $(\omega t + \phi)$ is called **phase** of the motion.

- The value of phase at $t = 0$ is ϕ. So, ϕ is called **phase constant** or **phase angle.**
- The function containing sine or cosine term is known as **sinusoidal function.**

Two SHM may have the same A (amplitude) and ω (angular frequency) but different phase angle as shown below.

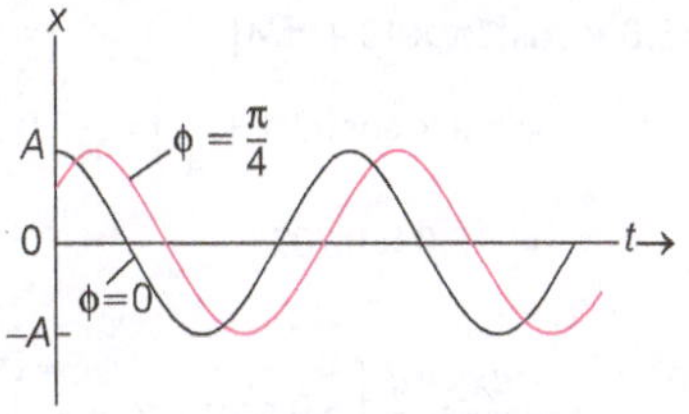

Phase determination

(iv) Angular Frequency

Angular frequency of a body executing periodic motion is equal to the product of frequency of the particle with factor 2π.

It is denoted by ω and its **SI unit is radian per second.**

$$\omega = 2\pi\nu = \frac{2\pi}{T} \qquad \left(\because \nu = \frac{1}{T}\right)$$

where, ν is the frequency and T is the time period.

Two SHMs may have the same amplitude (A) and phase angle (ϕ) but different angular frequency ω.

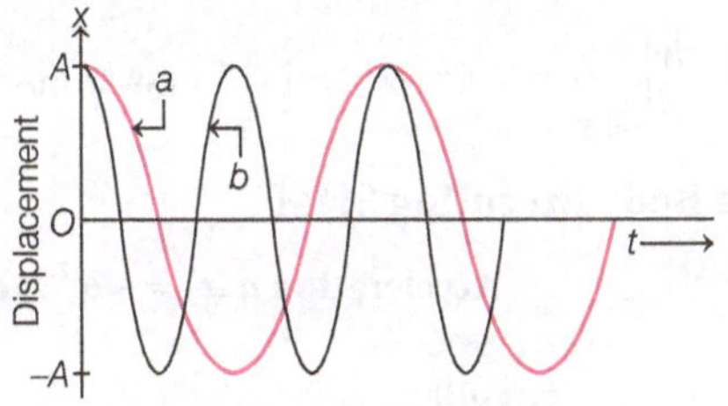

Two SHM having same amplitude and phase

In the above wave diagram, curve (b) has half the period and twice the frequency of the curve (a).

(v) Velocity

The velocity of a particle executing SHM at any instant, is defined as the time rate of change of its displacement at that instant.

$$\text{Velocity, } v = \omega\sqrt{A^2 - x^2}$$

At mean position, $x = 0$

$\therefore \quad v = \omega A \quad$ [maximum velocity]

At extreme position $\quad x = A$

$\therefore \quad v = 0 \quad$ [minimum velocity]

The velocity can also be calculated as

$$v(t) = \frac{d}{dt}[x(t)] = \frac{d}{dt}[A\cos(\omega t + \phi)]$$

$$\boxed{\text{Velocity, } v(t) = -\omega A \sin(\omega t + \phi)}$$

TEACHER TIP

During SHM, the speed of the particle will be maximum at the mean position and minimum (zero) at the extreme positions.

Velocity amplitude is given by $v_{max} = A\omega$

(vi) Acceleration

The acceleration of the particle executing SHM at any instant is defined as the time rate of change of its velocity at that instant.

$$\boxed{\text{Acceleration, } a = -\omega^2 x}$$

At mean position, $x = 0$

$\therefore \quad a = 0 \quad$ [minimum acceleration]

At extreme position $x = A$,

$\therefore \quad a = -\omega^2 A \quad$ [maximum acceleration]

The acceleration can also be calculated as

$$a(t) = \frac{d}{dt}[v(t)] = \frac{d}{dt}[-\omega A \sin(\omega t + \phi)]$$

$$\boxed{\text{Acceleration, } a(t) = -\omega^2 A\cos(\omega t + \phi)}$$

Example 5. **A simple harmonic motion is represented by $x = 12\sin(10t + 0.6)$. Find out the amplitude, angular frequency, frequency, time period and initial phase, if displacement is measured in metre and time in seconds.**

Sol. Given equation, $x = 12\sin(10t + 0.6)$

On comparing with $x(t) = A\sin(\omega t + \phi)$

We have,

(i) Amplitude, $A = 12$ m

(ii) Angular frequency, $\omega = 10$ rad / s

(iii) Frequency, $\nu = \dfrac{\omega}{2\pi} = \dfrac{10}{2\pi} = 1.59$ Hz

(iv) Time period, $T = \dfrac{2\pi}{\omega} = \dfrac{1}{1.59} = 0.628$ s

(v) Initial phase, $\omega t + \phi|_{t=0} = 10t + 0.6|_{t=0}$

$= 0.6$ rad

Example 6. **A particle executes SHM with a time period of 2 s and amplitude 5 cm. Find**
(i) displacement (ii) velocity and
(iii) acceleration after (1/3) s starting from the mean position.

Sol. Here, $T = 2$ s, $A = 5$ cm, $t = \dfrac{1}{3}$ s

(i) For the particle starting from mean position, (i.e. $\phi = 0$) displacement is

$$x = A\sin\omega t = A\sin\frac{2\pi}{T}t$$

$$= 5\sin\frac{2\pi}{2}\times\frac{1}{3} = 5\sin\frac{\pi}{3}$$

$$= 5\times\frac{\sqrt{3}}{2} = 4.33\text{ cm}$$

(ii) Velocity, $v = \dfrac{dx}{dt} = \dfrac{d(A\sin\omega t)}{dt} = A\omega\cos\omega t$

$$= \frac{2\pi A}{T}\cos\frac{2\pi}{T}t = \frac{2\pi\times 5}{2}\cos\frac{\pi}{3}$$

$$= 5\times 3.14\times 0.5 \quad \left[\because \cos\frac{\pi}{3} = 0.5\right]$$

$$= 7.85\text{ cm s}^{-1}$$

(iii) Acceleration, $a = \dfrac{dv}{dt} = \dfrac{d(A\omega\cos\omega t)}{dt}$

$$= -A\omega^2\sin\omega t$$

$$= -\frac{4\pi^2 A}{T^2}\sin\frac{2\pi}{T}t$$

$$= -\frac{4\times 9.87\times 5}{4}\sin\frac{\pi}{3}$$

$$= -9.87\times 5\times\frac{\sqrt{3}}{2} = -42.73\text{ cm s}^{-2}$$

$\therefore$ $|a| = 42.73$ cm s^{-2}

Example 7. **A body oscillates with SHM according to the equation, $x = (5.0\text{ m})\cos[(2\pi\text{ rad s}^{-1})t + \pi/4]$. At $t = 1.5$ s, calculate displacement, speed and acceleration of the body.** **NCERT**

Sol. Equation of SHM,

$$x(t) = (5.0\text{ m})\cos[(2\pi\text{ rad s}^{-1})t + \pi/4]$$

Time, $t = 1.5$ s

$$x(t) = 5.0\times\cos[2\pi\times 1.5 + \pi/4]$$

$$= 5.0\times\cos\left(3\pi + \frac{\pi}{4}\right) = -5.0\cos\frac{\pi}{4}$$

$$= -5.0\times 0.707$$

$$x(t) = -3.535\text{ m}$$

$$v = \frac{dx}{dt} = \frac{d}{dt}\left[5.0\cos\left(2\pi t + \frac{\pi}{4}\right)\right]$$

$$= -5.0\times\sin\left(2\pi t + \frac{\pi}{4}\right)\times 2\pi$$

$$= -10\pi\sin\left(2\pi t + \frac{\pi}{4}\right)$$

$$\therefore \left.\frac{dx}{dt}\right|_{t=1.5} = -10\pi\sin\left(3\pi + \frac{\pi}{4}\right) = 10\pi\times 0.707$$

$$= 22.22\text{ m/s} \quad [\because \sin(3\pi + \theta) = -\sin\theta]$$

$$a = \frac{dv}{dt} = \frac{d}{dt}\left[-10\pi\sin\left[2\pi t + \frac{\pi}{4}\right]\right]$$

$$= -10\pi\times 2\pi\cos\left(2\pi t + \frac{\pi}{4}\right)$$

$$\left.\frac{dv}{dt}\right|_{t=1.5} = -20\pi^2\cos\left(3\pi + \frac{\pi}{4}\right) = 139.56\text{ m/s}^2$$

Displacement, Velocity and Acceleration of a Body Executing SHM

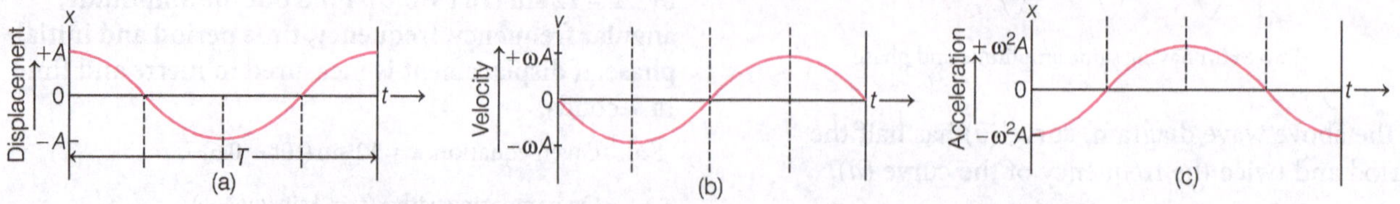

Displacement $x(t) = A\cos\omega t$	Velocity $v(t) = -\omega A\sin\omega t$	Acceleration $a(t) = -\omega^2 A\cos\omega t$
Sinusoidal in nature, x varies from $-A$ to A.	Sinusoidal in nature, $v(t)$ varies from $-\omega A$ to ωA.	Sinusoidal in nature. $a(t)$ varies from $-\omega^2 A$ to $\omega^2 A$.
It has zero phase difference.	It has a phase difference of $\dfrac{\pi}{2}$ w.r.t. $x(t)$	It has a phase difference of π w.r.t. $x(t)$.

Quick Test 1

Conceptual Questions

1. State the conditions when motion of a particle can be an SHM.

2. If a hollow pipe passes across the centre of gravity of the earth, then what changes would take place in the velocity and acceleration of a ball dropped in the pipe?

3. Can velocity and acceleration be in the same direction in a SHM?

4. Which of the following relationships between the acceleration a and the displacement x of a particle involve simple harmonic motion? NCERT

(i) $a = 0.7x$ (ii) $a = -200x^2$

(iii) $a = -10x$ (iv) $a = 100x^3$

5. The maximum acceleration of a simple harmonic oscillator is a_0 and the maximum velocity is v_0. What is the displacement amplitude?

Numerical Questions

6. The piston in the cylinder head of a locomotive has a stroke (twice the amplitude) of 1.0 m. If the piston executes simple harmonic motion with an angular frequency of 200 rad/min, then what is its maximum speed?

7. A particle is in linear simple harmonic motion between two points *A* and *B*, 10 cm apart. Take the direction from *A* to *B* as the positive direction and give the signs of velocity, acceleration and force on the particle when it is NCERT

(i) at the end *A*.
(ii) at the end *B*.
(iii) at the mid-point of *AB* going towards *A*.
(iv) at 2 cm away from *B* going towards *A*.
(v) at 3 cm away from *A* going towards *B*.
(vi) at 4 cm away from *B* going towards *A*.

8. A man stands on a weighing machine placed on a horizontal platform. The machine reads 50 kg. By means of a suitable mechanism, the platform is made to execute harmonic vibrations up and down with a frequency of 2 vibrations per second. What will be the effect on the reading of the weighing machine? The amplitude of vibrations of platform is 5 cm. (Take, $g = 10\ \text{ms}^{-2}$)

9. A particle executes SHM of amplitude 25 cm and time period 3 s. What is the minimum time required for a particle to move between two points located at a distance of 12.5 cm on either side of the mean position ?

Answers

6. 100 m/min 8. 10.5 kgF 9. 0.5 s

For Solutions, See QR Code on Pg. 458

13.3 Force and Energy in SHM

Force Law for Simple Harmonic Motion

It states that simple harmonic motion is the motion executed by a particle subjected to a force, which is proportional to the displacement of the particle and is always directed towards the mean position.

Using Newton's second law of motion, the force on a body of mass m during SHM is given by

$$F(t) = ma(t)$$

$$= -m\omega^2 x(t) \qquad [\because a(t) = -\omega^2 x(t)]$$

$$\Rightarrow \boxed{\text{Restoring force, } F(t) = -kx(t)} \qquad \ldots\text{(i)}$$

where, $k = m\omega^2$ or $\omega = \sqrt{\dfrac{k}{m}}$

The force law is expressed by Eq. (i) and can be taken as an alternative definition of simple harmonic motion.

Example 8. **Two identical springs of spring constant k are attached to a block of mass m and to fixed supports as shown in figure. Show that when the mass is displaced from its equilibrium position on either side. It executes a simple harmonic motion. Find the period of oscillations.** NCERT

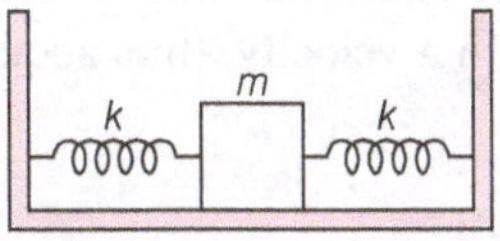

Sol. Force exerted by left spring, trying to pull the mass towards the mean position.

$$F_1 = -kx$$

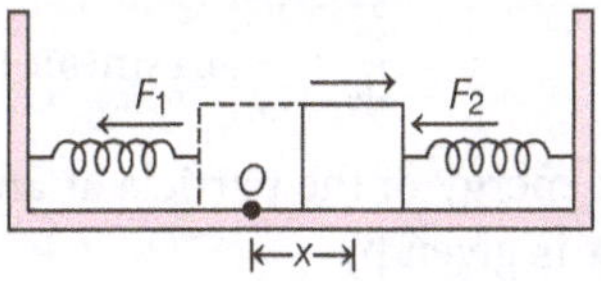

Similarly, force exerted by the right spring, trying to push the mass towards the mean position,

$$F_2 = -kx$$

The net force acting on the mass due to both the springs,

$$F = F_1 + F_2 = -2kx$$

Thus, the force acting on the mass is proportional to its displacement x and is directed towards its mean position. Hence, the motion of the mass m is simple harmonic.

Comparing the equation, $F = -2kx$ with $F = -k'x$.

We have, force constant $k' = 2k$.

$\therefore$ The time period of oscillation,

$$T = 2\pi\sqrt{\frac{m}{k'}} = 2\pi\sqrt{\frac{m}{2k}}$$

Example 9. **The vertical motion of a huge piston in a machine is simple harmonic with a frequency of 0.50 s^{-1}. A block of 10 kg is placed on the piston. What is the maximum amplitude of the piston's SHM for the block and the piston to remain together?**

Sol. As, $\nu = \frac{1}{2\pi}\sqrt{\frac{k}{m}}$

$\therefore$ $k = 4\pi^2 m\nu^2$

For maximum displacement, $y_{max} = A$

Maximum restoring force,

$$F = -kA = -mg$$

or $$A = \frac{mg}{k} = \frac{mg}{4\pi^2 m\nu^2} = \frac{g}{4\pi^2\nu^2}$$

$$= \frac{9.8}{4 \times (3.14)^2 \times (0.50)^2} = 0.99 \text{ m}$$

Energy in Simple Harmonic Motion

A particle executing SHM posseses both kinetic energy and potential energy. When a body is displaced from its equilibrium position by doing work upon it, it acquires potential energy. When the body is released, it begins to move back with a velocity, thus acquiring kinetic energy.

Kinetic Energy

At any instant, the displacement of a particle executing SHM is given by

$$x = A\cos(\omega t + \phi)$$

$\therefore$ Velocity, $$v = \frac{dx}{dt} = -\omega A\sin(\omega t + \phi)$$

Hence, kinetic energy of the particle at any displacement x is given by

$$K = \frac{1}{2}mv^2 = \frac{1}{2}m\omega^2 A^2 \sin^2(\omega t + \phi)$$

But, $A^2\sin^2(\omega t + \phi) = A^2[1 - \cos^2(\omega t + \phi)]$

$$= A^2 - A^2\cos^2(\omega t + \phi) = A^2 - x^2$$

Thus, $$K = \frac{1}{2}m\omega^2(A^2 - x^2)$$

$$\boxed{K = \frac{1}{2}k(A^2 - x^2)} \quad [\because k = m\omega^2]$$

Kinetic energy is maximum at mean position and zero at extreme positions. While the overall motion has a period T, the kinetic energy oscillates with a period of $\frac{T}{2}$.

Potential Energy

When the displacement of a particle from its equilibrium position is x, then restoring force acting on it given as

$$F = -kx$$

If we displace the particle further through a small distance dx, then work done against the restoring force is given by

$$dW = -Fdx = -kxdx$$

The total work done in moving the particle from mean position ($x = 0$) to displacement x is given by

$$W = \int dW = -\int_0^x kx\,dx$$

$$= -k\left[\frac{x^2}{2}\right]_0^x = -\frac{1}{2}kx^2$$

This work done against the restoring force is stored as the potential energy of the particle. Hence, potential energy of a particle at displacement x is given by

$$U = -W = \frac{1}{2}kx^2 = \frac{1}{2}m\omega^2 x^2$$

$$\boxed{\text{Potential energy, } U = \frac{1}{2}kx^2}$$

$$= \frac{1}{2}m\omega^2 A^2\cos^2(\omega t + \phi)$$

$$\boxed{U = \frac{1}{2}kA^2\cos^2(\omega t + \phi)}$$

Thus, potential energy of a particle executing simple harmonic motion is also periodic with period $T/2$.

Potential energy is zero at the mean position and maximum at the extreme position.

Total Energy

At any displacement x, the total energy of a harmonic oscillation is given by

$$E = K + U = \frac{1}{2}k(A^2 - x^2) + \frac{1}{2}kx^2$$

$$\text{Total energy, } E = \frac{1}{2}kA^2$$

$$E = \frac{1}{2}m\omega^2 A^2$$

$$= 2\pi^2 m\nu^2 A^2 \qquad [\because \omega = 2\pi\nu]$$

During SHM, total energy of a particle is independent of time or displacement. It depends upon the mass (m), amplitude (A) and frequency (ν) of vibration of the particle.

Hence, **in the absence of any frictional force, the total energy of a harmonic oscillator is conserved.**

Graphical Representation of Energy in SHM

At mean position, $x = 0$

(i) Kinetic energy, $K = \frac{1}{2}k(A^2 - 0^2) = \frac{1}{2}kA^2$

(ii) Potential energy, $U = \frac{1}{2}k(0^2) = 0$

Hence, at **mean position, the entire mechanical energy is in the form of kinetic energy.**

At extreme positions, $x = \pm A$

(i) Kinetic energy, $K = \frac{1}{2}k(A^2 - A^2) = 0$

(ii) Potential energy, $U = \frac{1}{2}kA^2$

Hence, **at the two extreme positions, the energy is totally potential, i.e. kinetic energy is zero.**

From above results, the graph for kinetic energy K, potential energy U and total energy E with displacement x is given below.

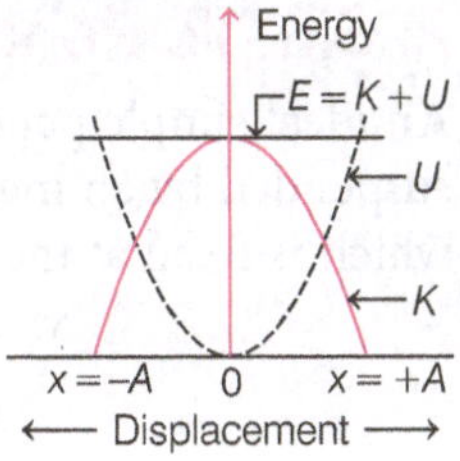

Plot for variation of energies K, U and E of a harmonic oscillator with time t is given below.

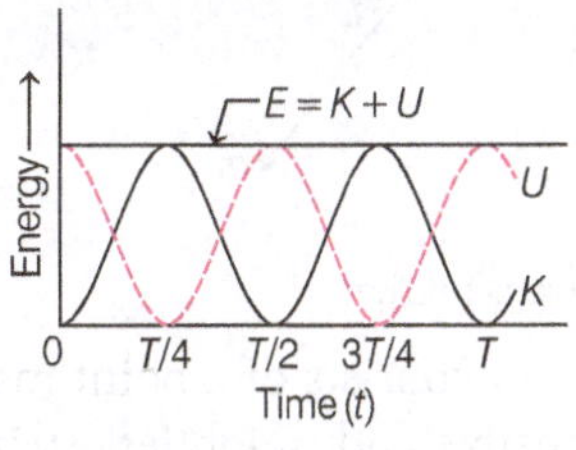

From the graph, we note that PE or KE completes two vibrations in a time during which SHM completes one vibration (i.e. PE and KE both repeat after a period $T/2$). **Thus, the frequency of PE or KE is double than that of SHM but the total energy remains constant at all t or x.**

Example 10. **A block whose mass is 1 kg is fastened to a spring. The spring has a spring constant of 50 Nm^{-1}. The block is pulled to a distance x = 10 cm from its equilibrium position at x = 0 on a frictionless surface from rest at t = 0. Calculate the kinetic, potential and total energies of the block when it is 5 cm away from the mean position.** NCERT

Sol. Given, $m = 1\text{kg}, k = 50\text{ Nm}^{-1}$,

$A = 10\text{ cm} = 0.1\text{m}, x = 5\text{ cm} = 0.05\text{ m}$

Kinetic energy, $K = \frac{1}{2}k(A^2 - x^2)$

$$K = \frac{1}{2} \times 50 \times [(0.1)^2 - (0.05)^2] = 0.1875\text{ J}$$

Potential energy of a block,

$$U = \frac{1}{2}kx^2 = \frac{1}{2} \times 50 \times (0.05)^2 = 0.0625\text{ J}$$

Total energy, $E = K + U = 0.1875 + 0.0625$

$E = 0.25\text{ J}$

Example 11. **A body of mass 0.2 kg and its velocity 1s after it passes through its mean position be 6 m/s executes SHM. Find out the total energy and potential energy of the body, if time period of the body is 8 s during the SHM ?**

Sol. Given, $m = 0.2\text{ kg}, T = 8\text{ s}$,

$$\omega = \frac{2\pi}{T} = \frac{2\pi}{8} = \frac{\pi}{4}\text{ rad/s}$$

When $t = 1\text{ s}, v = 6\text{ m/s}$

$$v(t) = \omega A\cos\omega t$$

$$6 = \frac{\pi}{4} \times A\cos\left(\frac{\pi}{4} \times 1\right)$$

$$\Rightarrow \quad 6 = \frac{\pi}{4} \times A \times \frac{1}{\sqrt{2}}$$

$$A = \frac{4\sqrt{2} \times 6}{\pi} = \frac{24\sqrt{2}}{\pi}\text{ m}$$

The total energy of the body

$$E = \frac{1}{2}m\omega^2 A^2 = \frac{1}{2} \times 0.2 \times \left(\frac{\pi}{4}\right)^2 \times \left(\frac{24\sqrt{2}}{\pi}\right)^2$$

$$= \frac{230.4}{32} = 7.2\text{ J}$$

Potential energy, $\text{PE} = E - \text{KE} = 7.2\ \frac{1}{2}\text{mv}^2$

$$= 7.2 - \frac{1}{2} \times 0.2 \times (6)^2 = 7.2 - 3.6$$

Potential energy $= 3.6$ J

13.4 Some Systems Executing Simple Harmonic Motion

1. Oscillation of Mass-Spring System

A mass m attached to a massless spring executes SHM when displaced by a small displacement x. The motion is driven by the restoring force (F) as shown below.

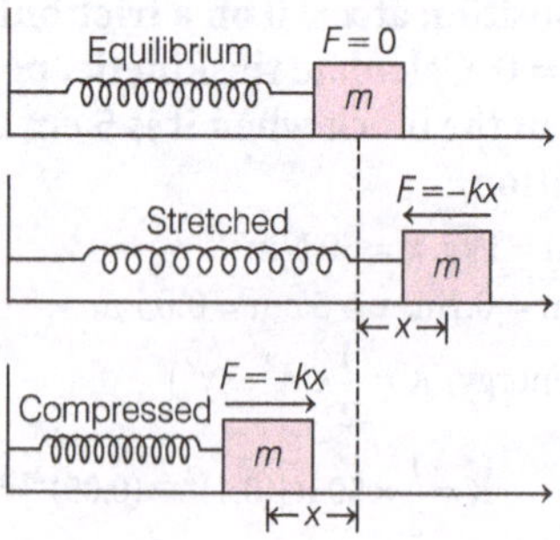

Three different positions of the oscillation due to a spring

where, k is the spring constant of the spring.

The **time period of the oscillating mass** is given by

$$T = \frac{2\pi}{\omega} = \frac{2\pi}{\sqrt{k/m}}$$

or
$$\text{Time period, } T = 2\pi\sqrt{\frac{m}{k}}$$

Frequency of oscillation can also be calculated as

$$\text{Frequency, } \nu = \frac{1}{T} = \frac{1}{2\pi}\sqrt{\frac{k}{m}}$$

Oscillation of Spring Combination

(i) **Series Combination** If two springs of spring constants k_1 and k_2 are connected in series, the equivalent spring constant (k) of the combination is given by

$$\frac{1}{k} = \frac{1}{k_1} + \frac{1}{k_2}$$

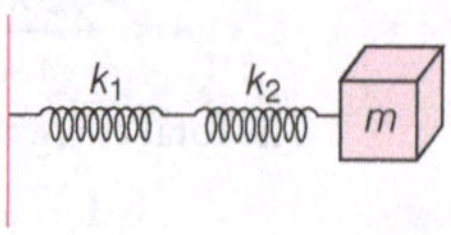

$$\Rightarrow \quad k = \frac{k_1 k_2}{k_1 + k_2}$$

So, $$T = 2\pi\sqrt{\frac{m(k_1 + k_2)}{k_1 k_2}}$$

(ii) **Parallel Combination** If two springs of spring constants k_1 and k_2 are connected in parallel, the equivalent spring constant (k) of the combination is given by

$$k = k_1 + k_2$$

So, $$T = 2\pi\sqrt{\frac{m}{k_1 + k_2}}$$

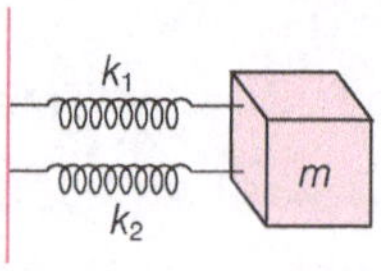

Example 12. A 5 kg collar is attached to a spring of spring constant 500 Nm^{-1}. It slides without friction over a horizontal rod. The collar is displaced from its equilibrium position by 10.0 cm and released. Calculate

(i) the period of oscillation,

(ii) the maximum speed and

(iii) maximum acceleration of the collar.

Sol. Draw the figure containing collar of 5 kg attached to a spring of spring constant 500 N /m.

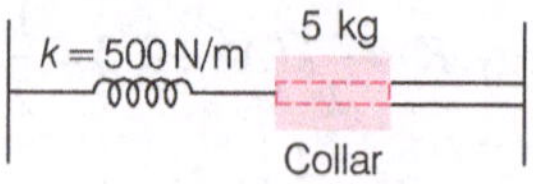

(i) Given, $m = 5$ kg, $k = 500$ N/m, $A = 10$ cm $= 0.1$m

The period of oscillation is given by

$$T = 2\pi\sqrt{\frac{m}{k}} = 2\pi \times \sqrt{\frac{5}{500}} = 0.628 \text{ s}$$

(ii) Maximum speed of the collar, $v_{max} = \omega A$

$$v_{max} = \sqrt{\frac{k}{m}} \cdot A = \sqrt{\frac{500}{5}} \times 0.1 = 1 \text{ m/s}$$

(iii) Maximum acceleration of the collar,

$$a_{max} = \omega^2 A = \frac{k}{m} \cdot A = \frac{500}{5} \times 0.1 = 10 \text{ m/s}^2$$

2. Simple Pendulum

An ideal simple pendulum consists of a point mass suspended by an inextensible and weightless string which is fixed at the other end as shown in figure.

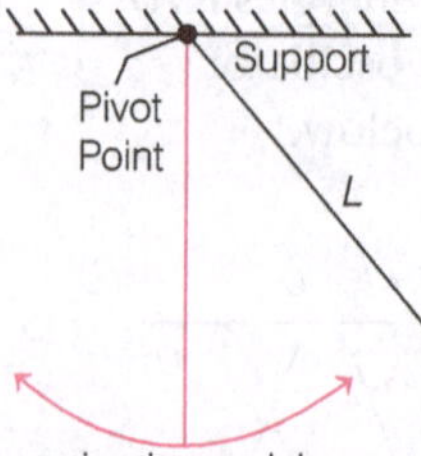

a simple pendulum

An ideal simple pendulum consists of a point mass (m) suspended by an inextensible and weightless string of length (L) which is fixed at the other end as shown in figure.

If the simple pendulum is displaced by a small angle, it will execute SHM.

The time period of the simple pendulum is given by

$$T = 2\pi\sqrt{\frac{L}{g}}$$

where, g is the acceleration due to gravity.

TEACHER TIP

The time period of the simple pendulum does not depend on the amplitude, mass and the material of the bob. It depends on the length L and acceleration due to gravity g.

The time period of a second's pendulum is 2 s.

Example 13 **What is the length of a simple pendulum, which ticks seconds?** NCERT

Sol. Given, $T = 2$s

and $g = 9.8 \text{ m/s}^2$

$$T = 2\pi\sqrt{\frac{L}{g}} = 2\pi\sqrt{\frac{L}{9.8}}$$

$$2^2 = 4\pi^2 \times \frac{L}{9.8}$$

$$\Rightarrow \quad L = \frac{9.8}{\pi^2} = 0.992 \text{ m}$$

$$\simeq 1.0 \text{ m}$$

Quick Test 2

Conceptual Questions

1. What is the ratio between the distance travelled by the oscillator in one time period and amplitude? *NCERT Exemplar*

2. How much is KE for displacement equal to half the amplitude?

3. A simple pendulum is transferred from earth to the surface of moon. How will its time period be affected?

4. A spring controlled wrist watch is taken from Earth to Moon. What shall be the effect on the watch?

5. Justify the following statements

(i) The motion of an artificial satellite around the earth cannot be taken as SHM.

(ii) The time period of a simple pendulum will get doubled if its length is increased four times.

Numerical Questions

6. If the length of a simple pendulum is increased by 25%, then what is the change in its time period?

7. A body of mass 12 kg is suspended by coil spring of natural length 50 cm and force constant $2.0 \times 10^3 \text{ Nm}^{-1}$. What is the stretched length of the spring? If the body is pulled down further stretching the spring to a length of 5.9 cm and then released, then what is the frequency of oscillation of the suspended mass? (Neglect the mass of the spring)

8. A spring compressed by 0.1 m develops a restoring force 10 N. A body of mass 4 kg is placed on it. Deduce

(i) the force constant of the spring.

(ii) the depression of the spring under the weight of the body (take $g = 10$ N/kg)

(iii) the period of oscillation.

9. A spring balance has a scale that reads from 0 to 50 kg. The length of the scale is 20 cm. A body suspended from this spring, when displaced and released, oscillates with a period of 0.60 s. What is the weight of the body? *NCERT*

Answers

6. 12.5% 7. 2.06 s^{-1}

8. (i) 100 Nm^{-1} (ii) 0.4 m (iii) 1.26 s

9. 219.13 N

For Solutions, See QR Code on Pg. 458

Mind Map

Oscillations

Periodic Motion

It refers to motion that repeats itself at regular intervals of time.
e.g. Revolution of planets around sun.

Time Period and Frequency

The motion repeats after a fixed period is referred as time period (T).
Frequency The number of cycles completed per unit time is called the frequency (f), given by $f = 1/T$

Periodic Functions

These are functions that repeat their values in regular intervals, known as the period. A function $f(x)$ is periodic if

$$f(x + T) = f(x) \text{ for all } x$$

Energy in SHM

In SHM, the total energy of the system remains constant and oscillates between kinetic energy (KE) and potential energy (PE).

Kinetic Energy
A particle has kinetic energy due to its velocity in simple harmonic motion.

Kinetic energy, $K = \frac{1}{2}k(A^2 - x^2)$

Potential Energy
When a particle displaces from its equilibrium position, then it does work against restoring force which store in the form of potential energy.

Potential energy, $U = \frac{1}{2}M\omega^2 x^2$

Total Energy

- Total mechanical energy of a harmonic oscillation is independent of time or displacement, while depends on the maximum displacement.

Total energy, $E = \frac{1}{2}kA^2$

- **Velocity** At any instant, the rate of change of displacement with respect to time of particle executing SHM is known as its velocity.
  $v = \omega\sqrt{A^2 - x^2}$
  At mean position, $x = 0$, $v = \omega A$
  At extreme position, $x = A$,
  $v = 0$ (Minimum velocity)
  $v(t) = -\omega A \sin(\omega t + \phi)$
- **Acceleration** At any instant, the rate of change of velocity with respect to time of particle executing SHM is known as acceleration. $a = \omega^2 x$
  At mean position, $x = 0$, $a = 0$
  At extreme position, $x = A$, $a = -\omega^2 A$
  $a(t) = -\omega^2 A\cos(\omega t + \phi)$

Oscillatory Motion

It refers to a type of motion where an object moves back and forth about an equilibrium position in a regular manner.
e.g. Motion of piston of engine.

Simple Harmonic Motion

Motion where the restoring force is directly proportional to the displacement.
The motion of a particle executing SHM can be expressed by the following equations,

$$x(t) = A\cos(\omega t + \phi)$$
$$y(t) = A\sin(\omega t + \phi)$$

where, $\omega = 2\pi f = \frac{2\pi}{T}$

Represents the rate of oscillation in radians per second.

Simple Harmonic Motion (SHM) and Circular Motion

Simple Harmonic Motion (SHM) and circular motion can be visualised as the projection of uniform circular motion onto one of the axes in a plane. This connection provides an elegant way to analyse SHM using the geometry of circular motion.

Charteristics of SHM

- **Amplitude** The maximum displacement of particle executing SHM.

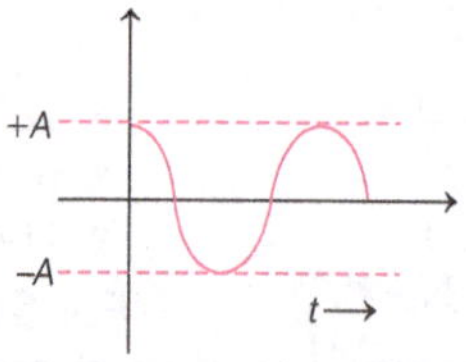

- **Phase** Phase of a oscillating particle is that quantity which refers to the position and direction of motion of the particle at that instant.
  $x = A\cos(\omega t + \phi)$
  where, ϕ is phase difference.

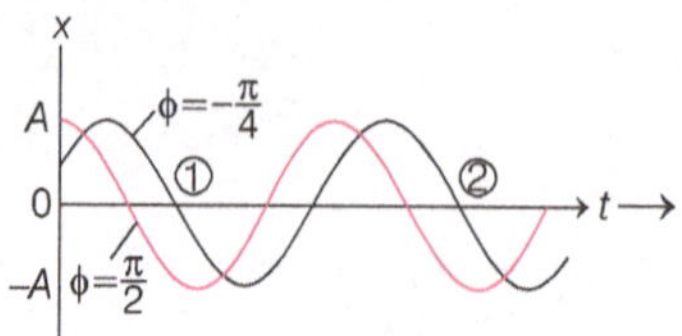

Simple Pendulum

- If a point mass is suspended with a massless, inextensible and perfectly flexible string from a rigid support, the arrangement is called simple pendulum.
- Restoring force acting on the bob,
  $F = -mg\sin\theta$
- If θ is very small,
  $F = -mg\frac{x}{L}$
- Acceleration of bob,
  $a = \frac{F}{m} = -\frac{gx}{L}$
- Time period, $T = 2\pi\sqrt{\frac{L}{g}}$

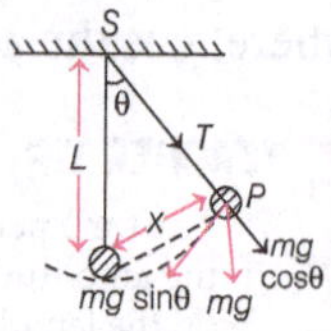

- **Effective length**
  Time period of pendulum depend on its effective length $T \propto \sqrt{L}$ or $T^2 \propto L$

- Time period of simple pendulum suspended from moving vehicle with horizontal acceleration,
  $T = 2\pi\sqrt{\frac{L}{g}} = 2\pi\sqrt{\frac{L}{\sqrt{g^2 + a^2}}}$
- Simple pendulum suspended from the roof of a vehicle, which moves without friction down an inclined plane of inclination θ
  $T = 2\pi\sqrt{\frac{L}{g\cos\theta}}$
- If simple pendulum is brought inside a liquid, then effective acceleration,
  $g' = g\left[1 - \frac{\sigma}{\rho}\right]$

Motion of a Body Attached to a Spring

- Let a particle of mass m is executing SHM with angular frequancy ω, then
- acceleration of the body is,
  $a = \frac{F}{m}$ or $a = -\omega^2 x$

Time period, $T = 2\pi\sqrt{\frac{m}{k}}$

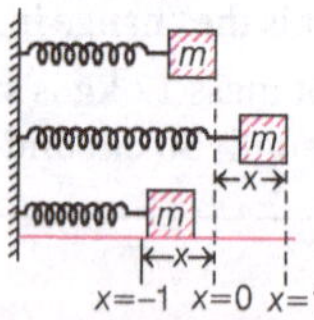

Damped Oscillation

- Oscillation of a body whose amplitude goes on decreasing with time.
- Damped force $F_d = -br$, $r = dx/dt$
- Displacement of damped oscillator.
  $x = x_m e^{-bt/2m}\cos(\omega t + \phi)$
- Amplitude decrease with time as
  $x = x_m e^{-(bt/2m)}$

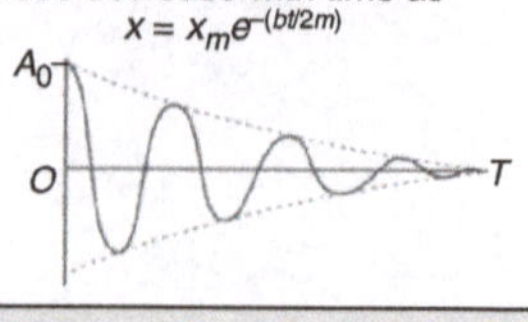

EXAM PATTERN QUESTIONS

Objective Type Questions

Multiple Choice Questions (MCQs)

1. The periodic function $f(t) = A\sin(\omega t)$ repeats itself with periodic function of

(a) 2π (b) 3π
(c) π (d) $\pi/2$

2. The displacement of a particle is represented by the equation $y = \sin^3 \omega t$. The motion is **NCERT Exemplar**

(a) non-periodic
(b) periodic but not simple harmonic
(c) simple harmonic with period $2\pi/\omega$
(d) simple harmonic with period π/ω

3. The displacement of a particle in SHM varies according to the relation $x = 4(\cos\pi t + \sin\pi t)$. The amplitude of the particle is **Competency Based Que.**

(a) -4 (b) 4 (c) $4\sqrt{2}$ (d) 8

4. At extreme position, velocity of the particle executing SHM that has amplitude A is

(a) $\omega^2 A$ (b) 0 (c) ωA (d) $\frac{\omega A}{2}$

5. A body of mass 400 g connected to a spring with spring constant 10 Nm^{-1}, executes simple harmonic motion, time period of oscillation is

(a) $4\pi \times 10^{-1}$ s (b) 0.3π s
(c) 2 s (d) 5×10^{-1} s

6. The period of a particle in linear SHM is 8 s. At t = 0, it is at mean position. The ratio of the distance travelled by it at t = 1 s and t = 2 s is

(a) 3.2 :1 (b) 0.41 :1 (c) 2.4 :1 (d) 1.6 :1

7. The periodic time of a time executing simple harmonic motion is 3s. After how much interval from t = 0, its displacement will be half of its amplitude?

(a) $\frac{1}{8}$ s (b) $\frac{1}{6}$ s (c) $\frac{1}{4}$ s (d) $\frac{1}{3}$ s

8. Two equations of two SHM $y = a\sin(\omega t - \alpha)$ and $y = a\cos(\omega t - \alpha)$. The phase difference between the two is

(a) 0° (b) α°
(c) 90° (d) 180°

9. A particle is oscillating according to the equation $x = 7\cos(0.5\pi t)$, where t is in second. The point moves from the position of equilibrium to maximum displacement in time.

(a) 4s (b) 2s (c) 1s (d) 0.5s

10. The relation between acceleration and displacement of four particles are given below **NCERT Exemplar**

(a) $a_x = +2x$ (b) $a_x = +2x^2$
(c) $a_x = -2x^2$ (d) $a_x = -2x$

Which one of the particle is exempting simple harmonic motion.

11. A particle is acted simultaneously by mutually perpendicular simple harmonic motion $x = a\cos\omega t$ and $y = a\sin\omega t$. The trajectory of motion of the particle will be **NCERT Exemplar**

(a) an ellipse (b) a parabola
(c) a circle (d) a straight line

12. The displacement of a particle varies with time according to the relation $y = a\sin\omega t + b\cos\omega t$. **NCERT Exemplar**

(a) The motion is oscillatory but not SHM
(b) The motion is SHM with amplitude $a + b$
(c) The motion is SHM with amplitude $a^2 + b^2$
(d) The motion is SHM with amplitude $\sqrt{a^2 + b^2}$

13. Natural length of the spring is 40 cm and its spring constant is 4000 Nm^{-1}. A mass of 20 kg is hung from it. The extension produced in the spring is ($g = 9.8\ ms^{-2}$) **Competency Based Que.**

(a) 4.9 cm (b) 0.49 cm (c) 9.4 cm (d) 0.94 cm

14. Two springs of force constants k_1 and k_2 are connected to a mass m as shown in figure. The frequency of oscillation of the mass is f. If both k_1 and k_2 are made four times their original values, the frequency of oscillation becomes **Competency Based Que.**

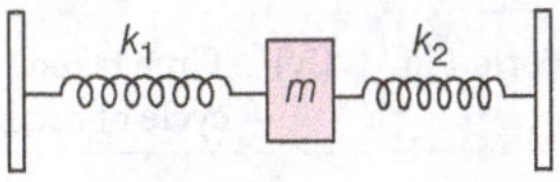

(a) $f/2$ (b) $f/4$ (c) $4f$ (d) $2f$

15. The fundamental frequency of a stretched string is ν_0. If the length is reduced by 35% and tension increased by 69% the fundamental frequency will be

(a) $0.2\nu_0$ (b) $0.5\nu_0$ (c) $2.0\nu_0$ (d) $1.6\nu_0$

16. Motion of an oscillating liquid column in a U-tube is **NCERT Exemplar**

(a) periodic but not simple harmonic
(b) non-periodic
(c) simple harmonic and time period is independent of the density of the liquid
(d) simple harmonic and time period is directly proportional to the density of the liquid

17. **The velocity-time diagram of a harmonic oscillator is shown in the adjoining figure. The frequency of oscillation is**

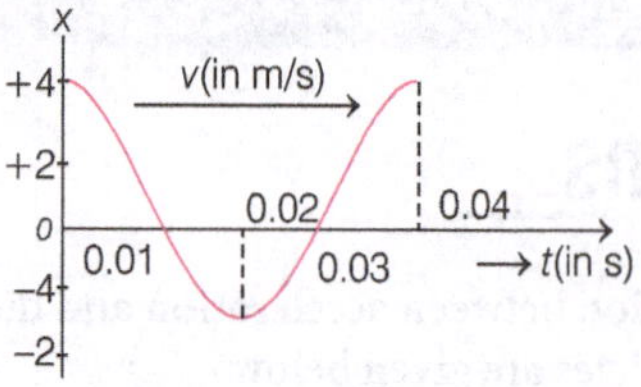

(a) 25 Hz (b) 50 Hz (c) 12.25 Hz (d) 33.3 Hz

18. **A body performs SHM. Its kinetic energy K varies with time t as indicated by graph** **Competency Based Que.**

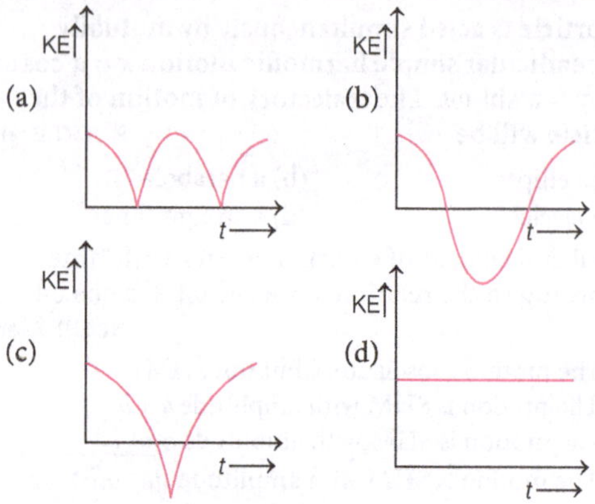

19. **Match the following columns.**

Column I	Column II
A. Simple Harmonic Motion (SHM)	(i) Energy remains constant, oscillates between kinetic and potential energy
B. Frequency of SHM	(ii) The number of complete oscillations per unit time
C. Amplitude of SHM	(iii) Maximum displacement from the equilibrium position
D. Time Period of SHM	(iv) Time taken for one complete cycle of oscillation

(a) (A)-(iv), (B)-(ii), (C)-(iii), (D)-(i)
(b) (A)-(i), (B)-(ii), (C)-(iii), (D)-(iv)
(c) (A)-(ii), (B)-(iv), (C)-(i), (D)-(iii)
(d) (A)-(iii), (B)-(i), (C)-(iv), (D)-(i)

20. **Match the following columns.**

Column I	Column II
A. Restoring Force in SHM	(i) It is proportional to the displacement
B. Displacement in SHM	(ii) Maximum value occurs at the extreme positions
C. Velocity in SHM	(iii) Maximum value occurs at the equilibrium position
D. Acceleration in SHM	(iv) It is always directed towards the mean position

(a) (A)-(iv), (B)-(ii), (C)-(iii), (D)-(i)
(b) (A)-(i), (B)-(iii), (C)-(ii), (D)-(iv)
(c) (A)-(ii), (B)-(i), (C)-(iii), (D)-(iv)
(d) (A)-(i), (B)-(iv), (C)-(iii), (D)-(ii)

Assertion–Reason

Directions *(Q.No. 21-27) In the following questions, two statements are given- one labelled Assertion (A) and the other labelled Reason (R). Select the correct answer to these questions from the codes (a), (b), (c) and (d) as given below.*

(a) Both Assertion and Reason are true and Reason is the correct explanation of Assertion.
(b) Both Assertion and Reason are true but Reason is not the correct explanation of Assertion.
(c) Assertion is true but Reason is false.
(d) Assertion is false but Reason is true.

21. **Assertion (A)** The periodic time of a hard spring is less as compared to that of a soft spring.

Reason (R) The periodic time depends upon the spring constant, which is large for hard spring.

22. **Assertion (A)** In SHM, acceleration is always directed towards the mean position.

Reason (R) In SHM, the body has to stop momentarily at the extreme position and move back to mean position. **Competency Based Que.**

23. **Assertion (A)** The spring constant of a spring is k. When it is divided into n equal parts, then spring constant of one piece is nk.

Reason (R) The spring constant is independent of material used for spring. **Competency Based Que.**

24. **Assertion (A)** $x(t) = A\sin(\omega t)$ is periodic but cannot represent an oscillatory motion.

Reason (R) $\sin\theta$ is a sinusoidal periodic function. **Competency Based Que.**

25. **Assertion (A)** In simple harmonic motion, the velocity is maximum when acceleration is minimum.

Reason (R) Displacement and velocity of SHM differ is phase by $\pi/2$.

26. **Assertion (A)** The percentage change in time period is 1.5%, if the length of simple pendulum increases by 3%.

Reason (R) Time period is directly proportional to length of pendulum.

27. Assertion (A) Consider motion for a mass spring system under gravity, motion of M is not a simple harmonic motion unless Mg is negligibly small.

Reason (R) For simple harmonic motion, acceleration must be proportional to displacement and is directed towards the mean position. **Competency Based Que.**

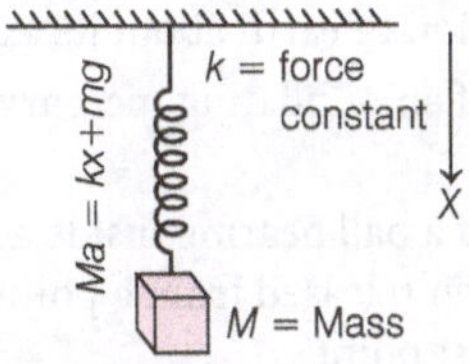

Case Based Questions

Directions *(Q.Nos. 28-29) These questions are case study based questions. Read the following paragraph and answer the questions on the basis of same.*

28. A system of two blocks is attached with a spring and stretched by two equal and opposite forces as shown in the figure. Let the maximum stretch of spring towards each block is $\frac{x}{2}$. **Competency Based Que.**

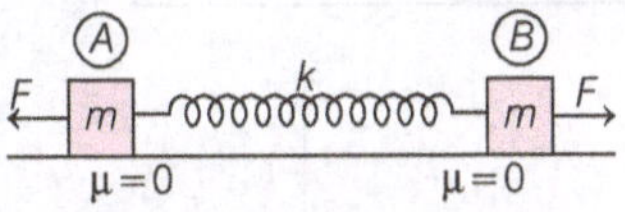

(i) The magnitude of spring force on block B is

(a) kx (b) $\frac{kx}{2}$

(c) $2kx$ (d) None of these

(ii) The equation of SHM for block B, when F from both blocks is removed, is

(a) $F_{SHM} = -m\omega^2 x$

(b) $F_{SHM} = -\frac{m\omega^2 x}{2}$

(c) $F_{SHM} = -kx$

(d) None of the above

(iii) In SHM,

(a) PE is stored due to elasticity of system

(b) KE is stored due to inertia of system

(c) Both KE and PE are stored by virtue of elasticity of system.

(d) Both (a) and (b)

(iv) I. Time period of a spring-mass system depends on its amplitude.

II. Time period of a spring-mass system depends on its mass.

III. Time period of a spring-mass system depends on spring constant.

Choose the correct option regarding the above statements.

(a) I and II (b) I and III

(c) II and III (d) All of these

29 An ideal simple pendulum consists of a heavy point body (bob) suspend by a weightless, inextensible and perfectly flexible string from a rigid support about which it is free to oscillate.

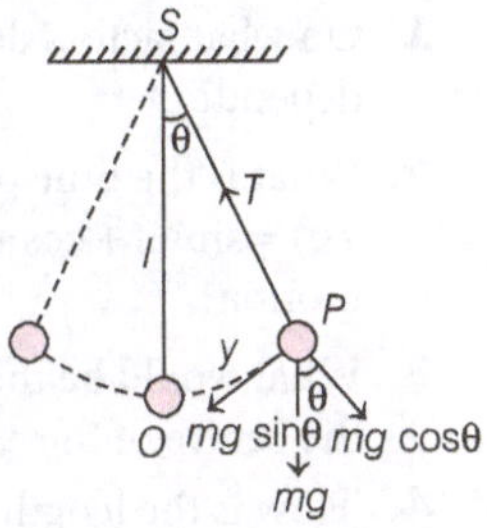

But in reality neither point mass nor weightless string exist, so we can never construct a simple pendulum strictly according to the definition.

Suppose simple pendulum of length l is displaced through a small angle θ from it's mean position. Consider m as of the bob is m and linear displacement from mean position is x.

(i) The period of a simple pendulum is doubled, when

(a) its length is doubled

(b) the mass of the bob is doubled

(c) its length is made four times

(d) the mass of the bob and the length of the pendulum are doubled

(ii) The period of oscillation of a simple pendulum of constant length at earth surface is T. Its period inside a mine is

(a) greater than T (b) less than T

(c) equal to T (d) cannot be compared

(iii) A pendulum suspended from the ceilling of a train has a period T, when the train is at rest. When the train is accelerating with a uniform acceleration a the period of oscillation will

(a) increase (b) decrease

(c) remain unaffected (d) become infinite

(iv) Which of the following statement is not true? In the case of a simple pendulum for small amplitudes the period of oscillation is

(a) directly proportional to square root of the length of the pendulum

(b) inversely proportional to the square root of the acceleration due to graivity

(c) dependent on the mass, size and material of the bob

(d) independent of the amplitude

(v) The time period of a second's pendulum is 2 s. The spherical bob which is empty from inside has a mass of 50 g. This is now replaced by another solid bob of same radius but having different mass of 100 g. The new time period will be

(a) 4 s (b) 1 (c) 2 s (d) 8 s

Subjective Questions

Very Short Answer Type Questions

1. On what factors does the energy of a harmonic oscillator depend?

2. What is the time period for the function $f(t) = \sin\omega t + \cos\omega t$ may represent the simple harmonic motion?

3. What would be the time period of a simple pendulum at the centre of the earth?

4. How is the length of second's pendulum related with acceleration due to gravity of any planet ?

5. There are two springs, one delicate and another hard or stout one. For which spring, the frequency of the oscillator will be more ?

6. Define the restoring force and it characteristic in case of an oscillating body.

Short Answer Type Questions

7. A body of mass m is situated in a potential field $U(x) = U_0\,(1 - \cos\alpha x)$ where, U_0 and α are constants. Find the time period of small oscillations.

8. One end of a U-tube containing mercury is connected to a suction pump and the other end to atmosphere. A small pressure difference is maintained between the two columns.

Show that when the suction pump is removed, the column of mercury in the U-tube executes simple harmonic motion

9. Show that the motion of a particle represented by $y = \sin\omega t - \cos\omega t$ is simple harmonic with a period of $2\pi/\omega$.

10. Let us take the position of mass when the spring is unstreched as $x = 0$ and the direction from left to right as the positive direction of X-axis. Given x as a function of time t for the oscillating mass, if at the moment we start the stopwatch ($t = 0$), the mass is

(i) at the mean position

(ii) at the maximum stretched position and

(iii) at the maximum compressed position.

In what way do these functions for SHM differ from each other, in frequency, in amplitude or the initial phase?

11. A mass of 2 kg is attached to the spring of spring constant 50 Nm^{-1}. The block is pulled to a distance of 5 cm from its equilibrium position at $x = 0$ on a horizontal frictionless surface from rest at $t = 0$. Write the expression for its displacement at anytime t.

12. Which of the following examples represent (nearly) simple harmonic motion and which represent periodic but not simple harmonic motion?

(i) The rotation of earth about its axis.

(ii) Motion of an oscillating mercury column in a U-tube.

(iii) Motion of a ball bearing inside a smooth curved bowl, when released from a point slightly above the lower most point.

(iv) General vibrations of polyatomic molecule about its equilibrium position.

13. Figures depict four x-t plots for linear motion of a particle. Which of the plots represent periodic motion? What is the period of motion (in case of periodic motion)?

(i)
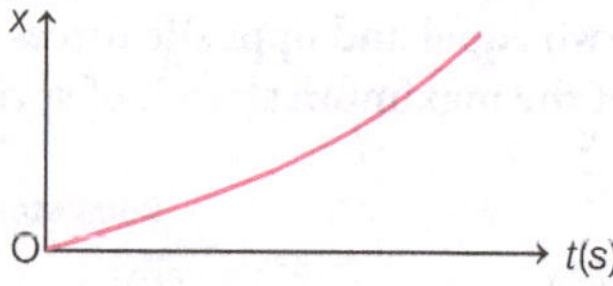

(ii)
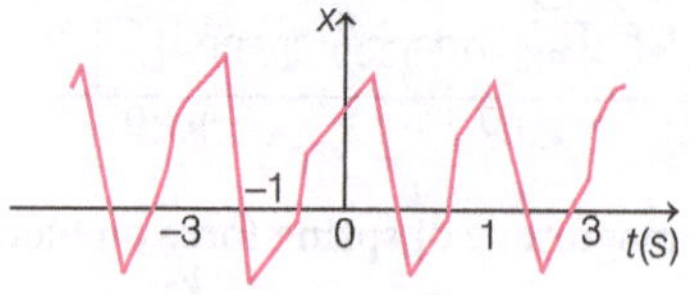

(iii)
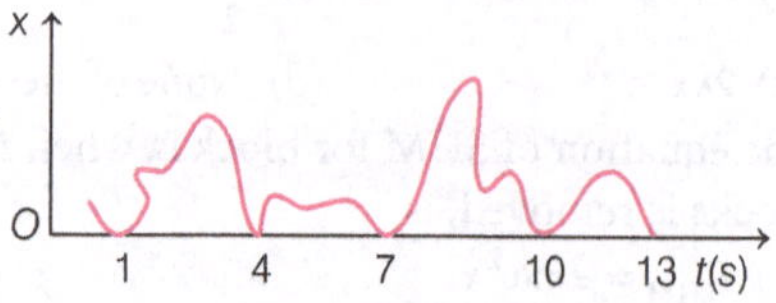

(iv)
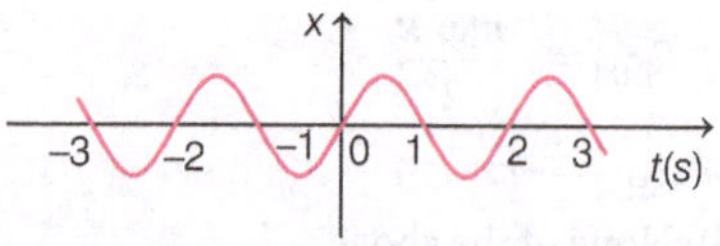

14. Find the displacement of a simple harmonic oscillator at which its PE is half of the maximum energy of the oscillator.

15. What is the effect on the time period of a simple pendulum when

(i) it is immersed in a liquid of density σ.

(ii) the temperature of wire through which the bob is suspended increased?

Long Answer Type Questions

16. Write down the differential equation for SHM. Give its solution. Hence, obtain expression for the time period of SHM.

17. (a) The relation between the acceleration a and displacement x of a particle executing SHM is $a = -\left(\frac{p}{q}\right)y$, where p and q are constants. What will be the time period of oscillation of the particle? If p is doubled and q is halved, then find the value of new time period of oscillation. **Competency Based Que.**

(b) Show that for a particle in linear SHM, the average kinetic energy over a period of oscillation equals the average potential energy over the same period. **NCERT**

18. Find the time period of mass M when displaced from its equilibrium position and then released for the system shown in figure.

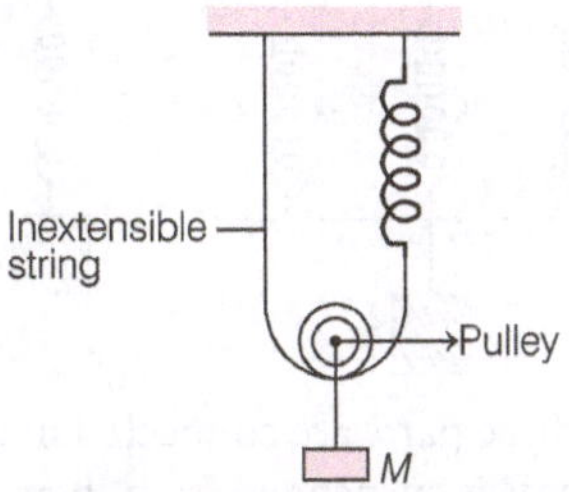

19. Show that for small oscillations, the motion of a simple pendulum is simple harmonic. Derive an expression for its time period.

20. Fig. (a) shows a spring of force constant k clamped rigidly at one end and a mass m attached to its free end. A force F applied at the free end stretches the spring. Fig. (b) shows the same spring with both ends free and attached to a mass m at either end. Each end of the spring in Fig. (b) is stretched by the same force F. **Competency Based Que.**

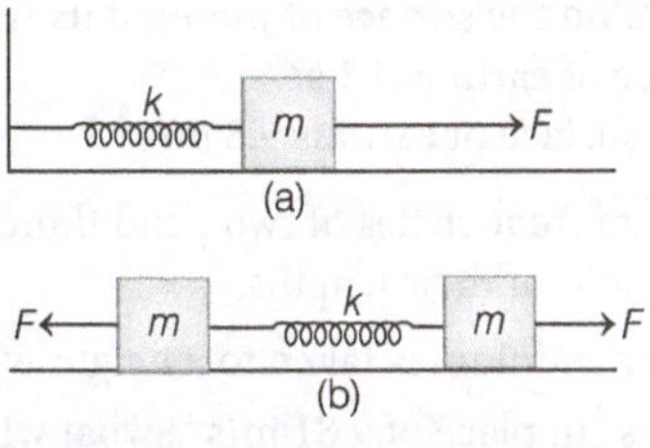

(i) What is the maximum extension of the spring in both the cases?

(ii) If the mass in Fig. (a) and the two masses in Fig. (b) are released, then what is the time period of oscillation in each case? **NCERT**

21. A simple pendulum of length l and having a bob of mass M is suspended in a car. The car is moving on a circular track of radius R with a uniform speed v. If the pendulum makes small oscillations in a radial direction about its equilibrium position, then what will be its time period? **NCERT**

Numerical Problems

Simple Harmonic Motion

22. The time period of a body executing SHM is 1s. After how much time will its displacement be $\frac{1}{\sqrt{2}}$ of its amplitude ?

23. Two particles are executing SHM. The equation of their motion are $y_1 = 10\sin\left(\omega t + \frac{\pi T}{4}\right)$ and $y_2 = 25\sin\left(\omega t + \frac{\sqrt{3}\pi T}{4}\right)$. What is the ratio of their amplitude? **Competency Based Que.**

24. Find the period of vibrating particle (SHM), which has acceleration of 45 cm s^{-2}, when displacement from mean position is 5 cm.

25. The vertical motion of a huge piston in a machine is approximately SHM with a frequency of 0.5 s^{-1}. A block of 10 kg is placed on the piston. What is the maximum amplitude of the piston's SHM for the block and piston to remain together?

26. The displacement equation for a particle executing simple harmonic motion is

$$y = 0.2\sin 50\pi(t + 0.01) \text{ metre}$$

where, y is the displacement at instant t. Calculate the amplitude, time period, maximum velocity, initial phase and initial displacement.

27. A body describes simple harmonic motion with an amplitude of 5 cm and a period of 0.2 s. Find the acceleration and velocity of the body when the displacement is (i) 5 cm, (ii) 3 cm and (iii) 0 cm.

28. Figures corresponds to two circular motions. The radius of the circle, the period of revolution, the initial position and the sense of revolution (i.e. clockwise or anti-clockwise) are indicated on each figure.

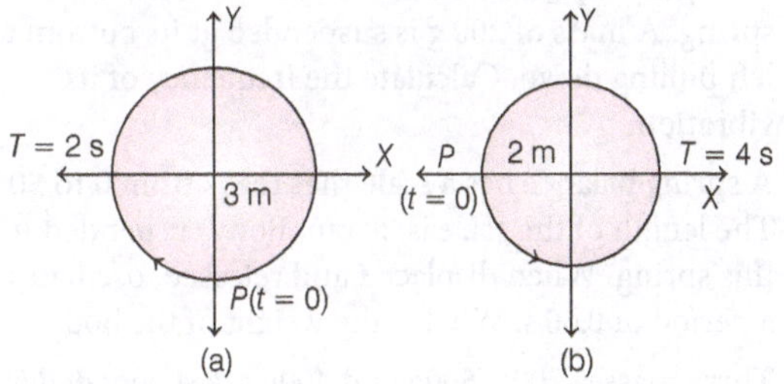

Obtain the corresponding simple harmonic motions of the X-projection of the radius vector of the revolving particle P, in each case.

29. Which of the following function of time represent (i) simple harmonic (ii) periodic but not simple harmonic and (iii) non-periodic motion? Give period for each case or periodic motion (ω is any positive constant).

(a) $\sin\omega t - \cos\omega t$ (b) $\sin^3 \omega t$

(c) $3\cos\left(\frac{\pi}{4} - 2\omega t\right)$ (d) $\cos\omega t + \cos 3\omega t + \cos 5\omega t$

(e) $\exp(-\omega^2 t^2)$ (f) $1 + \omega t + \omega^2 t^2$

30. Plot the corresponding reference circle for each of the following simple harmonic motions. Indicate the initial ($t = 0$) position of the particle, the radius of the circle and the angular speed of the rotating particle. For simplicity, the sense of rotation may be fixed to be anti-clockwise in every case (x is in cm and t is in second). **NCERT**

(a) $x = -2\sin\left(3t + \frac{\pi}{3}\right)$

(b) $x = \cos\left(\frac{\pi}{6} - t\right)$

(c) $x = 3\sin\left(2\pi t + \frac{\pi}{4}\right)$

(d) $x = 2\cos\pi t$

Mass- Spring System

31. A spring of force constant 1200 Nm^{-1} is mounted on a horizontal table. A mass of 3.0 kg is attached to the free end of the spring, pulled sideways to a distance of 2.0 cm and then released. **NCERT**

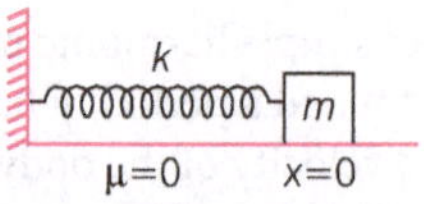

(i) What is the frequency of oscillation of the mass? [1]

(ii) What is the maximum acceleration of the mass. [1]

(iii) What is the maximum speed of the mass? [1]

32. A 40 g mass produces on extension of 4 cm in a vertical spring. A mass of 200 g is suspended at its bottom and left pulling down. Calculate the frequency of its vibration.

33. A spring balance has a scale that reads from 0 to 50 kg. The length of the scale is 20 cm. Body suspended from this spring. When displaced and released, oscillates with a period of 0.60 s. What is the weight of the body ?

34. Three masses 700g, 500g and 400g are suspended at the end of a spring as shown and are in equilibrium. When the 700g mass is removed, the system oscillates with a period of 3 s. Find the period of oscillation, when the 500 g mass is also removed. **Competency Based Que.**

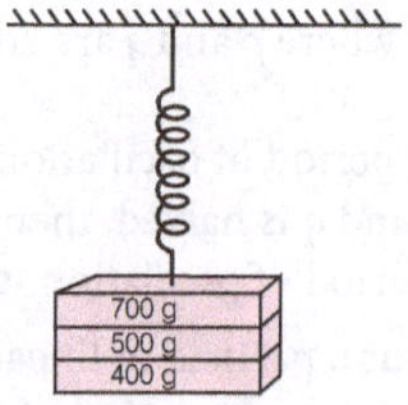

35 The time period of a body suspended from a spring is $T = 1.5$ s. It the spring is divided into three parts of equal length, what will be the time period of oscillations in the following cases

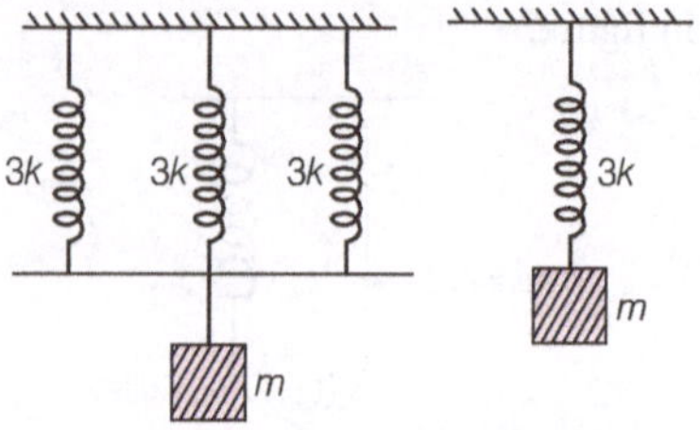

(a) all the three parts are connected in parallel and the same mass is suspended from them

(b) the same mass is suspended from one part of spring ?

36. A body weighing 10 g has a velocity of 6 cms^{-1} after one second of its starting from mean position. If the time period is 6 s, then find the kinetic energy, potential energy and the total energy.

Simple Pendulum and Energy

37. The acceleration due to gravity on the surface of moon is 1.7 m/s^2. What is the time period of a simple pendulum on the surface of moon, if its time period on the surface of earth is 3.5 s? (g on the surface of earth is 9.8 m/s^2.) **NCERT**

38. The ratio of frequencies of two pendulums are 2 : 3. Find the ratio of their lengths.

39. A second pendulum is taken to a height where value of g is 4.36 m/s^2 in place of 9.81 m/s^2, what will be the new time period ?

40. The total energy of a particle executing SHM is 80 J. What is the potential energy when the particle is at a distance of 3/4th of amplitude from the mean position?

41. The length or a second pendulum on the surface of earth is 1 m. What will be the length of a second pendulum on the moon? **NCERT Exemplar**

Hints & Solutions

Objective Type Questions

1. (*a*) A periodic function repeats itself after a time period T.

and $f(t) = f(t+T)$

As, $\sin(\omega t) = \sin(\omega t + 2\pi)$

$\therefore$ Period of function is 2π.

2. (*b*) Given equation of motion is

$$y = \sin^3 \omega t \Rightarrow \sin 3\theta = 3\sin\theta - 4\sin^3\theta$$

$$\Rightarrow \quad 4\frac{dy}{dt} = 3\omega\cos\omega t - 4\times[3\omega\cos\omega t]$$

$$\Rightarrow \quad 4\times\frac{d^2y}{dt^2} = -3\omega^2\sin\omega t + 12\omega\sin 3\omega t$$

$$\Rightarrow \quad \frac{d^2y}{dt^2} = -\frac{3\omega^2\sin\omega t + 12\omega^2\sin 3\omega t}{4}$$

$\Rightarrow \dfrac{d^2y}{dt^2}$ is not proportional to y.

Hence, motion is not SHM.

As the expression is involving sine function, hence it will be periodic.

3. (*c*) Given, equation $x(t) = 4(\cos\pi t + \sin\pi t)$

$$= 4\sqrt{2}\left(\sin\frac{\pi}{4}\cos\pi t + \cos\frac{\pi}{4}\sin\pi t\right)$$

$$= 4\sqrt{2}\sin\left(\pi t + \frac{\pi}{4}\right)$$

Hence, amplitude $= 4\sqrt{2}$

4. (*b*) Velocity of the particle executing SHM is given as

$$v = \omega\sqrt{A^2 - x^2}$$

At extreme position, $x = A \Rightarrow v = 0$

5. (*a*) Here, $m = 400\text{ g} = 400\times10^{-3}$ kg

As, $R = 10\text{ Nm}^{-1}$

$$T = 2\pi\sqrt{m/R}$$

$$= 2\pi\sqrt{\frac{400\times10^{-3}}{10}} = 4\pi\times10^{-1}\text{s}$$

6. (*b*) $t_1 = 1\text{ s}, t_2 = 2\text{s}$

Now, $y_1 = a\sin(\omega t_1) = a\sin(\omega\times1)$

$$y_1 = a\sin\omega$$

$$y_2 = a\sin(\omega\times2) - a\sin\omega = a\sin 2\omega - a\sin\omega$$

$$\frac{y_2}{y_1} = \frac{\sin 2\omega - \sin\omega}{\sin\omega} = \frac{\sin 2\omega}{\sin\omega} - 1$$

$$\frac{y_2}{y_1} = \frac{2\sin\omega\cos\omega}{\sin\omega} - 1 = 2\cos\omega - 1$$

$$\frac{y_2}{y_1} = 2\cos\left(\frac{2\pi}{T}\right) - 1 = 2\cos\frac{2\pi}{8} - 1 = 0.41 : 1$$

7. (*c*) Given that

time period $(T) = 3$ s.

The equation for SHM is given by

$$Y = A\sin\omega t \text{ and } \omega = 2\pi f = \frac{2\pi}{T}$$

Let after time t, the displacement is half its amplitude.

$$\frac{A}{2} = A\sin\left(\frac{2\pi}{3}t\right)$$

$$\sin\left(\frac{\pi}{6}\right) = \sin\left(\frac{2\pi t}{3}\right)$$

$$\frac{\pi}{6} = \frac{2\pi t}{3}$$

or $\quad t = \dfrac{1}{4}$ s

8. (*c*) $X = a\sin(\omega t - \alpha) = a\cos(\omega t - \alpha - \pi/2)$

Another equation is

$$Y = b\cos(\omega t - \alpha)$$

$\therefore$ The phase difference $= (X - Y)$ at $t = 0$

$$a\cos(\omega\cdot0 - \alpha - \pi/2) - b\cos(\omega\cdot0 - \alpha)$$

$$= \frac{\pi}{2} = 90^\circ$$

9. (*c*) $\omega t = 0.5\pi\, t \Rightarrow \omega = 0.5\pi \Rightarrow T = 4\text{ s}$.

Required time $= \dfrac{T}{4} = 1$ s

10. (*d*) For motion to be SHM acceleration of the particle must be proportional to negative of displacement.

i.e., $\quad a \propto -(y \text{ or } x)$

We should be clear that y has to be linear.

11. (*c*) Given, $\quad x = a\cos\omega t \quad$ ...(i)

$y = a\sin\omega t \quad$ ...(ii)

Squaring and adding Eqs. (i) and (ii),

$$x^2 + y^2 = a^2(\cos^2\omega t + \sin^2\omega t) = a^2$$

$$\Rightarrow \quad x^2 + y^2 = a^2 \quad [\because \cos^2\omega t + \sin^2\omega t = 1]$$

This is the equation of a circle.

Clearly, the locus is a circle of constant radius a.

12. (*d*) According to the question, the displacement

$$y = a\sin\omega t + b\cos\omega t$$

Let $\quad a = A\sin\phi$ and $b = A\cos\phi$

Now, $a^2 + b^2 = A^2\sin^2\phi + A^2\cos^2\phi = A^2$

$$\Rightarrow \quad A = \sqrt{a^2 + b^2}$$

$$y = A\sin\phi.\sin\omega t + A\cos\phi.\cos\omega t$$

$$= A\sin(\omega t + \phi)$$

$$\frac{dy}{dt} = A\omega \cos\ (\omega t + \phi)$$

$$\frac{d^2y}{dt^2} = -A\omega^2 \sin(\omega t + \phi) = -Ay\omega^2 = (-A\omega^2)y$$

$$\Rightarrow \quad \frac{d^2y}{dt^2} \propto (-y)$$

Hence, it is an equation of SHM with amplitude $A = \sqrt{a^2 + b^2}$.

13. (a) In equilibrium, $kx = mg$

$\therefore$ Extension, $x = \frac{mg}{k}$

$$x = \frac{20 \times 9.8}{4000}$$

$$x = 0.049 \text{ m}$$

$$x = 4.9 \text{ cm}$$

14. (d) Frequency of oscillation, $f = \frac{1}{2\pi}\sqrt{\frac{k_1 + k_2}{m}}$

and $f' = \frac{1}{2\pi}\cdot 2\sqrt{\frac{k_1 + k_2}{m}} = 2f$

15. (c) $\nu_0 = \frac{1}{2L}\sqrt{\frac{T}{M}}$ Frequency in new condition

$$\nu = \frac{1}{2(65\% \text{of } L)}$$

$$\sqrt{\frac{T + 69\% \text{ of } T}{M}} = 2\nu_0$$

16. (c) Consider the diagram in which a liquid column oscillates. In this case, restoring force acts on the liquid due to gravity. Acceleration of the liquid column, can be calculated in terms of restoring force.

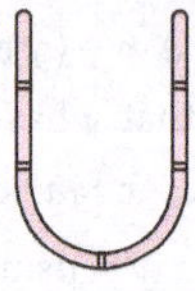

Restoring force,

f = Weight of liquid column of height $2y$

$\Rightarrow \quad f = -(A \times 2y \times \rho) \times g = -2A\rho g y \quad [\because \eta = \rho v]$

$\Rightarrow \quad f \propto -y$

$\Rightarrow$ Motion is SHM with force constant $k = 2A\rho g$.

$\Rightarrow$ Time period, $T = 2\pi\sqrt{\frac{m}{k}} = 2\pi\sqrt{\frac{A \times 2h \times \rho}{2A\rho g}} = 2\pi\sqrt{\frac{h}{g}}$

$$T = 2\pi\sqrt{\frac{l}{g}}, \text{ where } l = h$$

Which is independent of the density of the liquid.

17. (a) $f = \frac{1}{T} = \frac{1}{0.04} = 25$ Hz

18. (a) Kinetic energy varies with time but it is never negative.

19. (b) A → (i), B → (ii), C → (iii), D → (iv)

20. (a) A → (iv), B → (ii), C → (iii), D → (i)

21. (a) Time period of a hard spring is given by

$$T = 2\pi\sqrt{\left(\frac{m}{k}\right)} \text{ i.e. } T \propto \frac{1}{\sqrt{k}}$$

Since, spring constant is more for hard spring, hence hard spring has a less periodic time as compared to soft spring.

22. (a) Acceleration and displacement are in opposite phase.

23. (c) When a spring is cut into n equal parts, then spring constant k' of each part is given by $k' = nk$

Also, spring constant depends on the properties of the material of the spring.

24. (d) $x(t) = A\sin(\omega t)$ is a sinusoidal periodic function that can represent an oscillatory motion. Motion of a particle in SHM can be represented by this function.

25. (b) $x = a\sin\omega t$ and $v = \frac{dx}{dt} = a\omega\cos\omega t$

It is clear phase difference between x and a is $\pi/2$.

26. (c) Time period of simple pendulum of length l,

$$T = 2\pi\sqrt{\frac{l}{g}} \Rightarrow T \propto \sqrt{l} \Rightarrow \sqrt{\frac{\Delta T}{T}} = \frac{1}{2}\frac{\Delta l}{l}$$

$$\therefore \quad \frac{\Delta T}{T} = \frac{1}{2} \times 3 = 1.5\%$$

27. (d)

28. (i) (a) $f_s = kx$ = Tension in the spring

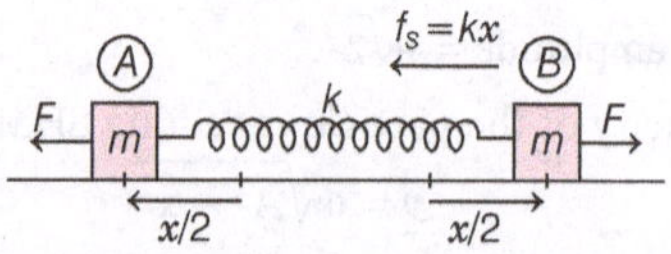

Spring force on block $B = kx$

(ii) (b) Equation of SHM $F_{SHM} = -m\omega^2 \frac{x}{2}$

Here, centre of spring length will not oscillate.

(iii) (d) In SHM, potential energy depends on its spring behaviour and kinetic energy on its inertial behaviour. In case of mass m oscillating on spring. KE is due to m and PE is due to spring.

(iv) (c) $F_s = -kx$ (spring force) ...(i)

$F = -m\omega^2 x$ (for SHM condition) ...(ii)

On comparing Eqs. (i) and (ii),

$$\omega = \sqrt{\frac{k}{m}} \Rightarrow T = 2\pi\sqrt{\frac{m}{k}} \qquad \left(\because T = \frac{2\pi}{\omega}\right)$$

$$\Rightarrow T \propto \sqrt{m} \Rightarrow T \propto \frac{1}{\sqrt{k}}$$

So, T does not depends on the amplitude of the oscillation T, it depends on m and k.

29. (i) (c) $T = 2\pi\sqrt{\frac{l}{g}} \Rightarrow T \propto \sqrt{l}$

(ii) (a) Inside the mine g decreases.

Hence, from $T = 2\pi\sqrt{\frac{l}{g}}$; T increases

(iii) (b) Initially time period, $T = 2\pi\sqrt{\frac{l}{g}}$

When train accelerates, the effective value of g becomes $\sqrt{(g^2 + a^2)}$ which is greater than g.

Hence, new time period becomes less than the initial time period.

(iv) (c) For small oscillations T is dependent on the mass, shape and material of the bob.

(v) (c) $T = 2\pi\sqrt{\frac{l}{g}}$ (independent of mass)

Subjective Questions

1. The energy of a simple harmonic oscillator depends on the mass of the particle, frequency and amplitude of oscillation.

2. $T = 2\pi/\omega$

3. The time period of a simple pendulum at the centre of the earth would be infinite.

4. Length of the second pendulum proportional to (acceleration due to gravity).

5. We have, $\nu = \frac{1}{2\pi}\sqrt{\frac{k}{m}} = \frac{1}{2\pi}\sqrt{\frac{g}{l}}$

So, when a hard spring is loaded with a mass m. The extension l will be lesser w.r.t. delicate one. So, frequency of the oscillation of the hard spring will be more and if time period is asked it will be lesser.

6. A force which takes the body back towards the mean position in oscillation is called restoring force

Characteristic of Restoring Force

The restoring force is always directed towards the mean position and its magnitude at any instant is directly proportional to the displacement of the particle from its mean position of that instance.

7. Given potential energy associated with the field,

$$U(x) = U_0(1 - \cos \alpha x) \quad \text{..... (i)}$$

Now, force $F = -\frac{dU(x)}{dx}$

[$\because$ for conservative force F, we can write $F = \frac{-dU}{dx}$]

[We have assumed the field to be conservative]

$$F = -\frac{d}{dx}(U_0 - U_0 \cos \alpha x) = -U_0\,\alpha \sin \alpha x$$

$$F = -U_0\,\alpha^2 x \quad \text{...(ii)}$$

[$\because$ for small oscillations αx is small, $\sin \alpha x \approx \alpha x$]

$\Rightarrow \quad F \propto (-x)$

As, U_0, α being constant.

$\therefore$ Motion is SHM for small oscillations.

Standard equation for SHM

$$F = -m\omega^2 x \quad \text{...(iii)}$$

Comparing Eqs. (ii) and (iii), we get

$$m\omega^2 = U_0\alpha^2$$

$$\omega^2 = \frac{U_0\alpha^2}{m} \quad \text{or} \quad \omega = \sqrt{\frac{U_0\alpha^2}{m}}$$

$\therefore$ Time period, $T = \frac{2\pi}{\omega} = 2\pi\sqrt{\frac{m}{U_0\alpha^2}}$

8. Let area of cross-section of each arm of the U-tube be A. When a small pressure difference is maintained between two columns, then liquid column falls through height h in one arm.

Now, difference in liquid column in two arms = $2h$

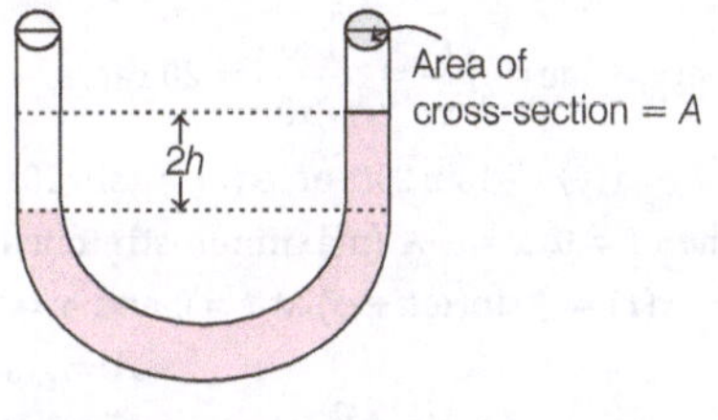

Density of mercury column = ρ

Acceleration due to gravity = g

Restoring force,

$F = -$ Weight of mercury column in excess of one arm

$= -(\text{Volume} \times \text{Density} \times g)$

$= -(A \times 2h \times \rho \times g)$

$= -2A\rho h = -k \times$ Displacement in one arm (h)

Clearly, $2A\rho g$ = constant = k (say) [as, $F = -kx$]

$$F \propto -h$$

Hence, motion is SHM, $k = 2A\rho g$

$\therefore$ Time period, $T = 2\pi\sqrt{\frac{m}{k}} = 2\pi\sqrt{\frac{m}{2A\rho g}}$

where, m = mass of the mercury column of length l.

If ρ_{H_2} is density of mercury, then

$$\Rightarrow \quad T = 2\pi\sqrt{\frac{Al\rho}{2A\rho g}} = 2\pi\sqrt{\frac{l}{2g}}$$

9. We have to convert the given combination of two harmonic functions to a single harmonic (sine or cosine) function.

Given, displacement function is

$$y = \sin \omega t - \cos \omega t$$

$$= \sqrt{2}\left(\frac{1}{\sqrt{2}} \cdot \sin \omega t - \frac{1}{\sqrt{2}} \cdot \cos \omega t\right)$$

$$= \sqrt{2}\left[\cos\left(\frac{\pi}{4}\right)\cdot \sin \omega t - \sin\left(\frac{\pi}{4}\right)\cdot \cos \omega t\right]$$

$$= \sqrt{2}\left[\sin\left(\omega t - \frac{\pi}{4}\right)\right] = \sqrt{2}\left[\sin\left(\omega t - \frac{\pi}{4}\right)\right]$$

Comparing with standard equation,

$y = a\sin(\omega t + \phi)$, we get $= \omega = \frac{2\pi}{T} \Rightarrow T = \frac{2\pi}{\omega}$

Clearly, the function represents SHM with a period

$$T = \frac{2\pi}{\omega}$$

10. Assuming the standard equation, $x(t) = A\sin(\omega t + \phi)$

(i) When $t = 0$, $x = 0$ [mean position]

$\Rightarrow \quad 0 = A\sin(\omega \times 0 + \phi)$

$A\sin\phi = 0$ [as, $A \neq 0$]

or $\sin\phi = 0 \quad \therefore \phi = 0$

$\therefore$ Required fucntion is

$$x(t) = A\sin(\omega t + 0) \text{ or } x(t) = A\sin\omega t$$

where, $\omega = \sqrt{\frac{k}{m}} = \sqrt{\frac{1200}{3.0}} = 20$ rad/s

$\therefore \quad x(t) = A\sin 20t$ or $x(t) = 2\sin 20t$

(ii) When $t = 0$, $x = +A$ (maximum stretched position)

$x(t) = A\sin(\omega t + \phi)$ at $t = 0$ and $x = +A$

$+A = A\sin(\omega \times 0 + \phi)$

or $1 = \sin\phi \Rightarrow \phi = \frac{\pi}{2}$

$\therefore \quad x(t) = A\sin\left(\omega t + \frac{\pi}{2}\right)$

$= A\cos\omega t = A\cos 20t = 2\cos 20t$

(iii) When the spring is at maximum compressed position.

At $t = 0$, $x(t) = -A$

$\Rightarrow -A = A\sin(\omega \times 0 + \phi)$ or $-1 = \sin\phi$

or $\phi = \frac{3r}{2}$

$\therefore \quad x(t) = A\sin\left(\omega t + \frac{3\pi}{2}\right) = -A\cos\omega t = -2\cos 20t$

So, the equations only differ in initial phase and in no other factors.

11. Consider the diagram of the spring block system. It is a SHM with amplitude of 5cm about the mean position as shown.

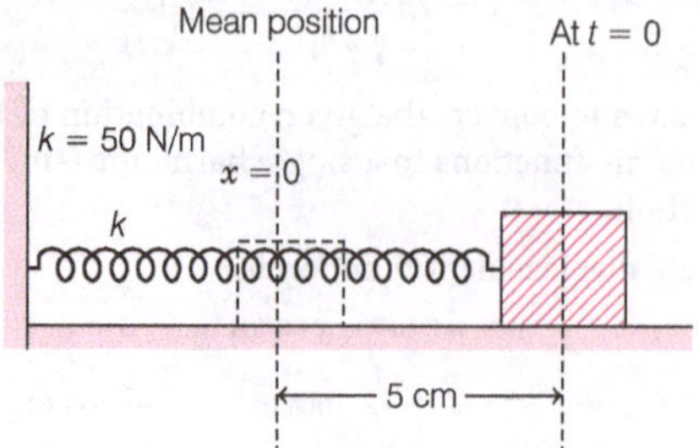

Given, spring constant $k = 50$ N/m

m = mass attached = 2 kg

$\therefore$ Angular frequency,

$$\omega = \sqrt{\frac{k}{m}} = \sqrt{\frac{50}{2}} = \sqrt{25} = 5 \text{ rad/s}$$

Assuming the displacement function is

$$y(t) = A\sin(\omega t + \phi)$$

where, ϕ = initial phase

But given at $t = 0$, $y(t) = +A$

$y(0) = +A = A\sin(\omega \times 0 + \phi)$

or $\sin\phi = 1 \Rightarrow \phi = \frac{\pi}{2}$

$\therefore$ The desired equation is

$$y(t) = A\sin\left(\omega t + \frac{\pi}{2}\right) = A\cos\omega t$$

Putting $A = 5$ cm, $\omega = 5$ rad/s

we get, $y(t) = 5\sin 5t$

where, t is in second and y is in centimetre.

12. (i) There is no to and fro motion which is a must for a periodic motion to be SHM. Hence, rotation of earth about its axis is not SHM.

(ii) This is a periodic motion and as it follows $F = -kx$ (about mean position, to and fro motion), hence it is SHM.

(iii) A periodic motion, oscillatory in nature (about lower most point as mean position) follows SHM force law, hence it is SHM.

(iv) A polyatomic molecule has a number of natural frequencies. So, in general, its vibration is a superposition of SHM of a number of different frequencies. Thus, superposition is periodic but not necessarily SHM.

13. (i) No repetition of motion. It is a unidirectional, linear but non-uniform motion of the particle.

(ii) Motion repeats after every 2s, hence periodic with time period 2 s.

(iii) Repetition of one position or a few positions (but not all) is not enough for motion to be periodic, the entire motion during one period must be repeated successively. Hence, the given x-t plot is not periodic, though there is repetition of a single position ($x = 0$ at every 3s) but other positions are not repeated.

(iv) Clearly, the motion repeats itself after every 2 s. Hence, periodic motion having a time period of 2 s.

14. Let us assume that the required displacement be x.

$\therefore$ Potential energy of the simple harmonic oscillator

$$= \frac{1}{2}kx^2$$

where, k = force constant = $m\omega^2$

$\therefore \quad PE = \frac{1}{2} m\omega^2 x^2 \quad ...(i)$

Maximum energy of the oscillator

$$TE = \frac{1}{2} m\omega^2 A^2 \quad [\because x_{max} = A] \; ...(ii)$$

where, A = amplitude of motion

Given, $PE = \frac{1}{2} TE$

$$\Rightarrow \frac{1}{2} m\omega^2 x^2 = \frac{1}{2}\left[\frac{1}{2} m\omega^2 A^2\right]$$

$$\Rightarrow x^2 = \frac{A^2}{2}$$

or $$x = \sqrt{\frac{A^2}{2}} = \pm \frac{A}{\sqrt{2}}$$

Sign ± indicates either side of mean position.

15. (i) Let ρ = density of the material of the pendulum bob.

σ = density of the liquid in which the pendulum bob is immersed such that $\rho > \sigma$. Let it is made oscillate with a time period T'. The effective value of g in the liquid is given by

$$g' = f\left(1 - \frac{\sigma}{\rho}\right) = g\left(\frac{\rho - \sigma}{\rho}\right)$$

$$\therefore \quad T' = 2\pi\sqrt{\frac{l}{g'}} = 2\pi\sqrt{\frac{1}{g\frac{(\rho - \sigma)}{\rho}}}$$

$$= T\sqrt{\frac{\rho}{\rho - \sigma}} \quad \left(\because T = 2\pi\sqrt{\frac{l}{g}}\right)$$

where T = time period of the simple pendulum when it oscillates in air.

or $$\frac{T'}{T} = \sqrt{\frac{\rho}{\rho - \sigma}}$$

$$\therefore \quad \rho > \sigma \text{ or } \rho - \sigma > 0$$

$$\therefore \quad \frac{\rho}{\rho - \sigma} > 1$$

or $$\frac{T'}{T} > 1 \text{ or } T' > T$$

i.e. its time period increases.

(ii) When the temperature of the wire with which the bob of the pendulum is suspended increases, the length of the wire increases due to thermal expansion. As $T \propto \sqrt{l}$, so T will also increases as shown below.

Let l = original length of the wire

$d\theta$ = rise in its temperature

α = coefficient of linear expansion of the material of the wire

If l' = new length

and dl = increases in its length $l' - l$, then

$$dl \propto l$$
$$\propto d\theta \text{ or } dl \propto l d\theta$$

If T' = its period of oscillation, then

$$T' = 2\pi\sqrt{\frac{l'}{g}} = 2\pi\sqrt{\frac{l(1 + \alpha d\theta)}{g}}$$

$$= T\sqrt{(1 + \alpha d\theta)} \quad \left(\because T = 2\pi\sqrt{\frac{l}{g}}\right)$$

$$= T(1 + \alpha d\theta)^{1/2} = T\left(1 + \frac{1}{2}\alpha d\theta\right)$$

(Using Binomial expansion)

$$\text{Increases in time period} = T' - T = \frac{T\alpha d\theta}{2}$$

16. Differential equation of SHM, $\frac{d^2x}{dt} = -\omega^2 x$

General solution to this equation is

$$x = A\sin(\omega t) + B\cos(\omega t)$$

On putting the boundary conditions specific to this situation, we get $x = A\sin(\omega t + \delta)$.

To find the time period of SHM, consider that a particle of mass m is moving in a field where the potential energy is given by $U(x) = U_0(1 - \cos ax)$.

$$\Rightarrow \frac{dU}{dx} = U_0 a \sin ax$$

$$F = -\frac{dU}{dx} \Rightarrow F = -U_0 a \sin ax$$

For small x, $F = -U_0 a^2 x$

$$\because \quad F = -kx$$

$$K = U_0 a^2$$

$$\therefore \quad \omega = \sqrt{\frac{k}{m}}$$

$$T = \frac{2\pi}{\omega}$$

$$T = 2\pi\sqrt{\frac{m}{U_0 a^2}}$$

17. (a) Here, $a = \left(\frac{-p}{q}\right)y = -\omega^2 y$, where ω is the angular frequency of particle executing SHM. So,

$$\omega = \sqrt{p/q} \text{ or } \frac{2\pi}{T} = \sqrt{\frac{p}{q}}$$

$$\Rightarrow \quad T = 2\pi\sqrt{\frac{q}{p}}$$

when p is doubled and q is halved, then

$$T' = 2\pi\sqrt{\frac{q/2}{2p}} = 2\pi\sqrt{\frac{q}{p}} \times \frac{1}{2} = \frac{T}{2}$$

New time period becomes half of first time period.

(b) Let $x = A\sin\omega t$

$$\Rightarrow \quad v = \frac{dx}{dt} = \frac{d}{dt}(A\sin\omega t) = A\omega\cos\omega t$$

$\because$ Kinetic energy, KE $= \frac{1}{2}mv^2$

$\because$ Average kinetic energy

$$= \frac{1}{T}\int_0^T \frac{1}{2}mv^2 dt = \frac{1}{4}mA^2\omega^2 \quad \text{...(i)}$$

and average potential energy

$$= \frac{1}{T}\int_0^T \frac{1}{2}kx^2 dt = \frac{1}{4}mA^2\omega^2 \quad \text{...(ii)}$$

From Eqs. (i) and (ii),
we can say that for a particle in linear SHM, the average kinetic energy over a period of oscillation equals the average potential energy over the same period.

18. For the calculation purpose, in this situation we will neglect gravity because it is constant throughout and will not effect the net restoring force.

Let in the equilibrium position, the spring has extended by an amount x_0.

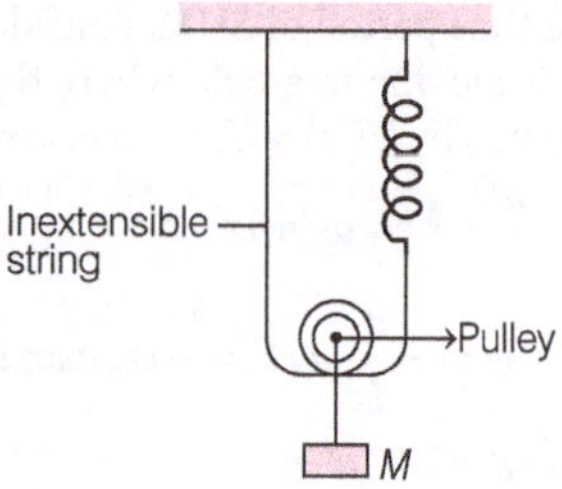

Now, if the mass is given a further displacement downwards by an amount x. The string and spring both should increase in length by x.

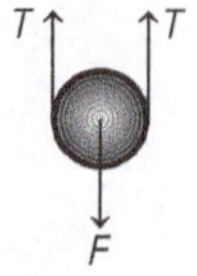

But, string is inextensible, hence the spring alone will contribute the total extension $x + x = 2x$, to lower the mass down by x from initial equilibrium mean position x_0. So, net extension in the spring $(= 2x + x_0)$.

Now force on the mass before pulling (in the x_o extension case)

$$F = 2T$$

But $\quad T = kx_0 \quad$ [where k is spring constant]

$$\therefore \quad F = 2kx_0 \quad \text{...(i)}$$

When the mass is lowered down further by x,

$$F' = 2T'$$

But new spring length $= (2x + x_0)$

$$\therefore \quad F' = 2k(2x + x_0) \quad \text{...(ii)}$$

Restoring force on the system.

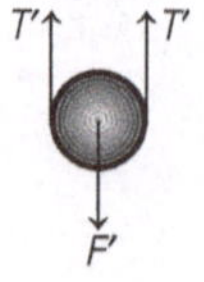

$$F_{\text{restoring}} = -[F' - F]$$

Using Eqs. (i) and (ii), we get

$$F_{\text{restoring}} = -[2k(2x + x_0) - 2kx_0]$$
$$= -[2 \times 2kx + 2kx_0 - 2kx_0]$$
$$= -4kx$$

or $\quad Ma = -4kx$

where, $\quad a =$ acceleration $\quad$ (As, $F = ma$)

$$\Rightarrow \quad a = -\left(\frac{4k}{M}\right)x$$

k, M being constant.

$$\therefore \quad a \propto -x$$

Hence, motion is SHM.

Comparing the above acceleration expression with standard SHM equation $a = -\omega^2 x$, we get

$$\omega^2 = \frac{4k}{M}$$

$$\Rightarrow \quad \omega = \sqrt{\frac{4k}{M}}$$

$$\therefore \text{ Time period, } T = \frac{2\pi}{\omega} = \frac{2\pi}{\sqrt{\frac{4k}{M}}} = 2\pi\sqrt{\frac{M}{4k}}$$

19. An ideal simple pendulum consists of a point mass suspended by an inextensible and weightless string which is fixed at the other end. But this type of pendulum is not possible to make practically.

So practically, a simple pendulum is obtained by suspending a small metal bob by a long and fine cotton thread from a support as given in the figure along side.

Expression for Time Period of a Simple Pendulum

Consider a simple pendulum, a small bob of mass m tied to an inextensible massless string of length L.

In the equilibrium position, the bob of a simple pendulum lies vertically below the point of suspension. If the bob is slightly displaced on the either side and then released, it begins oscillation about the mean position.

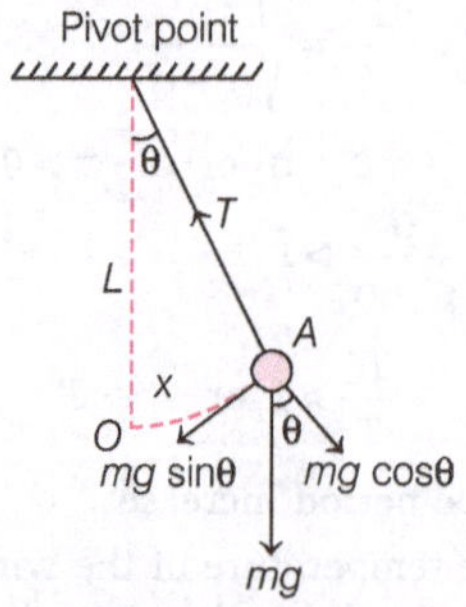

Let us consider that at any instant during oscillation, the bob lies at position A when its displacement is $OA = X$ and the thread makes an angle θ with the vertical.

The forces acting on the bob are

(i) **Weight mg** of the bob acting vertically downwards.

(ii) **Tension T** along the string.

The force mg has two rectangular components.

(i) The component $mg\cos\theta$ acting along the thread is balanced by the tension T in the thread.

(b) The tangential force $mg\sin\theta$ will provide the restoring torque, which tends to bring the bob back to its mean position. Thus, the restoring torque of the force $mg\sin\theta$ about the pivot point is given by

$$\tau = -(mg\sin\theta)L = -mgL\sin\theta \quad \text{...(i)}$$

where, **the negative sign shows that the torque acts to reduce θ.** L is the length of the simple pendulum. For rotation, the torque can be given as

$$\tau = I\alpha \quad \text{...(ii)}$$

where, I = pendulum's moment of inertia about the pivot point

α = angular acceleration about the pivot point

From Eqs. (i) and (ii), we get

$$-mgL\sin\theta = I\alpha$$

$$\Rightarrow \quad \alpha = \frac{-mgL\sin\theta}{I}$$

If θ is in radian, sin θ can be expressed as

$$\sin\theta = \theta - \frac{\theta^3}{3!} + \frac{\theta^5}{5!} - \dots$$

Now, if θ is small, sin θ can be approximated by θ

$$\therefore \quad \alpha \approx \frac{-mgL\theta}{I}$$

Therefore, **the angular acceleration of the pendulum is proportional to the angular displacement θ but in opposite sign.** Thus, as the pendulum moves to the right, it's pull to the left increases until it stops and begins to return to the left.

Similarly, when it moves towards left, its acceleration to the right tends to return it to the right and so on as it swings to and fro as SHM. Hence, the motion of a simple pendulum swinging through small angles is approximately SHM.

Equation $\alpha = \frac{-mgL}{I}\theta$ is the angular analogue of equation $a = -\omega^2 x$.

On comparing these equations, we have

$$\omega = \sqrt{\frac{mgL}{I}} \Rightarrow \frac{2\pi}{T} = \sqrt{\frac{mgL}{I}}$$

$$\Rightarrow \quad T = 2\pi\sqrt{\frac{I}{mgL}} \quad \text{...(iii)}$$

where, T = time period of pendulum.

All the masses of a simple pendulum are centered in the mass m of the bob (taken as a point) which is at a distance of L from the pivot point. Therefore, $I = mL^2$. On putting this value in Eq. (iii)

$$T = 2\pi\sqrt{\frac{mL^2}{mgL}} = 2\pi\sqrt{\frac{L}{g}}$$

$\Rightarrow$ Time period of pendulum, $T = 2\pi\sqrt{\frac{L}{g}}$

20. (i) For **Case** (a), as we know that, $F = -kx \Rightarrow |F| = kx$

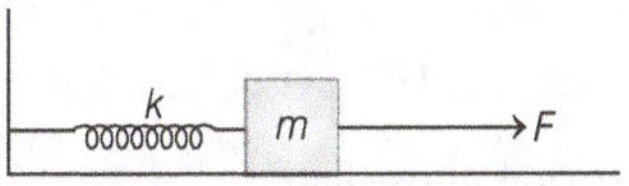

$$\therefore \text{ So,} \quad x = \frac{F}{k}$$

Case (b)

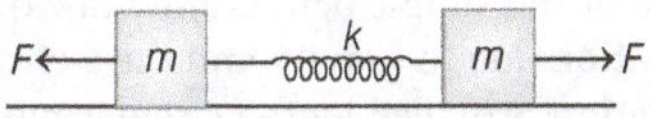

If x' is the extension in the spring, then drawing free body diagram of either mass (as the system under applied force is under equilibrium).

$$kx' = F$$

$$\therefore \quad x' = \frac{F}{k}$$

In both the cases, extension is the same $\left(\frac{F}{k}\right)$.

(ii) The period of oscillation in case (a),

As, $\quad F = -kx$

where, x = given extension

But $\quad F = ma$

$$\therefore \quad ma = -kx \Rightarrow a = -\left(\frac{k}{m}\right)x \quad \text{...(i)}$$

$$a \propto -x \quad \left[\text{as, } \frac{k}{m} \text{ is a constant}\right]$$

On comparing Eq. (i) with $a = -\omega^2 x$, we get

$$\therefore \quad \omega = \sqrt{\frac{k}{m}}$$

Period of oscillation,

$$T = \frac{2\pi}{\omega} = 2\pi\sqrt{\frac{m}{k}}$$

Time period of oscillation in case (b)

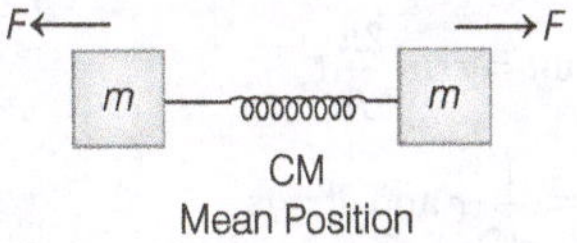

The system is divided into two similar systems with spring divided in two equal halves. $k' = 2k$

Hence, $\quad F = -k'x$

$k' = 2k$ (on cutting a spring in two halves, its k doubles)

$$\Rightarrow \quad F = -2kx$$

But $\quad F = ma$

$$\therefore \quad ma = -2kx$$

$$\Rightarrow \quad a = -\left(\frac{2k}{m}\right)x \quad \text{...(ii)}$$

$$\Rightarrow \quad a \propto -\text{displacement}$$

$$\left[\text{as } \frac{2k}{m} \text{ is a constant}\right]$$

On comparing Eq. (ii) with $a = -\omega^2 x$, we get

$$\omega = \sqrt{\frac{2k}{m}}$$

Time period of oscillation,

$$T = \frac{2\pi}{\omega} = 2\pi\sqrt{\frac{m}{2k}}$$

21. The bob of the simple pendulum will experience the acceleration due to gravity and the Centripetal acceleration provided by the circular motion of the car.

Acceleration due to gravity = g

Centripetal acceleration = $\frac{v^2}{R}$

where, v is the uniform speed of the car and R is the radius of the track.

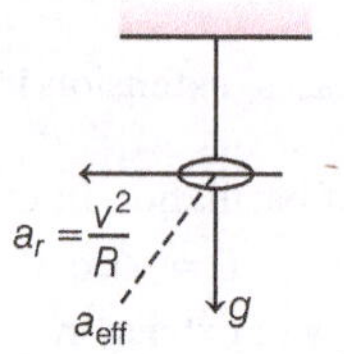

$\therefore$ Effective acceleration, $g_{eff} = \sqrt{g^2 + \left(\frac{v^2}{R}\right)^2}$

$\therefore$ Time period of the simple pendulum,

$$T = 2\pi\sqrt{\frac{l}{g_{eff}}} = 2\pi\sqrt{\frac{l}{\left(g^2 + \left(\frac{v^2}{R}\right)^2\right)^{1/2}}}$$

$$= 2\pi\sqrt{\frac{l}{\left(g^2 + \frac{v^4}{R^2}\right)^{1/2}}}$$

22. $y = r\sin\omega t = r\sin\frac{2\pi}{T}t$

Here, $y = \frac{1}{\sqrt{2}}r$ and $T = 1\text{s}$

$\therefore \frac{1}{\sqrt{2}}r = r\sin\frac{2\pi}{T}t \Rightarrow 2\pi t = \frac{\pi}{4} \Rightarrow t = \frac{1}{8}$ s.

23. $\frac{a_1}{a_2} = \frac{10}{25} = \frac{2}{5}$

24. Here, $y = 5$ cm and acceleration $a = 45 \text{ cm s}^{-2}$

We know $a = \omega^2 y$

$\therefore 45 = \omega^2 \times 5$ or $\omega = 3 \text{ rad s}^{-1}$

and $T = \frac{2\pi}{\omega} = \frac{2\pi}{3} = 2.095$ s.

25. Given, $\nu = 0.5 \text{ s}^{-1}$, $g = 9.8 \text{ ms}^{-1}$

$a = \omega^2 y = (2\pi\nu)^2 y = 4\pi^2\nu^2 y$

a_{max} at the extreme position i.e. $r = y$

$a_{max} = 4\pi^2\nu^2 r$ and $a_{max} = g$ to remain in contact.

or $r = \frac{g}{4\pi^2\nu^2} = \frac{9.8}{4\pi^2 \times (0.5)^2} = 0.993$ m

26. The displacement of the particle is

$$y = 0.2\sin 50\pi\,(t + 0.01) \text{ metre}$$

The general equation of SHM is

$$y = A\sin(\omega t + \phi)$$

Comparing Eqs. (i) and (ii), we get

Amplitude, $A = 0.2$ m

$\omega = 50\,\pi$

$\therefore$ Periodic time, $T = \frac{2\pi}{\omega} = \frac{2\pi}{50\pi} = 0.04$ s

Maximum velocity, $v_{max} = \omega A = 50\pi \times 0.2$

$= 10 \times 3.14 = 31.4$ m/s

Initial phase (i.e. at $t = 0$), $\phi = 50\pi \times 0.01 = 0.5\pi$

Displacement of particle at the start (i.e. at $t = 0$) is obtained by putting $t = 0$ in equation (i) i.e., initial displacement

$$y = 0.2 \sin 50\pi(t + 0.01)$$

$$= 0.2\sin 50\pi \times 0.01 = 0.2\sin\frac{\pi}{2} = 0.2 \text{ m}$$

27. Given, amplitude, $A = 5$ cm $= 0.05$ m,

Time period, $T = 0.2$ s

(i) When displacement is $x = 5$ cm $= 0.05$ m.

Acceleration, $a = -\omega^2(x) = -\left(\frac{2\pi}{T}\right)^2(x)$

$= -\left(\frac{2\pi}{0.2}\right)^2(0.05) = -5\pi^2 \text{m/s}^2$

Velocity, $v = \omega\sqrt{A^2 - x^2}$

$= \left(\frac{2\pi}{T}\right)\sqrt{(0.05)^2 - (0.05)^2}$

$= \left(\frac{2\pi}{T}\right) \times 0 = 0$

(ii) When displacement is $x = 3$ cm $= 0.03$ m

Acceleration, $a = -\left(\frac{2\pi}{0.2}\right)^2(0.03) = -3\pi \text{ m/s}^2$

and velocity, $v = \omega\sqrt{A^2 - x^2}$

$= \left(\frac{2\pi}{0.2}\right)\sqrt{(0.05)^2 - (0.03)^2} = 0.4\pi$ m/s

(iii) When displacement is $x = 0$,

acceleration, $a = -\omega^2 x = 0$

Velocity, $v = \omega\sqrt{A^2 - x^2}$

$= \left(\frac{2\pi}{0.2}\right)\sqrt{(0.05)^2 - (0)^2} = 0.5\pi$ m/s

28. If the particle moves from P to P' in time-interval t, then angle moved by position vector (or radius vector) is

$$\theta = \omega t = \frac{2\pi}{T}t = \frac{2\pi}{2}t = \pi t \text{ rad}$$

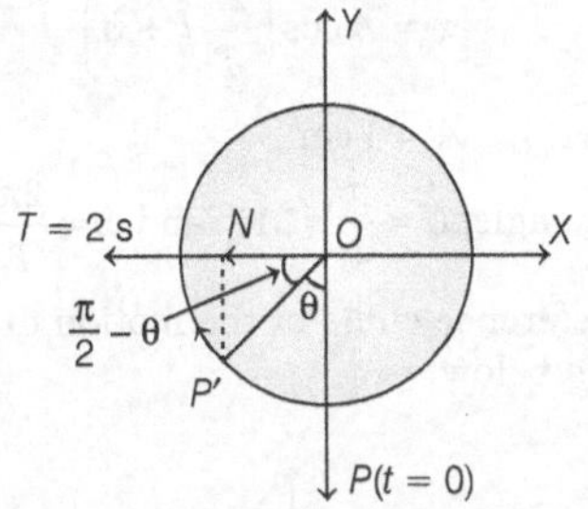

Displacement suffered by the particle,

$$ON = OP' \cos\left(\frac{\pi}{2} - \theta\right)$$

$$= OP' \sin\theta$$

But $ON = -x(t)$

As it is left to mean position O, hence, negative sign.

$\Rightarrow \quad -x(t) = 3\sin\theta \qquad [\because OP = 3 \text{ cm}]$

or $\quad x(t) = -3\sin\theta$

or $\quad x(t) = -3\sin\pi t$ as $\theta = \pi t$

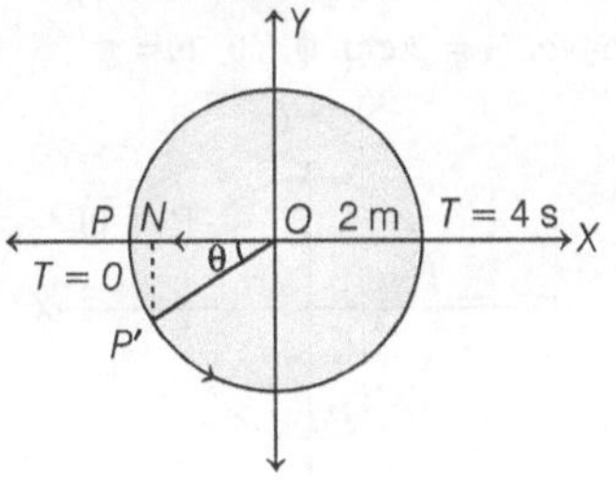

If the particle moves from P to P' in the time-interval t.

Angle swept by radius vector

$$\theta = \omega t = \frac{2\pi}{T}t = \frac{2\pi}{4}t = \frac{\pi t}{2} \text{ rad}$$

Displacement, $\quad ON = OP' \cos\theta$

or $\quad -x(t) = 2\cos\frac{\pi t}{2} \qquad [\because OP = 1\text{cm}]$

Negative sign to indicate left to mean position.

$$\Rightarrow \quad x(t) = -2\cos\left(\frac{\pi t}{2}\right)$$

29. (a) Assuming $x(t) = \sin\omega t - \cos\omega t$

$$= \sqrt{2}\left[\frac{1}{\sqrt{2}}\sin\omega t - \frac{1}{\sqrt{2}}\cos\omega t\right]$$

$$= \sqrt{2}\left[\cos\frac{\pi}{4}\sin\omega t - \sin\frac{\pi}{4}\cos\omega t\right]$$

$$= \sqrt{2}\sin\left(\omega t - \frac{\pi}{4}\right)$$

Clearly, the above equation is of the form

$$x = A\sin(\omega t \pm \phi)$$

represents SHM.

Again, if $t = \dfrac{2\pi}{\omega}$ is the period of SHM, then

$$x\left(t + \frac{2\pi}{\omega}\right) = \sqrt{2}\sin\left[\omega\left(t + \frac{2\pi}{\omega}\right) - \frac{\pi}{4}\right]$$

$$= \sqrt{2}\sin\left(\omega t + 2\pi - \frac{\pi}{4}\right)$$

$$= \sqrt{2}\sin\left(\omega t - \frac{\pi}{4}\right) = x(t)$$

Hence, the period $T = \dfrac{2\pi}{\omega}$

and $\quad$ phase angle $= -\dfrac{\pi}{4}$ or $\left(2\pi - \dfrac{\pi}{4}\right)$

(b) Periodic but not SHM

The given function is

$$\sin^3\omega t = 1/4[3\sin\omega t - \sin 3\omega t]$$

The terms $\sin\omega t$ and $\sin 3\omega t$ individually represents simple harmonic motion (SHM). However, the super position of two SHMs is periodic and not simple harmonic.

Its period is $2\pi/\omega$ (LCM of time periods)

(c) $x(t) = 3\cos\left(\dfrac{\pi}{4} - 2\omega t\right) = 3\cos\left(2\omega t - \dfrac{\pi}{4}\right)$

As $\quad \cos(-\theta) = \cos\theta$

The above equation is of the form

$$x(t) = A\cos(\omega t \pm \phi)$$

Hence, SHM with period $T = \dfrac{2\pi}{2\omega} = \dfrac{\pi}{\omega}$

(d) $x(t) = \cos\omega t + \cos 3\omega t + \cos 5\omega t$

$\cos\omega t$ represents SHM with period $= \dfrac{2\pi}{\omega} = T$ (say)

$\cos 3\omega t$ represents SHM with period $= \dfrac{2\pi}{3\omega} = \dfrac{T}{3}$

$\cos 5\omega t$ represents SHM with period $= \dfrac{2\pi}{5\omega} = \dfrac{T}{5}$

The minimum time after which the combined function repeats its value is T. Hence, the given function represents periodic function but not SHM, with period T.

(e) $x(t) = \exp(-\omega^2 t^2)$

The given function is an exponential function. It decreases monotonically, i.e. $x(t) \to 0$ as $t \to \infty$

There is no repetition of the values. Hence, it represents a non-periodic function.

(f) $x(t) = 1 + \omega t + \omega^2 t^2$

Here, $\quad$ as $t \to \infty$, $x(t) \to \infty$

No repetition of values. Hence, it represents non-periodic function.

30. (a) Given, $x = -2\sin\left(3t + \frac{\pi}{3}\right) = 2\cos\left(3t + \frac{\pi}{3} + \frac{\pi}{2}\right)$

$$= 2\cos\left(3t + \frac{5\pi}{6}\right)$$

On comparing with standard equation for SHM,

$x = A\cos\left[\frac{2\pi}{T}t + \phi\right]$, we get amplitude $A = 2$ cm

Phase angle, $\phi = \frac{5\pi}{6} = 150°$

Angular velocity, $\omega = \frac{2\pi}{T} = 3$ rad/s

This corresponding reference circle is plotted as below.

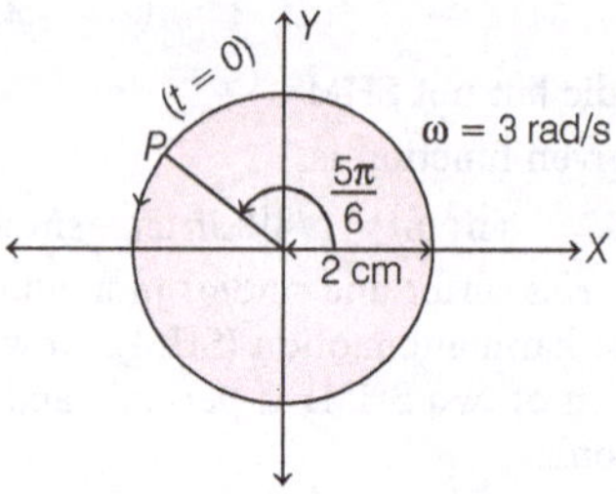

(b) $x = A\cos\left(\frac{2\pi}{T}t + \phi\right)$ is the standard SHM equation.

The given equation,

$$x = \cos\left(\frac{\pi}{6} - t\right) = \cos\left(t - \frac{\pi}{6}\right)$$

[as $\cos(-\theta) = \cos\theta$]

On comparison, amplitude $A = 1$ cm

Phase angle, $\phi = -\frac{\pi}{6} = -30°$

Angular velocity, $\omega = \frac{2\pi}{T} = 1$ rad/s

The reference circle is plotted below.

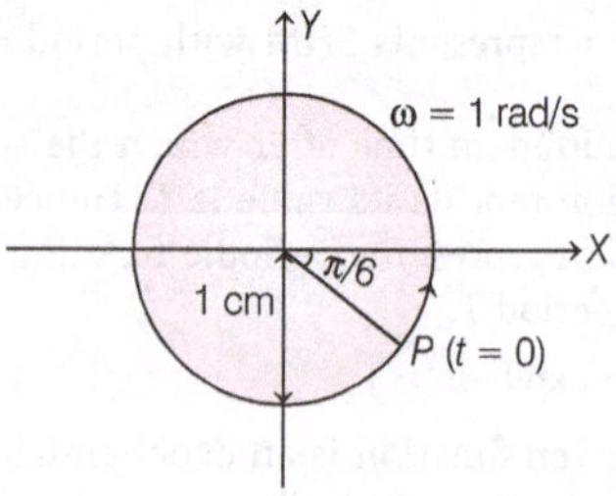

(c) Given equation

$$x = 3\sin\left(2\pi t + \frac{\pi}{4}\right) = 3\cos\left[\left(2\pi t + \frac{\pi}{4}\right) - \frac{\pi}{2}\right]$$

$$\left[\because \cos\left(\frac{\pi}{2} - \theta\right) = \sin\theta\right]$$

or $x = 3\cos\left(2\pi t - \frac{\pi}{4}\right)$

On comparing with standard SHM equation,

$$x = A\cos\left(\frac{2\pi}{T}t + \phi\right)$$

We get, $A = 3$ cm

Phase angle, $\phi = \frac{\pi}{4} = 315°$ and $\omega = \frac{2\pi}{T} = 2\pi$ rad/s

The reference circle of the motion of the particle is plotted below.

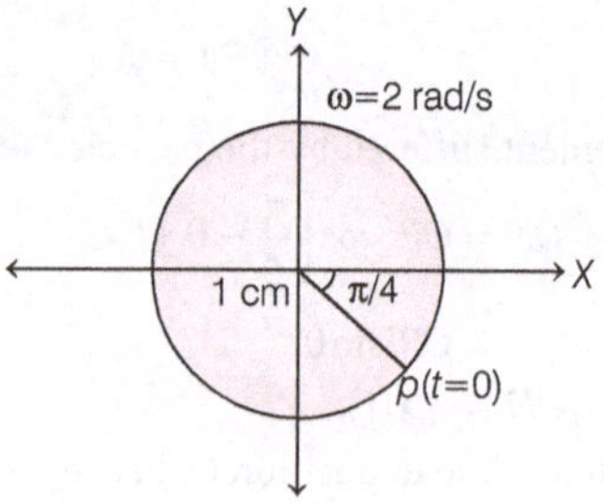

(d) For $x = 2\cos \pi t$

Comparing it with

$$x = A\cos(\omega t + \phi)$$

We have, $A = 2$ cm, $\phi = 0$, $\omega = \pi$

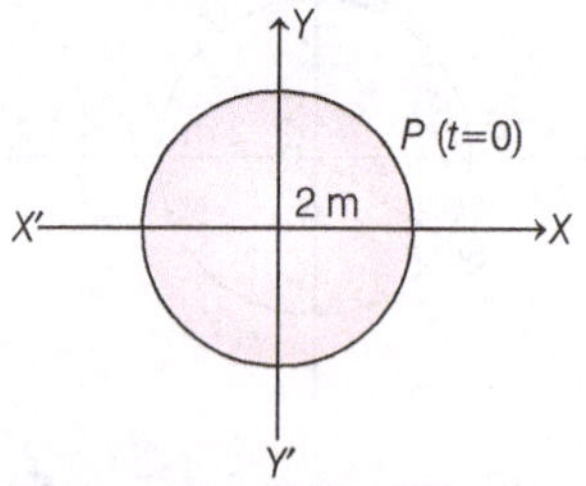

31. Here, $k = 1200$ Nm^{-1}, $m = 3.0$ kg

and $A = 2.0$ cm $= 2.0 \times 10^{-2}$ m

(i) Frequency of oscillation of the mass,

$$\nu = \frac{1}{2\pi}\sqrt{\frac{k}{m}} = \frac{1}{2 \times 3.14}\sqrt{\frac{1200}{3.0}}$$

$$= \frac{1}{2 \times 3.14} \times 20 = 3.18\text{s}^{-1} \approx 3.2\text{s}^{-1}$$

(ii) Angular frequency,

$$\omega = \sqrt{\frac{k}{m}} = \sqrt{\frac{1200}{3.0}} = 20\text{ s}^{-1}$$

$\therefore$ Maximum acceleration of the mass

$$= \omega^2 A = (20)^2 \times 2.0 \times 10^{-2} = 8.0\text{ms}^{-2}$$

(iii) Maximum speed of the mass

$$= \omega \cdot A = 20 \times 2.0 \times 10^{-2} = 0.40\text{ ms}^{-1}$$

32. Here, $mg = 40\ g = 40 \times 980$ dyne; $l = 4$ cm.

say k is the force constant of spring, then

$$mg = kl \text{ or } k = mg/l$$

$$k = \frac{40 \times 980}{4} = 9800 \text{ dyne cm}^{-1}$$

When the spring is loaded with mass $m = 200$ g

$$\nu = \frac{1}{2\pi}\sqrt{\frac{k}{m}} = \frac{1}{2\pi}\sqrt{\frac{9800}{200}} = 1.113 \text{ s}^{-1}$$

33. Here, $m = 50$ kg, $l = 0.2$ m

We know, $mg = kl$

or $$k = \frac{mg}{l} = \frac{50 \times 9.8}{0.2} = 2450 \text{ Nm}^{-1}$$

$T = 0.60$ s and M is the mass of the body, then using

$$T = 2\pi\sqrt{\frac{M}{k}} \Rightarrow M = \frac{2450 \times (0.60)^2}{4\pi^2} = 22.34 \text{ kg}$$

Weight of body, $Mg = 22.34 \times 9.8 = 218.93$ N

34. When mass 700 g is removed, the left out mass $(500 + 400)$ g oscillates with a period of 3 s.

$$\therefore \quad 3 = t = 2\pi\sqrt{\frac{(500+400)}{k}} \quad \text{...(i)}$$

When 500 g mass is also removed, the left out mass is 400 g.

$$\therefore \quad t' = 2\pi\sqrt{\frac{400}{k}} \quad \text{...(ii)}$$

Dividing Eq. (i) by Eq. (ii), we get

$$\Rightarrow \quad \frac{3}{t'} = \sqrt{\frac{900}{400}} \Rightarrow t' = 2 \text{ s}$$

35. If force constant of a spring of length l is k, then the force constant of a spring of length $\frac{1}{n}$ will be nk.

$\left(\text{since } k \propto \frac{1}{l}\right)$. In initial state

$$T = 2\pi\sqrt{\left(\frac{m}{k}\right)} \quad \text{...(i)}$$

(a) When spring is divided into 3 parts, therefore force constant of each part is $3k$.

In parallel combination of springs, the net force constant.

$$k' = k_1 + k_2 + k_3 = 3k + 3k + 3k = 9k$$

Time period, $$T' = 2\pi\sqrt{\left(\frac{m}{k'}\right)} \quad \text{...(ii)}$$

Dividing Eq. (ii) by Eq. (i), we get

$$\frac{T'}{T} = \sqrt{\left(\frac{k}{k'}\right)} = \sqrt{\left(\frac{k}{9k}\right)} = \frac{1}{3}$$

$$T' = \frac{T}{3} = \frac{1.5}{3} = 0.5 \text{ s}$$

(b) If mass is suspended from one part, then

$$\frac{T'}{T} = 2\pi\sqrt{\left(\frac{m}{k_1}\right)} = 2\pi\sqrt{\left(\frac{m}{3k}\right)} \quad \text{...(iii)}$$

Dividing Eq. (iii) by Eq. (i), we get

$$\frac{T'}{T} = \sqrt{\frac{1}{3}} \text{ or } T' = \frac{T}{\sqrt{3}} = \frac{1.5}{\sqrt{3}} = \frac{1.5\sqrt{3}}{3}$$

$$= 0.5 \times 1.732 = 0.866 \text{ s.}$$

36. Here, $m = 10$ g, $T = 6$ s

$$\omega = \frac{2\pi}{T} = \frac{2\pi}{6} = \frac{\pi}{3} \text{ rad s}^{-1}$$

When $t = 1$ s, $v = 6 \text{ cms}^{-1}$

As $\quad v = A\omega \cos \omega t$

$$6 = A \times \frac{\pi}{3} \cos \frac{\pi}{3} \times 1 = A \times \frac{\pi}{3} \cos 60°$$

$$= A \times \frac{\pi}{3} \times \frac{1}{2} = \frac{\pi A}{6}$$

or $$A = \frac{36}{\pi} \text{ cm}$$

Total energy, $E = \frac{1}{2} mA^2 \omega^2$

$$= \frac{1}{2} \times 10 \times \left(\frac{36}{\pi}\right)^2 \times \left(\frac{\pi}{3}\right)^2 = 720 \text{ erg}$$

$$\text{Kinetic energy} = \frac{1}{2} mv^2 = \frac{1}{2} \times 10 \times 6^2 = 180 \text{ erg}$$

$\therefore$ Potential energy = Total energy − Kinetic energy
$= 720 - 180 = 540$ erg

37. Time period on the surface of earth,

$$T = 3.5 \text{ s}, g = 9.8 \text{ ms}^{-2}$$

For simple pendulum, $T = 2\pi\sqrt{\frac{l}{g}}$

$$3.5 = 2\pi\sqrt{\frac{l}{9.8}} \quad \text{...(i)}$$

On moon $g' = 1.7 \text{ ms}^{-2}$ and if T is time period

then $$T' = 2\pi\sqrt{\frac{l}{1.7}} \quad \text{...(ii)}$$

Dividing Eq. (ii) by Eq. (i), we get

$$\frac{T'}{3.5} = \sqrt{\frac{9.8}{1.7}}$$

or $$T' = \sqrt{\frac{9.8}{1.7}} \times 3.5 = 8.4 \text{ s}$$

38. Frequency, $n \propto \frac{1}{\sqrt{l}}$

$$\Rightarrow \quad \frac{n_1}{n_2} = \sqrt{\frac{l_2}{l_1}}$$

$$\Rightarrow \quad \frac{l_1}{l_2} = \frac{n_2^2}{n_1^2} = \frac{3^2}{2^2} = \frac{9}{4} = 9:4$$

39. Time period of a second pendulum,

$$T = 2\text{ s}$$

$$\frac{T}{T'} = \sqrt{\frac{g'}{g}}$$

$$\frac{2}{T'} = \sqrt{\frac{4.36}{9.81}}$$

$$T' = 3\text{ s}$$

40. $$\frac{U}{E} = \frac{\frac{1}{2}m\omega^2 y^2}{\frac{1}{2}m\omega^2 a^2} = \frac{y^2}{a^2} \Rightarrow \frac{U}{80} = \frac{\left(\frac{3}{4}a\right)^2}{a^2} = \frac{9}{16}$$

$$\Rightarrow \quad U = 45\text{ J}$$

41. A second pendulum means a simple pendulum having time period, $T = 2\text{ s}$

For a simple pendulum, $T = 2\pi\sqrt{\frac{l}{g}}$

where, l = length of the pendulum and g = acceleration due to gravity on surface of the earth.

$$T_s = 2\pi\sqrt{\frac{l_e}{g_e}} \quad \text{...(i)}$$

On the surface of the moon,

$$T_m = 2\pi\sqrt{\frac{l_m}{g_m}} \quad \text{...(ii)}$$

Dividing Eq. (i) by Eq. (ii), we get

$$\therefore \quad \frac{T_s}{T_m} = \frac{2\pi}{2\pi}\sqrt{\frac{l_e}{g_e}} \times \sqrt{\frac{g_m}{l_m}}$$

$T_s = T_m$ to maintain the second pendulum time period.

$$\therefore \quad 1 = \sqrt{\frac{l_e}{l_m} \times \frac{g_m}{g_e}} \quad \text{...(iii)}$$

But the acceleration due to gravity at moon is (1/6)th of the acceleration due to gravity at earth, i.e. $g_m = \frac{g_e}{6}$

Squaring Eq. (iii) and putting this value,

$$1 = \frac{l_e}{l_m} \times \frac{g_e/6}{g_e} = \frac{l_e}{l_m} \times \frac{1}{6}$$

$$\Rightarrow \quad \frac{l_e}{6l_m} = 1$$

$$\text{or} \quad l_m = \frac{1}{6}l_e = \frac{1}{6} \times 1 = \frac{1}{6}\text{ m}$$

QR Code for Quick Test 1

QR Code for Quick Test 2

SELF ASSESSMENT TEST

Multiple Choice Questions (MCQs)

1. The period of a simple pendulum, whose bob is a hollow metallic sphere is T. The period is T_1 when the bob is filled with sand, T_2 when it is filled with mercury and T_3. when it is half filled with mercury. Which of the following is true?

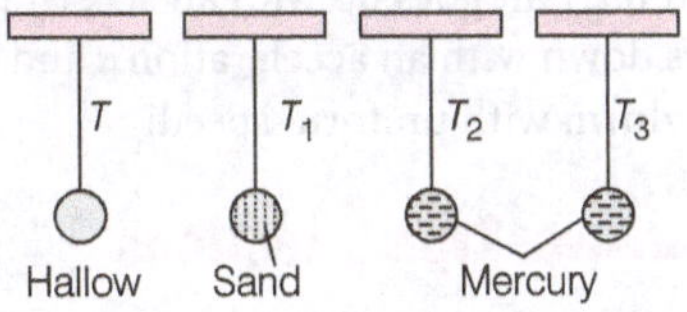

(a) $T = T_1 = T_2 > T_3$ (b) $T_1 = T_2 = T_3 > T$
(c) $T > T_3 > T_1 = T_2$ (d) $T = T_1 = T_2 < T_3$

2. A pendulum clock that keeps correct time on the earth is taken to the moon it will run (it is given that $g = g/6$)
(a) at correct rate (b) 6 times faster
(c) $\sqrt{6}$ times faster (d) $\sqrt{6}$ times slowly

3. A spring with 10 coils has spring constant k, is exactly cut into two halves, then each of these new springs will have a spring constant
(a) $k/2$ (b) $3k/2$
(c) $2k$ (d) $3k$

4. Equations $y_1 = A\sin\omega t$ and $y_2 = \frac{A}{2}\sin\omega t + \frac{A}{2}\cos\omega t$ represent SHM. The ratio of the amplitudes of the two motions is
(a) 1 (b) 2
(c) 0.5 (d) $\sqrt{2}$

5. Match the Column I with Column II.

Column I	Column II
A. 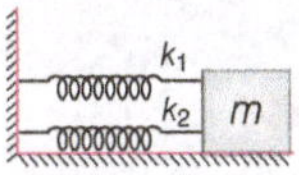	P. $T = 2\pi\sqrt{\frac{m(k_1 + k_2)}{k_1 k_2}}$
B. 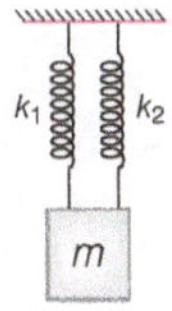	Q. $T = 2\pi\sqrt{\frac{2m}{k}}$
C. 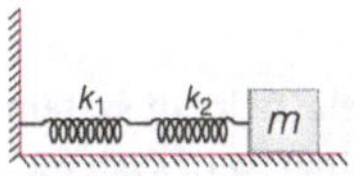	R. $T = 2\pi\sqrt{\frac{m}{2k}}$
D. 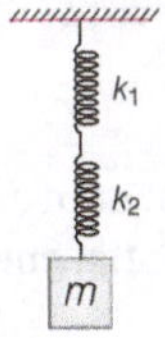	S. $T = 2\pi\sqrt{\frac{m}{k_1 + k_2}}$

(a) A-P, B-Q, C-S, D-R (b) A-S, B-R, C-P, D-Q
(c) A-R, B-P, C-S, D-Q (d) A-P, B-R, C-Q, D-S

Assertion-Reason

Direction *(Q. Nos. 6-7) In the following questions, two statements are given-one labelled Assertion (A) and the other labelled Reason (R). Select the correct answer to these questions from the codes (a), (b), (c) and (d) as given below.*

(a) Both Assertion and Reason are true and Reason is the correct explanation of Assertion.
(b) Both Assertion and Reason are true but Reason is not the correct explanation of Assertion.
(c) Assertion is true but Reason is false.
(d) Assertion is false but Reason is true.

6. **Assertion (A)** If the amplitude of a simple harmonic oscillator is doubled, its total energy becomes four times.
Reason (R) The total energy is directly proportional to the square of amplitude of vibration of the harmonic oscillator.

7. **Assertion (A)** The graph of total energy of a particle in SHM w.r.t position is a straight line with zero slope.
Reason (R) Total energy of particle in SHM remains constant throungout its motion.

Case Based Questions

Directions *(Q.No. 8) This question is case study based question. Read the following paragraph and answer the questions on the basis of same.*

8. A particle executing SHM posseses both kinetic energy and potential energy. When a body is displaced from its equilibrium position by doing work upon it, it acquires potential energy. When the body is released, it begins to move back with a velocity, thus acquiring kinetic energy. Both kinetic and potential energies of a particle in SHM vary between zero and their maximum values.

(i) In SHM,

(a) PE is stored due to elasticity of system
(b) KE is stored due to inertia of system
(c) Both KE and PE are stored by virtue of elasticity of system
(d) Both (a) and (b)

(ii) The expression for the displacement of an object in SHM is $x(t) = A\cos(\omega t)$. The potential energy at $t = T/4$ is

(a) $\frac{1}{2}kA^2$ (b) $\frac{1}{8}kA^2$
(c) $\frac{1}{4}kA^2$ (d) zero

(iii) For an SHM, if the maximum potential energy becomes double, choose the correct option.

(a) Maximum kinetic energy will become double
(b) The total mechanical energy will become double
(c) Both (a) and (b)
(d) Neither (a) nor (b)

(iv) A block is in simple harmonic motion as shown in the figure on a frictionless surface. i.e. $\mu = 0$. Choose the correct option.

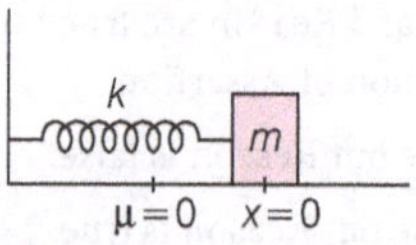

(a) The kinetic energy varies between a maximum value and zero.
(b) The potential energy varies between a maximum value and zero.
(c) Total energy remains constant.
(d) All of the above

(v) In simple harmonic motion, let the time period of variation of potential energy is T_1 and time period of variation of position is T_2, then relation between T_1 and T_2 is

(a) $T_1 = T_2$
(b) $T_1 = 2T_2$
(c) $2T_1 = T_2$
(d) None of the above

Very Short Answer Type Questions

9. What is the force equation of an SHM?

10. What will be the shape of the graph between length (L) and time period (T) of a simple pendulum ?

Short Answer Type Questions

11. Will a pendulum clock gain or lose time when taken to the top of a mountain?

12. A simple pendulum is suspended in a stationary lift has a time period T. What will be the effect on its time period if (i) lift goes up with an acceleration a, (ii) lift moves down with an acceleration a and (iii) lift moves up or down with uniform speed?

Long Answer Type Questions

13. Obtain an expression for the velocity of a particle executing SHM, when its velocity is
(i) maximum and (ii) minimum.

14. Answer the following questions.

(i) Time period of a particle in SHM depends on the force constant k and mass m of the particle $T = 2\pi\sqrt{\frac{m}{k}}$. A simple pendulum executes SHM approximately. Then, why is the time period of a pendulum independent of the mass of the pendulum?

(ii) The motion of a simple pendulum is approximately simple harmonic for small angle oscillations. For larger angles of oscillation, a more involved analysis shows that T is greater than $2\pi\sqrt{\frac{l}{g}}$. Think of a qualitative argument to appreciate this result.

(iii) A man with a wristwatch on his hand falls from the top of a tower. Does the watch give correct time during the free fall?

(iv) What is the frequency of oscillation of a simple pendulum mounted in a cabin that is freely falling under gravity?

Answers

1. (d) 2. (d) 3. (c) 4. (d) 5. (b)
6. (a) 7. (a)
8. (i) (d), (ii) (d), (iii) (c), (iv) (d), (v) (c)

14

CHAPTER

Waves are disturbance that transfer energy from one point to another. It is a fundamental concept in Physics and play a crucial role in various phenomena, from sound and light to seismic activity and ocean tides. Waves can be classified based on their nature, medium and the direction of energy transfer.

▼ **YOUR STUDY GOALS**

▼ **YOUR PRACTICE GOAL**

- Objective Type Questions (27 Qs, MCQs, A-R, Matching)
- Case Based Questions (2)
- Subjective Questions (4 VSAs, 6 SAs, 4 LAs)
- Numerical Problems (2)

Waves

14.1 Waves and their Superposition

Wave is a periodic disturbance that propagates energy and momentum from one place to other without any bulk motion of the matter of a medium. It can occur whenever a system is disturbed from its equilibrium position.

Types of Waves

We usually deal with three types of waves. They are as follows

(i) **Mechanical Waves** The waves which require medium for their propagation are called mechanical waves. These waves are also called **elastic waves** because their propagation depends on the elastic properties of the medium.
e.g. Waves on string and spring, water waves, sound waves, seismic waves etc.

(ii) **Electromagnetic Waves** The waves which do not require medium for their propagation are called electromagnetic wave. These waves are also called **non-mechanical waves**.
e.g. Visible and ultraviolet light, X-rays, radio and television waves, microwaves, etc.

All the electromagnetic waves travel through the vacuum at the same speed c, given as

$$c = 29{,}97{,}92{,}458 \text{ m/s} \quad \text{(speed of light)}$$
$$\simeq 3 \times 10^8 \text{ m/s}$$

(iii) **Matter Waves** The waves which associated with moving constituents of matter, electrons, protons, neutrons, atoms and molecules are called matter waves. These waves are also called **de-Broglie waves.**
e.g. Matter waves associated with electrons are employed in electron microscopes.

Dual Nature of Light

Light wave is an electromagnetic wave. Every radiation that we get from the sun comes under electromagnetic waves. Actually, light shows dual nature. Light behaves as wave, as well as particle.

In the same way, a moving particle could behave as wave. **Matter wave is the wave associated with a moving particle.**

Characteristics of Wave Motion

(i) When a wave motion passes through a medium, particles of the medium only vibrate simple harmonically about their mean position.

(ii) Energy is transferred from one place to another without any actual transfer of the particles of the medium.

(iii) In wave motion, the phase of particles of medium keeps on changing.

(iv) In a given medium, the wave velocity remains constant, while the particle velocity changes continuously during its vibration about the mean position.

(v) For the propagation of a mechanical wave, the medium must posses the properties of inertia, elasticity, less friction between particles and uniform density.

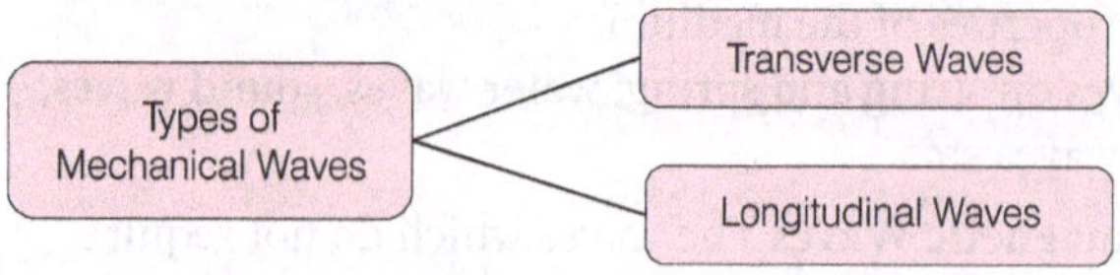

Transverse Waves

The waves in which the particles of the medium execute simple harmonic motion about their mean position in a direction perpendicular to the direction of wave propagation are called transverse waves.

e.g. Waves in string, ripples on the surface of water, movement of string of stringed musical instruments like sitar, guitar, etc.

Transverse wave travels in the form of crests (C, C') and troughs (T, T') as shown below.

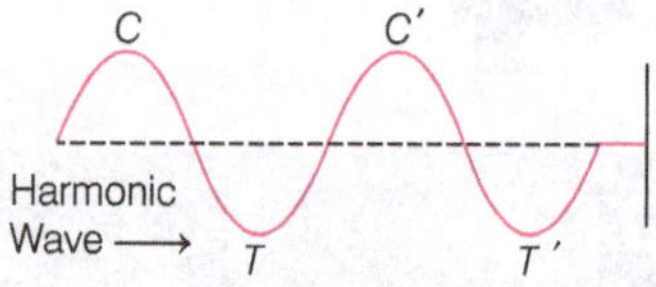

Transverse wave along the stretched string

- **Crest** is the highest point of a wave, representing the maximum displacement above the equilibrium position.
- **Trough** is the lowest point of a wave, representing the maximum displacement below the equilibrium position.

Note Transverse waves can propagate only in those media which can sustain shearing stress, such as solids and not in fluids (liquids and gases).

Longitudinal Waves

The waves in which the particles of the medium execute simple harmonic motion about their mean position along the direction of propagation of the wave are called longitudinal waves.

e.g. Waves in spring, sound waves, vibration of air column in organ pipes, etc.

These waves travel in the form of compressions (C) and rarefactions (R) as shown below.

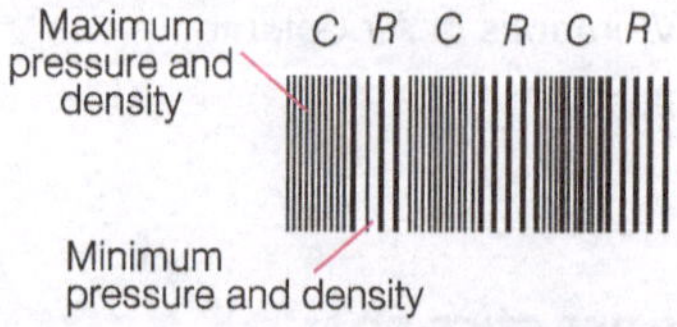

Longitudinal waves can be produced in a cylinder containing a liquid or air by moving its piston back and forth.

Due to continuous pushing and pulling of the piston in a simple harmonic manner, a sinusoidal wave travels in the cylinder in the form of **compressions** and **rarefactions**, (marked C, R, C, R, etc.) resulting a temporary reduction in volume and consequent increase in density.

- **Compression** is a region where particles are close together, resulting in higher pressure.

- **Rarefaction** is a region where particles are spread apart, resulting in lower pressure.

Note Longitudinal waves can be transmitted through all elastic mediums such as solids, liquids and gases.

Characteristics of Medium of Propagation

(i) In a medium like steel, both transverse and longitudinal waves can propagate, while air can sustain only longitudinal waves.

(ii) Some waves in nature are neither transverse nor longitudinal but a combination of the two. For example, waves in an ocean are the combination of both longitudinal and transverse waves.

(iii) Transverse and longitudinal waves travel with different speeds, when they propagate the same medium.

(iv) In a wave motion, only the disturbance travels through a medium. The medium does not travel with the disturbance.

(v) Waves may be one, two or three-dimensional. Mode of dimension will be according to the propagation of energy in one, two or three dimension.

(vi) Transverse waves along a string are one-dimensional, ripples on water surface are two-dimensional and sound waves produced from a point source are three-dimensional.

Displacement Relation in a Progressive Wave

If during the propagation of a progressive wave, the particles of the medium perform SHM about their mean position, then the waves is known as a plane progressive wave.

Equation

The displacement of a plane progressive wave travelling in positive x-direction is given by

$$\text{Displacement, } y(x, t) = A\sin(kx - \omega t + \phi) \quad \ldots\text{(i)}$$

The above equation can also be represented by using linear combination of sine and cosine functions such as

$$y(x,t) = a\sin(kx - \omega t) + b\cos(kx - \omega t)$$

where, $A = \sqrt{a^2 + b^2}$ and $\phi = \tan^{-1}\left(\frac{b}{a}\right)$ ...(ii)

The wave travelling in the negative direction of X-axis can be represented by

$$y(x,t) = a\sin(kx + \omega t + \phi) \quad \ldots\text{(iii)}$$

where,

$y(x,t)$ = displacement of vibrating element or particle as a function of position x and time t.

a = amplitude of the vibrating element or particle

ω = angular frequency of the wave

x = position of vibrating element

k = angular wave number.

$(kx - \omega t + \phi)$ = phase of a vibrating element at time t and position x. ϕ is phase constant at $x = 0, t = 0$.

The plot for a plane simple harmonic wave travels from the origin along the positive direction of X-axis from left to right as shown in the figure.

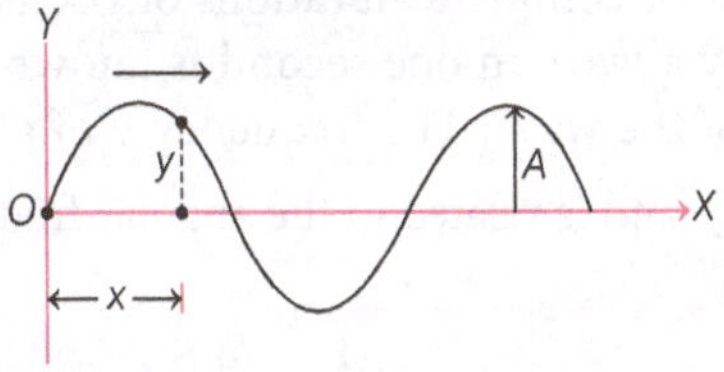

Amplitude

The magnitude of the maximum displacement of the particles from the equilibrium position is known as amplitude (A). The displacement (y) varies between A and $-A$.

Phase

The argument of the sine or cosine function i.e. $(kx - \omega t - \phi)$ is called the phase of the wave.

Wavelength

The minimum distance between two particles having the same phase is called its wavelength. In other words, wavelength is the distance between two consecutive crests or troughs. It is denoted by λ as shown below.

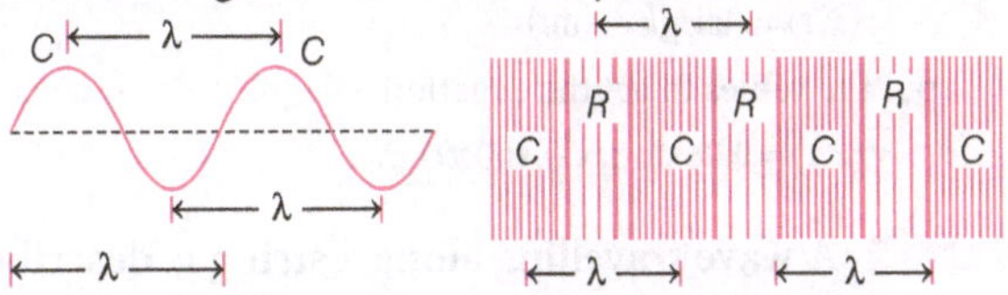

(a) Transverse wave (b) Longitudinal wave

Angular Wave Number

The number of wavelengths in distance 2π is called angular wave number or **propagation constant.** It is denoted by k and its SI unit is rad/m.

$$\text{Angular wave number, } k = \frac{2\pi}{\lambda}$$

Time Period and Angular Frequency

The time taken by a wave to travel a distance equal to one wavelength is known as the **time period** of wave.

$$T = \frac{2\pi}{\omega}$$

where, ω is called the **angular frequency**, SI unit is rad/s.

Angular frequency (ω) is a measure of how quickly an object moves through an angle in rotational or oscillatory motion. It is typically expressed in radians per second (rad/s). It is given by, $\omega = 2\pi f$.

Frequency

The number of complete vibrations or oscillations produced by a wave in one second is known as the frequency of the wave. The frequency ν of a wave is defined as $\frac{1}{T}$ and is related to the angular frequency ω.

$$\text{Frequency, } \nu = \frac{1}{T} = \frac{\omega}{2\pi}$$

Its SI unit is hertz (Hz).

Example 1 **If a progressive wave travelling in positive *x*-direction having the amplitude of 6 cm, frequency 200 Hz and velocity is 400 m/s, then write the equation of that progressive wave.**

Sol. Given, $A = 6\,\text{cm} = 0.06\,\text{m}$

$$\nu = 200\ \text{Hz}$$

$$k = \frac{2\pi}{\lambda} = \frac{2\pi}{v/\nu} \qquad \left[\because \lambda = \frac{v}{\nu}\right]$$

$$k = \frac{2\pi\nu}{v} = \frac{2\pi \times 200}{400} = \pi\,\text{m}^{-1}$$

$$\omega = 2\pi\nu = 2\pi \times 200 = 400\,\pi\ \text{rad/s}$$

The standard equation of the progressive wave is

$$y(x,t) = A\sin(kx - \omega t)$$

put the values to get the equation

$$y(x,t) = 0.06\sin(\pi x - 400\pi t)\ \text{m}$$

Example 2 **A wave travelling along a string is described by $y(x,t) = 0.005\sin(80.0x - 3.0t)$ in which the numerical constants are in SI units (0.005 m, 80.0 rad m^{-1} and 3.0 rad s^{-1}). Calculate**

(i) the amplitude of particle,

(ii) the wavelength and

(iii) the period and frequency of the wave. Also, calculate displacement *y* of the particle at a distance $x = 30.0$ cm and time $t = 20$ s? NCERT

Sol. Given, $y(x,t) = 0.005\sin(80.0x - 3.0t)$

Then, $y(x,t) = A\sin(kx - \omega t)$

Now, compare the given equation with standard equation to find out all the physical quantities.

$$A = 0.005\ \text{m}$$

$$k = 80.0\ \text{rad/m}$$

$$\omega = 3.0\ \text{rad/s}$$

The physical quantities by using the given fundamental physical quantities.

(i) Amplitude, $A = 0.005\ \text{m} = 5\ \text{mm}$

(ii) Wavelength, $\lambda = \frac{2\pi}{k} = \frac{2\pi}{80} = 7.85\ \text{cm}$

(iii) Time period, $T = 2\pi/\omega = \frac{2\pi}{3} = 2.09\ \text{s}$

and frequency, $\nu = \frac{1}{T} = \frac{1}{2.09}$

$$= 0.478 \simeq 0.48\ \text{Hz}$$

Now, the displacement *y* of the particle at a distance.

$$x = 30.0\ \text{cm} = 0.3\ \text{m and time } t = 20\ \text{s}$$

$$y\,(0.3, 20) = 0.005\sin(80 \times 0.3 - 3.0 \times 20)$$

$$y\,(0.3, 20) = 0.005\sin(24 - 60)$$

$$= 0.00495\ \text{m} \simeq 5\ \text{mm}$$

Speed of a Travelling Wave

Wave speed (v) is defined as the distance travelled by the disturbance in one time period. It only depends on the properties of the medium and it independent of time and position.

$$\therefore \quad \text{Speed of travelling wave, } v = \frac{\omega}{k} = \nu\lambda = \frac{\lambda}{T}$$

Its SI **unit is m/s** and **dimensional formula is** $[\text{LT}^{-1}]$.

Speed of a Transverse Wave on Stretched String

The speed of a transverse wave in terms of tension (T) and mass per unit length (or linear mass density) μ of a string is given by

$$v = \sqrt{\frac{T}{\mu}} = \nu\lambda$$

Note Speed of a transverse wave in a solid is given by $v = \sqrt{\frac{\eta}{\rho}}$, where, η is the modulus of rigidity and ρ is the density of a solid.

Example 3 **A steel wire has a length of 12 m and a mass of 2.10 kg. What will be the speed of a transverse wave on this wire when a tension of 2.06×10^4 N is applied?** NCERT Exemplar

Sol. Given, $L = 12$ m, $M = 2.10$ kg, $T = 2.06 \times 10^4$ N

Mass per unit length, $\mu = \frac{M}{L} = \frac{2.10}{12}$

Speed of transverse wave, $v = \sqrt{\frac{T}{\mu}}$

$= \sqrt{\frac{2.06 \times 10^4 \times 12}{2.10}} \approx 343$ m/s

Speed of a Longitudinal Wave (Speed of Sound)

Speed of sound in any elastic medium is given by

$$v = \sqrt{\frac{\text{Elasticity of the medium}}{\text{Density of the medium}}}$$

(i) **In solids** the speed of sound is given by $v = \sqrt{\frac{Y}{\rho}}$

where, Y is the Young's modulus of the material and ρ is the density.

(ii) **In liquid and gaseous medium** the speed of sound is given by $v = \sqrt{\frac{B}{\rho}}$

where, B is the Bulk modulus of the medium.

Speed of Sound in Different Media

Medium	Speed (m s^{-1})
Gases	
Air (0°C)	331
Air (20°C)	343
Helium	965
Hydrogen	1284
Liquids	
Water (0°C)	1402
Water (20°C)	1482
Sea water	1522
Solids	
Aluminium	6420
Copper	3560
Steel	5941
Granite	6000
Vulcanized rubber	54

Note The velocity of sound is maximum in solids and minimum in gases.

Example 4 **Speed of sound in mercury at a certain temperature is 1450 m/s. Find the bulk modulus of mercury if its density 13.6×10^3 kg / m^3.**

Sol. Given, $v = 1450$ m/s, $\rho = 13.6 \times 10^3$ kg / m^3

$\because \quad v = \sqrt{\frac{B}{\rho}}$

$B = v^2\rho = (1450)^2 \,(13.6 \times 10^3)$

$\approx 2.86 \times 10^{10}$ N/m^2

Speed of Electromagnetic Waves

In vacuum, the speed of propagation (c) of all types of electromagnetic waves, is given by

$$c = \frac{1}{\sqrt{\mu_0 \varepsilon_0}}$$

Here, μ_0 = permeability of vacuum and

ε_0 = permittivity of vacuum.

In any other material medium, the speed of propagation (v) of electromagnetic waves, is given by

$$v = \frac{1}{\sqrt{\mu\varepsilon}}$$

where, μ is permeability of the medium and ε is permittivity of the medium.

Speed of Mechanical Waves

Speed of all mechanical waves can be given by

$$\text{Speed of mechanical waves, } v = \sqrt{\frac{E}{\rho}}$$

where, E is the (appropriate) elastic constant and ρ is the density of the medium. The speed is thus, dependent only on the properties of the medium.

Newton's Formula for Speed of Sound

Newton assumed that when sound propagates through air, temperature remains constant. i.e. the process is isothermal. For isothermal process, bulk modulus (B) = pressure (p) of the gas.

The speed of sound in gas is given by $v = \sqrt{\frac{B}{\rho}} = \sqrt{\frac{p}{\rho}}$

where, ρ is density of the gas.

Example 5 **Estimate the speed of sound in air at STP. The mass of 1 mole of air is 29.0×10^{-3} kg.** NCERT

Sol. We know that, volume of any gas at STP is 22.4 litre.

Density of air at STP is

$$\rho_0 = \left(\frac{\text{mass}}{\text{volume at STP}}\right)_{\text{for one mole of air}}$$

$$= \frac{29.0 \times 10^{-3} \text{ kg}}{22.4 \times 10^{-3}} = 1.29 \text{ kgm}^{-3}$$

According to Newton's formula,

$$\text{Speed of sound, } v = \left[\frac{1.01 \times 10^5 \text{Nm}^{-2}}{1.29 \text{ kgm}^{-3}}\right]^{1/2} = 280 \text{ ms}^{-1}$$

- According to the Newton's formula, the speed of sound in air at STP is 280 ms^{-1}. But the experimental value of the speed of sound in air at STP is 332 ms^{-1}. Newton could not explain this large difference. Newton's formula was corrected by Laplace.

Laplace Correction

Laplace modified Newton's formula by assuming that propagation of sound in gaseous medium is an adiabatic process. For adiabatic process, $B = \gamma p$.

The speed of sound in gas is given by

$$v = \sqrt{\frac{B}{\rho}} = \sqrt{\frac{\gamma p}{\rho}} = \sqrt{\frac{\gamma RT}{M}} \qquad \left[\because p = \frac{RT}{V} \text{ and } M = \rho \times V\right]$$

where, T is temperature, M is molar mass of the gas, and γ is adiabatic constant.

- For air: $\gamma = 1.41 \Rightarrow v_{\text{air}} = \sqrt{1.41} \times 280 \approx 332$ m/s

$$v \propto \sqrt{T}$$

$$\text{and } v \propto \frac{1}{\sqrt{p}}$$

- Speed of sound in gas is independent of pressure at constant temperature.
- With increase in humidity, density of air decreases and hence speed of sound increases.

Example 6. The ratio of densities of nitrogen and oxygen is 14 : 16. Find the temperature at which the speed of sound in nitrogen will be same at that in oxygen at 55°C.

Sol. Given, $\frac{\rho_N}{\rho_O} = \frac{14}{16}$, $T_O = 55°\text{C} = 328 \text{ K}$, $T_N = ?$

Since, $v = \sqrt{\frac{\gamma RT}{M}}$

At same speed, $\frac{T_N}{T_O} = \frac{M_N}{M_O} = \frac{\rho_N}{\rho_O}$

$$\frac{T_N}{328} = \frac{14}{16}$$

$$T_N = 287 \text{ K} = 14°\text{C}$$

14.2 Principle of Superposition of Waves

This principle states that when two or more pulses overlap, the resultant displacement is the algebraic sum of the displacements due to each pulse.

If $y_1, y_2, y_3, \ldots$ are the displacements at a particular position at a particular time due to individual waves, then the resultant displacement at that position is given by $y = y_1 + y_2 + y_3 + \ldots$

Three important applications of superposition principle are

(i) Interference of waves (ii) Stationary waves

(iii) Beats

Interference of Wave

It is a phenomenon that occurs when two or more waves travelling along same medium, overlap, their displacements combine according to the principle of superposition resulting in new wave pattern depending on the phase relationship between the interacting wave. The nature of resultant wave can be classified into two main types

Constructive interference occurs when waves interfere in phase (crest to crest or trough to trough).

Destructive interferene occurs when waves interfere out of phase (crest to trough).

In generalised, form for constructive interference,

Phase difference, $\phi = 2n\pi$

Path difference, $\Delta x = n\lambda$

For destructive interference.

Phase difference, $\phi = (2n+1)\pi$

Path difference, $\Delta x = (2n+1)\lambda/2$

where, $n = 0, 1, 2, \ldots$

and λ is the wavelength.

The phenomenon of constructive and destructive interference are shown in the figures (a) and (b), respectively.

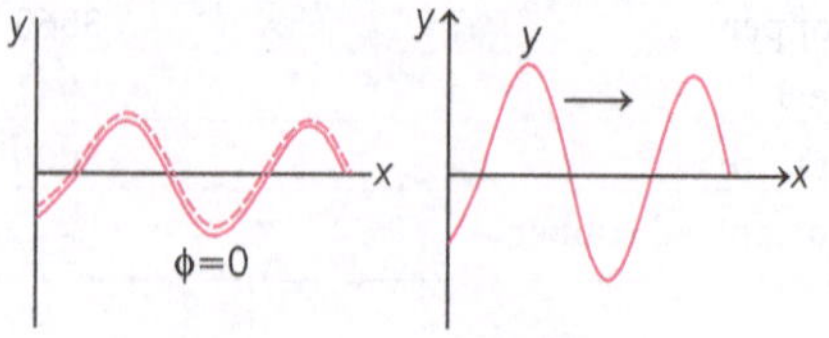

(a) Constructive interference

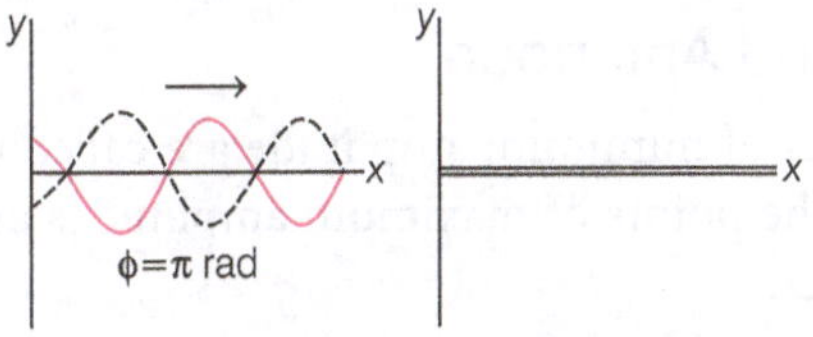

(b) Destructive interference

(i) In constructive interference, if a wave meets a crest of another wave of same frequency at the same point, then the magnitude of the displacement is the sum of the individual magnitudes as shown in Fig. (a).

(ii) In destructive interference, if a crest of one wave meets a trough of another wave, then the magnitude of the displacements is equal to the difference in the individual magnitudes as shown in Fig. (b).

(iii) If two sinusoidal waves of the same amplitude and wavelength travel in the same direction along a stretched string, they interfere to produce a resultant sinusoidal wave travelling in that direction.

(iv) For interference between sources of amplitudes A_1, A_2 and associated intensities I_1, I_2 as $I \propto A^2$.

$$\frac{I_{max}}{I_{min}} = \left(\frac{\sqrt{I_1}+\sqrt{I_2}}{\sqrt{I_1}-\sqrt{I_2}}\right)^2$$

When $I_1 = I_2 = I_0$, then $I_{resultant} = 4I_0 \cos^2(\phi/2)$ where, ϕ is the phase difference.

(v) These principles are valid for sound and light waves as well provided sources must be coherent i.e. these phase differences must not change with passage of time.

Example 7 **Two waves of equal frequencies have their amplitudes in the ratio of 3 : 5. They are superimposed on each other. Calculate the ratio of I_{max}/I_{min}.**

Sol. $$\frac{A_1}{A_2} = \frac{3}{5}$$

$$\Rightarrow \sqrt{\frac{I_1}{I_2}} = \frac{3}{5}$$

Now, $$\frac{I_{max}}{I_{min}} = \left(\frac{\sqrt{I_1}+\sqrt{I_2}}{\sqrt{I_1}-\sqrt{I_2}}\right)^2$$

$$= \left(\frac{\sqrt{I_1/I_2}+1}{\sqrt{I_1/I_2}-1}\right)^2$$

$$= \left(\frac{3/5+1}{3/5-1}\right)^2 = \frac{64}{4} = \frac{16}{1}$$

Quick Test 1

Conceptual Questions

1. What is the quantity transmitted with propagation of longitudinal waves through a medium? *NCERT Exemplar*
2. Is Newton's law of motion applicable for material waves? Is this applicable for electromagnetic waves?
3. Does a vibrating source always produce sound?
4. How speed of sound waves in air varies with humidity? *NCERT Exemplar*

Numerical Questions

5. The displacement of an elastic wave is given by the function $y = 3\sin\omega t + 4\cos\omega t$ where, y is in cm and t is in second. Calculate the resultant amplitude. *NCERT Exemplar*
6. Sound waves of wavelength λ travelling in a medium with a speed of v m/s enter into another medium where, its speed is $2v$ m/s. What is the wavelength of sound waves in the second medium? *NCERT Exemplar*
7. A steel wire has a length of 12.0 m and a mass of 2.10 kg. What should be the tension in the wire so that speed of a transverse wave on the wire equals the speed of sound in dry air at 20°C = 343 ms^{-1}? *NCERT*
8. A string of mass 2.50 kg is under a tension of 200 N. The length of the stretched string is 20.0 m. If the transverse jerk is struck at one end of the string, how long does the disturbance take to reach the other end ? *NCERT*
9. At what temperature (in °C) will the speed of sound in air be 3 times its value at 0°C? *NCERT Exemplar*

Answers

5. 5 6. 2λ 7. 2.06×10^4 N 8. 0.50s 9. 2184°C

For Solutions, See QR Code on Pg. 483

14.3 Reflection of Waves

When waves are incident on a boundary between two media, a part of incident waves return back into the initial medium known as **reflected waves,** while the remaining is partly absorbed and partly transmitted into the second medium known as **refracted waves.**

Reflection from Rigid End

When the incident wave reaches a fixed end, then there is phase change of π. Due to reflection from rigid end, crest (C) reflects as trough (T) and *vice-versa* as shown in figure.

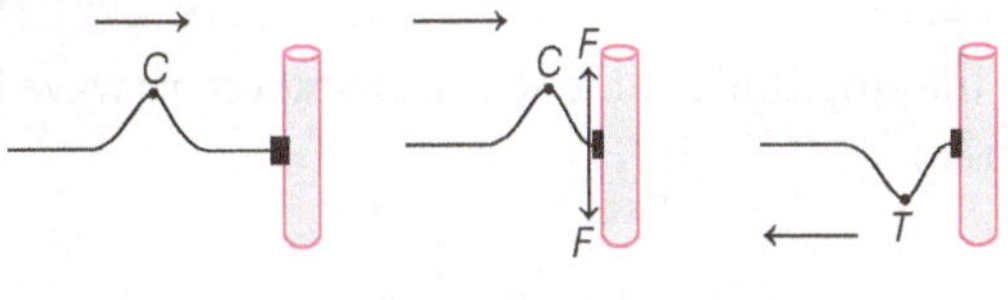

At the rigid boundary, the net displacement is zero.

Reflection from Free End

When a wave or pulse is reflected from a free end, then there is no change of phase. Due to reflection from free end, crest (C) reflects as crest (C) and trough (T) reflects as trough (T) as shown below.

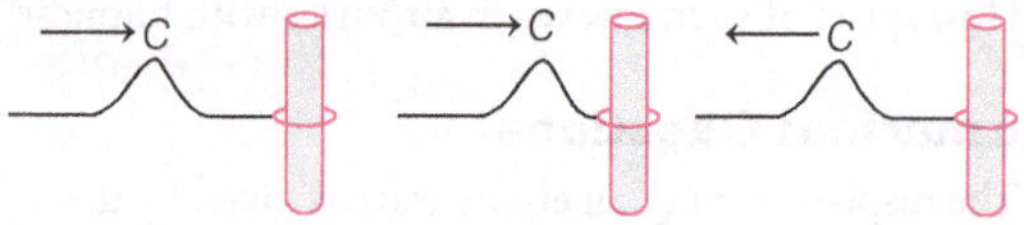

Equation

Let the incident travelling wave,

$$y(x, t) = A \sin(kx - \omega t)$$

At the rigid boundary, the reflected wave is given by

$$y_r(x, t) = A \sin(kx - \omega t + \pi)$$
$$= -A \sin(kx - \omega t)$$

At an open boundary, the reflected wave is given by

$$y_r(x, t) = A \sin(kx - \omega t + 0)$$
$$= A \sin(kx - \omega t)$$

At the rigid boundary, $y' = y + y_r = 0$ at all times.

Standing or Stationary Waves

If two waves of same type having same amplitude and same frequency/wavelength, travelling with same speed in opposite directions along a straight line, their superposition gives rise to a new type of wave called standing or stationary wave.

The resultant waves do not propagate in any direction, there is no transfer of energy in the medium.

Equation of Standing Wave

Consider incident (y_1) and reflected (y_2) wave equations as given below.

$y_1(x, t) = A \sin(kx - \omega t)$ (for wave along +ve X-axis)

$y_2(x, t) = A \sin(kx + \omega t)$ (for wave along –ve X-axis)

Resultant wave, $y(x, t) = y_1(x, t) + y_2(x, t)$

$$= A[\sin(kx - \omega t) + \sin(kx + \omega t)]$$

$$\boxed{\text{Net resultant wave, } y(x, t) = 2A \sin kx \cos \omega t}$$

Here, the amplitude of the standing/stationary wave is $2A \sin kx$.

Node and Anti-node

The points of minimum amplitude are called **nodes,** whereas the points of maximum amplitudes are called **anti-nodes.**

- The distance between two successive nodes or anti-nodes is $\dfrac{\lambda}{2}$.
- The distance between a node and adjacent anti-node is $\dfrac{\lambda}{4}$.

Normal Modes

Stationary waves can oscillate at specific natural frequencies, rathers than any arbitrary frequencies, called normal modes of oscillation.

Now, let us determine these normal modes for a stretched string fixed at both ends.

From above equation for **nodes,** the amplitude is zero for values of kx that give $\sin kx = 0$

$\sin kx = 0 \Rightarrow kx = n\pi$ where, $n = 0, 1, 2, 3, 4, \ldots$

$$\Rightarrow \boxed{\text{For nodes, } x = \frac{n\pi}{k}}$$

$$x = \frac{n\pi}{2\pi/\lambda} = \frac{n\lambda}{2} \text{ where, } n = 0, 1, 2, 3 \ldots$$

For **anti-nodes,** the maximum value of amplitude is $2a$ which occurs for values of kx that give $|\sin kx| = 1$

$$\Rightarrow kx = \left(n + \frac{1}{2}\right)\pi;\ n = 0, 1, 2, 3 \ldots$$

$$\Rightarrow \boxed{\text{For anti-nodes, } x = (2n+1)\frac{\lambda}{4}}$$

$$\boxed{n = 0, 1, 2, \ldots} \quad \left(\because k = \frac{2\pi}{\lambda}\right)$$

Example 8 The two individual wave functions are $_1$ = (5 cm) sin (4x – t) and $_2$ = (5 cm) sin (4x + t) where, x and y are in centimetres. Find out the maximum displacement of the motion at x = 2.0 cm. Also, find the positions of nodes and anti-nodes.

Sol. Given, $y_1 = (5 \text{ cm}) \sin(4x - t)$

$$y_2 = (5 \text{ cm}) \sin(4x + t)$$

The resulting wave $y = (2A \sin kx) \cos \omega t$

Now, compare the given equation.

$$y_1 = (5\text{ cm})\sin(4x - t) \text{ with}$$
$$y_1 = A\sin(kx - \omega t).$$
$$A = 5\text{ cm}, k = 4 \text{ and } \omega = 1\text{ rad/s}$$
$$y = (2A\sin kx)\cos\omega t$$
$$y = (10\sin 4x)\cos t$$

The maximum displacement of the motion at position $x = 2.0$ cm

$$y_{max} = 10\sin 4x|_{x=2.0}$$
$$= 10\sin(4\times 2) = 10\sin(8\text{ rad})$$
$$y_{max} = 9.89\text{ cm}$$

The wavelength can be determined by using the relation between wavelength and wave number.

$$k = \frac{2\pi}{\lambda} = 4$$
$$\Rightarrow \quad \lambda = \frac{2\pi}{4} = \frac{\pi}{2}\text{ cm}$$

Nodes at $x = \frac{n\lambda}{2} = n\times\left(\frac{\pi}{4}\right)$ cm,

where, $n = 0, 1, 2, \ldots$

Anti-nodes at $x = (2n+1)\frac{\lambda}{4}$

$$= (2n+1)\times\left(\frac{\pi}{8}\right)\text{ cm},$$

where $n = 0, 1, 2, \ldots$

Vibration of String Fixed at Both Ends

When a string is fixed at both ends, transverse standing waves are formed. The frequency of vibration is given by

$$\nu = \frac{nv}{2L} \quad \text{for } n = 1, 2, 3, \ldots$$

Here, v is the speed of the wave.

Modes of Vibration

The manner in which the string vibrates and gives rise to a standing wave is known as mode of vibration of the string.

- The mode of vibration in which string will vibrate in one segment or the lowest possible natural frequency is called **fundamental mode** or **first harmonic.**

For first mode, $n = 1 \Rightarrow \nu_1 = \frac{v}{2L}$ (first harmonic)

- The mode of vibration in which string will vibrate in two segments is called **second harmonic** or **first overtone.**

For second mode, $n = 2 \Rightarrow \nu_2 = \frac{2v}{2L} = 2\nu_1$ (second harmonic or first overtone)

- For third mode, $n = 3 \Rightarrow \nu_3 = \frac{3v}{2L} = 3\nu_1$ (third harmonic or second overtone)

Figure below shows the first four harmonics of a stretched string fixed at both ends

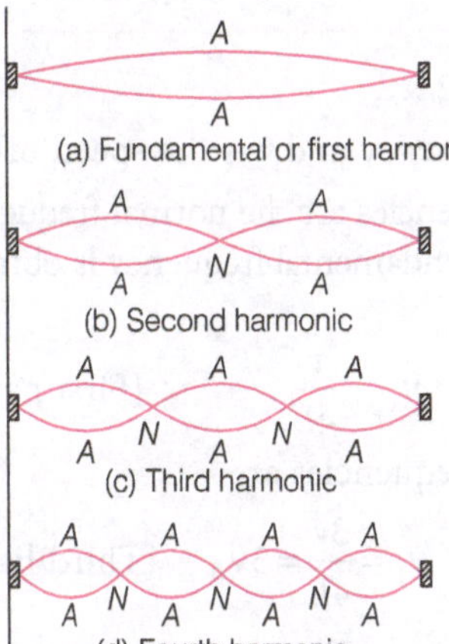

(a) Fundamental or first harmonic
(b) Second harmonic
(c) Third harmonic
(d) Fourth harmonic

> **Harmonics** The frequencies which are integral multiples of the fundamental frequency are called harmonics.
>
> **Overtones** The harmonics other than the first or fundamental note which are actually produced by the instrument are called overtones.
>
> All harmonics are overtones but all overtones are not harmonics.

Example 9. A guitar string is 100 cm long and has a fundamental frequency of 125 Hz. Where should it be pressed to produce a fundamental frequency of 200 Hz ?

Sol. Fundamental frequency of a string fixed at both end is

$$\nu = \frac{v}{2L}$$
$$\nu = \frac{1}{2L}\sqrt{\frac{T}{\mu}} \qquad \left[\because v = \sqrt{\frac{T}{\mu}}\right]$$

As T and μ are fixed

$$\frac{\nu_1}{\nu_2} = \frac{L_2}{L_1}$$
$$\Rightarrow \quad L_2 = \frac{\nu_1}{\nu_2}L_1$$
$$\Rightarrow \quad L_2 = \frac{125\text{ Hz}}{200\text{ Hz}}\times 100$$
$$= \frac{125}{2} = 62.5\text{ cm}$$

Vibration of a String Fixed at one End

If one end of the string is fixed, transverse stationary waves are formed. **Anti-node will be formed at the free end and node at the fixed end.** The frequency of vibration for nth mode is given by

$$\text{Frequency of the vibration, } \nu_n = \frac{(2n+1)}{4L} v$$

where, $n = 0, 1, 2 \ldots\ldots$.

where, ν is frequency and v is the speed of the wave.

The above frequencies are the normal frequencies of vibration. The fundamental frequency is obtained when $n = 0$.

$$\nu_0 = \frac{v}{4L} \qquad \text{[First harmonic]}$$

The overtone frequencies are

$$\nu_1 = \frac{3v}{4L} = 3\nu_0 \qquad \text{[Third harmonic]}$$

$$\nu_2 = \frac{5v}{4L} = 5\nu_0 \qquad \text{[Fifth harmonic]}$$

$$\nu_3 = \frac{7v}{4L} = 7\nu_0 \qquad \text{[Seventh harmonic]}$$

$\nu_0 : \nu_1 : \nu_2 : \nu_3 \ldots = 1:3:5:7:\ldots$

Here, we see that only odd harmonics are present. (i.e. contains odd multiples of the fundamental frequency).

The figure given below shows shapes of the string.

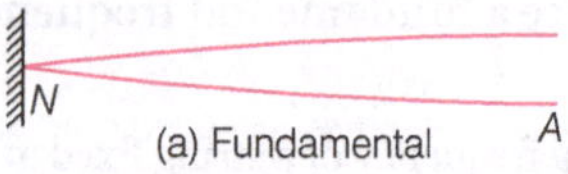

(a) Fundamental

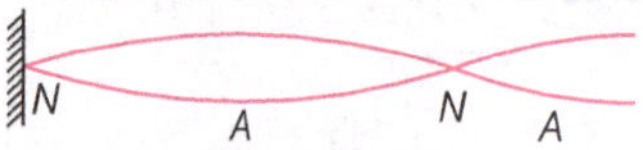

(b) First overtone

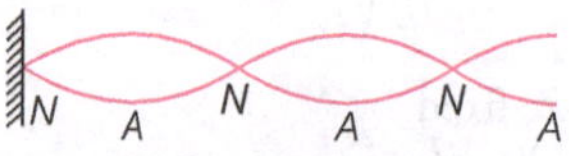

(c) Second overtone

Laws of Transverse Vibration of String

- For a given string under a tension (T), the frequency of the vibrating string is inversely proportional to the vibrating length (L) of the string.

  i.e. $\nu \propto \frac{1}{L}$

- The frequency of the uniform string of given length is proportional to square root of tension (T) in the string

  i.e. $\nu \propto \sqrt{T}$

- For a given vibrating length and tension of the string, the frequency of the vibrating string is inversely proportional to the square root of the mass per unit length of the string.

  i.e. $\nu \propto \frac{1}{\sqrt{\mu}}$

- The fundamental frequency of a vibrating string is determined by a device known as **sonometer.**
- The laws of vibration of a string are also verified by using sonometer.

Example 10. **A 50 cm long wire of mass 20 g supports a mass of 1.6 kg as shown in figure. Find the fundamental frequency of the portion of the string between the wall and the pulley. Take, $g = 10 \text{ m/s}^2$.**

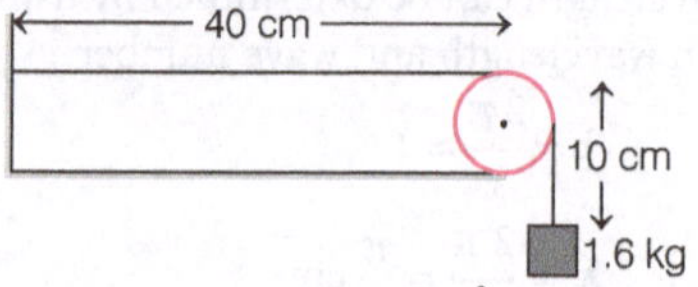

Sol. Here, mass/length, $m = \frac{20 \times 10^{-3}}{50/100} = 0.04 \text{ kg/m}$

$$T = 1.6 \text{ kg} = 1.6 \times 10 \text{ N} = 16 \text{ N}$$

Length that vibrates, $L = 50 - 10 = 40 \text{ cm} = 0.4 \text{ m}$

$$\therefore \nu = \frac{1}{2L}\sqrt{\frac{T}{m}} = \frac{1}{2 \times 0.4}\sqrt{\frac{16}{0.04}} = \frac{20}{0.8} = 25 \text{ Hz}$$

Example 11. **Two identical wires of length L and 2L vibrate with fundamental frequencies 100 Hz and 150 Hz, respectively. What is the ratio of their tensions?**

Sol. Let, $\mu_1 = \mu_2 = \mu \Rightarrow \nu_1 = 100 = \frac{1}{2L}\sqrt{\frac{T_1}{\mu}}$

$$\nu_2 = 150 = \frac{1}{2(2L)}\sqrt{\frac{T_2}{\mu}} \Rightarrow \frac{\nu_1}{\nu_2} = \frac{100}{150} = 2\sqrt{\frac{T_1}{T_2}}$$

$$\frac{T_1}{T_2} = \left(\frac{1}{3}\right)^2 = \frac{1}{9} \Rightarrow T_2 = 9\,T_1$$

14.4 Vibrations of Air Column

Organ pipe is the simplest musical instrument in which sound is produced by setting an air column into vibrations. Longitudinal stationary waves are formed on account of superposition of incident and reflected longitudinal waves.

Closed Organ Pipe

When an organ pipe is closed at one end, longitudinal stationary waves are formed. The frequency of the waves in nth mode is given by

$\Rightarrow$ Frequency, $\nu_n = (2n+1)\dfrac{v}{4L}$; $n = 0, 1, 2, 3, \ldots$

For fundamental frequency, $n = 0$ and $\nu_0 = \dfrac{v}{4L}$

The higher frequencies are odd harmonics i.e. $\dfrac{3v}{4L}, \dfrac{5v}{4L}$, etc.

Thus, in a closed end pipe, only odd harmonics are present.

Figure below shows odd harmonics of air column with one end closed and the other is open.

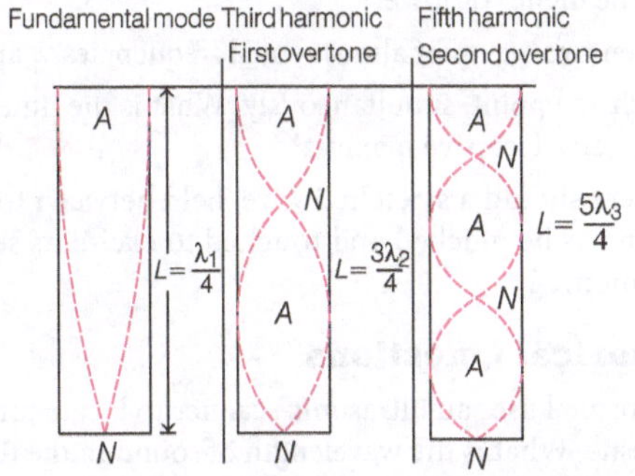

- If the external frequency is close to one of the natural frequencies, the system is said to be in **resonance**.
- The standing waves in closed organ pipe is similar to the standing wave on a string fixed at one end.

Open Organ Pipe

For a pipe opened at both ends, each (i.e. an open organ pipe) end is an anti-node. It is then easily seen that an open air column at both ends generates all harmonics. The equation for the frequency will be same as that of string fixed at both ends.

Frequency, $\nu_n = \dfrac{nv}{2L}$ for $n = 1, 2, 3, \ldots$

At both ends, anti-nodes will present and nodes will be alternate to anti-nodes. The diagram shows the vibration in both end open organ pipe.

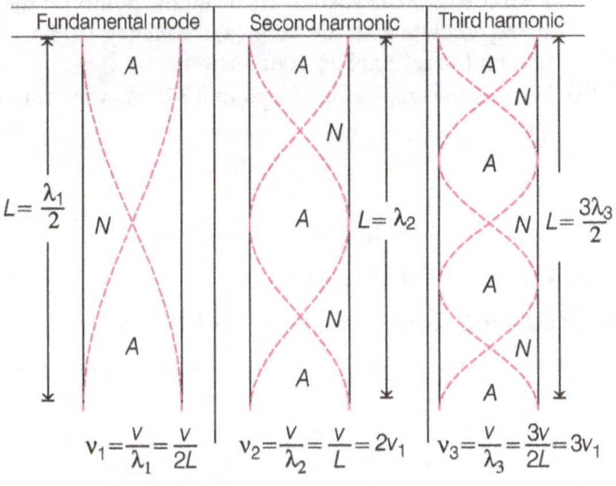

$\Rightarrow$ $\nu_1 : \nu_2 : \nu_3 : \ldots = 1 : 2 : 3 : \ldots$

- The sound produced by open organ pipe is more shriller than that produced by closed organ pipe.
- The quality of sound produced by an open organ pipe is better than that produced by the closed organ pipe.

Example 12. **A pipe 30.0 cm long is opened at both ends. Which harmonic mode of the pipe resonates with a 1.1 kHz source? Will resonance with the same source be observed, if one end of the pipe is closed? Take the speed of sound in air as 330 ms^{-1}.** NCERT

Sol. Here, $L = 30.0$ cm $= 0.3$ m

Let nth harmonic of open pipe resonate with 1·1 kHz source,

i.e. $\nu_n = 1.1$ kHz $= 1100$ Hz

As, $\nu_n = \dfrac{nv}{2L}$

$\therefore \quad n = \dfrac{2L\nu_n}{v} = \dfrac{2 \times 0.30 \times 1100}{330} = 2$

i.e. 2nd harmonic resonates with open pipe.

If one end of pipe is closed, its fundamental frequency can be put as $n = 0$ in $\nu = (2n+1)\dfrac{v}{4L}$

$$\nu_1 = \frac{v}{4L} = \frac{330}{4 \times 0.3} = 275 \text{ Hz}$$

As odd harmonics alone are produced in a closed organ pipe, therefore possible frequencies are $3\nu_1 = 3 \times 275 = 825$ Hz, $5\nu_1 = 5 \times 275 = 1375$ Hz and so on. As the source frequency is 1100 Hz, therefore, no resonance can occur when the pipe is closed at one end.

14.5 Beats

This phenomenon arises from interference of waves having nearly same frequencies. The periodic variation in the intensity of sound wave caused by the superposition of two sound waves of nearly same frequencies and amplitude travelling in the same direction is called beats.

One rise and one fall in the intensity of sound constitutes **one beat** and the number of beats per second is called **beat frequency**.

Beat frequency, $\nu_{beat} = \nu_1 - \nu_2$.

e.g. Suppose ν_A is the known frequency of tuning fork A and ν_B is the unknown frequency of tuning fork B. When both tuning forks A and B are sounded together, they produce beats of frequency ν, then $\nu_B = \nu_A \pm \nu$.

- If B is loaded with wax, its frequency decreases i.e. $\nu_B = \nu_A - \nu$.
- If B is filled with wax, its frequency increases i.e. $\nu_B = \nu_A + \nu$.

Note • The difference in frequencies of two sources must be less than 10 Hz to produce beats.
• As the tuning fork is loaded with wax, there will be decrease in the frequency. In case of filing, the frequency increases.

Example 13. **Two sitar strings A and B playing the note 'Dha' are slightly out of tune and produce beats of frequency 5 Hz. The tension of string B is slightly increased and the beat frequency is found to decrease to 3 Hz. What is the original frequency of B, if the frequency of A is 427 Hz?** NCERT

Sol. Here, frequency of $A = 427$ Hz

As number of beats/second $(m) = 5$ Hz

$\therefore$ Possible frequencies of B are (427 ± 5) Hz $= 432$ Hz or 422 Hz.

When tension of B is increased, its frequency increases. Number of beats/s decreases to 3.
Therefore, m is negative.
Hence, original frequency of $B = 427 - 5 = 422$ Hz.

Example 14. **Consider the two identical piano strings, each tuned exactly to the 420 Hz. The tension in any one of the strings is increased by 2.0%. If they are now struck, what is the beat frequency between the fundamentals of the two strings? Take, length of the strings = 65 cm.**

Sol. If ν_1, v_1, T_1 and ν_2, v_2, T_2 are the frequencies, velocity and tension in the first and second strings respectively, then

$$\frac{\nu_2}{\nu_1} = \frac{v_2/2L}{v_1/2L} = \frac{v_2}{v_1}$$

$$\Rightarrow \quad \frac{\nu_2}{\nu_1} = \frac{\sqrt{T_2/\mu}}{\sqrt{T_1/\mu}} = \sqrt{\frac{T_2}{T_1}}$$

Given that the tension in one string is 2.0% larger than the other

i.e. $$T_2 = T_1 + \frac{2}{100} T_1 = 1.02\, T_1$$

The ratio of frequencies, $$\frac{\nu_2}{\nu_1} = \sqrt{\frac{1.02\, T_1}{T_1}} = 1.01 \text{ Hz}$$

Now, solve for the frequency of the tightened string.

$$\nu_2 = 1.01\, \nu_1 = 1.01 \times 420 = 424.2 \text{ Hz}$$

[Given, $\nu_1 = 420$ Hz]

Thus, the beat frequency is

$$\nu_{beat} = \nu_2 - \nu_1 = 424.2 - 420 = 4.2 \text{ Hz}$$

Quick Test 2

Conceptual Questions

1. In a hot summer day, pitch of an organ pipe will be higher or lower?

2. When two waves of almost equal frequencies ν_1 and ν_2 reach at a point, simultaneously. What is the time interval between successive maxima? NCERT Exemplar

3. Where should a stretched wire, held between to fixed supports be plucked and touched to excite its second harmonic ?

Numerical Questions

4 A hospital uses an ultrasonic scanner to locate tumours in a tissue. What is the wavelength of sound in the tissue in which the speed of sound is 1.7 kms^{-1}? The operating frequency of the scanner is 4.2 MHz. NCERT

5. A metre-long tube open at one end, with a movable piston at the other end, shows resonance with a fixed frequency source (a tuning fork of frequency 340 Hz) when the tube length is 25.5 cm or 79.3 cm. Estimate the speed of sound in air at the temperature of the experiment. The edge effects may be neglected. NCERT

6. A tuning fork A, marked 512 Hz, produces 5 beats per second, where sounded with another unmarked tuning fork B. If B is loaded with wax, the number of beats is again 5 per second. What is the frequency of the tuning fork B when not loaded? NCERT Exemplar

7. A steel rod 100 cm long is clamped at its middle. The fundamental frequency of longitudinal vibrations of the rod are given to be 2.53 kHz. What is the speed of sound in steel? NCERT

8. (i) For the wave on a string described by $y = 0.06 \sin(2\pi/3) x \cos(120\pi t)$, do all the points on the string oscillate with the same (a) frequency, (b) phase, (c) amplitude? Explain your answers.
(ii) What is the amplitude of a point 0.375 m away from one end? NCERT

Answers

4. 4.04×10^{-4} m *5.* 346.8ms^{-1} *6.* 517 Hz
7. 5.06 km/s *8.* (ii) 0.042

For Solutions, See QR Code on Pg. 483

Mind Map

Waves

Transverse Waves

When particle of a medium vibrate perpendicular to the direction of propagation of wave, the wave is called transverse wave.

Example Waves produced in strings of musical instrument, visible light, etc.

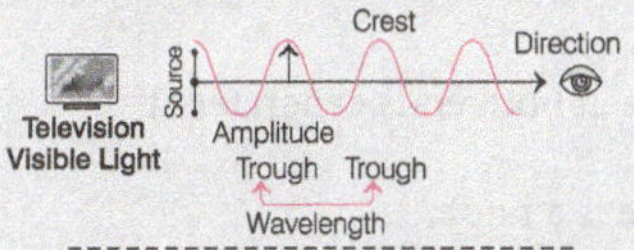

- **Speed of a transverse wave,** $v=\sqrt{\frac{T}{\mu}}$
  Here, $T=$ tension in string

Longitudinal Waves

When particles of medium vibrate in the direction of propagation of wave, the wave is called longitudinal wave.

Examples Spring waves, sound waves, etc.

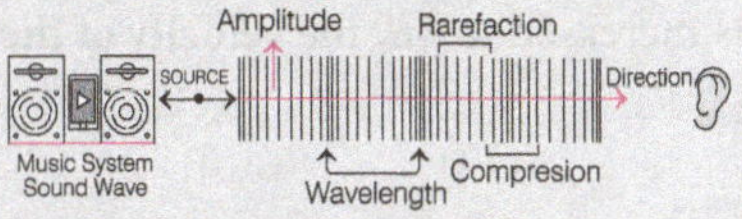

- **Speed of a longitudinal wave (sound wave),**

$$v=\sqrt{B/\rho}=\sqrt{\frac{Y}{\rho}}$$

Here,
$Y=$ Young's modulus of the material,
$B=$ Bulk modulus and
$\rho=$ Density of the material

Principle of Superposition

It states that when two or more waves overlap in a medium, the resulting displacement at any point is the algebraic sum of the displacement caused by the individual waves at that point

Standing Waves

Standing waves is a stationary wave pattern formed by the interference of two waves travelling in opposite directions.

Reflection of a Waves

Reflection of a wave occurs when a wave encounters a boundary and bounces back into the original medium without changing its frequency.

Beats

Beats are the periodic variations in sound intensity caused by the interference of two waves of slightly different frequencies, resulting in alternating constructive and destructive interference

Mechanical Waves

- The waves which require medium for their propagation are called mechanical or elastic waves.
  Example Sound waves, seismic waves, water waves, etc.

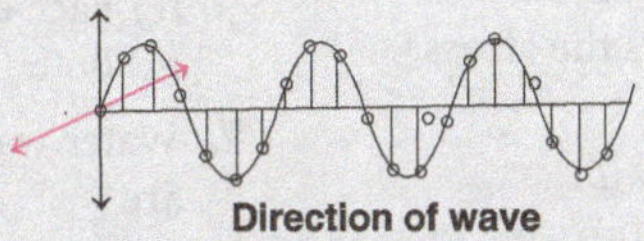

Direction of wave

Electromagnetic Wave

These type of waves travel in the form of oscillating electric and magnetic fields are called electromagnetic waves.

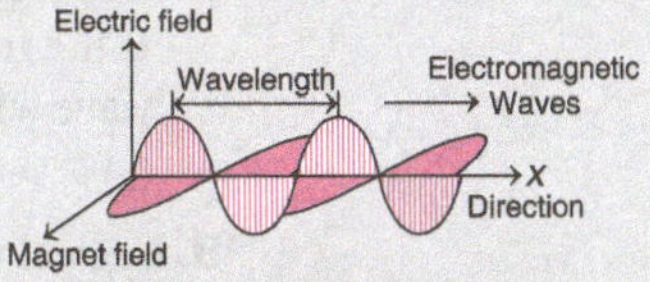

Matter waves

Matter waves are associated with microscopic particles i.e. electrons, protons and other fundemental particles.
It represent wave like nature of moving particle.

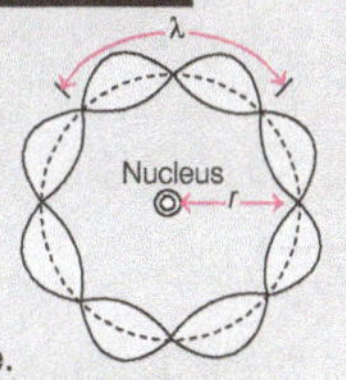

Vibration in an Air Column

Vibration in an air column occurs when sound waves resonate within a hollow tube, creating standing waves with nodes and antinodes determined by the tube's length and whether its ends are open or closed.

Open Organ Pipe

- For a pipe opened at both ends, each end is an anti-node.

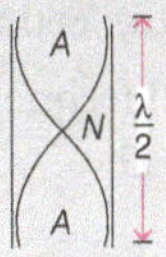

- Frequency, $f=n\frac{v}{2L}$
- **Fundamental Tone**
  If we blow air on one end of an organ pipe gently, then an anti-node is formed on both ends in between them.
  $L=\frac{\lambda}{2}$ or $\lambda=2L$, $f=\frac{v}{\lambda}=\frac{v}{2L}$

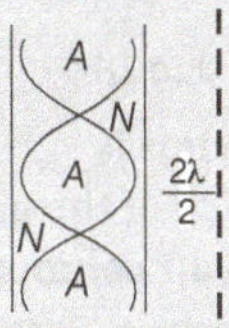

- **First Overtone**
  $L=2\frac{\lambda}{2}$ or $\lambda=L$, $f=\frac{v}{\lambda}=\frac{v}{L}$

Vibration in String

A standing wave in a string is formed when two waves of the same frequency and amplitude travel in opposite directions, creating fixed nodes and antinodes along the string.

- A stretched string having length L fixed at both ends, then boundary conditions.
  $L=\frac{n\lambda}{2}$, $n=1, 2, 3....$

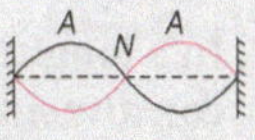

- Possible wavelength,
  $\lambda=\frac{2L}{n}$, $n=1, 2, 3....$
- Frequencies, $f=\frac{nv}{2L}$, $n=1, 2, 3....$

Modes of Vibration

The manner in which the string vibrates and give rise to a standing wave is known as mode of vibration of the string.

$$L=\frac{n\lambda}{2},\ f=\frac{nv}{2L}$$

- **First Mode of Vibration** The mode of vibration in which string will vibrate in one segment or the lowest possible natural frequency (fundamental mode),
  $L=\frac{\lambda}{2}$ and $f=\frac{v}{2L}$

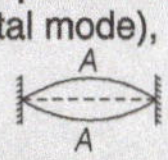

- **Second Mode of Vibration** The mode of vibration in which string will vibrate in two segments called second harmonic.
  $L=\lambda$ and $f=\frac{v}{L}$

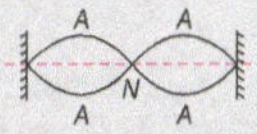

Normal Modes

- Normal modes of oscillation is the set of natural frequencies at which a system vibrates.
- Point having zero amplitude are called **nodes** and the point having largest amplitude are known as **anti-nodes**.

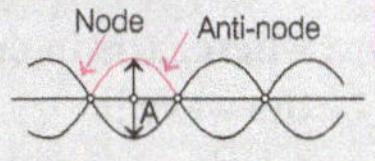

- **For Node,** $x=\frac{n\pi}{k}$
  $x=n\lambda/2$
- **For Anti-node,** $x=(2n+1)\frac{\lambda}{4}$

Closed Organ Pipe

- Frequency, $f=(2n+1)\frac{v}{4L}$
  $n=0, 1, 2, 3 ...$
- **Fundamental Tone** If we blow at open mouth of organ pipe gently, then the lowest frequency is produced.
  $L=\frac{\lambda}{4}$ or $\lambda=4L$ or $f=\frac{v}{4L}$

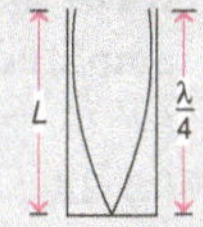

- **First Over Tone**
  $L=\frac{3\lambda}{4}$ or $\lambda=\frac{4L}{3}$

∴ Frequency of the node produced,
$f=\frac{3v}{4L}$

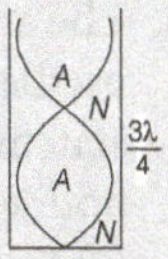

- It is also called **third harmonics.**

EXAM PATTERN QUESTIONS

Objective Type Questions

Multiple Choice Questions (MCQs)

1. **In a longitudinal wave, the elastic property of the constituents of the medium that determines the stress under compressional strain is**

(a) Young's modulus (*Y*) (b) bulk modulus (*B*)
(c) shear modulus (*S*) (d) Either (b) or (c)

2. **A student plotted the following four graphs representing the variation of velocity of sound in a gas with the pressure p at constant temperature. Which one is correct?**

(a) 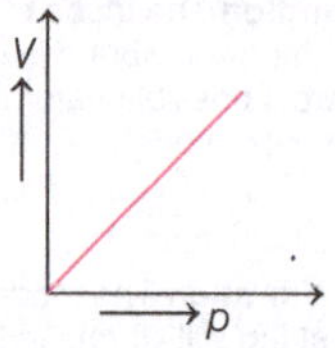

(b) 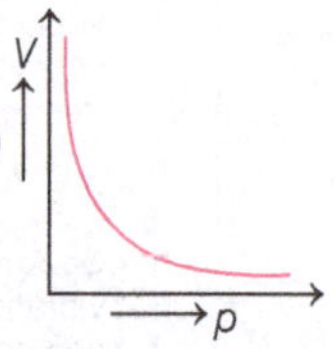

(c) 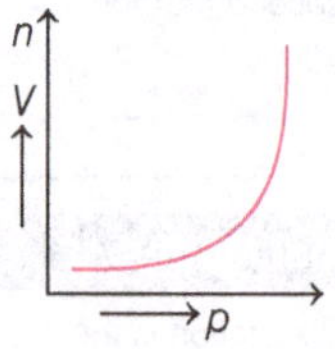

(d) 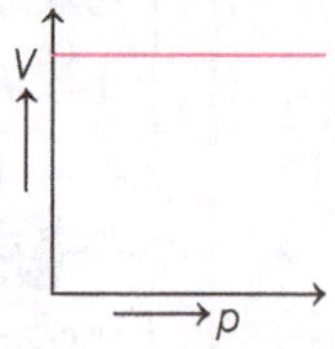

3. **A wave equation is given by**

$$y = 4\sin\left[\pi\left(\frac{t}{5} - \frac{x}{9} + \frac{1}{6}\right)\right]$$

where, x is in cm and t is in second. The wavelength of the wave is

(a) 18 cm (b) 9 cm (c) 36 cm (d) 6 cm

4. **The equation of a progressive wave can be given by $y = 15\sin(660\pi t - 0.02\pi x)$ cm. The frequency of the wave is**

(a) 330 Hz (b) 342 Hz (c) 365 Hz (d) 660 Hz

5. **Two waves of equal amplitude A and equal frequency travel in the same direction in a medium. The amplitude of the resultant wave is**

(a) 0 (b) *A*
(c) 2*A* (d) between 0 to 2*A*

6. **The air column in a pipe open at both ends is oscillating with certain frequency. Which of the given statement(s) is/are correct for the open air column at both ends?** **Competency Based Que.**

(a) Each end of the pipe acts as an anti-node.
(b) An open air column at both ends generates all harmonics.
(c) Each end of the pipe is a node.
(d) Both (a) and (b)

7. **Water waves produced by a motorboat sailing in water are** **NCERT Exemplar**

(a) neither longitudinal nor transverse
(b) both longitudinal and transverse
(c) only longitudinal
(d) only transverse

8. **The frequency of a sound wave is n and its velocity is v. If the frequency is increased to 4n, the velocity of the wave will be**

(a) *v* (b) 2*v* (c) 4*v* (d) *v* / 4

9. **A steel wire has linear mass density 6.9×10^{-3} kg m^{-1}. If the wire is under a tension of 60 N, then the speed of the transverse waves on the wire is** **Competency Based Que.**

(a) 63 ms^{-1} (b) 75 ms^{-1} (c) 73 ms^{-1} (d) 93 ms^{-1}

10. **Let a wave $y(x, t) = a\sin(kx - \omega t)$ is reflected from an open boundary and then the incident and reflected waves overlaps. Then the amplitude of resultant wave is.** **Competency Based Que.**

(a) $2a\cos(kx)$ (b) $2a\sin(kx)$
(c) $2a\sin\left(\frac{kx}{2}\right)$ (d) $a\sin(kx)$

11. **At nodes in stationary waves,**

(a) change in pressure and density are maximum
(b) change in pressure and density are minimum
(c) strain is zero
(d) energy is maximum

12. **Following two wave trains are approaching each other.**

$$y_1 = a\sin 2000\,\pi t$$
$$y_2 = a\sin 2008\,\pi t$$

The number of beats heard per second is/are

(a) 8 (b) 4 (c) 1 (d) zero

13. **The speed of a wave in a medium is 760 m/s. If 3600 waves are passing through a point, in the medium in 2 min, then its wavelength is**

(a) 13.8 m (b) 25.3 m
(c) 41.5 m (d) 57.2 m

14. A wave of frequency 500 Hz has velocity 360 m/sec. The distance between two nearest points 60° out of phase, is
(a) 0.6 cm (b) 12 cm (c) 60 cm (d) 120 cm

15. A sound wave travels in air with a speed of 340 m/s. If the wavelength of the wave is 2 m, what is the frequency of the wave?
(a) 170 Hz (b) 340 Hz (c) 680 Hz (d) 85 Hz

16. A tuning fork produces sound waves in air at 20°C. The speed of sound at this temperature is 343 m/s. When the air temperature increases to 30°C, what will be the percentage increase in the frequency if the speed of sound is now 349 m/s ?
(a) 0% (b) 1.75% (c) 1.6% (d) 2.0%

17. A standing wave is formed on a string of length 1.2 m fixed at both ends. The wave speed is 240 m/s and the frequency of oscillation is 100 Hz. How many loops (antinodes) are formed on the string?
(a) 1 (b) 2 (c) 3 (d) 4

18. Match the Column I with Column II.

Column I		Column II
1. Resonance	P.	Stationary wave with nodes and antinodes
2. Principle of superposition	Q.	Amplitudes increases when frequency matches natural frequency
3. Beats	R.	Frequency difference between two waves
4. Standing wave	S.	Resultant displacement is the sum of individual displacements

(a) 1 → Q, 2 → S, 3 → R, 4 → P
(b) 1 → Q, 2 → R, 3 → S, 4 → P
(c) 1 → P, 2 → Q, 3 → R, 4 → S
(d) 1 → R, 2 → Q, 3 → P, 4 → S

19. Match Column I with Column II.

Column I		Column II
1. Wave number (k)	P.	Energy carried by a wave
2. Phase difference	Q.	$\frac{2\pi}{\lambda}$
3. Intensity of wave	R.	Determines constructive or destructive interference
4. Transverse wave in a string	S.	Depends on tension and linear mass density
5. Fundamental frequency of a string	T.	$\frac{1}{2L}\sqrt{\frac{T}{\mu}}$

(a) 1 → P, 2 → Q, 3 → R, 4 → S, 5 → T
(b) 1 → Q, 2 → R, 3 → P, 4 → S, 5 → T
(c) 1 → R, 2 → Q, 3 → P, 4 → S, 5 → T
(d) 1 → T, 2 → S, 3 → R, 4 → P, 5 → Q

Assertion and Reason

Directions (Q.Nos. 20-27) *In the following questions, two statements are given- one labelled Assertion (A) and the other labelled Reason (R). Select the correct answer to these questions from the codes (a), (b), (c) and (d) as given below.*
(a) Both Assertion and Reason are true and Reason is the correct explanation of Assertion.
(b) Both Assertion and Reason are true but Reason is not the correct explanation of Assertion.
(c) Assertion is true but Reason is false.
(d) Assertion is false but Reason is true.

20. Assertion (A) Sound waves cannot propagate through vacuum but light waves can.
Reason (R) Sound waves cannot be polarised but light waves can be polarised.

21. Assertion (A) Transverse waves are possible in solids and strings (under tension) but not in fluids.
Reason (R) Solids and strings have no zero shear modulus, i.e. they can sustain shearing stress but fluids yield to shearing stress and hence they do not have shape of their own.

22. Assertion (A) Longitudinal waves can be propagated through solids and fluids both.
Reason (R) Solids as well as fluids have non-zero bulk modulus, i.e. they can sustain compressive stress and longitudinal waves involve compressive stress (pressure).

23. Assertion (A) Speed of sound is more in liquids and solids than gases.
Reason (R) Liquids and solids have higher densities than gases.

24. Assertion (A) Compression and rarefaction involves change in density and pressure.
Reason (R) When particles are compressed, density of medium increases and when they are rarefied, density of medium decreases.

25. Assertion (A) It is not possible to have interference between the waves produced by two violins.
Reason (R) For interference of two waves, the phase difference between the wave must remain constant.

26. Assertion (A) In a stationary wave, nodes are points of maximum displacement.
Reason (R) At the nodes, destructive interference of the two waves occurs.

27. **Assertion (A)** The speed of a transverse wave on a string increases when the tension in the string is increased.
Reason (R) The speed of a wave in a medium is inversely proportional to the square root of the density of the medium.

Case Based Questions

Directions (Q.Nos. 28-29) *These questions are case study based questions. Read the following paragraph and answer the questions on the basis of same.*

28. **Ultrasound is an example of longitudinal wave having high frequency. These types of waves are the one in which the individual particles of the medium execute simple harmonic motion about their mean positions along the direction of propagation of the wave.**

Ultrasound is used to investigate the internal organs of a human body as it can penetrate into matter.

Figure below shows how ultrasound is used to produce an image of the heart.

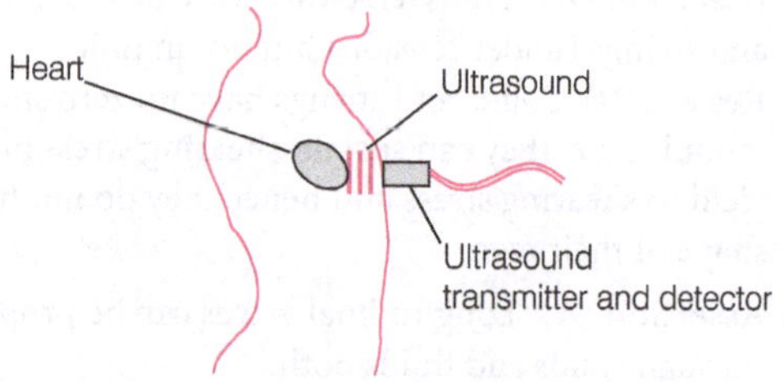

(i) What is the frequency range of ultrasound?
(a) 20 Hz (b) 20 kHz
(c) Less than 20 Hz (d) More than 20 kHz

(ii) Which of these can produce ultrasound?
(a) Bats (b) Dolphins
(c) Porpoises (d) All of these

(iii) When ultrasound wave passes through a body, then the particles in the body have motion in
(a) forward and backward direction
(b) parallel to direction of motion
(c) perpendicular to direction of motion
(d) Both (a) and (b)

(iv) There are small bubbles of gas in a body. When the body is kept in the path of ultrasound, then
(a) bubbles gets expanded (b) bubbles gets contracted
(c) Both (a) and (b) (d) No change occur

Or **The ultrasound of wavelength 1.2×10^{-3} m has a speed of 1500 m/s in a human body. The frequency is**
(a) 1.25×10^{-6} Hz (b) 1.25×10^{6} Hz
(c) 1.2×10^{-4} Hz (d) 2×10^{6} Hz

29. **Organ pipes are the musical instruments which are used for producing musical sound by blowing air into the pipe. Longitudinal stationary waves are formed on account of superimposition of incident and reflected longitudinal waves.**

Equation of standing wave $y = 2a \cos \frac{2\pi vt}{\lambda} \sin \frac{2\pi x}{\lambda}$

Frequency of vibration, $n = \frac{v}{\lambda}$

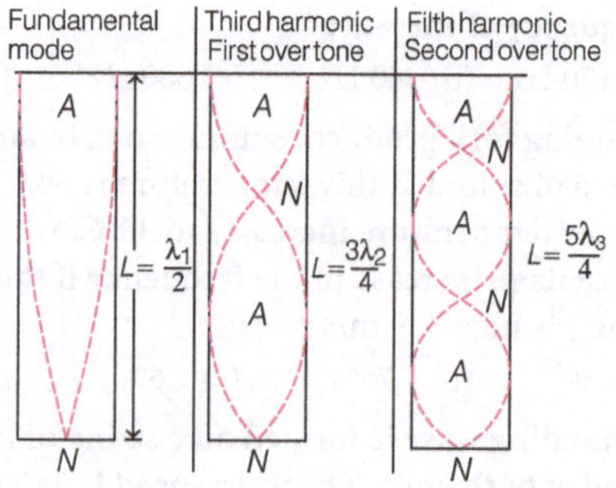

(i) A tube closed at one end and containing air is excited. It produces the fundamental note of frequency 512 Hz. If the same tube is open at both the ends, the fundamental frequency that can be produced is
(a) 1024 Hz (b) 512 Hz
(c) 256 Hz (d) 128 Hz

(ii) A closed pipe and an open pipe have their first overtone identical in frequency. Their lengths are in the ratio
(a) 1 : 2 (b) 2 : 3
(c) 3 : 4 (d) 4 : 5

(iii) The first overtone in a closed pipe has a frequency
(a) same as the fundamental frequency of an open tube of same length
(b) twice the fundamental frequency of an open tube of same length
(c) same as that of the first overtone of an open tube of same length
(d) None of the above

(iv) An empty vessel is partially filled with water, then the frequency of vibration of air column in the vessel
(a) remains same (b) decrease
(c) increases
(d) first increases, then decreases

Or **It is desired to increase the fundamental resonance frequency in a tube which is closed at one end. This can not be achieved by**
(a) replacing the air in the tube by hydrogen gas
(b) increasing the length of the tube
(c) decreasing the length of the tube
(d) opening the closed end of the tube

Subjective Questions

Very Short Answer Type Questions

1. What are harmonics?

2. If an explosion takes place at the bottom of lake or sea, will the shock waves in water be longitudinal or transverse?

3. The formula for time period T for a loaded spring is

$$T = 2\pi\sqrt{\frac{\text{displacement}}{\text{acceleration}}}$$

Does the time period depend on length of the spring?

4. Why the shape of pulse is distorted during propagation in a dispersive medium?

Short Answer Type Questions

5. Two sources of intensities I and $4I$ produce interference. Find the intensity at points where phase difference be (i) zero (ii) $\pi/2$ (iii) π.

6. Show that when a string fixed at its two ends vibrates in 1 loop, 2 loops, 3 loops and 4 loops, the frequencies are in the ratio 1 : 2 : 3 : 4. **NCERT Exemplar**

7. What is the direction of oscillations of the particles of a medium through which (i) transverse and (ii) longitudinal wave is propagating?

8. State few important use of phenomenon of beats.

9. The displacement of particle in SHM may be given by $y = a\sin(\omega t + \phi)$ show that if the time t is increased by $\frac{2\pi}{\omega}$, the value of y remains the same.

10. In a sound wave, a displacement node is a pressure anti-node and *vice-versa.* Explain, why?

Long Answer Type Questions

11. A tuning fork of frequency 200 Hz is in resonance with a sonometer wire. How many beats will be heard if tension in the wire is increased by 2%? **Competency Based Que.**

12. If c is rms speed of molecules in a gas and v is the speed of sound waves in the gas, show that c/v is constant and independent of temperature for all diatomic gases. **NCERT Exemplar**

13. Explain, why (or how)

(i) bats can ascertain distances, directions, nature and sizes of the obstacles without any eyes? **[1]**

(ii) a violin note and sitar note may have the same frequency, yet we can distinguish between the two notes? **[1]**

(iii) solids can support both longitudinal and transverse waves but only longitudinal waves can propagate in gases? **[1]**

(iv) the shape of a pulse gets distorted during propagation in a dispersive medium? **NCERT [2]**

14. Use the formula, $v = \sqrt{\frac{\gamma p}{\rho}}$ to explain, why the speed of sound in air

(i) is independent of pressure? **[1]**

(ii) increases with temperature? **[2]**

(iii) increases with humidity? **[2] NCERT**

Numerical Problems

Progressive Waves

15. A progressive wave of frequency 500 Hz is travelling with a velocity of 360 m/s. How far apart are two points 60° out of phase ?

16. In the given progressive wave,

$$y = 5\sin(100\pi t - 0.4\pi x)$$

where, y and x are in metre and t is in seconds. What is the

(i) amplitude, **[1]** (ii) wavelength, **[1]**

(iii) frequency, **[1]** (iv) wave velocity and **[1]**

(v) particle velocity **NCERT Exemplar [1]**

17. Stationary waves are set up by the superposition of two waves given by $y_1 = 0.05\sin(5\pi t - x)$ and $y_2 = 0.05\sin(5\pi t + x)$, where x and y are in metre and t in second. Calculate the amplitude of a particle at a distance of $x = 1$ m.

18. A stone dropped from the top of a tower of height 300 m in high splashes into the water of a pond near the base of the tower. When is the splash heard at the top, given that the speed of sound in air is 340 ms^{-1}? (Take, $g = 9.8$ m s^{-2}) **NCERT**

19. Two tuning forks A and B give 5 beats/s. A resounds with a closed column of air 15 cm long and B with an open column of air 30.5 cm long.
Calculate their frequencies. Neglect end correction.

Stationary Waves in Strings and Pipes

20. Earthquakes generate sound waves inside the earth. Unlike a gas, the earth can experience both transverse (S) and longitudinal (P) sound waves. Typically the speed of S wave is about 4.0 kms^{-1} and that of P wave is 8.0 kms^{-1}. A seismograph records P and S waves from an earthquake. The first P wave arrives 4 min before the first S wave. Assuming the waves travel in straight line, at what distance does the earthquake occur? **NCERT**

21. One end of a long string of linear mass density 8.0×10^{-3} kg m^{-1} is connected to an electrically driven tuning fork of frequency 256 Hz. The other end passes over a pulley and is tied to a pan containing a mass of 90 kg. The pulley end absorbs all the incoming energy so that reflected waves at the end have negligible amplitude. At $t = 0$, the left end (fork end) of the string $x = 0$ has zero transverse displacement ($y = 0$) and is moving along positive y-direction. The amplitude of the wave is 5.0 cm. Write down the transverse displacement y as function of x and t that describes the wave on the string. **NCERT**

22. A transverse harmonic wave on a string is described by $y(x, t) = 3.0\sin(36t + 0.018x + \pi/4)$
Where, x and y are in cm and t in seconds. The positive direction of x is from left to right.

(i) Is this a travelling wave or a stationary wave? If it is travelling, what are the speed of its propagation? **[1½]**

(ii) What are its amplitude and frequency? **[1]**

(iii) What is the initial phase at the origin? **[1]**

(iv) What is the least distance between two successive crests in the wave? **NCERT [1½]**

23. A source of frequency 250Hz produces sound waves of wavelength 1.32 m in a gas at STP. Calculate the change in the wavelength, when temperature of the gas is 40°C.

24. For the harmonic travelling wave
$y = 2\cos 2\pi(10t - 0.0080x + 3.5)$ where, x and y are in cm and t is in second. What is the phase difference between the oscillatory motion at two points separated by a distance of

(i) 4 m (ii) 0.5 m (iii) $\frac{\lambda}{2}$ **[3]**

(iv) $\frac{3\lambda}{4}$ (at a given instant in time)? **[1]**

(v) What is the phase difference between the oscillation of a particle located at $x = 100$ cm, at $t = T$ s and $t = 5$ s? **NCERT Exemplar [1]**

25. The pattern of standing waves formed on a stretched string at two instants of time are shown in figure. The velocity of two waves superimposing to form stationary waves is 360 m/s and their frequencies are 256 Hz.

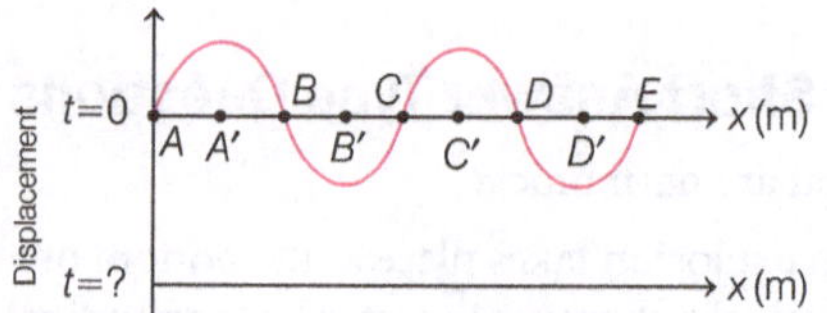

(i) Calculate the time at which the second curve is plotted. **[1]**

(ii) Mark nodes and anti-nodes on the curve. **[1]**

(iii) Calculate the distance between A' and C'. **NCERT Exemplar [1]**

26. The wave pattern on a stretched string is shown in figure. Interpret what kind of wave this is and find its wavelength?

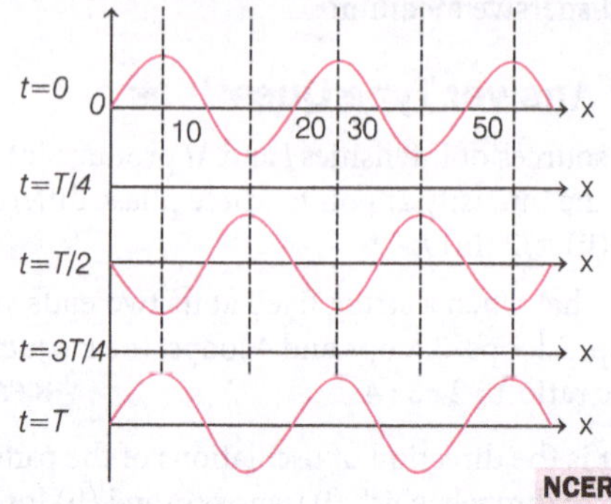

NCERT Exemplar

27. A pipe 20 cm long is closed at one end. Which harmonic mode of the pipe is resonantly excited by a 430 Hz source? Will the same source be in resonance with the pipe if both ends are open? (Speed of sound in air is 340 ms^{-1}) **NCERT**

28. A tuning fork vibrating with a frequency of 512 Hz is kept close to the open end of a tube filled with water shown in figure. The water level in the tube is gradually lowered. When the water level is 17 cm below the open end the maximum intensity of sound is heard.

If the room temperature is 20°C, then calculate

(i) speed of sound in air at room temperature. **[1]**

(ii) speed of sound in air at 0°C. **[1]**

(iii) If the water in the tube is replaced with mercury, will there be any difference in your observations? **NCERT Exemplar [1]**

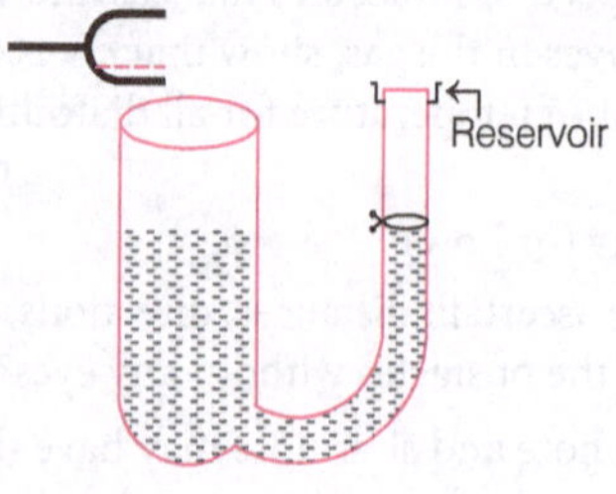

Hints & Solutions

Objective Type Questions

1. (b) 2. (d) 3. (a) 4. (a) 5. (d)
6. (d) 7. (b) 8. (a)

9. (d) Given, $\mu = 6.9 \times 10^{-3}$ kg/m

Tension, $T = 60$ N

The speed of wave on the wire is given by

$$v = \sqrt{\frac{T}{\mu}} = \sqrt{\frac{60\text{N}}{6.9\times10^{-3}\text{ kg m}^{-1}}}$$

$$= 93 \text{ m/s}$$

10. (b) We have,

$$y_1 = a\sin(kx - \omega t)$$
$$y_2 = a\sin(kx + \omega t)$$

From principle of superposition, standing wave equation is obtained as

$$y(x, t) = y_1 + y_2 = a[\sin(kx - \omega t) + \sin(kx + \omega t)]$$
$$= 2a\sin kx \cos \omega t \quad \text{...(i)}$$

On comparing Eq. (i) with

$$y(x, t) = A(x)\cos \omega t$$

Amplitude, $A(x) = 2a\sin(kx)$.

11. (b) 12. (b)

13. (b) Frequency of wave,

$$n = \frac{3600}{2\times60}\text{ Hz} \Rightarrow \lambda = \frac{v}{n} = \frac{760}{30} = 25.3 \text{ m}.$$

14. (b) The distance between two points i.e., path difference Δ between them is

$$\Delta = \frac{\lambda}{2\pi}\times\phi = \frac{\lambda}{2\pi}\times\frac{\pi}{3} = \frac{\lambda}{6} = \frac{v}{6n} \quad (\because v = n\lambda)$$

$$\Rightarrow \quad \Delta = \frac{360}{6\times500} = 0.12\text{ m} = 12\text{ cm}$$

15. (a) The relationship between speed, frequency and wavelength is

$$v = \lambda f$$

Here, $v = 340$ m/s and $\lambda = 2$ m

$$f = \frac{v}{\lambda} = \frac{340}{2} = 170 \text{ Hz}$$

16. (a) The frequency of a sound wave is given by $f = \frac{v}{\lambda}$.

The wavelength λ depends on the source and does not change with temperature.

Hence, the frequency will remain the same irrespective of changes in the speed of sound.

Percentage increases in frequency = 0%.

17. (a) The wavelength λ is given by

$$\lambda = \frac{v}{f} = \frac{240}{100} = 2.4 \text{ m}$$

For a standing wave, the condition for wavelength is $L = n\frac{\lambda}{2}$, where n is the number of loops.

Substituting $L = 1.2$ m and $\lambda = 2.4$ m

$$1.2 = n\frac{2.4}{2}, n = 1$$

18. (a) 1 → Q, 2 → S, 3 → R, 4 → P.

19. (b) 1 → Q, 2 → R, 3 → P, 4 → S, 5 → T.

20. (b) 21. (a) 22. (a) 23. (b) 24. (a)

25. (a) Since the initial phase difference between the two waves coming from different violins changes, therefore the waves produced by two different violins does not interfere because two waves interfere only when the phase difference between them remains constant throughout.

26. (d) Nodes are points of minimum displacement (not maximum) because they result from destructive interference. Hence, the Assertion is false, but the Reason is true.

27. (b) The speed v of a transverse wave on a string is given by $v = \sqrt{\frac{T}{\mu}}$, where T is the tension and μ is the linear mass density. As tension increases, speed increases. The Reason talks about wave speed in general but does not apply specifically to tension in a string. Hence, while both A and R are true, R is not the correct explanation of A.

28. (i)-(d), (ii)-(d), (iii)-(d), (iv)-(c) or (b)

29. (i) (a)Fundamental frequency of open pipe is double that of the closed pipe.

$$f_0 = 2f$$
$$f_0 = 2\times512 = 1024 \text{ Hz}$$

(ii) (c) If is given that

First overtone of closed pipe = First overtone of open pipe

$$\Rightarrow \quad 3\left(\frac{v}{4l_1}\right) = 2\left(\frac{v}{2l_2}\right)$$

where l_1 and l_2 are the lengths of closed and open organ pipes, hence $\frac{l_1}{l_2} = \frac{3}{4}$

(iii) (d) First overtone for closed pipe $= \frac{3v}{4l}$

Fundamental frequency for open pipe $= \frac{v}{2l}$

First overtone for open pipe $= \frac{2v}{2l}$.

(iv) (c) For closed pipe in general

$$n = \frac{v}{4l}(2N-1) \Rightarrow n \propto \frac{1}{l}$$

i.e., if length of air column decreases frequency increases.

Or

(*b*)

Subjective Questions

1. Harmonics are the notes of frequencies which are integral multiple of the fundamental frequency.
2. Explosion at the bottom of lake or sea create enormous increase in pressure of medium (water). A shock wave is thus a longitudinal wave travelling at a speed which is greater than that of ordinary wave.
3. Although length of the spring does not appear in the expression for the time period, yet the time period depends on the length of the spring. It is because, force constant of the spring depends on the length of the spring.
4. A medium is said to be dispersive, if speed of a wave in medium depends on frequency of wave. A pulse consists of a large number of waves of different frequencies. These waves travel in dispersive medium with different speeds, so the waves speed out by different amounts. As a result, the shape of pulse gets distorted while propagating in a dispersive medium.
5. If A_1 and A_2 be the amplitudes of waves, intensities of wave will be $I_1 = A_1^2, I_2 = A_2^2$ and resultant intensity

$$I_R = A_1^2 + A_2^2 + 2A_1A_2 \cos\phi = I_1 + I_2 + 2\sqrt{I_1 I_2}\cos\phi$$

Here $I_1 = I, I_2 = 4I$

$$I_R = I + 4I + 2\sqrt{I \times 4I}\cos\phi = 5I + 4I\cos\phi$$

(i) $\phi = 0, \quad \therefore I_R = 5I + 4I\cos 0° = 5I + 4I = 9I$

(ii) $\phi = \frac{\pi}{2}, \quad \therefore I_R = 5I + 4I\cos\frac{\pi}{2} = 5I + 0 = 5I$

(iii) $\phi = \pi, \quad \therefore I_R = 5I + 4I\cos\pi = 5I - 4I = I$

6. When the string vibrates in loop *n*, its frequency,

$$\nu_n = \frac{nv}{2L}$$

where, *L* is the length of the string and *v* is the velocity of the wave.

$\because \quad \nu_n \propto n$

$\therefore$ When the string fixed at its both ends vibrates in 1 loop, 2 loops, 3 loops and 4 loops, the frequencies are in the ratio of 1 : 2 : 3 : 4.

7. (i) In transverse waves, particles of the medium oscillate in a direction perpendicular to the direction of propagation of waves.
   (ii) In longitudinal waves, particles of the medium oscillates in the direction of propagation of waves.
8. (i) The phenomenon of beats is used for matching the frequencies of different musical instruments by artist.
   (ii) The speed of an airplane can be determined by using Doppler RADAR. The phenomenon of beats, arising due to the difference in frequencies produced by the source and received at the source after reflection from the airplane, allows us to calculate the velocity of the airplane.
   (iii) The unknown frequency of a sound note can be determined by using the phenomenon of beats.
9. The displacement at any time *t* is

$$y = a\sin(\omega t + \phi)$$

$\therefore$ displacement at any time $\left(t + \frac{2\pi}{\omega}\right)$ will be

$$y = a\sin\left[\omega\left(t + \frac{2\pi}{\omega}\right) + \phi\right] = [a\sin\{(\omega t + \phi) + 2\pi\}]$$

$$y = a\sin(\omega t + \phi) \quad [\because \sin(2\pi + \phi) = \sin\phi]$$

Hence, the displacement at time *t* and $\left(t + \frac{2\pi}{\omega}\right)$ are same.

10. **Node** It is a point where the amplitude of oscillation is zero, i. e. displacement is minimum. As pressure is inversely related with displacement, i. e. when displacement will be minimum, pressure will be maximum.

Anti-node At this point, displacement is maximum, i. e. amplitude of oscillation will be maximum and hence, pressure will be minimum as it is inversely related.

Therefore, a displacement node is nothing but a pressure antinode and *vice-versa*.

11. Since, we know that,

$$v = \sqrt{\frac{T}{\mu}}$$

$$\Rightarrow \quad v^2 = \frac{T}{\mu} \quad \text{...(i)}$$

(on squaring both sides of above equation)

Now, differentiate the above equation, we get

$$2v\,dv = \frac{dT}{\mu} \quad \text{...(ii)}$$

On dividing Eq. (ii) by Eq. (i), we get

$$\frac{2dv}{v} = \frac{dT}{T}$$

$$\Rightarrow \quad \frac{dv}{v} = \frac{1}{2}\frac{dT}{T}$$

$$\Rightarrow \quad \frac{dv}{v} = \frac{1}{2} \times \frac{2}{100} \quad \left\{\because \frac{dT}{T} = 2\%\right\}$$

$$\Rightarrow \quad \frac{dv}{v} = \frac{1}{100} = 1\%$$

$$\frac{dF}{F} = \frac{dv}{v} = 1\%$$

$$\therefore \quad dF = \frac{1}{100} \times F = \frac{1}{100} \times 200 = 2$$

$\therefore$ Number of beats = 2 beats/second.

12. From kinetic theory of gases,

$p = \frac{1}{3}\rho c^2$, where c is rms speed of molecules of gas.

$$\Rightarrow \quad c = \sqrt{\frac{3p}{\rho}} \quad \text{...(i)}$$

$$v = \text{speed of sound in the gas} = \sqrt{\frac{\gamma p}{\rho}} \quad \text{...(ii)}$$

From Eqs. (i) and (ii), we get

$$\frac{c}{v} = \sqrt{\frac{3p}{\rho} \times \frac{\rho}{\gamma p}} = \sqrt{\frac{3}{\gamma}}$$

For diatomic gases, $\gamma = 1.4$ = constant

$$\Rightarrow \quad \frac{c}{v} = \sqrt{\frac{3}{1.4}} = 1.46 = \text{constant}$$

13. (i) Bats emit ultrasonic waves of large frequencies. These waves will be reflected by the obstacles in their path. The reflected rays received by the bat will give idea about the obstacle, i.e. distance, direction, size and nature.

(ii) As overtones produced and relative strengths of notes are different in two notes of violin and sitar. Although frequencies are same, we will distinguish by their strengths.

(iii) The reason behind is that solids have both the elasticity of volume as well as shape, whereas gases have only the volume elasticity.

(iv) A sound pulse is a combination of waves of different wavelength. As waves of different λ travel in a dispersive medium with different velocities, therefore the shape of pulse get distorted.

14. (i) Effect of pressure,

v = speed of sound in a gas $= \sqrt{\frac{\gamma p}{\rho}}$

p = pressure, ρ = density $= \frac{M}{V}$

$$\Rightarrow \quad v = \sqrt{\frac{\gamma pV}{M}}$$

When T is constant, pV = constant

$\Rightarrow \quad v$ = constant

Hence, velocity of sound is independent of the change in pressure of the gas provided temperature remains constant.

(ii) Formula for velocity, $v = \sqrt{\frac{\gamma p}{\rho}}$

According to standard gas equation,

$$pV = RT$$

$$\Rightarrow \quad p = \frac{RT}{V}$$

$$\Rightarrow \quad v = \sqrt{\frac{\gamma \times RT}{pV}} = \sqrt{\frac{\gamma RT}{M}}$$

where, $M = pV$ = molecular weight of the gas

$$\Rightarrow \quad v \propto \sqrt{T}$$

Hence, v increases with temperature.

(iii) Due to presence of water vapours in air, density changes. Hence, velocity of sound changes with humidity.

Let ρ_m = density of moist, ρ_d = density of dry air

v_m = velocity of sound in moist air

v_d = velocity of sound in dry air

$$v_m = \sqrt{\frac{\gamma p}{\rho_m}}, \; v_d = \sqrt{\frac{\gamma p}{\rho_d}}$$

$$\frac{v_m}{v_d} = \sqrt{\frac{\rho_d}{\rho_m}} \quad \text{as } \rho_d > \rho_m \Rightarrow v_m > v_d$$

15. Given, $v = 360$ m/s, $\nu = 500$ Hz

and $\Delta\phi = 60^\circ = \frac{\pi}{3}$

$\because$ The velocity of a wave

$$v = \nu\lambda$$

$$\lambda = \frac{v}{\lambda} = \frac{360}{500} = 0.72 \text{ m}$$

As, $$\Delta\phi = \frac{2\pi}{\lambda} \times \Delta x$$

$$\Delta x = \Delta\phi \times \frac{\lambda}{2\pi}$$

$$= \frac{\pi}{3} \times \frac{0.72}{2\pi}$$

$$\Delta x = 0.12 \text{ m}$$

16. Comparing with the standard form of equation,

$$y = a\sin[\omega t - kx]$$

(i) Amplitude, $a = 5$ m

(ii) $\omega = \frac{2\pi}{T} = 100\pi$

$$k = \frac{2\pi}{\lambda} = 0.4\,\pi$$

$$\Rightarrow \quad \lambda = \frac{2}{0.4} = \frac{20}{4} = 5 \text{ m}$$

(iii) Frequency, $\omega = 2\pi\nu = 100\pi \quad \Rightarrow \nu = 50$ Hz

(iv) Wave velocity, $v = \nu\lambda = 50 \times 5 = 250$ m/s

(v) Particle velocity $= \frac{dy}{dt} = a\omega\cos(\omega t - kx)$

$$\left(\frac{dy}{dt}\right)_{\max} = a\omega = 5 \times 100\pi = 500\pi \text{ m/s}$$

17. The equation of stationary wave is

$$y = y_1 + y_2$$

$$= 0.5\sin(5\pi t - x) + 0.05\sin(5\pi t + x)$$

$$= 0.1\sin 5\pi t\cos x = (0.1\cos x)\sin 5\pi t$$

The amplitude of the wave, $R = 0.1\cos x$

$\therefore$ The displacement of the particle situated at $x = 1$ m, is

$$R = 0.054 \text{ m}$$

18. Given, $h = 300$ m, $g = 9.8\ \text{m/s}^2$, $v = 340\ \text{ms}^{-1}$

t_1 = time taken by stone to strike the water surface

$$t_1 = \sqrt{\frac{2h}{g}} = \sqrt{\frac{300}{4.9}} = 7.82\text{ s} \quad \left(\text{As } h = 0 + \frac{1}{2}gt_1^2\right)$$

t_2 = time taken by the splash's sound to reach top of the tower

$$t_2 = \frac{h}{v} = \frac{300}{340} = 0.882\text{ s} \quad \left[\because v = \frac{h}{t_2}\right]$$

Total time, t = time to hear splash of sound

$$= t_1 + t_2 = 7.82 + 0.882 = 8.702\text{ s}$$

19. Frequency of A,

$$\nu_1 = \frac{v}{4l_1} = \frac{v}{4 \times 0.15} = \frac{v}{0.6}$$

Frequency of B,

$$\nu_2 = \frac{v}{2l_2} = \frac{v}{2 \times 0.305} = \frac{v}{0.61}$$

Beat frequency, $\nu_{\text{beat}} = \nu_1 - \nu_2$

$$\Rightarrow \quad 5 = \frac{v}{0.6} - \frac{v}{0.61}$$

$$\Rightarrow \quad 5 = \frac{(0.61 - 0.60)v}{0.6 \times 0.61}$$

$$\Rightarrow \quad v = \frac{5 \times 0.6 \times 0.61}{0.01} = 183\ \text{ms}^{-1}$$

$$\therefore \quad \nu_1 = \frac{v}{0.6} = \frac{183}{0.6} = 305\text{ Hz}$$

$$\nu_2 = \frac{v}{0.61} = \frac{183}{0.61} = 300\text{ Hz}$$

20. Let v_1, v_2 be the velocities of S wave and P wave and t_1, t_2 be the time taken by these waves to reach the seismograph.

l = distance of occurrence of earthquake from the seismograph

$$v_1 t_1 = v_2 t_2$$

$$\Rightarrow \quad v_1 = 4\ \text{km s}^{-1}, v_2 = 8\ \text{km s}^{-1}$$

$$\Rightarrow \quad 4t_1 = 8t_2 \Rightarrow t_1 = 2t_2 \quad \text{...(i)}$$

$$t_1 - t_2 = 4\text{ min} = 240\text{ s} \quad \text{...(ii)}$$

On solving Eqs. (i) and (ii), we get $t_2 = 240$ s

$$\Rightarrow \quad t_1 = 2t_2 = 2 \times 240 = 480\text{ s}$$

$$\Rightarrow \quad l = v_1 t_1 = 4 \times 480 = 1920\text{ km}$$

21. $\nu = 256$ Hz, $T = m \times g$, $T = 90 \times 9.8 = 882$ N

$$\mu = \frac{m}{L} = 8.0 \times 10^{-3}\ \text{kgm}^{-1}$$

Amplitude, $a = 5\text{ cm} = 0.05$ m

Velocity of the transverse wave,

$$v = \sqrt{\frac{T}{\mu}} = \sqrt{\frac{882}{8 \times 10^{-3}}} = 3.32 \times 10^2\ \text{m/s}$$

$$\omega = 2\pi\nu = 2 \times 3.14 \times 256 = 1.61 \times 10^3\ \text{rad/s}$$

$$\lambda = \frac{v}{\nu} = \frac{3.32 \times 10^2}{256}$$

$$k = \frac{2\pi}{\lambda} = \frac{2 \times 3.14 \times 256}{3.32 \times 10^2} = 4.84\ \text{m}^{-1}$$

As wave propagating along positive X-axis,

$$y = a\sin(\omega t - kx) = 0.05\sin(1.61 \times 10^3 t - 4.84x)$$

Here x, y are in metre and t is in second.

22. Given equation is $y(x, t) = 3.0\sin(36t + 0.018x + \pi/4)$

Comparing with standard equation

$$y(x, t) = a\sin(\omega t + kx + \phi)$$

(i) The given equation represents a transverse harmonic wave travelling from right to left (i.e. along negative X-axis). It is not a stationary wave.

By comparing, we get $\omega = 36$ rad/s, $k = 0.018$ cm

$$\therefore \text{ Speed of wave, } v = \frac{\omega}{k} = \frac{36}{0.018} = 2000\text{ cm/s}$$

(ii) By comparing amplitude, $a = 3$ cm

$$\Rightarrow \quad 2\pi\nu = 36 \Rightarrow \nu = \frac{36}{2\pi} = 5.73\text{ Hz}$$

(iii) Initial phase, $\phi = \dfrac{\pi}{4}$

(iv) $\omega = 36$, $k = \dfrac{2\pi}{\lambda} = 0.018$

$$\Rightarrow \lambda = \text{least distance} = \frac{2\pi}{k} = \frac{2\pi}{0.018}\text{ cm}$$

$$= 349.1\text{ cm}$$

23. We have, $\nu_0 = 250$ Hz, $T_0 = 273$ K

$$T_1 = 273 + 40 = 313\text{ K}; \ \lambda_0 = 1.32\text{ m}$$

$\therefore$ Speed of sound, $v_0 = \nu_0 \cdot \lambda_0 = 250 \times 1.32 = 330$ m/s

As we know that,

Speed of sound, $v \propto \sqrt{T}$

$$\text{Thus,} \quad \frac{v_1}{v_0} = \sqrt{\frac{T_1}{T_0}}$$

$$v_1 = v_0\sqrt{\frac{T_1}{T_0}} = 330\sqrt{\frac{313}{273}} = 353.34\text{ m/s}$$

$$\because \quad v_1 = \nu_0\,\lambda_1$$

$$\lambda_1 = \frac{353.34}{250} = 1.41\text{ m}$$

$\therefore$ Change in the wavelength,

$$\Delta\lambda = \lambda_1 - \lambda_0 = 1.41 - 1.32 = 0.09\text{ m}$$

24. Given equation is $y = 2\cos 2\pi(10t - 0.0080x + 3.5)$

Comparing with standard equation,

$$y = a\cos(\omega t - kx + \phi)$$

$$a = 2\text{ cm}, \ \omega = \frac{2\pi}{T} = 20\pi, \ T = 0.1\text{ s}$$

$$k = \frac{2\pi}{\lambda} = 0.008 \times 2\pi$$

$$\Rightarrow \quad \lambda = \frac{2\pi}{2\pi \times 0.008} = 1.25 \text{ m}$$

$$\phi = 2\pi \times 3.5 = 7\pi \text{ rad}$$

(i) $\phi_1 = \frac{2\pi}{\lambda} \times 4 = \frac{2\pi}{1.25} \times 4 = 6.4\pi \text{ rad}$

(ii) $\phi_2 = \frac{2\pi}{\lambda} \times x = \frac{2\pi}{1.25} \times 0.5 = 0.8\pi \text{ rad}$

(iii) When $x = \lambda/2$

$$\phi_3 = \frac{2\pi}{\lambda} \times \lambda/2 = \pi \text{ rad}$$

(iv) When $x = \frac{3\lambda}{4}$; $\phi_4 = \frac{2\pi}{\lambda} \times \frac{3\lambda}{4} = \frac{3\pi}{2}$ rad

(v) At $t = T$; $\phi = \frac{2\pi}{T} = \frac{2\pi}{0.1} = 20\pi$ rad

and at $t = 5$ s; $\phi' = \frac{2\pi}{0.1} \times 5 = 100\pi$ rad

$\therefore$ Phase difference, $\phi' - \phi = 100\pi - 20\pi = 80\pi$ rad

25. Here, $v = 360$ m/s, $\nu = 256$ Hz

(i) In the figure, second curve represents all the particles passing simultaneously through mean position. This happens at $t = \frac{T}{4}\left(\because T = \frac{1}{256}\text{s}\right)$

$$= \frac{1}{4 \times 256} \text{ s} = 9.8 \times 10^{-4} \text{ s}$$

(ii) Nodes are at points A, B, C, D, E and antinodes are at A', B', C', D'

(iii) Distance between A' and C'

$$= \frac{2\lambda}{2} = \lambda = \frac{v}{\nu} = \frac{360}{256} = 1.41 \text{ m}$$

26. The wave pattern shown, represent stationary wave.

t	x (cm)
0	0
$\frac{T}{2}$	10
T	20

At the above time and position and similarly for next interval and position. These points are at rest and called nodes.

Distance between successive nodes $= \frac{\lambda}{2} = 10$ cm

$$\Rightarrow \quad \lambda = 20 \text{ c}$$

27. Given, $L = 20$ cm $= 0.2$ m, $\nu_n = 430$ Hz, $v = 340$ m/s

It will behave as closed organ pipe

$$\nu_n = (2n-1)\frac{v}{4L}, \text{ where } n = 1, 2, 3, \ldots$$

$$\Rightarrow \quad 430 = (2n-1)\frac{v}{4L} = (2n-1) \times \frac{340}{4 \times 0.2}$$

$$\Rightarrow (2n-1) = \frac{430 \times (0.8)}{340} \Rightarrow 2n = \frac{(430)(0.8)}{340} + 1$$

$$\Rightarrow \quad n = \frac{43 \times 4}{340} + \frac{1}{2} = \frac{2 \times 172 + 340}{340 \times 2}$$

$$= \frac{684}{680} = 1.006$$

Hence, it will be the 1st normal mode or harmonic mode of vibration.

In a pipe open at both ends,

$$\nu_n = n \times \frac{v}{2l} = \frac{n \times 340}{2 \times 0.2} = 430$$

$$\Rightarrow \quad n = \frac{430 \times 2 \times 0.2}{340} = \frac{43 \times 2 \times 2}{340} = 0.5$$

As n is not integer, hence open organ pipe cannot be in resonance with the source.

28. (i) $\nu = \frac{v}{4l}$

$$\Rightarrow \quad v = (\nu)(4l) = (512)\left(\frac{4 \times 17}{100}\right) \text{ m/s} = 348.16 \text{ m/s}$$

(ii) $v_0 = v_t\sqrt{\frac{T_0}{T}} = 348.16\sqrt{\frac{273}{273 + 20}} = 336.1$ m/s

(iii) There will not be any change in resonance length, as frequency will remain same. As mercury acts as reflector, intensity may change to some extent.

QR Code for Quick Test 1

QR Code for Quick Test 2

SELF ASSESSMENT TEST

Objective Type Questions (MCQs)

1. The frequency of the first hormonic of a string stretched between two points is 100 Hz. The frequency of the third overtone is

(a) 200 Hz (b) 300 Hz
(c) 400 Hz (d) 600 Hz

2. If $n_1, n_2, n_3 ......$ are the frequencies of segments of a stretched string, the frequency n of the string is given by

(a) $n = n_1 + n_2 + n_3 + ...$
(b) $n = \sqrt{n_1 \times n_2 \times n_3 \times ......}$
(c) $\frac{1}{n} = \frac{1}{n_1} + \frac{1}{n_2} + \frac{1}{n_3} + ...$
(d) None of the above

3. The equation of stationary wave along a stretched string is given by $y = 5\sin\frac{\pi x}{3} \cos 40\,\pi t$, where x and y are in centimetres and t in second. The separation between two adjacent nodes is

(a) 6 cm (b) 4 cm
(c) 3 cm (d) 1.5 cm

4. A pipe open at both ends produces a note of frequency f_1. When the pipe is kept with $\frac{3}{4}$th of its length in water, it produced a note of frequency f. The ratio $\frac{f_1}{f_2}$ is

(a) $\frac{3}{4}$ (b) $\frac{4}{3}$
(c) $\frac{1}{2}$ (d) 2

5. Match the equations of waves mentioned in Column II with waves mentioned in Column I.

Column I	Column II
(A) Plane progressive wave moving in $+x$-direction	(p) $y = A\sin(\omega t + kx)$
(B) Incident waves $y = A_i \sin(\omega t - kx)$ reflected from rarer medium surface	(q) $y = A\sin(\omega t - kx)$
(C) Incident wave $y = A_i \sin(\omega t - kx)$ reflected from denser medium surface	(r) $y = -A\sin(\omega t + kx)$
(D) Stationary wave	(s) $y = 2A\sin\omega t\cos kx$

(a) A-p,B-q,C-s,D-r
(b) A-s,B-r,C-p,D-q
(c) A-r,B-p,C-s,D-q
(d) A-q,B-p,C-r,D-s

Assertion-Reason

Directions (Q.Nos. 6-7) *In the following questions, two statements are given- one labelled Assertion (A) and the other labelled Reason (R). Select the correct answer to these questions from the codes (a), (b), (c) and (d) as given below.*

(a) Both Assertion and Reason are true and Reason is the correct explanation of Assertion.
(b) Both Assertion and Reason are true but Reason is not the correct explanation of Assertion.
(c) Assertion is true but Reason is false.
(d) Assertion is false but Reason is true.

6. Assertion (A) Compression and rarefaction involve changes in density and pressure.

Reason (R) When particles are compressed, density of medium increases and when they are rarefied, density of medium decreases.

7. Assertion (A) Where two vibrating tuning forks having frequencies 256 Hz and 512 Hz are held near each other, beats cannot be heard.

Reason (R) The principle of superposition is valid only if the frequencies of the oscillators are nearly equal.

Very Short Answer Type Question

8. Where will a person hear maximum sound, at node or anti-node?

9. What is the distance between a node and an adjoining anti-node in a stationary wave?

Short Answer Type Questions

10. A vessel is placed below a water tap. We can estimate the height of the water level reached in the vessel from a distance simply by listening to the sound. Why?

11. What is standing wave? Give its characteristics.

12. Equation of a plane progressive wave is given by $y = 0.6\sin 2\pi\left(t - \frac{x}{2}\right)$. On reflection from a denserm, medium, its amplitude becomes $\frac{2}{3}$ of the amplitude of incident wave. What will be equation of reflected wave?

Long Answer Type Questions

13. Two open organ pipes on sounding together produce 5 beats/second. If the length of the smaller pipe be 66 cm, calculate the length of larger organ pipe. (Speed of sound in air 330 m/s).

14. A bat emits ultrasonic sound of frequency 100 kHz in air. If the sound meets a water surface, then what is the wavelength of (i) the reflected sound, (ii) the transmitted sound? Speed of sound in air is 340 ms^{-1} and in water 1486 ms^{-1}.

Answers

1. (c) *2.* (c) *3.* (c) *4.* (c) *5.* (d)

6. (a) *7.* (c)

12. $-0.4 \sin 2\pi\left(t + \frac{x}{2}\right)$

13. 67.3 cm

14. (i) 3.4×10^{-4}m (ii) 1.49×10^{-3} m

SAMPLE QUESTION PAPER 1

A Highly Simulated Sample Question Paper for CBSE Class XI Examination

PHYSICS

Time : 3 Hours **Max. Marks : 70**

General Instructions

1. There are 33 questions in all. All questions are compulsory.
2. This question paper has five sections : Section A, Section B, Section C, Section D and Section E.
3. All the sections are compulsory.
4. Section A contains sixteen questions, twelve MCQ and four Assertion Reasoning based of 1 mark each, **Section B** contains five questions of two marks each, **Section C** contains seven questions of three marks each, **Section D** contains two case study based questions of four marks each and **Section E** contains three long answer questions of five marks each.
5. There is no overall choice. However, an internal choice has been provided in one question in Section B, one question in Section C, one question in each CBQ in Section D and all three questions in Section E. You have to attempt only one of the choices in such questions.
6. Use of calculators is not allowed.
7. You may use the following values of physical constants where ever necessary
   i. $G = 6.67 \times 10^{-11} \text{Nm}^2/\text{kg}^2$
   ii. $R = 8.314 \text{J mol}^{-1}\text{K}^{-1}$
   iii. $k_B = 1.38 \times 10^{-23} \text{J/K}$
   iv. $\sigma = 5.67 \times 10^{-8} \text{Wm}^{-2}\text{K}^{-1}$
   v. $N_A = 6.023 \times 10^{23} \text{mol}^{-1}$

Section-A

1. The displacement-time graphs of two moving particles make angles of 30° and 45° with the *X*-axis. The ratio of their velocities is

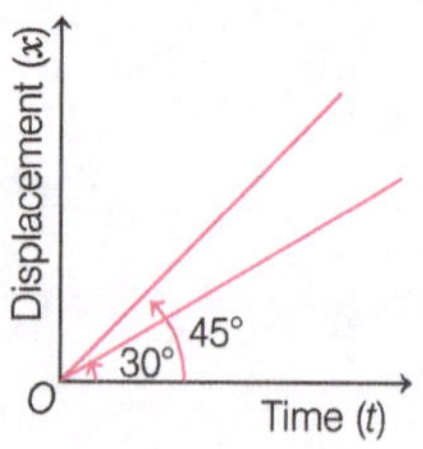

(a) $1:\sqrt{3}$ (b) 1:2 (c) 1:1 (d) $\sqrt{3}:2$

2. Which one of the following statements is true?

(a) A scalar quantity is the one that is conserved in a process
(b) A scalar quantity is the one that can never take negative values
(c) A scalar quantity is the one that does not vary from one point to another in space
(d) A scalar quantity has the same value for observers with different orientation of the axes

3. Conservation of momentum in a collision between particles can be understood from

(a) conservation of energy
(b) Newton's first law only
(c) Newton's second law only
(d) Both Newton's second and third law

4. A ball is travelling with uniform translatory motion. This means that

(a) it is at rest
(b) the path can be a straight line or circular and the ball travels with uniform speed
(c) all parts of the ball have the same velocity (magnitude and direction) and the velocity is constant
(d) the centre of the ball moves with constant velocity and the ball spins about its centre uniformly

5. **In figure, pressure inside a spherical drop is more than pressure outside. (S = surface tension and r = radius of bubble)**
The extra surface energy if radius of bubble is increased by Δr is
(a) $4\pi r\,\Delta r\,S$ (b) $8\pi r\,\Delta r\,S$ (c) $2\pi r\,\Delta r\,S$ (d) $10\pi r\,\Delta r\,S$

6. **Two water pipes of diameters 2 cm and 4 cm are connected with the main supply line. The velocity of flow of water in the pipe of 2 cm diameter is**
(a) 4 times that in the other pipe
(b) $\frac{1}{4}$ times that in the other pipe
(c) 2 times that in the other pipe
(d) $\frac{1}{2}$ times that in the other pipe

7. **Choose the correct option.**
(a) Zeroth law gives the concept of temperature
(b) Temperature measures the 'hotness' of the body
(c) Heat flows from higher temperature to lower temperature until thermal equilibrium is attained
(d) All of the above

8. **Due to the change in main voltage, the temperature of an electric bulb rises from 3000 K to 4000 K. What is the percentage rise in electric power consumed?**
(a) 216 (b) 100 (c) 150 (d) 178

9. **The angular velocity of a wheel increases from 100 rps to 300 rps in 10 s. The number of revolutions made during that time is**
(a) 600 (b) 1500 (c) 1000 (d) 2000

10. **Radius of a soap bubble is increased from R to $2R$. Work done in this process in terms of surface tension is**
(a) $24\,\pi R^2 S$ (b) $48\,\pi R^2 S$ (c) $12\pi R^2 S$ (d) $36\pi R^2 S$

11. **If the force and displacement of particle in the direction of force are doubled, then work done would be**
(a) double (b) 4 times (c) half (d) 1/4 times

12. **Match the law with its description.**

Law	Description
A. Netwon's law of gravitation	1. Gravitational force is directly proportional to the product of masses and inversely proportional to the square of the distance.
B. Universal law of gravitation	2. Gravitational force acts between two bodies regardless of their size or shape.
C. Kepler's first law	3. A planet moves in an elliptical with the Sun at one focus.
D. Kepler's third law	4. The square of the time period is proportional to the cube of the average distance of the planet from the Sun.

(a) A-1, B-2, C-3, D-4
(b) A-2, B-1, C-4, D-3
(c) A-1, B-3, C-4, D-2
(d) A-3, B-2, C-1, D-4

For questions 13 to 16, two statements are given -one labelled Assertion (A) and other labelled Reason (R). Select the correct answer to these questions from the options as given below.

(a) If both Assertion and Reason are true and Reason is correct explanation of Assertion.
(b) If both Assertion and Reason are true but Reason is not the correct explanation of Assertion.
(c) If Assertion is true but Reason is false.
(d) If both Assertion and Reason are false.

13. **Assertion (A)** At highest point of a projectile, dot product of velocity and acceleration is zero.
Reason (R) At highest point, velocity and acceleration are mutually perpendicular.

14. **Assertion (A)** When a body is dropped or thrown horizontally from the same height, it would reach the ground at the same time.
Reason (R) Horizontal velocity has no effect on the vertical direction.

15. **Assertion (A)** In isothermal process, whole of the heat energy supplied to the body is converted into internal energy.
Reason (R) According to the first law of thermodynamics, $\Delta Q = \Delta U + \Delta W$.

16. **Assertion (A)** Longitudinal waves can be propagated through solids and fluids both.
Reason (R) Solids as well as fluids have non-zero bulk modulus, that is they can sustain compressive stress and longitudinal waves involve compressive stress (pressure).

Section-B

17. **(a) Is rms speed same as the average speed? Write an expression of rms and average speed.**
(b) Why does molecular motion increase at 0 K?

18. **A particle at the end of a spring executes simple harmonic motion with a period t_1, while the corresponding period for another spring is t_2. What is the period of oscillation when the two springs are connected in series?**

19. **0.15 kg of ice at 0°C is mixed with 0.30 kg of water at 50°C in a container. The resulting temperature is at 6.7°C. Find heat of fusion of ice.**
(Given, specific heat of water is 4186 $Jkg^{-1}K^{-1}$)

20. Determine the tensions T_1 and T_2 in the strings shown in following figure:

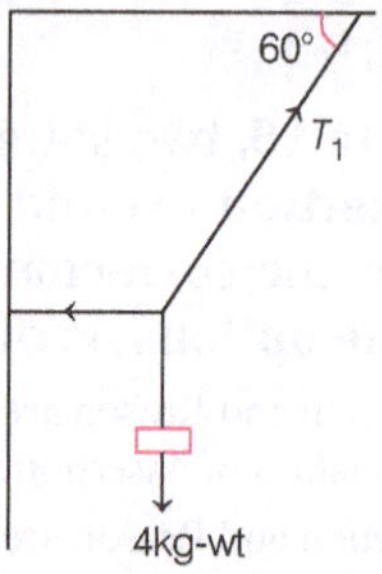

21. Two particles are projected from the same point with same speed u at an angle of projection α and β from horizontal. If the maximum heights attained by them are h_1 and h_2 respectively for same range R, then find the relation between h_1, h_2 and R.

Or A bullet fired at an angle of 30° with the horizontal hits the ground 3 km away. By adjusting its angle of projection, can one hope to hit a target 5 km away? Assume the muzzle speed to be fixed and neglect air resistance.

Section-C

22. Derive an expression for the moment of inertia of a thin uniform rod about an axis through its centre and perpendicular to its length. Also, determine the radius of gyration about the same axis.

Or From a uniform disc of radius R, a circular section of radius $\frac{R}{2}$ is cut out. The centre of the hole is at $\frac{R}{2}$ from the centre of the original disc. Locate the centre of gravity of the resulting flat body.

23. A smooth rod of length l rotates freely in a horizontal plane with angular velocity ω about a stationary vertical axis O. The moment of inertia of the rod is equal to I relative the axis. A small ring of mass m is located on the rod close to the rotation axis and is tied to it by a thread. When the thread is burnt, the ring starts sliding radially outwards along the rod. Find the velocity of the ring relative to the rod as a function of its distance r from the rotation axis.

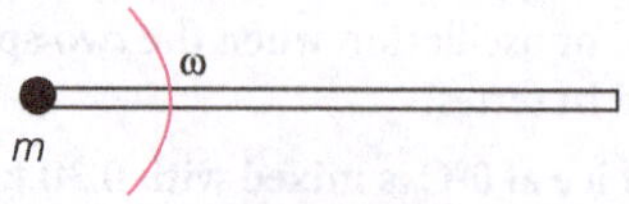

Smooth rod rotating freely with a ring

24. (a) A man standing near the top of an old wooden step ladder feels unstable. Why?

(b) Why does a belly dancer fold her arms and bring the stretched leg close to the other leg?

(c) What is instantaneous rotational power? Write its expression.

25. The p-V diagram of an ideal gas two different masses m_1 and m_2 are drawn (as shown) at constant temperature T. State whether $m_1 > m_2$ or $m_2 > m_1$?

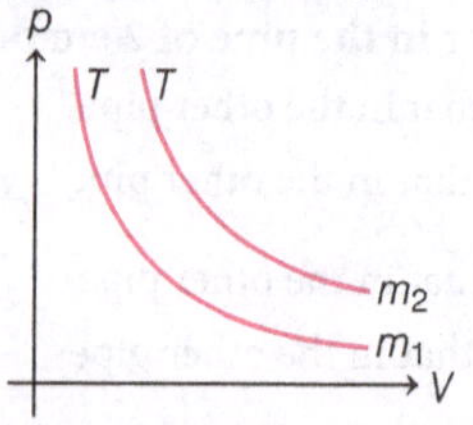

26. A man standing on a hill top projects a stone horizontally with speed v_0 as shown in the given figure. Taking the coordinate system as given in the figure, find the coordinates of the point, where the stone will hit the hill surface.

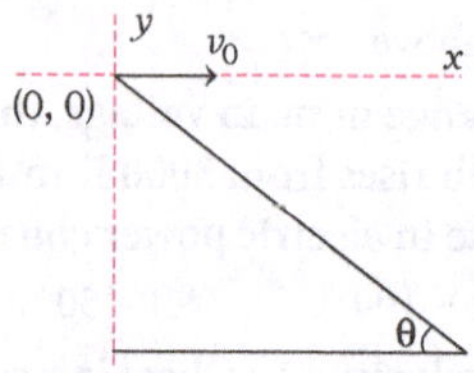

27. Identify the thermodynamic process in which

(a) work done is zero,

(b) heat interaction is zero,

(c) the p-V diagram is rectangluar hyperbola.

Write the thermodynamic equation for each of the above processes.

28. (a) If C and R denote capacitance and resistance, then find the dimension of CR.

(b) Check whether the following quantities are dimensionless or not.

(i) $\frac{\text{Work}}{\text{Energy}}$ (ii) $\sin\theta$ (iii) $\frac{\text{Momentum}}{\text{Time}}$

Section-D

29. Read the following paragraph and answer the questions that follow.

The centre of gravity of a rigid body is a point through which the total weight of the body act. Centre of gravity can lie within the body or not. For small objects, centre of mass always coincides with centre of gravity.

But in case of large bodies whose dimensions are comparable to the size of earth, centre of mass and centre of gravity will be at different locations.

(i) Where will be the centre of gravity of the following rigid body?

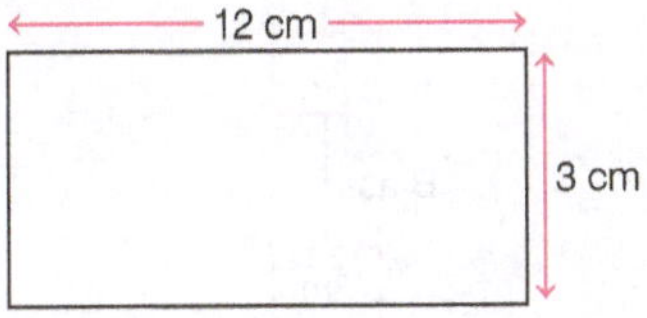

(a) (6,3) (b) (6,6)
(c) (6,1.5) (d) (1.5,3)

(ii) In which of the following figures, the centre of gravity has correct position?

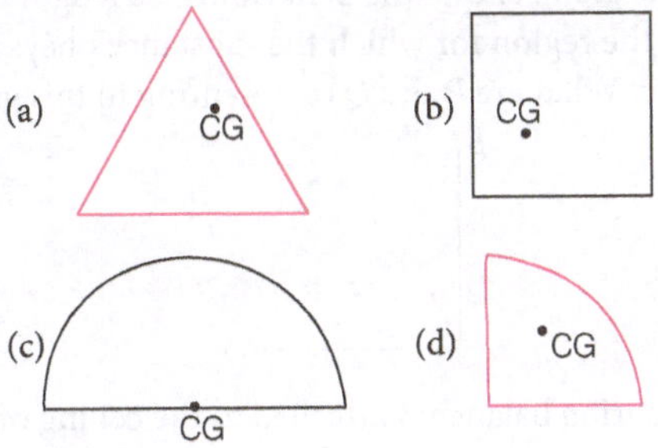

(iii) The centre of gravity and the centre of mass of a body coincide when
(a) g is negligible (b) g is variable
(c) g is constant (d) g is zero

Or

In the given figure, balancing of a cardboard on the tip of a pencil is done. The point of support, G is the centre of gravity.

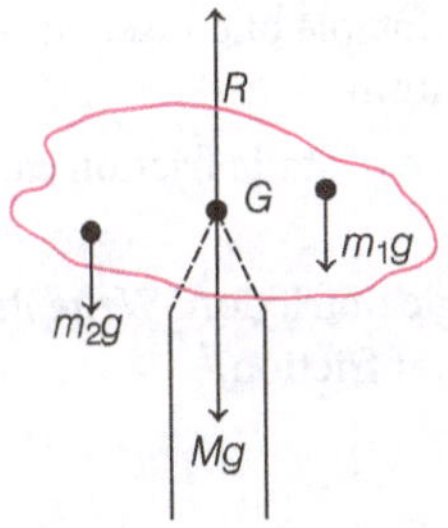

If the $\mathbf{F}_{\text{net, ext}}$ is zero on the cardboard, it means
(a) $R = Mg$ (b) $m_1 g = Mg$
(c) $m_2 g = Mg$ (d) $R = m_1 / g$

(iv)

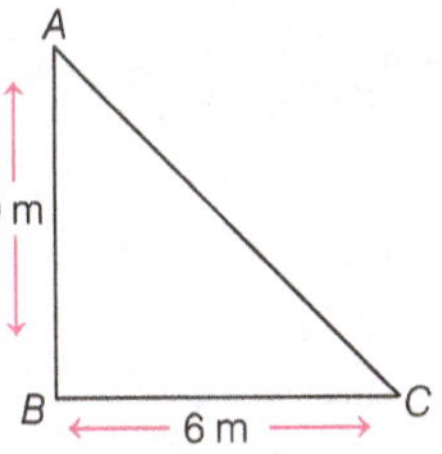

A triangle is shown in the figure. The position of centre of gravity is
(a) (4m, 5m) (b) (3m, 4m)
(c) (2m, 3m) (d) (3m, 2m)

30. **Read the following paragaph and answer the questions that follow**

For a dynamic system in thermal equilibrium, the total energy is distributed equally amongst all the degree of freedom and the energy associated with each molecule per degree of freedom is $\frac{1}{2} k_B T$

where, $k_B = 1.38 \times 10^{-23} \text{JK}^{-1}$ is Boltzmann constant and T is absolute temperature of system on the kelvin scale. For a monoatomic gas in thermal equilibrium at temperature T, the average value of translational energy of the molecule is

$$\langle E_t \rangle = \left\langle \frac{1}{2} m v_x^2 \right\rangle + \left\langle \frac{1}{2} m v_y^2 \right\rangle + \left\langle \frac{1}{2} m v_z^2 \right\rangle$$

Translational energy of the molecules,

$$\langle E_t \rangle = \frac{3}{2} k_B T$$

(i) Molecules of CO at moderate temperature have energy
(a) $\frac{7}{2} k_B T$ (b) $\frac{5}{2} k_B T$
(c) $\frac{3}{2} k_B T$ (d) $\frac{1}{2} k_B T$

(ii) Law of equipartition of energy is used to
(a) predict the specific heats of gases
(b) predict the specific heats of solids
(c) Both (a) and (b)
(d) Neither (a) nor (b)

(iii) Diatomic molecule (rigid rotator) has
(a) 3 translational degrees of freedom
(b) 2 rotational degrees of freedom
(c) Both (a) and (b)
(d) All of the above

(iv) Choose the correct option
(a) Each translational mode contricutes $\frac{1}{2} k_B T$ average energy
(b) Each rotational mode contributes $\frac{1}{2} k_B T$
(c) Vibrational mode contributes $\frac{1}{2} k_B T$ average energy.
(d) All of the above

Or

The mean kinetic energy of one mole of gas per degree of freedom (on the basis of kinetic theory of gases) is

(a) $\frac{1}{2}kT$ (b) $\frac{3}{2}kT$

(c) $\frac{3}{2}RT$ (d) $\frac{1}{2}RT$

Section-E

31. (i) Mention any two conditions under which the weight of a person can become zero.

(ii) Calculate the period of revolution of the neptune around the sun, given that diameter of its orbit is 30 times the diameter of the earth's orbit around the sun. Assume both the orbits to be circular.

Or (i) What do you mean by binding energy of a satellite? Write an expression for it.

(ii) Calculate the escape velocity for an atmospheric particle 1600 km above the earth's surface. (Given, radius of earth = 6400 km and $g = 9.8\ \text{m/s}^2$)

(iii) To break a wire, a force of $10^6\ \text{Nm}^{-2}$ is required. If the density of the material is $3 \times 10^3\ \text{kgm}^{-3}$, then calculate the length of the wire which will break by its own weight.

(iv) A body is rotating with angular velocity, $\omega = (3\hat{\mathbf{i}} - 4\hat{\mathbf{j}} - \hat{\mathbf{k}})$. What is the linear velocity of a point having position vector $\mathbf{r} = (5\hat{\mathbf{i}} - 6\hat{\mathbf{j}} + 6\hat{\mathbf{k}})$?

32. (i) When the load of a wire is increased from 3 kg-wt to 5 kg-wt, the length of that wire changes from 0.61 mm to 1.02 mm. Calculate the change in the elastic potential energy of the wire.

(ii) If the ratio of diameters, lengths and Young's moduli of steel and brass wires shown in the figure are p, q and r respectively, what will be the corresponding ratio of increase in their lengths?

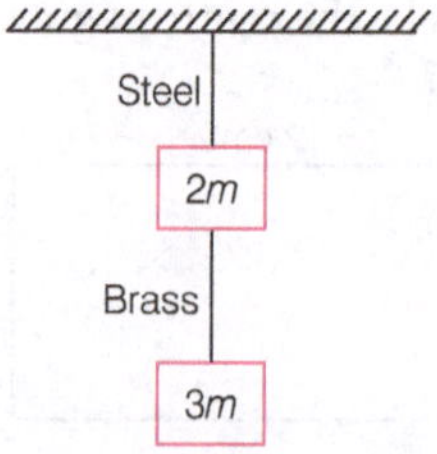

Or

(i) State Stoke's law and derive its expression dimensionally.

(ii) The graph shows the behaviour of a length of wire in the region for which the substance obeys Hooke's law. What are P and Q representing in this graph?

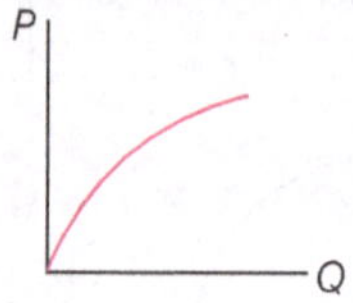

33. (i) A spring balance is attached to the ceiling of a lift. A man hangs his bag on the spring and the spring reads 49 N, when the lift is stationary. What will be the reading of the spring balance, if the lift moves downward with an acceleration of $5\ \text{ms}^{-2}$?

(ii) A body tied to a string is made to revolve in a vertical circle. Derive an expression for the velocity and tension in an string at any point. Hence, find the tension at the bottom and the top of the circle.

(a) Explain the need for banking of curved tracks.

(b) State principle of conservation of angular momentum.

Or (a) Why is force of static friction called a self adjusting force?

(b) Define angle of friction. Write its relation with coefficient of friction.

Answers

1. (a) **2.** (d) **3.** (d) **4.** (c) **5.** (b)

6. (a) **7.** (c) **8.** (a) **9.** (d) **10.** (a)

11. (b) **12.** (a) **13.** (a) **14.** (a) **15.** (d)

16. (a) **19.** $334 \times 10^5\ \text{J kg}^{-1}$ **20.** 45.26 N, 22.63 N **21.** Or 3464 m **23.** $\frac{\omega_0 r}{\sqrt{1+\frac{mr^2}{I}}}$

29. (i) (c), (ii) (d), (iii) (c) Or (a) (iv) (c)

30. (i) (b), (ii) (c), (iii) (c), (iv) (d) Or (d)

31. Or (ii) 12528.5 m/s (iii) 34 m (iv) $-18\mathbf{j} - 13\hat{\mathbf{j}} + 2\hat{\mathbf{k}}$

32. (i) $-16 \times 10^{-3}\ \hat{\mathbf{j}}$

33. (i) 24N

SAMPLE QUESTION PAPER 2

A Highly Simulated Sample Question Paper for CBSE Class XI Examination

PHYSICS

Time : 3 Hours **Max. Marks : 70**

General Instructions

1. There are 33 questions in all. All questions are compulsory.
2. This question paper has five sections : Section A, Section B, Section C, Section D and Section E.
3. All the sections are compulsory.
4. Section A contains sixteen questions, twelve MCQ and four Assertion Reasoning based of 1 mark each, **Section B** contains five questions of two marks each, **Section C** contains seven questions of three marks each, **Section D** contains two case study based questions of four marks each and **Section E** contains three long answer questions of five marks each.
5. There is no overall choice. However, an internal choice has been provided in one question in Section B, one question in Section C, one question in each CBQ in Section D and all three questions in Section E. You have to attempt only one of the choices in such questions.
6. Use of calculators is not allowed.
7. You may use the following values of physical constants where ever necessary
   i. $G = 6.67 \times 10^{-11} Nm^2/kg^2$
   ii. $R = 8.314 J mol^{-1} K^{-1}$
   iii. $k_B = 1.38 \times 10^{-23} J/K$
   iv. $\sigma = 5.67 \times 10^{-8} Wm^{-2} K^{-1}$
   v. $N_A = 6.023 \times 10^{23} mol^{-1}$

Section-A

1. The solid angle subtended by the periphery of an area 1 cm^2 at a point situated symmetrically at a distance of 5 cm from the area is

(a) 2×10^{-2} steradian
(b) 4×10^{-2} steradian
(c) 6×10^{-2} steradian
(d) 8×10^{-2} steradian

2. The damping force on an oscillator is directly proportional to the velocity. The unit of the constant of proportionality is

(a) kg ms^{-1} (b) kg ms^{-2} (c) kg s^{-1} (d) kg s

3. The coordinates of object with respect to a frame of reference at $t = 0$ are (– 1, 0, 3). If $t = 5$ s, its coordinates are (– 1, 0, 4), then the object is in

(a) motion along Z-axis
(b) motion along X-axis
(c) motion along Y-axis
(d) rest position between $t = 0$ s and $t = 5$ s

4. Which of the following statements is true for a car moving on the road?

(a) With respect to the frame of reference attached to the ground, the car is at rest
(b) With respect to the frame of reference attached to the person sitting in the car, the car is at rest
(c) With respect to the frame of reference attached to the person outside the car, the car is at rest
(d) None of the above

5. The relation between the vectors **A** and –2**A** is that,

(a) both have same magnitude
(b) both have same direction
(c) they have opposite directions
(d) None of the above

6. The component of a vector **r** along X-axis will have maximum value if

(a) **r** is along positive Y-axis
(b) **r** is along positive X-axis
(c) **r** makes an angle of 45° with the X-axis
(d) **r** is along negative Y-axis

7. A body of mass 2 kg travels according to the law $x(t) = pt + qt^2 + rt^3$ where, $q = 4\text{ ms}^{-2}$, $p = 3\text{ms}^{-1}$ and $r = 5\text{ ms}^{-3}$. The force acting on the body at $t = 2\text{s}$ is

(a) 136 N (b) 134 N (c) 158 N (d) 68 N

8. A particle is pushed by forces $2\hat{i} + 3\hat{j} - 2\hat{k}$ and $5\hat{i} - \hat{j} - 3\hat{k}$ simultaneously and it is displaced from point $\hat{i} + \hat{j} + \hat{k}$ to point $2\hat{i} - \hat{j} + 3\hat{k}$. The work done is

(a) 7 units (b) −7 units (c) 10units (d) −10 units

9. Two masses are joined with a light rod and the system is rotating about the fixed axis as shown in the figure. The MI of the system about the axis is

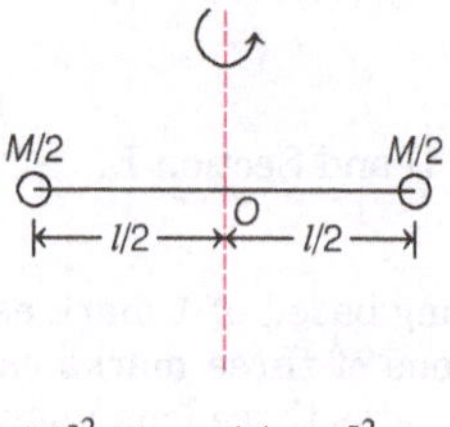

(a) $Ml^2/2$ (b) $Ml^2/4$ (c) Ml^2 (d) $Ml^2/6$

10. The graph shows the behaviour of a length of wire in the region for which the substance obeys Hook's law. P and Q represent

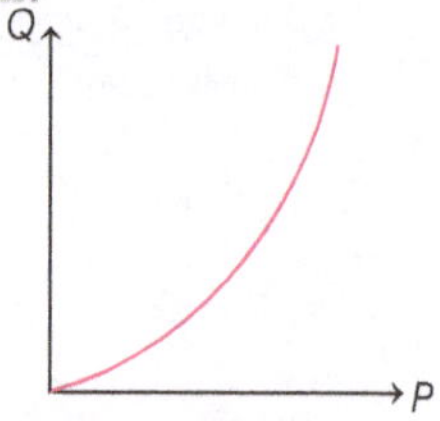

(a) P = applied force, Q = extension

(b) P = extension, Q = applied force

(c) P = extension, Q = stored elastic energy

(d) P = stored elastic energy, Q = extension

11. A system is provided with 200 cal of heat and the work done by the system on the surroundings is 40 J. Then its internal energy

(a) increases by 600 J (b) decreases by 800 J

(c) increases by 800 J (d) decreases by 50 J

12. Match the system of measurement with its characteristic.

System of Measurement	Characteristic
A. MKS System	1. Used widely in engineering and science
B. CGS System	2. Uses metre, kilogram, and second as base units
C. FPS System	3. Uses foot, pound and second as base units
D. SI System	4. Internationally accepted system with seven base units

(a) A-2, B-3, C-1, D-4 (b) A-4, B-2, C-3, D-1

(c) A-2, B-4, C-3, D-1 (d) A-1, B-2, C-4, D-3

For questions 13 to 16, two statements are given-one labelled Assertion (A) and the other labelled Reason (R). Select the correct answer to these questions from the codes (a), (b), (c) and (d) as given below.

(a) If both Assertion and Reason are true and Reason is correct explanation of Assertion.

(b) If both Assertion and Reason are true but Reason is not the correct explanation of Assertion.

(c) If Assertion is true but Reason is false.

(d) If both Assertion and Reason are false.

13. **Assertion (A)** Moon has no atmosphere.

Reason (R) The escape speed for the moon is much smaller. Gas molecules, if formed on the surface of the moon having velocities larger than escape speed will escape the gravitational pull of the moon.

14. **Assertion (A)** The dimensional method cannot be used to obtain the dependence of the work done by a force **F** on the angle θ between force **F** and displacement x.

Reason (R) All trigonometric functions are dimensionless.

15. **Assertion (A)** A body of mass 10 kg is placed on a rough inclined surface ($\mu = 0.7$). The surface is inclined to horizontal at angle 30°. Acceleration of the body down the plane will be zero.

Reason (R) Work done by friction is always negative.

16. **Assertion (A)** Smaller drop of liquid resists deforming forces better than the larger drops.

Reason (R) Excess pressure inside a drop is directly proportional to its surface area.

Section-B

17. (i) Action and reaction are equal and opposite. Why cannot they cancel each other?

(ii) According to Newton's third law, every force is accompanied by an equal and opposite force. How can a movement ever take place?

18. There are two spheres of same radius and material at same temperature but one being solid while the other hollow. Which sphere will expand more, if they are heated to same temperature?

19. A liquid X of density 3.36 g/cm^3 is poured in a U-tube in right arm with height 10 cm, which contains Hg. Another liquid Y is poured in left arm with height 8 cm.

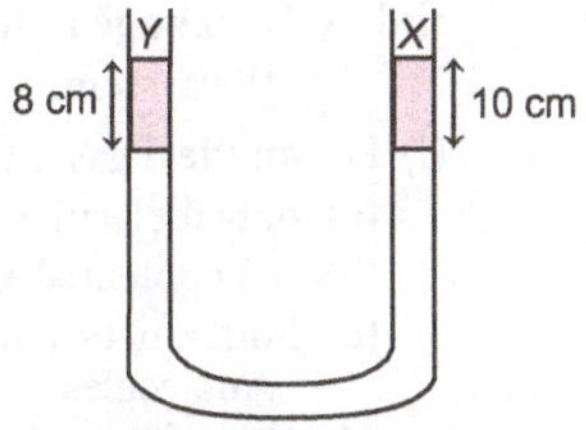

Upper levels of X and Y are same. What is the density of Y? (Given, density of Hg = 13.6 g/cc)

20. A silver atom in a solid oscillates in SHM in a certain direction with a frequency of $10^{12}\,s^{-1}$. What is the force constant of the bonds connecting one atom with the other? (Molecular weight of silver = 108)

21. The figure given below is the part of a horizontal stretched net. In this section, AB is stretched with a force of 10 N, then find the force in the section BC.

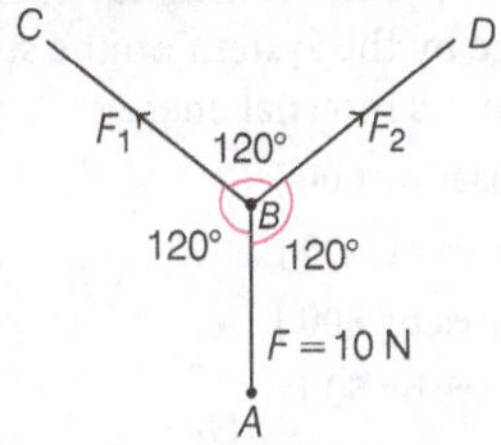

Or

A force of 98 N is required to just start moving a body of mass 100 kg over ice. What is the coefficient of static friction?

Section-C

22. (i) 10 mol of an ideal gas at constant temperature, 500 K is compressed from 50 L to 5L. Calculate the work done in this process. (Given, $R = 8.31\,J\,mol^{-1}K^{-1}$)

(ii) An electric heater supplies heat to a system at a rate of 50W. If the system performs work at a rate of 30 J/s. At what rate is the internal energy increased?

Or

A spherical body of volume V and density σ is suspended from a string, the other end of the string is connected to the roof of a sealed container filled with an ideal fluid of density ρ. If the container accelerates towards right with a constant acceleration a, then find the force exerted by the liquid on the body, when body is in equilibrium w.r.t. fluid.

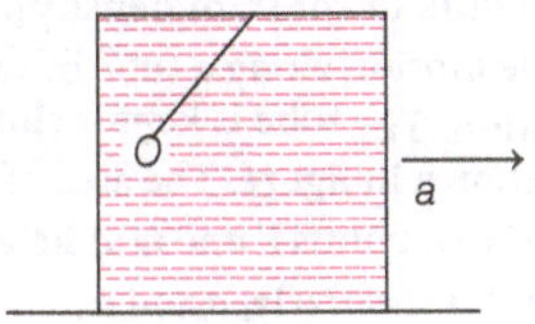

23. Two simple harmonic motions are represented by $y_1 = 5\,(\sin 2\pi t + \sqrt{3}\cos 2\pi t)$ units and $y_2 = 5\sin\left(2\pi t + \frac{\pi}{4}\right)$ units, calculate the ratio of their amplitudes.

24. A monkey of mass 40 kg climbs on a rope which can withstand a maximum tension of 600 N. Determine in the following cases whether the rope will break or not.

(i) The monkey climbs up with an acceleration of $6\,ms^{-2}$.

(ii) The monkey climbs down with an acceleration of $4\,ms^{-2}$.

(iii) The monkey climbs up with a uniform speed of $5\,ms^{-1}$. (Take, $g = 10\,ms^{-2}$)

Ignore the mass of the rope.

25. A block of wood of mass 5 kg is resting on the surface of a rough inclined plane making angle 60° as shown in figure. If the coefficient of static friction is 0.3, calculate the forces.

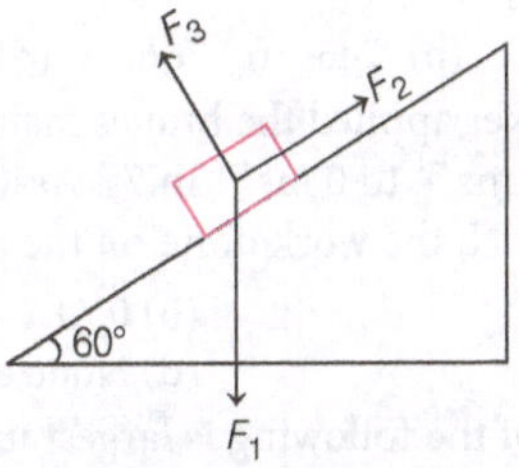

26. A man of mass 50 g stands on a frame of mass 30 g. He pulls on a light rope which passes over a pulley. The other end of the rope is attached to the frame. For the system to be in equilibrium, what force man must exert on the rope?

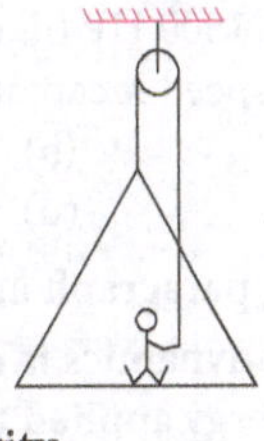

27. (i) Define capillarity.

(ii) Find the height of liquid, if a capillary tube has a base radius of 0.05 cm and surface tension 0.073 Nm^{-1}

(iii) At what speed will the velocity of a stream of water be equal to 20 cm of mercury column? (Take, $g = 10\,ms^{-2}$)

28. (i) If frequency (F), velocity (v) and density (D) are considered as fundamental units. Then find the dimensional formula for momentum.

(ii) Which group of Physics has recently came into existence?

Section-D

29. **Read the following paragraph and answer the questions that follow.**

Two bikers having same racing skills are competing against each other. Biker 1 has a bike of 1500 HP while Biker 2 has a bike of 1000 HP. Biker 1 defeated biker 2 in a race by 10 seconds.

Later biker 1 explained biker 2 that he can also win if he had 1500 HP bike. Moreover the weight also has a huge impact on the speed of the bike. More power and less weight makes a bike faster whereas less power and more weight makes a bike go slower.

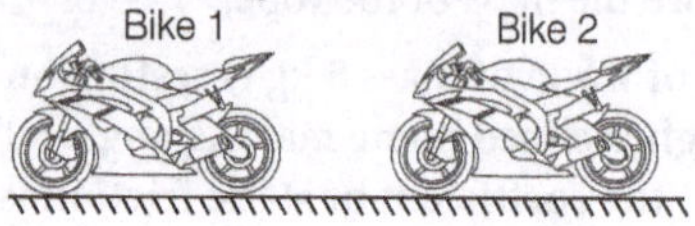

(i) 1 Horse power (HP) .... watt

(a) 446 (b) 746 (c) 766 (d) 674

(ii) If the biker applied the brakes instantly, he goes from 10 ms^{-1} to 0 ms^{-1} in 7s. Assume that brakes apply 70 N, the work done on the road is equal to

(a) 700 J (b) 0.7 J
(c) zero (d) None of these

(iii) Which of the following is largest unit of power?

(a) Watt (b) HP (c) Joule (d) erg

Or

The 1500 HP engine produce ...... joule per second energy.

(a) 1.1×10^6 (b) 3.8×10^6
(c) 1.1×10^4 (d) 3.8×10^4

(iv) If the weight of 1500 HP bike is 100 kg, then find the maximum speed it can attain.

(a) 380 km/h (b) 360 km/h
(c) 340 km/h (d) 400 km/h

30. **Read the following paragraph and answer the solution.**

First law of thermodynamics is a statement of conservation of energy applied to any system in which energy transfer from or to the surroundings is taken into account.

It states that heat given to a system is either used in doing external work or it increases the internal energy of the system or both.

i.e. Heat supplied, $\Delta Q = \Delta U + \Delta W$

where, ΔQ = heat supplied to the system by the surroundings,

ΔW = work done by the system on the surroundings

and ΔU = change in internal energy of the system.

(i) For an ideal gas, internal energy depends on

(a) only molecular kinetic energy
(b) only potential energy of the molecules
(c) Both kinetic and potential energies of the molecules
(d) None of the above

(ii) The internal energy of a system could be changed

(a) by extracting heat from the system
(b) by doing work done on the system
(c) if system do some work on the surroundings
(d) All of the above

(iii) $(\Delta Q - \Delta W)$ is

(a) path dependent (b) path independent
(c) equal to ΔU (d) Both (b) and (c)

(iv) A system is provided with 200 cal of heat and the work done by the system on the surroundings is 40 J. Then, its internal energy

(a) increases by 600 J
(b) decreases by 800 J
(c) increases by 800 J
(d) decreases by 50 J

Or

Using first law of thermodynamics, which is true for isothermal expansion of an ideal gas,

(a) $\Delta U = +ve$ (b) $\Delta Q = +ve$
(c) $\Delta W = +ve$ (d) Both (b) and (c)

Section-E

31. (i) An object placed on a ground is in stable equilibrium. If object is slightly pushed, then what will be the effect on the position of centre of gravity?

(ii) Why is it easier to open a tap with two fingers than with one finger?

Or

(i) Define terminal velocity.

(ii) A capillary tube A is dipped in water and another identical tube B is dipped in soap solution. Draw the diagram showing the nature of liquid columns in both the tubes and explain.

(iii) What happens when a capillary tube of insufficient length is dipped in a liquid?

32. (i) **An ideal liquid of constant density ρ flows in a streamline motion along a tube of variable cross-section. The tube is kept inclined in the vertical plane as shown in figure. The area of cross-section of the tube at two points P and Q at heights of h_1 metre and h_2 metre are respectively, a_1 and a_2.**

The velocity of the liquid at point P is 1 ms^{-1}. Find the expression for work done per unit volume by the pressure.

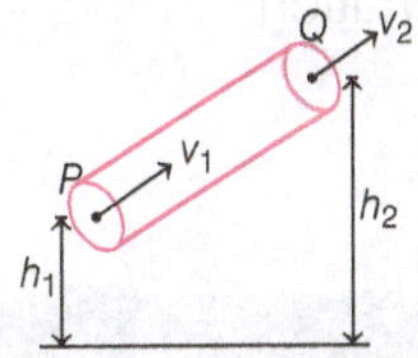

(ii) A venturimeter is connected to two points in the mains where its radii are 20cm and 10cm respectively and the levels of water column in the tubes differ by 10 cm. How much water flows through the pipe per minute?

Or

(i) A metallic ball has a radius of 9.0 cm at 0°C. Calculate the change in its volume when it is heated to 90°C. Given that coefficient of linear expansion of metal of ball is 1.2×10^{-5} K^{-1}.

(ii) Two rods of the same area of cross-section, but of lengths l_1 & l_2 and conductivities K_1 & K_2 are joined in series. Find the equivalent conductivity of the given combination.

33. (i) Determine the ratio of the kinetic energy required to be given to the satellite to escape earth's gravitational field to the kinetic energy required to be given, so that the satellite moves in a circular orbit just above earth atmosphere.

(ii) Two satellites A and B go round a planet P in circular orbits in circular orbits having radii $4R$ and R respectively. If the speed of the satellite A is $3v$, what will be the speed of the satellite B?

(iii) For a satellite, escape velocity is 11 kms^{-1}. If the satellite is launched at an angle of 60° with the vertical, then what will be the escape velocity?

Or

(i) Two containers of equal volume contain the same gas at pressures p_1 and p_2 and absolute temperatures T_1 and T_2, respectively. When both the vessels are joined together, the gas reaches a common pressure p and common temperature T. Determine the ratio p/T.

(ii) At a given temperature, equal masses of monoatomic and diatomic gases are supplied equal quantities of heat. Which of the two gases will suffer larger temperature rise?

Answers

1. (b)	**2.** (c)	**3.** (a)	**4.** (b)	**5.** (c)
6. (b)	**7.** (a)	**8.** (b)	**9.** (b)	**10.** (c)
11. (c)	**12.** (a)	**13.** (a)	**14.** (a)	**15.** (c)
16. (c)	**19.** 0.3 g/cc	**20.** 7.1 N/m	**21.** 10 N	**22.** (i) -9.6×10^4J (ii) 20 W
23. 2 : 1	**25.** 50.8 N	**26.** 40 g	**27.** (ii) 2.98 cm (iii) 7.37 m/s	
28. Dv^4F^{-3}	**29.** (i) (b), (ii) (c), (iii) (b), Or (a), (iv) (b)		**30.** (i) (a), (ii) (d), (iii) (d), (iv) (d) Or (c)	
31. (ii) 2726.58 Litres/minute				

SAMPLE QUESTION PAPER 3

A Highly Simulated Sample Question Paper for CBSE Class XI Examination

PHYSICS

Time : 3 Hours **Max. Marks : 70**

General Instructions

1. There are 33 questions in all. All questions are compulsory.
2. This question paper has five sections : Section A, Section B, Section C, Section D and Section E.
3. All the sections are compulsory.
4. Section A contains sixteen questions, twelve MCQ and four Assertion Reasoning based of 1 mark each, **Section B** contains five questions of two marks each, **Section C** contains seven questions of three marks each, **Section D** contains two case study based questions of four marks each and **Section E** contains three long answer questions of five marks each.
5. There is no overall choice. However, an internal choice has been provided in one question in Section B, one question in Section C, one question in each CBQ in Section D and all three questions in Section E. You have to attempt only one of the choices in such questions.
6. Use of calculators is not allowed.
7. You may use the following values of physical constants where ever necessary
   i. $G = 6.67 \times 10^{-11} Nm^2/kg^2$
   ii. $R = 8.314 J mol^{-1} K^{-1}$
   iii. $k_B = 1.38 \times 10^{-23} J/K$
   iv. $\sigma = 5.67 \times 10^{-8} Wm^{-2} K^{-1}$
   v. $N_A = 6.023 \times 10^{23} mol^{-1}$

Section-A

1. The angle between particle velocity and wave velocity in a transverse wave is

(a) zero (b) $\pi/4$
(c) $\pi/2$ (d) π

2. The mass of 22.4 L of any gas is equal to its molecular weight in grams at

(a) 270 K and 1 atm
(b) 273 K and 1 atm
(c) 273 K and 10 atom
(d) 270 K and 10 atm

3. A body of mass 5 kg is thrown vertically up with a kinetic energy of 490 J. The height at which the kinetic energy of the body becomes half of the original value is

(a) 12.5 m (b) 10 m
(c) 2.5 m (d) 5 m

4. Find the centre of mass of a uniform *L*-shaped lamina (a thin flat plate) with dimensions as shown in the figure below. The mass of the lamina is 3 kg.

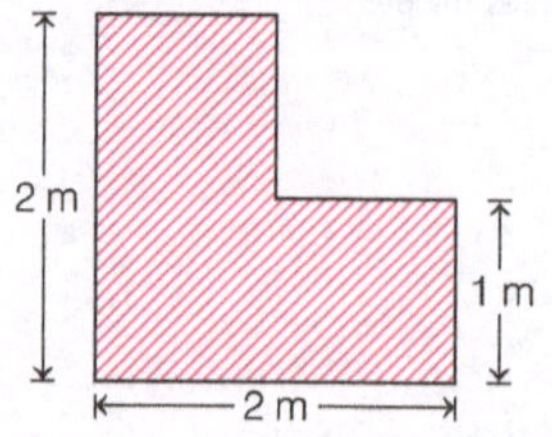

(a) (5/6) m, (5/6) m (b) (3/4) m, (3/4)m
(c) (5/8) m, (5/8) m (d) (3/5) m, (3/5) m

5. A player throws a ball upwards with an initial speed of $29.4 ms^{-1}$. To what height does the ball rise? (Take, $g = 9.8 ms^{-2}$ and neglect air resistance).

(a) 44.1 m (b) 46 m
(c) 55 m (d) 60 m

6. A constant retarding force of 50 N is applied to a body of man 20 kg moving initially with a speed of 15 ms^{-1}. How long does the body take to reverse its velocity?

(a) 10 s (b) 11 s (c) 12 s (d) 13 s

7. The periodic function $f(t) = A\sin\omega t$ repeats itself

(a) 2π (b) 3π

(c) π (d) $\pi/2$

8. In a two-dimensional motion, instantaneous speed v_0 is a positive constant. Then, which of the following are necessarily true?

(a) The average velocity is not zero any time

(b) Average acceleration must always vanish

(c) Displacements in equal time intervals are equal

(d) Equal path lengths are traversed in equal intervals

9. Three particles each of mass m are kept at vertices of an equilateral triangle of side L. The gravitational potential at the centre due to these particles is

(a) $-\frac{3Gm}{L}$ (b) $\frac{-9Gm}{\sqrt{3}L}$

(c) $-\frac{3\sqrt{3}Gm}{L}$ (d) Both (b) and (c)

10. $pV = \mu RT$ can be rewritten as

(a) $pV = k_B NT$ ($N \rightarrow$ total number of molecules in the perfect gas)

(b) $p = k_B nT$ ($n \rightarrow$ number density)

(c) $p = \rho RT / M_0$ ($\rho \rightarrow$ mass density and $M_0 \rightarrow$ molar mass

(d) All of the above

11. Centre of mass of the given system of particles will be at

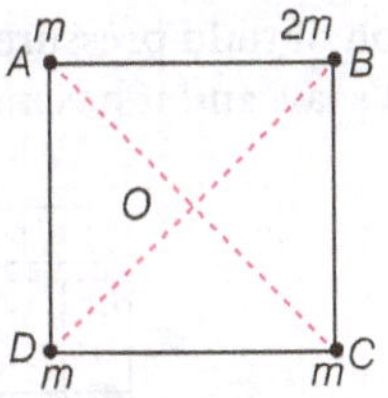

(a) OD (b) OC

(c) OB (d) AO

12. Match the kinematic equation with its corresponding quantity.

Kinematic Equation	Quantity
A. $v = u + at$	1. Equation for final velocity with constant acceleration
B. $s = ut + \frac{1}{2}at^2$	2. Equation for displacement with constant acceleration
C. $v^2 = u^2 + 2as$	3. Equation relating final velocity, initial velocity acceleration and displacement
D. $s = \frac{v+u}{2} \times t$	4. Equation for displacement using average velocity

(a) A-1, B-2, C-3, D-4 (b) A-4, B-2, C-3, D-1

(c) A-3, B-2, C-4, D-1 (d) A-1, B-4, C-3, D-2

For questions 13 to 16, two statements are given-one labelled Assertion (A) and the other labelled Reason (R). Select the correct answer to these questions from the codes (a), (b), (c) and (d) as given below.

(a) If both Assertion and Reason are true and Reason is correct explanation of Assertion.

(b) If both Assertion and Reason are true but Reason is not the correct explanation of Assertion.

(c) If Assertion is true but Reason is false.

(d) If both Assertion and Reason are false.

13. Assertion (A) In isothermal process for ideal gas change in internal energy is zero.

Reason (R) No heat is supplied to system or rejected by system, in an isothermal process.

14. Assertion (A) Pressure has the dimensions of energy density.

Reason (R) Energy density $= \frac{\text{Energy}}{\text{Volume}}$

15. Assertion (A) As we go up the surface of the earth, we feel light weighed than on the surface of the earth.

Reason (R) The acceleration due to gravity decreases on going up above the surface of the earth.

16. Assertion (A) The value of a_x depends on $\frac{dv}{dt}$.

Reason (R) Acceleration means rate of change of distance.

Section-B

17. (a) 10 mol of an ideal gas at constant temperature 500 K is compressed from 50 L to 5L. Calculate the work done in this process. (Given, $R = 831$ J mol^{-1} K^{-1})

(b) An electric heater supplies heat to a system at a rate of 50W. If the system performs work at a rate of 30 J/s. At what rate is the internal energy increased?

18. What will be mass of air in a room that measures 5.0 m × 8.0 m × 3.0 m? (The density of air is $\frac{1}{800}$ times of that of water)

19. How can we locate the centre of mass of rigid bodies of regular geometrical shape and having uniform mass distribution? Give examples.

20. When is a rigid body said to be in equilibrium? State the necessary conditions for a body to be in equilibrium.

21. Find the moment of inertia of a ring which is formed by bending a thin wire of mass M and length L about its axis.

Or A hollow cylinder and solid sphere of mass m and radius r are rotating about an axis passing through its centre. If torques of equal magnitude are applied to them, then find the ratio of angular accelerations produced.

Section-C

22. A solid cylinder of mass 10 kg rotates about its axis with angular speed of 100 rad/s. The radius of cylinder is 0.5 m. What is the kinetic energy associated with the rotation of the cylinder? What is the magnitude of angular momentum of the cylinder about its axis?

Or

A solid cylinder rolls up an inclined plane of angle of inclination 30°. At the bottom of inclined plane, the centre of mass of cylinder has a speed of 5 ms^{-1}. How far will the cylinder go up the plane?

23. A block of wood of mass 5 kg is resting on the surface of a rough inclined plane making angle 60° as shown in figure. If the coefficient of static friction is 0.3, calculate the forces.

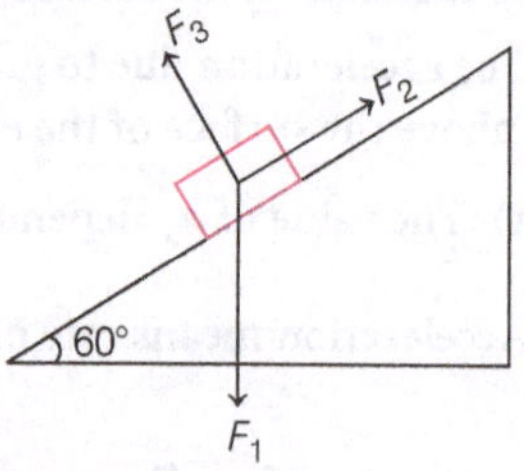

24. (a) Define terminal velocity.

(b) A capillary tube A is dipped in water and another identical tube B is dipped in soap solution. Draw the diagram showing the nature of liquid columns in both the tubes and explain.

(c) What happens when a capillary tube of insufficient length is dipped in a liquid?

25. A uniform rod of length L and density ρ is being pulled along a smooth floor with a horizontal acceleration α as shown below. What is the magnitude of the stress at the transverse cross- section through the mid-point of the rod?

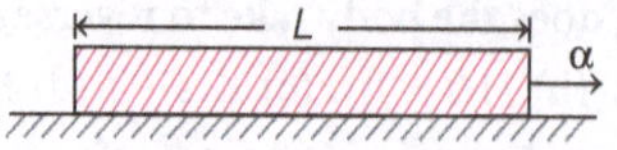

26. Figure shows two bars of iron and brass having same length and same area of cross-section in steady state. Determine temperature at common junction. Given that $K_{iron} = 79\ Wm^{-1}K^{-1}$ and $K_{brass} = 109\ Wm^{-1}K^{-1}$

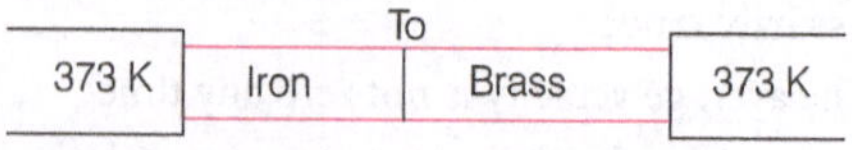

27. Identify the force which

(a) produces a work done on a body independent on the path followed,

(b) produces a work done on a body dependent on the path followed,

(c) binds any two bodies in this universe.

Write one example of each of the above forces.

28. (a) A bowler throws a ball giving it a horizontal velocity and a small downward velocity. Determine the resultant speed of the ball at the bottom.

(b) If the speed of a projectile at the maximum height is $\frac{1}{2}$ of its initial speed, then show that $\frac{4}{\sqrt{3}}$ is the ratio of range of projectile to the maximum height attained.

Section-D

29. Read the following paragraph and answer the questions that follow

The transmission of fluid pressure in a closed system is based on Pascal's law and it has many applications in daily life.

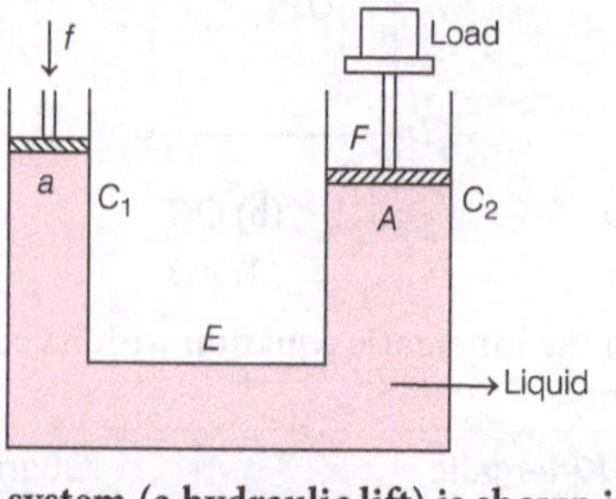

One such system (a hydraulic lift) is shown in figure, which consists of two cylinders C_1 and C_2 connected to each other by a pipe E. These cylinders are fitted with water-tight frictionless pistons of different cross-sectional areas. These cylinders and the pipe contain a liquid.

Suppose, a downward force f is applied on the smaller piston of cross-sectional area a. Then, pressure exerted on the liquid,

$$p = \frac{f}{a}$$

and upward force on a larger piston, $F = \frac{A}{a} f$

(i) A hydraulic lift has 2 limbs of areas A and $2A$. Force F is applied over limb of area A to lift a heavy car. If distance moved by piston P_1 is x, then distance moved by piston P_2 is

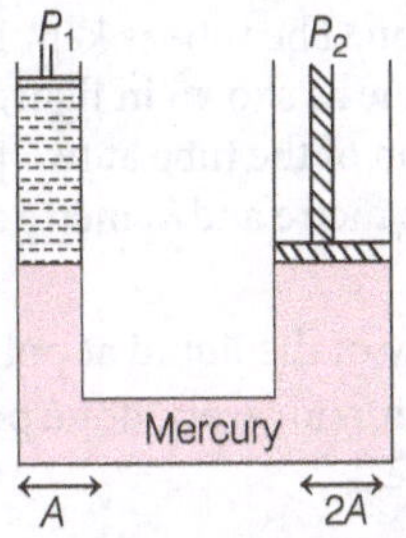

(a) x (b) $2x$ (c) $\frac{x}{2}$ (d) $4x$

(ii) In which of the following figure, the force acting on the base of the vessel is maximum.

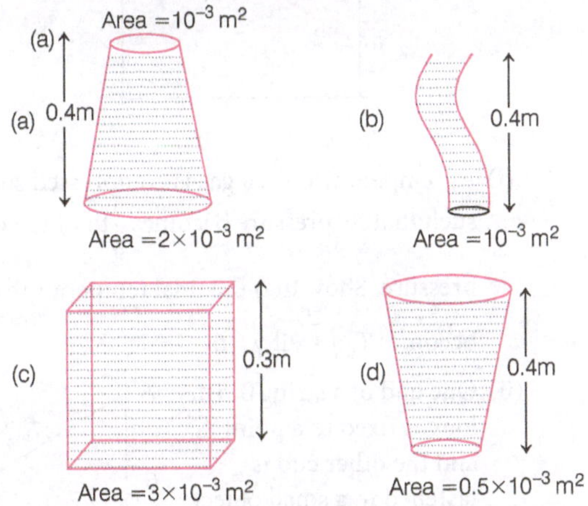

(iii) Pressure at a point inside a liquid does not depend on

(a) the depth of the point below the surface of the liquid
(b) the nature of the liquid
(c) the acceleration due to gravity at that point
(d) total weight of fluid in the beaker

Or

Three vessels filled with a liquid are shown in the figure. Three points A, B and C are given in the liquid. Choose the correct option for $P_A > P_B > P_C$, where P_A, P_B and P_C are the pressures at points A, B and C

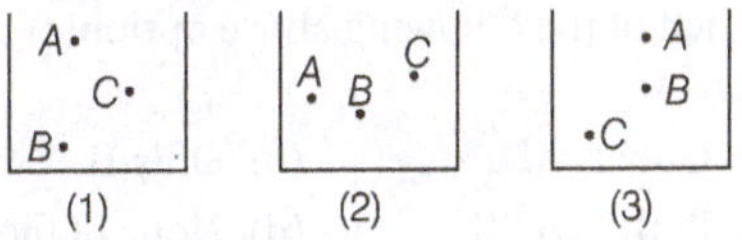

(a) in the vessel (1) and (2)
(b) in the vessel (2) and (3)
(c) in the vessel (1) and (3)
(d) only in vessel (3).

(iv)

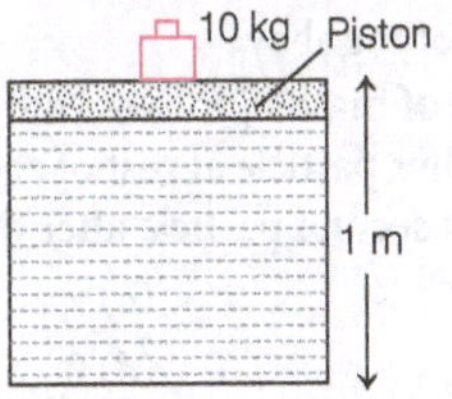

A container of area 0.02 m² is filled with water. If a weight is placed on the piston, then the pressure at the bottom of the container is

(a) 14500 N/m² (b) 14700 N/m²
(c) 13800 N/m² (d) 16400 N/m²

30. **Read the following paragraph and answer the questions that follow**

A collision is an isolated event in which two or more colliding bodies exert strong forces on each other for a relatively short time. For a collision to take place, the actual physical contact is not necessary.

At the time of collision, the two colliding objects are deformed and may be momentarily at rest with respect to each other. If the initial velocities and final velocities of both the bodies are along the same straight line, then it is called a one-dimensional collision or head-on collision.

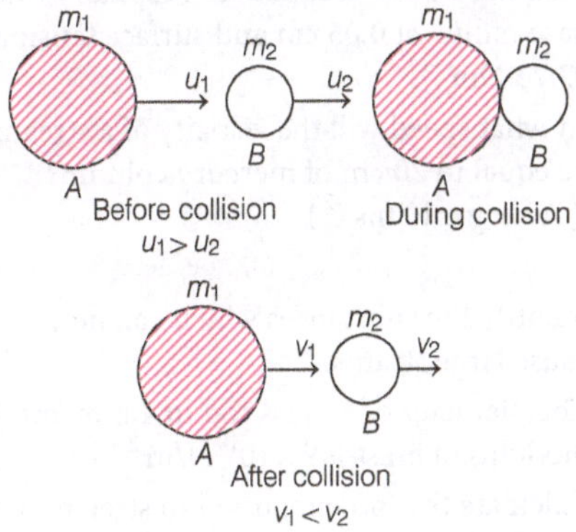

(i) In elastic collision,

I. initial kinetic energy is equal to the final kinetic energy.

II. kinetic energy during the collision time Δt is constant.

Which of the following above option(s) is/are correct?

(a) Only I (b) Only II

(c) Both I and II (d) None of these

(ii) In an inelastic collision,

(a) conservation of momentum is not followed

(b) conservation of mechanical energy is not followed

(c) conservation of mechanical energy is followed

(d) None of the above

(iii) A particle of mass m_1 moves with velocity v_1 collides with another particle at rest of equal mass. The velocity of second particle after the elastic collision is

(a) $2v_1$ (b) v_1

(c) $-v_1$ (d) 0

(iv) A molecule in a gas container hits a horizontal wall with speed 200 ms^{-1} at an angle 30° with the normal and rebounds with the same speed. Which statement is true?

(a) Momentum is conserved

(b) Elastic collision

(c) Inelastic collision

(d) Both (a) and (b)

Or

A particle of mass 1g moving with a velocity $\mathbf{v}_1 = 3\hat{\mathbf{i}} - 2\hat{\mathbf{j}} \text{ms}^{-1}$ experiences a perfectly elastic collision with another particle of mass 2 g and velocity $\mathbf{v}_2 = 4\hat{\mathbf{j}} - 6\hat{\mathbf{k}} \text{ ms}^{-1}$. The velocity of the particle is

(a) 2.3ms^{-1} (b) 4.6 ms^{-1}

(c) 9.2 ms^{-1} (d) 6 ms^{-1}

Section-E

31. (i) Find the height of liquid, if a capillary tube has a base radius of 0.05 cm and surface tension 0.073 Nm^{-1}.

(ii) At what speed will the velocity of a stream of water be equal to 20 cm of mercury column? (Take, $g = 10 \text{ ms}^{-2}$)

Or

(i) Identify the substances which can be stretched to cause large strains.

(ii) The diameter of a brass rod in 4 mm and Young's modulus of brass is $9 \times 10^{10} \text{N/m}^2$.

Calculate the force required to stretch by 0.1% of its length.

(iii) To what depth must a rubber ball be taken in deep sea, so that its volume is decreased by 0.1%? (Take, density of sea water $= 10^3 \text{ kgm}^{-3}$, bulk modulus of rubber $= 9 \times 10^8 \text{ Nm}^{-2}$ and $g = 10 \text{ms}^{-2}$)

(iv) The upper end of a wire of radius 4 mm and length 100 cm is clamped and its other end is twisted through an angle of 30°. Then, find angle of shear.

32. (i) A venturimeter is connected to two points in the mains where its radii are 20cm and 10cm respectively and the levels of water column in the tubes differ by 10 cm. How much water flows through the pipe per minute?

(ii) An ideal liquid of constant density ρ flows in a streamline motion along a tube of variable cross-section. The tube is kept inclined in the vertical plane as shown in figure. The area of cross-section of the tube at two points P and Q at heights of h_1 metre and h_2 metre are respectively, a_1 and a_2.

The velocity of the liquid at point P is 1 ms^{-1}. Find the expression for work done per unit volume by the pressure.

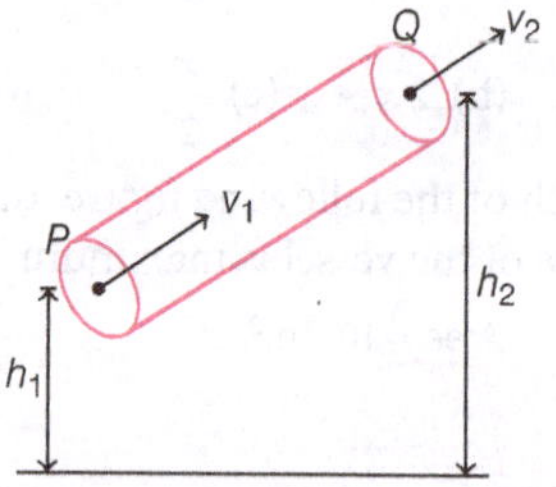

Or

(i) At temperature T_0, a gas is compressed suddenly such that its pressure becomes $\frac{1}{q}$th of the original pressure. Show that the final temperature of gas becomes $T_0 q^{\frac{1-t}{t}}$, if $\gamma = t$.

(ii) One end of a string 0.5m long is fixed to a point A and the other end is fastened to a small object of weight 8N. The object is pulled aside by a horizontal force F, until it is 0.3 m from the vertical through A. Find the magnitudes of the tension T in the string and the force F.

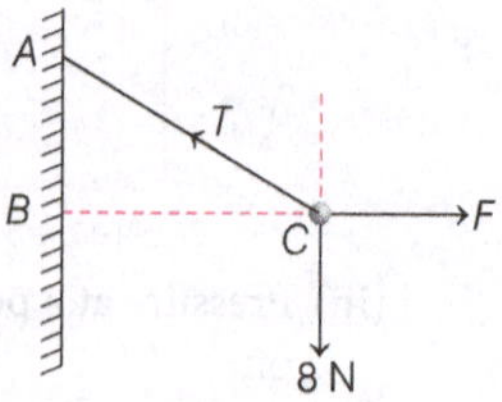

33. (a) Prove that the mass of a planet m can be measured by equation $M = \frac{gR^2}{G}$

where, g = acceleration of gravity on planet, R = radius of planet and G = gravitational constant.

(b) The mean radius of the earth is R, its angular speed on its own axis is ω and the acceleration due to gravity at the earth's surface is g.
Prove that the radius of the orbit of geo-stationary satellite is $\left[\frac{gR^2}{\omega^2}\right]^{1/3}$.

(c) Gravitational force between point masses m and M separated by a distance is F. Now if a point mass $5m$ is placed next to m, what will be the
(i) force on M due to m
(ii) and total force on M?

Or

(a) State two advantages of friction in daily life.
(b) A 100 kg gun fires a ball of 1 kg horizontally from a cliff of height 500 m.
It falls on the ground at a distance of 400m from the bottom of the cliff. What will be the recoil velocity of the gun?

Answers

1. (c)	**2.** (b)	**3.** (d)	**4.** (a)	**5.** (a)
6. (c)	**7.** (a)	**8.** (d)	**9.** (c)	**10.** (d)
11. (c)	**12.** (a)	**13.** (c)	**14.** (a)	**15.** (a)
16. (c)	**17.** (a) -9.6×10^4 J (b) 20 W		**18.** 150 kg	

22. 6250 J, 125 kg-m^2s^{-1} *Or* 1.91 m
23. 50.8 N
26. 315 K
29. (i) (c), (ii) (c), (iii) (d) Or (d) (iv) (b)
30. (i) (a), (ii) (c), (iii) (b), (iv) (d), Or (b)
31. (i) 2.98 cm (ii) 7.37 ms^{-1} *Or* (ii) 360 πN (iii) 90 m (iv) 0.12°
32. (i) 2728.7 litre/min Or, (ii) 6N
33. (c) 6 F *Or* (b) 0.4 m/s